AN EXEGETICAL SUMMARY OF
LUKE 12–24

AN EXEGETICAL SUMMARY OF LUKE 12–24

Second Edition

Richard C. Blight

SIL International

Second Edition
© 2007, 2008 by SIL International

Library of Congress Catalog Card Number: 2008924475
ISBN: 978-155671-213-5

Printed in the United States of America

All Rights Reserved
No part of this publication may be reproduced, stored in a retrieval system, or transmitted in any form or by any means without the express permission of SIL International. However, brief excerpts, generally understood to be within the limits of fair use, may be quoted without written permission.

Copies of this and other publications
of SIL International may be obtained from

International Academic Bookstore
SIL International
7500 West Camp Wisdom Road
Dallas, TX 75236-5699, USA

Voice: 972-708-7404
Fax: 972-708-7363
academic_books@sil.org
www.ethnologue.com

PREFACE

Exegesis is concerned with the interpretation of a text. Exegesis of the New Testament involves determining the meaning of the Greek text. Translators must be especially careful and thorough in their exegesis of the New Testament in order to accurately communicate its message in the vocabulary, grammar, and literary devices of another language. Questions occurring to translators as they study the Greek text are answered by summarizing how scholars have interpreted the text. This is information that should be considered by translators as they make their own exegetical decisions regarding the message they will communicate in their translations.

The Semi-Literal Translation

As a basis for discussion, a semi-literal translation of the Greek text is given so that the reasons for different interpretations can best be seen. When one Greek word is translated into English by several words, these words are joined by hyphens. There are a few times when clarity requires that a string of words joined by hyphens have a separate word, such as "not" (μή), inserted in their midst. In this case, the separate word is surrounded by spaces between the hyphens. When alternate translations of a Greek word are given, these are separated by slashes.

The Text

Variations in the Greek text are noted under the heading TEXT. The base text for the summary is the text of the fourth revised edition of *The Greek New Testament*, published by the United Bible Societies, which has the same text as the twenty-sixth edition of the *Novum Testamentum Graece* (Nestle-Aland). Dr. J. Harold Greenlee researched the variants and has written the notes for this part of the summary. The versions that follow different variations are listed without evaluating their choices.

The Lexicon

The meaning of a key word in context is the first question to be answered. Words marked with a raised letter in the semi-literal translation are treated separately under the heading LEXICON. First, the lexicon form of the Greek word is given. Within the parentheses following the Greek word is the location number where, in the author's judgment, this word is defined in the *Greek-English Lexicon of the New Testament Based on Semantic Domains* (Louw and Nida 1988). When a semantic domain includes a translation of the particular verse being treated, **LN** in bold type indicates that specific translation. If the specific reference for the verse is listed in *A Greek-English Lexicon of the New Testament and Other Early Christian Literature* (Bauer, Arndt, Gingrich, and Danker 1979), the outline location and page number is given. Then English equivalents of the Greek word are given to show how it is translated by commentators who offer their own translations of the whole text and, after a semicolon, all the versions in the list of abbreviations for translations. When reference is made to "all versions," it refers to only the versions in the list of translations. Sometimes further comments are made about the meaning of the word or the significance of a verb's tense, voice, or mood.

The Questions

Under the heading QUESTION, a question is asked that comes from examining the Greek text under consideration. Typical questions concern the identity of an implied actor or object of an event word, the antecedent of a pronominal reference, the connection indicated by a relational word, the meaning of a genitive construction, the meaning of figurative language, the function of a rhetorical question, the identification of an ambiguity, and the presence of implied information that is needed to understand the passage correctly. Background information is also considered for a proper understanding of a passage. Although not all implied information and background information is made explicit in a translation, it is important to consider it so that the translation will not be stated in such a way that prevents a reader from arriving at the proper interpretation. The question is answered with a summary of what commentators have said. If there are contrasting differences of opinion, the different interpretations are numbered and the commentaries that support each are listed. Differences that are not treated by many of the commentaries often are not numbered, but are introduced with a contrastive 'Or' at the beginning of the sentence. No attempt has been made to select which interpretation is best.

In listing support for various statements of interpretation, the author is often faced with the difficult task of matching the different terminologies used in commentaries with the terminology he has adopted. Sometimes he can only infer the position of a commentary from incidental remarks. This book, then, includes the author's interpretation of the views taken in the various commentaries. General statements are followed by specific statements, which indicate the author's understanding of the pertinent relationships, actors, events, and objects implied by that interpretation.

The Use of This Book

This book does not replace the commentaries that it summarizes. Commentaries contain much more information about the meaning of words and passages. They often contain arguments for the interpretations that are taken and they may have important discussions about the discourse features of the text. In addition, they have information about the historical, geographical, and cultural setting. Translators will want to refer to at least four commentaries as they exegete a passage. However, since no one commentary contains all the answers translators need, this book will be a valuable supplement. It makes more sources of exegetical help available than most translators have access to. Even if they had all the books available, few would have the time to search through all of them for the answers.

When many commentaries are studied, it soon becomes apparent that they frequently disagree in their interpretations. That is the reason why so many answers in this book are divided into two or more interpretations. The reader's initial reaction may be that all of these different interpretations complicate exegesis rather than help it. However, before translating a passage, a translator needs to know exactly where there is a problem of interpretation and what the exegetical options are.

Acknowledgments

Ronald L. Trail wrote four volumes of the *Exegetical Summaries*. Because of this experience he did an excellent job of editing this volume.

Matthew E. Carlton took time to read this volume and offer many valuable suggestions while writing his next book, *The Translator's Reference Translation of the Gospel of Luke*.

J. Harold Greenlee has spent most of his life teaching and writing about New Testament Greek. He wrote five volumes of the *Exegetical Summaries*. Since retiring he has provided textual comments for a number of the summaries, including this one.

ABBREVIATIONS

COMMENTARIES AND REFERENCE BOOKS

Asterisks indicate books that translators may find especially helpful as they study the text of Luke. A dagger indicates that a knowledge of Greek is required.

AB*	Fitzmyer, Jospeph A. *The Gospel According to Luke.* 2 vols. Garden City, N.Y.: Doubleday, 1981 and 1985.
Alf	Alford, Henry. *The Four Gospels.* The Greek Testament, vol. 1. 1874. Reprint. Chicago: Moody, 1968.
Arn*	Arndt, William F. *Luke.* St. Louis: Concordia, 1984.
BAGD	Bauer, Walter. *A Greek-English Lexicon of the New Testament and Other Early Christian Literature.* Translated and adapted from the fifth edition, 1958 by William F. Arndt and F. Wilbur Gingrich. Second English ed. revised and augmented by F. Wilbur Gingrich and Frederick W. Danker. Chicago: University of Chicago Press, 1979.
Bai	Bailey, Kenneth E. *Poet & Peasant and Through Peasant Eyes.* Reprint (2 vols. in 1). Grand Rapids: Eerdmans, 1983.
BECNT*	Bock, Darrell L. *Luke.* 2 vols. Baker Exegetical Commentary on the New Testament. Grand Rapids: Baker Books, 1994 and 1996.
Blm	Blomberg, Craig. *Interpreting the Parables.* Downer Grove, Ill.: InterVarsity Press, 1990.
BNTC	Leaney, A. R. C. *A Commentary on the Gospel According to St. Luke.* 2d ed. Black's New Testament Commentary. London: Adam and Charles Black, 1966.
Crd	Creed, John Martin. *The Gospel According to St. Luke.* London: MacMillan, 1930.
EGT	Bruce, Alexander Balmain. *The Synoptic Gospels.* Expositor's Greek Testament, vol. 1. 1910. Reprint. Grand Rapids: Eerdmans, 1997.
Gdt	Godet, F. *A Commentary on the Gospel of St. Luke.* 2 vols. 1870. Reprint. Edinburgh: T. & T. Clark, 1957.
Hlt	Hiltgren, Arland J. *The Parables of Jesus.* Grand Rapids: Eermans, 2000.
Hu	Hultgren, Arland J. *The Parables of Jesus.* Grand Rapids: Eerdmans, 2000.
ICC*	Plummer, Alfred. *A Critical and Exegetical Commentary on the Gospel According to S. Luke.* The International Critical Commentary. Edinburgh: T. & T. Clark, 1896.
Kst	Kistemaker, Simon J. *The Parables of Jesus.* Grand Rapids: Baker, 1950.

LN*	Louw, Johannes P., and Eugene A. Nida. *Greek-English Lexicon of the New Testament Based on Semantic Domains*. New York: United Bible Societies, 1988.
Lns*	Lenski, R. C. H. *The Interpretation of St. Luke's Gospel*. Minneapolis: Augsburg, 1946.
MGC	Pate, C. Marvin. *Luke*. Moody Gospel Commentary. Chicago: Moody Press, 1995.
My	Meyer, Heinrich August Wilhelm. *Critical and Exegetical Handbook to the Gospels of Mark and Luke*. [American Edition.] New York: Funk and Wagnalls, 1884.
NAC	Stein, Robert H. *Luke*. New American Commentary. Nashville, Tenn.: Broadman, 1992.
NIBC	Evans, Craig A. *Luke*. New International Biblical Commentary. Peabody, Mass.: Hendrickson, 1990.
NIC	Geldenhuys, Norval. *Commentary on the Gospel of Luke*. New International Commentary on the New Testament. Grand Rapids: Eerdmans, 1951.
NICNT	Green, Joel B. *The Gospel of Luke*. New International Commentary on the New Testament. [Replacement.] Grand Rapids: Eerdmans, 1997.
NIGTC*†	Marshall, I. Howard. *The Gospel of Luke*. The New International Greek Testament Commentary. Grand Rapids: Eerdmans, 1978.
NIVS	Barker, Kenneth, ed. *The NIV Study Bible*. Grand Rapids: Zondervan, 1985.
NTC*	Hendriksen, William. *Exposition of the Gospel According to Luke*. New Testament Commentary. Grand Rapids: Baker, 1978.
Pnt	Pentecost, J. Dwight. *The Parables of Jesus*. Grand Rapids: Zondervan, 1982.
Rb	Robertson, Archibald Thomas. *The Gospel According to Luke*. Word Pictures in the New Testament, vol. 2. Nashville, Tenn.: Broadman, 1930.
Su	Summers, Ray. *Commentary on Luke*. Waco, Texas: Word, 1972.
TG*	Bratcher, Robert G. *A Translator's Guide to the Gospel of Luke*. London, New York: United Bible Societies, 1982.
TH*	Reiline, J., and J. L. Swellengrebel. *A Handbook on The Gospel of Luke*. New York: United Bible Societies, 1971.
TNTC	Morris, Leon. *Luke*. Revised Edition. Tyndale New Testament Commentaries. Grand Rapids: Eerdmans, 1988.
WBC*	Nolland, John. *Luke*. 3 vols. Word Biblical Commentary. Dallas: Word Books, 1989 and 1993.

GREEK TEXT AND TRANSLATIONS

GNT	The Greek New Testament. Edited by B. Aland, K. Aland, J. Karavidopoulos, C. Martini, and B. Metzger. Fourth ed. London, New York: United Bible Societies, 1993.
CEV	The Holy Bible, Contemporary English Version. New York: American Bible Society, 1995.
GW	God's Word. Grand Rapids: World Publishing, 1995.
HCSB	Holman Christian Standard Bible. Nashville, Tennessee: Holman Bible Publishers, 2000.
KJV	The Holy Bible. Authorized (or King James) Version. 1611.
NASB	New American Standard Bible. La Habra, Calif.: Lockman Foundation, 1995.
NCV	New Century Version. Dallas: Word Publishing, 1991.
NET	The NET Bible. New English Translation, New Testament. Version 9.206. WWW.BIBLE.COM: Biblical Studies Press, 1999.
NIV	The Holy Bible, New International Version. Grand Rapids: Zondervan, 1984.
NLT	The Holy Bible, New Living Translation. Wheaton, Ill.: Tyndale House, 1996.
NRSV	The Holy Bible: New Revised Standard Version. New York: Oxford University Press, 1989.
REB	The Revised English Bible. Oxford: Oxford University Press and Cambridge University Press, 1989.
TEV	Good News Bible, Today's English Version. Second ed. New York: American Bible Society, 1992.

GRAMMATICAL TERMS

act.	active		mid.	middle
fut.	future		opt.	optative
impera.	imperative		pass.	passive
imperf.	imperfect		perf.	perfect
indic.	indicative		pres.	present
infin.	infinitive		subj.	subjunctive

EXEGETICAL SUMMARY OF LUKE 12–24

DISCOURSE UNIT: 12:1–13:21 [NIGTC]. The topic is readiness for the coming crisis.

DISCOURSE UNIT: 12:1–13:9 [NICNT, WBC]. The topic is vigilance in the face of eschatological crisis [NICNT], preparing for the coming judgment [WBC].

DISCOURSE UNIT: 12:1–48 [BECNT]. The topic is discipleship: trusting God.

DISCOURSE UNIT: 12:1–12 [BECNT, NAC, NICNT, NIGTC, Su, WBC; GW, NASB, NET, NIV, NLT]. The topic is Jesus speaking to his disciples [GW], God knows and cares [NASB], warnings and exhortations [NAC], warnings and encouragements [NIV], a warning against hypocrisy [NLT], a warning against hypocrisy and blasphemy [Su], persecution and identification with God's purpose [NICNT], the need to avoid hypocrisy, fear God, and confess Jesus [BECNT], fear God, not man [NET], fearless confession [NIGTC], the need for a clear–cut acknowledgment of Jesus [WBC].

DISCOURSE UNIT: 12:1–7 [NCV]. The topic is a command to not be like the Pharisees.

DISCOURSE UNIT: 12:1–3 [TNTC; CEV, HCSB, NRSV, TEV]. The topic is the leaven of the Pharisees [TNTC], warnings [CEV], a warning against hypocrisy [NRSV, TEV], beware of religious hypocrisy [HCSB].

DISCOURSE UNIT: 12:1 [AB]. The topic is the leaven of the Pharisees.

12:1 **During-which-things**[a] **the myriads**[b] **of-the crowd having-been-gathered-together**[c] **so-as to-trample-on**[d] **one-another, he-began to-say to his disciples first, Pay-attention-to**[e] **yourselves from the leaven,**[f] **which is hypocrisy,**[g] **of-the Pharisees.**

LEXICON—a. The phrase ἐν οἷς 'during which things' is translated 'under these circumstances' [NASB], 'in connection with which things' [Lns], 'during this period' [WBC], 'meanwhile' [AB; GW, NET, NIV, NLT, NRSV, REB], 'in the meantime' [BECNT, NTC; KJV], 'at this juncture' [Arn], 'in these circumstances' [HCSB], not explicit [CEV, NCV, TEV].

b. μυριάς (LN 60.8) (BAGD 2. p. 529): 'countless, innumerable' [LN]. The plural form is translated 'myriads' [BAGD, Lns, WBC], 'thousands' [AB; CEV, GW, NLT, NRSV, TEV], 'tens of thousands' [Arn], 'many thousands' [HCSB, NET, NIV, REB], 'so many thousands' [BECNT, NTC; NASB, NCV], 'an innumerable (multitude of people)' [KJV]. This noun is used hyperbolically [AB, EGT, ICC, Lns, My, NIC, Rb, TH] for the large number of the people in the crowd [AB, EGT, Lns]. This refers

to a very large and indefinite number [BAGD, LN, TG, TH, TNTC]. The article with this noun refers to what was usual [NIGTC, TH, TNTC].
c. aorist pass. participle of ἐπισυνάγω (LN 15.126) (BAGD p. 301): 'to be gathered together' [BAGD, LN, Lns; KJV], 'to gather together' [NASB], 'to gather' [Arn, BECNT, NTC, WBC; GW, NCV, NET, NIV, NRSV, REB], 'to gather closely' [AB], 'to crowd together' [TEV], 'to come together' [HCSB], 'to crowd around Jesus' [CEV], 'to grow' [NLT]. It is implied that the crowds increased in size since the time the crowd was first mentioned at 11:29 [Gdt, ICC, MGC, NAC, NIC, NIGTC]. The passive form has an intransitive meaning [TH].
d. pres. act. infin. of καταπατέω (LN 19.52) (BAGD 1.b. p. 415): 'to trample on' [LN], 'to tread on' [BAGD]. The phrase 'so as to trample on one another' is translated 'insomuch that they trode one upon another' [HCSB, KJV], 'so that they were treading on each other' [Lns], 'that they were trampling on each other' [NTC], 'so that they trampled/were trampling on one another' [Arn, BECNT; NET, NIV, NRSV, REB], 'they were actually trampling on one another' [AB], 'and they were trampling one another' [WBC], 'they were stepping on each other' [CEV, NCV, TEV; similarly GW, NASB], 'were milling about and crushing each other' [NLT]. There were so many people that all were trying to get near enough to Jesus to hear what he was saying [NTC].
e. pres. act. impera. of προσέχω (LN 27.59) (BAGD 1.b. p. 714): 'to pay attention to, to be on one's guard against' [BAGD, LN], 'to beware of' [BAGD]. The phrase 'pay attention to yourselves from' is translated 'beware of' [AB, Arn, BECNT, Lns, WBC; KJV, NASB, NCV, NLT, NRSV], 'be on your guard against' [NTC; HCSB, NET, NIV, REB; similarly TEV], 'be sure to guard against' [CEV], 'watch out for' [GW]. The use of the present imperative indicates that they were to constantly be on their guard [NET]. See this word at 21:34.
f. ζύμη (LN 5.11, **88.237**) (BAGD 2. p. 340): 'leaven' [AB, Arn, BAGD, BECNT, Lns, WBC; KJV, NASB, REB], 'yeast' [BAGD, LN (5.11), NTC; GW, HCSB, NCV, NET, NIV, NLT, NRSV, TEV], 'pretense' [**LN** (88.237)], 'hypocrisy' [LN (88.237)], 'dishonest teaching' [CEV]. Leaven was old sour dough that was stored away to be used as a rising agent in new dough [AB, NAC]. The sour dough was stored in fermenting juices until it was mixed with fresh dough [WBC].
g. ὑπόκρισις (LN 88.227) (BAGD p. 845): 'hypocrisy' [AB, Arn, BAGD, BECNT, LN, Lns, NTC, WBC; all versions except CEV, NCV], 'pretense' [BAGD, LN], 'outward show' [BAGD], 'they are hypocrites' [NCV], 'their way of fooling people' [CEV].

QUESTION—During what things did Jesus warn his disciples?

This refers to the time the Pharisees were plotting against Jesus as Luke reported in 11:53–54 [AB, Alf, Crd, EGT, My]. This is not only connected to the summary in 11:53–54, but to all that precedes in 11:37–54 [Lns, TH], so that while all this was happening the crowd was still gathering [TH]. It means 'during this period' [WBC]

QUESTION—What is meant by the word πρῶτον 'first'?

1. 'First' is a temporal marker that indicates Jesus first spoke to his disciples before addressing the crowd [AB, Alf, Arn, BAGD, Crd, ICC, Lns, MGC, NAC, NICNT, NIGTC, NTC, Rb, Su, TG, TH, TNTC, WBC]: First Jesus spoke to his disciples and said, 'Beware of the leaven'. In this chapter, Jesus began to speak to his disciples. At 12:13 someone in the crowd interrupted his teaching and received an answer that was addressed to the listening audience. Then at 12:22 Jesus again spoke to his disciples. Finally, at 12:54 Jesus began speaking to the crowd in general [Crd]. Jesus spoke primarily to his disciples and not directly to the listening crowd [AB, Alf, ICC, Lns, MGC, NICNT, Su, TG, TH, WBC].
2. 'First' indicates the first thing he spoke to his disciples [NIC]: Jesus first of all said to his disciples, 'Beware of the leaven'. This is what they should heed above all, since sincerity is basic for religion [NIC].
3. 'First' is part of the words Jesus spoke to his disciples [Gdt, My]: Jesus said to his disciples, 'First of all beware of the leaven'.

QUESTION—What is the meant by the metaphor of leaven?

The *image* in this metaphor is leaven. The *point of similarity* is a pervasive influence [Arn, NIGTC, TH, WBC], a slow, insidious, and constant penetration [TNTC], a secret and penetrating power [Lns], a process of spreading throughout the whole [NIBC, Su]. Leaven is the symbol of every good or bad principle that has the power of assimilation [AB, Gdt, NICNT], but it is used with a bad sense here [AB]. Some take leaven to be a symbol of evil and the point of similarity includes this negative aspect of leaven [BNTC, ICC, TH, TNTC]. The figure draws on the penetrating power of the yeast, on its secretive working, and also upon its corrupting influence [NICNT].

1. The *topic* of the metaphor is the hypocrisy of the Pharisees [AB, Crd, EGT, Lns, MGC, NAC, NIBC, NIC, NICNT, NTC, Su, TG, TH, TNTC, WBC; GW, KJV, NASB, NET, NIV, NLT, REB, TEV]. Jesus immediately explained leaven by saying 'which is hypocrisy'. This is a warning that the disciples should not become hypocritical like the Pharisees rather than a warning that they should not be taken in by their hypocrisy [Lns, TH]. This is a different warning from Matt. 16:11–12 where leaven is compared with the teaching of the Pharisees and Sadducees [AB, Crd, ICC], and different from Mark 8:14 [NTC] where the leaven of the Pharisees and Herod is an evil disposition [NIVS]. Like leaven pervades all things, so the hypocrisy of the Pharisees pervades all things [TH]. The hypocrisy of the Pharisees was spreading through society like leaven spreads through the dough [Su]. The implication is that the disciples should be sincere [NTC]. They should not conceal their allegiance to Jesus and should not fear what may happen to them because of that allegiance [NIGTC].

2. The *topic* of the metaphor is the hypocritical nature of the evil doctrines and principles of the Pharisees [Arn, BNTC, My; CEV, and possibly NCV]. It is to be connected with the previous conversation with the Pharisees at the table at 11:37–52 [My]. 'Be sure to guard against the dishonest teaching of the Pharisees! It is their way of fooling people' [CEV], 'Beware of the yeast of the Pharisees, because they are hypocrites' [NCV]. Leaven is the symbol of the inner corruption that was hidden by the Pharisees' hypocrisy [BNTC]. Leaven is a style of teaching that is characterized by hypocrisy [My]. This then is similar to the warning in Matt. 16:11–12.

DISCOURSE UNIT: 12:2–9 [AB]. The topic is an exhortation to fearless confession.

12:2 And (there) is nothing having-been-concealed[a] that will- not -be-revealed,[b] and hidden[c] that will- not -be-made-known.[d]
LEXICON—a. perf. pass. participle of συγκαλύπτω (LN 28.81) (BAGD p. 773): 'to be concealed' [Arn, BAGD, LN, NTC; NIV], 'to be covered' [BAGD; GW, HCSB, KJV], 'to be covered up' [AB, Lns, WBC; NASB, NRSV, REB, TEV], 'to be covered over' [BECNT], 'to be kept secret' [LN], 'to be hidden' [CEV, NCV, NET], not explicit [NLT].
  b. fut. pass. indic. of ἀποκαλύπτω (LN 28.38) (BAGD 1. p. 773): 'to be revealed' [Arn, BAGD, BECNT, LN, Lns, NTC, WBC; KJV, NASB, NET, NLT], 'to be disclosed' [LN; NIV], 'to be made fully known' [LN], 'to be exposed' [GW], 'to be uncovered' [AB; HCSB, NRSV, REB, TEV], 'to be shown' [NCV], 'to be found out' [CEV].
  c. κρυπτός (LN 28.69) (BAGD 1. p. 454): 'hidden' [Arn, BAGD, BECNT, LN, NTC, WBC; HCSB, NASB, NIV, REB], 'secret' [AB, BAGD, LN, Lns; CEV, GW, NCV, NET, NLT, NRSV, TEV]. This noun is also translated as a verb: 'to be hid' [KJV].
  d. fut. pass. indic. of γινώσκω (LN 28.1) (BAGD 2.a. p. 161): 'to be known' [Arn, BAGD, LN, Lns; CEV, KJV, NASB], 'to become known' [AB, WBC; NRSV], 'to be made known' [BECNT, NTC; GW, HCSB, NCV, NET, NIV, REB, TEV], 'to be made public' [NLT].
QUESTION—How is this saying connected with the previous verse?
  1. This is a continuation of Jesus' warning about hypocrisy in 12:1 [Arn, BECNT, Gdt, ICC, Lns, My, NAC, NIBC, NIC, NICNT, NIGTC, NIVS, NTC, TH, TNTC, WBC]. Most translations have Jesus' words continue from 12:1 and it is all in one paragraph to the end of 12:3 [Lns, NTC, WBC; all versions except KJV]. The statement is a general one, and it is applied here to the futility of hypocrisy [Lns]. Jesus used a proverbial saying to show that any kind of hypocrisy will not work because all will finally be revealed. This is a warning to the disciples, but it also applies to the Pharisees [BECNT, Gdt, Su]. Hypocrisy is useless because the time is coming when it will be exposed [ICC, TH]. It is futile to conceal evil since it will be uncovered in this life [Su]. It may come to light partly in

this life, but fully at the final judgment [Arn, NIC, NTC], and therefore hypocrisy is folly [NTC]. This refers to the future judgment [NAC, NIGTC, TG, TNTC, WBC] when hypocrites will be unmasked [NIGTC], and the passive implies that God will reveal it and make it known [NAC, TG; NET]. This tells why they must heed Jesus' warning to beware of hypocrisy [My, TH].

2. This begins a separate collection of wisdom-sayings [AB, Crd]. These further sayings of Jesus come from different occasions in Jesus' ministry to make the point that the truth concerning a person's inner self will become known. The sayings are placed here as a commentary on the subject of hypocrisy [AB].

12:3 Therefore/because[a] what (things) you-said in the darkness[b] will-be-heard in the light,[c] and what you-spoke to the ear[d] in the inner-rooms[e] will-be-proclaimed upon the housetops.[f]

LEXICON—a. ἀνθ' ὧν (LN 89.23) (BAGD p. 74): 'therefore' [BECNT, WBC; HCSB, KJV, NRSV, REB], 'wherefore' [Lns, NTC], 'so then' [NET, TEV], 'accordingly' [AB; NASB], 'because' [BAGD, LN], 'instead of' [Arn], not explicit [CEV, GW, NCV, NIV, NLT].

b. σκοτία (LN 28.71) (BAGD 1. p. 757): 'darkness' [BAGD, LN]. The phrase ἐν τῇ σκοτίᾳ 'in the darkness' [Lns, WBC; KJV] is also translated 'in darkness' [Arn], 'in the dark' [AB, BECNT, NTC; all versions except KJV], 'in secret' [BAGD, LN], 'in private, privately, secretly' [LN]. The darkness refers to the night [TH]. To say something in the dark means to say it in secret [NIGTC].

c. φῶς (LN 28.64) (BAGD 1.a. p. 871): 'light' [BAGD, LN]. The phrase ἐν τῷ φωτί 'in the light' [Arn, BECNT, Lns, NTC, WBC; HCSB, KJV, NASB, NCV, NET, NLT, NRSV] is also translated 'when it is day' [CEV], 'in the daylight' [GW, NIV], 'in broad daylight' [AB; REB, TEV], 'in the open' [BAGD], 'in public' [LN], 'publicly' [BAGD, LN, TG]. What is said in the darkness of the night will be repeated in the light of day [TH].

d. οὖς (LN **28.73, 33.91**) (BAGD 1. p. 595): 'ear' [BAGD, LN]. The phrase πρὸς τὸ οὖς λαλέω 'to speak to the ear' [WBC; KJV] is also translated 'to tell into the ear' [Arn], 'to utter for the ear' [Lns], 'to whisper' [AB, BECNT, **LN** (33.91), NTC; CEV, GW, NASB, NCV, NET, NLT, NRSV, REB], 'to whisper in the/an ear' [BAGD; HCSB, NIV], 'to whisper in private' [TEV], 'to say privately' [**LN** (28.73)].

e. ταμεῖον (LN 7.28) (BAGD 2. p. 803): 'inner room' [LN; NASB, NCV, NIV], 'inner chamber' [WBC], 'secret room' [Arn, BAGD, Lns], 'closed room' [CEV, TEV], 'closet' [KJV], 'private room' [BECNT; GW, HCSB, NET], 'behind closed doors' [AB, NTC; NLT, NRSV, REB], 'innermost, hidden' [BAGD]. It is a room that is not readily accessed by outsiders [AB].

f. δῶμα (LN 28.64) (BAGD p. 210): 'housetop' [BAGD, LN]. The phrase ἐπὶ τῶν δωμάτων 'upon the housetops' [KJV, NASB] is also translated 'on the housetops' [AB, Arn, BECNT, Lns; HCSB], 'on the rooftops' [WBC], 'from the housetops' [NTC; CEV, GW, NCV, NET, NRSV, REB, TEV], 'from the housetops for all to hear' [NLT], 'from the roofs' [NIV], 'publicly' [BAGD, LN], 'in public' [LN]. This could be taken literally [Arn]. People would go up on their flat roofs to rest and converse and they could talk from one house to the next [TG]. A speaker could best be heard from a housetop [TH, TNTC]. It refers to making something known publicly [NIGTC; NET].

QUESTION—Does the phrase ἀνθ ὧν mean 'therefore' or 'because'?

1. It indicates the result or application of the principle stated in 12:2 [AB, BNTC, Lns, My, NAC, NIGTC, NTC; HCSB, NASB, NET, REB, TEV]: therefore. This is a warning to those who have something to hide, but it is a motivation for those who do what is right [BECNT]. This refers to the final judgment [TNTC, WBC]. One's true character will be revealed on Judgment Day [MGC]. This may partly come to pass in this life, but it will completely happen at the Day of Judgment [NIC]. Probably he is thinking of how futile it is to conceal one's evil deeds in this life [Su].
2. It indicates the ground for stating 12:3 [ICC, Rb, TH]: it is true that there is nothing hidden that will be made known because.... Hypocrisy will be unmasked [ICC].
3. It indicates the proper alternative [Arn, Gdt]: instead of concealing what you spoke in darkness, let it be heard in the light. The future tense forms 'will be heard' and 'will be proclaimed' are to be taken as imperatives and he is saying that instead of being hypocrites like the Pharisees, they were to proclaim the true message Jesus has taught them [Arn].

DISCOURSE UNIT: 12:4–12 [TNTC; NRSV]. The topic is being ready for judgment [TNTC], an exhortation to fearless confession [NRSV].

DISCOURSE UNIT: 12:4–7 [CEV, HCSB, TEV]. The topic is the one to fear [CEV], whom to fear [TEV], fear God [HCSB].

12:4 And I-say to-you my friends, do- not -be-afraid of the (ones who) kill the body and after these (things) not having anything more to-do.[a] **12:5** But I-will-show[b] you someone you-should-fear. Fear the (one who) after the killing[c] has authority[d] to-throw into hell.[e] Yes, I-say to-you, fear this (one).

LEXICON—a. aorist act. infin. of ποιέω (LN 42.7): 'to do' [LN]. The phrase 'not having anything more to do' is translated 'who have no more that they can do' [KJV, NASB], 'who have nothing more they can do' [NTC; NET, REB], 'who are not able to do anything further' [Arn], 'who have nothing further they can do' [WBC], 'who do not have a thing further to do' [Lns], 'they can't do anything more' [GW], 'who can do no more' [AB; NIV], 'who can do nothing more' [BECNT; HCSB, NRSV], 'there is nothing else they can do' [CEV], 'they cannot do any more to you'

[NLT], 'who can do nothing more to hurt you' [NCV], 'who cannot do anything worse' [TEV].
  b. fut. act. indic. of ὑποδείκνυμι (LN 28.47) (BAGD 2. p. 844): 'to show' [AB, Arn, BAGD, BECNT, LN, Lns, NTC, WBC; GW, HCSB, NIV, REB, TEV], 'to make known' [LN], 'to warn' [BAGD; NASB, NET, NRSV], 'to forewarn' [KJV], 'to tell' [NLT], not explicit [CEV]. Here 'to show' constitutes a warning or an exhortation [NET].
  c. aorist act infin. of ἀποκτείνω (LN 20.61): 'to kill' [LN]. The phrase τὸν μετὰ τὸ ἀποκτεῖναι 'the one who after the killing' is translated 'who, after killing' [Lns, NTC; TEV], 'the one/him who, after he has killed' [KJV, NASB, NRSV, REB], 'the one who after he kills' [WBC], 'him/the one who after killing you' [Arn; GW], 'the one who has the power to kill you' [NCV], 'God, who has the power to kill people' [NLT], 'not only can he take your life' [CEV], 'him/the one who, after the killing' [AB, BECNT; NET], 'him who, after the killing of the body' [NIV], 'he who…after death' [HCSB].
  d. ἐξουσία (LN 76.12) (BAGD 2. p. 278): 'authority' [AB, Arn, BECNT, Lns, WBC; HCSB, NASB, NET, NRSV, REB, TEV], 'power' [BAGD, LN; GW, KJV, NCV, NIV, NLT]. This noun is also translated as a verb: 'to be able to' [CEV]. It refers to a judge who has the right and authority to punish with hell [TG]. Instead of fearing those with no real authority, one should fear the Judge who will judge a person after death [BECNT].
  e. γέεννα (LN **1.21**) (BAGD p. 153): 'hell' [Arn, BAGD, **LN**; all versions], 'Gehenna' [AB, BAGD, BECNT, LN, Lns, WBC]. This is the place where the dead are punished for their sins [LN]. The rubbish dumps in the valley of Gehenna were continually burning and this valley became a symbol for the place where the unrighteous would forever be punished after death [ICC, MGC, NAC, WBC].

QUESTION—In 12:4, what is referred to by ταῦτα 'these things' in the phrase 'and after these things not having anything more to do'?

The plural 'these things' may refer to the details involved in killing the body [EGT, ICC], or to the different ways of killing the body [EGT, ICC, My]. It means 'after they have actually killed the body' [TH]. It is translated in the singular: 'after that' [NTC, WBC; CEV, GW, HCSB, KJV, NASB, NCV, NET, NIV, NRSV, REB], 'after this' [BECNT, Lns], 'afterward' [AB; TEV].

QUESTION—What is the important thing here that people cannot do after killing the body?

The cannot kill the soul [AB, MGC, NIBC, NIGTC, NTC], as in the parallel passage in Matt. 10:28 [AB, NIBC, NIGTC]. Killing the body is their absolute limit [Lns].

QUESTION—Who is the one they should fear?

They should fear God [AB, BECNT, Crd, Gdt, ICC, Lns, NAC, NIBC, NIC, NIGTC, NIVS, NTC, Su, TG, TH, TNTC, WBC; CEV, HCSB, NASB, NET, NLT, TEV]. The next verses about trusting in God's care implies that here it is fearing God's displeasure [Su]. The final authority for people is God, not Satan [NIGTC]. This fear means to be in awe of the majesty and holiness of God [NTC], and have a healthy respect, not a cringing dread [WBC]. Or, it is a terrifying fear of God's holy wrath [Lns].

QUESTION—Does the phrase 'fear the one who after the killing' mean that God is the one who kills the body?

1. Some translate the phrase so that the one who kills the body is not specified and it could mean that after the killing had taken place, God is the one who casts the person into hell [AB, BECNT, MGC; HCSB, NET, NIV]. The unspecified one could be God who kills the person, or it could simply mean that after a killing has taken place, God is the one who casts the person into hell [NET]. It refers to being killed by another human being [AB]. After a person has been killed, God will judge that person [BECNT, MGC].

2. Most translate so that it is God who both kills and casts into hell [Arn, Lns, NIGTC, NTC, Su, TG, TH, WBC; CEV, GW, KJV, NASB, NCV, NLT, NRSV, REB, TEV]. God has the authority and power to kill a person and also to throw that person into hell [Su, TG].

12:6 (Are) not five sparrows sold (for) two assarion[a]? And not one of them has-been forgotten[b] before God. 12:7 But[c] even the hairs of-your head have- all -been-counted. Do- not -be-afraid. You-are-more-valuable[d] (than) many[e] sparrows.

TEXT—In 12:7, instead of μὴ φοβεῖσθε 'do not be afraid', some manuscripts evidently read μὴ οὖν φοβεῖσθε 'therefore do not be afraid' although GNT does not mention this variant. Μὴ οὖν φοβεῖσθε 'therefore do not be afraid' is read by KJV.

LEXICON—a. ἀσσάριον (LN 6.77) (BAGD p. 117): 'assarion' [BAGD, BECNT, LN, WBC], 'as' [Lns], 'penny' [AB, Arn, LN; CEV, HCSB, NCV, NET, NIV, NLT, NRSV, TEV], 'cent' [BAGD, NTC; GW, NASB], 'pence' [REB], 'farthing' [KJV]. This was a Roman copper coin worth one-sixteenth of a denarius [AB, BAGD, BECNT, LN, MGC, NAC, NICNT, NIGTC, Su, WBC; NET]. It was worth about less than half an hour's wage for a common laborer [NET]. It was the smallest unit of money [TG].

b. perf. pass. participle of ἐπιλανθάνομαι (LN **29.17**) (BAGD 2. p. 295): 'to be forgotten, to be neglected, to be overlooked' [BAGD, LN]. The phrase 'has been forgotten before God' is translated 'is forgotten before God' [Arn; KJV, NASB, NET], 'has been forgotten in the sight of God' [Lns], 'is forgotten in God's sight' [AB, NTC; HCSB, NRSV], 'is forgotten by God' [BECNT, **LN**; NIV, TEV], 'is overlooked by God' [REB], 'has escaped God's notice' [WBC], 'God does not forget' [CEV, GW, NCV, NLT]. God remembers each one of them and he cares for them [TG]. The phrase ἐνώπιον τοῦ θεοῦ 'before God' implies that each bird is present to God's mind [AB, ICC].

c. ἀλλά (LN 89.125) (BAGD 3. p 38): 'but' [BAGD, LN]. The phrase ἀλλὰ καί 'but even' [Arn, BECNT; KJV, NCV, NRSV] is also translated 'but also' [BAGD], 'even' [CEV, GW, TEV], 'indeed' [HCSB, NASB, NIV], 'indeed, even' [AB, WBC], 'more than that, even' [REB], 'yea, even' [Lns], 'in fact' [NTC], 'in fact, even' [NET], 'and' [NLT].

d. pres. act. indic. of διαφέρω (LN 65.6) (BAGD 2.b. p. 190): 'to be more valuable than' [BAGD, LN; NASB, NET, NLT], 'to be of more value than' [BECNT, NTC; KJV, NRSV], 'to be worth more than' [Arn, BAGD, LN, WBC; GW, HCSB, NIV, REB], 'to be worth much more than' [CEV, NCV, TEV], 'to be worth far more than' [AB], 'to excel' [Lns]. See this word at 12:24.

e. πολύς (LN 59.1): 'many' [AB, Arn, BECNT, LN, Lns, WBC; all versions except NLT, REB], 'any number of' [NTC; REB], 'a whole flock of' [NLT]. The adjective 'many' should not be taken to mean that although they were more valuable than *many* sparrows, yet they were not more valuable than *all* sparrows [NTC]. The 'many' is in contrast with the 'one' in the previous verse [NIGTC].

QUESTION—What was the reason sparrows were sold?

Sparrows were small birds used as food [AB, Arn, BECNT, ICC, Lns, MGC, NAC, NIGTC, NIVS, NTC, WBC]. The noun refers to a sparrow [AB, Arn, BECNT, Lns, NTC, WBC; all versions], but it was sometimes used generically for any variety of small perching birds and songbirds [ICC, TH]. Actually, sparrows were not eaten and this refers to those small birds that were used for food [NIGTC]. These birds were caught and sold in the market to be killed, skinned, and roasted [NTC]. They were a cheap food for the poor [AB, BECNT, MGC, NAC, WBC]. They were considered to be delicacies [NTC]. The penny (assarion) coin was of little value and the birds were sold in the market two for a penny (Matt. 10:30). However, when someone bought two pennies' worth, an extra bird was thrown in for free so that the purchaser got five for two pennies [EGT, Su, TNTC]. The price is mentioned to indicate that sparrows were of very little value [TH]. Not even the one sparrow that is tossed in for free is forgotten by God [Su, TNTC].

QUESTION—What relationship is indicated by ἀλλὰ καί 'but even'?

It is used to intensify Jesus' point [BAGD, NTC]. The preceding clause is a settled matter and this conjunction forms a transition to something new or this is to be taken as ascensive 'and not only this, but also' [BAGD]. It means 'but little as you might expect it' [ICC]. The clause contrasts with the previous verse and also goes beyond it: 'but more than that, even…' [TH]. God is concerned not only with birds, he is concerned especially with people [BECNT]. This is a second example of the omniscience of God [NAC]. Now he turns to the hairs on their heads, something even smaller and more insignificant than the sparrows and this gives greater force to the argument that since God's providential care includes such small and insignificant things, how much more will he care for his own children [Lns].

QUESTION—What should the disciples learn from the fact that God has counted all the hairs of their heads?

God cares enough that he knows the smallest details about his people [NIGTC, TNTC].

QUESTION—How does the command that they were not to be afraid relate to the context?

The preceding verses in 12:4–5 emphasize the fact that the disciples needed to fear God but not men, while the present two verses offer them comfort by describing the extent of God's fatherly concern for them [NIGTC]. These verses give another reason why the disciples should not fear men [Lns]. If they are killed by men, it will not be without God's consent [Gdt]. The previous verse tells them to fear God because he controls the destiny of those who die and here they are told not to fear how God will care for them in this life [BECNT]. They are not to fear God's care over them [NET]. The lives of the disciples may have little value in the estimation of those who will persecute and kill them, but the disciples are to be encouraged by the fact that they are precious in God's estimation [NIBC]. The sparrows are bought and killed and people can be persecuted and killed, but none of this is apart from God's attention and care [NICNT].

DISCOURSE UNIT: 12:8–12 [CEV, HCSB, NCV, TEV]. The topic is telling others about Christ [CEV], acknowledging Christ [HCSB], confessing and rejecting Christ [TEV], don't be ashamed of Jesus [NCV].

12:8 **And I-say to-you, everyone who confesses**[a] **me before**[b] **men, also the Son of-Man**[c] **will-confess him before the angels of-God.** **12:9** **But the (one) having-denied**[d] **me before men will-be-denied before the angels of-God.**

LEXICON—a. aorist act. subj. of ὁμολογέω (LN 33.274) (BAGD 4. p. 568): 'to confess' [BAGD, LN], 'to acknowledge' [BAGD], 'to profess' [LN]. The phrase 'everyone who confesses me before men' [Arn, BECNT; NASB; similarly NTC; KJV] is also translated 'whoever shall confess me in front of men' [Lns], 'whoever acknowledges me before men' [NET, NIV; similarly AB, WBC; HCSB, NRSV, REB], 'every person who acknowledges him in front of others' [GW], 'if anyone acknowledges me publicly here on earth' [NLT], 'all those who stand before others and say they believe in me' [NCV], 'if you tell others that you belong to me' [CEV], 'those who declare publicly that they belong to me' [TEV]. It means to openly express one's allegiance to a person [LN]. Although 'before men' could be translated 'before people', 'men' is used because of the word play with 'the Son of Man' [NICNT; NET], and because of the contrast with angels [Lns; NET].

b. ἔμπροσθεν (LN 83.33) (BAGD 2.b. p. 257): 'before' [AB, Arn, BAGD, BECNT, LN, NTC, WBC; KJV, NASB, NCV, NET, NIV, NRSV, REB], 'in front of' [BAGD, LN, Lns; GW], 'in the presence of' [BAGD], not explicit [CEV, NLT, TEV]. 'Before men' emphasizes the fact that the confession is made publicly [Lns, NICNT, NIGTC, TG, TH; NLT, TEV], when faced with hostility [NICNT]. For the translation of the whole phrase see a. above.

c. υἱὸς τοῦ ἀνθρώπου 'Son of Man'. This title for Christ occurs at 5:24; 6:5, 22; 7:34; 9:22, 26, 44; 11:30; 12:8, 40; 17:22, 24, 26; 18:8, 31; 19:10; 21:27, 36; 22:22, 48, 69; 24:7. See the discussions of this title at 5:24, 6:5, and 9:22.

d. aorist mid. (deponent = act.) participle of ἀρνέομαι (LN **34.48**) (BAGD 3.a. p. 107): 'to deny' [BAGD, LN], 'to repudiate, to disown' [BAGD]. The phrase 'the one having denied me before men' is translated 'the one/he who denies me before men' [Arn, BECNT, NTC; NASB, NET; similarly HCSB, KJV], 'he that denied me in front of men' [Lns], 'whoever denies me before others' [NRSV], 'the one who denies me before people' [WBC], 'he who disowns me before men' [NIV], 'everyone who disowns me in the sight of men' [AB], 'whoever disowns me before others' [REB], 'those people who tell others that they don't know me' [GW], 'all who stand before others and say they do not believe in me' [NCV], 'if anyone denies me here on earth' [NLT], 'those who reject me publicly' [TEV], 'if you reject me' [CEV], 'whoever shows people that he does not know me' or 'whoever refuses to admit that he does know me' [**LN**].

QUESTION—What is involved in confessing Jesus before men?

Confessing Jesus is to tell what one knows to be the truth about Jesus, and here it presupposes that such a person really has faith in Jesus [Arn]. It means that the person believes that Jesus is the Messiah [ICC, NIC, NIVS], and acknowledges Jesus to be his Lord [Gdt, Su]. It means that the person openly proclaims that he is a follower of Christ [ICC, NIC, TG], and publicly acknowledges his faith and allegiance to Christ [TH; NCV]. This verb involves a public confession accompanied by a life of obedience to God [NAC].

QUESTION—Why did Jesus refer to himself as the Son of Man here?

The title Son of Man suggests Jesus' role in the final judgment [BECNT, NIBC, NIGTC]. The writers of the Gospels felt free to interchange the titles Son of Man, Christ, and Lord with the personal pronoun [NAC].

QUESTION—What is involved in Jesus confessing a person before God's angels?

Jesus will acknowledge that such disciples are his loyal followers [ICC, NAC, NIC, NIVS, Su; CEV], and that they belong to him [NCV, NTC]. When he confesses the disciples before the angels, it assumes that it is also done in the Father's presence [NIC, NTC]. The reference to angels is a circumlocution for 'God' [NAC]. Jesus will be at God's side before the angels who are witnesses to the confession [BECNT]. God's angels are members of the heavenly court [AB, NICNT, NIGTC, WBC], but it does not have to refer specifically to a court at judgment [WBC]. This will happen on the final Day of Judgment [AB, Arn, Lns, NIBC, NIC, TG, TH, TNTC; NET]. Or, it is not limited to the Day of Judgment and can be temporal as well [Su]. This occurs at judgment, either at death or the final Judgment Day [WBC].

QUESTION—What is involved in denying Jesus before men?

Denying Jesus is to state something about him that a person knows is not the truth [Arn]. It means to deny that Jesus is the Messiah [NIC], or the Lord [Su], or God [TNTC]. It means to deny one's allegiance to Jesus [TH], to deny that he is a follower of Jesus [NIC, TG, TNTC], and to repudiate Jesus' claims [TNTC]. Denial can be through a person's conduct that does not match his profession [Arn]. This is not a momentary denial like that of Peter's denial; instead, it refers to renouncing Jesus by either failing to decide for him or eventually totally renouncing him [NET].

DISCOURSE UNIT: 12:10–12 [AB]. The topic is the Holy Spirit.

12:10 **And everyone who will-say a-word^a against the Son of-Man, it-will-be-forgiven^b him. But the (one) having-blasphemed^c against the Holy Spirit will- not -be-forgiven.**

LEXICON—a. λόγος (LN 33.98) (BAGD 1.a.γ. p. 477): 'word' [BAGD, LN], 'statement' [BAGD]. The phrase 'everyone who will say a word against' [Arn, Lns] is also translated 'everyone/anyone who speaks a word against' [BECNT, NTC; HCSB, NASB, NET, NIV, NRSV, REB; similarly WBC; KJV, TEV], 'anyone who speaks against' [NCV; similarly NLT], 'anyone who will speak out against' [AB], 'who says something against' [GW], 'if you speak against' [CEV]. This refers to deliberately saying something that is hostile or disrespectful to Jesus [TG].

b. fut. pass. indic. ἀφίημι (LN 40.8) (BAGD 2. p. 126): 'to be forgiven' [BAGD, LN]. The phrase 'it will be forgiven him' [WBC; KJV, NASB] is also translated 'it shall be remitted' [Lns]. Instead of 'it' being the thing forgiven him, most translate with the person himself being forgiven: 'will be forgiven' [AB, Arn, BECNT, NTC; GW, HCSB, NET, NIV, NRSV, REB], 'can be forgiven' [CEV, NCV, TEV], 'may be forgiven' [NLT]. The future tense refers to the time of the final day of judgment [NIGTC, TG, TH], or it is merely predictive of the future [Lns]. The passive voice implies that God is the one who forgives [AB, Lns, NAC, TG, TH]. Of course, such forgiveness is conditioned on repentance [Lns, NAC, NIGTC, NTC, TNTC; probably CEV, NCV, NLT, TEV].

c. aorist act. participle of βλασφημέω (LN 33.400) (BAGD 2.b.γ. p. 142): 'to blaspheme' [BAGD, LN], 'to defame, to revile' [LN]. The phrase 'the one having blasphemed against' is translated 'the one who blasphemes against' [NTC, WBC; HCSB, KJV, NASB, NET, NIV], 'whoever blasphemes against' [NRSV], 'he who blasphemed against' [Lns], 'anyone who speaks blasphemies against' [NLT], 'he who blasphemes' [Arn, BECNT], 'the person who dishonors' [GW], 'him who slanders' [REB], 'anyone who reviles' [AB], 'whoever says evil things against' [TEV], 'anyone who speaks against' [NCV], 'if you speak against' [CEV].

QUESTION—What is meant by saying a word against the Son of Man and why could this sin be forgiven?
   It means to deliberately say something hostile or disrespectful about Jesus [TG]. An example is saying that Jesus broke the Sabbath laws, or that Jesus was leading people astray when he ignored traditional regulations [Su]. It is an act of an unbeliever who speaks in ignorance about who Jesus is [Arn, NAC]. A person who rejects Jesus in his state of humiliation could be forgiven since Jesus' glory as the Son of God had not yet been clearly manifested [NIC]. This refers to the Jews' rejection of Jesus before the resurrection [MGC, NIBC]. Blasphemy against Jesus is an instant rejection that may later be repented of [BECNT]. The person who does not yet believe in Jesus may later believe and be forgiven and saved [WBC]. Jesus brought up this example of forgiveness to show the greatness of the sin of blasphemy against the Holy Spirit [EGT, Gdt].
QUESTION—What is meant by blaspheming the Holy Spirit and why can it not be forgiven?
   The blasphemy against the Holy Spirit is attributing the works of the Holy Spirit to Satan [Gdt, Rb, Su]. An act of blasphemy against the Holy Spirit is recorded in 11:15 where some said that Jesus was casting out demons by the power of Beelzebul instead of by the power of God's Spirit [Gdt, ICC, Lns, NIVS, NTC, Su]. It can be done through actions that oppose the Spirit as well as by words [AB, ICC, NAC]. Rather than by words, one blasphemes against the Spirit by denying or rejecting the manifest saving intervention of God and this rejection is the set of one's life, not just a few words spoken on one occasion [TNTC]. It is an obstinate rejection of the testimony that the Spirit gives to Jesus and his message [NET]. It is rejecting the Holy Spirit speaking through the apostles as described in 12:11–12 [Crd, EGT, NIGTC]. Blasphemy against the Spirit is a fixed rejection of the Spirit's testimony about God's work through Jesus [BECNT]. Blasphemy against the Spirit refers to the Jews' persistent rejection of the post-resurrection preaching of the disciples who were empowered by the Holy Spirit [MGC, NIBC, NIC]. The Holy Spirit brings about repentance and those who are so hardened that they blaspheme the Spirit reject the Spirit and his work [Lns, NTC]. A few commentators refer this to apostasy [Arn, NICNT, WBC]. The person who repudiates his experience of salvation, which was brought about by the Spirit, is not able to be forgiven for his apostasy [WBC]. Blasphemy against the Spirit refers to apostasy in the face of persecution [NICNT].

12:11 And when they-bring[a] you before the synagogues and the rulers and the authorities, do- not -worry-about[b] how or what you-should-defend-yourself[c] or what you-should-say.
   LEXICON—a. pres. act. subj. of εἰσφέρω (LN 15.194) (BAGD 1. p. 233): 'to bring' [BAGD, BECNT, Lns, NTC, WBC; HCSB, KJV, NASB, NET, NRSV], 'to take' [Arn], 'to bring to trial' [CEV], 'to bring to be tried' [TEV], 'to drag in' [BAGD], 'to hale' [AB]. This active verb is also

translated passively, thus avoiding the indefinite 'they': 'to be put on trial' [GW], 'to be brought' [NCV, NIV, REB], 'to be brought to trial' [NLT]. The authorities were the ones who would take them to court [TG].

b. aorist act. subj. of μεριμνάω (LN 25.225) (BAGD 1. p. 505): 'to worry about' [AB, BAGD, LN, NTC; all versions except KJV, TEV], 'to worry' [Arn], 'to be worried about' [WBC; TEV], 'to be anxious about' [BAGD, BECNT, LN], 'to be distracted' [Lns], 'to take thought' [KJV]. They might have doubts about the course they should pursue [Arn]. See this word at 10:41; 12:22, 25, 26.

c. aorist mid. (deponent = act.) subj. of ἀπολογέομαι (LN 33.345) (BAGD p. 95): 'to defend oneself' [BAGD, LN, NTC; CEV, GW, HCSB, NCV, NIV, NRSV, TEV], 'to make one's defense' [AB, Lns, WBC; NET], 'to conduct one's defense' [REB], 'to speak in one's defense' [Arn; NASB], 'to say in one's defense' [NLT], 'to answer' [BAGD; KJV], 'to reply' [BECNT]. This is an oral defense in a court setting [TG].

QUESTION—How is this verse related to the preceding ones?

This is an example of the worst situation that the disciples could be in [Lns], yet even so, they should not be afraid of committing the sin of blasphemy against the Holy Spirit [ICC], of the sin of hypocrisy and fear of people [Lns], of denying that they are followers of Jesus [NIC]. They should not be afraid because the Holy Spirit himself will direct them as to what they say [ICC, NIC, Su].

QUESTION—What are the distinctions between τὰς συναγωγάς 'the synagogues', τὰς ἀρχάς 'the rulers', and τὰς ἐξουσίας 'the authorities'?

The word συναγωγάς 'synagogues' refers to the many local Jewish courts held in synagogues [Gdt, ICC, Lns, NIGTC, Su, TG, TH, TNTC]. Here 'before the synagogue' refers to the council assembled in the synagogue [TH]. Most translate this as a location and the one preposition ἐπί 'before' that governs all three of the nouns is translated to reflect the difference between a place and the people: 'in' [CEV, GW, NLT, TEV] or 'into' [AB, Arn; NCV] *synagogues*, and 'before' [AB, Arn; CEV, NCV, NLT, TEV] or 'in front of' [GW] *rulers, and authorities*. Synagogue courts were the lowest Jewish courts [Su] and were responsible for maintaining discipline [ICC, NIGTC]. The courts consisted of twenty-three elders to try cases [Lns] and these courts had authority to excommunicate from the synagogue [Arn, ICC], or to administer a physical punishment of scourging with rods [Arn, Lns, Su]. The words ἀρχάς 'rulers' and ἐξουσίας 'authorities' are generic terms for those who exercised rule [Lns] and they refer to Gentile civil authorities [AB, BECNT, EGT, Gdt, MGC, TG; NET], or to Gentile courts [NAC, NIGTC]. Or, the two terms could refer to both Jews and Gentiles [ICC, NTC, Su, TNTC]. These terms refer to courts higher than the local synagogue [Su]. The Sanhedrin would be included in these terms [Arn]. There is little or no difference between the two terms for authorities in this context [TG, TH] and they are not being used to designate two kinds of authorities [TG]. They were leaders and other powerful people [NCV], the magistrates and other authorities in Roman administration [WBC]. They had the power to decree severer punishments than the synagogue courts [Lns].

QUESTION—What are the distinctions between πῶς 'how' and τί 'what' they should defend themselves and how is this connected with the following clause ἢ τί εἴπητε 'or what you should say'?

How they are to defend themselves concerns the method of their defense [BNTC, Lns, NTC, Su, TH; GW]. It concerns the general form of a speech [Gdt, ICC, NIGTC]. *What* they are to defend themselves concerns the content of their defense [Gdt, ICC, Lns, NIGTC, Su, TH]. The second *what* clause 'or what you should say' is redundant [NIGTC; NET]. Or, it is different in that the first clause concerns their defense in court and the second clause refers to bearing their testimony and preaching the gospel at the trial [Gdt]. The two 'what' clauses are treated differently in the translations.

1. Some keep the two 'what' phrases separate as in the Greek [Arn, Lns, WBC; KJV, NASB]: do not worry about how or *what* you should speak in defense or *what* you should say.
2. Some combine the two 'what' phrases and puts them in the last clause [AB, NTC; CEV, GW, HCSB, NCV, NET, NIV, NRSV, REB, TEV]: do not worry about how you should defend yourselves or about *what* you should say.
3. One combines the two 'what' phrases and put them in the first clause [BECNT]: do not worry about how or *what* you reply or say.
4. One combines everything [NLT]: do not worry about what to say in your defense.

12:12 Because the Holy Spirit will-teach[a] you in the same hour what is-necessary[b] to-say.

LEXICON—a. fut. act. indic. of διδάσκω (LN 33.224): 'to teach' [AB, Arn, BECNT, LN, Lns, NTC, WBC; all versions except CEV, REB], 'to instruct' [REB], 'to tell' [CEV]. This describes the Spirit's verbal inspiration when it was needed [Lns, NIGTC]. The Spirit will illumine their minds and sharpen their power of speech [NTC], and enable them to speak of their faith in Christ [MGC].

b. pres. act. indic. of δεῖ (LN **71.21**) (BAGD 5. p. 172): 'is necessary' [BAGD, BECNT, Lns, WBC], 'should' [**LN**, NTC; NIV, TEV], 'ought' [LN; KJV, NASB, NRSV], 'must' [AB, BAGD; GW, HCSB, NCV, NET], 'have to' [Arn], 'needs to be said' [NLT], not explicit [CEV, REB].

QUESTION—What kinds of words would it be necessary to say?

The Spirit would teach them to fit their defense to whatever charges were brought forward [Su]. Their reply will be adequate to prevent any counter response by their opponents [BECNT]. This does not mean that they will always escape punishment [Lns, TNTC], but they will not dishonor Christ by any confusion, mistakes, ignorance, or other handicaps [Lns]. They will be taught that confession of Christ has priority over self-defense [WBC]. This is not a promise to pastors and teachers in their ministry but to Christians facing martyrdom [NAC].

DISCOURSE UNIT: 12:13-34 [NICNT; NASB]. The topic is faithfulness concerning possessions [NICNT], covetousness denounced [NASB].

DISCOURSE UNIT: 12:13-21 [BECNT, NAC, NIGTC, Su, TNTC, WBC; CEV, GW, HCSB, NCV, NET, NIV, NLT, NRSV, TEV]. The topic is a rich fool [CEV], the parable of the rich fool [BECNT, NAC, NIGTC, TNTC; HCSB, NIV, NLT, NRSV, TEV], the parable of the rich landowner [NET], a story about material possessions [GW], the folly of preoccupation with possessions [WBC], a warning against greed [Su], Jesus warns against selfishness [NCV].

DISCOURSE UNIT: 12:13-15 [AB]. The topic is a warning against greed.

12:13 And someone from the crowd said to-him, Teacher, tell my brother to-divide^a the inheritance^b with me.

LEXICON—a. aorist mid. infin. of μερίζω (LN **63.23**) (BAGD 1.b. p. 504): 'to divide' [Arn, BAGD, BECNT, **LN**, Lns, WBC; all versions except CEV, GW], 'to share' [AB, BAGD, NTC], 'to give someone his share' [CEV, GW].

   b. κληρονομία (LN 57.40) (BAGD 1. p. 435): 'inheritance' [BAGD, LN]. The phrase 'the inheritance' [Arn, BECNT, Lns, NTC, WBC; HCSB, KJV, NET, NIV] is also translated 'the family inheritance' [AB; NASB, NRSV], 'the family property' [REB], 'the inheritance that our father left us' [GW], 'the property our father left us' [NCV, TEV], 'our father's estate' [NLT], 'what our father left us when he died' [CEV].

QUESTION—What was the problem about the inheritance?

   According to Jewish law in Deut. 21:17, the division would be two-thirds of the inheritance to the elder son and one-third to the younger son [EGT, NIVS, TG]. The man who addressed Jesus was the younger brother [Arn, Gdt, NICNT, NIGTC, TG]. This man felt that an injustice was being done concerning the inheritance and wanted Jesus to rule against his brother [ICC, NIC, TNTC], but there is no indication that the brother wanted arbitration [ICC, TNTC]. Probably the brother was also present [NIC]. Probably the heirs were expected to live together in order to keep the land intact [MGC, NIGTC] and the younger brother wanted to get his share and be independent [NIGTC]. The elder brother probably had refused to give his younger brother the share that he should receive [Arn, BECNT, NIGTC, WBC]. It is not clear whether the brother was keeping the entire inheritance for himself or was preventing the younger brother from using the share that should come to him [Lns].

12:14 And he-said to-him, Man,^{a} who appointed me a-judge^b or arbitrator^c over you (plural)?

TEXT—Instead of κριτὴν ἢ μεριστήν 'judge or arbitrator', some manuscripts read δικαστὴν ἢ μεριστήν 'judge or arbitrator', some manuscripts read ἄρχοντα καὶ δικαστήν 'ruler and judge', some manuscripts read κριτήν 'judge', and some manuscripts read μεριστήν 'arbitrator'. GNT reads κριτὴν ἢ μεριστήν 'judge or arbitrator' with a B decision, indicating that the text is almost certain.

LEXICON—a. ἄνθρωπος (LN 9.24) (BAGD 1.a.γ. p. 68): 'man' [Arn, BAGD, BECNT, LN, Lns, NTC, WBC; KJV, NASB, NET, NIV], 'sir' [AB], 'friend' [HCSB, NLT, NRSV, TEV], not explicit [CEV, GW, NCV, REB]. This was a form of address that was fitting for strangers and was neither hostile nor especially friendly [TG]. Jesus used this term gently in 5:20, but here it is spoken harshly and implied disapproval [AB, Alf, Arn, Bai, BECNT, EGT, ICC, My, NIC, NICNT, TH, TNTC; NET].

b. κριτής (LN 56.28) (BAGD 1.a.α. p. 453): 'judge' [AB, Arn, BAGD, BECNT, LN, Lns, NTC, WBC; GW, HCSB, KJV, NASB, NET, NIV, NLT, NRSV]. This noun is also translated as a verb: 'to judge' [NCV, REB, TEV]. The question 'who appointed me a judge or arbitrator over you?' is translated 'who gave me the right to settle arguments between you and your brother?' [CEV].

c. μεριστής (LN **63.25**) (BAGD p. 505): 'arbitrator' [BAGD, NTC; HCSB, NASB, NRSV], 'arbiter' [AB], 'divider' [Arn, BAGD, **LN**, Lns, WBC; KJV]. The phrase 'arbitrator over you' is translated 'an arbiter between you' [BECNT; NIV], 'an arbitrator between you two' [NET], '(set me over you) to arbitrate' [REB], 'to decide between you' [NCV], 'to decide such things as that' [NLT], 'to divide your inheritance' [GW], 'to divide the property between you two' [TEV].

QUESTION—What is meant by Jesus' question, 'Who appointed me?'

It is a rhetorical question that indicates no one had appointed him to be the brothers' judge or arbitrator [BECNT, Gdt, TG, TH]. There were already Jewish judges appointed for property disputes and Jesus did not have that kind of appointment [ICC, Lns]. This point is not Jesus' legal standing but that Jesus had not come to deal with what were trivial problems in light of his ministry [MGC, NAC, NIBC, Su, TNTC].

QUESTION—What is the difference between κριτής 'judge' and μεριστής 'arbitrator'?

1. They are two different functions [EGT, Gdt]. A judge decided a case and an arbitrator carried out the judgment [EGT, Gdt].
2. The two terms refer to the same function in this instance [ICC, TG, TH]. A judge who decides concerning a partition is an arbitrator [ICC, WBC]. It can be translated 'who appointed me to decide about the division?' [TH], 'no one has made me a judge with the authority to divide the property between you and your brother' [TG].

QUESTION—Who are the referents Jesus addressed with the plural 'you'?

1. They are the two brothers [TG; CEV, GW, NET, NIV, TEV].
2. They are all those in the crowd [Bai]. It seems that Jesus is addressing the question not only to the two brothers, but to the whole crowd, and he is

telling them that he will not be the judge or arbitrator for any of them [Bai].

12:15 **And he-said to them, Watch-out^a and keep^b from all greediness,^c because not in the abounding^d to-anyone is his life, (not) from his possessions.**

TEXT—Instead of πάσης πλεονεξίας 'all greediness', some manuscripts read τῆς πλεονεξίας 'greediness', although GNT does not mention this variant. Τῆς πλεονεξίας 'greediness, covetousness' is read by KJV.

LEXICON—a. pres. act. impera. of ὁράω (LN 30.45) (BAGD 2.b. p. 578): 'to watch out' [BECNT, NTC, WBC; HCSB, NET, NIV, TEV], 'to be watchful' [Arn], 'to be on one's guard' [BAGD], 'to pay attention' [LN], 'to see to it' [Lns], 'to be careful' [GW, NCV], 'to take care' [AB; NRSV], 'to take heed' [KJV], 'to beware' [NASB, NLT, REB]. The phrase 'watch out and keep from' is translated 'don't (be greedy)' [CEV].

b. pres. mid. impera. of φυλάσσομαι, φυλάσσω (LN **13.154**) (BAGD 2.a. p. 868): 'to keep from' [**LN**], 'to avoid' [BAGD, LN], 'to be careful not to' [LN], 'to be on guard against' [AB, BAGD, BECNT, NTC, WBC; HCSB, NASB, NIV, NRSV, REB], 'to guard against' [Arn, Lns; NCV, NET], 'to guard from' [GW, TEV], 'to look out for' [BAGD], 'to beware of' [KJV]. The phrase 'keep from all greediness' is translated 'don't be greedy' [NLT].

c. πλεονεξία (LN 25.22) (BAGD p. 667): 'greediness' [BAGD], 'greed' [LN], 'covetousness' [Arn, BAGD, LN; KJV], 'avarice' [BAGD, LN]. The phrase πάσης πλεονεξίας 'all greediness' is translated 'all greed' [HCSB], 'all covetousness' [Lns], 'all kinds/types/forms of greed' [BECNT; NCV, NET, NIV, NRSV], 'every kind/form of greed' [AB, WBC; GW, NASB, TEV], 'greed of every kind' [REB], '(don't) be greedy' [CEV], '(don't) be greedy for what you don't have' [NLT]. Greed is a strong desire to possess more [AB, Arn, BAGD, BECNT, Gdt, ICC, Rb, Su, TG], more than needed [AB], more than what is right and appropriate [Arn, Su]. It is the desire to get more without reference to one's needs or to the situation of others [WBC]. It is a lust for more and more that is never satisfied and accumulating wealth becomes the focus of the person's whole life [NAC]. Jesus warned against all kinds of greed [Alf, NIGTC] because the kind of greed exhibited by the brother is not the only kind or even the worst [Alf]. Or, since greed is a great desire to possess things, 'all greed' means having a great desire for anything and everything [TG].

d. pres. act. infin. of περισσεύω (LN 59.52) (BAGD 1.a.β. p. 650): 'to abound' [LN], 'to be in abundance' [BAGD, LN]. This difficult clause 'not in the abounding to anyone is his life, (not) from his possessions' is translated 'when there is abundance for someone, his life is not due to his possessions' [Lns], 'it is not through abundance that a man's possessions sustain his life' [Arn], 'it is not in the abundance for someone of his possessions that his life consists' [WBC], 'a man's life does not consist in the abundance of his possessions' [NIV; similarly KJV, NET, NRSV], 'not even when one has an abundance does his life consist of his possessions' [NASB], 'even when someone has more than enough, his possessions do not give him life' [REB], 'life is not about having a lot of material possessions' [GW], 'one's life does not depend upon one's belongings, even when they are more than sufficient' [AB], 'one's life is not from the abundance of his possessions' [BECNT], 'one's life is not in the abundance of his possessions' [HCSB], 'life is not measured by how much one owns' [NCV], 'owning a lot of things won't make your life safe' [CEV], 'your true life is not made up of the things you own, no matter how rich you may be' [TEV], 'real life is not measured by how much we own' [NLT].

QUESTION—Who is Jesus speaking to now?
1. Jesus now spoke to all those present in the crowd [AB, Alf, Bai, BECNT, ICC, Lns, MGC, My, NIGTC, Su, TH, WBC; CEV, GW]. Jesus knew that greed was at the root of the brother's request and so he took this opportunity to warn the crowd about greed [Alf, ICC].
2. Jesus continued speaking to the two brothers [NIC].

QUESTION—What is meant by a person's ζωή 'life'?
It is an existence that is humanly meaningful [MGC, NIGTC, Su] and satisfying [WBC]. Greed can cause a person to be concerned about the wrong things in life and ignore the really important thing, being rich towards God [NIGTC]. Life is a metaphor for salvation [NICNT].

DISCOURSE UNIT: 12:16–21 [AB]. The topic is the parable of the rich fool.

12:16 **And he-spoke a-parable**[a] **to them, saying, The farm of-a-certain rich man produced-a-good-crop.**[b] **12:17** **And he-was-thinking within himself saying, What should-I-do, because I-do- not -have (a place) where I-will-store**[c] **my crops**[d]**?**

LEXICON—a. παραβολή (LN 33.15) (BAGD 2. p. 612): 'parable'. See translations of this word at 5:36.
  b. aorist act. indic. of εὐφορέω (LN **23.204**) (BAGD p. 327): 'to produce a good crop' [NIV], 'to produce a good harvest' [LN], 'to bear good crops' [BAGD; TEV], 'to produce good/fine crops' [GW, NLT], 'to produce a big crop' [CEV], 'to produce an abundant crop' [NET], 'to produce abundant crops' [AB], 'to produce a bountiful crop' [WBC], 'to produce bumper crops' [NTC], 'to grow a good crop' [NCV], 'to yield a good harvest' [REB], 'to yield plenty of fruit' [**LN**], 'to bear well' [Lns], 'to be fruitful' [BAGD], 'to be very productive' [BECNT; HCSB, NASB], 'to produce abundantly' [NRSV], 'to bring forth plentifully' [KJV], 'to have borne well' [Arn].
  c. fut. act. indic. of συνάγω (LN **85.48**) (BAGD 1. p. 782): 'to store' [AB, Arn, BECNT, **LN**, NTC; CEV, GW, HCSB, NASB, NET, NIV, NRSV, REB], 'to gather' [BAGD], 'to gather together' [Lns, WBC], 'to keep in a

place' [LN], 'to keep' [NCV, TEV], 'to bestow' [KJV]. Verse 17 is translated: 'In fact, his barns were full to overflowing' [NLT].
  d. καρπός (LN 3.33) (BAGD 1.a. p. 404): 'crop' [Arn, BAGD, LN, Lns, NTC, WBC; GW, HCSB, NASB, NCV, NET, NIV, NRSV, TEV], 'harvest' [LN], 'yield' [BECNT], 'produce' [AB; REB], 'grain' [LN], 'fruit' [LN; KJV], 'everything' [CEV], not explicit [NLT].
QUESTION—What relationship is indicated by ὅτι 'because'?
  This indicates that the reason he was asking himself about what he should do to store his crop was that he didn't have a place to store it all [AB, BECNT, Lns, MGC, NIGTC].

12:18 And he-said, This I-will-do, I-will-tear-down my barns[a] and I-will-build larger (ones) and there I-will-store all the grain and my goods.[b] 12:19 And I-will-say to-my soul,[c] Soul, you-have many goods stored-up for many years. Rest,[d] eat, drink, be merry.[e]

TEXT—In 12:18, instead of τὸν σῖτον 'the grain', some manuscripts read τὰ γενήματά μου 'my produce'. GNT does not mention this variant. Τὰ γενήματά μου 'my produce' is read by KJV.
LEXICON—a. ἀποθήκη (LN7.25) (BAGD p. 91): 'barn' [AB, BAGD, BECNT, LN, NTC, WBC; all versions], 'storehouse' [BAGD, LN, Lns], 'granary' [Arn]. His barns were warehouses to store things [AB, TG], or they were sheds or bins [TG].
  b. ἀγαθός (LN 57.33) (BAGD 2.b.b. p. 3): 'good' [AB, BAGD, LN]. The plural substantive τὰ ἀγαθά 'the goods' is translated 'goods' [Arn, BAGD, BECNT, LN, NTC; GW, HCSB, KJV, NASB, NET, NIV, NRSV], 'other goods' [AB; CEV, NCV, REB, TEV], 'good things' [Lns, WBC], 'possessions' [LN]. The phrase 'all the grain and my goods' is translated 'everything' [NLT]. The grain would be wheat or barley and his goods would be the moveable things he owned. However, in the next verse, the word 'goods' includes all of his grain [TH]. The other things would be other than farm produce [AB, NAC], the things that belong to a wealthy farm [Lns]. Or, this probably does not cover more than 'the good crop' mentioned in 12:16 and does not include the other things the farmer owned [WBC].
  c. ψυχή (LN 26.4) (BAGD 1.b.a. p. 893): 'soul, inner life' [BAGD], 'inner self, mind, being' [LN]. The soul is the immaterial part of a person which animates his body [Lns]. It means the whole person [Bai, Hlt]. 'Soul' is used as a synecdoche for his whole self and it is a Semitic substitute for 'myself' [AB]. It is the self, but with reference to the life-force giving life to the body [WBC]. However, in 12:20 the word means the 'life' that can be taken away from this man [TH]. The phrase 'I will say to my soul, Soul' [Arn, BECNT, Lns, NTC, WBC; KJV, NASB, NRSV] is also translated 'I will say to myself' [CEV, GW, HCSB, NET, NIV, REB], 'I can say to myself' [NCV], 'I will say to myself, Friend' [AB], 'I'll sit

back and say to myself, My friend' [NLT], 'I will say to myself, Lucky man!' [TEV].
   d. pres. mid. impera. of ἀναπαύομαι, ἀναπαύω (LN 23.80) (BAGD 2. p. 59): 'to rest' [BAGD, LN], 'to take one's ease' [BAGD]. The imperative is translated 'rest' [NCV], 'take your rest' [Arn, WBC], 'continue to rest' [Lns], 'relax' [NET, NRSV], 'take your ease' [BECNT; KJV, NASB], 'take it easy' [AB, NTC; HCSB], 'take life easy' [GW, NIV, REB, TEV], 'live it up' [CEV]. A person takes it easy after eating well [AB].
   e. pres. pass. impera. of εὐφραίνω (LN 25.131) (BAGD 2. p. 327): 'to be merry, to enjoy oneself' [BAGD], 'to be glad' [BAGD, LN], 'to be happy, to be cheered up' [LN]. The imperative is translated 'be merry' [AB, BECNT, WBC; KJV, NASB, NIV, NRSV], 'be of good cheer' [Arn], 'continue to be of good cheer' [Lns], 'enjoy life' [NCV], 'enjoy yourself' [CEV, GW, HCSB, REB, TEV], 'have a good time' [NTC], 'celebrate' [NET]. See this word at 15:23, 24, 29, 32; 16:19.

QUESTION—Why would the rich man want to tear down his barns in order to build new ones?

Instead of building additional barns to what he already had, he planned to tear down the old barns to make room for larger ones and thus retain all the present agricultural land for his crops [NICNT]. He didn't plan to destroy the materials that were used in his old barns, rather he would dismantle the barns and use the material in the new barns [TG, TH]. The parable ignores the problem of where the farmer would store his crops and goods while he was replacing the barns [Hlt].

QUESTION—Why did he tell his soul to eat, drink, and be merry?

The three verbs symbolize carefree and luxurious living [AB], leisure and self-indulgence, the product of greed [BECNT]. To eat and drink in the context of 'be merry' means to feast [TH]. These words were already a traditional saying [NIGTC]. This man was selfish and thought only of his own enjoyment [Arn].

12:20 **And God said to-him, Foolish (one), this night they-demand-back^a your soul from you. Now what you-prepared^b to-whom will-it-be?**

LEXICON—a. pres. act. indic. of ἀπαιτέω (LN 33.165) (BAGD 1. p. 80): 'to demand back, to ask back' [BAGD], 'to ask back' [LN]. The phrase 'they demand back your soul from you' is translated 'thy soul they are demanding from thee' [Lns], 'your soul is being demanded of you' [NTC], 'your soul is being demanded of you' [NTC], 'your life is being demanded of you' [NRSV; similarly AB; HCSB], 'your life will be demanded from you' [NIV], 'your life will be demanded back from you' [NET], 'your life will be taken from you' [NCV], 'your soul is required of you' [BECNT; KJV, NASB], 'you will be required to give up your soul' [Arn], 'you will be asked to give back your soul' [WBC], 'you must surrender your life' [REB], 'you will have to give up your life' [TEV], 'I will demand your life from you' [GW], 'you will die' [CEV, NLT]. The present tense indicates the imminence of the action [Lns, TH], the immediate future [Gdt].

b. aorist act. indic. of ἑτοιμάζω (LN 77.3) (BAGD 1. p. 316): 'to prepare' [BAGD, LN], 'to make ready' [LN]. The clause 'what you prepared to whom will it be' is translated 'who will get all that you have prepared?' [AB], 'who will get what you've accumulated?' [GW], 'the things you have prepared, whose will they be?' [BECNT; HCSB, NRSV; similarly WBC], 'the things you have prepared for yourself, whose shall they be?' [NTC], 'who will get what you have prepared for yourself?' [NET, NIV], 'who will get those things you have prepared for yourself?' [NCV], 'who will be the owner of what you have prepared?' [Arn], 'who will own what you have prepared' [NASB], 'who will get what you have stored up?' [CEV], 'whose shall those things be which thou hast provided?' [KJV], 'the money you have made, who will get it now?' [REB], 'who will get all these things you have kept for yourself?' [TEV], 'who will get it all?' [NLT]. This refers to the man's harvest and wealth [Lns]. See this word at 12:47.

QUESTION—How and when did God speak to the man?

God spoke in a dream [AB], or within his conscience [EGT]. Or, in this story God directly spoke to the man [Alf, NIGTC]. Since this is a parable, one need not ask how he spoke to the man [ICC].

1. God immediately spoke after the man's thoughts of 12:18–19 [AB, Lns, NAC, NIC, TH]. 'What you prepared' refers to the man's wealth and the ripening harvest for which he was making plans to build larger barns [Lns]. His plans would never be realized [AB]. If God spoke to him that day, 'this night' refers to the coming night [TH].

2. From the aorist tense of 'what you prepared', we are to understand that God spoke to him after his plans in 12:18 had been carried out and the new barns were built [Bai, NIGTC].

QUESTION—Why was this man a fool?

The rich man did not include God in his plans [Hlt, NICNT, NIGTC, WBC]. He thought that the future was in his control [Su]. He thought he was in control of everything and had no need of God [NTC, Pnt]. It was senseless to think that he could nourish his soul on food alone [Su]. He had no thought for those who were in need [NIGTC].

QUESTION—Who will demand the man's soul in the phrase τὴν ψυχήν σου ἀπαιτοῦσιν ἀπὸ σοῦ 'they demand back your soul from you'?

1. The subject 'they' is an indefinite pronoun [Arn, Gdt], an impersonal plural pronoun [Crd, ICC, Rb, WBC]. The phrase is equivalent to the passive voice [AB, Arn, Crd, NTC, WBC; KJV, NASB, NCV, NET, NIV]: your soul will be demanded back. Some translate with the rich man as subject [CEV, NLT, REB, TEV]: you will die.

2. This acts as a passive verb that implies that God is the actor [Bai, BECNT, BNTC, MGC, NAC, NIC, NTC, Rb, TG, TH, TNTC; GW]: I,

God, will demand your soul from you. The impersonal plural form is a special use of the plural that indicates that the actor is God without mentioning his name [TG, TH]. God requires his soul by means of death [NIC]. The man's soul was loaned to the man and God, the owner, wants the loan returned [Bai].
3. Since God is the speaker, the word 'they' implies that angels were the actors [Alf, Lns, NIGTC]: the angels will demand your soul from you. The plural form 'angels', is a way of referring to the angel of death [NIGTC].

QUESTION—What is meant by the verb ἀπαιτέω 'to demand back'?
1. It means to ask for something to be returned [LN (33.136)] and this gives the picture of one's life being a loan [BAGD (p. 80), Bai, Lns, NICNT, NIGTC; NET]. This is the meaning of the verb at 6:35. Only a few translations make the idea of a loan explicit [WBC; NET]. A person's life force, which gives one the power to act, is a trust from God and God may ask that it be returned at any time [WBC]. He was a disobedient debtor [Lns]. His life was a loan from God and he must account for God's will in his actions [NICNT].
2. There is no indication that one's life is being taken back [BECNT, Lns, NTC; all versions except NET].

QUESTION—What is meant by the question 'what you prepared to whom will it be?'

This is a rhetorical question [AB]. It will not be the man, but the heirs who would be dividing up the things he had heaped up [NTC]. He doesn't know who will win the power struggle to get what he left behind [Bai]. The point is that his possessions were totally lost to him [Arn, MGC]. The one person who will not own them is that man who pursued possessions [BECNT, EGT, MGC]. When a person dies, the goods that he had stored up are of no help to him [NIGTC].

12:21 Thus[a] (it is with) the (one) storing-up-treasure[b] for-himself and not being-rich[c] toward God.

TEXT—Some manuscripts omit this verse, and some manuscripts include this verse and add ταῦτα λέγων ἐφώνει, Ὁ ἔχων ὦτα ἀκούειν ἀκουέτω 'saying these things he cried, The one having ears to hear, let him hear'. GNT includes this verse without the addition with an A decision, indicating that the text is certain.

LEXICON—a. οὕτως (LN 61.9) (BAGD 1.b. p. 597): 'thus' [Arn, BAGD, LN], 'so' [BAGD, LN], 'in this way' [LN], 'in this manner' [BAGD], 'so is' [KJV, NASB], 'so it is with' [WBC; NET, NRSV], 'so it will be with' [AB], 'so it is for' [BECNT], 'so it goes with' [NTC], 'this is what happens to' [CEV], 'that's how it is when' [GW], 'that is how it is with' [HCSB, REB], 'this is how it will be for' [NCV], 'this is how it will be with' [NIV], 'yes' [NLT], 'and Jesus concluded, This is how it is with' [TEV].

b. pres. act. participle of θησαυρίζω (LN 65.11) (BAGD 1. p. 361): 'to store up treasure' [BAGD, WBC; HCSB, NASB, NRSV], 'to accumulate treasure' [BECNT], 'to gather treasure' [Arn], 'to store up riches' [NET], 'to lay up treasure' [KJV], 'to pile up treasure' [AB; REB], 'to pile up riches' [TEV], 'to hoard up riches' [NTC], 'to treasure material possessions' [GW], 'to store up earthly wealth' [NLT], 'to store up things' [NCV, NIV], 'to store up everything' [CEV].

c. pres. act. participle of πλουτέω (LN 57.25) (BAGD 2. p. 674): 'to be rich' [BAGD, LN]. The phrase καὶ μὴ εἰς θεὸν πλουτῶν 'and not being rich toward God' is translated 'and is/are not rich toward God' [BECNT; HCSB, KJV, NASB, NCV], 'but is/are not rich toward God' [NET, NIV, NRSV], 'but is not rich with God' [AB], 'and does not become rich with God in view' [WBC], 'but is not rich in God's sight' [NTC], 'but are not rich in God's sight' [TEV], 'but are poor in the sight of God' [CEV], 'and remains a pauper in the sight of God' [REB], 'and his riches don't serve God' [GW], 'but not have a rich relationship with God' [NLT], 'and is not rich in his relations to God' [Arn].

QUESTION—What relationship is indicated by οὕτως 'thus'?

It indicates a comparison [AB, BECNT, NTC, WBC; KJV, NASB, NET, NRSV]: what happened to that rich man is like what happens to a person who stores up treasures for himself. It introduces the parable's moral [BAGD, MGC, TH], meaning [NIGTC], or conclusion [Su]. It is an application [BECNT, Gdt, Hlt, NAC, TG, WBC] that differs from the parable alone [Hlt]. It doesn't mean that every person of this kind will die suddenly, but that the inner details describe what God considers to be a fool [Lns]. The rich man was an example of someone who wrongly used his possessions [Hlt]. It does not forbid planning or possessing wealth, rather it describes the outcome when a person takes wealth and uses it totally for himself [BECNT]. Every one bent on collecting riches for himself will lose his happiness by unexpected death [My].

QUESTION—What is meant by εἰς θεὸν πλουτῶν 'being rich toward God'?

It is being rich in spiritual things [EGT, NIC, Su], the things that please God [Hlt, ICC]. It refers to living in fellowship with God [NIC] and serving him [Bai, NAC, NIC]. It is laying up treasure in heaven, as in 12:33 and 18:22 [Hlt, NAC, NIGTC]. The riches are found in being in union with God and they consist of God's forgiveness, peace, and salvation [Lns]. It means being rich in the sense of doing what really counts in God's sight [AB], in the presence of God [Gdt], with God in view [WBC]. The man stored up treasure for himself and did not store up what really counted in God's sight [AB]. The riches that pleased the man are contrasted with the riches that please God [Arn]. One of the things he should have done was to use some of his wealth to help the poor [AB, Gdt, MGC, WBC].

DISCOURSE UNIT: 12:22–34 [BECNT, NAC, NIGTC, Su, TNTC, WBC; GW, HCSB, NET, NIV, NLT, NRSV]. The topic is seeking the kingdom

[TNTC], trust in God as a way of life [Su], teaching about money and possessions [NLT], care and anxiety [NAC], call to avoid anxiety [BECNT], the cure for anxiety [HCSB], do not worry [NIV, NRSV], stop worrying [GW], an exhortation not to worry [NET], earthly possessions and heavenly treasure [NIGTC], the generous provider requires generous disciples [WBC].

DISCOURSE UNIT: 12:22–32 [AB]. The topic is worry about earthly things.

DISCOURSE UNIT: 12:22–31 [CEV, NCV, TEV]. The topic is worry [CEV], don't worry [NCV], trust in God [TEV].

12:22 And he-said to his disciples, Because-of this[a] I-say to-you, Do not worry-about[b] the life[c] what you-will-eat, nor the body what you-will-wear. **12:23** Because the life is more-than[d] food and the body (more than) clothing.

TEXT—In 12:22, instead of τοὺς μαθητὰς αὐτοῦ 'his disciples', some manuscripts read τοὺς μαθητάς 'the disciples'. GNT reads τοὺς μαθητὰς [αὐτοῦ] 'his disciples' with a C decision and places αὐτοῦ 'his' in brackets, indicating that the Committee had difficulty making the decision.

TEXT—In 12:22, instead of τῇ ψυχῇ 'the life', some manuscripts read τῇ ψυχῇ ὑμῶν 'your life'. GNT does not mention this variant. Τῇ ψυχῇ ὑμῶν 'your life' is read by KJV.

TEXT—In 12:23, some manuscripts omit γάρ 'because'. GNT does not mention this variant. Γάρ 'because' is omitted by KJV.

LEXICON—a. The phrase διὰ τοῦτο 'because of this' is translated 'for this reason' [AB, Arn, Lns; NASB], 'so' [GW, NCV, NLT], 'on this basis' [WBC], 'and so' [TEV], 'therefore' [BECNT, NTC; HCSB, KJV, NET, NIV, NRSV], 'this is why' [REB], not explicit [CEV].

b. pres. act. impera. of μεριμνάω (LN 25.225) (BAGD 1. p. 505): 'to worry about'. See translations of this word at 10:4 and 12:11. The present imperative indicates a constant attitude [BECNT], a course of action [Lns]. This word also occurs at 10:41; 12:25, 26.

c. ψυχή (LN 23.88) (BAGD 1.a.b. p. 893): 'life' [AB, Arn, BAGD, LN, Lns, NTC; CEV, HCSB, KJV, NASB, NET, NIV, NRSV], 'everyday life' [NLT], 'yourself' [BECNT], 'soul' [WBC], not explicit [GW]. The phrase 'the life, what you will eat' is translated 'the food you need to live' [NCV], 'the food you need to stay alive' [TEV], 'food to keep you alive' [REB]. The article in the phrase τῇ ψυχῇ 'the life' is to be taken as equivalent to the possessive pronoun 'your' [AB, Lns, NTC, TH, WBC; CEV, KJV, NASB, NET, NIV, NRSV]. This is the same Greek word translated 'soul' in 12:19. This refers to the physical life which must be sustained by food [TH].

d. πλεῖον, πολύς (LN 78.28) (BAGD II.2.c. p. 689): 'more than' [Arn, BAGD, BECNT, LN, Lns, WBC; CEV, GW, HCSB, KJV, NASB, NCV, NIV, NRSV, REB], 'worth more than' [NTC], 'much more important than' [TEV]. The phrase 'the life is more than food' is translated 'life means more than food' [AB], 'there is more to life than food' [NET], 'life consists of far more than food' [NLT].

QUESTION—In 12:22, what relationship is indicated by διὰ τοῦτο 'because of this'?

This verse is an inference from the preceding parable [TH]. It is a conclusion related to the rich man's conduct and his fate [AB]. On account of the wrong attitudes characterized by greed and selfishness, Jesus now treats the sin of worrying about the sufficiency of what a person owns [Arn]. It refers back to the preceding warning about greed [NIC], or the preceding teaching about the folly of storing up material possessions [Alf, Gdt, NAC, NIGTC]. It explains that life doesn't depend on riches [ICC]. A disciple should not try to avoid anxiety by amassing possessions, rather he must trust God to meet his needs [BECNT].

QUESTION—In 12:23, what relationship is indicated by γάρ 'because'?

This indicates the reason Jesus told them not to worry [BECNT, Lns, MGC, NAC, NIGTC]. Life is more than food and clothing, so if one is overly concerned about those things, he will miss the most important thing in life, which is his relationship with God [BECNT]. Since life is more important than food, they should be concerned about the whole of life and not the material aspects of supporting it [NIGTC]. God has given us what is the greater (the life and the body), so we need not doubt that he will provide what is of lesser importance (food that sustains life, and clothing that keeps the body warm and alive) [EGT, Gdt, ICC, NIC, NTC, Su].

12:24 Consider[a] the crows[b] that they-do- not -sow nor reap, they have no storeroom[c] nor barn, and-yet[d] God feeds[e] them. How-much more you are-valuable-than[f] the birds.

LEXICON—a. aorist act. indic. of κατανοέω (LN 30.4) (BAGD 2. p. 415): 'to consider' [BAGD, BECNT, NTC, WBC; GW, HCSB, KJV, NASB, NET, NIV, NRSV], 'to consider closely, to think about very carefully' [LN], 'to carefully consider' [Lns], 'to think of' [REB], 'to look at' [AB, BAGD; CEV, NCV, NLT, TEV], 'to observe' [Arn]. This means to observe the crows in order to draw a lesson from them [NIGTC, Su].

b. κόραξ (LN **4.43**) (BAGD p. 444): 'crow' [BAGD, **LN**; CEV, GW, TEV], 'raven' [AB, Arn, BAGD, BECNT, LN, Lns, NTC, WBC; HCSB, KJV, NASB, NET, NIV, NLT, NRSV, REB], 'bird' [NCV]. Crows and ravens belong to the same family, ravens differing from crows in that they are larger [ICC, LN]. Many members of the crow family are represented in Palestine [ICC; NET]. In English, 'crow' is generally used for the whole family [NET].

c. ταμεῖον (LN 7.32) (BAGD 1. p. 803): 'storeroom' [BAGD, LN]. This is the same word translated 'inner-room' in 12:3. The phrase ταμεῖον οὐδὲ ἀποθήκη 'storeroom or barn' [AB, WBC; GW, HCSB, NASB, NET, NIV] is also translated 'storerooms or barns' [NCV], 'storehouse or barn' [BECNT; KJV, NRSV, REB], 'storehouses or barns' [CEV], 'storage rooms or barns' [TEV], 'storeroom nor granary' [Arn, Lns, NTC], 'barns' [NLT]. A storeroom was a room for storing provisions and a barn was a special building for storing grain [Arn]. Or, the two nouns are synonyms and together mean 'storehouses of any kind' [TH], 'places to keep their crops' [TG].

- d. καί (LN 89.92, 91.12): 'and' [BECNT, LN (89.92), Lns; KJV], 'and yet' [Arn; NASB, NRSV], 'yet' [AB, LN (91.12), NTC, WBC; GW, NCV, NET, NIV, REB], 'yet' [HCSB], 'but' [CEV, NCV], 'because' [NLT], not explicit [TEV]. The conjunction is concessive [NIGTC, TH]: 'and yet they do not starve, for God feeds them' [TH].
- e. pres. act. indic. of τρέφω (LN 23.6) (BAGD 1. p. 825): 'to feed' [AB, Arn, BAGD, BECNT, NTC, WBC; all versions except CEV], 'to provide food for' [BAGD, LN], 'to nourish' [Lns], 'to take care of' [CEV].
- f. pres. act. indic. of διαφέρω (LN 65.6) (BAGD 2.b. p. 190): 'to be more valuable than'. See translations of this word at 12:7.

QUESTION—What is the point of using crows in the example?

This shows how comprehensive God's care is [BECNT]. Crows and ravens were of no value, different from the previously mentioned sparrows which were used as food [Lns, NIGTC]. Ravens were unclean (Lev. 11:15) and yet God provided for even them [AB, Arn, BECNT, NICNT, NIGTC, NTC, TNTC, WBC]. The references to sowing and reaping, storeroom and barn are connected with the story of the rich man who died in spite of possessing everything, while the crows which lacked such things live by God's care [Gdt]. Since God cares for even crows or ravens, he will surely care for the disciples who are so much more valuable to him [BECNT, Lns, NIC, NICNT, NIGTC, Su].

12:25 And who of you (by) worrying^a is-able to-add a-cubit^b upon his lifespan/stature?^{c} **12:26** Therefore if you-are- not -able (to do) a-little-thing,^{d} why do-you-worry about the rest?^{e}

TEXT—In 12:25, instead of πῆχυν 'cubit' some manuscripts read πῆχυν ἕνα 'one cubit'. GNT does not mention this variant. Πῆχυν ἕνα 'one cubit' is read by KJV.

LEXICON—a. pres. act. participle of μεριμνάω (LN 25.225) (BAGD 1. p. 505): 'to worry about'. See translations of this word at 10:41 and 12:11. This word also occurs at 12: 22, 26.
- b. πῆχυς (LN 81.25) (BAGD p. 657): 'cubit' [Arn, BAGD, LN, NTC; HCSB, KJV], 'a half yard' [Lns], 'hour' [BECNT; GW, NET], 'a single hour' [NASB, NIV, NRSV], 'day' [REB], 'a single moment' [NLT], 'a moment of time' [AB], 'any time' [NCV], 'a small amount' [WBC], not explicit [CEV, TEV]. Originally this noun was the word for 'forearm' and then it was used as a measurement of length, a cubit being about eighteen inches [BAGD]. 'Cubit' is used here in a temporal sense to mean a small amount [AB, Lns, WBC] in regard to length of life [Lns]. This is a metaphorical use of a measurement of length to indicate a period of time

[Crd, NIGTC]. Or, it is used literally as a measurement of length [Gdt, NIC, Rb, Su, TNTC].

c. ἡλικία (LN 67.151, 81.4) (BAGD1.a. 2. p. 345): 'lifespan' [NTC], 'span of life' [AB, BECNT, LN (67.151), WBC; NRSV], 'life's span' [NASB], 'lifetime' [LN (67.151), Lns], 'life' [GW, NCV, NET, NIV, NLT, REB], 'age' [Arn, BAGD (1.a.), LN (67.151)], 'stature' [BAGD (2.), LN (81.4); KJV], 'height' [LN (81.4); HCSB]. The phrase 'to add a cubit upon his lifespan' is translated 'make you live longer' [CEV], 'live a bit longer' [TEV]. In 2:52 and 19:3 this word refers to stature, but here to one's length of life [NAC].

d. ἐλάχιστος (LN 65.57) (BAGD 2.a. p. 248): 'a very little thing' [BAGD; NASB], 'this very little thing' [NTC; NIV], 'even a little thing' [HCSB], 'even a very little thing' [Lns; REB], 'even the little things' [NCV], 'such a very little thing as this' [NET], 'little things like that' [NLT], 'small things' [CEV], 'a small thing like that' [GW], 'such a very small thing' [WBC], 'so small a thing as that' [NRSV], 'even such a small thing' [TEV], 'even a tiny little thing' [AB], 'such a trivial thing' [BECNT], 'very small, quite unimportant, insignificant' [BAGD], 'of very little importance' [LN], 'what is very insignificant' [Arn], 'that thing which is least' [KJV].

e. λοιπός (LN 63.21) (BAGD 2.b.β. p. 480): 'rest' [BAGD, LN], 'other' [LN]. The phrase τῶν λοιπῶν 'the rest' [AB, BECNT, Lns, NTC; HCSB, KJV, NET, NIV, NRSV, REB] is also translated 'other things' [WBC; GW, TEV], 'the remaining things' [Arn], 'other matters' [NASB], 'everything else' [CEV], 'the big things' [NCV], 'bigger things' [NLT].

QUESTION—What is added to what?

1. This refers to adding more time to a person's lifetime [AB, Alf, Arn, BECNT, BNTC, Crd, ICC, Lns, MGC, NAC, NIGTC, NTC, TH, WBC; all versions except HCSB, KJV]: to add more time to his lifespan. The length of time is a moment [NLT], an hour [BECNT; GW, NASB, NET, NIV, NRSV], a day [REB], any time at all [NCV]. The farmer was concerned about providing for his financial future [MGC]. The rich man failed to secure a prolongation of life [Arn, ICC]. Neither worrying nor the activity resulting from such concern can guarantee a gain in longevity [WBC]. Few would consider adding 18 inches to their height and that would not be a small thing [AB, ICC, NAC, NIGTC] or desirable [Lns], but length of life is an important item of worry [BECNT].

2. This refers to adding length to a persons' height [Gdt, NIC, Rb, Su, TNTC; HCSB, KJV]: to add a cubit to his stature. Jesus commonly used absurd, exaggerated illustrations to make his point more impressive [Su].

QUESTION—Why is such an addition called a little thing?

Adding a brief moment to a lifetime of seventy or eighty years does not amount to much [BECNT, MGC, NTC, TG].

QUESTION—What does 'the rest' refer to?
This is worry concerning such things as food [ICC, WBC], clothing [ICC, NIGTC, WBC], bodily necessities [ICC], and material things that cannot add to our lives [MGC]. Worry is futile [NAC].

12:27 Consider the wild-flowers[a] how they grow. They-do- not -work nor spin.[b] But I-say to-you, not-even Solomon in all his glory[c] clothed-himself like one of-these.

TEXT—Instead of πῶς αὐξάνει· οὐ κοπιᾷ οὐδὲ νήθει 'how they grow; they do not work nor spin', some manuscripts read πῶς οὔτε νήθει οὔτε ὑφαίνει 'how they neither spin nor weave', and some manuscripts read πῶς αὐξάνει· οὐ κοπιᾷ οὔτε νήθει οὔτε ὑφαίνει 'how they grow; they do not work nor spin nor weave'. GNT reads πῶς αὐξάνει· οὐ κοπιᾷ οὐδὲ νήθει 'how they grow; they do not work nor spin' with a B decision, indicating that the text is almost certain.

LEXICON—a. κρίνον (LN 3.32) (BAGD p. 451): 'wild flower' [LN; CEV, HCSB, TEV], 'flower' [GW, NET], 'lily' [AB, Arn, BAGD, BECNT, Lns, NTC, WBC; KJV, NASB, NCV, NIV, NLT, NRSV, REB]. This designation for the white lily can also be used for any of the beautiful flowers that grow in the Palestinian fields in the spring [AB], such as a type of lily [BAGD, Gdt, LN, Lns, MGC, TNTC, WBC], the purple or scarlet anemone [AB, Arn, BAGD, BECNT, Gdt, ICC, LN, MGC, TH], the scarlet Martagon [ICC], gladiolus [BAGD, LN], poppy [AB, LN], daisy [AB, LN, MGC], autumn crocus [AB, BAGD], and Turk's cap lily [BAGD]. It is probably not what is now called lilies [TNTC]. Instead of referring to any particular kind of flower, it may refer to all the beautiful wild flowers visible in the fields [Arn, ICC, MGC, NIGTC, NTC, TG, TH, TNTC].

b. pres. act. indic. of νήθω (LN 48.2) (BAGD p. 537): 'to spin' [AB, Arn, BAGD, BECNT, LN, Lns, NTC, WBC; GW, KJV, NASB, NET, NIV, NRSV], 'to spin thread' [HCSB], 'to weave' [REB]. The clause 'they do not work nor spin' is translated 'they don't work or make clothes for themselves' [NCV, TEV], 'they don't work or make their clothing' [NLT], 'they don't work hard to make their clothes' [CEV].

c. δόξα (LN 87.23) (BAGD 2. p. 204): 'glory' [Arn, BECNT, LN, Lns, WBC; KJV, NASB, NET, NLT, NRSV], 'splendor' [AB, BAGD, NTC; HCSB, NIV, REB], 'greatness' [LN], 'majesty' [GW]. The phrase 'in all his glory' is translated 'with all his wealth' [CEV, TEV], 'with his riches' [NCV]. This refers to the magnificence and splendor which surrounds a king [Arn], especially his outward appearance [TH]. This describes the finest clothing the king had [NTC]. Solomon was the wealthiest of all Israel's kings [BECNT], and was legendary for his wealth and fine clothing [AB, WBC].

QUESTION—What is meant by πῶς αὐξάνει 'how it grows'?
>In this context, it means that the flowers do not toil on their part nor do they receive human care [NTC]. Or, instead of referring to the process of growing, it means the results of their growing in regard to their appearance [TH].

QUESTION—Why is work and spinning mentioned?
>These verbs describe how clothing is made [TH, TNTC]. Men had to work hard on growing plants and women had to spin the cloth [ICC, TH].

12:28 And if God thus clothes the grass[a] in a-field, existing today and tomorrow being-thrown into an-oven,[b] how-much more you, (you) of-little-faith.[c]

LEXICON—a. χόρτος (LN 3.15) (BAGD p. 884): 'grass' [AB, Arn, BAGD, BECNT, LN, Lns, NTC, WBC; all versions except CEV, NLT], 'flowers' [NLT], 'small plants' [LN], 'everything that grows (in the fields)' [CEV].

b. κλίβανος (LN 7.74) (BAGD p. 436): 'oven' [Arn, BAGD, BECNT, LN, Lns, WBC; KJV, NRSV, TEV], 'incinerator' [GW], 'furnace' [AB, NTC; HCSB, NASB], 'stove' [REB], 'fire' [CEV, NCV, NIV], not explicit [NLT]. The phrase 'being thrown into an oven' is translated 'is tossed into the fire to heat the oven' [NET]. This was a clay oven used for baking bread. It was dome-shaped and was heated by burning wood or dried grass [LN].

c. ὀλιγόπιστος (LN 31.96) (BAGD p. 563): 'of little faith' [BAGD, LN]. This adjective is translated 'O you of little faith' [BECNT; KJV, NIV], 'you of little faith' [HCSB, NRSV], 'O people of little faith' [AB], 'you people of little faith' [WBC; NET], 'you people who have so little faith' [GW], 'O men of little faith' [Arn, NTC], 'men of little faith' [Lns], 'you men of little faith' [NASB], 'you have so little faith' [NLT], 'you have such little faith' [CEV], 'how little faith you have' [REB], 'what little faith you have' [TEV], 'Don't have so little faith!' [NCV].

QUESTION—Why is attention now changed from the wild flowers to grass?
1. 'Grass' now describes the wild flowers [Lns, MGC, NIGTC, NTC, TH, TNTC; NLT]. With the verb 'clothes' it is seen that Jesus was still speaking of the lilies, which have a grassy foliage and can rightly be referred to as grass [Lns]. By calling the flowers 'grass', the contrast is sharpened between the flowers and God's children [MGC]. No particular flower is in view and so it can be referred to in different ways [TNTC]. 'Grass' means all of those plants which are uncultivated [NTC]. The designation 'grass' includes different kinds of wild short-living vegetation and includes the lilies [TH].
2. This is another example added to the example of the lily [AB, Arn, BECNT, NAC, NICNT]. The illustration of the flower is now reduced to one of grass for the sake of the argument from the least to the greater [AB, NAC].

QUESTION—Why would grass be thrown into an oven?
  Grass was used as fuel [Arn, BECNT, Gdt, ICC, Lns, NIGTC, NTC, TG, WBC], since wood was scarce [Arn, ICC, Lns, NTC, WBC]. Grass was thrown into the fire that heated the ovens [NAC; NET], not thrown into an oven to be baked [NET]. Grass was burned in clay ovens to bake bread [TG]. All sorts of grass, wild flowers, and chaff from harvest were used [WBC]. Being thrown into the oven indicates its insignificance and transitory nature [BECNT, NAC].
QUESTION—What will be much more for people?
  How much more he will clothe you [AB, BECNT, Lns, MGC, NTC, TNTC; GW, KJV, NASB, NCV, NET, NIV, NRSV, TEV]. Since God clothes the lowly flowers so gorgeously, he will surely give common garments to his greater creatures [Lns, NTC]. Or, how much more he will take care of you [TG, WBC; NLT]. Or, how much more he will provide for you [NIGTC].
QUESTION—What was the purpose of calling them people of little faith?
  It shows Jesus' surprise at their little faith [TG], and this also functions as a rebuke [TG, TH]. Not only is this a criticism, it also served to encourage them because Jesus does not reject them [Arn]. Some of the disciples had shown their anxiety [TNTC]. This refers to their lack of faith that God would provide for their material existence [AB, Su, WBC].

12:29 **And you, do- not -be concerned-about^a what you-will-eat and what you-will-drink, and do- not –be-worrying.^b**

LEXICON—a. pres. act. impera. of ζητέω (LN 25.9) (BAGD 1.c. p. 339): 'to be concerned about' [TEV], 'to concern yourself about' [GW], 'to be overly concerned about' [NET], 'to set one's mind on' [REB], 'to worry about' [NLT], 'to consider' [BAGD], 'to think about' [NCV], 'to set one's heart on' [NTC; NIV], 'to desire' [LN], 'to seek' [Arn, BECNT, Lns; KJV, NASB], 'to seek continually' [AB], 'to have as one's constant consideration' [WBC], 'to strive for' [HCSB, NRSV], not explicit [CEV]. It probably implies that the person makes an attempt to realize one's desire [Lns]. It means 'to be intent on', 'to be preoccupied with' [TH], 'to seek' [NIGTC]. The translation 'seek' should not imply that a person should make no attempt to obtain food and drink, rather it means not to be unduly concerned about such things [NET, TNTC]. It refers to making this the aim of one's life [NIC].

  b. pres. mid./pass. (deponent = act.) impera. of μετεωρίζομαι (LN **25.232**) (BAGD 1. p. 514): 'to worry' [BAGD; CEV, GW, NASB, NCV, NET, NIV], 'to live in a state of constant worry' [NTC], 'to be concerned about' [**LN**], 'to be anxious' [AB, BAGD, LN, WBC; HCSB, REB], 'to be of anxious mind' [BECNT], 'to be filled with anxiety' [Arn], 'to be upset' [TEV], 'to be of doubtful mind' [KJV], 'to be in suspense' [Lns]. The clause is translated 'and don't worry whether God will provide it for you' [NLT]. The present tense indicates that they were worrying and should stop it [GW, NASB, NCV, NRSV]: don't keep worrying. This is a rare word that usually means 'to raise up' [NIGTC], 'to be raised on high, to be elated, to be overweening' [AB], 'to be lifted up' [BECNT, ICC]. It may be taken as a metaphor for ships being tossed about in the sea, with the resultant meaning 'to be tossed with cares, to waver anxiously' [ICC, NIC], 'to be in suspense' about where to obtain food and drink [Lns]. It means to be worked up over something [BECNT]. This worry is about the things mentioned in the previous clause [Lns; NET]. This refers to the emotion that accompanies being concerned about food and drink [TH]. Here it means 'do not make yourselves anxious' [Alf, Crd, NIC]. In the passive it means 'to worry' [MGC, NIGTC]. It is a synonym for the verb μεριμνάω 'to worry' in 12: 22, 25, 26 [NAC, TH].

12:30 Because these (things) all the nations^a of-the world are-concerned-about,^b and your Father knows that you-need^c these (things).
LEXICON—a. ἔθνος (LN 11.37) (BAGD 1., 2. p. 218): 'nation' [BAGD (1.)]. The phrase τὰ ἔθνη τοῦ κόσμου 'the nations of the world' [BECNT, WBC; KJV, NASB, NET, NRSV] is also translated 'the nations of this world' [Arn], 'the people in the world' [NCV], 'the pagans of this world' [AB; TEV], 'the pagan world' [NIV], 'people who don't know God' [CEV], 'the Gentiles' [REB], 'the Gentiles of the world' [Lns], 'the Gentile world' [HCSB], 'worldly people' [NTC], 'everyone in the world' [GW], 'most people' [NLT]. The plural form τὰ ἔθνη 'the nations' has an extended meaning that refers to those who do not belong to the Jewish or Christian faith, that is, the heathen or the pagans [LN].
  b. pres. act. indic. of ἐπιζητέω (LN 25.9) (BAGD B.2.a. p. 292): 'to be concerned about' [GW, TEV], 'to occupy the mind' [REB], 'to have as one's constant consideration' [WBC], 'to worry about' [CEV], 'to dominate the thoughts' [NLT], 'to desire' [LN], 'to wish for' [BAGD], 'to eagerly seek' [HCSB, NASB], 'to seek' [Arn, BECNT], 'to seek after' [Lns; KJV], 'to try to get' [NCV], 'to constantly crave' [NTC], 'to pursue' [NET], 'to run after' [AB; NIV], 'to strive after' [NRSV]. This has virtually the same meaning as ζητέω 'to be concerned about' in 12:29 and the present tense indicates a habitual attitude [NTC, TH].
  c. pres. act. indic. of χρῄζω (LN 57.39) (BAGD p. 885): 'to need' [AB, Arn, BECNT, LN, NTC, WBC; all versions except KJV, NLT], 'to have need of' [BAGD, Lns; KJV]. This verb is also translated as a noun: 'your needs' [NLT].
QUESTION—What relationship is indicated by γάρ 'because'?
  It indicates that the reason they should not be worried is that if they did worry, they would be like the heathen who seek after material things [NIGTC], and they had reason to be different [BECNT].
QUESTION—What does πάντα 'all' modify?
  1. It modifies the preceding the preceding word ταῦτα 'these things' [AB, Gdt, ICC, NAC, NIGTC, TH; HCSB, KJV, NASB, NIV, NRSV, REB,

TEV]: all these things the nations of the world are concerned about. 'These things' refer to such things as eating and drinking [TH].
  2. It modifies the following words τὰ ἔθνη 'the nations' [BECNT, BNTC, Lns, WBC; GW, NCV, NET]: these things all the nations of the world are concerned about. The word order connects it with the nations, but the difference is insignificant [BECNT].

QUESTION—How is the second sentence 'And your Father knows that you need these things' related to the preceding text?
  1. This relates to the preceding sentence in 12:30 [BECNT, ICC, Lns, NIC, NIGTC, WBC; GW, KJV, NASB, NCV, NET, NIV, NLT, NRSV, REB]. It clarifies the thought [WBC]. Unlike the heathen nations, they need not worry about such things, because their Father knows what they need [NIGTC]. Knowing of those needs, their Father will supply them [Lns, TNTC]. The disciples do not need to be disturbed about these needs [ICC].
  2. This relates directly with the 12:29 [TG; TEV]. The first part of 12:30 is parenthetical and this sentence continues with 12:29 and gives a reason why they should not be concerned [TG].

12:31 Instead, be-concerned-about[a] his kingdom,[b] and these (things) will-be-provided[c] to-you.

TEXT—Instead of τὴν βασιλείαν αὐτοῦ 'his kingdom', some manuscripts read τὴν βασιλείαν τοῦ θεοῦ 'the kingdom of God', some manuscripts read τὴν βασιλείαν τοῦ θεοῦ καὶ τὴν δικαιοσύνην αὐτοῦ 'the kingdom of God and his righteousness', and one important manuscript reads τὴν βασιλείαν 'the kingdom'. GNT reads τὴν βασιλείαν αὐτοῦ 'his kingdom' with a B decision, indicating that the text is almost certain. Τὴν βασιλείαν τοῦ θεοῦ 'the kingdom of God' is read by KJV.

TEXT—Instead of ταῦτα 'these things', some manuscripts read ταῦτα πάντα 'all these things'. GNT does not mention this variant. Ταῦτα πάντα 'all these things' is read by KJV.

LEXICON—a. pres. act. impera. of ζητέω (LN 25.9) (BAGD 2.a. p. 339): 'to be concerned about'. The phrase ζητεῖτε τὴν βασιλείαν αὐτοῦ 'be concerned about his kingdom' [GW] is also translated 'be concerned with his kingdom' [TEV], 'have his kingdom as your constant consideration' [WBC], 'make the Kingdom of God your primary concern' [NLT], 'set your minds on his kingdom' [REB], 'seek God's kingdom' [BECNT; NCV; similarly Arn, Lns, NTC; HCSB, KJV, NASB, NIV], 'seek for his kingdom' [AB], 'pursue God's kingdom' [NET], 'strive for his kingdom' [NRSV], 'put God's work first' [CEV]. This word repeats the verb ζητέω in 12:29 and the sense of the verb ἐπιζητέω in 12:30, and all have the same meaning [TH; NET]. With the conjunction πλήν 'instead', it has the idea 'what you should be concerned about instead is his kingdom' [TH].
  b. βασιλεία (LN 37.64) (BAGD 3.g. p. 135): 'kingdom' [AB, Arn, BAGD, BECNT, Lns, NTC, WBC; all versions except CEV], 'royal reign'

[BAGD], 'reign' [LN], '(God's) work' [CEV]. God's kingdom is the realm in which Jesus rules and to which his disciples belong [NET].
  c. fut. pass. indic. of προστίθημι (LN **57.78**) (BAGD 2. p. 719): 'to be provided' [BAGD, **LN**; GW, HCSB, TEV], 'to be given' [Arn, BAGD, LN; NCV], 'to be one's as well' [CEV], 'to be given as well' [NET, NIV, NRSV], 'to be given in addition' [AB, WBC], 'to be granted as an extra gift' [NTC], 'to be added to' [BECNT, Lns; KJV, NASB], 'the rest will come as well' [REB]. This passive verb is also translated actively with God as the subject: 'to give' [NLT].

QUESTION—What is meant by being concerned about God's kingdom?
  Since this is addressed to believers, this means that they are to seek the spiritual benefits of the God's kingdom instead of material things of the world [NIVS]. Their concern is to be under God's rule [BNTC], to be concerned with the values that matter in God's kingdom [TG, TH], to live the way members of God's kingdom should live [BECNT, TG]. They must always desire to more fully enter into union with God [Lns]. They are to seek the blessings of the kingdom [NAC, NIGTC], and in this way gain treasure in heaven instead of earthly possessions [NAC]. They are to be concerned with God's rule in their own hearts and in all of society [MGC, NTC, Su, TNTC]. God's kingship should dominate their lives so that they will seek to spread its influence [AB]. The present tense 'be desiring' indicates that this is to be habitual with them [BECNT, ICC, TH]. When they seek the kingdom of God instead of seeking material things, the material things will be given to them in addition [NIGTC, Su]. The passive 'will be provided' implies that God is the one who will give them these things [TG].

DISCOURSE UNIT: 12:32–34 [CEV, TEV]. The topic is treasures in heaven [CEV], riches in heaven [TEV].

12:32 Do- not -fear little flock,[a] because your Father was-well-pleased[b] to-give[c] you the kingdom.

LEXICON—a. ποίμνιον (LN 11.31) (BAGD 2.b. p. 684): 'flock' [AB, Arn, BAGD, BECNT, LN, Lns, NTC, WBC; all versions except CEV], 'group of disciples' [CEV]. This is a figurative extension of a flock of sheep to refer to the followers of Christ who need his care and guidance [LN].
  b. aorist act. indic. of εὐδοκέω (LN 25.87) (BAGD 1. p. 319): 'to be well pleased' [BAGD; NET], 'to be pleased' [Arn, BECNT, LN; GW, NIV, TEV], 'to be (your Father's) good pleasure' [KJV, NRSV], 'to take pleasure in' [LN, NTC], 'to delight' [HCSB,] 'to please' [Lns], 'to want to' [CEV, NCV], 'to choose' [REB], 'to choose gladly' [NASB], 'to determine in his pleasure' [WBC]. The phrase 'your Father was well pleased' is translated 'it gives your Father great happiness' [NLT]. This means that their Father had resolved or decided to do this [TG, TH]. This refers to God's will [BECNT, Lns, NICNT]. The aorist tense indicates that this was a decision made in the past [Arn, Lns, TG, WBC; NASB, NIV, REB]. Or, the aorist tense may indicate present action [NTC; CEV,

GW, KJV, NCV, NET, NLT, NRSV, TEV]. Or, it may be a timeless aorist [Rb]. What was God's pleasure is still his pleasure, and will ever remain so [NTC].

c. aorist act. infin. of δίδωμι (LN 90.90): 'to give, to make someone experience something' [LN]. The phrase δοῦναι ὑμῖν τὴν βασιλείαν is translated 'to give you the kingdom' [Arn, BECNT; all versions; similarly Lns, NTC, WBC].

QUESTION—Is this verse part of the preceding paragraph or the following paragraph?

1. This closes the preceding verses [AB, BECNT, Su; GW, NASB, NCV]. Although transitional, it is closely connected with the preceding command to be concerned with God's kingdom [Su].
2. This begins the paragraph consisting of 12:32–34 [EGT, NIBC, NICNT; CEV, NCV, NET, NIV, NRSV, REB, TEV]. This paragraph functions as the climax of Jesus' argument [NICNT].
3. This is a unit by itself [NLT].

QUESTION—Why did Jesus call his disciples a little flock?

The picture of a flock was already used in the OT for Israel [AB, BECNT, NAC, TNTC, WBC]. Jesus compared his disciples to a flock of sheep and he is like a shepherd to them [Alf, TG]. It implies that Jesus will care for them like a shepherd cares for his flock [Lns, TNTC]. They are a small flock because their numbers are few [Lns, NIC, TNTC]. They are few in relation to the nations of the world [NIC], and even in relation to the Jewish nation [Lns]. The use of 'flock' implies that like sheep they are defenseless [NIC], weak, and helpless [NIC, NIGTC], and since they were liable to fear danger, they needed to be commanded not to be afraid [NIGTC]. Their small number would cause them to fear their vulnerability [WBC]. They were not to fear the future in regard to food and clothing [EGT], or the loss of their part in the kingdom [EGT]. They were not to fear the coming persecution for being Jesus' disciples [BECNT]. The command functioned as a word of reassurance [NAC].

QUESTION—In what sense did their Father give them the kingdom?

1. The disciples have already received God's kingdom [AB, Arn, BECNT, Lns, NAC, NICNT, Su]. God gives the kingdom to those who seek it [NIC]. God had determined that as people joined his flock, they would receive this gift [Lns]. The kingdom has already been given them and this refers to Jesus' ministry among them [NICNT]. This means that God made them a part of his kingdom [AB, NAC]. The kingdom is God's reign in their hearts [Su]. This refers to the kingdom blessings that come with pursuing the kingdom [BECNT].
2. The disciples would receive God's kingdom in its fullness in the future [NIC, NIGTC, TG, TH]. They already participate in the blessings of the kingdom in principle, but at the end of the age they will receive it in its fullness when they live with God and rule forever [NIC]. The persecuted group of disciples will be glorified in the future kingdom [NIGTC]. Here

their reception of the kingdom will be at the end of the world [TG] when God will let them reign where he reigns [TG, TH].

DISCOURSE UNIT: 12:33–34 [AB; NCV]. The topic is treasure in heaven [AB], don't trust in money [NCV].

12:33 Sell your possessions and give alms.[a] Make[b] for-yourselves purses[c] not becoming-old,[d] a-never-decreasing[e] treasure in the heavens, where a-thief does- not -approach[f] nor a-moth destroys.[g]

LEXICON—a. ἐλεημοσύνη (LN 57.112) (BAGD p. 250): 'alms' [BAGD, LN]. The phrase 'give alms' [Arn, BECNT, Lns, WBC; KJV, NRSV] is also translated 'give to charity' [NTC; NASB, REB], 'give to the poor' [HCSB, NCV, NET, NIV], 'give to those in need' [NLT], 'give them away as alms' [AB], 'give the money to the poor' [CEV, GW, TEV]. They are to give the money that they get from selling their possessions [AB, NIGTC, TH]. See this word at 11:41.

b. aorist act. impera. of ποιέω (LN 42.29) (BAGD I.1.c.a. p. 682): 'to make' [Arn, BAGD, LN, Lns, WBC; CEV, GW, HCSB, NRSV], 'to get' [NCV], 'to provide for oneself' [AB, BAGD, BECNT, NTC; KJV, NET, NIV, REB, TEV]. The whole clause is translated 'this will store up treasure for you in heaven' [NLT]. The verb means 'to get' or 'to try to acquire' [TH].

c. βαλλάντιον (LN 6.144) (BAGD p. 130): 'purse'. See the next lexical item for translations of this word. See this word also at 10:4, 22:35.

d. pres. pass. participle of παλαιόω (LN 67.103) (BAGD 2. p. 606): 'to become old' [BAGD], 'to be made old' [LN]. The phrase βαλλάντια μὴ παλαιούμενα 'purses not becoming old' is translated 'bags which wax not old' [KJV], 'purses that do/will not grow old' [Arn, BECNT], 'purses that age not' [Lns], 'purses that do/will not wear out' [AB; NCV, NET, NIV, NRSV, REB, TEV], 'purses that will never wear out' [NTC], 'moneybags that won't grow old' [HCSB], 'moneybags that never wear out' [CEV], 'money belts which do not wear out' [NASB], 'wallets that don't wear out' [GW], 'treasure-sacks which will not age' [WBC], not explicit [NLT]. This refers to a money bag that business owners used [BECNT]. It probably refers to sacks of treasure that will not deteriorate with age [WBC]. Or, this means a treasure that will not be lost through death [AB].

e. ἀνέκλειπτος (LN **13.99**) (BAGD p. 64): 'never decreasing' [LN], 'inexhaustible' [BAGD, LN; HCSB], 'unfailing' [BAGD, Lns, WBC; NASB, NRSV], 'never-failing' [REB], 'imperishable' [Arn]. The phrase 'a never decreasing treasure' is translated 'a treasure which can never decrease, a treasure which will never fail' [**LN**], 'a treasure that never decreases' [NET; similarly TEV], 'a treasure that will not be exhausted' [NIV], 'a treasure that does not fail' [BECNT; similarly AB; KJV], 'a treasure that will never give out' [NTC], 'a treasure that never loses its value' [GW], 'the treasure that never runs out' [NCV], 'treasure that is safe' [CEV], 'the purses of heaven have no holes in them' [NLT].

f. pres. act. indic. of ἐγγίζω (LN 15.75) (BAGD 5.a. p. 213): 'to approach' [Arn, BAGD, BECNT, LN; KJV, NET], 'to come near' [BAGD, LN, Lns; HCSB, NASB, NIV, NRSV], 'to draw near' [WBC], 'to get near' [AB; REB], 'to reach' [NTC]. The phrase 'where a thief does not approach' is translated 'where thieves can't steal' [NCV], 'where thieves can not steal it' [CEV], 'no thief can get to them' [TEV], 'your treasure will be safe—no thief can steal it' [NLT]. The clause 'where a thief does not approach nor a moth destroys' is translated 'in heaven thieves and moths can't get close enough to destroy your treasure' [GW]. The sense is that a thief gets to it in order to take it away [NAC]. A thief cannot get near the treasure that is located in heaven [TH].

g. pres. act. indic. of διαφθείρω (LN 20.40) (BAGD 1. p. 190): 'to destroy' [AB, Arn, BAGD, BECNT, Lns, WBC; all versions except KJV], 'to destroy utterly' [LN], 'to spoil' [BAGD], 'to ravage' [NTC], 'to corrupt [KJV]. Treasure is not only money and jewels, it includes costly clothing that moths would destroy [BECNT, MGC, NAC, TG, TH, WBC].

QUESTION—Are all of the disciples commanded to sell all of their possessions?

1. It does not literally mean to sell all of their possessions and give all of the proceeds to the poor [Arn, EGT, Gdt, ICC, Lns, NTC, TNTC]. This presents a new attitude [NIGTC] or principle [ICC] that the disciples are to have concerning their possessions [NIGTC]. The disciples' possessions are not to dominate their thoughts, because if they are trusting in riches, they will not be trusting in God [TNTC]. They are to be ready to part from their possessions [ICC], if this is God's will [Arn]. This contrasts with the selfish spirit of the rich man in 12:17–19 [Lns, NTC].

2. It is a command to be taken literally by part of the disciples [My]. This is not required of all Christians, but the command is given to the apostles who needed perfect release from their temporal possessions in order to fulfill their office [My].

QUESTION—What is meant by the phrase 'a never decreasing treasure in heaven'?

1. The phrase explains the meaning of the metaphor about the purses [NIGTC, NTC, TH, TNTC; CEV, GW]. 'Purses' are used as a metonymy for what they contain [NAC, TH]: provide for yourselves wealth that never ends, that is, provide for yourselves a never decreasing treasure in heaven. One should use the money he possesses to lay up treasure in heaven and then, unlike money, his heavenly treasure will not be lost at death [NAC].

    1.1 The verb ποιέω 'make' goes with both 'purses' and 'treasure' and is translated 'make yourselves wallets…make a treasure for yourselves' [GW], 'make…make sure' [CEV], 'make…gather' [TH], 'provide yourselves with purses…with a treasure' [BECNT].

    1.2 The phrase is in apposition with 'purse' and indicates that such purses are receptacles for heavenly treasure [NIGTC, NTC, TNTC]: make for

yourselves purses that do not wear out, purses that contain a never decreasing treasure in heaven. These purses will not perish so as to lose the treasure they hold [NIGTC]. There will always be more and more [NTC].
2. The phrase is distinct from the previous phrase [Lns]. Making purses has to do with what they are to do with earthly wealth, not where they are to store heavenly treasure, and the treasure in heaven is obtained when their hearts are in the kingdom of heaven [Lns].

QUESTION—What is the reason for mentioning a thief and a moth?
A contrast is intended. Earthly treasures, which in the case of money can be stolen by thieves, and in the case of expensive clothing can be ruined by moths, are insecure and can be lost. Heavenly treasure is forever secure [NIGTC].

12:34 **Because where your treasure is, there also your heart will-be.**
QUESTION—What relationship is indicated by γάρ 'because'?
This verse indicates the grounds for obeying the exhortations in 12:32–33 [BECNT, ICC, MGC, NIGTC, NTC]. It gives the general principle behind the preceding command [TH].

QUESTION—What is the connection between one's treasure and heart?
The word 'heart' is a figure for one's feelings, concerns, and interest [TG], the seat of the emotions and desires [TH], one's thoughts, ideals, inclinations, and deeds [NIC], one's interests and concerns [Su], one's affections [NIGTC], one's priorities [BECNT], one's commitment [MGC]. The word 'treasure' is used figuratively for what is valued [BECNT]. When one's treasure is in heaven, then one's heart will be set on heavenly things [AB]. When a person's heart is set on earthly wealth his heart is not really related to God [NIGTC].

DISCOURSE UNIT: 12:35–59 [Su]. The topic is a caution to watchfulness in the impending crisis.

DISCOURSE UNIT: 12:35–48 [BECNT, NAC, NICNT, NIGTC, WBC; CEV, GW, NASB, NET, NIV, NLT]. The topic is watchfulness [NIV], the watchful servants [NAC], the faithful and unfaithful servants [CEV], faithfulness within the household of God [NICNT], be in readiness [NASB], a call to faithful stewardship [NET], a call to be ready and faithful stewards [BECNT], the coming of the Son of Man [NIGTC], be ready for the Lord's coming [NLT], be ready and alert, and on the job for the Master [WBC], the Son of Man will return when you least expect him [GW].

DISCOURSE UNIT: 12:35–46 [AB]. The topic is sayings about vigilance and faithfulness.

DISCOURSE UNIT: 12:35–40 [TNTC; HCSB, NCV, NRSV, TEV]. The topic is the coming of the Son of Man [TNTC], watchful servants [NRSV, TEV], always be ready [NCV], ready for the Master's return [HCSB].

12:35 **Let your waists be-girded[a] and the lamps[b] burning.**

LEXICON—a. perf. pass. participle of περιζώννυμαι (LN 49.15) (BAGD 1. p. 647): 'to be girded' [BAGD, LN]. The clause Ἔστωσαν ὑμῶν ὀσφύες περιεζωσμέναι 'let your waists be girded' [WBC] is also translated 'let your loins be girded' [Arn, BECNT], 'let your loins be girded about' [KJV], 'let your loins be as having been girded' [Lns], 'be dressed in readiness' [NASB], 'get dressed for service' [NET], 'be dressed, ready for service' [NCV, NIV], 'be dressed for service' [NLT], 'be dressed for action' [NRSV], 'always be dressed so that you are ready for action' [NTC], 'be ready for whatever comes, dressed for action' [TEV], 'be ready for action' [GW, REB], 'be ready for service' [HCSB], 'be ready' [CEV], 'keep your aprons on' [AB].

b. λύχνος (LN 6.104) (BAGD 1. p. 483): 'lamp' [AB, Arn, BAGD, LN, Lns, NTC, WBC; all versions except KJV, NLT], 'light' [KJV]. The clause 'and the lamps burning' is translated 'be well prepared' [NLT]. In the setting of the palace of a master, these would be fine lamps made of a bowl with a snout for the wick [Lns]. The lamps would enable them to be ready to move about in the darkness [BECNT]. It is implied that it is nighttime [EGT, Gdt, My, NIGTC, TH]. Having the lamps burning signifies watchfulness [AB, BECNT; NET], and being alert for some attack [MGC]. See this word at 8:16; 11:33.

QUESTION—What is meant by the command to let their waists be girded?

The figure is that of men who have pulled up their long outer garments and tucked the material under their belts so that their clothes will not get in the way of their movements [Arn, NTC, TG]. In leisure, the long robe hung down loosely, but for active work or travel it was tied in place with a belt [NIGTC, WBC]. In the story, they should be properly dressed to honor the master at his arrival, although it might also hint of the activity involved with the arrival of the master [WBC].

12:36 **And you (should be) like men waiting-for their master when he-returns from the wedding-feasts,[a] in-order-that having-come and having-knocked immediately they-may-open (the door) for-him.**

LEXICON—a. γάμος (LN 34.68) (BAGD 1.b. p. 151): 'wedding feast' [BECNT; CEV, NASB, NLT, TEV], 'marriage feast' [NTC], 'wedding banquet' [BAGD; HCSB, NIV, NRSV], 'wedding party' [AB; NCV, REB], 'wedding celebration' [Arn; NET], 'wedding' [LN, Lns; GW, KJV], 'banquet' [WBC]. This plural form of the noun was commonly used for a single celebration [Arn].

QUESTION—What were the disciples to be waiting for?

Addressed directly to the disciples, it is already apparent that the parable is about their Lord's return after he leaves them [Lns]. They were to be ready for the return of Jesus (12:40) [AB, WBC], his return from heaven [NTC], the second coming [BECNT, MGC, NAC, NIC], the coming of the Son of Man [TG]. Some refer the wedding feast in the story to the eschatological banquet [AB], the marriage supper of the Lamb when Jesus ascended to heaven after his death [Lns]. Others think that the wedding feast is just a descriptive detail without any reference to the eschatological messianic banquet [BECNT, NAC, NIGTC]. This would not be marriage supper of the Lamb, since the master does not return to his servants until after the feast [NAC]. Or, this was addressed to people in general, telling them to be ready for a crisis in which they would called to account to God concerning their responsibilities [Su, TNTC].

QUESTION—What is meant by γάμος 'wedding feast'?
1. This refers to a wedding feast [Alf, Arn, BECNT, BNTC, Gdt, ICC, Kst, Lns, MGC, My, NIC, NTC, Pnt, Rb, Su, TG, TNTC, WBC; all versions]. This would be some friend's wedding, not the master's [Gdt, ICC]. Or, the master was the groom who had been to a supper with his friends [WBC]. At that time wedding celebrations could last for seven days and so the time of the master's return was not known [MGC, TG].
2. This refers to some feast, not necessarily connected with a wedding [TH, WBC]. In the plural, it refers to a party or banquet [TH].

QUESTION—Why would their master want a group of servants ready to open the door at his coming?

An ordinary man would need just one man to open the door, but the master had a palace and when he returned with many others accompanying him, the master wanted his many slaves to be ready to receive the group with great ceremony [Lns].

12:37 **Blessed[a] (are) those slaves, whom the master having come will-find keeping-awake.[b] Truly I-say to-you that he-will-gird-himself[c] and make-them -recline,[d] and having-come-beside[e] (them) he-will-serve[f] them. 12:38 And-if in the second or-if in the third watch[g] he-comes and he-finds (it) thus, blessed are those.**

LEXICON—a. μακάριος (LN 25.119) (BAGD 1.b. p. 485): 'blessed' [GW, KJV, NASB, NET, NRSV], 'fortunate' [CEV], 'happy' [LN; REB, TEV]. The phrase 'blessed are' is translated 'will be blessed' [HCSB, NCV], 'it will be good for' [NIV], 'there will be special favor for' [NLT]. See this word at 1:45; 6:20; 7:23; 10:23; 11:27; 12:43; 14:14; 23:29.

b. pres. act. participle of γρηγορέω (LN 27.56) (BAGD 1. p. 167): 'to be awake' [Arn, BAGD; GW, REB], 'to be awake and ready' [CEV, TEV], 'to be watchful' [LN], 'to be watching' [Lns; KJV, NCV, NIV], 'to be ready and waiting' [NLT], 'to be waiting' [BECNT], 'to be alert' [LN; HCSB, NET, NRSV], 'to be on the alert' [AB, NTC, WBC; NASB]. It means to be ready for action [NIGTC].

c. fut. mid. indic. of περιζώννυμαι (LN 49.15) (BAGD 2.a. p. 647): 'to gird oneself' [Arn, BAGD, BECNT, LN, Lns, WBC; KJV, NASB], 'to fasten one's belt' [NRSV], 'to hitch up one's robe' [REB], 'to take off one's coat' [TEV], 'to change one's clothes' [GW], 'to dress oneself to serve' [NTC; NCV, NET, NIV], 'to put on an apron' [AB; NLT], 'to get ready'

[CEV, HCSB]. This means to put a belt or sash around oneself [LN]. The master will tie up his robe around his waist as a servant would do [Su].
d. fut. act. indic. of ἀνακλίνω (LN 17.24) (BAGD 1.b. p. 56): 'to cause to recline' [BAGD], 'to cause to recline to eat' [LN], 'to make/have someone recline at the table' [AB, Lns, NTC, WBC; HCSB, NASB, NIV], 'to make/have someone sit down' [Arn; CEV, TEV], 'to make someone sit down at the table' [GW], 'to tell someone to sit at the table' [NCV], 'to have someone sit down to eat' [LN; NRSV], 'to make someone sit down to meat' [KJV], 'to seat someone' [NLT], 'to seat someone at table' [REB], 'to have someone take his place at the table' [NET], 'to recline at the table (with)' [BECNT]. The master would make them take their places at the table as though they were masters [Su]. Or, the master will recline with them at the table in order to share the meal with them [BECNT]. See this word at 9:14.
e. aorist act. participle of παρέρχομαι (LN **15.86**) (BAGD 3. p. 626): 'to come' [AB, Arn, BAGD, BECNT, LN, Lns, WBC; HCSB, NET, NIV, NRSV, REB], 'to come up' [NASB], 'to come forth' [KJV], 'to arrive' [**LN**], 'to go ahead' [NTC], not explicit [CEV, GW, NCV, NLT, TEV]. This verb is redundant in this context [NIGTC]. The master will come to where they are at the table [Gdt, TH] to serve them the food that they had prepared for him [Gdt]. He will come to each of the seated slaves in turn [Alf].
f. fut. act. indic. of διακονέω (LN 35.19) (BAGD 1. p. 184): 'to serve' [AB, Arn, BECNT, LN, WBC; CEV, GW, HCSB, KJV, NCV, NLT, NRSV], 'to wait on someone' [Lns, NTC; NASB, NET, NIV, REB, TEV], 'to wait on someone at table' [BAGD]. He will serve them a meal [NIGTC, TG, TH].
g. φυλακή (LN 67.196) (BAGD 4. p. 868): 'watch' [Arn, BAGD, BECNT, LN, Lns, NTC, WBC; KJV, NASB, NET, NIV], 'a fourth of the night' [LN]. The phrase 'if in the second or if in the third watch' is translated 'if it is the middle of the night or before dawn' [REB], 'in the middle of the night or just before dawn' [NLT], 'during the middle of the night or near dawn' [NRSV], 'if in the middle of the night, or even near dawn' [HCSB], 'if in the middle of the night or toward morning' [GW], 'about midnight or shortly before dawn' [AB], 'even though late at night or early in the morning' [CEV], 'even if it is midnight or later' [NCV], 'even if at midnight or even later' [TEV].

QUESTION—In what way will the slaves be blessed?

The master reverses their normal roles and serves the slaves a meal [AB, Alf, EGT, Lns, MGC, NIVS, Su, TNTC; NET]. Here the meaning is 'how fortunate' or 'how good it will be for them' [TG]. Being slaves, they would merely be doing their duty, so their blessedness depends solely on what the returning master decides to do for them [Lns]. This is not a true-to-life situation, but things are different in God's kingdom [TNTC, WBC].

QUESTION—What time was the second or third watch?

1. This refers to the Roman practice of dividing the night into four periods of three hours each [Alf, EGT, Lns, MGC, My, NAC, NTC, Pnt, Su, TG]. The four watches were 6–9, 9–12, 12–3, and 3–6 [NAC, Su, TG]. Jesus did not rule out the possibility of returning at the first or fourth watch and could have named them instead [Lns]. The second and third watches were the times most people find it hard to remain awake [EGT].
2. This refers to the Jewish practice of dividing the night into three periods of four hours each [Arn, Crd, ICC, NIGTC, NIVS, TH, WBC]. The three watches were 6–10, 10–2, and 2–6. The first hour is not mentioned as a possibility since the wedding feast would extend into the first watch [ICC, NIVS]. These watches are mentioned to show the zeal of the servants in remaining at their posts until the night was past [Crd].

12:39 And know^a this, that if the master-of-the-house had-known at-what hour the thief was-coming, he-would- not -have-allowed^b his house to-be-broken-into.^c

TEXT—Following ἔρχεται 'was coming', some manuscripts add ἐγρηγόρησεν ἂν καί 'he would have watched and'. GNT does not mention this variant. Ἐγρηγόρησεν ἂν καί 'he would have watched and' is read by KJV.

LEXICON—a. pres. act. impera. of γινώσκω (LN 28.1) (BAGD 6.c. p. 161): 'to know' [Arn, BAGD, BECNT, LN, WBC; HCSB, KJV, NLT, NRSV], 'to realize' [Lns; GW], 'to understand' [NET, NIV], 'to be assured' [NTC], 'to remember' [NCV, REB], 'to be sure' [NASB, TEV], 'to consider' [AB], not explicit [CEV].

b. aorist act. indic. of ἀφίημι (LN 13.140) (BAGD 4. p. 126): 'to allow' [BAGD, LN, WBC; NASB, NCV], 'to let' [AB, BAGD, BECNT, LN, Lns; CEV, GW, HCSB, NET, NIV, NRSV, REB, TEV], 'to permit' [Arn, NTC; NLT], 'to suffer' [KJV]. The way in which he would not let this happen is by taking the necessary precautions of locking the door and probably staying awake [TG], or by assigning his servants to stand guard at the gate [Pnt].

c. aorist pass. infin. of διορύσσω (LN **19.41**) (BAGD p. 199): 'to be broken into' [AB, Arn, BAGD, BECNT, **LN**, NTC, WBC; HCSB, NASB, NET, NIV, NLT, NRSV, REB], 'to be broken through' [BAGD, LN, Lns; KJV]. This passive form is also translated actively with the thief as the subject: 'to break into' [CEV, GW, TEV], 'to enter' [NCV]. The thief would dig through the mud-brick wall [AB, Arn, BECNT, ICC, MGC, NAC, TH, TNTC, WBC], or burrow through the clay wall [NIGTC], or break through the door or window [Lns], or sneak through the gate [Pnt].

QUESTION—How is the mention of a thief connected with the preceding story?

Following the picture of servants being ready for the return of their master, a new illustration is used of a master being ready when a thief comes to the house [EGT, TH]. This reinforces the command to be ready [BECNT]. The common theme of the two illustrations is being ready [BECNT, EGT, Gdt], and being watchful [Lns, Su, TH]. The first parable is about the possibility of delay in the coming of the master and this parable is about the sudden and unexpected coming of a thief [NIGTC]. The first parable is about the blessedness of being watchful and this added parable is a warning about failing to watch [BECNT, Lns, NIGTC].

QUESTION—Is the verb γινώσκετε 'know' in the first phrase 'know this' an imperative or indicative?
    1. It is an imperative [AB, Arn, BECNT, BNTC, Lns, NTC, TH, WBC; KJV, NASB, NCV, NET, NIV, NLT, NRSV, REB]: know this! This is something they must know [TH].
    2. It is indicative [Gdt, ICC; GW, TEV]: you know this. The knowledge they already possess is the grounds for the exhortation in 12:40 [Gdt].

12:40 Also you be ready,^a because in-what hour you-do- not -think the Son of-Man^b is-coming.

TEXT—Following ὑμεῖς 'you', some manuscripts add οὖν 'therefore'. GNT does not mention this variant. Οὖν 'therefore' is read by KJV.
LEXICON—a. ἕτοιμος (LN 77.2) (BAGD 2. p. 316): 'ready, prepared' [BAGD, LN]. The phrase γίνεσθε ἕτοιμοι 'be ready' [BECNT, Lns; GW, HCSB, KJV, NASB] is also translated 'you must be ready' [AB, WBC; NCV, NET, NIV, NRSV, TEV], 'hold yourselves in readiness' [REB], 'you must be ever ready' [NTC], 'always be ready' [CEV], 'you must be ready all the time' [NLT], 'prove yourselves ready' [Arn]. The present imperative γίνεσθε 'be' is durative [NTC; CEV, NLT, REB], meaning to be ever ready [Lns], to keep on being ready [Rb], to constantly be ready [NIC, NIGTC]. To be ready to prevent a thief from unexpectedly breaking into his house, he must be ready all the time [WBC].
    b. υἱὸς τοῦ ἀνθρώπου 'Son of Man'. This title for Christ occurs at 5:24; 6:5, 22; 7:34; 9:22, 26, 44; 11:30; 12:8, 40; 17:22, 24, 26; 18:8, 31; 19:10; 21:27, 36; 22:22, 48, 69; 24:7. See the discussions of this title at 5:24, 6:5, and 9:22.

QUESTION—In what respect were the disciples to be ready?
In the parallel passage in Matt. 24:42–44, the setting is the Second Coming of Christ and here it also refers to the second coming [Arn, Gdt, Lns, MGC, NAC, NIC, NICNT, NIVS, NTC, Su, WBC]. They are to be ready to receive and welcome the Son of Man [TH]. They must not be taken by surprise [TG]. They must be ready for his second coming by believing in him and obeying him [NIC].

QUESTION—What relationship is indicated by ὅτι 'because' in the last clause 'because in what hour you do not think the Son of Man is coming'?
It indicates the reason for always being ready [BECNT]. One doesn't know when he will come [CEV]. It is a time when they don't expect him [NTC, TH; NCV, NET, NIV, NRSV], when they least expect him [GW, NLT, REB]. Those on watch for his coming may come to expect him at some time

they think is especially appropriate [Lns]. It is implied that it would be a long time before he would come and so there would be some who would no longer be looking for him [NET]. The reason the disciples are included in this warning is answered in the following parable [BECNT].

DISCOURSE UNIT: 12:41–48 [TNTC; HCSB, NCV, NRSV, TEV]. The topic is the responsibility of servants [TNTC], who is the trusted servant? [NCV], the faithful or the unfaithful servant [NRSV, TEV], rewards and punishment [HCSB].

12:41 **And Peter said, Lord, do-you-speak this parable with-regard-to[a] us or also with-regard-to all?**
TEXT—Following εἶπεν δέ 'and said', some manuscripts add αὐτῷ 'to him'. GNT does not mention this variant. Αὐτῷ 'to him' is read by KJV.
LEXICON—a. πρός (LN 89.7) (BAGD III.5.a. p. 710): 'with regard to' [LN], 'with reference to' [BAGD], 'for' [AB, BECNT; CEV, GW, NET, NLT, NRSV, REB], 'to' [Arn, Lns, NTC, WBC; HCSB, KJV, NASB, NCV, NIV], 'to apply to' [TEV].
QUESTION—What parable was Peter referring to and what did he mean by his question?
> It is possible that both of the preceding parables are intended [NIGTC]. It applies to the parable of 12:39–40, but the answer will also include the previous parable as well [WBC]. Perhaps the promise of the high rewards in 12:37 was in mind [Gdt, ICC]. Peter wanted to know if this parable was told for the sake of the Apostles (and possibly other leaders among the disciples) alone or whether all of the disciples were included [AB, Alf, Crd, Gdt, ICC, NIGTC, TH, WBC], or all the people who were then present [Su]. Or, he wanted to know if it concerned only the disciples or also the others in the crowd around them [AB, Arn, BECNT, Lns, MGC, NAC, NICNT, TG]. Or, he couldn't understand how disciples could be in danger of suffering loss at the coming of the Son of Man, so he wanted to know if the possibility of suffering loss concerned only the unbelievers in the crowd [NIC]. Since Jesus had been speaking especially to his disciples from verse 22 on, Peter wondered if Jesus meant that some of the disciples would not be ready to welcome him [NTC].

12:42 **And the Lord said, Who then is the faithful[a] wise[b] steward[c] whom the master will-put-in-charge[d] over his servants[e] to-give the food-allowance[f] at (the) proper-time?**
TEXT—Instead of ὁ πιστὸς οἰκονόμος ὁ φρόνιμος 'the faithful wise steward' some manuscripts read ὁ πιστὸς οἰκονόμος καὶ φρόνιμος 'the faithful steward and wise' although GNT does not mention this variant. Ὁ πιστὸς οἰκονόμος καὶ φρόνιμος 'the faithful and wise steward' is read by KJV.
TEXT—Some manuscripts omit τό 'the' before σιτομέτριον 'food allowance'. GNT does not deal with this variant in the apparatus but places τό 'the' in brackets in the text. Τό 'the' is omitted by KJV (since 'their', representing

the definite article, is italicized, indicating that τό 'the' is not in its Greek text source). Some versions might not distinguish between these two readings.

LEXICON—a. πιστός (LN 31.87) (BAGD 1.a.α. p. 664): 'faithful' [AB, Arn, BAGD, BECNT, LN, NTC, WBC; all versions except NCV, REB], 'dependable' [BAGD, LN], 'trustworthy' [BAGD, LN, Lns], 'trusted' [NCV], 'trusty' [REB], 'reliable' [LN]. He must be trustworthy in his service to the master [Lns].

b. φρόνιμος (LN 32.31) (BAGD p. 866): 'wise' [BAGD, BECNT, LN, WBC; CEV, KJV, NCV, NET, NIV, TEV], 'sensible' [BAGD, Lns, NTC; HCSB, NASB, NLT, REB], 'prudent' [AB, Arn; NRSV], 'skilled' [GW]. He must be sensible in managing his master's estate [Lns].

c. οἰκονόμος (LN 46.4) (BAGD 1.a. p. 560): 'steward' [Arn, BAGD, BECNT, LN, WBC; KJV, NASB, REB], 'steward-slave' [Lns], 'manager' [AB, BAGD, NTC; GW, HCSB, NET, NIV, NRSV], 'manager of a household' [LN], 'servant' [CEV, NCV, NLT, TEV]. The steward was a slave (12:43) whom the master assigned the task of managing his whole estate [BECNT, Lns, NICNT, NIGTC, NIVS, TH, TNTC]. See this word at 16:1.

d. fut. act. indic. of καθίστημι (LN 37.104) (BAGD 2.a. p. 390): 'to put in charge' [BAGD, LN, NTC; CEV, GW, HCSB, NASB, NET, NIV, NRSV, TEV], 'to give the responsibility of managing' [NLT], 'to appoint' [BAGD, LN, WBC; REB], 'to designate' [LN], 'to set over' [BECNT, Lns], 'to put over' [AB], 'to place over' [Arn], 'to make ruler' [KJV], not explicit [NCV]. It is implied that the master is leaving home for a while [TG].

e. θεραπεία (LN **46.6**) (BAGD 2. p. 359): 'servants' [BAGD, NTC; CEV, GW, NCV, NIV, REB, TEV], 'household servants' [**LN**; HCSB, NET], 'slaves' [NRSV], 'household' [BECNT; KJV, NLT], 'staff' [AB], 'service' [Lns], not explicit [WBC]. The noun refers to the group of servants who work in the household [WBC; NET]. It refers to the domestic staff [AB, BNTC, Gdt].

f. σιτομέτριον (LN **5.3**) (BAGD p. 752): 'food allowance' [AB, BAGD, NTC; NIV], 'allowance of food' [NET, NRSV], 'a due amount of food rations' [**LN**], 'a measure of food' [BECNT], 'food ration' [Arn, WBC], 'allotted food' [HCSB], 'food supplies' [CEV], 'rations' [NASB, REB], 'share of food' [GW, TEV], 'their food' [NCV], 'due portion' [Lns], 'portion of meat' [KJV], not explicit [NLT]. The noun means a measured allowance of food [NIGTC]. In large Roman households food rations were served out daily, weekly, or monthly [BECNT, ICC]. The rations consisted of food such as grain [BECNT].

QUESTION—Did Jesus answer Peter's question?

Peter's question does not seem to be answered because it was asked from curiosity and what Peter should be concerned about was to be a faithful and wise manager [NTC]. The counter-question indicates that it is enough for

Peter to recognize that he is a steward with responsibilities [ICC, TH]. Along with the following parable, Jesus indicated that he particularly meant his parable for those whom he appoints as leaders to care for others [NIC]. The preceding parables applied especially to the Apostles and other leaders among the disciples [NIGTC, Rb]. Only when 12:47–48 is reached is it clear how Peter's question is answered [WBC]. Indirectly, the answer was that the parable was intended for all the people, but for the disciples in a special way [Arn]. The parable is for all, but each individual must be responsible for the station assigned to him [Lns].

QUESTION—What is the intent of asking 'Who then is the faithful wise steward'?

It is a way to introduce the parable by asking 'What kind of person is a faithful and wise servant?' [TG]. The question invites the hearer to examine himself as to whether he fills the specifications [Lns]. If there is such a steward, then he will be blessed (12:43) [BECNT].

12:43 Blessed[a] (is) that slave whom his master having-come will-find doing thus.[b] 12:44 I-say to-you truly[c] that he-will-put- him -in-charge over all his possessions.[d]

LEXICON—a. μακάριος (LN 25.119) (BAGD 1.b. p. 485): 'blessed'. See translations of this word at 12:37. As in 12:37, this word has no religious connotation in the story [NIGTC]. This word also occurs at 1:45; 6:20; 7:23; 10:23; 11:27; 12:37; 14:14; 23:29.

b. οὕτως (LN 61.9): 'thus, in this way' [LN], The phrase 'doing thus' is translated 'doing so' [BECNT, Lns; NIV], 'doing just so' [WBC], 'so doing' [NTC; KJV, NASB], 'doing this' [TEV], 'thus engaged' [Arn], 'doing his work' [NCV], 'doing their job' [CEV], 'doing this job' [GW], 'has done a good job' [NLT], '(finds him) working' [HCSB], '(finds) at work' [NET, REB; similarly AB; NRSV]. 'Thus' refers to doing what his master had commanded him [NTC, TG], carrying out his duties [TG; NET], being faithful [BECNT, Lns; CEV], and being sensible [Lns]. What he was doing is described in 12:42 [Lns].

c. ἀληθῶς (LN 70.3) (BAGD 1. p. 37): 'truly' [AB, BAGD, BECNT, LN, Lns, NTC, WBC; NASB, NRSV], 'of a truth' [Arn; KJV], 'surely' [CEV], 'indeed' [TEV], not explicit [REB]. The phrase 'I say to you truly' is translated 'I tell you the truth' [HCSB, NCV, NET, NIV], 'I assure you' [NLT], 'I can guarantee this truth' [GW]. This word makes the saying particularly solemn [NIGTC]. See this word at 9:27.

d. pres. act. participle of ὑπάρχω (LN 57.16) (BAGD 1. p. 838): 'to belong to' [BAGD, LN]. The phrase τὰ ὑπάρχοντα means 'possessions' [BAGD, LN], 'property' [LN]. The phrase 'all his possessions' [Arn, BECNT, Lns, NTC; HCSB, NASB, NET, NIV, NRSV] is also translated 'all his property' [GW, TEV], 'all his master's property' [REB], 'all his goods' [WBC], 'all he possesses' [AB], 'all that he has' [KJV], 'all he owns' [NLT], 'everything he/the master owns' [CEV, NCV]. See this word at 11:21.

QUESTION—What is meant by referring to the man as ὁ δοῦλος ἐκεῖνος 'that slave'?

Most appear to take 'that' to refer to the slave who is the steward in 12:42 [BECNT, NAC, NIBC, NTC, Su, TH; GW, NCV, NLT, REB, TEV]. Or, 'that slave whom' refers to 'that sort of slave' [Lns, NIGTC, WBC] and the reference is broadened to include all slaves who do thus [CEV]. This is one type of steward and there are two other types described in the following verses [BECNT]. In the application of the parable, it refers to any disciple whom God has given some responsibility [BECNT, Lns, MGC, NIBC, NIC]. It refers to all believers who are faithful [NTC] and prepared for the Lord's second coming [NAC]. It refers to the end time judgment [WBC].

QUESTION—Didn't the slave already have the responsibility of being a steward?

Probably his position as steward in the previous verse consisted of serving the master as a subordinate who was temporarily in charge, so here he is appointed to be permanently in control [MGC, NIGTC]. Now his responsibilities are more permanent and include not only management of the house, but the whole estate [BECNT, Lns]. The master will give the slave a share in all of his own power and wealth [AB].

12:45 But if that slave says in his heart, My master delays to-come, and he-begins to-beat the men-servants[a] and the woman-servants, and both to-eat and to-drink[b] and to-become drunk,

LEXICON—a. παῖς (LN 87.77) (BAGD 1.a.γ. p. 604): 'servant, slave' [BAGD, LN]. The phrase with both the masculine and feminine forms of the word, τοὺς παῖδας καὶ τὰς παιδίσκας 'the men servants and the woman servants' is translated 'the male and female servants' [WBC], 'the male and female slaves' [HCSB], 'the menservants and maidservants' [Arn, BECNT, Lns; NIV], 'the menservants and maids' [REB], 'the menservants and maidens' [KJV], 'the servants and maids' [AB], 'the men and the women servants' [NTC], 'the slaves, both men and women' [NASB], 'the other slaves, (both) men and women' [NET, NRSV], 'the other servants, men and women' [NCV], 'the other servants, both the men and the women' [TEV], 'the other servants' [GW, NLT], 'all the other servants' [CEV].

b. pres. act. infin. of πίνω (LN 23.34) (BAGD 1. p. 658): 'to drink' [AB, Arn, BAGD, BECNT, LN, Lns, NTC, WBC; all versions except NLT]. The phrase 'to eat and to drink and to become drunk' is translated 'partying and getting drunk' [NLT].

QUESTION—Why would the slave who was the steward begin to beat the servants?

The steward thought that he could act as the master and dominate the others [NIGTC]. He abused those under him to the extent of beating them [Lns]. He would probably beat them with his hand or with a stick [TG]. The master had delayed so long that the steward began to think he would be able to cover up his actions before his master returned [WBC].

QUESTION—What is meant by the steward eating and drinking and becoming drunk?

This combination of verbs refers to feasting [TG]. The verbs 'to eat and to drink' are translated 'partying' [NLT] or feasting [TH], and together the two verbs were a phrase meaning gluttony [TH]. The parallel passage in Matthew 24:49 says 'eats and drinks with drunken revelers' and the three verbs together were a proverbial way of describing such conduct [AB, NIGTC]. Perhaps the steward was using what he should have been giving them [ICC].

12:46 the master of-that slave will-come on a-day which he-does- not -expect[a] and at an-hour which he-does- not -know,[b] and he-will-cut-in-pieces[c] him and will-assign (him) his place with the unbelievers/ unfaithful.[d]

LEXICON—a. pres. act. indic. of προσδοκάω (LN 30.55) (BAGD 3. p. 712): 'to expect' [AB, Arn, BAGD, BECNT, LN, Lns, NTC, WBC; HCSB, NASB, NET, NIV, NRSV, REB, TEV], 'to look for' [KJV]. The object of 'expect' is the master [Arn, BECNT, TH, WBC]. The phrases 'on a day which he does not expect and at an hour which he does not know' is translated 'on a day and at a time when the servant least expects him' [CEV], 'when that servant is not ready and is not expecting him' [NCV], 'unannounced and unexpected' [NLT], 'at an unexpected time' [GW].

b. pres. act. indic. of γινώσκω (LN 28.1) (BAGD 6.a.α. p. 161): 'to know' [Arn, BAGD, BECNT, LN; HCSB, NASB, NRSV, TEV], 'to know about' [WBC], 'to foresee' [NET], 'to figure on' [NTC], 'to be aware of' [KJV, NIV], 'to realize' [Lns], 'to suspect' [AB], 'to be told' [REB]. See a. above for translations of the two verbs by CEV, GW, NCV, NLT.

c. fut. act. indic. of διχοτομέω (LN **19.19**) (BAGD p. 200): 'to cut in two' [Arn, BAGD, **LN**, Lns, WBC; NET], 'to cut in sunder' [KJV], 'to cut in pieces' [HCSB, NASB, NCV, NIV, NRSV, REB, TEV], 'to cut to pieces' [NTC], 'to tear apart' [NLT], 'to dismember' [AB, BECNT], 'to severely punish' [GW]. This active verb is also translated passively: 'to be punished' [CEV]. This verb may be used figuratively for punishing severely [BAGD, LN].

d. ἄπιστος (LN 31.98) (BAGD 2. p. 85): 'unbelieving' [BAGD, LN], 'unfaithful' [BAGD], 'untrustworthy' [LN]. The clause τὸ μέρος αὐτοῦ μετὰ τῶν ἀπίστων θήσει 'will assign him a place with the unbelievers/unfaithful' is translated 'will appoint him his portion with the unbelievers' [KJV], 'will assign him a place with the unbelievers' [HCSB, NASB, NIV], 'will assign him a place with the faithless' [REB], 'will assign his lot with the unfaithful' [Arn], 'will allocate him his place with the faithless' [WBC], 'will assign him a fate fit for the faithless' [AB], 'will put his portion with the unfaithful' [BECNT], 'will place together with the faithless' [Lns], 'will assign him a place with the unfaithful'

[NTC; NET], 'will assign him a place with unfaithful people' [GW], 'will put him with the unfaithful' [NRSV], 'will banish him with the unfaithful' [NLT], 'will be thrown out with the servants who cannot be trusted' [CEV], 'will send him away to be with the others who don't obey' [NCV], 'make him share the fate of the disobedient' [TEV].

QUESTION—Why is the clause 'and at an hour which he does not know' added to the clause 'a day he does not expect'?

The two clauses are synonymous [TG; CEV, GW] and the second is added for the sake of emphasis [Lns, NAC]. The parallelism of day and hour were a stereotyped phrase [NIGTC]. The steward did not know the day because his master had not told him when he would return [TH].

QUESTION—Does it mean that the master will literally cut him in two?

1. It refers to a literal execution [Arn, Crd, ICC, Lns, Rb, WBC]. Such extreme actions are general in parables [Lns, WBC]. He will be cut in two with a saw [Lns].
2. It is used metaphorically (hyperbolically [MGC]) for severe punishment [AB, BECNT, EGT, Gdt, MGC, NAC, NICNT, TG, TNTC; CEV, GW]. It could be understood as scourging his back with a rod [EGT, Gdt].

QUESTION—Does ἄπιστος mean 'unbelieving' or 'unfaithful'?

1. This refers to people who were unbelievers [AB, BECNT, Lns, MGC, NAC, TH, WBC; HCSB, KJV, NASB, REB]. This is a way of referring to the last judgment and means that he will suffer what unbelievers suffer [TH]. This verse is not part of the story but is an application concerning the ultimate destiny of unbelievers [WBC]. Here the word 'unfaithful' contrasts with the faithful servant, but in the context of such a severe punishment, it must refer to unbelievers and so to be placed with such people means to receive the same punishment and total rejection as all unbelievers [BECNT]. It is a place of eternal punishment [NAC].
2. This refers to servants who were unfaithful [Arn, EGT, Gdt, ICC, NTC, Rb; CEV, GW, NCV, NET, NLT, NRSV, TEV]. There is no point for the parable to refer to unbelievers, so this means unfaithful servants, those who abused the trust the master placed in them [ICC]. They were unfaithful to their trust [Arn]. They were unreliable [NTC, Rb], the same as the 'hypocrites' in the parallel passage in Matt. 24:51 [NTC; NET].

DISCOURSE UNIT: 12:47–48 [AB]. The topic is the servant's reward.

12:47 And that slave, the (one) having-known the will of-his master and not having-prepared[a] or having-done[b] according-to his will, will-be-beaten[c] (with) many (blows).

LEXICON—a. aorist act. participle of ἑτοιμάζω (LN 77.3) (BAGD 1. p. 316): 'to prepare' [Arn, BAGD, LN, Lns], 'to prepare himself' [HCSB, KJV, NRSV], 'to make preparations' [WBC], 'to make ready' [BECNT, LN], 'to be ready' [CEV, NCV], 'to get ready' [NTC; GW, NASB, NET, NIV], 'to get himself ready' [TEV], 'to anticipate' [AB], not explicit [NLT,

REB]. He was not prepared for the master's coming [Gdt, Lns]. See this word at 12:20.
  b. aorist act. participle of ποιέω (LN 42.7) (BAGD I.2.b.α. p. 682): 'to do' [Arn, BAGD, LN, Lns; all versions except CEV, NASB, REB], 'to be willing to do' [CEV], 'to act' [AB, BAGD, BECNT, LN, NTC, WBC; NASB], 'to accomplish, to perform' [LN], 'to carry out' [REB].
  c. fut. pass. indic. of δέρω (LN **19.2**) (BAGD p. 175): 'to be beaten' [BAGD, LN], 'to be whipped, to be punished with a beating' [LN]. The phrase 'to be beaten with many blows' [WBC; NCV, NIV] is also translated 'to be beaten with many stripes' [KJV], 'to be beaten with many lashes' [Arn], 'to be flayed with many lashes' [Lns], 'to stand many blows' [AB], 'to be punished with a hard beating' [**LN**], 'to be punished with a heavy whipping' [TEV], 'to receive many blows of the lash' [NTC], 'to receive a hard beating' [GW], 'to receive a severe beating' [BECNT; NET, NRSV], 'to be beaten hard' [CEV], 'to receive many blows' [BAGD], 'to receive many lashes' [NASB], 'to be flogged severely' [REB], 'to be severely beaten' [HCSB], 'to be severely punished' [NLT]. This is figurative language and refers to punishment in hell [Lns].

QUESTION—How is this verse and the following one connected with the preceding parable?

These verses give a conclusion to the preceding parable [NIGTC, Su, TG], or an application of it [Su]. The preceding verse indicates that the fate of unbelievers is to be punished in hell and this verse indicates that there are differences of punishment in hell [Lns]. Or, this adds two more degrees of unfaithfulness and describes their punishments [BECNT, NIVS]. The master of the parable is the same as the master here and he symbolizes Christ [NTC]. This retains the same picture of servant and master as the parable [NIGTC]. The parable ended with 12:46 [Arn, NIBC, NTC, Su]. This verse is included in a separate discourse unit [AB], or in a separate paragraph [NTC, WBC; CEV, GW, NCV, NIV, REB, TEV]. Verse 12:47 is included in the paragraph before it and 12:48 is made into a separate paragraph [NLT]. This explains why such severe punishment was applied in the preceding parable [EGT, My, NTC]. This is a warning that punishment is certain for those who do not do their duty [TNTC]. With privileges come responsibilities [TG].

QUESTION—Who is referred to as 'that slave' at the beginning of 12:47?

The word 'that' refers to the following words, 'the one having known the will of his master' and not backward to the slave in 12:45–46 [BECNT, Lns, NAC, TH]. The aorist verbs in the sentence are timeless so as to state the fact of the verbs, not the time of them [Lns]. 'That slave' refers to the class of slaves to which the steward in 12:45 belongs [My].

12:48 But the (one) not having-known and having-done (things) worthy of-blows will-be-beaten (with) few (blows). And everyone to whom much was-given,[a] much will-be-demanded[b] from him, and to-whom they-entrusted[c] much, even-more they-will-ask[d] (from) him.

LEXICON—a. aorist pass. indic. of δίδωμι (LN 57.71) (BAGD 3. p. 193): 'to be given' [AB, Arn, BECNT, LN, Lns, NTC, WBC; all versions except CEV], 'to be entrusted with' [BAGD]. The phrase 'to whom much was given' is translated '(if) God has been generous to you' [CEV]. The implied object of the verb is abilities or opportunities [TG]. The passive voice implies that God is the one who gives and demands in this clause [AB, NAC, NICNT, NIGTC, TG, TH; CEV].
- b. fut. pass. indic. of ζητέω (LN 33.167) (BAGD 2.c. p. 339): 'to be demanded' [BAGD, LN; NCV, NIV], 'to be required' [AB, Arn, BECNT, NTC, WBC; HCSB, KJV, NASB, NET, NLT, NRSV, TEV], 'to be expected' [GW, REB], 'to be sought' [Lns]. The phrase 'much will be demanded from him' is translated 'he will expect you to serve him well' [CEV]. The passive voice implies that God is the one who will require this [NAC, NICNT, NIGTC, TG, TH].
- c. aorist mid. indic. of παρατίθεμαι (LN 35.47) (BAGD 2.b.α. p. 623): 'to entrust' [Arn, BAGD; NASB], 'to give' [BAGD, LN], 'to commit' [BECNT; KJV], 'to deposit' [Lns], '(if) he has been more than generous' [CEV]. This middle voice is also translated as a passive: 'to be entrusted' [AB, NTC; GW, HCSB, NET, NIV, NRSV, REB], 'to be trusted with' [NCV], 'to be given' [NLT, TEV], 'to be handed over' [WBC].
- d. fut. act. indic. of αἰτέω (LN 33.163): 'to ask' [Arn, BECNT, LN, Lns; KJV, NASB], 'to demand' [LN]. This active voice is also translated as a passive: 'to be asked' [WBC; NET, NIV], 'to be demanded' [AB, NTC; GW, NRSV, REB], 'to be expected' [HCSB, NCV], 'to be required' [NLT, TEV]. The phrase 'even more they will ask from him' is translated 'he will expect you to serve him even better' [CEV]. This verb is a synonym of the preceding verb ζητέω 'to be demanded' [TH; NLT, TEV].

QUESTION—Why wouldn't the slave have known his master's will and why would he still be worthy of receiving a beating?

It is implied that this slave had not known the will of his master [Lns, TH; NET] and because of this did not prepare [Lns]. It may be that he was a lower slave who had not received explicit orders from the master [EGT, Gdt, Su]. Such a slave is nevertheless responsible to a certain extent [Gdt]. Ignorance is never absolute [NTC]. The slave could have known his master's will if he had wanted to [Arn, ICC]. Even without explicit orders, he had a moral standard of obedience to the master [My]. It is important to know God's will and we should endeavor to find out about it [TNTC].

QUESTION—What is the function of the last sentence?

This sentence states the principle on which the evaluations of the degrees of punishment is based [BECNT, NAC, NIBC, Su]. It states the grounds for the fate of the two slaves [Lns]. This is an application of the picture of the slaves and master to the disciples and God [CEV].

QUESTION—What is meant by the use of the third person plural form of the verbs παρέθεντο...αἰτήσουσιν 'they entrusted...they will ask'?
1. This is a universal application of a principle, so this means 'people' [Lns, Su; KJV]. Some translations supply 'they' [Lns; NASB], or 'men' [KJV]. This applies universally among men and it is right for them to do so [Lns]. This gives a human sense of justice [Su].
2. The third person is used as an impersonal plural [BECNT]. It is used as a substitute for the passive form [AB; GW, NCV, NET, NIV, NLT, NRSV, REB, TEV]. It refers to the master of the illustrations [BECNT]. It is to be applied as a reference to God [NAC, NIGTC; CEV].

QUESTION—What is the difference between being *given* πολύ 'much' and being *entrusted with* πολύ 'much' so that περισσότερον 'even more' will be asked from the second?
1. The two parts are not synonymous [Gdt, Lns; NET]. The first verb 'being given' refers to an assigned position and can be applied to the commission given to believers in general, while the verb 'entrusted' refers to the higher light given to the apostles [Gdt]. The second verb 'entrusted' implies a certain responsibility that requires faithfulness [NET]. The second verb means that something has been deposited with someone to do business with, and the return of that deposit along with the interest gained are asked for [Lns].
2. The two parts are virtually synonymous [Crd, My, NIGTC; NLT, REB, TEV]. In the second part the word περισσότερον 'even more' refers to 'more than had been committed to him' [My]. Perhaps περισσότερον 'even more' means that more will be asked of the person who is given more than the person who has been given little [Crd, NIGTC; NLT]. This is translated 'much more is required from those to whom much more is given' [NLT], 'the more he has had entrusted to him the more will be demanded of him' [REB], 'much more is required from the person to whom much more is given' [TEV].

DISCOURSE UNIT: 12:49–14:24 [BECNT]. The topic is knowing the nature of the time.

DISCOURSE UNIT: 12:49–59 [BECNT, NICNT, NIGTC; NASB, NLT]. The topic is the coming crisis [NIGTC], recognizing the coming crisis [NICNT], knowing the time [BECNT], Jesus causes division [NASB, NLT].

DISCOURSE UNIT: 12:49–53 [AB, BECNT, NAC, TNTC, WBC; CEV, GW, HCSB, NCV, NET, NIV, NRSV, TEV]. The topic is fire on the earth [TNTC], Jesus, the great divider [NAC], Jesus as the cause of division [BECNT; NCV, NRSV, TEV], Jesus will cause conflict [GW], not peace, but trouble [CEV], not peace, but division [HCSB, NET, NIV], the prospect of fire, baptism, and division [WBC], the enigma of Jesus' mission [AB].

12:49 I-came to-throw[a] fire upon the earth, and how/what I-wish that/if already it-was-ignited.[b]

LEXICON—a. aorist act. infin. of βάλλω (LN 39.15): 'to throw' [LN]. The idiom πῦρ βάλλω 'to throw fire' [Lns; GW] is also translated 'to cast fire (upon/on)' [AB, Arn, BECNT, NTC, WBC; NASB], 'to set fire (to)' [CEV, NCV, REB], 'to set on fire' [TEV], 'to send fire (on)' [KJV], 'to bring fire (on)' [HCSB, NET, NIV], 'to bring fire (to)' [NLT, NRSV], 'to bring division (into)' [**LN**]. 'Fire' is at the beginning of the Greek sentence, thus making the word emphatic [ICC, Lns, NAC, TH]. The picture is that of throwing a fire brand to the earth [Gdt].

b. aorist pass. indic. of ἀνάπτω (LN **14.65**) (BAGD p. 60): 'to be ignited' [LN], 'to be kindled' [Arn, BAGD, BECNT, LN, Lns, NTC, WBC; KJV, NASB, NET, NIV, NRSV, REB, TEV], 'to be started' [GW], 'to be burning' [NCV], 'to be set ablaze' [HCSB], 'to be ablaze' [AB], 'to be on fire' [CEV], 'to be completed' [NLT].

QUESTION—What is meant by throwing πῦρ 'fire' upon the earth?

1. Fire is a symbol of judgment [BECNT, MGC, NAC, NIBC, NICNT, NIGTC, NIVS, NTC, Su, TG, TH, TNTC, WBC]. This symbol for judgment has already been used at 3:16 [TH]. The fire was smoldering throughout Jesus' ministry and would flare up at his death and what would follow [Su]. The fire of judgment would separate good from evil, resulting in division among people [NAC, NIVS] and persecution of the righteous [NIGTC]. Or, judgment upon unbelief would be kindled at Jesus' death, but this judgment would be borne by Jesus for the salvation of others [NTC, TNTC].
2. Fire is a symbol of removal of evil, both by judgment of unbelievers and purification of believers [Alf, NIC]. The gift of the Holy Spirit would separate mankind with its purifying and separating work, thus causing the division which is brought about by the fullness of the Holy Spirit entering believers [NIC].
3. Fire is a symbol of discord and contention [Arn, Crd, ICC, LN, Lns, WBC]. It means 'I came to bring division into the world' [LN (39.15)]. The discord described in the following verses must come about before God's kingdom could come [Crd]. Jesus' ministry would cause divisions and he knew that his death would be the cause of controversy and argument and wished that it had already been accomplished [WBC]. The death of Jesus would set the world on fire by causing strife and one of the functions of the good news of the cross may be described as fire [Lns].
4. Fire is a symbol of faith and spiritual fervor [EGT, Gdt, My, Rb]. The enthusiasm of the disciples would cause others to oppose them [EGT, Rb]. Jesus' presence brought about spiritual excitement with a subsequent division between believers and unbelievers [Gdt]. The fire would be kindled by Jesus' death [My].

LUKE 12:49

QUESTION—What is meant by 'how/what I wish that/if already it was ignited'?
1. It means that the fire has not yet been ignited [AB, Alf, Arn, BECNT, BNTC, Crd, EGT, Lns, MGC, My, NAC, NIGTC, NTC, Rb, TG, TH, TNTC, WBC; all versions except KJV]: how I wish that the fire were already was ignited. The word τί is to be taken as equivalent to πῶς 'how' and the word εἰ equivalent to ὅτι 'that' [Rb]. This expresses Jesus' impatient desire to have God's judgment begin [TG]. Jesus must undergo the baptism before the fire can be kindled [TH]. The fire would be ignited when Jesus died on the cross [Lns, TNTC].
2. It means that the fire was already ignited [Gdt, ICC, NICNT; KJV]: what have I to wish for if the fire is already ignited? It is translated 'What more have I to desire, if it be already kindled?' and although it was already kindled in Christ's ministry, it was not yet blazing to its full extent [ICC]. It means 'What more have I to seek, since it is already kindled?' and this shows Jesus' satisfaction that the inevitable division described in 12:1–12 was already beginning to happen [Gdt].

12:50 And I-have a-baptism[a] to-be-baptized (with), and how I-am-distressed/constrained[b] until it-is-accomplished.[c]

LEXICON—a. βάπτισμα (LN 24.82) (BAGD 3. p. 132): 'baptism' [BAGD, LN]. The idiom βάπτισμα βαπτίζομαι 'to be baptized with a baptism' means to suffer or undergo a difficult experience or ordeal [LN]. The phrase 'I have a baptism to be baptized with' [Arn, BECNT, Lns; HCSB, KJV] is also translated 'I have a baptism with/in which to be baptized' [AB, NTC, WBC; NRSV], 'I have a baptism to receive' [TEV], 'I have a baptism to go through' [GW], 'I have a baptism to suffer through' [NCV], 'I have a baptism to undergo' [NASB, NET, NIV, REB], 'there is a terrible baptism ahead of me' [NLT], 'I must undergo an ordeal' [LN], 'I am going to be put to a hard test' [CEV]. 'Baptism' is at the beginning of the Greek sentence, thus making the word emphatic [Lns, NAC, TH].

b. pres. pass. indic. of συνέχομαι (LN **90.65**) (BAGD 5. p. 789): 'to be distressed' [BAGD, BECNT, **LN**; NASB, NET, NIV, TEV], 'to be troubled' [LN], 'to feel very troubled' [NCV], 'to be under stress' [NRSV], 'to be overwhelmed with anguish' [NTC], 'to be under a heavy burden' [NLT], 'to be straitened' [Lns; KJV], 'to be hard pressed' [AB], 'to have to suffer a lot of pain' [CEV], 'to be afflicted' [Arn], 'to suffer' [GW], 'to be taken up (with it)' [WBC], 'to be under constraint' [REB]. This passive verb is also translated actively: '(how it) consumes me' [HCSB].

c. aorist act. subj. of τελέω (LN 13.126) (BAGD 2. 811): 'to be accomplished' [AB, BAGD, LN, NTC, WBC; KJV, NASB, NLT], 'to be completed' [NIV, NRSV], 'to be carried out, to be performed' [BAGD], 'to be finished' [Arn, BECNT, Lns; HCSB, NET], 'to be over' [CEV, GW, NCV, TEV], 'to be fulfilled' [BAGD, LN].

QUESTION—What is meant by the baptism?

Baptism is a metaphor for the difficulties and sufferings Jesus must experience [My, NTC, TG, TH], even to bringing about his death [Alf, BECNT, BNTC, Crd, ICC, Lns, MGC, NIBC, NIC, NIVS, WBC]. The metaphor means to be overwhelmed by the disaster of his coming passion [WBC]. It was God's judgment on the sin that Jesus bore for sinners [BECNT, Lns, MGC, Su; NET].

QUESTION—What is meant by 'how I am distressed/constrained until it is accomplished'?

1. This refers to Jesus' mental anguish about what was to happen [Alf, Arn, BECNT, Crd, EGT, Gdt, ICC, Lns, MGC, My, NAC, NIC, NIVS, NTC, TG, TH, TNTC; NASB, NCV, NET, NIV, NLT, NRSV, TEV]. Jesus was distressed because he wanted to do more than he would be able to do before he died [BECNT]. Or, Jesus was distressed because he wanted to get it over with [NIVS, TG]. Whenever Jesus thought of his coming Passion he was assailed by sorrow and wished that it would soon be accomplished [Arn]. His suffering and death would be so severe that Jesus wished it were finished, yet he would not hesitate because of that [Lns]. Only by receiving this baptism would the fire be kindled [NAC]. Although Jesus longed to do his Father's will, his human will desired a shortened waiting period for the baptism [ICC].
2. This means that Jesus was dominated by the thought of his baptism [AB, NIGTC, Su, WBC; REB]. He was totally occupied with the events that would bring about redemption for men and nothing else mattered to him [Su].

12:51 **Do-you-think that I-came to-bring**[a] **peace on the earth? No, I-tell you, but rather division.**[b]

LEXICON—a. aorist act. infin. of δίδωμι (LN 90.51): 'to bring' [BECNT; CEV, GW, NET, NIV, NLT, NRSV, TEV], 'to bring about, to cause, to produce' [LN], 'to establish' [Arn; REB], 'to give' [Lns, NTC, WBC; HCSB, KJV, NCV], 'to put' [AB], 'to grant' [NASB].

b. διαμερισμός (LN **39.14**) (BAGD p. 186): 'division' [BECNT, **LN**, Lns, NTC, WBC; GW, HCSB, KJV, NASB, NET, NIV, NRSV, TEV], 'dissension' [Arn, BAGD; REB], 'discord' [AB], 'disunity' [BAGD], 'strife and division' [NLT], 'opposition, hostility' [LN]. This noun is also translated as a verb phrase: 'to divide' [NCV], 'to make people choose sides' [CEV].

QUESTION—Didn't Jesus come to bring peace?

Peace is used here of a sense of undisturbed harmony [Lns, TG], of concord and agreement [TG]. This is a paradox since it is clear that peace is a goal of Jesus' ministry [WBC]. However there will be conflict before that peace is realized [WBC]. This statement was a way to emphasize one aspect of the truth, not to state a universally valid truth [NTC]. Jesus' offer of peace causes people to choose to receive it or reject it and so they take sides

[BECNT, TG]. The ones who choose Jesus' side will be hated and persecuted by the ones who choose against him [NIC]. The people are divided about their relationships with Jesus [Su]. They are divided over the claims of Christ [MGC] and the gospel [NIGTC].

12:52 Because from now (on) there-will-be five in one house/family[a] having-been-divided,[b] three against two and two against three. **12:53** They-will-be-divided father against son and son against father, mother against the daughter and daughter against the mother, mother-in-law against her daughter-in-law and daughter-in-law against the mother-in-law.

TEXT—In 12:53, instead of τὴν πενθεράν 'the mother-in-law', some manuscripts read τὴν πενθερὰν αὐτῆς 'her mother-in-law'. GNT does not mention this variant. Τὴν πενθερὰν αὐτῆς 'her mother-in-law' is read by KJV; some versions might not distinguish between the two readings.

LEXICON—a. οἶκος (LN 10.8): 'house' [Arn, BECNT, Lns], 'family' [AB, LN, NTC; CEV, GW, NCV, NIV, NLT, REB, TEV], 'household' [LN, WBC; HCSB, KJV, NASB, NET, NRSV].

b. perf. pass. participle of διαμερίζω (LN **90.51**) (BAGD 2. p. 186): 'to be divided' [AB, Arn, BAGD, BECNT, **LN**, Lns, NTC, WBC; all versions except NLT], 'to be split apart' [NLT]. This is a division between opposing and hostile parties [LN].

QUESTION—Is there a significance in the number five?

This gives the number of the people involved in the relationships described in the next verses, the mother and mother-in-law being the same person [Arn, BECNT, Crd, EGT, Gdt, ICC, MGC, NIC, NTC, TH, TNTC]. The family is comprised of father, mother, their son and their daughter and the son's wife [TH]. It was the custom for a son to bring his wife to live in his father's house [Lns, TH]. The daughter would have been unmarried since if she had married she would be living in her husband's house [Lns]. The three would be the daughter, the son, and his wife, and they would be against the father and mother [Su, TH].

QUESTION—Are the five people in one house or in one family?

1. The five people are located in one house [BNTC, Lns, TH]: there will be five in one house.
2. Instead of talking about the location, the five people are members of one family [AB, LN, NTC, WBC; all versions]: there will be five in one family.

DISCOURSE UNIT: 12:54–59 [NAC, TNTC; CEV, GW, NIV]. The topic is the signs of the times [TNTC], the signs of the time and settling with one's opponents [NAC], interpreting the times [NIV], knowing what to do [CEV], using good judgment [GW].

DISCOURSE UNIT: 12:54–56 [AB, BECNT, WBC; HCSB, NCV, NET, NRSV, TEV]. The topic is the signs of the times [AB], reading the signs [NET], interpreting the time [HCSB, NRSV], understanding the times [NCV, TEV], reading the times like the weather [BECNT], interpreting the present time [WBC].

12:54 **And also he-was-saying to-the crowds, When you-see the cloud rising in (the) west, immediately you-say, A rainstorm is-coming, and it-happens thus.** **12:55** **And when (you see) a-south-wind blowing, you say, It-will-be hot, and it-happens.**

TEXT—In 12:54, some manuscripts omit τήν 'the' before νεφέλην 'cloud'. GNT does not deal with this variant in the apparatus but places it in brackets in the text, indicating doubt about including it. Τήν 'the' is omitted by KJV.

TEXT—In 12:54, instead of ἐπί 'in', some manuscripts read ἀπό 'from'. GNT does not mention this variant. Ἀπό 'from' is read by KJV.

QUESTION—Whom did Jesus address in these verses?

Jesus not only spoke to his disciples with the preceding words, he καί 'also' spoke to the crowds with the following words [Alf, Arn, Lns]. Jesus now turned to the larger crowd at this point and continued to address them until 13:9 [BECNT]. It implies that Jesus was speaking to the crowd in contrast to his former speaking to his disciples [NIGTC, TG]. It is implied that Jesus' disciples understood the significance of his coming, but the crowds didn't [AB, NAC]. It does not mean that Jesus turned from his disciples to address the crowds, rather he widened the scope of his address [WBC]. The disciples were not immune from being hypocrites too [NICNT].

QUESTION—How did people know when a rainstorm was coming?

In Israel, west is the direction of the Mediterranean Sea, the normal place for rain clouds to develop [Arn, BECNT, EGT, Gdt, Lns, MGC, NAC, NIC, NICNT, TG, TH, TNTC, WBC; NET], and then the clouds would condense over the hills of central Israel [AB].

QUESTION—How did people 'see' the wind and know when it was going to be hot?

The verb 'you see' of 12:54 is implied here [Alf, ICC, My, TH, WBC; NASB, NET, NRSV]: when you see a south wind blowing. The wind can be seen by the objects it moves [ICC]. Some supply the verb 'you feel' [NCV, TEV]. In Israel, south is the direction of the Arabian desert where warm air would come from [Gdt, Lns, MGC, NIC, NICNT, NIGTC, TG; NET]. The wind was from the desert in the southwest [BECNT], the southeast [AB, Arn, Lns, NAC]. The word for 'south' was used for southerly or even southwesterly winds that carried the heat from the desert [WBC].

12:56 **Hypocrites,[a] you-know (how) to-interpret[b] the-appearance[c] of-the earth and the sky, but how (is it) you-do- not -know (how) to-interpret this time?[d]**

TEXT—Instead of πῶς οὐκ οἴδατε δοκιμάζειν 'how do you not know to interpret' some manuscripts read πῶς οὐ δοκιμάζειν 'how do you not interpret' and one manuscript reads οὐ δοκιμάζετε 'do you not interpret'. GNT reads πῶς οὐκ οἴδατε δοκιμάζειν 'how do you not know to interpret'

LUKE 12:56

with a B decision, indicating that the text is almost certain. Πῶς οὐ δοκιμάζειν 'how do you not interpret' is read by KJV.

LEXICON—a. ὑποκριτής (LN 88.228) (BAGD p. 845): 'hypocrite' [AB, Arn, BAGD, BECNT, LN, Lns, NTC, WBC; all versions except CEV], 'pretender' [BAGD, LN]. This noun is also translated as a clause: 'are you trying to fool someone?' [CEV]. See this word at 6:42; 13:15.

  b. pres. act. infin. δοκιμάζω (LN 27.45) (BAGD 1. p. 202): 'to interpret' [AB, NTC, WBC; HCSB, NET, NIV, NLT, NRSV, REB], 'to examine' [BAGD, LN], 'to analyze' [NASB], 'to test' [Arn, LN, Lns], 'to discern' [BECNT; KJV], 'to understand' [NASB], 'to predict' [CEV], '(look at) to predict the weather' [TEV], 'to forecast the weather by judging' [GW]. To 'interpret' the appearance of the earth and sky is to determine their character [Arn].

  c. πρόσωπον (LN 24.24) (BAGD 1.d. p. 721): 'appearance' [Arn, BAGD, LN, WBC; all versions except CEV, KJV, TEV], 'face' [Lns; KJV], 'situation' [BECNT]. The phrase 'the appearance of' is translated 'the look of' [AB, NTC], 'by looking at' [CEV], '(you can) look at' [TEV]. It refers to changes in the weather, the appearance of clouds, and any other weather signs [TG]. Perhaps there were other signs of rain or heat from how the hills appeared [Alf].

  d. καιρός (LN 67.145) (BAGD 3. p. 395): 'time' [BAGD; KJV], 'age, era' [LN]. The phrase 'this time' [HCSB] is also translated 'this present time' [WBC; NASB, NIV], 'the present time' [BECNT; NET, NRSV], 'these present times' [NLT], 'the present critical hour' [NTC], 'this fateful hour' [REB], 'this particular time' [Arn], 'the season that is here' [AB], 'this season of time' [Lns], 'the time in which you are living' [GW], 'what's going on right now' [CEV].

QUESTION—Why were these people hypocrites?

They pretended that they did not understand what was happening at the present time because they refused to do so [AB, Arn, ICC, Lns, NAC, NIC, NIGTC, TG, TH, WBC]. Since they were intelligent enough to interpret the weather, they should have been able to interpret the present time, yet they were unwilling to do so [AB, Gdt, NIC, NIGTC, TG, TNTC]. They would not act on their knowledge of the signs [Lns]. They pretended to be religious, but ignored what was important [NTC, TNTC]. Here the word translated 'hypocrite' does not mean someone who plays a role, but someone who was unable to discern the meaning of the signs that were plain to see [NICNT].

QUESTION—What is the function of the question in 12:56?

It is a rhetorical question [TG], indicating reproach [MGC, NIGTC]. Beginning the question with 'hypocrites' implies that they refused to recognize the meaning of what was happening in the ministry of Jesus at that time [TG]. The question indicates surprise at their actions [Lns, TH]. It is possible to treat this as a statement, 'but you do not know how to interpret this time', instead of a rhetorical question. However, the sense is the same either way [BECNT].

QUESTION—What does 'this time' refer to?

It means the time in which God was acting through Jesus [BECNT, TH], the time of Jesus' presence and ministry [NIGTC, WBC]. It was the time in salvation history marked by the coming of God's kingdom in Jesus ministry [NAC]. The time of Jesus' ministry was a significant era, a critical time [AB].

DISCOURSE UNIT: 12:57–59 [AB, BECNT, WBC; HCSB, NCV, NET, NRSV, TEV]. The topic is clearing your debts [NET], settle your problems [NCV], settling accounts [HCSB], settling accounts with the accuser [AB, BECNT], settling with your opponent [NRSV, TEV], under accusation and on the way to the court of justice [WBC].

12:57 **And why indeed/also for yourselves do-you- not -judge[a] (what is) right?[b]**

LEXICON—a. pres. act. indic. of κρίνω (LN 30.108) (BAGD 4.a.α. p. 451): 'to judge' [AB, Arn, BAGD, BECNT, LN, Lns, NTC; all versions except CEV, NCV, NLT], 'to make a judgment' [WBC], 'to evaluate' [LN], 'to determine' [BAGD], 'to decide' [NCV, NLT], 'to understand' [CEV]. This verb is the equivalent of δοκιμάζω 'to interpret' in 12:56 [NIGTC, WBC] and refers to discerning what is fitting to do in the circumstances [NIGTC]. It refers to reflecting about the wise course of action [BECNT].

c. δίκαιος (LN 66.5) (BAGD 5. p. 196): 'right' [AB, Arn, BAGD, BECNT, LN, Lns, NTC; all versions except CEV, TEV], 'proper' [LN]. This noun is also translated as an adjective: 'right (judgment)' [WBC]. The phrase 'what is right' is translated 'the right thing to do' [CEV, TEV].

QUESTION—What brought on this question about judging what is right?

This rhetorical question is a challenge for the hypocrites to interpret this present time (12:56) [AB, Lns, WBC]. They could do so if they wanted, since 'this time' is clearly marked by the preaching of John, his baptism, the person of Jesus and his preaching and miracles [Lns]. The right thing includes thinking for themselves instead of letting the scribes and Pharisees doing it for them, letting their consciences be their guide, and learning to think for themselves about religious matters [NTC]. This rhetorical question criticizes them for being unwilling to decide what was the right thing to do [TG], the right things being implied in the following parable in 12:58–59 [TH]. The right thing is reconciliation with God by conversion [Gdt]. In view of the coming time of crisis (12:56), it is wise to settle difficulties at once [Lns, Su].

QUESTION—What relationship is indicated by καί 'indeed, also, even'?

The conjunction καί is translated 'indeed' [WBC], 'even' [KJV, NASB], or 'also' [Lns], but the rest of the translations do not make the word explicit. The phrase δὲ καί 'and indeed' functions to emphasize the following phrase ἀφ' ἑαυτῶν 'for yourselves' [TH]. It can focus on what they should do on their own, apart from information or teaching from others [ICC, NIVS; NASB, NTC]. Or, it may mean what they should do this as well as something else [ICC, Lns]: 'of yourselves also, as readily as in the case of the weather' [ICC], 'moreover on top of what I thus ask, why do you not also of yourselves judge' [Lns].

12:58 Because as you-go-away with your accuser[a] to a-ruler,[b] make an-effort on the way to-come-to-a-settlement[c] with him, lest he-drag[d] you to the judge, and the judge will-hand-over you to the officer,[e] and the officer will-throw you into prison.

LEXICON—a. ἀντίδικος (LN 56.11) (BAGD p. 74): 'accuser' [BECNT, LN, WBC; NET, NLT, NRSV], 'opponent' [AB, BAGD, NTC; GW, NASB, REB], 'adversary' [Arn; HCSB, KJV, NIV], 'enemy' [NCV], 'opponent at law' [Lns], 'someone who accuses (you) of something' [CEV], 'someone who brings a lawsuit (against you)' [TEV]. This refers to an opponent in a lawsuit [BAGD, TH], a legal adversary [NIGTC], about a debt [TH].

b. ἄρχων (LN **56.29**) (BAGD 2.a. p. 114): 'ruler' [Lns; GW, HCSB], 'magistrate' [AB, Arn, BECNT, NTC; KJV, NASB, NET, NIV, NRSV], 'official' [BAGD, LN, WBC], 'judge' [BAGD, **LN**]. The phrase 'you go away with your accuser to a ruler' is translated 'you are going with your opponent to court' [REB], 'your enemy is taking you to court' [NCV], 'you are taken to court' [CEV], 'and takes you to court' [TEV], 'you are on your way to court' [NLT]. This noun refers to a minor government official who serves as a judge [LN]. The ruler also acted as a judge [Lns].

c. perf. pass. infin. of παλλάσσομαι (LN **40.3**) (BAGD 2.a. p. 80): 'to come to a settlement' [BAGD], 'to reach a settlement' [REB], 'to be reconciled' [NIV], 'to come to an agreement' [**LN**], 'to settle' [AB, BECNT, NTC; GW, HCSB, NASB, NET], 'to settle it' [NCV], 'to settle the issue' [**LN**], 'to settle the dispute' [TEV], 'to settle the matter' [NLT], 'to settle things' [CEV], 'to settle the case' [NRSV], 'to be released' [WBC], 'to be delivered (from)' [KJV], 'to be free of' [Arn], 'to be wholly rid of (him)' [Lns]. This refers to an action that is directed toward getting free from the debt that is assumed in the illustration [BECNT]. 'You', the guilty party, must propose terms that the accuser will agree to and thus avoid the court proceedings [TH]. The object is not to be reconciled with each other, but to satisfy the accuser so that he will go away for good [NIGTC].

d. pres. act. subj. of κατασύρω (LN **15.179**) (BAGD p. 419): 'to drag' [AB, Arn, BAGD, **LN**, NTC; GW, HCSB, NASB, NET, NIV, REB], 'to drag off' [WBC], 'to hale' [Lns; KJV], 'to take' [NCV], 'to ruin' [BECNT], not explicit [NLT]. This active verb is also translated as a passive: 'to be dragged' [CEV, NRSV, TEV]. This action is done by force [BAGD, LN]. The action of being dragged away implies that the person is shamed and in the Septuagint it can mean to be ruined [BECNT, ICC].

e. πράκτωρ (LN **37.92**) (BAGD p. 697): 'officer' [Arn, BECNT, **LN**; GW, KJV, NASB, NCV, NET, NIV, NLT, REB], 'court officer' [Lns], 'bailiff' [BAGD, LN, WBC; HCSB], 'jailer' [AB; CEV], 'constable' [NTC], 'the

LUKE 12:58

police' [TEV]. This was an officer of a court who carried out the judge's orders [BAGD, LN, NTC, TH] and was in charge of the prison [TH]. This was a civil official who functioned like a bailiff and was in charge of a debtor's prison [BECNT, NAC, NIGTC; NET]. This refers to the constable of a debtor's jail [AB].

QUESTION—What relationship is indicated by the first conjunction γάρ 'because'?

Here the point of judging in 12:57 is explained with an illustration of a legal dispute [BECNT, EGT, Gdt, Lns, NTC; GW]. A person must judge what is right because of the legal situation into which he might fall [BECNT]. They should act thus with God because it is what they would do with a human adversary [Gdt]. It indicates a reason why they should judge for themselves (12:57) [Gdt].

QUESTION—Is it significant that the 'you' in 12:57 is plural, while in the illustration in 12:58–59, 'you' is singular?

Each individual is now addressed [ICC]. The singular form emphasizes the individual application [BECNT]. Each person should be reconciled to God [NTC].

QUESTION—Who will drag you to court?

1. The accuser is the one who will drag you to the judge [NIGTC, TG, TH]. The grammar of most translations also seems to indicate this.
2. The ruler is the one who will drag you to the judge [My, Su]. The accuser would go to the ruler and demand that he arrest you and then that ruler would drag you before the judge [Su].

12:59 I-say to-you, you-will- not-at-all -get-out from-there, until you-pay-back even the last lepton.[a]

LEXICON—a. λεπτόν (LN 6.79) (BAGD 2. 472): 'lepton' [BECNT, LN, Lns, WBC], 'tiny coin' [LN], 'small copper coin' [BAGD], 'cent' [AB; CEV, HCSB, NASB], 'penny' [Arn; GW, NET, NIV, NLT, NRSV, REB], 'mite' [NTC; KJV]. This was the smallest coin in use [NAC, NICNT, TNTC; NET]. See this word at 21:2.

QUESTION—What is the last lepton that must be paid back?

It refers to the complete amount that the judge orders you to pay [TG]. It refers to the complete amount that is owed to the accuser [Lns, MGC, NICNT, NIGTC, TH, WBC]. It is called a fine [GW, TEV]. The debt might be paid off by sale of property [NICNT], or his family and friends might pay the debt [BECNT]. Generally, it was not likely that he could get out of the debtor's prison [BECNT]. Or, the full payment of the debt will no longer be possible and the condemnation lasts forever [NIC].

QUESTION—What is this parable about?

'This present time' in 12:56 is identified in this parable as being the time on the way to the law court and only swift action can avoid the steps of the judicial process [WBC]. As they would act in an ordinary case of debtor and creditor, so they should act with repentance in regard to the coming judgment day [EGT]. They must settle affairs in this world before God settles with them in the next life [NIBC]. A person should consider the nature of 'this time' and make the right response to his spiritual indebtedness to God [BECNT]. The religious application is that everyone should be reconciled to God while there is still time [NAC, NTC]. The point of the parable is to do what 12:57 says before it is too late [TH]. It indicates that the sinner needs to seek forgiveness from God before the day of judgment [MGC, NIC, NICNT, TNTC]. The prison represents hell and any payment there will be impossible [Lns].

DISCOURSE UNIT: 13:1–9 [AB, BECNT, NAC, NICNT, NIGTC, TNTC, WBC; NASB, NIV]. The topic is repentance [TNTC], the need to repent [NAC, NIGTC, WBC], a call to repent [NASB], repent or perish [NIV], a warning concerning repentance and fecundity [NICNT], lessons for Israel [BECNT], timely reform; the parable of the barren fig tree [AB].

DISCOURSE UNIT: 13:1–5 [Su; CEV, GW, HCSB, NCV, NET, NLT, NRSV, TEV]. The topic is a call to repentance [Su; NET, NLT], turn back to God [CEV], change your hearts [NCV], Jesus tells people to turn to God and change the way they think and act [GW], repent or perish [HCSB, NRSV], turn from your sins or die [TEV].

13:1 And at the same time some arrived/were-present[a] reporting to-him about the Galileans whose blood Pilate mingled[b] with their sacrifices.

LEXICON—a. imperf. act. indic. of πάρειμι (LN 13.86, **85.23**) (BAGD 1.a. p. 624): 'to arrive' [BECNT, LN (13.86), NTC], 'to come' [BAGD, LN (13.86); HCSB, REB], 'to be present' [AB, Arn, **LN** (85.23), Lns, WBC; KJV, NASB, NET, NIV, NRSV], 'to be there' [NCV, TEV]. The phrase 'some arrived/were present reporting to him' is translated 'some people reported to Jesus' [GW], 'Jesus was told' [CEV], 'Jesus was informed' [NLT].

b. aorist. act. indic. of μίγνυμι, μείγνυμι (LN **63.10**) (BAGD 1. p. 499): 'to mingle' [AB, BAGD, LN, Lns, NTC, WBC; KJV, NRSV], 'to mix' [Arn, BAGD, BECNT, LN; HCSB, NASB, NCV, NET, NIV, REB]. The phrase 'whose blood Pilate mixed with their sacrifices' is translated 'whom Pilate had killed while they were offering sacrifices to God' [TEV], 'Pilate caused them to be killed while they were offering sacrifices to God' [LN], 'Pilate ordered them to be slain while they were sacrificing' [LN], 'Pilate had given orders for some people from Galilee to be killed while they were offering sacrifices' [CEV], 'whom Pilate had executed while they were sacrificing animals' [GW], 'Pilate had murdered some people from Galilee as they were sacrificing at the Temple in Jerusalem' [NLT].

QUESTION—Who were the persons who reported the death of the Galileans?
1. They arrived and came up to Jesus at that time [AB, Alf, BECNT, Crd, ICC, NIBC, NIC, NIGTC, NTC, TH]. They were probably messengers who came from Jerusalem to bring the news [Alf, NIGTC]. The present

LUKE 13:1 73

participle ἀπαγγέλλοντες 'reporting' indicates their purpose for coming [TH]. The verb 'reporting' usually refers to recent news [BECNT]. They had not been in the crowd that Jesus had been addressing, but possibly had arrived in time to hear his last words and thought that this news could be regarded as a sign [ICC]. Or, this passage is not connected with the preceding discourse [Alf].

2. They were already present among the crowd at that time [Arn, EGT, Lns, MGC, My, Su, WBC]. The imperfect 'were present' indicates that they had come previously and were now present [Lns]. Some think that this does not refer to a recent arrival. They were present while Jesus was speaking in 12:54–59 [EGT]. They could have been some of the crowd, some of the Pharisees, or some of the Twelve Apostles [Su]. Perhaps when they heard Jesus speak of the signs of times, they wondered if the slaughter of the Galileans was one of the signs [Arn].

QUESTION—Why did Pilate kill the Galileans and who were they?

The reason the Galileans were killed was that they were known for being rebellious [NIGTC], they may have broken some important Roman law [NIVS], they probably were involved in some activities against the Romans [WBC], such as plotting to overthrow the Roman rule in Palestine [TG]. Pilate did not kill them personally but ordered that they be killed [AB, TG; CEV]. Pilate caused them to be killed while they were engaged in offering their sacrifices in the outer court at the temple [AB, My]. The Galileans were probably pilgrims who had come to Jerusalem for a feast, possibly the Passover [AB, BECNT], because the Passover feast was the only occasion in which the sacrificial animals were slaughtered by the people themselves instead of by the priests [BECNT, MGC, NIGTC]. Since they are compared with the group of eighteen people who perished in 12:4, the logic of the sequence suggests that there were probably less than eighteen in this massacre [WBC]. The number need not be more than a couple [NIGTC].

QUESTION—Is the clause 'the Galileans whose blood Pilate mixed with their sacrifices' to be taken literally?

1. The Galileans were killed in the act of slaughtering their sacrificial animals with the result that their blood actually mingled with the blood from the sacrifices [Arn, ICC, NIC, Su, TG, TNTC, WBC; all versions]. This is a horrible detail concerning their deaths [TNTC].

2. The verb 'mixed' was an idiom that meant two events occurred together without the blood from the men physically mixing with the blood of the animals [BECNT, LN, MGC, NIBC, NIGTC]. It is to be understood figuratively [LN, MGC, NIBC]. If taken literally as a slaughter within the Temple grounds during a sacrifice, it would probably have brought about an insurrection by the Jews, so this should be taken as a literary device, meaning that not only was the blood of sacrificed animals shed at that time, but the blood of the Galileans was shed also [NIBC].

LUKE 13:2–3

13:2 And answering he-said to-them, Do-you-think that these Galileans were sinners beyond^a all the Galileans because they-have-experienced^b these (things)? **13:3** No, I-tell you, but unless you-repent, all (of) you-will-perish^c likewise.

TEXT—In 13:2, instead of εἶπεν 'he said', some manuscripts read ὁ Ἰησοῦς εἶπεν 'Jesus said'. GNT does not mention this variant. Ὁ Ἰησοῦς εἶπεν 'Jesus said' is read by KJV.

LEXICON—a. παρά (LN 78.29) (BAGD III.3. p. 611): 'beyond' [Arn, BAGD, LN, Lns], 'above' [KJV], 'more than' [BAGD, LN], 'in comparison to' [BAGD], 'to a greater degree than' [LN]. The phrase 'were sinners beyond all the Galileans' is translated 'were greater sinners than all the other Galileans' [NTC, WBC; NASB], 'were greater sinners than all the others in Galilee' [AB], 'were more sinful than all others from Galilee' [NCV], 'were more sinful than all Galileans' [HCSB], 'were worse sinners than all the other Galileans' [BECNT; NET, NIV, NRSV, TEV], 'were worse sinners than everyone else in Galilee' [CEV], 'were worse sinners than other people from Galilee' [NLT], 'were more sinful than other people from Galilee' [GW], 'must have been greater sinners than anyone else in Galilee' [REB].

  b. perf. act. indic. of πάσχω (LN 90.66) (BAGD 3.b. p. 634): 'to experience' [BAGD, LN], 'to suffer' [AB, Arn, BAGD, BECNT, LN, Lns, NTC, WBC; HCSB, KJV, NASB, NET, NIV, NLT, NRSV, REB], 'to endure' [BAGD], 'to be killed' [TEV]. This active voice is also translated passively: 'of what happened to them' [CEV], 'this happened to them' [GW, NCV]. They did not suffer in the sense of being only wounded, they were actually killed [TG].

  c. fut. mid. indic. of ἀπόλλυμι (LN 20.31): 'to perish' [AB, Arn, BECNT, Lns, NTC, WBC; KJV, NASB, NET, NIV, NLT, NRSV], 'to die' [GW, TEV], 'to be killed' [CEV], 'to be destroyed' [LN; NCV], 'to come to the (same) end' [REB].

QUESTION—What relationship is indicated by ὅτι 'because' in the last clause of 13:2?

This indicates the reason why the people might think the murdered Galileans were the worst sinners [BECNT, NIGTC, TH]. Calamities were commonly thought to be the result of past sin [AB, BECNT, NAC, NIC, NIGTC, TNTC, WBC], and this was what the audience assumed [Gdt, MGC].

QUESTION—What is meant by perishing ὁμοίως 'likewise'?

  1. The manner of their death will also be violent and sudden [AB, Alf, Arn, BECNT, Crd, EGT, Gdt, MGC, NAC, NIGTC, TG, TNTC, WBC; NRSV]: you will be killed in the same manner. This refers to a tragic death such as what would take place when Jerusalem would be destroyed in A.D. 70 [Crd, NAC], or perishing in the final judgment [NAC]. This would be the fate of the nation [Gdt] and Jews actually did perish by the Roman swords [Alf]. Or, the comparison is with dying tragically and perishing ultimately before God [BECNT]. Disaster will come to all who

do not repent [WBC]. They will perish in a similar way in the context of the last judgment [AB, MGC, NIGTC].
2. They will come to the same end, that is, they will die [Lns, NIGTC, NTC, Su, TH; CEV, GW, HCSB, NET, NIV, NLT, REB]: you too will die as well. It is not that they are to fear some form of cruel death, but they must fear the danger of dying in an unrepentant state and thus perish in death [Lns; NET]. They cannot escape God's judgment just because they were descended from Abraham [NTC]. Regardless of the fate of those Galileans, it was just as certain that Jesus' hearers would perish if they did not repent [Su].

13:4 Or those eighteen upon whom the tower[a] in Siloam fell and killed them, do-you-think that they were offenders[b] beyond all the men living-in Jerusalem? **13:5** No, I-tell you, but unless you-repent all (of) you-will-perish in-the-same-way[c].

LEXICON—a. πύργος (LN 7.23) (BAGD 1. p. 730): 'tower' [AB, Arn, BAGD, BECNT, LN, Lns, NTC, WBC; all versions]. The word is generic for any type of tower that was used for military purposes or used by watchmen who were protecting a harvest [LN].

b. ὀφειλέτης (LN 88.300) (BAGD 2.c.β. p. 598): 'offender' [Arn, BAGD, LN; NET, NRSV], 'debtor' [BECNT, Lns, WBC], 'culprit' [NASB], 'sinner' [BAGD, LN; KJV, NLT]. The phrase 'they were offenders beyond all the men' is translated 'they were more sinful than all the others' [NCV], 'they were more sinful than other people' [GW], 'they were more sinful than all the people' [HCSB], 'they were more guilty than all the other people' [AB, NTC], 'they were more guilty than all the others' [NIV], 'they must have been more guilty than all the other people' [REB], 'they were worse than everyone else' [CEV], 'they were worse than all the other people' [TEV]. The noun ὀφειλέτης 'debtor' is used in the sense of 'sinner' [EGT, Lns, NAC, NIGTC, TG, TH] and corresponds to the noun ἁμαρτωλοί 'sinners' in 13:2 [TH].

c. ὡσαύτως (LN 64.16) (BAGD p. 899): 'in the same way' [BAGD, LN], 'the same way' [AB, Lns], 'in the same manner;' [Arn], 'in a similar manner' [BECNT], 'similarly' [BAGD, NTC], 'as (they did)' [NRSV, TEV], 'like' [REB], 'just as' [WBC], 'likewise' [BAGD; KJV, NASB], 'also' [CEV, NLT], 'as well' [HCSB, NET], 'too' [GW, NCV, NIV]. This adverb is equivalent to ὁμοίως 'likewise' in 13:3 [NIGTC, TG, TH] and most translate the two adverbs the same [CEV, GW, KJV, NASB, NET, NIV, NLT, TEV]. Or, here the adverb is stronger than the one in 13:3 [BECNT, EGT, ICC, WBC], in that in 13:3 ὁμοίως means 'in like manner' and here ὡσαύτως means 'in the same manner' [ICC]. The two words are translated differently: 'likewise...similarly' [NTC], 'in a similar manner...just as they did' [WBC], 'as they did...just as they did' [NRSV], 'as they were...too' [NCV], 'the same end...an end like theirs'

[REB], 'likewise...the same way' [Lns], 'likewise...in a similar manner' [BECNT], 'in a similar way...in the same way' [AB].

QUESTION—What relationship is indicated by the conjunction ἤ 'or' at the beginning of 13:4?

This conjunction introduces another question to describe a similar case to the one treated in 13:1–2 [NIC, TH]. Jesus reinforces his point by giving an example of his own [NIGTC]. This applies not only to Galileans but to everyone [Alf, NTC]. It serves to emphasis the seriousness of the need for repentance [MGC, NIC].

QUESTION—What was the tower in Siloam and why did it collapse?

The reference to '*the* tower in Siloam' indicates that everyone knew about the tower and what happened to it [TH]. Probably the tower was one of the fortifications constructed in the wall that surrounded Jerusalem [AB, Lns, NAC, NIC, NIGTC, NIVS, Su, TG, WBC]. Siloam was the name of a pool or reservoir for the city of Jerusalem near the junction of the south and east walls of Jerusalem [AB, BECNT, Gdt, Lns, MGC, NAC, NIBC, NIC, NIGTC, NTC, Su, WBC]. Siloam was a district of the city in which the pool of Siloam was located [Alf]. Or, Siloam was a suburb of Jerusalem and the tower was located in the walls of Jerusalem by that suburb [Alf, TG, TH]. The phrase ἐν τῷ Σιλωάμ 'in the Siloam' means that the tower was 'in the neighborhood of Siloam' [TH]. Perhaps the tower collapsed because it was in a state of disrepair [Lns]. Or, perhaps it collapsed in the process of constructing an aqueduct to improve the water supply to Jerusalem [MGC, NIGTC]. Or, perhaps the 'tower' was just a temporary scaffolding [NIBC].

DISCOURSE UNIT: 13:6–9 [Su; CEV, GW, HCSB, NCV, NET, NLT, NRSV, TEV]. The topic is the parable of the barren fig tree [Su; HCSB, NLT, NRSV], the parable of the unfruitful fig tree [TEV], a story about a fig tree [CEV], the useless tree [NCV], a story about a fruitless tree [GW], a warning to Israel to bear fruit [NET].

13:6 **And he-was-speaking this parable:**[a] **A-certain (man) had a-fig-tree which had-been-planted in his vineyard, and he-came seeking**[b] **fruit on it and he-did- not -find (any).** **13:7** **And he-said to the vinedresser,**[c] **Behold (it is) three years since I-have-come seeking fruit on this fig-tree and I-did- not -find (any). Therefore cut-down (the tree). Why is-it- even -using-up**[d] **the soil?**

TEXT—In 13:7, some manuscripts omit οὖν 'therefore'. GNT reads οὖν 'therefore' with a C decision and encloses this word in the text in brackets, indicating that the Committee had difficulty making the decision.

LEXICON—a. παραβολή (LN 33.15) (BAGD 2. p. 612): 'parable' [AB, BAGD, BECNT, LN, Lns, NTC, WBC; HCSB, KJV, NASB, NET, NIV, NRSV, REB, TEV], 'story' [CEV, NCV], 'illustration' [GW, NLT]. See this word at 5:36, 6:39; 14:7.

b. pres. act. participle of ζητέω (LN 27.41) (BAGD 1.a.β. p. 338): 'to seek' [Arn, BAGD, BECNT, Lns; KJV], 'to look for' [AB, BAGD, LN, NTC,

WBC; all versions except CEV, KJV, NLT], 'to see (if)' [NLT], 'to try to find' [LN]. The phrase 'he came seeking fruit' is translated 'he went out to pick some figs' [CEV]. Figs are not visible from a distance because of the foliage, so the man had to approach the tree to look for the fruit [NTC]. It is implied that the tree was mature and might be expected to have fruit [NIGTC]. The present participle indicates that he came to seek the figs from time to time [TG; NLT]. Or, it is translated so that it refers to this particular time [CEV].
  c. ἀμπελουργός (LN **43.21**) (BAGD p. 47): 'vinedresser' [BAGD, **LN**, Lns; REB], 'gardener' [AB, BAGD; CEV, GW, NCV, NLT, NRSV, TEV], 'vineyard keeper' [Arn, BECNT, NTC; NASB], 'vineyard worker' [WBC; HCSB], 'dresser of his vineyard' [KJV], 'worker who tended the vineyard' [NET], 'man who took care of the vineyard' [NIV].
  d. pres. act. indic. of καταργέω (LN 76.26) (BAGD 1.a. p. 417): 'to use up' [AB, BAGD, BECNT, NTC, WBC; GW, NASB, NIV, TEV], 'to exhaust' [BAGD], 'to deplete' [NET], 'to take up' [Lns], 'to take goodness from' [REB], 'to waste' [BAGD; HCSB, NCV, NRSV], 'to cumber' [KJV]. The question 'Why is it even using up the soil?' is translated 'Why does it make the ground useless?' [Arn], 'Why should it take up space?' [CEV], 'It's taking up space we can use for something else' [NLT].
QUESTION—What is indicted by the reference to three years?
  It indicates that it was a mature tree [Arn, NIGTC, TNTC]. The three years does not refer to the time from planting the tree, but the time from which it would be expected to bear fruit [BECNT, EGT, NTC, TNTC, WBC; NET]. Fig trees normally produce figs two times each year, in May and in late August [Hlt, TG]. Or, fig trees bear fruit annually [BECNT, NIGTC].
QUESTION—What is meant by the fig tree 'using up' the soil?
  1. This refers to the space it used up [EGT, Hlt, Lns, Pnt, Rb, TG, TNTC; CEV, NLT]. It wasted valuable space because another tree that would produce fruit could be planted in its place [TG]. The ground was of no use [Rb].
  2. This refers to the nourishment it used up [Alf, ICC; NET, REB]. It made good soil useless [ICC].
  3. This refers to both the space and the nourishment [Bai, BECNT, Kst, MGC, NIC, NIGTC, NTC]. The fig tree took up space and it also took nourishment from the ground [NIGTC].

13:8 And answering he-says to-him, Master, leave it also this year, until I-dig around it and put-on manure, **13:9** and if indeed it-produces fruit in the future[a] (good). But if not, cut- it -down.
LEXICON—a. τὸ μέλλον (LN 67.135) (BAGD 2. p. 501): This participle is used absolutely as 'the future' [BAGD, LN]. Translations specify the time as 'next year' [BAGD; all versions except KJV, NET, REB], 'the coming year' [BECNT, WBC], 'next season' [REB], 'afterward' [NTC], 'in the

future' [Arn], 'later on' [AB], 'soon after' [Lns], not explicit [KJV]. It refers to the next fig season [TH; NET].

QUESTION—What will be the result if the fig tree bears fruit?

The apodosis of the initial 'if' clause in 13:9 is not explicit because the vinedresser breaks off because of his emotion at the prospect of the tree finally producing figs [Lns, NTC]. Most translations supply the implied apodosis: 'good' [NCV], 'fine' [NASB, NIV, NLT], 'well' [KJV], 'very well' [NET], 'well and good' [NRSV, REB], 'so much the better' [TEV]. Another solution is to indicate the missing apodosis by a dash [Lns, NTC]. Still another solution is to turn the protasis into a statement: 'Perhaps it will bear fruit in the coming year' [WBC], 'Perhaps it will bear fruit next year' [HCSB], 'Perhaps it will bear fruit later on' [AB], 'Maybe it will have figs on it next year' [CEV], 'Maybe next year it'll have figs' [GW]. It is implied that if the condition is fulfilled, the tree will remain [BECNT].

QUESTION—What is the point of this parable?

Many treat this parable as an allegory and identify the participants. The owner of the vineyard and fig tree is God [BECNT, Gdt, ICC, Lns, My, Pnt]. The vinedresser is Jesus [Gdt, Lns, My, Pnt]. A lone view is that the owner is God as judge and the vinedresser is God in regard to his mercy [Hlt]. The fig tree is the Jewish nation [BECNT, Crd, Gdt, ICC, Lns, NAC, NIC, Pnt] and also any individual person [ICC]. The lack of fruit stands for the need of repentance [WBC]. Cutting down the tree stands for judgment [BECNT]. The parable means that unless the repentance called for in 13:3–5 happens, it will be too late [TH]. God is patient, but this will not last forever and the opportunity to be saved will be withdrawn [BECNT, NTC]. There is a strict time limit available for the required repentance [ICC, WBC]. This is Israel's last chance [NAC, NIC], and if they do not repent of sin and unbelief they will face God's judgment [NAC] and they will be removed from their privileged position as God's chosen people [NIC]. The people in the audience have the opportunity to repent so they can enter God's kingdom and live fruitful lives, but the offer will come to an end and then the unrepentant will face judgment [MGC, NICNT]. The outcome is left open since it is left up to the responses of those that are represented in it [BECNT]. Or, all of the items are merely natural details of the parable that dramatize the central lesson that Israel's failure to bear fruit for God in bringing Gentiles to the experience of redemption would result in having that responsibility taken away from them and given to the Gentiles [Su]. The guilt from a person's lack of repentance is greater than that which is implied the two preceding situations [AB].

DISCOURSE UNIT: 13:10–17:10 [NICNT]. The topic concerns who will participate in the kingdom.

DISCOURSE UNIT: 13:10–14:35 [WBC]. The topic is reversals now and to come.

DISCOURSE UNIT: 13:10–21 [NICNT]. The topic is the unsettling presence of the kingdom.

DISCOURSE UNIT: 13:10–17 [AB, BECNT, NAC, NIGTC, Su, TNTC, WBC; CEV, GW, HCSB, NASB, NCV, NET, NIV, NLT, NRSV, TEV]. The topic is healing on the Sabbath [NET], Jesus heals on the Sabbath [NASB, NCV, NLT], healing a woman on the Sabbath [CEV], healing a daughter of Abraham [HCSB], the healing of the crippled woman on the Sabbath [AB, BECNT, NAC, NIGTC, Su, TNTC; GW, NIV, TEV], Jesus heals a crippled woman [NRSV], releasing the one bound by Satan on the Sabbath [WBC].

13:10 And he-was teaching in one of-the synagogues on the Sabbaths.
13:11 And behold (there came) a-woman having a-spirit of-illness[a] eighteen years and she-was bent-over[b] and not able to-straighten-up[c] completely.

LEXICON—a. ἀσθένεια (LN 23.143) (BAGD 1.a. p. 115): 'illness' [BAGD, LN], 'disability' [LN], 'infirmity' [Arn; KJV], 'weakness' [Lns, WBC]. The phrase πνεῦμα ἔχουσα ἀσθενείας 'having a spirit of illness' is translated 'who had a sickness caused by a spirit' [NASB], 'who had a spirit that caused weakness' [BECNT], 'who had been disabled by a spirit' [HCSB, NET], 'who had an evil spirit in her that made her crippled' [NCV], 'who had been crippled by a spirit' [NIV], 'who had been crippled by an evil spirit' [CEV, NLT], 'with a spirit that had crippled her' [NRSV], 'possessed by a spirit that had crippled her' [REB], 'had an evil spirit that had kept her sick' [TEV], 'who had an evil spirit in her that had kept her in a state of infirmity' [NTC], 'infirm and afflicted by a spirit' [AB], 'who was possessed by a spirit…The spirit had disabled her' [GW].

b. pres. act. participle of συγκύπτω (LN **17.32**) (BAGD p. 775): 'to be bent over' [AB, BAGD, BECNT, **LN**, WBC; CEV, HCSB, NET, NIV, NRSV, TEV], 'to be bent double' [BAGD, NTC; NASB, NLT, REB], 'to be bent together' [Lns], 'to be bent' [Arn], 'to be doubled up' [LN], 'to be hunched over' [GW], 'to be bowed together' [KJV], '(her back) was always bent' [NCV]. This condition was the result of the illness [TH], of the spirit's possession [TG]. This describes a curvature of the spine [Su]. Probably the physical cause was that there was a fusion of her spinal bones [MGC, NIBC, NIC, NIGTC, NIVS, NTC, TNTC, WBC], but the spiritual cause was a demonic spirit [MGC].

c. aorist act. infin. of ἀνακύπτω (LN **17.33**) (BAGD 1. p. 56): 'to straighten up' [AB, BAGD, **LN**, NTC, WBC; CEV, HCSB, NIV, TEV], 'to straighten oneself up' [NET], 'to straighten oneself' [Arn, BECNT], 'to stand erect' [BAGD], 'to stand up straight' [GW, NLT, NRSV, REB], 'to lift up oneself' [KJV], 'to bend back' [Lns].

QUESTION—What is meant by the plural form τοῖς σάββασιν 'the Sabbaths'?
  1. It is singular in meaning [AB, Arn, BECNT, ICC, Lns, NIGTC, NTC, TH, WBC; all versions]. This does not refer to any specific Sabbath and could

be translated 'on a Sabbath' [TH]. The singular meaning is supported by the reference to one synagogue [NIGTC].
2. It could be plural in meaning and may imply that that Jesus was teaching a course in a particular synagogue for weeks [EGT].

QUESTION—How is the presence of the woman indicated?

Most supply 'there was (a woman)' [BECNT, TH; KJV, NASB], '(a woman) was there' [Arn; CEV, GW, HCSB, NCV, NET, NIV, REB], 'was present' [AB], 'there appeared' [NRSV], 'he saw' [NLT], '(a woman) there' [TEV]. With the exclamation 'behold', it implies that the woman was not in the synagogue from the start, but she slowly made her way to where Jesus was teaching [Lns, NTC].

QUESTION—What was a 'spirit of illness'?

The woman was possessed or controlled by an evil spirit that caused the illness [AB, Crd, ICC, Lns, MGC, NIC, NICNT, NIVS, NTC, Rb, TG, TH; CEV, GW, NASB, NCV, NET, NIV, NLT, NRSV, REB, TEV]. Her muscular powers were paralyzed by a demon [My]. She was demon possessed [Lns, NAC, NTC]. Demon possession varied greatly and often it inflicted some kind of physical hurt [Lns]. Or, since the evil spirit affected her physical condition and not her behavior, it may be better to refer to this to demonic influence rather than demon possession [Arn, BECNT, NICNT, NIGTC]. Or, this was not a case of possession by an evil spirit but an illness ultimately traced to Satanic influence as all illnesses are [NIBC]. Her illness was not due to possession, but due to the power Satan was permitted to have [Alf].

QUESTION—How far could the woman straighten when it says she could not straighten up εἰς τὸ παντελές 'to the complete'?

If this phrase qualifies the negation, then the rendering is 'she could not straighten up at all', but if the phrase qualifies just the verb 'stand upright', then the appropriate meaning would be 'she could not straighten up completely' [LN (78.47)].
1. The phrase qualifies the negation [AB, BECNT, BNTC, EGT, Lns, My, NIGTC, NTC, TG, WBC; all versions except NET]: the woman could not at all stand upright. The severity of the case favors this interpretation [BECNT, NIGTC, WBC].
2. The phrase qualifies the verb [Alf, Arn, Crd, ICC, My; NET]: the woman could not stand upright completely. The proximity to the verb favors this interpretation [NET].

13:12 And having-seen her Jesus called[a] and said to-her, Woman,[b] you-have-been-set-free[c] from your illness. **13:13** And he-placed-upon her (his) hands. And immediately she-was-restored[d] and she-was-praising[e] God.

LEXICON—a. aorist act. indic. of προσφωνέω (LN 33.308) (BAGD 2. p. 720): 'to call' [LN], 'to call out' [BAGD], The phrase 'called and said' [BECNT] is also translated 'he called her and said' [REB], 'he called to her and said' [Arn], 'he called her to him and said' [Lns, NTC; KJV,

NET], 'he called her to come to him and said' [GW], 'he called her over and said' [CEV, NASB, NCV, NLT, NRSV], 'he called her forward and said' [NIV], 'he called out to her' [HCSB, TEV], 'he called out and said' [WBC], 'he addressed her and said' [AB].

b. γυνή (LN 9.34): 'woman' [AB, Arn, BECNT, LN, Lns, NTC, WBC; all versions except CEV, REB], 'lady' [LN], not explicit [CEV, REB]. Used as a form of address, γυνή 'woman' was used in speaking politely to a female person [LN]. This form of address was the proper way to address the woman [TG] and did not sound unkind [TH].

c. perf. pass. indic. of ἀπολύω (LN 37.127) (BAGD 1. p. 96): 'to be set free' [BAGD, LN; NIV, NRSV], 'to be released' [BAGD, NTC, WBC], 'to be loosed' [Lns; KJV], 'to be rid of' [AB; REB], 'to be freed' [Arn, BECNT; NASB, NET], 'to be free' [GW, HCSB, NCV, TEV], 'to be healed' [NLT], 'to be well' [CEV]. The perfect tense does not reach into the past but starts from the moment Jesus freed her and extends indefinitely into the future [Lns]. It indicates a new and permanent condition [MGC, NIGTC, TH]. The woman has been freed and is now in that state of freedom [Arn]. The passive voice implies that God has freed her [NICNT, WBC]. Or, since the synagogue leader complained that Jesus had healed the woman on the Sabbath (13:14), it is not to be taken as a divine passive here [NAC]. The woman was set free from the bond of Satan and from her illness [NIVS].

d. aorist pass. indic. of ἀνορθόω (LN 17.33) (BAGD 72): 'to be restored' [BAGD], 'to be straightened up' [LN]. The phrase 'she was restored' [HCSB], is also translated 'she was made straight' [BECNT; KJV], 'she was made erect again' [NASB], 'she was raised upright' [NTC], 'she was straightened up' [Lns], 'she became erect' [Arn], 'she became erect once more' [BAGD]. The passive voice is also translated actively: 'she straightened up' [AB; NET, NIV, REB], 'she straightened herself up' [LN; TEV], 'she stood up straight' [CEV, GW, NRSV], 'she became erect again' [WBC], 'she was able to stand up straight' [NCV], 'she could stand straight' [NLT]. The passive implies that God had restored her [AB, BECNT].

e. imperf. act. indic. of δοξάζω (LN 33.357) (BAGD 1. p. 204): 'to praise' [Arn, BAGD, BECNT, LN; CEV, GW, NCV, NET, NIV, NRSV, REB, TEV], 'to glorify' [AB, BAGD, LN, Lns, NTC, WBC; HCSB, KJV, NASB], 'to praise and to thank' [NLT]. The imperfect tense means that her praising was a prolonged act [AB, TH]. The imperfect tense is ingressive to indicate that she *began* to praise God [Arn, Lns, NAC, NTC, Su, WBC; HCSB, NASB, NCV, NRSV, REB], for what Jesus had done [Su]. She praised God because she recognized the connection between Jesus and the act of God's power in healing her [BECNT, NICNT]. See this word at 5:25; 7:16.

QUESTION—What is the connection between the two verbs in the phrase 'Jesus *called out* and *said* to her'?

    1. These verbs describe two separate acts [EGT, Lns, NIC, NICNT, NIGTC, NTC, TH; all versions except TEV]: Jesus called her to come to him and then said the following words. The woman was at the back of the synagogue on the side where women sat and Jesus called her to the front where he addressed her [NICNT, NTC].

    2. This was one act [AB, BECNT, BNTC, WBC; HCSB, TEV]: Jesus called out to her, saying the following words.

QUESTION—When and why did Jesus place his hands on the woman to cure her?

Jesus probably placed his hands on the woman as he was speaking to her [Lns, NAC, NIGTC, NTC, TH], and the healing immediately followed [NIGTC]. Or, Jesus first spoke to the woman and then placed his hands on her [EGT, NICNT, NTC, TNTC; NET, NIV, NLT]. He spoke to her as she was approaching and then the cure happened when Jesus placed his hands on her [EGT]. Perhaps the evil spirit was cast out at Jesus' words and then Jesus completed the cure with his touch [TNTC]. Or, the woman was cured when Jesus spoke to her [Alf, Arn] and then Jesus touched her to give her the strength to stand up after all those years of stiffening [Alf], or to strengthen her faith [Arn]. Jesus touched the woman's curved spine [Su], or he touched either her head or shoulders [Lns, TG]. The laying on of hands symbolized God's will to heal [Lns]. This act informed the skeptical audience that Jesus' power healed the woman [BECNT].

13:14 And responding[a] the synagogue-leader,[b] being-indignant[c] that/because Jesus healed on-the Sabbath, was-saying to the crowd, There-are six days in which it-is-necessary[d] to-work. Therefore come on them (and) be-healed[e] and not on-the day of-the Sabbath.

LEXICON—a. aorist pass. (deponent = act.) participle of ἀποκρίνομαι (LN 33.28) (BAGD 2. p. 93): 'to respond' [NTC, WBC; HCSB], 'to answer' [BAGD, Lns; KJV], 'to reply' [BAGD], 'to speak, to address' [LN], 'to speak up' [Arn; TEV], not explicit [AB, BECNT; CEV, GW, NCV, NET, NIV, NRSV]. This verb is also translated 'in response' [NASB]. The synagogue leader was responding to the fact that the healing took place on the Sabbath and he was not giving an answer to anything that had been said [ICC, Lns, NIGTC, NTC].

    b. ἀρχισυνάγωγος (LN **53.93**) (BAGD p. 113): 'synagogue leader' [GW, NCV], 'leader of the synagogue' [AB, BAGD, LN; HCSB, NRSV], 'president of the synagogue' [BAGD, **LN**; NET, REB], 'ruler of the synagogue' [Arn, NTC, WBC; similarly Lns; NIV], 'leader in charge of the synagogue' [NLT], 'synagogue official' [NASB], 'man in charge of the meeting place' [CEV].

    c. pres. act. participle of ἀγανακτέω (LN 88.187) (BAGD p. 4): 'to be indignant' [BAGD, BECNT, LN, Lns, NTC; HCSB, KJV, NASB, NET,

NIV, NLT, NRSV, REB], 'to be angry' [BAGD, LN; CEV, NCV, TEV], 'to be irritated' [GW], 'to be annoyed' [AB, WBC], 'to be vexed' [Arn].
d. pres. act. indic. of δεῖ (LN 71.21) (BAGD 3. p. 172): 'it is necessary' [BAGD, BECNT, Lns], 'ought' [LN; KJV, NRSV], 'should' [LN; HCSB, NASB, NET, TEV], 'has to' [AB, Arn; NCV], 'must' [NTC, WBC], 'can' [CEV, GW], not explicit [NIV, NLT, REB]. The statement that 'it was necessary' relates to the fact that God had commanded that work be done on six days of the week [Lns], and this was prescribed in the Jewish law [TG, TH]. The synagogue leader considered healing to be labor that was prohibited on the Sabbath [BECNT]. The verb is used in a general way and refers to being allowed by the law to work [TG].
e. pres. pass. impera. of θεραπεύω (LN 23.139) (BAGD 2. p. 359): 'to be healed' [Arn, BAGD, BECNT, LN, Lns, NTC, WBC; all versions except NASB, NRSV, REB], 'to get healed' [NASB], 'to be cured' [AB; NRSV, REB]. It means 'come to get yourselves healed' [Gdt]. It sounds as though anyone could come on a weekday be healed, but he forgot that the woman had been coming for eighteen years without being healed [Rb].

QUESTION—Does the conjunction ὅτι indicate what the leader was indignant about or the reason he was indignant?
  1. It indicates what he was indignant about [AB, BECNT, Lns, MGC, NIGTC, WBC; GW, NLT, TEV]: being indignant *that* Jesus healed on the Sabbath.
  2. It indicates the reason why he was indignant [Arn, NTC, Su, TH; CEV, HCSB, KJV, NASB, NCV, NET, NIV, NRSV]: being indignant *because* Jesus healed on the Sabbath

QUESTION—Why did the synagogue leader rebuke the crowd instead of Jesus?
  The leader was hesitant to directly rebuke Jesus, so he spoke to the crowd attending worship service in the synagogue [NIGTC]. He probably lacked the nerve to speak directly to Jesus [Alf, Gdt, NIC, NTC]. By rebuking the crowd, the leader was indirectly rebuking Jesus [Arn, EGT, ICC, NIC, Rb]. Since Jesus had performed the work of healing, he was the one being rebuked [BECNT]. The leader was indirectly criticizing Jesus and was also warning the crowd about Jesus [AB]. The leader implied that the woman had come to the synagogue in order to be healed, so he was rebuking her too [Lns]. He meant that if anyone wanted to be healed, that person should return on another day and not join Jesus in breaking Sabbath laws [Su]. By addressing the people he was publicly challenging Jesus' authority as a teacher and he was making himself out to be the authorized interpreter of Scripture [NICNT].

13:15 **And the Lord answered him and said, Hypocrites,[a] does not each of-you on-the Sabbath untie his ox or donkey from the stall[b] and having-led-it-away it drinks?**

LEXICON—a. ὑποκριτής (LN 88.228) (BAGD p. 845): 'hypocrite'. See translations of this word at 6:42 and 12:56.

b. φάτνη (LN **7.64**, 6.137) (BAGD p. 854): 'stall' [BAGD, **LN** (7.64), NTC; GW, KJV, NASB, NET, NIV, NLT, REB, TEV], 'manger' [AB, Arn, BAGD, BECNT, LN (6.137), Lns, WBC; NRSV], 'feeding trough' [HCSB], not explicit [CEV, NCV]. This noun refers to a feeding trough as in 2:6 [AB, TG]. But by metonymy the part (manger) can represent the whole so that this can refer to a stall [NET]. It refers to a stall where animals are fed [LN].

QUESTION—Why did Jesus address the leader of the synagogue with the plural designation 'hypocrites'?

With the plural form, 'hypocrites', Jesus included the synagogue leader and all others who agreed with him [Alf, Arn, ICC, Lns, NAC, NIC, NICNT, NIGTC, NTC, Rb, Su, TG, TH, TNTC, WBC], not all the people in general [WBC]. It appears from 13:17 that there were some in the crowd who shared the leader's attitude [Alf, Gdt, Su, TG]. The plural refers to the whole party that this leader represented [EGT, Gdt]. It is a use of apostrophe in which such people were addressed although they were not present [Gdt]. The leader was a hypocrite in that he pretended to be rebuking the people when he really intended the rebuke for Jesus [ICC, TNTC]. The leader made it seem that he was zealous to uphold the Law while his real motive was to discredit Jesus [ICC, NTC, TNTC]. However, by applying the term hypocrite to a class of people, the focus is on their inconsistency and this is shown in the example Jesus now gives about supplying for the needs of their animals but not the needs of humans [Alf, Arn, BECNT, NIVS, NTC, WBC]. They were hypocrites by 'working' on the Sabbath to water their animals, but would not allow someone to do the 'work' of healing suffering people on the Sabbath [Lns, Su]. Such hypocrites put religious traditions before mercy and compassion [NAC].

13:16 And this (woman) being a-daughter[a] of-Abraham whom Satan bound[b] behold ten and eight years, was-it- not -necessary (that she) be-set-free from this bond on-the day of the Sabbath?

LEXICON—a. θυγάτηρ (LN **10.31**) (BAGD 2.b.α. p. 364): 'daughter' [BAGD, LN], 'female descendant' [BAGD, **LN**]. The phrase 'a daughter of Abraham' [AB, Arn, BECNT, Lns, NTC, WBC; HCSB, KJV, NASB, NCV, NET, NIV, REB] is also translated 'a descendant of Abraham' [GW, TEV], 'belongs to the family of Abraham' [CEV], 'this dear woman' [NLT]. This indicates that she was a member of God's people [TG, TH], one of God's chosen people [AB].

b. aorist act. indic. of δέω (LN 18.3, **23.157**) (BAGD 1.b. p. 177): 'to bind' [Arn, BAGD, BECNT, LN (18.3), Lns, NTC, WBC; CEV, HCSB, KJV, NASB, NET, NIV], 'to keep physically incapacitated, to cause physical hardship' [**LN** (23.157)], 'to keep tied up' [AB], 'to keep in this condition' [GW]. This active voice is also translated passively: 'to be bound by' [REB], 'to be held by' [NCV]. This is a figurative use of the verb and means 'to be bound with sickness' [TH]. The aorist tense functions like a pluperfect here, indicating that the situation has now come to an end [TH]. Satan has kept her bound and now she is free [NIGTC].

QUESTION—Why was it necessary for the woman to be healed on the Sabbath?

Since it was right to heal on the week days, how much more is it right that the expression of God's love and mercy be done on the Sabbath [NAC]. No other day was more appropriate for healing [NET]. This is a minor to major argument [BECNT, EGT, ICC, Lns, NIGTC]. The woman is more important than an animal, a daughter of Abraham is more privileged than an ordinary woman, being bound by Satan is a greater disaster than being bound in a stall, eighteen years is longer than one Sabbath day, and the need to be freed from a demon is greater than the need to be provided with water [Gdt, Lns]. If an animal which they themselves had bound for a few hours should be loosed on the Sabbath, how much more a daughter of Abraham whom Satan has bound for eighteen years [ICC]. What is right for cattle is all the more right for a woman [BECNT, NIBC, NIGTC] and especially an Israelite woman [MGC]. To heal the woman was not only allowed, it was obligatory [WBC]. She has already suffered for eighteen years, so she should be released immediately [NIGTC, NTC].

QUESTION—Who had bound the woman, Satan (13:16) or the spirit of illness (13:11)?

Satan had bound the woman by means of his servant, the spirit of illness [My]. All evil is to be traced to Satan [Su].

13:17 And (as/because) he was-saying these (things), all the (ones who) opposed him were-being-put-to-shame,[a] and all the crowd was-rejoicing over all the wonderful[b] (things) being-done by him.

LEXICON—a. imperf. pass. indic. of καταισχύνω (LN 25.194) (BAGD 2. p. 410): 'to be put to shame' [Arn, BAGD, BECNT, LN, NTC, WBC], 'to be humiliated' [LN; HCSB, NASB, NET, NIV], 'to be disgraced' [LN], 'to be ashamed' [Lns; KJV, NCV, TEV], 'to feel ashamed' [GW], 'to be struck with shame' [AB], 'to be covered with confusion' [REB]. The passive voice is also translated actively with Jesus' words as the subject: 'to make ashamed' [CEV], 'to shame' [NLT]. They were not ashamed because they had been convinced, but because they were confounded [Alf].

b. ἔνδοξος (LN 79.19) (BAGD 2. p. 263): 'wonderful' [AB, LN; CEV, NCV, NET, NIV, NLT, REB, TEV], 'glorious' [BAGD, BECNT, LN, Lns, NTC, WBC; HCSB, KJV, NASB], 'splendid' [BAGD, LN], 'miraculous' [GW].

QUESTION—What relationship is indicated by the use of the participial phrase ταῦτα λέγοντος 'saying these things'?

The participle indicates the time when the opponents were put to shame: 'when' [Su; KJV, NCV, NET, NIV] or 'as' [AB, BECNT, ICC, NTC, TH, WBC; GW, NASB]: when he said these things, the ones who opposed him were put to shame. However, what he said also involved the means or reason the opponents were put to shame [BECNT, BNTC, Lns, NIC, NTC; NLT, TEV]: by saying these things, the ones who opposed him were put to shame. Jesus' words exposed their false attitude [NIC] and exposed them as being hypocrites [Lns].

QUESTION—What were the wonderful things Jesus was doing?

This included the healing of the crippled woman [AB]. This refers to much more than the healing of the woman [ICC, NTC, TNTC]. The present tense 'being done by Jesus' indicates that Jesus continued to do many other wonderful things in that locality [Lns, My].

DISCOURSE UNIT: 13:18–30 [TNTC]. The topic is the kingdom of God.

DISCOURSE UNIT: 13:18–21 [BECNT, NAC, NIGTC, Su; CEV, GW, HCSB, NASB, NCV, NET, NIV]. The topic is the kingdom of God [NET], a mustard seed and yeast [CEV], the parables of the mustard seed and leaven [BECNT, NAC, NIGTC, Su; HCSB, NASB, NIV], stories about a mustard seed and yeast [GW, NCV].

DISCOURSE UNIT: 13:18–19 [BECNT, NAC, NIGTC, Su, WBC; NASB, NIV]. The topic is the kingdom of God being like a mustard seed [WBC], the parable of the mustard seed [AB, TNTC; NLT, NRSV, TEV].

13:18 **Then/therefore he-was-saying, What is the kingdom of-God like, and to-what shall-I-compare it?**

QUESTION—Does the beginning conjunction οὖν mean 'then' or 'therefore'?

1. The conjunction is continuative [Arn, ICC, TH, WBC; KJV, NCV, NIV, NLT, REB; probably CEV, GW, TEV]: then he said this. After the interruption by the hypocritical opponents, Jesus continued his teaching [ICC].
2. The conjunctive indicates result [AB, BECNT, BNTC, Lns, My, NIC, NICNT, NIGTC, NTC, Rb, Su, TNTC; HCSB, NASB, NET, NRSV]: therefore he said this. This indicates a connection to the preceding event but it is not clear how it is related [Su]. It is not clear whether he is responding to the case of the woman (13:11), or to the enthusiasm of the crowd (13:17), or to something that Luke did not record [Rb]. It illustrates the implications to be derived from the healing of the woman [BECNT, NICNT]. This legitimatizes the healing by connecting it to kingdom activity [NICNT]. This is a comment on what had just happened in the synagogue [NIGTC]. The opposition of the leader of the synagogue and his friends did not mean that God's kingdom would fail, while the enthusiasm of the crowd showed that God's kingdom was indeed making an impact [NTC, TNTC]. Because of the joy shown by the people [Lns, My], Jesus felt justified in expressing the optimism for the establishment of the kingdom [My].

QUESTION—What is the function of the question?

It is a rhetorical question that is used to gain the attention of the listeners [NIC, NTC, TG]. Both parts of the question mean the same thing and the doubling is for the sake of emphasis [Lns]. Perhaps the two questions indicated that two comparisons were to follow [NIGTC].

13:19 It-is like a-mustard seed, which a-man having-taken (it) threw[a] (it) into his-own garden.[b] And it-grew and became into a-tree,[c] and the birds[d] of-the sky nested[e] in its branches.

TEXT—Instead of εἰς δένδρον 'into a tree', some manuscripts read δένδρον 'a tree', some manuscripts read εἰς δένδρον μέγα 'into a great tree', and some manuscripts read δένδρον μέγα 'a great tree'. GNT reads εἰς δένδρον 'into a tree' with a B decision, indicating that the text is almost certain. Versions might not distinguish between εἰς δένδρον 'into a tree' and δένδρον 'a tree', nor between εἰς δένδρον μέγα 'into a great tree' and δένδρον μέγα 'a great tree'. Εἰς δένδρον μέγα 'into a great tree' or δένδρον μέγα 'a great tree' is read by KJV.

LEXICON—a. aorist act. indic. of βάλλω (LN 15.215) (BAGD 1.a. p. 130): 'to throw' [Arn, BAGD, LN, Lns, WBC; NASB], 'to cast' [KJV], 'to plant' [NTC; NIV, TEV], 'to sow' [AB, BECNT; HCSB, NET, NRSV, REB]. The phrase 'having taken it threw into' is translated 'plants/planted' [CEV, GW, NCV, NLT]. That the man threw the seed indicates his careless confidence in its growth [WBC]. Or, this has a weakened sense of 'throw' and simply means 'to put' [TH]. It was a deliberate sowing [AB].

b. κῆπος (LN **1.97**) (BAGD p. 430): 'garden' [AB, Arn, BAGD, BECNT, **LN**, Lns, NTC, WBC; all versions except TEV], 'field' [TEV]. The choice of 'garden' gives a more exact location than 'the earth' (Mark 4:31) or 'field' (Matt 13:31) [EGT]. Knowing the potential growth, the man may have planted the seed in a field bordering the garden plot [Kst].

c. δένδρον (LN 3.2) (BAGD p. 174): 'tree' [AB, Arn, BAGD, BECNT, LN, Lns, NTC, WBC; all versions except CEV], 'bush' [LN]. The phrase 'it grew and became a tree' is translated 'the seed grows as big as a tree' [CEV]. The mustard plant remained a herb, but it became a tree-sized plant [Su] and in popular speech it could be called a tree since it could reach a height of ten to twelve feet [Kst]. Calling the plant a tree is an exaggeration to emphasize the great size of the mustard plant [EGT].

d. πετεινόν (LN 4.41) (BAGD p. 654): 'bird' [BAGD]. The phrase πετεινὰ τοῦ οὐρανοῦ 'birds of the sky' is an idiom used to designate wild birds in contrast with domesticated birds such as chickens [LN]. See this phrase at 8:5.

e. aorist act. indic. of κατασκηνόω (LN 6.147) (BAGD 2. p. 418): 'to nest' [BAGD, LN, WBC; CEV, GW, HCSB, NASB, NCV, NET], 'to make nests' [BECNT; NRSV, TEV], 'to build nests' [AB], 'to lodge' [NTC; KJV], 'to make their habitation' [Arn], 'to tent' [Lns], 'to find shelter' [NLT], 'to roost' [REB], 'to perch' [NIV].

QUESTION—What is being compared in this parable?
The *image* is the growth of a mustard seed. The *topic* is the growth of the kingdom of God. The *point of comparison* is the growth from something small to a something large [Arn, BECNT, Crd, EGT, Gdt, Hlt, ICC, Kst, Lns, MGC, NIBC, NIC, TG, WBC]. The parable is not a comparison between a mustard seed and the kingdom of God, rather, it illustrates a situation that is similar in both cases [NIGTC]. The comparison applies to the whole story, not just to a mustard seed and it has the idea, 'what happens to the kingdom of God is like what happens when a man takes a mustard seed and plants it in his garden' [NIGTC, Su, TG], 'it is like what happens when someone plants a mustard seed' [CEV], 'it is like this...' [TEV]. However, most simply keep a direct comparison: 'it is like a mustard seed' [AB, BECNT, Lns, NTC, WBC; all versions except CEV, TEV]. The emphasis is not so much on the growth as on the certainty that something that appears to be small and insignificant in the beginning will end up big and mighty [NAC, NIGTC, NTC, TNTC]. The point is that the kingdom of God is destined to become a large thing [Lns, NIC, Su], worldwide in size [NIGTC]. A mustard seed grows quickly and the kingdom will grow slowly so there is no emphasis on the time the growth takes [NIC].
QUESTION—Why is the detail about birds nesting in its branches given?
1. This detail emphasizes the large size of the mustard plant and the great size of the kingdom [NAC, Su].
2. This adds another point to the parable by comparing people with birds [AB, BECNT, EGT, ICC, Kst, Lns, MGC, NIC, NIGTC, NTC, TNTC, WBC]. By the preaching of the gospel the kingdom will take hold in the world and many lives will be transformed [MGC]. People from all nations will find a place in God's kingdom [BECNT, ICC, NIC, NIGTC, NTC, TNTC]. The Gentiles would be coming into the kingdom [EGT, WBC]. Men in general would seek shelter in the kingdom [AB]. Or, since the plant is the kingdom, the birds are not members of the kingdom and their contact with it is only temporary as they enjoy some of the blessings of the church [Lns].

DISCOURSE UNIT: 13:20–21 [AB, TNTC, WBC; NLT, NRSV, TEV]. The topic is the parable of the yeast [AB, TNTC; NLT, NRSV, TEV], the kingdom of God is like leaven [WBC].

13:20 And again he-said, To-what shall-I-compare the kingdom of-God? **13:21** It-is like leaven,ª which a-woman having-taken (it) hid^b in three satas^c of-flour^d until (the) whole was-leavened.^e
LEXICON—a. ζύμη (LN 5.11) (BAGD 1. p. 340): 'leaven'. See translations of this word at 12:1. Leaven was old fermented dough that was added to a new batch of dough in order to start the process of fermentation [NIGTC].
  b. aorist act. indic. of ἐγκρύπτω (LN 85.50) (BAGD 1.d. p. 454): 'to hide' [BAGD, BECNT, Lns, WBC; KJV, NASB, NCV], 'to put' [LN, NTC], 'to mix (into)' [CEV, GW, HCSB, NIV, NRSV], 'to mix (with)' [AB;

NET, REB, TEV], 'to use (by a woman making bread)' [NLT]. The meaning 'to hide' does not fit the process of mixing the leaven in the dough [TG]. Perhaps the woman was confident that when she put in her special leaven, it would permeate the dough without even being mixed in [WBC]. The use of the verb 'hid' means that the leaven was hidden from view and it worked secretly and invisibly [Lns]. The use of 'hid' conforms with the hiddenness of the kingdom [Hlt]. 'Hiding' the leaven from view does not give the purpose, but the result of her action [BAGD, TH]. This action presumes that it was mixed in the dough [AB; CEV, GW, NET, NIV, NRSV, REB, TEV]. Specifically this means that she mixed the leaven in the dough by kneading the dough [TH]. The process of leavening the whole batch of dough would take place overnight [NIGTC].

c. σάτον (LN 81.23) (BAGD p. 745): 'saton' [LN, WBC], 'peck' [NASB], 'measure' [AB, Arn, BAGD, BECNT, LN, Lns, NTC; KJV, NET, NRSV, REB], 'a large tub' [NCV], 'a bushel' [TEV], 'batch' [LN; CEV], 'a large amount' [GW, NIV, NLT], '50 pounds' [HCSB]. A *satan* (plural, *sata*) is a Hebrew measure for grain and is equivalent to about a peck and a half [AB, BAGD, LN]. Its equivalent is one ephah in Gen. 18:6, Judg. 6:19, and 1 Sam. 1:24 [WBC].

d. ἄλευρον (LN 5.9) (BAGD 35): 'flour' [AB, Arn, BECNT, WBC; all versions except KJV], 'wheat flour' [BAGD, LN, NTC], 'wheat' [Lns], 'meal' [KJV]. It was ground wheat [Su].

e. aorist pass. indic. of ζυμόω (LN **5.12**) (BAGD p. 340): 'to be leavened' [Arn, BAGD, BECNT, Lns, WBC; KJV, NASB, NRSV, REB], 'to have risen' [**LN**], 'to be fermented' [AB]. The phrase 'the whole was leavened' is translated 'all the dough rises' [CEV], 'all the dough had risen' [NET], 'the whole batch of dough rises' [TEV], 'the whole batch had risen' [NTC], 'it made all the dough rise' [NCV], 'it worked all through the dough' [NIV], 'it spread through the entire mixture' [HCSB], 'the yeast worked its way through all the dough' [GW], 'the yeast permeated every part of the dough' [NLT].

QUESTION— How many people would three *sata* of flour feed and why would the woman use such a great quantity of wheat flour?

The amount of flour was almost five gallons, enough to feed about 160 people [NIGTC], or 150 people [NICNT], or 100 people [Blm; NET]. In Gen. 18:6, Sarah used three *sata* to prepare more than a sufficient amount of bread for the three visitors, and in 1 Sam. 25:18 Abigail used five *sata* to prepare bread for David and his band of followers [WBC]. Hyperbole is being used [Hlt]. The point of the parable is that only a small amount of leaven was needed for leavening a large quantity of dough [TNTC]. The large amount of dough emphasizes the effective penetrating power of the leaven [NTC].

QUESTION—What is the point of the parable?

The *image* is a small amount of leaven affecting a large mass of dough [TG]. Here yeast is not a symbol of evil influence, but the pervading influence of

goodness [BECNT, Crd, Lns, MGC, Pnt, Su, TH, TNTC]. The *point of comparison* is the manner of the unobserved extension of yeast in the dough and of the kingdom in the world until the whole is affected [AB]. They both transform from within and the process is unseen [BNTC].
1. Some focus on the process involved in changing the world [AB, Arn, BNTC, Gdt, Hlt, Lns, MGC, NIGTC, NIVS, NTC, TNTC, WBC]. Instead of focusing on the extension of the kingdom throughout the world, this treats the kingdom's transforming power in the world by Christ's work in the hearts of people [NTC, TNTC]. The hidden power of the kingdom will affect the whole [AB]. The gospel works an inner change by removing superstition and social evils, thus lifting all to a higher plane [Lns]. It speaks of the powerful influence of the kingdom which will one day change the world [MGC]. The kingdom of God will transform the whole of creation [Hlt].
2. Some focus on the end result of the spreading influence [BECNT, Blm, EGT, Hlt, Kst, NAC, NIC, Su, WBC]. The aorist tense of 'was leavened' indicates that the focus is on the end result, not the process [NAC]. Matching the focus of the parable of the mustard seed, this parable focuses on the contrast between the start and the finish of the kingdom, not the process of the growth [BECNT]. The kingdom is relatively insignificant at its beginning, but it will become a great power in the world [EGT, Su], and be present everywhere [BECNT]. This does not indicate that the kingdom will some day dominate the world, but that in the end, the kingdom will be much greater than any of the crowd could imagine [Blm]. The insignificant beginning has the irresistible result of the kingdom transforming the lives of all saved persons to perfect holiness [NIC].

DISCOURSE UNIT: 13:22–17:10 [AB, NAC]. The topic is the second mention of the journey to Jerusalem [NAC], from the second to the third mention of Jerusalem as destination [AB].

DISCOURSE UNIT: 13:22–14:35 [NIGTC]. The topic is the way of the kingdom.

DISCOURSE UNIT: 13:22–35 [NASB]. The topic is teaching in the villages.

DISCOURSE UNIT: 13:22–30 [AB, BECNT, NAC, NICNT, NIGTC, Su, TNTC, WBC; CEV, GW, HCSB, NCV, NET, NIV, NLT, NRSV, TEV]. The topic is teaching on the road to Jerusalem [Su], the narrow door [BECNT, NAC; CEV, GW, NCV, NET, NIV, NLT, NRSV, TEV], the narrow way [HCSB], the entry to the kingdom [NIGTC], who will be saved? [NICNT], is it true that those who are saved will be few? [WBC], who are in the kingdom? [TNTC], reception and rejection in the kingdom [AB].

13:22 And he-was-traveling throughout cities and villages teaching and making (his) way[a] to Jerusalem. **13:23** And someone said to-him, Lord, (are) the (ones) being-saved[b] few? And he-said to them, **13:24** Strive[c] to-enter through the narrow[d] door, because many, I tell you, will-try[e] to-enter and they-will- not -be-able-to.

LEXICON—a. πορεία (LN **15.18**) (BAGD 1. p. 692): 'way' [LN], 'journey, trip' [BAGD]. The phrase 'and making his way to' [HCSB] is also translated 'and journeying to/toward' [Arn, WBC; KJV], 'and proceeding on his way to' [NASB], 'always pressing on toward' [NLT], 'as Jesus was on his way to' [CEV], 'as he traveled toward' [NCV], 'as he made his way to/towards' [NIV, NRSV, REB], 'and making his way to/toward' [AB, BECNT, Lns, NTC; NET, TEV], 'on his way to' [GW]. Jesus was teaching on his way to Jerusalem [WBC]. He was not in a hurry so he stopped along the way to teach people at various places [NTC, TNTC]. At 9:21 it relates the beginning of this journey to Jerusalem [AB, Lns, NIC, NICNT, TH] and now Jesus was stopping at the villages the seventy disciples had been sent to (10:1) [Lns].

b. pres. pass. participle of σῴζω (LN **21.27**) (BAGD 2.b. p. 798): 'to be saved' [BAGD, LN]. The present participle 'being saved' [HCSB] is also translated 'are being saved' [Arn; NASB], 'going to be saved' [CEV, GW, NIV], 'are to be saved' [AB; REB], 'will be saved' [NCV, NET, NLT, NRSV, TEV], '(those who) are saved' [BECNT, WBC], '(that) be saved' [KJV]. This verb is also translated as a noun: 'the saved' [NTC]. The present participle describes those being saved then or at any time [Lns]. Or, the participle looks to the future [BECNT, NIGTC]. Or, the participle indicates that the saving is something that continues up to the time of death or to the Judgment Day [Arn]. The question is perhaps about the total number of persons who will ultimately be saved [NTC]. They are saved from being punished on the Day of Judgment [TG]. They are saved from sin and damnation by being placed in God's kingdom [Lns]. Perhaps the present tense 'being saved' indicates that some of the people thought the kingdom was on the verge of appearing [BNTC].

c. pres. mid./pass. (deponent = act.) impera. of ἀγωνίζομαι (LN **68.74**) (BAGD 2.b. p. 15): 'to strive' [AB, Arn, NTC; KJV, NASB, NRSV], 'to make every effort' [**LN**, WBC; HCSB, NIV, REB], 'to try hard' [GW, NCV], 'to work hard' [NLT], 'to work' [BECNT], 'to do everything possible' [LN], 'to do all (you) can' [CEV], 'to do (your) best' [NET, TEV], 'to strain every nerve' [BAGD]. The present tense indicates that striving was to be continual [BECNT, ICC]. This verb implies a wholehearted effort [TNTC]. The effort they are to make is to repent [NAC]. They are to strive by letting nothing stop them from entering by way of repentance [Lns]. They are to work hard at listening and responding to Jesus' message [BECNT]. The opponents they are to strive against are Satan, sin, and their old natures [NTC].

d. στενός (LN **81.19**) (BAGD p. 766): 'narrow' [AB, Arn, BAGD, BECNT, **LN**, NTC, WBC; all versions except KJV], 'strait' [KJV]. The narrow door is the only door there is to enter the kingdom [AB]. The image of a door is the entrance into a house [NIGTC, TG, TH] where there is a banqueting hall [NIGTC], and this pictures entrance into the kingdom of God [MGC, NIGTC, TG, TH].

e. fut. act. indic. of ζητέω (LN 68.60): 'to try' [LN, WBC; all versions except KJV, NASB], 'to seek' [AB, Arn, BECNT, NTC; KJV, NASB], 'to seek to do something' [LN].

QUESTION—How did the questioner get the idea that only a few would be saved?

The reason he thought that only a few might be saved was because of Jesus' stringent teachings [My, NTC, WBC; NET]. The question arose because Jesus had said that he had come to divide families and that judgment was near [BECNT]. It may have been because the man realized how many people were opposing Jesus and how few were following him [NIC, NIVS]. Perhaps he thought that only Jews could be saved [ICC, Su]. There was a debate among the Jews whether all or only a minority of the Jews would be saved on the day of judgment [BNTC, MGC, Su].

QUESTION—Why will many people not be able to enter the narrow door?

1. They will not be able to enter because they will wait too long and the door will be shut [BECNT, Gdt, ICC, Lns, MGC, NIC, NIGTC, NTC, TNTC, WBC]. It is explained in 13:25 that they will be knocking on the closed door and in 13:26–27 it describes how futile their effort will be [Gdt]. The future tense of 'will try' indicates that they did not try until it was too late [ICC, TNTC]. They are not then striving to enter, but later they will be seeking in vain to enter after the time of salvation is past when the door is shut [ICC, NIC].

2. They will not be able to enter because they seek entrance by another door [Alf, Su]. They must seek to enter at the narrow door because many will seek to enter elsewhere and will not be able [Alf].

3. The door is too narrow for all to get through [Arn, EGT]. This illustrates the fact that the door is so narrow that there will only be enough time for the strongest to get in by pushing others aside. A person has to be in dead earnest to get in [EGT]. Or, it means that self-denial is required since the door will not allow someone to bring all the baggage he might like to have [Arn].

13:25 When[a] the master-of-the-household[b] has-arisen and he-closes the door and you-begin to-stand outside and to-knock (on) the door saying, Lord open for-us, and/then answering he-will-say to-you, I-do- not -know[c] you from-where you-are.

TEXT—Instead of κύριε 'Lord', some manuscripts read κύριε, κύριε 'Lord, Lord'. GNT does not mention this variant. Κύριε, κύριε 'Lord, Lord' is read by KJV.

LEXICON—a. ἀφ' οὗ ἄν. This Greek phrase 'from (the time) when' is translated 'from which time' [BECNT], 'when' [Arn, Lns; NCV], 'but when' [NLT], 'after' [WBC; GW], 'when once' [NTC; NRSV, REB],

'once' [CEV, HCSB, NASB, NET, NIV], 'especially once' [AB], not explicit [TEV].
   b. οἰκοδεσπότης (LN 57.14) (BAGD p. 558): 'master of the household' [LN], 'master of the house' [AB, Arn, BAGD; KJV, REB], 'head of the house' [NASB, NET, NLT], 'owner of the house' [NTC; CEV, NCV, NIV, NRSV], 'householder' [BECNT, NTC], 'homeowner' [GW, HCSB], 'house-lord' [Lns].
   c. perf. act. indic. of οἶδα (LN 28.1) (BAGD 1.c. p. 556): 'to know' [BAGD, LN], 'to be acquainted with' [LN]. The phrase 'I do not know you from where you are' is translated 'I do not know you, whence you are' [Lns; KJV], 'I don't know you or where you come from' [AB; HCSB, NCV, NIV], 'I do not know where you are from' [Arn, BECNT, WBC; NASB], 'I do not know where you come from' [NTC; NET, NRSV, REB], 'I do not know you' [NLT], 'I don't know who you are' [GW], 'I don't know a thing about you' [CEV].
QUESTION—What is the 'when' clause connected to?
   1. The 'when' clause ends with 'he closes the door' and it modifies the following clause [BECNT, WBC; CEV, NCV, NET, NIV, REB]: *when the master of the household has arisen and he closes the door, then you begin to stand outside and knock on the door and say....*
   2. The 'when' clause ends with 'open for us' and modifies the following clause [Arn, BNTC, EGT, NIGTC, NTC, TH; NASB, NRSV]: *when the master of the household has arisen and he closes the door, and you begin to stand outside and to knock on the door, saying, Lord open for us, then answering he will say to you...from where you are.* The difficulty with the grammar is the clause καὶ ἀποκριθεὶς ἐρεῖ ὑμῖν 'and answering he will say to you'. In spite of the initial conjunction καί 'and', the clause probably forms the apodosis of the 'when' clause [NIGTC]. The word καί 'and' here has the meaning of 'then' and begins the apodosis [EGT].
   3. The 'when' clause ends at the end of the verse and modifies 13:26 [Alf, Gdt, My]. The main clause begins with 'then' in 13:26 [Alf].
   4. The 'when' clause ends with an implied clause and the next sentence begins with 'you begin to stand outside' [GW, NLT]. The verse is translated 'After the homeowner gets up and closes the door, it's too late. You can stand outside, knock at the door...' [GW], 'but when the head of the house has locked the door, it will be too late. Then you will stand outside knocking...' [NLT].
   5. The 'when' clause consists of 13:25 and modifies the preceding clause in 13:24 [AB, ICC, Lns, Rb]: *they will not be able to enter when the master of the household has arisen and closes the door...from where you are.* Verse 13:26 then begins a new sentence [ICC].
QUESTION—What is meant by the verb ἄρξησθε 'you begin' in the phrase 'you begin to stand outside and knock'?
   They were outside the door all the time and the verb 'you begin' indicates the new situation of being locked out [TH]. The verb 'you begin' is to be

taken with both verbs 'to stand outside' and 'to knock'. They expect the door to be opened as soon as they get there, but after standing a while they try knocking [EGT]. The verb 'you begin' seems to be redundant [NIGTC] and is omitted by many [AB, WBC; CEV, GW, HCSB, NCV, NIV, NLT, REB, TEV].

QUESTION—Does the application of the illustration mean that Jesus doesn't know such people?

The verb here has its secondary meaning of 'to recognize' or 'to treat with good will' [NIC]. The master of the house does not know them nor whence they are, indicating that they had not been at the door when it stood open [Lns]. He speaks in irony when he claims not to know those people or their origins and this means that he will not recognize them as members of his household [NICNT]. Although the wording seems to say he doesn't know where they live, the following two verses show that this refers to their relationship with the master of the household and it means 'You are not my friends' [TG], 'I do not know of any relationship with you' [TH], 'I do not acknowledge you' [Arn, NIGTC].

13:26 Then you-will-begin to-say, We-ate and we-drank before[a] you and you-taught in our streets. **13:27** And he-will-say saying to-you, I do- not -know you from-where you-are. Go-away from me all workers[b] of-unrighteousness.

TEXT—In 13:27, instead of ἐρεῖ λέγων ὑμῖν 'he will say, saying to you' some manuscripts read ἐρεῖ, λέγω ὑμῖν 'he will say, I say to you', some manuscripts read ἐρεῖ ὑμῖν 'he will say to you', and some manuscripts read ἐρεῖ 'he will say'. GNT reads ἐρεῖ λέγων ὑμῖν 'he will say, saying to you' with a C decision, indicating that the Committee had difficulty making the decision. Some translations seem to follow the reading ἐρεῖ, λέγω ὑμῖν 'he will say, I say to you' [BECNT, Lns; KJV, NASB, NET, NLT]. Some translations seem to follow the reading ἐρεῖ ὑμῖν 'he will say to you' [AB, WBC; NCV]. Some translations seem to follow the reading ἐρεῖ 'he will say' [NTC; CEV, GW, NIV, NRSV, REB, TEV].

TEXT—In 13:27, instead of οὐκ οἶδα ὑμᾶς πόθεν ἐστέ 'I do not know you, from where you are' some manuscripts read οὐκ οἶδα πόθεν ἐστέ 'I do not know from where you are', some manuscripts read οὐκ οἶδα ὑμᾶς 'I do not know you', and some manuscripts read οὐδέποτε εἶδον ὑμᾶς 'I never saw you'. GNT reads οὐκ οἶδα ὑμᾶς πόθεν ἐστέ 'I do not know you, from where you are' with a C decision, indicating that the Committee had difficulty making the decision.

LEXICON—a. ἐνώπιον (LN 83.33) (BAGD 2.a. p. 270): 'before' [Arn, BAGD, LN], 'in front of' [LN], 'in the presence of' [BAGD], 'in your presence' [Lns, NTC, WBC; HCSB, KJV, NASB, NET], 'with' [AB, BECNT; GW, NCV, NIV, NLT, NRSV, REB, TEV]. The clause 'we ate and we drank before you' is translated 'we dined with you' [CEV].

LUKE 13:26–27

b. ἐργάτης (LN 41.21) (BAGD 2. p. 307): 'worker' [LN], 'doer' [BAGD, LN]. This noun means someone who characteristically engages in a particular activity [LN]. The phrase 'all workers of unrighteousness' [Arn, Lns, WBC] is also translated 'all you workers of unrighteousness' [BECNT; HCSB], 'all doers of evil' [AB], 'all you who do evil' [NCV, NLT], 'all you evildoers' [NASB, NET, NIV, NRSV], 'all ye workers of iniquity' [KJV], 'all you wicked people' [TEV], 'all you evil people' [GW], 'you evil people' [CEV], 'all you wrongdoers' [NTC], 'all of you, you and your wicked ways' [REB]. This indicates the reason he has rejected them [NIGTC, TH]. They had not accepted the righteousness Jesus had offered them [Arn].

QUESTION—What is meant by eating and drinking before him?

They had been his guests [EGT, My]. They were his acquaintances [AB, Arn], neighbors [Arn], or friends [TG]. They were claiming that the master was one of them, a native Jew [Lns]. Physically, they had been close to Jesus, but they had not responded with repentance to his message [BECNT, NAC]. Pharisees had given hospitality to Jesus while rejecting his teachings [Su]. This shows that the householder represents Jesus, not God [BECNT, NICNT].

13:28 There[a] will-be weeping and gnashing[b] of-the teeth when you-will-see Abraham and Isaac and Jacob and all the prophets in the kingdom of-God, but you being-thrown-out[c] outside. **13:29** And they-will-come from east and west and from north and south and they-will-recline-to-eat[d] in the kingdom of-God.

LEXICON—a. ἐκεῖ (LN 83.2): 'there, at that place' [LN], 'in that place' [NASB], 'there (will/shall be)' [AB, Arn, BECNT, Lns, NTC, WBC; HCSB, KJV, NET, NIV, NLT, NRSV, REB], 'then' [CEV, GW], not explicit [NCV, TEV]. The word indicates a location relatively far from the speaker [LN]. It refers to their position outside the door [EGT, NIGTC, Rb]. The picture has been dropped and 'there' no longer refers to the door in the preceding verses [ICC, Lns]. It could mean 'there in your exclusion' [ICC], and refers to the place where they were banished [ICC, My]. Or, instead of a local meaning it has a temporal meaning [TH].

b. βρυγμός (LN **23.41**) (BAGD p. 148): 'gnashing' [Arn, BAGD, BECNT, **LN**, Lns; HCSB, KJV, NASB, NET, NIV, NLT, NRSV], 'grinding' [AB, NTC, WBC; REB]. This noun is also translated as a verb: 'to gnash' [TEV], 'to grit' [CEV], 'to grind (your teeth) with pain' [NCV]. It is the action of the teeth striking together [BAGD], or grinding together [LN]. The phrase 'there will be gnashing of teeth' is translated 'you will be in extreme pain' [GW]. It is a sign of emotion such as pain, suffering, or anger [LN].

c. pres. pass. participle of ἐκβάλλω (LN 15.220) (BAGD 1. p. 237): 'to be thrown out' [BAGD, LN]. The phrase 'to be thrown out outside' is translated 'to be thrown out' [AB, Arn, NTC; GW, HCSB, NASB, NET,

NIV, NLT, NRSV, TEV], 'to be thrown outside' [Lns, WBC; CEV, NCV], 'to be thrust out' [KJV], 'to be cast out' [BECNT], 'to be driven away' [REB].

d. fut. pass. indic. of ἀνακλίνομαι (LN 17.23) (BAGD 2. p. 56): 'to recline to eat, to be at table, to sit down to eat' [LN], 'to recline at a meal' [BAGD], 'to recline at table' [AB, Lns, NTC], 'to recline at the table' [HCSB, NASB], 'to sit at the table' [BECNT], 'to sit down at the table' [NCV], 'to sit down at the feast' [TEV], 'to sit down to feast' [CEV], 'to eat' [GW, NRSV], 'to sit down' [Arn, WBC; KJV], 'to take their places' [NLT], 'to take their places at the feast' [NIV], 'to take their places at the banquet' [REB], 'to take their places at the banquet table' [NET]. This refers to a future heavenly banquet [NIGTC, TG], the eschatological banquet God prepares for his chosen ones [AB]. The banquet is a metaphor for describing the kingdom of God [NAC].

QUESTION—Why did the people outside weep and gnash their teeth?

1. This was a sign of their mental state. They wept in sorrow [MGC, NIGTC], and hopelessness [NTC], and grief [NTC], because of their loss [NIGTC]. It was a sign of their despair [TG] and great distress because of their loss [Su, TG]. It indicates their remorse at being rejected [BECNT; NET]. They gnashed their teeth as a reaction to their rage [Gdt, NIGTC, NTC, TNTC], their anger [NIGTC, NTC, TH] against the master [NIGTC, TH] at being excluded from the kingdom [NTC, TH] and seeing the patriarchs, the prophets, and the Gentiles in the kingdom [NTC].

2. This was a sign of their pain [Lns, NAC, TG; GW, NCV] since they are now in hell [Lns]. It indicates the pangs of conscience [NIC].

QUESTION—How could the people outside see the patriarchs and prophets inside at the banquet?

Perhaps they saw them enter [TH]. Perhaps there was an opening in the door [NIGTC]. Instead of physical sight, this would indicate knowledge of their presence in heaven [Lns]. They were made aware of this [NTC].

QUESTION—How could they be thrown out if they had not been allowed to enter?

This is an unfortunate use of the word in the parable [WBC]. It means that when they had tried to get in they were prevented [TH]. They were driven away from the door to forever be outside [Arn]. In an outward way the Jews were in the kingdom but in reality they were outside [Lns]. It refers to their exclusion [ICC, NAC, TG]. They tried to get inside, so their exclusion was spoken of as being cast out [ICC, TH]. It means that they were barred, kept out, not allowed to enter [TG]. Their being thrown out doesn't fit the illustration, so the thought is now of the last judgment [NIGTC].

QUESTION—If the door has been shut, how will people from all directions come to sit at the table?

The shut door is no longer a part of the picture and the master's house in the parable is now changed to what it represents, the kingdom of God [EGT, Lns, NICNT, WBC]. These people are the Gentiles [Alf, Arn, BECNT, Crd,

Gdt, ICC, Lns, MGC, My, NIC, NIGTC, NTC, Su, TNTC], who have accepted the invitation [Su]. Or, these are the displaced Jews [WBC].

13:30 And behold there-are last[a] (ones) who will-be first[b] and there-are first (ones) who will-be last.

LEXICON—a. ἔσχατος (LN 87.66) (BAGD 2. p. 313): 'last' [AB, Arn, BAGD, BECNT, LN, Lns, NTC, WBC; GW, HCSB, KJV, NASB, NET, NIV, NRSV, REB, TEV], 'least important' [LN; CEV], 'most insignificant' [BAGD], 'those who have the lowest place in the life' [NCV], 'some who are despised now' [NLT].

b. πρῶτος (LN 87.45) (BAGD 1.c.β. p. 726): 'first' [AB, Arn, BAGD, BECNT, Lns, NTC, WBC; GW, HCSB, KJV, NASB, NET, NIV, NRSV, REB, TEV], 'foremost' [BAGD, LN], 'prominent' [BAGD, LN], 'most important' [CEV], 'those who have the highest place in the future' [NCV], 'some will be greatly honored then' [NLT].

QUESTION—What is meant by the reversal of those who are first and those who are last and does this apply to all in each type?

This is a proverbial saying that probably was repeated with various applications [BECNT, ICC, NIGTC]. The future tense 'will be' indicates that this will occur in the age to come [NIGTC], at the end times when the fullness of the kingdom comes [BECNT]. In this context it probably refers to the Jews as the first who become last and to the Gentiles as the last who become first [Crd, EGT, Gdt, NIBC, NIC, NIGTC, NTC, Su, TG, TH, TNTC]. Those who supposedly ranked first will be excluded from the kingdom while those who supposedly ranked last will be inside the kingdom [Lns, TG]. The Gentiles were called the last because they were far from the kingdom and far from the means of grace enjoyed by the Jews [Lns, NTC]. Or, there is also a possibility that both the first and the last will ultimately be in heaven and this is talking about degrees of glory so that some are first in honor and prestige and some are last in reputation [NTC]. By saying 'there are first ones and there are last ones' it can mean that there are many of each type but it doesn't mean all, so it is possible that some of the first will remain first and some of the last will remain last [BECNT, ICC, Lns, NAC, NTC]. Some translations include the word 'some' [AB, NTC; GW, NASB, NET, NLT, NRSV, REB]: some who are first now will be last then…some who are last now will be first then.

DISCOURSE UNIT: 13:31–35 [BECNT, NAC, NICNT, Su, TNTC, WBC; GW, NCV, NET, NIV, NLT, NRSV, TEV]. The topic is going to Jerusalem [NET], the lament over Jerusalem [NRSV], Jesus' sorrow for Jerusalem [NIV], Jesus grieves over Jerusalem [NLT], Jesus' love for Jerusalem [TEV], Jesus warns Jerusalem [GW], a warning concerning Herod and the lament over Jerusalem [NAC], rejecting a warning about danger from Herod [Su], the entwined fates of Jesus and Jerusalem [NICNT, WBC], lament for the nation as Jerusalem nears [BECNT], prophets perish in Jerusalem [TNTC], Jesus will die in Jerusalem [NCV].

LUKE 13:31

DISCOURSE UNIT: 13:31–33 [AB, NIGTC, TNTC; CEV, HCSB]. The topic is Jesus and Herod [CEV, HCSB], a warning against Herod [NIGTC], Herod's desire to kill Jesus and Jesus' departure from Galilee [AB], that fox Herod [TNTC].

13:31 **In the same hour some Pharisees approached saying to-him, Depart**[a] **and go from-here, because Herod wants to-kill you.**

LEXICON—a. aorist act. impera. of ἐξέρχομαι (LN 15.40): 'to depart out of' [LN]. The phrase 'depart and go from here' is translated 'depart and travel away from here' [Arn], 'get thee out and depart hence' [KJV], 'go away, leave here' [NASB], 'get up and go from here' [BECNT], 'get thee out and be going from here' [Lns], 'get out and move on from here' [NTC], 'get out of here and go somewhere else' [GW], 'you must get out of here and go somewhere else' [TEV], 'leave this place and go somewhere else' [NIV], 'leave this place and be on your way' [REB], 'leave here and move on' [AB], 'go off and get away from here' [WBC], 'go, get out of here' [HCSB]. Taking the two verbs 'depart' and 'go' to contain a redundancy this phrase is translated 'go away from here' [NCV], 'get away from here' [NET, NRSV], 'you had better get away from here' [CEV], 'get out of here if you want to live' [NLT]. The imperative 'depart' is to be taken as advice rather than a command, meaning 'you had better get out' [TH].

QUESTION—Why would the Pharisees warn Jesus?

They were concerned about the threat to Jesus' life if he remained in Herod's territory [AB, MGC, NIC, TG, TNTC]. They were only some of the Pharisees and they were sympathetic towards Jesus' ministry [AB, NAC]. Or, they opposed Jesus and gave this warning so that Jesus would leave the area [NIGTC, Su]. They wanted to frighten Jesus so that he would go on to Judea where he would be in the power of the Sanhedrin [Gdt, ICC, Lns, My, NIVS]. The next verse seems to indicate that Jesus took them to be agents of Herod [EGT, NIGTC].

13:32 **And he-said to-them, Go tell this fox,**[a] **Behold I-cast-out demons and I-perform healings today and tomorrow and on-the third (day) I-will-be-finished.**[b]

LEXICON—a. ἀλώπηξ (LN **88.120**) (BAGD 2. p. 42): 'fox' [AB, Arn, BAGD, BECNT, LN, Lns, NTC, WBC; all versions], 'wicked person, cunning person' [**LN**]. The word is used figuratively of crafty people [BAGD].

b. pres. mid./pass. indic. of τελειόω (LN 68.31) (BAGD 1. p. 809): 'to be finished' [WBC], 'to finish (my) work' [NRSV, TEV], 'to reach (my) goal' [AB, BAGD, NTC; NASB, NCV, NIV, REB], 'to be at the goal' [Lns], 'to accomplish (my) purpose' [NLT], 'to complete (my) work' [HCSB, NET], 'to complete (my) task' [BECNT], 'to be through' [CEV], 'to succeed fully, to be completely successful' [LN]. Some take this to be passive: 'to be brought to the goal' [Arn], 'to be perfected' [KJV]. The present tense is the prophetic present tense [Rb] and has the sense of the

LUKE 13:32

future tense [AB, Arn, Gdt, NIGTC, Rb]. Some translate with the future tense [AB, Arn; CEV, GW, KJV, NCV, NET, NIV, NLT, TEV].

QUESTION—When Jesus called Herod a fox, what was the point of comparison in the metaphor?

1. The point of comparison is craftiness or cunningness [AB, Arn, BAGD, EGT, Gdt, ICC, Lns, MGC, My, NAC, NIVS, NTC, TG, TH, WBC]. Herod was using others to scare Jesus out of his territory [NTC]. Herod feared that Jesus popularity would cause political trouble for him [NTC]. He didn't have the courage to have such an influential teacher killed, so he used the report of his intentions to cause Jesus to leave his jurisdiction [Arn, ICC].
2. The point of comparison is that of destructiveness [BECNT, BNTC]. Both a fox and Herod were destroyers [BNTC]. This interpretation is strengthened by the fact that Herod had already ordered the death of John the Baptist and now wanted to kill Jesus [BECNT].
3. The point of comparison is insignificance [Crd]. Compared to a lion, a fox is insignificant and so was Herod insignificant as a ruler [Crd].
4. The point of comparison was a combination of characteristics [MGC, NIC, NICNT, Rb, WBC; NET]. Both a fox and Herod were sly and cowardly [Rb, WBC], or cunning and weak [NIC]. The main idea is the destructiveness of Herod who had killed John the Baptist and was now opposed to Jesus. Yet it also refers to the insignificance of Herod since he lacked real power and had to use cunning to accomplish his plans [NET]. Herod was impotent in carrying out his desire to destroy God's agent [NICNT].

QUESTION—What was the intent of Jesus' message to Herod?

Jesus' message meant that he was going on with his work in spite of Herod [Crd, Lns, NIGTC, TH, TNTC]. He would not stop his ministry for fear of Herod [AB]. He would not be hurried [Arn]. Jesus also gave examples that he was performing the signs of the Messiah [ICC] and that he was actually helping Herod's subjects [Gdt, NTC]. Jesus' command may indicate that the Pharisees were to take the message back to Herod, or it may only be a rhetorical way of saying that it didn't matter to Jesus whether or not Herod heard about what he had said about him and his threats [TNTC]. The command to go tell Herod was only rhetorical and Jesus did not intend for the Pharisees to actually go with the message [NAC].

QUESTION—What is meant by 'today and tomorrow, and on the third day'?

1. The refers literally to three days [My].
2. This was a way of referring to a short time [AB, EGT, Gdt, Lns, TG, TH]. It was not to be taken literally and Jesus was saying that he would continue his activities for only for a limited time [TG]. It would just be a short time when Jesus would cross the Jordan River on the direct road to Jerusalem [Lns].
3. This was a figurative way of referring to a definite time that had been determined [BECNT, BNTC, ICC, Lns, MGC, NIGTC, NTC, WBC]. The

Messiah's course had been determined and would not be changed by Herod's threats [ICC]. The two days refer to a short time and they will be followed by some certain event [BNTC]. The 'third day' was the day appointed by God, the day of his death on the cross [NTC]. Since it is clear that it would take more than three days before he entered Jerusalem, it means that at the end of the quick succession of events Jesus would enter Jerusalem and complete his task of ministry by his death [BECNT]. Each period of time is replaced by another at the proper point, so Jesus would disregard the danger and carry out his ministry as long as it was determined [WBC].

QUESTION—What would be finished on the third day?
1. Jesus would be finished with his work of casting out demons and healing people [My, NIC, TH; CEV].
2. This refers to reaching his goal [AB, BECNT, Gdt, Lns, MGC, NAC, NIC, NIGTC, NTC; NET]. Although it might refer to reaching Jerusalem as the goal of his journey, it is possible that it means reaching the end or goal of his life [AB]. Reaching Jerusalem represents what will happen to this prophet, his death [BECNT]. Jesus' mission was to perform miracles until the goal God had set for him, his death in Jerusalem [Lns]. The goal is Jesus' death [Arn, Gdt, NIC, NIGTC]. Jesus goal was the redemption of his people and would be reached by means of his death [NTC].
3. This refers to Jesus being made perfect [ICC, Rb; KJV]. This is what Hebrews 2:10 refers to, the full perfection of his humanity [ICC].

QUESTION—Where is the end of Jesus' message to Herod?
1. The message ends in 13:32 and 13:33 is a comment to his audience [AB, BNTC, TG, TH; CEV, HCSB, NASB, NCV, NIV, REB, TEV].
2. The message ends in 13:33 [BECNT; NET, NRSV].

13:33 Nevertheless[a] it-is-necessary for-me to-travel[b] today and tomorrow and the (one) following, because it-is- not -possible[c] (for) a-prophet to-die[d] outside Jerusalem.

LEXICON—a. πλήν (LN 89.130) (BAGD 1.b. p. 669): 'nevertheless' [LN, Lns; KJV, NASB, NET], 'in any case' [NIV], 'moreover' [BECNT], 'except' [LN], 'only' [BAGD], 'but' [AB, LN, NTC; CEV, GW], 'yet' [HCSB, NCV, NRSV, TEV], 'however' [Arn, BAGD; REB], 'yes' [NLT], 'indeed' [WBC]. This indicates a contrast that is true irrespective of other considerations [LN].

b. pres. mid./pass. infin. of πορεύομαι, πορεύω (LN 15.18) (BAGD 1. p. 692): 'to travel' [Arn, LN; HCSB], 'to be journeying' [BAGD], 'to journey' [Lns; NASB], 'to walk' [KJV], 'to be on (my) way' [BAGD, LN; GW, NRSV, TEV], 'to continue on (my) way' [NTC, WBC], 'to go on (my) way' [CEV, NET, REB], 'to go (my) way' [BECNT], 'to keep on (my) way' [AB], 'to proceed on (my) way' [NLT], 'to keep going' [NIC].

c. pres. mid./pass. (deponent = act.) indic. of ἐνδέχεται (LN 71.4) (BAGD p. 263): 'to be possible' [BAGD, LN]. The phrase 'it is not possible' [Arn,

BECNT, **LN**, WBC; GW, HCSB] is also translated 'it is impossible' [AB; NET, NRSV], 'it cannot be that' [KJV, NASB], 'it is unthinkable' [**LN**; REB], 'it is not right' [TEV], 'it would never do' [NTC], 'it is not permissible' [Lns]. The clause is translated 'for surely no prophet can die outside Jerusalem' [NIV], 'after all, Jerusalem is the place where prophets are killed' [CEV], 'for it wouldn't do for a prophet of God to be killed except in Jerusalem' [NLT].
  d. aorist mid. infin. of ἀπόλλυμι (LN 20.31): 'to die' [LN; GW], 'to be killed' [CEV, NCV, NET, NIV, NLT, NRSV], 'to perish' [AB, Arn, BECNT, WBC; HCSB, KJV, NASB], 'to meet death' [REB]. The verb refers to the destruction of objects or persons [LN].

QUESTION—What relationship is indicated by the initial conjunction πλήν 'nevertheless'?

It indicates an emphatic explanation of what he had just said [BECNT]. Jesus had to continue on in his journey to Jerusalem, but he was not going because of fear of Herod, rather it fitted into his own plans [ICC, NIC, NICNT], and God's schedule [MGC], or God's plan of salvation [Arn]. In spite of the fact that Jesus would soon reach his goal, it won't happen until he reaches Jerusalem [Lns]. This gives the other side of the case, that although he must continue his work a short time, yet he must continue on to Jerusalem where he was to die [EGT]. Although the time was short for Jesus, it nevertheless was true that he would continue his journey without anyone forcing him to bring his work and journey to a hasty end [Gdt].

QUESTION—What relationship is indicated by ὅτι 'because' which begins the last clause?

It indicates that the reason Jesus is not concerned about Herod's threat is that he has no fear of perishing before he reaches Jerusalem [Gdt, Lns]. It is not destined that Herod would kill Jesus since he would be killed in Jerusalem [AB].

QUESTION—What is meant by it not being possible for a prophet to die outside Jerusalem?

This is spoken in irony [Arn, BECNT, Gdt, ICC, Lns, NIC, NTC, Rb, TG, TNTC, WBC], or sarcasm [Su]. It was not an existing proverb or general rule that all prophets perished in Jerusalem [NIGTC, WBC]. Prophets were killed in Jerusalem as is stated in the next verse, but not all prophets and not even John the Baptist were killed there [Lns, NIGTC]. However, in no other place were so many prophets killed and it was appropriate that Jesus, the greatest prophet of all, would have to perish there [Lns, NIGTC]. Jesus spoke of what generally happened [Arn]. This statement implies that Jesus was a prophet [AB, BECNT, TG].

DISCOURSE UNIT: 13:34–35 [AB, NIGTC, TNTC; CEV, HCSB]. The topic is Jesus' lament over Jerusalem [AB, NIGTC, TNTC; HCSB], Jesus' love for Jerusalem [CEV].

13:34 Jerusalem Jerusalem, the (one) killing the prophets and stoning the (ones who) had-been-sent[a] to her, how-often I-wanted to-gather-together[b] your children[c] just-as a-hen (gathers) her chicks under the wings, and you-did- not -want.[d]

LEXICON—a. perf. pass. participle of ἀποστέλλω (LN 15.66): 'to be sent' [AB, Arn, BECNT, LN, Lns, NTC, WBC; all versions except NLT, TEV]. The phrase 'the ones having been sent' is translated 'the messengers God has sent' [TEV], 'God's messengers' [NLT]. The use of the passive indicates that it was God who sent them [Lns, NICNT].

  b. aorist act. infin. of ἐπισυνάγω (LN 15.126) (BAGD p. 310): 'to gather together' [AB, BAGD, BECNT, LN, NTC; GW, HCSB, KJV, NASB, NET, NIV, NLT, NRSV], 'to gather' [Arn, Lns, WBC; CEV, NCV, REB], 'to put (my) arms around' [TEV].

  c. τέκνον (LN **11.63**) (BAGD 2.f.α. p. 808): 'child' [BAGD]. The phrase 'your children' [AB, Arn, BECNT, Lns, NTC, WBC; all versions except CEV, NCV, TEV] is also translated 'your people' [**LN**; CEV, NCV, TEV]. The plural here is used figuratively for the inhabitants of the city [BAGD, LN].

  d. aorist act. indic. of θέλω (LN 25.1): 'to want' [LN]. The phrase 'you did not want' is translated 'you would not' [NTC; KJV], 'you did not will' [Lns], 'you were not willing' [Arn; GW, HCSB, NIV, NRSV], 'you didn't want it' [WBC], 'you did not wish it' [BECNT], 'you would not have it' [AB; NASB], 'you would not let me' [CEV, NCV, NLT, REB, TEV], 'you would have none of it' [NET].

QUESTION—What is signified by the vocative, 'Jerusalem, Jerusalem'?

The repetition of the name makes this emphatic [Su, TH]. It indicates intense emotion [NTC; NET]. It expresses Jesus' sorrow over the fate of Jerusalem [Arn, BECNT, ICC, Lns, NAC, NTC, Su]. It indicates Jesus' love and concern for Jerusalem [Lns]. Addressing the city stands for addressing its inhabitants and means 'O you people of Jerusalem' [TH]. Jerusalem represents the nation in this verse [BECNT, NTC]. Since Jerusalem was the capital and religious center for the Jews, Jesus was addressing the nation as a whole [Gdt, Lns, NTC]. The following phrase 'your children' refers first to the inhabitants of Jerusalem [Gdt, TG], but the fate of the inhabitants of Jerusalem involves the other people of the country [Gdt]. By extension the children of Jerusalem refers to the whole nation [Lns, NTC, TH, WBC].

QUESTION—What is indicated by the use of the present tense of 'killing' and 'stoning'?

The present tense indicates that these acts were habitual [TH], their characteristic conduct [AB, ICC, Lns]. Jerusalem was always ready to kill God's messengers [NIGTC].

QUESTION—Is there a difference between the 'prophets' who were killed and the 'ones having been sent' who were stoned?

  1. Both descriptions refer to the same people [Arn, ICC, NIGTC, TG, TH, WBC]. This is rhetorical parallelism [WBC]. The prophet speaks God's

message and the messenger is one whom God sends to proclaim his message [TG]. The second clause is a more definite description of the first [ICC].
2. The first clause describes only a part of those referred to in the second clause [Lns, NIGTC]. The ones which were sent refers to a wider group which includes the prophets and all those who assisted in the work of the prophets [Lns].

QUESTION—Is it significant that the sentence is addressed to Jerusalem in the second person, but the description that is inserted following the vocatives is in the third person ('the one…to her')?

The changes from second person to third person to second person is a Semitism [Lns, NIGTC, TH]. Some translations leave the third person participles in the third person but change 'to her' to 'to you' [AB, BECNT]. Some translations change the third person participles to second person (you who kills…and stones) and change 'to her' to 'to you' [GW, NCV, NET, NIV, TEV]. Or 'the one' is changed to 'your people' and 'to her' is changed to 'to you' [CEV].

QUESTION—Why would Jesus want to gather together the people of Jerusalem?

Like a hen gathers her chicks under her wings to protect them from danger, Jesus wanted to protect the Jews from danger [AB, Arn, BAGD, BECNT, NAC, NIC, NIGTC, NTC, Su, WBC; NET] and care for them [AB, BECNT; NET]. The impending danger is the coming judgment [NIC]. He would protect them by leading them into the kingdom [NIGTC]. By leading the people to repentance, he would avert the fall of Jerusalem in A.D. 70 and their condemnation at the Final Judgment [Arn].

QUESTION—Does ποσάκις 'how often' imply that Jesus had ministered in the city of Jerusalem many times?

The synoptic Gospels do not record frequent visits to Jerusalem, but the Gospel of John does refer to several visits [Arn, NIGTC, Su]. Without being in the city, many times Jesus yearned to gather the people of Jerusalem to himself [MGC, NAC]. Many think that in addressing Jerusalem, Jesus was including the whole nation [Lns, NTC, TH].

13:35 Behold your house[a] is-left[b] to-you. And I-say to-you, You-will- not - see me until it-will-come[c] when you-say, Having-been-blessed (be/is) the (one) coming in (the) name (of the) Lord.

TEXT—Following ὁ οἶκος ὑμῶν 'your house', some manuscripts add ἔρημος 'desolate'. GNT reads ὁ οἶκος ὑμῶν 'your house' with a B decision, indicating that the text is almost certain. Ἔρημος 'desolate' is added by KJV, NASB, NIV.

TEXT—Instead of λέγω δέ 'and I say', some manuscripts read λέγω 'I say' and some manuscripts read ἀμὴν δὲ λέγω 'and truly I say'. GNT does not deal with these variants in the apparatus, but uses brackets, reading λέγω [δέ] '[and] I say', indicating difficulty making the decision. Ἀμὴν δὲ λέγω 'and truly I say' is read by KJV.

TEXT—Instead of ἕως ἥξει ὅτε εἴπητε 'until it will come when you say', some manuscripts read ἕως ἂν ἥξῃ ὅτε εἴπητε 'until it comes when you say', others read ἕως ἂν ἥξει ὅτε εἴπητε 'until it will come when you say', others read ἕως εἴπητε 'until you say', others read ἕως ἂν εἴπητε 'until you say', others read ἀπ' ἄρτι ἕως ἂν εἴπητε 'from now until you say', another reads ἕως ὅτε εἴπητε 'until when you say', and another reads ἀπ' ἄρτι ἕως ἂν ἥξει ὅτε εἴπητε 'from now until it comes when you say'. GNT uses brackets, reading ἕως [ἥξει ὅτε] εἴπητε 'until [it will come when] you say' with a C decision, indicating that the Committee had difficulty making the decision. Ἕως ἂν ἥξῃ ὅτε εἴπητε 'until it comes when you say' is read by KJV.

LEXICON—a. οἶκος (LN 7.2) (BAGD 1.a.γ. p. 560): 'house' [AB, Arn, BAGD, BECNT, LN, Lns, NTC, WBC; all versions except CEV, REB, TEV], 'city' [BAGD], 'temple' [LN; CEV, REB, TEV].

b. pres. pass. indic. of ἀφίημι (LN 85.62) (BAGD 3.a. p. 126): 'to be left' [BAGD, LN]. The phrase 'is left to you' [BECNT, Lns; NRSV] is also translated 'will be left to you' [Arn], 'is abandoned to you' [NTC; HCSB], 'is left to you desolate' [KJV, NASB, NIV], 'is left to you empty' [NLT], 'is left completely empty' [NCV], 'will be deserted' [CEV], 'will be abandoned' [GW, TEV], 'is abandoned' [AB, WBC], 'is forsaken' [NET], 'forsaken by God' [REB]. The parallel passage in Matt. 23:39 says that the house is desolate [BECNT]. The present tense indicates a prophecy of what was to take place in the future [Arn, TG; CEV, GW, TEV].

c. fut. act. indic. of ἥκω (LN 13.112) (BAGD 2. p. 344): 'to come' [BAGD], 'to happen' [LN]. The phrase 'until it will come when' is translated 'until the time comes when' [AB, WBC; HCSB, KJV, NASB, NRSV, REB, TEV], 'until the time arrives when' [NTC], 'until the time when' [CEV], 'until that time when' [NCV], 'till the day comes when' [Arn], 'until' [BECNT, Lns; GW, NET, NIV, NLT].

QUESTION—What is meant by their 'house' and in what way was it left?

1. Their house is the temple in Jerusalem [NIC; CEV, REB, TEV]. God will forsake the temple and the people and will not protect them and this will result in their complete destruction [NIC].

2. Their house is the city of Jerusalem [Alf, Arn, BAGD, ICC, Lns, MGC, NAC, NICNT, NIGTC, NIVS, NTC, Su, TH, TNTC, WBC]. This refers to the city and its inhabitants [NAC, NIGTC, NIVS]. God's judgment upon Jerusalem will come when he abandons the city to its foes and it is destroyed in A.D. 70 [MGC, NAC, WBC]. It is the place where the people lived [Arn]. Of course the temple is included [Lns, NTC]. The city will be left to them in the sense that God will abandon them and they will have to protect the city themselves [Arn, TH], but they will not be able to do so [Arn]. Jerusalem is to be abandoned by God and the result will be that

their enemies will destroy them [NIGTC]. Or, God left the city to them and they did as they pleased until the Jewish nation was finally driven from its capital and land [Lns, Su].
3. Their house is the nation of Israel [BECNT].

QUESTION—What point in history would they see Jesus again?
1. This refers to Jesus' triumphal entry into Jerusalem when the welcoming crowds actually said these words [AB, MGC, Su]. This prophecy probably merges two events into one: Jesus' reception by the Jews at his coming entry into Jerusalem and also his acceptance by Israel at the Second Coming [MGC].
2. This refers to the second advent when Jesus will return in splendor [BNTC, Gdt, NAC, NIBC, NIC, NICNT, NIGTC, NTC, TH, TNTC, WBC; NET]. In Matt. 23:39 Jesus spoke these words after the triumphal entry into Jerusalem where he was welcomed by the crowds but not by the Jewish leaders. Therefore, Jesus must have been speaking about his coming again as the Messiah [NAC, NIGTC]. At Jesus' second advent all people will see the glory of the Jesus and will acknowledge him as the Messiah, even if the unconverted remain unrepentant [NTC, TNTC], and it is too late for them to be redeemed [NIC].
3. This refers to converted Jews throughout this age [Arn, ICC, Lns]. The saved remnant of the Jewish nation will see Jesus through the eyes of faith [Arn, Lns].

QUESTION—Is the utterance, 'Blessed the one coming' a request or a statement?
1. It is a request [TG; NCV, NLT, REB, TEV]: may he be blessed. It means 'God bless him' [NCV, TEV].
2. It is a statement [AB, BECNT, Lns, NTC, WBC; CEV, GW, KJV, NASB, NET, NIV, NRSV]: he is blessed.

QUESTION—What is meant by 'the one coming in the name of the Lord'?
He is coming as a messenger or spokesman of the Lord [TG]. He is both sent and authorized by God to represent him [TH]. He will appear at the end time as the Messiah [WBC].

DISCOURSE UNIT: 14:1–24 [NICNT, TNTC; GW]. The topic is Jesus' attendance at a banquet [GW], dinner with a Pharisee [TNTC], the kingdom and the banquet [NICNT].

DISCOURSE UNIT: 14:1–14 [NIV]. The topic is Jesus at a Pharisee's house.

DISCOURSE UNIT: 14:1–6 [AB, BECNT, NAC, NICNT, NIGTC, Su, TNTC, WBC; CEV, HCSB, NASB, NCV, NET, NLT, NRSV, TEV]. The topic is a healing on the Sabbath [NCV], healing again on the Sabbath [NET], Jesus heals on the Sabbath [NASB, NLT], Jesus heals a sick man [CEV, TEV], the healing of the man with dropsy [AB, NAC, NIGTC, TNTC, WBC], Jesus heals the man with dropsy [NRSV], Jesus heals an insatiable thirst [NICNT], a Sabbath healing in a Pharisee's house [Su], another Sabbath healing and silence [BECNT], a Sabbath controversy [HCSB].

14:1 And it-happened when he went into a-house of-a-certain (one) of-the rulers[a] of-the Pharisees (on the) Sabbath to-eat bread[b] that/and they were closely-watching[c] him.

TEXT—Some manuscripts omit τῶν 'the' before Φαρισαίων 'Pharisees'. GNT does not deal with this variant in the apparatus places it in brackets in the text. Versions might not distinguish between these two readings.

LEXICON—a. ἄρχων (LN 37.56) (BAGD 2.a. p. 114): 'ruler' [BAGD, LN, Lns, WBC], 'leader' [Arn, BECNT; NASB, NET, NLT, NRSV]. The phrase 'a certain one of the rulers of the Pharisees' is translated 'one of the chief Pharisees' [KJV], 'an important Pharisee' [CEV], 'a prominent Pharisee' [AB; GW, NIV], 'a leading Pharisee' [NCV], 'one of the leading Pharisees' [NTC; HCSB, REB, TEV]. This man was one of the leading personalities [TH]. It is impossible to know what this prominent official's specific position was [AB, BECNT, NIGTC]. This designation could mean that he was a member of the Sanhedrin [Crd, NIBC, NIGTC, TNTC], or an official at a synagogue [Lns, NIGTC; NET], or a leading man among the Pharisees [Alf, ICC, My, NIGTC]. See this word at 8:41 and 18:18.

b. ἄρτος (LN 5.1) (BAGD 2. p. 110): 'bread, food' [BAGD, LN]. This word for bread can refer to any type of food [BAGD, LN]. The phrase 'to eat bread' [Arn, BECNT, Lns, WBC; KJV, NASB] is also translated 'to eat' [NTC; GW, HCSB, NCV, NIV], 'to eat a meal' [NRSV, TEV], 'to have a meal' [REB], 'to have dinner' [CEV], 'to dine' [NET], not explicit [NLT]. This probably was a dinner after the synagogue service [AB, NICNT, NIGTC]. It was a midday meal [AB, BECNT] since bread was the main course [BECNT]. Or, it was the main meal at the end of the day [Lns]. It was common to have guests for dinner on the Sabbath [TNTC]. This seems to be an elaborate meal at which other Pharisees and rabbis were invited, but probably Jesus' disciples were not invited [Arn, Lns].

c. pres. mid. participle of παρατηρέω (LN 24.48) (BAGD 1.a.b. p. 622): 'to watch closely' [BAGD, LN, Lns, NTC; HCSB, NASB, NET, NLT, NRSV, REB, TEV], 'to watch very closely' [GW, NCV], 'to carefully watch' [CEV], 'to watch' [Arn, BECNT, WBC; KJV]. This is also translated passively with Jesus as the subject: 'to be carefully watched' [NIV]. This is a durative imperfect tense, meaning that they were constantly watching him [Lns, TH], and doing this in a covert way [Lns].

QUESTION—Who were closely watching Jesus and why were they watching him?

Although the others had not yet been introduced in the narrative, the antecedent of the pronoun 'they' are the Pharisees mentioned in the description of the host [WBC], and 'they' is further defined in 14:3 where the lawyers and Pharisees are mentioned [NIGTC, NTC, Su, TH, TNTC,

WBC]. They were the host and his friends [NTC, TH]. Or, it is not clear that the host was included among those opponents of Jesus [NAC]. This verb is also translated in the passive and avoids the use of 'they': 'he was being carefully watched' [NIV]. They were watching to see what Jesus would do on the Sabbath [AB, BECNT, TG]. They were watching to see if Jesus broke any of their laws [MGC, NIBC, Su]. They hoped to see Jesus do something that they could find fault with [NAC]. They wanted to see if Jesus would do something that they could charge him with [NTC, TNTC].

QUESTION—Where is the apodosis of the ἐν 'when' clause?
1. The 'when' clause ends before the last clause of the verse [Arn, BNTC, EGT, ICC, Lns, NIGTC, NTC, TH; HCSB, KJV, NASB, NCV, NET, NIV, NRSV]: when he went into a house..., it happened that they were closely watching him. The word καί which begins the last clause of the verse indicates content and has the meaning 'that' so that it serves to introduce the apodosis [EGT, ICC, TH].
2. The 'when' clause includes the rest of the verse [AB, NICNT, WBC]: when he went into a house...and they were closely-watching him, it happened that there was a man in front of him.... The καί which begins the last clause of the verse means 'and' and introduces a coordinate clause with the 'when' clause.
3. The 'when' clause is changed to an independent clause [BECNT; CEV, GW, NLT, REB, TEV]: 'it happened that he entered into the house...and they were watching him. The καί which begins the last clause of the verse means 'and' and introduces a coordinate clause with the preceding clause.

14:2 And behold a-certain man suffering-from-dropsy[a] was in-front-of him. 14:3 And answering Jesus spoke to the lawyers[b] and Pharisees saying, Is-it-permitted[c] to-heal on-the Sabbath or not? 14:4 And they-were-silent. And having-taken-hold[d] (of him) he-healed him and sent-away[e] (him).

TEXT—In 14:3, some manuscripts omit ἢ οὔ 'or not'. GNT does not deal with this variant. Ἢ οὔ 'or not' is omitted by KJV.

LEXICON—a. ὑδρωπικός (LN **23.164**) (BAGD p. 832): 'suffering from dropsy' [BAGD, **LN**, WBC; NASB, NET, NIV, REB], 'afflicted with dropsy' [AB, Arn, NTC], 'with dropsy' [Lns; NCV], 'with swollen legs' [CEV]. This adjective is also translated as a descriptive phrase: 'who had dropsy' [BECNT; NRSV], 'which had the dropsy' [KJV], 'whose body was swollen with fluid' [GW, HCSB], 'whose arms and legs were swollen' [NLT], 'whose legs and arms were swollen' [TEV]. This is a swelling of the body because of the accumulation of lymph in the body tissues [LN] and it especially affects the legs [NET] and the arms [TG]. It may be described as an illness that made his arms and legs swell [NIBC, TG; NLT, TEV]. It is commonly called edema [AB, NICNT]. Such a person had an insatiable thirst even though his body already retained too much fluid [NICNT]. Dropsy was a serious symptom of some disease [AB, BECNT, Lns, NIVS, WBC], such as an illness which affected the heart [Lns, NICNT, WBC], the kidneys [Lns, NICNT], the liver, or the blood [Lns].

b. νομικός (LN 33.338) (BAGD 2. p. 541): 'lawyer' [AB, Arn, BECNT, LN, Lns, WBC; KJV, NASB, NRSV, REB], 'expert in the Law, interpreter of the Law' [LN], 'legal expert' [BAGD], 'law expert' [NTC; HCSB], 'expert on/in the law' [NCV, NLT], 'expert in religious law' [NET], 'teacher of the Law' [TEV], 'teacher of the Law of Moses' [CEV], 'expert in Moses' Teachings' [GW]. See this word at 7:30; 10:25; 11:45, 46, 52.

c. pres. act. indic. of ἔξεστι (LN 71.32) (BAGD 1. p. 275): 'to be permitted' [BAGD], 'must, ought to' [LN]. The phrase 'is it permitted' [NLT, REB] is also translated 'is it permissible' [Arn], 'is it right' [BECNT; CEV, GW], 'is it lawful' [AB, Lns, NTC, WBC; HCSB, KJV, NASB, NET, NIV, NRSV], 'is it right or wrong' [NCV], 'does our Law allow' [TEV]. See this word at 6:2, 9.

d. aorist mid. (deponent = act.) participle of ἐπιλαμβάνομαι (LN 15.43) (BAGD 1. p. 295): 'to take hold of' [AB, Arn, BAGD, LN, Lns, NTC; CEV, GW, NASB, NET, NIV], 'to take' [BECNT, WBC; HCSB, KJV, NCV, NRSV, REB, TEV], 'to grasp' [BAGD, LN], 'to touch' [NLT]. Most understand the verb to mean that Jesus placed his hands on the man. Perhaps it was some physical contact such as an embrace to show Jesus' compassion for the man [BECNT]. Probably Jesus grasped the man's hand to assure him that he sympathized with him and wanted to help [Arn]. However, it could mean that Jesus took the man aside to speak to him [TG], or that Jesus took on the man's case by accepting the task of healing him on the Sabbath [Su].

e. aorist act. indic. of ἀπολύω (LN 15.43) (BAGD 2.b. p. 96): 'to send away' [AB, BAGD; all versions except KJV], 'to dismiss' [Arn, BAGD, LN, WBC], 'to let go' [BECNT, NTC; KJV], 'to release' [Lns]. Jesus gave the man permission to go home [AB, TH]. Jesus told the man to go home [TG]. Jesus wanted the man to leave so that the Pharisees wouldn't be able to bother him [ICC], or Jesus wanted the man to be undisturbed so that he could think about how God had healed him through Jesus [Lns]. Or, this word means that Jesus released the man from his illness [NICNT].

QUESTION—How did the sick man happen to be in front of Jesus?

The sick man came to Jesus to be healed [ICC, TG]. He probably was not an invited guest at the meal [AB, Crd, ICC], because the word ἰδού 'behold' indicates that the man's presence was unexpected [ICC] and Jesus later sent him away [AB, NIBC]. It was common for people to walk in uninvited and probably Jesus had not yet reclined at the table [NTC]. Or, the man was also sitting at the meal and the inclusion of ἰδού 'behold' indicates surprise that such a man was present at the meal [BECNT]. Perhaps the Pharisees had arranged for the man to appear at the meal in order to get Jesus do something they could criticize [Arn, BECNT, Gdt, NIC, NIGTC].

QUESTION—In 14:3, what was Jesus answering?

Jesus was responding to the situation [Arn, Lns, WBC], to the unspoken challenge of his opponents [NIGTC, TNTC]. He answered their thoughts [BECNT, Crd, Gdt, ICC, NAC, NIC, Rb]. This is implied by the preceding verse where it states that they were closely watching him [ICC], or it is implicit by the man's presence [Gdt] The question of whether or not Jesus would heal the man was implicit in the sudden appearance of the man at the dinner [NIC]. Some do not translate this word [AB, BECNT; CEV, NCV, NET, NIV, NLT, NRSV, REB, TEV].

QUESTION—Why did the Pharisees and lawyers keep silent?

They didn't know what to say because they didn't want to break their own laws and say that healing of the Sabbath was permissible, yet they did not dare appear to be inhumane by saying that it was not permissible [ICC, MGC]. The rabbinic laws said that healing was permitted on the Sabbath only if one's life was in danger, yet the Law of Moses said nothing about this situation [TNTC]. Perhaps they had differences of opinion [BNTC]. Perhaps the nature of the illness made it uncertain as to whether or not the man's life was in danger [NIGTC]. Perhaps they felt that forbidding all healing on the Sabbath was difficult to prove that it really pleased God and was proper [Arn].

14:5 And he-said to them, Which of-you (having) a-son or an-ox fall into a-well, and won't immediately lift-out him on the Sabbath day? **14:6** And they-were- not -able to-make-a-reply against[a] these (things).

TEXT—In 14:5, before πρὸς αὐτόν 'to them', some manuscripts add ἀποκριθείς 'answering'. GNT does not deal with this variant. Ἀποκριθείς 'answering' is read by KJV.

TEXT—In 14:5, instead of υἱὸς ἢ βοῦς 'son or ox' some manuscripts read ὄνος ἢ βοῦς 'donkey or ox', others read ὄνος υἱὸς ἢ βοῦς 'donkey, son, or ox', and others read πρόβατον ἢ βοῦς 'sheep or ox'. GNT reads υἱὸς ἢ βοῦς 'son or ox' with a B decision, indicating that the text is almost certain. Ὄνος ἢ βοῦς 'donkey or ox' is read by Arn, WBC, and KJV.

TEXT—In 14:6, following ἀνταποκριθῆναι 'to reply', some manuscripts add αὐτῷ 'to him'. GNT does not deal with this variant. Αὐτῷ 'to him' is read by KJV.

LEXICON—a. πρός (LN90.33) (BAGD III.5.a. p. 710): 'against' [LN], 'with reference to' [BAGD]. Verse 14:6 is translated 'And they could make no reply to this' [NASB], 'And they were not able to reply to this' [Arn], 'And they were not able to reply to these things' [BECNT], 'And they could not reply to this' [NRSV], 'But they could not reply to this' [NET], 'They could not return an answer' [NTC], 'But they were not able to answer him about this' [TEV], 'And they could not answer him' [NCV], 'Again they had no answer' [NLT], 'And they could not answer him again to these things' [KJV], 'And to this they could find no answer' [AB; HCSB], 'To this they could find no reply' [REB], 'They were not able to give an answer back to this' [WBC], 'And they had no strength to reply to these things' [Lns], 'And they had nothing to say' [NIV], 'There was nothing they could say' [CEV], 'But they didn't say a thing' [GW].

QUESTION—What was the function of Jesus' question?

This was a rhetorical question that expected an affirmative answer [BECNT, NAC, TG]. Jesus justified his healing of the man with this question [NAC, NIGTC, TNTC]. Since the Pharisees would not answer the question about whether or not it was permitted to heal on the Sabbath, Jesus defended his action of healing by an appeal to their sense of compassion [BECNT]. The argument is that what we would do for our own sons or even animals, we should also do for others [Lns]. What the Pharisees would allow for their own benefit should be allowed to Jesus for the benefit of others [ICC].

QUESTION—Why couldn't they make a reply against these things?

In 14:4 they were silent because they did not want to answer, but here they were silent because they would only be able to answer in the affirmative, thus admitting that they were wrong [NTC]. They could not refute the implied criticism in Jesus' question [TH]. They knew that the Law allowed such deeds [TG]. Of course they would do so for their own son or their own ox, but the answer was not so clear to them about someone else's son or ox [AB]. The word ταῦτα 'these things' refers to what Jesus said in 14:5 and to all he said in the whole episode [BECNT].

DISCOURSE UNIT: 14:7–15 [NASB]. The topic is the parable of the guests.

DISCOURSE UNIT: 14:7–14 [AB, BECNT, NAC, NICNT, TNTC; CEV, HCSB, NET, NLT, NRSV, TEV]. The topic is an invitation to a banquet [TNTC], sayings concerning banquet behavior [AB, NAC], recasting meal etiquette [NICNT], how to be a guest [CEV], on seeking seats of honor [NET], a parable on humility [Su], teachings on humility [HCSB], Jesus teaches about humility [NLT], humility and hospitality [NRSV, TEV], lessons on humility and generosity [BECNT].

DISCOURSE UNIT: 14:7–11 [NIGTC, WBC; NCV]. The topic is the places of honor [NIGTC], when you are invited to a banquet [WBC], don't make yourself important [NCV].

14:7 And he-was-speaking a-parable[a] to the (ones who) were invited, noticing how they-were-choosing the places-of-honor,[b] saying to them, **14:8** When you-(singular)-are-invited by someone to wedding-feasts,[c] you-should- not -recline in the place-of-honor, lest a-distinguished[d] (person) (more than) you may-have-been-invited by him,

LEXICON—a. παραβολή (LN 33.15) (BAGD 2. p. 612): 'parable' [AB, Arn, BAGD, BECNT, LN, Lns, NTC, WBC; HCSB, KJV, NASB, NET, NIV, NRSV, REB, TEV], 'story' [NCV], 'illustration' [GW], 'advice' [NLT], not explicit [CEV]. By calling this a parable, it signifies that this is intended to teach a spiritual lesson [Arn]. The divine principle given in 14:11 makes the illustration a parable [EGT, Gdt, Lns, NIC, NIGTC].

Connected with the concluding advice, the narrative is to be understood metaphorically [ICC, TH]. See this word at 5:36; 6:39; 13:6.

b. πρωτοκλισία (LN 87.18) (BAGD p. 725): 'place of honor' [BAGD, LN], 'best place' [LN]. The two occurrences of this word in 14:7-8 are translated 'the places of honor...the place of honor' [GW, NET, NIV, NRSV, REB], 'the places of honor at the table...the place of honor' [NTC; NASB], 'seats of honor...the seat of honor' [BECNT], 'the best places to sit...the most important seat' [NCV], 'the best places...the best place' [HCSB, TEV], 'the first places...the first position' [WBC], 'the first places...the first place' [AB], 'the best seats...the best place' [CEV], 'near the head of the table...the best seat' [NLT], 'the chief seats...the chief seat' [Arn], 'the chief reclining places...the chief reclining place' [Lns], 'the chief rooms...the highest room' [KJV]. The noun literally means the 'first reclining places' [BNTC].

c. γάμος (LN 34.68) (BAGD 1.b. p. 151): 'wedding feast' [BECNT, NTC; CEV, NASB, NCV, NET, NIV, NLT, REB, TEV], 'wedding banquet' [Arn, BAGD; HCSB, NRSV], 'wedding' [LN, Lns; GW, KJV], 'banquet' [AB, WBC]. A wedding was specified because there is great formality in the dinner, involving a great deal of ranking the guests [ICC]. A 'wedding feast' represents all important social functions where people might try to seek special honor [EGT]. The word can be used generically for 'banquets' [AB, NAC, NICNT, NIGTC; NET], especially in the plural form [AB]. Or, this does not apply to the present dinner and actually refers to a wedding where there would be many guests and many chief places [Lns]. The parable applies to weddings and any other banquets [TNTC].

d. ἔντιμος (LN 87.6) (BAGD 1.a. p. 268): 'distinguished' [BAGD], 'honored, respected' [BAGD, LN]. The phrase 'a distinguished person more than you' is translated 'a person more distinguished than you' [AB, NTC; NASB, NET, NIV, NRSV; similarly HCSB, REB], 'someone more respected than you' [NLT], 'someone more important than you' [GW, NCV, TEV], 'someone more important' [CEV], 'a more honored person than you' [Arn], 'one more honored than thou' [Lns], 'a more eminent man than you' [BECNT], 'one who is more honorable than you' [WBC], 'a more honorable man than thou' [KJV]. This refers to someone of high social standing [TG], or anyone whom the host holds in honor [EGT]. Precedence was based on rank, reputation, or age [NAC], on rank and distinction [MGC, NIGTC].

QUESTION—What is the setting of this section?

Jesus had just healed the man with dropsy before the dinner had started and then he watched how the guests were taking their places [AB, BECNT, Gdt, ICC, MGC, NIC, NICNT, NTC, Su, TH]. Or, since this talks about a wedding, it is a separate occasion from the preceding dinner where the healing of the man with dropsy took place [Alf, NIBC].

QUESTION—Where was the place of honor?
The place of honor at a dinner would be the place beside the host [BAGD, BECNT, Pnt, Su, TG; NET]. It was at the middle place of each couch [MGC, NIGTC, TNTC], or at the head end of the table [MGC, NIGTC]. There would be a number of couches for three persons each and these couches would be arranged in a U-shape. The places of honor would be the central positions of the couches [Arn, ICC, NTC, TNTC]. Or, instead of the middle of the couch, it was at the left end of each couch because the person there had the fullest view of the table and guests [Lns]. Or, instead of picturing several places of honor, the second mention of 'the place of honor' with the singular form refers to the place for the most honored guest of all [WBC].

14:9 and having-come the (one) having-invited both you and him-will-say to-you, Give (your) place to-this (one), and then with-shame[a] you-will-begin[b] to-occupy the last[c] place.

LEXICON—a. αἰσχύνη (LN **25.189**): 'shame, disgrace' [LN]. The phrase 'with shame' [BECNT, Lns, WBC; KJV] is also translated 'with embarrassment' [NTC], 'in embarrassment' [AB], 'in humiliation' [HCSB], 'with disgrace' [Arn], 'in disgrace' [NASB, NRSV], 'ashamed' [NET], 'humiliated' [NIV], 'embarrassed' [GW], 'you will be ashamed' [**LN**], 'you will/would be embarrassed' [CEV, NCV, NLT, TEV], 'you will look foolish' [REB].

b. fut. mid. indic. of ἄρχομαι (LN 68.1): 'to begin, to commence' [LN]. The phrase 'you will begin to occupy' [Arn] is also translated 'you will begin to take' [KJV], 'you will begin to take up' [WBC], 'you would/will proceed to take' [AB; HCSB], 'you begin to head to' [BECNT], 'you will begin to hold' [Lns], 'you would start to take' [NRSV], 'you will have to take' [NLT], 'you will begin to move to' [NET], 'you proceed to occupy' [NASB], 'you will be taking and keeping' [NTC], 'you will have to take' [GW, NIV], 'you will have to move to' [NCV], 'you will have to sit in' [CEV, TEV], 'as you go to take' [REB]. The man's shame would be most keenly felt at the beginning of his move to the lowest place [EGT, My]. The verb indicates that this is a new and unexpected situation [TH]. Or, the verb 'will begin' is a filler verb with no special significance [Arn].

c. ἔσχατος (LN 87.66) (BAGD 1. or 2. p. 313): 'last, lowest, least important' [LN]. This may refer to location and mean 'the place in the farthest corner' [BAGD (1.)], or it may refer to rank and mean 'poorest' [BAGD (2.)]. The phrase 'the last place' [AB, Lns, WBC; NASB, NCV] is also translated 'the last seat' [BECNT], 'whatever seat is left at the foot of the table' [NLT], 'the lowest room' [KJV], 'the lowest place' [Arn, NTC; HCSB, NRSV, REB, TEV], 'the place of least honor' [GW], 'the least important place' [NET, NIV], 'the worst place' [CEV].

QUESTION—Where did the host come from?
>	The guests had taken their places before the host came in [EGT, Pnt]. When the host arrived he was accompanied by another guest whom the host intended to seat in a place of honor. Or, perhaps the host was there and saw what had happened, so he brought another invited guest over to take that place [NTC].

QUESTION—After the guest had to give up his place, why did he move to the last place?
>	The intermediate places of honor had already been filled [Arn, BECNT, Gdt, ICC, Lns, NIC, NTC, Rb, TNTC, WBC], or the humiliated person took the lowest seat because he did not want to experience a second humiliation [NTC]. His shame caused him to bypass the intermediate ranking seats [WBC].

14:10 But when you-are-invited, having-gone recline in the last place, so-that/then when the (one) having-invited you comes he-will-say to-you, Friend, go-up[a] to-a-higher (place). Then there-will-be honor[b] to-you before all the (ones) reclining-at-table-with you.

LEXICON—a. aorist act. impera. of προσαναβαίνω (LN **15.106**) (BAGD p. 711): 'to go up to, to move up to' [BAGD, LN], 'to come up to' [LN]. The phrase 'go up to a higher place' is translated 'go up higher' [WBC; KJV], 'go on up higher' [Lns], 'move up higher' [NTC; HCSB, NASB, NRSV], 'move up to a higher place' [AB], 'move up to a better seat' [BECNT], 'move up to a better place' [NIV], 'move up here to a better place' [NET], 'move here' [Arn], 'take a better seat' [CEV], 'move to a more honorable place' [GW], 'move up here to a more important place' [NCV], 'come up higher' [REB], 'come on up to a better place' [TEV], 'we have a better place than this for you' [NLT], 'come up higher, come up to a higher place, come up to a better seat, come up to a more important place' [**LN**]. This probably means that the man is invited to come up to where the host is seated [Gdt, ICC, NIGTC, TH].

b. δόξα (LN 87.4): 'honor, respect' [LN]. The phrase 'there will be honor to you' is translated 'there will be honor for you' [Lns], 'you will have honor' [Arn; NASB], 'you will be honored' [BECNT, NTC; CEV, HCSB, NET, NIV, NLT, NRSV], 'you will enjoy honor' [AB], 'this will bring you honor' [TEV], 'you will have glory' [WBC], 'thou shalt have worship' [KJV], '(all the other guests) will respect you' [NCV], '(all your fellow-guests) will see the respect in which you are held' [REB].

QUESTION—Why should someone take the last place?
>	Then there would be no place to go except up [TNTC].

QUESTION—Does ἵνα 'so that' indicate the result of taking the last place or the guest's purpose for taking the last place?
>	1. It indicates the result of taking the last seat [Alf, ICC, NAC, NIC; CEV, GW, NCV, NLT]: then you will be honored.

2. It indicates the purpose for taking the last seat [AB, BECNT, Lns, My, NTC, TH, WBC; KJV, NASB, NET, NIV, NRSV, REB, TEV]: so that you will be honored. It is the intended result [TH]. This is said in irony and indicates the way the Pharisee should go about obtaining the honor that he is greedy for [Lns]. Jesus is merely telling the people to take the way of modesty to obtain honor here on earth [Arn]. Or, if it indicates purpose, it is Christ's purpose in giving this advice, not the purpose that the guest is to have in taking the lowest seat [ICC].

14:11 Because[a] everyone exalting[b] himself will-be-humbled,[c] and the (one) humbling himself will-be-exalted.

LEXICON—a. ὅτι (LN 89.33): 'because' [LN, Lns], 'for' [AB, Arn, BECNT, NTC, WBC; all versions except CEV, GW, NCV], not explicit [CEV, GW, NCV].

b. pres. act. participle of ὑψόω (LN 87.20) (BAGD 2. p. 851): 'to exalt' [BAGD, LN]. The phrase in the first clause 'everyone exalting himself' is translated 'everyone who exalts himself' [AB, Arn, BECNT, NTC, WBC; HCSB, NASB, NET, NIV, REB; similarly Lns; KJV], 'all who exalt themselves' [NRSV], 'all/those who make themselves great' [NCV, TEV], 'those who honor themselves' [GW], 'if you put yourself above others' [CEV], 'the proud' [NLT]. The phrase in the second clause 'will/shall be exalted' [AB, Arn, BECNT, Lns, NTC, WBC; HCSB, KJV, NASB, NET, NIV, NRSV, REB] is also translated 'will be made great' [NCV, TEV], 'will be honored' [GW, NLT], 'you will be honored' [CEV].

c. fut. pass. indic. of ταπεινόομαι (LN 87.63) (BAGD 2.a. p. 804): 'to be humbled, to be humiliated' [BAGD], 'to be made to live like those of low status' [LN]. The phrase in the first clause 'will/shall be humbled' [AB, Arn, BECNT, Lns, NTC, WBC; GW, HCSB, NASB, NET, NIV, NLT, NRSV, REB, TEV] is also translated 'will be made humble' [NCV], 'shall be abased' [KJV], 'you will be put down' [CEV]. The phrase in the second clause 'the one humbling himself' [BECNT] is also translated 'the one humbling his own self' [Lns], 'the one/he who humbles himself' [AB, NTC, WBC; HCSB, NASB, NET, NIV; similarly Arn; KJV, REB], 'those who make themselves humble' [NCV], 'those who humble themselves' [NRSV, TEV], 'people who humble themselves' [GW], 'if you humble yourself' [CEV], 'the humble' [NLT].

QUESTION—What is the function of this verse?

It gives the moral of the parable [EGT]. It indicates that the preceding verses are more than rules of conduct at banquets or directions of good taste [Gdt, ICC, Lns, NIC]. The preceding parable concerns the need for humility in all relations [Arn, BECNT, Gdt, NIBC, NTC, TNTC]. The passives 'will be humbled' and 'will be exalted' implies that God is the one who will humble a person who exalts himself or God will exalt a person who humbles himself [BECNT, Lns, MGC, NAC, NICNT, NIGTC, TG, TH, WBC]. This extends to the eschatological reversal of pride and humility [BECNT]. Its message is that self-assertion is not enough in view of God's judgment [AB].

DISCOURSE UNIT: 14:12–14 [NIGTC, WBC; NCV]. The topic is the choice of guests [NIGTC], when you are going to give a luncheon or a dinner [WBC], you will be rewarded [NCV].

14:12 And also he-was-speaking to-the (one) having-invited him, When you-prepare a-luncheon[a] or a-dinner,[b] do- not -invite your friends or your brothers[c] or the (ones) related[d] to-you or rich neighbors, lest they also should-invite-in-return[e] you and it-becomes a-repayment[f] to-you.

LEXICON—a. ἄριστον (LN **23.23**, 23.22) (BAGD 2. p. 106): 'luncheon' [AB, NTC, WBC; NASB, NIV, NLT, NRSV], 'lunch' [**LN** (23.23); GW, HCSB, NCV, REB, TEV], 'noon meal' [BAGD, LN (23.23)], 'morning meal' [Lns], 'breakfast' [Arn], 'dinner' [BECNT; CEV, KJV, NET], 'meal, banquet, feast' [LN (23.22)]. There were two Jewish meals each day [WBC], and this was a late morning meal [BECNT, WBC], a noonday meal [AB, TH]. It was a breakfast or a lunch [Arn].

b. δεῖπνον (LN 23.25, 23.22) (BAGD 1. p. 173): 'dinner' [AB, Arn, BAGD, NTC, WBC; GW, HCSB, NASB, NCV, NIV, NLT, NRSV, TEV], 'supper' [BAGD, BECNT, LN (23.25); KJV, REB], 'evening meal' [Lns], 'main meal' [BAGD, LN (23.25)], 'banquet' [LN (23.22); CEV, NET], 'meal, feast' [LN (23.22)]. This was a late afternoon meal, usually the main meal of the day [AB, Arn, BECNT, NIGTC, NTC, WBC]. It contrasts with the preceding meal as to the kind of meal it is, not the time of day [NAC]. The previous term for a meal and this term for a meal overlap and the presence of rich neighbors as guests make it probable that both refer to an elaborate meal [NET]. Both the noon and the evening meals would be large meals or feasts [TH].

c. ἀδελφός (LN 10.49): 'brother' [LN]. The plural form is translated 'brothers' [AB, Arn, BECNT, Lns, NTC, WBC; all versions except CEV, GW, NCV], 'family' [CEV, GW, NCV]. The noun 'brothers' may mean blood brothers who are here contrasted with other relatives [AB, TG, TH]. Or, 'brothers' may be used in an extended sense to mean close family relatives who are then contrasted with more distant relatives [NIGTC, TG, TH].

d. συγγενής (LN 10.6) (BAGD p. 772): 'related' [BAGD, LN]. The phrase 'the ones related to you' is translated 'your relatives' [AB, Arn, BECNT, Lns, NTC; CEV, HCSB, NET, NIV, NLT, NRSV, TEV], 'your other relatives' [GW, NCV], 'your other relations' [REB], 'thy kinsmen' [KJV], not explicit [WBC]. Both 'brothers' and 'relatives' form one category [EGT] and some translations show this by translating this word as 'other relatives' [GW, NCV, REB].

e. aorist act. subj. of ἀντικαλέω (LN **33.317**) (BAGD p. 74): 'to invite in return' [BAGD], 'to invite back' [**LN**]. The phrase 'lest they also should invite in return you' is translated 'lest they invite you in return' [Arn], 'lest they also invite you in turn' [BECNT], 'lest they only invite you in turn' [AB], 'lest they invite you back' [NTC], 'lest they, too, invite thee again' [Lns], 'lest they also bid thee again' [KJV], 'in case they may invite you in return' [NRSV], 'in case they in turn call you' [WBC], 'otherwise, they will return the favor' [GW], 'otherwise they may also invite you in return' [NASB], 'they will only ask you back again' [REB], 'if you do, they will invite you in return' [CEV], 'if you do, they may invite you back' [NIV], 'so you can be invited by them in return' [NET], 'at another time they will invite you to eat with them' [NCV], 'for they will invite you back' [TEV], 'because they might invite you back' [HCSB], 'for (they will repay you) by inviting you back' [NLT].

f. ἀνταπόδομα (LN **57.155**) (BAGD p. 73): 'repayment' [BAGD, LN]. The phrase 'it becomes a repayment to you' is translated 'that will be your repayment' [NASB], 'there is a repayment to you' [WBC], 'you are repaid' [AB, BECNT], 'you get repaid' [**LN**], 'you will be repaid' [NCV, NIV, REB], 'you would be repaid' [HCSB, NRSV], 'you will be paid back' [CEV], 'a recompense be made thee' [KJV], 'they will repay you' [NLT], 'you receive a recompense' [Arn], 'you receive a return payment' [NTC], 'there be a due return for thee' [Lns], '(in this way) you will be paid for what you did' [TEV], not explicit [GW]. The repayment would be a return invitation to a banquet [WBC].

QUESTION—What does καί 'also' refer to?

The word 'also' indicates that Jesus made an additional statement [TH]. After speaking to the guests, Jesus turned to directly address the host [Lns, NIC, NTC, WBC].

QUESTION—Did Jesus mean that they were never to invite their families and friends to a banquet?

The present imperative μὴ φώνει 'do not invite' means that they were not to habitually invite them [BECNT, ICC, Lns, NAC, NTC], so Jesus was telling them not to *always* invite only their families and relatives [ICC, Lns]. It is a Semitic idiom to say 'not this, but that' with the meaning 'not so much this as rather that' [NAC, NIGTC].

QUESTION—What is the significance of being repaid when being invited back?

This return banquet is the sum total of his reward and it is implied that he will not receive a heavenly reward [NAC, NIGTC, NTC]. Such a person has not really given in a spirit of generosity, but has only made a trade [TG]. There was no opportunity to practice the requirement to show hospitality to those in need [NTC].

14:13 But when you-prepare a-banquet,ª invite (the) poor, (the) crippled, (the) lame, (the) blind.

LEXICON—a. δοχή (LN **23.27**) (BAGD p. 206): 'banquet' [BAGD, **LN**, Lns, WBC; GW, HCSB, NIV, NRSV], 'feast' [LN; CEV, KJV, NCV, TEV], 'elaborate meal' [NET], 'reception' [BECNT, NTC; NASB], 'party'

[REB], 'dinner party' [AB], 'dinner' [Arn], not explicit [NLT]. This noun is a general term for a meal that could be either a 'luncheon' or a 'dinner' [TH, WBC]. It is a major meal such as a reception [Arn, BECNT].

QUESTION—What is the significance of the categories of people they are to invite?

The list is not comprehensive, but it is used as an illustration of the types of people to invite [TH]. These are the kind of people who were in need and would not be able to pay him back [Arn, BECNT]. The lame people are a class included in the more general class of the crippled or maimed people [TH].

14:14 And you-will-be blessed,[a] because they-do- not -have (the means) to-repay you, because it-will-be-repaid to-you in the resurrection of-the righteous.[b]

LEXICON—a. μακάριος (LN 25.119) (BAGD 1.b. p. 486): 'blessed'. See translations of this word at 12:37. The passive implies that God is the one who will bless them [AB, BECNT, NAC, TG, TH; CEV, NET]. This word also occurs at 1:45; 6:20; 7:23; 10:23; 11:27; 12:43; 23:29.

b. δίκαιος (LN 88.12) (BAGD 1.b. p. 195): 'the righteous' [BAGD, BECNT, LN, Lns, NTC, WBC; HCSB, NASB, NET, NIV, NRSV, REB], 'the just' [Arn; KJV], 'the upright' [AB], 'the good people' [NCV, TEV], 'the godly' [NLT], 'those who have God's approval' [GW], 'his (God's) people' [CEV]. The righteous person is one who will be free of guilt at the last judgment [Lns]. They are righteous on the basis of Christ's atonement [NTC]. See this word at 1:6, 17; 2:25; 5:32; 15:7; 18:9; 20:20; 23:47, 50.

QUESTION—Why will such a person be blessed because the needy people cannot repay him?

This clause gives the reason for being blessed in negative terms, while the next clause 'because it will be repaid to you in the resurrection of the righteous' gives the reason in positive terms [TH]. This clause makes it clear that his hospitality was due to generosity and not self interest [Lns, MGC, NIGTC, TNTC]. He will be blessed because his good deeds are sure to be rewarded and if they cannot be rewarded by repayment from his banquet guests in the present world, they will surely be rewarded by God in the hereafter [ICC].

QUESTION—Does the phrase 'the resurrection of the righteous' imply that there will be a different resurrection of the unrighteous?

1. This implies that there will be two resurrections, the resurrection of the righteous and another resurrection of the rest [Alf, Gdt, ICC, My, WBC]. This is the first resurrection [Alf]. In this statement it is not implied that there is a distinction made between two resurrections, but 20:35 proves that this distinction was in the mind of Jesus [Gdt].

2. This does not indicate that there will be two resurrections [Arn, BNTC, Crd, EGT, Lns, NAC, NIGTC]. Here the focus is on those who are righteous among those who will be resurrected [Crd]. The unrighteous are

not in view since they have nothing to do with Jesus' teaching here [Lns]. This is the positive half of the resurrection of the righteous and the unrighteous (Acts 24:15) [NIGTC]. This is a shortened reference to the resurrection of the righteous and the unrighteous [NAC]. The unrighteous will also be raised, but in order to be condemned [Arn].

DISCOURSE UNIT: 14:15–24 [AB, BECNT, NAC, NICNT, NIGTC, Su, TNTC, WBC; CEV, HCSB, NCV, NET, NIV, NLT, NRSV, TEV]. The topic is the great banquet [CEV], the great supper [NIGTC], the parable of the great/large banquet [AB, BECNT, NAC, Su; HCSB, NET, NIV, NRSV], a story of the great feast [NCV, NLT, TEV], a wealthy householder and his invitation list [NICNT], who shall eat bread in the kingdom of God? [WBC], excuses [TNTC].

14:15 And having-heard these (things) a-certain (one) of-the (ones who) were-reclining-at-table-with (Jesus) said to-him, Blessed (is he) who will-eat bread^a in the kingdom of-God.

LEXICON—a. ἄρτος (LN 5.1) (BAGD 2. p. 111): 'bread, food' [BAGD, LN]. The phrase 'who will eat bread' [Arn, BECNT, Lns, WBC; HCSB, KJV, NASB, NRSV] is also translated 'who will be at the banquet' [CEV, GW], 'who will share in the meal' [NCV], 'who will share the meal' [AB], 'who will sit at the feast' [REB], 'who will sit down at the feast' [TEV], 'who will eat at the feast' [NIV], 'who will feast' [NET], 'who will partake in the feast' [NTC], 'to have a share (in the kingdom)' [NLT]. To 'eat bread' is an idiom for eating a full meal [Bai, NAC, NIGTC, WBC]. To eat bread in God's kingdom means to share the eternal bliss of salvation [BAGD].

QUESTION—How does this verse connect with its context?

The use of the word 'blessed' is taken up from the preceding verse where Jesus pronounced a blessing [BECNT, NIGTC, NTC]. The speaker may be a guest who wanted to extend the seeming limitation of blessedness in Jesus' statement to include all those who will be present at the heavenly banquet [NIGTC]. The thought of God's kingdom was suggested by the statement Jesus made about the resurrection of the righteous [AB, Arn, BECNT, ICC, Lns, NAC, NIC, TNTC, WBC], and by the setting of the banquet the guests were attending [BECNT, NAC, NIBC]. The Pharisees assumed that they would be the blessed ones at the banquet in the kingdom of heaven [BECNT, ICC, NIC, TNTC]. By preceding this verse with a section heading, many indicate that it is to be closely linked to the following parable [AB, Alf, Arn, BECNT, Blm, EGT, Gdt, ICC, NAC, NIC, NICNT, NIGTC, Su, TG, TNTC, WBC; CEV, NCV, NET, NIV, NLT, NRSV, TEV]. The remark by the guest in this verse provides the occasion for the following parable [AB, Arn, NIGTC, Su].

QUESTION—What is the significance of eating bread in the kingdom of God?

The Jews looked forward to the Messiah coming to rule and a messianic banquet would occur at the inauguration of his rule [Bai, Blm, BNTC, ICC,

NIC, NIVS, Su]. Jesus had previously spoken about reclining to eat at the feast in the kingdom of God at 13:29 [AB]. The kingdom of God refers to heaven [Arn]. To eat bread refers to being admitted to the banquet [Gdt], to dine with the saints in heaven [Lns]. The symbolism of a heavenly banquet refers to eschatological blessedness in the kingdom of God [NTC]. It means to enjoy the fellowship of God's coming rule [NET]. It describes salvation and receiving eternal life [NAC]. The guest talked about a future messianic rule, but Jesus considered God's kingdom to have already come in his presence and the parable is about men rejecting God's kingdom at the present time [Su].

DISCOURSE UNIT: 14:16–24 [NASB]. The topic is the parable of the dinner.

14:16 And he-said to-him, A-certain man was-preparing a-great dinner[a] and he-invited many. **14:17** And he-sent his slave[b] at-the hour of-the dinner to-say to-the (ones who) have-been-invited, Come, because now it-is ready.

TEXT—In 14:17, instead of ἕτοιμά ἐστιν 'it is ready' (with the singular verb), some manuscripts read the plural verb ἕτοιμά εἰσιν (with the same meaning) 'are ready', some manuscripts read ἕτοιμά ἐστιν πάντα 'everything is ready', and some manuscripts read πάντα ἕτοιμά ἐστιν 'everything is ready'. GNT reads ἕτοιμά ἐστιν 'it is ready' with a C decision, indicating that the Committee had difficulty making the decision. Ἕτοιμά ἐστιν πάντα 'all things are ready' is read by KJV.

LEXICON—a. δεῖπνον (LN 23.25) (BAGD 2. p. 173): 'dinner'. See translations of this word at 14:12.
   b. δοῦλος (LN 87.76): 'slave' [Arn, BECNT, LN, Lns, WBC; HCSB, NASB, NET, NRSV], 'bondservant' [LN], 'servant' [AB, NTC; CEV, GW, KJV, NCV, NIV, NLT, REB, TEV].

QUESTION—Why did the host send his slave to guests who had already been invited?

It was the custom among the Jews for the guests to have a double invitation [Bai, EGT, ICC, MGC, NAC, NICNT, NIVS, NTC, TNTC]. The first invitation had informed the guests the time of the coming dinner and then when that time had come, the slave went to summon them to the meal [MGC, NIC]. According to custom, the exact time had not been included in the invitation, and so they waited for a slave to come and tell them when it was actually time to go to the dinner [Arn, BECNT, BNTC, Hlt, Lns]. The slave had to go to the different homes to tell them [TG]. It is understood that the people who had been invited had accepted the invitation [BECNT, NTC, TNTC].

14:18 And all one-after-another began to-make-excuses. The first said to-him, I-bought a-field and I-need to-go-out to-see^a it. I-ask you, have me having-been-excused.^b

LEXICON—a. aorist act. infin. of ὁράω (LN 24.1) (BAGD 1.a. p. 220): 'to see' [LN], 'to look at' [BAGD]. The phrase 'to see it' [Arn, BECNT, WBC; GW, HCSB, KJV, NET, NIV, NRSV] is also translated 'to look at it' [NASB, NCV, TEV], 'to look it over' [NTC; CEV], 'to inspect it' [AB; NLT, REB].

    b. perf. pass. participle of παραιτέομαι (LN 33.163) (BAGD 1. p. 616): 'to excuse' [BAGD, LN]. The phrase 'I ask you, have me having been excused' is translated 'I ask you, have me excused' [WBC], 'I ask you to excuse me' [HCSB], 'I ask you, let me be excused' [Arn], 'I beg of you, have me be excused' [BECNT], 'I pray thee have me excused' [KJV], 'consider me excused' [BAGD, NTC], 'please consider me excused' [NASB], 'please excuse me' [CEV, GW, NCV, NET, NIV], 'he asked to be excused' [NLT], 'please accept my regrets' [NRSV], 'please convey my regrets' [AB], 'please accept my apologies' [REB, TEV]. He was asking to be excused from not keeping his prior commitment to attend [BECNT].

QUESTION—Were there only three people who had been invited?

There were many invited guests at this large banquet and it was clear that none of them wanted to attend [Arn, Su] and they all produced reasons why they should be released from their former acceptance of the invitations [TH]. Since this is a parable, the unlikely event occurred that all of the many guests refused to attend [NAC]. All of those who had been invited made excuses and the three excuses given here were typical of the kinds of excuses that were offered [Arn, EGT, Lns, NIC, NICNT, NIGTC, TNTC, WBC]. These three examples did not cover all of the excuses that were offered [EGT]. These three were the best of the many excuses offered [Lns]. The guests didn't want to attend and gave these ridiculous and humorous excuses [Su]. Or, the excuses were more or less valid [BNTC, EGT], as all excuses for not following Christ usually seem to be [BNTC]. Whether the excuses were weak or not, the point is that in this parable the invitation was refused by all of the invited guests [AB].

QUESTION—Did the slave have authority to excuse them?

The invited people spoke to the slave but their excuses were to be passed through him to the host [TH]. The slave was to excuse them on behalf of his master [Lns].

QUESTION—What was involved in the first excuse about the land?

The field was out of town and was to be used for planting [AB, TG]. The new owner acted like he had not examined the field before buying it [Su]. This excuse was a lie since anyone buying a piece of land would have examined it thoroughly before the sale [Bai, NIVS]. He must have seen it before buying it and further inspection could wait [ICC, NTC]. Some think that an inspection of the land was still required. The sale could have been on condition of a later inspection and approval [NIGTC]. An owner would want to become well acquainted with the land that he had bought [My]. However, dinners were held late in the afternoon and any legitimate inspection should have been done during the day, so the excuse was a great discourtesy [Bai, NIGTC]. The field could have been examined at another time [Arn, Hlt, NTC, TNTC].

14:19 And another said, I-bought five pair of-oxen and I-am-going to-test[a] them. I-ask you, have me having-been-excused. **14:20** And another said, I-married[b] a-woman and therefore I-am- not -able to-come.

LEXICON—a. aorist act. infin. of δοκιμάζω (LN 27.45) (BAGD 1. p. 202): 'to test' [BAGD, LN], 'to examine' [Arn, BAGD, LN; NET], 'to prove' [KJV], 'to try' [NCV], 'to try out' [AB, BECNT, NTC, WBC; CEV, HCSB, NASB, NIV, NLT, NRSV, REB, TEV], 'to see how well they plow' [GW]. He wanted to test the oxen for their usefulness [BAGD]. Testing them would be to see how they would pull together as yoked teams [Bai, TG].

b. aorist act. indic. of γαμέω (LN 34.66) (BAGD 1.a. p. 150): 'to marry' [BAGD, LN]. The phrased 'I married a woman' is translated 'I married a wife' [Arn], 'I have married a wife' [BECNT, WBC; KJV, NASB], 'I have just gotten married' [CEV, REB, TEV], 'I just got married' [NTC; HCSB, NCV, NET, NIV], 'I have just been married' [AB; NRSV], 'I recently got married' [GW], 'had just been married' [NLT].

QUESTION—What was involved in the second excuse about the five pairs of oxen?

The man was about to set out to examine the oxen when the slave came with the information about the dinner being ready [Lns, TH; NET]. This had been a major purchase and the man was naturally eager to see how they worked [EGT, NIGTC, WBC]. However, some consider this to be a lame excuse [EGT, NIC, NTC, TNTC, WBC]. The oxen were already purchased and any further testing could be done the next day [Hlt, NTC, TNTC, WBC]. The invited guest plainly did not want to attend the banquet [Arn]. The invited guest was implying that his animals were more important to him than the host [Bai].

QUESTION—What was involved in the third excuse about being newly married?

We are to presume that the marriage had been recent [AB, Bai, BECNT, NTC, WBC; CEV, GW, HCSB, NCV, NET, NIV, NLT, NRSV, REB, TEV] as indicated by the aorist 'I have married' along with his response to the invitation [BECNT]. The wedding could not have been the day of the banquet since in a small village, major events would not be scheduled on the same day [Bai]. It is not clear why the fact of being recently married prevented him from attending [NET]. The man would naturally prefer spending time with his bride [AB]. It was possible for the invited guest to take his wife with him to the banquet [Lns, NTC]. That he was 'not able' to attend was not true [Arn].

14:21 And having-arrived (back) the slave reported these (things) to his master. Then being-angry[a] the master-of-the-household said to-his slave, Go-out quickly into the streets[b] and lanes[c] of-the city and bring-in here the poor and (the) crippled and (the) blind and (the) lame.

TEXT—Instead of ὁ δοῦλος 'the slave', some manuscripts read ὁ δοῦλος ἐκεῖνος 'that slave', although GNT does not mention this variant. Ὁ δοῦλος ἐκεῖνος 'that slave' is read by KJV.

LEXICON—a. aorist pass. (deponent = act.) participle of ὀργίζομαι, ὀργίζω (LN 88.174) (BAGD p. 579): 'to be angry' [AB, Arn, BAGD, BECNT, LN, Lns, NTC, WBC; all versions except NET, REB, TEV], 'to be furious' [LN; NET, REB, TEV]. This is the ingressive aorist, he *became* angry [TH].

b. πλατεῖα (LN 1.103) (BAGD p. 666): 'street' [AB, Arn, BAGD, BECNT, Lns, NTC, WBC; all versions], 'wide street, avenue' [LN], 'wide road' [BAGD]. This refers to the main streets or public squares [NIGTC].

c. ῥύμη (LN 1.104) (BAGD, p. 737): 'lane' [AB, Arn, BAGD, BECNT, LN; KJV, NASB, NRSV], 'narrow street' [BAGD, LN], 'alley' [BAGD, LN, Lns, NTC, WBC; all versions except KJV, NASB, NRSV]. Lanes were the narrow cross streets of the wide main streets [Arn, Gdt]. Specifying both the wide and narrow streets indicates that the whole city was searched for guests [ICC, Lns].

QUESTION—Why was the master angry?

The invited guests had publicly insulted him by turning down his invitations after first accepting them [Bai]. The invited guests had treated him with indifference, contempt, and deceitfulness [NIC].

QUESTION—Why was the slave to go quickly?

The feast was already prepared for guests [Arn, BECNT, EGT, MGC, NIGTC, WBC; NET]. The host did not want to see the prepared food go to waste [Arn].

QUESTION—What is the significance of the list of people to be brought to the banquet?

This is the same list found in 14:13, although the order is reversed for the lame and the blind. The blind and the lame are specifics of the more generic term 'crippled' and it is significant that the crippled were banned from fully participating in Jewish worship [BECNT]. Such people were likely to be beggars who would be found in the city streets [NIGTC]. Those people could be brought to the banquet at once without a formal invitation since they were not likely to refuse [ICC, WBC]. They must be brought in because they might doubt that such a banquet could be for them [NTC].

14:22 And the slave said, Master, what you-commanded has-been-done, and there-is still room.[a] **14:23** And the master said to the slave, Go-out to the roads[b] and hedges[c] and urge[d] (them) to-come-in, in-order-that my house may-be-filled.

TEXT—In 14:22, instead of ὅ 'what', some manuscripts read ὡς 'as', although GNT does not mention this variant. Ὡς 'as' is read by KJV.

LEXICON—a. τόπος (LN 80.1) (BAGD 1.e. p. 822): 'room' [AB, Arn, BAGD, BECNT, LN, Lns, NTC; all versions], 'space' [LN, WBC]. There was still room for more people [TH; CEV, TEV].
- b. ὁδός (LN 1.99) (BAGD 1.a. p. 554): 'road' [Arn, BAGD, LN, Lns; GW, NCV, NIV, NRSV], 'highway' [AB, BAGD, BECNT, LN, NTC, WBC; HCSB, KJV, NASB, NET, REB], 'country road' [TEV], 'back road' [CEV], 'country lane' [NLT]. These were rural roads [NIGTC, Su]. It refers to a major and well-traveled road outside the city [Bai, BECNT, NTC, TNTC]. They were roads going from one town to another [Arn].
- c. φραγμός (LN 1.105) (BAGD 1. p. 865): 'hedge' [Arn, BAGD, BECNT, Lns; KJV], 'hedgerow' [AB, NTC, WBC], 'along the hedges' [NASB], 'along the hedgerows' [REB], 'behind the hedges' [NLT], 'fence row' [CEV], 'byway' [LN], 'path' [LN; GW], 'lane' [HCSB, NRSV, TEV], 'country road' [NET], 'country lane' [NCV, NIV]. This refers to a path along a fence, wall, or hedge [LN]. Fields were divided by hedgerows which served as fences [AB, EGT, Su]. Inter-village travel often was through narrow paths along stone walls or hedgerows [Bai]. Boundaries between fields were formed by rows of bushes, shrubs, or small trees and tramps and beggars were to be found along such boundaries [TG]. Hedges often grew alongside the country roads and derelicts could find shelter there [NIGTC, TNTC]. Poor people would construct rude shelters amid the bushes [Arn, NTC]. Hedges were around vineyards, and along highways, roads, and houses and travelers might stop to rest next to them [BECNT]. Highways and hedgerows probably were not separate places, rather the rural roads were lined at places with hedges or fences that surrounded the fields next to the roads [AB, TNTC, WBC]. Or, some make a distinction between the main roads and the smaller roads or paths between fields [Bai, EGT, Pnt; GW, NCV, NET, NIV, NRSV, TEV].
- d. aorist act. impera. of ἀναγκάζω (LN 37.33) (BAGD 2. p. 52): 'to urge' [BAGD, BECNT; GW, NCV, NET, NLT], 'to invite' [BAGD], 'to compel' [Arn, BAGD, LN, Lns, NTC, WBC; NASB, NRSV, REB], 'to force' [BAGD, LN], 'to make' [AB; CEV, HCSB, NIV, TEV]. This does not mean to compel people to come by force but by urgent invitation [BECNT, NIC, NIGTC], by persuasion [Bai, Crd, ICC, NTC, Rb, TNTC; NET]. Oriental courtesy directed that an invited guest first politely refused to come until being pressed to do so [Bai, NIGTC]. These people would be hesitant about entering the house of someone they did not know and needed to be urged to do so [Arn, BECNT, NAC]. Poor people would modestly resist such an invitation, so they were to be gently led into the house [AB].

QUESTION—When did the slave speak to his master?
> It is assumed that there was an interval of time between 14:21 and 14:22 [TH]. After receiving the command in 14:21, the slave followed those orders and then returned to make this report [BECNT, ICC, Lns, MGC, NIGTC, TG, TH, TNTC, WBC]. In a small village, it would not take long to gather the people [Arn, WBC]. The beginning of 14:22 'And the slave said' is translated 'Soon the servant said' [TEV], 'Later the servant said to him' [NCV], 'When the servant returned, he said' [CEV], 'After the servant had done this, he reported' [NLT]. Or, the slave had anticipated his master's wishes and immediately replied to the instructions given in 14:21 [My].

14:24 Because[a] I-say to-you (plural) that no-one of-those men having-been-invited will-taste[b] my dinner.

LEXICON—a. γάρ (LN 89.23): 'because' [LN], 'for' [AB, Arn, BECNT, LN, Lns, NTC; HCSB, KJV, NASB, NET, NLT, NRSV], not explicit [WBC; CEV, GW, NCV, NIV, REB, TEV].

b. fut. mid. (deponent = act.) fut. of γεύομαι (LN 23.3, 24.72) (BAGD 1. p. 157): 'to taste' [AB, Arn, BAGD, BECNT, LN (24.72), Lns, NTC, WBC; GW, KJV, NASB, NET, NRSV, REB, TEV]. 'to eat' [LN (23.3)], 'to partake of, to enjoy' [BAGD]. The phrase 'will taste my dinner' is translated 'will get a taste of my banquet' [NIV], 'will get even the smallest taste of what I had prepared for them' [NLT], 'will get even a bite of my food' [CEV], 'will eat with me' [NCV], 'will enjoy my banquet' [HCSB].

QUESTION—In the phrase 'I say to you (plural)', who is speaking and who is he speaking to?
> 1. The master in the story is speaking to his slave and to the people who had already been brought in from the streets and lanes of the city to attend the banquet (14:21), and the other slaves present [Arn, EGT, Gdt, ICC, Lns, NIGTC, TG, TH, TNTC]. By saying 'my dinner' it is implied that the speaker is still the host in the story [Arn]. The master in the story is speaking and this indicates that the host would not send food from the banquet to those people who had excused themselves from attending the banquet [NIGTC].
> 2. The plural 'you' has no place in the story and it is as though the person playing the part of the master in the story has stepped aside on the stage to address the audience and the master is to be identified as Jesus [Hlt, NICNT, WBC].
> 3. Jesus is speaking to those who were listening to the parable [AB, Alf, Bai, BECNT, NIC, NTC]. The parable was now ended and Jesus addressed those at the dinner he was attending [NTC]. Jesus now summarized the parable to say that the leaders among the Jews had missed the opportunity to sit at the table of God's blessing while others will end up at the meal [BECNT]. By saying 'my dinner', Jesus identifies himself with the host of the story and refers to the messianic banquet that ushers in the new age of

salvation [Bai]. The people are to be gathered from the roads and hedges γάρ 'because' the master wanted his house to be full and he had determined that none of those who were first invited were to taste his dinner [NTC], they had excluded themselves [Arn].

QUESTION—What was Jesus' purpose in telling this parable?

It was a warning to those Jews who were considered to be pious but who neither entered the kingdom nor allowed others to do so; they would be excluded from the kingdom of God and the way would be opened to the needy and the outsiders [NIGTC]. As Jesus called people to come into the kingdom of God, he was being snubbed by many who seemed to have a claim to attend the eschatological banquet, but the poor, crippled, blind, and lame were entering [WBC]. Those who refuse God's invitation of salvation will be excluded from the kingdom in its consummation and the church would expand to include the Gentiles [NTC]. The gospel proclaimed by Jesus, the apostles, and Christian workers could be rejected and such rejection would bring eternal disaster [Arn]. A person must respond to the summons to enter the kingdom in order to participate in it [NET].

DISCOURSE UNIT: 14:25–35 [BECNT, NAC, NICNT, NIGTC, Su, TNTC, WBC; GW, HCSB, NASB, NET, NIV, NLT]. The topic is counting the cost [NET], a teaching on the cost of discipleship [Su], the cost of being a disciple [GW, NIV, NLT], the cost of following Jesus [HCSB], conditions of discipleship [NAC, NICNT, NIGTC, TNTC], discipleship in the face of rejection [BECNT], the disciples tested [NASB], the disciple's fate and the possibility of failed discipleship [WBC].

DISCOURSE UNIT: 14:25–33 [AB, TNTC; CEV, NCV, NRSV, TEV]. The topic is being a disciple [CEV], conditions of discipleship [AB], the cost of discipleship [TNTC; NRSV], the cost of being a disciple [TEV], the cost of being Jesus' follower [NCV].

14:25 And large crowds were-accompanying[a] him, and having-turned he-said to them, 14:26 If someone comes to[b] me and does- not -hate[c] his-own father and mother and wife and children and brothers and sisters and also in-addition his-own life, he-can not be my disciple.[d]

LEXICON—a. imperf. mid./pass. (deponent = act.) indic. of συμπορεύομαι (LN 15.148) (BAGD 1. p. 780): 'to accompany' [BECNT, LN; NET, REB], 'to be with' [KJV], 'to go with' [BAGD, LN]. 'to go along with' [Lns, WBC; NASB, TEV], 'to walk along with' [CEV], 'to travel with' [Arn, NTC; GW, HCSB, NCV, NIV, NRSV], 'to travel along with' [AB], 'to follow' [NLT].

b. πρός (LN 84.18): 'to' [LN]. The phrase 'to come to me' [AB, Arn, BECNT, Lns, NTC, WBC; all versions except CEV, NLT] is also translated 'to come with me' [CEV], 'to want to be my follower' [NLT].

c. pres. act. indic. of μισέω (LN 88.198) (BAGD p. 522): 'to hate' [AB, Arn, BAGD, BECNT, LN, Lns, NTC, WBC; HCSB, KJV, NASB, NET,

NIV, NRSV, REB]. The clause 'if someone does not hate' is translated 'you must love me more than' [NLT], 'unless they love me more than they love…' [TEV], 'unless you love me more than you love…' [CEV], 'if anyone loves…more than me' [NCV], 'if people are not ready to abandon…' [GW].

 d. μαθητής (LN 36.38): 'disciple' [AB, Arn, BECNT, LN, Lns, NTC, WBC; all versions except NCV], 'follower' [LN; NCV]. 'Disciple' was the usual word for being a Christian [AB, NIBC]. A disciple is a learner, a pupil, whom Jesus instructs in the way to God [BECNT, WBC]. A disciple follows his teacher's lifestyle, habits, and way of thinking so as to become as much like him as possible [NIBC].

QUESTION—Why was a crowd accompanying Jesus?

The people thought that Jesus was the Messiah [ICC, NIC] and that the crisis of the kingdom was at hand [ICC]. They followed because of the blessings and wonderful things associated with the kingdom of God [AB, ICC]. They wanted to hear Jesus' teachings and see his miracles, or perhaps they wanted to find out if he really was the Messiah [Su]. From the teaching in this section, it appears that some, at least, wanted to become his disciples [Arn, BECNT, Lns]. The crowd may have included people traveling to Jerusalem for the Passover [Lns]. This was a neutral crowd from which Jesus might draw disciples [NICNT].

QUESTION—What is meant by hating one's family?

It is a hyperbole that exaggerates for emphasis and an equivalent statement that is less drastic is found in Matt. 10:37: 'Anyone who loves his father or mother more than me is not worthy of me' (NIV) [Arn, BECNT, Crd, NAC, NTC, TG, WBC]. This does not mean literal hatred and here it means loving one's family less than loving Christ [Arn, BECNT, EGT, NAC, NIBC, NIVS, NTC, TG, TNTC; CEV, NCV, NET]. This understanding is confirmed by the following command to hate oneself [Arn], and by other passages where they are commanded to love their neighbor [BECNT]. A disciple must be ready to act toward his family as though it were an object of hatred when they are opposed to Christ and loyalty to Christ is at stake [AB, ICC]. Where there is hate, there are no ties that bind the disciple from being a disciple [WBC]. The hyperbole has the sense of abandoning or renouncing one's family [MGC, NIGTC]. It refers to a feeling of alienation from the world's relationships [Alf]. Compared to one's devotion to Christ, every other devotion must be so secondary that it may be compared to hatred and rejection [Su, TNTC].

QUESTION—What is meant by hating one's life?

Jesus must be the first priority in one's life in order to be a disciple [BECNT; NET]. A disciple must not let family ties or personal desires take precedence over his loyalty to Jesus [TG]. He must be ready to give up his own life rather than give up the Lord [Su]. One's life includes one's worldly interests and affections, and even life itself [ICC]. It is the total of one's being and this concept is illustrated in the next verse [Arn, Su].

14:27 **Whoever does- not -carry**[a] **his-own cross and come after**[b] **me, can not be my disciple.**
TEXT—Before ὅστις 'whoever', some manuscripts add καί 'and'. GNT does not deal with this variant. Καί 'and' is read by KJV.
TEXT—Instead of τὸν σταυρὸν ἑαυτοῦ 'his own cross', some manuscripts read τὸν σταυρὸν αὐτοῦ 'his cross', although GNT does not mention this variant. Τὸν σταυρὸν αὐτοῦ 'his cross' is read by NTC, GW, KJV, NCV, NET, NIV, NRSV, REB (although the reading of versions other than KJV may be stylistic rather than textually based).
LEXICON—a. pres. act. indic. of βαστάζω (LN **24.83**) (BAGD 2.b.α. p. 137): 'to carry' [AB, BAGD, **LN**, NTC, WBC; all versions except HCSB, KJV], 'to bear' [Arn, BAGD, BECNT, Lns; HCSB, KJV]. This verb is virtually synonymous with αἴρω 'to take up' in 9:23 [TG].
b. ὀπίσω (LN 36.35) (BAGD 2.a.β. p. 575): 'after' [BAGD, LN]. The phrase 'to come after me' [Arn, BECNT, Lns, WBC; HCSB, KJV, NASB, TEV] is also translated 'to come with me' [CEV, REB], 'to follow me' [NTC; GW, NCV, NET, NIV, NLT, NRSV], 'to walk behind me' [AB]. To come after Jesus is the same as to follow him [NIGTC].
QUESTION—What is meant by carrying one's own cross?
They must be prepared to share Jesus' fate of being persecuted and being put to death [TG]. Up to this point Jesus had not informed his followers how he was to die [Su], yet they understood that carrying a cross was a sign of death [ICC, Su]. This was a current expression meaning 'to be put to death' [Arn]. Jesus' followers must be willing to hate their own lives (14:26) and even endure Roman crucifixion because of their loyalty to him [NIBC, NIC]. Some take the expression to be figurative for being willing to accept all the sacrifice, suffering, and persecution involved in being followers of Jesus [NIC]. It is being willing to experience suffering when being persecuted because of following Jesus and it is another way of hating oneself (14:26) [BECNT]. Here the expression is used figuratively for being rejected [NET]. The cross is the emblem for the humiliating and painful sufferings to be endured because of following Jesus [Gdt]. 'To carry one's cross' is an idiomatic expressions meaning to be prepared to endure severe suffering, even to the point of death [LN (24.83)].
QUESTION—What is the difference between 'to come *to* (πρός) me' in 14:26 and 'to come *after* (ὀπίσω) me' in this verse?
Both expressions are virtually equivalent to the verb ἀκολουθεῖν 'to follow' [TH]. The phrase 'to come to me' means to enter into discipleship [BECNT, NIGTC], to become Jesus' disciple [EGT, Lns, NAC, TG, TH]. Coming after Jesus refers to the process of discipleship, being ready to share Jesus' fate of being rejected by the world [BECNT]. It is concerned with the continuation of the relationship into which that the disciple has entered [NIGTC]. Although 'to come after me' is a variant of 'come to me', the expression 'to come to Jesus' is to turn from others while 'to come after Jesus' is to share the cross which is his [Lns]. To come after Jesus meant to

be willing to suffer [Arn]. There is a difference between coming to Jesus and being his disciple since after coming to Jesus, there are conditions associated with becoming a disciple [AB]. Both expressions are translated the same, 'to come with me' [CEV].

14:28 Because[a] who among you wanting to-build a-tower[b] (will) not first having-sat-down calculate[c] the cost, (to see) if he-has (enough) for completion? **14:29** Otherwise having-laid his foundation and not being-able to-finish, everyone seeing (it) may-begin to-ridicule[d] him **14:30** saying, This man began to-build and was- not -able to-finish.

LEXICON—a. γάρ (LN 89.23): 'because' [LN], 'for' [AB, Arn, BECNT, LN, Lns, NTC, WBC; HCSB, KJV, NASB, NET, NLT, NRSV], not explicit [CEV, GW, NCV, NIV, REB, TEV].

- b. πύργος (LN 7.23) (BAGD 1. or 2. p. 730): 'tower' [AB, Arn, BAGD (1.), BECNT, LN, Lns, NTC, WBC; all versions except NLT], 'watchtower' [LN], 'farm building' [BAGD (2.)], 'building' [NLT].
- c. pres. act. indic. of ψηφίζω (LN **60.4**) (BAGD p. 892): 'to calculate' [BAGD, **LN**, Lns; HCSB, NASB, REB], 'to compute' [Arn; NET], 'to figure out' [LN, NTC; CEV, GW, TEV], 'to count' [BECNT; KJV], 'to estimate' [NRSV], 'to reckon' [REB], 'to reckon up' [WBC], 'to decide how much' [NCV], 'to get estimates' [NLT].
- d. pres. act. infin. of ἐμπαίζω (LN 33.406) (BAGD 1. p. 255): 'to ridicule' [AB, BAGD, LN; NASB, NIV, NRSV], 'to make fun of' [BAGD, Lns; GW, HCSB, NCV, NET, TEV], 'to poke fun of' [NTC], 'to laugh at' [CEV, NLT, REB], 'to mock' [Arn, BAGD, BECNT, LN, WBC; KJV]. See this word at 18:32; 22:63; 23:11, 36.

QUESTION—What relationship is indicated by the initial conjunction γάρ 'because'?

It indicates the reason why a person who is not willing to take up his cross and follow Jesus cannot be a disciple; it is because that person is as little able to fulfill the requirement for being a disciple as the man who wants to build a tower without the necessary means is unable to build it [My]. It illustrates the need for counting the cost to follow Jesus [EGT, NIBC, Su]. One translation begins the verse 'But don't begin until you count the cost. For who would begin construction of a building without first...' [NLT]. The requirements for being a disciple involve making a conscious decision [TH]. The conjunction introduces two illustrations of what it means to count the cost in becoming a disciple [MGC]. Anyone who wants to be a disciple must be ready for the ultimate in self-denial, because anyone who begins a task without being prepared to pay the total cost will be shown to be foolish [NIGTC]. The decision to be a disciple is not to be hasty, but must be deliberately and thoroughly considered [Lns]. This illustration and the following one show that a person needs to examine himself and count the cost before committing himself to be a disciple of Jesus [Arn, Hlt, Pnt], he must determine whether he is ready to take on the commitment and sacrifice required to follow Jesus [BECNT]. For those who are already disciples, it points out that it is necessary to complete what has been commenced [Hlt].

QUESTION—What sort of building was a πύργος 'tower'?

It was probably a watchtower located in a vineyard [Arn, EGT, Su, TG, TH, WBC]. It guarded the vineyard against men who might steal from it or from animals that might damage it [Su]. It was a watchtower built to protect the house, land, or vineyard [AB, BECNT]. Or, it could be a tower for refuge from danger and merely an ornament in a garden [EGT]. The mention of a foundation indicates that the tower was quite substantial [BECNT]. The tower might even have contained a barn for produce and tools [BECNT, Hlt]. It might have been a farm building [BAGD, NIGTC, TNTC; NLT], or a building of some size since the foundation for it used up the man's resources [NIGTC].

14:31 Or what king going to-engage[a] another king in battle, not first having-sat-down will-consider if he-is able with ten thousand to-meet[b] the (one) having-come against him with twenty thousand? **14:32** And if-not,[c] while he is far-away having-sent an-ambassador[d] he requests[e] the (things) for peace.

LEXICON—a. aorist act. infin. of συμβάλλω (LN **15.79**) (BAGD 1.b. p. 777): 'to engage' [BAGD], 'to meet' [BAGD, LN]. The phrase πορευόμενος συμβαλεῖν εἰς πόλεμον 'going to engage in battle' is translated 'as he goes to engage in battle' [WBC], 'going to engage in war' [BECNT], 'going out to confront in battle' [NET], 'when he sets out to meet in battle' [NASB], 'going to clash in war with' [Lns], 'when he proceeds to clash in war with' [Arn], 'would march forth to engage (another king) in battle' [AB], 'is going to war against' [GW, HCSB], 'going out to wage war against' [NRSV], 'going to make war against' [KJV], 'setting out to wage war with' [NTC], 'to march to battle against' [REB], 'goes out to fight' [TEV], 'is going to fight' [NCV]. Some translations indicate that the king had not yet sent his army on its way to meet the other army: 'is about to go to war against' [NIV], 'would ever dream of going to war' [NLT], 'to defend himself against another king who is about to attack him' [CEV].

b. aorist act. inf. of ὑπαντάω (LN **55.3**) (BAGD p. 837): 'to meet' [AB, Arn, BAGD, BECNT, Lns, WBC; KJV], 'to encounter' [NASB], 'to meet in battle' [LN, NTC], 'to face' [NET, REB, TEV], 'to face in battle' [**LN**], 'to go out to battle' [CEV], 'to oppose' [BAGD; HCSB, NRSV], 'to fight against' [GW], 'to defeat' [NCV, NLT]. The verb 'to meet' in this context means 'to meet in battle' [BECNT; NET].

c. εἰ μή γε. This phrase 'if not' [BECNT, Lns; HCSB] is also translated 'or else' [KJV, NASB], 'otherwise' [WBC], 'if he cannot' [GW, NCV, NRSV, REB], 'if he isn't' [TEV], 'if he is not able' [Arn, NTC; NIV, NLT], 'if he cannot succeed' [NET], 'if he could not' [AB], 'if he thinks he won't be able to defend himself' [CEV]. This phrase indicates the alternative to meeting in battle [BECNT].

d. πρεσβεία (LN **37.87**) (BAGD p. 699): 'an ambassador' [BAGD, LN], 'a representative' [**LN**; NET], 'an emissary' [BECNT], 'a delegation' [AB, NTC, WBC; HCSB, NASB, NIV, NLT, NRSV], 'an embassy' [Arn, Lns], 'an ambassage' [KJV], 'ambassadors' [GW], 'envoys' [REB], 'messengers' [CEV, TEV], 'some people to speak to him' [NCV]. An 'embassy' is an abstract noun used for the specific noun 'ambassadors' [AB, NIGTC, TH]. The person is an ambassador who is sent to negotiate the terms of peace or surrender and secure an agreement that will stop the war [BECNT]. See this word at 19:14.

e. pres. act. indic. of ἐρωτάω (LN 33.161) (BAGD 2. p. 312): 'to request, to ask for' [BAGD, LN]. The phrase ἐρωτᾷ τὰ πρὸς εἰρήνην 'to request the things for peace' is translated 'to ask for terms of peace' [AB, NTC; GW, HCSB, NASB, NET, NIV, NRSV, TEV], 'to ask for peace' [CEV, NCV], 'to ask for terms' [REB], 'to ask terms of peace' [BECNT], 'to enquire about terms of peace' [Arn], 'to enquire for the terms of peace' [Lns], 'to sue for terms of peace' [WBC], 'to discuss terms of peace' [NLT], 'to desire conditions of peace' [KJV]. This includes the idea of accepting the terms and surrendering [AB, ICC, Lns].

QUESTION—What relationship is indicated by the initial conjunction ἤ 'or'?

This indicates a parallel example, not an alternative [TH]. The same point is now made on an even larger scale [NIGTC]. Note that instead of 'who among you' (14:28), this second illustration begins 'what king' since there was no king in the audience [NIGTC, WBC]. Israel had no king at that time [NAC], but one does not need to be a king to appreciate the lesson [NICNT].

QUESTION—How close are the two kings to entering into battle?

The first king has not yet sent out his army [TH; CEV, NIV, NLT; probably NCV]. The phrase 'going to meet' does not mean that the king is already marching to war, rather it signifies that this is his intention [TH], but the phrase 'the one having come against him' indicates that the other king is the one who has started the war [NTC, TH]. Or, the two armies are already marching against each other [WBC].

QUESTION—What is the point of this illustration?

1. This has the same point as the preceding parable about the builder [AB, Arn, BECNT, Blm, BNTC, Crd, Hlt, MGC, NIBC, NIC, WBC]. It is a second illustration concerning counting the cost in becoming a disciple of Jesus [BECNT, Hlt, MGC, NIBC, NIC]. It is necessary to examine a situation and consider it before acting [BECNT]. A person must first be sure that he will be able to finish what he undertakes before starting [NIC]. Both mean that one should not get involved in something he is unable to complete, but must carefully consider the commitment required to be a disciple of Christ [Blm]. He must see his discipleship through to the end [BNTC]. Both concern self-examination and counting the cost

[Arn]. A would-be disciple must not rush into the decision if he wants to avoid ridicule or surrendering to unconditional terms [AB, WBC].
2. The point is different from the lesson about the builder and pictures Jesus or God as the king they must face [Alf, NTC; NET]. Here it is about recognizing who is stronger and implies a warning to achieve peace with God, the stronger one [NET]. He cannot remain neutral, he must become reconciled with God [NTC].
3. The king is not God, but the prince of this world [Gdt, Pnt]. Before making a complete commitment to Christ, a disciple must consider the power of the enemy who is seeking to destroy the kingdom [Pnt]. This is a warning that if the would-be disciple is not ready to follow Jesus to the cross, he had better make peace with the Sanhedrin [Gdt].

14:33 In-this-way[a] therefore each of you who does- not -give-up[b] all his possessions[c] is- not -able to-be my disciple.

LEXICON—a. οὕτως (LN 61.9): 'in this way, so, thus' [LN]. The phrase οὕτως οὖν 'in this way therefore' is translated 'in the same way therefore' [HCSB, NET], 'in the same way then' [WBC], 'in the same way' [GW, NCV, NIV, TEV], 'so likewise' [KJV], 'thus therefore' [Lns], 'so therefore' [NRSV], 'so then' [Arn; CEV, NASB], 'so also' [BECNT; REB], 'so' [NLT], 'similarly therefore' [NTC], 'similarly then' [AB].
  b. pres. mid. indic. of ἀποτάσσομαι, ἀποτάσσω (LN 57.70) (BAGD 2. p. 100): 'to give up' [BAGD, **LN**, NTC, WBC; GW, NASB, NCV, NIV, NLT, NRSV, TEV], 'to give away' [CEV], 'to renounce' [BAGD, BECNT, Lns; NET], 'to leave behind' [REB], 'to forsake' [KJV], 'to bid farewell to' [Arn], 'to say good-bye to' [AB; HCSB]. The present tense indicates a continual readiness to give up one's possessions [NIGTC].
  c. pres. act. participle of ὑπάρχω (LN 57.16) (BAGD 1. p. 838): 'to belong to' [BAGD, LN]. The phrase πᾶσιν τοῖς ἑαυτοῦ ὑπάρχουσιν 'all the (things) of himself being possessed' is translated 'all his own possessions' [Lns; NASB, NET], 'all of his possessions' [Arn; HCSB], 'all that he has' [BECNT; KJV], 'all he has' [AB], 'everything he has' [NIV], 'all that belonged to him' [NTC], 'all his goods' [WBC], 'everything you own' [CEV], 'all your possessions' [NRSV, REB], 'everything you have' [NCV, TEV], 'everything' [GW, NLT].

QUESTION—What does οὕτως οὖν 'in this way therefore' refer to?
  1. This signals the application of the two parables about building a tower (14:28–30) and going to war (14:31–32) [Blm, ICC, Lns, Su, TNTC]. The two parables vary in the degree of consequences and this verse is even more severe as it goes beyond the point of the two parables and indicates that as people have to calculate their chances of success in human situations, even more so must they take seriously the results of their spiritual commitments [Blm]. Everyone wanting to follow Jesus must understand that this meant taking a total risk after counting the cost even if it meant humiliation and total loss [Su]. The two proverbs illustrated the

132   LUKE 14:33

teaching in 14:26–27 and now the command is given to renounce everything (as in 14:26–27) because the person will never get beyond the foundation or win against an overwhelming force unless he comes to Jesus without anything of his own [Lns]. Jesus wanted potential disciples to think about the price involved, they must renounce all that they had [TNTC].

2. This is the application of 14:26–27 [Hlt, NIC, NICNT, TG]. Although presented as an application of the two preceding parables, it continues the thought of 14:26–27 since the two parables speak about being prudent rather than giving up all that one has [Hlt]. The application goes back to 14:26–27 about placing one's loyalty to Jesus above all other relationships [TG]. This summarizes the previous two conditions in 14:26 and 14:27 for being a disciple [NIC, NICNT]. The word 'possessions' refers to all one has and means the abandonment of all other securities [NICNT].

3. This is a third condition for discipleship [AB, BECNT, NAC, WBC]. The first condition (14:26) is being willing to put all family relationships in subordination, the second (14:27) is to deny self, and the condition in this verse is to renounce all of one's material possessions [AB, BECNT]. Although elsewhere the words 'in the same way' introduces the application of a parable, this verse reaches back to 14:26–27 [WBC]. The two parables in 14:28–32 have been inserted before the third condition to show the need for advance self-probing before deciding to be disciples [AB].

QUESTION—Must every disciple literally give up all his possessions?

A disciple must be *ready* to renounce his possessions and many of the first disciples did so [ICC]. It means that a disciple must give Jesus full control of his life, including control over all that he possesses [NIC]. He must be ready to renounce everything that would prevent total commitment to discipleship [Blm, NIGTC, Su]. Preoccupation with property and wealth prevents one from accepting the demands Jesus makes of disciples [WBC]. It signifies complete surrender to Jesus [NIVS]. The word 'possessions' refers to all earthly attachments that would keep God from having first place in one's life [NET].

DISCOURSE UNIT: 14:34–35 [AB, TNTC; CEV, NCV, NRSV, TEV]. The topic is about salt [NRSV], the parable of salt [AB, TNTC], worthless salt [TEV], salt and light [CEV], don't lose your influence [NCV].

14:34 Indeed/therefore[a] salt (is) good.[b] But if even the salt should-become-tasteless,[c] with what will-it-be-seasoned?[d]

TEXT—Some manuscripts omit οὖν 'therefore'. GNT does not deal with this variant. Οὖν 'therefore' is omitted or not made explicit by all versions except NASB.

LEXICON—a. οὖν (LN 91.7, 89.50): 'indeed' [LN (91.7), NTC], 'now' [BECNT; HCSB], 'then' [AB, LN (89.50, 91.7), WBC], 'therefore' [Arn, LN (89.50), Lns; NASB], not explicit [all versions except NASB].

b. καλός (LN 65.22) (BAGD 2.a. p. 400): 'good' [AB, Arn, BAGD, BECNT, LN, NTC, WBC; all versions except NLT], 'good for seasoning' [NLT], 'excellent' [Lns], 'useful' [BAGD]. Here 'good' means that it is useful, a necessity for life [NIGTC]. It has a valuable function [BECNT].

c. aorist pass. subj. of μωραίνομαι (LN 79.44) (BAGD 2. p. 531): 'to become tasteless' [AB, BAGD, LN, NTC; NASB, REB], 'to lose its taste' [Arn, BECNT; GW, HCSB, NRSV], 'to lose its savor' [KJV], 'to lose its flavor' [NET, NLT], 'to lose its salty taste' [NCV], 'to lose its saltiness' [NIV, TEV], 'to no longer taste like salt' [CEV], 'to become insipid' [Lns, WBC].

d. fut. pass. indic. of ἀρτύω (LN **46.14**) (BAGD p. 11): 'to be seasoned' [Arn, BAGD, LN, NTC, WBC; KJV, NASB, REB], 'to restore its flavor' [GW, NET], 'to restore its saltiness' [BECNT; NRSV], 'to restore it' [NTC], 'to make it salty again' [NCV, NLT], 'to be made salty' [HCSB], 'to be made salty again' [AB; NIV], 'to be made to taste salty again' [CEV]. The question is also translated as a statement: 'there is no way to season it again' [**LN**], 'there is no way to make it salty again' [TEV].

QUESTION—What relationship is indicated by οὖν 'indeed, therefore'?

1. It indicates a connection of some kind to the preceding verses [AB, ICC, Lns, NIGTC, WBC]. It is loosely connected, but it indicates a further comment [AB]. This is a further conclusion from the foregoing verses [Lns]. This makes the same point as the two parables, that a person who cannot sustain the course will come under judgment [NIGTC]. Perhaps this refers to previous utterances like this one [ICC].

2. It indicates emphasis [NTC]: indeed.

3. It is difficult to interpret and can be left untranslated. This is a general truth that is left up to the audience to draw the inference and could be introduced with 'remember' or 'you all know' [TH].

QUESTION—In what way is salt good?

Salt is good for seasoning food [AB, Arn, BECNT, NAC, NIGTC, NTC, Su, WBC; NET], or preserving food [AB, Arn, BECNT, NIGTC, NTC, Su, WBC; NET], or enhancing the fertility of the soil [Crd, NIC, WBC; NET], or destroying the fertility of the soil [WBC]. Salt had a catalytic effect on burning fuel in a baker's oven [BECNT, WBC]. Here its seasoning effect is in focus [NAC, NIGTC, WBC; NLT].

QUESTION—Can salt lose its flavor?

Although pure salt does not lose it saltiness, much of the salt at that time was impure and the salt would dissolve and leave flavorless salt-like crystals [Arn, MGC, NAC, NIGTC, NTC, TG, TNTC, WBC]. However, the issue of realism is not the issue [AB, NAC, WBC]. It is not necessary to explain how this could be possible since Jesus sometimes used impossible examples [Lns; NET].

14:35 It-is neither suitable for soil nor for (the) manure-pile,ª they-throw it out. The (one) having ears to-hear let-him-hear.

LEXICON—a. κοπρία (LN **8.77**) (BAGD p. 443): 'manure pile' [LN, NTC; CEV, GW, HCSB, NASB, NET, NIV, NRSV, TEV], 'dung heap' [AB, BAGD, LN, WBC; REB], 'dunghill' [Arn, BECNT; KJV], 'rubbish heap' [BAGD], 'manure' [Lns; NCV], 'fertilizer' [NLT].

QUESTION—How is good salt suitable for soil?

Salt makes the soil more fertile [MGC, TG]. Salt was used as a fertilizer for some vegetables [AB, WBC]. Salt was used to wilt seeds for fertilizer and improve the soil at deeper levels [BECNT]. Or, salt has a negative effect on soil and would ruin it [NAC].

QUESTION—How is good salt suitable for a manure pile?

Adding salt to manure was practiced in Palestine [Arn, Crd]. It is possible that salt could be used as a means of slowing down fermentation of the dung [BECNT, NIGTC, WBC]. Another way to take this is that many things that have deteriorated and become corrupt were useful to add to the soil or manure heap, but tasteless salt did not even have that much use [ICC]. Such salt is fit for nothing, not even the lowest service imaginable [Arn].

QUESTION—What is the point of this illustration?

The point is that the disciple who cannot stay the course is as useless as salt that has lost it flavor [NIGTC, TG]. Salt represents the disciples themselves [Arn, BECNT, EGT, ICC, Lns, NIBC, NIC, NIGTC, NTC, WBC]. In a similar passage at Matthew 5:13, the disciples are called the salt of the earth. Jesus' followers must not be mere nominal disciples, but be wholeheartedly devoted to him [NTC]. Discipleship is a good thing, but a person who tries to be a disciple without being disencumbered or without bearing his cross is represented by the salt without flavor and he becomes useless like the builder who could not complete the tower or the king who went to a battle he could not win [WBC]. Salt is valuable only when it has the quality of seasoning, and disciples are valuable only when they possess the attributes of true disciples, especially in the matters of unselfishness and self-sacrificing loyalty to Jesus [NIC]. Disciples without a spirit of self-devotion are like savorless salt [ICC]. A disciple who returns to his old love, refuses to bear his cross, and again trusts in his possessions is as unnatural as salt that has lost its saltiness and will have a worse fate than the pagans at the judgment [Lns]. Those disciples who were set to oppose the work of the Holy Spirit in their lives could not be renewed to repentance anymore than salt could be restored after losing its saltiness [NTC]. Or, some take salt to represent the qualities desired in disciples [ICC, Su, TH]. Salt stands for the self-sacrifice mentioned in 14:26–27 and 24:33 [ICC], for one's readiness to renounce relatives, comfortable lives, or even life for the sake of being Jesus' disciple [Su]. It probably stands for discipleship [TH].

QUESTION—What is meant by the concluding exhortation, 'The one having ears to hear, let him hear'?

It indicates the gravity of the teaching [NICNT]. Those who discern the meaning of what he has said should apply it to themselves [Su]. The welfare of their souls depends on it [NIC]. This is a call for a positive decision [AB, Su]. The audience was challenged to get the point that discipleship requires their wholehearted devotion to Jesus [MGC]. It indicates that attention to the preceding words will be rewarded [ICC]. See this same exhortation at 8:8.

DISCOURSE UNIT: 15:1–32 [BECNT, NAC, NICNT, NIGTC, TNTC, WBC; REB]. The topic is three parables of the lost [TNTC], the parables of the lost sheep, the lost coin, and the gracious Father [NAC], finding the lost [REB], rejoicing at the finding of the lost [NICNT], the pursuit of sinners [BECNT], the gospel for the outcast [NIGTC], that which was lost is found [WBC].

DISCOURSE UNIT: 15:1–10 [NCV, NET]. The topic is a lost sheep, a lost coin [NCV], the parable of the lost sheep and coin [NET].

DISCOURSE UNIT: 15:1–7 [AB, BECNT, Su, WBC; CEV, GW, HCSB, NASB, NIV, NLT, NRSV, TEV]. The topic is one sheep [CEV], the lost sheep [GW, NASB, TEV], the parable of the lost sheep [AB, BECNT, Su; HCSB, NIV, NLT, NRSV], the joy of finding the one lost sheep [WBC]

DISCOURSE UNIT: 15:1–3 [NIGTC]. The topic is the introduction.

DISCOURSE UNIT: 15:1–2 [TNTC]. The topic is the sinners gather.

15:1 And all the tax-collectors and the sinners[a] were drawing-near[b] to-him to-listen to-him. **15:2** And both the Pharisees and the scribes were-complaining[c] saying, This (one) welcomes[d] sinners and eats-with them.

- TEXT—In 15:1, instead of ἐγγίζοντες πάντες 'drawing near all', some manuscripts read πάντες ἐγγίζοντες 'all drawing near' and some manuscripts read ἐγγίζοντες 'drawing near'. GNT reads ἐγγίζοντες πάντες 'drawing near all' with an A decision, indicating that the text is certain.
- TEXT—In 15:2, instead of οἵ τε Φαρισαῖοι καί 'both the Pharisees and' some manuscripts read οἱ Φαρισαῖοι καί 'the Pharisees and'. GNT does not mention this alternative. Οἱ Φαρισαῖοι καί 'the Pharisees and' is read by KJV.
- LEXICON—a. ἁμαρτωλός (LN 88.295) (BAGD 2. p. 44): 'sinner' [AB, Arn, BAGD, BECNT, LN, NTC, WBC; CEV, GW, HCSB, KJV, NASB, NCV, NET, NIV, NRSV, REB], 'open sinner' [Lns], 'notorious sinner' [NLT], 'outcast' [LN; TEV]. This is a person who customarily sins and here it may refer to anyone who was not concerned about obeying the religious laws [LN].
  b. pres. act. participle of ἐγγίζω (LN 15.75) (BAGD 1. p. 213): 'to draw near' [AB, BECNT, LN, Lns, WBC; KJV]. 'to come near' [BAGD, LN; NASB, NRSV], 'to come (to listen)' [GW, NCV, NET, NLT, TEV], 'to

136   LUKE 15:1-2

approach' [Arn, BAGD, LN; HCSB,], 'to crowd around' [CEV], 'to crowd in' [REB], 'to gather around' [NTC; NIV].

c. imperf. act. indic. of διαγογγύζω (LN 33.383) (BAGD p. 182): 'to complain' [BAGD, LN; GW, HCSB, NCV, NET, NLT], 'to grumble' [AB, BAGD, BECNT, LN, NTC, WBC; NASB, NRSV, TEV], 'to murmur' [Arn, Lns; KJV, REB], 'to mutter' [NIV]. This probably took place in Jesus' presence [TH]. They complained among themselves [NIVS]. They probably spoke aloud to each other and pointed at Jesus [Rb]. The imperfect tense is inceptive, they *began* to complain [CEV, NASB, NCV, REB, TEV]. Or, it is durative, they *kept* complaining [AB, Arn, Lns, NTC, TNTC]. They were voicing their disapproval [Arn]. See this words at 19:7.

d. pres. mid./pass. (deponent = act.) indic. of προσδέχομαι (LN 34.53) (BAGD 1.a. p. 712): 'to welcome' [AB, BAGD, LN, NTC; GW, HCSB, NCV, NET, NIV, NRSV, REB, TEV], 'to receive' [Arn, BAGD, BECNT, LN, Lns, WBC; KJV, NASB], 'to accept' [LN], 'to associate with' [NLT], 'to be friendly with' [CEV]. He welcomed such people into his company [TH]. The present tense indicates that it was Jesus' habit to welcome them [Lns, Rb]. Jesus willingly conversed with them and gave helpful instructions [Arn].

QUESTION—What is the function of πάντες 'all' in regard to the tax collectors and the sinners?

The use of 'all' is hyperbolic for 'very many' [AB, BECNT, Lns, My, NAC, NIGTC, TH, WBC]. It may be hyperbole and mean 'very many' or it may mean literally all of this kind of people who were present in the particular area [ICC, Rb].

QUESTION—What is meant by the imperfect verb phrase ἦσαν ἐγγίζοντες 'were drawing near'?

1. The imperfect form describes their habitual action [Alf, Arn, Gdt, Lns, NAC, NIC, NIGTC, NTC, Rb, WBC; NLT]. This describes the general circumstances connected with Jesus' ministry [NIGTC, WBC].
2. The imperfect form describes a particular occasion [My, TH]. This is closely connected to the preceding scene [My].

QUESTION—Where did Jesus eat with the sinners?

Such people probably invited Jesus to eat with them in their homes [Lns, TH]. To the Pharisees, eating with sinners was even more terrible than welcoming them to his presence [Arn, BECNT, EGT, Gdt, ICC, Lns, NTC, TNTC].

DISCOURSE UNIT: 15:3–7 [TNTC]. The topic is the lost sheep.

15:3 And he-told this parable[a] to them, saying,

LEXICON—a. παραβολή (LN 33.15) (BAGD 2. p. 612): 'parable' [AB, Arn, BAGD, BECNT, LN, Lns, NTC, WBC; HCSB, KJV, NASB, NET, NIV, NRSV, REB, TEV], 'story' [CEV, NCV], 'illustration' [GW, NLT]. This parable extends to 15:10 [EGT, Lns]. In one translation, the second part of

LUKE 15:3 137

the parable is separated from the first by adding 'Jesus told the people another story' (15:8) [CEV]. This actually introduces three parables [AB, Pnt]. Perhaps Luke used this word collectively as a parabolic discourse to include all three [MGC, NAC, NIGTC, Pnt]. A parable teaches a religious lesson, so this is more of an illustration than a parable [Arn].

DISCOURSE UNIT: 15:4–7 [NIGTC]. The topic is the lost sheep.

15:4 What man of you having[a] one-hundred sheep and having-lost[b] one from them is- not -leaving[c] the ninety-nine in the wilderness[d] and goes[e] after the (one) having-been-lost until he-finds it?

LEXICON—a. pres. act. participle of ἔχω (LN 57.1) (BAGD I.2.a. p. 332): 'to have' [Arn, BAGD, BECNT, LN, NTC, WBC; all versions], 'to possess' [BAGD, LN], 'to own' [LN]. The herd would be a normal size for an average shepherd [BECNT, NIGTC] and this man probably owned all of the sheep [Alf, BECNT, NIC, NICNT, NIGTC]. Or, in the case of a hundred sheep, the shepherd probably would not be the sole owner, and this verb means 'to hold in his charge or keeping' [Bai].

b. aorist act. participle of ἀπόλλυμι (LN 57.68) (BAGD 2.b. p. 95): 'to lose' [Arn, BAGD, BECNT, LN, NTC, WBC; all versions except CEV, NLT]. This verb is also translated with the sheep as the subject: 'to get lost' [CEV], 'to stray away and be lost' [NLT]. The verb does not imply that the shepherd was negligent, rather he discovered that one of the sheep was missing [Hlt, TG, TH]. The sheep was lost by straying from the flock [Lns, TG].

c. pres. act. indic. of καταλείπω (LN 85.65) (BAGD 2.a. p. 413): 'to leave' [Arn, BAGD, BECNT, LN, NTC, WBC; all versions except GW], 'to leave behind' [BAGD, LN], 'to leave grazing' [GW].

d. ἔρημος (LN 1.86) (BAGD 2. p. 309): 'wilderness' [Arn, BAGD, BECNT, LN, WBC; KJV, NLT, NRSV, REB], 'lonely place' [LN], 'field' [CEV], 'open field' [HCSB, NCV], 'open country' [NTC; NIV], 'pasture' [GW, TEV], 'open pasture' [NASB, NET]. This 'wilderness' was a place that was fit for pasturing sheep [Alf, Arn, ICC, Lns, Rb, TH, WBC]. It would be an open place where sheep could graze [EGT, ICC, NIC, TG] and is to be contrasted with tilled fields [Arn, Gdt].

e. pres. mid./pass. (deponent = act.) indic. of πορεύομαι (LN 15.34) (BAGD 1. p. 692): 'to go away, to leave, to depart' [LN]. The phrase πορεύομαι ἐπί 'to go after' [Arn, BAGD, BECNT, NTC, WBC; HCSB, KJV, NASB, NIV, NRSV, REB] is also translated 'to go look for' [CEV, NET], 'to go looking for' [TEV], 'to look for' [GW], 'to go out and look for' [NCV], 'to go and search for' [NLT].

QUESTION—What type of question is this?

It is a rhetorical question with the obvious answer being that anyone would leave the flock to look for the lost sheep [BECNT, EGT, NICNT, NIGTC, TH, TNTC]. Any good shepherd would do this [AB, NTC]. This question is addressed to a man, which parallels the question addressed to a woman in the next parable at 15:8 [Hlt, NIGTC, WBC]. This was addressed to the Pharisees and scribes who did not personally tend to sheep, and so the question was hypothetical and easy to answer [Lns].

QUESTION—Does a good shepherd leave ninety-nine sheep to go looking for one lost sheep?

We can assume that he did not leave the ninety-nine sheep untended, rather he left them in the care of a fellow shepherd or helper [Bai, BECNT, NIGTC]. Another shepherd could divide his attention between both flocks for a time [WBC]. The sheep were feeding in the wilderness and the shepherd left them there in care of some servant [Arn]. Or, the man was counting the sheep as they entered the sheepfold and he left the sheep securely in the fold when he went to look for the missing sheep [MGC, NAC, NIGTC, Su]. The point of the number of sheep is that the lost sheep received special attention over all the many other sheep that were safe in the flock [BECNT, ICC].

15:5 And having-found (it) he-puts-on[a] (it) on his shoulders rejoicing. **15:6** And having-come to the house he-calls-together (his) friends and neighbors saying to-them, Rejoice-with[b] me, because I-found my sheep the (one) having-been-lost.

LEXICON—a. pres. act. indic. of ἐπιτίθημι (LN 85.51) (BAGD 1.a.α. p. 302): 'to put on' [BAGD, LN, Lns, NTC; CEV, GW, HCSB, NCV, NIV, TEV], 'to lay on' [BAGD, LN; KJV, NASB, NET, NRSV], 'to place on' [Arn, BECNT, LN, WBC], 'to lift on' [REB], 'to lift to' [AB], 'to carry on' [NLT]. Carrying a sheep was an unusual act [TH] and it expressed his joy over finding the sheep [Arn, TH; CEV, TEV]. Or, carrying a sheep was a normal practice of shepherds [BECNT, NIGTC]. This was a necessity because the sheep would not walk [EGT], being exhausted [Alf, Lns, NAC]. Perhaps he would have to carry the sheep because it would helplessly lie there and not move on its own [AB, Bai, WBC], being frightened and disoriented [WBC]. The sheep would be placed over the shepherd's shoulders with its stomach at the back of his neck and the feet would be tied together in front of his face [NTC].

b. aorist pass. (deponent = act.) impera. of συγχαίρω (LN **25.126**) (BAGD 1. p. 775): 'to rejoice with' [BAGD, **LN**]. The phrase 'rejoice with me' [Arn, BECNT, Lns, WBC; HCSB, KJV, NASB, NET, NIV, NLT, NRSV, REB] is also translated 'be happy with me' [NCV], 'celebrate with me' [AB], 'let's celebrate' [CEV, GW, TEV].

QUESTION—Where did the shepherd go with the sheep he was carrying?

The shepherd carried the sheep home with him [Alf; CEV, GW, NCV, NIV, NLT, REB, TEV]. Or, instead of carrying the sheep home on his shoulders, the man probably took it to where the flock was before he himself returned home [TG, WBC]. Then perhaps the whole flock was brought back home that evening [Arn].

QUESTION—What was involved in calling together his friends and neighbors to his house?
>They were called for a celebration [EGT, MGC, NIBC, NICNT, NTC, TH], probably a feast [Hlt, NICNT, NIGTC]. The shepherd invited his friends and all the others living in his neighborhood [Hlt].

15:7 I-tell you that thus[a] there-will-be joy in heaven over one sinner repenting (more/rather) than over ninety-nine righteous[b] (ones) who have no need[c] of-repentance.[d]

LEXICON—a. οὕτως (LN 61.9) (BAGD 1.b. p. 597): 'thus' [BAGD, BECNT, LN, Lns], 'in this way' [LN], 'in this manner' [Arn, BAGD], 'in the same way' [WBC; all versions except GW, KJV, NRSV], 'likewise' [KJV], 'similarly' [AB, NTC], 'just so' [NRSV], not explicit [GW]. In the same way as described in the parable, there will be joy [Lns].
- b. δίκαιος (LN 88.12) (BAGD 1.b. p. 195): 'righteous'. See translations of this word at 1:6 and 14:14. This word also occurs at 1:17; 2:25; 5:32; 12:57; 18:9; 20:20; 23:47, 50.
- c. χρείαν (LN 57.39): 'need' [LN]. The phrase 'who have no need of repentance' [BECNT, NTC, WBC] is also translated 'who have no need to repent' [NET], 'who do not need to repent' [NIV, REB, TEV], 'such as do not have need of repentance' [Lns], 'who do not need repentance' [Arn; HCSB], 'who need no repentance' [KJV, NASB, NRSV], 'who don't need to change' [NCV], 'who need no reform' [AB], 'who do not need conversion' [NTC], 'who don't need to' [CEV], 'who already have turned to God' [GW], 'and haven't strayed away' [NLT].
- d. μετάνοια (LN 41.52) (BAGD p. 512): 'repentance'. See translations of this word in the preceding item. See this word at 3:3, 8; 5:32; 24:47.

QUESTION—What is the function of οὕτως 'thus'?
>Along with the phrase 'I tell you that', this indicates Jesus' application of the parable [Arn, BECNT, Gdt, Hlt, Lns, NICNT, NIGTC, TNTC, WBC], or the conclusion of the argument [Gdt].

QUESTION—What is meant by the comparison between one sinner and the ninety-nine righteous people?
1. There is more joy over the repentant sinner than the joy felt over the righteous people who have no need for repentance [AB, Alf, Arn, Bai, BECNT, Gdt, Lns, My, NIGTC, TH, TNTC, WBC; all versions]. There is joy over the righteous, but there is more joy over the repenting sinner [TNTC]. There already is a constant joy over the righteous who long ago had repented, but when a sinner repents and joins the ranks of the righteous, there is a great wave of joy expressed [Lns]. Or, when one of one hundred of God's children goes astray and then repents, there is special rejoicing [Arn]. Or, the comparison stays within the framework of the parable and says that there is more joy when something is found than when there is no change of status [BECNT].

2. There is joy over the repentant sinner rather than over the self-righteous people who think they have no need to repent [ICC, NTC, Rb]. There will be joy over converts, but not over the ninety-nine self-righteous sinners who do not repent [NTC].

QUESTION—What is referred to by the future tense of 'there will be joy in heaven'?

    1. It happens at the time a sinner repents [Arn, BECNT, Hlt, NAC, TH, WBC]. There is no significance between the future tense here and the present tense 'there is joy' in 15:10 [TH]. It is a 'proverbial' future used to refer to the present time [NAC]. It is a logical future [WBC]. Whenever a sinner repents, there is joy in heaven [Arn, Hlt].

    2. It refers to the future Judgment Day [AB, MGC].

QUESTION—Who rejoices in heaven?

This refers to God [EGT, Hlt, NAC, NIBC, NIGTC, NIVS, NTC, Pnt, Su, TNTC, WBC], and perhaps it includes angels as in 15:10 [Hlt, NIGTC, NTC]. Or, this does refer to both God and the angels [Arn, Gdt]. Or, this refers to angels [AB, Lns, MGC]. Or, it could be that both 'heaven' here and its parallel 'the angels of God' in 15:10 are expressions used to avoid a direct mention of God [BECNT, MGC].

QUESTION—Who are the ninety-nine who have no need of repentance?

    1. This assumes that there really are such righteous people [Arn, BECNT, Blm, Gdt, Lns, My, NIGTC, Rb, Su, WBC; GW].

    1.1 Since 'more than' indicates that there is also joy over the ninety-nine righteous people, it cannot be referring to the self-righteous Pharisees; rather it refers to those who already have repented and were a constant source of joy while the conversion of a sinner brought a forth a sudden burst of joy in heaven [Lns, NIGTC]. The righteous are those who are already right with God [Blm]. There is no extra rejoicing over those who have not fallen because they are already safe [Arn].

    1.2 The righteous are those who have not strayed like the tax collectors and sinners and do not need to repent as such people do. But this statement is merely completing the logic of the contrast and is not to be taken to mean that that there are any who have no need of repentance [WBC].

    1.3 For the sake of argument, Jesus accepted the claims of the Pharisees [My, Rb, Su]. Then Jesus condemns them for their criticism over his efforts to save the lost sheep [Rb]. In effect Jesus was saying 'If you are righteous and these are sinners who are repenting, God rejoices more over one of them than over all of you' [Su].

    2. This was spoken ironically and implies that there really are no such righteous people [Alf, EGT, Hlt, ICC, NAC, NIVS, NTC, TG, TH]. The ninety-nine people represented the Pharisees and scribes who thought they were righteous [NTC]. It refers to people who thought that they had no need to repent or who appeared to others as having no need of repentance [TG, TH]. Since Jesus was responding to the Pharisees' objections to fellowshipping with sinners when he used the terms 'the righteous' and

'those who have no need of repentance', he was just voicing the opinion of the Pharisees and scribes [TG]. Probably this detail should not be pressed in the parable [NAC].

DISCOURSE UNIT: 15:8–10 [AB, BECNT, NIGTC, Su, TNTC, WBC; CEV, GW, HCSB, NASB, NIV, NLT, NRSV, TEV]. The topic is one coin [CEV], the lost coin [NIGTC, TNTC; GW, NASB, TEV], the parable of the lost coin [AB, BECNT, Su; HCSB, NIV, NLT, NRSV], the joy of finding the lost coin [WBC].

15:8 Or what woman having ten drachmas[a] if she-loses one drachma, (will) not light a-lamp and sweep the house and search carefully[b] until she-finds (it)? **15:9** And having-found (it) she-calls-together friends and neighbors saying, Rejoice with-me, because I-found the drachma which I-lost. **15:10** Thus I-say to-you, there-is joy before/among[c] the angels of-God over one sinner repenting.

LEXICON—a. δραχμή (LN **6.76**) (BAGD p. 206): 'drachma' [Arn, BAGD, BECNT, LN, Lns, WBC], 'coin' [**LN**; CEV, GW], 'silver coin' [AB, NTC; HCSB, NASB, NCV, NET, NIV, NRSV, REB, TEV], 'valuable silver coin' [NLT], 'piece of silver' [KJV]. This was a Greek silver coin [BAGD, LN] of about the same value as the denarius, the wage paid to a laborer for a day's work [Arn, BECNT, Gdt, ICC, LN, Lns, MGC, NIGTC, NIVS, NTC, TNTC; NET]. The woman may have been poor and the ten coins may have been her savings [TNTC], or the coins may have been strung together as an ornament [MGC, TNTC]. She probably had them tied up in a rag and the knot may have worked loose [NTC]. It was only a modest amount of money [AB, BECNT, EGT, NICNT, TH], but if she only had ten, even one coin was of value to the woman [EGT]. The one coin was a significant part of her savings [WBC].

b. ἐπιμελῶς (LN **30.41**) (BAGD p. 296): 'carefully' [AB, Arn, BAGD, **LN**, Lns, NTC; CEV, GW, HCSB, NASB, NCV, NIV, NRSV, TEV], 'thoroughly' [LN; NET], 'diligently' [BAGD, BECNT, WBC; KJV], '(look) in every corner' [NLT, REB].

c. ἐνώπιον (LN **83.33**) (BAGD 5.a. p. 270): 'before' [AB, Arn, BAGD, BECNT, LN, Lns, WBC], 'in the presence of' [NTC; HCSB, KJV, NASB, NCV, NET, NIV, NLT, NRSV], 'among' [BAGD; REB]. The phrase 'before the angels of God' is translated 'God's angels (are happy)' [CEV, GW], 'the angels of God (rejoice)' [TEV].

QUESTION—What is indicated by the opening conjunction ἤ 'or'?

This introduces a second parable that is also in the form of a question [TH], and it shows that it is a companion parable to the preceding one [NIGTC, TG]. It is a continuation of the question form and also implies an affirmative answer [Lns]. Perhaps the words 'of you' used in the question in 15:4 are not included here because no women were present in the audience [Bai, Gdt, ICC]. Both parables have the same point [AB, Arn, NIBC, Su, WBC]. In ordinary life, we search for what is lost and Jesus should not be criticized for doing the same thing for people who have fallen away [Arn]. Also, God takes special delight when a sinner who has been lost from his people has been found [WBC].

QUESTION—Are the numbers for the sheep and the coins significant?

There is a change of proportions for the three parables: one out of a hundred for the sheep, one out of ten for the coins, and one out of two for the sons, and this progressively shows the value that Jesus places on the lost sinner [Lns]. No comparison is intended between the different numbers [NAC].

QUESTION—Why would the woman have to light a lamp and sweep the floor?

The house probably had no windows and it was always dark inside [AB, Arn, BECNT, EGT, Gdt, ICC, MGC, NAC, NICNT, NIGTC, NTC, TNTC]. It probably had a dirt floor [Bai, NTC]. Probably the light from the lamp in the dark house was not sufficient to illumine the floor [Su]. She used a broom made of a handful of straw or stems to sweep every dark corner of the floor in hope of bringing the coin to light [Su].

QUESTION—How are the friends and neighbors the woman invited different from those the shepherd invited?

The friends and neighbors that the woman invited are the feminine forms of the nouns [AB, BECNT, EGT, Hlt, ICC, Lns, NTC, TG, TH, WBC]. However this is of no relevance in this context [TH]. It indicates the propriety of a woman calling together her woman friends and neighbors and this has no other significance [EGT, ICC, Lns].

QUESTION—Was the rejoicing done before the angels or by them?

1. This means that God rejoiced in the presence of the angels [AB, Arn, My, NAC, NTC, Rb, Su, TG, TNTC, WBC; probably KJV, NASB, NCV, NIV, NLT, NRSV]. This is the same as 'joy in heaven' (15:7), both being a circumlocution for referring to God [NAC, Su]. God is pictured as sitting on his throne [Arn], surrounded by angels [Arn, My, NTC], and he allows them to see his joy [Arn, My]. It certainly refers to God in the presence of his angels and perhaps it implies that the angels also rejoiced [AB].

2. This means that God's angels rejoiced [Gdt, ICC, Lns, TG, TH; CEV, GW, REB, TEV]. This means 'in the judgment of the angels', the angels' estimate of the facts is different from that of the Pharisees [ICC]. The expression does not mean someone other than the angels is rejoicing, it means the rejoicing is done by the angels [TG].

3. This means that God and angels rejoice together [BECNT, EGT, Hlt, MGC, NIGTC; NET]. The angels rejoiced along with God [MGC, NIGTC].

DISCOURSE UNIT: 15:11–32 [AB, BECNT, NIGTC, Su, TNTC, WBC; CEV, GW, HCSB, NASB, NCV, NET, NIV, NLT, NRSV, TEV]. The topic is two sons [CEV], the father and his two sons [WBC], the parable of the prodigal son [AB; NASB], the parable of the prodigal and his brother [NRSV], the lost son [GW, TEV], the parable of the lost son [NIGTC, Su, TNTC; HCSB, NIV,

NLT], the parable of the compassionate father [NET], the parable of the forgiving father [BECNT], the son who left home [NCV].

15:11 And he-said, A-certain man had two sons. **15:12** And the younger of-them said to-(his) father, Father, give me the part^a of-the property^b belonging^c (to-me). And he-distributed^d the property^e to-them.

LEXICON—a. μέρος (LN **63.14**) (BAGD 1.a. p. 505): 'part' [BAGD, **LN**, Lns], 'portion' [AB, BECNT, WBC; KJV], 'share' [Arn, NTC; all versions except KJV].
  b. οὐσία (LN **57.19**) (BAGD p. 596): 'property' [AB, Arn, BAGD, BECNT, **LN**, Lns, WBC; CEV, NCV, NRSV, REB, TEV], 'estate' [LN, NTC; HCSB, NASB, NET, NIV, NLT], 'wealth' [BAGD, LN], 'goods' [KJV].
  c. pres. act. participle of ἐπιβάλλω (LN **57.3**) (BAGD 2.c. p. 290): 'to belong to' [BAGD, **LN**; NET, NRSV], 'to fall to' [Arn, BAGD, Lns; KJV, NASB], 'to be due to' [WBC], 'to come to' [AB, BECNT; HCSB]. The phrase 'the part belonging to me' is translated 'my share' [NTC; CEV, GW, NCV, NIV, NLT, REB, TEV]. This implies that it was his by right or by inheritance [NET].
  d. aorist act. indic. of διαιρέω (LN **57.91**) (BAGD p. 183): 'to distribute' [BAGD, LN; HCSB], 'to divide' [AB, Arn, BAGD, BECNT, **LN**, Lns, NTC, WBC; all versions except HCSB].
  e. βίος (LN **57.18**) (BAGD 3. p. 142): 'property' [BAGD, LN, NTC; CEV, GW, NCV, NIV, NRSV, TEV], 'estate' [AB, BECNT, WBC; REB], 'possessions' [LN], 'assets' [HCSB, NET], 'livelihood' [LN], 'living' [Arn, Lns; KJV], 'wealth' [NASB, NLT]. This refers to the resources possessed by someone as a means of living [LN]. The word means 'life' or 'means of subsistence' and the estate was what supported the life of the family [WBC]. The request is for a portion of what the father's life will leave the son [BECNT]. This noun is the equivalent of οὐσία 'property' in the preceding clause [TH]. There is no distinction implied [Alf] and both nouns are translated the same [CEV, GW, NCV, TEV]. See this word at 21:4.

QUESTION—How young was the youngest son and what part of the property belonged to him?

The son is presumed to be unmarried, perhaps about twenty years old [AB], or late teens [BECNT, MGC, NIGTC], but this is not relevant to the parable [NAC]. In the OT law at Deut. 21:17, the elder son was entitled to twice as much of the inheritance as the younger son [AB, Arn, Lns, NAC, NIGTC]. The son was anticipating the division of the property that would be his when his father died [Gdt]. His share was what he was due to receive when his father died [TG]. The parable takes his share to be due at the time of the request [TH]. The father was not required to do this, but the parable depends on the fact that he does so [EGT]. A father had the choice of disposing of his property by a will to be executed after his death, or as a gift to his children while he was still alive [AB]. Some say that it was not unusual for a father to divide his estate to his children before his death [Arn, ICC]. Others say that it was unusual [NIVS], and it was not right for children to divide their father's inheritance before his death [Bai, Hlt, Lns, NICNT, Pnt, WBC]. The unreasonable request must have grieved the father, but he converted one-third of his property to cash and gave it to the younger son [NTC].

QUESTION—How did the father distribute his property to his two sons?

The son wanted the equivalent value of the property in the form of money [Gdt]. This division required that a considerable part of the holdings of the estate be sold and converted to cash [NTC]. When the father gave the younger son his share in money, he also made over the rest of the inheritance to the elder son [Hlt, NICNT, NIGTC, TH; HCSB], while retaining the legal right of using and enjoying the fruits or profits of the property during his lifetime [Hlt, NIGTC]. Or, the elder son would not take possession of his share of the inheritance until his father's death [NTC]. In dividing the estate, it does not mean that the father gave all of the property over to both sons, since the dividing would be accomplished by giving a third to his younger son and this was probably the case since throughout the parable it appears that the father still possessed the property [AB]. Or, both sons received their shares and the elder son kept his share at home where he was still under the control of his father [Alf, BECNT, TNTC]. Perhaps it means that the elder son was assigned capital goods but not a claim to their produce while the father remained alive [WBC]. It is not relevant to speculate whether the father was wise or foolish in submitting to the younger son's request [NAC].

15:13 And after not many days having-gathered-together[a] everything the younger son went-on-a-journey[b] to a-country far-away[c] and there he-wasted[d] his property[e] living recklessly.[f]

LEXICON—a. aorist act. participle of συνάγω (LN 15.125) (BAGD 1. p. 782): 'to gather together' [BAGD, LN]. The phrase 'to gather together everything' [Lns; NASB] is also translated 'to gather all together' [KJV], 'to gather up everything' [WBC], 'to gather everything' [Arn], 'to gather up all that was his' [NCV], 'to gather together all he had' [AB; HCSB, NET, NRSV], 'to gather all he had' [NTC], 'to gather his possessions' [GW], 'to pack up everything he owned' [CEV], 'to pack all his belongings' [NLT], 'to get together all he had' [NIV], 'to gather together all that he had and turn it into cash' [BECNT], 'to turn the whole of his share into cash' [REB], 'to sell his part of the property' [TEV].

b. aorist act. indic. of ἀποδημέω (LN **15.47**) (BAGD 1. p. 90): 'to go on a journey' [BAGD, **LN**; NASB], 'to journey (to)' [WBC], 'to leave on a journey' [NET], 'to take a journey' [KJV], 'to take a trip' [NLT], 'to travel' [HCSB, NCV, NRSV], 'to leave (for)' [CEV, GW], 'to leave home' [AB, BECNT, Lns; REB, TEV], 'to go away' [NTC], 'to set off' [NIV], 'to emigrate' [Arn].

c. μακρός (LN **81.14**) (BAGD 2. 488): 'far away, distant' [BAGD, **LN**]. The phrase 'a country far away' [TEV] is also translated 'a distant country' [NTC; HCSB, NASB, NET, NIV, NRSV, REB], 'a distant land' [AB, BECNT, WBC; NLT], 'a faraway country' [Arn], 'a far country' [Lns; KJV], 'a foreign country' [CEV], 'far away from home' [GW], 'far away to another country' [NCV]. This refers to a land outside of Israel [Hlt, MGC, NICNT], a Gentile land where dispersed Jews lived [AB]. He wanted to be far away from his father so he could live like he wanted to without restraint [NIC, Su].

d. aorist act. indic. of διασκορπίζω (LN **57.151**) (BAGD p. 188): 'to waste' [BAGD, **LN**; CEV, GW, KJV, NCV, NLT, TEV], 'to squander' [AB, Arn, BAGD, BECNT, LN, Lns, NTC, WBC; HCSB, NASB, NET, NIV, NRSV, REB]. This probably means that he lived extravagantly as a spendthrift [NTC, TH], squandering his wealth [NTC]. This describes a reckless waste of his money [EGT]. This includes living in dissolute pleasures [NIGTC]. The way he did this is described in the next phrase [NAC, NIVS].

e. οὐσία (LN 57.19) (BAGD p. 596): 'property' [AB, Arn, BAGD, LN, Lns, WBC; NRSV], 'estate' [HCSB, NASB], 'substance' [KJV], 'possessions' [BECNT], 'everything he had' [GW], 'money' [CEV, NCV, NLT, TEV], 'cash' [REB], 'wealth' [NTC; NET, NIV]. This has the same reference as 'everything' and could be translated 'it' or 'his money' [TH]. See this word at 15:12.

f. ἀσώτως (LN **88.97**) (BAGD p. 119): 'recklessly' [**LN**], 'loosely, dissolutely' [BAGD]. The phrase 'living recklessly' is translated 'in reckless living' [TEV], 'in foolish living' [HCSB, NCV], 'by living extravagantly' [NTC], 'in/on wild living' [CEV, NIV, NLT], 'with a wild lifestyle' [NET], 'on a wild lifestyle' [GW], 'living in disorderly fashion' [Arn], 'living a dissolute life' [AB, BECNT], 'in dissolute living' [NRSV, REB], 'by living dissolutely' [WBC], 'with loose living' [NASB], 'with riotous living' [KJV], 'by living prodigally' [Lns].

QUESTION—How long a time is 'after not many days'?

The phrase is a litotes [AB, BECNT, MGC, NAC, NIGTC, WBC] and many translate this in its positive form: 'after a few days' [BECNT; GW, NET, TEV], 'a few days later' [TH; NLT, NRSV, REB].

QUESTION—In what sense did the younger son gather everything together before he traveled to a country far away?

1. He packed up everything he owned to take with him on the trip [NIC, NIVS, TNTC; CEV, NLT]. He departed with all of his possessions so that he had nothing to come back to [NIVS, TNTC].
2. He converted all the property he inherited into cash [AB, BECNT, Crd, Hlt, MGC, NAC, NIGTC, TG, TH, WBC; REB, TEV]. Instead of 'to gather together', here it means 'to turn into cash' [NAC, NIGTC]. He sold all of the property that he had inherited [TH]. This phrase was used by Plutarch to refer to converting an inheritance into cash and this meaning may be intended here [AB, WBC]. This probably indicates that he brought together everything he possessed in order to convert it to cash [AB]. The

way he converted his inheritance to cash is not described, whether it involved a sale of the land or such [NAC].

QUESTION—What is meant by living recklessly?

1. This refers to wasting his money foolishly [Bai, Hlt, NTC, TH, TNTC; HCSB, NCV]. He spent his money extravagantly [NTC, TH, TNTC]. The word itself does not indicate whether he wasted his money in moral or immoral ways [Bai, Hlt].

2. This refers to wasting his money in immoral ways [AB, Arn, BECNT, Lns, MGC, NAC, NIC, NIGTC, NTC, WBC; NASB, NRSV, REB]. He lived a life that was dissolute [AB, Arn, BECNT, NTC, WBC; NASB, NRSV, REB], unrestrained [Arn, NTC], undisciplined, debauched [BECNT], profligate [AB, BECNT, NIC], and sinful [NIC]. He was not so far away that news about his conduct would not reach his father and brother [Arn]. The way he wasted his money is described in 15:30 [NAC], where the elder brother said that his brother had spent his money on prostitutes [AB, BECNT, Lns, MGC], although his elder brother may have exaggerated [NIVS]. Probably it means spending his money recklessly on dissolute pleasures [NIGTC],

15:14 And having-spent everything of-his there-came a-severe[a] famine throughout that country, and he began to-go-without.[b] **15:15** And having-gone[c] he-hired-himself-out-to[d] one of-the citizens of that country, and he-sent him into his fields to-feed[e] pigs,

LEXICON—a. ἰσχυρός (LN 78.16) (BAGD 2. p. 383): 'severe' [AB, Arn, BAGD, LN, NTC, WBC; GW, HCSB, NASB, NET, NIV, NRSV, REB, TEV], 'great' [BECNT, LN; NLT], 'mighty' [KJV], 'strong' [Lns], 'bad' [CEV]. The phrase 'severe famine' is translated 'there was no food anywhere' [NCV]. The noun 'strong' is used figuratively for 'severe' [TH].

b. pres. pass. infin. of ὑστερέω (LN 57.37) (BAGD 2. p. 849): 'to go without' [BAGD], 'to lack' [BAGD, LN], 'to be in need, to be in want' [LN]. The phrase 'he began to go without' is translated 'he began to be in need' [BECNT, NTC; NET, NIV, NRSV, REB], 'he began to be in want' [AB, Lns, WBC; KJV], 'he began to suffer want' [Arn], 'he was left without a thing' [TEV], 'he began to be impoverished' [NASB], 'he began to starve' [NLT], 'he had nothing' [HCSB], 'he had nothing to live on' [GW], 'soon he had nothing to eat' [CEV], 'the son was poor and hungry' [NCV]. He lacked the things he needed in order to live, especially food [TH]. He began more and more to be in want [ICC]. This suggests that not only was he without funds, he was without friends to help him [Su]. The famine would give people an excuse for not being able to help him [TNTC].

c. aorist pass. (deponent = act.) participle of πορεύομαι (LN 15.10): 'to go' [AB, Arn, BECNT, LN, Lns, NTC, WBC; KJV, NASB, NET, NIV, NRSV, REB], 'to move' [LN], not explicit [CEV, GW, NCV, NLT]. The

phrase 'having gone he hired himself to' is translated 'he went to work for' [HCSB, TEV]. This verb refers to a change of place and here it is especially a change of situation [TH].
   d. aorist pass. indic. of κολλάομαι, κολλάω (LN 34.22) (BAGD 2.b.α. p. 441): 'to hire oneself out to' [AB, BAGD, BECNT, NTC; NASB, NIV, NRSV], 'to join oneself to' [Arn, BAGD, LN, WBC; KJV], 'to join' [BAGD, LN], 'to attach oneself to' [Lns; REB], 'to work for' [NET], 'to go to work for' [CEV, HCSB, TEV], 'to get a job from/with' [GW, NCV], 'to persuade someone to hire him' [NLT]. The verb suggests that the man was not seeking a worker during this time of famine, but the son forced himself on him [Arn, Bai, EGT, Lns], and the man gave him the lowliest job [Lns]. He had to beg for work, probably receiving nothing more that food [TH]. Or, this is merely an idiom for beginning to work for someone [NET].
   e. pres. act. infin. of βόσκω (LN 44.1) (BAGD 1. p. 145): 'to feed' [AB, BAGD, BECNT, NTC, WBC; GW, HCSB, KJV, NASB, NET, NIV, NRSV], 'to look after' [LN], 'to take care of' [LN; CEV], 'to herd' [Arn, LN], 'to pasture' [Lns], 'to tend' [BAGD], 'to mind' [REB]. His work was to look after the pigs while they were feeding [TH]. The verb is in the present continuative, indicating that every day he was feeding the pigs [NTC].

QUESTION—What kind of man was the citizen of that country?
   The fact that the man raised pigs indicates that the he was a Gentile [AB, BECNT, Hlt, MGC, NAC, NIBC, NIGTC, Su].

QUESTION—What is the relevance of the son feeding pigs?
   Pigs were considered unclean by the Jews and this suggests how degraded the son's situation was [AB, Arn, BNTC, Hlt, NIBC, NIGTC, NTC, Pnt]. The job would be degrading for anyone, but it was an abomination to a Jew [ICC]. This was the lowest job that a Jew could have [BECNT, Gdt, TNTC]. It was humiliating [NIC, NTC], and an insult [NET]. This crushed the son's pride and conscience [Lns] and it shows how desperate he was [TH, TNTC].

15:16 **and he-was-longing[a] to-be-satisfied[b] with the carob-pods[c] that the pigs were-eating, and no-one was-giving (the pods/anything) to him.**
   TEXT—Instead of χορτασθῆναι ἐκ 'to be satisfied with', some manuscripts read γεμίσαι τὴν κοιλίαν αὐτοῦ ἀπό 'to fill his stomach with' and one manuscript reads γεμίσαι τὴν κοιλίαν καὶ χορτασθῆναι ἀπό 'to fill the stomach and to be satisfied with'. GNT reads χορτασθῆναι ἐκ 'to be satisfied with' with a B decision, indicating that the text is almost certain. Γεμίσαι τὴν κοιλίαν αὐτοῦ ἀπό 'to fill his stomach with' is read by Arn, Bai, NIGTC, NTC, WBC; KJV, NASB, NIV, REB.
   LEXICON—a. imperf. act. indic. of ἐπιθυμέω (LN 25.12) (BAGD p. 293): 'to long to' [AB, BAGD, LN, NTC; HCSB, NET, NIV], 'to desire' [Arn, BAGD, Lns], 'to desire very much' [LN], 'to deeply desire' [BECNT], 'to be glad to' [CEV, NASB, NRSV, REB], 'to have liked to' [WBC], 'to

want to' [NCV], 'to wish' [TEV]. The phrase 'he was longing to be satisfied' is translated 'he would fain have filled his belly' [KJV]. This clause is translated 'The boy became so hungry that even the pods he was feeding the pigs looked good to him' [NLT].

 b. aorist pass. infin. of χορτάζομαι (LN 23.15) (BAGD 2.a. p. 884): 'to be satisfied' [BAGD], 'to be filled' [BAGD, Lns], 'to have his fill' [AB], 'to be fed' [BAGD], 'to eat' [CEV, NCV, NET], 'to eat his fill' [HCSB], 'to fill himself' [NRSV, TEV], 'to have his fill' [BECNT]. Here it refers to the result of being satisfied and means 'to eat one's fill' [LN]. It means not only to eat, but to appease his hunger [TH]. Others take the alternate text: 'to fill his belly' [WBC; KJV, REB], 'to fill his stomach' [Arn, NTC; NASB, NIV].

 c. κεράτιον (LN 3.46) (BAGD p. 429): 'carob pod' [AB, BAGD, BECNT, LN, Lns, NTC, WBC; HCSB], 'carob tree pod' [Arn], 'bean pod' [TEV], 'pod' [NCV, NET, NIV, NLT, NRSV, REB], 'husk' [KJV], 'what (the pigs were eating)' [CEV, GW]. The pods were hornlike bean pods of the carob tree [EGT, NIC, NIVS]. They were shaped like a bean pod, but were larger and curved like a horn [Alf]. The pods were the sweet beans of the carob or locust tree [TH; NET]. They contained seeds in a sweet gelatinous substance [Su]. In extreme cases poor people would eat these pods, but they were regarded as animal food [Su]. Or, although this carob pod is usually taken to refer to St. John's Bread which has a sweet pulp, it could have been a wild variety of carob which was smaller and had black, bitter berries [Bai, NIGTC].

QUESTION—What was it that people didn't give him?

 1. No one gave him the pods that the pigs ate [Arn, ICC, My, TG; HCSB].

 2. No one gave him anything to eat [AB, Bai, BECNT, EGT, MGC, NICNT, NTC, Pnt, Su, WBC; CEV, GW, NASB, NCV, NET, NIV, NLT, NRSV, REB, TEV]. The clause is also logically placed first: 'No one in the country would give him any food, and he was so hungry that he would have eaten what the pigs were eating' [GW]. No one would give him anything better than the pods [EGT]. Unable to eat the pods, he was reduced to begging, yet no one would give him anything [Pnt].

QUESTION—Did he eat the carob pods he was longing to eat?

 1. This was an unfulfilled desire to eat the pods [AB, Arn, BECNT, Hlt, Lns, My, NAC, NTC, Pnt, Rb, TG, TH, TNTC]. The addition 'but no one was giving anything to him' indicates that no one would give him the pods to eat [Lns, NTC, TNTC; TEV]. The imperfect tense 'he was longing' implies that his desire was not fulfilled [AB, Bai, Lns] (but this pod was eaten by some and this linguistic point is not compelling [NIGTC]). It is not known why he didn't just take the food [NTC]. When he drove the pigs home, it was the job of others to put out the food for the pigs and they would not give him any [Arn, My]. He didn't dare take the food away from the pigs [Pnt]. Perhaps his inability to eat the pig's food was

psychological [AB, NAC]. Probably he was given some food from his master's house, but not enough to do away with his intense hunger [Arn].

2. He not only desired the pods, but he ate them [Alf, Bai, EGT, NIBC, Su]. He could easily eat the pods of the pigs under his care, but no one gave him anything better [EGT]. No one gave him food that was fit for humans, but he did eat the pigs' food [Su]. He was unable to satisfy his hunger with the carob pods which had no nourishment because no matter how much he ate, he was not filled, yet no one was feeding him regularly [Bai].

15:17 And having-come[a] to himself he-said, How-many hired-workers[b] of-my father (there are) having-more-than-enough[c] bread, but here I am-perishing with-hunger.[d]

TEXT—Some manuscripts omit ὧδε 'here'. GNT does not deal with this variant. ⁰Ωδε 'here' is omitted by KJV.

LEXICON—a. aorist act. participle of ἔρχομαι (LN 13.50) (BAGD I.2.c. p. 311): 'to come' [BAGD, LN]. The phrase 'having come to himself' [Lns] is also translated 'coming to himself' [WBC], 'he came to himself' [AB, Arn, Lns; KJV, NRSV], 'he came to his senses' [BECNT, NTC; all versions except KJV, NCV, NRSV], 'he realized what he was doing' [NCV]. He came to recognize his situation for what it was [TH].

b. μίσθιος (LN **57.174**) (BAGD p. 523): 'hired worker' [**LN**; NET, TEV], 'hired man' [BAGD, LN, Lns, NTC; GW, NASB, NIV, NLT], 'hired hand' [AB, BECNT, WBC; HCSB, NRSV], 'hired laborer' [Arn], 'hired servant' [KJV, REB], 'servant' [NCV], 'day laborer' [BAGD], 'worker' [CEV]. This refers to a laborer who was paid a wage at the end of the day and does not refer to the household servants [AB, BECNT, Hlt]. He was an employee at the time and he was comparing himself to his father's employees [Su].

c. pres. mid. indic. of περισσεύω (LN **57.24**) (BAGD 2.b. p. 651): 'to have more than enough' [LN], 'to receive something in great abundance' [BAGD]. The phrase 'having more than enough bread' is translated 'get more than enough bread' [BAGD], 'have more than enough bread' [NASB], 'have bread enough and to spare' [KJV, NRSV], 'have an abundance of bread' [WBC], 'have bread in abundance' [Arn], 'are abounding in bread' [Lns], 'abound in food' [BECNT], 'have more than enough food' [HCSB], 'have food to spare' [NIV], 'have food enough to spare' [NET, NLT], 'have more food than they can eat' [GW, REB], 'have more than they can eat' [NTC; TEV], 'have more than enough to eat' [AB], 'have much more than they can eat' [**LN**], 'have plenty of food' [NCV], 'have plenty to eat' [CEV]. The middle voice here is to be taken as active, not passive [TH]. The noun 'bread' is not being contrasted with the pods; the contrast is their having plenty to eat and his starving condition [ICC].

d. λιμός (LN 23.31) (BAGD 1. p. 475): 'hunger' [BAGD, LN]. The phrase 'I am perishing with hunger' [Lns; KJV] is also translated 'I perish of hunger' [Arn], 'I am being destroyed by hunger' [BECNT], 'I am dying of/with hunger' [AB, BAGD, NTC; HCSB, NASB, NET, NLT, NRSV], 'almost dying of hunger' [NCV], 'I am perishing in a famine' [WBC], 'I am starving to death' [CEV, GW, NIV, REB], 'I am about to starve' [TEV].

QUESTION—In what way did he come to himself?

1. This implies that he had been beside himself [Alf, ICC, Su]. This is the same as the English idiom 'he came to his senses' [AB, Arn, BECNT, Hlt, MGC, NICNT, NTC, TNTC, WBC; CEV, GW, HCSB, NASB, NET, NIV, NLT, REB, TEV]. He realized his situation and came to a sane mind [EGT]. He realized how foolishly had had acted [Hlt, NIC]. He realized what course of action to take to remedy his plight [Su]. This was the first step to repentance [Hlt, NIC]. This is repentance in a qualified sense since it does not seem to be remorse for his sins at this point but only coming to the realization that he has no other option [Bai].

2. This is an idiom meaning that he repented [Bai, Gdt, Lns, MGC, NAC, NIGTC]. He realized that his wrongdoing had brought about his desperate state and this phrase means that he repented [NIGTC]. Repentance is a change of feeling from which springs a resolution (15:18) [Gdt]. He not only started to think more clearly, he also had a moral renewal that involved repentance as can be seen in his confession of sin in 15:18 and 21 [NAC]. This describes his conversion [Lns].

QUESTION—What is meant by asking himself, 'how many' of the workers had enough to eat?

The use of 'many' implies that there were many workers working at his father's home [Rb]. He was thinking of the many hired men there were at this father's house [Lns]. This does not mean that he thought that some of the workers did not have enough—he knows that all of them were well taken care of [TG]. Instead of 'how many', it is translated 'My father's workers have plenty to eat' [CEV], 'All my father's hired workers have more than they can eat' [TEV], 'All of my father's servants have plenty of food' [NCV], 'At home even the hired men have food enough to spare' [NLT].

15:18 Having arisen^a I-will-go to my father and I-will-say to-him, Father, I-have-sinned against heaven^b and before^c you. **15:19** I-am no-longer worthy^d to-be-called^e your son. Make^f me as one of-your hired-workers.

TEXT—In 15:19, before οὐκέτι 'no longer', some manuscripts add καί 'and', although GNT does not mention this variant. Καί 'and' is read by KJV.

LEXICON—a. aorist act. participle of ἀνίσταμαι (LN 15.36) (BAGD 2.d. p. 70): 'to arise' [Arn, Lns, NTC; KJV], 'to rise' [BAGD], 'to rise up' [BECNT], 'to get up' [AB; HCSB, NASB, NET, NRSV, TEV], 'to depart' [LN], 'to leave' [LN; NCV], 'to get ready' [BAGD], 'to set out' [BAGD; NIV], 'to set off' [WBC], '(I will go) at once' [GW, REB], not explicit [CEV, NLT]. This verb indicates the beginning of the action expressed by the following verb [BAGD]. Although this word is somewhat redundant here, it functions to mark the beginning a decisive change of direction in the son's life [WBC]. 'Rising I will go' is an Aramaic expression meaning 'I will go at once' [BECNT, NIGTC]. Or, he will rise from his despair [ICC].

b. οὐρανός (LN **12.16**) (BAGD 3. p. 595): 'heaven' [BAGD]. The phrase 'I have sinned against heaven' [AB, Arn, BECNT, NTC, WBC; GW, HCSB, KJV, NASB, NET, NIV, NLT, NRSV] is also translated, 'I did sin against the heaven' [Lns], 'I have sinned against God in heaven' [CEV], 'I have sinned against God' [NCV, REB, TEV]. This mention of heaven was a way the Jews used in order to avoid mentioning a name for God and it refers to 'God' [BAGD, **LN**]. See this word at 20:4.

c. ἐνώπιον (LN **90.20**) (BAGD 5.b. p. 271): 'before, against' [BAGD], 'in the sight of' [**LN**]. The phrase 'and before you' [AB, Arn, BECNT, WBC; KJV, NRSV] is also translated 'and against you' [CEV, GW, NET, NIV, NLT, REB, TEV], 'and in your sight' [Lns, NTC; HCSB, NASB], 'and have done wrong to you' [NCV]. The expression 'before you' is parallel with the preceding 'against heaven' and so it is equivalent to 'against' [TH]. Both Greek prepositions are translation variants of a single Hebrew word meaning 'against' [WBC]. Or, he sinned before his father in that he did it within his father's knowledge, thus grieving him [Arn]. Or, he sinned in his father's judgment of how he had behaved [EGT].

d. ἄξιος (LN **65.17**) (BAGD 2.a. p. 78): 'worthy' [Arn, BAGD, BECNT, LN, Lns, NTC, WBC; HCSB, KJV, NASB, NCV, NET, NIV, NLT, NRSV], 'fit' [BAGD; REB, TEV], 'good enough' [CEV]. This adjective is also translated as a verb: 'to deserve' [AB; GW]. He was morally unfit [NIGTC]. He had forfeited all his former rights to sonship and inheritance [BECNT].

e. aorist pass. infin. of καλέω (LN **33.131**) (BAGD 1.a.δ. p. 399): 'to be called' [AB, Arn, BAGD, BECNT, LN, Lns, NTC, WBC; all versions]. This pertains to what his father called him [ICC]. He was not fit to be regarded as a son [NIGTC].

f. aorist act. infin. of ποιέω (LN **13.9**) (BAGD I.1.b.ι. p. 682): 'to make' [BAGD, LN], 'to cause to be' [LN]. The phrase 'make me as' [Lns, NTC; KJV, NASB] is also translated 'make me like' [HCSB, NIV], 'make me' [BECNT; GW], 'instate me as' [WBC], 'treat me as' [AB, Arn; CEV, REB, TEV], 'treat me like' [NET, NRSV], 'let me be like' [NCV], 'please take me on as' [NLT].

QUESTION—What is involved in saying that he sinned against οὐρανόν 'heaven'?

In such expressions, 'heaven' is used as a circumlocution for God [AB, BAGD, Crd, EGT, Hlt, MGC, NAC, NIC, NIGTC, NTC, TG, TH, TNTC, WBC; NET]. The Jews used the holy name of God as little as possible [Arn]. Heaven is used as a metonymy for the one who is in heaven, specifically,

God [TH]. He had sinned against God's fifth commandment about not taking the name of God in vain [NAC]. His filial misconduct was displeasing to God [ICC]. God had given him a loving and kind father [NTC].

QUESTION—How did he sin against his father?

He had dishonored his father [NAC]. It was wrong to spend everything without leaving something to help his father in his old age, or perhaps his whole attitude towards his father was wrong and he had failed to honor his father according to the commandment [TNTC]. He had squandered the money that the father had saved for him and had ignored any moral or legal obligation he had to his father [Hlt, NIGTC].

QUESTION—What is meant by the request 'make me as one of your hired workers'?

He did not ask to be received as a family member but only sought the minimal burden of being treated as a day worker, the lowest class of laborers [BECNT]. Rather than asking to be treated as one of the workers, he was asking to be put in the same position as the workers [TH]. He was asking for a job as a day laborer [AB, TH, TNTC].

15:20 And having-arisen he-came[a] to his father. And while he was being-away[b] (at) a-distance his father saw him and felt-compassion[c] and having-run fell[d] upon his neck and kissed him. **15:21** And the son said to-him, Father, I-sinned against heaven and before you, no-longer I-am worthy to-be-called your son.

TEXT—In 15:21, before οὐκέτι 'no longer', some manuscripts add καί 'and', although GNT does not mention this variant. Καί 'and' is read by KJV.

TEXT—In 15:21, following υἱός σου 'your son', some manuscripts add ποίησόν με ὡς ἕνα τῶν μισθίων σου 'make me as one of your hired servants'. GNT rejects this addition with an A decision, indicating that the text is certain.

LEXICON—a. aorist act. indic. of ἔρχομαι (LN 15.81) (BAGD II. p. 311): 'to come' [BAGD, BECNT, LN]. The phrase 'came to' [Arn, WBC; KJV, NASB] is also translated 'started back to' [CEV, TEV], 'set out for' [REB], 'went to' [Lns, NTC; GW, HCSB, NCV, NET, NIV, NRSV], 'went back to' [AB], 'returned home to' [NLT]. The 'going' of 15:19 becomes 'coming' as the scene shifts to the father's perspective [WBC].

b. pres. act. participle of ἀπέχω (LN 85.16) (BAGD 2. p. 85): 'to be away from' [BAGD, LN]. The phrase αὐτοῦ μακρὰν ἀπέχοντος 'he was being away at a distance' is translated 'he was still a long distance away' [NLT], 'he was still some distance away' [BECNT], 'he was still at a distance' [GW], 'he was still a long way off' [AB, NTC; CEV, HCSB, NASB, NCV, NIV, REB], 'he was still far off' [NRSV], 'he was still far away' [Arn], 'he was still a long way from home' [NET, TEV], 'he being still far off' [Lns], 'he was yet a great way off' [KJV]. He was still far away from his father's house [TH; NET], but close enough to be recognized by his father [TH]. Perhaps the father was a considerable

LUKE 15:20–21

distance from the house [Pnt]. The father saw his son in the distance and with a parent's intuition realized who he was [Arn]. Measuring the distance misses the point of the story [AB, ICC].

c. aorist pass. (deponent = act.) indic. of σπλαγχνίζομαι (LN 25.49) (BAGD p. 762): 'to feel compassion for' [LN; NASB], 'to be filled with compassion' [Lns; HCSB, NIV, NRSV], 'to be filled with love and compassion' [NLT], 'to have compassion' [WBC; KJV], 'to have great affection for' [LN], 'to have/feel pity' [AB, Arn, BAGD, BECNT], 'to have sympathy' [BAGD], 'to feel sorry for' [CEV, GW, NCV], 'his heart went out to him' [NTC; NET, REB], 'his heart was filled with pity' [TEV]. He pitied his son who was dressed in rags and looked like a beggar [Arn, EGT]. See this word at 7:13; 10:33.

d. aorist act. indic. of ἐπιπίπτω (LN 34.64) (BAGD 1.b. p. 297): 'to fall upon' [BAGD]. The phrase 'fell upon his neck' [Arn, Lns, WBC; KJV] is also translated 'embraced him' [NASB, NLT], 'he hugged him' [CEV, NCV, NET], 'he put his arms around him' [GW, NRSV], 'he threw his arms around his neck' [AB, NTC; HCSB], 'embraced him about the neck' [BECNT], 'threw his arms around him' [NIV, TEV], 'flung his arms around him' [REB].

QUESTION—How did the father kiss his son and what was the significance of this?

The father kissed his son on the cheeks [TG]. The verb may mean that he kissed him many time [EGT, Lns, MGC, My, NTC, Rb, TNTC], he covered his face with kisses [Lns]. It was a sincere greeting, not just politeness [TNTC]. It expressed the father's affection, joy, and acceptance of his son [BECNT, NAC]. It signified that the father forgave his son [AB, MGC, NIGTC, TNTC] and wanted to restore the broken relationship [NIGTC].

QUESTION—Why didn't the son finish what he had decided to tell his father about not being worthy and being given a job as a worker?

His father interrupted him [BNTC, Crd, Hlt, Lns, NIGTC, Pnt, Rb, Su, TG]. Or, the forgiveness and acceptance by the father prevented the son from going on [Alf, Bai, Gdt, My].

15:22 **And the father said to his slaves,[a] Quickly[b] bring-out a-robe,[c] the best, and clothe him, and give a-ring[d] for his hand and sandals[e] for the feet,**

TEXT—Some manuscripts omit ταχύ 'quickly'. GNT does not deal with this variant. Ταχύ 'quickly' is omitted by KJV.

LEXICON—a. δοῦλος (LN 67.110): 'slave' [Arn, LN, Lns, WBC; HCSB, NASB, NRSV], 'servant' [AB, BECNT, NTC; all versions except NASB, NRSV]. This is a different word than μίσθιος 'hired worker' used in 15:17–18 and means a slave who was a permanent servant in the household [NAC, NIGTC, Su].

b. ταχύς (LN 67.110) (BAGD 2.b. p. 807): 'quickly' [Arn, BAGD, LN, NTC, WBC; NASB, NRSV], 'quick' [AB, Lns; HCSB, NIV, NLT], 'hurry' [CEV, GW, NCV, TEV], 'immediately' [BECNT], 'at once, without delay' [BAGD].

c. στολή (LN 6.174) (BAGD p. 769): 'long, flowing robe' [BAGD, LN]. The phrase στολὴν τὴν πρώτην 'a robe, the best' is translated 'a robe, the best one' [NTC; NRSV], 'a robe, the best we have' [REB], 'a festal robe, the best' [Lns], 'the best robe' [AB, Arn, BECNT, WBC; GW, HCSB, KJV, NASB, NET, NIV, TEV], 'the best clothes' [CEV, NCV]. They were to bring the robe from the house [EGT]. It was the best robe the father had [Alf, Bai, ICC, My, WBC], a robe of the finest quality [AB, Alf, Crd, EGT, Lns, MGC, Rb, Su], the most beautiful [TH]. It was the best robe in the house [Arn, ICC, TH]. It was a long outer garment [My, TG, TH]. The robe was reserved for notable guests [NAC]. It would be worn on grand occasions [Arn, Bai, BECNT, Lns]. Putting it on the son would assure that he would be given the proper respect by the slaves [Bai].

d. δακτύλιος (LN **6.190**) (BAGD p. 170): 'ring' [BAGD, **LN**]. The phrase δότε δακτύλιον εἰς τὴν χεῖρα αὐτοῦ 'give a ring for his hand' is translated 'give him a ring for his hand' [Lns], 'provide a ring for his hand' [WBC], 'give him a ring for his finger' [AB, BECNT; CEV], 'get a ring for his finger' [NLT], 'put a ring on his hand' [Arn, NTC; KJV, NASB], 'put a ring on his finger' [GW, HCSB, NCV, NET, NIV, NRSV, REB, TEV]. The Greek word χεῖρα usually means 'hand' or any relevant part of it [NET], and here it obviously means 'finger' [TG]. Usually a ring was made of gold or silver and had the owner's signet for sealing documents [LN]. The ring was a sign of honor and perhaps authority [Hlt, ICC, Lns, MGC, NAC, NIGTC, NIVS, NTC, Pnt, TG, TH, TNTC]. The father was giving his son the privilege of exercising the authority to transact business in the father's name [Pnt]. Or, this would not be the Father's signet ring, but it would be a sign of honor [WBC]. It did not transfer authority to him nor give him a higher position than that of his elder brother [BECNT].

e. ὑπόδημα (LN 6.182) (BAGD p. 844): 'sandal' [AB, BAGD, BECNT, LN, Lns, WBC; all versions except KJV, TEV], 'shoe' [KJV, TEV]. Wearing sandals indicated that a person was a freeman and not a slave [Alf, Arn, Bai, EGT, ICC, Lns, MGC, NAC, NIGTC, NIVS, Pnt, Rb, TG, TNTC]. Or, instead of marking his position as a free man, it merely implies that the son had arrived barefoot [BECNT, WBC; NET].

QUESTION—How did the slaves enter the picture?

Perhaps the slaves had seen their master running to greet his son and had followed him [Arn, Bai, EGT], or they met the father as he returned home [EGT]. Or, it can be presumed that this scene took place after the father and son returned home [TH].

15:23 and bring the fattened[a] calf, kill[b] (it), and having-eaten let-us-be-merry,[c]

LEXICON—a. σιτευτός (LN **44.2, 65.8**) (BAGD p. 752): 'fattened' [BAGD, BECNT, Lns, NTC; GW, HCSB, NASB, NET, NIV], 'grain-fattened' [**LN** (44.2)], 'fatted' [AB, Arn, WBC; KJV, NRSV, REB], 'fat' [NCV], 'prize' [**LN** (65.8); TEV], 'best' [CEV], '(the calf) we have been fattening in the pen' [NLT].

  b. aorist act. impera. of θύω (LN **20.72**) (BAGD 2. p. 367): 'kill' [BAGD, BECNT, **LN**, NTC; all versions except CEV, HCSB], 'to make the kill' [WBC], 'to slaughter' [AB, Arn, BAGD, LN, Lns; HCSB], 'to prepare' [CEV]. Although this verb normally means 'to sacrifice', here it means 'to slaughter' [Arn, ICC]. Or, the calf was first to be sacrificed [Pnt].

  c. aorist pass. subj. of εὐφραίνω (LN **25.131**) (BAGD 2. p. 327): 'to be merry, to enjoy oneself' [BAGD], 'to be glad' [BAGD, LN], 'to be happy, to be cheered up' [LN]. The phrase 'having eaten let us be merry' is translated 'eating, let us make merry' [Lns], 'eating, let us rejoice' [BECNT], 'let us eat and be merry' [Arn; KJV], 'let us eat and make merry' [WBC], 'let us eat and celebrate' [NTC; NASB, NET, NRSV], 'let us feast and be merry' [AB], 'let us celebrate with a feast' [GW, HCSB, REB, TEV], 'we must celebrate with a feast' [NLT], 'let's have a feast and celebrate' [NIV], 'so we can eat and celebrate' [CEV], 'so we can have a feast and celebrate' [NCV]. The participle φαγόντες 'having eaten' is equivalent here to 'let us eat and', while 'to be merry' especially refers to the enjoyment of a meal [NIGTC]. See this word at 12:19, 29; 16:19.

QUESTION—What was distinctive about a fattened calf?

The calf was different from other calves which were in the pasture since it was fattened for some festive occasion [NIGTC, NTC, Su, TH]. It was given extra food to fatten it [TG]. It would be standing in a stall [Alf]. There was only one such calf kept for a special occasion [Gdt, ICC]. The fact that it was a calf indicates that a large gathering was planned for [Bai, Hlt, NICNT] and it would take hours of preparation [BECNT, WBC]. The purpose of the banquet was to reconcile the son to the whole community [Bai].

15:24 because this my son was dead and he-lived-again,[a] he-had-been lost and he-was-found.[b] And they-began to-be-merry.

LEXICON—a. aorist act. indic. of ἀναζάω (LN **23.93**) (BAGD 2. p. 53): 'to live again' [LN], 'to come back to life' [AB, LN, Lns; CEV, GW, REB], 'to come to life again' [BAGD; NASB], 'to come back to life again' [WBC], 'to be alive again' [NTC; HCSB, KJV, NCV, NET, NIV, NRSV], 'to become alive' [Arn], 'to now be alive' [TEV], 'to now live' [BECNT], 'to return to life' [NLT]. This is a hyperbole that describes in figurative language a person who had been separated from all contact with his family and later been found to be alive and well [LN].

b. aorist pass. indic. of εὑρίσκω (LN 27.27): 'to be found' [AB, Arn, BECNT, LN, Lns, NTC, WBC; all versions], 'to now be found' [TEV].

QUESTION—What relationship is indicated by the beginning conjunction ὅτι 'because'?

It indicates the reason for the celebration [BECNT, EGT, Lns, MGC, NTC, TG]. Or, it indicates the reason for the father's joy [NIGTC, Su].

QUESTION—In what sense had the son been dead and returned to life?
   1. This refers to the father's viewpoint [EGT, Hlt, ICC, Lns, NICNT, NIGTC, Su, TG, TH, WBC]. The father had considered his son to be dead, but had now found that his son was alive [Su, TH]. 'Dead' means 'dead to me' [ICC]. He was as though he were dead [TG]. Since the son had probably announced that he never intended to return, he was as good as dead [NIGTC].
   2. This refers to the moral or spiritual state of the son [BAGD, BNTC, Gdt, Lns, MGC, My, NTC]. Life apart from God is spiritual death and conversion is gaining true life [Lns]. The son had been morally dead or depraved [BAGD].
   3. This may refer to the father's relationship to his son and/or to the spiritual state of the son [AB, Arn, Gdt, NAC, NIC]. The son was either thought to be dead because he was no longer in his father's household, or he was morally dead because of his dissolute life [AB]. Because of his son's disappearance, the father speaks of his son as being as good as dead to him, but now his son stands there alive before him, so the application of the parable gives a spiritual meaning to the words [Arn, NAC, NIC], and spiritually he was dead in sin and he was alive in the sense of having life in God's kingdom [NAC].

QUESTION—In what sense had the son been lost and found?

This repeats the previous thought [ICC, TG, TH], being a parallelism with no special distinction between the two [Crd]. The words *lost* and *found* connect this parable with the two preceding parables [AB, NAC, NIGTC; NET].
   1. This refers to the father's viewpoint [BECNT, EGT, Hlt, ICC, Su, TG, WBC]. Lost and found means the same as being dead and alive [Su]. The son was lost to the father [BECNT, ICC, WBC], his whereabouts unknown [EGT] and his father never expected to see him again [BECNT]. The son was as though he had lost himself [TG].
   2. This is to be taken in the spiritual sense [BNTC, Lns, NTC]. The son was lost to God and found by God in his conversion [Lns].
   3. This may refer to the father's relationship to his son and/or to the spiritual state of the son [AB, Arn, Gdt, NAC].

QUESTION—When did they begin to be merry?

An interval had to take place to prepare the feast which is the setting for the second part of the parable [ICC]. The father's orders had been carried out with this result [NTC].

15:25 And his son, the older (one), was in (the) field. And coming as he-drew-near to-the house, he-heard music and dancing. **15:26** And having-summoned[a] one of-the servants[b] he-was-inquiring what these[c] (things) could be.

LEXICON—a. aorist mid. participle of προσκαλέομαι, προσκαλέω (LN 33.308) (BAGD 1.a. p. 715): 'to summon' [BAGD; HCSB, NASB], 'to call' [AB, Arn, BECNT, NTC, WBC; KJV, NET, NIV, NRSV, TEV], 'to call to' [GW, NCV, REB], 'to call to oneself' [BAGD, LN, NTC], 'to call over' [CEV], not explicit [NLT].

b. παῖς (LN 87.77) (BAGD 2.a.γ. p. 604): 'servant' [Arn, BAGD, BECNT, WBC; all versions except NET, NRSV], 'servant boy' [AB, NTC], 'lad' [Lns], 'slave' [LN; NET, NRSV]. This noun is a variant of δοῦλος 'slave' in 15:22 [NIGTC, TH]. This has the same sense as παῖς 'servant' in 7:7 [AB]. Since it was a large estate, there were different kinds of workers and this noun is meant to indicate a kind of worker that was different from a δοῦλος 'slave' [Arn], perhaps a young servant or a special servant [BECNT], perhaps a slave who was a house servant [TG; NET] in distinction from a field hand [TG]. Or, he probably was a young boy and not a servant at all [Bai].

c. τοῦτο (LN 92.29): 'this' [LN]. The phrase 'what these things could be' [NASB] is also translated 'what this could be' [NTC], 'what this might be' [WBC], 'what was happening' [GW, NET], 'what was going on' [NIV, NLT, NRSV], 'what this could mean' [Arn], 'what it was all about' [AB], 'what it meant' [REB], 'what all this meant' [NCV], 'what these things meant' [BECNT; GW, HCSB], 'what these things might be' [Lns], 'What's going on?' [TEV], 'What's going on here?' [CEV]. He wanted to know what this noise meant or what the people were doing [TG].

QUESTION—What was the music and dancing that the elder son heard?

There were at least several musical instruments [Lns, Su], probably including flutes [BECNT, ICC], given by a band of musicians [Arn, BECNT], and perhaps it included singing [BECNT; NET]. The dancing was a circular dance on the green [Rb]. The dancing was performed by professional entertainers who had been hired for the occasion [Arn], not by the guests [ICC, TNTC]. It was a choral dance by performers and included gestures and clapping of hands [Lns]. Perhaps it was clapping, singing, and dancing by men [NIGTC]. The combination produced the loud, boisterous, and joyous sound that the son heard [Bai].

QUESTION—In 15:26, what is indicated by the imperfect form ἐπυνθάνετο 'he was enquiring'?

The son asked more than one question [Arn]. He asked a series of questions [Bai, BECNT]. He *began* to enquire [Lns, TH].

15:27 And he-said to-him, Your brother has-come, and your father killed the fattened calf because he-has-received-back[a] him being-in-good-health.[b]

15:28 And he-was-angry and did- not -want to-enter, but his father having-come-out was-pleading^c with-him.

TEXT—In 15:28, instead of δέ 'but', some manuscripts read οὖν 'therefore', although GNT does not mention this variant. Οὖν 'therefore' is read by KJV.

LEXICON—a. aorist act. indic. of ἀπολαμβάνω (LN **34.53**) (BAGD 2. p. 94): 'to receive back' [Arn, **LN**, Lns, NTC; NASB], 'to receive' [BECNT, WBC; KJV], 'to get (him) back' [AB, BAGD; NET, NRSV, TEV], 'to have back' [HCSB, NIV, REB], not explicit [CEV, GW, NCV].

b. pres. act. participle of ὑγιαίνω (LN 23.129) (BAGD 1. p. 832): 'to be in good health' [BAGD], 'to be healthy' [BAGD, LN], 'to be well' [LN], 'safe and sound' [AB, BECNT, Lns, NTC, WBC; all versions except GW, NCV, NLT], '(to receive him back) in health' [Arn], '(to come home) safely' [NCV], '(his) safe return' [GW, NLT].

c. imperf. act. indic. of παρακαλέω (LN 33.315, 33.168) (BAGD 1.b., 5. p. 617): 'to plead with' [AB, NTC; HCSB, NASB, NIV, NRSV, REB], 'to appeal to' [LN (33.168); NET], 'to entreat' [BECNT, WBC; KJV], 'to urge' [Arn], 'to beseech' [Lns], 'to beg' [NLT], 'to beg him to go/come in' [CEV, GW, NCV, TEV], 'to try to conciliate, to try to consol' [BAGD (5.)], 'to invite' [BAGD (1.b.), LN (33.315)]. The imperfect tense means that he *began* to plead with his son [Lns, NTC; NASB, NRSV], or that he *kept on* pleading with him [BECNT, ICC, Rb, TG, TH]. He asked him to join the celebration in the house [Hlt, MGC, NAC].

QUESTION—Why did the father kill the fattened calf?

The father had the calf killed in order to have a banquet and he had the banquet because he wanted to celebrate the fact that he had his younger son back with him [TG]. The father did not directly kill the calf, he ordered his slave to kill it [TH].

15:29 And answering he-said to his father, Behold so-many years I-serve^a you and never have-I-disobeyed a-command of-yours, and never did-you-give me (even) a-young-goat^b in-order-that I-might-be-merry^c with my friends. **15:30** But when this son of-yours the (one) having-eaten-up^d your property^e with prostitutes came, you-killed the fattened calf for-him.

LEXICON—a. pres. act. indic. of δουλεύω (LN 35.27) (BAGD 2.a. p. 205): 'to serve' [AB, Arn, BAGD, BECNT, LN; KJV, NASB], 'to work hard' [NLT], 'to serve like a slave' [BAGD; NCV], 'to work like a slave' [CEV, GW, NET, NRSV, TEV], 'to slave (for)' [Lns, NTC, WBC; HCSB, NIV, REB]. The son felt that he had a position like that of a mere slave [Bai, ICC, Lns, NIC, NIGTC, Rb, TG, TNTC; NET]. Or, this does not indicate his attitude, but it makes a contrast with what the younger brother had done [WBC].

b. ἔριφος (LN **4.19**) (BAGD p. 309): 'young goat' [NTC; HCSB, NASB, NCV, NIV, NLT, NRSV], 'little goat' [CEV, GW], 'kid' [Arn, BAGD, BECNT, **LN**, Lns; KJV, REB], 'he-goat' [BAGD, LN], 'goat' [AB,

WBC; NET, TEV]. This was a cheap animal in comparison with a fattened calf [Alf, Arn, BECNT, EGT, Hlt, ICC, MGC, My, NIGTC, NIVS, TG, TH, TNTC, WBC].
- c. aorist pass. subj. of εὐφραίνω (LN 25.131) (BAGD 2. p. 327): 'to be merry'. See this word at 12:19; 15:23; 16:19.
- d. aorist act. participle of κατεσθίω (LN **57.150**) (BAGD 2. p. 422): 'to eat up' [BAGD], 'to waste' [LN]. This is a figurative extension of 'to eat up' and means 'to waste' [**LN**]. The phrase 'having eaten up your property' is translated 'consumed your estate' [WBC], 'devoured your property' [NTC; NRSV], 'devoured your estate' [AB], 'devoured your living' [Arn, Lns; KJV], 'devoured your livelihood' [BECNT], 'devoured your wealth' [NASB], 'devoured your assets' [HCSB, NET], 'wasted your money' [CEV], 'wasted all your money' [NCV], 'wasted all your property' [TEV], 'squandered your property' [NIV], 'squandering your money' [NLT], 'spent your money' [GW], 'running through your money' [REB].
- e. βίος (LN 57.18) (BAGD 3. p. 142): 'property'. See this word at 15:12.

QUESTION—What is the significance of referring to his brother as 'this son of yours, the one having eaten up your property with prostitutes'?

The elder son was expressing his contempt for his brother [Alf, EGT, Gdt, ICC, My, NIGTC, TG, TH], his scorn [AB, Alf, Su], his anger [BECNT]. He avoided referring to him as 'my brother' [AB, Arn, BECNT, ICC, Lns, NIGTC, NIVS, NTC; NET].

QUESTION—Had all of the father's property been used up?

This was an hyperbole since the younger son had spent only the part that had been given him [TG]. It was untrue, because only part of the father's money had been given to the younger son as his share of the inheritance [NTC]. The father's property had been destroyed in the sense that the Father was poorer because the son's part no longer contributed to the family fortunes [NIGTC, WBC].

QUESTION—How did the elder brother know that his brother wasted his money on prostitutes?

We are not told how the news reached him [AB, Crd]. In the parable, it is just something that he knows [NAC]. Or, this was a matter of conjecture [Bai, EGT, Hlt, ICC, Rb, TNTC], but it was a probability [NIGTC]. From the expression 'he wasted his property living recklessly' in 15:13, it appears that the elder brother was right in his appraisal of his brother's life of debauchery [Su].

15:31 **And he-said to-him, Child,[a] you are always with me, and everything (that is) mine is yours. 15:32 But it-was-necessary[b] to-be-merry and to-rejoice, because this brother of-yours was dead and he-lived, and was-lost and was-found.**

LEXICON—a. τέκνον (LN 10.36) (BAGD 1.a.β. p. 808): 'child' [BAGD, LN, Lns, WBC], 'my child' [Arn, BECNT, NTC; GW]. The sex of the child is made clear by the context [BAGD]: 'my boy' [REB], 'son' [AB, BAGD;

HCSB, KJV, NASB, NCV, NET], 'my son' [CEV, NIV, NRSV, TEV], 'dear son' [NLT]. This word τέκνον 'child' is more affectionate than υἱός 'son' [AB, ICC, NIGTC, WBC].
   b. imperf. act. indic. of δεῖ (LN 71.21) (BAGD 2., 6.a.): 'to be necessary' [BAGD], 'it was necessary' [Lns], 'ought, should' [BAGD (2.), LN], 'we should' [CEV], 'it was fitting' [BECNT], 'it was appropriate' [NET], 'we had to' [AB, BAGD (6.a.), LN, WBC; HCSB, NASB, NCV, NIV, NLT, NRSV, TEV], 'we just had to' [NTC], 'there had to be' [Arn], 'we have something (to celebrate)' [GW], 'to be meet' [KJV], 'how could we fail to' [REB]. It was a moral necessity [BECNT, Lns]. It was the right and proper thing to do [NTC]. The imperfect tense reaches back to the beginning of the celebration that had begun several hours ago [Arn]. The imperfect tense reaches from the past to the present joy [Lns].

QUESTION—What is the significance of the father saying that his son was always with him?
   Since the eldest son had never left his father, there was no occasion to welcome him home with a special feast [Alf, Gdt]. This implies that the eldest son had never been dead and lost [AB].

QUESTION—What is meant by saying all that was the father's was the son's?
   Since the younger son had taken his share, all that that remained of the estate belonged to the elder son [TG, TH]. All of the present the estate had been given to the elder son, including the house, fields, and animals [Lns]. Any particular gift given to the son wouldn't mean anything since it was already the son's [Gdt]. Anytime the son had wanted a party he could have had it since he owned everything [BECNT, ICC]. If he had not had a celebration with his friends, it was because he had not asked [ICC, NIGTC, Pnt]. The father said this to reassure his elder son that his place with his father was as secure as ever and his claim on his part of the inheritance was not changed at all [BECNT, NTC, TNTC, WBC]. Or, although not in charge of the estate at the present time, the son would legally inherit the estate since it had been promised to him [AB, NAC, NIGTC]. Although the father had not yet retired and turned over control of the estate, the elder son was the owner and there had not been any special occasion for celebrating [Arn].

QUESTION—What was the necessity for the celebration?
   The occasion for the present celebration had come by the return of the younger son [CEV]. Implicitly, this is an appeal to the eldest son to join in the celebration [WBC].

DISCOURSE UNIT: 16:1–18:30 [REB]. The topic is the instruction of the disciples.

DISCOURSE UNIT: 16:1–31 [BECNT, NICNT, NIGTC, TNTC, WBC]. The topic is kingdom economics [NICNT], generosity: handling money and possessions [BECNT], warnings about wealth [NIGTC], the use and abuse of riches [WBC], teaching, mostly about money [TNTC].

DISCOURSE UNIT: 16:1–18 [GW, NASB, NLT]. The topic is the story of the shrewd manager [NLT], the unrighteous steward [NASB], Jesus speaks about dishonesty [GW].

DISCOURSE UNIT: 16:1–15 [NIV]. The topic is the parable of the shrewd manager.

DISCOURSE UNIT: 16:1–13 [BECNT, Su; CEV, HCSB, NCV, NET, NRSV, TEV]. The topic is a dishonest manager [CEV, HCSB], the shrewd manager [TEV], the parable of the shrewd steward [Su], the parable of the crafty steward [BECNT], the parable of the clever steward [NET], the parable of the dishonest manager [NRSV], true wealth [NCV].

DISCOURSE UNIT: 16:1–9 [NICNT, NIGTC, TNTC]. The topic is the use of wealth to make friends [NICNT], the prudent steward [NIGTC], the unjust steward [TNTC].

DISCOURSE UNIT: 16:1–8 [NAC, WBC]. The topic is the parable of the dishonest manager.

DISCOURSE UNIT: 16:1–8a [AB]. The topic is the parable of the dishonest manager.

16:1 And also he-was-saying to the disciples, A-certain man was rich who had a-steward,ᵃ and this (one) was-accusedᵇ before-him as wastingᶜ his possessions.ᵈ

TEXT—Instead of τοὺς μαθητάς 'the disciples', some manuscripts read τοὺς μαθητὰς αὐτοῦ 'his disciples'. GNT does not deal with this variant. Τοὺς μαθητὰς αὐτοῦ 'his disciples' is read by KJV.

LEXICON—a. οἰκονόμος (LN **46.4**) (BAGD 1.a. p. 560): 'steward' [Arn, BAGD, BECNT, LN, Lns, WBC; KJV, REB], 'manager' [AB, BAGD, NTC; HCSB, NASB, NET, NIV, NRSV], 'a manager of a household' [**LN**], 'a business manager' [GW], 'a manager to take care of business' [CEV, NCV], 'a manager to handle his affairs' [NLT], 'a servant who managed his property' [TEV]. See this word at 12:42.

b. aorist pass. indic. of διαβάλλω (LN **33.426**) (BAGD p. 181): 'to be accused' [**LN**, NTC, WBC; GW, KJV, NCV, NIV], 'to have charges brought' [BAGD, LN], 'to be denounced' [Lns], 'to be reported' [NASB], 'to be maliciously reported' [Arn]. This passive is also translated with the master as the subject: 'he was told' [CEV, TEV], 'who was informed of accusations that' [NET], 'who received an accusation' [HCSB], 'he received complaints that' [REB], 'he heard complaints' [AB]; or with the master as the indirect object: 'charges were brought to him' [NRSV], 'a report was brought to him' [BECNT], 'a rumor went around' [NLT]. This does not refer to legal charges, but to reports made to the master by friends and acquaintances [NET]. It was a secret denunciation [Lns]. The accusation proceeded from a hostile intent [Alf, BAGD, BECNT, EGT, Lns, NIGTC]. The accusations were caused by sinister motives of the steward's enemies [Arn]. Evidently the charges were true since the master took them seriously [AB, Arn, BECNT, Lns, NIGTC] and the steward did not deny the charges [Alf, Hlt].

c. pres. act. participle of διασκορπίζω (LN 57.151) (BAGD p. 188): 'to waste' [Arn, BAGD, BECNT, LN; CEV, GW, KJV, NET, NIV, TEV], 'to squander' [AB, BAGD, LN, Lns, NTC, WBC; HCSB, NASB, NRSV, REB]. The phrase 'as wasting his possessions' is translated 'of cheating him' [NCV], 'was thoroughly dishonest' [NLT]. This refers to a wasteful use of the property [AB]. See this word at 15:13.

d. pres. act. participle of ὑπάρχω (LN 57.16) (BAGD 1. p. 838): 'to belong to' [BAGD, LN]. The phrase τὰ ὑπάρχοντα 'possessions' [LN, Lns, NTC; HCSB, NASB, NIV] is also translated 'property' [AB, Arn; GW, NRSV, REB], 'assets' [NET], 'money' [CEV, TEV], 'goods' [BECNT, WBC; KJV], not explicit [NCV, NLT].

QUESTION—At the beginning of the verse, what is the function of καί 'also'?

'Also' modifies 'he was saying' and the phrase is a transition formula [EGT]. This is a continuation of the preceding passage [Alf, Arn, EGT, NIC, NIGTC, WBC], but there is a widening of the audience to include the disciples [WBC]. At that same time he also said this to his disciples [ICC, Lns]. Or, this indicates a change of audience, but there is not necessarily a temporal connection with the preceding parable [BECNT]. Jesus now dealt with the life of those who have been found [Lns] and this parable applies to his disciples [Alf, Arn, ICC, Lns, NTC]. This was primarily addressed to his disciples, but it was spoken in the hearing of the Pharisees (16:14) [AB, Crd, MGC, NIGTC, Rb, TNTC, WBC]. The next parable in this chapter was directed to the Pharisees [Arn].

QUESTION—What position did the steward have?

Usually a steward was a slave whom the master put in charge of the estate in order to relieve himself of routine management [TNTC]. He could have been a slave who had been trained for this role [NET]. Or, in this parable the steward must have been a freeman [Alf, Arn, Gdt, Hlt, ICC, Lns, NTC, TNTC], since he could enter into agreements that were binding upon the master [TNTC] and he was merely discharged [Lns]. A steward kept his master's affairs in order and ruled the estate in its financial affairs [Su, WBC]. Probably the steward managed the estate while the master lived in town [Arn, Gdt, ICC, MGC, NIGTC]. But it is also possible that the master also lived on the estate [WBC].

QUESTION—How did the steward waste his master's possessions?

It is not stated whether he wasted his master's possessions by fraud or by extravagant living [EGT]. It was by misappropriating funds for his own purposes [TNTC]. The present participle indicates that the steward was in the process of doing his crooked work [Lns]. He could have been taking part of the funds from transactions he made in his master's name [ICC, WBC]. Or, it was probably by neglect of duty since there is no indication that he had to pay compensation for misappropriating funds [NIGTC]. It was a case of careless mismanagement [Arn, NICNT, NTC, Pnt, Su] and incompetence [BECNT]. If the owner had thought that his steward was dishonest, instead of merely incompetent, he would have had him arrested and punished [NIC]. The steward was given the opportunity to make arrangements for his departure and to get his books in order before he departed, all this implying that he had not been guilty of embezzlement [NTC].

16:2 And having-called[a] him he-said to-him, What[b] (is) this I-hear about you? Give[c] the account of your management,[d] because no longer are-you-able[e] to-be-steward.

LEXICON—a. aorist act. participle of φωνέω (LN **33.107**) (BAGD 2.b. p. 870): 'to call' [Arn, BAGD, BECNT, **LN**, Lns, WBC; KJV, NASB], 'to call (him) in' [AB, NTC; CEV, HCSB, NCV, NET, NIV, NLT, TEV], 'to call for' [GW], 'to summon' [BAGD, LN; NRSV], 'to send for' [REB].

b. τί (LN 92.14): 'what' [LN]. The clause 'What is this (that) I hear about you?' [AB, BECNT, WBC; all versions except KJV, NLT] is also translated 'What is this I am hearing about you?' [NTC], 'How is it that I hear this of thee?' [KJV], 'How do I hear this concerning thee!' [Lns], 'What's this I hear about your stealing from me?' [NLT], 'Why do I hear this about you?' [Arn].

c. aorist act. impera. of ἀποδίδωμι (LN 90.46) (BAGD 1. p. 90): 'to give' [BAGD, LN]. The phrase ἀπόδος τὸν λόγον 'give the account' is translated 'give an account' [HCSB, KJV, NIV], 'give an accounting' [NASB], 'give due account' [Lns], 'give me an accounting' [NRSV], 'render the account' [Arn], 'turn in the account' [BECNT; NET], 'draw up for me an account' [AB], 'hand over the account' [WBC]. The phrase 'give an account of your management' is translated 'Turn in a complete account of your handling of my property' [TEV], 'Surrender the account books' [NTC], 'Tell me what you have done!' [CEV], 'Give me a report of what you have done with my money' [NCV], 'Get your report in order' [NLT], 'Produce your accounts' [REB], 'Let me examine your books' [GW].

d. οἰκονομία (LN **46.1**) (BAGD B.1.a. p. 559): 'management' [AB, BAGD; HCSB, NASB, NIV, NRSV], 'management of the household' [BAGD, **LN**], 'stewardship' [Arn, BECNT, Lns, WBC KJV], 'administration' [NET]. See c. above for NTC; CEV, GW, NCV, NLT, REB, TEV.

e. pres. mid./pass. (deponent = act.) indic. of δύναμαι (LN 74.5): 'to be able' [LN]. The clause 'no longer are you able to be steward' is translated 'you are no longer able to be a steward' [BECNT], 'you can no longer be (my) steward/manager' [AB, Lns, NTC; HCSB, NASB, NET], 'you cannot be (my) steward/manager any longer' [Arn; NCV, NIV, NRSV, REB, TEV], 'thou mayest be no longer steward' [KJV], 'you may no longer act as steward' [WBC], 'you are no longer going to work for me' [CEV], 'it's obvious that you can't manage my property any longer'

[GW], 'you are going to be dismissed' [NLT]. He cannot be steward any longer because he is being fired [TG].

QUESTION—What is meant by the master's question, 'What is this I hear about you?'

This is a demand for an explanation [NTC, TG], and it is evident that the steward cannot clear himself [NTC]. Most take this to be a question, 'What is this that I hear about you?' [AB, Bai, BECNT, BNTC, My, NTC, TH, WBC; all versions except KJV]. It is implied that both the master and the steward know about what has been reported [TH]. The question suggests that the master already believes the charges [AB, BECNT; NET]. The question means 'why have you followed such a course?' [Arn]. It may also be translated 'Why do I hear this about you?' and it asks for the basis of the report by demanding the steward to produce his books to show the truth or falsehood of the accusation [Alf, ICC]. Or, this expresses the master's indignant surprise, not a request for information [NTC]. It is an exclamation by the master who had thought that his steward had been honest and capable [Lns].

QUESTION—Why was the steward told to give the account of his management?

Since the master had already decided to dismiss the steward, this is a request for a final accounting of the state of affairs [Bai, EGT, Gdt, Lns, NAC, NIGTC, NTC, Rb, Su, TH, TNTC]. The owner needed to know what was now on hand after such mismanagement [Pnt]. This is a request for inventory of the master's possessions and an account of the transactions that had been made, listing the debtors and the amounts they owed [AB]. The statement of accounts would benefit the person who would be appointed to be the new steward [MGC, NIGTC]. This accounting would help the master and the new steward see the extent of wastefulness and disorder the business was in [NIC]. It would expose the steward's dishonesty [MGC]. The account would verify that the charges were true, as the master expects [BECNT]. Or, this indicates that the master wanted to examine the accounts to see if the accusation was true [Alf, ICC]. 'Your account' means 'the account you owe me' [Arn].

16:3 And the steward said within himself, What shall-I-do, because/that[a] my master is-taking-away[b] the management from me? I-am- not -strong (enough) to-dig,[c] I-am-ashamed[d] to-beg.[e]

LEXICON—a. ὅτι (LN 89.33): 'because' [Arn, LN], 'since' [LN, NTC, WBC; HCSB, NASB, NCV, NET], 'for' [KJV], 'seeing that' [Lns], 'now that' [NRSV, REB], not explicit [AB, BECNT; CEV, GW, NIV, TEV]. This conjunction means 'that' and gives the content of his soliloquy [BECNT].
   b. pres. mid. indic. of ἀφαιρέω (LN **68.47**) (BAGD 3. p. 124): 'to take away' [BAGD, **LN**, Lns, NTC, WBC; HCSB, KJV, NASB] 'to take' [Arn, BECNT]. The phrase 'is taking away the management from me' is translated 'is taking my job away from me' [AB; GW, NCV], 'is taking

away my job' [NIV], 'is taking away my position from me' [NET], 'is taking the position away from me' [NRSV], 'is going to dismiss me from my post/job' [REB, TEV], 'is going to fire me' [CEV], 'I'm through here' [NLT].
  c. pres. act. infin. of σκάπτω (LN **19.55, 43.3**) (BAGD 1. p. 753): 'to dig' [AB, Arn, BAGD, BECNT, LN (19.55), Lns, NTC, WBC; GW, HCSB, KJV, NASB, NET, NIV, NRSV, REB], 'to dig ditches' [**LN** (19.55); CEV, NCV, NLT, TEV], 'to work the soil' [**LN** (43.3)]. 'to till the ground' [LN (43.3)].
  d. pres. mid. indic. of αἰσχύνομαι (LN 25.190) (BAGD 1. p. 25): 'to be ashamed' [AB, Arn, BAGD, BECNT, LN, Lns, NTC, WBC; all versions except NLT, REB], 'to be too proud' [NLT, REB]. The steward thought that being a professional beggar would be below his station in life [Su].
  e. pres. act. infin. of ἐπαιτέω (LN **33.173**) (BAGD p. 282): 'to beg' [AB, Arn, BAGD, BECNT, **LN**, Lns, NTC, WBC; all versions]. The present tense means begging over and over, and implies begging for alms [ICC, Lns]. This means being a professional beggar, the obvious alternative to physical labor for a living [TH].
QUESTION—How and when did the steward say this?
  This is what he was thinking [TG; GW]. The steward said this to himself [CEV, NLT], he debated inwardly [TH]. This is what the steward did as he thought the matter over after leaving his master [ICC, Rb]. It was when he had time to consider a plan of action [TNTC].
QUESTION—What was he considering when he asked himself 'What shall I do?'
  The question was not about rendering an account of his management; it was about his personal future [TH]. Being fired from his job would make it impossible to get a job as a steward somewhere else [TG, WBC]. His options were not appealing [BECNT].
QUESTION—What wasn't he strong enough to do?
  He wasn't strong enough to dig ditches [LN; CEV, NCV, NLT, TEV]. Digging ditches was a proverbial saying for doing any heavy manual labor [Alf, Su, TH]. He wasn't strong enough for digging in the fields, a form of agricultural labor [EGT, TH]. He had been trained for a white-collar job, not for hard, physical labor [AB]. He was not willing to do hard physical labor, the labor of uneducated people [BECNT].

16:4 I-know what I-can-do, so-that when I-am-removed[a] from the management they-may-receive[b] me into their houses. **16:5** And having-summoned each one of-the debtors[c] of-his master he-said to-the first, How-much do-you-owe[d] my master?
LEXICON—a. aorist pass. subj. of μεθίστημι (LN 15.9) (BAGD 1. p. 499): 'to be removed' [AB, Arn, BAGD, LN, WBC; HCSB, NASB], 'to be dismissed' [NRSV], 'to be discharged' [Lns] 'to be put out of' [KJV, NET]. The phrase 'when I am removed from the management' is

translated 'when I'm discharged from my position' [NTC], 'after/when I've lost my job' [CEV, GW], 'when I lose my job' [NCV, NIV], 'when my job is gone' [TEV], 'when I am dismissed' [REB], 'when I leave' [NLT].
- b. aorist mid. (deponent = act.) subj. of δέχομαι (LN 34.53) (BAGD 1. p. 117) 'to receive' [BAGD, LN, Lns, WBC; KJV], 'to welcome' [AB, LN, NTC; all versions except KJV, NLT, REB], 'to have as a guest' [LN], 'to take (me) in' [Arn; REB]. The phrase 'they may receive me into their houses' is translated 'I'll have plenty of friends to take care of me' [NLT].
- c. χρεοφειλέτης (LN 57.222) (BAGD p. 885): 'debtor' [AB, Arn, BAGD, LN, Lns, NTC, WBC; GW, KJV, NASB, NET, NIV, NRSV, REB]. The phrase 'each one of the debtors' is translated '(all) the people who were in debt' [CEV, TEV], 'everyone who owed money' [NCV], 'each person who owed money' [NLT].
- d. pres. act. indic. of ὀφείλω (LN 57.219) (BAGD 1. p. 598): 'to owe' [AB, Arn, BAGD, LN, Lns, NTC, WBC; all versions], 'to be indebted' [BAGD], 'to be in debt' [LN].

QUESTION—How is the exclamation 'I know what I can do' to be understood?

It is a dramatic use of the aorist [AB, Arn, NAC; NET]. It indicates that he had suddenly arrived at a solution [Alf, BECNT, ICC, Lns, MGC, NAC, TG, TH; NET]. It is like exclaiming 'I've got it!' when arriving at a solution [Arn, BECNT, NTC, TNTC]. The aorist tense of the verb indicates that his knowledge was an achieved state [WBC], he had come to know this [Hlt]. He had decided a moment ago what he will do and this is best expressed as 'I know what I will do' [NIGTC].

QUESTION—Who will receive the steward into their houses?

The subjects are his master's debtors [Alf, Crd, ICC, My, NIGTC, TH, WBC]. According to his plan, they will be friendly to him and help take care of him after he loses his job [TG]. They would give him shelter [Alf, Gdt]. He would become an honored member of the households [Arn]. This does not mean that he will have permanent residence in their houses [EGT]. Probably he thought that he could become a house guest successively in a number of homes, although this would last only during the time of his immediate pressing problems [WBC]. They would take care of him until something better turned up [Lns]. He hoped that they would take care of him or employ him [BECNT]. In view of the plural 'houses', it does not appear that he thought they would give him some permanent position such as a steward [WBC].

QUESTION—Who were the master's debtors he summoned?

Probably they were merchants who had received goods on credit from the master's estate and had given promissory notes to the steward [Gdt, Lns, My, NIC, NIGTC]. The quantities owed were large and it appears that they were traders who bought from the master and still owed him [Lns]. They were large-scale business associates [WBC]. The men in the two examples must have been wealthy outsiders, but the master's books could have included different types of debtors [BECNT]. They may have included tenants of the master's estate who paid their rents in kind [Bai, NIGTC, NTC, TH]. The debts were in terms of agricultural items and this indicates that the master sold food or lent money in exchange for commodities or he rented out land with the rent payments being made with produce [BECNT]. The 'first' debtor was the one who came first [TH], the first one described in the parable [EGT]. The two instances of meeting with the debtors were examples of the many debtors the steward dealt with [AB, Arn, Crd, Hlt, Lns, MGC, NIGTC, NTC, Su].

QUESTION—Why did the steward have to ask the debtor how much he owed?

The steward had promissory notes from each debtor, but this question advances the story [AB]. The steward had a record of the debt, but when a debtor had to state the amount owed, he would better appreciate the reduction the steward would give him [BECNT].

16:6 And he-said, One-hundred baths[a] of-olive-oil.[b] And he-said to-him, Take your accounts[c] and having-sat-down quickly[d] write fifty. 16:7 Then to-another he-said, And you, how–much do-you-owe? And he-said, One-hundred cors[e] of-wheat. He-says to-him, Take your accounts and write eighty.

LEXICON—a. βάτος (LN **81.20**) (BAGD p. 137): 'bath' [Arn, BAGD, **LN**, Lns, WBC]. This was a liquid measure of uncertain amount since different standards were used in different times [NIGTC]. The measure was between eight and nine gallons [BAGD, LN, Lns, NAC], about eight gallons [TH], about nine gallons [WBC], or 8.75 gallons [Arn, BECNT, ICC]. The numbers of the amounts can be kept by translating one hundred 'barrels' [LN; CEV, TEV], 'containers, large jars' [LN], 'jars' [REB], 'jugs' [AB; NRSV], or 'measures' [BECNT, NTC; HCSB, KJV, NASB, NET]. Or, some use equivalent measures and translate 'eight hundred gallons' [GW, NCV, NIV, NLT]. This quantity represents the yield of a very large olive grove [WBC], nearly 150 olive trees [BECNT], or, 450 olive trees [NIVS]. Its value would be about one thousand denarii [BECNT].

b. ἔλαιον (LN 6.202) (BAGD 1. p. 247): 'olive oil' [AB, BAGD, LN, WBC; all versions except HCSB, KJV, NASB], 'oil' [Arn, BECNT, Lns, NTC; HCSB, KJV, NASB]. Olive oil was used as food, medicine, fuel in lamps, and as perfume when mixed with sweet-smelling substances [LN].

c. γράμμα (LN **33.39**) (BAGD 2.b. p. 165): 'account' [**LN**], 'record of debt' [LN], 'promissory note' [BAGD]. Even a single copy was referred to in the plural [BAGD, Lns, NIGTC, WBC; all versions]. The phrase 'your accounts' is translated 'your account' [NTC; REB, TEV], 'your bill' [Arn, BECNT; CEV, KJV, NASB, NCV, NET, NIV, NRSV], 'your invoice' [HCSB], 'thy writing' [Lns], '(tear up) that bill' [NLT], 'your contract' [WBC], 'your bond' [AB], 'the ledger' [GW]. This refers to a promissory note [AB, NIGTC] that indicated the total owed, without specifying the principal and the interest [AB].

d. ταχέως (LN 67.110) (BAGD 1.a. p. 806): 'quickly' [Arn, BAGD, BECNT, LN, Lns, NTC, WBC; CEV, HCSB, KJV, NASB, NCV, NET, NIV, NRSV], 'at once, without delay' [BAGD], 'quick!' [GW], 'hurry' [AB], 'be quick about it' [REB], not explicit [NLT, TEV]. Some translate this adverb so as to modify 'sit down' [BECNT, NTC, WBC; HCSB, KJV, NASB, NCV, NET, NIV, NRSV], or 'write' [Arn, Lns; CEV], or both [GW, REB].

e. κόρος (LN 81.21) (BAGD 445): 'cor' [Arn, BAGD, LN, Lns, WBC]. This measure is uncertain since different standards were used in different times [AB, ICC, NIGTC]. This was a dry measure of between ten and twelve bushels [BECNT, LN; NET], ten bushels [Arn, BNTC, ICC, Lns, NTC, Pnt, Rb, TG, TH, TNTC], about eleven bushels [Bai, NIC], about twelve bushels [Su]. The numbers of the amounts can be kept by translating a hundred 'measures' [BECNT, NTC; HCSB, KJV, NASB, NET, REB], or 'containers' [NRSV]. Or, some use equivalent measures and translate 'a thousand bushels' [AB; CEV, GW, NCV, NIV, NLT, TEV]. This would be the yield of about 100 acres [NIVS, TNTC].

QUESTION—What did the debtors owe?

The debtors may have purchased the oil and grain from the master and had not yet paid the bill or perhaps it means that the master had loaned them money and they had to pay it back in produce [Arn].

QUESTION—Why didn't the steward change the bills instead of having the debtors do it?

The directions to take his accounts imply that the steward took the bill from a drawer or strongbox [Lns, NTC] and handed it to the debtor [TH]. Although the contract was kept by the steward [WBC] it had been handwritten by the debtor [BECNT, Lns, NTC, WBC]. The new note needed to be written in the debtor's own hand so that it would appear to be the original one [BECNT, Lns]. This could mean that the debtor destroyed the old bill and wrote a new one [Arn, Lns, NIGTC, TH], or he erased the original amount on the bill and wrote in the lower amount [Arn].

QUESTION—What was the purpose for telling the first debtor to change the bill quickly?

Perhaps the steward didn't want the debtor to have time to figure out the strategy behind the steward's actions [NTC]. He had to finish before his master found out what he was doing [Bai].

QUESTION—Is there any reason why the first debtor had his bill reduced from 100 baths to 50 and the second debtor had his bill reduced from 100 cors to 80?

Probably the difference of commodities accounts for the different discounts [TNTC; NET]. Perhaps olive oil was more valuable than grain and therefore received a higher commission [BECNT, Lns]. The values of 50 baths of olive oil and 20 cors of wheat was about the same [Bai, NIGTC]. The steward knew the kind of people each of the debtors were and what it would take to accomplish his purpose of gaining their goodwill [Gdt, ICC]. The circumstances for the differences are irrelevant to the story [Arn]. We can assume that there was an array of deductions as he dealt with the many other debtors not mentioned [BECNT, TNTC].

QUESTION—What did the debtors think about changing the amounts they owed?

They probably did not think they were acting dishonestly and thought the steward had talked his master into reducing the amounts they owed [NTC].

QUESTION—What was behind the actions of reducing the amounts owed to his master?

1. The steward falsified the amounts legally owed to his master [Alf, Bai, EGT, Gdt, ICC, Lns, My, NIC, NTC, Pnt, Rb].
2. The steward removed the illegal interest due his master [Gdt, NIGTC, TNTC].
3. The steward removed his own commission and the master suffered no loss [AB, MGC].

16:8a **And the master praised**[a] **the steward of-unrighteousness**[b] **because he-acted wisely.**[c]

LEXICON—a. aorist act. indic. of ἐπαινέω (LN **33.354**) (BAGD p. 281): 'to praise' [AB, Arn, BAGD, **LN**, Lns, NTC, WBC; CEV, GW, HCSB, NASB, NCV, TEV], 'to commend' [BECNT; KJV, NET, NIV, NRSV], 'to applaud' [REB], 'to admire' [NLT].

b. ἀδικία (LN 88.21) (BAGD 2. p. 18): 'unrighteousness' [BAGD], 'unjust deed, what is unjust' [LN]. This noun in the genitive case is translated as an adjective modifying 'steward': 'unrighteous' [BAGD, BECNT, LN, Lns; HCSB, NASB], 'unjust' [Arn; KJV], 'dishonest' [AB, NTC, WBC; all versions except HCSB, KJV, NASB]. This unrighteousness is specifically his dishonesty [TH].

c. φρονίμως (LN **32.31**) (BAGD p. 866): 'wisely' [BAGD, **LN**; KJV], 'shrewdly' [BAGD, BECNT, Lns, NTC, WBC; NASB, NET, NIV, NRSV], 'prudently' [AB, Arn], 'astutely' [HCSB]. The phrase 'because he acted wisely' is translated 'for being smart' [NCV], 'for being so clever' [GW], 'for acting so astutely' [REB], 'for being so shrewd' [NLT], 'for doing such a shrewd thing' [TEV], 'for looking out for himself so well' [CEV]. It refers to having common sense and forethought [TG].

QUESTION—In what way was the steward dishonest?

He was previously dishonest in his management of the estate [BECNT, ICC, NAC; NET]. This describes wasting his master's possessions (16:1) [BECNT, MGC]. He was dishonest throughout the story, including his dealings with the debtors [Arn, Hlt, NIC, NTC, Su, TNTC, WBC].

QUESTION—In what way was the steward wise?

He was wise in planning ahead [NTC]. He was wise in making plans for being aided by the grateful debtors [ICC, NIGTC]. He was wise in using his own wealth (commissions) to ensure the future [AB]. The praise was a recognition of the steward's cleverness, not his crookedness [Alf, EGT, NIC, NICNT, NTC, Pnt, Su, WBC]. The master had heard of the trick his steward had done and could not help admiring the way the steward had prudently dealt with the dishonest debtors [Arn]. The master praised the steward for his shrewdness, and the narrator of the parable is the one who describes the steward as being dishonest [NIC, NICNT]. Shrewdness is not a moral quality [NAC, TH].

DISCOURSE UNIT: 16:8b–13 [AB]. The topic is three applications of the parable.

16:8b Because^a the sons^b of-this age are more-wise^c in-respect-to^d their-own generation^e than the sons^f of-the light.

LEXICON—a. ὅτι (LN 89.33): 'because' [LN, Lns; TEV], 'for' [AB, Arn, BECNT, NTC, WBC; HCSB, KJV, NASB, NET, NIV, NRSV, REB], 'and it is true that' [NLT], not explicit [GW]. This conjunction is also translated 'yes' [NCV], 'That's how it is' [CEV].

b. υἱός (LN **11.16**): 'son' [LN]. 'Son of' is an idiom for people belonging to a particular class [NIGTC]. The phrase οἱ υἱοὶ τοῦ αἰῶνος τούτου 'the sons of this age' is an idiom for people who hold to the value system of the world [LN]. It is translated 'the sons of this age' [Arn, BECNT, WBC; HCSB, NASB], 'the children of this age' [NRSV], 'the sons of this eon' [Lns], 'people of this age' [LN], 'the people of this world' [**LN**, NTC; CEV, NET, NIV, TEV], 'the children of this world' [AB; KJV, REB], 'the citizens of this world' [NLT], 'worldly people' [GW, NCV], 'non-religious people' [LN]. The phrase 'this age' was commonly used to mean 'the present evil order of things' [Arn]. They are people who are concerned with worldly matters [TG], they are driven by secular values [Hlt].

c. φρόνιμος (LN 32.31) (BAGD p. 866): 'more wise' [BAGD, LN], 'wiser' [Arn; KJV], 'smarter' [NCV], 'shrewder' [Lns], 'more shrewd' [BECNT, NTC, WBC; NASB, NET, NIV, NLT, NRSV], 'much more shrewd' [TEV], 'more clever' [GW], 'more astute' [HCSB, REB], 'more prudent' [AB]. The phrase 'are more wise' is translated 'look out for themselves better than' [CEV].

d. εἰς (LN 90.23): 'with respect to, with reference to, concerning' [LN], 'in relation to' [NASB], 'among' [WBC], 'with' [NCV], 'toward' [Arn], 'in' [Lns; KJV], 'in dealing with' [AB, BECNT, NTC; HCSB, NET, NIV, NRSV, REB], 'when it comes to dealing with' [GW]. The phrase 'in respect to their own generation' is translated 'in handling their affairs' [TEV], 'look out for themselves' [CEV], not explicit [NLT].

e. γενεά (LN **10.4**) (BAGD 1., 2. p. 154): 'generation' [BAGD (2.)], 'clan, kind' [BAGD (1.)]. The phrase τὴν γενεὰν τὴν ἑαυτῶν 'their own generation' [AB, BECNT, Lns, WBC; NRSV] is also translated 'their generation' [KJV], 'their contemporaries' [NET], 'people like themselves' [LN], 'their own kind' [**LN**, NTC; NASB, NCV, NIV, REB], 'their own people' [HCSB], 'their class' [Arn], 'others' [GW], 'themselves' [CEV], not explicit [NLT, TEV]. There are two groups, the sons of this age and the sons of the light, and a person in one group is surrounded by a number of contemporaries like himself, which form his generation [Gdt].

f. υἱός (LN 11.16): 'son' [LN]. The phrase τοὺς υἱοὺς τοῦ φωτὸς 'the sons of the light' is an idiom for people who are living according to God's truth which has been revealed to them [LN]. It is translated 'the sons of the light' [BECNT, LN], 'the sons of light' [Arn, Lns, WBC; HCSB, NASB], 'the children of the light' [LN; KJV], 'the children of light' [AB; NRSV, REB], 'the people of the light' [NIV], 'the people of light' [NET], 'the people who belong to the light' [CEV, TEV], 'the people who have the light' [NTC], 'the people of God' [LN], 'the godly' [NLT], 'spiritual people' [NCV], 'spiritually minded people' [GW]. 'Light' is a symbol of the kingdom of God and sons of light are the people who belong to the kingdom of God [TH]. This is a designation for Christian disciples [AB, Hlt]. They are people who are concerned with the values of the kingdom of God [TG].

QUESTION—What relationship is indicated by ὅτι 'because'?

1. It is part of the parable and gives the master's analysis of the situation. The master's comment is to the effect 'Now there was a man who knew how to take care of himself! As a man of the world, he knew what real values are and how to deal with the men of his own time. One of these 'sons of light' would never have known how to do that' [Su].
2. It is a comment about the parable that ended with 16:8a and indicates the grounds for the master's praise of the steward [Arn, ICC, Lns, NIBC, NIGTC, NTC, TH]: the master was right in praising the steward's shrewdness because worldly people are the shrewdest people. The steward did what is expected of worldly people [NIGTC]. With the words 'And I say to you' (16:9) Jesus makes an application of the parable, but 16:8b, although not part of the narrative, is added to put the parable in the right light by informing the listeners that the parable is to be taken only as pertaining to the shrewdness of worldly people [Lns]. In addition, it points to the parable's lesson [BECNT]. Probably 16:8b is an expansion of the original parable either by Luke, or someone before him, and here it adds a lesson from the parable [WBC].
3. It is a comment about the parable that ended with 16:8a and it indicates that Jesus told the example of shrewdness because it illustrates the point he wanted to make [AB, BECNT, Gdt, MGC, NTC, Rb, WBC; NET]. This gives the reason for the master's comments and also points to the parable's lesson [BECNT]. Luke draws the lesson from the story that

Christians seem less effective in dealing with their own situation than the worldly-wise people are [WBC].

QUESTION—What is meant by 'their own generation'?

1. It means their own kind of people [AB, Alf, Arn, EGT, Gdt, ICC, My, NIGTC, NTC, TH]. People of the world are more prudent in dealing with their own kind than Christians are in dealing with other Christians [ICC]. Worldly people often show more wisdom in their dealings with one another than Christians do in matters affecting their salvation [NTC], or the coming kingdom [TH], or the eschatological situation [NIGTC]. He is not telling the disciples to become worldly minded or crooked [NTC].

2. It means all the people then living [Lns, NIC], the people of their time [Su]. In matters of their own generation, worldly people are shrewder than Christians. But this does not criticize the Christians, it merely states that the parable has been taken from what is common among people of this age and is to be understood in that way [Lns]. Or, this is a criticism of Christians who often acted unwisely towards others with the result that people are unnecessarily repulsed by them instead of being drawn to them [NIC].

QUESTION—What is the point of the parable?

Christians are to act as prudently with regard to divine things as worldly people act with regard to earthly things [NAC]. The disciples are to look ahead and plan for the future [NTC]. This is a challenge to be shrewd enough to recognize and seize whatever opportunity there is in the midst of a threat and it is especially pertinent to the events brought about by Jesus' ministry [WBC]. God's children should be as diligent in considering the long-term effect of their actions as those who do not know God are in protecting their earthly well-being [BECNT]. Worldly people have more wisdom in acting towards the children of the generation to which they belong than Christians do in acting towards toward those of the generation to which Christians belong [Gdt]. Or, because of the phrase 'in respect to their own generation' this means that in affairs where sons of this age have to be dealt with, worldly people show more cleverness than do the children of God [AB, Arn]. Christians can learn something from the children of this world in the matter of prudence [AB, NIBC]. Christians often lack wisdom to use what they have, in contrast with worldly people who use their possessions for their different ends [TNTC].

DISCOURSE UNIT: 16:9–18 [NAC]. The topic is sayings on stewardship.

DISCOURSE UNIT: 16:9–13 [WBC]. The topic is serving God and using mammon.

16:9 And I say to-you, Make friends for-yourselves by-means-of[a] the wealth[b] of-unrighteousness, in-order-that when it-gives-out[c] they-may-welcome[d] you into the eternal tents.[e]

TEXT—Instead of ἐκλίπῃ 'it gives out', some manuscripts read ἐκλίπητε 'you give out', although GNT does not mention this variant. Ἐκλίπητε 'you give out' is read by KJV.

LEXICON—a. ἐκ (LN **89.77**) (BAGD 3.f. p. 235): 'by means of' [BAGD, BECNT, **LN**, NTC, WBC; HCSB, NASB, NRSV], 'by' [Lns], 'by how you use' [NET], 'from' [LN], 'with' [Arn; TEV], 'of' [KJV], not explicit [GW]. This relationship is also expressed by a verb: 'use' [AB; NIV, REB], '(I tell you) to use' [CEV], '(make friends) using' [NCV], 'use to benefit others' [NLT].
- b. μαμωνᾶς (LN **57.34**) (BAGD p. 490): 'wealth' [BAGD], 'riches' [LN]. The phrase τοῦ μαμωνᾶ τῆς ἀδικίας 'the wealth of unrighteousness' [NASB] is also translated 'the mammon of unrighteousness' [Lns, NTC, WBC; KJV], 'unrighteous mammon' [Arn, BECNT], 'the mammon of dishonesty' [AB], 'worldly wealth' [**LN**; NET, NIV, REB, TEV], 'worldly riches' [NCV], 'worldly resources' [NLT], 'wicked wealth' [CEV], 'dishonest wealth' [NRSV], 'unrighteous money' [HCSB]. The phrase 'by means of the wealth of unrighteousness' is translated 'although wealth is often used in dishonest ways, you should make use of it (to make friends)' [GW]. This noun is an Aramaic word and seems to mean 'that in which someone trusts' and it came to be a term for money or wealth [Arn, BECNT, MGC, NIGTC, WBC]. It has strong negative connotations [LN]. The noun can refer to wealth of any kind with either a good or bad sense, and the addition 'of unrighteousness' indicates that it is worldly wealth in contrast with heavenly treasure [NIGTC].
- c. aorist act. subj. of ἐκλείπω (LN **57.46**) (BAGD p. 242): 'to give out' [BAGD, **LN**], 'to fail' [LN]. The phrase 'it gives out' [AB, Lns; TEV] is also translated 'it runs out' [NET], 'it fails' [Arn, BECNT, WBC; HCSB, NASB], 'it is gone' [NTC; CEV, NIV, NRSV], 'are gone' [NCV], 'money is a thing of the past' [REB], '(when) life is over' [GW], 'ye fail' [KJV], not explicit [NLT].
- d. aorist mid. (deponent = act.) subj. of δέχομαι (LN 34.53) (BAGD 1. p. 177): 'to welcome' [LN, NTC; HCSB, NRSV], 'to receive' [Arn, BAGD, BECNT, Lns, WBC; KJV, NASB]. This active verb is also translated as a passive: 'to be welcomed' [AB; CEV, GW, NCV, NET, NIV, TEV], 'to be received' [REB]. This clause is translated 'your generosity stores up a reward for you' [NLT].
- e. σκηνή (LN 7.9) (BAGD p. 754): 'tent' [BAGD, LN], 'dwelling' [BAGD]. The phrase τὰς αἰωνίους σκηνάς 'the eternal tents' [Lns] is also translated 'the everlasting tents' [Arn], 'eternal dwellings' [BECNT, WBC; HCSB, NASB, NIV], 'the eternal homes' [NET, NRSV], 'the eternal home' [TEV], 'an eternal home' [CEV, GW, REB], 'everlasting

habitations' [NTC; KJV], 'dwellings that are everlasting' [AB], 'those homes that continue forever' [NCV], 'in heaven' [NLT].

QUESTION—What is signified by the initial 'And I say to you'?

Jesus now gives his application of the parable [Alf, Arn, EGT, Gdt, ICC, Lns, My, NIGTC, TG, TH, WBC]. This is a second application that follows the first one in 16:8b [AB, BECNT, Su]. Not only is prudence necessary, so is generosity [BECNT]. The parable referred to material possessions and now Jesus speaks of the right use of material things [NIC]. The master in the parable praised the steward for planning ahead, and Jesus tells his disciples to plan ahead [My]. The 'I' is emphatic and 'I say to you' balances what the master said to the steward in the parable [ICC, Su].

QUESTION—What is 'the wealth of unrighteousness'?

It is the wealth that is gained in a wicked and sinful world and it does not mean wealth that is gained by dishonest means [TG]. It seems to mean mammon or money that tends to lead to dishonesty rather than possessions that have been acquired dishonestly [AB, MGC]. It is the kind of wealth that that is often accumulated by unrighteous means and used in unrighteous ways [NIC, TH, TNTC]. Money that is commonly used for wrong purposes is to be used by the disciples in a proper and beneficial way [Arn]. It is called unrighteous because people who set out to attain wealth can become selfish and take advantage of others, and be unfaithful to God [BECNT]. It is unrighteous in that money circulates among sinful people and it is used in sinful ways for sinful purposes with the result that it has the quality of unrighteousness no matter who possesses it [Lns]. This worldly wealth is in contrast with heavenly treasure [NIGTC].

QUESTION—Who are the ones they are to make friends with?

1. The friends are needy people [Alf, Arn, BECNT, EGT, Gdt, ICC, MGC, NICNT, NIGTC, NIVS, NTC, Rb, TNTC, WBC]. This implies that the money is to be used for almsgiving and in other ways to help the poor [Arn, BECNT, MGC, NIGTC].
2. The friends are angels [My].
3. The friends are God and Christ [Lns]. What we do for others, we do for Christ and he is the one who will receive us into heaven [Lns].

QUESTION—What relationship is indicated by ἵνα 'in order that'?

It expresses the purpose the disciples are to have in making friends [NASB, NCV, NET, NIV, NRSV, REB, TEV]: make friends *so that* they may welcome you. Helping the needy not only is an act of kindness, it also promotes our own interests [Arn]. Or, it expresses Jesus' purpose in giving this advice [ICC, Rb].

QUESTION—How will the wealth give out?

It can mean when their wealth gives out, or when their wealth is no longer of any value, or when their wealth can do them no good [BECNT, TG], but whatever it refers to, it means that money does not last [BECNT]. It means there will be none left [AB, ICC, NIGTC, NTC]. It means when it is no longer of any use, which happens when we die [Arn, Crd, EGT, Lns, TNTC,

WBC; GW], or when the new age comes [Crd], or when Jesus returns to judge the world [Arn].

QUESTION—Who are the 'they' who will welcome them into heaven?
1. The needy friends they gain by means of their wealth will welcome them [Alf, Arn, Gdt, MGC, NIC, NIVS, NTC, Rb, WBC]. Those people that were helped while on earth and have since died will be welcoming the new arrivals in heaven [Alf, NTC]. The parable at 16:4 indicates that the people they have helped have become their friends and will testify that they showed themselves to be children of God [Arn].
2. The angels will welcome them [My]. As ministering spirits, their duties include welcoming the saved into the Messiah's kingdom [My].
3. Angels will welcome them, but the word 'angels' is used as a circumlocution for the name of God [NIGTC].
4. God and Christ will receive them into heaven [Lns]. They are the ones we make friends with and they alone can receive us into heaven [Lns].
5. God will welcome them [BECNT, Crd, NAC, NIC, TH, TNTC]. This is the common Jewish use of the plural to refer to God without mentioning his name [TH, TNTC]. Human friends cannot provide them with an eternal habitation [BECNT].
6. The ones who will welcome them are not intended to be specified [AB; CEV, GW, NCV, NET, NIV, REB, TEV]. This is an indefinite third person plural used as a substitute for the passive 'you will be welcomed' and there is no need to take this as the divine passive [AB].

QUESTION—What is meant by 'eternal tents'?

The eternal tents contrast with the uncertain and temporary houses the steward would be welcomed into in the parable [ICC]. Although a tent is usually a temporary shelter, it refers to something permanent and perhaps 'tent' is used as in the OT to refer to a place where the presence of God dwells [NIGTC]. The tents of Abraham and Isaac represent a glorified Canaan [Gdt]. These are the dwelling places in the age to come [TH]. The reference is to heaven [Lns, MGC, TG], or heavenly mansions [MGC].

DISCOURSE UNIT: 16:10–13 [NICNT, NIGTC, TNTC]. The topic is the rule of wealth [NICNT], faithful stewardship [NIGTC], God and mammon [TNTC].

16:10 The (one) (who is) faithful in little[a] also is faithful in much,[b] and the (one) (who is) unrighteous[c] in little also is unrighteous in much.[d]

LEXICON—a. ἐλάχιστος (LN 65.57) (BAGD 2.a. p. 248): 'very small, quite unimportant' [BAGD], 'of least importance, of very little importance' [LN]. The phrase 'is faithful in little' [BECNT] is also translated 'is faithful in very little' [Lns; HCSB, NET, NRSV], 'is faithful in a very little thing' [NASB], 'is faithful in what is very little' [Arn], 'is faithful in little things' [AB], 'is faithful in the smallest thing' [WBC], 'is faithful in small matters' [TEV], 'is faithful in that which is least' [KJV], 'you are faithful in small matters' [NLT], 'is trustworthy in a very small matter' [NTC], 'can be trusted with a little' [NCV], 'can be trusted with very

little' [GW, NIV], 'can be trusted in little matters' [CEV], 'can be trusted in small matters' [REB].
  b. πολύς (LN 59.11) (BAGD I.2.c.α. p. 688): 'much' [AB, Arn, BAGD, BECNT, LN, Lns; HCSB, KJV, NASB, NET, NIV, NRSV], 'a lot' [GW, NCV], 'something great' [WBC], 'important matters' [NTC; CEV], 'great matters' [REB], 'large matters' [NLT, TEV].
  c. ἄδικος (LN 88.20) (BAGD 1. p. 18): 'unrighteous' [LN], 'untrustworthy' [BAGD]. The phrase 'is unrighteous in little' is translated 'is unrighteous in very little' [Lns; HCSB], 'is unrighteous in a very little thing' [NASB], 'is unrighteous in the smallest thing' [WBC], 'is unjust in the least' [KJV], 'is untrustworthy in a very small matter' [NTC], 'is unfaithful in little' [BECNT], 'is dishonest with a little' [NCV], 'is dishonest with very little' [GW, NIV], 'is dishonest in a very little' [NET, NRSV], 'is dishonest in what is little' [Arn], 'is dishonest in little things' [AB], 'is dishonest in little/small matters' [CEV, REB, TEV], 'you cheat even a little' [NLT]. When a general comparison is made with the term 'faithful' the noun which is usually 'unrighteous' means 'unfaithful' [BECNT].
  d. πολύς (LN 59.11) (BAGD I.2.c.α. p. 688): 'much' [AB, Arn, BAGD, BECNT, LN, Lns; HCSB, KJV, NASB, NET, NIV, NRSV], 'a lot' [GW, NCV], 'important matters' [NTC; CEV], 'large matters' [TEV], 'something great' [WBC], 'great matters' [REB], 'greater responsibilities' [NLT].

QUESTION—How is this connected with the preceding verse?

The point of the preceding parables is explained in 16:10–18 [Rb]. This verse begins a section to modify the impression that Jesus had been praising a dishonest action [BNTC, EGT, NTC]. The steward had been dishonest in money matters, but the listeners are not to think that it does not matter whether or not they are honest in money matters [EGT]. Or, 16:10–11 has no connection at all with the preceding parable [WBC].

QUESTION—What is the person faithful about?

'Little' and 'much' refer to the things that are entrusted to us to administer [Lns]. This concerns being honest, trustworthy, and dependable in administering the things of the master [TG]. This is a quality needed by a steward [NAC]. It describes the dishonest steward's responsibilities [MGC]. The main application is still that of being a steward who manages the property of a master [TG]. It is clear from 16:11 that money is what the 'least thing' refers to [NICNT, WBC], but the 'much' is revealed in a more riddling way [WBC]. The least things concern acquiring and using worldly goods and the much refers to being responsible in matters connected with eternal and true riches [NIC, Pnt, Su]. This refers to things like handling money and a specific illustration of this follows in the next verse [BECNT]. This refers to small and large responsibilities [NIGTC]. It deals with the little things in life and the big things, with handling ordinary possessions and valuable goods [AB].

LUKE 16:10

QUESTION—What is meant by being unrighteous about little and much?
Here 'unrighteous' is the opposite of being faithful and means being unfaithful [BECNT, MGC, TH], untrustworthy [NTC, TH], and dishonest [AB, Arn, NIGTC, TH; CEV, GW, NCV, NET, NRSV, REB, TEV].

16:11 Therefore if you-were not faithful with unrighteous wealth, who will-entrust[a] the true[b] (riches) to-you?

LEXICON—a. fut. act. indic. of πιστεύω (LN 35.50) (BAGD 3. p. 662): 'to entrust' [Arn, BAGD, BECNT, LN, Lns, NTC, WBC; NASB, NET, NRSV], 'to put in the care of' [LN], 'to trust (you) with' [AB; CEV, GW, HCSB, NCV, NIV, NLT, REB], 'to commit to (your) trust' [KJV]. This active voice is also translated passively: 'to be trusted with' [TEV].
  b. ἀληθινός (LN 72.1) (BAGD 3. p. 37): 'true' [BAGD, LN]. The phrase τὸ ἀληθινὸν 'the true' is translated 'the true riches' [NTC; KJV, NASB, NCV, NET, NRSV], 'true riches' [BECNT; NCV, NIV], 'true wealth' [CEV, TEV], 'real wealth' [AB], 'wealth that is real' [GW], 'the wealth that is real' [REB], 'the true riches of heaven' [NLT], 'that which is of real value' [Arn], 'that which is of true value' [WBC], 'what is genuine' [HCSB], 'the genuine thing' [Lns].

QUESTION—What relationship is indicated by the initial οὖν 'therefore'
It indicates an inference or application of the general principle stated in 16:10 [Gdt, Lns, MGC, NIGTC, NTC, Su, TH]. The handling of money is a specific example of faithfulness [BECNT].

QUESTION—What is the unrighteous wealth the disciples are expected to be faithful with?
The 'unrighteous wealth' means 'worldly wealth', not wealth that has been dishonestly acquired [NIGTC]. It is a gift from God [NIC]. See the discussion in 16:9 where unrighteous wealth has the same meaning [ICC, NAC, TH; NET]. Being 'faithful' refers to being entrusted as stewards [NIGTC]. In the light of 16:9, this could refer to making friends with this wealth [My].

QUESTION—Who is the one who would not entrust them with the true riches?
There is no one who would entrust them with true wealth [TH], 'you cannot be trusted' [TG]. This implies that God would not entrust true riches to them [Arn, BECNT, NAC, NIGTC, WBC].

QUESTION—What are the true riches?
It is the opposite of money or wealth, and means that which is heavenly and spiritual [Arn], that which is of true value [WBC]. The true wealth is used metaphorically [TH] for spiritual wealth [EGT, MGC, Su, TG, TH], one's heavenly reward [NAC]. It refers to all of our spiritual and heavenly wealth [Lns]. This refers to the heavenly treasure in the age to come, that which is of a permanent quality [NIGTC]. It refers to the spiritual blessing of future service in God's kingdom [BECNT].

16:12 And if you-were not faithful with the (thing) belonging-to-another,ᵃ who will-give you the (thing) of-yours?ᵇ

TEXT—Instead of ὑμέτερον 'your', some manuscripts read ἡμέτερον 'our', others read ἐμόν 'my', and others read ἀληθινόν 'true'. GNT reads ὑμέτερον 'your' with an A decision, indicating that the text is certain.

LEXICON—a. ἀλλότριος (LN **92.20**) (BAGD 1.b.α. p. 40): 'belonging to another' [LN]. The phrase τῷ ἀλλοτρίῳ 'the belonging to another' is translated 'what belongs to another' [BAGD; NRSV, REB], 'what belongs to someone else' [**LN**; CEV, HCSB, TEV], 'things that belong to someone else' [NCV], 'that which is another's' [BECNT; NASB; similarly Lns; KJV], 'someone else's wealth' [GW], 'other people's money' [NLT], 'someone else's property' [NTC; NET, NIV], 'another's goods' [AB], 'in the sphere of what belongs to somebody else' [Arn], 'in the use of what belongs to another' [WBC].

b. ὑμέτερος (LN 92.9): 'your' [LN]. The phrase τὸ ὑμέτερον 'the yours' is translated 'that which is yours' [Arn], 'that which is your own' [BECNT; KJV, NASB], 'what is your own' [Lns, NTC; HCSB, NRSV], 'things of your own' [NCV], 'what belongs to you' [TEV], 'anything of your own' [REB], 'your own' [GW, NET], 'money of your own' [NLT], 'property of your own' [NIV], 'goods of your own' [AB], 'what is to be your own' [WBC], 'something that will be your own' [CEV].

QUESTION—What is meant by being faithful with the things belonging to another?

This suggests that the worldly wealth mentioned in 16:11 is equated with what belongs to another [NIGTC, NTC, TH]. Or, this broadens the scope of money to the affairs of another [BECNT]. Worldly riches do not really belong to us because we have them for a little while and then have to relinquish them [Arn]. It has been entrusted to us by God [NAC, NIC, NIGTC, Su, WBC].

QUESTION—What is meant by being given the things of yours?

This could refer to material things or to spiritual realities [MGC]. It is what God has given a person as inheritance [ICC, My, TH]. It is the treasure in heaven [Arn, My, NIGTC, WBC], it is the salvation of Messianic kingdom [My, NTC]. Spiritual treasures belong to the disciples because they are members of the household of God [Arn]. If you cannot take care of the things in this life that God has given, you cannot expect anything from God in the future life [BECNT, ICC].

16:13 No slaveᵃ is-able to-serveᵇ two masters, because either he-will-hateᶜ the one and he-will-loveᵈ the other, or he-will-be-devoted-toᵉ one and he-will-despiseᶠ the other. You-are- not -able to-serve God and wealth.

LEXICON—a. οἰκέτης (LN 46.5) (BAGD p. 557): 'slave' [BAGD; CEV, NRSV, REB], 'house slave' [BAGD], 'household slave' [HCSB], 'house servant' [LN, Lns], 'household servant, personal servant' [LN], 'servant' [AB, BECNT, NTC, WBC; GW, KJV, NASB, NCV, NET, NIV, TEV],

'no one' [Arn; NLT]. This means a household servant [Arn, TNTC] and it has reference to the dishonest steward of the household in the preceding parable [Arn].
- b. pres. act. infin. of δουλεύω (LN 35.27) (BAGD 2.a. p. 205): 'to serve' [AB, Arn, BAGD, BECNT, LN, NTC; all versions except CEV, HCSB, TEV], 'to be the slave of' [CEV, HCSB, TEV], 'to be slave to' [Lns], 'to give slave service to' [WBC]. This is not serving in general, but serving as a slave [TH].
- c. fut. act. indic. of μισέω (LN 88.198) (BAGD 1. p. 522): 'to hate' [AB, Arn, BAGD, BECNT, LN, Lns, NTC, WBC; all versions except CEV], 'to detest' [BAGD, LN]. The pair of *love and hate* is translated as showing degrees of love: 'you will like one more than the other' [CEV]. 'Hate' means to love less, as in 14:26 [Arn], to reject strongly [TH].
- d. fut. act. indic. of ἀγαπάω (LN **25.43**) (BAGD 1.a.α. p. 4): 'to love' [AB, Arn, BAGD, BECNT, **LN**, Lns, NTC, WBC; all versions except CEV], 'to regard with affection' [LN], 'to be grateful to' [BAGD], 'to like' [CEV]. This love is based on sincere appreciation and high regard [LN]. It means to prefer strongly [TH].
- e. fut. mid. indic. of ἀντέχομαι, ἀντέχω (LN 34.24) (BAGD 1. p. 73): 'to be devoted to' [AB, BAGD, BECNT, NTC, WBC; GW, HCSB, NASB, NET, NIV, NLT, NRSV, REB], 'to adhere to' [LN], 'to cling to' [Arn], 'to be loyal to' [CEV, TEV], 'to hold to' [Lns; KJV], 'to follow' [NCV].
- f. fut. act. indic. of καταφρονέω (LN 88.192) (BAGD 1. p. 420): 'to despise' [AB, Arn, BAGD, BECNT, LN, Lns, WBC; all versions except CEV, NCV], 'to scorn' [BAGD, LN], 'to look down on' [NTC], 'to refuse to follow' [NCV]. The pair of *being devoted and despising* is translated as showing degrees of devotion 'you will be more loyal to one than to the other' [CEV]. To 'despise' means to honor less [Arn].

QUESTION—How is this verse connected with the preceding one?

The person who was put in charge of unrighteous wealth must not serve it, but God [Alf]. This saying occurs in the Sermon on the Mount in Matthew 6:24. Some see this verse in Luke as an independent saying spoken at a different time than the preceding verse [EGT, TG]. Others see it as a natural conclusion to the preceding verse and think that the occurrence in Matthew is out of place [ICC]. Or, Jesus was repeating the words he spoke at the Sermon on the Mount and the saying fits in both places [NTC]. This gives the third application of the parable about the unjust steward in 16:1–8 [MGC, NIBC]. The steward in the preceding parable had two masters, the owner of the estate and the money he was worshipping [Gdt].

QUESTION—Why can't a slave serve two masters?

The force of the verb 'to serve as a slave' means that the slave is the absolute property of a master who has full unrestricted command over him and it is impossible to have two masters in this sense [Arn, MGC, Su]. At that time, a slave worked for only one master [ICC, TG]. Or, a slave might work for two men in partnership, but the point is that a slave cannot give to two masters the exclusive loyalty and service that is inherent in the practice of slavery [NIGTC]. It is psychologically impossible to give wholehearted devotion to two masters [NTC]. The slave cannot serve two masters at the same time with the same devotion [AB]. This assumes that a slave cannot serve two masters who have opposite views and wills [Su]. Proper service to one master will be less satisfactory than to the other master [WBC]. To be a servant to two masters is possible, but to be a slave at the absolute disposal of two different masters is impossible [ICC].

QUESTION—Why would a slave hate one master and love the other?

The conjunction γάρ 'because' shows the impossibility of serving two masters from the slave's viewpoint [Lns]. These two verbs deal with the emotions of the slave [AB, Arn]. To 'hate' means to reject strongly and to 'love' means to prefer strongly [TH].

QUESTION—How is being devoted to one and despising the other different from the previous contrast of hate and love?

This second contrast is less strong than the first contrast, and the conjunction 'or' may mean 'or if not actually hating and loving them, he will at least he will be devoted to one and despise the other' [Gdt, ICC, NIGTC]. Or, this contrast is as strong as the first contrast [TH]. These two verbs deal with evaluations made by the slave [AB, Arn]. Pairing the contrasting verbs is done for a rhetorical effect [BECNT; NET]. The words are practically synonymous with the first pair but are in reversed order according to the common Greek use of chiasm [NAC, TH, WBC].

QUESTION—What makes it impossible to serve both God and wealth?

Wealth is treated as an idolatrous threat to God [BECNT]. This is a moral impossibility because each claims the slave's undivided service [ICC, NIGTC]. Now that the two masters are identified, it is clear why it is impossible to serve them both [NICNT]. Wealth is personified [AB, BECNT, NICNT, Su]. Wealth represents the material things and God represents the spiritual [Su]. Wealth is represented as a power that may gain control of people [TH]. Because of collocation differences between serving God and serving wealth, it may be necessary to use different verbs each, or the order can be reversed to 'you cannot have both God and money as masters' [TG].

DISCOURSE UNIT: 16:14–31 [NICNT]. The topic is Jesus' polemic against the Pharisees, lovers of money.

DISCOURSE UNIT: 16:14–18 [BECNT, Su; CEV, HCSB, NET, NRSV, TEV]. The topic is some sayings of Jesus [CEV, TEV], the law and the kingdom of God [NRSV], kingdom values [HCSB], responses to the Pharisees' scoffing [BECNT], more warnings about the Pharisees [NET], a rebuke to the insincere [Su].

DISCOURSE UNIT: 16:14–17 [NCV]. The topic is God's law cannot be changed.

DISCOURSE UNIT: 16:14–15 [AB, NIGTC, TNTC, WBC]. The topic is the covetous Pharisees [TNTC], a reproof to the Pharisees [AB, NIGTC], lovers of money and seekers of honor [WBC].

16:14 And the Pharisees being lovers-of-wealth[a] were-hearing all these (things) and they-were-sneering-at[b] him.

LEXICON—a. φιλάργυρος (LN **25.108**) (BAGD p. 859): 'lover of wealth' [**LN**], 'lover of money' [Arn, BECNT, NTC, WBC; HCSB, NASB, NRSV], 'money-lover' [Lns]. This noun is also translated as an adjective: 'avaricious' [AB, BAGD], 'covetous' [KJV]. The phrase 'being lovers of wealth' is translated 'who loved money' [GW, NCV, NET, NIV, REB], 'who dearly loved their money' [NLT], 'really loved money' [CEV], 'because they loved money' [TEV]. This was their constant characteristic [ICC, TH]. It suggests that the reason for their ridiculing Jesus was that they loved money [TG, TH; TEV].

b. imperf. act. indic. of ἐκμυκτηρίζω (LN **33.409**) (BAGD p. 243): 'to sneer at' [AB, **LN**, NTC; NIV], 'to scoff at' [BECNT; HCSB, NASB, NLT, REB], 'to show contempt for' [LN], 'to ridicule' [BAGD, LN, WBC; NET, NRSV], 'to make fun of' [CEV, NCV, TEV], 'to mock' [Arn], 'to make sarcastic remarks about' [GW], 'to deride' [KJV], 'to turn up one's nose in derision' [Lns]. The imperfect tense indicates that they were sneering at Jesus while they were listening to him [TH]. Apparently no words were spoken, but their disdain was apparent in their faces [Lns, Rb]. Or, they spoke about Jesus among themselves [CEV, GW].

QUESTION—Why were the Pharisees ridiculing Jesus?

They loved money and scoffed at his statements about the danger of trying to love both God and money [Su]. They considered their wealth to be a proof that God had blessed them for their observance of the Law and they ridiculed Jesus, pointing out that he was just a poor teacher with poor disciples and because of that he was preaching against riches [ICC, NIC]. It was easy to speak of money with disdain when one lacks it as Jesus did [Gdt].

16:15 And he-said to-them, You are the (ones who) justify[a] yourselves before men, but God knows your hearts. Because the (thing) highly-esteemed[b] among men (is) an-abomination[c] before God.

LEXICO—a. pres. act. participle of δικαιόω (LN **88.16**) (BAGD 2. p. 197): 'to justify' [AB, Arn, BAGD, BECNT, Lns, NTC, WBC; GW, HCSB, KJV, NASB, NET, NIV, NRSV], 'to vindicate' [BAGD], 'to show to be right, to prove to be right' [LN], 'to make (yourselves) look good' [CEV, NCV], 'to make (yourselves) look right' [TEV], 'to like to look good' [NLT], 'to impress others with (your) righteousness' [REB].

b. ὑψηλός (LN **65.9**) (BAGD 2. p. 850): 'highly esteemed' [KJV, NASB], 'highly prized' [NET], 'highly valued' [NIV], 'highly regarded' [NTC], 'highly admired' [HCSB], 'considered of great value' [TEV], 'very valuable' [LN], 'exalted' [Arn, BAGD, BECNT, WBC], 'high' [Lns], 'important' [CEV, GW, NCV], 'prized' [NRSV], 'admirable' [REB]. The phrase 'the things highly esteemed among men' is translated 'what is of highest human value' [AB], 'what this world honors' [NLT].

c. βδέλυγμα (LN **25.187**) (BAGD 1. p. 137): 'an abomination' [AB, Arn, BECNT, Lns, WBC; KJV, NLT, NRSV], 'what is abhorrent' [LN], 'what is detestable' [BAGD, LN]. This noun is also translated as an adjective: 'abhorrent' [**LN**], 'worthless' [CEV], 'disgusting' [NTC; GW], 'detestable' [NASB, NIV, REB], 'utterly detestable' [NET], 'revolting' [HCSB], 'hateful' [NCV], 'worth nothing' [TEV].

QUESTION—In what respect were the Pharisees justifying themselves before men?

This was not a matter of self-justification by argument, it was their attitude of being only interested in the impression they make on others [WBC]. They attempted to justify themselves by their external behavior [NAC, NIGTC]. They endeavored to appear to very pious with their outward devotion to God and the Law [Su]. They gave alms to impress people [BECNT, Crd, My, NIC]. The Pharisees attempted to give an appearance of righteousness since their avaricious dealings brought about criticisms [Arn].

QUESTION—What relationship is indicated by ὅτι 'because' which begins the last sentence?

It is difficult to see the connection of 'because' [NIGTC]. Perhaps the consequence of God knowing their hearts is implicit: God knows your hearts *and judges you* because what you highly esteem he abhors [Gdt, NIGTC]. It indicates a reason for an implied step: 'God knows your hearts *and he sees your avaricious tendencies and your hollow pretensions to holiness, and he condemns them, because*, etc.' [Arn]. It explains the importance of the fact that God knew their hearts [Lns]. God knows their hearts *and he sees not as man sees, because* that which is highly esteemed among men, is an abomination before God [ICC]. It indicates the reason Jesus can make this complaint about them [BECNT].

DISCOURSE UNIT: 16:16–18 [WBC; NIV]. The topic is additional teachings [NIV], the demands of the law and the prophets, and those of the gospel of the kingdom of God [WBC].

DISCOURSE UNIT: 16:16–17 [AB, NIGTC, TNTC]. The topic is the law and the kingdom [NIGTC], the law and the prophets [TNTC], two sayings about the Law [AB].

16:16 The Law and the Prophets (were)[a] until John. Since then the kingdom of-God is-being-announced-as-good-news[b] and all forcibly-(enter)/are-forcibly-(urged-to-enter)/forcibly-(oppose)[c] into/towards it.

LEXICON—a. The implied verb is translated 'were' [BECNT; HCSB, KJV, REB], 'were in force' [GW, NET], 'were in effect' [NRSV, TEV], 'were proclaimed' [NTC; NASB, NIV], 'were preached' [NCV], 'were your guides' [NLT], 'extended to' [Arn], not explicit [Lns]. The phrase 'the Law and the Prophets were' is translated 'people had to obey the Law of

Moses and the Books of the Prophets' [CEV], 'there was only the law and the prophets' [WBC], '(up to John) was the law and the prophets' [AB]. It cannot mean that the Scriptures were in existence until John, since they continued to exist after the coming of John; therefore it means something like 'were in force', 'were valid', or 'had authority' [TG].

b. pres. pass. indic. of εὐαγγελίζω (LN 33.215) (BAGD 2.b.α. p. 317): 'to tell the good news, to announce the gospel' [LN], 'to preach' [BAGD]. The phrase 'the kingdom of God is being announced as good news' is translated 'the good news of the kingdom of God is announced' [WBC], 'the good news of the kingdom of God is proclaimed' [Arn; NRSV, REB], 'the good news of the kingdom of God has been proclaimed' [HCSB, NET], 'the good news of the kingdom of God is preached' [BECNT; NLT], 'the gospel of the kingdom of God is being preached' [NTC], 'the good news of the kingdom of God is being preached' [NIV], 'the kingdom of God is being preached as good news' [Lns], 'the Good News about the kingdom of God is being told' [NCV, TEV], 'people have been telling the Good News about the kingdom of God' [GW], 'the kingdom of God is preached' [KJV], 'the kingdom of God has been preached' [NASB], 'God's kingdom has been preached' [CEV], 'the kingdom of God is being preached;' [AB]. The present tense indicates that the preaching was still going on [AB, TH]. See this expression at 4:43, 8:1. The verb occurs at 1:19; 2:10; 3:18; 4:18, 43; 7:22; 8:1; 9:6, 20:1.

c. pres. mid./pass. indic. of βιάζομαι (LN 20.10) (BAGD 2.d. p. 140): 'to use violence' [LN], 'to enter with violence' [BAGD]. The basic sense is to apply force [BECNT]. This clause is translated in the middle voice as 'everyone is forcing his way into it' [NASB, NIV], 'everyone forces their way in' [TEV], 'everyone forces a way in' [REB], 'everyone is trying to force their way into it' [GW], 'everybody tries to force his way into it' [Arn], 'everyone tries to enter it by force' [NCV, NRSV], 'everyone is trying hard to get in' [CEV], 'every man presseth into it' [KJV], 'everybody is vigorously pressing forward into it' [NTC], 'everyone is energetically pressing into it' [Lns], 'eager multitudes are forcing their way in' [NLT], 'everyone takes vigorous steps to enter it' [WBC]. The phrase is translated in the passive voice as 'everyone is pressed to enter it' [AB], 'everyone is urged insistently into it' [BECNT], 'everyone is strongly urged to enter it' [HCSB], 'everyone is urged to enter it' [NET].

QUESTION—What are the Law and the Prophets?

The Hebrew Scriptures were divided into the Law (the Torah, the first five books of Moses) and the Prophets (the rest of the Scriptures) [Arn, TG]. The expression was used to refer to the whole Old Testament [ICC, Lns, MGC, NIBC, NTC, TH, TNTC]. It refers to the OT dispensation and may point to the time when only the books of the Law and the prophets existed [ICC]. It refers to OT preaching [AB]. It refers to the OT period or age, not the Scriptures, since the next verse indicates that the OT did not cease with the coming of the kingdom [NAC].

LUKE 16:16

QUESTION—What is meant by μέχρι Ἰωάννου 'until John'?
1. This means up to, but excluding John [Lns, MGC, My, NAC, NIC, NICNT, NIGTC, NTC, Su, TG, TH, WBC]. It means up to the time when John came but it does not include the ministry of John [TH]. John directed people to the Messiah who was actually present [NTC]. John began proclaiming the coming of the kingdom of God and Jesus and the disciples preached that the kingdom had come in the person of Jesus [NIC]. The ministry of John was the beginning of the preaching of the gospel [NIGTC, TG].
2. This means up to and including John [AB, Arn, BECNT, TNTC]. John was a transition figure in terms of his function as a pointer of the way in the old era [BECNT]. John belongs at the end of the old era [Arn, BECNT].

QUESTION—What is meant by the last clause?
1. The verb is in the middle voice, indicating that they act for themselves [Alf, BNTC, Crd, Gdt, ICC, Lns, My, NAC, NIC, NIGTC, NIVS, NTC, Rb, Su, TH, TNTC, WBC].
   1.1 This refers to those who accept the gospel and describes their intense desire to enter the kingdom [Alf, Crd, Gdt, LN, Lns, My, NAC, NIC, NIGTC, NTC, Rb, TH, TNTC, WBC]. In response to the preaching of the gospel, everyone tries hard to enter the kingdom [TH]. The picture is of a dense crowd of people pressing through the gate that is now open, and this has the sense of people hastening to enter it [Gdt]. This refers to the fierce eagerness with which people accepted the gospel [NIVS]. Seeing the value of entering the kingdom, people are ready to force their way into it in contrast with the Pharisees who did not want to enter [TNTC]. This indicates the need for vigorously pressing forward to enter the kingdom with earnest endeavor and self-denial and this echoes the command to strive to enter through the narrow door in 13:24 [NIC, NTC]. It involves the radical choice described in 16:13 [WBC]. The idea is of energy, not violence, and refers to the decisiveness brought about in those who accept the preaching of the kingdom [Lns]. 'Everyone' is used in the sense of 'anyone who wishes to enter must strive to do so' [NIGTC]. The word 'everyone' is restricted by its context and refers only to those who enter the kingdom [Lns], or those who want to embrace the good news [WBC].
   1.2 This refers to both those who accept the gospel and those who do not [Arn, ICC]. Everybody excitedly tries to get into the kingdom and receive its blessings. Some repent and enter the narrow gate, but others try to force their way in without repenting of their sins and have to remain outside [Arn].
   1.3 This refers to those who do not accept the gospel and unsuccessfully try to force their way into the kingdom by some other way than faith [Su]. They intended to force their way into the kingdom and would not accept Jesus' teaching about the kingdom, just as in the time of the Old

Testament such people had rejected God's way in preference to their own [Su].
1.4 A widely held view is that many people want to use violence and even military force to establish what they thought God's Kingdom on earth would be [LN (20.11)].
2. The verb is in the passive voice, indicating something that is done to all [AB, BECNT, NICNT; HCSB, NET]. All people did not enter the kingdom, so this must have the softened sense of the passive and mean that all people were urged to enter it [HCSB, NET]. All are warned and urgently invited to enter the kingdom [BECNT]. They are forced into the kingdom by a demanding and urgent invitation [AB].
3. This means all opponents treat the kingdom violently and oppress it [BNTC, MGC]. People such as the Pharisees tried to hinder the working of the kingdom [BNTC, MGC], and demons tried to hinder as well [MGC].

16:17 **But it-is easier[a] (for) the heaven and the earth to-pass-away[b] than (for) one stroke-of-a-letter[c] of-the Law to-drop[d] (out).**

LEXICON—a. εὔκοπος (LN 22.39) (BAGD p. 321): 'easier' [AB, Arn, BAGD, BECNT, LN, Lns, NTC, WBC; all versions except CEV, NLT]. The comparative construction is changed to an absolute statement: 'Heaven and earth will disappear before...' [CEV], 'It is stronger and more permanent than heaven and earth' [NLT].
  b. aorist act. infin. of παρέρχομαι (LN 13.93) (BAGD 1.b.α. p. 626): 'to pass away' [AB, Arn, BAGD, BECNT, LN, Lns, WBC; HCSB, NASB, NCV, NET, NRSV], 'to pass' [KJV], 'to cease to exist' [LN], 'to come to an end' [BAGD; REB], 'to disappear' [BAGD, NTC; CEV, GW, NIV, TEV], not explicit [NLT].
  c. κεραία (LN 33.37) (BAGD p. 428): 'stroke, part of a letter' [LN], 'horn, projection, serif' [BAGD]. The phrase 'one stroke of a letter' [AB; HCSB, NASB, NRSV] is also translated 'one tiny stroke of a letter' [NET], 'the tiniest hook on a letter' [NTC], 'the projecting part of one letter' [WBC], 'the smallest part of a letter' [NCV], 'one particle of a letter' [Lns], 'one tittle' [Arn; KJV], 'one jot' [BECNT], 'one letter' [REB], 'the smallest letter' [CEV], 'a comma' [GW], 'the least stroke of a pen' [NIV], 'the smallest point' [NLT], 'the smallest detail' [TEV].
  d. aorist act. infin. of πίπτω (LN 68.49) (BAGD 2.b.δ. p. 660): 'to drop out' [AB, WBC; HCSB, NIV], 'to drop (from)' [GW], 'to be dropped' [NRSV], 'to fall' [BECNT, Lns], 'to fail' [Arn, BAGD, LN; KJV, NASB], 'to become invalid, to come to an end' [BAGD], 'to become void' [NET], 'to be done away with' [TEV], 'to be changed' [NCV], 'to lose its force' [NTC; NLT, REB].

QUESTION—What relationship is indicated by δέ 'but'?
  It indicates a contrast [Arn, BECNT, Gdt, ICC, Lns, NIC, TH]. The contrast is between the end of the legal economy and the permanence of the law,

since Jesus abolished the law by fulfilling it [Gdt]. A new dispensation is entered, *but* God's revelation under the old covenant is not set aside since it remains absolutely authoritative in a moral and spiritual sense [NIC]. Or, It is an additional comment on the relation of the kingdom of God to the law [AB] The situation described in 16:16 does not imply that the law is no longer valid [TH]. The law cannot be flouted by the person who rushes to enter the kingdom [Arn]. Everything in the Law will be fulfilled [TG].

QUESTION—What is meant by τὸν οὐρανὸν 'heaven'?

'Heaven' means the sky [AB, MGC]. The phrase 'heaven and earth' refers to the whole created universe [AB, NAC, NIGTC].

QUESTION—How easy is it for heaven and earth to pass away?

This comparison speaks of the permanence of the Law and implies that heaven and earth are also permanent [NIGTC]. Or, heaven and earth will pass away some day (2 Pet. 3:12) [AB, NAC], because they are the sum of the material and corruptible creation [AB]. They seem eternal, but they will finally pass away (Matt. 5:18; Mark 13:31) [Su].

QUESTION—What is meant by 'one small stroke of a letter'?

It refers to the small additions to the Hebrew letters that distinguish one letter from another [AB, Arn, BECNT, Gdt, ICC, Lns, NAC, NIBC, NIC, NTC, Su, TG, TH, TNTC, WBC; NET]. It could refer to the scribal ornaments added to various letters in the Torah [BECNT, NIGTC]. This means that not one small part of a letter will drop out of the text [NET]. Or, this is a hyperbole, because only a statement can be fulfilled [NAC]. Here it means the most insignificant detail of the law and emphasizes the continuing validity of the law [MGC, NIGTC, Su, TNTC]. Nothing is insignificant in the Law [NIBC].

QUESTION—In what way will the Law be permanent?

'To drop out' means to become devoid of authority [ICC, NIC] and this says that the moral elements of the Law are indestructible when the gospel confirms them by giving them a new sanction [ICC, NTC]. The 'Law' is used in the same sense as 'the Law and the Prophets' in 16:16 and refers to the entire Old Testament [Lns, My]. This refers to the moral Law, not the ceremonial and civil laws, and it is binding on all people throughout all ages [Arn, NAC, NIC]. The ethical content of the Law is in focus as shown by the following verse [WBC]. Or, it means that the Law will be fulfilled to the minutest detail [Gdt, NIBC, TG, TNTC]. The ministry of Jesus fulfilled the Law [NIVS]. Or, the Law points to the kingdom and therefore it does not fail since it is transformed and fulfilled in Jesus [BECNT]. Every part of the Law will realize its purpose [Su]. The Law will reach its goal when the kingdom has come [NET].

DISCOURSE UNIT: 16:18 [AB, NIGTC, TNTC; NCV]. The topic is the law concerning divorce [AB, NIGTC, TNTC], divorce and remarriage [NCV].

16:18 Everyone divorcing his wife and marrying another commits-adultery,[a] and the (man) marrying (the woman) having-been-divorced by/from[b] (her) husband commits-adultery.

TEXT—Following the second καί 'and', some manuscripts add πᾶς 'everyone'. GNT does not deal with this variant. Πᾶς 'everyone' is probably read by KJV.

LEXICON—a. pres. act. infin. of μοιχεύω (LN 88.276) (BAGD 2.a. p. 526): 'to commit adultery' [AB, BAGD, BECNT, LN, Lns, NTC, WBC; all versions except CEV, NCV], 'to be guilty of adultery' [NCV]. This is also translated as an evaluation of the divorce: 'it is a terrible sin' [CEV]. This verb means more than engaging in forbidden sexual intercourse, it means to do anything that destroys the divine institution of marriage [Lns].

b. ἀπό (LN 90.7, 89.122): 'by' [Arn, LN (90.7)], 'from' [AB, BECNT, LN (89.122), Lns, NTC, WBC; HCSB, KJV, NASB, NET, NRSV, REB]. The phrase 'divorced by/from her husband' is translated 'divorced in this way' [GW], 'a divorced woman' [CEV, NCV, NIV, NLT, TEV].

QUESTION—How is this verse connected with the preceding one?

This has an entirely different topic and it is an isolated saying of divorce [AB]. Since this law about divorce is not found in the OT, it cannot be an example of the preceding verse [AB, TG, TH]. Most look for a connection. It is an example of the durability of the moral law [ICC, NIBC]. There is no obvious reason for inserting this statement here, but perhaps it is an example of the insincere way in which men treat the law [Su]. Perhaps this is an example of how the moral law continues in spite of human attempts to evade it by legalizing divorce [ICC, NTC]. It is an example of the immutability of the Law, picked perhaps because of the Pharisees' laxity about divorce [Arn]. This illustrates that the law continued to be valid, but in a new and more demanding form given it by Jesus [Gdt, NIGTC, WBC].

QUESTION—What makes remarriage after divorce adultery?

In spite of a divorce, the woman is still the wife of her first husband [Arn]. Remarriage is unfaithfulness to the original vows [BECNT].

QUESTION—How does this categorical statement against divorce harmonize with Matt. 5:32 and 19:9 where adultery on the part of the wife is a justified cause for divorce?

Here Jesus was stating the general principle without mentioning allowed exemptions [Arn, MGC]. Matthew and Paul took this statement as somewhat hyperbolic when they wrote about divorce [NAC].

QUESTION—Does the second clause indicate whether the woman was divorced by her husband or the woman obtained a divorce from her husband?

The preposition means 'having been divorced *from* her husband' and it does not indicate which one initiated the divorce [TH]. The possibility of a woman divorcing her husband is not regarded here [NAC]. It refers to the divorce described in the preceding clause [Arn; GW].

DISCOURSE UNIT: 16:19–31 [AB, BECNT, NAC, NIGTC, Su, TNTC, WBC; CEV, GW, HCSB, NASB, NCV, NET, NIV, NLT, NRSV, TEV]. The topic is the rich man and Lazarus [AB, BECNT, NAC, NIGTC, Su, TNTC; CEV, GW, HCSB, NASB, NCV, NET, NIV, NLT, NRSV, TEV], the outcome of life for the rich man and Lazarus [WBC].

16:19 And a-certain man was rich, and he-was-clothing-himself with-purple-cloth[a] and fine-linen, every day being-merry sumptuously.[b]

LEXICON—a. πορφύρα (LN 6.169) (BAGD p. 694): 'purple cloth' [BAGD, LN]. The phrase 'purple cloth and fine linen' is translated 'purple and fine linen' [AB, Arn, BECNT, Lns, NTC, WBC; HCSB, KJV, NASB, NET, NIV, NRSV], 'purple and the finest linen' [REB], 'the finest clothes' [NCV], 'expensive clothes' [CEV, GW], 'the most expensive clothes' [TEV]. The phrase 'he was clothing himself with purple cloth and linen' is translated 'was splendidly clothed' [NLT]. The purple cloth was dyed from a dye obtained from the purple shellfish murex [LN, NIGTC], which was found along the Phoenician coast [MGC].

b. λαμπρῶς (LN **88.255**) (BAGD 466): 'sumptuously' [BAGD], 'luxuriously, with ostentation, showing off' [LN]. The phrase 'being merry sumptuously' is translated 'making merry splendidly' [Lns], 'joyously living in splendor' [NASB], 'rejoiced in living luxuriously' [**LN**], 'made merry in a splendid manner' [WBC], 'enjoying himself in splendor' [Arn], 'lived in luxury' [NCV, NIV, NLT], 'lived in great luxury' [TEV], 'living in dazzling splendor' [NTC], 'ate sumptuously' [BECNT], 'feasted sumptuously' [AB; NET, NRSV, REB], 'feasting lavishly' [HCSB], 'fared sumptuously' [KJV], 'ate the best food' [CEV], '(every day) was like a party to him' [GW]. He enjoyed himself by eating sumptuously [NAC]. This refers to the feasts that rich men gave [NIGTC, TH]. He celebrated life with daily feasts as only a rich man could [BECNT].

QUESTION—How was the rich man dressed?

The imperfect tense of 'was clothing himself' implies that this was his habitual conduct [NIGTC, TH]. The purple cloth was a purple outer garment [Alf, Arn, BECNT, Crd, Gdt, Hlt, ICC, My, NTC, Rb, TG, TH, TNTC, WBC], an upper garment [TH], a long robe [Lns, NICNT], a mantle [NIGTC]. It was an expensive process to obtain purple dye from the shellfish and such a purple outer garment was often reserved for royalty [NTC]. The color purple was used by kings and nobles [Lns, MGC]. It would be a costly wool mantle, the kind a king would wear [Gdt, NIGTC]. Probably it was fine wool that was dyed with imported purple [AB]. The linen garment was an undergarment [AB, Alf, Arn, BECNT, Crd, Gdt, Hlt, ICC, My, NAC, NICNT, NTC, Rb, TG, TH, TNTC, WBC] a tunic next to the body [Lns]. Fine linen was a product from Egypt [AB, ICC, NAC].

16:20 And a-certain poor-man, Lazarus by-name, had-been-laid[a] at his gate,[b] being-covered-with-sores[c] **16:21** and desiring to-be-fed from the (things) falling[d] from the table of-the rich-man. But[e] also the dogs came (and) were-licking his sores.

TEXT—In 16:20, instead of πτωχὸς δέ τις ὀνόματι Λάζαρος ἐβέβλητο 'and a certain poor man, Lazarus by name, was laid', some manuscripts read πτωχὸς δέ τις ἦν ὀνόματι Λάζαρος ὃς ἐβέβλητο 'and there was a certain poor man, Lazarus by name, who was laid'. GNT does not deal with this variant. Πτωχὸς δέ τις ἦν ὀνόματι Λάζαρος ὃς ἐβέβλητο 'and there was a certain poor man, Lazarus by name, who was laid' is read by KJV.

TEXT—In 16:21, instead of τῷ πιπτόντων 'the things falling', some manuscripts read τῶν ψιχίων τῶν πιπτόντων 'the crumbs the ones falling' and some manuscripts read τῶν πιπτόντων ψιχίων 'the falling crumbs'. GNT reads τῷ πιπτόντων 'the things falling' with a B decision, indicating that the text is almost certain. Τῶν ψιχίων τῶν πιπτόντων 'the crumbs the ones falling' is read by KJV.

TEXT—In 16:21, following πλουσίου 'rich man', some manuscripts add καὶ οὐδεὶς ἐδίδου αὐτῷ 'and no one was giving to him'. GNT rejects this addition with an A decision, indicating that the text is certain.

LEXICON—a. pluperf. pass. indic. of βάλλω (LN 15.215, 85.34) (BAGD 1.b. p. 131): 'to be thrown' [BAGD, LN]. The pluperfect passive form of this verb could mean that he was thrown down [NICNT], 'was thrown at' the gate, that is, men just dropped him there [Lns]. But the verb has weakened meanings such as 'was laid at' [KJV, NASB, NCV, NET, NIV], 'had been laid at' [Arn, NTC], 'was brought to' [CEV], 'was left at' [HCSB], 'used to be brought to' [TEV], 'was regularly brought to' [GW], 'was positioned at' [WBC]. Or the passive absolute simply means that the man was lying before the door [BAGD, NIGTC]. The pluperfect indicates the result of being laid down, not the action [TH]: 'lay at' [BECNT; NLT, NRSV, REB], or 'squatted at' [AB]. The verb suggests that he was too ill to move [BECNT]. There is no roughness implied [ICC].

b. πυλών (LN 7.48) (BAGD 1. p. 729): 'gate' [Arn, BAGD, BECNT, LN, NTC, WBC; all versions except NLT, TEV], 'portal' [Lns], 'door' [AB, LN; NLT, TEV]. The gate would be a wide entrance opening into the large courtyard of the palace [Gdt, Lns]. It was a high and ornate gate of a mansion [BECNT], an impressive gateway [Arn].

c. perf. pass. participle of ἑλκόομαι, ἑλκόω (LN **23.180**) (BAGD p. 251): 'to be covered with sores' [AB, Arn, BAGD, **LN**, NTC; all versions except KJV], 'to be full of sores' [BECNT, LN; KJV], 'to have many sores' [LN], 'diseased' [NLT], 'to suffer from ulcers' [Lns], 'in an ulcerated condition' [WBC]. The medical cause of the sores is unknown, but it is clear that they caused a health problem that kept him from employment [WBC]. Probably these were surface ulcers or abscesses [BECNT]. Lazarus was covered with ulcerous boils in contrast with the rich man who was covered with purple and linen garments [Su].

d. pres. act. participle of πίπτω (LN 15.118) (BAGD 1.a. p. 659): 'to fall' [BAGD, LN]. The phrase 'the things falling' [Lns] is also translated 'the things which fell' [WBC], 'what fell' [Arn, BECNT; HCSB, NET, NIV, NRSV], 'the scraps that fell' [NTC; CEV, GW], 'scraps that dropped' [AB], 'scraps' [NLT, REB], 'the crumbs which fell' [KJV], 'the crumbs which were falling' [NASB], 'the bits of food that fell' [TEV], 'the small pieces of food that fell' [NCV]. This refers to the crumbs that fell from the table [Su]. Perhaps they were the pieces of bread which the guests used to wipe their hands and then threw under the table [BECNT, NICNT, NIGTC]. Or, it was the food that was thrown away after the meal [Lns, TH].

    e. ἀλλά (LN 89.125) (BAGD 3. p. 3): 'but' [BAGD, LN]. The phrase ἀλλὰ καί 'but also' is translated 'but instead' [WBC; HCSB], 'but even' [Arn], 'and' [CEV, GW, NCV], 'moreover' [BECNT; KJV], 'in addition' [NET], 'besides, even' [NASB], 'yes, even' [NTC], 'yea, even' [Lns], 'even' [NIV, NRSV, TEV], 'too' [AB], not explicit [NLT, REB]. This conjunction is not adversative, it merely adds a striking detail [Lns]. It adds another touch to the sorrow [TH], it was the culmination of his misery [NAC, TH].

QUESTION—Why was the poor man lying at the gate?

He was probably crippled and had been carried to the gate [BECNT, MGC]. Presumably Lazarus was begging near the outer gate, not at the actual door of the building [WBC]. Probably his desire for scraps from the table was not met [Arn, BECNT, NAC, NIC, NTC, WBC]. What little food he received was given him by others [Arn, NIC]. Or, since Lazarus remained there instead of seeking another location, perhaps scraps were thrown out into the street for scavenger dogs to eat and the servant boy who did this could have given some to Lazarus [Lns]. Perhaps he shared bits of meat with the dogs, yet it was not enough to satisfy his hunger [ICC]. He had been laid there, probably because he was unable to walk [Lns, NTC].

QUESTION—What is the significance of the dogs licking his sores?

    1. This was an undesirable situation [AB, Arn, BECNT, Crd, Gdt, Hlt, ICC, MGC, My, NAC, NICNT, NIGTC, NTC, TG, TH, TNTC, WBC; NET]. The misery endured by Lazarus is brought out by adding that he had to put up with these dogs [TH]. Instead of being fed, even the dogs came to add to his misery [My]. 'But also' has the sense of 'and worse of all' the dogs aggravated his sores by licking them [NIGTC]. Street dogs licking the sores would be degrading, and would prevent the sores from healing [Hlt]. These were big, unclean pariah dogs from the streets [NTC]. The wild dogs were ceremonially unclean and since Lazarus could not avoid them, he was rendered unclean himself [BECNT]. He was too weak to avoid the dogs [Arn, ICC]. Or, the dogs belonged to the house and after they had eaten scraps from the table, they came out to lick the sores [WBC].

    2. This was a desirable situation [Lns, Su]. The dogs were his only friends as they licked his sores to clean them and ease the pain [Lns]. The dogs

licked his sores as they would their own and thus showed more concern for the poor man than the rich man had [Su].

16:22 And it-happened the poor-man died and he was-carried-away[a] by the angels to Abraham's bosom.[b] And also the rich-man died and he-was-buried.

LEXICON—a. aorist pass. infin. of ἀποφέρω (LN 15.202) (BAGD 1.a.α. p. 101): 'to be carried away' [AB, Arn, BAGD, LN, NTC, WBC; HCSB, NASB, NRSV, REB], 'to be carried' [KJV, NET, NLT, TEV], 'to be taken up' [BECNT], 'to be taken away' [BAGD, LN], 'to be borne away' [Lns]. The passive is also translated actively with the angels as the subject: 'to carry' [GW, NCV, NIV], 'to take' [CEV].

b. κόλπος (LN 1.16) (BAGD 1. p. 442): 'bosom' [BAGD, LN]. The noun indicates the region of a body from the breast to the legs [LN]. The phrases '(22) to Abraham's bosom…(23) and Lazarus in his bosoms' is translated 'into/to Abraham's bosom…and/with Lazarus in his bosom' [BECNT; KJV, NASB], 'into Abraham's bosom…and Lazarus at his bosom' [BECNT], 'to the bosom of Abraham…and Lazarus in his bosom' [BECNT, Lns, WBC], 'to the arms of Abraham…with Lazarus at his side' [NCV], 'to Abraham's side…with Lazarus at/by his side' [HCSB, NET, NIV], 'to be with Abraham…with Lazarus by his side' [NRSV], 'to be with Abraham…with Lazarus close beside him' [REB], 'to be with Abraham…and Lazarus' [GW], 'to be with Abraham…Lazarus with Abraham' [NLT], 'to sit beside Abraham at the feast in heaven…with Lazarus at his side' [TEV], 'to the place of honor next to Abraham…and Lazarus at his side' [CEV]. The second reference to bosom in 16:23 is in the plural, but with no change of meaning from the singular form in 16:22 [WBC]. Or, the plural κόλποις 'bosoms' at 16:23 could mean 'in the folds of Abraham's garment' [Arn].

QUESTION—What did the angels carry away?

They carried away Lazarus' soul after death [AB, Alf, Arn, Crd, Gdt, ICC, Lns, NTC, Rb, TH; NLT], not his body [TH]. The story does not mention that his body was buried, but assumes that it was [Arn]. That he died implies that his soul separated from his body [ICC]. Perhaps the burial was so obscure and dismal that it was best not to mention it [Lns, NTC]. He was left unburied [AB]. Or, since this is a parable, the whole man, body and soul, was carried away [EGT, My]. Or, it is possible that this does not refer to the normal fate of the righteous, but to Lazarus' translation to heaven like Enoch and Elijah [Hlt, WBC] and the fact that the angels carried him to heaven implies his bodily ascension into heaven [Hlt].

QUESTION—What is meant by 'Abraham's bosom'?

Although the phrase is not a synonym for Paradise, this is where Abraham was thought to be [BECNT, ICC, My, NIGTC]. The phrase means 'heaven' [LN (1.16), Lns, Rb]. Abraham's bosom is a Jewish idiom meaning the presence of God [Pnt].

1. This is a metaphor suggested by a child lying in its parent's bosom or lap [Crd, Lns, NIC, NIGTC]. This is a picture of a child being laid on Abraham's bosom and being embraced by him, and it is a metaphor for being in heaven where Abraham is and also being in intimate association with the father of believers [Lns].
2. The metaphor suggests the position of a guest reclining next to the host at a banquet [Arn, Gdt, MGC, NIGTC, NTC, TG, TH, TNTC; CEV, NET, TEV]. The picture is of a feast in which the favored person reclines with his head on Abraham's bosom [NTC, TNTC]. The context of the rich man feasting and Lazarus starving before they died favors this interpretation [MGC, TNTC].
3. This perhaps combines both of the above so that this pictures the poor man enjoying close fellowship with Abraham at the messianic banquet [NIGTC, WBC].

16:23 And in Hades[a] being in torments,[b] having-lifted-up[c] his eyes he-sees from far-away[d] Abraham and Lazarus in his bosoms.

TEXT—Some manuscripts omit the first word in this verse, καί 'and'. GNT reads καί 'and' with an A decision, indicating that the text is certain.

LEXICON—a. ᾅδης (LN 1.19) (BAGD 1. p. 17): 'Hades' [Arn, BAGD, BECNT, LN, Lns, WBC; HCSB, NASB, NRSV, REB, TEV], 'the underworld' [BAGD], 'the world of the dead' [LN], 'the place of the dead' [NCV, NLT], 'death's abode' [AB], 'hell' [CEV, GW, KJV, NET, NIV]. See this word at 10:15.

b. βάσανος (LN 24.90) (BAGD 1. p. 134): 'torment' [BAGD, LN], 'severe pain, severe suffering' [LN]. The phrase 'being in torments' [Lns; KJV] is also translated 'being in torment' [Arn, BECNT, WBC; HCSB, NASB], 'as he was in torment' [NET], 'was tormented' [AB], 'where he was in torment' [NIV, REB], 'where he was being tormented' [NRSV], 'in torment' [NLT], 'he was in much pain' [NCV], 'where he was in great pain' [TEV], 'he was suffering terribly' [CEV], 'he was constantly tortured' [GW]. In 16:24 it says that he was suffering in a flame and the picture of hell as a place of fire is stated throughout Scripture [NTC]. Or, the suffering was more mental than physical, an anguish brought on by realizing that he would eternally be separated from righteous people and from God [Arn, BECNT].

c. aorist act. participle of ἐπαίρω (LN 24.34) (BAGD 1. p. 281): 'to lift up' [BAGD, LN]. The phrase 'having lifted up his eyes' is translated 'he lifted up his eyes' [BECNT, Lns; KJV, NASB], 'he lifts up his eyes' [Arn], 'he raised his eyes' [WBC], 'he looked up' [AB; CEV, GW, HCSB, NET, NIV, NRSV, REB, TEV], not explicit [NCV, NLT]. The picture seems to have Lazarus positioned in a place above the rich man [WBC]. Ancient people thought Hades was deep in the earth and Paradise was high above the earth [TG]. However, the statement that the rich man 'lifted up his eyes' was a stereotyped expression and need not indicate that Abraham was located above him [NIGTC].

d. μακρόθεν (LN 83.30) (BAGD p. 488): 'far away' [BAGD, LN; NASB, NCV, NIV, NRSV, REB, TEV], 'far off' [CEV, NET], 'afar off' [KJV], 'from afar' [Arn, BECNT, Lns, WBC], 'a long way off' [HCSB], 'in the distance' [GW], 'in the far distance' [NLT], 'at a distance' [AB], 'from a distance' [BAGD]. Abraham was far away, yet within hearing distance [EGT, TH].

QUESTION—Where are the places of Hades and Abraham's bosom?
1. Hades is the intermediate abode of the dead, so that both the rich man and Lazarus are in Hades, but in different sections of it [AB, Alf, Arn, Gdt, ICC, My, NICNT, NIGTC, Rb, WBC]. Hades is the place where all those who have died go until the time of the final judgment [ICC, NIGTC, WBC]. The rich man is said to be in Hades, but Abraham is considered to be there also [Alf, NIGTC]. Hades includes both Gehenna and Paradise [Alf, Arn, Gdt, ICC]. Torment is a feature of the intermediate state as well as the final state in hell [NIGTC].
2. Hades means hell in the parable, the place of torment, and Abraham was not in Hades but in Paradise [BNTC, EGT, Hlt, Lns, NTC, Su, TG, TNTC; CEV, GW, KJV, NET, NIV]. Hades is the final abode of the lost [Su]. Hades is hell and Paradise is heaven and there are no intermediate places [Lns]. This noun is used for the Hebrew word *Sheol* and it is practically equivalent to hell [TG].

QUESTION—How could the rich man see Lazarus?
The details are not to be taken literally [Arn, BECNT, EGT, ICC, Lns, NAC, NIGTC]. Lifting his eyes, seeing people far away, the mention of a finger and tongue cannot be taken literally since we are told that the rich man's body had been buried [NTC]. The story requires that communication by shouting be possible [NIGTC]. The rich man and Lazarus and Abraham are seen in bodily terms since this is the only way they can be visualized and these details are not be to be taken literally [Lns, NIGTC].

16:24 And calling he said, Father[a] Abraham, have-mercy[b] on-me and send Lazarus in-order-that he-may-dip the tip of-his finger (in) water and may-cool my tongue, because I-am-suffering[c] in this flame.

LEXICON—a. πατήρ (LN 10.20) (BAGD 1.b. p. 635): 'father' [AB, Arn, BAGD, BECNT, Lns, NTC, WBC; all versions except CEV, REB], 'my father' [REB], 'ancestor, forefather' [LN], not explicit [CEV]. This is an honorary title or a form of respectful address [BAGD]. Being a Jew, the rich man is speaking to the father of his race [AB, NAC, NIBC, Su, TG]. This may indicate the basis on which he feels he can make his plea [Hlt, WBC].

b. aorist act. impera. of ἐλεάω (LN 88.76) (BAGD p. 249): 'to have mercy' [AB, BAGD, BECNT, LN, Lns, WBC; GW, HCSB, KJV, NASB, NCV, NET, NRSV], 'to be merciful' [BAGD, LN], 'to show mercy' [BAGD,

LN], 'to have pity' [CEV, NIV], 'to have some pity' [NLT], 'to take pity' [NTC; REB, TEV], 'to show pity' [Arn]. The use of the aorist tense points to a specific act of mercy which the rich man spells out [TH]. He is asking for gracious help in his time of helplessness [NIGTC]. See this word at 17:13; 18:38.

c. pres. pass. indic. of ὀδυνάομαι, ὀδυνάω (LN **24.92**) (BAGD 1. p. 555): 'to suffer' [GW, NCV], 'to suffer terribly' [**LN**; CEV], 'to be in pain' [WBC], 'to be in great pain' [AB, LN; TEV], 'to be in agony' [NTC; HCSB, NASB, NIV, NRSV, REB], 'to be in anguish' [BECNT; NET, NLT], 'to be anguished' [Lns], 'to suffer torment' [BAGD], 'to be tormented' [Arn; KJV].

QUESTION—How could the rich man speak with Abraham?

Since the rich man's soul is in torment and not his body, this account is a picture of the rich man's terrible situation [Arn]. In reality, the damned cannot see or speak with the blessed in heaven and the conversation is put in the parable to teach the hearers what Abraham could answer every unbeliever in hell [Lns].

QUESTION—What did the rich man think would happen if Abraham showed him mercy?

Even though the flames could not be put out, he was suffering so terribly that even the smallest alleviation would be welcome [Arn, EGT, ICC]. The water would have been on Abraham's side of the chasm, so Lazarus would have to dip his finger in water before he came over to where the rich man was [TH].

16:25 And Abraham said, Child,ᵃ remember that you-received your good (things) during your life, and likewise Lazarus (received) the bad (things). But now he-is-comfortedᵇ here, and you are-suffering.

LEXICON—a. τέκνον (LN 10.28) (BAGD 1.b. p. 808): 'child' [Arn, BAGD, Lns, WBC; GW, NASB, NCV, NET, NRSV], 'descendant' [LN], 'my child' [AB; REB], 'son' [BECNT, NTC; HCSB, KJV, NIV, NLT], 'my son' [TEV], 'my friend' [CEV].

b. pres. pass. indic. of παρακαλέω (LN 25.150) (BAGD 4. p. 617): 'to be comforted' [AB, Arn, BAGD, BECNT, Lns, NTC; HCSB, KJV, NASB, NCV, NET, NIV, NLT, NRSV], 'to be consoled' [LN, WBC]. God is the one who comforts him [AB, NAC]. The passive voice is also translated actively with Lazarus as the subject: 'to have consolation' [REB], 'to have peace' [GW], 'to be happy' [CEV], 'to enjoy himself' [TEV]. This refers to the mental comfort Lazarus received in his new situation [BECNT].

QUESTION—Why did Abraham call the rich man his child?

Abraham acknowledged the racial relationship claimed by the rich man who had called him, 'Father' [ICC, NAC, NTC, TG, TH, TNTC, WBC]. This is a gentle refusal [EGT, ICC]. This makes the reply tender, in spite of being firm [BECNT, TNTC].

16:26 And in (addition to) all these (things) a-great chasm[a] has-been-fixed[b] between us and you, so-that the (ones who) want to-come-over from (here) to you are- not -able, neither from-there to us may-they-cross-over.

LEXICON—a. χάσμα (LN 1.54) (BAGD p. 879): 'chasm' [BAGD, LN]. The phrase 'a great chasm' [AB, Arn, Lns, WBC; HCSB, NASB, NET, NIV, NLT, NRSV] is also translated 'a vast chasm' [NTC], 'a great gulf' [KJV, REB], 'a big pit' [NCV], 'a deep pit' [TEV], 'a deep ditch' [CEV], 'a wide area' [GW]. It is a deep and impassible valley or space between two points [LN]. It is a yawning gorge [NTC]. Here it is unbridgeable gulf between the place of bliss and the place of torment [AB, BECNT, NIBC].
- b. perf. pass. indic. of στηρίζω (LN **85.38**) (BAGD 1. p. 768): 'to be fixed' [AB, Arn, BAGD, **LN**, Lns, NTC, WBC; HCSB, KJV, NASB, NET, NIV, NRSV, REB], 'to be established' [BAGD, LN]. The passive voice is also translated actively: 'there is' [CEV, NCV], 'is lying' [TEV], 'is separating' [NLT], 'separates' [GW]. The perfect tense indicates that this is a permanent situation [ICC, Lns, TH]. The passive voice implies that God has fixed the chasm [AB, BECNT, Gdt, Hlt, MGC, NAC, WBC].

QUESTION—What things are referred to in the phrase 'in addition to all these things'?

These are the things described in 16:25 [Lns]. These things are the moral aspects described in 16:25 [TH], what has been done according to God's justice [NAC]. Verse 16:25 shows that on equitable grounds, alleviation of the rich man's sufferings is not possible [ICC]. It is retributive justice [NIGTC]. If the rich man wanted to argue that the principle of equity had been carried too far, 16:26 is an additional reason to show that it impossible to change things [EGT].

QUESTION—What relationship is indicated by ὅπως 'in order that'?

It indicates the purpose God had in fixing the chasm between the two locations [Alf, Arn, EGT, ICC, Lns, NAC, NTC, TH]. It is practically the same as result [NIGTC].

16:27 And he-said, Then[a] I-ask you, father, that you-send him to the house of my father, **16:28** because[b] I-have five brothers, in-order-that[c] he-may-warn them, in-order-that[d] they not also come to this place of-torment.[e]

LEXICON—a. οὖν (LN 89.50): 'then' [AB, Arn, LN, Lns, NTC, WBC; all versions except KJV, NLT], 'therefore' [LN; KJV], not explicit [BECNT; NLT]. It has the meaning 'in that case' [TH]. Since his former request cannot be granted, he makes this request concerning his brothers [BECNT, EGT, Lns, NIGTC, WBC].
- b. γάρ (LN 89.23): 'because' [LN; HCSB], 'for' [Arn, BECNT, LN, Lns, NTC, WBC; KJV, NASB, NET, NIV, NLT, NRSV], not explicit [AB; CEV, GW, NCV, REB, TEV].
- c. ὅπως (LN 89.59): 'in order that' [LN, Lns; NASB], 'so that' [BECNT, LN], 'that' [AB, Arn, WBC; KJV, NRSV], 'to' [NET], not explicit [NTC; CEV, GW, NCV, NIV, REB, TEV]. This conjunction is also translated as

a verb phrase: 'and I want him to' [NLT]. This gives the purpose for sending Lazarus [My, NIGTC, TH].

d. ἵνα (LN 89.59): 'in order that' [Arn, LN], 'so that' [WBC; GW, NASB, NCV, NET, NIV, NRSV, REB, TEV], 'to' [HCSB]. The phrase 'in order that not' is translated 'lest' [AB, BECNT, Lns, NTC; KJV], 'so (they) won't' [CEV, NLT].

e. βάσανος (LN 24.90) (BAGD 1. p. 134): 'torment'. See translations of this word at 16:23.

QUESTION—How did the rich man think Lazarus could be sent to his five brothers?

Perhaps he thought that Lazarus could appear to the five brothers in a vision or a dream [AB, BECNT, MGC], but he didn't think Lazarus would be resurrected in order to go to them [BECNT]. Or, Lazarus would rise from the dead to go to them [TEV].

QUESTION—Was the rich man's father still alive?

This does not assume that his father was still alive, but it indicates that the five brothers still lived together in their father's house [TG]. He does not speak about warning his father, so probably the father had died and the five brothers lived together because they had decided not to divide their shares of the inheritance [NIGTC].

QUESTION—What relationship is indicated by γάρ 'because' in the clause 'because I have five brothers'?

It explains why Lazarus should be sent to the rich man's father's house [TH]. This is a parenthetical clause [NIGTC, TH]. The clause is enclosed in dashes [Lns; NASB, NRSV], in parentheses [NET], or it is treated as a separate sentence [GW].

QUESTION—What did the rich man want Lazarus to warn his brothers about?

They must be warned of what awaits them [TNTC]. It is implied that the brothers led the same kind of life he had and would share his fate if they did not repent [Hlt, Su]. He knew that his brothers needed to repent and needed to be warned that the way he had lived had ended in disaster [BECNT]. He wanted to warn them that there was life after death and there will be retribution for sinful conduct [AB]. The brothers needed to have someone from the dead warn them that their present way of life would bring them into torment and they needed to change their ways so they wouldn't end up where the rich man was [NIGTC, TG]. The brothers must be warned to repent [NAC, NIC] and do good deeds such as using their wealth to help people like Lazarus [NAC]. Perhaps the rich man thought that only a warning from someone who had died and had found out about the fact of eternal punishment could save them from such a fate [BECNT].

QUESTION—What is the relationship of ἵνα 'in order that' in the clause 'in order that they not also come to this place of torment'?

This indicates the purpose of the warning [NAC, NIC]. The rich man thought such a warning would keep them from coming to the place where he ended up [NIGTC, TH]. The rich man thought that if God had properly warned him, he would have escaped the place of torment and he implied that he hadn't had a fair chance [ICC, TNTC].

16:29 And Abraham says, They-have^a Moses and the Prophets. Let-them-listen^b to-them. 16:30 But he-said, No,^c father Abraham, but if someone from (the) dead^d should-go to them they-will-repent.^e

LEXICON—a. pres. act. indic. of ἔχω (LN 57.1) (BAGD I.2.d. p. 332): 'to have' [AB, Arn, BAGD, BECNT, LN, Lns, NTC, WBC; GW, HCSB, KJV, NASB, NET, NIV, NRSV, REB], 'to have at one's disposal' [BAGD]. The phrase 'they have Moses and the prophets' is translated 'they have the law of Moses and the writings of the prophets' [NCV], 'your brothers can read what Moses and the prophets wrote' [CEV], 'your brothers have Moses and the prophets to warn them' [TEV], 'Moses and the prophets have warned them' [NLT].

b. aorist act. impera. of ἀκούω (LN 24.52, 36.14) (BAGD 4. p. 32): 'to listen' [AB, BAGD, BECNT, NTC, WBC; GW, HCSB, NIV, NRSV, REB, TEV], 'to hear' [Arn, LN (24.52), Lns; KJV, NASB], 'to pay attention to and obey' [LN (36.14)], 'to pay attention to' [CEV], 'to learn from' [NCV], 'to respond to' [NET]. The clause is translated 'your brothers can read their writings anytime they want to' [NLT].

c. οὐχί (LN 64.2) (BAGD 2. p. 598): 'no' [AB, Arn, BAGD, BECNT, LN, NTC, WBC; all versions except CEV, KJV, TEV], 'nay' [KJV], 'no, that's not enough' [CEV], 'that is not enough' [TEV], 'no, on the contrary' [Lns].

d. νεκρός (LN 23.121) (BAGD 2.a. p. 535): 'dead' [BAGD, LN]. The phrase 'from the dead' [Arn, BECNT, Lns, NTC, WBC; CEV, HCSB, KJV, NASB, NCV, NET, NIV, NRSV] is also translated 'comes back from the dead' [GW], 'will come back from the dead' [AB], 'is sent to them from the dead' [NLT], 'someone from the dead visits them' [REB], 'were to rise from death and go to them' [TEV].

e. fut. act. indic. of μετανοέω (LN 41.52) (BGD p. 512): 'to repent' [Arn, BAGD, BECNT, LN, Lns, WBC; HCSB, KJV, NASB, NET, NIV, NRSV, REB], 'to turn from their sins' [NLT], 'to be converted' [NTC], 'to listen and turn to God' [CEV], 'to reform their lives' [AB], 'to believe and change their hearts and lives' [NCV], 'to turn to God and change the way they think and act' [GW].

QUESTION—In what sense did they have Moses and the prophets?
They had the writings of Moses and the writings of the prophets [Arn, TNTC; NLT], or their teachings [GW]. Moses wrote the Pentateuch and in a broad sense of the term, the prophets wrote all the other books of the OT [Arn, Lns]. This means the Law and the Prophets, that is, the whole OT [Alf, EGT, Hlt, NAC, NIVS, Su, TNTC]. They had the writings in the sense that the passages from the writings of Moses and the prophets were read and explained in the synagogue [TH]. They could have it read to them [TG].

QUESTION—In what sense were they to listen to the writings of Moses and the prophets?

'Listen' especially refers to listening to the Scriptures that were regularly read and explained in the synagogue [NIGTC, TG, TH]. 'To listen' means to obey the writings [BECNT, TH], to respond to them [BECNT], to heed them [NAC]. They were to hear so as to receive the message in their hearts [Lns]. They were to listen and also obey what they heard [TH]. The Scriptures had sufficient instructions so they could learn about the way should live in relation to God and people [Su]. The Law and the prophets told of God's requirements for fellowship with him, and told how people were acceptable to him [Pnt].

QUESTION—Why did the rich man say 'No' to Abraham?

He disagreed with Abraham and meant 'no, they would not listen to Moses and the prophets' [My, TH], 'they will not believe or be persuaded' [Alf], 'no, that is not enough' [EGT, ICC, NIGTC; CEV]. From his personal experience he knew that his brothers would not take the Scriptures any more seriously than he had done and something more was needed [Arn, BECNT, EGT, ICC, MGC, NIGTC, TNTC].

16:31 And he-said to-him, If they-do- not -listen-to Moses and the Prophets, neither will-they-be-persuaded[a] if someone should-come-back-to-life[b] from (the) dead.

LEXICON—a. fut. pass. indic. of πείθω (LN 33.301) (BAGD3.a. p. 639): 'to be persuaded' [Arn, BAGD, LN, Lns, WBC; GW, HCSB, KJV, NASB], 'to be convinced' [AB, BAGD, LN, NTC; NET, NIV, NRSV, TEV], 'to believe' [BECNT], 'to listen to' [CEV, NCV, NLT], 'to pay heed' [REB].

b. aorist act. subj. of ἀνίσταμαι (LN 23.93): 'to come back to life, to live again, to be resurrected' [LN]. The phrase 'to come back to life from the dead' is translated 'to come back from the dead' [CEV, NCV], 'to rise from the dead' [AB, Arn, BECNT, NTC, WBC; HCSB, KJV, NASB, NET, NIV, NLT, NRSV, REB], 'to rise up from the dead' [Lns], 'to rise from death' [TEV], 'to come back to life' [GW].

QUESTION—What would they not be persuaded to do?

They would not be persuaded to repent [EGT, ICC, My, NAC, TG]. They would not be persuaded of the truth of the Good News [Arn]. They would not be persuaded that someone had really risen from the dead [Lns]. The verb implies conversion and salvation [NIBC].

QUESTION—What is the significance of ignoring the request to send Lazarus and instead making a general statement of the possibility of someone being resurrected?

Even a far mightier miracle than the rich man asked would be ineffectual [EGT, ICC]. The resurrection of another Lazarus later did not persuade the unbelieving Jews [Alf, Arn, NAC, TNTC]. The rich man had asked for a mere visit from Lazarus to warn his brothers, and now Abraham spoke of someone coming back to life [BECNT]. This probably alludes to Jesus' later resurrection [BECNT, Hlt, MGC, NAC, NIC, Su, TNTC; NET].

QUESTION—Why wouldn't people be persuaded by the miracle of someone being raised from death?

For people who had already hardened themselves against God's message in the OT, even the resurrection of a person would not make an impact on their hearts [NIGTC, NTC, Su, WBC]. Their wills prevent them from believing the empirical evidence [BECNT].

DISCOURSE UNIT: 17:1–19 [WBC]. The topic is a fitting response to the demands and working of the kingdom of God.

DISCOURSE UNIT: 17:1–10 [BECNT, NAC, NICNT, NIGTC, TNTC; CEV, NASB, NET, NIV, NLT, NRSV]. The topic is instructions [NASB], some sayings of Jesus [NRSV], teachings addressed to the disciples [NAC, NIGTC], teachings about forgiveness and faith [NLT], faith and service [CEV], faithful service [NICNT], teaching about service [TNTC], false teaching, forgiveness, and service [BECNT], sin, faith, duty [NIV], sin, forgiveness, faith, and service [NET].

DISCOURSE UNIT: 17:1–6 [WBC]. The topic is dealing with sin in the disciple community.

DISCOURSE UNIT: 17:1–4 [Su, TNTC; GW, HCSB, TEV]. The topic is sin [TEV], warnings from Jesus [HCSB], forgiving others [TNTC], offending and forgiving [Su], causing others to lose faith [GW].

DISCOURSE UNIT: 17:1–3a [AB]. The topic is a warning against stumbling blocks.

17:1 **And he-said to his disciples, It-is impossible (for) the traps/stumbling-blocks[a] not to-come, nevertheless woe[b] (to him) through whom it-comes.**

TEXT—Instead of τοὺς μαθητὰς αὐτοῦ 'his disciples', some manuscripts read τοὺς μαθητάς 'the disciples', although GNT does not mention it. Τοὺς μαθητάς 'the disciples' is read by KJV.

TEXT—Instead of πλὴν οὐαί 'nevertheless woe', some manuscripts read οὐαὶ δέ 'but woe'. GNT does not mention this variant. Some translations might not distinguish between these two words.

LEXICON—a. σκάνδαλον (LN 6.25, 25.181, 88.306) (BAGD 2. p. 753): 'trap' [BAGD (1.), LN (6.25)], 'stumbling block' [BAGD (3.)], 'offense' [BAGD (3.), LN (25.181)], 'temptation to sin' [BAGD (2.)], 'that which causes someone to sin, one who causes someone to sin' [LN (88.306)]. The phrase 'it is impossible for the trap/stumbling block not to come' is translated 'impossible it is for fatal traps not to come' [Lns], 'it is impossible for things which cause one to stumble not to come' [WBC], 'it is inevitable that stumbling blocks come' [NASB], 'stumbling blocks are sure to come' [NET], 'occasions for stumbling are bound to come' [NRSV], 'there are bound to be causes of stumbling' [REB], 'it is impossible but that offenses will come' [KJV], 'it is impossible that offenses should not occur' [Arn], 'offenses will certainly come' [HCSB], 'things that cause people to sin are bound to come' [NIV], 'there will always be temptations to sin' [NLT], 'temptations are bound to come' [NTC], 'it is impossible for enticements not to come' [BECNT], 'it is impossible that scandals not occur' [AB], 'things that make people fall into sin are bound to happen' [TEV], 'there will always be something that causes people to sin' [CEV], 'things that cause people to sin will happen' [NCV], 'situations that cause people to lose their faith are certain to arise' [GW].

b. οὐαί (LN 22.9) (BAGD 1.a. p. 591): 'woe' [BAGD], 'alas (for you)' [BAGD], 'disaster, horror' [LN]. The phrase 'woe to' [Arn, BECNT, Lns, NTC, WBC; HCSB, KJV, NASB, NET, NIV, NRSV] is also translated 'woe betide' [AB; REB], 'how horrible it will be' [GW], 'how terrible it will be' [NLT], 'how terrible for' [NCV, TEV], 'is in for trouble' [CEV]. Such a person will be subject to God's wrath [BECNT]. See this word at 6:24; 10:13; 11:42; 21:23; 22:22.

QUESTION—What is meant by σκάνδαλον 'traps/stumbling-blocks'?

It refers to causing others to fall into sin [MGC]. It has the meaning of enticement to sin, or more specifically, to apostasy [AB, TH]. It refers to anything that causes one to lose or lessen his allegiance to Jesus [MGC, NAC].

1. The literal meaning of the noun σκάνδαλον is a trap or snare [Arn, ICC, LN (6.25), Lns, NTC], a bait-stick of a trap [TNTC], a trigger spring of a trap [Arn, Crd]. The trap is baited and when the bait is touched, the stick holding the bait springs the trap [Lns]. The idea of a snare by which someone is entrapped into sin is the figurative meaning in the NT [Crd], not the idea of a stumbling-block [Crd, Lns], nor offense [Lns]. It is used figuratively from the bait stick triggering off trouble or hindrances, the worst of which are temptations to sin [TNTC]. It is used figuratively in the sense of a person being entrapped in sin [Crd]. It is someone's act or attitude that leads another into sin and may be referred to as an offense that is a stumbling block for someone's faith [Arn]. It pictures temptation to sin [NTC].

2. The literal meaning is a stumbling-block [BECNT, NIBC, NICNT, NIGTC, TG, WBC]. Figuratively it is something that causes people to stumble in the sense that they are led into sin [NIGTC]. It pictures putting an obstacle in someone's way and thus enticing him to go in a wrong direction [BECNT]. It is a 'cause of offense' [NIGTC, Su]. The origin of the term is the Greek imagery of a trap, but probably it is used here in the Septuagintal use that means 'things that cause one to stumble' [WBC]. The danger is offending others by causing them to sin [Su].

17:2 It is-better for-him if a-stone of-a-mill[a] is-hung around his neck and he-had-been-thrown into the sea than that he-should-cause-to-stumble[b] one of-these little[c] (ones).

TEXT—Instead of λίθος μυλικός 'stone of a mill', some manuscripts read μύλος ὀνικός 'millstone of a donkey' ('millstone turned by a donkey'). GNT does not mention this variant. Some translations might not distinguish between these two phrases.

LEXICON—a. μυλικός (LN **7.70**) (BAGD p. 529): 'of a mill' [**LN**], 'belonging to a mill' [BAGD]. The phrase 'a stone of a mill' is translated 'a millstone' [AB, Arn, BECNT, Lns, NTC, WBC; HCSB, KJV, NASB, NET, NIV, NRSV, REB], 'a large millstone' [NLT, TEV], 'a heavy stone' [CEV], 'a large stone' [GW, NCV]. This was the upper stone in a grinding mill where grain was crushed [BECNT, NTC]. It was a heavy top stone that was turned by a donkey [Gdt, NAC, NICNT, NTC] and in the middle of it was a hole so that it could be rotated [NIGTC] and through which grain was fed [NTC]. Or, it was not so large as to need a donkey to turn it [EGT]. Hanging this heavy stone around one's neck would make drowning certain [BECNT, NIGTC, NTC]. The body would be beyond recovery and never be able to cause a little one to stumble [Lns].

b. aorist act. subj. of σκανδαλίζω (LN 88.304) (BAGD 1.a. p. 753): 'to cause to stumble' [AB, BECNT, WBC; HCSB, NASB, NRSV], 'to offend' [Arn; KJV], 'to entrap' [Lns], 'to cause to sin' [BAGD, LN, NTC; NCV, NET, NIV, TEV], 'to cause to lose his faith' [GW], 'to cause the downfall of' [REB], 'to harm' [NLT].

c. μικρός (LN 87.58, 79.125) (BAGD 1.c. p. 521): 'little' [LN (79.125)], 'unimportant' [LN (87.58)], 'humble' [BAGD]. The phrase 'little ones' [AB, Arn, BECNT, Lns, NTC, WBC; all versions except CEV] is also translated 'my little followers' [CEV].

QUESTION—Who are 'these little ones'?

'These' identifies them as being present in the audience [NIGTC]. It could mean that they were young in faith or young in age [NIVS]. The little ones are immature believers [Arn, Gdt, TG, TNTC], people who are beginners in the Christian life [BECNT, Gdt, ICC, TG], inexperienced believers [Lns], insignificant and unimportant believers [BNTC, ICC, NIC, NTC, TH], weaker disciples [NIC, TH], the weak, lowly, and vulnerable ones who were drawn to Jesus [WBC]. Or, it refers to disciples in a general sense [TH]. This does not refer to children only [Arn, BECNT], it refers to adult Christians [MGC]. It can be applied to any disciple that is being led astray [BECNT, NAC]. Matt. 18:6 identifies them as the children Jesus used for examples of the childlike nature of the citizens of the kingdom, although it may be that Luke dropped the idea of children and means all believers who were spiritually immature [Su].

QUESTION—Why would it be better for a person to drown than to cause a little one to stumble?

Causing one of these little ones to sin morally or spiritually gets one into a worse predicament than if he were drowned [WBC]. Drowning is to be preferred to the unspecified punishment awaiting a person who causes a little one to sin [TG]. The punishment of one who causes offense to another is so terrible that it would be better if he could die a violent death before he could offend that person [NIC]. A harsh death is preferable to the consequences of leading a little one astray [Arn, BECNT, MGC, Su]. This emphasizes the fearful judgment awaiting anyone who acts as a stumbling block [NIGTC].

17:3a Pay-attention-to[a] yourselves/one-another.

LEXICON—a. pres. act. impera. of προσέχω (LN 27.59) (BAGD 1.b. p. 714): 'to pay attention to' [BAGD, LN], 'to be on one's guard against' [LN]. The command 'pay attention to yourselves' is translated 'give attention to yourselves' [Arn], 'take heed to yourselves' [BECNT, Lns; KJV], 'watch yourselves' [NET, NIV], 'watch what you do' [TEV], 'be on your guard' [AB, BAGD, WBC; HCSB, NASB, NRSV, REB], 'be careful' [NCV], 'be careful what you do' [CEV], 'watch yourself' [GW], 'constantly be looking out for one another' [NTC], 'I am warning you' [NLT]. The present imperative indicates keeping a constant watch [BECNT; NET]. See this word at 12:1.

QUESTION—Does ἑαυτοῖς mean 'yourselves' or 'one another' and how is this command connected?

1. It means let each of you pay attention to himself [AB, Arn, BECNT, Crd, EGT, Gdt, ICC, MGC, My, NAC, NIBC, NIGTC, WBC; CEV, GW, NCV, NET, NIV, REB, TEV]. They are to take heed to themselves lest they offend the little ones [EGT, MGC]. They are warned against leading others into sin [Arn]. They must be careful what they teach others [BECNT]. They are to take care lest offenses occur in their own circle [My].

   1.1 This is most closely linked to the preceding warning [AB, Arn, BECNT, EGT, Gdt, ICC, MGC, My, NAC, NIBC; CEV, GW, NCV, NET, NIV, REB, TEV]. It comes as a conclusion to 17:1–2 [AB, MGC, NAC, NIBC; CEV, GW, NCV, NIV, REB, TEV]: so take pay attention to yourselves. Its warning tone is more appropriate with the preceding verses [BECNT]. It is the end of the preceding paragraph and a new paragraph begins at 17:3b [AB, BECNT; CEV, GW, NCV, NET, NIV, REB, TEV].

   1.2 This serves as a link between the two sections [NIGTC].

2. It means let each of you take heed to one another [Lns, NTC]. They are to guard each other [Lns], or look out for each other [NTC]. Instead of an anticlimax to the preceding warning, this is an introduction to the following instructions [Lns]. This interpretation is linked with the following verses [NTC].

LUKE 17:3b–4

DISCOURSE UNIT: 17:3b–4 [AB]. The topic is forgiveness.

17:3b If your (singular) brother sins rebuke[a] him, and if he-repents[b] forgive him. **17:4** And if he-sins towards[c] you seven-times (during) the day and seven-times he-returns[d] to you saying, I-repent, you-will-forgive him.

TEXT—In 17:3, following ἁμάρτῃ 'sins', some manuscripts add εἰς σέ 'against you'. GNT rejects this addition with an A decision, indicating that the text is certain. Εἰς σέ 'against you' is read by KJV.

TEXT—In 17:4, following the second occurrence of ἑπτάκις 'seven times', some manuscripts add τῆς ἡμέρας 'of the day'. GNT does not mention this variant. Τῆς ἡμέρας 'of the day' is read by KJV.

LEXICON—a. aorist act. impera. of ἐπιτιμάω (LN 33.419) (BAGD 1. p. 303): 'to rebuke' [AB, Arn, BAGD, BECNT, LN, Lns, WBC; HCSB, KJV, NASB, NET, NIV, NLT, NRSV, TEV], 'to reprove' [NTC; REB], 'to warn' [NCV], 'to correct' [CEV, GW]. He is to tell the sinner that what he is doing is wrong and he should stop doing it [TG].

    b. aorist act. subj. of μετανοέω (LN 41.52) (BAGD p. 512): 'to repent' [BAGD, LN]. The phrase 'if he repents' [Arn, BECNT, Lns, NTC, WBC; HCSB, KJV, NASB, NET, NIV, NLT, REB, TEV] is also translated 'if there is repentance' [NRSV], 'if he is sorry and stops sinning' [NCV], 'if he reforms his conduct' [AB], 'if he changes the way he thinks and acts' [GW], '(forgive) the ones who say they are sorry' [CEV]. Since this involves a personal wrong to be righted, it does not mean repentance toward God [WBC]. The sinner recognizes the presence of the sin and acknowledges his error [BECNT]. See this word at 10:13, 11:32; 13:3, 5; 15:7, 10; 16:30.

    c. εἰς (LN 90.59): 'towards' [LN]. The phrase 'if he sins towards you' is translated 'if he sins against you' [AB, BECNT, NTC, WBC; HCSB, NASB, NCV, NET, NIV, TEV], 'if he commit sin against thee' [Lns], 'if the same person sins against you' [NRSV], 'if he will sin against you' [Arn], 'if thy brother trespass against thee' [KJV], 'if he wrongs you' [GW, NLT, REB], 'if one of them mistreats you' [CEV]. It refers to wronging someone or doing something bad to someone [TG].

    d. aorist act. subj. of ἐπιστρέφω (LN 15.90) (BAGD 1.b.α. p. 301): 'to return' [LN; NASB, NET], 'to turn around' [BAGD], 'to turn back' [AB, BAGD; NRSV], 'to turn again' [KJV, NLT], 'to turn' [Arn, BECNT, Lns, WBC], 'to come back' [NTC; GW, HCSB, NIV, REB], 'to come' [TEV], not explicit [CEV, NCV]. The turning is in the context of one person speaking to another [TH].

QUESTION—Who is the brother?

1. He is a fellow disciple [AB, BECNT, MGC, NAC, NIGTC, WBC; CEV, GW, NCV, NET, NLT, NRSV].
2. He is a fellowman [Su]. Here, brother is more general than a physical brother or even a spiritual brother [Su].

QUESTION—What is the sin that you should rebuke?
1. The situation is when your brother sins against you [My, NAC, NIGTC, Su, TG, TH; KJV]. This is implied from 'if he sins against you seven times' in the next verse [TG, TH]. He mistreats you [CEV], he wrongs you [GW, NLT, REB].
2. It concerns any sin [BECNT, Lns]. It is any open sin and is not specified as it is in the next verse [Lns]. Probably it is some sin that the disciple had witnessed or had been the object of [BECNT].

QUESTION—How should one rebuke his brother?
He is to show his brother that he has sinned [Arn, Lns] and tell him how deadly the guilt of that sin is [Lns]. The rebuke is a loving and honest confronting of the sin while maintaining their relationship [BECNT].

QUESTION—What happens after sinning seven times?
The number 'seven times' is not to be taken literally, and the phrase indicates unlimited forgiveness [ICC, MGC, NAC, NIC, NIGTC, NTC, Su, TH, WBC]. Forgiveness is to be habitual [TNTC]. The situation is not repeating the same sin seven times in a row, it indicates committing seven different sins in a single day [Lns].

QUESTION—What is meant by the use of the future tense of 'you will forgive him'?
The future tense has the force of an imperative here [AB, Arn, BECNT, Lns, NIC, NIGTC, NTC, TH, WBC; all versions except KJV].

DISCOURSE UNIT: 17:5–10 [GW, HCSB]. The topic is the apostles' request for more faith [GW], faith and duty [HCSB].

DISCOURSE UNIT: 17:5–6 [AB, TNTC; NCV, TEV]. The topic is faith [AB, TNTC; TEV], how big is your faith? [NCV].

17:5 And the apostles said to-the-Lord, Add^a to-us faith.
LEXICON—a. aorist act. impera. of προστίθημι (LN 59.72) (BAGD 2. p. 719): 'to add' [LN, Lns], 'to grant' [BAGD]. The clause 'add to us faith' is translated in regard to quantity: 'increase our faith' [AB, Arn, BECNT, NTC; HCSB, KJV, NASB, NET, NIV, NRSV, REB], 'give us more faith' [GW, NCV], 'grant additional faith to us' [WBC], 'make our faith greater' [TEV], 'we need more faith; tell us how to get it' [NLT]. It is also translated in regard to quality: 'make our faith stronger' [CEV].

QUESTION—Is this verse connected with what precedes?
1. This is connected with the preceding commands [Arn, Lns, NIC, NICNT, NIVS, NTC, TNTC, WBC]. The apostles thought that a lot of faith was required to forgive in the manner Jesus told them to do [Lns, NIC, TNTC]. They asked for an increase of faith so that they could comply with what Jesus had commanded [Arn, NICNT, NIVS, WBC]. They didn't think they had enough faith to have the strength needed to avoid causing others to stumble and always being ready to forgive [Lns, NTC].

2. There seems to be no connection [AB, Gdt, ICC, NIGTC]. This must be a different occasion [ICC]. Probably Luke's source at this point was a list of sayings of Jesus [NIGTC]. There must have been a display of Jesus' power that is not recorded and this indicates the apostles' reaction to that miracle [Gdt].

QUESTION—What is meant by the request 'add to us faith'?
1. They asked to be given more faith than they already had [AB, Alf, Arn, BECNT, BNTC, Gdt, Lns, MGC, My, NAC, NIBC, NIC, NIGTC, NIVS, NTC, Rb, Su, TNTC, WBC; all versions except CEV]. Since they were the apostles, a certain amount of faith was present, and they were asking for even more [AB]. This refers to their daily faith in facing practical problems [Su], in meeting the preceding commands given by Jesus [Arn, My], and in faithfully serving God [BECNT, NIC]. They asked for an increase of faith, but Jesus' answer refers to the importance of the quality of their faith, not its quantity [Arn, NIC]. To have more faith is to have stronger faith [Lns]. They wanted to have their faith increased in quality [ICC, My, NIBC, TG; CEV, NET]. They wanted a genuine faith in Jesus' promises [ICC], a stronger faith [CEV], an increase of the depth of their faith [NET]. They wanted the kind of faith that would remain firm in the face of opposition, and enable them to forgive those who repented [NIBC].
2. They asked to be given faith in addition to the gifts they had already received as apostles [Crd, TH]. In addition to other gifts of grace, they asked for faith to trust in Jesus' miracle-working power [TH].

17:6 And the Lord said, If you-have faith like[a] a-mustard seed, you-could-say to-this mulberry-tree,[b] Be-uprooted[c] and be-planted[d] in the sea. And it-would-obey[e] you.

TEXT—Instead of the present tense εἰ ἔχετε 'if you have' (a condition of fact), some manuscripts read the imperfect tense εἰ εἴχετε 'if you had' (a condition contrary to fact), although GNT does not mention it. Εἰ εἴχετε 'if you had' is read by KJV.

TEXT—Some manuscripts omit ταύτῃ 'this'. GNT does not deal with this variant in the apparatus, but brackets it in the text, indicating difficulty in making the decision.

LEXICON—a. ὡς (LN 64.12) (BAGD II.3.b. p. 897): 'like' [Arn, BAGD, BECNT, LN; NASB], 'as' [LN, Lns, WBC; KJV], 'the size of' [AB; GW, HCSB, NCV, NET, NRSV], 'as small as' [NTC; NIV, NLT], 'as big as' [TEV], 'no bigger than' [CEV, REB], 'no greater than' [BAGD].

b. συκάμινος (LN **3.6**) (BAGD p. 776): 'mulberry tree' [AB, BAGD, **LN**, Lns, NTC; all versions except KJV, NET], 'black mulberry tree' [NET], 'sycamine tree' [Arn, BECNT; KJV], 'sycamore' [WBC]. Whatever kind of tree it was, it was a relatively large tree [AB, NAC]. The black mulberry has a vast root system and it could live up to six hundred years [BECNT, NIC; NET].

c. aorist pass. impera. of ἐκριζόω (LN 43.11) (BAGD 1. p. 245): The imperative is translated 'be uprooted' [AB, Arn, BAGD, BECNT, LN, Lns, NTC, WBC; HCSB, NASB, NIV, NRSV], 'be rooted up' [REB], 'be pulled out by the roots' [BAGD, LN; NET], 'be plucked up by the root' [KJV]. This imperative passive is also translated as active with God as the actor: 'may God uproot you' [NLT]; as reflexive: 'pull yourself up by the roots' [GW, TEV], 'dig yourself up' [NCV], 'to pull itself up, roots and all' [CEV].

d. aorist pass, impera. of φυτεύω (LN 43.5) (BAGD p. 870): The imperative is translated 'be planted' [AB, BAGD, BECNT, LN, Lns, NTC, WBC; KJV, NASB, NET, NIV, NRSV, REB], 'be plunged' [Arn]. This imperative passive is also translated as active with God as the actor: 'may God throw you (into the sea)' [NLT]; as reflexive: 'plant yourself' [GW, NCV, TEV], 'to plant itself' [CEV]. To be planted right into the sea is more than to be pitched into the sea [Lns].

e. aorist act. indic. of ὑπακούω (LN 36.15) (BAGD 1. p. 837): 'to obey' [AB, Arn, BAGD, BECNT, LN, Lns, NTC, WBC; all versions except CEV], 'it would' [CEV].

QUESTION—What is implied by the conditional clause 'if you have faith like a mustard seed'?

1. This implies that they did not have that much faith [AB, Gdt, ICC, MGC, My, NIC, NICNT, NTC, TG, TH; NET]. If they had the faith Jesus was speaking of (but they didn't) they could command the mulberry tree (but because of their lack of faith they couldn't) [TG]. They had some faith, but it was too little faith [Gdt, TNTC]. Jesus is speaking of faith in an ideal sense, as it ought to be [My].

2. This implies that they did have that much faith [EGT, Lns, Rb, Su]. If they had this faith (and they did), they could say (but they didn't since they are not using their faith) [Lns]. Without adding to the faith they already had, their faith was enough to accomplish tremendous things [Su]. Jesus encouraged them to use the faith they had in order to put forth its power [Lns].

QUESTION—What is the point of similarity in the phase 'like a mustard seed'?

1. This refers to the size of the mustard seed [AB, Gdt, Lns, My, NTC, TG, TH; CEV, GW, HCSB, NCV, NET, NIV, NLT, NRSV, REB, TEV]. This stresses the very small size of the seed and it brings out the potential of great results that can come from a very small thing [Su].

2. This refers to the living quality of the mustard seed [ICC, NIC, NTC]. They don't need more faith, but the right kind of faith, that is, a vigorous and living faith [NIC]. Although very small, the mustard seed contains the germ of life which makes it shoot up into a tree, and if the disciples had faith of the same quality of life, no problem would be too difficult for them [NIC]. Jesus was pointing out that they didn't need additional faith, rather they must examine themselves to see if they had genuine faith [ICC].

QUESTION—Why would a mulberry tree be chosen for being uprooted in this illustration?

There is no significant reason for picking out the mulberry tree, it could have been the nearest large object that Jesus could point to for using in his illustration [Su]. The συκάμινος 'mulberry tree' is different from the συκομορέα 'sycamore tree' that Zacchaeus climbed in 19:4, but the names became confused in early translations [NIGTC].

QUESTION—Who would do the uprooting and the planting of the tree?

1. Most use the passive form in the command to the tree without indicating an agent [AB, Arn, BAGD, LN; HCSB, KJV, NASB, NET, NIV, NRSV, REB].
    1.1 The implied agent of the passive is the tree itself obeying the command [BECNT]. The fact that the command is in the aorist while the action is a future condition means that the tree was ready to obey even before the command was given [BECNT].
    1.2 The implied agent of the passive is God who will do such astounding things concerning the things he has promised to do [Lns; NET, NLT].
2. It is best understood as reflexive, meaning that the tree itself should pull itself up by the roots and plant itself in the sea [TH; CEV, GW, NCV, TEV].

QUESTION—How could a tree be planted in the sea?

Of course this is a human impossibility [AB, EGT, Lns, TG]. It was presented as a paradox [BECNT]. There is no reason suggested why anyone would want to plant a tree in the sea and this absurd illustration indicates that it was not to be taken literally [NIGTC].

QUESTION—Was Jesus teaching how to move a tree?

It would be tempting God to order trees to be transplanted in the sea unless one is assured that such was God's will. Jesus was teaching them that the power of faith is as unlimited as God's power [Arn]. The figure of uprooting and planting is a hyperbole to indicate that faith can do amazing things and this was not intended to be taken literally [BECNT]. The figure taught that genuine faith would effect things beyond all expectation [AB]. The lesson is that God can do a lot with a little faith [Arn, BECNT], and faith is not a question of quantity but of its presence [BECNT]. No task that Jesus assigned to them would be impossible as long as they remained trusting in him [NTC]. The way to increase faith is to have it and also experience how it produces great results [BECNT, Lns, WBC]. The apostles had faith, therefore they should use the promises to which faith is directed [Lns].

DISCOURSE UNIT: 17:7–10 [AB, Su, TNTC, WBC; NCV, TEV]. The topic is being slaves to whom no favor is owed [WBC], unprofitable servants [AB, TNTC], being good servants [NCV], a servant's duty [TEV], believing and serving [Su].

17:7 And who among you having a-slave[a] plowing or tending-sheep, will-say to-him (after) he-has-come-in[b] from the field, Immediately[c] having-come, recline?[d]

LEXICON—a. δοῦλος (LN 87.76): 'slave' [Arn, LN, Lns, WBC; HCSB, NASB, NET, NRSV], 'bondservant' [LN], 'servant' [AB, BECNT, NTC; CEV, GW, KJV, NCV, NIV, NLT, REB, TEV]. Identifying the worker as a slave indicates that he was just performing his duties [NIVS, Pnt].

    b. aorist act. participle of εἰσέρχομαι (LN 15.93) (BAGD 1.e. p. 233): 'to come in' [BAGD, BECNT, LN, Lns, NTC; CEV, HCSB, NASB, NCV, NIV, NRSV, REB, TEV], 'to come' [Arn, WBC; GW, KJV, NET], 'to return' [AB]. The slave would be coming in from the field at the end of a day of work when it was time for an evening meal [BECNT, TG].

    c. εὐθέως (LN 67.53): 'immediately' [BECNT, LN; NASB], 'at once' [AB, Arn, Lns, NTC; HCSB, NET, NRSV], 'straight away' [REB], 'right away' [LN, WBC], 'hurry' [TEV], 'now' [LN; NIV], 'by and by' (= 'immediately' in the seventeenth century) [KJV], not explicit [CEV, GW, NCV, NLT].

    d. aorist act. impera. of ἀναπίπτω (LN 17.23) (BAGD 1. p. 59): 'to recline' [BAGD, LN], 'to recline at table' [Lns, NTC], 'to sit at the table' [BECNT], 'to sit down to eat' [AB, LN, WBC; HCSB, NASB, NCV, NIV], 'to sit down and eat' [NLT], 'to sit down for a meal' [NET], 'to sit down' [Arn], 'to have something to eat' [CEV, GW], 'to eat his meal' [TEV], 'to sit down to meat' [KJV], 'to take your place at the table' [NRSV]. The meals were eaten while reclining on one's side on the floor with the feet away from the low table [NET].

QUESTION—How is this connected with the preceding verse and who is referred to in the phrase 'who among you'?

    1. Jesus continued speaking to the apostles [Arn, Lns, NIGTC, Pnt, TH, TNTC]. He was speaking to the same disciples that he spoke to in 17:1 [Bai, MGC, NTC]. By giving the conditional force of '*if* you have a slave', Jesus wanted them to put themselves into the position of someone who has a slave working for him [Arn, Lns]. It is not clear, but if it belongs to the preceding verse, it may mean that even if the apostles use their little faith to accomplish great things, they must be humble because they were only doing their assigned work [Arn, Su]. If someone has such faith, he may be tempted to have spiritual pride [TNTC]. It is a warning to church leaders against thinking their ministry to the church entitled them to some reward [NIGTC]. Some translate so as to refer to a third person instead of to 'you' [GW].

    2. This is not connected with the preceding verses and comes from some other occasion when Jesus was speaking to his followers [TG], or to a mixed audience that included well-to-do persons [ICC]. The setting of a settled life on a farm with a slave to work in the field hardly fits the band of disciples who were traveling with Jesus [WBC]. This question does not

indicate that the listeners were of a wealthy class, rather it appeals to their knowledge of the servant-master relationship [Bai].

QUESTION—Who would say such a thing to his slave?

The question's expected answer is that none of them would do so [AB, Bai, BECNT, Blm, Hlt, MGC, NAC, NICNT, NIGTC, TH, WBC].

QUESTION—What does the adverb εὐθέως 'immediately' modify?
1. It modifies 'will say' [Alf; KJV]: will immediately say to him, Come and recline.
2. It modifies 'come' [AB, Arn, Bai, BECNT, EGT, ICC, NTC, WBC; HCSB, NASB, NET, NIV, NRSV]: will say, Come immediately and recline.
3. It modifies 'recline' [Lns; REB]: will say, Come and immediately recline.

QUESTION—Would the master be inviting the slave to sit down alongside him to eat?

This was an invitation from the master to join his meal as an honored guest [Hlt]. It appears that the slave would sit at the master's table in the translation 'Come here at once and take your place at the table' [NRSV]. The master invited his slave to sit by his side at the table and even attended to his needs and praised him for doing his duties [NIC]. Or, it appears likely that the master was telling the slave to eat at once, but not inviting him to share the same meal with him [Bai, TG]. He was inviting the slave to eat before he did [Blm].

17:8 But will–he- not -say to-him, Prepare[a] something I-may-eat and having-girded-yourself[b] serve me until I-eat and drink, and after these (things) you may-eat and drink? **17:9** He-does- not -have gratitude[c] to-the slave because he-did the (things) having-been-ordered[d] (does he)?

TEXT—In 17:9, following διαταχθέντα 'having been ordered', some manuscripts add οὐ δοκῶ 'I think not', and some manuscripts add αὐτῷ; οὐ δοκῶ 'to him? I think not'. GNT rejects both of these additions with a B decision, indicating that the text is almost certain. Αὐτῷ; οὐ δοκῶ 'to him? I think not' is read by KJV.

LEXICON—a. aorist act. impera. of ἑτοιμάζω (LN 77.3) (BAGD 1. p. 316): 'to prepare' [BAGD, LN], 'to make ready' [LN]. The phrase 'prepare something I may eat' is translated 'prepare something for me to eat' [HCSB, NASB, NCV], 'prepare what I am to eat' [WBC], 'prepare my supper' [NTC; NIV, REB], 'prepare supper for me' [NRSV], 'prepare my dinner' [AB], 'prepare what I shall eat for dinner' [BECNT], 'get ready what I shall eat for dinner' [Arn], 'get my supper ready' [TEV], 'get my dinner ready' [NET], 'get dinner ready for me' [GW], 'fix me something to eat' [CEV], 'make ready what I shall dine on' [Lns], 'make ready wherewith I may sup' [KJV], 'he must first prepare his master's meal' [NLT]. The main meal of the day was eaten in the evening [Lns]. A full and formal meal was served in the evening [BECNT, NIGTC], in contrast with the slave's simple supper afterwards [NIGTC].

b. aorist mid. participle of περιζώννυμαι (LN 49.15) (BAGD 2.a. p. 647): 'to gird oneself' [Arn, BAGD, BECNT, LN, Lns; KJV], 'to hitch up one's robe' [REB], 'to gird oneself suitably' [WBC], 'to properly clothe oneself' [NASB], 'to dress up properly' [NTC], 'to put on one's apron' [AB; NRSV, TEV], 'to get ready (to serve me)' [CEV, HCSB, NCV], 'to make oneself ready' [NET], 'to get oneself ready' [NIV], not explicit [GW, NLT]. After preparing the meal, the slave must gird himself to serve it [BECNT, TH]. To gird oneself involved putting a belt or sash around the waist [LN]. It was necessary to gird himself so that his tunic would not interfere with his movements [Arn]. Or, he would gird himself with an apron [AB; NET, NRSV, TEV], or towel [NET].

c. χάρις (LN 33.350) (BAGD 5. p. 878): 'gratitude' [BAGD], 'thanks' [BAGD, LN]. The phrase 'to have gratitude' is translated 'to thank' [AB, BECNT, Lns, NTC; GW, HCSB, KJV, NASB, NET, NIV, NRSV], 'to express thanks' [WBC], 'to be grateful' [Arn; REB]. This is also translated with the slave as the subject: '(not even) to be thanked' [NLT], 'to deserve thanks' [TEV], 'to deserve special thanks' [CEV], 'to get any special thanks' [NCV]. This does not refer to a verbal thanks, but to placing the master in debt to his slave [Bai, NICNT] as though the slave had some special merit [Bai].

d. aorist pass. participle of διατάσσω (LN 33.325) (BAGD p. 189): 'to be ordered' [BAGD, LN], 'to be commanded' [BAGD, LN]. The phrase 'because he did the things having been ordered' is translated 'because he did what was commanded' [BECNT, WBC; similarly Arn; HCSB, KJV, NASB], 'because he did the things he was ordered to do' [Lns], 'because the latter did what he had been ordered to do' [NTC], 'because he did what he was told to do' [NET, NIV], 'for doing what was commanded' [NRSV], 'for doing what his master commanded' [NCV], 'for obeying orders' [TEV], 'for carrying out his orders' [AB; REB], 'for doing what they are supposed to do' [CEV], 'because he is merely doing what he is supposed to do' [NLT], 'for following orders' [GW].

QUESTION—What is the function of the question in 17:8?

The question in 17:8 anticipates a positive answer [AB, BECNT, Hlt, Lns, NAC, TH; NET]. It gives the answer implied by the rhetorical question in 17:7 [EGT, TH].

QUESTION—What is the function of the question in 17:9?

The negative μή 'not' in the question indicates that a negative answer is anticipated [AB, Arn, Bai, BECNT, Hlt, Lns, MGC, NAC, NIGTC, TG, TH; NET]. This emphasizes the point of the parable, that slaves must do what they are ordered and must not think that their master is indebted to them for doing so [Bai, BECNT, Lns, NIGTC]. This verse serves as a transition between the parable and the application [Blm].

17:10 So also you, when you-do all the (things) having-been-ordered you, say, We-are unworthy[a] slaves, we-have-done (only)[b] what we-were-obligated[c] to-do.

LEXICON—a. ἀχρεῖος (LN 65.33) (BAGD p. 128): 'unworthy' [NASB, NCV, NIV], 'worthless' [BAGD, BECNT, LN; GW, NRSV], 'unprofitable' [AB, Lns, NTC; KJV], 'useless' [BAGD, LN], 'undeserving of special praise' [NET], 'not worthy of praise' [NLT], 'to whom no favor is owed' [WBC], 'deserve no credit' [REB], 'good-for-nothing' [HCSB], 'merely (servants)' [CEV], 'ordinary (servants)' [TEV].

  b. Some translations supply 'only' [AB, WBC; HCSB, NASB, NCV, NET, NIV, NRSV, REB, TEV], 'merely' [NTC], 'simply' [CEV, NLT],

  c. imperf. act. indic. of ὀφείλω (LN 71.25) (BAGD 2.a.β. p. 598): 'to be obligated' [BAGD], 'to be under obligation, ought' [LN]. The phrase 'what we were obligated to do' is translated 'what was our duty' [NET], 'that which/what was our duty to do' [Arn; KJV], 'our duty' [AB, NTC; CEV, GW, HCSB, NIV, NLT, REB, TEV], 'what we ought to do' [WBC], 'that which/what we ought to have done' [NASB, NRSV], 'what we were obligated to do' [BECNT], 'what we were under obligation to do' [Lns], 'the work we should do' [NCV]. In this context it refers to all that Jesus told his disciples to do, not God's laws in general [TG]. Or, this does refer to the OT commandments [NAC, NIGTC].

QUESTION—What is meant by οὕτως καὶ ὑμεῖς 'so also you'?

This applies the parable to those who were listening [BECNT, Hlt, MGC, Su, TG]. The audience is either the disciples mentioned in 17:1 or the apostles mentioned in 17:5 [AB]. It draws a parallel between the slave in the preceding verse and those listening to Jesus [TH]. This refers to God's commands to his servants [NIGTC]. The disciples are like the slave to whom no thanks are due [My]. It is translated 'That's how it should be with you' [CEV].

QUESTION—What is meant by God's servants being ἀχρεῖος 'unworthy'?

The sense of the Greek word ἀχρεῖος is debated, but whatever the sense of the word, it must be understood contextually [BECNT]. They are 'unworthy' [Hlt, MGC, NAC, NIGTC, Pnt, TG, TH; NASB, NCV, NIV]. They are unworthy of praise since they do not deserve praise, thanks, or rewards [Hlt, TG, TH; NET]. At best, they have only done what they should have and no more than that [NAC, TH]. They are 'worthless' [BECNT, NICNT; GW, NRSV]. The slaves do not bring anything 'worthy' to their tasks and this shows their humility before God [BECNT]. No favor is due them [NICNT]. They are 'unprofitable' [AB, Arn, Gdt, ICC, Lns, NIC, NTC; KJV]. They are 'unprofitable' because their master received no more than his due [Arn, Gdt, ICC, Lns]. They have nothing to glory about [NIC]. They deserve no special thanks nor do they have any special claims on the Lord [Lns]. They know that what they have managed to do is still inadequate [AB]. The translations 'useless' and 'worthless' are not correct since the slave in the parable did his duty and was not worthless, rather the meaning is that they are servants to whom nothing is owed, having only done their duty [Bai, Blm, TNTC].

DISCOURSE UNIT: 17:11–19:27 [NAC, NICNT]. The topic is the third mention of the journey to Jerusalem [NAC], responding to the kingdom [NICNT].

DISCOURSE UNIT: 17:11–18:14 [AB]. The topic is the time from the third mention of Jerusalem as his destination to the end of the Lucan travel account.

DISCOURSE UNIT: 17:11–18:8 [BECNT, NIGTC]. The topic is faithfulness in looking for the king, the kingdom, and the kingdom's consummation [BECNT], the coming of the Son of Man [NIGTC].

DISCOURSE UNIT: 17:11–21 [NASB]. The topic is the cleansing of ten lepers.

DISCOURSE UNIT: 17:11–19 [AB, BECNT, NAC, NICNT, NIGTC, Su, TNTC, WBC; CEV, GW, HCSB, NCV, NET, NIV, NLT, NRSV, TEV]. The topic is the ten lepers [HCSB], ten men with leprosy [CEV], healing ten lepers on the border of Samaria and Galilee [Su], the healing of ten lepers and a Samaritan's faith [BECNT], the response of faith to the healing mercy of God [WBC], Jesus cleanses ten lepers [NRSV], Jesus heals ten men [TEV], ten healed of leprosy [NIV, NLT], ten men with a skin disease are healed [GW], the cleansing of ten lepers [AB, TNTC], the grateful leper [NET], the grateful Samaritan [NAC, NIGTC], gratitude from a foreign leper [NICNT], be thankful [NCV].

17:11 And it-happened in the going to Jerusalem he was-traveling through (the) middle[a] of-Samaria and Galilee. **17:12** And (as) he entered into a-certain village[b] ten leprous[c] men who stood at-a-distance[d] met[e] him.

- TEXT—In 17:11, instead of ἐν τῷ πορεύεσθαι 'in the going', some manuscripts read ἐν τῷ πορεύεσθαι αὐτόν 'in his going/as he was going'. GNT does not mention this variant. Ἐν τῷ πορεύεσθαι αὐτόν 'in his going/as he was going' is read by KJV.
- TEXT—In 17:12, some manuscripts omit αὐτῷ 'him'. GNT does not deal with this variant in the apparatus, but brackets it in the text, indicating difficulty in making the decision.
- LEXICON—a. μέσος (LN 83.10) (BAGD 2. p. 507): 'middle' [BAGD, LN]. The phrase 'through the middle of' is translated 'through the midst of' [KJV], 'along the border between' [NTC; CEV, GW, NIV, TEV], '(he reached) the border between' [NLT], 'along between' [BECNT, WBC; NET], 'between' [AB; HCSB, NASB], 'through between' [Lns], 'through the area/region between' [Arn; NCV, NRSV], 'through the borderlands of' [REB].
  - b. κώμη (LN 1.92) (BAGD 1. p. 461): 'village' [BAGD, LN]. This is an unimportant center of population and contrast with πόλις 'city' [LN]. See this word at 5:17.

LUKE 17:11–12   213

- c. λεπρός (LN 23.162) (BAGD 472): 'leprous' [BAGD, LN]. The phrase 'leprous men' [Arn, Lns, NTC, WBC; NASB] is also translated 'men that were lepers' [KJV], 'men with leprosy' [CEV, NET, REB], 'men who had leprosy' [NIV], 'lepers' [AB, BECNT; NLT], 'men with a skin disease' [GW], 'men who had a skin disease' [NCV], 'men with serious skin diseases' [HCSB], 'men suffering from a dreaded skin disease' [TEV]. See a description of λέπρα 'leprosy' at 5:12.
- d. πόρρωθεν (LN **83.31**) (BAGD p. 694): 'at a distance' [Arn, BAGD, BECNT, **LN**, NTC; CEV, GW, HCSB, NASB, NET, NIV, TEV], 'far away' [LN], 'far off' [Lns, WBC], 'afar off' [KJV], 'some way off' [REB]. The phrase 'who stood at a distance' is translated 'they did not come close' [NCV], 'keeping their distance' [NRSV], 'they kept their distance' [AB].
- e. aorist act. indic. of ἀπαντάω (LN **15.78**) (BAGD p. 80): 'to meet' [Arn, BECNT, **LN**, Lns, NTC, WBC; GW, HCSB, KJV, NASB, NCV, NET, NIV, REB, TEV], 'to happen to meet' [AB], 'to draw near' [LN], 'to approach' [NRSV], 'to come toward' [BAGD; CEV], not explicit [NLT]. The lepers may have come together in a group when they heard that Jesus was approaching [ICC].

QUESTION—Where was Jesus traveling?

1. He went along the border area between the provinces of Samaria and Galilee [AB, Alf, Arn, BAGD, BNTC, Crd, EGT, Gdt, ICC, Lns, My, NAC, NIC, NICNT, NIGTC, NTC, Su, TH, TNTC, WBC; all versions except KJV]. Jesus was traveling along the border where the two provinces met, probably on the Galilean side of the border [Lns]. As Jews often did when traveling to Jerusalem, Jesus avoided the land of the Samaritans by traveling eastward along the border of Samaria towards Perea [ICC, NIC, NICNT]. Samaria is probably mentioned before Galilee because of the emphasis put on the Samaritan in 17:16 [MGC].
2. He was going through the midst of both provinces, first through Samaria, and then through Galilee [Rb; KJV]. Jesus was going to Ephraim (John 11:54), north through the midst of Samaria, and then through Galilee so as to cross the Jordan near Bethshean where he would join the Galilean caravan down through Perea to Jerusalem [Arn, Rb, TNTC].

QUESTION—What is the significance of the lepers standing at a distance?

The Jewish law required lepers to avoid physical contact with other people, but they stayed near to villages in order to receive charitable gifts [NIGTC]. Contact with a leper made people unclean [Lns]. The separation was required in Lev. 13:46 and Num. 5:2–3 [AB, Arn, ICC, MGC, NAC, NIGTC, WBC]. They were outside the village, but near the road [Su]. The lepers stopped at a distance from Jesus, but near enough to call to him [TH].

17:13 And they raised[a] (their) voice saying, Jesus, Master,[b] have-mercy[c] (on) us.

LEXICON—a. aorist act. indic. of αἴρω (LN 33.78) (BAGD b. p. 24): 'to raise the voice, to cry out, to speak loudly' [LN], 'to lift up' [BAGD]. The phrase αὐτοὶ ἦραν φωνήν 'they raised their voice' is translated 'they raised their voices' [AB, LN, WBC; HCSB, NASB, NET], 'they lifted the voice' [Lns], 'they lifted up their voices' [Arn, NTC; KJV], 'they shouted' [CEV, GW, TEV], 'they called out' [BECNT; NIV, NRSV, REB], 'they called to' [NCV], 'crying out' [NLT].

b. ἐπιστάτης (LN 87.50) (BAGD p. 300): 'master' [AB, Arn, BAGD, BECNT, LN, Lns, NTC, WBC; all versions except GW], 'leader' [LN], 'teacher' [GW]. See this word at 5:5; 8:24, 45; 9:33, 49.

c. aorist act. impera. of ἐλεάω (LN 88.76) (BAGD p. 249): 'to have mercy' [AB, BAGD, BECNT, LN, Lns, WBC; GW, HCSB, KJV, NASB, NCV, NET, NLT, NRSV], 'to be merciful, to show mercy' [BAGD, LN], 'to have pity' [Arn; CEV, NIV, TEV], 'to take pity on' [NTC; REB]. See this word at 16:24, 18:38.

QUESTION—Why did they shout 'Jesus, Master'?

The ten men stood at a distance and had to raise their voices to attract Jesus' attention [BECNT, Lns]. They knew who Jesus was, perhaps because Jesus had previously visited the village or someone had informed them of his coming [Su]. They had heard about him [BECNT]. When they called him 'Master', it indicated submission rather than the intimate relationship of being disciples [TH]. 'Master' was equivalent to 'Rabbi' [Lns, NTC]. It was a term of respect [TG].

QUESTION—What is implied by the lepers' request for Jesus to have mercy on them?

It is implied that they were asking Jesus to heal them [BECNT, Lns, NAC, Su, TG, TH, TNTC; NET]. They hoped that Jesus' feeling of compassion would move him to heal them [TG].

17:14 And having-seen (them) he-said to-them, Having-gone, show[a] yourselves to-the priests. And it-happened while they were-going they-were-cleansed.[b]

LEXICO—a. aorist act. impera. of ἐπιδείκνυμι (LN 24.25) (BAGD 1. p. 291): 'to show' [AB, Arn, BAGD, BECNT, **LN**, Lns, NTC, WBC; all versions except TEV]. The phrase 'show yourselves to the priests' is translated 'let the priests examine you' [TEV].

b. aorist pass. indic. of καθαρίζω (LN 23.137) (BAGD 1.b.α. p. 387): 'to be cleansed' [Arn, BAGD, BECNT, Lns, NTC; KJV, NASB, NET, NIV], 'to be made clean' [AB, WBC; GW, NRSV, REB, TEV], 'to be healed and made ritually pure or acceptable' [LN], 'to be healed' [CEV, HCSB, NCV]. The phrase 'they were cleansed' is translated 'their leprosy disappeared' [NLT]. See this word at 4:27; 5:12; 7:22.

QUESTION—Why did Jesus merely tell them to go and show themselves to the priests?

Instead of telling them 'Be cleansed!' as he did to another leper in 5:13, Jesus told them to go and show the priests that they were healed [NTC]. This was an implicit promise to heal them [Lns, TH]. By simply telling them to go do this, Jesus was putting their faith to the test [Lns, NIC, TNTC]. Showing oneself to a priest was a normal procedure when a person was cured of leprosy since a priest had to certify that they were truly healed before they could resume an ordinary life in contact with other people [Lns, NIC, TG, TNTC].

QUESTION—Why is the plural form used in the command to show themselves to the *priests*?

The plural noun 'priests' is used because there were ten men [AB, NAC]. The ceremonies described in 5:14 would be too much for one priest to handle for ten men [Lns]. The plural is used because each of the healed lepers would go to the priest near his own home town [BECNT, ICC, My]. Or, each would go to the priest appropriate for that person, whether Jew or Samaritan [Lns, NIGTC]. Although sacrifices had to be offered at the main temple, other aspects of the law could be carried out wherever a priest might be found [NIGTC].

QUESTION—When were the lepers cleansed?

The men had started out in obedience to Jesus' command when they were cleansed [ICC]. Since one turned back to thank Jesus, it is implied that they were only a short distance away when the healing took place [Lns]. The phrase 'while they were going' means 'as they set off' [WBC]. The following verse shows that being cleansed meant being healed [NIGTC].

17:15 And one of them, having-seen[a] that he-was-healed, returned praising[b] God with a-loud voice, **17:16** and he-fell[c] on (his) face at his feet thanking him. And he was a Samaritan.

LEXICON—a. aorist act. participle of ὁράω (LN 24.1): 'to see' [AB, Arn, BECNT, LN, Lns, NTC, WBC; all versions except CEV, REB], 'to discover' [CEV], 'to find' [REB].

b. pres. act. participle of δοξάζω (LN 33.357) (BAGD 1. p. 204): 'to praise'. See translations of this word at 13:13. This word also occurs at 5:25; 7:16.

c. aorist act. indic. of πίπτω (LN 17.21) (BAGD 1.b.α. p. 659): 'to fall down' [BAGD]. The phrase 'he fell on his face' [Arn, BECNT, Lns, NTC; NASB] is also translated 'he fell down on his face' [WBC; KJV], 'he fell face down on the ground' [NLT], 'he fell with his face to the ground' [NET], 'he fell face downward' [HCSB], 'he fell' [AB], 'he bowed down' [CEV, NCV], 'he bowed' [GW], 'he threw himself down' [REB], 'he threw himself (at Jesus' feet)' [NIV], 'he threw himself to the ground' [TEV], 'he prostrated himself' [NRSV]. This idiom indicates complete prostration [NET]. It showed his humility [TNTC]. It was an act of submission to Jesus' authority and an act of reverence [NICNT].

QUESTION—How did he see that he was healed?
  He felt a current of health rush through every tissue of his body [NTC].

QUESTION—Why did the healed man praise God instead of Jesus?
  He praised God as the one who had healed him [BECNT, TNTC]. He praised God for healing him through Jesus [Lns, NTC]. He realized the Jesus had carried out God's will [Arn]. In the next verse he thanked Jesus [TH], realizing that God had healed him through Jesus [NET].

QUESTION—What is the significance of this man being a Samaritan?
  Samaritans were despised by the Jews, yet only this Samaritan returned from the ten who had been healed [BECNT, ICC], and he might have been expected to be the last one to thank a Jew [TNTC]. This was an aside in the telling of the story [NICNT]. It is not known how many of the other nine were Jews [ICC]. Or, it is implied that the other nine were all Jews [BECNT, Lns, NIGTC, Su]. This shows that Jesus is the Savior of all men [Arn].

17:17 And answering Jesus said, Were not ten cleansed? But the nine where (are they)? 17:18 Were-there- not -found^a (any others) having-returned to-give praise to-God except this foreigner?^{b}

LEXICON—a. aorist pass. participle of εὑρίσκω (LN 27.33) (BAGD 2. p. 325): 'to be found' [BAGD, LN]. The phrase 'were there not found any others having returned' is translated 'were there not found, having turned back' [Lns], 'were not any of them found to return' [Arn], 'were none found to return' [NTC], 'was none of them found to return' [NRSV], 'was no one found to return' [NIV], 'was no one found to turn back' [NET], 'was no one found who returned' [NASB], 'was no one found returning' [REB], 'was no one found who would return' [BECNT], 'can it be that none has been found to come back' [AB], 'didn't any return' [HCSB], 'why was/is (this foreigner the only one) who came back' [CEV, TEV], 'is (this Samaritan the only one) who came back' [NCV], 'does (only this foreigner) return' [NLT]. This is best taken as a question [TH]. This clause is normally taken as a question, but the syntax is better taken as a statement [WBC]: 'they have not been found returning' [WBC], 'there are not found that returned' [KJV], '(only this foreigner) came back' [GW]. Here, 'find' is used in the sense of 'appear' [TH]. The verb does not refer to a search, rather, it is a substitute for 'to be' [ICC, TG, TH].

  b. ἀλλογενής (LN **11.76**) (BAGD p. 39): 'foreigner' [BAGD, BECNT, **LN**, Lns, NTC, WBC; all versions except KJV, NCV], 'stranger' [AB; KJV], 'alien' [Arn], 'Samaritan' [NCV]. It means a non-Israelite [TH]. The Samaritans were regarded as Israelites of doubtful descent, that is, as half-foreign [WBC]. Or, Samaritans were not even partly descended from Jews, they were Gentiles [Alf, Lns]. Not being of the house of Israel, the man was a foreigner [AB], a non-Israelite [NIGTC, TG, TH].

QUESTION—What was it that Jesus answered?

Jesus responded to the situation in which only one returned to thank God [BECNT, Lns, MGC, NIGTC]. Jesus responded to the words of thanks with this series of three questions [BECNT, NIGTC]. This is Jesus' comment on the whole incident and it is addressed to the bystanders, not the Samaritan [ICC]. Perhaps Jesus addressed his disciples or the other people who were there [TG].

17:19 And he-said to-him, Having arisen, go. Your faith has-saved[a] you.

LEXICON—a. perf. act. indic. of σῴζω (LN 23.136, 21.27) (BAGD 1.c. p. 798): 'to save' [LN (21.27)], 'to save or free from disease' [BAGD], 'to heal, to cure, to make well' [LN (13.136)]. The clause 'your faith has saved you' [Arn, BECNT, Lns, WBC] is also translated 'your faith has brought you salvation' [AB], 'your faith has made you well' [NTC; CEV, GW, HCSB, NASB, NET, NIV, NLT, NRSV, TEV], 'your faith has cured you' [REB], 'thy faith hath made thee whole' [KJV], 'you were healed because you believed' [NCV]. This clause is identical to the ones in 7:50; 8:48; 18:42.

QUESTION—Where was the man to go?

The Samaritan was to continue on his journey to the priests to be legally pronounced clean [Lns].

QUESTION—In what way was this man saved?

1. The verb σέσωκέν 'has saved' refers to saving the man from leprosy [ICC, Lns, My, NTC, TG, TH; all versions]: your faith has healed you. The man was healed because he believed in Jesus [TG]. His faith was the instrumental cause of being saved from leprosy, but this was not yet faith that justified him and saved his soul [Lns]. This refers to the man's faith that Jesus was a divine, miraculously powerful teacher, but he did not yet recognize him to be the Messiah [My]. His faith was in Jesus' implied promise to heal the men in 17:14 [TH].

2. The verb σέσωκέν 'has saved' refers to saving the man's soul [Alf, Arn, BECNT, Gdt, MGC, NAC, NIBC, NIC, NICNT, NIGTC, WBC]. The man's faith had saved him from not only his sickness but saved him in the fullest sense of the word because he believed in Jesus [NIC]. The man's faith was the means of his cure and of his salvation [NIGTC]. The Samaritan had already been healed as were the other nine, but at this time the Samaritan's faith brought him full salvation [Arn, MGC]. The faith of the other nine men brought them healing, but their faith was incomplete because their faith did not issue in gratitude [NIGTC].

DISCOURSE UNIT: 17:20–18:8 [NTC, WBC]. The topic is faithfulness at the coming of the Son of Man [NICNT], who will be ready when the Son of Man comes? [WBC].

DISCOURSE UNIT: 17:20–37 [BECNT, NAC, TNTC; CEV, HCSB, NIV, NLT, NRSV, TEV]. The topic is God's kingdom [CEV], the coming of the kingdom [HCSB], the coming of the kingdom of God [NIV, NRSV, TEV], the coming kingdom of God [NAC, TNTC; NLT], a question about the consummation [BECNT].

DISCOURSE UNIT: 17:20–23 [NCV]. The topic is God's kingdom within you.

DISCOURSE UNIT: 17:20–21 [AB, NICNT, NIGTC, Su, WBC; GW, NET]. The topic is the Pharisees' question about the kingdom of God [GW], when is the kingdom [NICNT, WBC], the coming of the kingdom [AB, NIGTC; NET], the true nature of the kingdom of God [Su].

17:20 And having-been-asked by the Pharisees when the kingdom of-God comes[a] he-answered them and said, The kingdom of-God is- not -coming with observation.[b]

LEXICON—a. pres. mid./pass. (deponent = act.) indic. of ἔρχομαι (LN 15.81) (BAGD I.2.b. p. 311): 'to come' [BAGD, LN], 'to appear' [BAGD]. The phrase 'when (it) comes' [BECNT] is also translated 'when it is coming' [Lns], 'when it was coming' [Arn; NASB, NET, NRSV], 'when it will come' [HCSB, NCV], 'when it would come' [AB, NTC, WBC; CEV, GW, NIV, TEV], 'when will it come?' [NLT, REB], 'when it should come' [KJV]. The present tense of ἔρχεται 'comes' can be equivalent to a future, 'when will it come?' [NIGTC, TH]. This is a temporal question: 'when is it coming?' [BECNT].

b. παρατήρησις (LN **24.48**) (BAGD p. 622): 'observation' [BAGD]. The phrase 'is not coming with observation' is translated 'cometh not with observation' [KJV], 'does not come accompanied by observation' [Lns], 'it is not by observation that it comes' [AB], 'doesn't come in such a way that it can be closely watched' [**LN**], 'does not come in such a way as to be seen' [TEV], 'does not come in such a way that it can be observed' [Arn], 'does not come with your careful observation' [NIV], 'people can't observe the coming' [GW], 'you cannot tell by observation when (it) comes' [REB], 'isn't something you can see' [CEV], 'is coming, but not in a way that you will be able to see with your eyes' [NCV], 'is not coming with something observable' [HCSB], 'does not come with outward display' [NTC], 'is not coming with signs to be observed' [BECNT; NASB, NET], 'is not coming with things that can be observed' [NRSV], 'will not come in a way that allows for advance observation' [WBC], 'isn't ushered in with visible signs' [NLT].

QUESTION—What is meant by the coming of the kingdom of God?

The coming of the kingdom refers to when God will exercise his rule in full [Arn, TH]. It can be stated 'When will God establish his Kingdom on earth?' or 'When will God begin to rule over mankind?' [TG]. The Pharisees expected the establishment of an outward, earthly, and visible kingdom in which they would have a prominent place [NTC]. Jesus had proclaimed that the kingdom was at hand and the Pharisees wanted to know when it would

LUKE 17:20 219

come. Perhaps it was a test so that if Jesus fixed a date and there was no sign of the kingdom, they would be able to say that he was not who he claimed to be [ICC]. In light of the following verse, the Pharisees expected an answer such as 'The kingdom will come when you see so-and-so taking place' [NIGTC]. They wanted a timetable and thought that there would be unusual signs that would announce it was about to come [TG]. They wanted to know how they would know that the kingdom will come or has come [WBC].

QUESTION—What is meant by 'the kingdom of God is not coming with observation'?

1. The kingdom is not coming in such a way that it can be observed [Arn, EGT, Gdt, ICC, Lns, My, NTC, Su, TNTC; CEV, GW, NCV, REB, TEV]. It would not come with a visible development [My]. It is not a kingdom that comes with a grand spectacle [Lns], with proclamations, marching armies, martial music, and other outward show [NTC]. Since the kingdom was God's spiritual rule in the hearts of his subjects [Su], there was no observable phenomena that earthly kingdoms have, such as the coming of a king with his triumphant armies, and lands coming under his rule [Arn, Su]. Nor would there be displays of comets and catastrophes in nature at the time it comes [Arn]. It does not come with people watching the grand spectacle of its arrival [Lns].

2. The kingdom is not coming in such a way as to have signs to be observed before it comes [AB, Alf, BECNT, Crd, MGC, NAC, NIC, NIGTC, Rb, TG, TH, WBC; NASB, NET, NLT, NRSV]. They were asking about general apocalyptic signs so they could calculate the arrival of the kingdom [BECNT]. 'Observation' refers to watching for signs of the coming of the kingdom in order to predict the time when it would arrive [NAC]. The signs would occur on earth and in heaven [MGC]. This might be translated 'The coming of the Kingdom of God will not be preceded by visible signs' [TG], or 'There are no signs that can tell you when God is going to rule' [TH]. It doesn't come with the observation of supernatural signs, the political situation, or the configuration of stars [WBC]. At other times Jesus did speak of signs that would precede his coming and those who are spiritually alert would be able to tell when the time was approaching. However, the actual moment of the advent will arrive suddenly and unexpectedly [NIC]. A spiritual kingdom is slow in producing its conspicuous material effects and begins in ways that cannot be dated [ICC].

17:21 Nor will-they-say, Behold here (it is), or, There (it is), because behold the kingdom of-God is among/inside[a] you.

TEXT—Instead of ἤ, Ἐκεῖ 'or, There' some manuscripts read ἤ, Ἰδού, ἐκεῖ 'or, Behold, there'. GNT does not mention this variant. Ἤ, Ἰδού, ἐκεῖ 'or, Behold, there' is read by KJV.

LEXICON—a. ἐντός (LN 83.9, 83.17) (BAGD p. 269): 'among' [BAGD, LN (83.9)], 'inside' [BAGD, LN (83.17)]. The phrase 'is among/inside you' is translated 'is among you' [AB; HCSB, NLT, NRSV, REB], 'is in your midst' [Arn, BECNT, WBC; NASB, NET], 'is here with you' [CEV], 'is inside you' [Lns], 'is within you' [NTC; GW, KJV, NCV, NIV, TEV].

QUESTION—In the light of 17:23, will they or will they not say, 'here it is' or 'there it is'?

In this verse, it means that they will not say this with any reason [EGT, ICC], and in 17:23 when they say it, it is a groundless statement [ICC]. Since there are no visible signs, they will not be able to point it out as being here or there [MGC]. Jesus is saying that there is no need to look here and there to find the kingdom [BECNT]. Although they say these words in 17:23, they will be mistaken [NIGTC].

QUESTION—Was the kingdom of God among them or inside them?

1. The kingdom was already among them, in their midst [AB, Alf, Arn, BECNT, BNTC, ICC, MGC, My, NAC, NIBC, NIGTC, NIVS, TH, TNTC; CEV, HCSB, NASB, NET, NLT, NRSV, REB]. The Pharisees were being addressed and the kingdom was not in their hearts, but it was in their midst [Arn, ICC]. The reason for not looking for signs of the coming of the kingdom is that it was already in their midst [NAC], since Jesus the King was present and God's reign had already begun [BECNT, NAC]. The kingdom was present in the midst of the Pharisees in the person of Jesus [Arn, NIBC], or in the person of both Jesus and his disciples [ICC]. The kingdom was present in the person and ministry of Jesus [MGC, TNTC].
2. The kingdom will come suddenly in the future and be there in their midst without any advance warning [WBC]. This view is best related to the first part of 17:21 and makes room for 17:22–37 [WBC].
3. The kingdom was within a person, in one's heart [Crd, EGT, Gdt, Lns, NTC, Rb; GW, KJV, NCV, NIV, TEV]. The pronoun 'you' is general and does not mean 'you Pharisees' or any definite person [Lns], it means 'a person' or 'one' [NTC]. It is within or inside a person in the sense that whenever God is truly honored as King, there one finds his kingdom or kingship [NTC]. The kingdom was in the hearts of the believers scattered among the Pharisees [Lns].

DISCOURSE UNIT: 17:22–37 [AB, NICNT, NIGTC, Su, WBC; GW, NASB, NET]. The topic is the day of the Son of Man [AB, NIGTC, Su, WBC], the coming of the Son of Man [NET], the second coming foretold [NASB], Jesus teaches about the time when he will come again [GW], where is the kingdom? [NICNT].

17:22 And he-said to the disciples, (The) days will-come[a] when you-will-desire[b] to-see[c] one/the-first of-the days of-the Son of-Man[d] and you-will-not -see (it).

LEXICON—a. fut. mid. (deponent = act.) indic. of ἔρχομαι (LN 15.81) (BAGD I.1.b.α. p. 311): 'to come' [BAGD, LN]. The phrase 'the days will come' [Arn, NTC, WBC; KJV, NASB] is also translated 'the days are coming'

[HCSB, NET, NRSV], 'there will come days' [BECNT, Lns], 'the time will come' [CEV, GW, NCV, REB, TEV], 'the time will be coming' [AB], 'the time is coming' [NIV, NLT]. It means the time will arrive when this will happen [NTC].
  b. fut. act. indic. of ἐπιθυμέω (LN 15.12) (BAGD p. 293): 'to desire' [Arn, BAGD, BECNT; KJV, NET], 'to desire very much' [LN], 'to long' [AB, BAGD, LN, Lns, NTC, WBC; CEV, GW, HCSB, NASB, NIV, NLT, NRSV, REB], 'to wish' [TEV], 'to want very much' [NCV].
  c. aorist act. infin. of ὁράω (LN 90.79) (BAGD 1.b. p. 578): 'to experience' [BAGD, LN]. The phrase 'to see one of the days' [AB, Arn, BECNT, Lns, NTC, WBC; all versions except NLT] is also translated 'to share in the days' [NLT].
  d. υἱὸς τοῦ ἀνθρώπου 'Son of Man'. This title for Christ occurs at 5:24; 6:22; 7:34; 9:22, 26, 44; 11:30; 12:8, 40; 17:22, 24, 26; 18:8, 31; 19:10; 21:27, 36; 22:22, 48, 69; 24:7. See the discussions of this title at 5:24, 6:5, and 9:22.

QUESTION—What is the significance of the plural ἡμέραι 'days' in the phrase 'there will come days'?

There will be days of tribulation that will make them long for the advent that will bring an end to their sorrows [Arn, EGT, Gdt, ICC, My, NIC, Su, TH]. Again and again things will happen that will make them long for help from the Son of Man [Lns]. This is a warning of the difficult times the disciples will experience before the end [Su]. It is translated to the effect that 'the time will come' [AB, NTC; CEV, GW, NCV, NIV, NLT, REB, TEV].

QUESTION—What is meant by 'one of the days of the Son of Man'?

This is a longing for the time of his Messianic glory in the future [Arn, BNTC, Crd, EGT, Gdt, ICC, Lns, NIGTC, NTC, TH, TNTC].
  1. It has reference to one of the days [Arn, Gdt, ICC, Lns, TG, TH]: you will desire to see one of the days of the Son of Man. It has the idea of 'you will desire to see the Son of man, if only for one of his days' [TH], or 'to see at least one of the days when the Son of Man will present himself in all his power and glory' [TG]. It means 'Oh for one day of heaven in this time of trouble!' [ICC]. Even one day would be a breathing spell in their afflictions [Lns]. It means 'you will desire to have me at your side in my glory, even if only for a day' [Arn].
  2. It has reference to the first of the days [BECNT, NIC, NTC]: you will desire to see the first of the days of the Son of Man. The word μία 'one' may be a Semitism for 'the first' and this then means that they will desire to see the beginning of the Messianic era [NTC]. The use of 'one' means the beginning of a broad period of days [BECNT].
  3. It is not clear that this concerns a period of time over which Christ would reign, but the sense is centered on the coming of the Messiah and his kingdom [AB, MGC, NAC, NICNT, TNTC].

17:23 And they-will-say to-you, Behold, there (he/it is) or, Behold here (he/it is). Do- not -go-out[a] and run-after[b] (them).

TEXT—Instead of ἰδοὺ ἐκεῖ, ἤ, ἰδοὺ ὧδε· 'behold there, or, behold here;' some manuscripts read ἰδοὺ ὧδε, ἤ, ἰδοὺ ἐκεῖ· 'behold here, or, behold there', some manuscripts read ἰδοὺ ὧδε, ἰδοὺ ἐκεῖ 'behold here, behold there', some manuscripts read ἰδοὺ ὧδε ἢ ἐκεῖ 'behold here or there', some manuscripts read ἰδοὺ ὧδε, ἰδοὺ ἐκεῖ ὁ Χριστός 'behold here, behold there (is) the Christ', and some manuscripts read ἰδοὺ ὧδε, μὴ διώξητε· ἢ ἰδοὺ ἐκεῖ ὁ Χριστός· 'behold here, do not pursue; or behold there (is) the Christ;'. GNT reads ἰδοὺ ἐκεῖ, [ἤ,] ἰδοὺ ὧδε 'behold there, [or,] behold here' with a C decision and brackets ἤ 'or', indicating that the Committee had difficulty making the decision to include this word. Ἰδοὺ ὧδε, ἤ, ἰδοὺ ἐκεῖ 'behold here, or, behold there' is read by KJV.

LEXICON—a. aorist act. impera. of ἀπέρχομαι (LN 15.37) (BAGD 2. p. 84): 'to go out' [BECNT; NET, NLT, TEV], 'to go' [BAGD, NTC; CEV, NIV, NRSV, REB], 'to go after' [KJV], 'to follow' [HCSB], 'to go away' [Lns; NASB, NCV], 'to leave' [Arn, LN], 'to head off' [WBC], 'to run off' [AB], not explicit [GW]. They are not to leave their ordinary occupations and run after them [TH].

b. aorist act. impera. of διώκω (LN 15.158) (BAGD 4.a. p. 201): 'to run after' [BAGD, LN]. The phrase 'don't go out and run after them' is translated 'do not go away or pursue after' [Lns], 'do not go away, and do not run after them' [NASB], 'do not go out or chase after them' [NET], 'do not leave or follow them' [Arn], 'do not go out or pursue them' [BECNT], 'do not go, do not set off in pursuit' [NRSV], 'don't follow or run after them' [HCSB], 'do not go running off in pursuit' [REB], 'do not run off in pursuit of it' [AB], 'do not go running off after them' [NTC; NIV], 'don't go after them, nor follow them' [KJV], 'don't run after those people' [GW], 'don't go looking for him' [CEV], 'don't go out looking for it' [TEV], 'don't head off; don't go in pursuit' [WBC], 'don't believe such reports or go out to look for him' [NLT], 'stay where you are; don't go away and search' [NCV].

QUESTION—What is it that people are claiming to be here or to be there?
 1. They are claiming to have found the Son of Man present at some particular place [BECNT, NAC, NTC, Su, TH; GW, NCV, NET, NIV, NLT]: there *he* is, here *he* is. They may claim that they are the Messiah or that some contemporary person is the divine Helper they were looking for [Arn].
 2. They are claiming that the Kingdom of God is present [AB, Arn, Lns, MGC, NTC, WBC]: there *it* is, here *it* is. 'It' refers both to the Messiah and his kingdom [MGC]. This concerns the possibility that the Son of Man has turned up in some remote place [WBC].

QUESTION—What is the significance of the command not to go out and run after them?

This refers going out to the people who say 'here' or 'there' [AB, Arn, ICC, Lns, NTC, TH]: do not run after them. These people will pose as prophets or even as manifestations of Christ and will call people to follow them [Lns]. They must not pursue the claims that the Son of Man is present [BECNT]. They are not to go out to look for the Son of Man [BECNT, NTC, WBC]. People will believe that the Son of Man has already come and is hiding somewhere. The disciples are not to go running after such people in search of Christ since the time of Christ's arrival will not be known and when he does come again it will be visible all over the world [NTC]. Or, it means that they are to have nothing to do with such seduction [AB].

DISCOURSE UNIT: 17:24–37 [NCV]. The topic is when Jesus comes again.

17:24 Because as the lightning flashing out-of the (one part) under[a] the sky shines[b] to the (other part) under (the) sky, thus will-be the Son of-Man in his day.[c] **17:25** But first it-is-necessary (for) him to-suffer[d] many (things) and to-be-rejected[e] by this generation.[f]

TEXT—Instead of ἡ ἀστραπὴ ἀστράπτουσα 'the lightning flashing' some manuscripts read ἡ ἀστραπὴ ἡ ἀστράπτουσα 'the lightning the one flashing/that flashes'. GNT does not mention this variant. Ἡ ἀστραπὴ ἡ ἀστράπτουσα 'the lightning the one flashing/that flashes' is read by KJV.

TEXT—Instead of ὁ υἱὸς τοῦ ἀνθρώπου ἐν τῇ ἡμέρᾳ αὐτοῦ 'the Son of Man in his day' some manuscripts read καὶ ὁ υἱὸς τοῦ ἀνθρώπου ἐν τῇ ἡμέρᾳ αὐτοῦ 'the Son of Man also in his day', some manuscripts read ἡ παρουσία τοῦ υἱοῦ τοῦ ἀνθρώπου 'the coming of the Son of Man', and some manuscripts read ὁ υἱὸς τοῦ ἀνθρώπου 'the Son of Man'. GNT reads ὁ υἱὸς τοῦ ἀνθρώπου [ἐν τῇ ἡμέρᾳ αὐτοῦ] 'the Son of Man [in his day]' with a C decision and brackets ἐν τῇ ἡμέρᾳ αὐτοῦ 'in his day', indicating that the Committee had difficulty making the decision to include this phrase.

LEXICON—a. ὑπό (LN 83.51) (BAGD 2.a.β. p. 843): 'under' [BAGD, LN]. Perhaps the sky is thought of as the upper limit of space so that lightning is under it [NIGTC]. 'Under the sky/heaven' means 'on earth' [TH, WBC], but the picture of being under the vault of heaven can include the sky [WBC].

b. pres. act. indic. of λάμπω (LN **14.37**) (BAGD 1.a. p. 466): 'to shine' [BAGD, **LN**; KJV], 'to give light' [LN]. The phrase 'flashing out of the one part under the sky, shines to the other part under the sky' is translated 'when it flashes out of one part of the sky, shines to the other part of the sky' [NASB], 'shines out of one part under the heaven unto the other part under the heaven' [Lns], 'blazes forth, flashing from one part under the heaven to another part under the heaven' [Arn], 'flashes from one end of the sky to the other' [GW], 'that flashes from one side of the heavens to the other lights up the sky' [BECNT], 'flashes and lights up the sky from one end to the other' [AB; NIV], 'flashes from horizon to horizon and lights up the sky' [HCSB], 'lights up the sky from one end to the other' [NTC], 'which flashes across the sky and lights it up from one side to the other' [NCV, TEV], 'flashes and lights up the sky from one side to the other' [NET, NRSV], 'that flashes across the sky' [NLT], 'flashing across the sky' [CEV], 'a lightning-flash that lights up the earth from end to end' [REB], 'when it flashes, lights up the earth from one end of heaven to the other end of heaven' [WBC]. It flashes and lights up one region/side/point under the sky to the other [TH]. This means from one place on earth to another place on earth [NIGTC]. The point is that lightning covers the sky and is seen by everyone [AB, BECNT].

c. ἡμέρα (LN 67.178) (BAGD 2.b.β. p. 347): 'day' [BAGD, LN]. The phrase 'the Son of Man in his day' [AB, BECNT, Lns, NTC, WBC; HCSB, KJV, NASB, NET, NIV, NRSV, REB, TEV] is also translated 'the Son of Man on his day' [Arn], 'the day of the Son of Man' [CEV, GW], 'when the Son of Man comes again' [NCV], 'when the Son of Man returns' [NLT].

d. aorist act. infin. of πάσχω (LN 24.78) (BAGD 3.b. p. 634): 'to suffer' [BAGD, LN], 'to endure' [BAGD]. The phrase 'to suffer many things' [AB, Arn, BECNT, Lns, NTC, WBC; HCSB, KJV, NASB, NCV, NET, NIV] is also translated 'to suffer a lot' [GW], 'to suffer terribly' [CEV, NLT], 'to suffer much' [TEV], 'to endure much suffering' [NRSV, REB]. See this word at 9:22.

e. aorist pass. infin. of ἀποδοκιμάζω (LN 30.117) (BAGD 2. p. 91): 'to be rejected' [Arn, BAGD, BECNT, LN, Lns, NTC, WBC; all versions], 'to be repudiated' [AB]. See this word at 9:22.

f. γενεά (LN 11.4) (BAGD 2. p. 154): 'generation' [BAGD], 'contemporaries' [BAGD], 'those of the same generation, those of the same time' [LN]. The phrase 'by this generation' [AB, Arn, BECNT, Lns, NTC, WBC; HCSB, NASB, NET, NIV, NLT, NRSV, REB], is also translated 'of this generation' [KJV], 'by the people of his day' [GW], 'by the people of today' [CEV], 'by the people of this day' [TEV], 'by the people of this time' [NCV]. It refers to the contemporary generation of Jews [BAGD] and generalizes the current response to both John and Jesus [BECNT]. 'This generation' is practically identical to 'the men of this generation' in 7:31 [TH]. It means Jesus' contemporaries [Gdt, NAC]. See this word at 1:48, 50; 7:31; 9:41; 11:29, 50; 16:8; 21:32.

QUESTION—What relationship is indicated by γάρ 'because'?

The reason that the disciples did not need to hunt for the Son of Man's appearance is that his coming will be very obvious [BECNT, Lns, MGC, NIGTC]. It explains why the Son of Man will not appear there or here [Gdt, TH].

QUESTION—What is the similarity between the coming of the Son of Man and the flashing of lightning?

Both the Son of Man's coming and lightning are universally visible [AB, Arn, BECNT, Crd, Gdt, ICC, Lns, NAC, NIC, NIGTC, NTC, Rb, Su, TG,

TH, TNTC, WBC]. They are evident [NLT], public [NIVS], and obvious [TNTC; NET]. Or, they appear suddenly [AB, Arn, Gdt, ICC, NIC, NIVS, TH; NET] and unexpectedly [NIVS]. Or, the comparison is with their brightness [BNTC], their shining [NCV], since the Son of Man will shine with the brightness he had at the transfiguration [BNTC].

QUESTION—What is meant by 'his day'?
This refers to the coming of the Son of Man [TG], or the day when he is revealed [NIGTC]. It refers to the day the Son of Man will come and appear in glory [TG, TH]. This is Christ's second coming [Arn]. This is an application of the OT 'day of the Lord' [WBC].

17:26 And just-as it-was in the days of-Noah, thus will-it-be also in the days of-the Son of-Man. **17:27** They-were-eating, they-were-drinking,[a] they-were-marrying, they-were-being-given-in-marriage[b] until the day Noah entered into the ark[c] and the flood came and destroyed[d] all.

LEXICON—a. imperf. act. indic. of πίνω (LN 23.34) (BAGD p. 658): 'to drink' [AB, Arn, BAGD, BECNT, LN, Lns, NTC, WBC; all versions except NLT]. The phrase 'they were eating, they were drinking' is translated 'the people enjoyed banquets and parties' [NLT]. This verb pertains to consuming liquids, especially water and wine [LN].

b. imperf. pass. indic. of γαμίζω (LN **34.72**) (BAGD 2. p. 151): 'to be given in marriage' [AB, Arn, BAGD, BECNT, **LN**, NTC, WBC; KJV, NASB, NET, NIV, NRSV], 'to be married' [BAGD]. This passive verb is also translated actively with 'people' as the subject: 'giving in marriage' [HCSB], 'to give their children to be married' [NCV]. The phrases 'they were marrying, they were being given in marriage' are translated 'getting married' [CEV, GW], 'they...married' [REB], 'men and women married' [TEV], 'enjoyed...weddings' [NLT], 'they were marrying, they were being married (up to the day)' [Lns].

c. κιβωτός (LN 6.44) (BAGD 1. p. 431): 'ark' [AB, Arn, BAGD, LN, NTC, WBC; HCSB, KJV, NASB, NET, NIV, NRSV, REB], 'ship' [GW], 'boat' [BECNT; NCV, NLT, TEV], 'big boat' [CEV]. The core meaning of the noun is a box or chest, and it was applied to the type of boat Noah constructed [LN]. It was a boat about 450 feet long, 75 feet wide, and 45 feet high [TG].

d. aorist act. indic. of ἀπόλλυμι (LN 20.31) (BAGD 1.a.α. p. 95): 'to destroy' [AB, Arn, BAGD, BECNT, LN, NTC, WBC; GW, HCSB, KJV, NASB, NET, NIV, NLT, NRSV], 'to kill' [NCV, TEV], 'to drown' [CEV], 'to make an end of' [REB]. The 'all' who were destroyed refers to those who participated in the activities of the first part of this verse [TG].

QUESTION—What is meant by 'in the days of Noah'?
This refers to Noah's lifetime [NIGTC]. It more specifically refers to the days before Noah entered the ark [Gdt, Lns, NTC, TG, TH, WBC], or the days during which he was building the ark [NTC].

LUKE 17:26–27

QUESTION—What is meant by 'in the days of the Son of Man'?
This expression is not a natural way of speaking, but it is stated so as to parallel 'in the days of Noah' [NIGTC, WBC]. It means the time period in which the revealing of the Son of Man takes place [WBC]. The plural 'days' refers to the days immediately preceding his coming [BECNT, Lns, NAC, NIGTC, TH], while the singular 'the day' in 17:24 refers to his actual coming [Lns].

QUESTION—What is the function of 17:27?
This verse details the comparison mentioned in the preceding verse [BECNT, NIGTC].

QUESTION—What is the significance of the two verbs 'they were marrying, they were being given in marriage'?
This first describes the viewpoint of the men, 'they were marrying', and then the viewpoint of the women, 'they were being given in marriage' [NIGTC, TH]. The young girls were being given in marriage by their parents [Gdt].

QUESTION—What is the point of listing the activities of the people in the days of Noah?
It indicates that the people were going about their normal lives [MGC, NIGTC] and communicates the familiar rhythm of life [WBC]. The imperfect tenses of these verbs indicate the steady flow of their normal lives [TH], and indicate the repetitive nature of these activities [Arn, BECNT, ICC]. These four imperfect verbs describe how people were living and they make an effective contrast with the three aorists describing what suddenly happened at the time Noah entered the ark [NTC]. Until the Son of Man comes, life will go on normally like in the times of Noah. Although the people in Noah's time were sinful, these activities were not sinful in themselves, the people were just so taken up in these activities that they paid no attention to the warnings of Noah [Arn, Lns, NICNT, Su, TG, TNTC, WBC]. The people were wholly taken up in these things [ICC]. They went on with their activities as though Noah's warnings meant nothing to them [Lns].

17:28 Likewise just-as it-was in the days of-Lot they-were-eating, they-were-drinking, they-were-buying, they-were-selling, they-were-planting, they-were- building.ᵃ

TEXT—Instead of καθώς 'just as', some manuscripts read καὶ ὡς 'also as'. GNT does not mention this variant. Καὶ ὡς 'also as' is read by KJV.

LEXICON—a. imperf. act. indic. of οἰκοδομέω (LN 45.1) (BAGD 1.b.β. p. 558): 'to build' [BAGD, LN; all versions], 'to construct' [LN], 'to erect buildings' [BAGD].

QUESTION—What relationship is indicated by ὁμοίως 'likewise'?
This indicates a second comparison parallel with the comparison in 17:26–27 [EGT, Lns, Su, TH, TNTC]. This intensifies the first comparison and both highlight the final judgment and the swift doom of the unbelieving [Lns]. This comparison uses the example of judgment by fire while the first

example is of judgment by water [Lns, NTC, Su]. In both comparisons, the faithful person heeded God's warning and the indifferent multitudes perished [NTC].

QUESTION—Is there any significance in using six activities here and only four activities in the case of the people of Noah's time?

Here the description is more extensive, but no special meaning is to be drawn from this fact [TH]. The two mentions of marriage in the preceding comparison are omitted, perhaps because Sodom was not noted for its marrying [NAC]. This comparison adds commercial practices [NICNT]. This describes the same moral conditions of living as there were in Noah's days [TG]. The focus is on the people being unprepared and attached to earthly pursuits [NAC, NICNT, NIGTC].

17:29 And (on) the day Lot went-out from Sodom, it/he-rained[a] fire and sulfur[b] from heaven[c] and destroyed all. 17:30 In-the-same-way[d] it-will-be (on) the day the Son of Man is-revealed.[e]

LEXICON—a. aorist act. indic. of βρέχω (LN 14.10, 14.11) (BAGD 2.a. or 2.b. p. 147): 'to rain' [BAGD (2.b.), LN (14.10)], 'to cause it to rain' [BAGD (2.a.), LN (14.11)]. The phrase 'it/he rained fire and sulfur' is translated 'it rained fire and sulfur' [Lns; KJV, NASB, NRSV], 'fire and sulfur rained' [GW, REB], 'fire and sulfur/brimstone rained down' [AB, NTC, WBC; HCSB, NCV, NET, NIV, TEV], 'fire and burning sulfur rained down' [NLT], 'fiery flames poured down' [CEV], 'he rained down fire and sulfur' [BECNT], 'he let fire and brimstone rain down' [Arn].

b. θεῖον (LN **2.26**) (BAGD p. 353): 'sulfur' [BAGD, BECNT, **LN**, WBC; GW, HCSB, NCV, NET, NIV, NLT, REB, TEV], 'brimstone' [AB, Arn, LN, Lns; KJV, NASB], 'burning sulfur' [NLT]. This noun is also translated as an adjective modifying 'fire': 'fiery (flames)' [CEV]. It is implied that the sulfur is on fire and 'fire and sulfur' could be taken as a hendiadys and be translated 'burning sulfur' [WBC]. Sulfur is a yellow substance that burns intensely and is accompanied by an unpleasant odor [TG].

c. οὐρανός (LN 1.5) (BAGD 1.b. p. 594): 'heaven' [AB, Arn, BAGD, BECNT, Lns, NTC, WBC; HCSB, KJV, NASB, NET, NIV, NLT, NRSV, TEV], 'sky' [LN; CEV, GW, NCV, REB].

d. κατὰ τὰ αὐτά (LN 64.16): 'in the same way' [LN]. The phrase κατὰ τὰ αὐτά ἔσται 'in the same way it will be' is translated 'it will be the same' [NET], 'it will be just the same' [NASB], 'it will be like that/this' [AB, WBC; HCSB, NIV, NRSV, REB], 'this/that is how it will be' [NCV, TEV], 'the same will happen' [CEV], 'so it will be' [NTC], 'even thus shall it be' [KJV], '(the day) will be like that' [GW], 'like these things' [BECNT], 'according to these things will it be' [Lns], 'things will be the same' [Arn], 'yes, it will be business as usual right up to the hour' [NLT]. See this phrase at 6:23.

e. pres. pass. indic. of ἀποκαλύπτω (LN 28.38) (BAGD 4. p. 92): 'to be revealed' [AB, Arn, BAGD, BECNT, LN, Lns, NTC, WBC; all versions except CEV, NCV, NLT]. The passive voice is also translated actively with 'the Son of Man' as subject: 'to appear' [CEV], 'to come' [NCV], 'to return' [NLT]. The present tense is the prophetic present indicating a future event [Lns, Rb].

QUESTION—Who rained fire and sulfur from heaven?
   1. This has an impersonal reference [Gdt, Lns; KJV, NASB, NRSV]: it rained fire and sulfur from heaven. With the location 'from heaven' it best to take the subject in a neuter sense [Gdt].
   2. This is translated with fire and sulfur being the subject: [AB, NTC, WBC; CEV, GW, HCSB, NCV, NET, NIV, NLT, REB, TEV]: fire and sulfur rained from heaven.
   3. This has a personal reference [Arn, BECNT, ICC, NIGTC, TH]: he (God) rained fire and sulfur from heaven. Gen. 19:24 indicates that the subject is the Lord [Arn].

QUESTION—In 17:30, what is the similarity involved?
Normal human activity will go on until the day in question [TG, TNTC; NLT]. It will be an unexpected doom [Arn, NAC; NET]. Both judgment and deliverance are involved [WBC].

QUESTION—In what way will the Son of Man be revealed?
This refers to when he comes [Lns, NAC, NIVS, TH; CEV, NCV, NLT] and appears in glory [NTC, TG, TH]. He will come from heaven [MGC]. By the use of 'revealed' it is implied that the Son of Man has been reigning all along, although not visibly [Arn, ICC, NIC]. Or, instead of the Son of Man being the subject, the *day* of the Son of Man will be revealed [BECNT].

17:31 On that day (the one) who will-be on the roof and his property^a (will be) in the house, must- not -go-down to-take^b them-away. And the (one) in a-field likewise must- not -turn-back^c to the (things) behind/back.

LEXICON—a. σκεῦος (LN 57.20) (BAGD 1.a. p. 754): 'property' [BAGD], 'goods' [BECNT, LN, NTC; NASB, NET, NIV], 'belongings' [AB, LN, WBC; GW, HCSB, NCV, NRSV, REB], 'any belongings' [TEV], 'stuff' [KJV], 'equipment' [Arn], 'utensils' [Lns], 'anything' [CEV], not explicit [NLT].
   b. aorist act. infin. of αἴρω (LN 15.203): 'to take away' [BECNT, LN, Lns, WBC; KJV, NET, NRSV], 'to carry away, to carry off' [LN], 'to take out' [NASB], 'to get' [Arn, NTC; CEV, GW, HCSB, NCV, NIV, TEV], 'to fetch' [REB], 'to pack' [NLT], 'to pick up' [AB].
   c. aorist act. impera. of ἐπιστρέφω (LN 15.90) (BAGD 1.b.α. p. 301): 'to turn back' [BAGD, LN], 'to return' [LN]. The phrase ἐπιστρεψάτω εἰς τὰ ὀπίσω 'turn back to the things behind' is translated with ὀπίσω taken as 'behind': 'turn back for what is behind' [AB], 'turn to what he had left behind' [Arn], 'return for the things behind' [Lns], 'go back to the house for anything' [CEV], 'go back for anything' [NIV]. Or, ὀπίσω is taken as

the adverb 'back': 'turn back' [BECNT, NTC, WBC; GW, HCSB, NASB, NET, NRSV, REB], 'return back' [KJV], 'go back to the house' [TEV], 'go back home' [NCV], 'return to town' [NLT].

QUESTION—Why would someone be on the roof of his house?

Roofs of houses were flat and reached by outside steps [AB, MGC, NAC, NTC, TG, WBC]. People went to their rooftops for rest [NIGTC, TG], to catch the breeze [MGC], and to have conversation after the work day was finished [TG]. The flat roof could be used for a living space [BECNT].

QUESTION—Why shouldn't a person go down from the roof to take his things?

A person would go down by an exterior staircase and not through the house, so it would take more time to go into the house to gather things [AB, MGC, NIBC, TG, WBC]. This means that a person must flee immediately without taking time to go into the house to gather up his belongings [TG].

QUESTION—Why shouldn't someone in the field go back to his things at home?

This means that the man working in his field must flee at once and not waste time in going back home to gather up his possessions [TG]. From the previous instructions about coming down from the rooftop, it is implied that the purpose one would have in going back to his house is to gather up his possessions before fleeing [NIGTC, WBC].

QUESTION—Are these instructions to be taken literally?

1. Literal flight is the proper action to take [BECNT, BNTC, NAC, TG; NET]. A catastrophe is so imminent that there is no time to waste in fleeing to safety [BNTC, TG]. Imminent danger must be avoided by fleeing at once in order to escape the terrible consequences [BECNT]. This does not mean that someone may escape judgment at the return of the Son of Man, the point is that there will be no time to prepare when he returns since it will be too late then [NAC].

2. A metaphorical application is intended about one's attitude toward earthly possessions [Arn, Crd, Gdt, ICC, Lns, My, NIC, NICNT, NIGTC, NTC, Rb, Su, TH, TNTC]. There will be no opportunity for flight when the Son of Man appears, so this has to be taken metaphorically [Lns, NIGTC, NTC]. The point is that attachment to earthly things will lead to disaster [Crd, NIC, NIGTC]. In Matthew 24:17 Jesus said similar things with a warning to flee before the destruction of Jerusalem, but it is possible to use similar instructions literally for one situation and figuratively for another [NIC, TNTC]. Here nothing is said about flight, and the point is an attitude of readiness for the Son of Man's coming by being indifferent to all worldly interests [ICC]. We are to have a whole-hearted devotion to the Son of Man that is not complicated by a desire for material things [TNTC].

17:32 Remember[a] Lot's wife.

LEXICON—a. pres. act. impera. of μνημονεύω (LN 29.7) (BAGD 1.a. p. 525): 'to remember' [AB, Arn, BAGD, BECNT, LN, Lns, NTC, WBC; all versions except CEV, NLT], 'to remember what happened to' [CEV, NLT]. This refers to remembering something that is known generally [TH]. It means more than just recollecting something, it includes paying heed to it and being warned by it [MGC, NIGTC].

QUESTION—What are they to remember about Lot's wife?
1. This is in connection with a literal flight in time of danger [TG]. Gen. 19:26 tells what happened to Lot's wife and this is added as a warning by giving an example of what happened to a person who did not flee at once [TG]. She looked back with longing to be where she used to be [NET].
2. This is in connection to a metaphorical understanding of the preceding command. Lot's wife is an example of someone who turned back [TH]. She did not want to abandon her earthly possessions [ICC, Lns, My]. She was not willing to give up everything at the time of judgment [NICNT]. This is a warning against the danger of falling back into worldliness and sin with the result of judgment [NIGTC]. One must not look back and yearn for possessions that had been left behind [NTC].

17:33 Whoever seeks[a] to-preserve[b] his life will-lose[c] it, but whoever loses[d] (it) will-preserve[e] it.

TEXT—Instead of ὃς ἐὰν ζητήσῃ τὴν ψυχὴν αὐτοῦ περιποιήσασθαι 'whoever seeks to preserve his life', some manuscripts read ὃς ἐὰν ζητήσῃ τὴν ψυχὴν αὐτοῦ σῶσαι 'whoever seeks to save his life' and some manuscripts read ὃς ἂν θελήσῃ ζωογονῆσαι τὴν ψυχὴν αὐτοῦ 'whoever wishes to keep alive his life'. GNT reads ὃς ἐὰν ζητήσῃ τὴν ψυχὴν αὐτοῦ περιποιήσασθαι 'whoever seeks to preserve his life' with a B decision, indicating that the text is almost certain. Ὃς ἐὰν ζητήσῃ τὴν ψυχὴν αὐτοῦ σῶσαι 'whoever seeks to save his life' is read by KJV.

LEXICON—a. aorist act. subj. of ζητέω (LN 68.60) (BAGD 2.b.γ. p. 339): 'to seek to do something, to try' [LN], 'to strive for, to aim at, to desire, to wish' [BAGD]. See the translation of this word in the phrase translated with the following word.

b. aorist mid. infin. of περιποιέομαι, περιποιέω (LN 21.24) (BAGD 1. p. 650): 'to preserve' [BAGD], 'to save' [BAGD, LN]. The phrase ζητέω τὴν ψυχὴν αὐτοῦ περιποιήσασθαι 'to seek to preserve his life' [Lns; REB] is also translated 'to seek to keep his life' [NASB], 'to try to keep his life' [NTC; NCV, NET, NIV], 'to seek to gain his life' [BECNT], 'to try to make his life secure' [HCSB, NRSV], 'to cling to this life' [NLT], 'to seek his life in order to gain full possession of it' [Arn], 'to try to retain his life as a possession for himself' [WBC], 'to seek to save his life' [KJV], 'to seek to save his own life' [LN], 'to try to save his own life' [TEV], 'to try to save his life' [AB; CEV, GW]. The middle voice of the verb indicates that the preserving of life is for the benefit of the subject [ICC, TH].

c. fut. act. indic. of ἀπόλλυμι (LN 57.68) (BAGD 1.b. p. 95): 'to lose' [AB, Arn, BAGD, BECNT, LN, Lns, NTC, WBC; all versions].

LUKE 17:33   231

d. aorist act. subj. of ἀπόλλυμι (LN 57.68) (BAGD 1.b. p. 95): 'to lose' [AB, Arn, BAGD, BECNT, LN, Lns, NTC, WBC; all versions except NCV], 'to give up their lives' [NCV].

e. fut. act. indic. of ζῳογονέω (LN 23.89) (BAGD 2. p. 341): 'to preserve' [BECNT, NTC, WBC; HCSB, KJV, NASB, NET, NIV], 'to preserve alive, to keep alive' [BAGD, LN], 'to save' [CEV, GW, NCV, NLT, TEV], 'to gain' [REB], 'to keep' [NRSV], 'to keep himself alive' [AB] 'to keep it alive' [Arn, Lns].

QUESTION—What is meant by seeking to preserve one's life?

Many point to the parallel passage in 9:24 for the meaning of this verse [AB, Alf, MGC, NAC, NICNT, NIVS, NTC, TG, TH]. In 9:24 this saying was applied to a daily taking up of one's cross to follow Jesus, but here it is applied to the coming judgment [WBC].

1. It means to hold on to what one considers to be his real life [NIGTC], to seek fullness of life and happiness in earthly things [NIC]. It is to seek to provide for the needs of this life [Crd], to devote one's thoughts and efforts to getting everything for his body [Lns]. It is valuing what is temporary and physical [Su].

2. It means trying to preserve one's physical life [BECNT]. If one seeks to avoid persecution, it will lead to a lack of commitment to God and a relationship with God defines life [BECNT].

QUESTION—What is meant by such a one losing his life?

He will forfeit his soul [Crd]. His soul will go to judgment [Arn, Lns, NIGTC]. He will be left behind in this perishing world [Gdt]. Or, he will never find true life and happiness [NIC].

QUESTION—In the second clause, what is meant by losing one's life?

This refers to physically losing one's life or being prepared to do so [Lns, TH, TNTC]. Or, it is to give up everything to lay hold of Jesus [Gdt].

QUESTION—What is meant by such a one preserving his life?

His body will die, but his soul will leave his body and will be saved to be reunited with the body at the resurrection and he will live in heaven forever [Lns]. He will enjoy true life in the fullest sense of the word [NIC].

17:34 I-say to-you, (On) that[a] night there-will-be two[b] in one bed, one will-be-taken[c] and the other will-be-left-behind.[d]

LEXICON—a. οὗτος, αὕτη (LN 92.29): 'this' [LN]. The phrase 'on that night' [AB, Arn, Lns, WBC; all versions except KJV, NET, NLT] is also translated 'in that night' [BECNT, NTC; KJV, NET], 'that night' [NLT].

b. δύο (LN 60.11): 'two' [Arn, BECNT, LN, WBC; HCSB, NASB, NRSV], 'two people' [NTC; CEV, GW, NCV, NET, NIV, NLT, REB, TEV], 'two men' [AB, Lns; KJV].

c. fut. pass. indic. of παραλαμβάνω (LN 15.177) (BAGD 1. p. 619): 'to be taken' [AB, BAGD, BECNT, NTC, WBC; all versions except NLT, TEV], 'to be taken away' [LN, Lns; NLT, TEV], 'to be accepted' [Arn].

d. fut. pass. indic. of ἀφίημι (LN 85.45): 'to be left behind' [LN, NTC, WBC; TEV], 'to be left' [AB, BECNT, Lns; all versions except TEV], 'to be abandoned' [Arn].

QUESTION—What does 'this night' refer to?

This verse goes back to 'the day' when the Son of Man is revealed in 17:30, but it does not prove that the return will be at night [NAC, Su, TH]. Or, it indicates that the coming of the Son of Man will occur at night [TG]. The Jewish day began with night and the first illustration takes place at night time [EGT]. 'Night' is part of the illustration since they are sleeping [ICC, NIGTC], but in conjunction with the two women grinding, it means whether people are sleeping or working when the Lord comes, this separation will take place [ICC]. The coming is certain, but the time of day is not [Lns]. When the Son of Man arrives, it will be night for some on earth and daylight for others [Gdt, NTC]. Or, both illustrations take place at the same time, a period just before dawn when some are still sleeping and others are up early to perform their daily tasks and that period of time is followed by the day of the Son of Man [NIGTC]. The time of day only provides background to the illustrations and does not indicate when the Son of Man will come [BECNT].

QUESTION—Who were the 'two' in one bed?

1. This refers to two men in one bed [AB, ICC, Lns, NAC, Su, TH]. The masculine gender of ὁ εἷς...ὁ ἕτερος 'the one...the other' indicates two males, not necessarily two adult men, possibly a man and his son [ICC, Su]. The following illustration concerning two women suggests that here the reference is to two men [AB].

2. This refers to a man and his wife [NIGTC, TNTC, WBC]. Both pronouns are masculine since either the man or his wife may be the one taken or left [NIGTC, TNTC], and if male and female pronouns had been used, a decision would have to be made as to which was taken and which was left [WBC].

17:35 There-will-be two grinding[a] at the same-(place/mill)/together, one will-be-taken, but the other will-be-left-behind.

LEXICON—a. pres. act. participle of ἀλήθω (LN 46.16) (BAGD 37): 'to be grinding' [BAGD, LN], 'to grind grain' [LN], 'grinding at the same place' [Arn; NASB], 'grinding at the same mill' [AB]. Or, taking ἐπὶ τὸ αὐτό to mean 'together': 'grinding together' [BECNT, Lns, NTC; KJV], 'together grinding wheat' [CEV], 'together grinding corn' [REB], 'grinding grain together' [GW, HCSB, NCV, NET, NIV], 'grinding meal together' [NRSV], 'grinding at the mill together' [WBC], 'grinding flour together at the mill' [NLT], 'grinding grain at the same place' [**LN**]. Since they are grinding at the same spot, they are grinding together [TH]. They were grinding at the same place because they used a hand mill that was operated by two women working together [BAGD, LN].

QUESTION—Who were the 'two' grinding?

The feminine gender of ἡ μία...ἡ ἑτέρα 'the one...the other' indicates two females [AB, BECNT, Su]. The females could be mother and daughter, mother and daughter-in-law, two sisters, or two female slaves [Su]. That they were together at the same place implies that they were working with the same instrument [TH]. The parallel passage in Matt. 24:41 says that they were grinding at the mill [BECNT]. The picture is of two women grinding grain, and they could be facing each other across a small millstone and turning the round flat grinding stone [Su], or they could be sitting side by side [Arn, Lns]. One woman would be turning the grinding stone while the other poured out the meal [MGC, NIGTC].

QUESTION—Which of the two suffers punishment in each illustration?

1. The person who is left is the one who suffers punishment [AB, Arn, BECNT, Gdt, ICC, Lns, MGC, NAC, NIC, NIGTC, NTC, TG, TH, TNTC]. One is taken from destruction (like Noah and Lot), the other is left to his fate or judgment (like the people of the world and the citizens of Sodom) [AB, BECNT, ICC, MGC, NAC, NIGTC]. Or, one is taken into the kingdom while the other is left outside [AB, ICC]. The following verse suggests that those who are left are left to the vultures as judgment [BECNT]. 'Taken' must refer to be taken to be with Christ [TNTC]. One is taken up to meet Christ and the unbeliever is left on earth to be judged [NIC]. The passive form of the verbs may indicate that the agent who takes away is God, who takes away his people from the scene of judgment [AB, NIGTC]. Or, the agent may be the angels as in Mark 13:27 and Matt. 24:31 [TG, TH]. Or, the agent is the Son of Man who is returning for his people [Lns].

2. The person who is taken away is the one who suffers punishment [Su]. The focus is on judgment and so it must mean that one is taken away for judgment, leaving the other to be reunited with the Son of Man. In the illustrations of Noah and Lot, it was the good men who were left and the evil ones were punished by being taken out of the world [Su].

17:37 And answering they-say to-him, Where,[a] Lord? And he-said to-them, Where the body[b] (is), there also the vultures[c] will-be-gathered.[d]

TEXT—Some manuscripts add verse 36, 'Two will be in a field; one will be taken and the other will be left'. GNT omits this verse with a B decision, indicating that the omission is almost certain. The verse is included by KJV. The verse in included in brackets by HCSB and NASB.

LEXICON—a. ποῦ (LN 83.6): 'where?' [AB, Arn, BECNT, LN, Lns, NTC, WBC; all versions except CEV, NCV, NLT], 'where will this be?' [NCV], 'where will this happen?' [CEV, NLT].

b. σῶμα (LN **8.1**) (BAGD 1.a. p. 799): 'body' [BAGD, BECNT, **LN**, Lns, WBC; KJV, NASB], 'a dead body' [BAGD; GW, NCV, NET, NIV, TEV], 'corpse' [AB, BAGD, NTC; CEV, HCSB, NRSV], 'carcass' [Arn; NLT, REB].

c. ἀετός (LN 4.42) (BAGD p. 19): 'vulture' [BAGD, BECNT, LN, NTC, WBC; all versions except CEV, KJV], 'buzzard' [CEV], 'eagle' [AB, Arn, BAGD, LN, Lns; KJV]. This refers to vultures [Arn, Gdt, ICC, NIGTC, NTC, TG, TH, TNTC, WBC], because eagles do not fly in flocks or feed on carrion [ICC]. However, it is a fact that eagles do gorge themselves on carrion [Lns].

d. fut. pass. indic. of ἐπισυνάγομαι, ἐπισυνάγω (LN 15.124) (BAGD p. 301): 'to be gathered' [BAGD, BECNT, LN; HCSB, NASB], 'to be gathered together' [Lns, WBC; KJV]. This passive is also translated actively: 'to gather' [Arn, NTC; GW, NCV, NET, NIV, NRSV, REB, TEV], 'to flock' [AB], 'there will be' [CEV], 'gathering' [NLT]. This describes the gathering of birds of prey around a dead body [BAGD]. They will be circling around in the sky [MGC, NICNT, Su, TNTC].

QUESTION—What is meant by the disciples' response 'Where?'

1. This is connected with the two preceding verses 17:34–35 [Arn, BECNT, Crd, Lns, NIC, Su, WBC; NET]. They wanted to know where the separation described in 17:34–35 would take place [Arn, BECNT, Lns, Su]. They asked where the judgment would take place [NET]. Even though the judgment will be visible to everyone, the Son of Man will return to some location and the question is where will the judgment be rendered when one is taken and the other is left behind [BECNT]. Or, they wanted to know where the unredeemed will be left [NIC]. Or, they wanted to know where the people of 17:34–35 were to be taken [WBC].

2. It refers the place where the events of 17:31–32 will take place since 17:34–35 doesn't describe the coming of the Son of Man [TG].

3. This is a question about where the second advent will take place [ICC, NIGTC, Su]. A question about a location doesn't proceed logically from the immediately preceding sayings, so this question takes up the point in 17:23 as to where the Messiah actually will appear [NIGTC].

QUESTION—What is meant by the Lord's answer?

1. This refers to the inevitable judgment that must come to the spiritually dead [Arn, Crd, ICC, Lns, NIC, NTC, TNTC]. Where a dead body is found there the vultures gather, and similarly where the spiritually dead are found, there the final judgment will overtake them [NIC, NTC, TNTC].

2. Once judgment is rendered, it is final and vultures will feast on the dead bodies [BECNT]. The disciples are not to worry about where the judgment will occur, because when it does come, it will be too late to do anything about it and all will see it [BECNT].

3. People will gather to the Son of Man for deliverance like vultures gather to feast on their prey [WBC].

4. This refers to the self-evident nature of the coming of the Son of Man [AB, NAC, NICNT, NIGTC, Su, TG, TH; NLT]. The Son of Man's presence will be made evident just as a dead body is made evident by vultures flying around it overhead [MGC, NICNT, NIGTC, Su]. Like the

eagles show up where the carrion is, so the day of the Son of Man will be inevitably revealed [AB, NAC]. 'Just as the gathering of vultures shows where there is a carcass nearby, so these signs indicate that the end is near' [NLT].

DISCOURSE UNIT: 18:1–14 [TNTC]. The topic is two parables about prayer.

DISCOURSE UNIT: 18:1–8 [AB, BECNT, NAC, NICNT, NIGTC, Su, TNTC, WBC; CEV, GW, HCSB, NASB, NCV, NET, NIV, NLT, NRSV, TEV]. The topic is a widow and a judge [CEV], the parable of the widow and the judge [TEV], the parable of the widow and the unjust judge [NRSV], the parable of the nagging widow [BECNT], the story of the persistent widow [HCSB, NIV, NLT], prayer and the parable of the persistent widow [NET], the parable of the unjust judge [AB, NAC, NIGTC, TNTC], an unjust judge and a just God [Su], faithfulness in anticipation [NICNT], speedy vindication for any who have faith [WBC], God will help his people [GW], God will answer his people [NCV], parables on prayer [NASB].

18:1 **And he-was-speaking a-parable to-them about (how) it-is-necessary (for) them to-pray always and not to-become-discouraged,**ᵃ

LEXICON—a. pres. act. infin. of ἐγκακέω (LN 25.288) (BAGD 1. p. 215): 'to become discouraged' [LN; HCSB, TEV], 'to lose heart' [LN, Lns, NTC; NASB, NET, NRSV, REB], 'to become weary' [BAGD], 'to grow weary' [Arn], 'to grow tired' [BECNT], 'to faint' [KJV], 'to give up' [AB, LN, WBC; CEV, GW, NIV, NLT], 'to lose hope' [NCV].

QUESTION—How was the subject of prayer brought up?

The disciples would be thinking of earnest prayer for the coming of the days of the Son of Man [Arn]. Prayer would be needed since there would be an interval before that day would come (17:22–37) [NIGTC]. There would be many difficult days before the coming of the Son of Man [NTC]. This is not about prayer in general, but prayer in connection with one's longing for the coming of the Son of Man (17:22) [WBC]. In reference to 18:8, such prayer is in regard to asking for God's justice and the return of the Son of Man who would bring justice [BECNT]. Or, prayer in general is meant here, not just prayer for Christ to return and deliver them [ICC, NIC]. Or, the original setting for this teaching is lost to us [AB].

QUESTION—What is meant by praying πάντοτε 'always'?

It does not mean to pray constantly without a break, but to pray persistently and not be tempted to stop when the answer is delayed [EGT]. It is not perpetual, continuous prayer, but prayer that continues on [AB, NAC, NIGTC]. It means to pray again and again [BECNT, NIGTC]. One doesn't give up if the prayer seems unanswered [AB, NIGTC, WBC].

QUESTION—What is meant by being discouraged?

One is not to become discouraged, thinking that God would not answer [TG, TNTC]. They must not stop believing that God will answer [TG]. Or, rather than the absolute sense of being discouraged and losing heart, it specifically means that they are not to give up praying [TH]. Persistence in prayer is required [BNTC, EGT], they are to keep praying in spite of a delayed answer [EGT].

18:2 saying, A-certain judge[a] was in a-certain city not fearing[b] God and not respecting[c] man.

LEXICON—a. κριτής (LN 56.28) (BAGD 1.a.α. p. 453): 'judge' [AB, Arn, BAGD, BECNT, LN, Lns, NTC, WBC; all versions]. This is a man appointed to judge in a small town, not an official of an organized judicial system [NIGTC]. However, the parable does not depend on whether the judge was an official of the judicial system or if he was merely a prominent person who took on such a task [AB].
- b. pres. pass. participle of φοβέομαι (LN **87.14**) (BAGD 2.a. p. 863): 'to fear' [AB, Arn, BAGD, BECNT, **LN**, Lns, WBC; all versions except NCV, NLT, REB], 'to have fear of' [REB], 'to show great reverence for, to show great respect for' [LN], 'to have reverence for' [NTC], 'to respect' [NCV]. The phrase 'not fearing God' is translated 'who was a godless man' [NLT].
- c. pres. pass. participle of ἐντρέπομαι, ἐντρέπω (LN 87.11) (BAGD 2.b. p. 269): 'to respect' [BAGD, LN; GW, HCSB, NASB, NET, TEV], 'to have respect for' [NTC; NRSV, REB] 'to stand in awe of' [Arn], 'to care about' [AB, WBC; CEV, NCV, NIV], 'to regard' [BECNT, Lns; KJV]. The phrase 'not respecting man' is translated 'with great contempt for everyone' [NLT].

QUESTION—What is meant by the judge not fearing God?

This does not primarily mean that the judge did not fear God's anger, rather it means that he did not respect, honor, and reverence God, in other words, he was irreverent and irreligious [TG]. He was without religious scruples [Arn]. He had no reverence for God's commands [NIC]. Or, he did not fear God's threats against unjust judges [Lns]. This probably indicates that he was a Gentile official [ICC]. Or, he was probably a Jew, since Romans stayed away from such matters [BECNT].

QUESTION—What is meant by the judge not respecting people?

The judge paid no heed to the opinions or interests of the citizens [NIC]. He was callous and insensitive to people's troubles, he did not care for their rights [TG]. He did not worry about what people thought of him [BECNT, NIVS]. He was not fair [AB]. He lacked moral and humane principles in general [Arn]. He had contempt for the people who came before him [Hlt].

18:3 And a-widow was in that city and she-was-coming[a] to him saying, Give-justice[b] to-me against my opponent.[c]

LEXICON—a. imperf. mid./pass. (deponent = act.) indic. of ἔρχομαι (LN 15.81): 'to come' [LN]. The imperfect tense in this verb is translated 'kept coming' [AB, Arn, Lns, NTC; all versions except KJV, NLT], 'came repeatedly' [NLT], 'used to come' [WBC], 'was coming again and again' [BECNT], 'came' [KJV].

b. aorist act. impera. of ἐκδικέω (LN 56.35) (BAGD 1. p. 238): 'to give justice' [LN], 'to procure justice' [BAGD]. The phrase 'give justice to me against my opponent' is translated 'give me justice against my adversary' [HCSB, NET], 'provide justice for me against my adversary' [Arn], 'give me my rights against my enemy' [NCV], 'avenge me of mine adversary' [KJV], 'give me legal protections from my opponent' [NASB], 'grant me justice against my opponent' [NTC; NRSV], 'grant me justice against my adversary' [NIV], 'give me justice' [GW], 'vindicate me against my antagonist' [WBC], 'vindicate me against my adversary' [BECNT], 'vindicate me of my opponent at law' [Lns], 'make sure that I get fair treatment in court' [CEV], 'see that I get justice over my opponent' [AB], 'pleading for her rights, saying, Help me against my opponent' [TEV]. This direct speech is also translated indirectly: 'appealing for justice against someone who had harmed her' [NLT], 'to demand justice against her opponent' [REB].

c. ἀντίδικος (LN 39.9) (BAGD p. 74): 'opponent' [AB, BAGD, NTC; NASB, NRSV, REB, TEV], 'opponent at law' [Lns], 'adversary' [Arn, BECNT; HCSB, NET, NIV], 'antagonist' [WBC], 'enemy' [LN; NCV], 'someone who had harmed her' [NLT], not explicit [CEV, GW]. Here 'opponent' is used in a legal sense [TG, TH], in a lawsuit [BAGD]. It appears that the widow is trying to initiate the suit, but her opponent appears as the aggressor [WBC].

QUESTION—What is indicated by the imperfect tense of ἤρχετο 'she was coming'?

The imperfect tense indicates repetition [BECNT, EGT, ICC, Lns, MGC, NAC, NIC, NIGTC, Rb, TH; NET].

QUESTION—What is meant by her request that the judge grant her justice?

The widow had been unjustly treated [Bai, Lns, NIC, NTC, Pnt]. Someone had taken advantage of her defenseless widowhood [TG]. It appears that she was a poor widow who had no influence [Lns]. Probably her opponent was some important person known by the judge [Su]. It probably was a money matter [Bai, Hlt]. She had been robbed of what little she had [Lns]. Perhaps someone had taken away what little she had or else had not given her what she was entitled to [NTC]. Perhaps she did not get her rightful share of her husband's property or perhaps she was being evicted from her home [Hlt]. She wanted protection against her enemy's lawless actions [Alf, Arn], and be preserved from his attacks [ICC]. She wanted the payment that was due her [Bai, NIGTC]. The decision could involve punishing her opponent [Lns, NTC], but the focus is on receiving what was due her [AB, NIGTC, NTC]. She was a plaintiff in some lawsuit [AB]. She had a lawsuit with her opponent and she wanted a just decision made and it is implied that the right was on her side [TG, TH]. An appeal for vengeance is possible with this verb, but more probably this is an appeal for protection or restoration of something [Gdt, WBC].

18:4 And he-was- not -willing[a] for a-time.[b] But after[c] these (things) he-said within himself, Even though I-do- not -fear God nor do-I-respect men,

LEXICON—a. imperf. act. indic. of θέλω (LN 25.1) (BAGD 2. p. 355): 'to will' [BAGD], 'to desire, to want' [LN], 'to wish' [BAGD, LN]. The phrase οὐκ ἤθελεν 'he was not willing' [Arn] is also translated 'he was unwilling' [NTC; HCSB, NASB], 'he would not' [Lns; KJV], 'he didn't want to' [WBC], 'he refused' [AB, BECNT; NET, NIV, NRSV, REB], 'the judge refused to act' [TEV], 'the judge refused to do anything' [CEV, GW], 'the judge refused to help her' [NCV]. The imperfect tense indicates that the judge continued to refuse as the widow continued to come before him [EGT, ICC]. The judge would not give a decision, he just did nothing [TG]. He would not defend the widow [TH]. The judge didn't want to give the widow justice, perhaps because he was just too lazy or perhaps her opponent was so powerful that he didn't want to offend him [NIGTC]. Or, instead of trying to speculate on the judge's reason, this is just a vital development in the story [NAC].

b. χρόνος (LN 67.78): 'time' [LN]. The phrase ἐπὶ χρόνον 'for a time' [AB, BECNT, Lns, WBC; REB] is also translated 'for some time' [Arn; NIV], 'for a long time' [TEV], 'for a while' [NTC; all versions except NIV, REB, TEV], 'at last' [NTC].

c. μετά (LN 67.48): 'after' [LN]. The phrase μετὰ ταῦτα 'after these' is translated 'after a while' [BECNT], 'afterwards' [Arn; KJV, NASB, NCV], 'later on' [WBC; NET], 'later' [AB; HCSB, NRSV], 'finally' [CEV, NIV], 'eventually' [NLT], 'in the end' [REB], 'at last' [TEV], 'then' [GW].

18:5 yet because this widow causes me trouble[a] I-will-give-justice to-her, lest to/in (the) end[b] coming she-may-strike- me -under-the-eye.[c]

LEXICON—a. κόπος (LN 22.7) (BAGD 1. p. 443): 'trouble' [BAGD, LN]. The phrase παρέχειν μοι κόπον 'causes me trouble' [Arn] is also translated 'troubles me' [KJV], 'is making me trouble' [Lns], 'bothers me' [BECNT; NASB], 'will continue to bother me' [NCV], 'keeps bothering me' [NIV, NRSV], 'keeps on bothering me' [NTC; CEV, NET], 'is a bother to me' [WBC], 'is a nuisance' [AB], 'is so great a nuisance' [REB], 'keeps pestering me' [HCSB], 'really annoys me' [GW], 'is driving me crazy' [NLT], 'all the trouble (this widow) is giving me' [TEV]. The judge felt badgered [NICNT].

b. τέλος (LN 68.12) (BAGD 1.d.γ. p. 812): 'end' [BAGD, LN]. The phrase εἰς τέλος 'in the end' [BAGD] is also translated 'finally' [BAGD], 'continually' [LN]. The phrase 'to the end/in the end coming' is translated 'she'll keep coming to me' [GW; similarly TEV], 'her persistent coming' [HCSB], 'by continually coming' [NASB, NRSV; similarly BECNT; KJV], 'with her constant requests' [NLT], 'with her persistence' [REB], 'she will continue (to bother me)' [NCV], 'in the end (she will wear me out) by her unending pleas' [NET], '(so that she won't) eventually (wear me out) with her coming' [NIV], 'she keep coming and finally (wear me out)' [AB], 'she may not continue to come and finally (make me miserable)' [Arn], 'she finally (wears me out) by her continual coming' [NTC], 'finally by coming (she will be knocking me out)' [Lns], not explicit [CEV].

   c. pres. act. subj. of ὑπωπιάζω (LN **25.245**) (BAGD 1. p. 848): 'to strike under the eye, to give a black eye' [BAGD], 'to be knocking (me) out' [Lns], 'to wear out by annoying' [**LN**], 'to wear (me) out' [AB, BECNT, NTC; all versions except KJV, NCV], 'to weary' [KJV], 'to annoy greatly' [BAGD], 'to make miserable' [Arn], 'to shame' [WBC]. This active verb is also translated passively: 'to be worn out' [NCV].

QUESTION—What was the trouble that the widow was causing?

The widow caused trouble for the judge by her persistent coming to try to get justice [AB]. She was destroying his personal ease and peace [Lns].

QUESTION—What is modified by εἰς τέλος 'to/in the end'?

1. The phrase means 'to the end' or 'continually' and modifies ἐρχομένη 'coming' [Alf, Bai, BECNT, EGT, Hlt, ICC, NIGTC, Su, TH; GW, HCSB, KJV, NASB, NCV, NLT, NRSV, REB, TEV]: lest by her unceasing coming she wears me out (or disgraces me).
2. The phrase means 'to the end' or 'to the uttermost' and modifies ὑπωπιάζῃ 'she may strike under the eye' [WBC]: lest by her coming she completely shames me.
3. The phrase is temporal and means 'in the end' or 'finally, at last' and modifies ὑπωπιάζῃ 'she may strike under the eye' and the verb is taken figuratively [AB, Arn, Lns; NET, NIV]: lest she finally wears me out.

QUESTION—What did the judge want to avoid by using the verb ὑπωπιάζω 'to strike under the eye'?

1. The verb is to be taken in the literal physical sense of the widow giving him a black eye [Gdt, My, NICNT]. The judge mockingly says that the woman might become so desperate that she would beat his face black and blue [My].
2. The verb is to be taken figuratively for wearing him out by her repeated coming [AB, Arn, Bai, BECNT, Blm, EGT, Hlt, ICC, Lns, MGC, NAC, NIC, NTC, Pnt, Rb, TG, TH, TNTC; all versions]. This verb's primary sense is to strike in the face as in boxing, but here it has a weakened sense of wearing him out or making him tired by her persistence [TH]. She was wearing him out emotionally [BECNT]. He didn't care what other people thought about him, but she was wearing him out [Bai, NAC]. It means to annoy greatly [ICC]. Her constant coming would destroy the judge's peace of mind and his patience [TG]. He was worn out by her continual coming and the point that annoyed him was her coming to plead for justice [NET].
3. The verb is taken figuratively for besmirching his character and causing him to be disgraced [NIGTC, WBC]. This metaphor is from boxing and means to defame or to disgrace [NIGTC]. He would be struck not in the

body but in his pride so that he would become embarrassed by her continual coming [WBC].

18:6 **And the Lord said, Listen-to**[a] **what the unrighteous judge says.**
LEXICON—a. aorist act. impera. of ἀκούω (LN 31.56): 'to listen to' [AB, LN, NTC; HCSB, NCV, NET, NIV, NRSV, TEV], 'to hear' [Arn, BECNT, Lns, WBC; KJV, NASB, REB], 'to heed, to pay attention and respond' [LN], 'to learn a lesson from' [NLT], 'to pay attention to' [GW], 'to think about' [CEV]. This means that they are to hear what the judge had said in the preceding verses, not what he will say, and it does not imply that the audience should imitate the judge's attitude or his actions [TH].
QUESTION—What is the point of listening to what the unrighteous judge said?
Attention is shifted from the plight of the widow to the judge's thoughts and conduct [AB]. This begins a lesser-to-greater argument [AB, Arn, BECNT, ICC, NAC, NIBC]. An unjust judge yielded to the pleas of an unknown widow who spoke to him at intervals, so how much more will a just God be ready to reward the cries of his chosen people who cry out to him day and night [ICC]. Even in the seemingly hopeless case of a widow appealing to a judge who did not know her, the unrighteous judge finally capitulated to her pleas, so how much better it must be for God's chosen people to find help from their God who is all-good [AB, BECNT, NAC, WBC]. God and the wicked judge are opposites in that God loves his people and will quickly grant them the help they need [NTC]. The parable has centered in what the judge says in 18:4–5, and 18:6 begins with δέ 'but', placing the unrighteous judge in contrast with the wholly righteous God, so that all is opposite except the fact of vindication which is alike in both the parable and reality [Lns].

18:7 **But (will) not**[a] **God do the justice**[b] **of-his chosen**[c] **(ones) the (ones who) cry-out**[d] **to-him day and night, and does-he-delay/is-he-patient**[e] **with them?**
TEXT—Instead of καὶ μακροθυμεῖ 'and does he delay' some manuscripts read καὶ μακροθυμῶν 'even delaying'. GNT does not mention this variant. Καὶ μακροθυμῶν 'even delaying' is read by KJV.
LEXICON—a. The two negatives οὐ μή 'not no' is translated 'will not?' [AB, Arn, BECNT, Lns, NTC; NASB, NIV, NRSV, REB, TEV; similarly CEV, GW, KJV, NET], 'won't (God) be sure to?' [WBC], 'don't you think?' [NLT]. This question is also translated as a statement of fact: 'God will always give what is right to his people' [NCV]. This combination of negatives οὐ μή 'not no' makes it an emphatic question that expects an emphatic 'yes' answer [AB, BAGD, EGT, Hlt, ICC, Lns, MGC, NIGTC, Su, TH, WBC].
b. ἐκδίκησις (LN 56.35) (BAGD p. 238): 'justice' [BAGD, LN], 'vengeance, punishment' [BAGD]. The phrase ποιήσῃ τὴν ἐκδίκησιν 'do the justice' is translated 'give justice (to)' [**LN**; GW, NET, NLT, REB], 'grant justice (to)' [HCSB, NRSV], 'furnish justice (to)' [Arn], 'give what is right' [NCV], 'bring about justice (for)' [NASB, NIV], 'see to it that justice is done' [BAGD, NTC], 'judge in favor of' [TEV], 'avenge'

[KJV], 'vindicate' [AB, WBC], 'work the vindication (of)' [Lns], 'make vindication (for)' [BECNT], 'protect' [CEV].
c. ἐκλεκτός (LN 30.93) (BAGD 1.b. p. 242): 'chosen' [BAGD, LN]. The phrase 'his chosen ones' [AB; CEV, NET, NIV, NRSV] is also translated 'his chosen' [REB], 'his chosen people' [GW, NLT], 'his elect' [Arn, BECNT, Lns, NTC, WBC; HCSB, NASB], 'his own elect' [KJV], 'his people' [NCV]. This designation is taken from the OT and applied to Christians here [MGC]. The elect are Jesus' disciples [AB, Arn]. God has chosen them to belong to him, to be his people [TH].
d. pres. act. participle of βοάω (LM 33.81) (BAGD 4. p. 144): 'to cry out (to)' [AB, BAGD, BECNT, LN, WBC; HCSB, NET, REB], 'to cry (to)' [Arn, Lns, NTC; KJV, NASB, NCV, NRSV], 'to cry out for help' [GW], 'to cry for help' [TEV], 'to plead (with)' [NLT], 'to pray' [CEV]. This refers to calling out to God in prayer [BAGD, TH]. It implies that they are being persecuted or are being afflicted [Arn, TH; NET]. They pray that God will deliver them from oppression [ICC]. Their constant entreaty to God indicates the need for rescue [BECNT]. They call to God for help [TH; GW, TEV]. They ask for justice [NET].
e. pres. act. indic. of μακροθυμέω (LN 25.168, **67.126**) (BAGD 3. p. 488): 'to delay long' [BAGD], 'to be patient' [LN]. The phrase μακροθυμεῖ ἐπ' αὐτοῖς is translated 'will he delay long over them?' [AB, BAGD; NASB; similarly BECNT], 'will he delay long in helping them?' [NRSV; similarly HCSB, NET], 'and will he delay in their case?' [Arn], 'will he be slow to help them?' [**LN**, NTC; TEV; similarly GW], 'will he keep putting them off?' [NIV, NLT], 'won't he be concerned for them?' [CEV], 'and is he waiting long over them?' [Lns]. This question is also translated as a statement: 'and he will not be slow to answer them' [NCV], 'to whom he listens patiently while they cry out' [REB], 'He will indeed show himself long-suffering with them' [WBC], 'though he bear long with them' [KJV].

QUESTION—What is meant when God ποιήσῃ τὴν ἐκδίκησιν 'does the justice'?

It means that God will render justice, he will do the just thing [Su]. It can mean that God will vindicate them by punishing the offenders, or, since there is no mention of opponents of the chosen ones, more probably it refers to rescuing those in trouble [NIGTC].

QUESTION—What is the meaning of the question 'does he delay with them?'

1. It means that God will not delay to do justice for his chosen ones [AB, Arn, Hlt, MGC, My, NIVS, NTC, Su, TG, TH; GW, HCSB, NASB, NCV, NET, NIV, NLT, NRSV, TEV]. The answer given in 18:8 is that God will do justice speedily [NTC, Su, TG, TH]. The expected answer to the question 'and does he delay with them?' is 'No, God won't be long in helping them' [Hlt, TH]. The contrast with the unrighteous judge is that the judge was slow to act, but God will act speedily [MGC, NTC, TG]. God will not permit a long delay [Arn]. The Lord is not slow in fulfilling

his promise, and once the proper time arrives, he will act quickly [Lns, NTC].
2. It means there will be a delay before he does justice for his chosen ones [BNTC, EGT, ICC, My, NIGTC, TNTC; KJV]. The καί 'and (does he delay)' is to be taken as 'while' and this clause describes the condition of God's chosen ones: 'God will do justice for his chosen ones, while he is slow to help them' [BNTC]. The chosen ones cry out day and night and God puts their patience to the test by not answering them at once, or they cry to God day and night even though it seems God delays in answering them [NIGTC]. It may seem that the answer to prayer is delayed, yet constant prayer is always answered [ICC].
3. It is a comment about God's patience with his chosen ones [Bai, WBC; REB]. God is slow to anger over them [Bai]. God does not lash out at the sins of his chosen people who may not deserve the vindication they ask for. Although he may discipline them, he will work for their vindication in the end [WBC].
4. It is a comment about God's patience with the opponents of his chosen ones [Crd, Rb]. This asks if God will not restrain his anger by being patient with those who mistreat his chosen ones [Crd]. The conjunction καί is to be taken as 'and yet' so that the answer is that God delays taking vengeance on behalf of his people not because of any indifference, but because of his patient forbearance with sinners [Rb].
5. It may be either that God will not delay or in God's patience he will restrict the enemies' power to persecute until the final vindication [BECNT]. It is clear there has been a lengthy delay and the final vindication has not yet taken place. So this may mean that vindication includes the initial forms of the Holy Spirit's provision and entry into the promises, or it means that God is patient in responding to persecution by the enemies of his people until the final vindication of his people [BECNT].

18:8 I-say to-you that he-will-do the justice[a] of-them with speed.[b] But the Son of-Man[c] having-come, will-he-find the faith[d] on the earth?

LEXICON—a. ἐκδίκησις (LN 56.35) (BAGD p. 238): 'justice' [BAGD, LN], 'vengeance, punishment' [BAGD]. See the phrase 'do the justice' at 18:7.

b. τάχος (LN 67.56) (BAGD p. 807): 'speed, quickness, swiftness' (BAGD). The phrase ἐν τάχει 'with speed' is translated 'soon' [BAGD, LN], 'very soon' [LN], 'in a short time' [BAGD]. The phrase 'he will do the justice of them with speed' is translated 'he will give them justice quickly' [GW], 'he will bring about justice for them quickly' [NASB], 'he will see that they get justice, and quickly' [NIV], 'he will give them justice speedily' [NET], 'he will provide justice for them in a hurry' [Arn], 'he will give them justice soon enough' [REB], 'he will swiftly grant them justice' [HCSB], 'he will quickly grant justice to them' [NRSV], 'he will grant justice to them quickly' [NLT], 'he will see to it

that justice is done for them, and quickly' [NTC], 'he will make haste to vindicate them' [AB], 'he will vindicate them speedily' [WBC], 'he will avenge them speedily' [KJV], 'he will make their vindication speedily' [BECNT], 'he will work their vindication with speed' [Lns], 'God will help his people quickly' [NCV], 'he will judge in their favor and do it quickly' [TEV], 'he will hurry and help them' [CEV].
  c. υἱὸς τοῦ ἀνθρώπου 'Son of Man'. This title for Christ occurs at 5:24; 6:5, 22; 7:34; 9:22, 26, 44; 11:30; 12:8, 40; 17:22, 24, 26; 18:31; 19:10; 21:27, 36; 22:22, 48, 69; 24:7. See the discussions of this title at 5:24, 6:5, and 9:22.
  d. πίστις (LN 31.102) (BAGD 2.d.α. p. 663): 'faith' [BAGD, LN], 'as true piety, genuine religion' [BAGD], 'faith, Christian faith' [LN]. The phrase 'will he find the faith?' [Lns] is also translated 'will he find faith?' [Arn, BECNT, WBC; GW, NASB, NET, NIV, NRSV, REB, TEV], 'shall he find faith?' [KJV], 'will he find that faith?' [AB, NTC; HCSB], 'will he find anyone with faith?' [CEV], 'will he find those who believe in him?' [NCV], 'how many will I find who have faith?' [NLT]. 'Faith' is used in the sense of true piety and genuine religion [BAGD].

QUESTION—What is meant by ἐν τάχει 'with speed'?
  1. God will do this soon, after a short interval of time [AB, Alf, Arn, Bai, BECNT, Hlt, ICC, Lns, MGC, NAC, NIBC, NIGTC, TH, TNTC, WBC]: he will do this *soon*. God is not like the unrighteous judge who had to be pestered before he gave in to the widow's persistence, God will answer soon [NIBC, NIGTC]. As God bears with such people, and it will seem that he is delaying, he really will act speedily [BECNT, ICC, MGC, NIGTC]. Although God delays, yet he will act swiftly when the moment comes [ICC]. In God's understanding and in the way faith reckons time, his coming will always be soon [NAC]. In relation to eternity, vindication is soon [NET]. Or, this refers to vindication in the final days of Jesus ministry [Bai]. The final redemption has not yet come because Christians have not prayed enough [Arn].
  2. When the time comes, God will suddenly act in a very short space of time [EGT, Gdt, NIC, NTC, TNTC]: he will do this *suddenly*. When the proper time comes, God will act suddenly [EGT]. At his coming, the various eschatological events will take place quickly [NTC].

QUESTION—What is the significance of the mention of the coming of the Son of Man?
  It is implied that his coming is linked to God's way of answering his people's cry for help [TG, TH]. This is the eschatological coming of the Son of Man to earth [Arn, BECNT, NIGTC, NTC]. In spite of the promised speed, the time will seem so long that the question must be asked [EGT, ICC].

244 LUKE 18:8

QUESTION—What is meant by the question about finding τὴν πίστιν 'the faith'?
1. The faith is Christian faith that is placed in Jesus [Arn, Crd, ICC, My, NAC, NIC, Pnt, TNTC; NET]. It refers to faith in Jesus as the Messiah and Savor [ICC, NIC]. The question does not imply that there will be no believers, rather, it implies that the characteristic of the people of the world will not be faith [TNTC]. Many of those who profess to believe in Jesus will give up so that they no longer will belong to the elect [My]. Jesus anticipated a negative answer and so indicated that his disciples should persist to believe in spite of opposition and rejection [Pnt]. The faith refers to saving faith and this implies that when he appears again, faith in him will not be evident on all sides [Arn].
2. The faith is the specific faith that vindication will come [AB, Alf, BNTC, Gdt, Lns, NICNT, NIGTC, NIVS, NTC, TG, WBC]. It is the particular kind of faith of which the widow is an example, a faith that perseveres [Gdt, Lns, NTC]. It is the faith that inspires persistent prayer and this statement intends to call the disciples to vigilance [AB]. With the article, this refers to the faithfulness that the disciples would express by persistent prayer in time of tribulation and this exhorts them to apply the lesson of the parable that God will act to vindicate them [NIGTC]. There will be believers on earth when he comes, but will there be that persevering faith that he has described, and this is asked so that the disciples would examine themselves [NTC]. The question leaves the answer up to the disciples in order to stimulate them to keep on crying out to him [Lns]. Neither a positive or a negative answer is implied, rather it indicates uncertainty, maybe anxiety, about the matter [TG].
3. The faith is the specific faith that the Son of Man will come [BECNT, EGT, NAC, TH]. This refers to a specific form of faith, the coming of the Son of Man [TH]. This refers to the Second Coming [EGT]. Jesus hopes that he will find his disciples still waiting for his coming and says this to exhort them to keep looking forward to that day [BECNT].

DISCOURSE UNIT: 18:9–19:27 [NICNT]. The topic is how to enter the kingdom.

DISCOURSE UNIT: 18:9–19:10 [NIGTC]. The topic is the scope of salvation.

DISCOURSE UNIT: 18:9–30 [BECNT, WBC]. The topic is humbly entrusting all to the Father [BECNT], entering the kingdom like a child [WBC].

DISCOURSE UNIT: 18:9–17 [NASB]. The topic is the Pharisee and the publican.

DISCOURSE UNIT: 18:9–14 [AB, BECNT, NAC, NICNT, NIGTC, Su, TNTC, WBC; CEV, GW, HCSB, NCV, NET, NIV, NLT, NRSV, TEV]. The topic is a Pharisee and a tax collector [CEV, GW], the parable of the Pharisee and the tax collector [AB, BECNT, NAC, NIGTC, Su, TNTC, WBC; HCSB,

NET, NIV, NLT, NRSV, TEV], a parable concerning the self–possessed [NICNT], being right with God [NCV].

18:9 **And also he-said this parable to/about^a some, the (ones who) have-confidence^b in themselves that/because^d they-are righteous^c and (who) were-despising^e the others.**

LEXICON—a. πρός (LN 90.25, 90.58): 'to' [AB, Arn, BECNT, LN (90.58), Lns, NTC; all versions except GW, KJV, REB], 'unto' [KJV], 'about' [LN (90.25)], 'it was aimed at' [REB]. The phrase 'he said to' is translated 'he addressed' [WBC], 'Jesus used this with' [GW]
  b. perf. act. participle of πείθω (LN 31.82) (BAGD 2.a. p. 639): 'to have confidence in' [LN], 'to be confident' [WBC; NET], 'to be confident of/in respect to' [Arn; NIV], 'to have great confidence' [NLT], 'to be self-confident' [AB], 'to trust in' [BAGD, BECNT, LN, NTC; HCSB, KJV, NASB, NRSV], 'to rest their trust on' [Lns], 'to depend on' [BAGD, LN], 'to rely on' [LN], 'to be sure' [GW, REB, TEV], 'to think' [CEV, NCV].
  c. ὅτι (LN 89.33, 90.21) (BAGD 3.a. p. 589): 'that' [Arn, BECNT, LN (90.21), Lns; CEV, GW, HCSB, KJV, NASB, NET, NRSV], 'because' [BAGD, LN (89.33), WBC], not explicit [AB, NTC; NCV, NIV, NLT, REB, TEV].
  d. δίκαιος (LN 88.12): 'righteous' [Arn, BECNT, LN, Lns, WBC; HCSB, KJV, NASB, NET, NRSV], 'self-righteous' [NTC], 'upright' [AB]. The phrase 'the ones having confidence in themselves that they are righteous' is translated 'who were confident of their own righteousness' [NIV], 'who were sure of their own goodness' [REB, TEV], 'who had great self-confidence' [NLT], 'some who were self-confident, regarding themselves as upright' [AB], 'who thought they were better than others' [CEV], 'who thought they were very good' [NCV], 'who were sure that God approved of them' [GW]. This refers to complying with God's commandments [TG]. See this word at 1:6, 17; 2:25; 5:32; 14:14; 15:7; 20:20; 23:47, 50.
  e. pres. act. participle of ἐξουθενέω (LN **88.195**): 'to despise' [Arn, BECNT, **LN**, WBC; KJV, TEV], 'to view with contempt' [NASB], 'to regard with contempt' [NRSV], 'to treat with contempt' [Lns], 'to regard as worthless' [AB], 'to scorn' [NLT], 'to look down on' [NTC; CEV, GW, HCSB, NCV, NET, NIV, REB].

QUESTION—What is meant by καί 'also'?
It is implied that this parable was spoken at the same time as the preceding one [NICNT, TG], and 'also' means in addition to the preceding parable [TG]. Or, the time of speaking this parable is not clear [NTC].

QUESTION—Was Jesus speaking to these people or about them?
  1. Jesus spoke this parable *to* them [AB, Alf, Arn, BECNT, BNTC, Crd, ICC, Lns, MGC, NIC, NIGTC, NTC, Pnt, TG, TH, WBC; all versions except REB]. He was speaking to the Pharisees [Crd, NIGTC, NTC, Pnt, Su], as is clear from 18:10 [NAC, NIGTC, Pnt]. Or, he was not addressing only Pharisees, but all to whom this description applies [AB, Alf, Arn,

BECNT, Lns, TNTC]. Here the audience still contained the disciples of 17:22, but it is widened so as to include those whose attitudes were like the Pharisee in the following parable [NICNT, TG, WBC]. Or, the parable was spoken on a different occasion and was addressed to a different audience [ICC]. He was not referring to all Pharisees [Arn, BECNT]. Or, Jesus would not have chosen to put a Pharisee in the parable if they had been present, and if he had been speaking about the Pharisees, this would not then be a parable. Here he was speaking to the people in his audience and this parable applied to some among them, [Alf, Gdt].
2. Jesus spoke this parable to the crowd *about* such people [Crd, EGT; REB]. Jesus spoke in reference to certain people who are described here [EGT].

QUESTION—Does ὅτι mean 'that' or 'because'?
1. It indicates the content of their confidence [AB, Arn, BECNT, BNTC, Crd, ICC, Lns, NAC, NIC, TG, TH; CEV, GW, HCSB, KJV, NASB, NET, NRSV]: they were confident *that* they were righteous. It does not mean 'because' since that would imply that they were in fact righteous [ICC].
2. It indicates the reason that they had confidence in themselves [BAGD, WBC]: they had confidence in themselves *because* they were righteous.
3. This is translated as their characteristics [NTC]: 'to some self-righteous persons, those who trusted in themselves and looked down on everybody else' [NTC].

QUESTION—Who are τοὺς λοιποὺς 'the others'?
The article is generic [TH]. This means 'all other people' [AB, ICC, Su, TH, WBC], 'everyone else' [NTC, TH; CEV, GW, HCSB, NCV, NET, NIV, NLT, REB, TEV].

18:10 Two men went-up to the temple to-pray, one a-Pharisee and the other a-tax-collector.ᵃ **18:11** The Pharisee having-stood by/to/about himself was-prayingᵇ these (things), God, I-thank you that I-am not like the rest of-men, swindlers,ᶜ unrighteous,ᵈ adulterers, or evenᵉ like this tax-collector.

TEXT—In 18:11, instead of πρὸς ἑαυτὸν ταῦτα 'to himself these things', some manuscripts read ταῦτα πρὸς ἑαυτόν 'these things to himself', some manuscripts read καθ' ἑαυτὸν ταῦτα 'according to himself these things', one version reads πρὸς ἑαυτόν 'to himself', and some manuscripts read ταῦτα 'these things'. GNT reads πρὸς ἑαυτὸν ταῦτα 'to himself these things' with a C decision, indicating that the Committee had difficulty making the decision. Some translations might not distinguish between the first three of these readings.

LEXICON—a. τελώνης (LN 57.184) (BAGD p. 812): 'tax collector' [BAGD, BECNT, LN, NTC, WBC; CEV, all versions except KJV, NLT], 'a dishonest tax collector' [NLT], 'toll collector' [AB], 'publican' [Arn, Lns; KJV]. A tax collector was generally irreligious and was the very opposite of a religious Pharisee [Su], and he wouldn't even be expected to be found

praying in the temple [TNTC]. Tax collectors are often paired with 'sinners' (5:30; 7:34; 15:1) [AB, MGC, NAC].
- b. imperf. mid./pass. (deponent = active) indic. of προσεύχομαι (LN 33.178) (BAGD p. 714): 'to pray' [BAGD, LN]. The phrase σταθεὶς πρὸς ἑαυτὸν ταῦτα προσηύχετο 'having stood by/to himself was praying these things' is translated 'standing by himself, was praying thus' [NRSV], 'stood over by himself and prayed' [CEV], 'stood apart by himself and prayed' [TEV], 'stood alone and prayed' [NCV], 'stood by himself and prayed this prayer' [NLT], 'stood and was praying thus to himself' [NASB], 'stood and prayed thus with himself' [KJV], 'stood and was directing a prayer to himself, as follows' [NTC], 'took a stand and went on praying these things for himself' [Lns], 'stood and prayed about himself like this' [NET], 'stood and prayed thus about himself' [WBC], 'took a stance and prayed thus about himself' [AB], 'stood up and prayed about himself' [NIV], 'stepped forth prominently, and in his heart he uttered this prayer' [Arn], 'took his stand and was praying like this' [HCSB], 'stood up and prayed this prayer' [REB], 'stood up and prayed' [GW].
- c. ἅρπαξ (LN **57.239**) (BAGD 2. p. 109): 'greedy' [CEV, HCSB, REB, TEV]. This adjective is also translated as a noun: 'swindlers' [BAGD; NASB], 'rogues' [BAGD], 'robbers' [AB, Arn, BAGD, **LN**, Lns, NTC, WBC; GW], 'thief' [NRSV], 'extortionists' [NET], 'extortioners' [KJV]; or as a verb: 'to steal' [NCV]. All three descriptions are included in a generic noun: 'I am not a sinner like everyone else' [NLT]. It refers to someone who robs others by charging exorbitant interest on loans [Su], or insofar as they took things that did not belong to them as when they overcharged people [Arn, NIBC]. It has the meaning of robber or swindler [NIGTC]. Instead of 'robber', here it means swindler [TH].
- d. ἄδικος (LN 88.20) (BAGD 1. p. 18): 'unrighteous' [LN, Lns; HCSB, NET], 'unjust' [BAGD, LN; KJV, NASB], 'dishonest' [CEV, GW, REB, TEV]. This adjective is also translated as a noun: 'evildoers' [AB, WBC], 'rogues' [NRSV], 'cheats' [NTC], 'devotees of unrighteousness' [Arn]; or as a verb: 'to cheat' [NCV]. It has the meaning here of swindler or cheat [NIGTC], lawbreaker, criminal [TG], untrustworthy [Su].
- e. καί (LN 89.93): 'even' [LN]. The phrase 'or even like' [AB, NTC, WBC; HCSB, NASB, NCV, NET, NRSV] is also translated 'or even as' [Lns; KJV], 'or also as' [Arn], 'or for that matter, like' [REB], 'not even like' [GW], 'especially like' [NLT], 'not like' [CEV, TEV].

QUESTION—What is the significance of 'going up' to the temple?

They went up from the lower part of Jerusalem [Crd, ICC, NIC, NICNT, NIGTC, TG, TH] to Mount Moriah on which the temple stood [AB, ICC, NAC, NIGTC, TG; NET]. The temple was a place where the public might pray, either in private or out loud [TNTC]. This was probably at one of the fixed hours of prayer [Arn, Bai, Crd, ICC, Lns]. An individual could pray in the temple at any time [NIGTC]. This would be the temple complex, and these two men were standing in the court of the men [Lns]. They went up to the temple courtyard [GW], temple complex [HCSB], specifically, the Court of Israel within the temple precincts [AB].

QUESTION—What is meant by the Pharisee σταθεὶς πρὸς ἑαυτὸν standing by/to/about himself?

Standing was the regular posture for prayer [ICC, NAC, NIGTC, NTC, Rb, TNTC]. This position also allowed the Pharisee to be seen in his devotions by others [Rb, TH]. He would be standing up in front by the stone barrier that divided the priests' court from the court of the men [Lns].

1. The phrase πρὸς ἑαυτὸν means 'by himself' and it is connected to 'having stood', indicating that the Pharisee stood apart by himself and prayed [Bai, NICNT, NIGTC; CEV, NCV, NLT, NRSV, TEV]. The Pharisee despised the others and therefore stood apart by himself [Bai, NICNT]. It may be implied that his prayer was spoken aloud to preach to the less fortunate around him [Bai].
2. The phrase πρὸς ἑαυτὸν means 'to himself' and it is connected to 'was praying', indicating that the Pharisee stood up and then prayed to himself [Alf, Arn, Crd, Gdt, ICC, My, NIC, NTC, Rb, Su, TH; HCSB, KJV, NASB].
   2.1 This means that he prayed silently [Alf, Arn, ICC, My, NIC, TH]. Perhaps his lips moved and only he could hear the words of his prayer [Arn]. He would not want others to hear his boastful and critical prayer [ICC].
   2.2 This means that in effect he was only talking to himself [Gdt, NTC, Rb, Su]. Instead of speaking to God, he was actually congratulating himself [Gdt]. The prayer was outwardly addressed to God, but inwardly he was talking to himself about himself and the prayer never reached God [NTC].
3. The phrase πρὸς ἑαυτὸν means 'about himself' and it is connected to 'was praying', indicating that the Pharisee stood up and then prayed to God about himself [AB, Lns, NAC, WBC; NET, NIV]. That he was praying to God is clear from the beginning of his prayer [WBC]. Probably he was praying out loud [NET]. His praying was 'for himself', that is, in favor of himself and amounted to boasting about himself [Lns].

QUESTION—In saying 'I am not like other men', did the Pharisee think that he was the only righteous man in the world?

The Pharisee thought that only he and other Pharisees were the people who were righteous [TH, WBC]. He was using hyperbole since he could not mean that all other people were like the 'other men' [TG]. It refers to the usual type of men, not everyone [Arn].

QUESTION—What is meant by adding 'or even like this tax collector'?

The phrase picks out the tax collector as being the epitome of sinners [EGT, Lns, Rb]: or even worse of all, like this tax collector. Or, the tax collector was not any worse than the others in the list, but he is included at this point because in his unclean state he had dared to pray in the temple [NIGTC]: or even this one close by. The tax collector was in the same class as the others [TH]. This emphatic reference to the tax collector may indicate that the Pharisee had seen his agony in prayer [Su]. Or, the Pharisee had applied all of the descriptions to the tax collector and then pointed him out, so the 'or' connects similar terms, not giving another class of sinner [Bai]: even like this tax collector. This does not indicate that the tax collector is worse or better than the others, it is just an offhand dismissal of another example of degradation [WBC].

18:12 **I-fast twice a week, I-tithe everything as-much-as I-get.**
QUESTION—How is this verse related to the preceding one?
   It continues the list of things for which the tax collector was thanking God [NIGTC]. After listing his negative virtues, he now lists some of his positive virtues [Arn]. It presents reasons why he considers himself better than others [BECNT, ICC].
QUESTION—What was significant about fasting twice a week?
   Fasting twice a week was more than the law required [Alf, Bai, BECNT, BNTC, Crd, EGT, ICC, Lns, NIC, NIGTC, NIVS, NTC, Su, TH, TNTC, WBC]. The pious were in the habit of fasting more often than the law required [TNTC]. A fast involved not eating or drinking from sunrise to sunset [NAC].
QUESTION—What did he tithe?
   'All that he got' refers to what he acquired, not his capital [Alf, Crd, ICC, MGC, NAC, NIVS, Rb]. He tithed his income [TH; CEV]. He went beyond the requirements of the law and even paid tithes on what he bought [NAC, NIGTC], perhaps in case the person who sold something to him had not tithed on it [NAC]. 'All' indicates that he did not make the common exceptions [TH]. The tithe was an offering to God and was usually given at the temple [TG].

18:13 **And the tax-collector having-stood at-a-distance[a] not even was-he-willing to-raise-up[b] the eyes to heaven, but was-beating[c] his chest saying, O God, have-mercy[d] on-me the sinner.**
LEXICON—a. μακρόθεν (LN **83.30**) (BAGD p. 488): 'at a distance' [LN, NTC; GW, NCV, NIV, NLT, TEV], 'at a great distance' [Arn], 'off at a distance' [CEV], 'from a distance' [BAGD], 'some distance away' [NASB], 'far off' [AB, BECNT, Lns, WBC; HCSB, NET, NRSV], 'afar off' [KJV]. The phrase 'having stood at a distance' is translated 'kept his distance' [REB].
   b. aorist act infin. of ἐπαίρω (LN **24.34**) (BAGD 1. p. 281): 'to lift up' [BAGD], 'to look' [LN]. The phrase 'raise up the eyes to heaven' is translated 'raise his eyes to heaven' [AB, Arn, WBC; HCSB, REB], 'raise his face to heaven' [TEV], 'lift his eyes to heaven' [BECNT; NLT], 'lift up his eyes to heaven' [NTC; KJV, NASB], 'look up to heaven' [GW, NCV, NET, NIV, NRSV], 'look up toward heaven' [CEV].

c. imperf. act. indic. of τύπτω (LN 19.1) (BAGD 1. p. 830): 'to beat, to strike' [BAGD, LN] The phrase 'was beating his chest' is translated 'was beating his breast' [NASB, NRSV], 'kept beating his breast' [NTC], 'repeatedly beat his breast' [Arn], 'beat his breast' [BECNT, WBC; NET, NIV], 'beat upon/on his breast' [REB, TEV], 'struck his breast' [AB], 'smote upon his breast' [KJV], 'was striking his breast' [Lns], 'kept striking his chest' [HCSB], 'beat his chest in sorrow' [NLT], 'beat on his chest because he was so sad' [NCV], 'he was so sorry for what he had done that he pounded his chest' [CEV], 'he became very upset' [GW]. The verb means to strike or hit something one or more times [LN]. See this word at 23:48.

d. aorist pass. impera. of ἱλάσκομαι (LN **88.75**) (BAGD 1. p. 375): 'to have mercy' [BAGD, **LN**; CEV, NCV, NIV, REB], 'to show mercy, to show compassion' [LN], 'to be merciful' [Arn, BECNT, NTC, WBC; GW, KJV, NASB, NET, NLT, NRSV], 'to have pity' [AB; TEV]. The phrase 'have mercy on me' is translated 'turn your wrath from me' [HCSB]. This is more than having an attitude of mercy, it involves an act of kindness [LN].

QUESTION—What is the significance of the tax collector standing at a distance?

Standing at a distance points out a contrast with the Pharisee who stood in front when he prayed [Arn, Su, TH]. He stood at a distance because he did not feel worthy to stand along with the others who were standing before God's altar [Bai]. He felt unworthy to go nearer to the sanctuary [Lns, NAC]. The tax collector stood to one side [Su]. He stood as far away from the sanctuary as possible [Lns, NTC], at the rear of the court of the men [Lns], or perhaps in the outer court of the temple complex [NIGTC]. He must have been in the court of Israel, since the Pharisee could hear him praying [ICC].

QUESTION—What is the significance of not being willing even to raise his eyes to heaven?

The tax collector felt unworthy to look up to God [Su, WBC]. He was ashamed of his sins [NTC]. Since one's eyes are normally directed towards the person being addressed, a person in prayer would look upward to where God was [TH]. Raising one's face toward heaven was the normal attitude in praying [NIBC, TG, TNTC]. The eyes would be closed [Rb]. By adding οὐδέ 'not even' strengthens the preceding οὐκ 'not' [ICC]. The use of 'even' means that he would not raise his eyes to heaven, much less express any confident or familiar attitude towards God [ICC]. He would not raise his eyes, still less raise his hands in prayer [Alf, MGC, My, NIGTC], as the Pharisee had prayed [Alf].

QUESTION—Why did he beat his chest?

This gesture consisted of striking his chest with his fists in rapid succession and this indicated extreme anguish or intense anger [Bai]. Here it was a sign of sorrow [AB, Arn, Bai, Lns, MGC, TG, TH, TNTC], grief over sins [EGT,

NAC, NIGTC], remorse [Pnt, WBC], contrition [AB, BECNT, Lns, NAC, NIGTC, Pnt, TH], repentance [TG], emotional distress [Su], despair [NTC], humility and shame [NICNT]. The imperfect tense here means that that he kept on beating his chest [Arn, ICC, Lns, NTC, Rb, TH, TNTC; HCSB].

QUESTION—How did the tax collector want God to show mercy on him?

He was asking for forgiveness [NIGTC, NIVS, WBC; NET]. God would show mercy to a sinner by forgiving him [NIGTC, TH]. This is not the usual word for being merciful, and here he was asking that his sin be expiated [Lns, Su] and that he be reconciled to God by the removal of his sin which alienated him from God [Su]. Literally, the Greek says 'God, be propitiated to me, a sinner', so the tax collector was pleading that the blood of his sacrifice be the basis on which God would let a sinner approach him [Pnt]. He was asking God to be appeased by the sacrifice he had offered for sin so that God would again extend his grace and favor to him [Lns]. He asked God to show mercy through atoning forgiveness [BECNT]. As he watched the smoke rising from the burnt offering, he longed that the atonement sacrifice would be applied to him [Bai]. He asked God to look on him as God looked upon the atonement cover because he was taking refuge under the propitiating blood [Pnt]. He asked that God be merciful by covering his sins and removing his wrath [NAC]. Or, he asked God to be merciful and gracious to him without including the Classical Greek sense of being appeased [AB].

QUESTION—What is meant by referring to himself as τῷ ἁμαρτωλῷ 'the sinner'?

It means 'sinner that I am' [Alf, TH], showing his intense self-abasement [Alf]. Or, the tax collector felt that he was the sinner of all sinners [Su], he was the well-known sinner [EGT], the open and notorious sinner [Lns]. He considered himself to be in a class by himself, the supreme sinner [ICC]. He was not comparing himself with others, but showed his intense self-abasement [Alf]. It is translated 'the sinner' [NTC; NASB], 'a sinner' [Arn, BECNT, WBC; GW, HCSB, KJV, NCV, NIV, NRSV, TEV], 'sinner that I am' [AB; NET, REB], 'I am such a sinner' [CEV], 'for I am a sinner' [NLT].

18:14 I-say to-you, This (one) went-down to his house having-been-justified[a] instead-of that (one). Because everyone exalting[b] himself will-be-humbled,[c] but the (one) humbling[c] himself will-be-exalted.[b]

LEXICON—a. perf. pass. participle of δικαιόω (LN 34.46, 56.34) (BAGD 2. p. 197): 'to be justified' [Arn, BAGD, BECNT, Lns, NTC; HCSB, KJV, NASB, NET, NRSV], 'to be justified before God' [NIV, NLT], 'to be acquitted' [LN (56.34)], 'to be acquitted of his sins' [REB], 'to be put right with someone' [LN (34.46)], 'to be right with God' [NCV], 'to be in the right with God' [TEV], 'to be upright in the sight of God' [AB, WBC], 'to have God's approval' [GW], 'to be pleasing to God' [CEV].

The past participle indicates that his justification occurred before he went down to his house [Lns], and this standing was permanent [NIC, Su, TH].
  b. pres. act. participle of ὑψόω (LN 87.20) (BAGD 2. p. 851): 'to exalt' [BAGD, LN]. The contrasting situations 'everyone exalting himself...but (the one humbling himself) will be exalted' are translated 'everyone who exalts himself...but...will be exalted' [AB, Arn, BECNT, Lns, NTC, WBC; HCSB, NASB, NET, NIV, REB], 'all who exalt themselves... but...will be exalted' [NRSV], 'everyone that exalts himself...but...shall be exalted' [KJV], 'all/those who make themselves great...but...will be made great' [NCV, TEV], 'everyone who honors himself...but...will be honored' [GW], 'the proud...but...will be honored' [NLT], 'if you put yourself above others...but...you will be honored' [CEV]. See this same clause at 14:11.
  c. fut. pass. indic. of ταπεινόομαι (LN 87.63) (BAGD 2.a. p. 804): 'to be humbled, to be humiliated' [BAGD], 'to be made to live like those of low status' [LN]. The contrasting situations 'will be humbled...but the one humbling himself' are translated 'will be humbled...but the one/he/who-ever who humbles himself' [AB, Arn, BECNT, Lns, WBC; HCSB, NASB, NET, NIV, REB], 'will be humbled...but all/those who humble themselves' [NRSV, TEV], 'shall be abased...but he that humbles himself' [KJV], 'will be humbled...but the person who humbles himself' [GW], 'will be made humble...but all who make themselves humble' [NCV], 'you will be put down...but if you humble yourself' [CEV], 'will be humbled...but the humble' [NLT]. See this same clause at 14:11.
QUESTION—What is meant by the tax collector being justified?
God had accepted the tax collector as being righteous [My, NIC]. God pronounced the tax collector, whose sins had been blotted out, to be righteous [NTC]. He was forgiven and God declared him to be righteous [Arn, NIVS]. God declared that the man was acquitted [Lns, NIGTC]. He was vindicated before God who forgave him and accepted him [BECNT]. He was set right with God [TH]. In this context it probably means that God had forgiven his sins [BNTC, EGT, NIC, Su, TG]. This does not have the sense of 'justification' as used by Paul [EGT].
QUESTION—What is meant by παρ' ἐκεῖνον 'instead of that one'?
  1. It contrasts the two men [AB, Arn, BECNT, ICC, Lns, TH, WBC; HCSB, KJV, NASB, NET, NIV, NRSV]: this one was justified instead of/rather than the former one.
  2. It has an exclusive sense [NIGTC, NTC; CEV, GW, NCV, NLT, REB, TEV]: this one was justified and the former one was not justified. The Pharisee was not accepted on the basis of his prayer [NIGTC].
QUESTION—What relationship is indicated by ὅτι 'because'?
This indicates the reason the Pharisee was rejected and the tax collector was accepted [BECNT, Lns, MGC, NIGTC, TNTC]. This indicates that the general rule held good in this instance [NIC]. This was an axiom or self-evident statement of what happened [Lns].

QUESTION—What is the sense of someone exalting himself and being humbled?

In this context it is not speaking of social rank or position among one's fellow men [Bai]. The one who elevates himself is one who considers himself to be righteous and looks down on others [Bai]. The humbling refers to the results of the final judgment [BECNT].

QUESTION—What is the sense of someone humbling himself and being exalted?

A person humbles himself by repenting of his sins [Lns, MGC]. God exalts such a one by justifying him and accepting him as his own [Lns]. God adopts him into his family [NTC]. The exaltation is at the final judgment [BECNT].

DISCOURSE UNIT: 18:15–19:27 [AB]. The topic is a synoptic travel account.

DISCOURSE UNIT: 18:15–17 [AB, BECNT, NAC, NICNT, NIGTC, Su, TNTC, WBC; CEV, GW, HCSB, NCV, NET, NIV, NLT, NRSV, TEV]. The topic is the little children and Jesus [NIV], Jesus and children [NIGTC, TNTC; NET], blessing the children [HCSB], Jesus blesses little children [AB, NAC; CEV, GW, NLT, NRSV, TEV], little children and kingdom children [Su], receiving children, receiving the kingdom [NICNT], children and faith [BECNT], entering the kingdom of God like a child [WBC], who will enter God's kingdom? [NCV].

18:15 **And they-were-bringing also/even babies[a] to-him in-order-that he-would-touch/hold[b] them. And having-seen (this) the disciples were-rebuking[c] them.**

LEXICON—a. βρέφος (LN 9.45) (BAGD 2. p. 147): 'baby' [AB, BAGD, LN, Lns, WBC; NASB, NCV, NET, NIV, REB, TEV], 'infant' [Arn, BAGD, BECNT, LN, NTC; GW, HCSB, KJV, NRSV], 'little child' [CEV, NLT]. This noun generally referred to children who still had to be carried [TG]. Possibly these babies were about a year old [NIC]. Or, in the next verse it suggests that the children were able to walk since they are also called παιδίον 'child' [TH]. The use of this word in 2 Tim. 3:15 shows that his noun can include early childhood beyond the toddler stage [BECNT].

b. pres. mid. subj. of ἅπτομαι, ἅπτω (LN 24.73) (BAGD 2.b. p. 103): 'to touch' [Arn, BAGD, BECNT, LN, Lns, NTC, WBC; HCSB, KJV, NASB, NCV, NET, NIV, NRSV, REB], 'to hold' [AB; GW], 'to place his hands on' [TEV], 'to touch and bless' [NLT], 'to bless' [CEV].

c. imperf. act. indic. of ἐπιτιμάω (LN 33.419) (BAGD 1. p. 303): 'to rebuke' [AB, Arn, BAGD, BECNT, LN, Lns, NTC, WBC; HCSB, KJV, NIV, REB], 'to reprove' [BAGD], 'to scold' [NET]. The phrase 'were rebuking them' is translated 'they scolded them for doing so' [TEV], 'they told the people not to do that' [GW], 'they sternly ordered them not to do it' [NRSV], 'they told them to stop' [NCV], 'they told the people to stop bothering him' [CEV], 'they told them not to bother him' [NLT]. The imperfect tense is conative, they *tried* to rebuke them [AB, BECNT,

NAC, NIGTC, NTC], as seen by Jesus' response in stopping them [BECNT].

QUESTION—Who were bringing babies to Jesus?

Presumably mothers were bringing their babies to Jesus [Arn, Gdt, TNTC]. In the command 'don't hinder them' the pronoun 'them' is masculine, so probably the fathers were included as well [TNTC]. Perhaps parents or other relatives brought then [NTC].

QUESTION—In the phrase 'they were bringing καί babies to him', does καί mean 'also' or 'even'?

1. It means 'also' [Alf, Arn, My, NIVS, Rb, TH; NIV]. In addition to the sick people they also brought babies to Jesus [Arn, TH].
2. It means 'even' [AB, BECNT, BNTC, EGT, Gdt, Lns, NIGTC, NTC, WBC; HCSB, NASB, NCV, NET, NRSV]. This indicates Jesus' great popularity, that even babies were brought to him [EGT, Gdt]. Little children were brought to Jesus, even including infants [NTC]. Jesus was concerned about even the infants [NIGTC].

QUESTION—What did they want when they brought their babies for Jesus to touch them?

1. They wanted Jesus to place his hands on their babies as he blessed them. In Matt. 19:13, the children were brought to Jesus for him to place his hands on them and pray for them. Touching the babies, means laying his hands on them [TNTC]. Their motive was for Jesus to bless their babies [ICC, NAC, NIC]. Touching the baby's head accompanied a prayer of blessing [TG]. The act was symbolic of blessing a person and it was joined with prayer to ask God's blessing on that person [Lns, NTC]. Touching the babies would bestow Jesus' blessings on them [Arn]. It was already a custom on the evening of the Day of Atonement for parents to bring their children to the elders or scribes for a prayer of blessing [BECNT, NIGTC]. There was nothing magical about touching the babies, it was just part of the blessing [NTC].
2. They wanted Jesus to hold the baby in his arms as he blessed the baby [AB, MGC; GW].

QUESTION—Why did the disciples rebuke the people for bringing babies to Jesus?

Probably the disciples thought Jesus was too busy or too tired to be bothered with insignificant children [NTC, TNTC]. It would be wasting Jesus' time [AB, Gdt, ICC, MGC, NIC], and abusing his kindness [AB, Gdt, ICC]. They considered this to be a sentimental act that was unnecessary [Arn]. They told the people not to bring their babies to Jesus [TG] and they stopped them from doing so [TH].

18:16 But Jesus called[a] them saying, Permit the children[b] to-come to me and don't hinder them, because the kingdom of-God is[c] of-such-ones.

LEXICON—a. aorist mid. indic. of προσκαλέομαι (LN 33.308): 'to call' [LN]. The phrase 'called them' is also translated 'called to them' [BECNT], 'called for them' [AB; NASB, NRSV], 'called for the children' [NCV, NET, NLT, REB], 'called them to him' [Lns; KJV], 'called them to himself' [Arn, NTC], 'invited them' [HCSB], 'offered them welcome' [WBC], 'called the infants to him' [GW], 'called the children to him' [NIV, TEV], 'called the children over to him' [CEV].

b. παιδίον (LN 9.42) (BAGD 2.a. p. 604): 'child' [Arn, BAGD, BECNT, LN, WBC; CEV, GW, NASB, NCV, NLT, REB, TEV], 'little child' [AB, Lns, NTC; HCSB, KJV, NET, NIV, NRSV]. Ordinarily, this noun refers to a child who is old enough to walk, but it is also used of John at eight days of age (1:59) and Jesus at forty days (2:27) [TG]. Jesus changed his reference from babies to children because babies cannot come to Jesus on their own [NAC].

c. pres. act. indic. of εἰμί (LN 13.1) 'to be' [LN]. The clause 'the kingdom of God is of such ones' is translated 'of such is the kingdom of God' [Lns; KJV], 'the kingdom of God belongs to such as these' [WBC; HCSB, NASB, NET, NIV, NLT, REB, TEV], 'the kingdom of God belongs to people who are like these children' [NCV], 'people who are like these children belong to God's kingdom' [CEV], 'to such as these is the kingdom of God' [BECNT], 'to such as these belongs the Kingdom of God' [AB, NTC], 'it is to such that the kingdom of God belongs' [Arn], 'it is to such as these that the kingdom of God belongs' [NRSV], 'children like these are part of the kingdom of God' [GW].

QUESTION—Who is the referent in the statement that Jesus called 'them'?

1. Jesus called the babies or children to himself [AB, Arn, Gdt, Lns, MGC, My, NTC, TH, TNTC, WBC; CEV, GW, NET, NLT, REB]: Jesus called for the children to come to him. He probably spoke to the children and said something like 'Come to me, little ones' [Lns]. Or, instead of addressing the children, he called them by speaking the following words [TH]. He was telling the parents to bring their children to him [AB]. Then he told his disciples not to hinder them [NTC; NET, NLT]. Or, he told the parents not to hinder their coming [EGT, Lns, My]. Or, he told both his disciples and the parents not to hinder their coming [WBC].

2. Jesus called the children to himself along with their parents [ICC, NIC, Rb]. In calling the children to himself, their parents were included as well [ICC]. Then he told his disciples not to hinder them [Gdt, ICC, Rb, TH].

3. Jesus called to his disciples [BECNT]: Jesus called out to his disciples, saying....

QUESTION—What is meant by the statement 'the kingdom of God is of such ones'?

The words 'of such' mean children in general, not just those who were present [MGC]. Or, the words 'of such' refers to the whole class of persons having a childlike nature [Su], which of course includes the children who are an example of the class [Lns]. The kingdom of God belongs to these children and also to all those who were like the children [WBC]. The children were representative of the members of the kingdom in regard to their childlike trust and reliance on their parents [BECNT]. It means that people who are like those children are the ones who are in the kingdom of God [TG, TH]. People who are childlike in character are the ones who are best fitted for the kingdom [ICC, Lns]. Children were lowly in society, helpless, without any claim of merit, and in need of constant attention from their parents [AB, MGC]. This does not mean that all children have received the kingdom simply because they are children, but they do have an innate quality that is essential for entering the kingdom [MGC, NAC]. A child must still come to Jesus to be in the kingdom [Rb].

18:17 Truly I-say to-you, whoever doesn't accept[a] the kingdom of-God as[b] a-child, by-no-means will-enter[c] into it.

LEXICON—a. aorist mid. (deponent = act.) subj. of δέχομαι (LN 31.51) (BAGD 3.b. p. 177): 'to accept' [AB, BAGD, LN; NCV, REB], 'to receive' [Arn, BECNT, LN, Lns, NTC, WBC; GW, KJV, NASB, NET, NIV, NRSV, TEV], 'to welcome' [HCSB], 'to get into' [CEV], not explicit [NLT].

b. ὡς (LN 64.12): 'as, like' [LN]. The phrase 'as a child' [Arn] is also translated 'as a little child' [AB, Lns, NTC; KJV, NRSV], 'as if you were a child' [NCV], 'as a little child receives it' [GW], 'like a child' [BECNT, WBC; CEV, NASB, NET, REB, TEV], 'like a little child' [HCSB, NIV], 'have their kind of faith' [NLT].

c. aorist act. subj. of εἰσέρχομαι (LN 15.93, 90.70) (BAGD 2.a. p. 233): 'to enter' [AB, Arn, BAGD, LN (15.93), Lns, NTC, WBC; all versions except NLT], 'to get into' [NLT], 'to come into' [BECNT], 'to begin to experience, to attain' [LN (90.70)], 'to come to enjoy' [BAGD].

QUESTION—What is meant by 'accepting the kingdom of God'?

It means to accept God's rule [TNTC], to accept God as their king [TG], to submit to God's rule [TG]. It means to receive the message and the messenger of the kingdom [NIGTC]. It means to accept the kingdom in its present manifestation through Jesus' ministry [NAC].

QUESTION—What is meant by accepting the kingdom as a child?

It means that a person must accept the kingdom of God *as a child accepts* the kingdom of God. This can be expressed as 'whoever doesn't accept the kingdom of God as a child receives it' [BNTC, WBC; GW] or 'whoever doesn't accept the kingdom of God as though he were a child' [Arn, BECNT, ICC, Lns, MGC; NCV, NLT]. It means to have a child's kind of faith [NLT]. This refers to being receptive [ICC, Lns, NIC, NIGTC, WBC] and trustful [Arn, BECNT, ICC, Lns, MGC, NIC, NIVS, WBC; NET] like little children are. A childlike character is humility [Arn, ICC, Lns, NAC, NIC, Su], being conscious of weakness [WBC], and having a wholehearted faith [ICC, NIC]. It refers to receiving the kingdom as readily and trustfully as a child receives a gift [NTC, TG].

QUESTION—When does a person enter the kingdom?
It means to become a citizen of God's kingdom in the present time [BECNT, Lns, TG]. By accepting the King, they enter his kingdom and become qualified to receive all of the blessings of the kingdom [BECNT]. Or, it refers to sharing the blessings of the kingdom at its final consummation [NAC, NIGTC, TH]. Or, the first part of 18:17 concerns receiving the present manifestation of the kingdom and the last part includes both the present and future manifestations of the kingdom [WBC].

DISCOURSE UNIT: 18:18–34 [NASB]. The topic is the rich young ruler.

DISCOURSE UNIT: 18:18–30 [BECNT, NAC, NICNT, Su, TNTC; CEV, GW, NET, NIV, NLT, NRSV, TEV]. The topic is the rich man [NLT, TEV], the rich ruler [NAC, TNTC; NIV, NRSV], the wealthy ruler [NET], a rich and important man [CEV], the rich ruler and Jesus [BECNT], the rich ruler and the way to eternal life [Su], the problem of power and wealth [NICNT], eternal life in the kingdom [GW]

DISCOURSE UNIT: 18:18–25 [NCV]. The topic is a rich man's question.

DISCOURSE UNIT: 18:18–23 [AB, NIGTC, WBC; HCSB]. The topic is the rich ruler [NIGTC], the rich young ruler [HCSB], the rich young man [AB], what must I do to inherit eternal life? [WBC].

18:18 And a-certain ruler[a] questioned him saying, Good[b] Teacher, what having-done will-I-receive[c] eternal life? **18:19** And Jesus said to-him, Why do-you-call me good? No-one (is) good except one—God.

LEXICON—a. ἄρχων (LN 37.56) (BAGD 2.a. p. 114): 'ruler' [Arn, BECNT, LN, Lns, NTC, WBC; HCSB, KJV, NASB, NET, NIV, NRSV, REB], 'authority' [BAGD], 'official' [BAGD; GW], 'magistrate' [AB], 'leader' [NCV], 'religious leader' [NLT], 'Jewish leader' [TEV], 'important man' [CEV]. See this word at 8:41; 14:1; 23:13.
  b. ἀγαθός (LN 88.1) (BAGD 1.b.a. p. 3): 'good' [AB, Arn, BAGD, BECNT, LN, Lns, NTC, WBC; all versions]. This refers to inner worth, especially one's moral quality [BAGD, LN, Su]. This means beneficial and here, morally beneficial [Lns]. In this verse, it has the sense of 'kind' or 'generous' while in 18:19 it refers to moral perfection [TH].
  c. fut. act. indic. of κληρονομέω (LN 57.131) (BAGD 2. p. 434): 'to receive' [BAGD, LN; TEV], 'to get' [NLT], 'to gain possession of' [BAGD, LN], 'to have' [CEV, NCV], 'to win' [REB], 'to inherit' [AB, Arn, BECNT, Lns, NTC, WBC; GW, HCSB, KJV, NASB, NET, NIV, NRSV], 'to be given' [LN]. This verb does not imply that the ruler thought that someone must die in order for him to inherit eternal life [TG]. See this same question asked by a lawyer at 10:25.

QUESTION—What kind of a ruler was the man?
This designation could mean that he was a member of the Sanhedrin [NAC, NIBC, NIGTC]. Or, it could mean one of the officers in the local synagogue

258   LUKE 18:18–19

[Gdt, Lns, My, NAC, NIBC, NTC, Su], perhaps the president of the synagogue [Gdt]. In the parallel account in Matt. 19:22, he is called a young man, so he would not have been a member of the Sanhedrin or a ruler of a synagogue [BECNT, ICC]. He was one of the lay-leaders of the Jews [WBC]. Either he had some government position or was a member of the local council [Arn]. He probably was an influential and wealthy man, perhaps a civic leader [BECNT; NET]. The word is used in a general sense to describe a member of an influential group that had some sort of ruling function [TH, TNTC].

QUESTION—What did the ruler mean by 'eternal life'?

This is the same question asked in 10:25. The ruler wanted to be assured that he was heading in the right direction for salvation at the close of the age [BECNT, NTC]. He was thinking of heaven [Arn]. Inheriting eternal life was another way of speaking about entering God's kingdom [NAC, NIBC, NICNT], and attaining the resurrection of the righteous [NIBC].

QUESTION—What is meant by Jesus' question, 'Why do you call me good?'

1. This was a rhetorical question that indicated that Jesus should not be called good [Su]. Jesus, in his incarnation, did not have a consciousness of sin, but in his humility he considered the attribute 'good' to be only applicable to God [Su].

2. This was a rhetorical question that indicated the ruler should think about the implications of calling Jesus good [Lns, NIC, TNTC, WBC]: you should realize that if you call me good, you are calling me God. If Jesus was good and if only God was good, then the ruler was saying something important about Jesus that he should reflect upon [Lns, TNTC]. Only if the ruler considered Jesus to be the Son of God, should he call him good [NIC]. God has an exclusive claim on the meaning of goodness and if the ruler has seen such goodness in the ministry of Jesus, he would realize that the kingdom of God was present [WBC].

3. This was a rhetorical question that rebuked the ruler for using the term 'good' in a superficial way [Arn, NIGTC, NTC]. The ruler thought that Jesus was a mere man and therefore he had no right to use the term 'good' which belonged only to God in an absolute sense [Arn]. The ruler's later refusal to obey Jesus shows that he didn't really take the goodness of Jesus seriously and he should not have used the word in an empty way [NIGTC]. If the ruler was to be saved, he must be confronted with the absolute standard of goodness [NTC].

4. This rhetorical question directed the ruler to focus on God so the he would be responsive to God [AB, BECNT, Gdt, ICC, MGC, NAC]. Jesus' statement that only God was good brings out God's unique holiness and righteousness and if the ruler wanted to follow the 'good' One, he must follow God and obey the instructions of the teacher from God [BECNT]. Only God is truly good and the source of goodness when it is found in others, so if the ruler recognized any goodness in Jesus, he must attribute

it to the right source [AB]. Jesus' goodness was the goodness of God working through him [Gdt, ICC, MGC].

18:20 **You-know the commandments, don't commit-adultery, don't murder,[a] don't steal, don't give-false-witness,[b] honor[c] your father and mother.**
18:21 **And he-said, All these (things) I-obeyed[d] from youth.[e]**

TEXT—In 18:20, following μητέρα 'mother', some manuscripts add σου 'your'. GNT does not mention this variant. Σου 'your' is added by KJV.

LEXICON—a. aorist act. subj. of φονεύω (LN 20.82) (BAGD p. 864): 'to murder' [AB, BAGD, BECNT, LN, WBC; all versions except KJV], 'to kill' [Arn, BAGD, Lns, NTC; KJV]. This verb means to intentionally and illegally take the life of someone [LN]. It is not a command against all killing, since God allowed killing in the cases of war and capital punishment [TH].

b. aorist act. subj. of ψευδομαρτυρέω (LN 33.271) (BAGD p. 892): 'to give false witness' [BECNT, LN; NET], 'to bear false witness' [AB, Arn, BAGD, Lns, NTC, WBC; HCSB, KJV, NASB, NRSV], 'to give false testimony' [BAGD; GW, NIV], 'to testify falsely' [LN; NLT], 'to give false evidence' [NRSV], 'to accuse anyone falsely' [TEV], 'to tell lies about others' [CEV], 'to tell lies about your neighbor' [NCV]. This has to do with presenting testimony in court [TH]. They are not to lie when they testify against someone [TG, TH]. It can also be used less specifically and simply mean that they are not to lie [TH].

c. pres. act. impera. of τιμάω (LN 87.8) (BAGD 2. p. 817): 'to honor' [AB, Arn, BAGD, BECNT, LN, Lns, NTC, WBC; all versions except CEV, TEV], 'to respect' [LN; CEV, TEV]. This involves both words and actions, and means about the same as saying that we are to obey our parents [Lns, TH].

d. aorist act. indic. of φυλάσσω (LN 36.19) (BAGD 1.f. p. 868): 'to obey' [LN; CEV, GW, NCV, NLT, TEV], 'to keep' [Arn, BAGD, LN, WBC; HCSB, KJV, NASB, NET, NIV, NRSV, REB], 'to observe' [AB, NTC], 'to guard' [BECNT], 'to watch' [Lns]. This claim was probably sincere [ICC, NAC, NIC, TNTC], but it was superficial [NAC, TNTC] and shows his ignorance of his own self and his duty [ICC, NIC, TNTC].

e. νεότης (LN 67.154) (BAGD p. 536): 'youth' [BAGD, LN]. The phrase ἐκ νεότητος 'from youth' is translated 'from my youth' [Arn; HCSB, NASB], 'from my youth on/up' [Lns; KJV], 'since my youth' [WBC; NET, NRSV], 'since childhood' [BECNT], 'since I was a child' [NTC; NLT], 'since I was a boy' [GW, NCV, NIV, REB], 'since I was a young man' [CEV], 'since I was a youth' [AB], 'ever since I was young' [TEV]. It can have the general sense, 'from childhood' [NTC], the first conscious days of his life [Lns]. Or, this probably means from the time he became a *bar mitzvah*, a 'son of the law' [MGC, TG], at the age of twelve or thirteen [TG, TH]. From the time he had reached religious and legal maturity he was accountable for obeying all the commandments of the Jewish Law [AB, NAC, NIBC].

QUESTION—What is implied by the statement, 'You know the commandments'?

It is implied that the ruler must obey the commandments in order to have eternal life [BECNT, Lns, MGC, NIC, NIGTC, Su]. In the parallel passage in Matthew 19:17, it says 'If you want to enter life, obey the commandments'. To earn eternal life, acts of righteousness are required [BECNT]. However, no one except Jesus has ever been able to be so perfect as to obey the commandments perfectly [Arn, NIC].

QUESTION—Is the choice of these five commandments significant?

Just enough commandments were listed to expose the self-righteousness of the ruler [Arn]. These five commandments deal with one's duty to fellowmen, and Jesus will bring out our duty to God in another way [TNTC]. These commandments were easier to judge whether they had been kept or not [NAC, NIGTC, Su]. These are the part of the Law where the ruler was surest of himself [Lns]. These commandments were chosen to show the ruler that he lacked love for people [MGC].

18:22 And having-heard (that), Jesus said to-him, Still one (thing) is-lacking[a] for-you. Sell all you-have and distribute[b] (to-the) poor, and you-will-have treasure[c] in the heavens, and come follow[d] me.

TEXT—Following ἀκούσας δέ 'and having heard', some manuscripts add ταῦτα 'these things'. GNT does not mention this variant. Ταῦτα 'these things' is read by KJV.

TEXT—Instead of τοῖς οὐρανοῖς 'the heavens', some manuscripts read οὐρανῷ 'heaven'. GNT does not deal with this variant in the apparatus, but brackets τοῖς 'the' in the text. Since the singular and plural of this word, with or without the definite article, are often translated the same, versions might not distinguish between these readings.

LEXICON—a. pres. act. indic. of λείπω (LN **57.44, 71.33**) (BAGD 2. p. 470): 'to be lacking' [LN]. The phrase 'still is lacking' is translated 'is still lacking' [BECNT; NRSV], 'is still missing' [AB], 'you still lack' [Arn, BAGD, **LN** (57.44), NTC; HCSB, NASB, NET, NIV, NLT, REB], 'yet lackest thou' [KJV], 'yet is lacking' [Lns], 'you still need' [GW], 'you still need to do' [**LN** (71.33); CEV, NCV, TEV], 'still remains for you to do' [WBC].

b. aorist act. impera. of διαδίδωμι (LN 57.94) (BAGD p. 182): 'to distribute' [AB, Arn, BAGD, LN, WBC; KJV], 'to distribute it' [HCSB, NASB], 'to distribute the proceeds' [NTC], 'to distribute the money' [GW, NRSV], 'to give out' [LN], 'to give' [BAGD, BECNT, Lns; NIV, REB], 'to give it' [NCV], 'to give the money' [CEV, NET, NLT, TEV].

c. θησαυρός (LN 65.10) (BAGD 2.b.α. p. 361): 'treasure' [AB, Arn, BAGD, BECNT, LN, Lns, NTC, WBC; all versions except CEV, TEV], 'wealth' [LN], 'riches' [LN; CEV, TEV].

d. pres. act. impera. of ἀκολουθέω (LN 36.31) (BAGD 3. p. 31): 'to follow' [Arn, BAGD, BECNT, LN, Lns, NTC, WBC; all versions except CEV], 'to be a disciple of' [LN], 'to be (my) follower' [CEV]. It is a call to discipleship [NIGTC, TG]. He would follow Jesus by sitting under his teaching and living the way Jesus showed [BECNT]. In following Jesus, the ruler must learn to deny himself in complete surrender [NTC].

QUESTION—What was the one thing still lacking?
1. There was one thing he must still do [Arn, BECNT, MGC, NAC, NIGTC, NTC, TG, TH, WBC; CEV, NCV, TEV]: you still need to do one more thing. In view of the following imperatives, this refers to something that must be done [TH]. In addition to obeying the commandments, he must do one more thing [TG]. This is something else he must do in his pursuit of eternal life [WBC]. The imperatives tell him to sell all that he has and distribute the money to the poor and then to follow Jesus [BECNT, TH]. This one thing is all-embracing [MGC, NIGTC]. This one thing was suited to the ruler's particular circumstances and his state of mind and it is not what every rich man must do [NTC].
2. There was one thing he still did not have [Gdt, ICC, Lns, Su; GW]: you still need one thing. Accepting the ruler's statement that he had obeyed the commandments, he still lacked detachment from his wealth [ICC]. He lacked the spirit of the Law which involves having a love that is ready to give everything [Gdt]. He lacked love and compassion for people in need and he needed to reject his own self-interest [Su]. Giving away his money was only a condition to entering a life of discipleship, so he lacked a commitment to follow Jesus [NIGTC]. This thing is a complete inward change [Lns].

QUESTION—If he sells everything, what does he have left to distribute to the poor?

He was to distribute the proceeds from what he sold [BECNT, NTC, TH; CEV, GW, HCSB, NASB, NCV, NET, NIV, NLT, NRSV]: sell everything and give the money you thus obtain to the poor.

QUESTION—What is the treasure in heaven that he would have?

In heaven he would be rich in spiritual and eternal possessions [TG]. The treasure consists of eternal life [NAC, NIGTC] and entering the kingdom [NAC]. The treasure is all the blessings associated with eternal life that come in both this age and the next [BECNT]. The treasure consists of blessings which are heavenly in character and can be experienced only in part before one gets to heaven [NTC]. By selling his earthly treasure, it would then be invested in heaven and he would no longer have an earthbound asset [WBC].

18:23 And having-heard these (things) he-became very-sad[a] because he-was very rich.

LEXICON—a. περίλυπος (LN 25.277) (BAGD p. 648): 'very sad' [AB, BAGD, LN, Lns, NTC, WBC; NASB, NCV, NET, NIV, TEV], 'extremely sad' [Arn; HCSB], 'sad' [BECNT; CEV, GW, NLT, NRSV], 'sorrowful' [LN], 'very sorrowful' [KJV], 'deeply grieved' [BAGD]. The phrase 'he became very sad' is translated 'his heart sank' [REB].

QUESTION—What is implied by the statement that the ruler became very sad?

It is implied that he refused to do what Jesus told him to do [AB, TNTC, WBC], because he loved money more than he loved God [NAC]. He may have wanted to follow Jesus' commands, but the cost seemed too great [ICC]. He went away, probably thinking that the requirement was not fair and none of the other rabbis would have made this demand upon him [NTC]. The ruler had a true religious interest, but it was overcome by his love for riches [Arn]. The great degree of his sadness matched the great extent of his wealth [MGC].

DISCOURSE UNIT: 18:24–30 [AB, NIGTC, WBC; HCSB]. The topic is riches and rewards [AB, NIGTC], possessions and the kingdom [HCSB], how hard it is for those who have money to enter the kingdom of God [WBC].

18:24 And having-looked-at him Jesus having-become very-sad[a] said, How with-difficulty[b] the (ones who) have wealth[c] enter[d] into the kingdom of-God. **18:25** Because it-is easier (for) a-camel to-go-through[e] (the) eye of-a-needle than (for) a-rich-person to-enter into the kingdom of-God.

TEXT—In 18:24, instead of ὁ Ἰησοῦς περίλυπον γενόμενον εἶπεν 'Jesus very sad having become said', some manuscripts read περίλυπον γενόμενον εἶπεν ὁ Ἰησοῦς 'very sad having become said Jesus' and some manuscripts read ὁ Ἰησοῦς εἶπεν 'Jesus said'. GNT reads ὁ Ἰησοῦς περίλυπον γενόμενον εἶπεν 'Jesus very sad having become said' with a C decision and places περίλυπον γενόμενον in brackets, indicating that the Committee had difficulty in making the decision to include that phrase.

TEXT—In 18:25, instead of κάμηλον 'camel', some manuscripts read κάμιλον 'rope'. GNT reads κάμηλον 'camel' with an A decision, indicating that the text is certain.

TEXT—In 18:25, instead of τρήματος βελόνης 'eye of a needle' some manuscripts read τρυμαλιᾶς ῥαφίδος 'eye of a needle'. GNT does not mention this variant. Most translations would not distinguish between these two phrases.

LEXICON—a. περίλυπος (LN 25.277) (BAGD p. 648): 'very sad'. See this word at 18:23. This word is omitted [Lns, NTC, WBC; GW, NASB, NCV, NIV, NLT, NRSV, REB].

b. δυσκόλως (LN 22.32) (BAGD p. 209): 'with difficulty' [BAGD], 'difficult, hard' [LN]. The phrase 'how with difficulty' [Lns] is translated 'how difficult it is for' [BECNT], 'how hard it is for' [AB, NTC, WBC; all versions except CEV, KJV, NCV], 'how hardly shall' [KJV], 'it is very hard for' [NCV], 'it's terribly hard for' [CEV], 'with what difficulty will…(enter into)' [Arn].

c. χρῆμα (LN 57.31) (BAGD 1. p. 885): 'wealth' [BAGD, LN], 'riches' [LN], 'property' [BAGD]. The phrase 'the ones having wealth' is translated 'those who have wealth' [HCSB, NRSV], 'those who are

wealthy' [NASB], 'those who possess wealth' [NTC], 'they that have riches' [KJV], 'those having riches' [Lns], 'those who have money' [AB, WBC], 'a man who has possessions' [BECNT], 'those that have possessions' [Arn], 'the wealthy' [REB], 'the rich' [NET, NIV], 'rich people' [CEV, GW, NCV, NLT, TEV].
- d. pres. mid./pass. (deponent = act.) indic. of εἰσπορεύομαι (LN 15.93) (BAGD 1. p. 233): 'to enter' [BAGD, LN], 'to go into' [BAGD, LN]. The phrase 'to enter into' [Arn, Lns; KJV] is also translated 'to enter' [AB, NTC, WBC; GW, HCSB, NASB, NCV, NET, NIV, NRSV, REB, TEV], 'to get into' [CEV, NLT], 'to come into' [BECNT]. Being present tense instead of future tense, it indicates what is apt to happen because of the riches [EGT]. It was possible to enter the kingdom now that Jesus was there [WBC]. The present tense has a timeless aspect [BECNT]. Or, this is a futuristic present tense [NIGTC, Rb]. The parallel passage at Mark 10:24 has a future tense. Entering the kingdom is another way of saying to be saved as the question in 18:26 indicates [BECNT, NIBC, NICNT].
- e. διά (LN 84.29): 'through' [LN]. The phrase 'to go through' [Arn, BECNT, Lns, NTC; all versions] is also translated 'to pass through' [AB], 'to go into' [WBC].

QUESTION—Who had become very sad according to the different manuscripts?
1. Jesus was very sad [HCSB]: Jesus looked at the rich ruler, and Jesus became very sad and said the following.
2. The rich ruler was very sad [AB, Arn, BECNT, TH; CEV, KJV, NET, TEV]: Jesus saw that the rich ruler had become very sad, and Jesus said the following. The parallel accounts in Matt. 19:22 and Mark 10:22 do say that the rich ruler went away sad.
3. The phrase is omitted [Lns, NAC, NTC, WBC; GW, NASB, NCV, NIV, NLT, NRSV, REB]: Jesus looked at the rich ruler and said the following.

QUESTION—Why is it difficult for rich people to enter the kingdom of God?
Although this statement is left unexplained, it is clear that the rich are tempted to trust in their own money instead of in God [MGC]. Those with wealth are tempted to rely on earthly things [Arn, TNTC] and they find it difficult to cast themselves on God's mercy [TNTC]. It is hard for them to divest themselves of their possessions [AB].

QUESTION—Does the impossibility of a camel going through the eye of a needle mean that it is impossible for the rich to enter the kingdom?
The illustration is a hyperbole to emphasize how difficult it is [AB, BECNT, MGC, NAC, WBC]. Humanly speaking, it is impossible for the rich to enter the kingdom since no one in his own strength is able to resist the temptation of earthly wealth [NIC]. It is impossible as long as the rich man trusts in his own riches [Lns]. By his own efforts, it is impossible [Arn, BECNT, Lns, NTC; NET] and it takes a miracle of God's grace for a rich person to enter the kingdom [Arn]. Jesus spoke in absolute terms without qualifying his statement so that the disciples would realize that salvation is not a human

achievement [NTC]. This is a grotesque or silly figure which uses the largest animal in Palestine with the smallest commonly known opening [AB, BECNT, MGC, NTC, TG]. It was probably already a proverbial saying [Arn, BECNT]. This dramatic comparison was intended to make the disciples take special notice of what he was about to say [NTC].

DISCOURSE UNIT: 18:26–30 [NCV]. The topic is who can be saved?

18:26 And the (ones who) heard said, Then[a] who is-able to-be-saved?[b]
18:27 And he-said, The (things) impossible[c] with men are possible[d] with God.

LEXICON—a. καί (LN 71.2): 'then' [Arn, BECNT, LN, NTC, WBC; all versions], 'well, then' [AB], 'and' [Lns]. This expresses surprise [LN, TH].

  b. aorist pass. infin. of σῴζω (LN 21.27) (BAGD 2.b. p. 798): 'to be saved' [AB, Arn, BAGD, BECNT, LN, Lns, NTC, WBC; all versions]. The passive indicates that God is the one who saves [Lns]. Entering the kingdom of God is now spoken of as being saved [BECNT, NICNT, NIGTC, WBC]. Inheriting eternal life (18:18) and entering the kingdom of God (18:25) are synonymous with being saved, all speaking of the same blessing from different angles [NTC].

  c. ἀδύνατος (LN 71.3) (BAGD 2.a. p. 19): 'impossible' [BAGD, LN]. The phrase 'the things impossible with men' [Lns] is also translated 'the things which are impossible with men/man' [Arn; KJV], 'the things that are impossible with people' [NASB], 'things that are impossible for man' [BECNT], 'the things that are impossible for people to do' [GW], 'what is impossible with men' [NTC; HCSB, NIV], 'what is impossible for men' [NET, REB], 'what is impossible for human beings' [AB, WBC], 'what is impossible for mortals' [NRSV], 'things that are not possible for people to do' [NCV], 'there are some things that people cannot do' [CEV], 'what is humanly impossible' [TEV], 'what is impossible from a human perspective' [NLT].

  d. δυνατός (LN71.2) (BAGD 2.c. p. 209): 'possible' [BAGD, LN]. The phrase 'are/is possible with God' [Arn, Lns, NTC; HCSB, KJV, NASB, NIV, NLT] is also translated 'are/is possible for God' [AB, BECNT, WBC; NET, NRSV, REB, TEV], 'are possible for God to do' [GW], 'God can do anything' [CEV], 'God can do things (that are not possible for people to do)' [NCV].

QUESTION—What is the significance of the question, 'Then who is able to be saved?'

  The word καί 'and, then' at the beginning of the question indicates astonishment at a statement that seems to say that no one can attain salvation [AB, Su, TH]. Jesus seemed to be saying that nobody can be saved and surely that could not be true [Lns]. It is a rhetorical question meaning 'If that is true, then nobody can be saved' [TG]. If rich people with all of their advantages can scarcely be saved, then there is no hope for the others [NAC, NIGTC,

Rb, Su]. Since wealth is a blessing from God and wealthy people are excluded from the kingdom, then no one can be saved [Gdt, MGC, NIC, NIGTC, Su, TNTC, WBC; NET]. Even poor people yearn to become rich, so Jesus was talking about all people [NTC]. Since everyone desires wealth, no one can be saved [ICC].

QUESTION—What is the application of the statement that God can do what people cannot do?

This speaks of God breaking through the mesmerizing effects of riches that control people [AB, ICC, NAC, NIGTC, WBC]. God is able to effect a change of perspective [BECNT]. God changes the most obstinate heart [Arn]. A person cannot save himself, but God can save him [TG]. God can save even the rich [Lns, NIC]. No one is able to save himself, but God, through Christ, is able to save anyone [NTC].

18:28 And Peter said, Behold we having-left our-own[a] (things) followed you. 18:29 And he-said to-them, Truly I-say to-you that there-is no-one who left[b] house or wife or brothers[c] or parents or children because-of[d] the kingdom of-God,

TEXT—In 18:28, instead of ἀφέντες τὰ ἴδια 'having left our own things', some manuscripts read ἀφήκαμεν πάντα καί 'have left all things and'. GNT does not mention this variant.

TEXT—In 18:29, instead of γυναῖκα ἢ ἀδελφοῖς ἢ γονεῖς 'wife or brothers or parents', some manuscripts read γονεῖς ἢ ἀδελφοῖς ἢ γυναῖκα 'parents or brothers or wife'. GNT does not mention this variant. Γονεῖς ἢ ἀδελφοῖς ἢ γυναῖκα 'parents or brothers or wife' is read by KJV.

LEXICON—a. ἴδιος (LN 57.4) (BAGD 3.b. p. 370): 'one's own' [BAGD, LN]. The phrase 'having left our own things' [BECNT, Lns] is also translated 'we have left what was ours' [WBC], 'we have left our possessions' [Arn], 'we have left all we had' [NTC; NIV, REB], 'we have left what we had' [AB; HCSB], 'we have left all' [KJV], 'we have left everything' [CEV, GW, NCV], 'we have left everything we own' [NET], 'we have left our own homes' [NASB], 'we have left our homes' [NLT, NRSV, TEV].

b. aorist act. indic. of ἀφίημι (LN 85.45) (BAGD 3.a. p. 126): 'to leave' [AB, BAGD, BECNT, LN, Lns, WBC; HCSB, KJV, NASB, NCV, NET, NIV, NRSV, TEV], 'to leave behind' [LN], 'to give up' [NTC; CEV, GW, NLT, REB], 'to forsake' [Arn]. This is the same verb as that used in 18:28. Leaving these things may refer to an outward act of separating from them, or it could be an inward separation [Lns].

c. ἀδελφός (LN 10.49): 'brother' [LN]. The plural form is translated 'brothers' [AB, Arn, NTC; all versions except KJV], 'brethren' [KJV], 'brother' [Lns], 'siblings' [BECNT, WBC]. The plural form of this word can include both brothers and sisters [NIGTC, TH]. The parallel passage in Matt. 19:29 has 'brothers or sisters'.

d. ἕνεκεν (LN 89.3) (BAGD p. 264): 'because of' [BAGD, LN; CEV, GW, HCSB], 'on account of' [Arn, BAGD, LN], 'for the sake of' [AB, BAGD, BECNT, Lns, NTC, WBC; KJV, NASB, NET, NIV, NLT, NRSV, REB, TEV], 'for' [NCV].

QUESTION—Why did Peter speak at this point?

Peter was speaking on behalf of his fellow disciples [BECNT, Crd, Gdt, MGC, NIC, TH]. 'We' includes at least Peter (the spokesman), John, and James [AB, NAC], or the Twelve [Lns, WBC]. This was said for information and it was not said in a boastful manner [Arn, BECNT]. Jesus had told the rich ruler to sell all he possessed and follow him, and here Peter reminded Jesus that the disciple had left everything to follow him [TG]. The disciples had already made the choice that the rich ruler failed to make [BECNT, NTC]. Peter wanted assurance that God's power had been exerted in behalf of the disciples so that they could have hope of entering the kingdom [ICC]. Peter wanted to know if they have the treasure in heaven that Jesus had spoken of in 18:22 [Lns, TG]. The implied question is 'Have we qualified for entry to the kingdom?' or 'What shall we get in return for our self-sacrifices?' [NIGTC].

QUESTION—What is meant by 'we, having left our own things'?

The pronoun 'we' is emphatic to contrast them with the rich ruler [Lns, Su, TH]. Their own things means the things they own [TH], everything [Su]. This probably includes their families with everything they had [NAC, TH]. In a more specific sense it means they left their possessions [NIGTC], their property [TH], their homes [Lns], their wives and children [TH], their own affairs and interests [Lns].

QUESTION—Did Jesus mean that some of his disciples were expected to leave their wives?

Instead of breaking up a marriage, this may mean that the disciple would renounce the possibility of marriage [BECNT, NAC, NIGTC]. If married, it could mean that they would travel without wife or children [BECNT]. This also includes the situation in which a disciple has been excluded from his family because he had chosen to follow Jesus [BECNT, ICC]. Departing from one's family in order to spread the gospel would have varying reactions according to whether the family members were disciples of Christ who approved of his actions or if they resented and renounced him [MGC].

QUESTION—What is meant by leaving all these things ἕνεκεν 'because of' the kingdom of God?

They left these things in order to serve the cause of the kingdom of God [TH]. Or, they left them in order to become a citizen of the kingdom [TG]. Because of what the kingdom was and what it meant to them they gave up all to follow Jesus [Su].

18:30 who will- not -receive-back[a] many-times-more[b] in this time and in the coming age[c] eternal life.

TEXT—Instead of ἀπολάβῃ 'receive back', some manuscripts read λάβῃ 'receive'. GNT does not deal with this variant. Versions might not distinguish between these two readings.

LEXICON—a. aorist act. subj. of ἀπολαμβάνω (LN 57.136) (BAGD 1. p. 94): 'to receive back' [LN, Lns], 'to receive' [AB, Arn, BAGD, BECNT, NTC, WBC; GW, HCSB, KJV, NASB, NET, NIV, TEV], 'to be given' [CEV], 'to get' [NCV], 'to get back' [NRSV], 'to be repaid' [NLT, REB].

b. πολλαπλασίων (LN **59.20**) (BAGD p. 687): 'many times more' [**LN**, Lns; HCSB, NET], 'many times as much' [AB, Arn, BAGD, LN, NTC, WBC; GW, NASB, NIV], 'many times over' [NLT, REB], 'manifold' [BAGD], 'manifold more' [KJV], 'very much more' [NRSV], 'much more' [CEV, NCV, TEV], 'more' [BECNT]. In the parallel passage at Mark 10:30 it says that they will receive a hundred times as much. This refers to receiving back many times more than that which was left behind [TH].

c. αἰών (LN 67.143) (BAGD p. 27): 'age' [BAGD, LN], 'era' [LN]. This refers to a particular period of history [LN]. The phrases ἐν τῷ καιρῷ τούτῳ...ἐν τῷ αἰῶνι τῷ ἐρχομένῳ 'in this time...in the coming age' are translated 'in this time...in the age to come' [BECNT, NTC], 'in this age...in the age to come' [AB, WBC; NET, NIV, NRSV, REB], 'in this time...in the eon that is coming' [Lns], 'in this present age...in the age to come' [TEV], 'at this time...in the age to come' [HCSB, NASB], 'in this life...in the age that is coming' [NCV], 'in this period...in the coming era' [Arn], 'in this present time...in the world to come' [KJV], 'in this life...in the world to come' [GW, NLT], 'in this life...in the future world' [CEV].

QUESTIONS—What will they receive back for what they left?

This at least refers to association with Jesus' new family [AB], the spiritual family of believers [Gdt, MGC, NAC, NICNT, NTC]. It refers to receiving the blessings enjoyed in Christian congregations [Arn, ICC]. This refers to spiritual benefits such as inward riches, friendships, and true happiness [NIC], peace of heart and mind [Arn, NTC]. At the Second Coming, this will be fully realized [NTC]. They will receive this from God [TG].

DISCOURSE UNIT: 18:31–20:47 [REB]. The topic is Jesus' challenge to Jerusalem.

DISCOURSE UNIT: 18:31–19:44 [BECNT]. The topic is turning to Jerusalem.

DISCOURSE UNIT: 18:31–34 [AB, BECNT, NAC, NICNT, NIGTC, Su, TNTC, WBC; CEV, GW, HCSB, NCV, NET, NIV, NLT, NRSV, TEV]. The topic is another prediction of Jesus' passion [NET], the third passion announcement [AB, BECNT, NAC, Su, TNTC], Jesus again tells about his death [CEV], the third prediction of his death [HCSB], Jesus speaks a third time about his death [TEV], Jesus again predicts his death [NIV, NLT], Jesus will rise from the dead [NCV], a third time Jesus foretells his death and resurrection [NRSV], for the third time Jesus foretells that he will die and come back to life [GW], the enigma of Jesus' suffering [NICNT], the passion draws near [NIGTC], everything written about the Son of Man will be carried out [WBC].

18:31 And having-taken-aside[a] the twelve he-said to them, Behold[b] we-are-going-up[c] to Jerusalem, and all the (things) written by the prophets about the Son of-Man[d] will-be-fulfilled.[e]

LEXICON—a. aorist act. participle of παραλαμβάνω (LN 15.180) (BAGD 1. p. 619): 'to take aside' [AB, Arn, BECNT, LN, Lns, NTC, WBC; all versions except KJV, NLT], 'to take along' [BAGD, LN], 'to take unto him' [KJV], 'to gather around' [NLT].

b. ἰδού (LN 91.13): 'behold' [Arn, BECNT; KJV, NASB], 'listen' [LN, NTC; HCSB, TEV], 'look' [LN, WBC; NET], 'see' [NRSV], 'pay attention' [LN], 'lo' [Lns], 'as you know' [NLT], not explicit [AB; CEV, GW, NCV, NIV, REB]. This indicates the importance of what he is about to say and in this context 'listen' is the right translation [NTC].

c. pres. act. indic. of ἀναβαίνω (LN 15.101) (BAGD 1.a.α. p. 50): 'to go up' [AB, Arn, BAGD, BECNT, LN, Lns, NTC, WBC; HCSB, KJV, NASB, NET, NIV, NRSV, REB], 'to ascend' [BAGD, LN], 'to go' [GW, NCV, NLT, TEV], 'to be on the way' [CEV]. The subject 'we' refers to Jesus and the Twelve [Lns]. They would travel up to the higher ground upon which Jerusalem was situated [MGC, NTC].

d. υἱὸς τοῦ ἀνθρώπου 'Son of Man'. This title for Christ occurs at 5:24; 6:5, 22; 7:34; 9:22, 26, 44; 11:30; 12:8, 40; 17:22, 24, 26; 18:8; 19:10; 21:27, 36; 22:22, 48, 69; 24:7. See the discussions of this title at 5:24, 6:5, and 9:22.

e. fut. pass. indic. of τελέω (LN 13.26) (BAGD 2. p. 811): 'to be fulfilled' [Arn, BAGD, BECNT, LN, NTC; NIV], 'to find fulfillment' [REB], 'to see fulfillment' [AB], 'to be accomplished' [BAGD, LN, Lns; KJV, NASB, NET, NRSV], 'to be carried out' [WBC], 'to come true' [GW, NLT, TEV], 'to happen' [CEV, NCV].

QUESTION—What was Jesus' purpose for taking the Twelve apostles aside?
There must have been a large number of people moving along the road when Jesus took the Twelve to a spot where they could be alone [Arn]. Jesus wanted to speak to them privately, away from the crowds [TG, TH]. He took the Twelve apart from the other disciples to speak with them [Arn, Lns]. He wanted to impress upon the twelve disciples the gravity of what would soon take place [NTC]. He reminded them of what awaited them [BECNT].

QUESTION—What things were written by the prophets?
This refers to the passages in the prophetic books of the Jewish Scriptures [TG]. Or, 'the prophets' refers to the entire OT [NAC]. The passages are not indicated, but presumably they are the passages concerning his suffering in

Deuteronomy, Isaiah, and the Psalms [Su]. Daniel 7:13 must have been one of the passages [WBC]. The prophets did not originate the message, rather, they were the instruments who wrote the message from God [Arn, ICC, Lns, MGC, NTC, TH]. It concerns everything written *through* the prophets [BECNT, Lns, NTC; HCSB, NASB].

QUESTION—In what way would they be fulfilled?

This means that all things will happen to the Son of Man as written by the prophets, rather than all things written by the prophets will be fulfilled by the Son of Man [EGT]. God would bring about the fulfillment [AB, TNTC].

18:32 Because he-will-be-delivered-up[a] to-the Gentiles and he-will-be-ridiculed[b] and he-will-be-mistreated[c] and he-will-be-spat-upon **18:33** and having-whipped[d] (him) they-will-kill him, and on-the third day he-will-rise-again.[e]

LEXICON—a. fut. pass. indic. of παραδίδωμι (LN 37.111) (BAGD 1.b. p. 614): 'to be delivered up' [BAGD, LN, WBC], 'to be delivered' [KJV], 'to be handed over' [AB, Arn, BAGD, LN, NTC; all versions except KJV, NASB], 'to be given over' [BECNT, Lns], 'to be turned over to' [NASB], 'to be betrayed' [LN].

b. fut. pass. indic. of ἐμπαίζω (LN 33.406) (BAGD 1. p. 255?): 'to be ridiculed' [AB, BAGD, LN, WBC], 'to be mocked' [Arn, BAGD, BECNT, LN, Lns, NTC; HCSB, KJV, NASB, NET, NLT, NRSV, REB], 'to be made fun of' [BAGD]. This passive verb is also translated actively with Jesus as the object: 'to mock' [NIV], 'to make fun of' [CEV, GW, TEV], 'to laugh at' [NCV]. See this word at 14:29; 22:63; 23:11, 36.

c. fut. pass. indic. of ὑβρίζω (LN 33.390) (BAGD p. 831): 'to be mistreated' [BAGD; NASB, NET], 'to be maltreated' [REB], 'to be treated shamefully' [BECNT; NLT], 'to be spitefully entreated' [KJV], 'to be outraged' [Lns], 'to be insulted' [AB, BAGD, LN, NTC, WBC; HCSB, NRSV], not explicit [Arn]. This passive verb is also translated actively with Jesus as the object: 'to mistreat' [CEV], 'to insult' [GW, NCV, NIV, TEV].

d. aorist act. participle of μαστιγόω (LN 19.9) (BAGD 1. p. 495): 'to whip' [BAGD, LN; GW, NLT, TEV], 'to flog' [AB, BAGD, WBC; HCSB, NIV, NRSV, REB], 'to flog severely' [NET], 'to scourge' [Arn, BAGD, BECNT, Lns, NTC; KJV, NASB], 'to beat' [CEV], 'to beat with whips' [NCV].

e. fut. mid. indic. of ἀνίσταμαι (LN 23.93): 'to rise again' [AB, Lns, NTC; KJV, NASB, NET, NIV, NLT, NRSV, REB], 'to rise' [Arn, BECNT, WBC; HCSB], 'to rise to life' [CEV, TEV], 'to rise to life again' [NCV], 'to come back to life' [LN; GW], 'to live again, to be resurrected' [LN].

QUESTION—Who will deliver up Jesus to the Gentiles?

1. The Jewish authorities will deliver Jesus to the Romans [Lns, MGC, NTC, Su, WBC; NET]. Since the Romans did not allow the Jews to carry out a death sentence, the Jewish authorities handed Jesus over to the Gentile

270   LUKE 18:32-33

  authority, Pilate, in order that Jesus could be crucified [NTC]. The
  Sanhedrin handed Jesus over to Pilate and his men [Lns].
2. God will deliver up Jesus [NAC, TH]. The delivering up is a fulfillment of
  prophecy [TH]. God will fulfill what was written by his prophets [NAC].
QUESTION—When was Jesus ridiculed?
  This happened in 22:63 when the soldiers blindfolded and told him to say
  who hit him, in 23:11 when Herod and his soldiers put a purple robe on Jesus
  as though he was royalty, and in 23:35–43 when the bystanders and the
  soldiers mocked Jesus for his inability to save himself from the cross.
QUESTION—When was Jesus mistreated and spat upon?
  This happened in Matthew 26:67 and 27:30 where the soldiers spit on him,
  and struck him with their fists.
QUESTION—When was Jesus whipped?
  This happened in Matthew 27:26 where Pilate had Jesus flogged before
  handing him over to be crucified. A person who was condemned to death
  was often flogged beforehand [BECNT, MGC, NTC, TG]. The condemned
  man was whipped thirty-nine times with a scourge made of nine ropes to
  which were attached bones, glass, and nails to increase the pain [MGC].

18:34 **And they understood[a] none of-these (things) and this word[b] had-been hidden[c] from them and they-were- not -comprehending[d] the (things) being-said.**
LEXICON—a. aorist act. indic. of συνίημι (LN 32.5) (BAGD p. 790): 'to
    understand' [Arn, BAGD, BECNT, LN, NTC, WBC; all versions], 'to
    comprehend' [AB, BAGD, LN], 'to grasp' [Lns]. The aorist gives a
    summary statement [Rb].
  b. ῥῆμα (LN 33.98) (BAGD 1. p. 735): 'word' [BAGD, LN, WBC],
    'statement' [LN], 'message' [AB], 'saying' [Arn; HCSB, KJV, NET],
    'utterance' [Lns], 'matter' [BECNT]. The phrase 'this word' is translated
    'what he said' [GW, NRSV], 'the meaning of what he said' [CEV], 'the
    meaning of this statement' [NTC; NASB], 'the meaning of the words'
    [TEV], 'the/its meaning' [NCV, NIV, REB], 'its significance' [NLT].
  c. perf. pass. participle of κρύπτω (LN 28.79) (BAGD 2.a. p. 454): 'to be
    hidden' [AB, Arn, BAGD, BECNT, LN, Lns; all versions except GW,
    REB], 'to be concealed' [BAGD, LN, NTC, WBC; REB]. The phrase
    'had been hidden from them' is translated 'was a mystery to them' [GW].
    See this word at 19:42.
  d. imperf. act. indic. of γινώσκω (LN 32.16) (BAGD 3.a. p. 161): 'to
    comprehend' [BAGD, LN; NASB], 'to understand' [BAGD, LN; CEV],
    'to perceive' [LN], 'to grasp' [NTC; HCSB, NET, NLT, NRSV, REB], 'to
    realize' [AB, Lns; NCV], 'to know' [Arn, BECNT, WBC; KJV, NIV,
    TEV], 'to know what was meant' [GW].
QUESTION—Why didn't they understand these things?
  Since Jesus' statement was so clear, perhaps this means that the Twelve
  could not understand how these events would fulfill Scripture, yet since there

is stress on it being hidden from them, perhaps it simply means that they could not believe that all of this could happen to Jesus [NIGTC]. It is not that they were unable to understand the words Jesus spoke, they could not understand that this could be the Messiah's destiny and God's plan [Arn, BECNT, My, NTC; NET]. They believed that Jesus was the Messiah and they could not accept the possibility of his death [BECNT, ICC, MGC, NIC, Su]. Perhaps they thought Jesus was speaking figuratively as he often did and talked of his dying in order to live in the same way he had already taught them [TNTC].

QUESTION—Why was this hidden from them?

This may mean that they were prevented from understanding since God's purpose was that they should not understand at this point [TNTC]. This explains that their lack of understanding was not their fault [TH]. God had not yet given them the ability to put these things together [BECNT]. Or, this passive does not indicate that it was God who hid it from them, rather it merely emphasizes their inability to understand [TG]. This does not mean that Jesus didn't want them to understand, it was hidden because of their own reluctance to accept what Jesus had said [Su]. Jesus' predictions were not useless, because when they had been fulfilled they would understand and their faith would be strengthened [Lns, NTC], and they would preach it [BECNT].

QUESTION—What is the significance of the last clause?

This repeats the thought of the first clause and here τὰ λεγόμενα 'the things being said' is equivalent to ῥῆμα τοῦτο 'this word' [TH]. Luke says the same idea three times to underscore it presence [BECNT]. This clause summarizes their perplexity [Su].

DISCOURSE UNIT: 18:35–19:46 [WBC]. The topic is reaching the city of destiny.

DISCOURSE UNIT: 18:35–43 [AB, BECNT, NAC, NICNT, NIGTC, Su, TNTC, WBC; CEV, GW, HCSB, NASB, NCV, NET, NIV, NLT, NRSV, TEV]. The topic is healing a blind man [NET], a blind man receives his sight [HCSB], a blind beggar receives his sight [NIV], the healing of the blind man at Jericho [AB, NAC, NIGTC, Su, TNTC], Jesus heals a blind man [NCV], Jesus heals a blind beggar [CEV, NLT, TEV], Jesus gives sight to a blind man [GW], Jesus heals a blind beggar near Jericho [NRSV], Bartimaeus receives sight [NASB], the irony of blindness [NICNT], healing by the Son of David [BECNT], Jesus, Son of David, have mercy on me [WBC].

18:35 **And it-happened as he drew-near[a] to Jericho a-certain blind-man was-sitting beside the road begging. 18:36 And having-heard a-crowd going-by[b] he was-inquiring[c] what this might-be.[d]**

LEXICON—a. pres. act. infin. of ἐγγίζω (LN 15.75) (BAGD 2. p. 213): 'to draw near' [AB, BECNT, LN, Lns, WBC; HCSB], 'to come near' [BAGD; GW, NCV, TEV], 'to come close' [CEV], 'to come nigh' [KJV],

'to approach' [Arn, BAGD, LN, NTC; NASB, NET, NIV, NLT, NRSV, REB].
- b. pres. mid./pass. (deponent = act.) participle of διαπορεύομαι (LN **15;22**) (BAGD p. 187): 'to go by' [BAGD, BECNT, NTC; GW, HCSB, NASB, NET, NIV, NRSV], 'to go past' [NLT, REB]. 'to pass through' [Arn, BAGD, **LN**, Lns], 'to pass by' [AB, **LN**; KJV, TEV], 'to pass along' [WBC], 'to walk by' [CEV], 'to come down the road' [NCV]. The sounds of an unusually large group of people on the way to Jerusalem aroused the beggar's curiosity [ICC]. As the people passed along, they would be making some noise as they walked and talked [Arn].
- c. imperf. mid./pass. (deponent = act.) participle of πυνθάνομαι (LN 33.181) (BAGD 1. p. 729): 'to inquire' [Arn, BAGD, BECNT, LN, Lns, NTC, WBC; HCSB, NASB], 'to ask' [AB, BAGD, LN; all versions except GW, HCSB, NASB], 'to try to find out' [GW]. The imperfect tense indicates that he repeatedly asked the people near him what the tramp of passing people was all about [Rb]. Or, the imperfect is inceptive, 'he *began* to inquire' [Lns; NASB]
- d. pres. act. opt. of εἰμί (LN 13.4): 'to be' [LN]. The phrase 'what this might be' [WBC] is also translated 'what it might be' [BECNT], 'what this was' [Lns, NTC; NASB], 'what was/is happening' [CEV, GW, NCV, NIV, NLT, NRSV, REB], 'what was going on' [AB; NET], 'what this/it meant' [Arn; HCSB, KJV], 'what is this?' [TEV].

QUESTION—Where did this incident take place?

Jesus was on his way to Jerusalem and was now approaching the town of Jericho, about 17 miles from Jerusalem [TG]. The beggar was at the side of the road, probably near the entrance to the city [NIGTC]. This was a strategic place for begging alms from the many religious travelers [Su]. There were two Jerichos. The old Jericho was the city spoken of in the OT and it was now largely abandoned, but about one and a-half miles past it was the New Jericho established by Herod the Great [Arn, BECNT, NIVS]. The beggar was situated on the road between the two Jerichos [Arn, NIVS, NTC, Su], at the approach to the New Jericho [BECNT]. Another explanation is that only one Jericho is involved and Jesus had passed through the city and on his way out he met Zacchaeus who invited him to stay at his house back in the city. It was when Jesus was going back into the city that he encountered the blind man [Lns].

18:37 And they-told him that Jesus the Nazarene is-going-by. **18:38** And he-called-out saying, Jesus Son of-David, have-mercy-on[a] me. **18:39** And the (ones) going-before[b] were-rebuking[c] him that he-should-be-silent, but he was-crying-out much more,[d] Son of-David, have-mercy-on me.

LEXICON—a. aorist act. impera. of ἐλεάω (LN 88.76) (BAGD p. 249): 'to have mercy (on)' [AB, Arn, BAGD, BECNT, LN, Lns, WBC; all versions except CEV, REB], 'to be merciful, to show mercy' [BAGD, LN], 'to

have pity (on)' [CEV, REB], 'to take pity (on)' [NTC]. See this word at 16:24, 17:13.
b. pres. act. participle of προάγω (LN 15.143) (BAGD 2.a. p. 702): 'to go before' [BAGD], 'to go in front of' [LN], 'to precede' [BAGD, LN]. The phrase 'the ones going before' is translated 'they which went before' [KJV], 'the crowds ahead of Jesus' [NLT], 'those leading' [Lns], 'those who led the way' [NASB, NIV], 'those in the lead' [AB], 'those who were in the lead' [WBC], 'the people leading the group' [NCV], 'the people/those in front' [NTC; HCSB, REB, TEV], 'those who were in front' [NET, NRSV], 'the people at the front of the crowd' [GW], 'those in front of him' [BECNT], 'those that walked at the head' [Arn], 'the people who were going along with Jesus' [CEV].
c. imperf. act. indic. of ἐπιτιμάω (LN 33.419) (BAGD 1. p. 303): 'to rebuke' [BAGD, LN], 'to reprove' [BAGD]. The phrase 'were rebuking him that he should be silent' is translated 'began rebuking him, that he be silent' [Lns], 'rebuked him that he should be quiet' [AB], 'rebuked him, saying that he should become silent' [Arn], 'rebuked him and told him to be quiet' [NIV], 'began to rebuke him that he should be quiet' [BECNT, WBC], 'rebuked him, that he should hold his peace' [KJV], 'were sternly telling him to be quiet' [NASB], 'told the man/him to be quiet' [CEV, GW], 'told him to keep quiet' [HCSB], 'warned the blind man to be quiet' [NCV], 'started to warn him to be quiet' [NTC], 'sternly ordered him to be quiet' [NRSV], 'scolded him and told him to be quiet' [TEV], 'scolded him to get him to be quiet' [NET], 'tried to hush the man' [NLT], 'told him to hold his tongue' [REB].
d. μᾶλλον (LN 78.28) (BAGD 1. p. 489): 'more' [BAGD, LN], 'to a greater degree' [LN]. The phrase πολλῷ μᾶλλον 'much more' [Arn, Lns] is also translated 'all the more' [AB, NTC, WBC; HCSB, NASB, NIV, REB], 'so much the more' [KJV], 'even more' [BECNT; NCV, NET], 'louder' [NLT], 'even louder' [CEV, GW], 'even more loudly' [BAGD; NRSV].

QUESTION—What is meant by the title 'Jesus the Nazarene'?

This means 'Jesus, the man from Nazareth' [BECNT, NIGTC, TG, TH; CEV, GW, NCV]. 'Nazarene' was added to distinguish Jesus from other men who were also named Jesus [Lns].

QUESTION—How did the blind man know that Jesus was the Son of David?

The blind man had no way of knowing Jesus' physical descent, but others must have told him that the man passing by was Jesus and that he was the anticipated Messiah [Su]. The blind man had heard reports about the miracles performed by Jesus and realized that he might be the Messiah because of the public stir he had created [BECNT]. He had learned about Jesus before and had come to believe that Jesus was the promised Messiah [Arn, NIC]. 'Son of David' was a title for the Messiah [BECNT, BNTC, Crd, Gdt, ICC, Lns, MGC, NIBC, NIC, NIGTC, NTC, Rb, Su, TH, TNTC, WBC].

QUESTION—What did the blind man ask Jesus to do?
: The blind man wanted Jesus to treat him compassionately [WBC]. He wanted Jesus to perform an act of mercy to him, the act being apparent by his need of sight [Lns]. Asking Jesus to have mercy on him was a way of asking Jesus to cure him of his blindness [BECNT, MGC, TG; NET].

QUESTION—Why did the people rebuke the blind man?
: The rebuke was not because he had called Jesus 'Son of David' [Arn, Gdt]. They thought that it was not proper to stop such an exalted person [Gdt]. They considered it to be impertinence [NIBC]. They thought he was asking for alms [Arn]. Perhaps they were in a hurry to go to Jerusalem, or thought it was undignified to have a beggar yelling out to Jesus, or they knew that Jesus wasn't yet ready to be proclaimed the Messiah [NTC], or it is useless to speculate [Lns].

18:40 And having-stopped Jesus commanded him to-be-brought^a to him. And having-come-near he asked him, 18:41 What do-you-want (that) I-should-do for-you? And he-said, Lord, that I-regain-sight.^b

TEXT—In 18:40, following ἐπηρώτησαν αὐτόν 'he asked him', some manuscripts add λέγων 'saying'. GNT does not mention this variant. Λέγων 'saying' is read by KJV.

LEXICON—a. aorist pass. infin. of ἄγω (LN 15.165) (BAGD 1.a. p. 14): 'to be brought' [BAGD, LN], 'to be led' [BAGD, LN]. The phrase 'commanded him to be brought to him' [WBC; KJV] is also translated 'commanded that he be brought to him' [Arn, BECNT], 'ordered him to be brought to him' [Lns], 'ordered the man to be brought to him' [AB, NTC; NIV, NRSV, REB], 'ordered the blind man to be brought to him' [NCV, TEV], 'ordered the beggar to be brought to him' [NET], 'commanded that he be brought to him' [HCSB, NASB], 'ordered that the man be brought to him' [NLT], 'ordered them to bring the man to him' [GW], 'told some people to bring the blind man over to him' [CEV]. 'To be brought' is the appropriate verb to use in regard to a blind man [WBC].

b. aorist act. subj. of ἀναβλέπω (LN 24.42) (BAGD 2.a.α. p. 51): 'to regain sight' [BAGD, LN, NTC; NASB], 'to see again' [AB, Arn, WBC; GW, NET, NRSV, TEV], 'to want sight back again' [REB], 'to receive sight' [Lns; KJV], 'to have sight' [BECNT], 'to be able to see' [LN], 'to see' [CEV, HCSB, NCV, NIV, NLT]. With the prefix ἀνα-, the verb means to look up or to see again [Arn, ICC].

QUESTION—What did the blind man mean by calling Jesus Κύριε 'Lord'?
: It probably meant no more than 'sir' to the blind man [AB, NIBC, TG], but Luke must have understood it as approaching the later Christian term of Lord [NIBC]. Or, the blind man understood Jesus' ministry as the Son of David and used the appropriate title of Lord [BECNT, Lns, MGC, NAC, NICNT, WBC]. Jesus was his Lord, his deity [MGC]. This is translated 'sir' by two versions [REB, TEV].

QUESTION—Had the blind man been able to see in the past, so that he wanted to regain his sight, or had he always been blind so that he wanted to see?

It is not possible to say [TG]. It is implied that he had once been able to see by those that translate with 'regain' or 'again' [AB, Arn, NTC, WBC; GW, NASB, NET, NRSV, REB, TEV]. The man has not been described as having been blind from birth, so it is likely that he wanted to receive back the sight that he once had [NET].

18:42 And Jesus said to-him, Regain-sight. Your faith has-saved[a] you.
18:43 And at-once he-regained-sight and was-following[b] him glorifying[c] God. And having-seen, all the people gave praise[d] to-God.

LEXICON—a. perf. act. indic. of σῴζω (LN 23.136, 21.27) (BAGD 1.c. p. 798): 'to save' [LN (21.27)], 'to save or free from disease' [BAGD], 'to heal, to cure, to make well' [LN (13.136)]. The clause 'your faith has saved you' [BECNT, Lns, WBC; KJV, NRSV] is also translated 'your faith has healed you' [HCSB, NET, NIV, NLT, REB], 'your faith has made you well' [NTC; GW, NASB, TEV], 'you are healed because you believed' [NCV], 'your eyes are healed because of your faith' [CEV], 'your faith has rescued you' [Arn], 'your faith has brought you salvation' [AB]. This clause is identical to the ones in 7:50; 8:48; 17:19.

b. imperf. act. indic. of ἀκολουθέω (LN 15.144): 'to follow' [AB, Arn, BECNT, LN, Lns, NTC, WBC; all versions except CEV], 'to go with' [CEV]. The imperfect tense can mean that he *began* to follow Jesus [Lns, NTC, Rb, WBC; HCSB, NASB], or that he *kept* following Jesus [AB, Rb]. See this word at 5:11, 27; 9:57.

c. pres. act. participle of δοξάζω (LN 33.357) (BAGD 1. p. 204): 'to glorify' [AB, LN, Lns, NTC, WBC; HCSB, KJV, NASB, NRSV], 'to praise' [Arn, BAGD, BECNT, LN; GW, NET, NIV, NLT, REB], 'to thank' [CEV, NCV], 'to give thanks to' [TEV]. He recognized God's marvelous work in the healing [WBC]. He glorified God by honoring and praising him, and by thanking him for healing him through his Messiah [NIGTC].

d. αἶνος (LN **33.354**) (BAGD p. 23): 'praise' [BAGD, LN]. The phrase 'gave praise to God' [AB, Arn, BECNT, NTC, WBC; HCSB, KJV, NASB, NET, REB] is also translated 'gave praises to God' [Lns], 'praised God' [**LN**; CEV, GW, NCV, NIV, NLT, NRSV, TEV]. This phrase is a close synonym to the preceding verb δοξάζω 'glorify' [TH, WBC].

QUESTION—In what sense did the man's faith save him?

God's power healed the man in response to his faith [NIGTC]. His faith was the means by which he received his sight [TNTC; NET]. This refers to his persistence in calling out to Jesus for help in spite of the crowd trying to keep him quiet [WBC]. The verb literally means 'has saved you' and here there is a suggestion that the man was not only saved from physical blindness, but also from spiritual blindness [MGC, Su]. It may have the meaning that his faith saved him [NTC]. His faith was the beginning of his salvation if he would continue to keep his faith in the Savior [Gdt]. He had entered the kingdom of God [NICNT].

QUESTION—In what sense did the man follow Jesus?

The man went with Jesus, accompanying him [TH]. He joined the band of disciples that was accompanying Jesus to Jerusalem [Arn, Lns, NIGTC, Su, WBC]. But it can also mean that he became Jesus' disciple [BECNT, MGC, NICNT, NIGTC, NTC].

DISCOURSE UNIT: 19:1–10 [AB, BECNT, NAC, NICNT, NIGTC, Su, TNTC, WBC; CEV, GW, HCSB, NASB, NCV, NET, NIV, NLT, NRSV, TEV]. The topic is Zacchaeus [CEV], Zacchaeus, the tax collector [AB, BECNT, NAC, NIGTC, TNTC; NIV], Jesus and Zacchaeus [NET, NLT, NRSV, TEV], Zacchaeus meets Jesus [GW, NCV], Jesus visits Zacchaeus [HCSB], Zacchaeus converted [NASB], the salvation of Zacchaeus in Jericho [Su], who is a son of Abraham? [NICNT], the Son of Man came to seek and to save the lost [WBC].

19:1 And having-entered Jericho he-was-passing-through.[a] **19:2** And behold (there was) a-man called[b] by-(the)-name Zacchaeus, and he was a-chief-tax-collector[c] and he (was) wealthy.

LEXICON—a. imperf. mid./pass. (deponent = act.) indic. of διέρχομαι (LN 15.21) (BAGD 1.a. p. 194): 'to pass through' [AB, BECNT, NTC; GW, HCSB, KJV, NASB, NET, NIV, NRSV, TEV], 'to begin to pass through' [Arn], 'to pass on through' [Lns], 'to go through' [BAGD; CEV, NCV], 'to travel around through' [LN], 'to make (his) way through' [NLT, REB], 'to be on (his) way through' [WBC]. This indicates that Jesus did not intend to stay in Jericho [TH, TNTC]. Jesus' destination was Jerusalem [NAC], so he entered Jericho only to go through it and leave at the other side of the city [TH]. He intended to go right through the city, but his plans were changed when he met Zacchaeus inside the city [ICC] and stayed the night in Jericho [BECNT].

b. pres. pass. participle of καλέω (LN 33.125) (BAGD 1.a.γ. p. 399): 'to be called' [BAGD, LN], 'to be named' [BAGD, LN]. The phrase 'a man called by the name of' [NASB] is also translated 'a man by the name' [WBC; NIV], 'a man whose name was' [BECNT], 'a man who was called' [Arn], 'a man called by name' [Lns], 'a man named' [AB, NTC; CEV, GW, HCSB, NCV, NET, NLT, NRSV, REB, TEV]. This phrase is unique and may be intended to call attention to his name [NIGTC]. The phrase is a Hebraism and the words 'by the name of' are superfluous [EGT]. The word ἰδού 'behold' adds interest and emphasis in introducing a new character into the account [NET].

c. ἀρχιτελώνης (LN 57.185) (BAGD p. 113): 'chief tax collector' [BAGD, BECNT, LN, NTC, WBC; HCSB, NASB, NET, NIV, NRSV, TEV], 'chief toll-collector' [AB], 'director of tax collectors' [GW], 'a very important tax collector' [NCV], 'superintendent of taxes' [REB], 'head publican' [Lns], 'chief among the publicans' [Arn; KJV]. This noun is also translated as a descriptive clause: 'he was in charge of collecting taxes' [CEV], 'he was one of the most influential Jews in the Roman tax-collecting business' [NLT].

QUESTION—What was a chief tax collector?

Zacchaeus was either the head of the local tax collectors or he was higher in rank than others [BECNT, TH]. Most take the description to indicate that he was the head of the local tax collectors [Arn, Gdt, Lns, MGC, NICNT, NIGTC, NIVS, Su, TG, TNTC; NET]. The tax collectors charged indirect taxes such as tolls, imposts, and customs [NIBC]. These tax collectors collected the custom duties of goods passing from Peraea into Judea [NAC, NIGTC]. There were important trade connections with Damascus, Tyre, Sidon, Caesarea, Joppa, and Egypt [NTC]. Jericho was a large frontier city and much of the carrier trade passed through it [Arn, ICC]. The city was a Roman regional tax center and Zacchaeus bid for and organized the collection of taxes from which he then took a cut [BECNT]. Zacchaeus would employ others to do the collecting of taxes while he passed on what was due the Roman government [TNTC]. The addition 'and he was wealthy' implies that that his wealth came from his activity as a chief tax collector [AB, BECNT, MGC, NIGTC]. His wealth probably was due to making a large profit on his transactions [NIGTC] since he received a commission from the taxes that were collected [BECNT; NET].

19:3 And he-was-trying^a to-see^b Jesus who he-is and was- not -able because-of^c the crowd, because he-was short in-stature. **19:4** And having-run-ahead to the front,^d he-climbed-up into a-sycamore-fig-tree^e in-order-to see him because he-was-about to-pass-through that (way).

LEXICON—a. imperf. act. indic. of ζητέω (LN 68.60): 'to try' [LN, Lns, NTC, WBC; GW, HCSB, NASB, NET, NLT, NRSV, TEV], 'to seek' [Arn, BECNT, LN; KJV], 'to want' [CEV, NCV, NIV], 'to be eager (to see)' [AB; REB]. The imperfect tense implies a continuous effort, although it was unsuccessful for a while [EGT].

b. aorist act. infin. of ὁράω (LN 24.1) (BAGD 1.c. p. 220): 'to see' [BAGD, LN]. The phrase 'to see Jesus who he is/was' [Arn, Lns, WBC; KJV] is also translated 'to see who Jesus was' [AB, BECNT, Lns; GW, HCSB, NASB, NCV, NIV, NRSV, TEV], 'to get a look at Jesus' [NET, NLT], 'to see what Jesus looked like' [REB], 'to see what he was like' [CEV].

c. ἀπό (LN **89.25**) (BAGD V.1. p. 87): 'because of' [BAGD, **LN**]. The phrase 'was not able because of the crowd' [BECNT; HCSB, NASB] is also translated 'he could not on account of/because of the crowd' [Arn; NIV], 'couldn't see Jesus because of the crowd' [GW, TEV], 'he could not see him for the crowd' [REB], 'was unable to see him on account of the crowd' [NTC], 'on account of/because of the crowd he could not' [AB; NRSV], 'because of the crowd he was not able' [WBC], 'could not for the press' [KJV], 'was not able due to the multitude' [Lns], 'he could not see over the crowd' [CEV, NET], 'he was not able to see above the crowd' [NCV], 'he was too short to see over the crowd' [NLT].

d. ἔμπροσθεν (LN 83.33): 'in front of, before' [LN]. The phrase 'having run ahead to the front' is translated 'having run forward to the front' [Lns], 'he ran ahead' [Arn, NTC; CEV, GW, NIV, NLT, NRSV], 'he ran on ahead' [AB; NASB, NET, REB], 'running ahead' [HCSB], 'running on ahead' [WBC], 'he ran before' [KJV], 'he ran ahead of the crowd' [TEV], 'he ran ahead to a place where Jesus would come' [NCV]. This refers to getting ahead of the front of the moving crowd [EGT, ICC, NIGTC], on the route the crowd was taking through the city [ICC].

e. συκομορέα (LN 3.7) (BAGD p. 776): 'sycamore-fig tree' [BAGD, LN, WBC; NIV], 'sycamore tree' [AB, NTC; all versions except GW, NET, NIV], 'fig-mulberry tree' [Arn, BAGD, Lns], 'fig tree' [GW]. This tree was somewhat like an oak tree in being easy to climb [Arn, NIGTC; NET] but it had evergreen leaves and bore an edible fruit [NIGTC]. Its branches spread out at a lower point than an American sycamore and its fruit is similar to small figs but grows out in clusters from the branches rather than on smaller twigs, quite different from a mulberry tree [Su]. Its leaves were like a mulberry tree [Arn, TH] and its fruit was like that of a fig tree [Arn].

QUESTION—What was Zacchaeus' motive for wanting to see Jesus?

Zacchaeus was trying to get a look at Jesus [TG]. He wanted to know which one in the crowd was Jesus [TG, TH]. It is implied that he had heard about Jesus but had never seen him [TH]. Never having seen Jesus before, he wanted to see which of all the people Jesus was [My, Rb, TH]. He had heard reports about Jesus and was curious to see such a person [Arn, BECNT] and learn what he looked like [Gdt]. Perhaps Zacchaeus was just curious [NIGTC]. He would not have yet been moved by a conviction of wrong doing in the way he had acquired his wealth [Crd]. Or, what follows shows that it was more than mere curiosity [Lns]. He wanted to see this man who had acted so sympathetically towards other tax collectors [NIC]. He was seeking the salvation that Jesus spoke about [NAC].

QUESTION—How are the two reasons in 19:3 related to the fact that he was not able to see Jesus?

The first reason was that there was a crowd around Jesus. The crowd was the source of the hindrance [ICC]. The crowd was too dense to penetrate [EGT, WBC] and the people would not make way for such an unpopular man [NICNT, TNTC]. Most translations simply imply that the crowd blocked Zacchaeus' view. The second reason explains why the crowd prevented him from being able to see Jesus. It builds on the first in that there were many people between Zacchaeus and Jesus and it turned out that Zacchaeus was too short to see over all those heads [EGT, MGC, NIGTC, TG]. The clause 'he was short in stature' refers to Zacchaeus, not Jesus [NAC, NIGTC]. Some use only one of the conjunctions: 'Zacchaeus was a small man, and he couldn't see Jesus because of the crowd' [GW], 'he was a little man and could not see Jesus because of the crowd' [TEV], 'he was not able because he was too short to see above the crowd' [NCV], 'being a short man he could not, because of the crowd' [NIV]. Some omit both conjunctions: 'Zacchaeus was a short man and could not see over the crowd' [CEV], 'he was too short to see over the crowd' [NLT].

19:5 **And as he-came to the place, having-looked-up Jesus said to him, Zacchaeus, having-hurried,[a] come-down, because today it-is-necessary (for) me to-stay[b] in your house. 19:6 And having-hurried he-came-down and welcomed[c] him with-joy.**

TEXT—In 19:5, instead of εἶπεν 'he said', some manuscripts read εἶδεν αὐτὸν καὶ εἶπεν 'he saw him and said'. GNT does not mention this variant. Εἶδεν αὐτὸν καὶ εἶπεν 'he saw him and said' is read by KJV.

LEXICON—a. aorist, act. participle of σπεύδω (LN 68.79) (BAGD 1.a. p. 762): 'to hurry, to hasten' [BAGD, LN], 'to do quickly' [LN]. This verb qualifies the imperative 'come down' [TH]. It is a participle that indicates the manner he is to come down [NET]. The phrase 'having hurried, come down' is translated 'with hastening climb down' [Lns], 'hurry down' [NTC; CEV, TEV], 'quickly come down' [BECNT], 'come down quickly' [NET], 'come down immediately' [NIV], 'hurry and come down' [AB, Arn; HCSB, NASB, NCV, NRSV], 'hurry and climb down' [WBC], 'make haste, and come down' [KJV], 'quick, come down' [NLT], 'be quick and come down' [REB], 'come down' [GW].

b. aorist act. infin. of μένω (LN 85.55) (BAGD 1.a.α. p. 503): 'to stay' [BAGD], 'to remain' [BAGD, LN]. The clause 'it is necessary for me to stay in your house' is translated 'it is necessary for me to remain at your house' [BECNT], 'I must stay at your house' [AB, WBC; GW, HCSB, NASB, NCV, NET, NIV, NRSV, REB], 'I must stay at your home' [NTC], 'I must stay in your house' [Arn; TEV], 'I must abide in/at thy house' [Lns; KJV], 'I must be a guest in your home' [NLT], 'I want to stay with you' [CEV]. The verb 'to stay' is the usual word for staying at a person's house, and here it refers to staying overnight [NIGTC, WBC]. Or, the stay is of an unspecified length [BECNT] and it could mean that he would just take a long rest at the house [ICC].

c. aorist mid. (deponent = act.) indic. of ὑποδέχομαι (LN 34.53) (BAGD p. 844): 'to welcome' [AB, BAGD, BECNT, LN, NTC, WBC; CEV, HCSB, NCV, NET, NIV, NRSV, REB, TEV], 'to welcome into his home' [GW], 'to receive' [Arn, BAGD, LN, Lns; KJV, NASB], 'to accept as a guest' [LN], 'to entertain as a guest' [BAGD], 'to take to his house' [NLT].

QUESTION—How did Jesus know Zacchaeus' name?
It might be due to Jesus' supernatural knowledge [Alf, Arn, BECNT, Lns, NAC, NIGTC], or he might have heard people calling to Zacchaeus by name [Arn, BECNT, Gdt, ICC], or he might have asked the people around him for his name [Alf, BECNT, ICC], or Jesus already knew his name [NIGTC]. For Luke, it was an unimportant detail [AB, NAC, Su].

QUESTION—What is meant by saying that it was necessary to stay at Zacchaeus' house?
>This implies that the necessity was imposed by God so that God's plan would be worked out [BECNT, Gdt, ICC, MGC, My, NAC, NIGTC, NIVS, TNTC, WBC]. Zacchaeus' salvation was part of God's plan [MGC]. Jesus saw that staying at Zacchaeus' house was part of his mission [Alf, NTC, TH, TNTC]. Jesus revealed that he must associate with people like him [NET]. When Jesus saw Zacchaeus' eager desire to see him, he knew that God had chosen him to be his host in Jericho [Gdt].

QUESTION—When and where did Zacchaeus welcome Jesus?
>This refers to receiving Jesus into his house as a guest [AB, MGC, NIGTC]. It implies that Zacchaeus was already home instead of standing at the base of the tree when he welcomed Jesus, so the expanded sentence would be 'Zacchaeus hurried down the tree and took Jesus to his home, where he welcomed him gladly' [TG]. Or, the reception started at the base of the tree and then Jesus and his disciples started back to the city with Zacchaeus [Lns].

19:7 And having-seen (this) all were-complaining[a] **saying, He-entered to-be-a-guest**[b] **with a-sinful man.**

LEXICON—a. imperf. act. indic. of διαγογγύζω (LN 33.383) (BAGD p. 182): 'to complain' [BAGD, LN; HCSB, NCV, NET], 'to grumble' [AB, BAGD, BECNT, LN, NTC, WBC; CEV, NASB, NRSV, TEV], 'to be displeased...to grumble' [NLT], 'to mutter' [NIV], 'to murmur' [Arn, Lns; KJV], 'to express disapproval' [GW]. This verb is also translated as a clause: 'there was a general murmur of disapproval' [REB]. The imperfect tense is inceptive, 'they *began* to complain' [Lns, NTC, WBC; CEV, GW, NASB, NCV, NIV, NRSV, TEV]. Or, it is durative, 'they *kept* complaining' [BECNT]. See this word at 15:2.

>b. aorist act. infin. of καταλύω (LN **34.61**) (BAGD 2. p. 414): 'to be a guest' [**LN**], 'to rest, to halt, to find lodging' [BAGD]. The phrase εἰσῆλθεν καταλῦσαι 'he entered to be a guest (with)' is translated 'he has gone in to be the guest (of)' [BECNT; NET], 'he went to be a guest (of)' [GW, TEV], 'he has gone to be the guest (of)' [NTC; NASB, NIV, NLT, NRSV, REB], 'he was gone to be a guest (with)' [KJV], 'he went in to lodge (with)' [Lns, WBC], 'he's gone to lodge (with)' [AB; HCSB], 'he went into the house to lodge there' [Arn], 'Jesus is staying (with)' [NCV], 'Jesus is going home to eat (with)' [CEV].

QUESTION—How many were complaining?
>Everyone in the crowd was complaining [BECNT]. All the people who watched Jesus go into the tax collector's house complained [TH]. It means people in general [EGT, NTC, TNTC]. Pharisees and all Jews in general considered lodging with a sinner to be sharing in his sins [NIGTC]. Or, 'all' is probably a hyperbole [AB, NAC, WBC]. 'All' must include some followers of Jesus [Arn, EGT].

QUESTION—In what way was Zacchaeus a sinful man?

They were not speaking of his personal character, but of his calling as a tax collector [BECNT, EGT, ICC]. Tax collectors were classed as open sinners because they aided the Roman government and because they were notorious in collecting excessive amounts to enrich themselves [Lns].

19:8 And having-stood^a Zacchaeus said to the Lord, Behold Lord, half of-my belongings^b I-give to-the poor, and if I-defrauded^c someone of-anything I-am-paying-back^d four-times.

LEXICON—a. aorist pass. participle of ἵσταμαι (LN 17.1) (BAGD II. 1.b. p. 382): 'to stand' [AB, BAGD, BECNT, LN, WBC; HCSB, KJV, NCV, NIV, NLT, NRSV, REB], 'to stand up' [NTC; CEV, GW, TEV], 'to take a stand' [Lns], 'to step up' [Arn], 'to stop' [NASB, NET].

b. pres. act. participle of ὑπάρχω (LN 57.16) (BAGD 1. p. 838): 'to belong to' [BAGD, LN]. The phrase μου τῶν ὑπαρχόντων 'my belongings' [Arn; TEV] is also translated 'my possessions' [Lns, NTC; HCSB, NASB, NCV, NET, NIV, NRSV, REB], 'my property' [CEV, GW], 'my wealth' [NLT], 'my goods' [BECNT, WBC; KJV], 'what I own' [AB].

c. aorist act. indic. of συκοφαντέω (LN 33.434) (BAGD 2. p. 776): 'to defraud' [BECNT; NASB, NRSV, REB], 'to cheat' [NTC; CEV, GW, NCV, NET, NIV, TEV], 'to extort' [AB, BAGD, Lns; HCSB], 'to obtain through extortion' [Arn], 'to make false charges' [LN], 'to take anything by false accusation' [KJV], 'to overcharge on taxes' [NLT], 'to unlawfully exact' [WBC]. This was the sin of the soldiers in 3:14 and they may have aided tax collectors in collecting taxes [NIGTC].

d. pres. act. indic. of ἀποδίδωμι (LN 57.154) (BAGD 2. p. 90): 'to pay back' [AB, BECNT; CEV, HCSB, NCV, NET, NIV, NRSV, TEV], 'to give back' [Arn, BAGD, LN, Lns, NTC; NASB, NLT], 'to repay' [WBC; REB], 'to return' [BAGD], 'to restore' [KJV]. The phrase 'I am paying back four times' is translated 'I'll pay four times as much as I owe' [GW].

QUESTION—What was involved in Zacchaeus standing up?

He took a position where everyone could hear him [TH]. It happened as soon as he came down from the tree [AB, ICC, MGC], Or, about to enter his house, he heard the grumbling and turned around to face the crowd [Rb]. Or, it was just as he entered the house while still in the presence of the crowd outside [Alf]. Or, he stood up at the dinner table [Su, TG; GW]. Or, the house must have been filled with people eager to hear Jesus and at some point Zacchaeus must have stepped forth to make this vow [Arn]. Or, this took place as they all left the house and the Lord was about to continue his journey to Jerusalem [NIC]. There is confusion about the time because it is not clear that the statement 'he entered to be a guest' (19:7) means that he had already entered the house and separated himself from the crowd [BECNT].

QUESTION—What is the meant by the use of the present tense of the verb δίδωμι 'I give'?
1. The present tense is futuristic, indicating his resolve to give to the poor [Arn, BECNT, Crd, EGT, ICC, MGC, NAC, NIGTC, TH, WBC; NET]. This shows his repentance and faith after meeting Jesus [BECNT]. His resolve is so firm that he says that he is in the process of giving already [NIC, TNTC]. This served as his thank offering for the change in his life [NAC].
2. It means that it already was his habit to give to the poor [AB, Gdt, NIBC, NICNT]. This denies the charge that he is a sinner [AB, Gdt, NIBC]. He was looking for Jesus' evaluation of his attitude towards money [NICNT].

QUESTION—Wasn't he sure that he had defrauded anyone?
He was admitting that he had cheated people [Alf, BECNT, ICC, Lns, MGC, My, NIGTC, NTC, Rb, Su, TG, TH, TNTC; NET]. The word 'if' is the condition of reality [Lns, MGC], and has the sense 'since I have extorted' [MGC]. As a tax collector, he had many opportunities to charge more duties on things than required by law [TG]. The conditional clause means 'from whomsoever I have wrongfully exacted anything' and what is in doubt is not the fact of extortion, but its extent [NIGTC]. Or, it means that he hadn't deliberately defrauded people, but if he discovers that he had been involved in such a case, he would make it right [AB].

QUESTION—What is the significance of paying back four times as much as he had defrauded?
Zacchaeus determined to make amends to the fullest possible measure [Lns]. The normal recompense for illegally acquiring money was the amount plus one fifth (Lev. 6:2–5) [NIGTC, NTC, WBC]. He was going to follow the harsher penalty that the Law imposed on rustlers (Exod. 22:1) [BECNT].

19:9 And Jesus said to/about him, Today salvation[a] came to-this house/household, because he also is a-son[b] of Abraham. **19:10** Because the Son of-Man[c] came to-seek[d] and to-save[e] the lost.[f]

LEXICON—a. σωτηρία (LN 21.26) (BAGD 2. p. 801): 'salvation' [BAGD, LN]. The phrase 'salvation came to this house' [Lns] is also translated 'salvation has come to this house' [AB, Arn, BECNT, NTC, WBC; HCSB, KJV, NASB, NCV, NIV, NRSV, REB, TEV], 'salvation has come to this home' [NLT], 'salvation has come to this household' [NET], 'you and your family have been saved' [CEV, GW]. This refers to Zacchaeus being forgiven of his sins [TG, TH]. This is a restoration to a sound relationship with God [AB]. Salvation has come in the sense that it has occurred [NAC, TH].

b. υἱός (LN 10.30) (BAGD 1.b.α. p. 833): 'son, descendant' [BAGD, LN]. The phrase 'he also/too is a son of Abraham' [Arn, BECNT, WBC; KJV, NASB, NET, NRSV] is also translated 'he too is Abraham's son' [Lns], 'even this man is a son of Abraham' [NTC], 'this man too is a son of Abraham' [AB; NIV, REB], 'this man also is a descendant of Abraham'

[TEV], 'this man also belongs to the family of Abraham' [NCV], 'this man has shown himself to be a son of Abraham' [NLT], 'you are a true son of Abraham' [CEV], 'you've shown that you, too, are one of Abraham's descendants' [GW].
c. υἱὸς τοῦ ἀνθρώπου 'Son of Man'. This title for Christ occurs at 5:24; 6:5, 22; 7:34; 9:22, 26, 44; 11:30; 12:8, 40; 17:22, 24, 26; 18:8, 31; 21:27, 36; 22:22, 48, 69; 24:7. See the discussions of this title at 5:24, 6:5, and 9:22.
d. aorist act. infin. of LN 27.41) (BAGD 1.a.α. p. 338): 'to seek' [Arn, BAGD, BECNT, Lns, NTC, WBC; all versions except CEV, NCV, NRSV], 'to seek out' [AB; NRSV], 'to look for' [BAGD, LN; CEV], 'to find' [NCV].
e. aorist act. infin. of σῴζω (LN 21.27) (BAGD 2.a.α. p. 338): 'to save' [AB, Arn, BAGD, BECNT, LN, Lns, NTC, WBC; all versions].
f. perf. act. participle of ἀπόλλυμαι (LN 21.32) (BAGD 2.a.α. p. 95): 'to be lost' [BAGD, LN; CEV]. The phrase τὸ ἀπολωλός 'the lost' [BECNT, WBC; HCSB, NET, NRSV, TEV] is also translated 'lost people' [NCV], 'that which is/was lost' [Arn; KJV, NASB], 'what was/is lost' [AB, NTC; NIV, REB], 'what has been lost' [Lns], 'those like him who are lost' [NLT], 'people who are lost' [TG; CEV, GW]. People are lost in sin and unbelief [NIC]. This singular noun is generic and means 'people who are lost' [TG].

QUESTION—Who was Jesus speaking to?
Normally, πρὸς αὐτόν means 'to him', but since the statement uses the third person 'this house' and 'he is', it could mean 'about him' [AB, BECNT, NIGTC].
1. Jesus was speaking to Zacchaeus [AB, Alf, BECNT, EGT, ICC, Lns, My, NAC, NTC, TG, TH; CEV, GW]. But Jesus intended that all who were there would listen and be benefited by what he said [BECNT, EGT, Lns, NAC, TG, TH]. Jesus spoke to the crowd by speaking to Zacchaeus [AB].
2. Jesus was speaking to the entire assembly about Zacchaeus [Arn, Gdt; probably NLT]. Jesus was looking at Zacchaeus as he was speaking to the crowd about him [Gdt].
3. The first clause was addressed to Zacchaeus and the second clause was addressed to the other people there [Su; probably HCSB, KJV, NASB, NCV, NET, NIV, NRSV, REB, TEV]. After addressing Zacchaeus, Jesus then spoke to the Twelve to say, Because the Son of Man came to seek and to save the lost [Su].

QUESTION—In what sense had salvation come to 'this house'?
1. The noun οἴκῳ 'house' refers to the building [AB, Gdt]. When Jesus entered the house, he brought salvation with him [Gdt]. The coming of Jesus is equivalent to the coming of the kingdom of God and this is to be equated with the coming of salvation [WBC].
2. The noun οἴκῳ 'house' refers to the family living in the building [Arn, BECNT, ICC, Lns, My, NIC, NICNT, NIGTC, NTC, TG, TH, TNTC;

CEV, GW, NET, NLT]. This probably means that salvation extended to the whole family [ICC; CEV, GW]. The covenant was still in effect, yet faith was necessary for each one in the family [NTC]. Nothing specific is said about the family, but evidently all believed and were saved [Arn, Lns].

QUESTION—What is meant by saying that salvation had come *because* Zacchaeus was also a descendant of Abraham?

1. This refers to the fact that Zacchaeus was a Jew by natural descent [AB, Alf, Arn, BECNT, EGT, ICC, My, NIGTC, TG, WBC]. A Jew, even though he is a tax collector and sinner is still a part of Israel and the Good Shepherd must seek such people [BECNT, NIGTC]. Jesus justified his interest in Zacchaeus by pointing out that he had come to the Jews as teacher and prophet [Arn]. Besides the religious leaders among the listeners being descendants of Abraham, Zacchaeus also was a descendant [TG]. As much as any other Jew, he was entitled to the blessings of Abraham that were now coming through Jesus [AB]. As a Jew, he has rights to God's promise if he takes advantage of those rights [BECNT].

2. This refers to Zacchaeus' spiritual relationship with Abraham because of his faith [Gdt, Lns, MGC, NAC, NIBC, NIC, NIVS, NTC, Su, TNTC; CEV, GW, NLT]. He was saved because he was a true son of Abraham [TNTC; CEV], since he followed the faith of Abraham [TNTC]. He had shown that he was a true son of Abraham [GW, NLT]. He had produced fruit in keeping with repentance and had exercised faith in Abraham's seed [NAC]. Because of being saved he became a son of Abraham [MGC].

QUESTION—At the beginning of 19:10, what relationship is indicated by γάρ 'because'?

This conjunction explains that salvation had come to this house because that was the purpose of Jesus' coming [BECNT, ICC]. This defends Jesus' coming to Zacchaeus' house [NICNT]. Visiting the home of Zacchaeus was in keeping with his mission [Arn]. It confirms the fact of Zacchaeus' salvation [Lns].

DISCOURSE UNIT: 19:11–21:38 [NIGTC]. The topic is the ministry in Jerusalem.

DISCOURSE UNIT: 19:11–28 [WBC]. The topic is going to a distant land to receive kingly power.

DISCOURSE UNIT: 19:11–27 [AB, BECNT, NAC, NICNT, NIGTC, Su, TNTC; CEV, GW, HCSB, NASB, NCV, NET, NIV, NLT, NRSV, TEV]. The topic is a story about ten servants [CEV, NLT], a story about three servants [NCV], the parable of the gold coins [TEV], the parable of the ten minas/pounds [AB, NAC, NIGTC, Su, TNTC; HCSB, NET, NIV, NRSV], a parable of money usage [NASB], a story about a king [GW], those who refuse the king [NICNT], a parable of stewardship [BECNT].

19:11 And (while) they were-listening-to these-things, adding[a] he-told a-parable because he was near Jerusalem and they thought that the kingdom of-God is-about to-appear[b] immediately.

LEXICON—a. aorist act. participle of προστίθημι (LN 59.72) (BAGD 1.c. p. 719): 'to add' [BAGD, LN], 'again, further' [BAGD]. The phrase 'adding he told' is translated 'he added and spoke' [KJV], 'Jesus went on to add' [AB], 'he went on tell' WBC; [HCSB, NASB, NIV, NRSV, REB], 'he went on to speak' [BECNT], 'Jesus continued and told' [TEV], 'he continued and spoke' [Arn], 'he furthermore spoke' [Lns], 'he/Jesus proceeded to tell' [NTC; NET], not explicit [CEV, GW, NCV, NLT]. The phase 'adding he told' is a Hebraism [AB, Arn, BECNT, Crd, EGT]. It means that Jesus went on to say something else to the things people had been listening to, namely a parable [NIGTC]

b. pres. pass. infin. of ἀναφαίνομαι (LN 24.23) (BAGD p. 63): 'to appear' [AB, BAGD, LN, WBC; CEV, GW, HCSB, KJV, NASB, NCV, NET, NIV, NRSV, TEV], 'to make an appearance' [Lns], 'to manifest itself' [Arn], 'to dawn' [REB], 'to begin' [NLT], 'to be near' [BECNT].

QUESTION—Who does 'they' refer to?

'They' refers to the audience who heard Jesus' words in 19:9–10 [ICC, Lns, My, NIC, TH], or, 19:7–10 [AB], or, 19:1–10 [BECNT].

QUESTION—How near were they to Jerusalem and why would the people think that the kingdom was about to appear?

Since they were close to Jericho, Jerusalem would be about 17 miles away [NIGTC, TNTC, WBC] with a rise of 3,300 feet in altitude [WBC]. It was a trip of about six hours to Jerusalem [BECNT, ICC, Lns]. Or, they were already approaching Jerusalem and the people were pondering the things Jesus had already told them, so it might be said that they were still listening to his words [NIC]. They had heard Jesus use the messianic title 'Son of Man' and that led them to expect that Jesus, the Messiah, would soon start his rule [Su]. Jesus was close to the destination he had announced in 18:31 [NIGTC], and people thought his arrival in Jerusalem would begin the establishment of his kingdom [Alf, BNTC, TH]. It was a common Jewish expectation that the full earthly kingdom of the Messiah would appear in Jerusalem [BECNT, MGC]. They probably envisioned a military takeover by Jesus and his band of followers [NIVS, WBC]. Then the kingdom would appear in great glory and earthly splendor [Lns].

19:12 Therefore he-said, A-certain man of-noble-birth[a] traveled to a-distant country to-receive[b] for-himself a-kingdom and (then) to-return. **19:13** And having-called ten of-his slaves he-gave them ten minas[c] and he-said to them, Do-business[d] until I-am-coming (back).

LEXICON—a. εὐγενής (LN 87.27) (BAGD 1. p. 319): 'well-born, high-born' [BAGD], 'of high status, important' [LN]. The phrase 'a man of noble birth' [AB, Arn, BECNT; NIV, REB] is also translated 'a man well-born' [Lns], 'a well-born man' [WBC], 'a man of high rank' [TEV], 'a very important man' [NCV], 'a nobleman' [BAGD, NTC; HCSB, KJV, NASB, NET, NLT, NRSV], 'a prince' [CEV, GW]. He had such rank and social position that he might legitimately aspire to rule over a kingdom [EGT].

b. aorist act. infin. of λαμβάνω (LN 37.65) (BAGD 1.c. p. 464): 'to receive' [BAGD, LN]. The phrase λαβεῖν ἑαυτῷ βασιλείαν 'to receive for himself a kingdom' is translated 'to receive to himself a kingdom' [BECNT], 'to receive a kingdom for himself' [Arn, NTC; KJV, NASB, NET], 'to take for himself a kingdom' [Lns], 'to receive for himself authority to be king' [HCSB], 'to obtain kingly power for himself' [BAGD], 'to get royal power for himself' [NRSV], 'to acquire kingship for himself' [WBC], 'to acquire for himself the title of king' [AB], 'to become a king' [LN], 'to be appointed king' [GW], 'to have himself appointed king' [NIV, REB], 'to be crowned king' [CEV, NLT], 'to be made king' [NCV, TEV].

c. μνᾶ (LN 6.81) (BAGD p. 524): 'mina' [BAGD, BECNT, Lns, WBC; HCSB, NASB, NET, NIV], 'one hundred denarii' [LN], 'a gold coin' [TEV], 'coin' [GW, NCV], 'pound' [AB, Arn, NTC; KJV, NRSV], 'pound of silver' [NLT], 'a quantity of money' [BAGD], 'some money' [CEV], 'a sum of money' [REB]. A mina was a Greek monetary unit worth 100 drachmas [Arn, BAGD, BECNT, NAC, NIGTC, NTC, TNTC], and one drachma was worth a Roman denarius [BECNT].

d. aorist mid. (deponent = act.) impera. of πραγματεύομαι (LN **57.197**) (BAGD p. 697): 'to do business' [AB, Arn, BAGD, **LN**, Lns, NTC; NASB, NCV, NET, NRSV], 'to conduct business' [BAGD, WBC], 'to be engaged in a business' [BAGD; HCSB], 'to invest' [GW, NLT], 'to earn more money' [CEV], 'to put money to work' [NIV], 'to earn (with)' [TEV], 'to trade (with)' [BECNT; REB], 'to occupy' [KJV].

QUESTION—What relationship is indicated by οὖν 'therefore'?

The Passover time drew pilgrims from all over and this was the time to expect any upheaval, so to counteract the thought of his leading a revolt, Jesus told a parable to show that the kingdom was not confined to a particular nation and its outward manifestation was not in the immediate future [NTC]. Jesus wanted his disciples to understand that Jerusalem was to be the location of his suffering, not his coming in glory, and that they needed to realize their responsibilities before that messianic coming [BECNT].

QUESTION—What did this man go to a distant country to receive?

He went to be named or appointed king of the region or province in which he lived [Arn, EGT, TG]. He would go to some Mediterranean ruler to receive the status of a vassal king [AB, BECNT]. He would be going to Rome to receive from the emperor the title of 'king' as a ruler of his region or country and then return home where he would exercise his authority [TG]. 'Kingdom' is to be understood as a kingly authority or kingship [MGC, NAC, TH], since what he brought back was the right and power to rule [NAC]. The fact that he went to a distant country indicates that he would be absent for a long time [AB, Arn, Gdt, ICC, Lns, NAC, TNTC, WBC].

QUESTION—When did this man call for his slaves?
He called for them before leaving on his journey to the distant country [AB, BECNT; CEV, GW, NLT, REB, TEV]. This is made explicit in some translation: 'before leaving' [CEV], 'before he left' [GW, NLT, TEV], 'but first' [AB; REB].
QUESTION—How many minas did each slave receive?
Each of the ten slaves received one mina [AB, Alf, Crd, EGT, Hu, Lns, MGC, Pnt, TH; NCV, NET].
QUESTION—What kind of business were the slaves told to do?
These were not ordinary slaves because a slave would not have the authority to make the business transactions involved [TNTC]. They were his agents whom he empowered to trade in his name [AB]. The money was a loan of capital and the master would expect to receive the profit when he returned [NIGTC]. Their business would be that of trading [ICC, Lns], or of a banker [ICC]. They wouldn't speculate with the money, rather they would trade with it to increase the amount as much as possible [Lns]. The type of business is not specified and it was up to each to pick the kind of business they were interested in [Su, TNTC], perhaps trading in food, clothing, or livestock [Su].

19:14 **But his citizens**[a] **were-hating**[b] **him and they-sent an-ambassador**[c] **after him saying, We-do- not -want this (one) to-be-a-king**[d] **over us.**
LEXICON—a. πολίτης (LN 11.68) (BAGD 2. p. 686): 'citizen' [BAGD, LN], 'fellow citizen' [BAGD]. The phrase 'his citizens' [Arn, BECNT, Lns; KJV, NASB, NET] is also translated 'the citizens of his own country' [GW], 'the citizens of his country' [NRSV], 'the people of his country' [CEV], 'the people in the kingdom' [NCV], 'his fellow citizens' [AB; REB], 'some of his fellow citizens' [WBC], 'his people' [NLT], 'his own people' [TEV], 'his subjects' [NTC; HCSB, NIV]. These were people in the country whom the nobleman wanted to rule over [NIGTC, TH]. They were his fellow citizens before he received his appointment to be their king [EGT, MGC].
  b. imperf. act. indic. of μισέω (LN 88.198) (BAGD 1. p. 522): 'to hate' [Arn, BAGD, BECNT, LN, Lns, NTC, WBC; all versions], 'to dislike' [AB]. The imperfect tense indicates that they continued to hate him [BECNT, Lns; NET]. Or, here this does not pertain to their personal feelings, but describes their rejection of his claim to become king and this hate was realized by sending their petition [NICNT].
  c. πρεσβεία (LN 37.87) (BAGD 699): 'ambassador' [BAGD, LN], 'representative' [LN], 'a delegation' [AB, BECNT, NTC, WBC; HCSB, NASB, NET, NIV, NLT, NRSV, REB], 'an embassage' [Lns], 'a group' [NCV], 'a message' [KJV]. This singular form is translated 'representatives' [GW], 'messengers' [CEV, TEV]. See this word at 14:32.
  d. aorist act. infin. of βασιλεύω (LN 37.64) (BAGD 1.a. p. 136): 'to be a king' [BAGD, LN], 'to rule' [BAGD, LN], 'to rein' [LN]. The phrase 'to

be king over us' [AB; NET] is also translated 'to become king over us' [Lns, NTC], 'to be our king' [CEV, GW, NCV, NIV, TEV], 'to be their king' [NLT], 'as our king' [REB], 'to rule over us' [BECNT, WBC; HCSB, NRSV], 'to reign over us' [KJV, NASB].

QUESTION—Where was the ambassador sent after him?

The citizens sent their representative to follow after him [GW] to that distant country [TH] to speak to the person who would appoint the nobleman to be king over the land the citizens lived in [My; GW].

QUESTION—What is the meant by referring to the nobleman as τοῦτον 'this one'?

It means 'he is no man of ours' [ICC]. It indicates their contempt for him [ICC, Su, TH]. It was used as a sneer [Arn], a derogatory reference [BECNT; NET]. His name was distasteful to them [Lns, Su].

19:15 **And it-happened when he-returned having-received**[a] **the kingdom he-said to-be-called**[b] **to-him these slaves to-whom he-had-given the money,**[c] **in-order-that he-might-know what they-had-earned.**[d]

TEXT—Instead of τί διεπραγματεύσαντο 'what they had earned', some manuscripts read τίς τί διεπραγματεύσατο 'who had earned what' and some manuscripts read τίς τί ἐπραγματεύσατο 'who had earned what'. GNT reads τί διεπραγματεύσαντο 'what they had earned' with a B decision, indicating that the text is almost certain. Most versions would probably not distinguish between the second and third readings, but τίς τί διεπραγματεύσατο 'who had earned what' is the reading of KJV which follows the Textus Receptus.

LEXICON—a. aorist act. participle of λαμβάνω (LN 37.65): 'to receive' [LN]. The phrase λαβόντα τὴν βασιλείαν 'having received the kingdom' [Arn, BECNT; KJV] is also translated 'after receiving the kingdom' [NASB, NET], 'after taking the kingdom' [Lns], 'having acquired the kingship' [WBC], 'having received the authority to be king' [HCSB], 'having received royal power' [NRSV], 'after he was appointed king' [GW], 'after he had been made king' [CEV], 'he was made king, however' [NIV], 'but he was made king' [NTC], '(he returned) with the title of king' [AB], '(he returned) however as king' [REB], 'the man became king' [NCV], 'the man was made king' [TEV], 'the king (called in)' [NLT]. The aorist tense of this participle 'having received' indicates an event prior to the verb 'he returned', which in turn is prior to the main verb 'he said' [TH].

  b. aorist pass. infin. of φωνέω (LN 33.307) (BAGD 2.b. p. 870): 'to be called' [BAGD, LN], 'to be summoned' [BAGD, LN]. The phrase 'he said to be called to him' is translated 'he commanded to be called unto him' [KJV], 'he ordered that...be called to him' [NASB], 'he ordered to be summoned before him' [NTC], 'he ordered to be summoned' [NRSV], 'he said to call' [BECNT], 'he said that...be called' [Arn, Lns], 'he asked for...to be summoned to him' [WBC], 'he had (those servants) summoned' [AB], 'he ordered (his servants) to appear before him' [TEV], 'he said, Call' [GW, NCV], 'he sent for' [NIV, REB], 'he called in' [CEV, NLT], 'he summoned' [HCSB, NET]. The passive voice implies that the order to call for the slaves is given through one or more intermediaries [TH]. Being king, he acted through the agency of others [WBC].

- c. ἀργύριον (LN 6.73) (BAGD 2.b. p. 104): 'money' [AB, Arn, BECNT, Lns, NTC, WBC; all versions except TEV], 'silver' [BAGD], 'silver money, silver coin' [BAGD, LN], not explicit [TEV].
- d. aorist mid./pass. (deponent = act.) indic. of διαπραγματεύομαι (LN 57.195) (BAGD p. 187): 'to earn' [BAGD, LN; CEV], 'to gain by trading' [BAGD]. The phrase 'what they had earned' is translated 'how much they had earned' [CEV, TEV], 'how much they earned with it' [NCV], 'what they had gained with it' [NIV], 'what profit each had made' [REB], 'what they had gained by trading' [BECNT; NRSV], 'what each had gained by doing business' [NTC], 'what they did gain by doing business' [Lns], 'how much every man had gained by trading' [KJV], 'how much they had earned by trading' [NET], 'how much they had made in business' [HCSB], 'how much each one has made by investing' [GW], 'what they had accomplished' [Arn], 'what business they had done' [WBC; NASB], 'what business they had done with it' [AB], 'what they had done with the money and what their profits were' [NLT].

QUESTION—How does this verse connect with the preceding one?

This resumes the main account of the parable [Su]. The attempts to prevent the nobleman from being made king failed [Arn, NIC, NTC]. Some indicate that the delegation was unsuccessful by adding the word 'however' to the fact that the man received the kingdom [NIV, REB], or by adding 'but' [NTC; NCV].

19:16 And having-come the first said, Lord, your mina earned[a] ten minas. **19:17** And he-said to-him, Excellent,[b] good slave, because in (the) smallest[c] (thing) you-were faithful, be having authority[d] over ten cities. **19:18** And the second came saying, Your mina, Lord, made five minas. **19:19** And he-said to-this (one) also, And you be over five cities.

LEXICON—a. aorist mid. (deponent = act.) indic. of προσεργάζομαι (LN 57.191) (BAGD p. 713): 'to earn in addition' [BAGD, LN], 'to make more' [BAGD, LN]. The phrase 'earned ten minas' [WBC] is also translated 'has earned ten more minas' [HCSB], 'has brought ten more minas' [BECNT], 'did make ten minas more' [Lns], 'has made ten minas more' [NASB, NET], 'has made ten more pounds' [NRSV], 'has won ten additional pounds' [Arn], 'has gained ten pounds' [KJV], 'has earned ten more' [AB, NTC; NIV], 'has earned ten times as much' [GW], 'has increased tenfold' [REB], 'I earned ten coins' [NCV], 'I have earned ten gold coins' [TEV], 'I have earned ten times as much' [CEV], '(reported) a tremendous gain—ten times as much' [NLT].

b. εὖγε (LN **65.23**) (BAGD p. 319): This exclamation is translated 'excellent' [AB, LN; NCV], 'splendid' [NTC], 'well' [Lns; KJV], 'well done' [BAGD, BECNT, LN, WBC; HCSB, NASB, NET, NIV, NLT, NRSV, REB, TEV], 'well done indeed' [Arn], 'fine' [**LN**], 'that's fine' [CEV], 'good job' [GW].

c. ἐλάχιστος (LN 87.66) (BAGD 2.a. p. 248): 'very little' [BAGD], 'least important' [LN]. The phrase ἐν ἐλαχίστῳ πιστὸς ἐγένου 'in the smallest thing you were faithful' is translated 'you have been faithful in a very little (thing)' [KJV, NASB], 'you were faithful in small matters' [TEV], 'you have been faithful in very little' [BECNT], 'you have been faithful in a very small matter' [WBC; HCSB, NET], 'you have been trustworthy in a very little thing' [AB], 'you have been trustworthy in a very small matter/thing' [NIV, NRSV], 'you have shown yourself trustworthy in a very small matter' [REB], 'in a very small matter you have been faithful' [NTC], 'thou didst prove faithful in a very little' [Lns], 'you showed yourself faithful in a very small matter' [Arn], 'you have shown that you can be trusted with a small amount' [CEV], 'you proved that you could be trusted with a little money' [GW], 'you have been faithful with the little I entrusted to you' [NLT], 'I can trust you with small things' [NCV]. The small matter refers to a small job or a small responsibility [TG]. The 'smallest thing' is in the sphere of money and there was not much money to start with [Arn].

d. ἐξουσία (LN 37.47) (BAGD 4.a. p. 278): 'authority' [BAGD, LN]. The phrase 'be having authority over' is translated 'be thou as having authority over' [Lns], 'have authority over' [HCSB, KJV], 'you are to be in authority over' [NASB], 'you are to have authority over' [AB], 'you will have authority over' [Arn, BECNT; NET], 'take charge of' [GW, NIV], 'be in charge of' [NTC], 'rule over' [NRSV], 'you will be given...to rule' [CEV], 'you are to be over' [WBC], 'you shall have charge of' [REB], 'I will put you in charge of' [TEV], 'I will let you rule over' [NCV], 'you will be governor of (ten cities) as your reward' [NLT].

QUESTION—What is meant by having authority over ten cities?

It could mean that the slave was elevated to being a ruler [Su]. He was to be a governor over ten cities and thus he would have much to do with the provincial revenues [EGT]. He did not receive the ten cities as his possessions, but he was given authority to administer affairs on behalf of his master [NIC]. The ten cities would be within the kingdom the nobleman had acquired [AB, Hu, MGC, NIBC]. It is possible that it means he was given a ten-city territory to trade in as a merchant [Su]

QUESTION—Why didn't the master say, 'Excellent, good slave' to the second slave?

The rewards were according to the amounts gained and the first slave was commended to a degree that the second was not [Hu]. The king's words to the second slave have been abbreviated, but the king's praise for the second is to be understood [WBC]. The second reward establishes the principle that the rewards were proportional to the profit made [BECNT, NTC, Su, TH, TNTC, WBC]. They were proportional to the degree of faithfulness [NTC]. The second was also trustworthy but had less ability, yet he could have done better [EGT]. The reward was according to faithfulness and diligence [NAC]. Or, the second was not necessarily less faithful, since the two could have been in different situations and the second could have been just as faithful in bringing only five minas [Lns]. The second was faithful, but not as successful as the first [Arn]. The two equally pleased their master and were rewarded in the same way according to their abilities [Su].

19:20 And the other (one) came saying, Lord, here-is[a] your mina which I-had being-put-away[b] in a-face-cloth.[c]

TEXT—Instead of ὁ ἕτερος 'the other', some manuscripts read ἕτερος 'another'. GNT does not mention this variant. 'Another' is translated by NTC; CEV, HCSB, KJV, NASB, NCV, NET, NIV, and TEV.

LEXICON—a. ἰδού (LN 91.13) (BAGD 2. p. 371): 'here is' [AB, BAGD, BECNT; all versions except GW, KJV, NLT], 'look' [LN, WBC; GW], 'behold' [KJV], 'lo' [Lns], not explicit [NTC; NLT].

b. pres. mid./pass. (deponent = act.) participle of ἀπόκειμαι (LN 85.53) (BAGD 1. p. 92): 'to put away' [BAGD, LN]. The phrase 'I had being put away' is translated 'I kept it laid away' [BAGD; NIV], 'I kept put away' [NASB], 'I had lying away' [Lns], 'I have kept laid up' [KJV], 'I kept it wrapped up' [REB], 'I have been keeping wrapped up' [NTC], 'I wrapped it up' [NRSV], 'I wrapped and hid' [NCV], 'I have kept stored' [BECNT], 'I have kept stored away' [AB, WBC], 'I kept it hidden' [TEV], 'I have kept it hidden away' [HCSB], 'I put away for safekeeping' [**LN**; NET], 'I've kept it for safekeeping' [GW], 'I kept it safe' [CEV], 'I hid it and kept it safe' [NLT].

c. σουδάριον (LN 6.159) (BAGD p. 759): 'face cloth' [BAGD, LN], 'a cloth' [BECNT; GW, HCSB], 'a piece of cloth' [NCV, NET, NIV, NRSV], 'sweat cloth' [Lns, WBC], 'handkerchief' [AB, BAGD, LN; CEV, NASB, REB, TEV], 'napkin' [LN, NTC; KJV], not explicit [NLT]. It was a scarf or neckcloth used to protect the back of one's head from the sun [BECNT, MGC, NIGTC]. It was a cloth used to wipe away perspiration [AB, Arn, Hu].

QUESTION—How are the ten slaves numbered?

Since there were ten slaves, there is a difficulty in calling the third ὁ ἕτερος 'the other' [ICC]. The first, the second, and another ('the third' [NLT, REB]) of the slaves the king summoned are representative of all ten [ICC, Lns, NIC]. For the purpose of the parable it was not necessary to include the reports of all ten slaves [BECNT, ICC, TG]. The 'other one' was the one that was different from the two described before him [Arn, BECNT, NIC; NET]. The three represent two classes, those who made good use of the money and those who did not [TNTC]. Or, the three represent the three types of responses [MGC]. Some gained very much, some gained less, and some gained nothing at all [ICC]. There were three classes: the faithful, the less faithful, and the unfaithful ones [NIC]. Or, instead of the third slave representing others of the ten, we can assume that the seven who are not mentioned were faithful to their master's instructions and received their rewards [Arn].

QUESTION—Why did he put away the mina in a face cloth?

He put it away in order to avoid squandering the money and he kept it carefully wrapped so that corrosion could not harm it [Su]. He was not confessing that he was at fault in doing so and in effect he was proclaiming that he had not lost or spent the money [ICC]. However, if he wanted to keep the money safe, he should have buried it [BECNT, MGC, NIGTC, TNTC], so he was actually careless in his treatment of the money [BECNT]. He had disobeyed his master's instructions to make a profit from the money [NICNT].

19:21 Because I-was-being-afraid-of[a] you, because you-are a severe[b] man, you-take what you-did- not -deposit[c] and you-reap[d] what you-did- not -sow.

LEXICON—a. imperf. pass. indic. of φοβέομαι (LN 25.252): 'to be afraid of' [AB, Arn, LN, WBC; all versions except KJV], 'to fear' [BECNT, Lns; KJV], 'to live in fear of' [NTC]. The imperfect tense indicates a continuing fear [Rb, TH]. He was in constant fear of his master [Lns, NTC].

b. αὐστηρός (LN **88.138**) (BAGD p. 122): 'severe' [BAGD, BECNT, **LN**; NET], 'exacting' [LN, WBC; NASB], 'strict' [BAGD], 'harsh' [NRSV], 'austere' [BAGD, Lns; KJV], 'stern' [AB, Arn, NTC], 'hard' [CEV, NCV, NIV, REB, TEV], 'hard to deal with' [NLT], 'tough' [HCSB], 'tough to get along with' [GW]. It means that the king was severe, strict, and exacting [AB, BECNT]. He was a ruthless business man [TG]. Matthew 25:24 uses hard or merciless, but here the meaning is severe or strict [Hu, NIBC].

c. aorist act. indic. of τίθημι (LN **57.217**) (BAGD I.1.b.γ. p. 816): 'to deposit' [BAGD, LN], 'to put in a bank' [**LN**]. The phrase 'you take what you did not deposit' [NRSV] is also translated 'you collect what you didn't deposit' [HCSB], 'you withdraw what you did not deposit' [NTC; NET], 'you carry off what you have not deposited' [AB, WBC], 'you seize what you do not deposit' [Arn], 'you draw out what you did not put in' [REB], 'you take out what you did not put in' [NIV], 'thou takest away what thou didst not put down' [Lns; KJV], 'you take up what you did not lay down' [NASB], 'you take what you did not lay down' [BECNT], 'you take what isn't yours' [CEV, GW, NLT, TEV], 'you take money that you did not earn' [NCV]. The present tense of 'you take away' indicates a habitual action [TH].

d. pres. act. indic. of θερίζω (LN 43.14) (BAGD 2.a. p. 359): 'to reap' [BAGD, LN], 'to harvest' [BAGD, LN]. The phrase 'you reap what you did not sow' [AB, BECNT, Lns, NTC; HCSB, KJV, NASB, NET, NIV,

LUKE 19:21 293

NRSV, REB] is also translated 'you harvest what you have not sown' [WBC], 'you reap what you did not plant' [TEV], 'you harvest crops you didn't plant' [CEV, NLT], 'you harvest grain you haven't planted' [GW], 'you gather food that you didn't plant' [NCV]. The present tense indicates that he habitually did this [TH].

QUESTION—What relationship is indicated by the initial γάρ 'because'?

The slave justified himself by stating the reason why he had he put away the mina for safe keeping [Arn, BECNT, NAC, NIGTC]. His constant fear of his master overrode a fear of being faithless to the trust of gaining money [Lns]. Fearing the exacting nature of his master, he did not trust his own ability and did not try to gain a profit from the mina for fear of the result of trying and failing [Su]. Since he considered the king to be a strict administrator, an unrelenting exploiter, and a cutthroat dealer [BECNT], he might have thought that if he earned money with the mina, the king would appropriate it all, but if he lost the mina in business dealings he would have to make good the loss [BECNT, ICC, MGC, NIBC, NIGTC]. This charge was not true since the king had proved himself to be magnanimous and generous towards the other slaves [Arn, NAC].

QUESTION—What relationship is indicated by the second ὅτι 'because'?

It indicates the reason he was afraid of his master. The slave regarded his master as a ruthless businessman [TG]. He feared that his master would require him to make good if he lost the mina [My]. He considered the king to be a strict man so he took care that the king would get back the exact deposit [ICC].

QUESTION—What is the significance of the two statements illustrating the master's severity?

He had called the king a hard man and now describes in what way he was hard [NAC, TH]. The two metaphors were proverbial sayings [AB, NIBC, NTC, TNTC, WBC]. They speak of making gain from other people's efforts [Crd, TH, TNTC]. They describe a grasping person who wants money without working to earn it [NIGTC]. This describes his master as one who made his servants slave for him in order to enrich himself with their profits [Lns]. The king is caricatured as one who exploits others [AB]. He describes the king as a fraud who uses exploitative business practices [NICNT], or a dishonest man [Su].

QUESTION—What is meant by the saying 'you take what you did not deposit'?

1. This is a saying drawn from financing [Arn, ICC, LN, MGC, NICNT, NIGTC, NTC, WBC; HCSB, NET, NRSV, REB]. It describes a person seeking an extremely high return of his investments [MGC, NIGTC]. It is a grasping scheme to get money that did not rightfully belong to him [Lns]. That this is a banking image is supported by the master's reference to interest in 19:23 [WBC].

2. This is a metaphor that is wider than financial actions [Crd, Su, TG, TH, TNTC]. It refers to a dishonest man who steals furtively, such as in the marketplace when someone would pick up the money or merchandise

another person had laid on a table and was looking away [Su]. It is a general statement meaning to get something for nothing [TG]. It refers to an unjust appropriation of another's labor [Crd].

19:22 He-says to-him, From your mouth^a I-will-judge^b you, evil^c slave. Did-you-know that I am a severe man, taking what I-did- not -deposit and reaping what I-did- not -sow? 19:23 And why did-you- not -give my money on a-table?^d And having-come I would-collect it with interest.^e

TEXT—In 19:22, instead of λέγει 'he says', some manuscripts read λέγει δέ 'and he says', although GNT does not mention this variant. Λέγει δέ 'and he says' is read by KJV.

LEXICON—a. στόμα (LBN 8.19) (BAGD 1.a. p. 770): 'mouth' [BAGD, LN]. The phrase ἐκ τοῦ στόματός σου 'from your mouth' is translated 'from your own mouth' [BECNT], 'out of your mouth' [Arn], 'out of your own mouth' [Lns, NTC, WBC; KJV, REB], 'by your own words' [AB; NASB, NCV, NET, NIV, NRSV], 'by what you have said' [GW, HCSB], 'by what you have just said' [CEV], '(I will use) your own words' [TEV], not explicit [NLT]. This noun is used as a metonymy for what the mouth utters [BAGD].

b. pres. act. indic. of κρίνω (LN 56.20) (BAGD 4.a.α. p. 451): 'to judge' [AB, Arn, BAGD, LN, Lns, NTC, WBC; GW, HCSB, KJV, NASB, NET, NIV, NRSV], 'to arrive at a verdict, to try a case, to act as a judge' [LN], 'to punish' [BAGD], 'to condemn' [BECNT; CEV, NCV, REB, TEV], not explicit [NLT]. The judgment would be against the slave so here it has the meaning 'condemn' [NAC]. This judicial term is used in a non-judicial setting and means to condemn [TH]. Depending on the accentuation in Greek, this verb may be taken as future [AB, Arn, BECNT, GNT; all versions except CEV, NLT] or present [Lns, NTC]. The sense is practically the same in either case since the verdict directly follows and the slave had already been addressed as 'evil slave' [Lns].

c. πονηρός (LN 88.110) (BAGD 1.b.α. p. 690): 'evil' [BAGD, BECNT, LN; CEV, GW, HCSB, NCV], 'wicked' [AB, BAGD, LN, Lns, NTC, WBC; KJV, NET, NIV, NLT, NRSV], 'bad' [TEV], 'worthless' [Arn, BAGD; CEV, NASB]. The phrase 'evil slave' is translated 'you scoundrel' [REB]. He was evil in that he had a grasping and self-interested nature [Su]. He was wicked because of his disobedience [AB]. He was bad in that he was irresponsible, inefficient, or lazy [TG].

d. τράπεζα (LN 57.215) (BAGD 4. p. 824): 'table' [BAGD], 'bank' [Arn, BAGD, BECNT, **LN**, Lns, NTC, WBC; all versions except NIV, REB], 'bank account' [AB], '(put) on deposit' [NIV, REB]. The 'table' refers to the table on which money-changers displayed their coins [BAGD]. There were no banks in the modern sense, so here the noun refers to the table of the money-lender [NTC, TNTC]. The word 'bank' has been derived from the word 'bench' [NTC]. The phrase 'on the table' is an idiom referring to the place where money is kept or managed, or credit is established, and can be called a bank [NET].

e. τόκος (LN **57.212**) (BAGD p. 821): 'interest' [AB, Arn, BAGD, BECNT, LN, Lns, NTC, WBC; all versions except KJV], 'usury' [KJV]. Moneylenders paid interest on money deposited with them, and they in turn lent the money out at a higher rate of interest [NTC].

QUESTION—How could the king judge and condemn the slave by the slave's own words?

The excuse the slave gave in 19:21 forms a basis for his condemnation [AB, BECNT]. The king did not try to defend himself from the false characterization given him by the slave, but judged the slave on his own terms and accusation [AB]. The hearers and readers of the parable know that the slave's statements about the king were false and he stood condemned because of that, but here the king was condemning the slave on the basis of the slave's own statements and in effect said, 'If what you said about me is true, you should at least have invested my money in a bank' [NAC]. If the slave thought that the king was so austere, he should have exerted himself all the more to obey him [NTC]. Since he had not acted from his own sense of duty, at least his fear of the king should have caused him to invest the money [Arn]. The slave was either trying to excuse his lack of obedience by lying about the king's character or if he believed it, he had seriously misjudged his king and had insulted him, but either way he had failed to obey him [BECNT].

QUESTION—In 19:22, what is the function of the question, 'Did you know…'?

This question indicates the basis for the condemnation [TH, TNTC]: you knew…so why didn't give m the money? Some translate the rhetorical question as a statement of fact, 'you knew that I am a severe man…' [Arn; CEV, GW, KJV, NCV, TEV] and this might be taken to mean that the king agreed with the slave's assessment. By repeating the slave's words, the king seemed to accept such an assessment of himself, but whether or not it is true, he did nothing to contradict it [NICNT]. In the parable, the king must correspond with Jesus, so this should be taken as a question rather than an agreement [Su]. By using the question, the king does not admit that the slave's description of him is correct [NIVS, Su, TNTC]. The question could be stated '(So) you knew, did you, that…?' [AB, BECNT, NTC, WBC; NET, NIV, NRSV]. The question is equivalent to a condition [NIGTC, Su] and it is translated as a conditional clause to the question in 19:23, 'If you knew that I am a severe man…, then why didn't you…' [HCSB, NLT]. For the purpose of argument, the king assumed the slave's assessment to be true and argued from that position [Su]. Another way to make a statement out of the question is to translate 'you said that you knew that I am a severe man…' [TH]. On the basis of what the slave had said about the king, the slave should have taken some other action [Su, TG].

QUESTION—In 19:23, what is the function of the question, 'Why did you not give...'?

This rhetorical question expresses astonishment [TH]. It indicates what the slave should have done [TG]. If what the slave had said was true, this is the deduction the slave should have made [Lns]. The question is introduced by 'why then' [AB, Arn, BECNT, NTC, WBC; GW, KJV, NASB, NCV, NET, NIV, NRSV, REB, TEV].

19:24 And he-said to-the (ones who) were-standing-nearby, Take from him the mina and give (it) to-the (one) having ten minas. 19:25 And they-said to-him, Lord, he-has ten minas.

TEXT—Some manuscripts omit verse 19:25. GNT includes this verse with an A decision, indicating that the text is certain. It is omitted by Crd.

QUESTION—Who were the ones standing by?

Since the master was a king, he would have a number of attendants present at all times [TG]. They were the king's attendants [Hu, ICC, TH, WBC; REB], including bodyguards [Hu], courtiers and gentlemen-at-arms [AB]. They were the same ones who were ordered to call the ten slaves in 19:15 [Lns]. There is no indication that the other nine slaves were present at the interview and this probably refers to lesser servants who were there [NIGTC]. Or, these would be the other slaves who had been entrusted with a mina and who had been gathered for an evaluation of their faithfulness [BECNT].

QUESTION—Why was the man who had ten minas given this extra one?

The slave who had proved most efficient in making a profit was rewarded with this additional mina to invest for his king [BECNT, ICC, Su, TNTC]. He was given the mina to trade with [WBC]. That he had ten minas does not refer to his total possessions, but to his profit, so that now he would have twelve minas altogether [BECNT, Hu]. When the master criticized the slave who had merely hidden the money, saying 'having come I would collect it with interest' (19:23), it appears that all of the money involved, both principle and interest, belonged to the master. Some have called this money a reward [NAC, NIGTC], or a gift [Lns] and this could be taken to mean that it was for the slave's own personal use. However, none have specifically contradicted the idea that giving the slave this extra mina rewarded him with this extra responsibility [BECNT, Su]. The slave was given this money to invest for his master [ICC].

QUESTION—In 19:25, who spoke and whom did they call 'Lord'?

1. The king's attendants were speaking to the king in the parable [AB, Arn, BECNT, Lns, MGC, NICNT, NIGTC, NTC, Su, TG, TH; CEV, GW, NCV, NET, NLT, and probably all other versions except KJV, NRSV]. The attendants were astonished at the king's unexpected action, which seemed to them to be an unfair decision [BECNT, NICNT, TH]. They seemed to think that the man already had all that he could manage [Su]. They would have given the mina to the one of the nine slaves who had

gained the least [Lns]. Their expression of amazement does not imply that they then disobeyed the king [TG].
2. The audience listening to the parable spoke to Jesus [Alf, Gdt, Hu, Rb; probably EGT, ICC; GW, KJV, NRSV which translate this within a parenthesis]. The people listening to Jesus interrupted him because of the sudden turn in the story when the one mina is given to the man who already had ten minas [Rb]. They would think that Jesus was spoiling the story by giving the mina to the man who seemed to need it the least [ICC]. If Jesus is speaking in the next two verses, he is giving the lesson of the parable [BECNT].

19:26 I-say to-you, that To-everyone having it-will-be-given,[a] but from the (one) not having even what he-has will-be-taken-away.[b]

TEXT—Instead of λέγω 'I say', some manuscripts read λέγω γάρ 'for I say', although GNT does not mention this variant. Λέγω γάρ 'for I say' is read by KJV.

TEXT—Following ἀρθήσεται 'shall be taken away', some manuscripts add ἀπ' αὐτοῦ 'from him', although GNT does not mention this variant. Ἀπ' αὐτοῦ 'from him' is read by KJV.

LEXICON—a. fut. pass. indic. of δίδωμι (LN 57.71): 'to be given' [LN]. The clause 'to everyone having it will be given' is translated 'to everyone who has it shall be given' [Lns; KJV], 'to everyone who has, more will be given' [AB, Arn, NTC, WBC; HCSB, NASB, NIV], 'to all those who have, more will be given' [NRSV], 'those who have will be given more' [NCV], 'to those who have something, even more will be given' [TEV], 'those who have something will be given more' [CEV], 'everyone who has will be given more' [NET, REB], 'everyone who has more shall be given' [BECNT], 'everyone who has something will be given more' [GW], 'to those who use well what they are given, even more will be given' [NLT]. The passive voice implies that God is the one who gives [Lns, TG].

b. fut. pass. indic. of αἴρω (LN 15.203): 'to be taken away, to be removed' [LN]. The phrase 'from the one not having even what he has will be taken away' is translated 'from the one who does not have, even what he does have will be taken away' [WBC; HCSB, NASB, NET; similarly Arn, Lns, NTC; KJV], 'from those who have nothing, even what they have will be taken away' [NRSV], 'those who do not have anything will have everything taken away from them' [NCV], 'as for the one who has nothing, even what he has will be taken away' [NIV], 'from the one who has nothing even what he has will be taken away' [AB], 'whoever has nothing will forfeit even what he has' [REB], 'everything will be taken away from those who don't have anything' [CEV], 'everything will be taken away from those who don't have much' [GW], 'those who have nothing, even the little that they have will be taken away from them' [TEV], 'from those who are unfaithful, even what little they have will be taken away' [NLT]. The passive voice implies that God is the one who takes away [Lns].

QUESTION—In the phrase 'I say to you that', does ὅτι 'that' indicate indirect speech or direct speech?

1. It indicates indirect speech [Arn, BECNT, Lns, NTC, WBC; NASB, NET, NIV, NLT, TEV]: I say to you that to everyone having....
2. It indicates direct speech [AB; CEV, GW, HCSB, NCV, NRSV, REB]: I say to you, 'To everyone having....'

QUESTION—Who is speaking here?

1. The king of the parable is speaking to those standing by him [Alf, BECNT, Crd, Gdt, MGC, My, NTC, TG, TH; CEV, NCV]. Understanding that the bystanders are the attendants of the king in the story makes the speaker in the next two verses to be the king in the parable [Arn, NTC]. Although 19:25 is an interruption by listeners of the parable, in this verse Jesus continues with the story of the king [Gdt]. The next verse also has the king as the speaker [BECNT, MGC, TG; CEV]. Since the next verse has the king in the parable as the speaker, so here too it must be the king [BECNT].
2. Jesus is speaking to those who were listening to his parable [ICC, WBC]. This verse is an aside by Jesus and then the following verse 19:27 returns to the king in the parable [WBC]. It depends on who was speaking in the preceding verse. The interruption in 19:25 came from Jesus' audience, so Jesus is replying to them [ICC].

QUESTION—What is meant by the statement 'to everyone having it will be given'?

Many supply 'more' so that it means 'to everyone having, more will be given' [AB, Arn, BECNT, NTC, WBC; all versions except KJV]. 'More' in the parable refers to more than the original distribution of minas and also a share in the king's rule [NICNT].

QUESTION—What is meant by the statement 'from the one not having even what he has will be taken away'?

This is similar to the saying in 8:18 'whoever has, it will be given to him, and whoever does not have, even what he seems to have will be taken from him' [AB, BECNT, TH; NET], and here the meaning is that the one who does not have (but 'had') loses what he appeared to have [BECNT]. The dead capital which was not invested had to be surrendered [Arn]. The unused gift is spoken of as not having it and it is taken away [ICC]. This means that when someone does not use what he has been given, God will take it away [TG].

19:27 But[a] these enemies of-mine the (ones who do) not want me to-rule over them, bring them here and kill[b] them before[c] me.

TEXT—Instead of τούτους 'these' some manuscripts read ἐκείνους 'those'. GNT does not mention this variant. 'Those' is translated by KJV, NIV, TEV, although the reading of versions other than KJV may be stylistic rather than textually-based.

LEXICON—a. πλήν (LN 89.130) (BAGD 1.b. p. 669): 'but' [BAGD, LN, Lns; HCSB, KJV, NASB, NIV], 'but as for' [BECNT, NTC, WBC; NET, NRSV, REB], 'nevertheless' [BAGD, LN], 'however' [Arn, BAGD], 'however, as for' [AB], 'now' [CEV, NCV], 'now, as for' [TEV], 'and now about' [NLT], not explicit [GW]. This conjunction indicates the validity of something irrespective of other considerations [LN].

b. aorist act. impera. of κατασφάζω (LN **20.72**) (BAGD p. 419): 'to kill' [**LN**; CEV, GW, NCV, NIV, TEV], 'to slay' [BECNT, WBC; KJV, NASB], 'to slaughter' [AB, Arn, BAGD, LN, Lns; HCSB, NET, NRSV, REB], 'to execute' [NLT], 'to strike down' [BAGD], 'to cut down' [NTC].

c. ἔμπροσθεν (LN 83.33) (BAGD 2.c. 257): 'before' [BAGD, LN], 'in front of' [BAGD, LN], 'in the sight of' [BAGD]. The phrase 'before me' [AB, Arn, BECNT, Lns, WBC; KJV, NCV] is also translated 'in front of me' [GW, NET, NIV], 'in my presence' [NTC; HCSB, NASB, NLT, NRSV, REB, TEV], 'while I watch' [CEV].

QUESTION—What relationship is indicated by πλήν 'but'?

It is a strong adversative [AB, Lns, MGC]. This contrasts the punishment of the disobedient slave with the punishment of the enemies of the king [ICC, MGC]. It indicates a sudden turn to discuss a different subject [TH]. It is an abrupt turn to the disloyal citizens who were mentioned in 19:14 [Crd]. Two groups, the faithful stewards and the ones who did not trust the master, have been dealt with and now the master deals with the rebels who openly rejected him [BECNT]. After judging the slaves, there remained only one more thing to do [Gdt]. This winds up the things the king must do at the start of his reign [EGT]. This is a natural action for a new king to establish his power [WBC].

QUESTION—Were τούτους 'these' enemies in the king's presence at the time?

They were absent because they had to be brought before him. They were present to the thoughts of the audience [ICC]. The hearers knew about these persons and their deeds [TH]. Some translate it 'those enemies' [KJV, NIV, TEV] and some leave the pronoun implicit [CEV, GW, NCV].

QUESTION—In what sense were these people enemies of the king?

They were disloyal [Crd], and rebellious [Lns, Su, TG].

QUESTION—What was to happen to the king's enemies?

They had to be arrested and brought before the king [TH]. They were to be killed by means of a sword [TH]. Perhaps this refers only to the leaders of the rebellious subjects [TG].

DISCOURSE UNIT: 19:28–23:56 [Su]. The topic is the ministry of the universal savior in Jerusalem.

DISCOURSE UNIT: 19:28–21:38 [AB, NAC]. The topic is Jesus' ministry in Jerusalem.

300　　　　　　　　　　LUKE 19:28

DISCOURSE UNIT: 19:28–48 [NICNT]. The topic is Jesus' arrival in Jerusalem.

DISCOURSE UNIT: 19:28–44 [Su, TNTC; CEV, GW, NASB, NIV, NLT]. The topic is Jesus' entry into Jerusalem [CEV], the king comes to Jerusalem [GW], the triumphal entry [TNTC; NASB, NIV, NLT], Sunday—a day of triumph [Su].

DISCOURSE UNIT: 19:28–40 [AB, BECNT, NAC, NICNT, NIGTC, Su, TNTC; HCSB, NCV, NET, NRSV, TEV]. The topic is the Messianic entry into Jerusalem [NAC, Su], going up to Jerusalem [NICNT], Jesus approaches Jerusalem [NIGTC], Jesus' controversial approach to Jerusalem [BECNT], Jesus enters Jerusalem as a king [NCV], the approach in triumph [TNTC], the triumphant approach to Jerusalem [TEV], the triumphal entry [HCSB, NET], Jesus' triumphal entry into Jerusalem [NRSV], the royal entry into the Jerusalem temple [AB].

19:28 And having-said these (things) he-was-traveling ahead/forward[a] going-up to Jerusalem.

LEXICON—a. ἔμπροσθεν (LN 83.33) (BAGD 1.b. p. 257): 'ahead, forward' [BAGD], 'ahead of, in front of, before' [LN]. The phrase 'he was traveling ahead/forward' is translated 'he went on ahead' [BECNT, NTC, WBC; HCSB, NIV, NRSV], 'he was going on ahead' [NASB], 'he continued on ahead' [NET], 'he kept moving ahead' [AB], 'he went before' [KJV], 'he went on before them' [Lns], 'he went on in front of them' [TEV], 'he went on' [CEV, NCV, NLT], 'he set out' [REB], 'he continued on his way' [GW].

QUESTION—What is the connection of this verse?
　1. This is most closely connected with the preceding parable [Alf, ICC, NIC, WBC]. At 19:11 the preceding parable began with an historical introduction, 'he told a parable because he was near Jerusalem', and now the parable has an historical conclusion with this verse [ICC].
　2. This is most closely connected with the following account [AB, Arn, BECNT, BNTC, Gdt, GNT, MGC, NAC, NICNT, NIGTC, NTC, Su, TG, TNTC; CEV, GW, HCSB, NASB, NCV, NET, NIV, NLT, NRSV, TEV].

QUESTION—Does ἔμπροσθεν mean 'before' or 'forward'?
　1. The word ἔμπροσθεν is to be interpreted as a preposition with αὐτῶν 'of them' understood and it indicates that others were following Jesus [AB, Gdt, ICC, Lns, NIGTC, NTC, TG, TNTC, WBC; KJV, NLT, TEV]: ahead of the disciples. Jesus was traveling along in front of his band of disciples [AB, Gdt, ICC, Lns, NIGTC, NTC, TNTC], his companions [WBC]. It should not be taken to mean that Jesus had left the others behind in order to enter the city alone [TG].
　2. The word ἔμπροσθεν is to be interpreted as an adverb, 'he went on forward', without focusing on the others who were following him [Arn, BECNT, EGT, TH; CEV, GW, NCV, NET, REB]. The word means either

'forward' or 'at the head' and it could be understood either way in this context, but 'forward' is to be taken when a choice must be made [Arn].

DISCOURSE UNIT: 19:29–40 [WBC]. The topic is making a royal approach to Jerusalem.

19:29 **And it-happened as he-came-near to Bethphage and Bethany at the mountain the (one) called of-Olives,**[a] **he-sent two of-the disciples**

TEXT—Instead of τῶν μαθητῶν 'of the disciples', some manuscripts read τῶν μαθητῶν αὐτοῦ 'of his disciples', although GNT does not mention this variant. Τῶν μαθητῶν αὐτοῦ 'of his disciples' is read by KJV.

LEXICON—a. ἐλαιών (LN 3.12) (BAGD p. 248): 'olive grove, olive orchard' [BAGD, LN]. The phrase πρὸς τὸ ὄρος τὸ καλούμενον Ἐλαιῶν 'at the mountain, the one called of Olives' is translated 'to the mount called Of Olives' [WBC], 'at the mount that is called Olives' [BECNT], 'at the mount called the mount of Olives' [KJV], 'at the hill called the Mount of Olives' [AB; NIV], 'at the place called the Mount of Olives' [HCSB, NET, NRSV], 'at the mount called Olive-place' [Lns], 'at the Mount of Olives (as it was called)' [GW], 'at the mountain which is called Olivet' [Arn], 'near the mount that is called Olivet' [NTC; NASB], 'at the hill called Olivet' [REB], 'at the Mount of Olives' [TEV], 'on the Mount of Olives' [CEV, NLT], '(towns) near the hill called the Mount of Olives' [NCV]. The phrase 'of Olives' describes the mount or hill as a place known for its olive trees [TH; NET]. 'Mount' means a hill, not a mountain [AB, TG; NCV, NIV, REB].

QUESTION—Where was Jesus when he sent his two disciples for the colt?

Bethany was a village Jesus had visited at different times and it was about one and a half miles east of Jerusalem [BECNT, TG], and it was situated on the slope of the Mount of Olives [AB, Arn]. Bethphage is not mentioned elsewhere in the Bible, but it is assumed that the two villages were close together [Lns, Su, TNTC, WBC]. It may have been a small suburb of Jerusalem or a separate village [NIC]. Although Bethany would have been further from Jerusalem than Bethphage, it is possible that the well-known Bethany was mentioned first in order to help indicate that the lesser known Bethphage was near it [MGC, NIGTC]. The two small villages were on a hill overlooking Jerusalem from the east [AB]. The Mount of Olives was a long ridge, not a mountain, and it was about 100 feet higher than Jerusalem [NET]. Jesus had started out from Bethany and the village of Bethphage was located a little to its side [Lns]. The situation is that when Jesus approached a spot between Bethphage and Bethany at the Mount of Olives, he stopped and sent two disciples to Bethphage [Arn]. Another view supports Lightfoot's contention that Bethphage was a district or precinct of Jerusalem that extended out to the Mount of Olives and even to the village of Bethany so that this verse speaks of Jesus coming to the district of Bethphage and to the village of Bethany where this district began [Gdt].

19:30 saying, Go into the village opposite,[a] in which entering you-will-find a-colt[b] having-been-tied, on which no-one of-men ever sat,[c] and having-untied it bring (it).

LEXICON—a. κατέναντι (LN 83.42) (BAGD 1. p. 421): 'opposite' [BAGD, LN], 'in front of, before, across from' [LN]. The phrase 'the village opposite' [AB, BECNT, WBC; REB] is also translated 'the village lying opposite' [Arn], 'the village opposite you' [NTC], 'the village ahead of you' [GW, HCSB, NASB, NET, NIV, NRSV], 'that village there ahead of you' [TEV], 'the village over against you' [HCSB], 'the village before you' [Lns], 'that village over there' [NLT], 'the town you can see there' [NCV], 'the next village' [CEV].

b. πῶλος (LN 4.33) (BAGD p. 731): 'colt' [AB, BAGD, BECNT, LN, Lns, NTC; all versions except CEV, GW, HCSB], 'foal' [Arn, LN], 'young donkey' [CEV, GW, HCSB], 'donkey' [WBC]. This refers to a young donkey [LN]. The noun could indicate a colt of a donkey or of a horse, but Matthew and John make it clear that it was a colt of a donkey [NAC, TNTC]. According to the pronouns it was a male colt [Lns].

c. aorist act. indic. of καθίζω (LN 17.12) (BAGD 2.a.α. p. 390): 'to sit' [BAGD, LN]. The phrase 'on which no one of men ever sat' [Lns] is also translated 'on which no one/person has ever sat' [NTC, WBC; HCSB], 'on which no one yet has ever sat' [NASB], 'upon/on which no man has ever sat' [Arn, BECNT], 'no one has ever sat on it' [GW], 'which no one has ever ridden' [NCV, NIV], 'on which no one has yet ridden' [AB; REB], 'that has never been ridden' [CEV, NET, NLT, NRSV, TEV].

QUESTION—What village was the one opposite them?

It is not certain whether it was Bethphage, Bethany, or even another village [ICC]. It was a village just ahead of them [NTC]. It was Bethphage [Arn, MGC, NAC, NIGTC, TG]. Or, they were in Bethphage and the two disciples were sent to Bethany [Su].

QUESTION—What is the significance of the colt having never been ridden before?

It may mean that the colt was unspoiled by previous use and therefore was fit for sacred purposes [Lns, NAC, NTC, TNTC]. It had not been defiled by use for unworthy purposes [Arn] and so it was fit for a king [AB, Arn, Gdt]. It was fitting that a king should ride on a new animal that no one else had ever ridden [Lns]. That may be correct, but perhaps it just indicated that they could identify the colt because it would be with its mother [Su]. This was a fulfillment of Zech. 9:9 [BNTC].

19:31 And if someone asks you, Why are-you-untying (it)? thus you-will-say, The Lord[a] has need[b] of-it. **19:32** And having-departed the (ones who) were-sent found (it) just-as he-told them. **19:33** And (as) they-were-untying the colt the owners[c] of-it said to them, Why are-you-untying the colt? **19:34** And they said, The Lord has need of-it.

TEXT—In 19:31, following ἐρεῖτε 'you will say', some manuscripts add αὐτῷ 'to him'. GNT does not mention this variant. Αὐτῷ 'to him' is read by KJV.

LEXICON—a. κύριος (LN 12.9): 'Lord' [AB, Arn, LN; all versions except NCV, REB, TEV], 'Master' [NCV, REB, TEV].

b. χρεία (LN 57.40) (BAGD 1. p. 885): 'need' [BAGD, LN]. The phrase 'has need of it' [AB, Arn, BECNT, WBC; NASB] is also translated 'has need of him' [Lns; KJV], 'needs it' [NTC; all versions except KJV, NASB].

c. κύριος (LN 57.12) (BAGD 1.a.α. p. 459): 'owner' [AB, Arn, BAGD, BECNT, LN, Lns, NTC, WBC; all versions], 'master' [LN].

QUESTION—What is meant by the use of the plural, the *owners* of the colt?

It can merely refer to the members of the family to which the donkey belonged [Arn, BECNT], or to the owner and his wife [BECNT]. Or, it refers to the owner and those with him [ICC]. That there were owners may indicate that the owners were poor people who had to share their donkey [TNTC].

QUESTION—What is the significance of the answer, 'The Lord has need of it'?

That the owners readily allowed the disciples to take the donkey can be explained if Jesus had prearranged to borrow the donkey or if the owners were believers ready to do whatever Jesus required [NAC]. It may be that the owners considered Jesus to be a rabbi who had the authority to make such a request [MGC]. Or, the owners of the donkey already honored Jesus as their Lord and they would let the colt be taken to Jesus without any opposition [Lns, NIC, NTC]. Being Lord, Jesus had the right to use the donkey [AB]. The word κύριος can mean 'Lord', 'master', or 'owner' and it is used both of Jesus and of the owners of the donkey. Jesus was using this title of sovereignty for himself [Gdt]. Or, it is doubtful that Jesus used the title 'Lord' of himself, but he was not the owner of the donkey, so it is possible, but unlikely, that he was talking about the Lord God and saying that the colt was needed in God's service [TNTC]. Perhaps the expression was a prearranged password so that the owners would know that it was being requested by Jesus [Su, TNTC].

19:35 And they-led it to Jesus and having-thrown[a] their garments[b] on the colt they-put-on[c] Jesus. **19:36** And (while) he was-going they-were-spreading[d] their garments on the road.

LEXICON—a. aorist act. participle of ἐπιρίπτω (LN **15.219**): 'to throw' [BECNT, **LN**, NTC, WBC; all versions except CEV, GW, KJV], 'to cast' [Arn, Lns; KJV], 'to toss' [AB], 'to put' [CEV, GW].

b. ἱμάτιον (LN 6.172) (BAGD 1. p. 376): 'garment' [BAGD, BECNT, WBC; KJV, NLT], 'coat' [LN; GW, NASB, NCV], 'robe' [LN, Lns; HCSB], 'cloak' [AB, Arn, LN, NTC; NET, NIV, NRSV, REB, TEV], 'some of their clothes' [CEV]. This refers to their outer garments [BECNT, Su, TH; NET].

c. aorist act. indic. of ἐπιβιβάζω (LN 15.98) (BAGD p. 290): 'to put someone on something' [BAGD], 'to cause to mount' [BAGD, LN]. The phrase 'they put on Jesus' is translated 'they put Jesus on it' [NASB, NCV, NIV], 'they put Jesus onto the mount' [WBC], 'they had Jesus get on it' [NET], 'they set Jesus on it' [BECNT, NTC; NRSV], 'they set Jesus thereon' [KJV], 'they helped Jesus onto it' [GW], 'they helped Jesus get on it' [CEV, HCSB, TEV], 'they mounted Jesus' [Lns], 'they made Jesus mount it' [AB, Arn], '(threw their garments over it) for him to ride on' [NLT], 'for Jesus to mount' [REB].

d. imperf. act. indic. of ὑποστρωννύω (LN **16.23**) (BAGD p. 847): 'to spread' [AB, Arn, BECNT, Lns, NTC; all versions except CEV, NRSV, REB], 'to spread out' [BAGD, **LN**] 'to spread in front of him' [CEV], 'to strew' [WBC], 'to lay' [REB]. The imperfect tense indicates that this act was kept up [AB, Lns, NTC; NRSV]. Perhaps people along the road kept spreading their robes on the ground as Jesus approached [Rb]. Or, perhaps people picked up the robes in the rear and laid them down again in front [Lns].

QUESTION—Who 'they' who put their garments on the colt?

This refers to the two disciples who brought the colt [AB, Su, TG, TH], and perhaps another [NTC], who placed their long, thin robes on the colt's back to provide a comfortable seat for Jesus [NTC]. Two or three of the disciples put their long outer robes on the colt and walked along in only their tunics [Lns]. Their outer robes served as a saddle for Jesus [NAC, Su]. They put on only as many garments it took to make a comfortable seat [Arn].

QUESTION—Who spread their garments on the road and why did they do this?

Luke's use of 'they' still refers to the disciples, but Mark 11:8 indicates that many others also spread out their garments [Arn]. Or, the subject is changed here from the two or three disciples who used their robes to make a saddle, to the rest of the disciples [NIGTC], to others [AB; NCV], to people [NET, REB, TEV], to the crowds [NLT], to the multitude [ICC, NTC], or to the people along the road [Lns, MGC]. They spread their own robes on the road to make a carpet for the colt to walk on [Arn, Su, TNTC], making a carpet of their clothes for Jesus to ride over [Lns]. This was an expression of submission [Lns], or respect [NIGTC]. It was a way to honor Jesus [Lns, NIC, NIGTC, TG, WBC]. They were honoring Jesus in the way triumphant conquerors were honored [TG].

19:37 And (as) he already was-nearing the descent[a] of-the Mount of Olives all the multitude of-the disciples rejoicing began to-praise God with-a-loud voice about all (the) miracles[b] which they-saw,

LEXICON—a. κατάβασις (LN **15.109**) (BAGD p. 409): 'descent, slope' [BAGD, **LN**]. The phrase 'he already was nearing the descent of the Mount' is translated 'as he was already drawing near to the descent of the Mount' [WBC], 'as he was now approaching the descent of the Mount' [NTC], 'when he was already close to the descent of the Mount' [AB], 'when he now was approaching the descent of the Mount' [Arn], 'by this time he was coming near the place where the road went down the Mount' [GW], 'when he came near the place where the road goes down the Mount' [NIV], 'as he was drawing near to the descent of the Mount' [Lns], 'as they reached the place where the road started down from the Mount' [NLT], 'as he approached the road leading down the Mount' [NET], 'now he came near the path down the Mount' [HCSB], 'as he was now approaching the path down from the Mount' [NRSV], 'when he was come nigh, even now at the descent of the mount' [KJV], 'as soon as he was approaching, near the descent of the Mount' [NASB], 'as he was now drawing near, at the descent of the Mount' [BECNT], 'when he reached the descent from the mount' [REB], 'when Jesus was starting down the Mount' [CEV], 'as he was coming close to Jerusalem, on the way down the Mount' [NCV], 'when he came near Jerusalem, at the place where the road went down the Mount' [TEV]. The noun 'descent' refers to the road leading down from the Mount of Olives [LN].

b. δύναμις (LN 76.7) (BAGD 4. p. 208): 'miracle' [AB, BAGD, LN, NTC; CEV, GW, HCSB, NASB, NCV, NIV, NLT], 'mighty deed' [Arn, LN], 'mighty work' [BECNT, WBC; KJV, NET], 'deed of power' [BAGD; NRSV], 'power work' [Lns], 'wonder' [BAGD], 'great thing' [REB, TEV]. See this word at 10:13.

QUESTION—Where was Jesus when he was nearing the descent of the Mount of Olives?

The road crossed the southern end of the Mount of Olives [Arn]. This was the road on the western slope of the Mount of Olives, leading to Kidron Valley [AB, TG], and on the other side of the valley was the city of Jerusalem [TG].

1. The participle ἐγγίζοντος 'nearing' refers to nearing the path that descended down the mountain [AB, Arn, ICC, Lns, NTC; GW, HCSB, NASB, NET, NIV, NLT, NRSV]. Jesus was nearing the crest where the road descends and suddenly the city came into view [Arn, WBC].
2. The participle refers to nearing the city of Jerusalem [BECNT, EGT, Gdt, TH; NCV, TEV]. In this case they could already be descending the road down from the Mount [EGT]. Jerusalem has been the goal of the journey [Gdt].

QUESTION—What miracles were they rejoicing about?

These are all the miracles reported in this book [AB, NIGTC]. They were the miraculous deeds Jesus did throughout his ministry [BECNT, TNTC, WBC]. The miracles enabled perceptive people to realize that the power of the kingdom of God was at work through Jesus [TNTC].

19:38 saying, Blessed[a] (is/be) the (one) coming, the king, in (the) name of-(the)-Lord. In heaven peace[b] and glory[c] in (the) highest.

TEXT—Instead of εὐλογημένος ὁ ἐρχόμενος, ὁ βασιλεὺς ἐν ὀνόματι κυρίου 'blessed (is) the one coming, the king, in (the) name of (the) Lord', some manuscripts read εὐλογημένος ὁ ἐρχόμενος βασιλεὺς ἐν ὀνόματι κυρίου 'blessed (is) the coming king in (the) name of (the) Lord', others read εὐλογημένος ὁ βασιλεὺς ἐν ὀνόματι κυρίου 'blessed (is) the king in (the) name of (the) Lord', others read εὐλογημένος ὁ ἐρχόμενος ἐν ὀνόματι κυρίου 'blessed (is) the one coming in (the) name of (the) Lord', and still others read ὁ ἐρχόμενος ἐν ὀνόματι κυρίου, εὐλογημένος ὁ βασιλεύς 'the one coming in (the) name of (the) Lord, blessed (is) the king'. The reading taken by GNT has a C decision, indicating that the Committee had difficulty making the decision. Εὐλογημένος ὁ ἐρχόμενος βασιλεὺς ἐν ὀνόματι κυρίου 'blessed (is) the coming king in (the) name of (the) Lord' is read by KJV.

LEXICON—a. perf. pass. participle of εὐλογέω (LN33.470) (BAGD 2.a. p. 322): 'to be blessed' [BAGD, LN]. The phrase 'blessed is the one coming, the king, in the name of the Lord' [NTC] is also translated 'blessed the king coming in the name of the Lord' [Lns], 'blessed is he who comes as king in the name of the Lord' [REB], 'blessed is he that comes in the name of the Lord, the King' [Arn], 'blessed is the coming one, the king; (the one who comes) in the name of the Lord' [WBC], 'blessed is the king who comes in the name of the Lord' [BECNT; CEV, GW, HCSB, NASB, NET, NIV, NRSV], 'blest be the king, the one coming in the name of the Lord' [AB], 'blessed be the King that cometh in the name of the Lord' [KJV], 'God bless the king who comes in the name of the Lord' [NCV, TEV], 'bless the King who comes in the name of the Lord' [NLT]. Jesus, the king, was coming as the representative of Jehovah, the great God [Arn, ICC].

b. εἰρήνη (LN 25.248) (BAGD 3. p. 227): 'peace' [BAGD, LN], 'freedom from worry' [LN]. The phrase 'in heaven peace' [NTC] is also translated 'peace in heaven' [AB, BECNT, Lns; all versions except NCV], 'there is peace in heaven' [NCV], 'there is to be peace in heaven' [WBC], 'in heaven there is peace' [Arn].

c. δόξα (LN 33.357, 87.4) (BAGD 3. p. 204): 'glory' [LN (33.357)], 'honor' [BAGD, LN (87.4)]. The phrase δόξα ἐν ὑψίστοις 'glory in the highest' [BECNT, NTC; KJV, NASB, NET, NIV] is also translated 'glory in the highest places' [Lns], 'glory in (the) highest heaven' [AB; GW, HCSB, NLT, NRSV, REB], 'let glory be proclaimed in the highest' [Arn], 'glory to God' [CEV, TEV], 'there is to be glory for God in highest heaven' [WBC], 'there is glory to God' [NCV].

QUESTION—Is the phrase Εὐλογημένος ὁ ἐρχόμενος 'Blessed the one coming' a statement or a request for God to bless him?

1. The passive 'blessed' is a statement [BECNT, WBC; CEV, GW, HCSB, NASB, NET, NIV, NRSV, REB]: he is blessed.
2. The passive 'blessed' is a request to God [AB, TG; KJV, NCV, TEV]: please bless him.

QUESTION—What is meant by 'peace in heaven'?
　It refers to the peace reserved in heaven for God's people [AB, Crd]. God was at peace with mankind [NTC, Su] and was blessing them through the Savior [Su]. There was peace in heaven in that God was being reconciled with the human race [Arn, BECNT, Gdt, TNTC]. God's plan is being fulfilled so there is peace in heaven [NAC]. Or, this is thanks to God for giving his people the peace of salvation [TG].
QUESTION—What is meant by 'glory in the highest'?
　It means 'let God now be glorified for what he accomplishes through his son' [Arn]. This is an exhortation to praise God for his goodness [TG].

19:39 And some of the Pharisees from the crowd said to him, Teacher, rebuke[a] your disciples. 19:40 And answering he-said, I-say to-you, if these will-be-silent, the stones will-cry-out.[b]

TEXT—In 19:40, following εἶπεν 'he said', some manuscripts add αὐτοῖς 'to them', although GNT does not mention this variant. Αὐτοῖς 'to them' is read by KJV.
LEXICON—a. aorist act. impera. of ἐπιτιμάω (LN 33.419) (BAGD 1. p. 303): 'to rebuke' [BAGD, LN], 'to reprove' [BAGD]. The clause 'rebuke your disciples' [AB, Arn, BECNT, Lns, NTC, WBC; HCSB, KJV, NASB, NET, NIV] is also translated 'restrain your disciples' [REB], 'order your disciples to stop' [NRSV], 'tell/command your disciples to be quiet' [GW, TEV], 'make your disciples stop shouting' [CEV], 'rebuke your followers for saying things like that' [NLT], 'tell your followers not to say these things' [NCV].
　b. fut. act. indic. of κράζω (LN 33.83) (BAGD 2.b.β. p. 448): 'to cry out' [AB, Arn, BAGD, BECNT, NTC, WBC; GW, HCSB, KJV, NASB, NCV, NET, NIV], 'to shout' [LN; CEV, TEV], 'to shout out' [NRSV], 'to shout aloud' [REB], 'to yell' [Lns], 'to burst into cheers' [NLT].
QUESTION—How did the Pharisees get to be in the crowd and why did they want the disciples rebuked?
　Up to this point only the disciples have been identified, but now we learn that there were Pharisees among them [NIGTC]. They had been with Jesus since the time they were mentioned in 13:31 [AB, NIBC]. There were Pharisees among those traveling on the road to Jerusalem [Su]. Or, they had come with the many people who had come out from Jerusalem to meet Jesus [Lns]. They happened to be on the roadside [Arn]. The Pharisees considered Jesus to be a law-breaker and when they saw that the people were identifying Jesus with the Messiah, they regarded the crowd's praise to be blasphemous [Arn, Su]. The Pharisees were offended by the homage directed toward Jesus and they also feared that such a tumult would cause trouble with Pilate [Gdt, ICC, NIC].
QUESTION—How is it possible for the stones to cry out?
　This is spoken in irony [BECNT, NICNT]. It is a rebuke for the Pharisees [Su; NET]. The significance of Jesus' reply was that it was impossible that

he not be honored as the Messiah on this occasion [EGT, Gdt, NIC]. This event was of such incomparable significance that if the people were silenced, then a miracle would have to take place so that the very stones on the ground would testify. In saying this, Jesus indirectly proclaimed himself to be the Messiah [Arn].

DISCOURSE UNIT: 19:41–48 [NAC, NIGTC]. The topic is a lament over Jerusalem and the cleansing of the temple [NAC], the fate of Jerusalem [NIGTC].

DISCOURSE UNIT: 19:41–44 [AB, BECNT, NICNT, NIGTC, Su, TNTC, WBC; HCSB, NCV, NET, NRSV, TEV]. The topic is Jesus' love for Jerusalem [HCSB], weeping over Jerusalem [AB, BECNT, NICNT, NIGTC, Su, TNTC, WBC], Jesus weeps over Jerusalem [NRSV, TEV], Jesus cries for Jerusalem [NCV], Jesus weeps for Jerusalem under judgment [NET].

19:41 And as he-came-near having-seen the city he-wept because-of[a] it **19:42** saying, If you-knew in this day even/also you the (things) with-respect-to[b] peace. But now it-was-hidden[c] from your eyes.

TEXT—In 19:42, instead of ἐν τῇ ἡμέρᾳ ταύτῃ καὶ σύ 'in this day, even you', some manuscripts read καὶ σὺ ἐν τῇ ἡμέρᾳ ταύτῃ 'even you in this day', others read καὶ σὺ καί γε ἐν τῇ ἡμέρᾳ ταύτῃ 'even you even/and indeed in this day', and still others read καὶ σὺ καί γε ἐν τῇ ἡμέρᾳ σου ταύτῃ 'even you even/and indeed in this your day'. GNT reads ἐν τῇ ἡμέρᾳ ταύτῃ καὶ σύ 'in this day, even you' with a B decision, indicating that the text is almost certain. Καὶ σὺ καί γε ἐν τῇ ἡμέρᾳ σου ταύτῃ 'even you even/and indeed in this your day' is read by KJV.

TEXT—In 19:42, instead of εἰρήνην 'peace', some manuscripts read εἰρήνην σου 'your peace' and some manuscripts read εἰρήνην σοι 'peace to you'. GNT reads εἰρήνην 'peace' with a B decision, indicating that the text is almost certain. Εἰρήνην σου 'your peace' is read by KJV.

LEXICON—a. ἐπί (LN 89.27): 'because of' [LN]. The phrase 'he wept because of it' is translated 'he wept over it' [Arn, WBC; HCSB, KJV, NASB, NET, NIV, NRSV, REB, TEV], 'he wept for it' [BECNT], 'he sobbed over it' [Lns], 'he cried for it' [NCV], 'he burst into tears over it' [NTC], 'he cried' [CEV], 'he began to cry' [GW, NLT]. The clause 'having seen the city, he wept because of it' is translated 'he wept at the sight of the city' [AB]. This means that Jesus burst into tears [Rb], or into sobbing [TNTC]. It was audible weeping [EGT, Rb], or wailing and sobbing [BECNT, ICC].

b. πρός (LN 89.7) (BAGD III.5.b. p. 710): 'with respect to' [LN], 'with regard to' [BAGD]. The phrase 'the things with respect to peace' is translated 'what would bring peace' [HCSB], 'what would bring you peace' [GW, NCV, NIV], 'what will bring them peace' [CEV], 'what would make for peace' [AB], 'the things for peace' [Lns], 'the things which/that make for peace' [BECNT; NASB, NET, NRSV], 'the things which belong unto thy peace' [KJV], 'the things that pertain to peace' [Arn, NTC], 'what concerns peace' [WBC], 'the way that leads to peace' [REB], 'the way of peace' [NLT], 'what is needed for peace' [TEV].

c. aorist pass. indic. of κρύπτω (LN 28.79) (BAGD 2.a. p. 454): 'to be hidden' [BAGD, LN], 'to be concealed' [BAGD, LN]. The phrase 'now it was hidden from your eyes' is translated 'now it/this is hidden from your eyes' [BECNT, WBC; HCSB, NIV], 'now they are hidden from your eyes' [Arn, NTC; KJV, NET, NRSV], 'now they have been hidden from your eyes' [NASB], 'now they were hid from thy eyes' [Lns], 'it is hidden from your sight' [REB], 'as it is, that is hidden from your sight' [AB], 'now it is hidden, so you cannot see it' [GW], 'now it is hidden from you' [NCV], 'now it is hidden from them' [CEV], 'now it is too late, and peace is hidden from you' [NLT], 'now you cannot see it' [TEV].

QUESTION—Why did Jesus weep?

The reason for Jesus' grief is explained in the next verse, it is the sad condition of the city [AB]. He wept because of his grief over Jerusalem or because he pitied it [TH]. He wept because of the terrible disasters that would come to the city [Arn, NAC, NIGTC, TH], or because of the judgment that was coming to this wicked city [Arn, Lns]. Jesus' grief was caused by the sight of the city and the thought of what might have been [ICC]. He wept for its lost opportunity [TNTC]. The words of the Pharisees in 19:39 proved to Jesus that the Jewish leaders were persisting in their rejection of him [NIC].

QUESTION—Who was Jesus speaking to in 19:42?

Jesus was addressing the city as though it were a person and 'Jerusalem' refers to the inhabitants of the city [TG]. The city stands for the nation of Israel [BECNT, NAC]. However, translating this as referring to the people of the city may bring up a problem in 19:44 where there is a reference to the city's stones, and the city having people within its walls [TG].

QUESTION—What is the meaning of the unfinished conditional sentence 'If you knew…'?

It is a contrary to fact condition that is not completed [BECNT, EGT, ICC, Lns, NAC, NIGTC, NTC]. The implied consequence to the condition is 'then the future would hold something better for you' [NIGTC], or 'your doom would be averted' [Arn], or 'it would be pleasing to me' [AB, BECNT, NIGTC]. This is translated as being broken off: 'If you knew this day what would bring peace—but now it is hidden from your eyes' [HCSB; similarly NIV]. Breaking off the sentence indicates strong emotion [ICC, NAC]. It is equivalent to a wish that could not be fulfilled [AB, Arn, BECNT, ICC, TH]. It is translated as a wish: 'Would that you, even you, had recognized this day what would make for peace!' [AB]. The word 'only' is supplied to indicate that it is a wish: 'If *only* you had known on this day!' [BECNT, NIGTC, NTC, TH, WBC; NET, NRSV, REB]. This is translated as a statement: 'I wish you knew today what would bring you peace' [NCV],

'It is too bad that today your people don't know what will bring them peace!' [CEV].

QUESTION—Does the phrase καὶ σύ mean 'even you' or 'also you'?

1. It means 'even you' [AB, Gdt, ICC, Lns, NAC, NIC, NIGTC, NTC, Rb; KJV, NASB, NET, NIV, NRSV]. It makes the word 'you' emphatic [NAC]. 'Even you inhabitants of Jerusalem' is in contrast with Jesus' disciples from Galilee and abroad [Gdt]. Jesus had made such efforts to bring peace to Jerusalem [Lns]. 'Even you' may be meant to draw attention to the significance of the name 'Jerusalem' as being the city of peace [NIGTC].
2. It means 'you also' as well as my disciples [Alf, Arn, EGT, My, TH, WBC]. It means 'you inhabitants of Jerusalem as well as my disciples who do know the things that make for peace' [Arn, EGT]. If only the people of Jerusalem would also welcome Jesus as did the crowd of his disciples when he had approached Jerusalem [WBC]. The disciples of Jesus would be saved by their knowledge, but the inhabitants of Jerusalem must know for themselves [EGT].
3. This phrase is not made explicit [BECNT; CEV, GW, HCSB, NCV, NLT, REB, TEV]. Probably they take the phrase to indicate that 'you' is emphatic.

QUESTION—What are 'the things with respect to peace'?

These are the conditions that produce peace [AB, TH; CEV, GW, HCSB, NCV, NIV, NRSV] and this especially includes salvation for God's people [EGT, NIGTC, TG]. This speaks of peace with God, the message of the gospel [BECNT]. This speaks of the messianic peace that is offered [NAC]. The necessary ingredient for peace is a right relationship with God [Crd, TNTC]. The things required for peace are the king who brings peace and the response of the people who should welcome the king [NICNT]. The things for peace are recognizing God's purpose and being committed to it [Su]. This concerns how they would have had a share in the peace of heaven that was being offered by Jesus [AB]. They needed to know that they could find true peace by accepting Jesus as king [NIBC].

QUESTION—Why were they blinded?

1. Blindness was the result of their inability to see [Arn, BECNT, Lns, NIC, TH, WBC]: it is hidden from your sight. This states a simple fact [Arn]. Their persistence in unbelief has blinded them to the opportunities for redemption and this is their own fault [NIC]. Their blindness resulted from their failure to respond [BECNT].
2. This blindness was brought about by God [AB, EGT, ICC, MGC, My, NAC, NIGTC, NTC]: God has hidden this from your sight. This is a theological passive [AB]. The city has a history of rejecting those whom God has sent to it and now God has given up Jerusalem [NIGTC]. This is a penalty for their long course of moral perversity [EGT], or their irresponsibility [AB]. When the sinners hardened themselves, God in turn hardened them [NTC].

19:43 Because days[a] will-come upon you and your enemies will-construct a-barricade[b] against-you and they-will-surround you and will-hem-in[c] you from-every-side[d]

LEXICON—a. ἡμέρα (LN 67.142) (BAGD 4.b. p. 347): 'day, time' [BAGD, LN]. The phrase 'days will come upon you' [Arn, Lns, NTC, WBC] is also translated 'the days will come upon/on you' [HCSB, KJV, NASB, NET, NIV, NRSV], 'days are coming upon you' [BECNT], 'a time will come upon you' [REB], 'the time is coming upon you' [AB], 'the time is coming' [NCV], 'the time will come' [CEV, GW, TEV], 'before long' [NLT].

b. χάραξ (LN **7.60**) (BAGD 2. p. 876): 'barricade' [**LN**], 'palisade' [BAGD, LN]. The phrase 'will construct a barricade against you and they will surround you' is translated 'will throw up a barricade against you, and surround you' [NASB], 'will throw up a palisade against you, encircle you' [NTC], 'will put a wall of palisades about you and will enclose you' [Arn], 'will surround you with barricades, blockade you' [TEV], 'will build an embankment against you, and surround you' [HCSB, NET], 'will build an embankment against you and encircle you' [NIV], 'will throw up an embankment against you, encircle you' [AB], 'will build walls around you to attack you. Armies will surround you' [CEV], 'will build a wall to surround you' [GW], 'will build a wall around you' [NCV], 'will cast a wall around you and will surround you' [BECNT], 'will build ramparts against your walls and encircle you' [NLT], 'will set up ramparts around you and surround you' [NRSV], 'will throw a rampart around thee and will encircle thee' [Lns], 'will set up siege mounds against you, and encircle you' [WBC], 'will set up siege-works against you; they will encircle you' [REB], 'shall cast a trench about thee, and compass thee round' [KJV].

c. fut. act. indic. of συνέχω (LN 19.45) (BAGD 3. p. 789): 'to press in, to crowd around' [LN], 'to press hard, to crowd' [BAGD]. The phrase 'will hem you in' [AB, BECNT, Lns, NTC; HCSB, NASB, NIV, NRSV, REB], is also translated 'will close in on you' [CEV, NET, TEV], 'will close you in' [GW], 'will hold you in' [NCV], 'will press you' [WBC], 'will bear down on you' [Arn], 'shall keep thee in' [KJV]. The phrase 'will hem you in from every side' is translated 'will close in on you' [NLT]. The verb indicates that the enemy will press its attack on the city [BECNT, NAC]. The verb indicates movement and refers to the attacks of the enemy against the city [TH].

d. πάντοθεν (LN **84.7**) (BAGD p. 608): 'from every side' [**LN**; CEV, NET], 'on every side' [AB, Lns, WBC; GW, HCSB, KJV, NASB, NIV, NRSV], 'on all sides' [BECNT; NCV], 'from all sides' [Arn], 'from all directions' [BAGD, LN, NTC], 'at every point' [REB], not explicit [NLT].

QUESTION—What relationship is indicated by ὅτι 'because'?
1. It indicates the reason Jesus fervently desired that they know the things concerning peace [Alf, ICC, NIGTC]: I wish you had known what could bring you peace, because now you must suffer terribly. Jesus wished that they knew, because the consequences for not knowing were so terrible [ICC, NIGTC].
2. It proves the fact that the things for peace were hidden from them [Lns, My]: it was hidden from your eyes, because the reverse of peace will come. The certainty of the terrible future proves that the things of peace have become hidden to them [My]. It states the evidence that Jerusalem did not know and that the things for peace were hidden from her [Lns].

QUESTION—What was the barricade and what is the significance of constructing a barricade around the city?

A χάραξ is a stake and the singular noun here is used collectively so that this means that palisades will surround the besieged city [Arn, TNTC]. The noun for a single stake came to refer to a palisade or a rampart, and here a palisaded mound [Alf, ICC]. They built a palisade of wooden stakes filled in with branches and earth, probably adding a ditch [Gdt]. The word can mean wooden barricades, or earthworks, or a combination of the two [NET]. The barricade is a palisaded wall or rampart [Lns]. Barricades or earthen mounds were placed around the city [BECNT]. This describes an embankment around the city [MGC]. This clearly describes the Roman attack on Jerusalem in A.D. 70 [BECNT]. The Romans erected a palisade and then it was burned down by the Jews, whereupon the Romans built a stone siege-dyke [EGT, ICC, NAC, NIGTC, TNTC]. The verb περικυκλώσουσίν 'they will surround' may refer to the building of the siege-dyke or may simply mean that that the siege-dyke extended all around Jerusalem [NAC, NIGTC]. This describes a siege of the city [BECNT, Su, TH, TNTC, WBC]. The rampart was a stronghold to protect the besiegers from attacks by the people in the city, and it surrounded the city so that no one could get out [TH]. The enemies would build the bank to protect themselves and serve as a base from launching attacks against the city [NTC, TNTC]. They did this for siege purposes and to cut off any way to escape from the city [Su, WBC].

19:44 And they-will-raze[a] you and your children within you, and they-will-not -leave[b] a-stone upon stone within you, because you-did- not -know the time of-your visitation.[c]

LEXICON—a. fut. act. indic. of ἐδαφίζω (LN **20.64**) (BAGD p. 217): 'to raze' [LN], 'to raze to the ground' [BAGD, LN], 'to dash to the ground, to kill' [BAGD]. To raze or tear down a population is used figuratively to mean to destroy or kill them [LN]. The clause 'they will raze you and your children within you' is translated 'they will throw down both you and the children within you' [WBC], 'shall lay thee even with the ground, and thy children within thee' [KJV], 'they will level you to the ground and your children within you' [NASB], 'they will bring you to the ground, you and your children within your walls' [REB], 'they will crush you to the ground, and your children with you' [NLT], 'they will crush you to the ground, you and your children within you' [NRSV], 'they will crush you and your children within you to the ground' [HCSB], 'they will cast to the ground you and your children in your midst' [Arn], 'they will dash you and your children within you to the ground' [AB, BECNT; similarly Lns; NET], 'they will dash to the ground you and your children along with you' [NTC], 'they will dash you to the ground, you and the children within your walls' [NIV], 'they will demolish you—you and your children within your walls' [NET], 'they will destroy you and all your people' [NCV], 'they will completely destroy you and the people within your walls' [TEV]. This verb collates differently in some translations when applied to a city and to the inhabitants within the city [Alf, BAGD, EGT, LN, NIGTC, TG, TH] and this clause is therefore translated 'they will raze you to the ground and kill those who live in you' [**LN**], 'they will level you to the ground and kill your people' [CEV, GW].

b. fut. act. indic. of ἀφίημι (LN **85.62**): 'to leave' [LN]. The clause 'they will not leave a stone upon stone within you' [AB; similarly Arn, BECNT, Lns, NTC; HCSB, KJV, NASB, NRSV] is also translated 'they will not leave within you one stone on top of another' [NET], 'they will not leave you one stone standing on another' [REB], 'they will not leave one stone on another' [NIV], 'one stone will not be left on top of another' [GW], 'not one stone in your buildings will be left on top of another' [CEV], 'not one stone will be left on another' [NCV], 'not a single stone will they leave in its place' [TEV], 'no stone in you will be left upon another' [WBC], 'your enemies will not leave a single stone in place' [NLT]. 'Leave' does not mean that they will take the stones away, but that they will not leave the stones where they belong [Su].

c. ἐπισκοπή (LN **34.51**) (BAGD 1. p. 299): 'visitation' [BAGD, LN], 'coming' [LN]. The phrase 'the time of your visitation' [AB, Arn, BECNT, WBC; HCSB, KJV] is also translated 'the time of your visitation from God' [NET, NRSV], 'the time of God's visitation' [REB], 'the time of God's coming to you' [NIV], 'the time of God's coming to save you' [**LN**], 'the time when God came to save you' [NCV, TEV], 'the time when God came to help you' [GW], 'the season of thy visitation' [Lns], 'the season when God in his grace visited you' [NTC], '(you did not see that) God had come to save you' [CEV], '(you rejected) the opportunity God offered you' [NLT]. This verb means to look upon someone either in blessing or in punishment [TH]. Here it has the positive meaning of blessing [Arn, BECNT, NIC, NIVS, TG, TNTC, WBC].

QUESTION—Is the statement about no stone being left on another to be taken literally?

This is figurative language for the thoroughness of the leveling of the city to the ground, but it does not literally refer to every single stone so that no part of the wall would still be standing [Arn]. In A.D. 70 the walls of Jerusalem were mostly leveled but some towers and at least one section of the wall were left standing [NIGTC]. This is stated as an hyperbole in regard to the city [NAC, NIC], but it literally happened to the temple [NIC]. It is an idiom for total destruction [NET].

QUESTION—Who are the city's children within it?

The city is figuratively referred to as a mother and its children are its inhabitants [AB, Lns, My]. They are inhabitants of all ages, not just the children [ICC, My, NIC, NIGTC, Su, TG]. This speaks of the fall of the nation of Israel and pictures the nation and its citizens dying. Since the next picture is of the razed city, this clause is best taken to be a picture of dead bodies [BECNT].

QUESTION—What relationship is indicated by the phrase ἀνθ' ὧν 'because'?

It indicates the reason for the destruction of Jerusalem by its enemies [BECNT, NAC, NIBC, TG, TNTC]. The reason is that the nation missed the opportunity to respond to God's visitation [BECNT].

QUESTION—What is meant by 'the time of your visitation'?

This is the time God appointed to bring aid and blessings, the time when the Son of God came to proclaim the message of salvation [Arn]. It is God's coming with grace and power [BECNT]. It is God's visit to them in the person of Jesus to bring salvation and blessing [NIC, NIVS]. The visitation was intended to be the opportunity of salvation preached by Jesus, but the visitation for blessing came to be the basis for judgment when it wasn't recognized [NIGTC]. The time of visitation was the whole of Jesus' ministry which was now coming to an end [WBC]. That the people did not know the time of visitation was not ignorance of the fact but it was their refusal to acknowledge that God had come to save them [TG, TNTC].

DISCOURSE UNIT: 19:45–24:53 [BECNT]. The topic is Jerusalem: the innocent one slain and raised.

DISCOURSE UNIT: 19:45–21:38 [TNTC]. The topic is Jesus in Jerusalem.

DISCOURSE UNIT: 19:45–21:4 [BECNT]. The topic is controversy in Jerusalem.

DISCOURSE UNIT: 19:45–48 [BECNT, NICNT, Su; CEV, GW, HCSB, NASB, NCV, NET, NIV, NLT, NRSV, TEV]. The topic is Jesus going to the temple [NCV, TEV], Jesus in the temple [CEV, NIV], preparing the temple for teaching [NICNT], cleansing the temple [BECNT; NET], cleansing the temple complex [HCSB], Jesus cleanses the temple [NRSV], Jesus clears the temple [NLT], traders driven from the temple [NASB], Jesus throws out the moneychangers [GW], Monday—a day of authority [Su].

DISCOURSE UNIT: 19:45–46 [AB, NIGTC, Su, TNTC, WBC]. The topic is the cleansing of the temple [AB, NIGTC, Su, TNTC], symbolic protest in the temple [WBC].

19:45 And having-entered into the temple[a] he-began to-expel[b] the (ones who) were-selling,

TEXT—Following τοὺς πωλοῦντας 'the ones selling', some manuscripts add ἐν αὐτῷ καὶ ἀγοράζοντας 'in it and buying'. GNT does not mention this variant. Ἐν αὐτῷ καὶ ἀγοράζοντας 'in it and buying' is added by KJV.

LEXICON—a. ἱερόν (LN 7.16) (BAGD 2. p. 372): 'temple' [Arn, BAGD, BECNT, LN, WBC; CEV, KJV, NASB, NRSV, REB], 'the Temple' [Lns; NCV, NLT, TEV], 'temple courts' [NET], 'temple courtyard' [GW], 'temple area' [AB, NTC; NIV], 'temple complex' [HCSB]. This noun refers to the Temple in Jerusalem, and the word includes the whole temple precinct with its buildings and courtyards [BAGD, LN].

b. pres. act. indic. of ἐκβάλλω (LN 15.44) (BAGD 1. p. 237): 'to expel, to drive out' [BAGD, LN], 'to send away' [LN]. This verb includes the idea of force [BAGD]. The phrase 'he began to expel' [WBC] is also translated 'he began to drive out' [Arn, NTC; NASB, NET, NIV, NLT, NRSV, REB, TEV], 'he started to drive out' [AB], 'he began to throw out' [Lns; GW, HCSB, NCV], 'he began to cast out' [BECNT; KJV], 'he started chasing out' [CEV].

QUESTION—When did this incident take place?

From the parallel passage in Mark 11:11–15, we learn that it was the day following the triumphal entry into Jerusalem [Gdt, ICC, NIC, NIVS, TNTC]. In Luke it could be taken to refer to the same day of the triumphal entry, but since Luke does not note the time, it is not in conflict with Mark [ICC].

QUESTION—In what part of the temple precincts did this incident take place?

It was not inside the sanctuary itself, but in one of the outer courts, the Court of the Gentiles where merchants carried on their businesses [AB, Arn, BECNT, Gdt, ICC, NAC, NIC, NIGTC, NTC, TG, TH; NET]. In this courtyard there would be much activity going on among buyers and sellers accompanied by the noise, filth, and stench produced by the many animals [NTC]. It was not necessary that the merchants be in courtyard [TNTC], and it is possible that they had been recently moved there for convenience [NET].

QUESTION—What was being sold in the temple?

People from distant places came to celebrate the Passover and they had to purchase animals for the Passover sacrifices. Sacrifices not only required animals, but wine, oil, and salt [NIGTC]. The other Gospels tell what was being sold: oxen, sheep, and pigeons [Su]. Also Temple officers were selling money by exchanging the foreign money brought by people from outside Judea for the image-less Judean coins that were required for paying the Temple tax [Su]. The term 'selling' is probably used broadly to include the money changers that are mentioned in Mark 11:15 and Matt. 21:12 who mention the two groups [BECNT]. Or, Luke mentions only the selling of the animals used for sacrifice and the things like wine and oil used for other offerings, leaving out any reference to the money-changers [AB, Arn, EGT, ICC, NAC, NIGTC]. The phrase 'the ones selling' is translated 'the people/those who were selling things there' [CEV, GW, NCV, NET, NRSV], 'the merchants' [TEV], 'the traders' [REB], '(to drive out) the merchants from their stalls' [NLT].

QUESTION—How did Jesus expel the ones who were selling?

The text is not explicit about the means of expelling them; but it could be by physical means or by an authoritative command [TG]. The first time he did this is described by John in 2:13–17 and at that time Jesus made a whip out of cords and used that to expel them, but we don't know that he did so at this time [NTC]. Matthew and Mark tell about Jesus upsetting tables and chairs and it must have been his intense indignation that caused the merchants to flee from him [Arn].

19:46 saying to-them, It-has-been-written 'And my house will-be a-house[a] of-prayer', but you made it a-cave[b] of-robbers.

TEXT—Instead of καὶ ἔσται ὁ οἶκός μου οἶκος προσευχῆς 'and my house will be a house of prayer', some manuscripts read ὁ οἶκός μου οἶκος προσευχῆς ἐστιν 'my house is a house of prayer'. GNT does not mention this variant. Ὁ οἶκός μου οἶκος προσευχῆς ἐστιν 'my house is a house of prayer' is read by KJV.

LEXICON—a. οἶκος (LN 7.2) (BAGD 1.a.b. p. 560): 'house' [BAGD, LN], 'temple' [LN]. The clause 'my house will be a house of prayer' [AB, Arn, BECNT, Lns, NTC, WBC; GW, HCSB, NASB, NET, NIV, NRSV, REB] is also translated 'my Temple will be a house of prayer' [TEV], 'my Temple will be a house for prayer' [NCV], 'my Temple will be a place of prayer' [NLT], 'my house should be a place of worship' [CEV], 'my house is the house of prayer' [KJV].

b. σπήλαιον (LN 1.57) (BAGD p. 762): 'cave, den' [BAGD, LN], 'hideout' [LN]. The phrase 'a cave of robbers' is translated 'a den of thieves' [HCSB, KJV, NLT], 'a den of robbers' [AB, Arn, BECNT, WBC; NET, NIV, NRSV], 'a robbers' den' [Lns, NTC; NASB], 'a gathering place for thieves' [GW], 'a hideout for thieves' [TEV], 'a hideout for robbers' [NCV], 'a place where robbers hide' [CEV], 'a bandits' cave' [REB].

QUESTION—What Scripture did Jesus refer to?

Jesus quoted Isaiah 56:7 'my house will be called a house of prayer for all nations' [Lns]. In this passage, Isaiah wrote what God said [TG, TH]. Instead of Mark's future tense 'will be called', Luke has 'it will be' so that here it is a legal stipulation instead of a prophecy of what shall happen for all nations as presented in Isaiah [WBC]. Here it means that the temple should be a place of appropriate worship [BECNT]. The quotation begins with καί 'and', indicating that the statement from the OT was taken from a context that had something else preceding it [Arn]. A translation can leave out this conjunction [TH], and most translations omit it [AB, Arn, BECNT, NTC, WBC; all versions except NASB]. The next sentence 'But you made it a cave of robbers' is Jesus' comment on the quote and recalls the words of Jeremiah 7:11 'Has this house, which bears my name, become a den of robbers to you?' [NTC, TG, TH]. Jesus used the passage from the prophets as the reason for his action [Arn, BECNT, NAC].

QUESTION—In what sense had God's house become a den of robbers?

It was legitimate to sell sacrificial animals, so it is implied that the selling was accompanied by greedy, commercial rivalry [NIGTC]. Their business had become a source of graft [WBC]. Worshippers who came for the Passover were being overcharged and cheated [MGC, NIBC]. It does not mean that they were robbing God's house, but that they had made it their den as they robbed others [Lns].

DISCOURSE UNIT: 19:47–48 [AB, NIGTC, Su, TNTC, WBC]. The topic is the beginning of a week of teaching [Su], Jesus teaches in the temple [NIGTC, TNTC], the leaders' rejection of Jesus' teaching [AB], hostility from the leaders, with adulation from the people [WBC].

19:47 **And he-was teaching daily in the temple. And the chief-priests and the scribes and (also) the prominent[b] (ones) of-the people were-seeking[a] to-kill him,**

LEXICON—a. imperf. act. indic. of ζητέω (LN 27.34): 'to search, to try to find out' [LN]. The phrase 'were seeking to kill him' is translated 'sought to destroy him' [KJV], 'looked for a way to kill him' [GW], 'kept looking for a way to kill him' [NRSV], 'were seeking to destroy him' [Arn, BECNT, Lns, WBC], 'were looking for a way to destroy him' [HCSB], 'were trying to destroy him' [NTC; NASB], 'were trying to kill him' [NIV], 'tried to have him killed' [CEV], 'wanted to kill him/Jesus' [NCV, TEV], 'wanted to bring about his death' [REB], 'were trying to assassinate him' [NET], 'began planning how to kill him' [NLT], 'kept looking for a way to do away with him' [AB]. The imperfect tense indicates that they attempted to do this, they were trying to find a way to kill Jesus [NTC, Rb; CEV, NASB, NET]. The tense indicates repetition, they kept trying to find a way [AB, BECNT, TG, TH]. This plan had been hatched when Lazarus had been raised from death [Arn]. Constantly they were on the lookout for an excuse to have Jesus killed [BECNT]. They were seeking some type of judicial murder [Lns].

b. πρῶτος (LN 87.45) (BAGD 1.c.β. p. 726): 'prominent' [BAGD, LN], 'important, foremost' [LN]. The phrase 'the prominent ones of the people' is translated 'the prominent leaders among the people' [NET], 'the leaders of the people' [AB, BECNT; GW, HCSB, NRSV, TEV], 'the leading men of the people' [Arn], 'the leading men among the people' [NTC], 'the leaders among the people' [NIV], 'some of the leaders of the people' [NCV], 'the leading men among the people' [NASB], 'the other leaders of the people' [NLT], 'the leaders of the People' [WBC], 'the chief of the people' [KJV], 'the foremost of people' [Lns], 'the leading citizens' [REB], 'some other important people' [CEV].

QUESTION—When did Jesus teach in the temple courtyard?

After expelling the sellers, Jesus kept teaching in the temple [Lns, TH]. He was teaching in the Temple from Sunday until he left the temple for good on Tuesday [Arn, Lns]. However, he spent his nights at Bethany or elsewhere outside the city [Lns].

QUESTION—Who were the three groups of men and why did they seek to kill Jesus?

The three groups composed the kind of men who were members of the Sanhedrin [AB, Arn, Gdt, MGC, NAC, NICNT, NIGTC, Su]. All three groups were members of the Sanhedrin, 'the prominent ones of the people' being the lay elders [Arn, Gdt, NIGTC]. The separate mention of the prominent ones of the people may indicate that the chief priests and scribes were the instigators of the plot and then the prominent ones yielded under pressure [Gdt]. Or, 'the prominent ones of the people' were not the 'elders' of the Sanhedrin referred to in 20:1, but were prominent leaders who were in full accord with the Sanhedrin [EGT, ICC, Lns, TH]. The prominent men are mentioned separately in the sentence and probably they were leading citizens [TH]. They are added as a sort of an afterthought and were socially important laymen who were in agreement with the religious professionals [EGT]. The construction of the sentence indicates that the chief priests and scribes were the real instigators and the chief laymen only yielded to their pressure [Gdt]. The chief priests opposed Jesus because he was taking over their special province, the Temple. The scribes opposed Jesus because he didn't accept their interpretation of the Law. The principal men opposed Jesus because they feared that he would become a popular revolutionist [Su].

19:48 and they-were- not -finding^a anything that they-might-do, because all the people hung-on^b him listening.

LEXICON—a. imperf. act. indic. of εὑρίσκω (LN **27.1**) (BAGD 2. p. 325): 'to find' [AB, Arn, BAGD, BECNT, **LN**, Lns, NTC; all versions except NCV, NLT], 'to discover' [BAGD, LN], 'to know' [NCV], 'to think of' [NLT], 'to work out' [WBC].

b. aorist mid. indic. of ἐκκρέμαμαι (LN **30.34, 68.15**) (BAGD 2. p. 242): 'to hang on' [BAGD], 'to pay close attention, to consider eagerly' [LN (30.34)], 'to continue intently' [LN (68.15)]. The phrase 'all the people hung on him listening' is translated 'all the people were hanging to him by hearing' [Lns], 'all the people hung on his words' [BECNT; NET, NIV], 'the people all hung on his words' [AB; REB], 'all the people hung on every word he said' [NLT], 'all the People hung upon his words' [WBC], 'all the people were hanging on his words' [NTC], 'all the people were hanging on to every word he said' [NASB], 'all the people hung on his lips as they listened' [Arn], 'all the people kept listening eagerly' [**LN** (68.15)], 'all the people paid close attention as they listened to him' [**LN** (30.34)], 'all the people were listening closely to him' [NCV], 'all the people were eager to hear him' [GW], 'everyone else was eager to listen to him' [CEV], 'all the people were very attentive to hear him' [KJV], 'all the people were captivated by what they heard' [HCSB], 'all the people were spellbound by what they heard' [NRSV], 'all the people kept listening to him, not wanting to miss a single word' [TEV].

QUESTION—What relationship is indicated by γάρ 'because' in the last clause?

This gives the reason they could find no way to have Jesus killed [NET]. They feared the people who were attracted to Jesus' teaching [Lns]. Jesus was too popular for them to act [BECNT]. Jesus was surrounded by too many people [NIBC]. They feared that the people would rise against the religious authorities [Arn]. These people were the pilgrims who had come from all parts of the country for the Passover, not the inhabitants of Jerusalem who followed the hostility of the religious leaders [Lns]. Or, they included the people of Jerusalem who would soon turn against Jesus [BECNT]. The 'People' were God's people who were taken up with Jesus' teaching [WBC].

DISCOURSE UNIT: 20:1–22:6 [Su]. The topic is Tuesday—a day of controversy and teaching.

DISCOURSE UNIT: 20:1–21:38 [NICNT, NIGTC]. The topic is teaching in the Jerusalem temple.

DISCOURSE UNIT: 20:1–19 [Su]. The topic is the controversy with the Sanhedrin over authority.

DISCOURSE UNIT: 20:1–8 [AB, BECNT, NAC, NICNT, NIGTC, TNTC, WBC; CEV, HCSB, NCV, NET, NRSV, TEV]. The topic is the authority of Jesus [NET], Jewish leaders question Jesus [NCV], a question about Jesus' authority [AB, BECNT, NAC, NICNT, NIGTC, TNTC, WBC; CEV, GW, NASB, NIV, NLT, TEV], the authority of Jesus questioned [HCSB, NRSV], the authority of Jesus challenged [GW, NASB, NIV, NLT].

20:1 **And it-happened on one of-the days (while) teaching the people in the temple and announcing-the-good-news,**[a] **the chief-priests and the scribes with the elders approached**[b]

TEXT—Instead of τῶν ἡμερῶν 'the days', some manuscripts read τῶν ἡμερῶν ἐκείνων 'those days'. GNT does not mention this variant. Τῶν ἡμερῶν ἐκείνων 'those days' is read by KJV.

LEXICON—a. pres. mid. participle of εὐαγγελίζω (LN 33.215) (BAGD 1. p. 317): 'to announce good news'. See translations of this word at 1:19 and 16:16. This word also occurs at 2:10; 3:18: 4:18, 43; 7:22; 8:1; 9:6.

b. aorist act. indic. of ἐφίσταμαι (LN 17.5) (BAGD 1.a. p. 330): 'to approach' [BAGD], 'to stand by' [BAGD, LN]. The verb 'approached' is translated 'came' [NRSV, TEV], 'came up' [BECNT, WBC; HCSB, NET], 'came up to him' [NTC; GW, NIV, NLT], 'came upon him' [Lns; KJV], 'confronted him' [NASB, REB], 'came up to talk with him'

[NCV], 'stepped up' [Arn], 'happened to be standing by' [AB], not explicit [CEV]. This verb often has a connotation of suddenness [BAGD, LN]. But it doesn't signify suddenness here [Alf].

QUESTION—Is there a distinction between 'he was teaching' and 'he was announcing the good news'?

1. No distinction between the two verbs is intended [AB, NAC, NIGTC, TNTC, WBC]. The first verb is explained by the second verb [NIGTC, TNTC]: he was teaching the people by announcing the good news. The two verbs are no different in content or substance [NAC].
2. The verbs are different activities [TH]: he was teaching the people and he was also announcing the good news. The difference is that teaching emphasizes explaining what is taught so that people can understand, while announcing the good news has the emphasis on preaching with an appeal to accept the message [TH].

QUESTION—How were the chief priests, scribes, and elders connected and what did they do?

They were all members of the seventy people comprising the Sanhedrin which had authority over all religious matters [AB, Arn, BECNT, MGC, NICNT, Su]. Listing the three groups indicates that they were an official delegation representing the whole body of the Sanhedrin [Arn, Gdt, NAC, NIC, NIGTC, NIVS, NTC, Rb, TNTC]. Probably most of the Sanhedrin was present in this group [Lns]. They suddenly stood there [Lns, Rb]. They came up to join the audience [TH]. They didn't crowd through the audience or interrupt Jesus as he was teaching since Mark 12:27 tells us that they waited until Jesus was walking to another place [Lns].

20:2 **and they-spoke saying to him, Tell us by what authority[a] you-do these (things), or who is the (one) having-given you this authority?**

LEXICON—a. ἐξουσία (LN 37.35) (BAGD 3. p. 278): 'authority' [BAGD, LN]. The phrase 'by what authority' [Lns, NTC, WBC; HCSB, KJV, NASB, NET, NIV, NRSV, REB] is also translated 'by what kind of authority' [Arn, BECNT], 'what authority do you have' [AB], '(tell us) what authority you have' [NCV], 'what right do you have' [CEV, TEV], 'what gives you the right' [GW], 'by whose authority' [NLT].

QUESTION—What is meant by the first question ἐν ποίᾳ ἐξουσίᾳ ταῦτα ποιεῖς 'by what authority do you do these things?'

They were asking what kind of authority Jesus possessed [Arn, BECNT, ICC, NIGTC, Su, TH]. It refers to the sphere or quality of Jesus' authority [BECNT], or the nature of his authority [Gdt, NICNT]. Was it rabbinic, prophetic, or what? [NIGTC]. Was his authority human or divine [Gdt, ICC], ecclesiastical or civil, assumed or conferred? [ICC]. His cleansing of the temple suggested that he was claiming to be a prophet, while his entry into Jerusalem suggested that he was claiming to be the Messiah [Su]. They wanted Jesus to declare publicly the source of his claim to have authority to teach and preach [AB].

LUKE 20:2

QUESTION—What does 'these things' refer to?
1. This refers to all that Jesus was doing [Arn, ICC, Lns, MGC, NAC, NIGTC, NTC, Su]. It refers to all Jesus had done in the Temple [NIGTC]. It refers to all Jesus had done since he arrived in Jerusalem, his entry as the Son of David, the cleansing of the Temple, his teaching, and his healing of blind and lame people in the Temple (Matt. 21:14) [Arn, Lns, Su]. It refers to his authority to forgive sins and to heal on the Sabbath, and to his right to demand total allegiance from his disciples [NAC].
2. This refers primarily to Jesus' teaching in the temple [BECNT, Crd, EGT, TH]. The broad reference to 'these things' centers on his teachings in general, although it does not exclude the temple cleansing [BECNT].
3. This refers primarily to his action of cleansing the temple of those who sold [TG, TNTC; NET]. The phrase 'these things' is stated in general terms but it primarily refers to cleansing the temple [TNTC].

QUESTION—What is the function of the second question introduced by ἤ 'or'?
This refers to the origin of Jesus' authority [Arn, Su, TH]. This question is not completely distinct from the first question [EGT, NAC, NTC, WBC]. This question recasts the first general question in terms of the person who authorized Jesus [AB, WBC]. It is an example of synonymous parallelism [NAC]. Besides asking for the kind of authority Jesus claimed, they wanted to know who gave him that kind of authority [NIGTC]. It anticipates the reply to the first question to be 'By the Messiah's authority', and asks who made him Messiah [ICC, TNTC]. The kind of authority Jesus had will appear when the giver of that authority is known [Lns]. They actually knew that Jesus claimed authority from God and wanted to demand unquestionable evidence for that claim [Su]. The purpose of the questions was to embarrass and discredit Jesus in the minds of the people who up to now had prevented them from having Jesus killed [ICC, NIC].

20:3 And answering he-said to them, I-also will-ask you a-word,[a] and you-tell me. **20:4** The baptism[b] of-John, was-it from[c] heaven[d] or from men?[e]

TEXT—In 20:3, instead of λόγον 'a word', some manuscripts read ἕνα λόγον 'one word'. GNT does not mention this variant. Ἕνα λόγον 'one word' is read by KJV.

LEXICON—a. λόγος (LN 33.98) (BAGD 1.a.b. p. 477): 'word' [BAGD, LN], 'question' [AB, BAGD, BECNT, LN, NTC, WBC; all versions except KJV], 'statement' [LN, Lns], 'matter' [Arn], 'thing' [KJV]. The exact sense of this noun is determined by its context [NTC].
b. βάπτισμα (LN 53.41) (BAGD 1. p. 132): 'baptism' [BAGD, LN]. The phrase 'the baptism of John' [Arn, BECNT, Lns, WBC; HCSB, KJV, NASB, NRSV, REB] is also translated 'John's baptism' [AB, NTC; NET, NIV, NLT], 'when John baptized people' [NCV], 'John's right to baptize' [TEV], '(who gave) John (the right) to baptize?' [CEV], 'John's (right) to baptize' [GW]. The phrase 'John's baptism' includes not only his act of baptizing, but also his whole ministry and message [NAC, NICNT].

c. ἐκ (LN 90.16): 'from' [LN]. The phrase 'was it from heaven' [Arn, BECNT, Lns, NTC; HCSB, KJV, NASB, NET, NIV, REB] is also translated 'did it come from heaven' [NLT, NRSV], 'did it come from God' [TEV], 'was that authority from God' [NCV], 'was it of heavenly origin' [AB], 'was it authorized from heaven' [WBC], 'did John's right to baptize come from heaven' [GW], 'who gave John the right to baptize? Was it God in heaven' [CEV]. The phrase refers to the baptism practiced by John [NET]. This refers to John's authority to baptize [TG].

d. οὐρανός (LN 12.16) (BAGD 3. p. 595): 'heaven' [BAGD, LN]. This location is used figuratively for God who lives there [BAGD, LN]. It is translated 'heaven' [GW, HCSB, KJV, NASB, NET, NIV, NLT, NRSV], 'God' [NCV, REB, TEV], 'God in heaven' [CEV]. 'From heaven' means 'from God' [AB, Arn, NIGTC].

e. ἄνθρωπος (LN 9.1): 'person, human being' [LN]. The phrase 'or from men' [Arn, BECNT, Lns, NTC; HCSB, NASB, NET, NIV] is also translated 'or of men' [KJV], 'or from man' [REB], 'or from humans' [GW], 'or from human beings' [TEV], 'or just from other people' [NCV], 'or did it only come from human beings' [WBC], 'or merely some human being' [CEV], 'or was it of human origin' [AB; NRSV], 'or was it merely human' [NLT].

QUESTION—Was Jesus refusing to answer their question?

There is an implied addition to what Jesus said: 'I also will ask you a question and you tell me, *and then I will tell you by what authority I do these things*' [NIGTC]. It becomes clear in 20:8 that Jesus would answer if they answered first [BECNT, WBC]. If Jesus' opponents would give an honest and correct answer to his question, they would have to accept that the greater one whom John had proclaimed was Jesus and therefore they would know that God had authorized him [ICC, Lns, NTC, TNTC]. They were teachers and therefore should speak first, so Jesus in effect says, 'You ask me to state my authority. I also will ask you for a statement' [ICC].

20:5 And they-discussed^a among themselves saying, If we say, From heaven, he-will-say, Why did-you- not -believe him? 20:6 But if we-say, From men, all the people will-stone us, because they-have-become-convinced^b John is a-prophet.

TEXT—In 20:5, following διὰ τί 'why', some manuscripts add οὖν 'then'. GNT does not mention this variant. Οὖν 'then' is read by KJV.

LEXICON—a. aorist mid. (deponent = act.) indic. of συλλογίζομαι (LN 33.157) (BAGD p. 777): 'to discuss' [BAGD, BECNT, **LN**; HCSB, NET, NIV, NRSV], 'to talk with, to speak with' [LN], 'to talk (this/it) over' [CEV, NLT], 'to talk about (this)' [GW], 'to jointly consider (the matter)' [Arn], 'to reason' [BAGD, Lns, NTC, WBC; KJV, NASB], 'to debate' [AB, BAGD], 'to argue' [NCV, REB], 'to start to argue' [TEV].

b. perf. pass. participle of πείθω (LN 33.301) (BAGD 4. p. 640): 'to be convinced' [AB, Arn, BAGD, BECNT, LN; GW, HCSB, NASB, NET,

NLT, NRSV, REB, TEV], 'to be certain' [BAGD], 'to think' [CEV], 'to be persuaded' [LN, Lns, NTC, WBC; KJV, NIV], 'to believe' [NCV]. The perfect tense indicates a settled state of being persuaded [EGT, Rb].

QUESTION—What did the men from the Sanhedrin do?

They withdrew to consider a way to answer [Arn]. They began whispering among themselves [NAC, NIGTC]. They were debating about the consequences of the answer, not the right answer [AB, Lns, TNTC]. They didn't believe that God had sent John and they were considering how to answer the question without getting into trouble with the masses [Arn, BECNT]. They couldn't give an honest answer of their real belief, and were discussing an answer that would play to the opinion of the people [BECNT].

QUESTION—Why would Jesus say, 'Why did you not believe him?'

If they had believed that John was a prophet from God, then they should have been baptized by John and accepted his message [NIGTC, TNTC]. John had preached about the coming king and identified that king to be Jesus, so if they had accepted John's message they would be forced to admit that Jesus was that king [Su]. If they said that John was from God, they faced the charge that they had not accepted John nor his message to repent and be baptized [MGC, NAC, NIGTC], nor his identification of Jesus as the Messiah [NIC, Su].

QUESTION—Why would the people stone them?

If the Jewish leaders said that John was not a prophet from God as the masses believed, the people would stone them for blasphemy against God who had sent John [Su]. Blasphemy might include insulting someone who acted on God's behalf [NICNT]. Stoning was the punishment for regarding a true prophet as a false one [BECNT, NIGTC].

20:7 **And they-answered (that they) didn't know from-where.**[a] **20:8** **And Jesus said to-them, Neither am- I -telling you by what authority I-do these (things).**

LEXICON—a. πόθεν (LN 84.6): 'from where' [LN]. The phrase 'they didn't know from where' [BECNT] is also translated 'they did not know whence' [Lns], 'they did not know whence it was' [Arn], 'they could not tell whence it was' [KJV], 'they did not know where it was from' [WBC], 'they did not know where it came from' [NASB, NCV, NET, NRSV], 'they did not know its origin' [AB; HCSB], 'they did not know where John's baptism came from' [NTC], 'they didn't know who gave John the right to baptize' [GW], 'they could not tell' [REB]. Instead of an indirect quotation, some translate with a direct quote: 'we don't know' [NLT], 'we don't know where it was from' [NIV, TEV], 'we don't know who gave John the right to baptize' [CEV].

QUESTION—Why did they say that they did not know?

They had the dilemma that there was no good public answer [BECNT]. They could not answer without putting themselves in an impossible position; they were unwilling to say that it was from God and they were afraid to say that it was from men [Su].

QUESTION—Why wouldn't Jesus answer their question?

He was not evading the question, but his questioners have forfeited any right to have their question treated as expressing their genuine interest in learning the truth [WBC]. The correct answer to Jesus' question would also have been the correct answer to their question, so by refusing to answer Jesus' question, they were already refusing to receive Jesus' answer [Lns]. In effect they were saying that as religious experts they had no opinion about the most important religious figure of their time [NET], and they were forfeiting the right to question Jesus about himself [NIC]. If they were incompetent to judge John, then they were incompetent to judge Jesus [AB, ICC, NAC]. Their refusal to answer Jesus' question canceled their right to receive an answer from him [ICC]. An answer was not necessary for the crowd or Luke's readers, so Jesus responded in kind [BECNT]. Jesus' response shows his indignation and contempt for their hypocritical evasion [Gdt].

DISCOURSE UNIT: 20:9–19 [AB, BECNT, NAC, NICNT, NIGTC, WBC; CEV, GW, HCSB, NCV, NET, NIV, NLT, NRSV]. The topic is the renters of a vineyard [CEV], the parable of the tenants [NET, NIV], the parable of the wicked tenants [AB, NAC, NIGTC, WBC; NRSV], the parable of the wicked vinedressers [BECNT], a story of the evil farmers [NLT], the parable of the vineyard owner [HCSB], a story about a vineyard [GW], a story about God's son [NCV], Jerusalem's unfaithful leadership [NICNT].

DISCOURSE UNIT: 20:9–18 [TNTC; NASB, TEV]. The topic is the parable of the wicked husbandmen [TNTC], the parable of the vine–growers [NASB], the parable of the tenants in the vineyard [TEV].

20:9 And he-began to-tell this parable to the people. A-certain man planted a-vineyard and leased[a] it to-farmers and he-went-away (for) a-long time.[b]

TEXT—Instead of ἄνθρωπός [τις] ἐφύτευσεν ἀμπελῶνα 'a certain man planted a vineyard', some manuscripts read ἄνθρωπος ἐφύτευσεν ἀμπελῶνα 'a man planted a vineyard', others read ἀμπελῶνα ἐφύτευσεν ἄνθρωπος 'a vineyard a man planted', and one manuscript reads ἀμπελῶνα ἄνθρωπος ἐφύτευσεν 'a vineyard a man planted'. GNT reads ἄνθρωπός [τις] ἐφύτευσεν ἀμπελῶνα 'a certain man planted a vineyard' with a C decision, and places τις 'a certain' in brackets, indicating that the Committee had difficulty making the decision.

LEXICON—a. aorist mid. indic. of ἐκδίδομαι (LN 57.177) (BAGD p. 238): 'to lease' [BAGD, LN], 'to rent out' [LN], 'to let out for hire' [BAGD, LN]. The phrase 'he leased it to farmers' [AB, WBC] is also translated 'he leased it to some farmers' [NCV], 'he leased it to tenant farmers' [HCSB, NET, NRSV], 'he leased it out to tenant farmers' [NLT], 'he leased it to vine-growers' [Lns], 'leasing it to sharecroppers' [NTC], 'he let it out to tenant farmers', [BECNT], 'he let it out to vine-growers' [REB], 'he let it forth to husbandmen' [KJV], 'he rented it out' [CEV], 'he rented it out to tenants' [Arn, **LN**; TEV], 'he rented it out to vine-growers' [NASB], 'he rented it to some farmers' [NIV], 'he let farmers grow crops on his land in exchange for a part of the harvest' [**LN**], 'he leased it to vineyard workers to obtain from them a share of the grapes from the vineyard' [GW].

b. ἱκανός (LN 59.12) (BAGD 1.b. p. 374): 'long' [BAGD], 'considerable' [BAGD, LN]. The phrase 'a long time' is translated 'for a long time' [all versions except GW, NLT], 'for a long while' [BECNT], 'for a considerable time' [Arn, Lns], 'for quite a time' [WBC], 'for a considerable period' [NTC], 'for quite some time' [AB], 'a long trip' [GW], '(he moved to another country to live) for several years' [NLT].

QUESTION—What is the function of the phrase ἤρξατο λέγειν 'he began to tell'?

It refers to a new turn in Jesus' activity [TH]. Jesus turned from speaking to the Pharisees to tell this parable to the people [Arn, EGT]. After a long pause after the plans of the Sanhedrin delegation were frustrated, Jesus began to speak to a different group of people [ICC]. He was speaking to the people about their leaders [NIGTC]. The word 'began' is not explicit in CEV, GW, NCV, NIV, NLT, REB, and TEV.

QUESTION—How was the rent paid?

The next verse shows that the rental was to be a part of the harvest, not cash [Lns]. It was a long lease and the payment was either a fixed amount of the product or a third or fourth part of it [ICC, TH].

QUESTION—How long a time was the owner away?

We are to understand it to be several years [ICC]. The owner was an absentee landowner, perhaps living outside Galilee or even Judea, and in a case of a new vineyard, it would take four years before the vines reached maturity [NIGTC].

20:10 **And at-the-right-time[a] he-sent a-slave to the farmers in-order-that they-will-give to-him from the fruit[b] of-the vineyard. But the farmers having-beaten[c] (him) sent- him -away empty-handed.[d]**

LEXICON—a. καιρός (LN 67.1) (BAGD 2.a. p. 395): 'time, occasion' [LN], 'right time' [BAGD]. The noun in the dative case here is translated 'in time' [BECNT], 'after a while' [AB], 'when the time came' [WBC], 'at the right time' [GW], 'at the proper time' [Arn, NTC], 'at the season' [KJV], 'in due season' [Lns], 'when the season came' [NRSV, REB], 'at harvest time' [HCSB, NASB, NIV], 'when harvest time came' [NET], 'when it was time to harvest the crop' [CEV], 'when it was time for the grapes to be picked' [NCV], 'when the time came to gather the grapes' [TEV], 'at grape-picking time' [NLT].

b. καρπός (LN 3.33) (BAGD 1.a. p. 404): 'fruit' [BAGD, LN]. The phrase ἀπὸ τοῦ καρποῦ τοῦ ἀμπελῶνος 'from the fruit of the vineyard' is translated 'from the fruit of the vine' [BECNT], 'of the fruit of the vineyard' [KJV], 'part of the fruit of the vineyard' [Lns], 'some fruit from/of the vineyard' [HCSB, NIV], 'of the produce of the vineyard' [Arn], 'some of the produce of the vineyard' [NASB], 'some of the grapes' [NCV], 'his share from the fruit of the vineyard' [WBC], 'his share of the grapes' [CEV], 'his share of the produce' [REB], 'his share of the produce of the vineyard' [NRSV], 'a share of the vineyard's produce' [AB], 'his share of the crop' [NLT], 'a share of the vintage' [NTC], 'his share of the harvest' [TEV], 'a share of the grapes from the vineyard' [GW], 'his portion of the crop' [NET].

c. aorist act. participle of δέρω (LN 19.2) (BAGD p. 175): 'to beat' [BAGD, LN; all versions except CEV, NLT, REB], 'to beat up' [CEV, NLT], 'to thrash' [REB], 'to strike, to whip' [LN]. This verb can refer to striking the slave on the face or body, or include a total physical beating [BECNT].

d. κενός (LN 57.42) (BAGD 1. p. 427): 'empty-handed' [AB, Arn, BECNT, LN, NTC, WBC; HCSB, NASB, NCV, NET, NIV, NLT, NRSV, REB], 'empty' [BAGD, LN, Lns; KJV], 'without anything' [LN; CEV], 'without a thing' [TEV], 'with nothing' [GW].

QUESTION—What was the right time?

It was the time for the fruit [ICC]. This is an expression for the harvest time [Hu, NIGTC]. Sufficient time was given for production [BECNT]. The time between the planting of the vineyard and the first harvest of the grapes would be five years [BECNT, TG, WBC].

QUESTION—Why should the farmers give anything to the slave sent by the owner?

The contract of the leasing of the vineyard stipulated that the owner would receive a share of the product [AB, NIVS, TG, WBC]. Many translate as if the share would be a part of the grapes themselves [NTC; all versions]. The slave was to carry back to the owner the portion of the vintage which the contract indicated would belong to him [NTC]. Or, the share would not be the actual grapes but a share of the money earned by the sale of the wine [TG, TH].

QUESTION—Why would the farmers beat the slave and send him away empty handed?

They sent the slave away without the owner's share of the harvest [TG], probably telling him that the owner's demand was unjust [ICC]. Probably they beat the slave because he refused to go away without receiving the rent [NIGTC]. However, this is a parable and the reason for the beating is that the storyteller decided that this should happen to symbolize the reality behind the story, that Israel had abused the OT prophets [NAC]. There was no mitigating circumstance for their atrocious actions, just as the prophets had been maltreated without cause [Lns]. The tenants had become so successful that they became arrogant and disregarded their contract, determined to keep all that they had produced [AB]. Or, he went away empty-handed because the vineyard was not producing fruit [NET].

20:11 And he-proceeded to-send another slave. But him-also having-beat and mistreated[a] (him) they sent-out empty-handed. **20:12** And he-proceeded to send a third (slave). And also this (one) having-wounded[b] (him) they threw-out.[c]

LEXICON—a. aorist act. participle of ἀτιμάζω (LN 88.127) (BAGD p. 120): 'to mistreat' [LN], 'to treat shamefully' [AB, BAGD, BECNT, LN; GW, HCSB, KJV, NASB, NIV, NLT, TEV], 'to treat outrageously' [NET, REB], 'to treat disgracefully' [NTC], 'to dishonor' [Arn, BAGD], 'to insult' [Lns; NRSV], 'to insult terribly' [CEV], 'to shame' [WBC], 'to show no respect for' [NCV].

    b. aorist act. participle of τραυματίζω (LN **20.28**) (BAGD p. 824): 'to wound' [Arn, BAGD, BECNT, **LN**, Lns, NTC, WBC; all versions except CEV, GW, NLT], 'to cover with wounds' [AB], 'to hurt' [LN], 'to injure' [GW]. This active verb is also translated passively with the slave as the subject: 'to be wounded' [NLT], 'to be beaten terribly' [CEV].

    c. aorist act. indic. of ἐκβάλλω (LN 15.220) (BAGD p. 236): 'to throw out' [BAGD, LN, Lns; GW, HCSB, NCV, NET, NIV, NRSV, TEV], 'to cast out' [BECNT; KJV, NASB], 'to fling out' [NTC; REB], 'to thrust out' [WBC], 'to drive away' [AB, Arn]. The active verb is also translated passively with the slave as the subject: 'to be thrown out' [CEV], 'to be chased away' [NLT].

QUESTION—How soon was the second slave sent?

The next slave may have been sent after the next year's harvest in hope that there was a better harvest and the tenants' attitude might have changed [NIGTC]. The three slaves may have been sent in successive years or during the same season for the same crop [AB, Arn, ICC], but this point is not vital [Arn]. The important point is that the punishment did not follow upon the first outrage [ICC].

QUESTION—In what way did they mistreat him?

It is not clear what they did, but whatever they did, they humiliated him [TG].

QUESTION—In what way did they wound him?

They wounded him by beating him [TG]. Probably they wounded him with some instrument that caused heavy bruises or wounds [TH].

QUESTION—What is the significance about the different treatments of the three slaves?

Each slave was treated worse than the one preceding him [Arn, BECNT, EGT, Gdt, Lns, NAC, TNTC]. The climax will be reached with the son's murder [NAC].

20:13 And the owner of-the vineyard said, What should-I-do? I-will-send my beloved son. Probably/perhaps[a] this (one) they-will-respect.[b]

TEXT—Before ἐντραπήσονται 'they will respect', some manuscripts add ἰδόντες 'having seen'. GNT does not mention this variant. Ἰδόντες 'having seen' is read by KJV.

LEXICON—a. ἴσως (LN **71.11**) (BAGD p. 384): 'probably' [BAGD, LN; GW], 'likely' [**LN**], 'surely' [CEV, NLT, TEV], 'perhaps' [AB, Arn, Lns, NTC, WBC; HCSB, KJV, NASB, NET, NIV, NRSV, REB], 'maybe' [NCV], 'it may be' [BECNT; KJV].
  b. fut. pass. indic. of ἐντρέπομαι, ἐντρέπω (LN **87.11**) (BAGD 2.b. p. 269): 'to respect' [AB, BAGD, BECNT, **LN**, Lns, NTC, WBC; all versions except KJV. 'to show respect to' [LN], 'to treat with respect' [Arn], 'to reverence' [KJV].
QUESTION—What is indicated by the owner's question, 'What should I do'?
  This indicates the owner's reflection over his uncertainty of what to do [BECNT]. Following this question an indication of the solution is added by some: 'I know' [NLT], 'I know what' [CEV]. His inner deliberation resulted in the decision to send his son [Gdt].
QUESTION—How certain is the word ἴσως 'probably'?
  It is more certain than 'perhaps', something like 'it may be', but it is not 'without a doubt' and indicates what may naturally and reasonably be expected [EGT]. It means undoubtedly [Gdt]. Or, it is closer to 'perhaps' than to 'surely' [Hu, NIGTC, TG]. The owner thought that he needed to send someone with sufficient rank and hoped that perhaps they will respect his son [BECNT]. The owner represents God in the matter of his long-suffering and mercy, not by his perplexity [ICC].

20:14 But having-seen him the farmers were-discussing[a] with one-another saying, This (one) is the heir. Let-us-kill him, in-order-that the inheritance[b] may-become ours.
TEXT—Instead of ἀλλήλους 'one another', some manuscripts read ἑαυτούς 'themselves'. GNT does not mention this variant. Ἑαυτούς 'themselves' is read by KJV.
TEXT—Before ἀποκτείνωμεν 'let us kill', some manuscripts add δεῦτε 'come'. GNT does not mention this variant. Δεῦτε 'come' is added by KJV.
LEXICON—a. imperf. mid./pass. (deponent = act.) indic. of διαλογίζομαι (LN 6.11) (BAGD 2. p. 186): 'to discuss' [AB, LN; HCSB, NRSV, REB], 'to converse' [LN], 'to talk it over' [GW], 'to talk the matter over' [NIV], 'to carry on a dialogue' [NTC], 'to consider and discuss' [BAGD], 'to reason' [Lns, WBC; KJV, NASB], 'to say' [BECNT; NCV, NET, NLT, TEV], 'to argue' [Arn]. The imperfect tense indicates that it took some time to come to a decision [TH].
  b. κληρονομία (LN 57.140) (BAGD 1. p. 435): 'inheritance' [AB, Arn, BAGD, BECNT, LN, Lns, NTC, WBC; GW, HCSB, KJV, NASB, NET, NIV, NRSV, REB], 'the vineyard' [CEV, NCV], 'the estate' [NLT], 'his property' [TEV]. The inheritance is what the son would inherit from his father [TG].
QUESTION—How could the tenants expect to get away with killing the son?
  They could claim self-defense by claiming they thought they were repelling a robber and had to kill him [TNTC].

QUESTION—Why did the tenants think they could get the inheritance by killing the heir?

The logic of their plan is hard to understand [BECNT]. The inheritance was the vineyard [TG]. They thought that if there was no other heir, the vineyard would become theirs when the owner died [AB, NAC, NTC, Su, TG]. They might have thought that the coming of the son indicated that the owner had died and the son had come to take possession of the vineyard [MGC, NTC, Su, TNTC], or, they might have thought that the owner had transferred the title to his son [AB, TNTC]. Or, they might claim possession of the land because they had cared for it while the owner was only an absentee landlord [TNTC], Or, if the title was uncertain, someone who had worked the land for three years was presumed to own it if there was no one to challenge them [TNTC]. Or, in the light of the owner's weak responses to their previous actions, they thought that if the son was removed, the vineyard might become theirs [Arn].

20:15 And having-thrown-out^a him outside the vineyard they-killed (him). Then what will-do the owner of-the vineyard to-them?

LEXICON—a. aorist act. participle of ἐκβάλλω (LN 15.220) (BAGD p. 236): 'to throw out' [BAGD, LN] The phrase ἐκβάλλω ἔξω 'to throw out outside' [Lns] is also translated 'to throw out of' [NTC; all versions except KJV, NLT, REB], 'to cast out of' [KJV], 'to cast outside' [BECNT], 'to thrust out of' [WBC], 'to fling out of' [REB], 'to drag out of' [NLT], 'to drive out of' [AB, Arn]. They took him outside the vineyard and then killed him [TG]. See this word at 2:12.

QUESTION—Was the son killed inside or outside of the vineyard?

In Mark 12:8 the son is said to have been killed in the vineyard and then his body was thrown out, but here in Luke and in Matt. 21:39 the order is reversed so that the son was thrown out of the vineyard and then killed. Probably the actual order was that the son was killed in the vineyard as in Mark, while the order in Luke and Matthew was changed to make the mention of his death the climax of the account [NIGTC]. Matthew and Luke changed the order found in Mark so as to picture the historical sequence of Jesus' execution which took place outside of the walls of Jerusalem [AB, EGT, MGC, NAC, Su, WBC; NET], but this point is doubtful [Arn, ICC, NIGTC]. Suggestions for explaining the difference are speculation and we can only recognize the variation in the order of the two events [BECNT].

QUESTION—What is the significance of the question?

Jesus did not expect them to answer since the purpose was to enliven the parable and focus their attention on the main point of the parable [TH], the appliction of the parable [TG]. The question brings out the point of accountability [BECNT]. Jesus broke off from telling the story to ask this question to those who were listening [NIGTC, TH]. The question is in the future tense as if Jesus and his listeners were witnesses to the event [TH].

20:16 He-will-come and will-destroy[a] these farmers and he-will-give[b] the vineyard to-others. And having-heard they said, May-it- never -happen.[c]

LEXICON—a. fut. act. indic. of ἀπόλλυμι (LN 20.31) (BAGD 1.a.α. p. 95): 'to destroy' [AB, Arn, BAGD, BECNT, LN, Lns, WBC; GW, HCSB, KJV, NASB, NET, NRSV], 'to put to death' [BAGD; REB], 'to kill' [BAGD, NTC; CEV, NCV, NIV, NLT, TEV].

b. fut. act. indic. of δίδωμι (LN 57.71): 'to give' [Arn, BECNT, LN, Lns, NTC, WBC; all versions except CEV, NLT, TEV], 'to turn over to' [TEV], 'to let someone have' [CEV], 'to lease' [AB; NLT].

c. aorist mid. (deponent = act.) opt. of γίνομαι (LN 13.107) (BAGD I.3.a. p. 158): 'to happen' [BAGD, LN]. The phrase Μὴ γένοιτο 'May it never happen' is translated 'May this never happen!' [NET], 'May it not come to pass!' [Arn], 'May this never be!' [NTC; NIV], 'May it never be!' [BECNT; NASB], 'Let this never happen!' [NCV], 'No—never!' [HCSB], 'Surely not!' [TEV], 'This must never happen!' [CEV], 'That's unthinkable!' [GW], 'Heaven forbid!' [AB, WBC; NRSV], 'God forbid' [Lns; KJV, REB], 'But God forbid that such a thing should ever happen' [NLT].

QUESTION—How would the owner destroy those wicked farmers?

Probably there would be an armed attack to kill them, or perhaps a legal process of trial for murder would take place [NIGTC].

QUESTION—Would the owner give away his vineyard to others?

The verb means 'to give', but in the parable it probably means that he will continue to own the vineyard and place it under the supervision of others [TG, WBC]. The context indicates that the meaning is 'to lease' [AB; NLT].

QUESTION—Why did the people react by exclaiming, 'May it never happen!'?

It is assumed that the people realized the application of the parable [BECNT, Lns, TH]. This is a strong statement of disagreement to the way the parable ended [BECNT, TG]. This was their reaction to the way the farmers treated the son [MGC]. They expressed their desire that this story would never happen in real life [Arn, Hu, NAC]. The people hoped that it would not come to such a terrible end that the heir would be killed and the farmers would have to be judged [Lns]. The people were reacting against the fact that the Jewish leaders would act in such a way towards God that they must be judged [NIGTC]. The destruction of the farmers foretold the destruction of Jerusalem and the Temple [Su]. That the vineyard, the privileges of the Jews, would be given to others, the Gentiles, made the people cry out in horror [NTC, TNTC]. Or, this refers of a new leadership within Israel and Luke's readers would know that it referred to the church [NIBC]. Or, this was the pious protest made by the members of the Sanhedrin who realized that the parable was directed towards them [Rb].

20:17 And having-looked-straight-at[a] them he-said, What then is this that-has-been-written, (The) stone which the builders rejected,[b] this (one) became for (the) head[c] of-(the)-corner?

LEXICON—a. aorist act. participle of ἐμβλέπω (LN 24.9) (BAGD 1. p. 254): 'to look straight at' [LN, NTC; CEV, GW, NET, REB], 'to look directly at' [LN; NIV], 'to fix one's gaze upon' [BAGD], 'to look at' [AB, Arn, BAGD, BECNT, WBC; HCSB, NASB, NCV, NLT, NRSV, TEV], 'to behold' [KJV], 'to give them a look' [Lns].
  b. aorist act. indic. of ἀποδοκιμάζω (LN 30.117) (BAGD 1. p. 90): 'to reject' [AB, Arn, BAGD, BECNT, LN, Lns, NTC, WBC; all versions except CEV, TEV], 'to reject as worthless' [TEV], 'to declare useless' [BAGD], 'to regard as unworthy' [LN], 'to toss aside' [CEV]. The verb means to reject something after examination [Arn], to reject as being useless [NIGTC] or worthless [TG].
  c. κεφαλή (LN 7.44) (BAGD 2.b. p. 430): 'head' [BAGD]. It is used figuratively for 'the uppermost part, extremity, end, point' [BAGD]. The phrase κεφαλὴν γωνίας 'the head of the corner' [Arn, BECNT, WBC; KJV] is also translated 'corner head' [Lns], 'the chief cornerstone' [NASB], 'the main cornerstone' [REB], 'the cornerstone' [AB, NTC; GW, HCSB, NCV, NET, NLT, NRSV], 'the capstone' [NIV], 'the most important (stone) of all' [CEV, TEV].

QUESTION—What was the point of Jesus looking straight at them before he spoke?
  Jesus gave them a meaningful look [TH]. It indicated that Jesus was going to say something with special meaning [NIGTC, TH]. It imparted impressiveness to what he was going to say [EGT], and made this a solemn occasion [NIGTC]. It added to the tension [Lns].

QUESTION—Why did Jesus ask, 'What then is this that has been written?' and where was it written?
  This was quoted from Psalm 118:22. The significance of Jesus' question is that if their wishes were fulfilled, how could this Scripture come to pass? [Alf, My]. What is written must be fulfilled and if the destruction he spoke about did not occur, how can they explain the passage in the Psalms? [Hu, ICC, TNTC]. The passage proves that Jesus' concluding statement was true [TG]. The link with the parable is not very direct and may be secondary [NIGTC]. Or, this quote stresses the coming of God's retribution to the evil tenants and the vindication of the murdered son [AB]. The rejection of the stone in the Psalm signifies the death of the son (Jesus) in the parable, those who are building and reject the stone signify the farmers (the Jewish leaders in the Sanhedrin) in the parable, and now the Psalm goes on to say that Jesus' death did not eliminate him, rather it made him what the new structure needed [Lns].

QUESTION—What is meant by the stone that was the head of the corner?
  It means that it was the most important stone [Su, TNTC; CEV, TEV], but it is not clear what exactly its function was [ICC, NIVS, TNTC, WBC]. It was

a large stone set at the corner of the foundation to be the cornerstone [AB, BECNT, Gdt, Lns, MGC, NAC, NICNT, NTC; GW, HCSB, NASB, NCV, NET, NLT, NRSV, REB]. This cornerstone was laid with special solemnity at the junction of two conspicuous walls [Gdt]. This was the large stone that binds together two sides of a building [Arn]. It was a stone that was crucial to a building's stability by bearing the weight of two intersecting walls [AB, BECNT, MGC, NAC, NICNT]. Or, the stone did not bear the weight of the building since it is not the whole foundation [Lns], but it is the cornerstone set at the chief corner to govern every angle in the foundation and the whole building [Lns, NTC].

20:18 Everyone having-fallen[a] upon that stone will-be-broken-into-pieces.[b] And upon-whomever it-falls,[c] it-will-crush[d] him.

LEXICON—a. aorist act. participle of πίπτω (LN 15.118) (BAGD B.1.a. p. 659): 'to fall' [Arn, BAGD, BECNT, LN, Lns, NTC, WBC; all versions except CEV, NLT], 'to stumble (over)' [CEV, NLT], 'to trip (over)' [AB].

b. fut. pass. indic. of συνθλάω (LN 19.39) (BAGD p. 790): 'to be broken to/into pieces' [AB, BECNT, LN; HCSB, NASB, NET, NIV, NLT, NRSV], 'to be dashed to pieces' [REB], 'to be smashed to pieces' [NTC], 'to be shattered' [Arn], 'to be cut to pieces' [TEV], 'to be broken' [GW, KJV, NCV], 'to be crushed' [BAGD, WBC], 'to be crushed together' [Lns], 'to get hurt' [CEV].

c. aorist act. subj. of πίπτω (LN 15.118) (BAGD B.1.a. p. 659): 'to fall' [AB, Arn, BAGD, BECNT, LN, Lns, NTC, WBC; all versions]. This is the same verb as item a. above.

d. fut. act. indic. of λικμάω (LN **19.47**) (BAGD p. 474): 'to crush' [AB, BAGD, BECNT, **LN**, NTC; GW, NLT, NRSV], 'to shatter' [WBC], 'to pulverize' [Lns], 'to grind to powder' [HCSB, KJV], 'to turn to dust' [Arn], 'to scatter like dust' [NASB]. This active verb is also translated passively with a person as the subject: 'to be crushed' [NCV, NET, NIV, REB], 'to be crushed to dust' [TEV], 'to be smashed to pieces' [CEV]. The stone will pulverize the man like winnowing the dust out of grain [ICC, Lns]. The person is crushed so fine that he becomes like chaff [BECNT, ICC]. This verb first meant 'to winnow' but being used as a metaphor it came to mean to scatter, flatten, destroy, or shatter [WBC].

QUESTION—How is this statement about 'that' stone connected with the previous quotation about the stone in the preceding verse?

This verse is an expansion of the previous verse [TH]. It elaborates the role of the stone, but the imagery is incompatible with the quotation from Psalm 118 [WBC]. The stone still represents Jesus, but the picture of the stone is now used in an entirely new and independent way [Lns]. The picture is changed considerably since instead of the stone being a cornerstone in a building, it is stone that someone can fall upon or a stone that can fall upon someone [BECNT, TH]. Now the picture does not concern the value of the stone, but its destructive power against a person [TNTC]. Now Jesus describes the stone's significance [BECNT]. This is an allegory that applies OT language from Isa. 8:14–15 to Jesus [Su]. The first half of the verse seems to be an adaptation of Isa. 8:14 and the second half of the verse seems to be an adaptation of Dan. 2:34–35 and 44–45 [AB, Arn, Gdt, Hu, ICC, MGC, NAC, NICNT, NIVS, WBC].

QUESTION—What is the imagery of a person falling upon a stone and being broken into pieces?

The picture is of a person falling from a height and being crushed upon an unyielding rock on the ground [WBC]. Or, the man runs against the stone in blind rage in order to remove or break it up, but instead he is shattered by it [Arn]. Or, this refers to a stone of stumbling (Isa. 8:14) and the picture is of a man stumbling over a stone and injuring himself [EGT, Hu, ICC, Lns, NIBC, NIC, Su]. Perhaps the man tripped when rushing toward his self-determined goals [Su], or he was blind [NIC]. The subject is a person in most commentaries and all translations, but some take the picture to have a different subject: it is of a pot falling upon a stone and breaking into pieces [NIGTC]. Jesus was a stumbling block because of the difficulty in accepting the rejected and crucified Jesus as the Messiah [NIBC]. Jesus was an offense to them [Hu]. This speaks of the inevitable judgment [AB, NAC].

QUESTION—What is the imagery of a stone falling upon a person and crushing him?

Now instead of a man being the actor, it is a stone [ICC]. The picture is of a stone falling from a height and shattering a person standing beneath it [Arn, Gdt, NIC, Su, WBC]. The subject is a person in most commentaries and all translations, but some take the picture to have a different subject: it is of a stone falling upon a pot and destroying it [NIGTC]. Or, it is of a stone used in a trap for small animals and when tripped, the snare would fall on the animal and kill it [Su]. This is a picture of the judgment authority that the Son will have as a ruling figure [BECNT], or a picture of the future judgment [EGT, Hu, TNTC].

DISCOURSE UNIT: 20:19–44 [TNTC]. The topic is attempts to trap Jesus.

DISCOURSE UNIT: 20:19–26 [TNTC; NASB, TEV]. The topic is tribute to Caesar [TNTC; NASB], the question about paying taxes [TEV].

20:19 And the scribes and the chief-priests sought to-lay[a] hands on him in the same hour, but/and they-feared the people, because they-knew that he-spoke this parable against[b] them.

LEXICON—a. aorist act. infin. of ἐπιβάλλω (LN 37.110) (BAGD 1.b. p. 289): 'to lay on' [BAGD]. The phrase ἐπιβάλλω τὰς χεῖρας 'to lay hands on' is an idiom for 'to seize' or 'to arrest' [LN]. Here the expression indicates either arresting someone or seizing someone in order to arrest him [NICNT]. This action is used here in a hostile sense [TH]. The phrase 'they sought to lay hands on him' [Arn, BECNT, Lns, WBC; KJV] is also translated 'they tried to lay hands on him' [NTC; NASB], 'they looked for a way to get their hands on him' [HCSB], 'they wanted to lay hands on him/Jesus' [AB; NRSV], 'they wanted to seize him' [REB], 'they looked for a way to arrest him' [NIV], 'they wanted to arrest him/Jesus' [CEV, GW, NCV, NET, NLT], 'they tried to arrest Jesus' [TEV]. The Jewish leaders were the initiators of the action, and they ordered others to lay hands on Jesus [TH]. See this phrase at 21:12.

b. πρός (LN 90.33) (BAGD III.5.a. p. 710): 'against' [LN], 'with reference to' [BAGD]. The phrase 'he spoke...against them' [BECNT, Lns; NASB] is also translated 'he had spoken against them' [NTC; KJV, NIV], 'he had told...against them' [HCSB, NET, NRSV, TEV], 'he had directed...against them' [AB], 'he had directed...at them' [GW], 'he was talking about them' [CEV], 'he had spoken with respect to them' [Arn], 'he had spoken with reference to them' [WBC], '(the story) was about them' [NCV], '(this parable) was aimed at them' [REB], 'he was pointing at them—that they were the farmers in the story' [NLT].

QUESTION—What is the function of καί in the clause '*but/and* they feared the people'?

This is the adversative καί, meaning 'but' in this context and it indicates that they refrained from laying hands on Jesus [EGT, Gdt, Rb; NET]. Many translate it as 'but' [AB, BECNT, NTC, WBC; all versions except KJV, NASB]. Or, the conjunction καί is used to indicate that the clause is parenthetic between what precedes and its explanation [TH]. Or, it indicates the state of mind in which the attempt was made 'and they did so in fear of the people' [Alf].

QUESTION—What relationship is indicated by γάρ 'because'?

1. This indicates the reason they tried to lay their hands on Jesus [Arn, BECNT, Gdt, NIGTC, NTC, TH]. Realizing that Jesus knew of their plans, they were angry and quickly consulted with one another as to what to do about him [Arn].
2. This indicates the reason they feared the people [ICC, NIC]. The Jewish leaders knew that the parable was directed towards them and this caused them to fear the people who had also heard the parable [ICC].

DISCOURSE UNIT: 20:20–26 [AB, BECNT, NAC, NICNT, NIGTC, Su, WBC; CEV, GW, HCSB, NCV, NET, NIV, NLT, NRSV]. The topic is paying taxes [CEV], taxes for Caesar [NLT], paying taxes to Caesar [NET, NIV], a question about taxes [GW], the question about paying taxes [NRSV], a question about tribute to Caesar [AB, BECNT, NAC, NIGTC, Su, WBC], is it right to pay taxes or not? [NCV], the question of Caesar's authority [NICNT], God and Caesar [HCSB].

20:20 And having-watched-closely[a] they-sent spies[b] pretending themselves to-be righteous/sincere,[c] in-order-that they-might-catch[d] (him) in-his word, so-that (they could) deliver him to-the rule[e] and the authority of-the governor.

LEXICON—a. aorist act. participle of παρατηρέω (LN 24.48) (BAGD 1.b. p. 622): 'to watch closely' [Arn, BAGD, LN; CEV, HCSB], 'to watch carefully' [NET], 'to observe carefully' [BAGD], 'to watch' [BECNT, NTC, WBC; KJV, NASB, NCV, NRSV], 'to keep a close watch' [NIV], 'to watch their opportunity' [REB], 'to watch their chance' [Lns], 'to watch for their opportunity' [AB; NLT], 'to look for an opportunity' [TEV], 'to watch for an opportunity (to send out some spies)' [GW].

b. ἐγκάθετος (LN **27.47**) (BAGD p. 215): 'spy' [AB, BAGD, BECNT, **LN**, Lns, NTC, WBC; all versions except NLT, REB, TEV], 'secret agent' [NLT], 'agent' [REB], 'suborned men' [Arn]. This is translated as a phrase: 'they bribed some men' [TEV]. This word refers to someone whose task is to obtain information surreptitiously [LN], someone who watches to see what someone does [BAGD]. They were agents hired with a secret commission, to catch Jesus in his words [TH]. They were people engaged in underhanded work [Arn]. They were imposters [TG].

c. δίκαιος (LN 88.12) (BAGD 1.b. p. 195): 'righteous' [BAGD, LN]. This pertains to the religious aspect of keeping God's laws [BAGD]. The phrase ὑποκρινομένους ἑαυτοὺς δικαίους εἶναι 'pretending themselves to be righteous' is translated 'who pretended to be righteous' [Arn, WBC; HCSB, NASB], 'hypocritically representing themselves to be righteous' [Lns], 'were to act like sincere religious people' [GW], 'which should feign themselves just men' [KJV], 'who pretended to be upright' [AB], 'who pretended to be good' [CEV], 'who pretended to be honest' [NIV, NRSV], 'pretending to be honest men' [NLT], 'in the guise of honest men' [REB], 'who pretended to be honorable men' [NTC], 'to pretend they were sincere' [TEV], 'pretending to be sincere' [BECNT], 'who pretended to be sincere' [NET], 'who acted as if they were sincere' [NCV]. See this word at 1:6, 17; 2:25; 5:32; 14:14; 15:7; 18:9; 23:47, 50.

d. aorist mid. (deponent = act.) subj. of ἐπιλαμβάνομαι (LN **27.32**) (BAGD 2.a. p. 295): 'to catch' [BAGD, **LN**]. The phrase 'in order that they might catch him in his word' is translated 'that they might catch him in some statement' [NASB], 'that they might take hold of his words' [KJV], 'in order to lay hold of him by a word' [Lns], 'their purpose was to lay hold on something he might say' [NTC], 'to seize on some word of his' [REB], 'in order that they might seize upon what he said' [BECNT], 'in order to seize him in an utterance' [Arn], 'so they could catch him in what he said' [HCSB], 'in order to catch him in his speech' [AB], 'so that they might catch him out in his speech' [WBC], 'they hoped to catch Jesus in something he said' [NIV], 'trying to catch Jesus saying something wrong' [CEV], 'they wanted to catch him saying the wrong thing' [GW], 'they wanted to trap Jesus in saying something wrong' [NCV], 'they sent them to trap Jesus with questions' [TEV], 'in order to trap him by what he said' [NRSV], 'they wanted to take advantage of what he might say' [NET], 'they tried to get Jesus to say something that could be reported' [NLT].

e. ἀρχή (LN 37.55, 37.56) (BAGD 3. p. 112): 'sphere of authority' [LN (37.55)], 'ruler' [BAGD (37.56), LN], 'authority' [BAGD]. The phrase τῇ ἀρχῇ καὶ τῇ ἐξουσίᾳ τοῦ ἡγεμόνος 'the rule and the authority of the governor' is translated 'the rule and the authority of the governor' [NASB], 'the power and authority of the governor' [KJV, NIV], 'the authority and power of the governor' [NCV], 'the authority and power of the Roman Governor' [TEV], 'the authority and jurisdiction of the governor' [BECNT; NET, REB], 'the jurisdiction and authority of the governor' [Lns; NRSV], 'the control and authority of the governor' [NTC], 'the jurisdiction and power of the governor' [WBC], 'the jurisdiction and authority of the prefect' [AB], 'the governor's rule and authority' [HCSB], 'the Roman governor' [CEV], 'the governor' [GW], 'the Roman government' [NLT], 'the government and the authority of the governor' [Arn].

QUESTION—What did the scribes and high priests watch?
1. They watched Jesus [BNTC, MGC, NICNT, NTC, WBC; CEV, KJV, NASB, NCV, NET, NIV, NRSV]. The verb refers to monitoring behavior [NICNT].
2. They watched for an opportunity [AB, Alf, EGT, Lns, Rb, Su, TG, TH; GW, NLT, REB, TEV]. They watched Jesus and everybody else in all affairs hoping for an opening for an attack on Jesus [Arn].

QUESTION—What did the spies pretend to be?
They pretended to be something they were not [TG, TH], as though they were not enemies [TNTC]. They disguised their true intentions [TG].
1. They pretended to be righteous [AB, Arn, BAGD, Lns, MGC, NAC, NIGTC, WBC; GW, HCSB, NASB]. They pretended to be loyal to the Jewish law [AB, MGC, NIGTC]. They were appearing to be men who strictly observed the Pharisaic regulations and were wondering whether righteous men ought to pay the tax [Lns].
2. They pretended to be sincere and honest [Arn, BECNT, EGT, ICC, NICNT, NTC, Su, TG, TH; CEV, NCV, NET, NIV, NLT, NRSV, REB]. They pretended to be sincere as they asked questions [TG]. They played the part of being scrupulous or conscientious in wanting to do the right thing [EGT, ICC, TH]. They came to Jesus pretending to have a genuine problem about paying the Roman tax [Arn, Su].

QUESTION—Who is the referent of 'they' in the phrase 'in order that they might catch him in his word'?
1. 'They' refers to the spies who asked the question [NAC, TH; CEV]: they sent the spies in order that the spies catch him in his word.
2. 'They' refers to the members of the Sanhedrin who sent the spies [AB, Alf, BECNT, Lns, My]: they sent the spies in order to catch him in his word.

QUESTION—What did they hope Jesus would say?
  They wanted Jesus to say something for which they could accuse him to the Roman governor [TG]. The members of the Sanhedrin knew that Pilate, the governor, would have to condemn Jesus if he were to be put to death [NIGTC]. If the governor tried Jesus and removed him, the Sanhedrin would be relieved of the responsibility in the eyes of the people [Lns, TNTC].

QUESTION—What is the meaning of τῇ ἀρχῇ καὶ τῇ ἐξουσίᾳ τοῦ ἡγεμόνος 'the rule and the authority of the governor'?
  The two nouns describe the governor's jurisdiction and his power [NIGTC], or his authority and jurisdiction, with the second noun ἐξουσία 'authority' having, in conjunction with ἀρχῇ 'rule', a reference to the domain or sphere of the governor's rule [NET]. They describe the governor's military power and judicial authority [Gdt]. The words τῇ ἀρχῇ καὶ τῇ ἐξουσίᾳ 'the ruler and the authority' are best considered a hendiadys where one of the words modifies the other, such as the supreme power of the governor [TH]. Or, the two words mean practically the same thing [TG]. This phrase should not be separated so as to mean something like 'to deliver him to the Government and in particular to the authority of the governor' (as does My), or 'to deliver him to the rule of the Sanhedrin and to the authority of the governor' [ICC].

20:21 **And they-questioned him saying, Teacher, we-know that rightly[a] you-speak and teach, and you-do- not -accept a-face,[b] but on-the-basis-of[c] truth you-teach the way[d] of-God.**

LEXICON—a. ὀρθῶς (LN 72.13) (BAGD p. 580): 'rightly' [BAGD, BECNT, Lns; KJV], 'correctly' [Arn, BAGD, LN; HCSB, NASB, NET], 'truthfully' [WBC]. The phrase 'rightly you speak and teach' is translated 'what you say and teach is right' [TEV], 'you speak and teach what is right' [NTC; NIV, NLT], 'you are right in what you say and teach' [GW, NRSV], 'what you say and teach is correct' [AB], 'what you say and teach is true' [NCV], 'what you speak and teach is sound' [REB]. The words 'we know that rightly you speak and teach…on the basis of truth you teach the way of God' is translated 'we know that you teach the truth about what God wants people to do' [CEV]. The pair of verbs 'you say and you teach' are redundant [NICNT, NIGTC]. This is a statement concerning the content of Jesus' speaking and teaching rather than the manner [TH]. It concerns his sound judgment in saying the right thing [EGT]. He teaches correctly [NIGTC]. He accurately presents God's way [BECNT]. He is orthodox [AB, NAC].

  b. πρόσωπον (LN 88.238) (BAGD 1.b. p. 721): 'face' [BAGD, LN]. The phrase λαμβάνω πρόσωπον 'to accept a face' means 'to show partiality' [LN]. The phrase 'you do not accept a face' [Lns] is also translated 'you do not show partiality' [BECNT; HCSB, NIV], 'you do not practice partiality' [Arn], 'you show no partiality' [NTC, WBC; NET], 'you are not partial to any' [NASB], 'you treat everyone with the same respect, no matter who they are' [CEV], 'you don't play favorites' [GW], 'you show deference to no one' [NRSV], 'you pay deference to no one' [REB], 'you show no favor to anyone' [AB], 'you pay no attention to who people are' [NCV], 'you pay no attention to anyone's status' [TEV], 'neither acceptest thou the person of any' [KJV], 'you are not influenced by what others think' [NLT].

    c. ἐπί (LN 70.4) (BAGD I.1.b.β. p. 286): 'on the basis of' [BAGD]. The phrase ἐπ' ἀληθείας 'on the basis of truth' is translated 'in truth' [Lns; NASB], 'in accordance with (the) truth' [BAGD; NET, NIV, NRSV], 'truly' [AB, BAGD, BECNT, WBC; KJV], 'actually, really' [LN], 'truthfully' [Arn, NTC; GW, HCSB], 'sincerely' [NLT], 'in all sincerity' [REB], '(you always teach) the truth' [NCV], 'teach the truth about (God's will)' [TEV]. Jesus taught in a true way, his teachings were the truth [TH].

    d. ὁδός (LN 41.16) (BAGD 2.b. p. 554): 'way' [BAGD, LN]. This word is used figuratively for 'way of life' [BAGD, LN], 'way to live' [LN], 'way of acting, conduct' [BAGD]. The phrase τὴν ὁδὸν τοῦ θεοῦ 'the way of God' [AB, Arn, BECNT, Lns, WBC; GW, HCSB, KJV, NASB, NET, NIV, NRSV] is also translated 'God's way' [NTC; NCV], 'the ways of God' [NLT], 'the way of life that God requires' [REB], 'what God wants people to do' [CEV], 'God's will for people' [TEV].

QUESTION—What did they mean when they said Jesus did not accept a face?

This is a Semitic idiom meaning that he was impartial or unbiased, he did not pay regard to outward appearances or factors such as a person's social status [NTC, TG]. It may be a statement of partiality in general or they may have applied this statement to partiality where Jews and Romans were concerned in the matter of taxes [Su]. Jesus was not afraid to challenge the Jewish leaders [BECNT].

QUESTION—What is meant by τὴν ὁδὸν τοῦ θεοῦ 'the way of God'?

It presents the image of walking in God's commandments to convey the thought of living out one's life in obedience to God [WBC]. It is a lifestyle of obedience to God [MGC]. It is the walk of righteousness with God [BECNT]. It means the kind of life that God requires from people [NIGTC]. It is the manner in which God wants people to think and to live [NTC]. In this context it may mean the Jewish faith or religion, or even the Law of Moses [TG].

20:22 Is-it-permitted[a] for-us to-pay a-tax[b] to-Caesar or not? 20:23 And having-perceived their craftiness[c] he-said to them, 20:24 Show me a-denarius. Of-whom has-it an-image[d] and inscription[e]? And they-said, Caesar.

TEXT—In 20:23, following πρὸς αὐτούς 'to them', some manuscripts add τί με πειράζετε; 'Why do you tempt me?' GNT does not mention this variant. Τί με πειράζετε; 'Why do you tempt me?' is read by KJV.

TEXT—In 20:24, instead of οἱ δὲ εἶπαν 'and they said', some manuscripts read ἀποκριθέντες δὲ εἶπαν 'and having answered they said/and they answered and said'. GNT does not mention this variant. Ἀποκριθέντες δὲ εἶπαν 'and having answered they said/and they answered and said' is read by KJV.

LEXICON—a. pres. act. indic. of ἔξεστι (LN 71.38) (BAGD 1. p. 275): 'to be permitted' [BAGD], 'must, ought to' [LN]. The question 'is it permitted' is translated 'is it right' [Arn, BECNT; GW, NCV, NET, NIV, NLT], 'is it lawful' [AB, Lns, NTC, WBC; HCSB, KJV, NASB, NRSV], 'is it against our Law' [TEV], 'are we or are we not permitted' [REB], 'should (we pay)' [CEV]. It asks what is permitted by the law [NIGTC]. This refers to the Mosaic Law [TG, TNTC], or to the way teachers of the Law interpreted it [TG].

b. φόρος (LN **57.182**) (BAGD p. 865): 'tax' [BAGD, BECNT], 'taxes' [Arn, NTC; all versions except KJV, NET], 'tribute tax' [**LN**; NET], 'tribute' [AB, BAGD, Lns, WBC; KJV]. The word is a general term that includes both tribute money and tax money [NICNT, NIGTC, WBC]. The word Luke uses means 'tribute', the money one nation pays to another [Lns, Su], but Matthew and Mark use a word that means a poll tax that every person had to pay [Lns]. This was a poll tax [AB, BECNT, ICC, MGC, NIC, NTC; NET]. Or, in the context of paying the tax to the emperor, the word is used in the narrower sense of tribute paid to Caesar [NICNT]. See this word at 23:2.

c. πανουργία (LN 88.270) (BAGD p. 608): 'craftiness' [Arn, BAGD, BECNT, LN, Lns, NTC; HCSB, KJV, NRSV], 'deceit' [NET], 'trickery' [AB, BAGD, WBC; NASB, NLT]. The phrase 'having perceived their craftiness' is translated 'knowing they were trying to trick him' [NCV], 'Jesus knew that they were trying to trick him' [CEV], 'he saw through their scheme' [GW], 'he saw through their trick' [REB, TEV], 'he saw through their duplicity' [NIV].

d. εἰκών (LN 6.96) (BAGD 1.a. p. 222): 'image' [AB, Arn, BAGD, LN, Lns, NTC, WBC; HCSB, KJV, NCV], 'likeness' [BAGD, BECNT, LN; NASB, NET], 'picture' [CEV, NLT], 'portrait' [NIV], 'face' [GW, TEV], 'head' [NRSV, REB]. Coins have been found from that time in history with the image of Caesar Tiberius [NIC]. On one side of the coin the emperor's head was sketched [NAC, TG]. The coin's specific name 'denarius' is retained in the translation because not all coins in use carried the image of Caesar [NET].

e. ἐπιγραφή (LN 33.46) (BAGD p. 291): 'inscription' [AB, Arn, BAGD, BECNT, LN, NTC, WBC; HCSB, NASB, NET, NIV, REB], 'superscription' [Lns; KJV], 'writing' [LN], 'name' [CEV, GW, NCV, TEV], 'title' [NLT, NRSV]. The coins with the emperor's image also had a superscription saying 'Tiberius Caesar Augustus, son of the divine Augustus' [AB, MGC, NAC, NIC, NIGTC, NTC]. The Emperor's name was inscribed around the image of his head [TG]. Or, the Emperor's name was inscribed on the other side of the coin from the emperor's image [NAC].

QUESTION—What was the issue about paying taxes to Caesar?

The Roman emperor at that time was named Tiberius, who ruled from A.D. 14–37. The name of the famed emperor Caesar was added to the name of the succeeding emperors and it became a common title for the reigning emperor [AB]. Here Caesar is used as a title [TH; NET]. Instead of 'Caesar' some translate the noun as 'the emperor' [CEV, GW], 'the Roman emperor' [REB, TEV], 'the Roman government' [NLT]. All of the tax money belonged to Caesar, the emperor of Rome [Su]. The taxes were demanded by the emperor [NIVS]. Of course the tax was not paid directly to Caesar but to the local tax collectors who represented the Roman government. Different from the indirect tax paid to tax collectors at toll-booths, this money went directly to the emperor [BECNT]. The taxes were direct taxes on land or personal property [TH]. Since there is no question of a payment being in accord with Caesar's law, 'is it permitted' asks if was in accord with God's law [TNTC]. Was it fitting for good Jews who worshipped God to pay tribute money to the emperor who had been proclaimed to be divine by the Roman senate? [Su]. It was a poll-tax the Roman government imposed on every Jew [AB, BECNT, ICC, MGC, NIC, NTC]. The law fixed the amount of tax as one denarius per person [NTC]. The image of Caesar on a coin was an abomination to an upright Jew [AB].

QUESTION—What was the craftiness that Jesus noticed?

Their question was presented as a pious request for advice in deciding what to do in a difficult matter of ethics, but their real intention was the destruction of Jesus by luring him into a trap he could not escape from [NTC]. Jesus realized that they were resorting to praise to achieve their goal [AB]. Their question was a trick to get Jesus into trouble whichever way he answered [TG, TNTC]. If Jesus answered that it was right to pay taxes to Caesar, then he would lose the support of Jewish patriots [NIC, NIGTC] and alienate many devout Jews [NTC]. But if he said that it was not right, then he would be in trouble with the Roman government [NIGTC] and would be charged with rebellion against the government [NIC, NTC]. Jesus' answer would have been the same for even sincere inquirers, but the method he used might have been different [Arn]. This was a question that bothered many Jews [NIC].

20:25 And he-said to them, Therefore^a give^b the (things) of-Caesar to-Caesar and the (things) of-God to-God. 20:26 And they-were- not -able to-catch^c (him) in-his word before^d the people and being-amazed^e at his answer they-were-silent.

LEXICON—a. τοίνυν (LN **89.51**) (BAGD p. 821): 'therefore' [**LN**; KJV], 'hence' [BAGD, LN], 'so' [BAGD, WBC], 'so then' [LN], 'then' [Arn, BECNT; NASB, NCV, NET, NIV, NRSV], 'well then' [Lns, NTC; GW, HCSB, NLT, TEV], 'very well then' [REB], not explicit [CEV].

b. aorist act. impera. of ἀποδίδωμι (LN 57.153) (BAGD 1. p. 90): 'to give' [BAGD], 'to pay' [BAGD, LN], 'to render' [LN]. The phrase 'give the

things of Caesar to Caesar' is translated 'duly give the things of Caesar to Caesar' [Lns], 'render unto Caesar the things which be Caesar's' [KJV], 'render the things of Caesar to Caesar' [BECNT], 'render to Caesar the things that are Caesar's' [NASB], 'give to the emperor the things that are the emperor's' [NRSV], 'give the emperor what belongs to the emperor' [GW], 'give to Caesar the things that are Caesar's' [WBC; NCV, NET], 'give to Caesar what is Caesar's' [NIV], 'give to Caesar what belongs to him' [NLT], 'give the Emperor what belongs to him' [CEV], 'what is due to Caesar render to Caesar' [NTC], 'pay to Caesar what belongs to Caesar' [REB], 'pay to the Emperor what belongs to the Emperor' [TEV], 'give back to Caesar the things that are Caesar's' [Arn; HCSB]. In connection with taxes, 'to give' means 'to pay' [Arn, BAGD, NAC, NIGTC], 'to pay what is due' [TNTC].
- c. aorist mid (deponent = act.) infin. of ἐπιλαμβάνομαι (LN 27.32) (BAGD 2.a. p. 295): 'to catch' [BAGD, LN]. For the phrase 'to catch him in his word' see 20:20.
- d. ἐναντίον (LN 83.33) (BAGD 1.a. p. 261): 'before' [Arn, BAGD, BECNT, LN, Lns; KJV, TEV], 'in front of' [LN; CEV, GW], 'in the presence of' [BAGD, NTC, WBC; NASB, NCV, NET, NLT, NRSV]. The phrase 'before the people' is translated 'in public' [HCSB], 'out in public' [REB].
- e. aorist act. participle of θαυμάζω (LN 25.213) (BAGD 1.a.β. p. 352): 'to be amazed' [LN, NTC; CEV, HCSB, NASB, NCV, NLT, NRSV, TEV], 'to be astonished' [AB, BAGD; NIV], 'to wonder' [BAGD, LN], 'to marvel at' [Arn, BECNT, LN, Lns, WBC; KJV], 'to be taken aback' [REB]. This verb is also translated with the answer as the subject: 'to surprise' [GW]. See this word at 1:21, 63; 2:18, 33; 4:22; 7:9; 8:25; 9:43; 11:14, 38; 24:12, 41.

QUESTION—What relationship is indicated by τοίνυν 'therefore'?

This indicates a strong conclusion [TH]. It indicates the obligation arising from recognizing Caesar's position [TNTC]. The coin indicates Caesar's rule over them, so the people should pay Caesar what was due to him [NIGTC].

QUESTION—What are the things of Caesar?

It does not mean to give back something, but to give what is due to a higher authority ordained by God, and this includes giving tribute, fear, and honor [Lns]. The term 'the things of Caesar' includes more than the payment of taxes and includes whatever he lawfully decreed, and this supports the principle of submission to political authority [NIGTC]. The clear answer is that they should pay the tax [Arn, BECNT, NIC, NTC], but there is a qualification in this statement that they were to give what was due to the emperor, so that the divine honor which the emperor claimed must be refused since it was not due him [NTC]. They were to pay what was due to Caesar [Lns, TH]. Since the name and face on the coin showed that it belonged to Caesar, he had the right to collect taxes from those who used his money [TG].

QUESTION—What are the things of God?
People are to recognize God's authority over them [Arn, NIGTC]. God's rights include contrition, faith, love, worship, obedience [Lns, NAC], service, gratitude, glory [NTC], and ourselves [Arn]. In giving Caesar his due, we must realize that Caesar's rights are limited and he has no rights in God's domain [TNTC]. The significance of Jesus' answer is that a person is law-abiding and pious not by withholding the taxes that Caesar demanded, but by actively giving God his due [WBC].

QUESTION—What is meant by the phrase 'before the people'?
The people had listened to the conversation and approved of Jesus' answer [Arn, EGT]. There were Jewish pilgrims standing around them who could testify to what Jesus said and thus prevent the Pharisees from twisting his word to denounce him before the authorities [Lns, TH].

DISCOURSE UNIT: 20:27–47 [NASB]. The topic is the question, Is there a resurrection?

DISCOURSE UNIT: 20:27–40 [AB, BECNT, NAC, NICNT, NIGTC, Su, TNTC, WBC; CEV, GW, HCSB, NCV, NET, NIV, NLT, NRSV, TEV]. The topic is marriage and the resurrection [NET, NIV], some Sadducees try to trick Jesus [NCV], a question about the resurrection [AB, BECNT, NAC, NIGTC, Su, WBC; NRSV], the question about rising from death [TEV], a discussion about the resurrection [NLT], the Sadducees and the resurrection [HCSB], the dead come back to life [GW], life in the future [CEV], the question of Moses' authority [NICNT], the seven brothers [TNTC].

20:27 **And having-approached some of-the Sadducees, the (ones) denying[a] (the) resurrection (saying) it-is- not -to-be, questioned him**

TEXT—Instead of οἱ ἀντιλέγοντες 'the ones denying', some manuscripts read οἱ λέγοντες 'the ones saying' and others read οἵτινες λέγουσιν 'who say'. GNT reads οἱ [ἀντι]λέγοντες 'the ones denying' with a C decision and brackets ἀντι 'against', indicating that the Committee had difficulty making the decision.

LEXICON—a. pres. act. participle of ἀντιλέγω (LN 33.455) (BAGD 1. p. 74): 'to deny, to speak against' [BAGD], 'to oppose, to speak in opposition to' [LN]. The phrase 'the ones denying the resurrection saying it is not to be' is translated 'which deny that there is any resurrection' [KJV], 'who deny that there is a resurrection' [Arn; REB], 'who contend that there is no resurrection' [NET], 'those who contested that there is no resurrection' [BECNT], 'who oppose the idea that there is a resurrection' [WBC], 'who claim there is no resurrection' [Lns], 'who say that there is no resurrection' [AB, NTC; HCSB, NASB, NIV, NRSV], 'who say there is no resurrection after death' [NLT], 'who say that people will never come back to life' [GW], 'who say that people will not rise from death' [TEV], 'who believed people would not rise from the dead' [NCV], 'did not believe that people would rise to life after death' [CEV].

QUESTION—Who were the Sadducees?
>The Sadducees were a small religious party composed mostly of Jewish priests [TG]. Not all priests were Sadducees, but the leaders among them were [Arn]. They were conservative, aristocratic, worldly-minded, and ready to cooperate with the Romans [TNTC]. They were the most religiously conservative sect of the time [BECNT]. They rejected the oral traditions that the Pharisees valued so much [AB, BECNT, NAC, TNTC]. They believed that the soul perishes along with the body [MGC, NTC]. They wanted to ridicule the idea of resurrection by posing a situation of levirate marriage that would result in one woman having seven husbands if there really was a resurrection [NIC, NTC, TNTC].

QUESTION—Does the phrasing 'some of the Sadducees, the ones denying the resurrection' imply that there were other Sadducees who accepted the belief in the resurrection?
>The words οἱ ἀντιλέγοντες ἀνάστασιν 'the ones denying the resurrection' should grammatically refer to the preceding τινες 'some', but it surely is meant to refer to the whole party of Sadducees [EGT, WBC]: some of the Sadducees, the party that denied the resurrection. It refers to the whole party of the Sadducees, not just the group that came to question Jesus [TH]. This was one of the cardinal doctrines of the Sadducee party [MGC]. Or, all of the Sadducees held that the resurrection was not an article of faith, but some might have believed it to be true [ICC].

20:28 saying, Teacher, Moses wrote to-us, if someone's brother dies having a-wife, and this (deceased brother) is childless, that his brother should-take[a] the wife and he-should-raise-up[b] a-seed/offspring (for) his brother.

TEXT—Instead of ἄτεκνος ᾖ 'is childless', some manuscripts read ἄτεκνος ἀποθάνῃ 'should die childless'. GNT does not mention this variant. Ἄτεκνος ἀποθάνῃ 'should die childless' is read by KJV.

LEXICON—a. aorist act. subj. of λαμβάνω (LN 34.66) (BAGD 1.c. p. 464): 'to take' [AB, Arn, BAGD, BECNT, Lns, NTC, WBC; HCSB, KJV], 'to marry' [LN; all versions except HCSB, KJV]. In this context it means to enter into a marriage relation [LN].

b. aorist act. subj. of ἐξανίστημι (LN 23.59) (BAGD 1. p. 272): 'to raise up' [BAGD], 'to beget, to become the father of' [LN]. The phrase 'and he should raise up a seed to his brother' is translated 'and raise up seed for his brother' [Arn, BECNT, Lns; KJV], 'and raise up children to his brother' [NASB], 'and raise up offspring for his brother' [AB, WBC], 'and raise up children for his brother' [NTC; NRSV], 'and have children for his brother' [GW, NCV, NET, NIV], 'and produce offspring for his brother' [HCSB], 'and have a child who will be the brother's heir' [NLT], 'and provide an heir for his brother' [REB], 'their first son would then be thought of as the son of the dead brother' [CEV], 'so that they can have children who will be considered the dead man's children' [TEV].

QUESTION—What was involved in Moses' command to the Jews?
> This refers to what Moses wrote in Deut. 25:5–6. It concerns the levirate requirement for a younger brother to beget a child by the widow of his deceased older brother and the reckoning of such an offspring as being the descendant of the older deceased brother [LN (23.59)]. The custom seemed to have died out in NT times and so the question was an academic one [Arn, TNTC], yet it concerned an OT law that could be used to reject the teaching of a resurrection [TNTC]. Or, perhaps it still was in effect [Crd]. The purpose of this levirate law was to keep alive the family name of a man who had died without having children [Su, TG, TNTC]. Or, this law pertained to brothers who lived together and its purpose was to keep the property in the family by raising up an heir to inherit the dead man's part [NIGTC].
> 1. The singular noun σπέρμα 'seed' is taken to mean a child, and presumably only the first son born of such a levirate marriage would be considered to be the son of the deceased first brother [Lns, NIC, Su; CEV, NLT, REB]. The first son born in this way would be legally the son of the dead brother, but all other children would be the younger brother's [Lns, Su].
> 2. The singular noun σπέρμα 'seed' is taken to mean children and presumably all of the children born of such a marriage would be considered to be children of the deceased first brother [AB, TNTC; GW, HCSB, KJV, NASB, NCV, NET, NIV, NRSV, TEV].

20:29 Therefore[a] there-were seven brothers. And the first having-taken a-wife died childless. **20:30** And the second **20:31** and the third took her, and likewise[b] also (all) seven died and did- not -leave-behind children. **20:32** And last[c] the woman died.

TEXT—In 20:30, instead of καὶ ὁ δεύτερος 'and the second', some manuscripts read καὶ ἔλαβεν ὁ δεύτερος τὴν γυναῖκα, καὶ οὗτος ἀπέθανεν ἄτεκνος 'and the second took the woman, and this one died childless'. GNT does not mention this variant. Καὶ ἔλαβεν ὁ δεύτερος τὴν γυναῖκα, καὶ οὗτος ἀπέθανεν ἄτεκνος 'and the second took the woman, and this one died childless' is read by KJV.

TEXT—In 20:32, instead of ὕστερον 'last', some manuscripts read ὕστερον δὲ πάντων 'and last of all'. GNT does not mention this variant. Ὕστερον δὲ πάντων 'and last of all' is read by KJV.

LEXICON—a. οὖν (LN 89.50): 'therefore' [LN; KJV], 'accordingly' [LN, Lns], 'then, so then' [LN], 'now' [AB, Arn, BECNT, NTC, WBC; HCSB, NASB, NET, NIV, NRSV, REB], 'well' [NLT], not explicit [CEV, GW, NCV, TEV].

b. ὡσαύτως (LN 64.16) (BAGD p. 899): 'likewise' [Arn, BAGD, BECNT], 'similarly' [BAGD, NTC], 'in the same way' [BAGD, LN; GW, HCSB, NIV, NRSV], 'in this way' [REB], 'in this same way' [NET], 'in like manner' [LN; KJV], 'the same thing happened' [CEV, NCV, TEV], 'and so on' [AB], 'and so it went' [NLT], 'as well' [WBC], 'moreover' [Lns].

c. ὕστερος (LN 61.16) (BAGD 2.b. p. 849): 'last' [BECNT, LN], 'last of all' [BAGD, LN, NTC; KJV, REB, TEV], 'at last' [CEV], 'finally' [AB, BAGD, LN, Lns; GW, HCSB, NASB, NCV, NET, NIV, NLT, NRSV], 'later on' [Arn, WBC]. The woman's death is necessary for the argument so that all the persons concerned would have been transferred into the other world [Lns].

QUESTION—What relationship is indicated by οὖν 'therefore' in 20:29?

This indicates a consequence of the levirate law [ICC, My]. This implies that the law that has been quoted gives rise to this dilemma [EGT, NIGTC]. It introduces an example of this law [Alf]. Assuming that married life continues in the hereafter, this presents a dilemma [NTC]. Or, the conjunction may merely be a particle of transition [ICC]. It marks a transition to the exposition of a specific case [TH]. The meaning is 'now begins the case' [AB].

QUESTION—Is the statement 'there were seven brothers' factual?

1. Although stated as a factual happening, it is a made-up story meant to show how foolish a belief in the resurrection really was [TG]. Two husbands would have been sufficient to make the point, but having seven husbands makes the story more interesting and makes belief in the resurrection appear even more absurd [NTC].
2. This is a factual case since the point could have been made with just two brothers instead of seven of them if it was just a made-up story [Lns].

QUESTION—What is implied in the statement 'And the second and the third took her.'?

Although there are two brothers as the subject, the verb ἔλαβεν 'took' is singular. This can be explained because the marriages with the second and third brothers are two distinct events [TH]. It is implied that the second brother died childless and then the third brother took her as wife and he also died childless [MGC, NAC, NIGTC, TH].

QUESTION—What is the meaning of ὡσαύτως 'likewise' in 20:31?

'Likewise' indicates that all the rest of seven married her in turn and each died without having children, so that none of the seven brothers could claim to be the real husband in terms of having fathered an heir [NIGTC]. Following 'likewise' it is implied that the *rest* of the seven brothers *took her as wife* [TH, WBC]. The implicit information is made explicit in some versions: 'The second one married his brother's widow, and he also died without having any children. The same thing happened to the third one. Finally, all seven brothers married that woman and died without having any children' [CEV], 'Then the second brother married the widow, and he died. And the third brother married the widow, and he died. The same thing happened with all seven brothers; they died and had no children' [NCV], 'His brother married the widow, but he also died. Still no children. And so it went one after another, until each of the seven had married her and died, leaving no children' [NLT].

346   LUKE 20:33

20:33 **The woman therefore in the resurrection of-which of-them does-she-become (the) wife? Because the seven had her (as) wife.**
QUESTION—What relationship is indicated by οὖν 'therefore'?
> It indicates a transition to the crucial question [TH; NET]. This is the point of the Sadducees' question [MGC]. They meant 'supposing for the sake of argument that there is a resurrection' [Lns, WBC].

QUESTION—What is the significance of the question?
> The question is 'will all seven together be her husband?', or 'which one of the seven be her husband, and why not another one?' [Lns]. The Sadducees are confident that no adequate answer can be given [BECNT].

QUESTION—What relationship is indicated by γάρ 'because'?
> This is intended to remind Jesus of the basic problem [NAC]. The fact that the woman had been the wife of all seven results in an unsolvable problem [WBC].

20:34 **And Jesus said to-them, The sons**[a] **of-this age marry and are-given-in-marriage,**[b]
TEXT—Before εἶπεν 'said', some manuscripts add ἀποκριθείς 'answering'. GNT does not mention this variant. Ἀποκριθείς 'answering' is read by KJV.

TEXT—Following τοῦ αἰῶνος τούτου 'of this age' some manuscripts add γεννῶνται καὶ γεννῶσιν 'are born and give birth'. GNT rejects this addition with an A decision, indicating that the text is certain.

LEXICON—a. υἱός (LN 11.16) (BAGD 1.c.d. p. 834): 'son' [BAGD, LN]. The phrase οἱ υἱοὶ τοῦ αἰῶνος τούτου 'the sons of this age' [Arn, BECNT, NTC, WBC; HCSB, NASB] is also translated 'the sons of this eon' [Lns], 'the children of this age' [AB], 'the children of this world' [KJV], 'the men and women of this age' [TEV], 'the men and women of this world' [REB], 'the people of this age' [NET, NIV], 'the people in this world' [CEV], 'the people here on earth' [NLT], 'those who belong to this age' [NRSV], 'in this world, people (get married)' [GW], 'on earth, people (marry)' [NCV].

b. pres. pass. indic. of γαμίζω (LN **34.72**) (BAGD 2. p. 151): 'to be given in marriage' [BAGD, **LN**]. The phrase 'marry and are given in marriage' [Arn, BECNT, Lns, NTC, WBC; HCSB, KJV, NASB, NET, NIV, NRSV] is also translated 'marry and are given to someone to marry' [NCV], 'marry and are married' [AB], 'get married' [CEV, GW], 'marry' [REB, TEV], 'marriage is for (people here on earth)' [NLT]. 'To be given in marriage' refers to a daughter being given in marriage by her father [Su].

QUESTION—Who are the sons of this age?
> It means all of the people who live in this world [Arn, TNTC]. The phrase refers to both men and women [TH]. The word 'sons' is used here to include women since it is the women who are given in marriage [TG, TH, WBC; NET]. The word αἰῶνος can mean either 'age' or 'world' and here it refers to mortal human beings in their earthly existence [AB]. The Jewish

expression 'this age' means 'this life' [MGC]. The flaw in the Sadducees' reasoning is that they were equating behavior in this age with behavior in the age to come [NAC].

20:35 but the (ones who) are-considered-worthy[a] to-attain[b] to-that age and the resurrection from the dead neither marry nor are-given-in-marriage.

LEXICON—a. aorist pass. participle of καταξιόω (LN 65.18) (BAGD 1. p. 415): 'to be considered worthy of' [AB, BAGD, LN, WBC; GW, NASB, NIV, NRSV], 'to be deemed worthy' [Lns], 'to be regarded as worthy' [NET], 'to be counted worthy' [HCSB], 'to be judged worthy' [REB], 'to be accounted worthy' [Arn, BECNT, NTC; KJV], 'to be worthy' [CEV, NCV, NLT, TEV].

    b. aorist act. infin. of τυγχάνω (LN 90.61) (BAGD 1. p. 829): 'to attain' [BAGD, BECNT, Lns, NTC, WBC; NASB], 'to experience' [BAGD, LN], 'to reach' [Arn], 'to take part in' [HCSB, NIV], 'to share in' [AB; NET], 'to obtain' [KJV]. The phrase 'the ones having been considered worthy to attain to that age and the resurrection from the dead' is translated 'those who are considered worthy of a place in that age and in the resurrection from the dead' [NRSV], 'those who have been judged worthy of a place in the other world, and of the resurrection from the dead' [REB], 'people who are considered worthy to come back to life and live in the next world' [GW], 'those who will be worthy to be raised from the dead and live again' [NCV], 'the men and women who are worthy to rise from death and live in the age to come' [TEV], 'in the future world no one who is worthy to rise from death (will either marry or die)' [CEV], 'But that is not the way it will be in the age to come. For those worthy of being raised from the dead won't be married then' [NLT].

QUESTION—In what way are they considered worthy?

God judges them to be worthy [AB, Lns, MGC, TG, TH]. The privilege to partake in the resurrection is bestowed by God on some unspecified basis [WBC]. They are accounted worthy to share in the resurrection of the righteous by virtue of God's grace, not from any merit of their own [NTC]. This implies that not all of the sons of this world will qualify to enter the kingdom that begins with the resurrection [BECNT, ICC].

QUESTION—What is meant by attaining to 'that age' and 'the resurrection from the dead'?

The second phrase modifies or explains the first: 'that age when the dead come to life again' [TH]. That age is the future world [CEV], or the age to come [NAC, NIGTC]. It is the age beyond the grave and was regarded as an age of bliss and glory [ICC]. The resurrection from the dead refers to those raised to everlasting life as in Dan. 12:2 where it speaks of people who sleep in the dust awakening to everlasting life or to shame and everlasting corruption [AB]. There is a distinction between ἡ ἀνάστασις τῆς ἐκ νεκρῶν 'the resurrection *from* the dead' and ἡ ἀνάστασις νεκρῶν 'the resurrection *of* the dead'. The latter phrase is more comprehensive and includes the resurrection of all the dead, while the 'resurrection *from* the dead' applies only to God's children [Arn, ICC] and implies that although the bodies of the unsaved will be resurrected, they will still continue in the sad state of spiritual death [Arn].

QUESTION—What is it about those worthy to be resurrected and attaining that age that prevents them from marrying?

They will not die, so marriage with a view to perpetuate the race will no longer be necessary [AB, BECNT, NTC]. Marriage and the entire marital relation is intended only for those of this world age [Lns, MGC]. The marriage relationship is transcended in a new level of personal relationship and it is no longer necessary for marriage to be used as a means for procreation [NIGTC]. The idea of the resurrection pertains to the next life, and the next life is not compatible with the levirate laws which pertain to this life [NIBC].

20:36 Because neither are-they-able any-longer to-die, because they-are like-angels[a] and they-are sons[b] of-God being sons[c] of-the resurrection.

TEXT—Instead of ἀποθανεῖν...δύνανται 'are they able...to die' some manuscripts read ἀποθανεῖν...μέλλουσιν 'are they going...to die'. GNT reads ἀποθανεῖν...δύνανται 'are they able...to die' with a B decision, indicating that the text is almost certain.

LEXICON—a. ἰσάγγελος (LN **12.29**) (BAGD p. 380): 'like an angel' [BAGD, LN]. The plural form is translated 'like angels' [AB, Arn, BECNT; HCSB, NASB, NCV, NLT, NRSV, REB, TEV], 'like the angels' [NTC; CEV, NIV], 'the same as the angels' [GW], 'equal to angels' [WBC; NET], 'equal unto the angels' [KJV], '(are) angel-like' [Lns].
  b. υἱός (LN 11.14): 'son' [LN]. The phrase 'sons of God' [Arn, BECNT, Lns, NTC, WBC; HCSB, NASB, NET] is also translated 'children of God' [AB; KJV, NCV, NLT, NRSV, REB, TEV], 'God's children' [CEV, GW, NIV].
  c. υἱός (LN 11.14): 'son' [LN]. The phrase 'being sons of the resurrection' [Arn, NTC, WBC; NASB, NET] is also translated 'being sons of resurrection' [BECNT], 'being children of the resurrection' [KJV, NRSV], 'as being sons of the resurrection' [Lns], 'raised up to new life' [NLT], 'since they are sons of the resurrection' [HCSB], 'since they are children of the resurrection' [NIV], 'since/because they share in the resurrection' [AB; REB], 'because they have risen from death' [TEV], 'because they have been raised from the dead' [NCV], 'because they have been raised to life' [CEV], 'who have come back to life' [GW].

QUESTION—What relationship is indicated by the first γάρ '*because* they can no longer die'?

This gives the reason that marriages are non-existent in heaven [AB, Arn, BECNT, Gdt, ICC, Lns, NAC, NIC, NICNT, NTC, TH, TNTC, WBC]: they neither marry nor are given in marriage because there is no longer death.

Marriage was instituted in order to preserve the human race [ICC], but in heaven there is no need for marriages and births [Arn].

QUESTION—What relationship is indicated by the second γάρ 'because they are like angels'?

1. This gives the reason they cannot die [Alf, Arn, ICC, MGC, NAC, NIC, NIGTC, TG, TH, WBC; HCSB, NASB, NET, NRSV]: they cannot die because they are like angels in this respect. They do not marry because they cannot die, and they cannot die because they are like the angels [ICC; NLT]. The point of similarity is immortality [ICC, NIC, NIGTC, TG; NET].
2. This gives the reason there will be no marriage in heaven [AB, Lns, NTC, Rb, TNTC]. This indicates that marriage is mortal and transitory in character [AB]. Disembodied spirits like angels do not marry [AB]. The point of similarity is the absence of sex and marriage in heaven [AB, Lns, Rb]. They will not become angels, but they will be like angels in regard to sex and marriage [Lns]. Marriage is especially in focus [TNTC].

QUESTION—What is the addition of the clause 'and they are sons of God' connected with?

This is coordinate with 'they are like angels' [AB, Alf, Arn; CEV, HCSB, NET, NRSV]. It gives another reason they cannot die [Arn; HCSB, NET]. Another reason for their immortality is that at the resurrection they will have glorified, heavenly bodies and share in God's divine nature [NIC]. Both state the idea of immortality in two different ways [TG]. This further defines what Jesus meant when he said that they would be like angels; their resurrection is proof of their sonship in the new and glorified nature which even their bodies will have [Lns].

QUESTION—What is meant by the participial phrase 'being sons of the resurrection' and how is it connected to what precedes?

They are sons of the resurrection in that they participate in the age to come and have immortal life [BECNT]. They are sons of the resurrection in the sense that they share in the resurrection [NIC, NIGTC, NIVS]. They are born of the resurrection [AB].

1. It gives the reason they are sons of God [Arn, Lns, MGC, NAC, NIGTC, TH; NCV, NIV, REB, TEV]: they are sons of God, because they have been raised from the dead. This explains why their full sonship has been realized and the mortal has been clothed with immortality [NAC].
2. It gives the reason they are like angels and are sons of God [CEV, HCSB].
3. It describes 'sons of God' [WBC; GW, NLT]: 'they are God's children who have come back to life'. Through resurrection they have been brought into the glories of the age to come [WBC]. They are resurrection sons, not physical sons of God and the line of relationships involved in physical life in this world of death will be no part in the age to come [Su]. 'Sons of the resurrection' explains the title 'sons of God' in that each of the resurrected ones is directly a child of God because his new body is an immediate work of God's power [Gdt]. Although believers are in a sense

sons of God in the present age, the fuller sense of sonship that will happen in the age to come is in view here [TNTC].

20:37 And that the dead are-raised,[a] even Moses revealed[b] at the bush, as he/it-speaks-about[c] (the) Lord the God of-Abraham and (the) God of-Isaac and (the) God of-Jacob.

LEXICON—a. pres. pass. indic. of ἐγείρω (LN 23.94): 'to be raised' [AB, Arn, BECNT, WBC; HCSB, KJV, NASB, NET, NLT, NRSV], 'to be raised up' [NTC], 'to be raised to life' [LN; NCV, REB, TEV], 'to be made to live again' [LN]. This passive verb is also translated actively with 'the dead' as the subject: 'to live again' [CEV]. 'to come back to life' [GW], 'to rise' [NIV], 'to arise' [Lns]. This passive verb implies that the dead are raised by God [AB, NAC].

b. aorist act. indic. of μηνύω (LN **33.209**) (BAGD p. 519): 'to reveal' [BAGD, **LN**], 'to inform' [BAGD, LN]. The phrase 'revealed at the bush' is translated 'revealed…in the passage about the bush' [NET], 'disclosed at the bush' [Lns], 'disclosed in the passage about/on the bush' [BECNT, NTC], 'showed at the bush' [KJV], 'showed in the passage about the burning bush' [NASB], 'showed in the passage about the bush' [GW], 'showed in the story about the bush' [NRSV], 'made known in the passage about the bush' [WBC], 'indicated in the account relating to the thorn bush' [Arn], 'revealed in the story of the burning bush' [AB], 'indicated in the passage about the burning bush' [HCSB], 'in the story about the burning bush, Moses clearly shows' [CEV], 'is shown…in the story of the burning bush' [REB], 'in the account of the bush…showed' [NIV], 'clearly showed….When he wrote about the burning bush, (he said)' [NCV], 'clearly proves….In the passage about the burning bush (he speaks of)' [TEV], 'proved this when he wrote about the burning bush' [NLT].

c. pres. act. indic. of λέγω (LN 33.69): 'to speak' [AB, LN, Lns; NRSV, TEV], 'to call' [Arn, BECNT, NTC; HCSB, KJV, NASB, NET, NIV, REB], 'to say' [LN; CEV, GW, NCV], 'to refer to' [NLT]. The subject of this verb is changed from Moses to the passage: 'it speaks about' [WBC]. The present tense 'speaks' is timeless [AB, NIGTC], and is equivalent to 'what stands written' [AB].

QUESTION—What issue did Jesus now address?

Jesus now proceeded to answer the objection that the Pharisees' previous question implied, that the teaching about the resurrection is inconsistent with the Mosaic law, and he showed that even Moses implied that there will be a resurrection [ICC]. Jesus referred to 'even' Moses, the very one who was supposed to be against this teaching [Gdt, ICC, My, Rb].

QUESTION—In what way did Moses show this?

Moses is referred to as the author of the account, not in regard to his role as participant [TH]. It means that Moses disclosed this when he wrote in

Exodus regarding the episode of God's appearance at the burning bush [Lns].

QUESTION—Who is the subject of the verb λέγει 'speaks' in the phrase 'speaks about the Lord the God of Abraham'?

1. Moses is the subject [BECNT, Lns; probably all versions]: as Moses speaks about the Lord being the God of Abraham. The significance of what Moses says does not mean that Moses gave God this title, but that Moses spoke about what God said about himself [Lns].
2. The passage about the bush is the subject [WBC]: as the passage speaks about the Lord being the God of Abraham. Although the words in Exodus are spoken by God, here it is simpler to take the verb impersonally as 'it (the text) says or speaks about' [WBC].

QUESTION—What is the reference to the bush?

The passage about the burning bush is Exodus 3:1–6. The OT Scriptures did not have chapter and verse numbers, so a passage had to be referred to by mentioning its contents [Arn, ICC, NAC, TNTC].

20:38 And^a he-is not God of-dead (persons) but of-living (persons), because^b all are-alive^c to-him.

LEXICON—a. δέ (LN 91.3): 'and' [LN], 'so' [LN; CEV, NLT], 'for' [KJV], 'now' [BECNT, Lns; NASB, NET, NRSV], 'indeed' [AB], 'but' [Arn], not explicit [NTC, WBC; GW, HCSB, NCV, NIV, REB, TEV]. The conjunction indicates a transition to a new thought [WBC; NET].

b. γάρ (LN 89.23, 91.1): 'because' [LN (89.23); HCSB, NCV], 'for' [AB, Arn, BECNT, LN (89.23), Lns, NTC, WBC; KJV, NASB, NET, NIV, NRSV, TEV], 'then' [LN (91.1)], 'this means that' [CEV], not explicit [GW, NLT, REB].

c. pres. act. indic. of ζάω (LN 23.88) (BAGD 3.b. p. 337): 'to be alive' [LN], 'to live' [BAGD, LN]. The phrase αὐτῷ ζῶσιν 'all are alive to him' [NTC] is also translated 'all are living to him' [HCSB; similarly Arn, BECNT; KJV, NASB, NCV], 'all are living for him' [Lns], 'all live before him' [NET], 'they are all alive to him' [NLT], 'to him they are all alive' [AB; similarly NIV, NLT, NRSV, TEV], 'so far as God is concerned all are alive' [WBC], 'everyone is alive as far as God is concerned' [CEV], 'in his sight all are alive' [REB], 'in God's sight all people are living' [GW].

QUESTION—How did God's words about himself prove that he is God of living persons?

The patriarchs Abraham, Isaac, and Jacob had died long before God said this to Moses. Since God told Moses that he is their God, this proves that these men were still alive since such a relationship presupposes living partners [BECNT, TH]. It means that even after the physical death of those men, they are still living and in the future they will share in the life of the resurrection [NIC]. The present tense verb in the phrase 'I *am* the God of Abraham' implies that Abraham still lives [Arn, ICC], because if Abraham had ceased to exist at his death, God would have ceased to be his God [ICC]. Only living people can have a God and God's promise that he will be the God of these patriarchs implies that he will maintain them as living beings [AB, NIGTC]. He meant that in some form they were still alive [Su]. Either these men must still be alive in some way or can expect that God will raise them from the dead [MGC, NIGTC].

QUESTION—What is meant by the last clause, 'because all are alive to him'?
This clause expresses the immortality of the soul [AB, MGC]. It gives an explanation of the preceding statement [Lns]. It is the grounds for the argument [NICNT]. The pronoun αὐτῷ 'him' in this phrase is in dative case. The dative case could be rendered 'by him' (by his power), or 'in him', or 'for him' (for his honor, or for his thought or judgment, meaning that God accounts them as living) [EGT]. It is the dative of reference, that is, in respect to God or in relation to him [My]. In relationship to God they are alive [Su, TG] and have a meaningful existence beyond death [Su]. In reference to us, they seem to die, but in reference to God, all live [Gdt, ICC, My, TH, TNTC]. The word 'all' refers to the patriarchs and probably all those who are righteous [MGC], whom God considers worthy of sharing in the resurrection and the age to come [AB, NIGTC]. 'All' refers to all who are mentioned in 20:35–36 [ICC]. No matter if they are physically alive or dead, all are alive to God [TH]. This clause indicates that God has taken the righteous dead alive to his own realm where they are awaiting the future resurrection [WBC].

20:39 **And answering some of-the scribes said, Teacher, you-spoke well.**[a]
20:40 **Because no-longer they-dared**[b] **to-question him (about) anything.**

TEXT—In 20:40, instead of γάρ 'because', some manuscripts read δέ 'and'. GNT does not mention this variant. Δέ 'and' is read by KJV.

LEXICON—a. καλῶς (LN 72.12) (BAGD 4.b. p. 401): 'well' [BAGD], 'rightly' [BAGD, LN], 'correctly' [LN]. The phrase 'you spoke well' is translated 'you have spoken well' [Arn, WBC; HCSB, NASB, NET, NRSV], 'you have answered well' [BECNT], 'thou hast well said' [KJV], 'excellently didst thou speak' [Lns], 'you have given a good answer' [CEV], 'you have put it well' [AB], 'your answer was good' [NCV], 'a good answer' [TEV], 'well spoken' [REB], 'well said' [NTC; NIV, NLT], 'that was well said' [GW].

b. imperf. act. indic. of τολμάω (LN 25.161) (BAGD 1.a. p. 821): 'to dare' [Arn, BAGD, BECNT, LN, Lns, NTC, WBC; all versions except NASB, NCV], 'to venture' [AB], 'to have the courage' [BAGD; NASB], 'to be brave enough' [BAGD; NCV].

QUESTION—What is involved in this shift from the Sadducees to the scribes?
These were members of other parties standing by and they were probably Pharisees [NIC, NIGTC, Rb, TNTC]. These are the scribes mentioned in 20:1 and 20:19 [AB]. These were Pharisee scribes who accepted Jesus' viewpoint about immortality and the resurrection [NIGTC, TG].

QUESTION—What did the scribes mean when they said Jesus spoke well?
Although they were hostile to Jesus, they felt compelled to commend Jesus' answer to the Sadducees [Lns]. The scribes expressed their approval of how Jesus had confronted the Sadducees [BECNT, Crd, ICC, NIC, TH]. They thought that Jesus had answered correctly in this matter [AB, BECNT, MGC, NIVS]. They approved of the way Jesus proved the doctrine of the resurrection, something they had not been able to do when they argued with the Sadducees [Lns]. They complemented Jesus because they were glad to have the Sadducees bested in the debate [NTC]. The word 'well' indicates that they approved of what Jesus said and that they marveled at the way he had handled the Sadducees' question [BECNT]. They were glad that Jesus had bested the Sadducees, but at the same time, they were not glad that Jesus had come out triumphant in an encounter [EGT].

QUESTION—Who no longer dared to question Jesus?
1. This refers to the Sadducees [Arn, Lns, NIC, NTC, Su, TH, TNTC, WBC]. The Sadducees who had questioned Jesus had been shown to be wrong about their views of the dead and the resurrection, so they did not venture to question him any more [NIC]. In Matthew 22:34–36 and Mark 12:28 we learn that the Pharisees and scribes did ask a further question. The conjunction γάρ 'because' is connected with 20:39 and explains why the scribes praised Jesus at this point—they had seen how he had silenced the Sadducees [Arn].
2. This refers to the scribes [AB, EGT, Gdt, ICC, My; NET]. They were opponents of Jesus, but some praised him because he always came out victorious and therefore they did not want to risk any more defeats [ICC]. The scribes could do nothing but flatter Jesus, seeing that they dared not offer more questions [EGT]. This means that they did not dare to *openly* question Jesus, since in 22:66–68 the scribes were among those who questioned Jesus at his trial [AB]. The conjunction γάρ 'because' is connected with 20:39 and gives the reason the scribes did not dare to question Jesus after seeing how the attempt to show up Jesus as being ignorant failed [Gdt; NET]. The scribes were so impressed with Jesus' ability, that they could do nothing but flatter Jesus because they dared not ask any argumentative question [EGT].
3. This refers to people in general [BECNT, MGC, NIGTC, Rb]. It refers to both the Sadducees and the unfriendly Pharisees [MGC, NIGTC]. It refers to all of Jesus' opponents [NICNT]. Every possible group had tried to best Jesus: Pharisees, nationalists, scribes, Sadducees, and leaders of the people [BECNT].

DISCOURSE UNIT: 20:41–47 [NIV, NLT]. The topic is whose son is the Messiah?

DISCOURSE UNIT: 20:41–44 [AB, BECNT, NAC, NICNT, NIGTC, Su, TNTC, WBC; CEV, GW, HCSB, NCV, NET, NRSV, TEV]. The topic is David's son [CEV], the question about David's son [AB, NAC, TNTC; NRSV], the question about the Messiah [HCSB, TEV], Jesus' question about Messiah [BECNT, Su, WBC], how can David's son be David's lord? [GW], is the Christ the son of David? [NCV], the question of the Messiah's authority [NICNT], the person of the Messiah [NIGTC], the Messiah: David's son and lord [NET]

20:41 **And he-said to them, How**[a] **(is it that) they-say the Messiah is David's son**[b]**?**

LEXICON—a. πῶς (Ln 92.16): 'how' [BECNT, LN; KJV], 'how is it that' [AB, Arn, WBC; NASB, NET, NIV], 'how can' [NTC; GW, HCSB, NRSV, REB], 'how can it be (said that)' [TEV], 'how do' [Lns], 'why' [CEV, NCV], 'why is it that' [NLT].

b. υἱός (LN 10.30): 'son' [BECNT, Lns, NTC, WBC; all versions except TEV], 'male descendant' [LN], 'descendant' [TEV]. It refers to a descendant of David [Arn]. He would be born of David's lineage [AB].

QUESTION—Who was Jesus addressing now?

Jesus was speaking to the scribes who in 20:39 had expressed their admiration for what Jesus had said [Alf, BECNT, EGT, Gdt, ICC, My, TH]. He was addressing the Pharisees [AB, Lns, NIGTC], because according to Matt. 22:41, the audience is composed of Pharisees [Lns, NIGTC]. The audience consisted of all those who were who were assembled, including all parties [Crd, WBC].

QUESTION—Who are the referents of λέγουσιν 'they say' in the question 'how do they say the Messiah is David's son'

This use of 'they' is odd, but in Mark 12:35 the subject of the verb is 'the scribes', so probably Jesus was speaking about the scribes to the crowd even though scribes were in the crowd [NIGTC]. The subject is the Pharisees, including both rabbis and lawyers [Rb]. It was a fact that Jesus' opponents believed that the Messiah would be a descendant of David [Arn, BECNT, NIGTC, Su] and there are many passages in the OT that caused them to believe this [BECNT, NIGTC]. Jesus asked why the scribes taught that the Messiah is David's son [BECNT]. The subject of the verb is people in general [Arn, Crd, TH]. The subject is indefinite [AB, Arn] and can be translated such as 'men say' or 'it is said' [Arn], 'how is it said' [AB; NIV], 'how can it be said' [TEV], 'why is it said' [NLT]. Jesus had been called the 'Son of David' by the blind man in 18:38 [Arn]

QUESTION—What is the function of Jesus' question beginning with πῶς 'how'?

This can be taken as a rhetorical question that denies that the Messiah can be David's son ('how is it possible that?'), or a request for an explanation of how the Messiah can be David's son and also David's lord ('in what sense?') [NIGTC]. Jesus was not trying to show that it was a false idea [Arn, MGC, NIBC], rather, he was affirming such a belief [MGC]. He wanted to lead his audience to a proper evaluation of what Scripture taught [Arn]. Jesus was challenging them to consider the implications of this sentence [Su]. Jesus was not *merely* David's descendant [NTC].

20:42 Because David himself says in (the) book of-Psalms, (The) Lord said to my Lord,[a] Sit at my right[b] **20:43** until[c] I-make your enemies a-footstool[d] for-your feet.

TEXT—In 20:42, instead of αὐτὸς γὰρ Δαυίδ 'because David himself', some manuscripts read καὶ αὐτὸς Δαυίδ 'and David himself'. GNT does not mention this variant. Καὶ αὐτὸς Δαυίδ 'and David himself' is read by KJV.

LEXICON—a. κύριος (LN 12.9) (BAGD 2.c.α. p. 459): 'Lord' [AB, Arn, BAGD, BECNT, LN, Lns, NTC, WBC; all versions].
- b. δεξιά (LN 87.34) (BAGD 2.b. p. 175): 'right' [BAGD, Lns], 'right hand' [AB, Arn, BECNT, LN, NTC, WBC; HCSB, KJV, NASB, NET, NIV, NRSV, REB], 'right side' [CEV, NCV, TEV]. This means to sit in the place of honor [AB, BAGD], to be granted a high honor, to be in a position of high status [LN]. The command 'sit at my right' is translated 'sit in honor at my right hand' [NLT], 'take the highest position in heaven' [GW].
- c. ἕως (LN 67.119) (BAGD I.1.b. p. 334): 'until' [AB, Arn, BAGD, BECNT, LN, Lns, NTC, WBC; all versions].
- d. ὑποπόδιον (LN 37.8) (BAGD p. 847): 'footstool' [BAGD, LN]. The phrase ἕως ὑποπόδιον τῶν ποδῶν σου 'until I make your enemies a footstool for your feet' [AB, BECNT, WBC; NASB, NET, NIV] is also translated 'until I make your enemies into a footstool for you' [CEV], 'until I make your enemies your footstool' [Arn, NTC; GW, HCSB, KJV, NRSV, REB], 'until I put your enemies as a footstool under your feet' [TEV], 'till I place thine enemies as a footstool of thy feet' [Lns], 'until I humble your enemies, making them a footstool under your feet' [NLT], 'until I put your enemies under your control' [NCV]. To make an enemy someone's footstool means to subject the enemy to someone so that he can put his foot on the subject's neck [BAGD].

QUESTION—What relationship is indicated by γάρ 'because' ?
This conjunction explains why Jesus had asked the question [Arn].

QUESTION—Where in the Psalms is this statement?
This is quoted from Psalm 110:1. Jesus referred to the traditional heading of the psalm, 'A Psalm of David', and the argument builds on the fact that David spoke these words [BECNT, WBC].

QUESTION—What is the meaning of εἶπεν κύριος τῷ κυρίῳ μου 'the Lord said to my Lord'?
In Hebrew, which was written only with consonants, the name for God was *YHWH* and to avoid violating the law about taking the name of God in vain, Jewish scholars later added to that name the vowels for another name for God they were allowed to pronounce, *Adonai* 'my Lord'. In the Greek translation of the Hebrew Scriptures, both of the names were written κύριος 'Lord' and also in this Greek text. In the Hebrew text, the distinction is clear that *YHWH* was speaking to *Adonai*. [NIGTC]. In the Psalm, 'The Lord' is Yahweh, the God of the Jews, and 'my Lord' is the king of Israel [BECNT, Lns, NTC, TG, WBC], the one chosen by God, and in the context of Jesus'

statement, 'my Lord' refers to the Messiah [MGC, TG]. It means 'the Lord (God) said to (David's) lord (the Messiah)' [MGC]. All translations stick to the Greek text 'the Lord said to my Lord' except two who try to show a distinction between the two titles: 'The *Lord* said to my *lord*' [AB, WBC].

QUESTION—What is meant by the idiom 'until I make your enemies a footstool for your feet'?

This is figurative language for the complete defeat and humiliation of the enemy [TG, WBC]. It pictures an enemy lying in the dust so the conqueror can place his feet on his neck [NTC]. Jesus referred to the intervention of God that would occur at the end of the age and therefore this is about the Messiah [WBC]. Then he shall reign as supreme in the universe [Lns].

20:44 Therefore David calls him Lord, then[a] how is-he his son?

LEXICON—a. καί (LN 91.12): 'then' [AB, LN, NTC; HCSB, KJV, NIV, REB, TEV], 'how is it then' [LN], 'so' [WBC; CEV, GW, NCV, NRSV], 'and' [Arn, BECNT, Lns; NASB], not explicit [NET, NLT].

QUESTION—What relationship is indicated by οὖν 'therefore'?

This indicates a conclusion to be drawn from the passage in the Psalms [NIGTC, TG]. It means 'as scripture shows' or 'as we have seen', David calls him Lord [TH]. It indicates the implied result of the preceding clause about David [NET].

QUESTION—What is meant by Jesus' question, 'How is he his son'?

It is clear that Jesus equated the Messiah with the one David called 'my Lord' in the Psalm [TG]. The question now is 'How can he be David's son if David calls him 'my Lord'?' Normally, a father has authority over his son [BECNT, MGC, NIBC; NET] and the son calls the father 'lord', not the other way around [AB, NAC]. How can the Messiah be at the same time David's son and David's divine Lord? [Lns]. Although grammatically, the question could be taken to mean that the Messiah was not David's son, such a response was not intended to be considered as a possibility [Crd, NIGTC, NTC]. Granted that the Messiah was David's son, then when David called his son 'my Lord', it indicates that the Messiah cannot *merely* be David's son in the sense of being David's descendant, he is more than that [NIGTC, NTC]. Both assertions were true, but one of them needs qualification, so the question asks in what sense was the Messiah David's son, the obvious answer being that his sonship stands in some lesser place than his lordship [BECNT; NET]. The Messiah has the characteristics of being an exalted figure and also of being the human descendant of David [NIGTC]. The answer must be that the Messiah is both human and divine [Arn, Gdt, Lns, Rb, Su]. The Messiah was David's son by physical descent and he was David's Lord because God had designated him *Adonai*, deity itself [Su].

QUESTION—What was the dilemma Jesus put his audience in?

They had considered David's son to be only human, and had never seen his deity, which is plainly disclosed in this Psalm. They knew that the Messiah would be David's son, and they dared not deny David's inspired word that the Messiah would be David's Lord (and thus very God), so they had no answer to give and refused to admit the deity of the Messiah [Lns]. To answer this question they would have to admit that the Messiah was the kind of person Jesus claimed himself to be [Su]. It was wrong for them to be offended when he spoke of himself as the Son of God [Arn]

DISCOURSE UNIT: 20:45–21:4 [NICNT]. The topic is the despotic authority of Jerusalem's leadership.

DISCOURSE UNIT: 20:45–47 [AB, BECNT, NAC, Su, TNTC, WBC; CEV, GW, HCSB, NCV, NET, NRSV, TEV]. The topic is Jesus and the teachers of the Law of Moses [CEV], warnings concerning the scribes [AB, NAC, TNTC; HCSB], Jesus accuses some leaders [NCV], Jesus' condemnation of the scribes [BECNT, Su, WBC], Jesus denounces the scribes [NRSV], Jesus disapproves of the example set by scribes [GW], Jesus warns against the teachers of the law [TEV], Jesus warns the disciples against pride [NET].

20:45 And (while) all the people were-listening he-said to his disciples, **20:46** Beware[a] of the scribes the (ones who) want to-walk-around in long-robes[b] and loving[c] greetings[d] in the marketplaces and best-seats[e] in the synagogues and places-of-honor[f] at the banquets,

TEXT—In 20:45, instead of τοῖς μαθηταῖς αὐτοῦ 'to his disciples', some manuscripts read τοῖς ἑαυτοῦ μαθηταῖς 'to his own disciples', others read τοῖς μαθηταῖς 'to the disciples', and one manuscript reads πρὸς αὐτούς 'to them'. GNT reads τοῖς μαθηταῖς αὐτοῦ 'to his disciples' with a C decision and places αὐτοῦ 'his' in brackets, indicating that the Committee had difficulty making the decision.

LEXICON—a. pres. act. impera. of προσέχω (LN 27.59) (BAGD 1.b. p. 714): 'to beware of' [AB, Arn, BAGD, BECNT, Lns, NTC, WBC; all versions except CEV, TEV], 'to be on guard against' [BAGD, LN; CEV, TEV]. This is a warning not to imitate such people [AB, BECNT, NICNT]. The present tense indicates that they were to be constantly on guard against such pride [NET].

b. στολή (LN 6.174) (BAGD p. 769): 'long robe' [AB, BECNT, LN; all versions except NCV, NIV, NLT], 'long garment' [Arn], 'flowing robe' [BAGD; NIV, NLT], 'long, flowing robe' [NTC], 'festal robe' [Lns], 'fancy clothes' [NCV], 'fine garb' [WBC].

c. pres. act. participle of φιλέω (LN 25.105) (BAGD 1.b. p. 859): 'to love' [BAGD, BECNT, LN, Lns, NTC, WBC; all versions except CEV], 'to be fond of' [AB, Arn], 'to like' [BAGD, LN; CEV].

d. ἀσπασμός (LN 33.20) (BAGD 1. p. 117): 'greeting' [BAGD, BECNT, LN; HCSB, KJV], 'greeting of respect' [AB], 'respectful greeting' [NASB], 'elaborate greeting' [NET], 'salutation' [Lns], 'formal salutation' [NTC]. This noun is also translated as a verb: 'to be greeted' [Arn, WBC; CEV, GW, NIV], 'to be greeted respectfully' [REB], 'to be greeted with respect' [NCV, NRSV, TEV], 'to have everyone bow to

them' [NLT]. This refers to formal greetings [BAGD]. See this word at 11:43.
e. πρωτοκαθεδρία (LN 87.18) (BAGD p. 725): 'best seat' [BAGD, LN; NET, NRSV], 'place of honor' [BAGD, LN], 'seat of honor' [LN; NLT], 'most important seat' [NCV, NIV], 'most prominent seat' [Arn], 'chief seat' [NTC; NASB, REB], 'prime seat' [WBC], 'highest seat' [KJV], 'first seat' [BECNT, Lns], 'reserved seat' [TEV], 'front seats' [AB; CEV, GW, HCSB]. This is the place of honor at the best seat in the synagogue [BAGD]. Probably it refers to the row of seats near the ark [BECNT, TG].
f. πρωτοκλισία (LN 87.18) (BAGD p. 725): 'place of honor' [LN, NTC; GW, HCSB, NASB, NET, NIV, NRSV, REB], 'seat of honor' [BAGD, LN; NLT], 'best seat' [BAGD, LN; CEV], 'most important seat' [NCV], 'best place' [TEV], 'first place' [AB, WBC], 'first seat' [BECNT], 'chief place' [Arn], 'chief room' [KJV], 'first reclining place' [Lns]. This noun has the same domain number as the preceding noun πρωτοκαθεδρία [LN] and both are translated the same [BECNT; NCV, NLT]. The two nouns are synonyms for the location of the seats reserved for the prominent people among the assembly [NICNT].

QUESTION—Who were the people listening to Jesus while he spoke to his disciples?

These were the people who had witnessed Jesus' conversation with the scribes [ICC, WBC]. The crowd consisted of the pilgrims who had come to Jerusalem for the Passover [Lns], but the scribes were still present to hear Jesus warn the people against them [Arn, Lns]. Jesus was addressing the Twelve who had positions of leadership, but other disciples were in the crowd [Su].

QUESTION—Does this condemnation apply to all scribes?

This is a condemnation of scribes as a class [Arn]. However, this doesn't mean that all scribes were selfish and unscrupulous like the kind pictured here [AB, Arn]. In view of the good response of some of the scribes in 20:39, this is taken to mean '*those* scribes who do such things' [WBC; NLT], and this translation is justified by the article τῶν following 'scribes' in the phrase 'the scribes, *the* (ones) wanting to-walk-around in long-robes' [Arn]. Although not all scribes fit the description, the wording is unqualified because it is a hyperbole that makes a more powerful statement than saying 'beware of some scribes' [NAC].

QUESTION—What is the significance of wanting to walk around in long robes?

The word στολή 'robe' is used for the outer cloak most people wore, but lawyers and officers used a more voluminous cloak with ornamentation which was a mark of distinction [AB]. They wanted to be recognized and treated as distinguished persons [Lns], as important people [TH]. The long robes signified that they were gentlemen of leisure [TNTC]. This describes the distinctive clothing denoting the high office the scribes considered themselves to have [WBC]. They wore long, flowing robes and had a long, fringed mantle reaching to their feet [BECNT]. This is a condemnation of their ostentatious style [BECNT, MGC, NAC, TG], and their pride [TG].

QUESTION—What is the significance of loving greetings in the marketplace?

They visited the crowded marketplaces in order to receive public recognition of their exalted status [NTC]. The greetings were given in recognition of their scribal position [WBC]. These were not simple and sincere greetings, but were long, elaborate greetings from people who curried their favor [Su]. The scribes wanted people to show them respect for their prominent position [NTC]. Jesus also rebuked the Pharisees for this love for attention in 11:43.

QUESTION—What is the significance of loving the best places in the synagogues and banquets?

They desired the recognition of being ushered to the best seats so people would see them receive such honor [Su]. Because of their scribal status they were honored with such seats [NTC, WBC]. Jesus had warned his disciples about this problem in 14:7–14.

20:47 **who devour^a widows' houses and for-pretense^b they-pray lengthy (prayers). These will-receive greater condemnation.^c**

LEXICON—a. pres. act. indic. of κατεσθίω (LN 88.145) (BAGD 2. p. 422): 'to devour, to eat up, to consume' [BAGD]. Here, this is a figurative extension of the meaning 'to eat up' (LN 23.11) and means to take total advantage of someone [LN]. It is figurative for 'destroy' and refers to appropriating the houses illegally [BAGD]. The phrase 'who devour widow's houses' [AB, Arn, BECNT, Lns, NTC; HCSB, KJV, NASB, NIV, NRSV] is also translated 'who devour widows' estates' [WBC], 'they devour widows' property' [NET], 'who eat up the property of widows' [REB], 'they cheat widows out of their homes' [CEV], 'they cheat widows and steal their houses' [NCV], 'they rob widows by taking their houses' [GW], 'they shamelessly cheat widows out of their property' [NLT], 'who take advantage of widows and rob them of their homes' [TEV].

b. πρόφασις (LN 88.230) (BAGD 2. p. 722): 'pretense' [LN], 'pretext, for appearance's sake' [BAGD]. This dative noun προφάσει 'for pretense' is translated 'in pretence' [Lns, WBC], 'for appearance's sake' [AB; NASB, REB], 'for the sake of appearance' [NRSV], 'for a show' [KJV], 'to make a show of' [TEV], 'to make themselves look good' [GW], 'then try to make themselves look good' [NCV], 'for a pretext' [Arn], 'under pretext' [BECNT], 'as/for a show' [NTC; NET, NIV], 'just for show' [HCSB], 'just to show off' [CEV], 'to cover up the kind of people they really are' [NLT].

c. κρίμα (LN 56.30) (BAGD 4.b. p. 450): 'condemnation' [BAGD, LN], 'punishment' [BAGD]. This means a 'judicial verdict' and mostly refers to the sentence of condemnation, yet it may include the subsequent punishment itself [BAGD]. The clause 'they will receive greater condemnation' [BECNT, WBC; NASB] is also translated 'they will receive the greater condemnation' [NRSV], 'these will receive a greater punishment' [HCSB, NCV], 'such men will receive a heavier sentence' [NTC], 'they will receive more abundant punishment' [Arn], 'they will receive a more severe punishment' [NET], 'they will incur the severest condemnation' [AB], 'their punishment will be the greater' [NLT], 'their punishment will be all the worse' [TEV], 'the sentence they receive will be all the more severe' [REB], 'these teachers will be punished most of all' [CEV], 'the same shall receive greater damnation' [KJV], 'these shall take more abundant judgment' [Lns], 'the scribes will receive the most severe punishment' [GW], 'such men will be punished most severely' [NIV]. See this word at 23:40.

QUESTION—What is meant by *devouring* widows' houses?
1. The scribes were cheating widows out of their houses and estates [AB, BAGD, BNTC, Lns, NAC, TG; CEV, GW, NCV, NLT, TEV]. They could do this while acting as executors of a widow's property [AB, NAC]. They may have acted legally, but not ethically [TG]. They took over the house as pledges for debts that could not be repaid [BNTC].
2. Perhaps they encouraged widows to make gifts beyond their means [Arn, NIC, TNTC]. They took advantage of kindhearted widows by constantly insisting that they give large amounts of gifts to the temples that were beyond their limited means [Arn, NIC]. They charged for services they rendered [Arn].
3. The scribes were abusing the hospitality of widows [Arn, ICC]. There were wealthy widows who were pious and weak and scribes accepted both hospitality and rich presents from them [ICC]. Being invited to meals, the scribes 'devoured' the property of the widows [Arn].
4. The scribes received money from credulous old widows as a payment for the long prayers they claimed to make on behalf of the widows [MGC].
5. Luke did not explain what he meant and no one can be sure [BECNT, NIBC, NICNT, NTC; NET]. Whatever they did, it was a crime of extortion [NTC]. By some kind of fraud and schemes they took advantage of defenseless widows [NIVS].

QUESTION—What is wrong with lengthy prayers?
Jesus wasn't condemning the length of their prayers, he condemned their motivation to look devout by praying long prayers [AB, Arn, NAC]. They appeared to be pious, but they were really not pious in the way they treated others so callously [BECNT]. This is how they covered up their robbery [Lns, TG]. Some closely connect this with the previous clause to show their hypocrisy [CEV, GW, NCV, NLT, TEV]: they devour the widows' houses and *then* for pretense they pray lengthy prayers. This ostentatious piety was used by the scribes as they prayed for the widows [AB, MGC; REB]: they devour the widows' houses *while* for pretense they pray lengthy prayers.

QUESTION—What is involved in their condemnation and what is being compared?

God will condemn them [AB, Arn]. This refers to the final eschatological judgment [AB, Lns]. All wrongdoing will be punished, but especially that which is cloaked in religious devotion [Arn]. God will punish them more severely than he would otherwise [TG]. God will punish them more severely than others who had not done so [TH, WBC]. God will punish them more severely than other Jews who did not claim greater piety and did not enjoy as many spiritual privileges as they do [NIC]. Those who are leaders of a religious community and use their position for personal profit will receive heavy punishment because God's punishment is given in proportion to their knowledge and guilt [Su].

DISCOURSE UNIT: 21:1–37 [REB]. The topic is warnings about the end.

DISCOURSE UNIT: 21:1–9 [NASB]. The topic is the widow's gift.

DISCOURSE UNIT: 21:1–4 [AB, BECNT, NAC, NIGTC, Su, TNTC, WBC; CEV, GW, HCSB, NCV, NET, NIV, NLT, NRSV, TEV]. The topic is a widow's offering [AB, NAC, NIGTC, TNTC; CEV, GW, NET, NIV, NLT, NRSV, TEV], the widow's gift [HCSB], the widow who gave all [BECNT], commending the pauper widow [Su], the giving of the rich and the poor [WBC], true giving [NCV].

21:1 And having-looked-up he-saw the wealthy (ones) putting their gifts[a] into the offering-box.[b] **21:2** And he-saw a-certain poor widow putting-in there two leptas.[c]

TEXT—In 21:2, following εἶδεν δέ 'and he said', some manuscripts add καί 'also', although GNT does not mention this variant. Καί 'also' is added by NTC; CEV, HCSB, KJV, NET, NIV, NRSV, TEV, although the readings of others than KJV may be stylistic rather than textually based.

LEXICON—a. δῶρον (LN 57.84): 'gift' [Arn, BECNT, LN, Lns, NTC, WBC; CEV, all versions except HCSB], 'offering' [HCSB], 'contribution' [AB].

b. γαζοφυλάκιον (LN **6.141**) (BAGD p. 149): 'offering box' [**LN**; CEV, NET], 'temple offering box' [GW], 'Temple money box' [NCV], 'contribution box' [BAGD], 'collection box' [NLT], 'treasury' [Arn, BECNT, WBC; KJV, NASB, NRSV], 'temple treasury' [AB, NTC; HCSB, NIV, REB, TEV].

c. λεπτόν (LN 6.79) (BAGD 2. 472): 'lepton' [LN, WBC], 'tiny coin' [LN; HCSB, REB], 'small coin' [AB; GW], 'very small coin' [NTC], 'copper coin' [BECNT; NASB, NCV], 'small copper coin' [BAGD; NET, NIV, NRSV], 'little copper coin' [TEV], 'mite' [Arn; KJV], 'penny' [CEV, NLT]. This was the smallest unit of money [AB, BECNT, TG]. Its value was one-hundredth of a denarius, the average daily wage [BECNT]. See this word at 12:59.

QUESTION—Where was Jesus?

Jesus was sitting down as he taught and he *looked up* to see what was going on around him [NIGTC]. Perhaps Jesus was taking a rest after his long discussions and was sitting down on a bench [Gdt, ICC, NIC, NTC], perhaps with his eyes downcast or closed [Arn, ICC]. In Mark 12:41 it says that Jesus had taken a position where he could watch people putting in their offerings, so Luke is telling about one incident that Jesus noticed [Su].

QUESTION—Why were there offering boxes in the Temple?

In addition to the tithe, people gave offerings for the support of the Temple and priests [Lns, Su]. The Treasury proper in the Temple was used for keeping legal documents, temple wealth, and the collected tithes and gifts, but in Luke the location here requires access by women [WBC]. Thirteen trumpet-mouthed boxes were placed in the Court of the Women for offerings [AB, BECNT, Gdt, ICC, Lns, NIVS, NTC, Su, TG, TNTC], and the room or area containing these boxes was apparently known as the Treasury [BECNT, ICC, Lns, NIGTC, TNTC]. The offering boxes were chests where gifts could be dropped and the receptacles were separately marked for their different purposes [AB, ICC, MGC, NTC]. The boxes were for contributions that were not obligatory [WBC]. The woman put her money into one of these receptacles [BNTC, Gdt, ICC, Lns, NIGTC, Su, TG, TH, TNTC]. Offerings were given for various purposes, and in relation to vows, the person declared the amount and purpose of the gift to the attending priest and it was therefore easy for Jesus to know the amounts given by the various people [NIGTC]. The offering boxes in the temple had trumpet-like openings into which money was thrown and coins might roll around as they went down, calling attention to large gifts [Su]. Jesus knew supernaturally that the two coins were all that the widow possessed [Arn, ICC, Lns].

21:3 And he-said, Truly I-say-to-you that this poor widow put[a] (in) more (than) all. **21:4** Because all these put into[b] the gifts from the (things) abounding[c] to-them, but this (widow) out-of her need[d] put (in) all the possessions[e] that she-had.

TEXT—In 21:4, following δῶρα 'gifts', some manuscripts add τοῦ θεοῦ 'of God'. GNT rejects this addition with a B decision, indicating that the text is almost certain. Τοῦ θεοῦ 'of God' is added by BECNT and KJV.

LEXICON—a. aorist act. indic. of βάλλω (LN 85.34) (BAGD 2.b. p. 131): 'to put' [BAGD, LN]. The phrase 'put in more than all' is translated 'has put in more than all' [Arn], 'has put in more than all the others' [CEV, NIV, TEV], 'has put in more than all of them' [BECNT; HCSB, NASB, NET, NRSV], 'dropped in more than all the others' [NTC], 'threw in more than all' [Lns], 'has cast in more than they all' [KJV], 'has given more than any of them' [REB], 'has given more than all the others' [GW], 'has given more than all the rest of them' [WBC; NLT], 'has contributed more than all the rest' [AB], 'gave more than all those rich people' [NCV].

b. εἰς (LN 84.22): 'into' [LN]. The phrase 'put into the gifts' is translated 'put into the offering' [WBC; NASB], 'have put in gifts' [HCSB], 'have cast in unto the offerings' [KJV], 'offered their gifts' [NET, TEV], 'gave their gifts' [NIV], 'have given their gifts' [AB], 'threw in for gifts' [Lns], 'gave what…' [CEV, GW, NCV], 'have given' [NLT, REB], 'have contributed' [NRSV], 'contributed to the donations' [Arn], 'have contributed into the gifts for God' [BECNT], 'dropped in something among the gifts' [NTC]. They added to the gifts that were already in the boxes [ICC].

c. pres. act. participle of περισσεύω (LN 59.52) (BAGD 1.a.β. p. 650): 'to abound, to be left over' [LN], 'to be in abundance' [BAGD, LN]. The phrase 'from the things abounding to them' is translated 'out of their abundance' [AB, NTC; KJV, NRSV], 'from their abundance' [BECNT], 'out of what abounds to them' [Lns], 'out of their surplus' [HCSB, NASB], 'out of their wealth' [NET, NIV], 'out of their leftovers' [WBC], 'only what they did not need' [NCV], 'what they could spare' [Arn; GW], 'from what they had to spare' [TEV], 'what they didn't need' [CEV], 'a tiny part of their surplus' [NLT], 'had more than enough' [REB].

d. ὑστέρημα (LN **57.38**) (BAGD 1. p. 849): 'need, want' [BAGD], 'what is needed' [LN], 'what is lacking' [**LN**]. The phrase 'out of her need' is translated 'in her need' [AB], 'out of her poverty' [NTC; HCSB, NASB, NET, NIV, NRSV], 'out of her want' [Lns], 'out of what she lacked' [WBC], 'of her penury' [KJV], 'from her poverty' [BECNT], 'in her poverty' [GW], 'in her want' [Arn], 'poor as she is' [NLT, TEV], '(she) is very poor' [CEV, NCV], 'with less than enough' [REB].

e. βίος (LN 57.18) (BAGD 3. p. 142): 'possessions, livelihood' [LN], 'property' [BAGD, LN]. The phrase 'all the possessions that she had' is translated 'everything she had' [CEV, NLT], 'all the living she had' [Lns; KJV], 'all the life that she had' [BECNT], 'her whole living' [NTC], 'the whole living she had' [Arn], 'all the livelihood that she had' [WBC], 'all she had to live on' [HCSB, NASB, NCV, NIV, NRSV, REB, TEV; similarly AB; GW, NET].

QUESTION—How could two leptas be more than what wealthy persons had put in?

This does not mean that she gave more money than others had [TG, TH].

1. 'More' means that the widow gave proportionately more than others [AB, BECNT, MGC, NIBC, NIGTC, TG, TNTC, WBC]. The wealthy had given only a small part of their wealth while the widow had given all that she had [NIGTC, TG].
2. 'More' means that what she did was more valuable than giving money [Gdt, Lns, NIC, NTC, Su, TH; NET]. What the widow did was more important in Jesus' view [NTC]. She gave the money sincerely at a great cost to herself [NET].

QUESTION—Who is the widow being compared with?

1. The widow had put in more than any one of them [REB].

2. The widow had put in more than all of them together [Lns, NAC, TNTC]. In Jesus' estimation, her two leptas amounted to more than the combined sum of all the wealthy givers [Lns].

QUESTION—Who were πάντες οὗτοι 'all these' who had put in their gifts?
Jesus referred to all the wealthy people who were in sight [EGT, ICC]. He pointed to them [EGT].

DISCOURSE UNIT: 21:5–38 [BECNT, NICNT, NIGTC; NIV, NLT]. The topic is the coming of the end [NICNT, NIGTC], Jerusalem's destruction and the end [BECNT], Jesus foretells the future [NLT], signs of the end of the age [NIV].

DISCOURSE UNIT: 21:5–36 [Su, TNTC]. The topic is the eschatological discourse [TNTC], teaching about judgment on Jerusalem and the world [Su].

DISCOURSE UNIT: 21:5–33 [GW]. The topic is Jesus teaching his disciples.

DISCOURSE UNIT: 21:5–19 [NCV]. The topic is the destruction of the temple.

DISCOURSE UNIT: 21:5–9 [NET]. The topic is the signs of the end of the age.

DISCOURSE UNIT: 21:5–7 [AB, TNTC]. The topic is the fate of the Jerusalem temple [AB], the sign [TNTC].

DISCOURSE UNIT: 21:5–6 [BECNT, NAC, NIGTC, WBC; CEV, HCSB, NRSV, TEV]. The topic is the destruction of the temple [NAC, NIGTC, WBC; CEV], the destruction of the temple foretold [HCSB, NRSV], Jesus speaks of the destruction of the temple [TEV], the setting [BECNT].

21:5 **And (while) some (were) talking about the temple that it-was-decorated^a with-beautiful stones^b and with-offerings^c he-said,**

LEXICON—a. perf. pass. indic. of κοσμέω (LN **79.12**) (BAGD 2.a.β. p. 445): 'to be decorated' [BAGD, **LN**], 'to be adorned' [BAGD, LN]. See the translation of the phrase in the next item of the Lexicon.

b. λίθος (LN 2.24) (BAGD 1.b. p. 474): 'stone' [BAGD, LN]. The phase λίθοις καλοῖς κεκόσμηται 'it was decorated with beautiful stones' [NCV] is also translated 'it was adorned with beautiful stones' [Arn, Lns, WBC; HCSB, NASB, NET, NIV, NRSV], 'it was adorned with goodly stones' [NTC; KJV], 'it had been adorned with fine stones' [AB], 'it was built with fine stones' [GW], 'it was adorned with noble stones' [BECNT], '(talked about) the beautiful stones used to build the temple' [CEV], '(talking about) the beautiful stonework of the Temple' [NLT], '(talked about) the beauty of its fine stones' [REB], '(were talking about) how beautiful it looked with its fine stones' [TEV].

c. ἀνάθημα (LN **53.18**) (BAGD p. 54): 'offering' [BAGD, **LN**], 'votive gift' [BAGD]. The phrase 'it was decorated...with offerings' is translated 'it was decorated with beautiful gifts' [GW], 'it was adorned with gifts'

[KJV], 'it was adorned with votive gifts' [NASB], 'it was adorned with votive offerings' [AB, Arn, Lns, NTC], 'it was adorned with offerings' [BECNT, WBC; NET], 'it was adorned with gifts dedicated to God' [HCSB, NIV, NRSV], 'it was decorated with gifts offered to God' [NCV], '(talked about) the gifts that had been placed in it' [CEV], '(talking about) the memorial decorations on the walls' [NLT], '(talked about) the beauty of its ornaments' [REB], '(were talking about) how beautiful it looked with the gifts offered to God' [TEV].

QUESTION—How is this connected with the preceding account?

There is no direct connection given in regard to time and place [ICC, TH]. Or, as Jesus continued teaching, some of his audience exclaimed about the temple [AB, BNTC]. Or, although the text seems to indicate that Jesus was still teaching in the temple, in Mark 13:1 it says that as Jesus was leaving the temple, one of his disciples spoke to him about the temple [Arn, Gdt, ICC, Lns, NIGTC, TNTC]. It may be a case of abbreviation in giving the setting [BECNT]. Luke leaves it unclear about who was speaking [BECNT, EGT, TG, TH, WBC]. But the reference to 'some' means some of Jesus' disciples [ICC, NICNT, Su, TG], since it is clear in 21:10–19 that Jesus was speaking to his disciples [TG].

QUESTION—What were the beautiful stones that decorated the temple complex?

The reference to stones means the material with which the temple buildings were erected [TH]. The stones were of good quality [BECNT]. They were huge marble stones [EGT]. The stones used in the building were enormous [ICC, Su], some being as much as sixty-seven feet long according to Josephus [AB, BECNT, TNTC]. There were columns of the portico that were white marble columns over forty feet high [ICC, Lns]. The temple was built with stones of white marble and the temple walls were set off with gold on its front and sides [NTC].

QUESTION—What were the offerings that decorated the temple?

These were special gifts from individuals used as decorative additions [Arn, Lns, TH]. In addition to the regular stone work, there were highly engraved and ornamented stones donated by wealthy worshipers [Su]. The 'offerings' may also have included gold used as an ornamental overlay [Su]. They were special gifts that were probably used to decorate the top of the walls [NTC]. At the entrance to the temple there was carved a huge grapevine with bunches of grapes to symbolize Israel [AB, Lns, MGC, Su], the bunches of grapes being as tall as a man [TNTC]. The offerings included gold and silver gates and gold-plated doors [BECNT].

21:6 These (things) which you-are-looking-at (the) days will-come in which a-stone will- not -be-left[a] upon a-stone which will- not -be-thrown-down.[b]

LEXICON—a. fut. pass. indic. of ἀφίημι (LN 85.62) (BAGD 3.a. p. 126): 'to be left' [BAGD, LN], 'to remain' [BAGD]. The clause 'there will not be left a stone upon a stone' is translated 'there will not be left one stone

upon another' [BECNT, NTC; KJV, NASB], 'not one stone will be left upon another' [Arn; HCSB, NCV, NET, NIV, NRSV, REB], 'not a stone of it will be left upon a stone' [AB], 'not one of these stones will be left on top of another' [GW], 'not one stone will be left on top of another' [NLT], 'there will not be left stone upon stone' [Lns, WBC], 'not a single stone here will be left in its place' [TEV], 'not one of them will be left in place' [CEV].
 b. fut. pass. indic. of καταλύω (LN **20.54**) (BAGD 1.a. p. 414): 'to be thrown down' [BAGD, BECNT, Lns, NTC, WBC; HCSB, KJV, NCV, NIV, NRSV, REB, TEV], 'to be torn down' [AB, Arn, **LN**; GW, NASB, NET], 'to be knocked down' [CEV], 'will be so completely demolished' [NLT]. The verb means to be destroyed by tearing down [LN].

QUESTION—When was the prophecy about the stones fulfilled?
 This was literally fulfilled when the Roman army destroyed Jerusalem in A.D. 70 [MGC, NIVS; NET]. Rather than a literal description of the destruction of the temple, it is a general description since the western wall still stands [BECNT]. This is to be interpreted as a hyperbole to emphasize the great destruction that will take place [NAC, NTC]. This prophecy would have been a shock to those who expected the Messianic kingdom to immediately begin with Jerusalem as its center [ICC].

DISCOURSE UNIT: 21:7–19 [CEV, HCSB, NRSV, TEV]. The topic is a warning about trouble [CEV], troubles and persecutions [TEV], signs and persecutions [NRSV], signs of the end of the age [HCSB].

DISCOURSE UNIT: 21:7–11 [BECNT, NAC, NIGTC, WBC]. The topic is the signs before the end [BECNT, NAC], deceptive signs of the end [NIGTC], the buildup to the coming devastation [WBC].

21:7 And they-questioned him saying, Teacher, then[a] when will- these (things) -happen[b] and what (will be) the sign[c] when these (things) are-about to-take-place[d]?

LEXICON—a. οὖν (LN 89.50) (BAGD 1.c.α. p. 593): 'then' [Arn, BAGD, LN, Lns, NTC, WBC], 'therefore' [LN; NASB], 'so' [HCSB], 'now' [BECNT], 'but' [KJV], not explicit [AB; all versions except HCSB, KJV, NASB].
 b. fut. mid. (deponent = act.) indic. of εἰμί (LN 89.50): 'to happen' [AB, LN, NTC; CEV, GW, NASB, NET, NIV], 'to take place' [NLT], 'to be' [Arn, BECNT, LN, Lns, WBC; HCSB, KJV, NRSV, REB, TEV].
 c. σημεῖον (LN 33.477) (BAGD 1. p. 747): 'sign' [AB, Arn, BAGD, BECNT, LN, Lns, NTC, WBC; all versions except CEV, TEV]. The phrase 'what will be the sign' is translated 'what will happen in order to show that the time has come' [TEV], 'how can we know' [CEV].
 d. pres. mid./pass. (deponent = act.) infin. of γίνομαι (LN 13.107): 'to take place' [AB, BECNT, NTC; CEV, HCSB, NASB, NCV, NIV, NRSV, TEV], 'to occur' [LN, Lns; GW], 'to happen' [Arn, WBC; REB], 'to

come to be' [LN], 'to come to pass' [KJV]. This clause is translated 'will there be any sign ahead of time' [NLT].

QUESTION—When did this conversation take place?

It happened while Jesus was sitting on the Mount of Olives with his disciples [BECNT, ICC, Lns, MGC, NIVS, NTC, Su]. By joining the accounts of Matthew, Mark, and Luke, it appears that the disciples had called attention to the beauty of the temple as they were leaving the temple and Jesus had told them that the temple was going to be destroyed. The disciples waited until they were walking up the Mount of Olives outside the city and had stopped to rest when they asked for an explanation [Su]. Or, Luke wanted this to appear that they were still in the temple precincts [WBC]. In this case, the audience includes the disciples and other people who were in the temple [NICNT, NIGTC].

QUESTION—What relationship is indicated by οὖν 'then'?

It indicates what is to be inferred from what Jesus had said [BECNT]. This question comes up because of what Jesus said in 21:6 [Alf].

QUESTION—What is meant by their questions, 'When will these things happen?' and 'What will be the sign when these things take place?'

1. The text indicates that 'these things' in both parts of the question refer to the events involved in the destruction of the temple as described in 21:6 [AB, Alf, EGT, Gdt, ICC, MGC, NAC, NIBC, TG, TH, TNTC]. They wanted to know the date when this was to happen [ICC]. In this setting, it appears that the sign would be a signal for the assault on Jerusalem [WBC]. The two questions amount to one question about when the temple would be destroyed [TG]. The answer in 21:8–24 is not about signs of the world's end but of the destruction of Jerusalem in A.D. 70 [NAC].

2. However, some refer to the parallel account in Matthew 24:3 where the double question is 'When will this happen and what will be the sign of your coming and of the end of the age?' and they find two events being involved. The plural 'these things' include the temple's destruction as the event in focus, but the end-time in people's minds was linked with the destruction of the temple so that Jesus' answer goes beyond what would happen to the temple and includes Jesus' coming at the end of the age [BECNT, NIGTC]. The disciples interpreted the destruction of the temple to mean the end of the world [NIC, NIVS, NTC]. They wanted to know the sign when the temple would be destroyed so that they could prepare for the time of its destruction, but their thoughts also turned to the end of the world when Jesus would return as Messiah [Arn]. 'These things' in connection with the sign refer to Jesus' return to render judgment at the end of this world age [Lns, NTC]. Luke used a deliberate ambiguity so that the sign could be taken to refer to the assault on Jerusalem, but as this account unfolds, Jesus' answer shows that the question was intended for the coming future of the world [WBC]. It seems that the question referred to the destruction of the temple, but the plural 'these things' may include eschatological connotations as well [NICNT; NET] and it turns out that

Jesus spoke of both the destruction of the temple and the coming of the End [NICNT].

QUESTION—How is the sign connected with 'these things' taking place?

They wanted to know what the signs would be that would indicate that these things were *about* to take place [Arn, BECNT, Lns, NTC; CEV, GW, HCSB, NASB, NCV, NET, NIV, NRSV, REB]. The sign would enable them to know when these things were going to happen [WBC]. When they saw the signs they would know that that the event would be about to take place [TH].

DISCOURSE UNIT: 21:8–11 [AB, TNTC]. The topic is the signs before the end [AB], the conflict of the nations [TNTC].

21:8 And he-said, Beware[a] (that) you- not -be-deceived.[b] Because many will-come[c] in my name saying, I am (he), and, The time has-drawn-near.[d] Do- not -go[e] after them.

TEXT—Instead of μὴ πορευθῆτε 'do not go', some manuscripts read μὴ οὖν πορευθῆτε 'therefore do not go'. GNT does not mention this variant. Μὴ οὖν πορευθῆτε 'therefore do not go' is read by KJV.

LEXICON—a. pres. act. impera. of βλέπω (LN 27.58) (BAGD 6. p. 143): 'to beware (that)' [BAGD, LN; NRSV], 'to watch out (that)' [BAGD, LN; HCSB, NET, NIV, TEV], 'to look out (not to)' [Arn], 'to take care (that)' [BAGD, NTC; REB], 'to see to it (that)' [BAGD, NTC; NASB], 'to see (that)' [BECNT, WBC], 'to make sure (that)' [AB], 'to take heed (that)' [KJV], 'to be careful (that)' [GW, NCV], 'don't let' [NLT], 'don't be' [CEV].

b. aorist pass. subj. of πλανάω (LN 31.8) (BAGD 2.c.d. p. 665): 'to be deceived' [Arn, BAGD, BECNT, LN, Lns, NTC; GW, HCSB, KJV, NIV], 'to be misled' [AB, BAGD, LN; NASB, NET, REB], 'to be fooled' [CEV, NCV, TEV], 'to be led astray' [WBC; NRSV]. This passive verb is also translated actively with 'anyone' as the subject: 'to mislead' [NLT]. This refers to a departure from the truth [AB, ICC], not just being mistaken [ICC]. They must not let themselves be tricked into to believing something that is not true [Lns]. They are not to be misled about what God is doing [BECNT].

c. fut. mid. (deponent = act.) indic. of ἔρχομαι (LN 15.81) (BAGD I.1.a.θ p. 311): 'to come' [LN], 'to appear' [BAGD]. The phrase 'will come in my name' [Arn, BECNT, Lns, NTC, WBC; HCSB, KJV, NASB, NCV, NET, NIV, NLT, NRSV] is also translated 'will come using my name' [AB; GW], 'will come claiming my name' [REB], 'will come and claim to be me' [CEV], 'many men, claiming to speak for me, will come' [TEV]. 'To come' means to appear on the scene [TH].

d. perf. act. indic. of ἐγγίζω (LN 15.75) (BAGD 5.b. p. 213): 'to draw near' [LN], 'to come near, to approach' [BAGD, LN]. The clause 'the time has drawn near' [AB, WBC; KJV], is also translated 'the time is near' [BECNT, NTC; GW, HCSB, NASB, NET, NIV, NRSV], 'the season has

come near' [Lns], 'the time has come near' [Arn], 'the time has come' [NCV, NLT, REB, TEV], 'now is the time' [CEV].
- e. aorist pass. (deponent = act.) impera. of πορεύομαι, πορεύω (LN 15.10) (BAGD 1. p. 692): 'to go' [BAGD, LN]. The phrase 'do not go after them' [Arn, BECNT, Lns, WBC; KJV, NASB, NRSV] is also translated 'do not follow them' [NTC; CEV, GW, HCSB, NCV, NET, NIV, REB, TEV], 'do not run after them' [AB], 'don't believe them' [NLT]. This implies following as a disciple [Lns, NIGTC, TH]. It might include literally following them into the wilderness [NIGTC].

QUESTION—What relationship is indicated by γάρ 'because'?

This indicates the grounds for the preceding warning that they are to beware that they not be deceived [Lns].

QUESTION—What is meant by many coming in Jesus' name?
1. Many will claim that their authority was derived from Jesus [AB, Su, TG; TEV]. They will claim to speak for Jesus [TG]. There will be false messiahs claiming to be the Lord's authorized representatives [Su]. The following clause 'I am (he)' means 'I am a representative of Jesus' since that person is not claiming to be the Messiah [AB].
2. Many will claim that they are the Messiah [Arn, BECNT, BNTC, EGT, Lns, MGC, NAC, NIBC, NIC, NIGTC, NIVS, TNTC, WBC; CEV, KJV, NLT]. They will claim Jesus' office, that is, they will claim to be the Messiah [Arn, WBC]. The following clause 'I am (he)' means 'I am the Messiah' [EGT, Lns, NAC, WBC; CEV, KJV, NLT]. They will claim to be what Jesus is, that is, that they are the Messiah [TNTC]. They will claim to be Jesus [CEV, GW], the Christ [CEV].

QUESTION—What time will be at hand?
1. This refers to the time before the destruction of the temple [BNTC, EGT, WBC].
2. This refers to the time for Jesus' return [ICC, Lns], the time for setting up the kingdom [AB, Alf, My], the time God appointed for the eschatological events to happen [TH], or the time for the end [BECNT, NIC, NIGTC, NIVS, TG]. Not saying that they themselves are the Messiah, they claim to figure out the date of Christ's coming and say that the time is at hand [Lns].

21:9 And when you-hear (about) wars and insurrections,[a] do- not -be-frightened. Because it-is-necessary (for) these (things) to-take-place first, but (it is) not immediately[b] the end.

LEXICON—a. ἀκαταστασία (LN 39.34) (BAGD 2. p. 30): 'insurrection' [BAGD, NTC; NLT, NRSV, REB], 'rebellion' [AB, LN; HCSB, NET], 'revolution' [GW, NIV, TEV], 'uprising' [Arn, WBC], 'riot' [CEV, NCV], 'disturbance' [NASB], 'commotion' [KJV], 'tumult' [Lns], 'chaos' [BECNT].
- b. εὐθέως (LN 67.53): 'immediately, right away' [LN]. The clause 'it is not immediately the end' [BECNT] is also translated 'the end will not come

immediately' [GW], 'the end will not follow immediately' [NASB, NLT, NRSV], 'the end will not follow at once' [AB; REB], 'the end will not come right away' [HCSB, NIV], 'the end is not there at once' [Arn], 'that is not immediately the end' [NTC], 'the fulfillment will not occur immediately' [WBC], 'the end will not come at once' [NET], 'the end will come later' [NCV], 'they do not mean that the end is near' [TEV], 'not at once the end' [Lns], 'the end is not by and by' [KJV], 'that isn't the end' [CEV].

QUESTION—What is meant by πόλεμος 'war'?

War refers to open warfare [LN (55.5)], or external strife [TH].

QUESTION—What is meant by ἀκαταστασίας 'insurrections'?

Insurrections refers to internal riots [TH]. People rise up to defy authority, intending to overthrow it or to act in complete opposition to its demands [LN (39.34)]. This refers to civil wars [NIGTC]. This refers to the calamities present in the world at this period, but the church will also have troubles [BECNT]. In a general sense, it means difficulties, hard times, or disorders [TG].

QUESTION—What might they be frightened of?

The disturbances might cause people to think the end was at hand and that they might not live to see it, or they might think that evil was so powerful that the end would never come [NIGTC]. This speaks of the terror of judgment [BECNT].

QUESTION—What things must take place first?

The appearance of false messiahs and national or political upheavals must occur [AB].

QUESTION—Why is it necessary for them to take place?

Wars and insurrections are included in God's plans and are ordered by him [BECNT, ICC, NAC, NIGTC]. Or, it is not that they are ordered by God, rather God knows that these things will happen and therefore they must happen [Arn]. They must take place due to the condition of the world's wickedness and God's judgments in dealing with such things [Lns]. They take place as the inevitable outcome of conflicts between men and nations [Su].

QUESTION—What is meant by τὸ τέλος 'the end'?

1. This is the end of the temple and Jerusalem [AB, Gdt, MGC, NAC, NIBC, WBC].
2. This is the end of the world [Arn, BECNT, BNTC, ICC, Lns, NIC, NIGTC, NIVS, NTC, TG], the final consummation [Arn]. Throughout the centuries this prophecy is being fulfilled [NTC]. The subject in 21:8–9 is the end of the age when the Messiah will return [TG].

DISCOURSE UNIT: 21:10–24 [NASB]. The topic is the things to come.

DISCOURSE UNIT: 21:10–18 [NET]. The topic is the persecution of disciples.

21:10 Then he-said to-them, Nation will-rise[a] against nation and kingdom against kingdom, **21:11** and there-will-be great[b] earthquakes and in-various places famines[c] and plagues,[d] and both dreadful-happenings[e] and from heaven[f] great signs there-will-be.

TEXT—In 21:11, instead of καὶ κατὰ τόπους λιμοί 'and in various places famines', some manuscripts read κατὰ τόπους καὶ λιμοί 'in various places, and famines'. GNT does not mention this variant. Κατὰ τόπους καὶ λιμοί '(earthquakes) in various places, and famines' is read by KJV.

LEXICON—a. fut. pass./mid. (intransitive) indic. of ἐγείρομαι (LN55.2) (BAGD p. 215): 'to rise' [BAGD], 'to rise up in arms against, to make war against' [LN]. The clause 'nation will rise against nation' [AB, Arn, BECNT, WBC; KJV, NASB, NIV, NRSV; similarly Lns] is also translated 'nation will be raised up against nation' [HCSB], 'nation will rise up in arms against nation' [NTC; NET], 'nation will fight against nation' [GW], 'nations will fight against other nations' [NCV], 'nation will go to war against nation' [REB], 'nations will go to war against one another' [CEV], 'countries will fight each other' [TEV]. The whole statement in this verse is translated 'nations and kingdoms will proclaim war against each other' [NLT].

b. μέγας (LN 78.2) (BAGD 2.a.γ. p. 494): 'great' [BAGD, LN], 'terrible, intense' [LN]. The two occurrences of this adjective in μεγάλοι 'great (earthquakes)' and μεγάλοι 'great (signs)' are translated 'great...great' [Arn, BECNT, Lns, NTC, WBC; KJV, NASB, NCV, NET, NIV, NLT, NRSV], 'great...frightening' [CEV], 'violent...great' [HCSB], 'severe... great' [AB; REB], 'terrible...' [GW, TEV].

c. λιμός (LN 23.33) (BAGD 2. p. 475): 'famine' [AB, Arn, BAGD, BECNT, LN, Lns, NTC, WBC; all versions except CEV, NCV], 'a lack of food' [NCV]. This noun is also translated as a verb clause: 'people will starve to death' [CEV].

d. λοιμός (LN **23.158**) (BAGD 1. p. 479): 'plague' [AB, BAGD, **LN**, WBC; HCSB, NASB, NET, NRSV, REB, TEV], 'pestilence' [Arn, BAGD, BECNT, LN, Lns, NTC; KJV, NIV], 'diseases' [BAGD], 'sicknesses' [NCV], 'dreadful diseases' [GW], 'epidemics' [NLT]. This refers to the occurrence of a widespread contagious disease [LN]. This noun is also translated as a verb phrase: 'people will suffer terrible diseases' [CEV].

e. φόβητρον (LN **25.258**) (BAGD p. 863): 'dreadful happening' [**LN**], 'terrifying happening' [LN]. The plural form is translated 'terrifying sights' [BAGD; GW, HCSB, NET], 'terrifying things' [NLT], 'fearful events' [NCV, NIV], 'fearful sights' [KJV], 'frightening phenomena' [Arn], 'dreadful portents' [BAGD, NTC, WBC; NRSV], 'dread portents' [AB], 'terrors' [BECNT, Lns; NASB, REB]. This noun refers to an object, event, or condition which causes fear [LN]. The clause 'there will be dreadful happenings and great signs from heaven' is translated 'all sorts of frightening things will be seen in the sky' [CEV], 'there will be strange and terrifying things coming from the sky' [TEV]. This refers to a

sight that is terrible and horrific [BECNT]. It refers to cosmic disturbances [TG], or to cosmic catastrophes [TH].
  f. οὐρανός (LN 1.5): 'heaven' [Arn, BECNT, Lns, NTC, WBC; HCSB, KJV, NASB, NCV, NET, NIV, NRSV], 'the heavens' [NLT], 'sky' [AB, LN; CEV, GW, REB, TEV]. The phrase ἀπ' οὐρανοῦ 'from the sky/heaven' [Arn, BECNT, Lns, WBC; GW, HCSB, KJV, NASB, NCV, NET, NIV, NRSV] is also translated 'in the sky' [AB; CEV, REB], 'in the heavens' [NLT], 'coming from the sky' [TEV], 'from the stars' [TNTC].

QUESTION—What is the function of the initial word τότε 'then'?
  This formula is used to emphasize what follows and does not indicate a new discourse [TH]. It introduces a solemn statement [ICC]. It is a fresh beginning [WBC]. It indicates a new subject concerning the persecutions the disciples will have to endure [TG]. It indicates a transition from the warnings in 21:8–9 to the following prophetic passage [Crd]. It marks a break so that the whole matter can be presented in detail [Lns].

QUESTION—What distinction is intended between ἔθνος 'nation' and βασιλεία 'kingdom'?
  An ἔθνος 'nation' is the largest unit into which the people of the world are divided on the basis of their constituting a socio-political community [LN (11.55)]. Βασιλεία 'kingdom' is an area or district ruled by a king [BAGD (p. 135), LN (1.82)]. There is no significant distinction intended since this is just a poetic way of speaking of countries in general [TG].

QUESTION—What is meant by ἀπ' οὐρανοῦ σημεῖα μεγάλα 'great signs from heaven'?
  The dreadful happenings and the great signs refer to the same occurrences from heaven [EGT, NTC; CEV, TEV]. The signs would be unusual phenomena. These signs could be comets, eclipses, meteors, and other phenomena, including those specified in 21:25–26 [Lns, NTC]. They were signs such as shooting stars [BECNT]. It is possible that instead of 'sky', 'heaven' means God [WBC]. These were signs that occurred before the fall of Jerusalem [AB, Gdt, MGC, NAC, NIC, NIGTC]. Or, this concerns the end of the age [BECNT, Lns, NTC].

QUESTION—In the phrase φόβητρά τε καὶ ἀπ' οὐρανοῦ σημεῖα μεγάλα 'both dreadful happenings and from heaven signs great', what does the adjective μεγάλα 'great' modify?
  1. 'Great' modifies signs [AB, Alf, Arn, BECNT, Lns, MGC, NTC, WBC; HCSB, KJV, NASB, NCV, NET, NIV, NLT, NRSV, REB]: dreadful happenings and great signs.
  2. 'Great' modifies both dreadful happenings and signs [EGT, TH]: great dreadful happenings and great signs. The words τε καὶ 'both and' closely connect φόβητρά 'dreadful happenings' with σημεῖα 'signs' so that μεγάλα 'great' modifies both nouns [Alf, EGT, TH].

QUESTION—What does the phrase ἀπ' οὐρανοῦ 'from heaven' modify?
It modifies both φόβητρά 'dreadful happenings' and σημεῖα 'signs' [AB, Alf, ICC, Lns, MGC, My, NIGTC, TG, TH; CEV, GW, KJV, NCV, REB, TEV]: from heaven there will be dreadful happenings and signs.

DISCOURSE UNIT: 21:12–19 [AB, BECNT, NAC, NIGTC, TNTC, WBC]. The topic is the coming persecution of the disciples [BECNT, NAC, NIGTC, TNTC, WBC], admonitions for the coming persecutions [AB].

21:12 And before all these (things) they-will-lay[a] their hands on you and they-will-persecute[b] (you), delivering[c] (you) to the synagogues and prisons, being-led-away[d] before kings and governors because-of[e] my name. **21:13** It-will-turn-out[f] for you for testimony.

LEXICON—a. fut. act. indic. of ἐπιβάλλω (LN 37.110) (BAGD 1.b. p. 289): 'to lay on' [BAGD]. The phrase ἐπιβάλλω τὰς χεῖρας 'to lay hands on' is an idiom meaning 'to seize' or 'to arrest' [LN]. See this phrase at 20:19.
  b. fut. act. indic. of διώκω (LN 39.45) (BAGD 2. p. 201): 'to persecute' [AB, Arn, BAGD, BECNT, LN, Lns, NTC, WBC; GW, HCSB, KJV, NASB, NET, NIV, NRSV, REB], 'to treat cruelly' [NCV]. This active verb is also translated passively: 'to be persecuted' [TEV], 'to be punished' [CEV]. The clauses 'they will lay hands on you and they will persecute you' are translated 'there will be a time of great persecution' [NLT]. See this word at 11:49.
  c. pres. act. participle of παραδίδωμι (LN 37.12) (BAGD 1.b. p. 614): 'to deliver' [BAGD], 'to hand over' [BAGD, LN], 'to turn over' [LN]. The phrase 'delivering you (up) to the synagogues and prisons' [Arn, Lns; NASB; similarly BECNT; KJV, NIV] is also translated 'handing you over to the synagogues and prisons' [NTC, WBC; NET; similarly AB; HCSB, NRSV], 'you will be dragged into synagogue and prisons' [NLT], 'they will hand you over to their synagogues and put you into their prisons' [GW], 'you will be handed over to synagogues and put in prisons' [REB], 'they will judge you in their synagogues and put you in jail' [NCV], 'you will be handed over to be tried in synagogues and be put in prison' [TEV], 'you will be tried in your meeting places and be put in jail' [CEV]. See this verb at 9:44.
  d. pres. pass. participle of ἀπάγω (LN 15.177): 'to be led away, to be led off' [LN]. The phrase 'being led away before kings' is translated 'being led before kings' [Arn, Lns], 'you will be led off to kings' [AB], 'being brought before kings' [KJV], 'you will be brought before kings' [BECNT, WBC; HCSB, NET, NIV, NRSV, TEV], 'you will be haled before kings' [REB], 'you will be accused before kings' [NLT], 'you will be placed on trial before kings' [CEV]. This passive verb is also translated actively: 'bringing you before kings' [NTC; NASB], 'they will drag you in front of kings' [GW], 'they will force you to stand before kings' [NCV]. It is implied that they will be brought before kings and governors in order to be tried by them [TG].

e. ἕνεκεν (LN 89.31) (BAGD p. 264): 'because of, on account of' [BAGD, LN], 'for the sake of' [BAGD]. This preposition marks cause, and often has the implication of purpose in the sense of 'for the sake of' [LN]. The phrase 'because of my name' [AB; GW, HCSB, NET, NRSV] is also translated 'on account of my name' [Arn; NIV], 'because of me' [CEV], 'because you follow me' [NCV], 'for your allegiance to me' [REB], 'for my name's sake' [NTC; KJV, NASB], 'for the sake of my name' [BECNT, Lns, WBC], 'for my sake' [TEV], '(you will be accused of) being my followers' [NLT]. It means 'because of the confession of me which you make' [WBC]. It explains why the disciples will experience persecutions [Lns]. They would face these troubles because they were proclaiming Jesus as Savior [Su], or because of their loyalty to Jesus [NTC].
  f. fut. mid. (deponent = act.) indic. of ἀποβαίνω (LN 89.41): The idiom ἀποβαίνω εἰς 'to go away into' means 'to result in, to lead to' [LN]. The clause 'it will turn out for you for testimony' [Lns] is also translated 'it shall turn to you for a testimony' [KJV], 'it will turn out for you to be an occasion for testifying' [Arn], 'this shall be for you to give testimony' [BECNT], 'this will result in your being witnesses to them' [NIV], 'it will lead to an opportunity for your testimony' [NASB], 'it will lead to an opportunity for you to witness' [HCSB], 'it will lead to your having to testify' [AB], 'this will give you an opportunity to testify' [NRSV], 'it will be your opportunity to testify to them' [GW], 'this will furnish you with an opportunity to testify' [NTC], 'this will be your chance to tell about your faith' [CEV], 'this will be your opportunity to testify' [REB], 'this will lead to an opportunity for you to witness' [WBC], 'this will give you an opportunity to tell about me' [NCV], 'this will be a time for you to serve as witnesses' [NET], 'this will be your opportunity to tell them about me' [NLT], 'this will be your chance to tell the Good News' [TEV].

QUESTION—What is meant by 'before all these things'?
  It is before the necessary wars and uprisings make their appearance [WBC]. 'These things' are the signs and events Jesus talked about in 21:10–11 [Alf, NTC, TG, TH], or 8–11, which include the destruction of the temple [NAC, NIBC, NIC, NICNT; NET]. The cosmic events are associated with the end, but persecution set in from the very beginning [NIGTC].

QUESTION—What is meant by delivering them to the synagogues and prisons?
  Synagogues were centers of Jewish life as well as places for worship, so Jewish law was administered in the synagogues and prison could be the result of an adverse judgment [TNTC]. This does not imply that prisons were located inside the synagogues. Rather, their trials in Jewish courts would take place in synagogues and when they were condemned they would be taken to the prisons [TG]. They would be examined in the synagogues and minor issues could result in beatings while more serious charges would result in being sentenced to prison [BECNT]. This and the next clause describe how the previous two clauses will be fulfilled [NAC].

QUESTION—How is delivering them to synagogues and prisons connected with bringing them before kings and governors?

This indicates that their persecutors would not just be Jews in the synagogues but Gentiles would also be included [Gdt, MGC, NICNT, TNTC, WBC]. This refers to their being tried in Gentile countries [TG]. The kings would be pagan, such as Felix, Festus, and the Roman emperor in Acts [Lns]. The kings would include Herod Agrippa I, Herod Agrippa II, and Herod Antipas, while governors would be Pontius Pilate, Felix, and Festus [NTC]. Or, instead of a contrast between Jewish and Gentile authorities, the contrast is between religious and civil authorities without regard to their nationalities [BECNT].

QUESTION—What is meant by 'it will turn out for you for testimony'?

1. This has the active sense of a testimony spoken by the disciples to the authorities [Arn, BECNT, Crd, Gdt, Lns, MGC, My, NAC, NIBC, NIC, NICNT, NTC, Su, TG, TH, TNTC, WBC; CEV, NCV, NLT, REB, TEV]: this will be an opportunity for you to witness to them. They will have the opportunity to speak publicly about the things they have experienced while they were with Jesus [TH]. Probably it refers to testifying to the truth of the gospel [Arn, ICC], or to their allegiance to Christ [MGC]. The persecutions would not take place in order for them to testify, but when they came it would provide the opportunity for them to give their testimonies [NTC, TG]. Verses 21:14–15 support this interpretation [Gdt, NICNT].

2. This has a passive sense of the disciples receiving a testimony about their innocence or good character [AB, Alf, EGT, ICC, Rb]: this will be a witness on your behalf in the day of judgment. 'For a testimony to you' means it will be a testimony about you for your credit, or for your honor [EGT]. It would be a testimony about their faithfulness or faithfulness to Jesus [Alf, Rb]. Their sufferings would be a testimony to their loyalty, or, more probably, to the truth of the gospel [ICC]. They would bear testimony in the sense that they would be called to act in such a way that would testify to their fidelity to Jesus or to what kind of people they really were [AB].

21:14 Therefore put[a] in your hearts not to-prepare to-defend (yourselves),
21:15 because I will-give you a-mouth[b] and wisdom which all the (ones who) oppose you will- not -be-able to-resist[c] or to-refute.[d]

LEXICON—a. aorist act. indic. of τίθημι (LN 30.76) (BAGD I.1.b.ε. p. 816): 'to put' [BAGD, LN]. The phrase τίθημι ἐν τῇ καρδίᾳ 'to place in the heart' is an idiom meaning 'to make up one's mind' [BAGD, LN, TH], 'to decide' [LN, NAC, NIGTC, TH], 'to resolve' [EGT, TH]. The phrase 'put in your hearts not to prepare' is translated 'you must determine in your hearts not to meditate in advance' [Arn], 'determine in your hearts not to prepare beforehand' [WBC], 'settle it in your hearts not to meditate before' [KJV], 'fix in your hearts not to meditate beforehand' [Lns], 'fix it in your hearts not to plan beforehand' [NTC], 'set your hearts not to contemplate how…' [BECNT], 'decide not to plan ahead of time' [**LN**], 'resolve not to prepare beforehand' [REB], 'make up your minds not to prepare beforehand' [NASB], 'make up your minds not to prepare ahead of time' [HCSB], 'make up your minds not to prepare in advance' [NRSV], 'make up your minds not to rehearse in advance' [AB], 'make up your minds not to worry ahead of time what you will say' [NCV], 'make up your minds ahead of time not to worry how…' [TEV], 'make up your minds not to worry beforehand how…' [GW, NIV], 'don't worry about how…' [NLT], 'be resolved not to rehearse ahead of time' [NET], 'don't worry about what you will say' [CEV].

b. στόμα (LN **33.105**) (BAGD 1.a. p. 770): 'mouth' [BAGD, LN]. The phrase ἐγὼ δώσω ὑμῖν στόμα 'I will give you a mouth' [BECNT, Lns, WBC; KJV] is also translated 'I myself shall supply you with lips' [AB], 'I will give you something to say' (**LN**), 'I will give you utterance' [Arn; NASB], 'I will give you the right words' [NLT], 'I will give you eloquence' [BAGD], 'I will give you (the) words' [GW, NET, NIV, NRSV], 'I will give you such words' [HCSB, REB, TEV]. The clause 'I will give you a mouth and wisdom' is translated 'I will give you the wisdom to know what to say' [CEV], 'I will give you such wisdom of speech' [NTC], 'I will give you the wisdom to say things' [NCV].

c. aorist act. infin. of ἀνθίστημι (LN 39.18) (BAGD 2. p. 67): 'to resist' [BAGD, BECNT, LN; HCSB, NASB, NIV, REB], 'to oppose' [BAGD; CEV, GW], 'to withstand' [AB, Arn, BAGD, WBC; NET, NRSV], 'to stand against' [Lns], 'to refute' [TEV], 'to gainsay' [KJV]. The phrase 'will not be able to resist or to refute' is translated 'will not be able to reply' [NLT].

d. aorist act. infin. of ἀντιλέγω, ἀντεῖπον (LN 33.455) (BAGD p. 73): 'to refute' [NASB, REB], 'to oppose, to speak in opposition to' [LN], 'to speak against' [Arn, Lns], 'to say in return' [BAGD], 'to contradict' [AB, BAGD, BECNT, WBC; HCSB, NET, NIV, NRSV, TEV], 'to prove wrong' [GW], 'to say that you are wrong' [CEV], 'to resist' [KJV].

QUESTION—What relationship is indicated by οὖν 'therefore'?

Since the disciples will be brought to court, this instructs them about their behavior during the trial [NIGTC, Su]. Persecution brings an opportunity to testify, so this is said to prevent anxiety about what to say in the courtroom [BECNT].

QUESTION—What is indicated by the presence of the pronoun ἐγώ 'I'?

This pronoun is emphatic [AB, Arn, EGT, ICC, Lns, My, NAC, NIGTC, Su, TH; REB]: I myself will do this.

QUESTION—What is meant by being given a mouth and wisdom?

1. Mouth is used figuratively for the power of speech [Arn, ICC, MGC, Su]. 'Mouth' is a metonym for what the mouth speaks [NTC], that is, utterance [EGT, Su], or words [NET]. The word 'mouth' refers to words and 'wisdom' refers to the right contents of what is said [Arn]. Wisdom is the

ability to make the right choice in what to say and how to act [ICC, Su]. Here this refers to eloquence of speech [BAGD, NTC, TNTC].
2. Mouth is used figuratively and the phrase στόμα καὶ σοφίαν 'mouth and wisdom' is a hendiadys meaning 'words of wisdom' [NTC, TG, TH]. It means wise words [TG].

21:16 And you-will-be-handed-over[a] even/also by parents and brothers and relatives and friends, and they-will-put-to-death (some) of-you, **21:17** and you-will-be hated[b] by all because-of[c] my name.

LEXICON—a. fut. pass. indic. of παραδίδωμι (LN 37.111) (BAGD 1.b. p. 614): 'to be handed over' [Arn, BAGD, LN, WBC; TEV], 'to be turned over' [BAGD, LN], 'to be delivered up' [BECNT], 'to be given up' [BAGD], 'to be betrayed' [LN, Lns, NTC; CEV, GW, HCSB, KJV, NASB, NET, NIV, NRSV]. This passive verb is also translated actively with the kinsmen as the subject: 'to betray' [NLT, REB], 'to turn against' [NCV]. The meaning here is 'to be betrayed' [TG].
  b. pres. pass. participle of μισέω (LN 88.198) (BAGD 3. p. 523): 'to be hated' [AB, Arn, BAGD, BECNT, LN, Lns, NTC, WBC; CEV, HCSB, KJV, NASB, NET, NRSV], 'to be detested' [BAGD, LN], 'to be abhorred' [BAGD], 'to be persecuted in hatred' [BAGD]. This passive verb is also translated actively with 'all' as the subject: 'to hate' [GW, NCV, NIV, NLT, REB, TEV]. The present tense indicates that the world will always hate them [EGT, NTC].
  c. διά (LN 89.26): 'because of' [LN], 'on account of, by reason of' [LN]. The phrase διὰ τὸ ὄνομά μου 'because of my name' [AB, BECNT, Lns, WBC; HCSB, NASB, NET, NRSV] is also translated 'on account of my name' [Arn], 'for my name's sake' [NTC; KJV], 'because of me' [CEV, NIV, TEV], 'because you follow me' [NCV], 'because you are committed to me' [GW], 'because of your allegiance to me' [NLT], 'for your allegiance to me' [REB]. See this phrase in 21:12.

QUESTION—What is meant by being handed over καί 'even/also' by their relatives?
  1. They will be betrayed by *even* their parents and families, who should be expected to protect them [AB, Arn, BECNT, EGT, ICC, Lns, NTC, WBC; all versions except CEV, KJV, TEV].
  2. Not only will they be persecuted (21:5–6) by their opponents and strangers, but *also* their close relatives will deliver them up for harsh treatment [MGC, My, TH].

QUESTION—Who will the relatives hand the disciples over to?
  The disciples' relatives will hand them over to the authorities in order that they be tried and punished [TG]. They will hand them over to the persecutors mentioned in the preceding verses [TNTC].

QUESTION—Who will put some of the disciples to death?
  The authorities to whom the disciples are handed over to will cause them to be put to death [TG, TH]. It is implied that the disciples will be found guilty

at their trials [TG]. They are the people carrying on the persecution [Arn]. Many will die as martyrs [NIC]. By specifying 'some' of them will be put to death, it is suggested that death will not be the normal experience of the disciples [NAC].

QUESTION—Who are the 'all' who will hate them?

'All' refers to people in general [NTC, TH], and it is an obvious exaggeration for the sake of emphasis [NAC, TG]. It is a rhetorical expression, because some in the community will love them [BECNT]. 'All' includes people in general regardless of rank, race, nationality, sex, or age [NTC]. It means all sorts of family and other intimate connections [NTC]. It means 'many' or 'all' of the people outside the Christian community [BECNT]. It means all outside the close circle of kinsmen and friends [AB].

QUESTION—What is meant by being hated 'because of my name'?

They will be hated because they profess to be loyal to Jesus [NIGTC], they confess their allegiance to Jesus [WBC], and they believe in Jesus and serve him [NIC]. They will be hated on account of proclaiming the message about Christ [Arn].

21:18 And a-hair of your head will- by-no-means -be-lost.^{a} 21:19 By your endurance^b acquire^c your souls.^{d}

TEXT—In 21:19, instead of the aorist imperative κτήσασθε 'acquire' some manuscripts read the future indicative κτήσεσθε 'you will acquire'. GNT reads the aorist imperative κτήσασθε 'acquire' with a C decision, indicating that the Committee had difficulty making the decision. The aorist imperative κτήσασθε 'acquire' is read by KJV. The future indicative κτήσεσθε 'you will acquire' seems to be translated by all versions except KJV. However, even accepting the imperative, the English translation will have to come out like the future indicative [AB].

LEXICON—a. aorist mid. subj. of ἀπόλλυμι (LN 27.29) (BAGD 2.b. p. 95): 'to be lost' [AB, BAGD, LN; GW, HCSB, REB, TEV], 'to perish' [Arn, BECNT, Lns, NTC, WBC; KJV, NASB, NET, NIV, NLT, NRSV]. The whole verse is translated 'But don't worry!' [CEV], 'But none of these things can really harm you' [NCV].

b. ὑπομονή (LN 25.174) (BAGD 1. p. 846): 'endurance' [AB, BAGD, BECNT, LN, NTC; GW, HCSB, NASB, NET, NRSV], 'patience' [Arn, BAGD, Lns; KJV], 'steadfastness' [BAGD, WBC], 'perseverance' [BAGD]. The phrase 'by your endurance' is translated 'by standing firm' [NIV, NLT, REB], 'stand firm' [TEV], 'by being faithful to me' [CEV], 'by continuing to have faith' [NCV]. This word refers to patient endurance [AB].

c. aorist mid. (deponent = act.) impera. of κτάομαι (LN **21.20**) (BAGD 1. p. 455): 'to acquire, to win, to procure for oneself, to get' [BAGD]. The idiom 'to acquire one's soul' or 'to acquire one's life' means to save oneself from grave danger or death [LN]. The words 'acquire your souls' is translated 'possess ye your souls' [KJV], 'secure your lives' [WBC],

LUKE 21:18-19 379

'gain your soul' [BECNT], 'you will gain your souls' [Lns; NRSV], 'you will win your souls' [NTC; NLT], 'you will gain your lives' [HCSB, NASB, NET, NIV], 'you will get possession of your lives' [Arn], 'you will make your lives secure' [AB], 'you will win yourselves life' [REB], 'you will save your lives' [GW, NCV], 'you will save yourselves' [**LN**; TEV], 'you will be saved' [CEV].

d. ψυχή (LN 23.88) (BAGD 1.c. p. 894): 'soul' [BAGD, BECNT, Lns, NTC; KJV, NLT, NRSV], 'life' [AB, Arn, BAGD, LN, WBC; GW, HCSB, NASB, NCV, NET, NIV, REB], 'you' [CEV]. The soul is the seat and center of the life that transcends the earthly existence [BAGD].

QUESTION—What is meant by the statement, 'not a hair of your head will perish'?

1. This refers to their physical safety with the implied qualification 'without God's permission' [Arn, NIC, NTC, TNTC]. They will not die until the time determined by God [Arn].
2. This refers to physical safety for the church in general although there will be some martyrs [Gdt, NICNT, TH, WBC].
3. This refers to spiritual safety [Alf, BECNT, BNTC, Crd, ICC, Lns, MGC, My, NAC, NIGTC, NIVS, Rb; NET]. This use of a proverbial saying expresses great security, but since they have just been told that some would be killed, its application concerns spiritual security and means that their eternal welfare is safe [ICC]. When they are persecuted and some are even killed, they are in God's care to the last hair of their heads [Lns]. This rhetorical remark means that final destruction is impossible for a disciple and this interpretation is supported by the next verse which says that clinging to Jesus is to have life even in the face of death [BECNT].

QUESTION—What is meant by acquiring their own souls?

1. This means that they will participate in eternal life, not that they will preserve their earthly lives [AB, Alf, Arn, BECNT, BNTC, ICC, Lns, NAC, NIC, NICNT, NIGTC, NTC, TG, TH]. They will reach true, real life [Arn, NIC, TG, TH], that is, eternal life [MGC, NAC, TG]. Whether persecution results in acquittal or in death, the lives of those who remain faithful will be preserved [NICNT].
2. This refers to saving their physical lives in the midst of danger [Gdt, TNTC, WBC]. Following the promise about not a hair being lost, this refers to their lives being saved in the midst of danger [WBC]. God's purpose determines whether they live or die, not the plans of their enemies [TNTC].

DISCOURSE UNIT: 21:20-24 [AB, BECNT, NAC, NIGTC, TNTC, WBC; CEV, HCSB, NCV, NET, NRSV, TEV]. The topic is the desolation of Jerusalem [NET], the destruction of Jerusalem foretold [HCSB, NRSV], Jesus speaks of the destruction of Jerusalem [TEV], the desolation coming upon Jerusalem [AB, NAC, TNTC, WBC], Jerusalem will be destroyed [CEV, NCV], a picture of the end: Jerusalem's destruction [BECNT], judgment upon Jerusalem [NIGTC].

21:20 **And when you-see Jerusalem being-surrounded[a] by armies, then know[b] that its devastation[c] has-drawn-near.**

LEXICON—a. pres. pass. participle of κυκλόω (LN 15.147) (BAGD 1. p. 456): 'to be surrounded' [AB, Arn, BAGD, BECNT, LN, NTC, WBC; CEV, HCSB, NASB, NET, NIV, NLT, NRSV, TEV], 'to be encircled' [BAGD, Lns; REB], 'to be compassed' [KJV], '(armies) all around' [NCV], '(armies) camped around' [GW]. The present tense 'being surrounded' indicates that the encircling is not yet accomplished, since if it had been, the following instruction about fleeing would be pointless [Arn, ICC, Lns, NIC, Rb, TH, TNTC].

  b. aorist act. impera. of γινώσκω (LN 32.16): 'to know, to come to understand, to comprehend' [LN]. This verb is translated as an imperative: 'know' [WBC; KJV, NET, NRSV], 'you must know' [CEV], 'realize' [Arn, Lns; GW], 'recognize' [HCSB, NASB], 'understand' [NTC]; or as a future tense: 'you will know' [LN (20.41); NCV, NIV, NLT, TEV], 'you will realize' [AB], 'then you know' [BECNT], 'then you may be sure' [REB]. The imperative means 'then you must know' referring to the future time when this will happen [TH].

  c. ἐρήμωσις (LN **20.41**) (BAGD p. 309): 'devastation, destruction' [BAGD]. The phrase 'its devastation has drawn near' [WBC] is also translated 'her devastation is near' [REB], 'its destruction has arrived' [NLT], 'her desolation has drawn near' [AB, Lns], 'its/her desolation has come near' [Arn, BECNT; HCSB, NET, NRSV], 'its/her desolation is near' [NTC; NASB, NIV], 'the desolation thereof is nigh' [KJV], 'it/she will soon be destroyed' [**LN**; CEV, NCV, TEV], 'the time is near for it to be destroyed' [GW].

QUESTION—How is this discourse unit connected with the rest of the chapter?
Jesus was answering the question about the sign asked for in 21:7 [Lns, NAC, NIBC, NICNT, NTC, Su]. This is the destruction mentioned in 21:6 and here the destruction includes the city as well as the temple [BECNT, TNTC]. The words 'when *you* see' indicates that it will happen in the lifetime of those listening to Jesus [TG], and this is addressed to all those who live in Jerusalem, not just the disciples [NIGTC]. This passage 21:20–24 refers to the destruction of Jerusalem in A.D. 70, not the end time [BECNT, ICC, NAC, NIC, TNTC]. Flight would be useless if this referred to the consummation of all things [NAC]. When the disciples asked about the destruction of the temple, Jesus first spoke about signs that the destruction of Jerusalem was coming, though not yet imminent (21:8–19). This verse is the second part of his reply in which he gives the sign immediately preceding the fall of Jerusalem [MGC, NAC, NIC]. Section 21:8–19 speaks of what would happen before the fall of Jerusalem [NAC, NTC], although those verses also have implications for the post A.D. 70

period [NTC]. Or, after the preceding general survey in 21:8–19 of the last times, Jesus then turns to the subject of the fall of Jerusalem. What will happen to Jerusalem is symbolical of what will happen to the unbelieving world when the last trumpet sounds [Arn]. Luke reworded the phrase 'abomination of desolation' from Mark 13:14 and Matt. 24:15 in order to keep his readers from confusing the fall of Jerusalem with the end time [NAC]. While Luke focuses on the near fulfillment in A.D. 70, Matthew and Mark focus on the parallel events of the end since the near destruction is like the end [BECNT; NET]. Matthew and Mark say that the tribulation of that period will be 'unprecedented in the creation', but this does not describe the fall of Jerusalem, horrible though it was. So here Luke is primarily thinking of Jerusalem's near future, not the final destruction at the end of the age [BECNT].

21:21 Then the (ones) in Judea must-flee to the mountains and the (ones) in (the) midst of-it must-get-out and the (ones) in the fields must- not -enter into it, **21:22** because these are days of vengeance[a] to-be-fulfilled[b] all the (things) having-been-written.

LEXICON—a. ἐκδίκησις (LN 39.33, 38.9) (BAGD p. 238): 'vengeance' [AB, Arn, BAGD, BECNT, Lns, WBC; GW, HCSB, KJV, NASB, NET, NLT, NRSV], 'retribution' [LN (39.33), NTC; REB], 'punishment' [BAGD, LN (38.9); CEV, NCV, NIV, TEV]. This verb means to repay harm with harm and assumes that retribution is called for since the initial harm was unjustified [LN].

b. aorist pass. infin. of πίμπλημι (LN **13.106**) (BAGD 1.b.α. p. 658): 'to be fulfilled' [BAGD, LN]. The clause τοῦ πλησθῆναι πάντα τὰ γεγραμμένα 'to be fulfilled all the things having been written' is translated 'in order to fulfill those things that have been written' [**LN**], 'so that all things which are written will be fulfilled' [NASB], 'to fulfill all the things that are written' [HCSB], 'that all things which are written may be fulfilled' [KJV], 'to bring about all that is written in the Scriptures' [NCV], 'that all the things that have been written be fulfilled' [Lns], 'that whatever is written may be fulfilled' [NTC], 'to fulfill all that is written' [BECNT; NET; similarly WBC], 'to make come true all that the Scriptures say' [TEV], 'for the fulfillment of all that is written' [Arn], 'in fulfillment of all that has been written' [NIV], 'as a fulfillment of all that is written' [NRSV; similarly AB], 'when all that stands written is to be fulfilled' [REB], 'and the prophetic words of the Scriptures will be fulfilled' [NLT], 'everything written about it will come true' [GW]. The whole verse is translated 'This time of punishment is what is written about in the Scriptures' [CEV].

QUESTION—What relationship is indicated by ὅτι 'because' in 21:22?

This gives the reason why the instructions about fleeing were given [Gdt, NIGTC]. It is the reason to avoid the city of Jerusalem [BECNT]. At this sign of the imminent devastation of Jerusalem, the city was the place to flee *from* rather than being a place of refuge [Su]. By referring to Judea, it is indicated that the siege of Jerusalem will influence the region around the city, although the worst conditions would be in the city itself [BECNT]. Those living in the war area of Judea around Jerusalem should flee to the mountainous areas beyond the Jordan in Perea [Lns], into the Trans Jordan or the remoter parts of Judea, such as the mountains near the Dead Sea [NIGTC].

QUESTION—What is meant by the phrase οἱ ἐν μέσῳ αὐτῆς 'the ones in the midst of it'?

'It' refers to Jerusalem [BNTC, EGT, TG, TH]. Grammatically this would refer back to Judea, but the context demands that it refer to Jerusalem [NIGTC]. This contrasts with 'the ones in the fields', that is, the ones outside Jerusalem, and so the ones in the midst of her refers to the people living in Jerusalem [BECNT].

QUESTION—What is meant by the days of vengeance?

The phrase refers to the handing out of justice, in this case retribution for the wrong that was done [Lns]. This is not Rome's vengeance, but God's vengeance and the Roman army was God's instrument [NAC]. This was the time when God would punish Jerusalem [NIGTC], and the people there would be punished for their sins [TNTC], for their unbelief and crimes against the gospel [Lns]. The inhabitants of Jerusalem were to be punished for their rebellion against God and his purposes for them [Su]. They had not recognized the day of God's visitation (19:44) [NIBC]. The culmination and completion of all of God's threats of judgment recorded in the Scriptures would happen when he squared the accounts of justice for the whole course of the history of Jerusalem [WBC].

QUESTION—How is the last clause τοῦ πλησθῆναι πάντα τὰ γεγραμμένα 'the to be fulfilled all the things having been written' related to the preceding clause 'these are days of vengeance'?

1. It indicates that the purpose of vengeance is to fulfill prophecy [AB, Arn, BECNT, LN, Lns, NTC, WBC; HCSB, KJV, NASB, NCV, NET, TEV]: these days of vengeance will come in order that all that is written will be fulfilled.
2. It indicates that this vengeance is a fulfillment of prophecy [EGT, NICNT, NIGTC, TH; GW, NIV, NRSV]: these are days of vengeance which fulfill all that is written. The days of vengeance are the days that were prophesied [CEV, REB].

QUESTION—What was written about this?

The words 'all things written' are limited by the context to all that is written about the coming judgment [TH]. There were many prophecies such as 1 Kings 9:6–9; Dan. 9:26; Micah 3:12 [NIGTC], Zech. 11:4–14; 14:2; Mal. 3:1 [Lns], Jer. 18:9–11; Dan. 9:27; Zech. 11:6; Mal. 3:1–2 [NTC]. Probably this refers to the prophecies concerning the destruction of Jerusalem under the Babylonians and other ancient enemies and though those prophecies had been fulfilled in the past, a greater and more meaningful fulfillment would take place under the viciousness of the Roman army [Su].

21:23 Woe[a] to-the (ones who) have (a child) in (the) womb and to-the (ones who) are-nursing in those days. Because there-will-be great trouble[b] on the land/earth[c] and judgment[d] (against) this people.

LEXICON—a οὐαί (LN 22.9) (BAGD 1.a. p. 591): 'woe, alas' [BAGD], 'disaster, horror' [LN]. The phrase 'woe to' [AB, Arn, BECNT, Lns, NTC, WBC; HCSB, KJV, NASB, NET, NRSV], is also translated 'alas for' [REB], 'it will be an awful time for' [CEV], 'how horrible it will be for' [GW], 'how terrible it will be for' [NCV, NLT, TEV], 'how dreadful it will be for' [NIV]. See this word at 6:24; 10:13; 11:42; 17:1; 22:22.

b. ἀνάγκη (LN **22.1**) (BAGD 2. p. 52): 'trouble' [**LN**], 'distress' [BAGD, LN], 'calamity' [BAGD]. The phrase 'there will be great trouble on the land' is translated 'there will be great distress upon/in the land' [BECNT, NTC; HCSB, KJV, NASB, NIV, NLT, REB], 'there will be great distress on the earth' [NET, NRSV], 'terrible distress will come upon this land' [TEV], 'great trouble will come upon this land' [NCV], 'there will be great calamity upon the land' [WBC], 'there shall be great anguish on the land' [Lns], 'the land will suffer very hard times' [GW], 'there will be great misery upon the land' [Arn], 'great will be the misery in this land' [AB], 'everywhere in the land people will suffer horribly' [CEV].

c. γῆ (LN 1.39, 1.79): 'land' [AB, Arn, BECNT, LN (1.79), Lns, NTC, WBC; all versions except NET, NRSV], 'region' [LN (1.79)], 'earth' [LN (1.39); NET, NRSV], 'world' [LN (1.39)].

d. ὀργή (LN 38.10) (BAGD 2.b. p. 579): 'judgment, anger' [BAGD], 'punishment' [LN]. The phrase 'there will be judgment against this/these people' [AB, Arn, NTC, WBC; HCSB, NET, NIV, NRSV] is also translated 'there will be a terrible judgment on this people' [REB], 'people will be punished' [CEV, GW], 'God's punishment will fall on this people' [TEV], 'there will be wrath to this people' [NASB], 'there will be wrath upon this people' [BECNT; KJV, NLT], 'there shall be wrath for this people' [Lns], 'God will be angry with these people' [NCV]. This refers to God's punishment based on his anger against someone [LN]. The wrath is provoked by the people of Jerusalem [ICC]. This word refers not to God's emotions, but to the expression of his anger in terms of judgment and punishment [TG]. See this word at 3:7.

QUESTION—Why did Jesus say 'Woe' for such women?

This is an expression of sorrow at the thought of the fate of such women [NIGTC]. The siege of the city will bring suffering for all, but it will be especially hard on pregnant women and women with young children [TNTC]. It would be difficult for such women to flee in a hurry [Su, TG]. Such women were less well equipped to handle such extreme hardship [MGC, NAC, WBC].

QUESTION—Does τῆς γῆς means that the trouble will be on 'the land' or 'the earth'?
1. The phrase τῆς γῆς means the land [Alf, BECNT, Gdt, Lns, MGC, NAC, NIC, NIGTC, TG, TH, TNTC, WBC; all versions except NET, NRSV]. The next phrase 'this people' refers to the Jews, so this refers to the land of Israel [BECNT, Crd, ICC, TG, WBC]. This refers to the territory of Judea [MGC, NIC, NIGTC, WBC]. The fate of Jerusalem affected the entire Jewish land [Lns]. This speaks of the fall of Jerusalem, so the land would be Judea [AB]. Distress on the land means that the people in the land will be in great distress [TG].
2. The phrase τῆς γῆς means the earth [Alf, My; NET, NRSV]. The general word 'earth' is used and the next phrase, 'and especially this people' defines what part of the earth will suffer God's wrath [My]. The trouble that comes on all the earth is not so distinctly the result of God's anger as that trouble which will come on the Jewish people [Alf].

21:24 And they-will-fall[a] by-(the) edge of-(the) sword and they-will-be-taken-captive[b] into all the nations, and Jerusalem will-be-trampled[c] by Gentiles until (the) times of-(the) Gentiles are-fulfilled.

LEXICON—a. fut. mid./pass. (deponent = act.) indic. of πίπτω (LN 23.105) (BAGD 1.b.α. p. 659): 'to fall' [BAGD]. The verb 'to fall down' is a euphemistic expression for a violent death and means 'to die' [LN]. The clause 'they will fall by the edge of the sword' [AB, BECNT, NTC; HCSB, KJV, NASB, NET, NRSV] is also translated 'they will fall by the mouth of the sword' [Arn, Lns, WBC], 'they will fall by the sword' [NIV, REB], 'they will be killed by the sword' [NCV], 'some will be killed by the sword' [TEV], 'some of them will be killed by swords' [CEV], 'they will be brutally killed by the sword' [NLT], 'swords will cut them down' [GW]. The noun στόμα means 'mouth, edge, point' of the sword [TH]. This clause refers to being killed in battle [BAGD, TG].

b. fut. pass. indic. of αἰχμαλωτίζω (LN **55.24**) (BAGD 1. p. 27): 'to be taken captive' [LN], 'to be captured' [BAGD, LN]. The clause 'they will be taken captive into all the nations' is translated 'they will be taken captive to all countries' [**LN**], 'they will be taken away as captives among all nations' [NRSV], 'they shall be led captive into all the Gentiles' [Lns], 'they will be led away captive into all the nations' [WBC; KJV, NASB; similarly HCSB, NET], 'be scattered as captives among all nations' [BAGD], 'they will be taken as prisoners to all the nations' [NIV; similarly Arn; NCV, TEV], 'will be carried off to foreign countries' [CEV], 'they will be carried off as captives into all the nations' [NTC; similarly AB; REB], 'they will be carried off into all nations as prisoners' [GW], 'sent away as captives to all the nations of the world' [NLT].

c. pres. pass. participle of πατέω (LN **20.22, 34.54**) (BAGD 1.a.γ. p. 635): 'to be trampled on' [BAGD, LN]. The clause 'Jerusalem will be trampled on by the Gentiles' [**LN** (20.22), Lns; HCSB, NIV, NRSV] is also translated 'Jerusalem will be trampled down by the Gentiles' [NET], 'Jerusalem will be trampled under foot by the Gentiles' [NASB, REB], 'Jerusalem will be overrun by foreign nations' [CEV], 'Jerusalem will be trodden down by Gentiles' [BECNT; KJV], 'Jerusalem will be trodden under foot by the Gentiles' [Arn], 'nations will trample Jerusalem' [GW], 'Jerusalem will be crushed by non-Jewish people' [NCV], 'Jerusalem will be conquered by the Gentiles' [**LN** (34.54)], 'Jerusalem will be conquered and trampled down by the Gentiles' [NLT], 'Jerusalem will be trampled upon by pagans' [AB], 'the heathen will trample over Jerusalem' [TEV]. This refers to the undisciplined swarming of a victorious army through a conquered city and can take on the meaning of mistreat, abuse, or tread contemptuously under foot [BAGD]. 'To trample' has a figurative extension meaning 'to conquer and keep under subjection' [LN (34.54)].

QUESTION—What is meant by καί 'and' in the clause '*and* they will be taken captive into all the nations'?

It cannot mean that the same people will be both killed and taken captive, so the idea is that some will be slain and others will be taken captive [NIGTC, TG; CEV, TEV]. Here 'and' introduces an alternative fate [AB, NIC, TH; NLT].

QUESTION—What is meant by Jerusalem being trampled on by the Gentiles?

Dropping the figure, it means it will be utterly destroyed [TH], or it could simply mean to be occupied by the Gentiles [EGT]. This refers not to one event, but to a future ongoing situation [TH]. The nation will be dominated by the Gentiles [NIC, TG].

QUESTION—What is meant by the times of the Gentiles?

Many suggestions have been given for this puzzling expression. It could mean the time that the Gentiles will execute God's judgments, the time that they will be supreme over Israel and exercise the privileges formerly belonging to Israel, or the time in which the Gentiles have the gospel preached to them [TNTC]. It could mean the time for executing God's judgments, the time for lording it over Israel, the time they will exist as Gentiles, the time for them to be subject to God's judgments, the time they have opportunities to turn to God, or the time they possess the privileges which the Jews had forfeited [ICC].

1. This refers to the time that the Gentile occupied and ruled the city of Jerusalem [AB, Arn, Crd, MGC, NIGTC, Su, TG; GW]. This is the time God has determined for their domination over Jerusalem [Arn, NIGTC, TG]. The Romans trampled upon Jerusalem and after they had their full opportunity to do this, the whole city was ruined [Su]. Or, 'nations will trample Jerusalem until the times allowed for the nations to do this are over' [GW]. This statement does not imply that Jerusalem will ever be free of Gentile rule, nor does it deny it [Arn]. Or, it suggests that Israel will repossess its land [MGC, NAC] after the second coming [MGC].
2. This refers to the time of Gentile prominence in God's plans for the world [Alf, BECNT, BNTC, Lns, My, NIC, NTC, TH, WBC]. This time began

with the destruction of Jerusalem and will end at Christ's second coming [BECNT, Lns, NIC, NTC]. This time will last until Christ comes to establish his eternal kingdom after the final judgment [NIC]. God is done with the Jews as a nation and his work is now with the non-Jews [Lns]. This is the current period in God's plan when the Gentiles are prominent, but this period will end with God judging the Gentile nations and then comes the restoration of Israel [BECNT]. 'Times of the Gentiles' is plural because of the length of time involved and because different Gentile nations will occupy Jerusalem [Lns].

3. This refers to the time that God offers the gospel to the Gentiles [EGT, Gdt]. The Jews had their day of grace and now the Gentiles will have their turn [EGT].

DISCOURSE UNIT: 21:25–38 [NASB]. The topic is the return of Christ.

DISCOURSE UNIT: 21:25–28 [AB, BECNT, NAC, NIGTC, TNTC, WBC; CEV, HCSB, NCV, NET, NRSV, TEV]. The topic is the coming of the Son of Man [AB, BECNT, NAC, NIGTC, TNTC; HCSB, NET, NRSV, TEV], when the Son of Man appears [CEV], the judgment of the nations and the coming of the Son of Man [WBC], don't fear [NCV].

21:25 And there-will-be signs in sun and moon and stars, and upon the earth distress[a] of-(the) nations in perplexity[b] (at the) sound of-sea and waves, **21:26** men fainting[c] from fear and expectation[d] of-the (things) coming-upon the world, because the powers[e] of-the heavens will-be-shaken.

LEXICON—a. συνοχή (LN **25.240**) (BAGD 2. p. 791): 'distress' [AB, Arn, BAGD, BECNT, **LN**, Lns, NTC, WBC; KJV, NET, NRSV], 'dismay' [BAGD; NASB], 'anguish' [BAGD; HCSB, NIV]. This noun is also translated as a verb: 'to be in despair' [TEV], 'to be deeply troubled' [GW], 'to be in turmoil' [NLT], 'to be afraid' [CEV, NCV], 'to stand helpless' [REB].

b. ἀπορία (LN **32.9**) (BAGD p. 97): 'perplexity' [AB, Arn, BAGD, BECNT, Lns, NTC; KJV, NASB, NIV], 'consternation' [**LN**], 'anxiety' [BAGD, **LN**, WBC], 'dismay' [NASB]. The phrase 'in perplexity' is translated 'and confused' [GW, NCV, NRSV], 'anxious over' [NET], 'afraid of' [TEV], 'bewildered by' [HCSB], 'perplexed by' [NLT], 'and they won't know what to do' [CEV], 'not knowing which way to turn' [REB]. People will be at a loss at what to do [BECNT, Lns].

c. pres. act. participle of ἀποψύχω (LN **23.184, 25.293**) (BAGD p. 102): 'to faint' [Arn, BAGD, BECNT, **LN** (25.184), NTC, WBC; all versions except KJV, NLT], 'to stop breathing' [AB], 'to expire' [Lns], 'to give up' [**LN** (25.293)], 'to be totally disheartened, to be completely discouraged, to lose heart' [LN (25.293)]. The phrase 'men fainting' is translated 'men's hearts failing them' [KJV], 'the courage of many people will falter' [NLT].

d. προσδοκία (LN 30.55) (BAGD p. 712): 'expectation' [Arn, BAGD, LN, Lns; NASB, NET], 'foreboding' [AB, BECNT, WBC; NRSV], 'apprehension' [NTC]. This noun is also translated as a verb: 'to look after' [KJV]. The phrase 'from...expectation of the things coming upon the world' [HCSB] is also translated 'because of what is happening to the world' [CEV], 'wondering what is happening to the world' [NCV], 'at the thought of all that is coming upon the world' [REB], 'as they wait for what is coming over the whole earth' [TEV], 'apprehensive of what is coming on the world' [NIV]. The phrase 'from fear and expectation of the things coming upon the world' is translated 'as they fearfully wait for what will happen to the world' [GW], 'because of the fearful fate they see coming upon the earth' [NLT].

e. δύναμις (LN 12.44): 'power' [LN]. The clause 'the powers of the heavens will be shaken' [BECNT, Lns, NTC, WBC; KJV, NASB, NCV, NET, NRSV] is also translated 'the powers of the heavens will be moved' [Arn], 'the powers of the universe will be shaken' [GW], 'every power in the sky will be shaken' [CEV], 'the celestial powers will be shaken' [HCSB, REB], 'the forces of heaven will be shaken loose' [AB], 'the heavenly bodies will be shaken' [NIV], 'the stability of the very heavens will be broken up' [NLT], 'the powers in space will be driven from their courses' [TEV].

QUESTION—How is the discourse unit 21:25–28 connected with the rest of the chapter?

This is connected with the preceding clause and indicates that the times of the Gentiles will last until this final event [Lns]. This happens after the times of the Gentiles comes to an end [Gdt, Lns, My, NIGTC, TH]. Jerusalem will be destroyed, but there is coming a time of universal upheaval when the other nations will experience God's judgment which will usher in the coming of the Son of man and final deliverance [WBC]. These events will occur over a long period of time, beginning with the destruction of Jerusalem and they only announce in a general way the approach of the end [Arn]. Or, these signs are not connected with the signs mentioned in 21:11, but are signs occurring at the winding up of the world [Lns].

QUESTION—What kind of signs will be in the sun, moon, and stars?

In the parallel passage in Matt. 24:29 it says that the sun will be darkened, and the moon along with it, and stars will fall from the sky [NTC].

QUESTION—What is meant by 'the powers of the heavens will be shaken'?

1. This appears to be a literal shaking of the heavenly bodies [Arn, BECNT, ICC, Lns]. The powers of heaven are not angels nor cosmic powers that hold up the heavens, rather they are the heavenly bodies, the stars [ICC]. God holds the universe in place and he will wind up the affairs of the world in this way [Lns].

2. This refers to personal heavenly forces who live in the heavens and their being shaken refers to their distress in the heavenly realms [NET].

3. This probably is a symbol of a climactic judgment on the nations [NAC, Su, WBC]. This describes the historical overthrow of earthly nations and empires [NAC].

21:27 **And then they-will-see the Son of Man[a] coming in/on a-cloud with power[b] and glory[c] great.**

LEXICON—a. υἱὸς τοῦ ἀνθρώπου 'Son of Man'. This title for Christ occurs at 5:24; 6:22; 7:34; 9:22, 26, 44; 11:30; 12:8, 40; 17:22, 24, 26; 18:8, 31; 19:10; 21:27, 36; 22:22, 48, 69; 24:7. See the discussions of this title at 5:24, 6:5, and 9:22.

b. δύναμις (LN 76.1): 'power' [AB, Arn, BECNT, LN, Lns, NTC, WBC; all versions].

c. δόξα (LN 76.13) (BAGD 1.a. p. 2203): 'glory' [AB, Arn, BECNT, Lns, NTC, WBC; all versions], 'brightness, splendor, radiance' [BAGD], 'glorious (power), amazing (might)' [LN].

QUESTION —What does τότε 'then' refer to?

This verse follows the terrifying events described in 21:25–26 [NIC, Su]. It refers not to the fall of Jerusalem, but to the time after the fulfillment of the times of the Gentiles [NIC, NIGTC]. It won't be until then [ICC].

QUESTION—Does ἐν mean that the Son of Man will come in or on a cloud?

1. He will come *in* a cloud [Arn, BNTC, Lns, NIGTC, NTC, TH; all versions except NLT]. He will come in the midst of a cloud, being enveloped by it [TH]. This cloud is that cloud that covered the Lord at his transfiguration [BECNT]. Since this is 'cloud' instead of 'clouds' it suggests that a cloud hides the glory associated with God from men as in 9:34 and here the picture is the Son of Man being accompanied by the glory of God [NIGTC].

2. He will come *on* a cloud [AB, BECNT, MGC, WBC; NLT]. This phrase is the same as in Mark 13:26, except Mark has the plural 'clouds'. Here this singular noun 'a cloud' is translated plural, 'on the clouds' [BECNT; NLT]. The cloud will be used as a heavenly chariot [TG].

QUESTION—What does πολλῆς 'great' modify in the phrase μετὰ δυνάμεως καὶ δόξης πολλῆς 'with power and glory great'?

1. 'Great' modifies glory [AB, Arn, BECNT, Lns, MGC, NTC, WBC; all versions except CEV, TEV]: with power and great glory. In Mark 13:26 'great' modifies 'power' while in Matthew and Luke it modifies 'glory' [BECNT].

2. 'Great' modifies both power and glory [TH; CEV, TEV]: with great power and great glory. In all three Gospels, 'great' is to be taken as modifying both power and glory [TH].

QUESTION—What is meant by the Son of Man coming *with* power and glory?

His power is made evident by what happens at his coming [Lns, NTC]. With his power he will conquer the entire hostile material order [Su]. 'Power' could be an allusion to angels accompanying him [Arn]. His glory consists of his attributes, such as his power, wisdom, holiness, and love [Lns, NTC]. His glory may refer to his radiance and brightness or to his majesty [TG].

21:28 And (when) these (things) begin to-occur stand-erect[a] and lift-up[b] your heads, because your redemption[c] draws-near.

LEXICON—a. aorist act. impera. of ἀνακύπτω (LN 17.33) (BAGD 2. p. 56): 'to stand erect, to raise oneself up, to straighten oneself' [BAGD], 'to straighten up' [LN]. The imperative is translated 'stand erect' [AB], 'stand up' [HCSB, NET, NIV, NRSV, TEV], 'stand straight' [NLT], 'stand up straight' [CEV], 'stand upright' [REB], 'stand' [GW], 'straighten up' [WBC; NASB], 'lift yourselves up' [Lns], 'look up' [Arn, BECNT, NTC; KJV, NCV]. This could mean either 'look up' or 'stand upright' and here it probably means the latter [TH].

b. aorist act. impera. of ἐπαίρω (LN **25.160**) (BAGD 1. p. 281): 'to lift up, to hold up' [BAGD]. The phrase 'lift up your heads' [Arn, **LN**, NTC; HCSB, KJV, NASB, NIV] is also translated 'raise your heads' [BECNT, Lns, WBC; NET, NRSV, TEV], 'hold your heads high' [AB; NCV, REB], 'be brave' [CEV], '(stand) with confidence' [GW], 'look up' [NLT]. The idiom ἐπαίρω τὴν κεφαλήν 'to lift up the head' means to demonstrate one's courage in the face of danger or adversity [LN], or to regain one's courage [BAGD]. Lifting the head is a sign of hope [NIGTC].

c. ἀπολύτρωσις (LN 37.128) (BAGD 2.a. p. 96): 'redemption' [BAGD], 'liberation, deliverance' [LN]. The clause 'your redemption draws near' [KJV] is also translated 'your redemption is drawing near' [Lns, NTC; NASB, NET, NIV, NRSV], 'your redemption is near' [BECNT; HCSB], 'your liberation is near' [REB], 'your deliverance is near' [AB], 'your deliverance is drawing near' [WBC], 'your deliverance approaches' [Arn], 'you will soon be free' [CEV], 'the time when you will be set free is near' [GW], 'the time when God will free you is near' [NCV], 'your salvation is near' [NLT, TEV].

QUESTION—What things are meant in the phrase 'And when these things begin to occur'?

1. This does not refer to the previous verse about the coming of the Son of Man [Lns, NIGTC, NTC, TG, TH]. It refers to the events described in 21:25–26 [NTC, TG, TH]. It is not clear how far back 'these things' refer to and probably we are to understand that deliverance is progressively closer the more the escalation of the signs appear until finally the Son of Man comes at the end [NIGTC]. 'These things' go back at least to 21:20 when Jerusalem would be encircled by the Roman army, and even the signs mentioned in 21:8–11 still continue [Lns]. For the disciples, the terrifying happenings in the sky and in the water will mean that the days of their suffering will soon be done with [NTC].

2. 'These things' include the appearance of the Son of Man [Arn, BECNT, MGC, NAC, Su; NET]. 'These things' cover 21:25–27 [BECNT, Su]. Or,

they cover 21:8–27 [NET]. It is his appearance that will cause the disciples to lift up their heads while the nations cower in fear [BECNT, MGC]. This is to be the reaction of the believers in general when the Messiah appears [Arn]. These are the things associated with the coming of the Son of Man, not the things associated with the fall of Jerusalem [NAC].

QUESTION—Who is to stand erect and lift up their heads?

The disciples to whom Jesus was speaking are representative of believers in general [Arn, ICC, NIC] since only those disciples who will be alive at the time of the appearance of these signs can fulfill this command [ICC, NIC].

QUESTION—What is meant by their ἀπολύτρωσις 'redemption'?

Here it refers to their release or deliverance and there is no notion of paying a ransom to redeem the people [AB, Arn, Lns]. They will be freed from the physical and spiritual assaults of all the forces of evil [Arn]. They will be released from such things as suffering and tribulation [Lns, NIGTC]. Their redemption will be accomplished at the crucifixion, so here Jesus speaks of the future unfolding of the full results of their redemption [TNTC]. This will be the completion of their redemption [Alf, NIGTC].

DISCOURSE UNIT: 21:29–33 [AB, BECNT, NAC, NIGTC, TNTC, WBC; CEV, HCSB, NCV, NET, NRSV, TEV]. The topic is the parable of the fig tree [AB, BECNT, NAC, TNTC; HCSB, NET], the lesson of the fig tree [NRSV, TEV], a lesson from a fig tree [CEV], new leaves herald the summer [WBC], the certainty of the end events [NIGTC], Jesus' words will live forever [NCV].

21:29 And he-told a-parable to-them, Consider^a the fig-tree and all the trees. **21:30** When already they-put-out (leaves), seeing (this) for yourselves you-know that already the summer is near.

LEXICON—a. aorist act. impera. of ὁράω (LN 30.45): 'to consider, to take notice of, to pay attention to' [LN]. This imperative is translated 'look at' [AB, Arn, BECNT, NTC, WBC; GW, HCSB, NCV, NET, NIV, NRSV, REB], 'behold' [KJV, NASB], 'see' [Lns], 'notice' [NLT], 'think of' [TEV], 'when you see (a fig tree)' [CEV].

QUESTION—Why is the phrase 'and all the trees' included?

The fig trees were made explicit because they were both popular and in abundance, but the illustration applies to all fruit trees in general [NTC]. Fig trees were especially suitable for the illustration since they lose their leaves in the winter [NIGTC, WBC]. Perhaps Luke generalized the reference to the fig tree for the readers who did not live in Israel [BECNT, ICC, NAC, NIGTC], or perhaps he is indicating that the fig tree is not to be taken as an eschatological symbol [NIGTC]. No special meaning is to be attached to the fig tree, this is just a parable of a general nature [TH]. The lesson he is teaching is not exclusive to the fig tree [AB, MGC]. The phrase 'and all the trees' is translated 'and all the other trees' [NCV, NET, TEV], 'or any other tree' [TG, TH; CEV, GW, REB].

QUESTION—What is meant by the phrase 'seeing this for yourselves you know'?

It means that they know without being told [ICC, TH]. It is translated 'you know without being told' [ICC, TH; GW, NLT], 'you can see for yourselves' [HCSB, NIV, NRSV], 'you can tell for yourselves' [AB], 'you know' [CEV].

21:31 So[a] you also, when you-see these (things) happening, you-know that the kingdom of-God is near.[b]

LEXICON—a. οὕτως (LN 61.9): 'so' [Arn, LN; CEV, KJV, NASB, NET, NIV, NRSV], 'just so' [NLT], 'thus' [BECNT, LN, Lns], 'in this way' [LN], 'in the same way' [WBC; GW, HCSB, NCV, REB, TEV], 'similarly' [NTC], 'so it is with you' [AB].

b. ἐγγύς (LN 67.61): 'near' [LN]. The clause 'the kingdom of God is near' [AB, Arn, BECNT, Lns, NTC, WBC; GW, HCSB, NASB, NET, NLT, NRSV, REB] is also translated 'God's kingdom is near' [NCV, NIV], 'the kingdom of God is nigh at hand' [KJV], 'God's kingdom will soon be here' [CEV], 'the Kingdom of God is about to come' [TEV]. This refers to being near in time, not in distance [LN].

QUESTION—What things are meant in the phrase 'when you see *these things* happening'?

These are the signs Jesus had been speaking of [Lns]. This takes up the phrase used in 21:28 [NIGTC, Su, TH], which in turn refers to 21:15f. [NIGTC, TH]. These things are mentioned in 21:25–26. [MGC, NAC, NTC, TG]. The coming of Christ is also considered a sign for those who think of the kingdom in terms of the restoration of Jerusalem in the millennial kingdom [MGC].

QUESTION—What is meant by the kingdom of God being near?

This is another way of saying that the coming of the Son of Man is near [EGT, NAC, TG]. All opposition to the reign of God will come to an end [Arn]. This is the kingdom in its consummation [BECNT, Su], in all its power [NET]. The kingdom of God is Christ's rule of glory that follows this present rule of grace [Lns]. It is Christ's reign in the new heaven and earth [NTC].

21:32 Truly I-say to-you this generation[a] will- never -pass-away[b] until all (these things) occur.[c]

LEXICON—a. γενεά (LN 11.41, 10.4, 67.144) (BAGD 2. p. 154): 'generation, contemporaries' [BAGD]. The phrase 'this generation' [AB, Arn, BECNT, Lns, NTC, WBC; GW, HCSB, KJV, NASB, NET, NIV, NLT, NRSV] is also translated 'the present generation' [REB], 'the people of this time' [NCV], 'the people now living' [TEV], 'some of the people of this generation' [CEV]. Generation means the sum total of those born at the same time, and it can also include all the rest of the people living at that same time [BAGD]. The noun means those of the same generation, those of the same time [LN (11.14)], or those of the same ethnic group

having the same cultural similarities [LN (10.4)], or it refers to a period of time about the length of a generation [LN (67.144)].
  b. aorist act. subj. of παρέρχομαι (LN 67.85) (BAGD 1.b.α. p. 626): 'to pass away, to come to an end, to disappear' [BAGD], 'to pass' [LN]. The phrase 'will not pass away' [Arn, BECNT, Lns, NTC; HCSB, KJV, NASB, NET, NIV, NRSV] is also translated 'will not have passed away' [WBC], 'will not pass from the scene' [NLT], 'will not disappear' [GW]. Some translate without including the negative 'not': '(it will all happen before)…passes away' [AB], 'will still be alive (when all this takes place)' [CEV], '(these things will happen while)…are still living' [NCV], 'will live (to see it all)' [NLT], '(all these things will take place) before the people now living have all died' [TEV].
  c. aorist mid. (deponent = act.) subj. of γίνομαι (LN 13.107): 'to occur' [LN], 'to happen' [AB, Arn, LN, WBC; NCV, NIV], 'to start happening' [CEV], 'to take place' [NTC; GW, HCSB, NASB, NET, NLT, NRSV, TEV], 'to come to pass' [BECNT], 'to be fulfilled' [KJV], '(will live) to see it' [REB].

QUESTION—What is meant by ἡ γενεὰ αὕτη 'this generation' and what things will occur?
  1. 'This generation' refers to the future generation that will see the signs of the coming of the Son of Man and 'these things' refers to 21:25–31 [AB, BECNT, NIBC]. 'This generation' refers to the generation that will see the signs of the end and the point is that the generation which sees the beginning of the end will still be alive at the finish of the age [BECNT]. This appears to be an independent saying that is not directly connected to the context [AB, NIBC].
  2. 'This generation' refers to Jesus' contemporaries and 'these things' refer to the destruction of the temple and Jerusalem (21:6–24) [EGT, Gdt, NIC]. In A.D. 70, everything predicted by Jesus in 21:6–24 concerning the destruction of Jerusalem has literally occurred [NIC]. It is to be noted that the period of the resulting Jewish dispersion would continue on through the centuries [NIC].
  3. 'This generation' refers to Jesus' contemporaries and 'these things' refer to all of the signs concerning the destruction of Jerusalem and the coming of the Son of Man (21:6–31) [Arn, ICC, Su, TG, TH, WBC]. Jesus meant that some of those people contemporary with him would still be alive at his coming [Su]. Jesus referred to the destruction of Jerusalem as a type of the end of the world, so the coming of the God's kingdom here refers to the destruction of Jerusalem [ICC]. The phrase 'these things' is the same as in 21:31 and 28, all referring to 21:25–26 [TG]. Jesus anticipated that everything would happen during a single generation, the generation of his contemporaries, and he was thus like the OT prophets who put together things that belong together in principle even though it turns out that they are separated by a long span of time [Arn, WBC].

4. 'This generation' refers to the Jews as a race and 'these things' refer to 21:6–31 [MGC, NTC]. Despite the fall of Jerusalem and the dispersion of the nation, there will still be Jews in the world when Christ returns. The Jewish race will continue to exist up to the fulfillment of the predicted events of the entire dispensation which will end with the Lord's return [NTC]. Despite times of suffering, God's promise is that he will preserve his chosen people and finally restore them [MGC].
5. 'This generation' refers to the type of Jewish people who were hostile to Jesus and 'these things' are all of the events and signs described in 21:8–31 [Lns, NAC, NICNT]. It might be expected that the type of Jews who opposed Jesus that day would come to an end with the destruction of the temple, but Jesus assures them that this type of Jews will continue to reject Jesus until his second coming [Lns]. 'This generation' is the final evil generation that is connected in descent and behavior with the generation of Jesus' day [NAC]. The disciples could expect hostility until the very end [NICNT].
6. Luke has used 'this generation' to refer to mankind [BNTC].
7. 'These things' refer to the kind of end that is accompanied by all the signs, and the mention of 'this generation' is used to emphasize the certainty of the end, not to indicate its time. This could mean that the end is as sure to come as that generation will continue to exist, or that this generation can be sure that the last events have begun and they will surely be brought to an end [NIGTC].

21:33 Heaven and earth will-pass-away,ᵃ but my words by-no-means will-pass-away.ᵇ

LEXICON—a. fut. mid. (deponent = act.) indic. of παρέρχομαι (LN 13.93): 'to pass away, to cease to exist, to cease' [LN]. The clause 'heaven and earth will pass away' [Arn, BECNT, NTC, WBC; HCSB, KJV, NASB, NET, NIV, NRSV, REB, TEV] is also translated 'heaven and earth will disappear' [NLT], 'the earth and the heavens will disappear' [GW], 'the sky and the earth will pass away' [AB], 'earth and sky will be destroyed' [NCV], 'the sky and the earth won't last forever' [CEV]. The present condition of heaven and earth is of a transient nature [NTC].

b. fut. mid. (deponent = act.) indic. of παρέρχομαι (LN 13.93): 'to pass away, to cease to exist, to cease' [LN]. The clause 'my words will not pass away' [AB, Arn, BECNT, WBC; KJV, NASB, NRSV] is also translated 'my words will never pass away' [NTC; HCSB, NET, NIV, REB, TEV], 'my words will never disappear' [GW], 'the words I have spoken will never be destroyed' [NCV], 'my words will remain forever' [NLT], 'my words will last forever' [CEV]. This verb is used in a slightly different sense than the sense in the preceding two occurrences in these two verses [NIGTC].

394 LUKE 21:33

QUESTION—Will heaven and earth pass away?

Jesus states that the physical heaven and earth will pass away [ICC, Lns], but this verb does not indicate whether it refers to their annihilation or to their transformation into a different kind of existence. From Rom. 8:19–23 and Rev. 21:1–5 we are to understand that the physical heaven and earth will be changed so completely that we will not recognize them [Lns]. This refers to the temporal creation as men know it [Su]. This phrase is also discussed in 16:17.

QUESTION—What is meant by Jesus' words not passing away?

This refers to the enduring validity of Jesus' words in both this age and the next [NIGTC]. What Jesus says will always be true [ICC, TG]. 'My words' refer to the totality of his teaching, not just to what he said in this passage [Lns, Su]. The prophecy Jesus just uttered is especially meant, but his words include everything he says [ICC]. No restriction of what words Jesus spoke should be made. Every word will be fulfilled and, being fulfilled, it will thus stand forever [Lns]. Or, 'my words' refers to what Jesus said in 21:6–28 about the second coming [NAC, TH], and he means that those words will never lose force or become invalid [TH].

QUESTION—What is the force of the double negatives οὐ μὴ παρέλθῃ '(this generation) will no not pass away' and οὐ μὴ παρελεύσονται '(my words) will no not pass away'?

The double negatives make the two statements emphatic [BECNT, Lns, NAC, NTC].

DISCOURSE UNIT: 21:34–38 [CEV, GW, HCSB, NET, NRSV, TEV]. The topic is a warning [CEV], no one knows when the earth and the heavens will disappear [GW], the need to watch [HCSB, TEV], an exhortation to watch [NRSV], be ready [NET].

DISCOURSE UNIT: 21:34–36 [AB, BECNT, NAC, NIGTC, TNTC, WBC; NCV]. The topic is an exhortation to vigilance [AB, NAC], application: call to watch [BECNT], be watchful and ready [NIGTC, TNTC], be ready all the time [NCV], the vigilant and prayerful will stand before the Son of Man [WBC].

21:34 **And pay-attention[a] to-yourselves lest your hearts be-burdened[b] with dissipation[c] and drunkenness and anxieties[d] of-life and that day come[e] upon you suddenly**

LEXICON—a. pres. act. impera. of προσέχω (LN 27.59) (BAGD 1.b. p. 714): 'to pay attention to, to be on one's guard against' [BAGD, LN], 'to beware of' [BAGD]. The phrase 'pay attention to yourselves' is translated 'take/give heed to yourselves' [Arn, BECNT, Lns; KJV], 'be on your guard' [AB; HCSB, NET, REB], 'be on guard' [NASB, NRSV], 'ever be on your guard' [NTC], 'beware' [WBC], 'watch out' [NLT], 'be careful' [NCV, NIV, TEV], 'make sure that (you don't)' [GW], not explicit [CEV]. They were to keep a constant check on their attitudes and conduct [Su]. They are to take care that they not become careless about the event

Jesus described and believe that the day would never come or that it makes no difference how one lives [BECNT]. They are to avoid anything that hinders their watchfulness [Arn] and the following list mentions some of such things [Arn, TH]. See this word at 12:1.

b. aorist pass. subj. of βαρέομαι, βαρέω (LN 22.18) (BAGD p. 133): 'to be burdened' [BAGD, LN], 'to be troubled' [LN]. The phrase 'lest your heart be burdened' [Arn] is also translated 'lest at any time your hearts be overcharged' [KJV], 'lest your hearts be loaded down' [NTC], 'lest your hearts be weighed down' [BECNT], 'lest perhaps your hearts be weighted down' [Lns], 'so that your hearts are not weighed down' [NET, NRSV], 'or your hearts will be weighed down' [NIV], 'so that your hearts will not be weighted down' [NASB], 'so that your minds are not dulled' [AB, WBC; HCSB], 'not to spend your time' [NCV], 'not to let yourselves become occupied with' [TEV], 'that you don't' [GW]. Some translate the phrase as a command: 'don't spend all of your time thinking about' [CEV], 'do not let your minds be dulled' [REB], 'don't let me find you living in' [NLT]. The verb refers to experiencing difficulties brought on by burdensome obligations [LN]. 'Weighed down' means that they would be insensitive and have a careless attitude about Jesus' return [BECNT].

c. κραιπάλη (LN 88.286) (BAGD p. 448): 'dissipation' [BAGD], 'drunken dissipation' [LN]. In connection with the following noun μέθη 'drunkenness', the phrase 'dissipation and drunkenness' [BECNT, NTC; NASB, NET, NIV, NRSV, REB] is also translated 'become drunk, hung over' [GW], 'drunken nausea and drunkenness' [Lns], 'carousing, drunkenness' [AB, WBC; HCSB], 'surfeiting and drunkenness' [Arn; KJV], 'careless ease and drunkenness' [NLT], 'feasting and drinking' [NCV, TEV], 'eating or drinking' [CEV]. Dissipation refers to dizziness or intoxication, with the results of 'drunken headache, hangover' [BAGD]. It is the after effects of drunkenness [Arn, NIGTC]. It is the nausea and headache caused by heavy drinking [ICC, Lns]. It is drunken behavior which is completely without moral restraint [LN]. It is losing control of their physical actions because of intoxicants [Su]. It is the excessive indulgence in pleasures [NTC]. This is revelry in drinking that leads to drunkenness [NAC].

d. μέριμνα (LN 25.224) (BAGD p. 504): 'anxiety, worry' [BAGD, LN]. The phrase 'anxieties of life' [Lns, NTC; NIV] is also translated 'worries of life' [WBC; HCSB, NASB], 'the worries of this life' [NET, NRSV, TEV], 'the cares of life' [BECNT; KJV], 'worrying about life' [CEV, GW], 'and worldly cares' [AB, Arn; REB], 'worrying about worldly things' [NCV], 'filled with the worries of this life' [NLT]. This is a feeling of apprehension or distress in view of possible danger or misfortune [LN]. This refers to distractions about earthly affairs such as food, clothes, shelter, and social life [Su]. The worries of life are described in 12:22–30 [Arn].

e. aorist act. subj. of ἐφίσταμαι (LN 13.119) (BAGD 1.b. p. 330): 'to come upon' [BAGD, LN], 'to overtake, to happen to' [LN]. The clause 'and that day come upon you suddenly' [Arn, BECNT, Lns] is also translated 'if you do, that day might come on you suddenly' [NCV], 'and that day will come on you suddenly' [NASB], 'so that that day comes upon you suddenly' [WBC], 'or that day will come on you unexpectedly' [HCSB], 'or that Day may suddenly catch you' [TEV], 'or that day will come upon you by surprise' [AB], 'so that day come upon you unawares' [KJV], 'then that day could suddenly catch you' [GW], 'so that the great day catches you suddenly' [REB], 'and that day catch you unexpectedly' [NRSV], 'and that day will close on you unexpectedly' [NTC; NIV], 'and that day close down upon you suddenly' [NET], 'don't let that day catch you unaware' [NLT]. The clause 'that day may come upon you suddenly like a snare' is translated 'that day will surprise everyone on earth' [CEV]. The use of the verb 'come upon' may be affected by the comparison 'like a snare' and it means 'to close upon, catch, fall upon' [TH]. The verb implies that some undesirable event will happen to someone or something [LN].

QUESTION—What is meant by their hearts being burdened with the three negative actions listed here?

Their 'hearts' refer to their minds and this means that they would not be sensitive to what is happening [TG]. Their 'hearts' refers to their thoughts and mental processes or to their emotions and they are warned not to become preoccupied and distracted by these things [TG]. The three actions are samples of the things that weigh the heart down [Arn, Lns]. The load on their hearts would prevent them from watching and from praying [Lns]. They would fail to be alert [WBC]. They could not perform effectively [Su].

QUESTION—Why were the disciples in danger of dissipation and drunkenness?

Even believers have ruined their lives by yielding to such temptations [NTC]. There was no indication that the apostles had alcoholic problems and this strong language indicates what can happen when a man under pressure surrenders to physical impulses [Su]. Although a warning of literal drunkenness is included, the main idea is probably metaphorical of the intoxicating attraction of the sinful world [NIGTC]. These words are symbols of various forms of spiritual degeneration [NIC].

QUESTION—What is meant by the day coming upon them suddenly?

This refers to the day of the Lord's return [ICC, NAC, NIC, NIVS, Su, TG, TH], 'the final day' [CEV], or the day of judgment [Arn, NIC]. It is the final day that includes the judgment on everyone without exception [NTC]. It is the time of destruction that anticipates the coming of the Son of Man [WBC]. It would come on them suddenly at a time when they least expected it and were not ready for it [TG]. This is a consequence of the preceding clause [TH]. It would be unexpected to those whose minds were dulled, but alert disciples would be able to trace the developments described in this chapter [WBC]. Worldly concerns would dull their attention to spiritual things and they would not be observing the signs [NIGTC]. At first glance it appears that the disciples would be alive on the day the Lord returns, and the reason for this is that every believer should fix his heart on that day and if this expectation is not realized by all the generations preceding the last generation when it actually happens, all will still meet the Lord at their death [Gdt]. This is primarily meant for the believers who would be alive at the last days, since all are called on to be prepared always [NIC].

21:35 like a-snare.ᵃ Because it-will-come upon all the (ones) residing/ sitting ᵇ on (the) face of-all the earth.

TEXT—Instead of ὡς παγίς· ἐπεισελεύσεται γάρ 'as a snare; for it will come upon' some manuscripts read ὡς παγίς γάρ ἐπεισελεύσεται 'for as a snare it will come upon'. GNT reads ὡς παγίς· ἐπεισελεύσεται γάρ 'as a snare; for it will come upon' with a B decision, indicating that the text is almost certain. Ὡς παγίς γάρ ἐπεισελεύσεται 'for as a snare it will come upon' is read by KJV.

LEXICON—a. παγίς (LN **6.23**) (BAGD 1. p. 602): 'snare, trap' [BAGD, LN]. The phrase ὡς παγίς 'like a snare' [Arn, BECNT, **LN**, WBC] is also translated 'as a snare' [Lns; KJV], 'like a trap' [AB, NTC; HCSB, NASB, NCV, NET, NIV, NRSV, REB, TEV], 'as in a trap' [NLT], '(catch you by surprise) like a trap that catches a bird' [GW], not explicit [CEV].

b. pres. mid./pass. (deponent = act) participle of κάθημαι (LN 85.63, 17.2) (BAGD 1.b. p. 389): 'to reside' [BAGD, LN (85.63)], 'to inhabit' [LN (85.63)], 'to sit' [LN (17.2)]. The phrase 'all the ones residing/sitting on the face of all the earth' is translated 'all the ones residing/dwelling on the face of all the earth' [WBC; NASB], 'all who live/dwell on the face of the whole earth' [BECNT; HCSB, KJV, NET, NIV, NRSV], 'all those who live/dwell on the face of the entire earth' [AB, NTC], 'all people who live on the earth' [GW], 'all people on earth' [NCV], 'everyone living on the earth' [NLT], 'all people everywhere on earth' [TEV], 'everyone on earth' [CEV], 'everyone, the whole world over' [REB], 'all who sit upon the face of the whole earth' [Arn], 'all those sitting on the face of all the earth' [Lns]. It means to remain for some time in a place, and often implies that it is a settled situation [LN (85.63)].

QUESTION—What is meant by the simile ὡς παγίς 'like a snare'?

The day could come suddenly like a snare suddenly catches a bird or animal [TG]. A snare catches a bird or animal in a noose or net [Lns]. The picture is of a net that suddenly encloses a covey of birds peacefully settled in a field [Gdt]. It expresses the unexpectedness of what happens [BECNT, NICNT, NIGTC, Su, TG, TH; HCSB, NIV]. It takes them by surprise [CEV, GW], by its suddenness [Arn, BECNT, NICNT, NTC, TH]. Only those who were not ready for that day would be caught in this snare [WBC].

QUESTION—What relationship is indicated by γάρ 'because'?
This indicates the reason for the warning [BECNT, My]: pay attention because it will come on everyone. It is because of the universal scope of that day [BECNT]. Here the final judgment is emphasized, not the judgment against Jerusalem [Crd].

QUESTION—Does καθημένους mean 'residing' or 'sitting' on the face of all the earth?

1. The verb κάθημαι means 'residing' here and refers to all of the people on earth [all commentaries except Alf, Lns, Su; all versions]. The day of the Lord will affect every person and so the disciples will not escape from it if they are not ready [NIGTC].
2. The verb κάθημαι has its primary meaning of 'sitting' here and refers to the people who are sitting at ease when the day comes [Alf, Lns, Su]. Of course all the people of the world will be affected by that day, but here the reference seems more limited to all those sitting at ease with no expectation of the Lord's return [Su]. Resting contentedly on earth, they care for nothing higher [Lns].

21:36 And be-alert[a] at every time praying that you-may-be-strong[b] to-escape[b] all these (things) (which) are-about to-happen and to-stand[c] before the Son of-Man.

TEXT—Instead of δέ 'and', some manuscripts read οὖν 'therefore'. GNT does not mention this variant. Οὖν 'therefore' is read by KJV.

TEXT—Instead of κατισχύσητε 'you may have strength', some manuscripts read καταξιωθῆτε 'you may be counted worthy'. GNT does not mention this variant. Καταξιωθῆτε 'you may be counted worthy' is read by Arn and KJV.

LEXICON—a. pres. act. impera. of ἀγρυπνέω (LN 27.57) (BAGD 1. p. 14): 'to be alert' [BAGD, LN; GW, HCSB, NRSV], 'to keep on the alert' [AB; NASB, REB], 'to stay alert' [NET], 'to watch out' [CEV], 'to be on watch' [NIV, TEV], 'to keep watch' [NTC; NLT], 'to watch' [Arn, BECNT, Lns; KJV], 'to stay awake' [WBC], 'to be ready' [NCV].

b. aorist act. subj. of κατισχύω (LN 74.10, 79.64) (BAGD 1. p. 424): 'to be strong enough, to be able, to be fully able' (being physically strong enough for some purpose) [LN (74.10)], 'to be able' (being capable of doing something) [BAGD, LN (79.64)]. The phrase ἵνα κατισχύσητε ἐκφυγεῖν 'that you may be strong to escape' is translated 'that you will be strong enough to escape' [NCV], 'that you may have strength to escape' [BECNT, NTC, WBC; HCSB, NASB, NET, NRSV], 'so that you have the power to escape' [GW], 'that you prevail to escape' [Lns], 'that you can escape' [CEV], 'that you may be able to escape' [NIV], 'that, if possible, you may escape' [NLT], 'that you will have the strength to go safely through' [TEV], 'for the strength to pass safely through' [REB], 'for the strength to come safely through' [AB].

c. aorist pass. infin. of ἵσταμαι (LN 17.1) (BAGD II.1.b. p. 382): 'to stand' [BAGD, LN]. The phrase σταθῆναι ἔμπροσθεν 'to stand before' [AB, BECNT, Lns, WBC; HCSB, KJV, NASB, NCV, NET, NIV, NLT, NRSV] is also translated 'to take your stand before' [Arn, NTC], 'to stand in front of' [GW], 'to stand in the presence of' [REB]. The clause 'and stand before the Son of Man' is translated 'and that the Son of Man will be pleased with you' [CEV]. This refers to taking one's stand in a way that a person appears before a judge [TH].

QUESTION—What are they to be alert about?

They are to be faithfully looking for the Lord's return [NET]. They are to be prepared for the coming of the Lord and praying is a means of doing this [NAC]. It reflects the uncertainty of the Lord's coming and they are to stay awake to pray [WBC]. This takes up the command in 21:34, 'pay attention to yourselves' [TH]. This concerns spiritual watchfulness [NIGTC]. They are to watch against sin and straying in their hearts and lives [NIC].

QUESTION—What does the phrase ἐν παντὶ καιρῷ 'at every time' modify?

1. It modifies the preceding verb 'be alert' [AB, Arn, BECNT, Lns, NTC, WBC; GW, HCSB, NASB, NCV, NET, NIV, NLT, NRSV]: be alert at every time and pray.
2. It modifies the following verb 'praying' [ICC, My, TH; CEV, KJV, REB]: be alert and at every time pray.

QUESTION—What is meant by κατισχύσητε 'you may be strong'?

1. It refers to being physically strong [TG, TH]. This speaks of being enabled to endure and survive the troubles and persecutions [TG].
2. It refers to inner strength so as to be able to do something. It means to be capable of doing something [BECNT, Lns, NAC; CEV]. They are to pray for God's strengthening so that they are faithful and able to endure the temptations and the pressures accompanying the end times [BECNT]. They are to be strong so as to keep the faith and not give up [NAC]. This is spiritual strength to resist growing slack in their watchfulness and to resist giving way to temptations such as those in 21:34 [Lns].

QUESTION—What is meant by escaping all these things which are about to happen?

This does not mean to avoid these things. It means being enabled to endure and survive those troubles and persecutions [Su, TG, TH]. It means to come through the events of the last days unscathed and not give up the faith [NIGTC]. They will not be overwhelmed by every temptation to slacken their watchfulness and not be caught in the worldly ways described in 21:34 [Lns]. 'All these things' refers to the signs in 21:25–26 along with the things mentioned in 21:34–35 [NAC].

QUESTION—What is meant by standing before the Son of Man?

1. The Son of Man will come as a judge [AB, Arn, BECNT, Lns, NAC, NIGTC, TG, TH]. The picture is that of appearing before a judge [TH]. To stand before him is to appear for judgment [TG]. This verb is dependent on the preceding verb 'you may be strong enough/able' [TH].

Here it means to secure a favorable verdict [BECNT, NIGTC]. They will escape his wrath and judgment [NAC]. It means to meet him without shame and without fear of rebuke, having resisted the pressures and cares of life (21:34) [Su]. They will face his judgment and come through with flying colors [AB]. They will stand safe from adverse judgment [Lns]. They will stand and remain with him without fear of being rejected [Arn].

2. This is not concerned specifically with being judged [Gdt, NIC, Su, TNTC, WBC]. They will stand before him as those whom he has redeemed and will not shrink away from him with shame [Gdt, NIC, Su]. Standing before him is an image of deliverance, not appearing before a judge, so after successfully enduring the trials of the last times they will safely arrive at the place of abiding security [WBC].

3. Angels will set them in the presence of the glorified Son of Man [Alf, My]. This will happen when the angels bring the elect from the whole earth to the Messiah who appears in glory [My].

DISCOURSE UNIT: 21:37-38 [AB, BECNT, NAC, NIGTC, Su, TNTC, WBC]. The topic is a summary statement of Jesus' activity during the week [Su], the ministry of Jesus in the temple [AB, BECNT, NAC, NIGTC, TNTC], days in the temple and nights on the mount of Olives [WBC].

21:37 And (during) the days he-was teaching in the temple, and (during) the nights he-went-out and he-was-spending-the-night[a] on the mountain (which) was-called of-olives. **21:38** And all the people were-getting-up-early (to come) to him in the temple to-listen to-him.

TEXT—Following 21:38, one manuscript adds the words of John 7:53–8:11. GNT rejects this addition with an A decision, indicating that the text is certain.

LEXICON—a. imperf. mid./pass. (deponent = act.) indic. of αὐλίζομαι (LN 67.194) (BAGD 1. p. 121): 'to spend the night' [BAGD, LN], 'to find lodging' [BAGD]. The phrase 'he was spending the night' is translated 'he would spend the night' [WBC; GW, HCSB, NASB, NIV, NRSV, REB, TEV], 'he would spend the nights' [AB], '(he returned) to spend the night' [NLT], 'he spent each night' [CEV], 'he abode' [KJV], 'he lodged' [BECNT], 'he would lodge' [NTC], 'he kept lodging' [Lns], 'he lodged in the open' [Arn], 'and stayed on' [NCV, NET]. It means to lodge in a place during the night [LN]. The verb is in the imperfect tense because he did this night after night [EGT].

QUESTION—When did this happen?

This covers the days from Jesus' arrival in Jerusalem to his arrest by the authorities [TG]. These two verses describe the time covered by chapters 22 and 23 [EGT]. It covers the day of the Triumphal entry and the next two days and it is a repetition of 19:47 with additional details [ICC]. This covers the time from Palm Sunday onward, but it doubtful that it covers Wednesday [Lns].

LUKE 21:37-38   401

QUESTION—Where did Jesus go at night?
It seems to say that Jesus camped out and slept outdoors on the Mount of Olives [Gdt, ICC]. He spent the nights in the open air [Gdt]. He would camp out on the hill [AB, Gdt, ICC]. He lodged in the open, probably forced to do this because of the large number of disciples [Arn]. The verb 'to lodge' can be used since he did this night after night [EGT]. In Matthew 21:7 it says that Jesus stayed at Bethany and the verb here does not necessarily imply sleeping outdoors [NIGTC]. The account in Matthew implies that he passed the night in a house in Bethany [EGT]. Since the town of Bethany is at the edge of the Olives, it is not clear whether Jesus slept in someone's house or outdoors [BECNT, NAC, TNTC]. At least some of the nights he probably spent in Gethsemane [Lns, Su], since Judas knew where to lead the soldiers to arrest Jesus [Su]. It is possible that he stayed outdoors and also in a home on different nights [NIGTC].

DISCOURSE UNIT: 22:1–24:53 [NIGTC]. The topic is the passion and the resurrection.

DISCOURSE UNIT: 22:1–23:56 [NAC, NICNT, TNTC, WBC]. The topic is Jesus' passion [NAC, WBC], the suffering and death of Jesus [NICNT], the crucifixion [TNTC].

DISCOURSE UNIT: 22:1–23:56a [AB]. The topic is the passion narrative.

DISCOURSE UNIT: 22:1–46 [REB]. The topic is the last supper.

DISCOURSE UNIT: 22:1–38 [AB, BECNT, NAC, NICNT, NIGTC]. The topic is the last supper [NAC, NICNT, NIGTC], betrayal and farewell [BECNT], the preliminary events [AB].

DISCOURSE UNIT: 22:1–13 [NASB]. The topic is preparing the Passover.

DISCOURSE UNIT: 22:1–6 [BECNT, TNTC; CEV, GW, HCSB, NCV, NET, NIV, NLT, NRSV]. The topic is the betrayal [TNTC], the plot to kill Jesus [NRSV], Judas becomes an enemy of Jesus [NCV], Judas' decision to betray Jesus [NET], Judas agrees to betray Jesus [NIV, NLT], Judas' plan to betray Jesus [BECNT], a plot to kill Jesus [CEV, GW, HCSB].

DISCOURSE UNIT: 22:1–2 [AB, Su, WBC; TEV]. The topic is a reference to Jesus' approaching death [Su], the conspiracy to arrest Jesus [AB, WBC], the plot against Jesus [TEV].

22:1 And the festival of-the unleavened[a] (bread), the (one) called Passover, was-coming-near.[b] **22:2** And the chief-priests and the scribes were-seeking[c] how they-might-destroy[d] him, because they-feared[e] the people.
LEXICON—a. ἄζυμος (LN 5.13) (BAGD 1.b. p. 20): 'unleavened' [BAGD, LN], 'without yeast' [LN], 'without fermentation' [BAGD]. The phrase 'the festival of the unleavened bread' is translated 'the Festival of Unleavened Bread' [Arn, Lns; GW, HCSB, NLT, NRSV, REB, TEV],

'the Feast of Unleavened Bread' [AB, BECNT, NTC, WBC; KJV, NASB, NCV, NET, NIV], 'the Festival of Thin Bread' [CEV].
- b. imperf. act. indic. of ἐγγίζω (LN 67.21) (BAGD 5.b. p. 213): 'to come near' [BAGD, LN], 'to be near' [CEV, GW, NRSV], 'to be close at hand' [AB], 'to draw near' [Arn, BECNT, Lns, WBC; HCSB, NLT], 'to draw nigh' [KJV], 'to approach' [BAGD, LN, NTC; NASB, NET, NIV, REB], 'it was almost time for' [NCV], 'the time was near for' [TEV]. Mark 14:1 states that it was two days away.
- c. imperf. act. indic. of ζητέω (LN 27.34) (BAGD 1.c. p. 339): 'to seek, to consider' [BAGD], 'to try to learn, to search, to try to find out' [LN]. The phrase 'were seeking how' [Arn, BECNT, Lns; NASB] is also translated 'sought how' [KJV], 'were seeking for some way' [AB], 'were looking for a/some way' [NTC; CEV, GW, HCSB, NIV, NRSV], 'were trying to find a/some way' [NCV, NET, TEV], 'were trying to devise some means of' [REB], 'were actively plotting' [NLT], 'were still seeking to work out how' [WBC]. The verb means to attempt to learn something by careful investigation or searching [LN]. The imperfect tense indicates that they continued to seek for a way to accomplish Jesus' death [ICC], and it is conative, meaning they were *trying* to find a way [Rb]. They were plotting how they might have Jesus killed [EGT, Gdt, Lns, NAC, NIGTC, Su]. This does not mean that they called a special meeting, since the imperfect tense indicates a continuing action [Arn]. They were on a constant watch for an opportunity [BECNT, ICC, NIGTC]. They had determined to put Jesus to death and their problem was how to bring it about [Lns, Su].
- d. aorist act. subj. of ἀναιρέω (LN 20.71) (BAGD 1.a. p. 55): 'to destroy' [Arn], 'to put to death' [BAGD, BECNT; HCSB, NASB, NET, NRSV], 'to put to death secretly' [TEV], 'to kill' [LN; GW, KJV, NCV], 'to execute' [LN], 'to get rid of' [CEV, NIV], 'to do away with' [AB, NTC, WBC; REB], 'to make away with' [Lns]. The phrase 'how they might destroy him' is translated '(plotting) Jesus' death' [NLT]. It means to get rid of someone by execution, often with legal or quasi-legal procedures [LN]. They planned a judicial murder [Lns].
- e. imperf. pass. indic. of φοβέομαι, φοβέω (LM 25.252) (BAGD 1.b.α. p. 863): 'to fear' [Arn, BAGD, BECNT, LN, Lns; KJV, NLT], 'to be afraid of' [AB, LN, NTC, WBC; CEV, GW, HCSB, NCV, NET, NIV, NRSV, REB, TEV].

QUESTION—What was the Festival of Unleavened Bread and how was it connected with the Passover?

This festival occurred about the beginning of April and lasted for seven days to celebrate God's deliverance of the Jews from slavery in Egypt [TG]. The festival's name came from the instructions God gave for a festival in Exod. 12:15 where they were instructed not to use yeast in making bread during that week [TG]. This festival week was called both 'Unleavened' and 'Passover', and the bread was made without yeast to commemorate the hurried event of the original Passover when there was not time to prepare leavened bread [Su]. The phrase 'the unleavened' probably refers to the unleavened cakes of bread [NTC]. The Passover was really a separate annual feast [AB, Arn, ICC, TNTC], but they were now merged and referred to as one [Arn, ICC, NICNT]. The Passover was a one day festival that was immediately followed by the seven day festival of unleavened bread and the two festivals were regarded and celebrated as one [BECNT, Lns, NAC, TG, TNTC]. In NT times the two names were used virtually interchangeably for the week-long festival [NIVS]. Verse 22:1 is translated 'The Festival of Unleavened Bread, which begins with the Passover celebration, was drawing near' [NLT].

QUESTION—What relationship is indicated by γάρ 'because'?

It indicates the reason they had to seek a safe way to have Jesus killed [Arn, Lns, NIGTC]. They were afraid of what the people might do [CEV]. Jesus was too popular for them to openly arrest [NET]. They didn't want to attract the attention of the people [TH]. They wanted to kill Jesus without starting a riot [NLT]. People were around Jesus from early in the morning until nighttime [Su]. Many of the pilgrims to the Passover Festival in Jerusalem supported Jesus and might riot [Gdt, TNTC]. This explains why they were perplexed about *how* to kill him [NIGTC, Su].

DISCOURSE UNIT: 22:3–6 [AB, Su, WBC; TEV]. The topic is the betrayal by Judas [AB, WBC], Judas agrees to betray Jesus [TEV], Judas's preparation for the betrayal [Su].

22:3 And Satan entered[a] into Judas the (one) called[b] Iscariot being of the number[c] of the Twelve. 22:4 And having-departed he-spoke-with the chief-priests and officers[d] how he-might-betray[e] him to-them.

LEXICON—a. aorist act. indic. of εἰσέρχομαι (LN 15.93) (BAGD 1.b.β. p. 232): 'to enter' [BAGD, LN], 'to go into' [LN]. The phrase 'entered into' [AB, Arn, Lns, WBC; KJV, NASB, NLT, NRSV, REB, TEV] is also translated 'entered' [NTC; GW, HCSB, NCV, NET, NIV], 'entered the heart of' [CEV], 'came into' [BECNT].

b. pres. pass. participle of καλέω (LN 33.129) (BAGD 1.a.γ. p. 399): 'to be called, to be named' [BAGD, LN]. The phrase 'Judas, the one called Iscariot' [NET] is also translated 'Judas, who was called Iscariot' [AB; NASB, REB], 'Judas, called Iscariot' [Arn, Lns, NTC, WBC; HCSB, NIV, NRSV, TEV], 'Judas surnamed Iscariot' [KJV], 'Judas Iscariot' [CEV, GW, NCV, NLT]. Since there were two disciples named Judas, the identifying phrase 'Iscariot, the man from Kerioth' had to be included [Arn]. Iscariot was not Judas' proper name but an additional name so that it means he was surnamed Iscariot [TH]. See the question about his name at 6:16.

c. ἀριθμός (LN 60.1) (BAGD 1. p. 106): 'number' [BAGD, LN]. The phrase 'being of the number of the twelve' [Lns; KJV] is also translated 'belonging to the number of the twelve' [NASB], 'who was of the number of the Twelve' [WBC], 'one of the number of the Twelve' [BECNT], 'who was numbered among the Twelve' [AB; HCSB], 'one of the Twelve/twelve' [NTC; NIV, REB], 'one of the twelve disciples' [TEV], 'one of the twelve apostles' [GW], 'who was one of the twelve' [Arn; NET, NRSV], 'who was one of the twelve apostles' [CEV, NLT], 'one of Jesus' twelve apostles' [NCV].

d. στρατηγός (LN 37.91) (BAGD 2. p. 770). 'officer' [Arn, BECNT, WBC; NASB], 'captain' [BAGD; KJV], 'official, commander' [LN]. Here the plural form στρατηγοῖς 'officers' is translated 'temple officers' [AB], 'officers of the temple guard' [NET, NIV, TEV], 'officers of the temple police' [CEV, NRSV], 'captains of the temple guard' [NTC; NLT], 'temple police' [HCSB], 'temple guards' [GW, REB] 'some of the soldiers who guarded the temple' [NCV]. The full phrase, found in 22:5, is στρατηγὸς τοῦ ἱεροῦ 'commander of the Temple guard' [LN], 'the captain of the temple' [BAGD].

e. aorist act. subj. of παραδίδωμι (LN 37.111) (BAGD 1.b. p. 614): 'to betray' [BECNT, LN, Lns, NTC; GW, KJV, NASB, NIV, NLT, NRSV, REB, TEV], 'to betray, handing him over' [NET], 'to hand over' [AB, BAGD, LN; HCSB, NCV], 'to turn over' [BAGD, LN], 'to deliver up' [WBC], 'to help arrest' [CEV]. This describes the formal identification by which Jesus could be legally arrested and includes the matter of when and how that would be done [Su]. It describes the actions of a person who is trusted as a friend, but helps the enemies of that one who trusts him [TG].

QUESTION—In what way did Satan enter into Judas?

Satan took possession of Judas [TG, TH], but not in the sense that Judas was like other demon-possessed people who were unable to control their own actions [ICC, Lns, TH, WBC]. This means that Judas became a tool of Satan in bringing about the arrest and death of Jesus and this was no sudden possession by Satan since there was a development in Judas' thinking about this betrayal [Lns, Su]. Satan made Judas his tool by filling his mind with thoughts of treachery and moving his will to act on them, so this is mental possession in which Judas gave Satan control of his mind, heart, and will [Lns]. Judas opened the door for Satan to gain control of him [ICC, NIC, Rb]. He yielded to Satan's influence [NTC].

QUESTION—Where did Judas depart from?

He left from where Jesus and his fellow disciples were located [TG, TH]. It was after Jesus' rebuke at the feast in Simon's house (John 12:4–6) [Rb].

QUESTION—Who were the στρατηγοῖς 'officers'?

This is a military term and refers to the Levite heads of the temple guards in and about the temple who kept order during the festivals [Arn, EGT, ICC, TG]. Their full title was στρατηγοὺς τοῦ ἱεροῦ 'officers of the temple' (22:52) and they would be the ones to make the arrest [ICC]. Officials included temple police and other officials such as accountants for the temple treasury, but whatever position they had, they were able to facilitate the arrest of Jesus [WBC]. They were leaders of the temple police [NAC, NIGTC]. Probably Judas had to first go to one of the members of the police force on duty at the temple, who would take him to the chief official in order to obtain an audience with the high priests [Lns].

22:5 And they-rejoiced and they-agreed to-give him money. **22:6** And he-consented,[a] and he-was-seeking an-opportunity[b] to-hand-over him to-them without[c] a-crowd.

LEXICON—a. aorist act. indic. of ἐξομολογέομαι, ἐξομολογέω (LN 33.351) (BAGD 1. p. 277): 'to consent' [BAGD, NTC; NASB, NIV, NRSV], 'to promise' [BAGD; KJV], 'to promise to do it' [GW], 'to agree' [AB, BECNT, WBC; CEV, NCV, NET, REB, TEV], 'to accept' [Arn], 'to accept (the offer)' [HCSB], 'to thank' [LN]. The middle voice of this verb means 'to confess', but this active form means 'to consent' [BECNT].

b. εὐκαιρία (LN 67.5) (BAGD p. 321): 'opportunity' [AB, Arn, BECNT, LN, WBC; GW, KJV, NET, NIV, NRSV, REB], 'favorable opportunity' [BAGD, LN], 'good opportunity' [NTC; NASB], 'good occasion, favorable time' [LN], 'best time' [NCV], 'a good chance' [CEV, TEV].

c. ἄτερ (LN **89.120**) (BAGD p. 120): 'without' [BAGD, **LN**], 'apart from' [BAGD, LN]. The phrase 'without a crowd' is translated 'apart from a/the crowd' [AB; NASB], 'in the absence of the multitude' [KJV], 'when the crowds were not around' [CEV, NLT], 'when the crowd was not present' [HCSB], 'when no crowd was present' [NET, NIV, NRSV], 'when there was no crowd' [GW], 'when he was away from the crowd' [NCV], 'in the absence of the/a crowd' [BECNT, NTC, WBC], 'without the presence of the crowd' [Arn], 'without the people knowing about it' [TEV], 'without collecting a crowd' [REB]. 'Without a crowd' means without a crowd being present [NIBC, TH, TNTC]. They wanted to avoid a public uproar [NET, Su, TNTC].

QUESTION—What was involved in the agreement?
It means that they came to an agreement with Judas to give him money [TH]. It was agreed that Judas would notify them of the time and place they could arrest Jesus when there was no crowd around him [Lns, Su]. The aorist tense implies that the money was paid at the time of the bargain [Lns, MGC] and Matt. 26:15–16 explicitly says that the money (30 shekels) was weighed out to Judas at this time [ICC, Lns, MGC]. Or, it implies that the money was not then paid to Judas, but afterwards when he had handed over Jesus [Alf].

DISCOURSE UNIT: 22:7–54a [Su]. The topic is Thursday—a day of joy and sorrow.

DISCOURSE UNIT: 22:7–38 [TNTC; NIV]. The topic is in the upper room [TNTC], the last supper [NIV].

DISCOURSE UNIT: 22:7–30 [NLT]. The topic is the last supper.

DISCOURSE UNIT: 22:7–18 [GW]. The topic is the Passover.

DISCOURSE UNIT: 22:7–14 [AB]. The topic is the preparation for the Passover meal.

DISCOURSE UNIT: 22:7–13 [BECNT, Su, TNTC, WBC; CEV, HCSB, NCV, NET, NRSV, TEV]. The topic is preparing for the meal [BECNT, Su, TNTC, WBC], the Passover [NET], the preparation of the Passover [HCSB, NRSV], Jesus prepares to eat the Passover meal [TEV], Jesus eats the Passover meal [NCV], Jesus eats with his disciples [CEV].

22:7 And the day[a] of-unleavened-bread came, in which it-was-necessary[b] to-slaughter/sacrifice[c] the Passover (lamb).

TEXT—Some manuscripts omit ἐν 'in'. GNT does not mention this variant in the apparatus but brackets it in the text, indicating doubt about including it. Most versions would probably not differentiate between including or omitting ἐν 'in'.

LEXICON—a. ἡμέρα (LN 67.178) (BAGD 2. p. 346): 'day' [AB, Arn, BAGD, BECNT, LN, Lns, NTC, WBC; HCSB, KJV, NCV, NET, NIV, NRSV, REB]. The phrase 'the day of unleavened bread came' is translated 'the day had come for the Festival of Thin Bread' [CEV], 'then came the first day of Unleavened Bread' [NASB], 'the day came during the Festival of Unleavened Bread when' [GW, TEV], 'now the Festival of Unleavened Bread arrived' [NLT].

b. δεῖ (LN 71.21, 71:34): 'to be necessary' [LN (71.34)]. It is translated 'it was necessary to' [WBC], 'it was necessary that' [Lns], 'had to be' [Arn, NTC; GW, HCSB, NASB, NCV, NET, NIV, NRSV, REB], 'must be' [KJV], 'was/were to be' [AB, BECNT; TEV]. The phrase 'in which it was necessary to slaughter' is translated 'it was time to kill' [CEV], 'when (the Passover lambs) were sacrificed' [NLT]. This means that it is something that should be done as the result of the law, custom, or circumstances: 'should, ought, to have to do.' [LN (71.21)]. The imperfect tense refers to the fact that it was a past obligation that continued into the present [Lns]. It was a necessity for a pious Jew [BECNT]. This was commanded in Exodus 12:5 where it says that the animal must be a one-year old male sheep or goat.

c. pres. pass. infin. of θύω (LN 20.72, 53.19) (BAGD 1., 4. p. 367): 'to be slaughtered' [AB, BAGD (4), LN (53.9), Lns; REB], 'to be killed' [Arn, BAGD (4), LN (53.9); CEV, GW, KJV, TEV], 'to be sacrificed' [BAGD (1), BECNT, LN (20.72), NTC; HCSB, NASB, NCV, NET, NIV, NLT, NRSV]. This passive verb is also translated actively: '(it was necessary) to slaughter' [WBC]. When an animal was sacrificed, it was slaughtered in a ritual manner as a sacrifice to God [LN (20.72)].

QUESTION—What was the day of unleavened bread?

The Festival of Unleavened Bread was a seven-day festival and it actually began on Nisan 15, not Nisan 14, which is the day Luke was speaking of since that was the day the lambs were sacrificed [WBC]. The phrase 'the day of unleavened bread' by itself would refer to Nisan 15 [NIGTC], or leave the impression that the feast of Unleavened Bread lasted for just one day [AB]. However, the added description indicates that Nisan 14 is meant [Gdt, Lns,

MGC, NIC, NIGTC, NIVS, NTC, Rb, Su]. It was Thursday morning [Arn, Lns, Su] and Nisan 14 was counted in with the other seven days [Lns]. On Nisan 14, the day of the Passover, the lambs were killed and all leaven or leavened cake was collected for burning on the following day, so this could be called 'the day' of unleavened bread [NIC, TNTC, WBC]. It was the day that the combined Passover and Unleavened Bread festivals began [TNTC]. It was the day of the eight-day-long festival on which the Passover lamb had to be killed [Arn]. The 'day' refers to the first day of the Feast of the Unleavened Bread, which was the Passover day [NET]. Or, the phrase 'the day of unleavened bread' is a generic designation of the week-long celebration from Nisan 15 to 21, and later the celebration was combined with Passover on Nisan 14 [MGC].

QUESTION—What is meant by πάσχα 'Passover'?

The text merely says πάσχα 'Passover', and this noun is used as a metonymy in which the name of the festival suggests the animal that was slain on that day [BECNT]. Exodus 12:5 commands that the animal must be a sheep or a goat. Most translations specify the animal to be a lamb [AB, Arn, BECNT, NTC, WBC; all versions except KJV]. In this whole account, the word 'Passover' is used with three meanings: the whole festival of Unleavened Bread (22:1), the Pascal lamb (22:7), and the Passover meal (22: 8) [Arn, Lns, NICNT].

QUESTION—Was the lamb slaughtered or sacrificed and does this refer to only one Passover lamb or many?

This singular word πάσχα 'Passover' refers to all of the lambs that were to be slain for the families to eat as they celebrated the festival [TG]. Some translations use the plural form 'lambs' [CEV, NCV, NLT, REB, TEV]. There would be a lamb for every family group of ten or more [Su]. Many avoid calling this a sacrifice, saying that the lamb was slaughtered or killed [AB, Arn, MGC, Su, TH, WBC; CEV, GW, KJV, REB, TEV]. On Nisan 14, a lamb selected for each household was slain between the ninth and eleventh hours in the temple court area and as many as 265,000 lambs were killed for Passover [MGC]. The lambs were slaughtered in the temple, but it was not offered as a sacrifice to God [TH, WBC], rather, the meat was taken away to be eaten at family meals in the evening [WBC]. Healthy lambs without blemish were taken to the temple to be slaughtered under the authority of the priests [Su]. Others describe this as a sacrifice, although the meat was taken home for the Passover meal [BECNT, ICC, NIGTC, NTC; HCSB, NASB, NCV, NET, NIV, NLT, NRSV]. Each head of a family group killed the sheep and the blood was caught in a bowl by a priest who then poured the blood at the foot of the altar of burnt-offerings [ICC]. After pouring the blood on the altar, a certain part of the lamb was given for the priestly sacrifice and the rest was wrapped in the skin and taken home for the Passover meal [MGC].

22:8 And he-sent Peter and John saying, Having-gone prepare the Passover[a] for-us in-order-that we-may-eat (it). **22:9** And they said to-him, Where do-you-want we-should-prepare (it)?

LEXICON—a. πάσχα (LN 51.7) (BAGD 3. p. 633): 'Passover' [Arn, BECNT, Lns, NTC, WBC; KJV, NASB, NET, NIV, NLT], 'Passover meal' [BAGD, LN; CEV, HCSB, NCV, NRSV, TEV], 'Passover supper' [AB; REB], 'Passover lamb' [GW]. Here the noun 'Passover' specifically means the Passover meal [BECNT, MGC, NIGTC].

QUESTION— How would Peter and John prepare the Passover?

This concerned preparing the meal to be eaten in celebrating the Passover Festival [LN (51.7)]. These two men were to take the lamb to the Temple to be sacrificed [BECNT, Lns, MGC, NAC, NTC, Su]. Perhaps the lamb had been purchased a few days earlier [NTC]. They would obtain a room of sufficient size for the disciples and arrange the furnishings and make it ready [BECNT, MGC, NAC, NIGTC, NTC, Su]. They would roast the lamb [NAC, Su], buy and prepare unleavened bread [NIGTC, NTC] and other food, sauces, and wine [BECNT, MGC, NAC, NIGTC, NTC, Su]. This might involve arranging for helpers to prepare the meal [NIGTC]. The owner supplied the room, with the cushions and furniture needed for the supper, but the two disciples would prepare what was needed for eating the Passover [MGC, NAC]. Perhaps the owner of the house already had the room provisioned for the feast so that the preparation could be done without a great deal of coming and going [WBC].

22:10 And he-said to-them, Behold, having-entered into the city a-man will-meet[a] you carrying a-jar[b] of-water. Follow him into the house into which he-enters **22:11** and you-will-say to-the house-master[c] of-the house, The teacher says to-you, Where is the guest-room[d] where I-may-eat the Passover with my disciples?

TEXT— In 22:10, instead of εἰς ἥν 'into which', some manuscripts read οὗ 'where'. GNT does not mention this variant. Οὗ 'where' is read by KJV.

LEXICON—a. fut. act. indic. of συναντάω (LN 13.120) (BAGD 1. p. 784): 'to meet' [AB, Arn, BAGD, BECNT, LN, Lns, NTC, WBC; all versions], 'to come upon' [LN]. There is no impliction that the man would come with the purpose of meeting them and the idea is 'you will meet', or 'you will find' the man [TH]. He will turn up in front of the disciples at the right time [WBC]. The two disciples were not to speak with the man [Lns], but to simply follow him to the house [BECNT, Lns].

b. κεράμιον (LN 6.128) (BAGD p. 428): 'jar' [Arn, BAGD, BECNT, LN, Lns, NTC, WBC; CEV, NCV, NET, NIV, NRSV, REB, TEV], 'jug' [AB; GW], 'earthenware vessel' [BAGD, LN], 'pitcher' [KJV, NASB, NLT]. It was an earthenware vessel for holding water and it may have been for washing hands before a meal [BECNT].

c. οἰκοδεσπότης (LN 57.14) (BAGD p. 558): 'master of the house' [BAGD], 'master of the household' [LN]. The phrase 'the house master of the house' is translated 'the householder of the house' [WBC], 'the master of the house' [AB, Lns], 'the owner of the house' [Arn, BECNT, NTC; GW, HCSB, NASB, NCV, NET, NIV, NRSV, TEV], 'the goodman of the house' [KJV], 'the householder' [REB], 'the owner' [CEV, NLT]. The added phrase τῆς οἰκίας 'of the house' is not needed [AB, EGT, WBC] since the noun οἰκοδεσπότης already means master of the house [WBC]. However the noun had lost its original force and the addition is justified [NIGTC].

d. κατάλυμα (LN 7.30) (BAGD p. 414): 'guest room' [AB, Arn, BAGD, BECNT, Lns, NTC, WBC; HCSB, NASB, NCV, NET, NIV, NLT, NRSV], 'guestchamber' [KJV], 'room' [LN; GW, REB, TEV], 'quarters, dining room' [LN]. The phrase 'where is the guest room in which I may eat' is translated 'where he can eat' [CEV]. This is the same word translated as 'inn' in 2:7.

QUESTION—What is the significance of meeting a man carrying a jar of water?

It was the work of women to carry water in a jar for a household and so if a man carried the water home in a jar he would be easy to identify [AB, Arn, BNTC, Lns, MGC, NAC, NIBC, NIC, NIGTC, NIVS, NTC, Su, TG, TNTC]. Normally, if a man carried water, it would be in a skin [NIGTC, NTC, TNTC]. The man was someone different from the owner of the house [AB]. Probably the man was a servant or slave [Alf, Arn, BECNT, ICC, NTC], or a relative or a friend [NTC]. Or, the man was the owner of the house himself [NIC]. This meeting may have been due to Jesus' divine knowledge [AB, Alf, Gdt], or it may have been part of a prearranged plan [NIC, NIGTC, Su, TG, TNTC]. Probably the man would be carrying the jar on his head [Lns, TG] or on his shoulder [TG].

QUESTION—What is implied in beginning the message with, 'The teacher says to you'?

The title 'teacher' was how Jesus was known to his disciples [NIGTC], so this probably indicates that the householder was a disciple [Arn, BECNT, ICC, MGC, NIGTC, NIVS, NTC]. Some suggest that this question was a prearranged formula for identifying the disciples as having been sent by Jesus [AB, NIGTC, TNTC].

QUESTION—What is implied by asking *where* the guest room was and what kind of a room was it?

This is a polite way to ask to see the room in order to prepare it for the Passover supper [NIGTC]. Probably this room was a nice room furnished with reclining couches for a meal [NET]. Probably the use of the room had been prearranged [NAC, NIC, Su, TNTC]. The arrangement with the householder had been kept secret from the disciples to prevent a premature betrayal by Judas [Lns, NIVS, Su, TNTC].

22:12 And-that (one) will-show you a-large upstairs-room[a] having-been-furnished/tiled.[b] Prepare (it) there. **22:13** And having-departed they-found (things) just-as he-had-told them and they-prepared the Passover.

LEXICON—a. ἀνάγαιον (LN 7.27) (BAGD p. 51): 'upstairs room' [LN, WBC], 'a room upstairs' [AB, BAGD; HCSB, NCV, NET, NRSV, REB, TEV], 'upper room' [Arn, BECNT, Lns, NTC; KJV, NASB, NIV]. The clause 'that one will show you a large upstairs room' is translated 'the owner will take you upstairs and show you a large room' [CEV, GW], 'he will take you upstairs to a large room' [NLT]. This was an extra room built onto the flat roof of a typical house [NIGTC, Su], and was reached by an outside staircase [Su]. It would be the best room in the house [Arn].

b. perf. pass. participle of στρώννυμι, στρώννυω (LN 46.9, 16.22) (BAGD p. 771): 'to be furnished, to be arranged' [LN (46.9)], 'to be paved' [BAGD], 'to be spread out' [LN (16.22)]. The phrase 'having been furnished/tiled' is translated 'furnished' [Arn, BECNT, NTC; GW, HCSB, KJV, NASB, NCV, NET, TEV], 'all furnished' [NIV], 'already furnished' [AB; NRSV], 'already setout' [WBC], 'all set out' [REB], 'ready for you to use' [CEV], 'that is already set up' [NLT], 'that has been tiled' [Lns].

QUESTION—Does στρώννυμι mean that the room was furnished or tiled?

1. The room was a furnished room [AB, Arn, BECNT, Gdt, ICC, NIGTC, NTC, TG, TH, TNTC, WBC; all versions]. It was furnished with couches [Arn, BECNT, NTC, Su; NET], table [NTC, Su, TG], cushions [MGC, NAC, NIGTC, TG], and rugs [Arn, NTC, Su, TG]. The verb means 'spread out' [ICC], and here it refers to couches or cushions in the room [ICC]. Probably it means that there were couches with coverings spread over them [TNTC].
2. The room had a tiled floor [Lns]. The verb means 'spread out' and refers to a beautiful tile floor, an unusual feature of houses [Lns].

DISCOURSE UNIT: 22:14–23 [CEV, HCSB, NASB, NRSV, TEV]. The topic is the Lord's supper [CEV, NASB, TEV], the institution of the Lord's Supper [NRSV], the first Lord's supper [HCSB].

DISCOURSE UNIT: 22:14–20 [BECNT, TNTC, WBC; NCV, NET]. The topic is the last supper [BECNT, TNTC, WBC], the Lord's supper [NCV, NET].

DISCOURSE UNIT: 22:14–18 [Su]. The topic the observance of the Passover supper.

22:14 And when the hour came, he-reclined[a] and the apostles with him.

TEXT—Instead of οἱ ἀπόστολοι 'the apostles', some manuscripts read οἱ δώδεκα ἀπόστολοι 'the twelve apostles' and some manuscripts read οἱ δώδεκα 'the twelve'. GNT does not mention the variants. Οἱ δώδεκα ἀπόστολοι 'the twelve apostles' is read by KJV.

LEXICON—a. aorist act. indic. of ἀναπίπτω (LN 17.23) (BAGD 1. p. 59): 'to recline' [BAGD, LN], 'to be at table, to sit down to eat' [LN]. The phrase 'he reclined' [BECNT] is also translated 'he reclined at the table' [HCSB, NASB, NIV], 'Jesus reclined at table' [AB, Lns, NTC, WBC], 'he/Jesus took his place at the table' [NET, NRSV, REB, TEV], 'were at table' [GW], 'he sat down' [KJV], 'sat down at the table' [NLT], 'he sat down to eat' [Arn], 'were sitting at the table' [NCV]. The whole verse is translated 'When the time came for Jesus and the apostles to eat' [CEV].

QUESTION—What hour came?

It was time to eat the Passover meal [BECNT, NIGTC, TG, TH, TNTC; GW]. This was after sundown [TG], after sunset on Thursday [Su] and with the appearance of the first star the Jewish Friday began [Lns]. The hour means not only evening time, but it also has a salvation-history connotation [AB, MGC]. In this setting, the hour refers to the time for celebrating the Passover, but to Luke's readers this could mean the hour that Jesus would complete his mission [NAC].

QUESTION—Why did Jesus and the apostles recline?

This was a formal meal, and they followed the Roman custom of reclining on couches stretching out from a low table [Su]. The verb probably was used more broadly than focusing on a particular posture and means to be at table [WBC].

DISCOURSE UNIT: 22:15–20 [AB]. The topic is the last supper.

22:15 **And he-said to them, With-desire^a I-desired to-eat this Passover with you before I suffer.^b**

LEXICON—a. ἐπιθυμία (LN **25.12**) (BAGD 2. p. 293): 'desire' [BAGD, LN]. This dative noun intensifies the verb [AB, TH]. The phrase ἐπιθυμίᾳ ἐπεθύμησα 'with desire I desired' is a Hebraism [Arn, BECNT, BNTC, ICC, Lns, TH] and it is translated 'with desire I have desired' [Lns; KJV], 'I have greatly desired' [**LN**], 'I have earnestly desired' [NASB, NET], 'I have eagerly desired' [NTC; NIV, NRSV], 'I wanted very much' [NCV], 'I have very much wanted' [CEV], 'I've had a deep desire' [GW], 'I have fervently desired' [Arn; HCSB], 'I have wanted so much' [TEV], 'how intensely have I desired' [AB], 'how I have longed' [WBC; REB], 'I have long desired' [BECNT], 'I have looked forward to this hour with deep longing, anxious (to eat)' [NLT]. Jesus had long desired to eat this Passover with his disciples and now it has happened [MGC].

b. aorist act. infin. of πάσχω (LN **24.78**) (BAGD 3.a.α. p. 634): 'to suffer' [BAGD, LN]. The phrase πρὸ με παθεῖν 'before I suffer' [AB, Arn, BECNT, Lns, NTC, WBC; all versions except NLT, REB] is also translated 'before my suffering' [**LN**], 'before my suffering begins' [NLT], 'before my death' [REB]. See this word at 24:46.

QUESTION—What is meant by τοῦτο τὸ πάσχα 'this Passover' and what was important about this particular Passover?

It refers to the Passover meal or supper [AB, Arn, BECNT, NAC, TG, TH; CEV, NCV, NLT, TEV]. Or, 'Passover' could refer to either the Passover meal or the Passover lamb and here the following verses make it probable that it refers to the Passover lamb [BECNT, NIGTC, WBC]. It was at this Passover meal that he had important things to tell his disciples [Arn] and would institute the Lord's Supper [Arn, NAC, NIBC]. Now he was bringing his work to a conclusion [NAC]. This was to be a farewell speech at the ending of Jesus' earthly ministry and the start of his saving work [BECNT].

QUESTION—What did Jesus mean by his suffering?

The suffering is unspecified, but it is implied that it will end with his death [TH]. The suffering includes his arrest, mistreatment, and crucifixion [TG]. It is the suffering of death [AB, MGC, NICNT; REB].

22:16 Because I-say to-you that by-no-means will-I-eat it until it-is-fulfilled[a] in the kingdom of-God.

TEXT—Instead of ὅτι οὐ μὴ φάγω 'that not not/by no means will I eat', some manuscripts read ὅτι οὐκέτι οὐ μὴ φάγω 'that again not not/by no means will I eat' and one important manuscript reads οὐκέτι μὴ φάγομαι 'no longer not I will eat'. GNT reads ὅτι οὐ μὴ φάγω 'that not not/by no means will I eat' with a B decision, indicating that the text is almost certain. Ὅτι οὐκέτι οὐ μὴ φάγω 'that again not not/by no means will I eat' is read by KJV.

LEXICON—a. aorist pass. subj. of πληρόω (LN 13.106) (BAGD 4.a. p. 671): 'to be fulfilled' [BAGD, LN]. The phrase 'by no means shall I eat it until it is fulfilled in (the kingdom of God)' is translated 'I will not eat it until it is fulfilled in' [BECNT; NRSV], 'I will in no wise eat it till it shall be fulfilled in' [Lns], 'I will never eat it until it is given its full meaning in' [TEV]. Many add an equivalent of 'again': 'I will not eat it again until it is fulfilled in' [NTC, WBC; HCSB, NET], 'I shall never again eat it until it is fulfilled in' [NASB], 'I will not any more eat thereof, until it be fulfilled in' [KJV], 'I won't eat it again until it comes to fulfillment in' [NLT], 'I won't eat it again until it finds its fulfillment in' [GW, NIV], 'never again shall I eat it until the time when it finds its fulfillment in' [REB], 'never again shall I eat it until it has found its fulfillment in' [AB], 'I shall certainly no longer do it until it has been fulfilled in' [Arn], 'I will not eat another Passover meal until it is given its true meaning in' [NCV], 'I will not eat another Passover meal until it is finally eaten' [CEV].

QUESTION—What relationship is indicated by γάρ 'because'?

It indicates the reason Jesus desired to eat this Passover with them [MGC, NIGTC, Su]. The reason is that he will not be able to do so again [NIGTC]. It explains that the next Passover that Jesus will eat with them will be the heavenly one [Lns].

QUESTION—Does the statement οὐ μὴ φάγω αὐτὸ ἕως ὅτου πληρωθῇ 'by no means shall I eat it until it is fulfilled' mean that he would not at the present time eat it with the disciples?

A literal translation of the Greek text seems to imply that Jesus would not even eat the present Passover meal, but what he is saying is that this was his last Passover with them and he would not eat another one until it is fulfilled in the kingdom of God [TG]. This strong negative statement does not refer to the present Passover that he is eating with them, but to future Passovers [AB, Alf, Crd, EGT, ICC, Lns, MGC, NAC, NICNT, NIGTC, NTC, Su, TG, TH, TNTC, WBC]. Jesus has just said that he desired to share this meal with them, so it means that he will not again sit at the Passover table until his return [BECNT]. Because of his forthcoming death, Jesus will not be able to share future Passovers with his disciples [NAC]. Many translate in agreement with the alternative reading having 'again', so that it means 'by no means shall I eat it *again* until it is fulfilled in the kingdom of God' [all versions except NRSV, TEV]. Although the text does not have οὐκέτι 'again', the addition of that word expresses the correct meaning: Jesus will eat this Passover, but he will eat no other Passover meal until he eats the one in heaven [AB, Lns]. Or, the meaning of the reading 'I shall not eat it' is uncertain. Perhaps 'it' refers to observing the entire Passover week and Jesus meant that before that week would be over, he would die as a Passover sacrifice. Or, it might mean that in spite of his desire to share this meal with them, his heaviness of heart would not allow him to eat at this time [Su]. The new age will begin with Jesus leading his people to the heritage of complete redemption and blessedness and this event was often represented by the symbol of the celebration of a Messianic banquet that was symbolized in the Passover celebrations [NIC]. The future Passover meal is picture language and we do not need to conclude that actual drinking and eating will occur in heaven [Arn]. Or, after Jesus' return, some sacrifices will be continued as a celebration or memorial, not as actual sacrifices [BECNT].

QUESTION—What is meant by 'until it is fulfilled in the kingdom of God'?

The Passover Festival refers to redemption and this will not become perfect until the kingdom of God has come [TH]. This refers to the final consummation and the messianic banquet [AB, Alf, Arn, BECNT, BNTC, Gdt, Lns, MGC, NAC, NIC, NIVS, NTC, Rb, Su, TG, TH, WBC]. The final results of Jesus' sacrifice will be realized at the time of consummation [BECNT]. It will be fulfilled when its typical and symbolical meaning has become fully realized in the new heaven and earth at the time when deliverance from all sin and evil has been accomplished [NTC]. In addition to being a memorial meal, the Passover was a prophecy pointing to the final deliverance of God's people at Jesus' second coming [AB, Arn]. The purpose of the Passover meal will be fully realized with the complete freedom of God's people [TG]. All that is prefigured about the Lamb of God being slain for our sins will reach its ultimate fulfillment then [Lns]. Or, Jesus will fulfill the typology of the Passover and the future Passover refers to the Lord's Supper [ICC]. This concerns the fulfillment of the Passover in heaven or in the new age brought about by Jesus' death, and here there is a hint of the Lord's Supper being a new Passover concerning fellowship between Jesus and his disciples [NIGTC].

22:17 And having-taken/received[a] a-cup, having-given-thanks[b] he-said, Take this and share[c] among yourselves.

TEXT—Instead of vv. 17, 18, 19, 20 some manuscripts read only vv. 17, 18, 19a through τὸ σῶμά μου 'my body'; some non-Greek manuscripts read vv. 19, 17, 18 only and in this order; two non-Greek manuscripts read v. 19a through τὸ σῶμά μου 'my body' plus vv. 17, 18; one non-Greek manuscript reads v. 19 plus μετὰ τὸ δειπνῆσαι 'after dining' from v. 20a, plus v. 17, plus τοῦτό μου τὸ αἷμα ἡ καινὴ διαθήκη 'this (is) my blood, the new covenant' from v. 20b, plus v. 18; and non-Greek manuscripts read vv. 19, 20 only. GNT reads vv. 17, 18, 19, 20 with a B decision, indicating that the text is almost certain.

LEXICON—a. aorist mid. (deponent = act.) participle of δέχομαι (LN **18.1**) (BAGD 2. p. 177): 'to take' [AB, Arn, BECNT, **LN**; all versions except CEV], 'to take hold of' [LN], 'to take in one's hand' [BAGD; CEV], 'to grasp' [BAGD], 'to receive' [Lns, NTC, WBC].

b. aorist act. participle of εὐχαριστέω (LN 33.349) (BAGD 2. p. 328): 'to give thanks' [AB, Arn, BAGD, BECNT, Lns, NTC, WBC; HCSB, KJV, NASB, NCV, NET, NIV, NRSV, REB], 'to give thanks to God' [CEV, TEV], 'to give thanks for it' [NLT], 'to thank' [LN], 'to speak a prayer of thanksgiving' [GW]. It is implied that Jesus thanked God [AB, TH]. The prayer would express gratitude for God's act of provision and salvation [BECNT].

c. aorist act. impera. of διαμερίζω (LN 57.89) (BAGD 1.b. p. 186): 'to share' [BAGD, WBC; CEV, GW, HCSB, NASB, NCV, NLT, REB, TEV], 'to distribute' [BAGD, LN], 'to divide' [AB, Arn, BAGD, BECNT, Lns, NTC; KJV, NET, NIV, NRSV], 'to give each in turn' [LN].

QUESTION—Is it implied that someone handed the cup to Jesus?
1. Jesus took hold of the cup [NIGTC, WBC]. The usual meaning is 'to receive from someone', but here it means 'to take hold of' [NIGTC], 'receiving' being a synonym for λαβών 'taking' [WBC].
2. Jesus received the cup from one of the disciples [AB, EGT, Gdt, NIC, Su, TG, TH]. This may mean that someone handed the cup to him [TG].

QUESTION—What was the cup that Jesus took hold of?
It was a cup full of wine [EGT, Gdt, ICC, Lns, My, NIC, NTC, Su, TG, TH; CEV, NLT]. As usual in a Passover feast, it was a fermented drink, a cup of real wine [Arn, Lns]. At Passover meals, four cups of wine were drunk [Arn, BECNT, NIBC, NICNT, TNTC; NET]. The cup was the first one since it followed the prayer of thanksgiving [BECNT, Gdt, MGC, NTC; NET]. It was either the first or second cup [AB, ICC, TNTC]. It was the second [NICNT]. It was either the first or third cup [NIVS]. It was the fourth or fifth cup [Lns].

QUESTION—How were the disciples to share the cup of wine?
The disciples would pass the cup from one man to the next and each one would drink a bit of the wine at his turn [ICC, TG, TH]. Or, instead of

drinking from a common cup, each would pour a bit of the wine from the cup of wine into his own cup [Gdt].

22:18 Because[a] I-say to-you that by-no-means will-I-drink from the now[b] from the fruit of-the vine[c] until the kingdom of-God comes.

TEXT—Some manuscripts omit ὅτι 'that'. GNT does not mention this variant in the apparatus but brackets it in the text, indicating difficulty in making the decision. Ὅτι 'that' is omitted by KJV.

TEXT—Some manuscripts omit ἀπὸ τοῦ νῦν 'from the now'. GNT does not mention this variant. Ἀπὸ τοῦ νῦν 'from the now' is omitted by KJV.

LEXICON—a. γάρ (LN 89.23): 'because' [LN], 'for' [AB, Arn, BECNT, LN, Lns, NTC, WBC; HCSB, KJV, NASB, NET, NIV, NLT, NRSV, REB], not explicit [CEV, GW, NCV, TEV].
   b. ἀπὸ τοῦ νῦν 'from the now'. This phrase is translated 'from now on' [AB, Arn, BECNT, Lns, NTC, WBC; GW, HCSB, NASB, NET, NRSV, TEV], 'from this moment' [REB], 'any more' [CEV], 'again' [NCV, NIV, NLT].
   c. ἄμπελος (LN 3.27) (BAGD 1.b. p. 46): 'vine' [BAGD], 'grapevine' [BAGD, LN]. The phrase τοῦ γενήματος τῆς ἀμπέλου 'the fruit of the vine' [AB, BECNT, Lns, NTC, WBC; HCSB, KJV, NASB, NCV, NET, NIV, NRSV, REB] is also translated 'the product of the vine' [Arn], 'wine' [CEV, GW, NLT, TEV].

QUESTION—What relationship is indicated by γάρ 'because'?
   1. This indicates the reason why the disciples were to share the contents of the cup among themselves and why they should not expect Jesus to join them in drinking the wine any more than he just had [ICC]. It explains why this meal, including the cup, was so important to Jesus [BECNT]. It is possible that this implies that Jesus had not drunk from the cup before handing it to the others and he was explaining why he himself would not drink from it until the coming of the kingdom, of God. Some think it is unclear whether Jesus drank some of the wine or not [AB, Arn, NAC]. Others think that Jesus did not taste the wine [BNTC, Su], since he was consecrating himself to the impending suffering [BNTC]. Most think that he did [BECNT, Gdt, ICC, Lns, MGC, NIBC, NIGTC, TG, TH, WBC]. The host always drank first [Lns]. 'From now on' implies that Jesus took the cups at this meal, but he will not take a cup after this meal until the kingdom comes [BECNT]. Jesus would die that very day [Lns].
   2. The conjunction γάρ 'because' appears only for the sake of parallelism with 22:16 which says '*Because* I say to you that by-no-means will I eat it until it is fulfilled in the kingdom of God' and it does not indicate a relationship with the previous verse [WBC]. This conjunction could be dropped in translation [WBC; CEV, GW, NCV, TEV].

DISCOURSE UNIT: 22:19–23 [Su]. The topic is the institution of the Memorial supper.

LUKE 22:19

DISCOURSE UNIT: 22:19–20 [GW]. The topic is the Lord's Supper.

22:19 And taking bread having-given-thanks he-broke[a] (it) and gave (it) to-them saying, This is my body being-given[b] for you. This do in my remembrance.[c]

TEXT—Some manuscripts end the verse after 'This is my body' and also omit 22:20. This is done by REB.

LEXICON—a. aorist act. indic. of κλάω (LN 19.34) (BAGD p. 433): 'to break' [AB, Arn, BAGD, BECNT, LN, Lns, NTC, WBC; all versions except NLT], 'to break in pieces' [NLT]. It means to break an object into two or more parts [LN].

   b pres. pass. participle of δίδωμι (LN 57.71) (BAGD 6. p. 193): 'to be given' [LN], 'to be given up, to be sacrificed' [BAGD]. The phrase τὸ ὑπὲρ ὑμῶν διδόμενον 'being given for you' is translated 'which is given for you' [AB, Arn, WBC; CEV, HCSB, KJV, NASB, NET, NRSV, REB, TEV], 'which is given up for you' [GW], 'given for you' [BECNT, NTC; NIV, NLT], 'which I am giving for you' [NCV], 'in the act of being given for you' [Lns]. The present participle denotes a relatively future action so that it means 'which is to be given' [AB, NAC, NIGTC] and his body is to be given as an offering in death as a sacrifice [AB, NIGTC].

   c. ἀνάμνησις (LN 29.11) (BAGD p. 58): 'remembrance' [BAGD], 'reminder' [BAGD, LN], 'means of remembering' [LN]. The phrase εἰς τὴν ἐμὴν ἀνάμνησιν 'in my remembrance' is translated 'in remembrance of me' [AB, BECNT, NTC, WBC; HCSB, KJV, NASB, NET, NIV, NLT, NRSV], 'for my remembrance' [Arn], 'for my own remembrance' [Lns], 'in memory of me' [TEV], 'to remember me' [GW, NCV], 'as a way of remembering me' [CEV].

QUESTION—What was the ἄρτος 'bread' that Jesus took?

It was the bread eaten at the beginning of the main meal [AB, NIGTC]. Here, this was unleavened Passover bread [MGC, WBC]. Jesus took the bread in his hands [CEV]. Being unleavened, it was not a plump 'loaf' of bread [Lns]. It was a large thin slice or sheet of unleavened bread which was designed to have pieces broken off so that it could be eaten [Arn, Lns, NTC]. It was unleavened bread cut in small thin wafers [BECNT]. It was round [TG].

QUESTION—What was the significance of the bread being broken by Jesus?

The verb κλάω 'to break' is used in the NT only of breaking bread at meals by tearing it apart [AB, BECNT, NIGTC, TNTC, WBC]. Jesus held the bread in his hand and gave pieces of it to his disciples as he broke them off [NTC]. Perhaps Jesus broke off a part of the loaf for each disciple or perhaps he broke the loaf in half and passed the halves in both directions for each disciple to break off an individual piece [Su]. The Textus Receptus for the parallel passage in 1 Cor. 11:24 has 'This is my body which is broken for you' [KJV], but GNT omits the verb 'broken' with an A rating so that it reads 'This is my body which is for you' [HCSB, NASB, NET, NIV, NRSV,

REB, TEV], '...it is for you' [NCV]. Some supply the verb 'given' in the Corinthian passage, probably taking the verb from this passage in Luke: '...which is *given* for you' [CEV, GW, NLT]. Some commentaries agree with the Textus Receptus text or at least with supplying the verb 'broken' and say that the broken bread is the symbol of Jesus' body being broken in his sacrificial death [EGT, NIC]. His body was broken in the sense of blood shedding [EGT]. However, most commentaries say that the bread was broken in order to distribute the bread and there is no symbolic significance in the act of breaking the bread [Arn, Lns, NICNT, Su, WBC]. The bones of the Passover sacrifice were never broken [Su] and in John 19:36 it is especially noted that the soldiers did not break Jesus' legs in fulfillment of the prophecy in Psalm 34:20 'not one of his bones will be broken' [Lns, Su]. Breaking the bread was a customary part of eating, but since the breaking is explicitly mentioned, it became a technical terms for the Lord's Supper [NIGTC]. Breaking of bread symbolized an experience of sharing and here breaking the one loaf indicated sharing with Jesus in God's redemption [Su].

QUESTION—What is meant by the statement τοῦτό ἐστιν τὸ σῶμά μου 'this is my body'?

As Jesus stood there with the bread in his heads, it was clear that his physical body and the bread were distinct [NTC, Su]. The bread represented Jesus [BECNT, MGC, NAC, NIVS, TNTC]. By 'body' he meant himself [AB]. Whether 'body' means the person as a whole or his flesh, Jesus is the sacrifice and it is he who is given for them [BECNT]. Some posit a miraculous transformation of the bread into the actual body of Jesus, others say that the bread remained bread but in some way Jesus' body was really present in it [Su]. The bread, now consecrated and blessed, was now bread of flesh and body, sacramentally one with Christ's body [Lns]. In view of the differences of understanding in the Christian community, it is advisable to translate 'This is my body' literally [TG].

QUESTION—In what sense was his body being given for the disciples?

The phrase ὑπὲρ ὑμῶν 'for you' may be taken merely as an unspecified 'on your behalf' [Su, TG, TH], or it may include a sacrificial and substitutionary force [BECNT]. It means for their advantage [ICC], for their sake [NICNT]. Jesus' body was given for them in the sense that it was sacrificed for them [AB, Arn, BNTC, MGC, TG, TH]. This looks forward to Jesus' vicarious gift of himself for their salvation [NAC, TNTC; NET]. The entire incarnation was redemptive and it was coming to the point where Jesus would say 'It is finished' [Su]. The fact that his body was being given for them means that he was to die for them [BECNT, NICNT, WBC]. It refers to the offering up of Jesus' body as a sacrifice on the cross [MGC, TG, TH].

QUESTION—What were they to do in his remembrance?

They were to perform this ceremony in remembrance of him [AB, Arn]. The word ποιέω 'to do' is used of repeating rites [NAC, NIGTC]. The word 'this' refers to the action of sharing the bread and perhaps includes using the words associated with this action [NIGTC]. It refers to breaking and eating the bread [TH]. They are to do this so that they will remember Jesus and the significance of his death [NIGTC]. They were to eat the bread as a way of remembering Jesus [CEV]. As they break the bread, the disciples are to remember what Jesus was about to do for them [BECNT]. Or, the act of breaking was part of this sacrament and symbolized that he gave his body in death on the cross [NTC]. This is to continually remind them of the redemption accomplished by Jesus' death [ICC, MGC]. They are to remember Jesus, along with his work and his presence among them [NAC].

22:20 And the cup likewise[a] after (they)-ate, saying, This cup (is) the new covenant[b] in my blood being-poured-out[c] for you.

TEXT—Instead of καὶ τὸ ποτήριον ὡσαύτως 'and the cup likewise', some manuscripts read ὡσαύτως καὶ τὸ ποτήριον 'likewise the cup also'. GNT does not mention this variant. Ὡσαύτως καὶ τὸ ποτήριον 'likewise the cup also' is read by HCSB and KJV.

LEXICON—a. ὡσαύτως (LN 64.16) (BAGD p. 899): 'likewise' [BAGD], 'similarly, in the same way' [BAGD, LN], 'in like manner' [LN]. The phrase 'the cup likewise' [Arn, BECNT, Lns; KJV], is also translated 'in the same way with the cup' [NRSV], 'in the same way he took the cup' [NTC; HCSB, NASB, NCV, NET, NIV], 'he did the same with the cup' [AB, WBC; GW], 'in the same way he gave them the cup' [TEV], 'he took another cup of wine' [NLT], 'he took another cup of wine in his hands' [CEV].

b. διαθήκη (LN 34.44) (BAGD 2. p. 183): 'covenant' [BAGD, LN], 'pact' [LN], 'decree' [BAGD]. The phrase ἡ καινὴ διαθήκη ἐν τῷ αἵματί μου 'the new covenant in my blood' [BECNT, Lns, NTC; NIV, NRSV] is also translated 'the new testament in my blood' [KJV], 'the new testament through my blood' [Arn], 'the new covenant with my blood' [AB], 'the new covenant established by my blood' [HCSB], 'the new covenant sealed with my blood' [WBC], 'God's new covenant sealed with my blood' [TEV], 'the new agreement that God makes with his people. This new agreement begins with my blood' [NCV]. The phrase 'this cup is the new covenant in my blood' is translated 'this is my blood...and with it God makes his new agreement' [CEV], 'this wine is the token of God's new covenant to save you—an agreement sealed with the blood (I will pour out for you)' [NLT], 'this cup (which is poured out for you) is the new covenant in my blood' [NASB, NET], 'this cup (that is poured out for you) is the new promise made with my blood' [GW]. This covenant is the verbal content of an agreement between two persons specifying reciprocal benefits and responsibilities [LN]. Or, it is a declaration of a person's will, not the result of an agreement between two parties [BAGD].

c. pres. pass. participle of ἐκχύννομαι, ἐκχέω (LN 23.112) (BAGD 1. p. 247): 'to be poured out' [BAGD, LN]. The phrase 'being poured out for you' is translated 'which is poured out for you' [AB, NTC, WBC; NCV, NIV, TEV], 'it is poured out for you' [CEV], 'I will pour out for you'

[NLT], 'that is in the act of being poured out for you' [Lns], 'which is shed for you' [Arn; KJV; similarly BECNT; HCSB], '(this cup) that is poured out for you' [GW, NRSV], '(this cup) which is poured out for you' [NASB, NET]. The phrase ἐκχύννεται τὸ αἷμα 'the blood pours out' is an idiom meaning 'to die', with the implication of having a sacrificial purpose, 'to die as a sacrifice, sacrificial death' [LN].

QUESTION—What cup is τὸ ποτήριον 'the cup'?

Four or five times during a Passover supper cups of wine were passed around [Lns]. It is the same cup as mentioned in 22:17 [TG, TH]. Or, the cup is here distinguished from the cup mentioned in 22:17 and from all of the cups used in the Passover meal [Su]. The addition 'after they ate' distinguished this cup from all the other cups that had been passed during the course of the Passover supper [Su]. The Passover meal began with the sharing of the bread, then came the eating and drinking of the Passover meal and after its conclusion, came this sacramental cup [Lns, NIGTC]. This was the third cup of the Passover and this was after the main course [BECNT, Gdt, MGC, NIGTC]. It was called the cup of blessing [Gdt, NIGTC]. During the meal the disciples drank out of their individual cups, but at this point Jesus shared his own cup with them [WBC]. The cup had already been passed around among the disciples during the meal, and now it had been refilled [Arn]. It is not important if a different cup was used each time or if one cup was refilled as needed [Lns].

QUESTION—What is meant by ὡσαύτως 'likewise'?

Jesus instituted the sacrament with a common cup that was used for all of the disciples [Lns]. What was done for the cup was similar as what was done for the bread in the preceding verse: Jesus took the cup, gave thanks for it, and gave it to his disciples [ICC, Su, TH]. 'Likewise' means that Jesus gave thanks for the cup and then spoke to the disciples [BECNT]. An interval separated this act from that in the preceding verse, so after conversation during the meal had taken free course, Jesus resumed the solemn attitude he had taken in breaking the bread [Gdt].

QUESTION—Was the physical cup a symbol of the new covenant?

'Cup' refers to its contents, that is, the wine contained in the cup [Lns, NIGTC, Su, TH, WBC]. 'This' cup refers to the contents alone [Lns]. 'This' refers to the cup, and the cup with its contents is the symbol of the new covenant brought about by Jesus' blood shed for the disciples [NIGTC]. The wine is symbolic of Jesus' blood [MGC].

QUESTION—What is meant by the new covenant?

In contrast with the old covenant made at Mount Sinai, this is the new covenant God now makes with his people [TG]. Jesus' death would establish a new way to approach God [TNTC]. The Old Covenant required fulfilling the Law, while the New Covenant required faith [My]. The Old covenant was written on tablets of stone and made almost exclusively between God and Israel, but the New Covenant was made in their hearts and was between God and all believers regardless of race [NTC]. The Old Covenant with

Israel was ratified and sealed by sprinkling the people with the blood of sacrificed animals (Exod. 24:7–8), but the New Covenant is ratified by the blood Jesus will shed at his death [AB, Su, TG]. This was the inauguration of a new era of salvation [BECNT].

QUESTION—What is poured out for them?
1. The cup is poured out for them [GW, NASB, NET, NRSV].
2. Jesus' blood is poured out for them [Arn, BECNT, ICC, Lns, MGC, NIGTC, NTC, Su, TG, TH, WBC; CEV, HCSB, KJV, NCV, NLT]. Grammatically the phrase goes with the cup, but semantically it refers to the blood [TH, WBC]. The words reflect the Jewish sacrificial system in which the blood of an animal sacrifice was offered for sins [TG]. The blood of sacrificial animals was poured out, but since Jesus' blood was not literally poured out, the imagery must be that of his impending violent death [WBC]. Jesus' blood literally poured out of his body from the wounds of thorns, nails, and sword [Su]. The death is a specific kind of death, a sacrificial death [Lns, MGC], and no other kind of death could establish the covenant [Lns]. The New Covenant is inaugurated by the sprinkling of blood and 'in' means through or by means of Jesus' blood [TH].

DISCOURSE UNIT: 22:21–38 [NET]. The topic is the final discourse.

DISCOURSE UNIT: 22:21–23 [AB, TNTC, WBC; GW, NCV]. The topic is Jesus' awareness of his betrayal [WBC], Jesus knows who will betray him [GW], Jesus foretells his betrayal [AB, TNTC], who will turn against Jesus? [NCV].

22:21 But behold[a] the hand[b] of-the (one) betraying me (is) with me on the table.

LEXICON—a. ἰδού (LN 91.13) (BAGD p. 371): 'behold' [Arn, BAGD, BECNT; KJV, NASB], 'lo' [Lns], 'look' [AB, BAGD, LN, NTC; HCSB, NET, TEV], 'see' [WBC; NRSV], 'listen, pay attention' [LN], not explicit [CEV, GW, NCV, NIV, NLT, REB]. This arouses the attention of the listeners [BAGD, LN] and also emphasizes the following statement [LN].

b. χείρ (LN 8.30): 'hand' [LN]. The phrase 'the hand...is with me on the table' [Arn, Lns, NTC; GW, KJV, NET] is also translated 'the hand is at the table with me' [HCSB], 'the hand is on the table with me' [WBC], 'the hand is with mine on the table' [NASB, NCV, NIV], 'the hand is with me at the table' [AB, BECNT], 'here at this table, sitting among us as a friend, is the man' [NLT], '(my betrayer) is here, his hand with mine on the table' [REB], '(the one who betrays me) is with me, and his hand is on the table' [NRSV], '(the one who betrays me) is here at the table with me' [CEV, TEV]. This is a synecdoche and 'hand' is used to represent the person of Judas [NAC, NIGTC].

QUESTION—What is the chronology of the institution of the Lord's Supper and Jesus' words in 22:21–23?

Luke spoke briefly of the traitor after the Supper and used statements taken from the accounts of his exposure found in the other Gospels. In the parallel passages this conversation appears to have occurred during the meal before the institution of the Lord's Supper. Matthew 26:20–29 and Mark 14:17–25 say that the Lord's Supper followed the announcement about the betrayer and John 13:21–30 reports that Judas left immediately after Jesus told him 'That which you do, do quickly' (John 13:27). Mark 14:26 tells about their departure to the Mount of Olives immediately after the Lord's Supper.

1. If Luke wrote in chronological order, Judas shared in the institution of the Lord's Supper, but doubt is raised because Matthew and Mark have the prophecy of the betrayal before the communion. However none of the Gospel writers specifically state that the events are in chronological sequence, so the actual sequence is uncertain [TNTC]. None of the Gospels exactly say if this happened before or after the Passover meal [NIC]. We cannot decide [Arn].
2. In Luke's account, 22:21–23 occurs in chronological order after 22:20 and indicates that Judas had participated in the Lord's Supper [Gdt, Su]. Luke signals no break in the sequence [NICNT, NIGTC]. In Luke, unlike Mark and Matthew, Jesus gives a farewell discourse to his disciples [AB, NAC].
3. It is not likely that Jesus spoke of his betrayal and of the Son of Man twice during the meal [BECNT]. There are various explanations. At this point Luke now returns to what took place while the Passover meal was still in progress so that what is said here actually took place before the institution of the Lord's Supper [NTC]. Probably Luke rearranged the sources so that he could make the meal prominent by treating it first and then reduced the betrayal account to a bare minimum and let it lead to a dramatic contrast with the following dispute about greatness [BECNT]. Luke cannot mean that 22:21 was spoken immediately after the institution of the Supper nor that Judas also received the Supper. Luke added the words about the traitor to the account of the Supper to show how Jesus would be brought to his sacrificial death [Lns].

QUESTION—What relationship is indicated by the beginning conjunction πλήν 'but'?

Many of the explanations appear to assume that the account in this verse follows that of the preceding verse. The conjunction indicates a restriction of 'for you' so as to exclude Judas [Gdt, ICC], or it indicates a transition from the meaning of his death to the manner of it, or it indicates a contrast between Christ's conduct and that of the traitor Judas [ICC]. It means 'notwithstanding': although my blood is shed for you, there is a traitor among you [My]. It indicates contrast [BECNT, Lns]. The conjunction separates the traitor from sharing in the association with Jesus that has just been described [BECNT, NIGTC].

QUESTION—What is meant by 'the hand of the one betraying me is with me on the table'?

It means that the traitor's hand is receiving bread and wine from Jesus' hand [TH]. His hand is now touching Jesus' hand on the table [EGT]. He had used his hand to dip into a dish with Jesus [Alf]. This describes close fellowship [TG, TH, TNTC]. It could be taken literally, but probably it merely means that the traitor was sharing the same meal with Jesus [ICC]. The traitor was near enough for Jesus to hand him a choice bit of food [Su].

22:22 Because indeed the Son of Man[a] goes/dies[b] according-to the (thing) having-been-determined,[c] but woe[d] to-that man by whom he-is-betrayed.

TEXT—Instead of ὅτι 'because', some manuscripts read καί 'and'. GNT does not mention this variant. Καί 'and' is read by KJV.

LEXICON—a. υἱὸς τοῦ ἀνθρώπου 'Son of Man'. This title for Christ occurs at 5:24; 6:5, 22; 7:34; 9:22, 26, 44; 11:30; 12:8, 40; 17:22, 24, 26; 18:8, 31; 19:10; 21:27, 36; 22: 48, 69; 24:7. See the discussions of this title at 5:24, 6:5, and 9:22.

  b. pres. mid./pass. (deponent = act.) indic. of πορεύομαι, πορεύω (LN 23.101) (BAGD 2.a. p. 692): 'to go' [BAGD, BECNT, Lns, NTC, WBC; KJV, NASB, NET, NIV, NRSV, REB] 'to go his way' [AB], 'to go on his way' [Arn], 'to go away' [LN; HCSB], '(what God has planned for the Son of Man) will happen' [NCV], 'to leave this life' [LN], 'to die' [BAGD, **LN**; CEV, TEV], 'to be going to die' [GW], 'must die' [NLT].

  c. perf. pass. participle of ὁρίζω (LN 37.96) (BAGD 1.a.α. p. 581): 'to be determined' [BAGD], 'to be appointed' [BAGD, LN], 'to be designated, to be assigned, to be given a task to' [LN]. The phrase κατὰ τὸ ὡρισμένον 'according to the thing having been determined' is translated 'according to what has been determined' [Lns], 'in accord with what has been determined' [WBC], 'as it has been determined' [AB, Arn, BECNT; HCSB, NASB, NET, NRSV], 'as it was determined' [KJV], 'as it has been decreed' [NTC; NIV], 'the way it has been planned for him' [GW], 'in the way that has been decided for him' [CEV], '(is going) his appointed way' [REB], 'in accordance with the divine decree' [BAGD], 'as God has decided' [TEV], 'since it is part of God's plan' [NLT], 'what God has planned (will happen)' [NCV].

  d. οὐαί (LN 22.9) (BAGD 1.a. p. 591): 'woe' [BAGD], 'disaster, horror' [LN]. The phrase 'woe to' [AB, Arn, BECNT, Lns, NTC, WBC; HCSB, KJV, NASB, NET, NIV, NRSV] is also translated 'alas for' [REB], 'it will be terrible for' [CEV], 'how terrible it will be for' [NCV, NLT], 'how terrible for' [TEV], 'how horrible it will be for' [GW]. This particle indicates a state of intense hardship or distress [LN]. See this word at 6:24; 10:13; 11:42; 17:1; 21:23.

QUESTION—What relationship is indicated by ὅτι 'because'?

This explains how the situation in 22:21 could have come to pass [ICC, NIC]. The presence of a betrayer is explained by the divine necessity for

Jesus' appointed destiny [Arn, NIGTC]. Or, instead of explaining 22:21, this reaffirms the truth of the divine necessity for Jesus' suffering [TH].

QUESTION—What is meant by the Son of Man πορεύεται 'going'?
1. It refers to Jesus' progress towards a goal [AB, Arn, BECNT, Lns, NTC, WBC; KJV, NASB, NCV, NET, NIV, NRSV, REB]. It refers to his progress through suffering to glory [Alf], to his progress to his destiny [AB]. What Jesus had begun in 9:51 was about to be accomplished [NAC]. The verb 'goes' includes living on earth, suffering, and dying [NTC].
2. It is a figurative extension of the meaning of πορεύομαι 'to go away', and means to depart from life and this serves as a euphemistic expression for dying [BAGD, EGT, ICC, **LN**, TG; CEV, GW, NLT, TEV]. Here the verb refers to his death [EGT, ICC, TG].

QUESTION—What is 'the thing' that had been determined?
This refers to the fact of Jesus' death rather than the manner of it [TH]. The passive tense indicates that God has determined this [AB, ICC, Lns, NAC, NIC, NIGTC, Su, TG, TH, TNTC, WBC; NCV, NLT, TEV]. This was established by God's eternal decree and was predicted by the prophets [NTC]. God did not determine the betrayal by Judas since that was Judas's own act, but God determined that his Son should not deliver himself from that betrayal [Lns].

QUESTION—What is meant by 'woe to that man'?
Although the Son of Man was destined to die, it does not relieve the instrument of his death of responsibility [BECNT, EGT, Lns, MGC, NIBC, NIC, NTC, TNTC, WBC]. It expresses Jesus' grief of the undefined, but unpleasant future that man has brought on himself [Su, TNTC]. It indicates sorrow and pity for the man who faces eternal damnation [NTC]. The betrayer will have to stand before God to answer for his act [BECNT].

22:23 And they began to-discuss[a] among themselves who then of them it-might-be who was-going-to-do this.

LEXICON—a. pres. act. infin. of συζητέω (LN 33.157, 33.440) (BAGD 2. p. 775): 'to discuss' [GW], 'to begin to discuss' [NTC; NASB], 'to speak with, to talk with, to converse' [LN (33.157)], 'to inquire' [Arn; KJV], 'to ask (each other)' [AB; NCV], 'to begin to ask (among themselves)' [REB, TEV], 'to begin to ask (each/one other)' [WBC; NLT], 'to begin to question (among themselves)' [NIV], 'to begin to question (one another)' [WBC; NET, NRSV], 'to begin to search (with themselves)' [Lns], 'to dispute' [BAGD, LN (33.440)], 'to debate' [BAGD], 'to argue' [BAGD; HCSB], 'to get into an argument' [CEV].

QUESTION—Why didn't the disciples know who the traitor was?
Judas had disguised his treachery so that no one suspected him [Gdt, ICC, TNTC]. They all had their hands on the table, so they were trying to discover whose hand it was [Rb]. They were appalled at such a dastardly deed and asked among themselves who would do such an act [NAC]. They discussed

the identity of the betrayer [BECNT]. Each one was afraid of the steadfastness of his own loyalty so they tried to determine which one of them was about to do this thing [Lns]. Each one had to face the possibility of being the one who betrays Jesus [WBC]. For all but Judas this indicates an attitude of wholesome self-distrust and for Judas it would be loathsome hypocrisy [NTC].

DISCOURSE UNIT: 22:24–38 [NASB]. The topic is the dialogue around the table [Su], who is the greatest?

DISCOURSE UNIT: 22:24–30 [AB, WBC; CEV, GW, HCSB, NCV, NRSV, TEV]. The topic is an argument about greatness [CEV, GW, HCSB, NRSV, TEV], be like a servant [NCV], Jesus' remarks on the disciples and their places in the kingdom [AB], Jesus' trials are to serve, while those who have shared Jesus' trials will gain royal stature [WBC].

DISCOURSE UNIT: 22:24–27 [TNTC]. The topic is a dispute as to the greatest.

22:24 And also there-arose a-dispute^a among them (as to) which of-them seems^b to-be greater.^c

LEXICON—a. φιλονεικία (LN 33.449) (BAGD 2. p. 860): 'dispute' [BAGD], 'heated quarrel' [LN]. The phrase 'there arose a dispute among them' [NTC; NASB; similarly HCSB; NIV, NRSV] is also translated 'there was a strife among them' [KJV] 'there arose strife among them' [Arn], 'there occurred a strife among them' [Lns], 'a dispute began' [REB], 'a dispute started among them' [NET], 'an invidious dispute developed among them' [AB], 'a quarrel broke out among the disciples. They argued about…' [GW], 'they began to argue among themselves' [NLT], 'the apostles began to argue about' [NCV], 'the apostles got into an argument' [CEV], 'an argument broke out among the disciples' [TEV], 'there came contention among them' [BECNT], 'a contention arose among them' [WBC].

b. pres. act. indic. of δοκεῖ (LN 31.30): 'to seem, to appear, to think' [LN]. The phrase 'which of them seems to be greater' is translated 'who of them seemed to be the greatest' [Arn; similarly AB, WBC], 'which of them was accounted to be greater' [Lns; similarly KJV], 'who should be considered the greatest' [GW, HCSB], 'which of them was to be considered the greatest' [BECNT; similarly NTC; NIV, REB], 'which of them was to be regarded as the greatest' [NET, NRSV; similarly NASB], 'which one of them should be thought of as the greatest' [TEV], 'which one of them was the greatest' [CEV], 'which one of them was the most important' [NCV], 'who would be the greatest in the coming Kingdom' [NLT].

c. μέγας (LN 87.22, 87.28) (BAGD 2.b.α. p. 498): 'greater' [LN (87.28)], 'great, important' [LN (87.22)]. This is being great in terms of status [LN], of rank and dignity [BAGD]. Although the form μείζων is comparative, the effect is superlative, the *greatest* among them [AB, Lns,

NAC, NIGTC, NTC, Rb; NET]. It means to be most important [AB]. There is a play on this one word: 'greatest' (22:24), 'greatest' (22:26), and 'greater' (22:27) [NAC]. See the preceding lexical item for translations of this word. See this word at 1:15, 32; 7:28; 9:46.

QUESTION—How is this verse connected with the previous one?

The question about which was the worst among them led to the question of which was the greatest among them [Alf, Gdt, NIBC, Su, WBC]. The word καί 'also' links this argument with the discussion in the previous verse [Gdt, NAC, NIGTC]. The words 'and also' indicate a transition to a new event in the same situation [TG]. Since Luke often disregards the sequence of time, there is some dispute as to where this incident occurred in the events of that evening and as to what caused the question of rank to be raised [Lns].

QUESTION—What is meant by *seeming* to be the greatest?

Here the verb 'seems' has the specific sense of having the reputation or being recognized as the greatest [TH]. The verb is used intransitively and refers to how the disciples would appear to people in general [AB, Gdt, MGC, NIGTC]. There is an implied 'ought' and it means who ought to be accounted as the greatest [ICC]. It is not who *appears* to be greater, but who is actually greater than the rest [Lns]. The dispute might well have been about who would have what role in the kingdom that Jesus brings since the topic of rule comes up in 22:29-30 [BECNT]. They were arguing about which one would have the highest rank in the kingdom [NIC, TG]. This doesn't say that they were vying for the top place in the kingdom, but they were very interested in who would get it [TNTC].

22:25 **And he-said to-them, The kings of-the nations lord-it-over[a] them and the (ones who) are-in-authority[b] (over) them are-called/call-themselves benefactors.[c]**

LEXICON—a. pres. act. indic. of κυριεύω (LN **37.50**) (BAGD 1. p. 458): 'to lord it over, to control' [BAGD], 'to rule' [BAGD, LN], 'to govern, to reign over' [LN]. The clause 'the kings of the nations lord it over them' is translated 'the kings of the Gentiles lord it over them' [Arn, Lns, NTC; NASB, NET, NIV, NRSV], 'the kings of this world reign over them' [**LN**], 'the kings of nations have power over their people' [GW], 'the kings of the Gentiles dominate them' [HCSB], 'the kings of the nations exercise their lordship over them' [WBC], 'the kings of the Gentiles exercise lordship over them' [KJV], 'the kings of the Gentiles exercise authority over them' [BECNT], 'the kings of the non-Jewish people rule over them' [NCV], 'among the Gentiles, kings lord it over their subjects' [REB], 'the kings of the pagans lord it over them' [AB], 'the kings of the pagans have power over their people' [TEV], 'foreign kings order their people around' [CEV], 'in this world the kings order their people around' [NLT]. The verb means to rule or reign over people and in some contexts it implies 'lording it over' [LN].

b. pres. act. participle of ἐξουσιάζω (LN **37.48**) (BAGD p. 279): 'to be in authority' [BAGD], 'to rule' [**LN**], 'to reign' [LN]. The phrase 'the ones being in authority' is translated 'those who exercise authority' [Arn, Lns, NTC; KJV, NIV], 'those in authority' [AB, WBC; GW, NET, NRSV, REB], 'those who have authority' [HCSB, NASB, NCV], 'those with authority' [BECNT], 'powerful rulers' [CEV], 'the rulers' [TEV], 'the great men' [NLT]. The verb means to rule or reign by exercising authority over people [LN], or to have the right or power over someone [BAGD].

c. εὐεργέτης (LN **35.15**) (BAGD p. 320): 'benefactor' [BAGD, **LN**]. The phrase 'are called benefactors' [Lns; HCSB, KJV, NASB, NET, NRSV] is also translated 'are given the title Benefactor' [REB], 'are styled Benefactors' [NTC], 'are called friends of the people' [NLT], 'like to be called friends of the people' [NCV], 'have themselves called benefactors' [WBC], 'call themselves everyone's friends' [CEV], 'claim the title Friends of the People' [TEV], 'call themselves friends of the people' [GW], 'call themselves Benefactors' [AB, Arn, BECNT; NIV]. This is someone who provides important help or assistance, and the word often is used as a title for princes or distinguished persons [LN]. It is a title for a prince or an outstanding benefactor [BAGD].

QUESTION—What is meant by κυριεύουσιν αὐτῶν 'lord it over them'?

It has a negative meaning of ruling and has the idea of 'lording it over them' by exercising overbearing authority and domineering over them [TH]. They make their political power felt [WBC]. They use their absolute power to exploit the people [Arn]. Or, this refers to the normal rule of kings and does not necessarily refer to singularly wicked kings who abuse their authority [NICNT].

QUESTION—What is meant by εὐεργέται καλοῦνται 'are called benefactors'?

1. The verb καλοῦνται is middle voice and means that they call themselves benefactors [AB, Arn, BECNT, ICC, MGC, NIC, TH, TNTC, WBC; CEV, GW, NIV, TEV]. They claim the title of Benefactor [Arn, ICC]. Earthly rulers are often conceited and claim this tile, looking for fame and honor [NIC]. When a king was generous to people, the required return was public recognition in various forms, including having himself called Benefactor [WBC]. This was a common title of respect and authority for princes and outstanding leaders [BECNT]. This title means the benefactor of the country or of mankind [ICC].

2. The verb καλοῦνται is in the passive voice and means that they are called benefactors by others [BNTC, Gdt, Lns, NIGTC, NTC, Su, WBC; HCSB, KJV, NASB, NCV, NET, NLT, NRSV, REB]. People rewarded benevolent rule by calling the ruler a benefactor [Su]. This does not mean that people voluntarily add such titles to the names of their kings in gratitude [Lns]. Benefactor is a flattering title that people used to honor even the harshest tyrants [Gdt].

22:26 But not thus with-you, but the (one who) is-greater among you let-him-become as the youngest[a] and the (one who) leads[b] as the (one who) serves.[c]

- LEXICON—a. νέος (LN 67.116) (BAGD 2.b.β. p. 536): 'younger, young' [BAGD, LN], 'the youngest' [AB, Arn, WBC; GW, HCSB, NASB, NET, NIV, NRSV, REB, TEV], 'the younger' [BECNT, Lns; KJV], 'the least important' [CEV], '(should take) the lowest rank' [NLT].
  - b. pres. mid./pass. (deponent = act.) participle of ἡγέομαι (LN 36.1) (BAGD 1. p. 343): 'to lead, to guide' [BAGD, LN], 'to direct' [LN]. The phrase ὁ ἡγούμενος 'the one who leads' [AB, Arn, Lns, WBC] is also translated 'he who takes the lead' [**LN**], 'whoever leads' [HCSB], 'the leader' [BAGD; CEV, NASB, NET, NLT, NRSV, TEV], 'your leader' [GW], 'the master' [**LN**], 'he that is chief' [KJV], 'the one who rules' [NIV, REB], 'the ruler' [BAGD, BECNT]. The verb refers to influencing others so as to cause them to follow a recommended course of action [LN].
  - c. pres. act. participle of διακονέω (LN 35.19) (BAGD 1. p. 184): 'to serve, to render service, to help' [LN], 'to wait on someone at table' [BAGD]. The phrase ὁ διακονῶν 'the one who serves' [AB, Arn, BECNT, WBC; HCSB, KJV, NET, NIV, NRSV, REB] is also translated 'the one ministering' [Lns], 'the/a servant' [CEV, GW, NASB, NLT, TEV], 'the waiter' [BAGD]. The verb means to render assistance or help by performing certain duties, often of a humble or menial nature [LN].

QUESTION—Is the clause 'but not thus with you' imperative or indicative?

1. It is imperative [AB, BECNT, Lns, MGC, NIGTC, NTC, TH, WBC; CEV, HCSB, KJV, NET, NIV, NLT, NRSV, REB]: but it must not be this way with you. The disciples should not act in this way [NIGTC], they should not be like those rulers in 22:25 [CEV]. They are not to lead through exercising power [BECNT]. Their manner of ruling must be transformed [NICNT].
2. It is indicative [Arn, My; GW, NASB, TEV]: but it is not this way with you. 'But you're not going to be that way!' [GW].

QUESTION—What is meant by a person who is greatest becoming the youngest?

A person who is youngest is usually obliged to perform the lowliest and menial service [Gdt, NIGTC]. In Jewish families the eldest son was preeminent and the youngest son was regarded as the least important and he was the one most naturally pressed into serving the rest [Su]. The youngest have no status that would require recognition [WBC]. Old age was regarded as honorable and the youngest was regarded with the least honor [NTC]. The youngest represent the people who have the least claim for ruling over others [NAC]. The 'youngest' usually refers to age, but here in contrast with the greater one, it refers to status [TG, TH] and the contrasts are between the greatest and the humblest, or the most important and the least important [TG]. The one considered the greatest among the disciples must assume the role of the youngest son and serve all the others [Su]. The greatest must behave as though he were called to menial service [NIGTC].

QUESTION—What is meant by a person who is a leader becoming a servant?

This is virtually a repetition of the meaning of the preceding sentence but using different words to make the matter clearer [Lns]. The leader must not press his authority, but is to behave as one who serves the people [WBC]. The person who wants to lead must first learn to be a servant [MGC]. The term leader was applied to church leaders and this nuance is present with the idea that church leaders must behave as servants [NIGTC].

22:27 **Because who (is) greater, the (one who) is-reclining-at-the-table or the (one who) serves[a]? (Is it) not the (one who) reclines-at-the-table? But I am among you as the (one who) serves.[b]**

LEXICON—a. pres. act. participle of διακονέω (LN 46.13): 'to serve' [Arn, BECNT, LN, NTC, WBC; all versions except GW, NLT, REB], 'to minister' [Lns], 'to wait upon' [LN]. This verb is also translated as a noun phrase: 'the servant' [GW], 'the servant who waits on him' [REB], 'the one waiting on him' [AB], '(is served by) his servants' [NLT]. Here the verb refers to table service [NIGTC, TH, WBC], or to serving food and drink to those who are eating [LN]. It describes a servant who washes the feet and cleanses the sandals of the one who eats at the table [Lns].

b. pres. act. participle of διακονέω (LN 35.19): 'to serve, to render service, to help' [LN]. The phrase 'I am among you as the one who serves' [BECNT, NTC; HCSB, KJV, NASB, NET, NIV, NRSV, TEV; similarly AB, Arn] is also translated 'I'm among you as/like a servant' [GW, REB], 'I am like a servant among you' [NCV], 'in your midst I am like the one who serves' [WBC], 'I have been with you as a servant' [CEV], 'I myself in your midst am as the one ministering' [Lns]. Here the verb means to render help by performing certain duties which are often of a humble or menial nature [LN]. Although the preceding use of 'serve' refers to waiting on someone at a meal, here it goes back to the general idea of service as in 22:26 [TH]. The whole of Jesus' ministry was one of serving his disciples [Gdt, ICC, NIC, NTC]. Or, this still has the meaning of being a table servant [AB, Arn, NIGTC, WBC]. Many point to John 13:4–16 where it tells how Jesus washed their feet [BECNT, Crd, Gdt, Lns, NIC, NIGTC, NTC, Rb, Su]. He might be referring to serving them by handing the cup to them [EGT]. Jesus was using figurative language to describe his self-denying course among them [Arn].

QUESTION—What relationship is indicated by γάρ 'because'?

This introduces an example [Lns, MGC, Su]. The preceding illustration of those in authority versus those who are ruled is changed to those who are served at the table versus those who serve them [Su]. This clinches the point of the preceding verse [NIGTC].

QUESTION—What kind of a person is ὁ διακονῶν 'the one who serves'?

This same term is also used in verses 26 and 27b, but here it has the more restricted meaning of one who waits upon a person who is eating at a table [Lns, NIGTC, TH, WBC].

QUESTION—What is the function of the question, 'Is not the one who reclines at the table'?

This is a rhetorical question that indicates that the answer is in the affirmative [TG, TH; NLT]. In secular life, everyone recognizes that the one being waited on is greater than the one who waits on him [NIGTC]. The answer is given according to normal ways of estimating roles in human society [AB, MGC, NAC].

QUESTION—What did Jesus mean by saying that he was among them as one who serves?

Jesus has reversed the secular opinion about the role of a servant [NIGTC, Su]. Jesus is great, yet he does not live like the world's leaders [BECNT]. In Jesus' dealing with them, he does the work of a servant [TG].

DISCOURSE UNIT: 22:28–30 [TNTC]. The topic is twelve thrones.

22:28 But you are the (ones who) have-remained[a] with me in my trials.[b]

LEXICON—a. perf. act. participle of διαμένω (LN 34.3) (BAGD p. 186): 'to remain' [Arn, BAGD, LN, Lns; NET], 'to remain true to' [NLT], 'to continue' [BECNT, LN; KJV], 'to stand by' [BAGD, NTC; GW, HCSB, NASB, NIV, NRSV], 'to stand firmly by' [REB], 'to stay with' [CEV, NCV, TEV], 'to stick with' [WBC]. It means to remain in an association with someone for a period of time [LN]. They had remained faithful to Jesus, or negatively, they had not abandoned him [TG]. The perfect tense emphasizes their constancy throughout the whole of Jesus' ministry [BECNT]. This situation had existed during his ministry and still did [NIGTC].

b. πειρασμός (LN 27.46, 88.308) (BAGD 2. p. 641): 'testing' [LN (27.46)], 'temptation' [BAGD, LN (88.308)]. The phrase τοῖς πειρασμοῖς μου 'my trials' [Arn, BECNT, NTC, WBC; HCSB, NASB, NET, NIV, NRSV, TEV] is also translated 'my times of trial' [REB], 'my time of trial' [NLT], 'all my troubles' [CEV], 'my struggles' [NCV], 'the troubles that have tested me' [GW], 'my temptations' [Lns; KJV].

QUESTION—What relationship is indicated by δέ 'but'?

This is a transition from Jesus' words of correction to a more genial style of addressing them [EGT]. Although ὑμεῖς 'you' is emphatic, no other persons are named to indicate with whom they are contrasted [TH]. The contrast is between these disciples and Jesus (22:27) [NIGTC], or, between these disciples and those who turned away (John 6:66–69) [Lns]. Or, it contrasts the deportment of the disciples when they were arguing about who was the greatest with their desire to stick with Jesus along the lowly roads of his trials [WBC]. In spite of the character defects the disciples had just displayed, they are praised for their faithfulness in the midst of trials [AB, Arn, BECNT, EGT, MGC, NIC, NTC].

QUESTION—What is meant by πειρασμοῖς 'trials'?

The verb πειρασμός can be described as either 'to try to learn the nature or character of someone or something by submitting such to thorough and extensive testing' [LN (27.46)] or 'to endeavor or attempt to cause someone to sin' [LN (88.308)]. Most refer to the aspect of being tested [Arn, EGT, ICC, Lns, TH, WBC; all versions except CEV, KJV, NCV]. He was put to the test by the difficulties he suffered [TH]. He was tested by the opposition and hatred of his opponents [AB, Lns]. Some include the idea of being tempted to fail the test, but not in the senses that the testing was given with the intent of trying to get Jesus to fail the test [EGT, ICC]. Experiences that tried his faith and patience were temptations to Jesus and even more to his disciples who were tempted to lose their confidence in him and their attachment to him who was so opposed by people of repute and influence [EGT]. The trials Jesus experienced during his ministry were temptations to abandon his work [ICC]. Some focus on the troubles that brought about the testing [Gdt, NIC, NICNT, NIGTC, TG, TNTC; CEV, GW]. It refers to difficulties caused by the indifference of the people and the hostility of the authorities [NIC]. It refers to being rejected by his fellow Jews [Gdt]. It refers to the many hardships involved in Jesus' ministry [TNTC]. It refers to dangers and tribulations, and behind it lies the idea of Satanic opposition [NAC, NIGTC]. A few speak of Satanic temptation [MGC, NIVS]. The trials include temptations by Satan (4:13), hardships (9:58), and being rejected (John 1:11) [NIVS].

22:29 **And-I assign[a] to-you just-as my Father has-assigned to-me a kingdom,**

LEXICON—a. pres. mid. indic. of διατίθεμαι (LN **37.105**) (BAGD 2. p. 189): 'to assign, to confer' [BAGD], 'to designate, to give the right' [LN]. The clause διατίθεμαι ὑμῖν καθὼς διέθετό μοι ὁ πατήρ μου βασιλείαν 'I assign to you, just as my Father has assigned to me a kingdom' is translated 'I on my part am assigning to you, even as my Father did assign to me, a kingdom' [Lns, NTC], 'I confer on you, just as my Father has conferred on me, a kingdom' [NRSV], 'I confer on you a kingdom, just as my Father conferred one on me' [NIV], 'I confer on you a kingship such as my Father has conferred on me' [AB], 'just as my Father has conferred royal rule upon me, I also confer it upon you' [WBC], 'I bestow on you a kingdom, just as my Father bestowed one on me' [HCSB], 'I now entrust to you the kingdom which my Father entrusted to me' [REB], 'I appoint unto you a kingdom, as my Father hath appointed unto me' [KJV], 'I appoint you even as my Father assigned to me a kingdom' [BECNT], 'I grant to you a kingdom, just as my Father granted to me' [NET], 'just as my Father has given me a kingdom, I also give you a kingdom' [NCV], 'as my Father has given me a kingdom, I'm giving it to you' [GW], 'just as my Father has given me the right to rule, so I will give you the same right' [TEV], 'I give you the right to rule just as my Father has given me the right to rule' [**LN** (37.105)], 'I will give you the right to rule, just as my Father has given me the right to rule as a king' [CEV], 'just as my Father has granted me a Kingdom, I now grant you the right (to eat and drink)' [NLT], 'just as my Father has granted me a kingdom, I grant you (that you may eat and drink)' [NASB], 'I appoint for you, just as my Father has appointed a kingdom for me, (that you shall eat and drink)' [Arn]. This is an appointment since Jesus continues to rule after his departure [BECNT]. The verb means 'to assign' [NIGTC]. It means to designate someone in a formal or official way for the role of ruling [LN].

QUESTION—What relationship is indicated by the conjunction καί 'and' at the beginning of 22:29?

It indicates the result of the disciples faithfully remaining with Jesus [AB, Gdt, MGC; CEV, GW, NET]: so, thus. This is their reward [AB, BECNT, ICC, NICNT].

QUESTION—What is the object of 'I assign to you'?

1. 'A kingdom' is the object of both 'I assign to you' and 'my Father has assigned to me' [AB, Alf, BECNT, Gdt, ICC, LN (37.105), Lns, My, NIGTC, NTC, Su, TG, TH, WBC; all versions except NASB, NLT]: I assign to you, just as my Father assigned to me, a kingdom. The disciples are promised a share in Jesus' rule [NIGTC]. Jesus gave them the same authority that his Father had given him [TG]. The present tense indicates that they are joining in the task at once, not later, and they will mediate for Jesus (as they do in Acts) and this form of leadership is service as explained in the preceding verses [BECNT]. Although the authority was given for the present time, the next verse indicates that the major manifestation of it is yet to come [NET]. Or, the next verse indicates that that this kingdom refers to the future form of the kingdom [NIVS]. When Jesus assigns them a kingdom, he means that they will share in his royal rule of the final manifestation of the kingdom [NTC]. This is not a reallocation of Jesus' authority but a sharing of his authority [NICNT]. This refers to participation in Jesus' eschatological rule rather than to any kind of independent rule [WBC].

2. 'That you may eat and drink at my table' (22:30) is the object of 'I assign to you' and 'a kingdom' is the object only of 'my Father has assigned to me' [Arn, Crd, NIC, TNTC; NASB, NLT]: just as my Father assigned to me a kingdom, I assign to you that you may eat and drink at my table in the kingdom. By the clause 'just as my Father assigned to me a kingdom', Jesus gives the reason why he has the right to promise his disciple the privilege of one day eating and drinking with him [NIC].

22:30 that you-may-eat and drink at my table in my kingdom, and you-will-sit on thrones judging[a] the twelve tribes of-Israel.

LEXICON—a. pres. act. participle of κρίνω (LN **37.46**, 56.30) (BAGD 4.b.β. p. 452): 'to judge' [Arn, BAGD, BECNT, LN (56.30), Lns, NTC, WBC; all versions except REB, TEV], 'to rule' [**LN** (37.46)], 'to rule over' [TEV]. This verb is also translated as a noun: '(sit on thrones as) judges' [AB; REB].

QUESTION—What relationship is indicated by ἵνα 'that'?
1. This indicates Jesus' purpose in assigning a kingdom to them [BECNT, ICC, My, TH].
2. This is explanatory [Lns, WBC]. It gives an example of what is included in this appointment to a kingdom [Lns].
3. This indicates the object of 'I assign to you' [Arn, Crd, NIC, TNTC; NASB, NLT].

QUESTION—What is meant by the disciples eating and drinking in Jesus' kingdom?

The kingdom is symbolized as a banquet at which Jesus' disciples will be present [TG]. Using the Jewish image of the messianic feast it symbolizes the inauguration of the messianic age in which Jesus will be honored as king and they will share his honor [Su]. It symbolizes their fellowship and acceptance in the messianic age [BECNT]. This is symbolic of the highest exaltation [Lns]. It is symbolic of the joys that they will experience in the new heaven and earth [Arn, NIC, NTC].

QUESTION—What is meant by the disciples sitting on thrones?

This is a symbolic way of indicating that the disciples would share in the glory of Jesus' rule as king [Su]. The disciples will be given places of honor at Jesus' side and he will make them rulers under and with him [Arn].

QUESTION—What is meant by the disciples judging the twelve tribes of Israel?

They will pass judgment on their fellow Jews according to their acceptance of Jesus as their king or their rejection of him [Su]. They will judge them according to how they have accepted or rejected what was proclaimed [ICC]. All judging will come to an end at the judgment of the last day [Lns]. Or, judging is to be taken in the general sense of governing and ruling [Arn, BNTC, Gdt, NICNT, TG, TNTC, WBC]. This does not refer to judging the Jews who persecuted them and killed Jesus, but, in conjunction with the thrones, judging has the sense of ruling [AB]. Or, this is to be taken metaphorically to refer to participating in the consummated kingdom where believers experience the blessings of the Lord's reign [NAC].

QUESTION—What is the significance of 'the twelve tribes of Israel'?

Gentiles will also be in the future kingdom, but a special honor will be given to the Apostles that they govern God's own people, the twelve tribes of Israel [Arn]. The Twelve apostles, having remained loyal to him, are going to receive a special reward among all the members of the new Israel and will be prominent in reflecting Jesus' glory [NTC]. Judas' defection is not taken into account and this speaks of twelve tribes having twelve apostles to rule over them [EGT]. The place of Judas would be filled by another [Lns]. There are twelve Apostles who will judge the twelve tribes, and the slot that Judas occupies will be later filled by Matthias [WBC]. Or, because of Judas' defection, Jesus did not say that *twelve* Apostles would judge the twelve tribes [AB, Lns]. The reference to the twelve tribes expresses the central place of Israel in the purposes of God [WBC]. The Church will judge the world of men and angels and the part of judgment allotted to the twelve is Israel [Gdt]. The reference is to the restored Israel in the millennial kingdom at the second coming of Christ [MGC]. They will judge the present Jews and the lost ten tribes by judging all the Gentiles [Lns]. The twelve tribes are the restored new Israel and are the total number of saved Israel gathered out of the twelve tribes and may include the chosen ones of both Jews and Gentiles [NTC].

DISCOURSE UNIT: 22:31–38 [BECNT; GW, NLT]. The topic is the last discourse [BECNT], Jesus' prediction of Peter's denial [GW, NLT].

DISCOURSE UNIT: 22:31–34 [AB, TNTC, WBC; CEV, HCSB, NCV, NRSV, TEV]. The topic is Satanic sifting and the denial of Jesus [WBC], Jesus' disciples will be tested [CEV], Jesus predicts Peter's denial [AB, TNTC; HCSB, NRSV, TEV], don't lose your faith [NCV].

22:31 Simon, Simon, behold[a] Satan asked-for[b] you (plural) to-sift[c] (you) like wheat.

TEXT—Before Σίμων Σίμων 'Simon, Simon', some manuscripts add εἶπεν δὲ ὁ κύριος 'and the Lord said'. GNT rejects this addition with a B decision, indicating that the text is almost certain. Εἶπεν δὲ ὁ κύριος 'and the Lord said' is added by CEV, GW, and KJV.

LEXICON—a. ἰδού (LN 91.13) (BAGD p. 371): 'behold' [Arn, BAGD, BECNT; KJV, NASB], 'lo' [Lns], 'look' [BAGD, LN], 'listen' [LN; GW, NRSV, TEV], 'listen to me' [CEV], 'pay attention' [LN; NET], 'look out' [WBC; HCSB], 'watch out' [NTC], 'take heed' [REB], 'beware' [AB], not explicit [NCV, NIV, NLT]. This emphasizes what he is going to say [NAC, TH]. What Jesus has to say is a warning to him [NTC].

b. aorist mid. indic. of ἐξαιτέομαι, ἐξαιτέω (LN **33.166**) (BAGD 1. p. 272): 'to ask for, to demand' [BAGD], 'to ask for with success, to ask and to receive' [LN]. The phrase 'asked for you' is translated 'has asked for you all' [WBC], 'hath desired to have you' [KJV], 'did ask to have you' [Lns], 'has asked to have all of you' [NLT], 'demanded to have you' [BECNT], 'has demanded to have you all' [NET], 'has demanded to have you apostles for himself' [GW], 'through request obtained you for himself' [Arn], 'has asked (to sift you)' [NTC; HCSB, NIV], 'has demanded (to sift all of you)' [NRSV], 'has demanded permission (to sift you)' [NASB], 'asked and received permission (to sift you)' [**LN**], 'has asked to test all of you' [NCV], 'has demanded the right to test each one of you'

[CEV], 'has received permission to test all of you' [TEV], 'has been given leave (to sift all of you)' [REB], 'has sought you all out' [AB]. This means that Satan demanded that God surrender the disciples to him [NIGTC]. Satan needed God's permission to carry out his attack on the disciples and it is understood that God did give his permission [WBC]. The aorist tense indicates that God did give Satan permission to do this [EGT, NIC, TH].

    c. aorist act. infin. of σινιάζω (LN **46.18**) (BAGD p. 751): 'to sift' [BAGD, LN], 'to shake in a sieve' [BAGD]. The phrase 'to sift you like/as wheat' [AB, **LN**, Lns, NTC, WBC; HCSB, KJV, NASB, NET, NIV, NLT] is also translated 'to sift all of you like wheat' [NRSV, REB], 'so he might sift you like wheat' [BECNT], 'to sift you as grain' [Arn], 'as a farmer does when he separates wheat from the husks' [CEV; similarly GW, TEV], 'as a farmer sifts his wheat' [NCV], 'to test you so as to separate the good from the bad' [**LN**], 'to test you' [**LN**].

QUESTION—What is the effect of repeating Simon's name?

The repetition gives emphasis to what follows [MGC, NTC, TH, TNTC]. Repeating his name does not indicate anger or censure [TG]. It causes Peter to realize the seriousness of the matter [BECNT, NIC]. It expresses deep concern [Lns, NTC, Su]. The solemn address expresses Jesus' affection for Simon [EGT]. Calling him Simon instead of Peter was appropriate in this situation since the name 'Peter' describes the rock-like nature of the apostle, which was lacking that night [Gdt, Lns, NIC, NTC]. Peter would revert back to his earlier behavior before he followed Jesus and had given him the new name of Peter [NAC].

QUESTION—What is meant by Σατανᾶς ἐξῃτήσατο ὑμᾶς 'Satan asked for you (plural)'?

The plural ὑμᾶς 'you' is the object of Satan's request [NIGTC]. Satan demanded that God surrender all of the disciples to him, and the aorist tense implies the success of the petition [NIGTC]. Satan demanded the opportunity to test Peter [Su]. The verb means 'has obtained you by asking' and indicates that the petition has been granted [Alf, Arn, EGT, ICC, NIC, NIGTC, TG, TNTC]. This means that God allowed Satan to test them all [ICC, TG]. Satan hoped that the apostles' loyalty to Christ and their faith in him might be shown to be unreal and he was given the right to test all of the disciples in regard to this [NIC]. Satan's request here is reminiscent of Satan's request to test Job [AB, Arn, BECNT, EGT, ICC, Lns, MGC, NAC, NIC, NICNT, NIGTC, Su, TG]. It shows that Satan can try out God's people only by God's permission [Lns]. Satan's request for bringing suffering into Job's life is different from this request because here this is about Satan trying to unsettle the disciples to the point that they become unfaithful [NAC].

QUESTION—What is meant by the metaphor 'to sift you like wheat'?

Sifting wheat is a repeated, swift, and violent shaking of the wheat in a sieve [Lns, NTC]. The point of sifting wheat is to separate off the rubbish [NIGTC]. There are various views about the details of sifting wheat. One explanation of the figure is that the heads and stalks of wheat were beaten and trampled on the threshing floor. Then small quantities of the broken mass were placed in a sieve to be violently shaken so that the wind would blew the chaff away, leaving behind the wheat [Su]. The vigorous shaking causes the chaff to rise to the surface so that it can be thrown away [NTC]. Two other explanations concern what passes through the sieve. Farmers used a double sieving process [WBC] and it is not clear if the grain is retained by this sieve or if the grain passes through the sieve [NAC, NIGTC, WBC]. One explanation is that the sifting was meant to hold back the larger pieces of strawy stuff while the wheat went through the sieve to form a pile of wheat below it [Lns]. Still another explanation is that the sifting was meant to hold back the wheat while the tiny waste materials such as sand went through the sieve. This metaphor of sifting the disciples like wheat was not phrased by Satan since his thought was that the disciples would be like the chaff that would be burned. Rather Jesus originated this metaphor to picture what the coming ordeal would be like for the disciples whom he likened to the wheat [Lns]. Satan wanted to make a last attempt to cast out the members of the apostles like chaff scattered by the wind [NIC]. The sifting of the disciples signifies severe trials [TNTC]. The question is whether the disciples would survive the testing [NIGTC, NTC]. Satan wanted to bring the disciples into difficulties in order to reveal their lack of integrity in their devotion to God [WBC]. He wanted to cause the sufferings coming to Christ to test the fidelity of the apostles [AB]. Satan would bring severe trials on the disciples in order to tempt them to become disloyal [Arn]. Satan received permission to put all of the disciples to the test in order to separate the good (or faithful) from the bad (or unfaithful) [TG]. The metaphor is filled out in some translations: 'Satan has demanded the right to test each one of you, as a farmer does when he separates wheat from the husks' [CEV], 'he wants to separate you from me as a farmer separates wheat from the husks' [GW], 'to test all of you, to separate the good from the bad, as a farmer separates the wheat from the chaff' [TEV]. The testing would happen that very night [NTC].

22:32 But I prayed for you (singular) that your faith may- not -fail.^{a} And when you have-returned^b strengthen^c your brothers.

    a. aorist act. subj. of ἐκλείπω (LN 68.36) (BAGD 242): 'to fail' [BAGD], 'to cease, to stop' [LN]. The phrase 'that your faith may not fail' [BECNT; HCSB, NET, NIV, REB; similarly GW, KJV, NLT, TEV] is also translated 'that your own faith may not fail' [NRSV], 'that your faith may not utterly fail' [NTC], 'that your faith might not give out' [AB, WBC], 'that your faith might not cease once for all' [Arn], 'that you will not lose your faith' [NCV], 'lest thy faith eclipse' [Lns], 'that your faith will be strong' [CEV]. The verb means 'that your faith may not run out', 'may not utterly fail' [NTC]. Here the verb means 'to disappear' [BECNT], 'to be wiped out once for all' [Arn].

b. aorist act. participle of ἐπιστρέφω (LN 41.51) (BAGD 1.b.β. p. 301): 'to return, to turn back' [BAGD]. 'to turn back to God' [LN]. The phrase 'when you have returned' is translated 'when you have turned again' [BECNT], 'when you have turned back' [WBC; HCSB, NET, NIV], 'when once you have turned back' [NRSV], 'when you turn back to me' [TEV], 'once you have returned to me' [NTC], 'when you have turned' [Arn], 'once having turned' [Lns], 'you yourself will turn back' [AB], 'when you have come back to me' [CEV], 'when you come back to me' [NCV], 'when you have repented and turned back to me again' [NLT], 'when you recover' [GW], 'when you are restored' [REB] 'when thou art converted' [KJV]. This does not refer to conversion in the absolute sense as if every bit of Peter's faith was destroyed, but it refers to turning back in repentance from a course that almost destroyed his faith [Lns].

c. aorist act. impera. of στηρίζω (LN 74.19) (BAGD 2. p. 768): 'to strengthen' [Arn, BAGD, BECNT, LN, NTC, WBC; GW, HCSB, KJV, NET, NIV, NRSV, TEV], 'to strengthen and build up' [NLT], 'to give strength to' [REB], 'to establish, to confirm' [BAGD], 'to make firm' [Lns], 'to make more firm' [LN], 'to help (your brothers) be stronger' [NCV], 'to reinforce' [AB], 'to help' [CEV]. Here 'strengthen' is used figuratively [BAGD] and it means to cause someone to become firmer and unchanging in attitude or belief [LN].

QUESTION—Why did Jesus change his address from Σατανᾶς ἐξῃτήσατο ὑμᾶς 'Satan asked for *you* (plural)' in 22:31 to ἐγὼ δὲ ἐδεήθην περὶ σοῦ 'but I prayed for *you* (singular)' in 22:32?

In both of these verses Jesus was addressing only Peter, although what he said applied to the other disciples who were present [NTC]. Simon is addressed as being the spokesman for the others [NIBC]. It means 'Simon, look to yourself and to the whole brotherhood of which you are the leading man' [EGT]. Simon was singled out because Jesus will give him a special commission in regard to the other apostles [TH]. Simon is addressed in these two verses, but clearly Satan had all of the disciples in view [WBC]. Jesus meant for all of them to know this, but 'I prayed for you (singular)' shows that Simon was involved in a special way, that is, in his strong denial of Jesus [BECNT, Lns]. Jesus prayed for all of the disciples, but he especially prayed for Peter who was to play a leading part in the events to come [NIC, NTC]. Peter was to be the means by which the others would be strengthened [Crd, NIGTC].

QUESTION—What is meant by Jesus' prayer 'that your faith may not fail'?

The conjunction ἵνα 'that' expresses both the purpose of the prayer and its content [NAC, NIGTC]. Jesus prayed that Peter would not stop believing in him [TH]. He prayed that Satan would not be able to destroy Peter's faith [NIGTC]. In the wake of his denials, Peter would be tempted to abandon his faith in Jesus altogether [NIBC]. Peter's faith proved to be weak and inadequate for the short time he was overpowered by fear, but he never ceased to love Jesus [EGT]. Peter's total renunciation of Jesus would be temporary [BECNT]. Jesus referred to the faith shown in Peter's statement of confidence that Jesus was the Messiah of God [Su]. The prayer was that in the end Peter's faith would prevail [NTC]. Peter's denials were lapses, not a total absence of faith [NET]. Or, since Peter was and would continue to be a believer all along [BECNT], 'faith' seems to have the sense of 'faithfulness' here [AB, BECNT, NAC, NIGTC]. This is not speaking of Peter losing the Christian faith by apostasy and regaining it by conversion, but it refers to Peter's fidelity to Jesus [NIGTC]. Peter's faithfulness and loyalty will be tested and found wanting, but in the long run, not totally wanting [AB].

QUESTION—What is meant by ποτε ἐπιστρέψας 'when you have returned'?

'Returned' implies both Peter's failure and his recovery [Su, TG]. This refers to when he turns back to Jesus after he had been sifted by Satan [TH]. It means turning to God as a penitent after sin [Alf, MGC]. It means turning from the fault of a temporary aberration [ICC]. He will return to his true self [EGT]. By the power of God he will be brought back to his former faith and loyalty [NIC]. Peter will repent of denying Jesus and turn back from that period of infidelity [AB, Lns]. Peter fell from faith when he denied Christ, but he repented and turned away from that disloyalty to again become a firm believer [Arn].

QUESTION—How would Peter strengthen his brothers?

This is a figurative expression for strengthening their faith [TH; NET], and courage [TH]. It is to make their faith or loyalty stronger [TG]. He is to make firm their commitment to Jesus [AB]. The other disciples will also be temporarily overwhelmed by the testing and he must help them become strong again in their faith and loyalty to Christ [NIC]. Peter's experience will enable him to be a help to the others [TNTC]. It does not mean that the other disciples will have a total failure of faith, but only that they may not recover as well as Peter will and will need Peter's help and encouragement [WBC]. Because Peter fell more deeply than the others fell, he would be the one to make the wavering faith of the others firm again [Lns]. This includes strengthening the faith of the early church [MGC, NICNT, Su].

22:33 And he-said to-him, Lord, with you I-am ready[a] to-go both- to prison -and[b] to death.

LEXICON—a. ἕτοιμος (LN 77.2) (BAGD 2. p. 316): 'ready, prepared' [BAGD, LN]. The phrase 'with you I am ready to go' [NTC; NASB] is also translated 'I am ready to go with you' [AB, Arn, WBC; all versions except NASB], 'together with thee I am ready to go' [Lns], 'I am ready to follow you' [BECNT]. The phrase μετὰ σοῦ 'with you' is made emphatic by its position at the beginning of the clause [ICC, My, TH]. That Peter was *prepared* to go with the Lord means that Peter was willing to suffer what Jesus had to suffer [TH].

b. καί...καί (LN 89.102): The sequence καί...καί are markers of a totality of two closely related elements 'both...and' [LN]. The phrase καὶ εἰς φυλακὴν καὶ εἰς θάνατον πορεύεσθαι 'to go both to prison and to death' [HCSB, NASB, NET] is also translated 'to go both into prison and to death' [Arn; KJV], 'to go to jail/prison and even to die' [CEV, NCV, NLT], 'to go even to prison and to death' [NTC], 'to go to prison and to death' [AB, WBC; NIV, NRSV, REB], 'to go into prison and into death' [Lns], 'to go to prison and to die' [GW, TEV], 'to follow to prison and to death' [BECNT],

QUESTION—What was Peter's declaration responding to?

This is Peter's reaction to the Lord's warning [Lns]. Peter understood that in the preceding verse Jesus had referred to his loyalty in the time of danger [Su, TG]. He was so sure of himself that he could not believe that he could ever be unfaithful to Jesus [NIC].

22:34 And he-said, I-tell you, Peter, a-rooster will- not -crow today until^a three (times) you-have-denied^b to-know me.

TEXT—Instead of ἕως 'until', some manuscripts read πρὶν ἤ 'before'. GNT does not mention this variant. Πρὶν ἤ 'before' is used by AB, BECNT, Lns, NTC, WBC; CEV, KJV, NCV, and NIV.

LEXICON—a. ἕως (LN 67.119) (BAGD I.1.b. p. 334): 'until' [BAGD, LN]. The phrase 'a rooster will not crow today until' is translated 'the rooster will not crow today until' [Arn; HCSB, NASB, NET], 'the cock will not crow this day until' [NRSV], 'the rooster/cock will not crow tonight until' [GW, REB, TEV], 'the rooster will not crow tomorrow morning until' [NLT], 'before the rooster crows today' [NIV], 'a cock will not crow this day before' [WBC], 'a rooster will not crow today before' [NTC], 'a cock will not crow today before' [AB, Lns], 'the cock shall not crow this day before that' [KJV], 'before the rooster crows this day' [NCV], 'today before the cock will crow' [BECNT], 'before a rooster crows tomorrow morning' [CEV].

b. aorist mid. (deponent = act.) subj. of ἀπαρνέομαι (LN 33.277) (BAGD p. 81): 'to deny' [BAGD, LN]. The phrase 'you have denied to know me' is translated 'you have denied that you know me' [WBC; NASB, NET, NRSV, REB], 'you have denied that you even know me' [NLT], 'you deny that you know me' [NTC; HCSB], 'you will deny that you know me' [BECNT; KJV, NIV], 'you will have denied that you know me' [AB, Arn], 'thou didst deny to know me' [Lns], 'you say that you don't know me' [GW], 'you have said that you do not know me' [TEV], 'you will say that you don't know me' [CEV, NCV]. The verb means that one does not know about someone or is not in any way related to him [LN].

QUESTION—Why did Jesus now call his disciple Peter instead of Simon?

Jesus now showed his tender concern for his friend by using his nickname [Su]. Peter thought that he was living up to his name of 'the rock-man', but this prediction lets him know that his confidence is misplaced [Arn]. Perhaps Jesus used his name in irony [NIGTC].

QUESTION—What is meant by using the crowing of a rooster as a marker of time?

The Jewish day began after sunset and ended at the following sunset [ICC, TG]. It was already nighttime when Jesus spoke to Peter [NICNT, TG] and he said that Peter would deny him before dawn of that same day [Arn, NIC, NICNT, NTC, WBC; NET]. The coming of dawn was referred to as 'cockcrow' and here Peter was informed that he would deny Jesus before the coming of dawn [Arn]. This means 'before the night is past' [ICC].

QUESTION—How does this correspond to the parallel passage in Mark 14:30, that says before the rooster crows *twice*, Peter would will deny Jesus three times?

In Luke it says that Peter would deny Jesus three times before the coming of dawn, and in Mark it says that there would be two cockcrows that night and before those two times, Peter will have denied Jesus three times [Arn]. Or, this does not refer to a crowing of an individual rooster. Two crowings were referred to in order to mark midnight and just before dawn and here Luke refers only to the crowing before dawn [Lns]. Roosters normally crow at the first light, but one might hear an individual rooster crow at any time after 2:30 A.M. [WBC]. Or, Luke abbreviated Mark's reference to two crowings [NIGTC]. Or, Mark meant that Peter's three denials would come so quickly that a rooster would not have crowed twice before the denials had happened [AB, MGC].

DISCOURSE UNIT: 22:35–38 [AB, TNTC, WBC; CEV, HCSB, NCV, NRSV, TEV]. The topic is the new rules for a time of crisis [WBC], the two swords [AB, TNTC], moneybags, traveling bags, and swords [CEV], purse, bag, and sword [NRSV, TEV], money-bag, backpack, and sword [HCSB], be ready for trouble [NCV].

22:35 **And he-said to-them, When I sent you without a-purse[a] and a-traveler's-bag[b] and sandals, you-did- not -lack anything (did you)? And they-said, Nothing.**

LEXICON—a. βαλλάντιον (LN 6.144) (BAGD p. 130): 'purse' [AB, Arn, BAGD, BECNT, LN, Lns, NTC, WBC; KJV, NCV, NIV, NRSV, REB, TEV], 'moneybag' [CEV, HCSB, NET], 'money belt' [NASB], 'wallet' [GW], 'money' [NLT]. It was used to carry money [Lns]. See this word at 10:4, 12:33.

b. πήρα (LN 6.145) (BAGD p. 656): 'traveler's bag' [BAGD, LN; NET, NLT], 'traveling bag' [CEV, GW, HCSB], 'bag' [BECNT, NTC, WBC; NASB, NCV, NIV, NRSV, TEV], 'pack' [REB], 'knapsack' [AB, Arn], 'scrip' [KJV], 'wallet' [Lns]. It was a bag in which travelers or beggars carried their possessions [LN]. It was used to carry food, clothes, and other things needed for a trip [Lns]. See this word at 9:3, 10:4.

QUESTION—Where does it tell about Jesus sending his apostles without these things?

These instructions given to the apostles about purse, traveler's bag, and sandals closely correspond to the instructions about purse, traveler's bag, and sandals given to the seventy disciples in 10:4, although the instructions given to the twelve apostles in 9:3 about staff, traveler's bag, bread, and silver are similar.

1. This verse refers to the instructions given to the Twelve in 9:3 [Arn, Gdt, NTC]. There is no essential difference in the instructions to the apostles and to the seventy, since in both cases precautionary measures about what might happen on the journey were ruled out by the instructions [NTC].
2. This verse refers to the instructions given to the seventy in 10:4 [AB, NIGTC, Su, TG, TH, TNTC, WBC]. It refers to the specific event of 10:4 [TH]. It implies that the twelve apostles also took part in the mission of the seventy or that the charge in 10:4 was originally addressed to the apostles [NIGTC]. Or, Luke had made the one instance of sending out the disciples into a double sending out [AB]. Perhaps this reflects a source used by Luke in which this list was associated with the sending of the apostles [WBC].
3. This verse reminds the apostles of the past missions of the apostles (9:3) and the seventy (10:4) [BECNT, Lns, MGC, NAC, NIBC, NIC, NICNT].

22:36 And he-said to-them, But now the (one who) has a-purse let-him-take (it), likewise also a-traveler's-bag, and the (one who) does- not -have (a sword/purse) let-him-sell his garment[a] and let-him-buy a-sword.[b]

TEXT—Instead of δέ 'and', some manuscripts read οὖν 'then'. GNT does not mention this variant. Οὖν 'then' is read by KJV.

LEXICON—a. ἱμάτιον (LN 6.172) (BAGD 2. p. 376): 'garment' [KJV], 'cloak' [AB, BAGD, LN, WBC; NET, NIV, NRSV, REB], 'robe' [BAGD, LN, Lns; HCSB], 'coat' [LN, NTC; GW, NASB, NCV, TEV], 'mantle' [Arn, BECNT], 'clothes' [CEV, NLT]. This noun is a generic term for any type of outer garment [BAGD, LN].

b. μάχαιρα (LN 6.33) (BAGD 1. p. 496): 'sword' [AB, Arn, BAGD, BECNT, LN, NTC, WBC; all versions], 'short sword' [Lns]. This was a Roman short sword [Lns]. It was a sword that men frequently wore [BECNT, NIGTC].

QUESTION—What relationship is indicated by ἀλλὰ νῦν 'but now'?

It indicates an emphatic contrast with the instructions mentioned in the preceding verse [EGT, NAC, TH, TNTC]. They were to be prepared for changed circumstances in their ministry [BECNT, ICC]. It contrasts the peaceable conditions of the mission in 10:4 with the impending crisis soon to occur [NIGTC]. Friends provided for them before, but now they will need these items to care for themselves [Lns].

QUESTION—Why will they need to take a purse and traveling bag?

They will no longer be welcomed and honored as they were before [NIC]. They will travel long hard roads that will require different preparations [MGC]. The purse and a traveling bag would provide what was needed in situations where the people were hostile and refused to provide hospitality [NIGTC]. As followers of their crucified leader, they will be despised and persecuted and they cannot depend on people providing for their needs as they had in the past [NIC]. In some places there will still be friends to welcome them and provide for them, but this will not happen in many places where they travel [Lns].

QUESTION—What does one not have in the phrase ὁ μὴ ἔχων 'the one not having'?

1. He does not have a sword [Arn, BECNT, Gdt, Lns, NIGTC, NTC, TH, WBC; all versions]. The person who has a sword should take along his purse and traveling bag, but the person who does not have a sword should even sell his needed garment to buy a sword because of the dire circumstances at hand [NIGTC].
2. He does not have a purse [Alf, ICC, My], or does not have a purse or traveler's bag [AB, MGC]. The person who has a purse can buy a sword without selling his garment [Alf]. Only the person who has no wallet would sell a necessary garment to buy anything [ICC]. The person who has a purse and knapsack is to take them along, while the one who does not have them must sell the clothing he has to get a sword [AB, ICC].

QUESTION—Why did Jesus tell the disciples to buy swords?

1. This was meant to be taken literally [Alf, EGT, Lns, Rb]. They would need swords for defense on the dangerous mountain roads [Lns, Rb]. There would be times when they needed protection so badly that a sword would be worth more to them then their outer robe [Lns]. Self protection would be needed for their altered situation in connection with the world [Alf].
2. This was meant to be taken figuratively [AB, Arn, BECNT, EGT, Gdt, ICC, MGC, My, NAC, NIBC, NIC, NICNT, NIGTC, NIVS, NTC, TNTC, WBC; NET]. Jesus did not mean that they were to repel force with force, nor that they were to use force to spread the gospel [ICC]. He did not mean that they were to be prepared for an anticipated messianic conflict, nor does it explain why they happened to have a sword in Gethsemane that very night [NIGTC]. That this is symbolic is seen in Jesus' rebuke of using a sword in 22:49–51 [NICNT]. Obtaining a sword is figurative for preparing to fight the opposition that they will be facing [NET]. This was a graphic way to make the disciples realize that they faced a situation of great peril [TNTC]. They will need all the courage they can muster [NTC]. This is a vivid way of letting them know that a supreme crisis was at hand and they must prepare for an approaching enemy [EGT]. Here the sword is a symbol of being prepared for opposition and indicates being ready and self-sufficient [BECNT]. This figuratively told them to be ready

442   LUKE 22:36

for hardship and self-sacrifice [NIGTC]. They must be mentally ready for bloody persecution [Arn]. The sword was a part of a traveler's equipment in the Roman world and the possession of a sword meant nothing more than protecting oneself. Since Satan had been given permission to sift the disciples (22:31), they would be without God's care and protection for a time and here Jesus gives a symbolic description of the kind of difficulties that they would experience. [WBC] They must be as determined and whole-hearted as a fighting man who gives up everything to possess a sword to continue the struggle with [NIC]. The purse, knapsack, and sword are all to be taken in a symbolic sense to indicate the kind of difficulties they will have to experience [WBC]. Or, the figure of the sword is to be taken figuratively for the spiritual conflict they would encounter at Jesus' crucifixion [MGC]. Taken metaphorically, they are to be spiritually armed to battle spiritual foes [NAC].

3. This was meant to be taken ironically [Su]. They had formerly found Jesus' way to be best, but now they were ready to abandon that way to and even join the revolutionaries to bring about the messianic kingdom. In effect, Jesus was saying to them, "Once you found my way completely adequate, but now, forget that; sell your clothes to buy a sword; join the Zealots; establish the kingdom of Israel" [Su].

22:37 Because I-say to-you that this (which) has-been-written must be-fulfilled[a] in me, And he-was-reckoned[b] with lawless (people). Because even the (thing which) concerns me has an-end.[c]

TEXT—Following ὅτι 'that', some manuscripts add ἔτι 'yet'. GNT does not mention this variant. Ἔτι 'yet' is added by KJV.

LEXICON—a. aorist pass. infin. of τελέω (LN 13.126) (BAGD 2. p. 811): 'to be fulfilled' [LN], 'to happen, to be accomplished' [LN]. The phrase 'this which has been written must be fulfilled in me' is translated 'this which is written must be fulfilled in me' [NASB; similarly NTC], 'what is written about me must be fulfilled in me' [HCSB], 'this saying which is written must be fulfilled in me' [Arn], 'this scripture must be fulfilled in me' [BECNT; NET, NRSV], 'this that has been written must be accomplished in me' [Lns; similarly KJV], 'the Scripture passage must find its fulfillment in me' [GW], 'this scripture must have its full meaning' [NCV], 'it is written…and this must be fulfilled in me' [NIV], 'there must be fulfilled in me this that stands written' [WBC], 'this must be fulfilled in me' [REB], 'must come true about me' [TEV], 'the time has come for this prophecy about me to be fulfilled' [NLT], 'this was written about me, and it will soon come true' [CEV], 'what has been written in Scripture must find its final sense in me' [AB]. The verb means to cause to happen for some end result [LN].

b. aorist pass. indic. of λογίζομαι (LN 31.1) (BAGD 1.b. p. 476): 'to be reckoned' [BAGD], 'to be considered' [BAGD, LN], 'to be regarded' [LN]. The phrase 'and he was reckoned with lawless persons' is translated 'and he was reckoned with the transgressors' [BECNT], 'and he was reckoned among transgressors' [KJV, REB], 'and he was reckoned together with lawless ones' [Lns], 'and he was counted with lawless people' [Arn, WBC], 'and he was counted among the lawless' [NRSV], 'and he was counted with the transgressors' [NET], 'he was counted with criminals' [GW], 'and he was counted among the outlaws' [HCSB], 'he was counted among those who were rebels' [NLT], 'and he was numbered with transgressors' [NTC; NASB, NIV], 'he was classed even with outlaws' [AB], 'he was considered a criminal' [CEV], 'he was treated like a criminal' [NCV], 'he shared the fate of criminals' [TEV]. The verb means to hold a view or to have an opinion with regard to something [LN].

c. τέλος (LN 67.66) (BAGD 1.a. p. 811): 'end' [BAGD, LN], 'termination' [BAGD]. The clause 'the thing which concerns me has an end' is translated 'the things concerning me have an end' [KJV], 'this concerning me has an end' [Lns], 'what concerns me is coming to an end' [WBC], 'all that concerns me comes now to its end' [AB], 'what is written about me has its completion' [BECNT], 'that which refers to me has its fulfillment' [NASB], 'what is written about me is being fulfilled' [NRSV], 'what is written about me is coming to its fulfillment' [HCSB], 'what is written about me is being fulfilled' [NET], 'what is written about me is reaching its fulfillment' [NIV], 'all that is written of me is reaching its fulfillment' [REB], 'that passage about me is reaching its fulfillment' [NTC], 'the prophecy about me, too, has its fulfillment' [Arn], 'whatever is written about me will come true' [GW], 'what was written about me is coming true' [TEV], 'everything written about me by the prophets will come true' [NLT], 'it was written about me, and it is happening now' [NCV], 'it will soon come true' [CEV]. This speaks of the consummation that happens when prophecy is fulfilled and here it perhaps means that the references in the Scriptures about Jesus were being fulfilled, although it could merely mean that Jesus' life's work was at an end [BAGD].

QUESTION—What relationship is indicated by the beginning γάρ 'because'?

It explains verse 22:36 [Lns, TH]. It explains the change to 'but now' in the preceding verse [ICC, NAC]. This indicates an explanation for the change from 'when I sent you' in 22:35 to 'now' in 22:36 [ICC, NICNT]. Now things are different and have become dangerous because people will deal with Jesus in the way implied in following quotation from Scripture [TH]. It indicates the reason the disciples must buy a sword if they don't already have one [CEV]. It indicates that the reason why the disciples must be ready to face the worst is because their master also will face the worst [Alf, EGT, NIC, NIGTC, WBC]. It explains that perilous times will come for them because Jesus will be cruelly treated and his followers will likewise have to suffer [Arn]. Jesus will be crucified between criminals and as a result he will be hated by the Jews and scorned by the Gentiles, so when the disciples come as messengers of the crucified Jesus, they will be treated accordingly [Lns].

QUESTION—Why must the scripture be fulfilled?

'Must' implies that this is God's plan [Arn, My, NAC, NICNT, NIGTC, NTC, TH; NET]. It concerns God's plan for the salvation of people [Arn]. God will fulfill his plan in Jesus [NAC]. Or, 'must' is impersonal and refers to what is necessary to accomplish the desired end. Here, it was necessary for Jesus to experience suffering and death in order to complete God's work of redeeming people [Su].

QUESTION—Where is the statement 'And he was reckoned with lawless persons' written?

This is a quotation from Isaiah 53:12 [AB, Arn, BECNT, Lns, NAC, NIGTC, Su, TG, TNTC, WBC]. The beginning καί 'and' is part of the quotation and is not connected to anything in this verse [Arn, ICC, Lns, My]. The beginning 'and' can be omitted in the translation of this quotation [AB, Arn, TH; CEV, GW, NCV, NLT]. In the Isaiah passage 'and' implies that in addition to other inflictions this will also be added [Lns].

QUESTION—What is meant by the statement μετὰ ἀνόμων ἐλογίσθη 'he was reckoned with lawless people'?

Jesus will be one with sinners and take their place [TNTC]. Or, the Jewish authorities condemned Jesus as a transgressor of their law and executed him as a transgressor between two lawbreakers [Su]. The lawless persons are the two criminals he was crucified between [BECNT, Lns, NIGTC]. The lawless people are godless and wicked people who broke God's law [TH]. The lawless people are the sinners Jesus associated with during his ministry and this attracted the hostility of the Jewish leaders [NICNT].

1. This has the abstract sense of being considered to be a lawless person [AB, Arn, BECNT, Lns, NIGTC, NTC, TH, WBC; CEV, GW, HCSB, KJV, NASB, NET, NIV, NLT, NRSV, REB]. Jesus was reckoned to be of the same class as those criminals [Lns].
2. This has the concrete sense being treated as a lawless person [MGC, TG; NCV, TEV]. Jesus was treated like a criminal by being condemned and executed [TG]. Jesus was about to die the death of a criminal [EGT]

QUESTION—What relationship is indicated by γάρ 'because' in the last clause?

This clause reinforces the first part of the verse [NAC]. It extends the argument from the fulfillment being necessary to the fact that it will certainly reach its conclusion [ICC, NIC]. This explains that the prophecy just quoted must be accomplished in Jesus [Lns].

QUESTION—What is meant by τὸ περ ἐμοῦ τέλος ἔχει 'the thing which concerns me has an end'?

1. It means that the things written about him will be fulfilled [BECNT, ICC, MGC, NICNT, NTC, TG; all versions except KJV]. The passage written about Jesus is reaching its fulfillment [Arn, BECNT, NTC, TG]. This emphasizes the idea of fulfillment that this verse begins with [BECNT].

2. It means that the things written about him have reached their goal in God's plan [Arn, EGT, ICC]. Jesus foretells that the end of his earthly ministry is near [Arn].
3. It means that the things that concern him will come to an end [Lns, My, NIGTC, TH, WBC]. The reckoning of Jesus with lawless people is one of the last things that concerns him in his earthly life, and in just a little while all that concerns him will be at an end, so that nothing further will happen to him to alter the impression left by his being reckoned among transgressors [Lns]. The end concerns Jesus' death [WBC]. This is equivalent to saying 'my life is drawing to an end' [NIGTC, TH], and this also shows that the Scripture is being fulfilled [NIGTC].

22:38 **And they-said, Lord, behold**[a] **here (are) two swords. And he-said to-them, It-is enough.**[b]

LEXICON—a. ἰδού (LN 91.13) (BAGD 2. p. 371): 'behold' [Arn, BAGD; KJV], 'lo' [Lns], 'look' [AB, BAGD, BECNT, LN, NTC, WBC; CEV, GW, HCSB, NASB, NCV, NET, NRSV, TEV], 'see' [NIV], not explicit [NLT, REB].
  b. ἱκανός (LN **59.44**) (BAGD 1.c. p. 374): 'enough, sufficient' [BAGD, LN]. The clause Ἱκανόν ἐστιν. 'It is enough.' [Arn, BECNT, **LN**, Lns; KJV, NASB, NET, NRSV] is also translated 'That is enough.' [GW, NCV, NIV, NLT, TEV], 'Enough!' [REB], 'Enough of that!' [AB, NTC, WBC; CEV, HCSB].

QUESTION—How is it that two of them already had swords?
  The instructions in 22:36 assume that some of them already had swords [NAC, WBC]. It was usual to wear swords, so this is not surprising [NIGTC]. They possessed swords in order to protect themselves from robbers on the journey to Jerusalem, or to protect themselves from attacks in the city [Alf, ICC]. Perhaps two of the disciples had secretly armed themselves because they had sensed danger for themselves and Jesus at this time, but since the noun for sword could also refer to knives, it more likely that this referred to the butcher knives that had been used for slaughtering and preparing the lamb for the Passover supper [Su]. Or, the swords had been hanging on the wall of the upper room and belonged to the owner of the house and Peter probably took one of them when they left the house [Lns].

QUESTION—What did Jesus mean when he said 'It is enough'?
  1. He meant that the subject did not need to be discussed any longer [AB, Alf, Arn, BECNT, ICC, Lns, MGC, NAC, NIBC, NIGTC, NTC, Rb, Su, TH, TNTC, WBC; CEV, HCSB, REB]. They had wrongly understood Jesus' instructions in 22:36 and thought that Jesus intended for all of the disciples to actually go and buy swords [AB, Arn, BECNT, NAC, NIC, NIGTC, NTC, Su, TNTC]. The disciples had so missed the point of what Jesus was talking about that he refused to explain further [AB, MGC]. It was enough of that kind of talk, the disciples were hopelessly astray [TNTC, WBC]. Jesus wanted to stop the discussion about the swords

[BECNT, Lns, NIGTC, TH] because of the disciples' misunderstanding [BECNT, Lns]. He simply intended to end the matter [Lns]. His answer was curt and decisive [NTC]. He spoke in frustration [NIBC]. It could be worded 'I give up!' [MGC]. Or, this is a rebuke meaning 'Enough of this kind of talk!' [NIGTC]. Or, it is spoken in sorrow, not impatience [ICC]. Sadly Jesus indicated that the subject had been sufficiently discussed, but later on they would realize the meaning of his instructions about swords [Arn].

2. He meant that two swords were sufficient for the group to have [BNTC, EGT, Gdt, TG]. Two swords were enough to fulfill his instructions [BNTC]. This is ironic, meaning that two swords are enough for the use they will have for any swords [Gdt]. They were enough for one who did not intend to fight [EGT]. The disciples had taken him literally and so he ironically said 'That's plenty!' and ended the conversation [NIVS].

DISCOURSE UNIT: 22:39–23:56 [BECNT, NAC]. The topic is the arrest and trial [NAC], the trials and death of Jesus [BECNT].

DISCOURSE UNIT: 22:39–23:56a [AB]. The topic is a the passion, death, and burial of Jesus.

DISCOURSE UNIT: 22:39–23:25 [NIGTC]. The topic is the arrest and trial of Jesus.

DISCOURSE UNIT: 22:39–46 [AB, BECNT, NAC, NICNT, NIGTC, Su, TNTC, WBC; CEV, GW, HCSB, NASB, NCV, NET, NIV, NLT, NRSV, TEV]. The topic is the agony [TNTC], Jesus prays [CEV], the prayer of Jesus [AB, NAC, NIGTC], on the Mount of Olives [NET], Jesus prays on the Mount of Olives [NIV, NLT, NRSV, TEV], the Garden of Gethsemane [NASB], the prayer in the garden [HCSB], Jesus prays in the Garden of Gethsemane [GW], the agony and prayer at Gethsemane [Su], Jesus on the Mount of Olives [NICNT], Jesus prays alone [NCV], preparation through prayer [BECNT], praying to be spared trial [WBC].

22:39 And going-out he-went according to habit[a] to the mountain of-olives, and also the disciples followed[b] him. **22:40** And coming to the place he-said to-them, Pray not to-enter into temptation/trial.[c]

TEXT—In 22:39, instead of οἱ μαθηταί 'the disciples', some manuscripts read οἱ μαηθται αὐτοῦ 'his disciples'. GNT does not mention this variant. Οἱ μαηθται αὐτοῦ 'his disciples' is read by KJV.

LEXICON—a. ἔθος (LN 41.25) (BAGD 1. p. 218): 'habit' [BAGD, LN], 'custom' [LN]. The phrase κατὰ τὸ ἔθος 'according to habit' is translated 'according to his custom' [Arn, BECNT, Lns], 'as was his custom' [WBC; NASB, NET, NRSV], 'as he often did' [CEV, NCV], 'as usual' [AB, NTC; HCSB, NIV, NLT, REB], 'as he usually did' [GW, TEV], 'as he was wont' [KJV].

b. aorist act. indic. of ἀκολουθέω (LN 15.156): 'to follow' [AB, Arn, BECNT, LN, Lns, NTC, WBC; GW, HCSB, KJV, NASB, NET, NIV, NRSV], 'to go along with' [LN], 'to go with' [CEV, NCV, TEV]. This active voice is also translated passively: 'to be accompanied by' [REB].

c. πειρασμός (LN 88.308) (BAGD 2.b. p. 641): 'temptation' [BAGD, LN]. The clause προσεύχεσθε μὴ εἰσελθεῖν εἰς πειρασμόν 'pray not to enter into temptation' is translated 'pray that you enter not into temptation' [AB; KJV], 'pray that you may not enter into temptation' [HCSB, NASB], 'pray that you do not come into temptation' [Arn, BECNT], 'pray that you will not fall into temptation' [NET, NIV, TEV], 'pray that you will not be overcome by temptation' [NLT], 'keep praying that you may not enter at all into temptation' [NTC], 'be praying not to enter into temptation' [Lns], 'pray that you won't be tempted' [GW], 'pray for strength against temptation' [NCV], 'pray that you may be spared the test' [REB], 'pray that you won't be tested' [CEV], 'pray that you may not come into the time of trial' [NRSV], 'pray not to enter into what will be a trial to you' [WBC].

QUESTION—What did Jesus go out of?
1. He went out of the house [ICC, NICNT, Su; NLT].
2. He went out of city [TH; GW, NCV, NET, TEV].
3. He went out of both the room and the city [Gdt].

QUESTION—Who were the disciples who accompanied Jesus?
These were the eleven apostles, not including Judas [AB, NAC, NTC, WBC]. Although Luke does not record the departure of Judas, it is evident that Judas did not accompany Jesus at this time because in 22:47 it speaks of Judas arriving with the group that came to arrest Jesus [WBC].

QUESTION—What was Jesus' habit?
During that week Jesus left the temple each night and lodged on the mount called Olivet (21:37–38) [AB, Su]. Throughout this week and perhaps at other times, Jesus spent the night on the slopes of this hill [TNTC]. Because of this habit, Judas knew where Jesus would likely be [NIGTC, Su, TNTC].

QUESTION—In 22:40, where was τοῦ τόπου 'the place' Jesus came to?
The Mount of Olives includes the slope and even the foot of the hill that begins immediately beyond the Kedron [Gdt]. No previous reference has been made to this place and it probably means 'the place he had in mind' [TH], or 'the place he planned to go' [My, TG]. It was Jesus' place of secret prayer [Rb]. It was the place at the Mount of Olives where Jesus usually spent the nights [Arn, NIC]. Mark and Matthew name the place as being Gethsemane, the place where Jesus usually stayed [Lns, MGC]. The walk to Gethsemane was about one mile [Arn]. This was only 140 feet higher than Jerusalem [NIGTC].

QUESTION—What is meant by εἰσελθεῖν εἰς πειρασμόν 'to enter into temptation'?
1. They are to ask God to keep them from being tempted or being put to the test [TG]. It refers to being tempted [Arn, BECNT, EGT, Gdt, Lns, MGC,

NIC, NTC, Su, TH; all versions except CEV, NRSV, REB]. They would be tempted to lose faith in Jesus [Gdt, Lns, MGC, NIVS], or to lose faith that he was the Messiah (22:9) by what would soon happen [Su]. They would be tempted to deny Jesus [BECNT, NTC], or to defect [NET]. The ordeals that were coming would tempt them to lose their faith in Jesus and think that God had abandoned them and that it was useless to cling to Jesus as their Lord [Lns]. Some refer to this as being tested [NICNT; CEV, NASB, REB]. Ordeals become temptations when the disciples listen to the devilish suggestion that God has abandoned them and that it is useless to continue being faithful to Jesus as their Lord [Lns].
2. It refers to experiencing severe ordeals [BNTC, WBC]. This concerns being spared troubles in the coming crisis that they would not be able to cope with [WBC].

22:41 And he withdrew/was-withdrawn[a] from them about (the) throw[b] of-a-stone and having-placed[c] the knees he prayed

LEXICON—a. aorist pass. indic. of ἀποσπάω (LN 15.214) (BAGD 3. p. 98): 'to withdraw' [BAGD], 'to draw away, to pull away' [BAGD, LN]. The phrase αὐτὸς ἀπεσπάσθη 'he withdrew/was withdrawn' is translated 'he withdrew' [AB, BECNT, NTC, WBC; GW, HCSB, NASB, NIV, NRSV, REB], 'Jesus walked on' [CEV], 'he walked away' [NLT], 'he went off' [TEV], 'he went away' [NCV, NET], 'he tore himself away' [Arn, Lns], 'he was withdrawn' [KJV].

b. βολή (LN **15.216**) (BAGD p. 144); 'a throw' [BAGD, LN]. The phrase ὡσεὶ λίθου βολήν 'about the throw of a stone' is translated 'about a stone's throw' [AB, Arn, BECNT, **LN**, Lns, NTC, WBC; GW, HCSB, NASB, NET, NIV, NLT, NRSV, REB], 'a stone's throw' [NCV], 'about a stone's cast' [KJV], 'about the distance of a stone's throw' [TEV], 'about the distance that a person might throw a stone' [**LN**], 'a little way' [CEV].

c. aorist act. participle of τίθημι (LN 17.19) (BAGD 1.1.b.a. p. 816); 'to put, to place' [BAGD, LN]. The phrase θεὶς τὰ γόνατα 'having placed the knees' is translated 'going to his knees' [BECNT], 'having knelt down' [Lns], 'he kneeled down' [KJV, NCV], 'he knelt down' [AB, Arn, NTC, WBC; all versions except KJV, NCV]. The phrase τίθημι τὰ γόνατα 'to place the knees' is an idiom for 'to kneel down before', and it implies an act of reverence or supplication [LN]. He placed his knees on the ground [AB].

QUESTION—What is meant by the aorist passive form of ἀπεσπάσθη 'he withdrew'?

1. The verb has an active intransitive meaning, 'he withdrew', or the middle meaning 'he drew himself away' [AB, Arn, BECNT, Crd, EGT, Lns, MGC, NIGTC, NTC, TH, WBC; all versions except KJV]. The verb is passive, but middle in sense: 'he tore himself away from them' [Arn, Lns]. Or, rather than the middle sense of 'he tore himself away', implying

that he acted with strong feeling, it does not necessarily mean more than that he simply withdrew [Crd, EGT].

2. This verb has the passive meaning,: 'he was drawn away' [Gdt, ICC; KJV]. The violence of his emotion drew Jesus away, his emotion being too strong to even tolerate the sympathy of his friends [ICC]. He was dragged away from the disciples by his anguish [Gdt].

QUESTION—How far away was a stone's throw away?

It was a figurative way of designating several yards [BECNT]. It was about 30 yards [TH], or about 100 feet away [TG]. It was still close enough for the disciples to see what Jesus did and to hear what he said [EGT, My, NTC]. Jesus left the group of disciples near the entrance and continued on for a distance that one can throw a stone. Luke does not tell about Peter, James, and John going along with him and they were only a few paces from Jesus as he prayed, so it was those three who heard what he said [Lns, NTC].

QUESTION—Why did Jesus kneel to pray?

This was an unusual attitude for prayer [NIGTC]. Although standing was the more common attitude for prayer, kneeling was more natural on occasions of special earnestness [Arn, EGT, ICC, NIGTC, TNTC, WBC]. It implied special urgency [EGT]. He knelt in humility before the Father [BECNT, NIGTC]. Parallel passages indicate that Jesus fell on his face in prayer, so we are to understand that Jesus first knelt while praying and then sank prostrate [Lns].

22:42 **saying, Father, if you-are-willing[a] take-away[b] this cup from me. Yet not my will[c] but yours be-done.**

LEXICON—a. pres. mid./pass. (deponent = act.) indic. of βούλομαι (LN 25.3) (BAGD 2.b. p. 146): 'to will' [BAGD, LN], 'to desire, to want' [LN]. The phrase εἰ βούλει 'if you are willing' [Lns, NTC; HCSB, KJV, NASB, NCV, NET, NIV, NLT, NRSV] is also translated 'if it is your will' [GW, REB], 'if you will' [Arn, BECNT, WBC; CEV, TEV], 'please' [AB]. It refers to decisions of the will after deliberation [BAGD]. This implies deliberate selection [ICC]. Rather than meaning 'if you are willing to grant me what I want', it means 'if you decide to do so' [TH]. It means 'if it can be in your plan' [Su].

b. aorist act. imper. of παραφέρω (LN 90.97) (BAGD 2,c. p. 623): 'to take away, to remove' [BAGD]. The phrase παρένεγκε τοῦτο τὸ ποτήριον ἀπ' ἐμοῦ 'take away this cup from me' is translated 'take this cup away from me' [AB, Lns, WBC; HCSB, NET], 'take this cup from me' [Arn; NIV, REB], 'remove this cup from me' [BECNT, NTC; KJV, NASB, NRSV], 'take away this cup' [NCV], 'take this cup of suffering from me' [LN], 'take this cup of suffering away from me' [GW, TEV], 'please take this cup of suffering away from me' [NLT], 'please don't make me suffer by having me drink this cup' [CEV], 'do not make me undergo this suffering' [LN]. The phrase παραφέρω τὸ ποτήριον ἀπό 'to take the

450   LUKE 22:42

cup from' is an idiom meaning to cause someone to not undergo some
trying experience [LN].

c. θέλημα (LN 25.2) (BAGD 1.a. p. 354): 'what is willed' [BAGD], 'wish,
desire' [LN]. The phrase μὴ τὸ θέλημά μου ἀλλὰ τὸ σὸν γινέσθω 'not
my will but yours be done' [AB, Arn, BECNT, NTC, WBC; HCSB, KJV,
NASB, NET, NIV, NRSV, REB] is also translated 'not my will but your
will be done' [TEV], 'your will must be done, not mine' [GW], 'let not
my will but thine go on being done' [Lns], 'I want your will, not mine'
[NLT], 'do what you want, and not what I want' [CEV, NCV].

QUESTION—What was the cup Jesus asked to be removed?

The cup was a metaphor for a person's fortune, whether good or bad [ICC].
It was the cup of destiny [AB, MGC]. The cup refers to Christ's suffering
[ICC, NAC, NIBC, NIGTC, NIVS, TG, TNTC; CEV, GW, NLT, TEV]. It
was a symbol of death [BNTC]. The OT background for this expression
emphasizes not simply destiny, but the infliction of punishment associated
with God's wrath [NIGTC]. It was a cup of wrath [BECNT, TNTC], the
wrath that Jesus would experience for us [NET]. The cup was the ordeal that
he was to suffer and this prayer reveals the dread and anguish Jesus felt
[Arn]. It was not about physical death in general but the particular death that
Jesus would suffer [NAC]. The cup was that impending terrible experience
Christ would go through and it culminated in his sense of complete
abandonment and his crucifixion [NTC]. Different from the deaths of later
courageous martyrs, Jesus would be made sin for us and die a death that
atoned for the world's sin and his whole nature shrank from such a contact
with sin [Lns]. The judgment on sin is death, spiritual as well as physical,
and spiritual death means being forsaken by God [NIC].

QUESTION—What is the significance of the last sentence 'Yet not my will but
yours be done'?

'Yet' looks at the request from another way and means 'if there is no other
way' [Su]. Whatever the Father determines, it is what Jesus wants [Lns].
Jesus' request was less significant than his desire to do God's will [BECNT].
This does not imply that Jesus' will is the opposite to the will of the Father
[TNTC]. The Father's will is in reference to his plan of salvation [AB].

**22:43 And an-angel from heaven appeared to-him strengthening[a] him.
22:44 And being in agony[b] he-was-praying more-fervently.[c] And his sweat
became[d] like drops of-blood falling-down upon the ground.**

TEXT—These two verses are omitted by some manuscripts, included by some
manuscripts, included but marked by some manuscripts to indicate doubt,
transposed by some manuscripts to follow Matt. 26.39, and one lectionary
manuscript transposes these two verses plus the phrase καὶ ἀναστὰς ἀπὸ
τῆς προσευχῆς 'and having arisen from the prayer' from the following
verse (45a) to follow Matt. 26.39. GNT favors the omission of these two
verses with an A decision, indicating that the omission is certain, but
includes these verses in the text in double brackets to indicate that the words

are included because of their antiquity and the position that they have traditionally had in the church. These verses are omitted by AB and WBC. They are included in brackets by HCSB and NRSV. They are translated as part of the text by Arn, BECNT, Lns, NTC; all versions except HCSB and NRSV.

LEXICON—a. pres. act. participle of ἐνισχύω (LN 79.66) (BAGD 2. p. 267): 'to strengthen' [Arn, BAGD, BECNT, LN, Lns, NTC; HCSB, KJV, NASB, NCV, NET, NIV, NLT, TEV], 'to give (him) strength' [GW, NRSV], 'to bring (him) strength' [NRSV], 'to help' [CEV].

b. ἀγωνία (LN **25.283**) (BAGD p. 15): 'agony' [Arn, BAGD, BECNT, Lns; KJV, NASB], 'agony of spirit' [NLT], 'anguish' [**LN**, NTC; GW, HCSB, NET, NIV, NRSV], 'anguish of spirit' [REB], 'great anguish' [TEV], 'intense sorrow' [LN], 'anxiety' [BAGD], 'great pain' [CEV], 'full of pain' [NCV]. This means a state of great mental and emotional grief and anxiety [LN]. The agony was caused by fear [EGT, ICC]. This noun may mean fear, but it could be that it was not fear of death but a concern for coming out victoriously in the coming battle [NIGTC].

c. ἐκτενής (LN 25.71) (BAGD p. 245): 'more fervently' [Arn, BECNT; HCSB, NLT, TEV], 'very fervently' [NTC; NASB], 'fervently' [BAGD], 'more earnestly' [KJV, NET, NIV, NRSV], 'earnestly' [LN], 'more urgently' [REB], 'more intensely' [Lns], 'so sincerely (that)' [CEV], 'even harder' [NCV], 'very hard' [GW].

d. aorist mid. (deponent = act.) indic. of γίνομαι (LN 13.107) (BAGD II.1. p. 160): 'to become, to be' [BAGD], 'to happen, to occur, to come to be' [LN]. The clause ἐγένετο ὁ ἱδρὼς αὐτοῦ ὡσεὶ θρόμβοι αἵματος 'his sweat became like drops of blood' [GW, HCSB, NASB] is also translated 'his sweat became like great drops of blood' [NRSV], 'his sweat became like thick drops of blood' [NTC], 'his sweat became like/as clots of blood' [Arn, Lns], 'his sweat was like drops of blood' [NCV, NET, NIV, REB, TEV], 'his sweat was as it were great drops of blood' [KJV], 'sweat came like drops of blood' [BECNT], 'his sweat (fell to the ground) like drops of blood' [CEV], 'his sweat (fell to the ground) like great drops of blood' [CEV].

QUESTION—Does ἀπ' οὐρανοῦ 'from heaven' modify the noun 'angel' or the verb 'appeared'?

1. The phrase modifies the noun 'angel' [AB; CEV, GW, HCSB, NASB, NCV, NET, NIV, NLT, NRSV, TEV]: an angel who came from heaven appeared to him.
2. The phrase modifies the verb 'appeared' [BECNT, NTC, TH; KJV]: an angel came from heaven to appear to him. In this case, the idea of 'coming' is added to 'appeared' [TH]. The angel appeared to him from heaven [BECNT].

452 LUKE 22:43–44

QUESTION—Who saw the angel and in what way did the angel strengthen Jesus?

Since the three disciples were chosen to be witnesses of Jesus' agony, undoubtedly they also witnessed the coming of the angel [Lns]. Or, probably the sleeping apostles did not see the angel and were informed of this by Jesus later [Arn]. This recalls the reports in Mark 1:13 and Matthew 4:11 about angels coming and ministering to Jesus at the conclusion of his temptation by Satan in the wilderness [Su]. Jesus was strengthened in regard to his moral and spiritual strength [TG]. Jesus was strengthened in his acceptance of the way of suffering in 22:42, or he was strengthened to accept the full implications of his prayer [NIGTC]. The angel strengthened Jesus to face the coming ordeal [BECNT]. Perhaps the angel strengthened Jesus by reminding him of God's purposes that were to be accomplished through his Passion, as Moses and Elijah had done in 9:31 [Arn]. The angel strengthened him for his battle in prayer to align his will with his Father's will not to take the cup away [WBC]. Or, this refers to physical strengthening [Alf]. Jesus' anguish demanded so much from his soul and body that the angel strengthened him so that he could complete the path of suffering and enabled him not to die before his work was finished [NIC]. This miraculous answer to Jesus' prayers gave strength to Jesus' human nature, but it was not that the angel exhorted Jesus, he strengthened his exhausted body by giving him new vitality [Lns].

QUESTION—Why was Jesus in agony after being strengthened by the angel?

Because of the angel's help, Jesus was enabled to pray more earnestly [MGC, NIGTC]. Although strengthened by this experience, it had not brought and end to the agony he experienced [Su]. Jesus' mind and body were strengthened to face the full horror of the wrath that was to come and so Jesus prayed more intensely [Lns].

QUESTION—What is meant by 'his sweat became like drops of blood falling-down upon the ground'?

1. This means that it was literally sweat and the sweat was falling to the ground like drops of blood would fall to the ground [AB, BECNT, MGC, NIC, NIGTC, Su; CEV, KJV, NCV, NET, NLT, REB, TEV]: his sweat was like drops of blood falling down upon the ground. This does not mean that his sweat changed into drops of blood or that there was a mixture of sweat with blood, rather it is a simile describing how great quantities of sweat trickled down and fell to the ground as though blood was running down from him [NIC]. The sweat *fell* like drops of blood [NIGTC]. Jesus' emotions were so intense that he sweated profusely and the sweat drops multiplied on his skin like flowing clumps of blood and dripped to the ground in this figurative description [BECNT]. The sweat was so profuse that it fell like blood spilling to the ground [MGC].

2. This means that his blood was literally mixed with his sweat and this bloody mixture was falling to the ground [Alf, Gdt, ICC, Lns, My, NTC]: his sweat became drops of blood falling upon the ground. The strain from

his combined anguish and intense supplication caused subcutaneous capillaries to dilate and burst so that blood and sweat mixed together in thick drops, giving a reddish color to the perspiration [Lns, NTC]. The blood thickened as it mingled with the sweat and both fell to the ground in little clots [Lns]. It was bloody sweat [ICC]. The sweat was *like* blood because it was highly colored by blood [Alf].

22:45 And rising from the prayer and coming to the disciples he-found them sleeping from the distress.ᵃ **22:46** And he-said to-them, Why are-you-sleeping? Get-up, pray that you may not enterᵇ into temptation/testing.

TEXT—In 22:45, instead of οἱ μαθηταί 'the disciples', some manuscripts read οἱ μαθηταὶ αὐτοῦ 'his disciples', although GNT does not mention this reading. Οἱ μαθηταὶ αὐτοῦ 'his disciples' is read by KJV.

LEXICON—a. λύπη (LN **25.273**) (BAGD p. 482): 'distress' [LN], 'grief' [BAGD], 'sorrow' [BAGD, LN]. The phrase κοιμωμένους ἀπὸ τῆς λύπης 'sleeping from distress' is translated 'sleeping from grief' [BECNT, WBC], 'sleeping from sorrow' [Lns, NTC; NASB], 'sleeping for grief' [Arn], 'sleeping for sorrow' [KJV], 'sleeping because of grief' [AB; NRSV], 'asleep because of their sadness' [NCV], 'asleep, worn out by their distress' [**LN**], 'asleep, worn out by grief' [NET, REB, TEV], 'asleep, exhausted from sorrow' [NIV], 'asleep, exhausted from grief' [NLT], 'sleeping, exhausted from their grief' [HCSB], 'asleep and overcome with sadness' [GW], 'they were asleep and worn out from being sad' [CEV]. The noun refers to a state of mental pain and anxiety [LN].

b. aorist act. subj. of εἰσέρχομαι (LN **90.70**) (BAGD 2.a. p. 233): 'to come into something' [BAGD], 'to begin to experience, to come into an experience' [LN]. The phrase προσεύχεσθε μὴ εἰσελθεῖν εἰς πειρασμόν 'pray that you may not enter into temptation' [NASB; similarly AB] is also translated 'pray that you will not begin to experience temptation/trial' [**LN**], 'pray that you will not fall into temptation' [NET, TEV], 'pray that you won't be tempted' [GW], 'pray that you do not come into temptation' [BECNT; similarly Arn], 'pray that you won't be tested' [CEV], 'pray that you may be spared the test' [REB], 'pray that you may not come into the time of trial' [NRSV], 'pray that you may not enter into what will be as trial to you' [WBC], 'pray for strength against temptation' [NCV], 'pray, so that you won't enter into temptation' [HCSB], 'pray so that you will not fall into temptation' [NIV], 'pray, that you may not enter into temptation' [NTC], 'pray, lest you enter into temptation' [Lns; KJV], 'pray, otherwise temptation will overpower you' [NLT]. This is a repeat of his instructions in 22:40 [BECNT, NAC, NIGTC, TH, TNTC, WBC]. They had failed the test by falling asleep, but now there will be further tests [TNTC].

QUESTION—What is meant by rising ἀπὸ τῆς προσευχῆς 'from the prayer'?
1. It means rising from the position of prayer [AB, Arn, BECNT, Lns, MGC, NICNT, NTC, WBC; all versions except GW, NCV]: Jesus arose from praying. Jesus had knelt to pray and now he stood up [NICNT].
2. It means rising 'after the prayer' [TH; GW, NCV]: after the prayer he got up. The preposition ἀπὸ 'from' has a temporal sense here [TH].

QUESTION—What is meant by κοιμωμένους ἀπὸ τῆς λύπης 'sleeping from grief'?
Their grief was the reason they went to sleep [Gdt, ICC, MGC, NAC, NIGTC, TG, TH]. They were emotionally exhausted [WBC]. After so much had happened in a long day and then thinking of Jesus' approaching death, they had become so emotionally drained they fell asleep [BECNT]. Prolonged grief and sorrow produces sleep [Gdt, ICC]. Troubled by what Jesus had told them, they had been praying until they were overcome by sleep [Su]. Verses 22:14–23 and 31–34 explain their grief [NAC].

QUESTION—What is meant by the rhetorical question 'Why are you sleeping'?
It functions as a rebuke [Arn, Lns, Su, TG]. It means 'You shouldn't be sleeping' [TG]. They should have fought off their drowsiness [Arn]. They should have kept awake, and could have if they had been earnestly praying [NTC]. The question is asked in astonishment [Su, TH]: 'how is it possible that you are asleep?' [TH]. Jesus was astonished that anyone could sleep after being told of the testing soon to come [Su].

QUESTION—Does 'pray that you may not enter into temptation/testing' give the content of the prayer or the purpose for praying?
1. It indicates the content of the prayer [AB, Arn, TNTC, WBC; CEV, GW, NASB, NCV, NET, NRSV, REB, TEV]: pray that you may not enter into temptation. They should pray that the trial would not destroy their faith [Arn].
2. It indicates the purpose for praying [BECNT, Lns, NTC; HCSB, KJV, NIV, NLT]: pray in order that you will not enter into temptation.

DISCOURSE UNIT: 22:47–23:56 [REB]. The topic is the trial and crucifixion of Jesus.

DISCOURSE UNIT: 22:47–54a [Su, TNTC, WBC; GW]. The topic is the arrest of Jesus [TNTC, WBC; GW], the betrayal and arrest [Su].

DISCOURSE UNIT: 22:47–53 [AB, BECNT, NAC, NICNT, NIGTC; CEV, HCSB, NASB, NCV, NET, NIV, NLT, NRSV, TEV]. The topic is Jesus is arrested [AB, NAC, NIGTC; CEV, NCV, NIV, TEV], Jesus confronts the arresting party [NICNT], Jesus is betrayed by Judas [NASB], betrayal and arrest [NET], Jesus is betrayed and arrested [BECNT; NLT, NRSV], the Judas kiss [HCSB].

22:47 (While) he was- still -speaking behold[a] a-crowd[b] (came), and the (one) called Judas one-of the twelve was-leading[c] them and he-approached

Jesus to-kiss him. **22:48** And Jesus said to-him, Judas, by-means-of-a-kiss are-you-betraying[d] the Son of-Man[e]?

TEXT—In 22:47, following ἔτι 'still', some manuscripts add δέ 'and'. GNT does not mention this variant. Δέ 'and' is added by KJV.

LEXICON—a. ἰδού (LN 91.13) (BAGD p. 371): 'behold' [Arn, BAGD, BECNT; KJV, NASB], 'look' [LN, NTC], 'lo' [Lns], 'listen, pay attention' [LN], 'suddenly' [AB; NET, NRSV], not explicit [WBC; CEV, GW, HCSB, NCV, NIV, NLT, REB, TEV]. This word functions to arouse the attention of the readers [BAGD, LN] and it also emphasizes the following statement [LN]. It suggests a sudden appearance of the crowd [AB, Lns, NIGTC, TH; NET, NRSV]. Here it indicates the commencement of an action [NIGTC]. It is used to indicate a transition, so it need not be translated [NET].

b. ὄχλος (LN 11.1): 'crowd' [AB, Arn, BECNT, LN, NTC, WBC; all versions except HCSB, KJV, NLT], 'multitude' [LN, Lns; KJV], 'mob' [HCSB, NLT].

c. imperf. mid./pass. (deponent = act.) indic. of προέρχομαι (LN **15.181**) (BAGD 2. p. 705): 'to lead' [BECNT, **LN**, NTC; all versions except KJV, NASB, REB], 'to show the way to' [LN], 'to go before' [BAGD, Lns; KJV], 'to precede' [NASB], 'to come on ahead' [WBC], 'to be at the head' [AB; REB], 'to walk at the head' [Arn]. Judas was not the leader in charge of the crowd, rather it meant that he was going before the crowd [NAC, NIGTC]. The verb means 'to go in front of' in order to show the way [LN, NIGTC]:

d. pres. act. indic. of παραδίδωμι (LN 37.11) (BAGD 1.b. p. 614): 'to betray' [Arn, BECNT, LN, Lns, NTC, WBC; all versions except NCV], 'to hand over' [AB, LN], 'to turn over to' [BAGD, LN], 'to give to (his enemies)' [NCV]. See this word at 22:4.

e. υἱὸς τοῦ ἀνθρώπου 'Son of Man'. This title for Christ occurs at 5:24; 6:5, 22; 7:34; 9:22, 26, 44; 11:30; 12:8, 40; 17:22, 24, 26; 18:8, 31; 19:10; 21:27, 36; 22:22, 69; 24:7. See the discussions of this title at 5:24, 6:5, and 9:22.

QUESTION—How big was the crowd that came?

It consisted of Judas, some of the chief priests and elders from the Sanhedrin, and some of the temple police, but it was not as numerous as the daytime crowds who surrounded Jesus while he taught at the temple [Su]. It consisted of Judas, temple police, Levites, and a detachment of Roman soldiers, thus making a rather large crowd [NTC]. Perhaps there were 200 Roman soldiers and as many temple police [Lns]. The large number of soldiers indicates that they feared resistance from Jesus' disciples [NIC].

QUESTIO—What is the significance of adding that Judas was one of the twelve?

Judas was a common name, so this addition identifies him more exactly [Arn]. This addition emphasizes the enormity of the betrayal [AB, BECNT, NIGTC, NTC].

QUESTION—Why would Judas kiss Jesus and did he actually kiss him?

Although not reported by Luke, Judas had arranged to show the soldiers which one of the group was Jesus by giving him a kiss [TNTC]. The kiss made the identification certain [BECNT]. It is clear in Jesus' following question that he recognized that the kiss would be used to betray him [TNTC]. Judas intended to kiss Jesus on a cheek or on both cheeks as a man kisses another man [TG]. A man would greet a close friend by bestowing a kiss on his cheek or forehead [Su]. It was a form of greeting [Gdt, NAC, TNTC]. Whether or not it was a usual greeting given to a rabbi [NTC], a kiss indicated friendship and affection [Lns, NTC]. Luke does not state whether Judas' plan to kiss Jesus was blocked by Jesus' question or if Judas actually kissed him [AB, NIGTC, TH, WBC]. The actual execution of the kiss is left to be inferred [EGT]. The two aorist verbs ἤγγισεν 'he approached' and φιλῆσαι 'to kiss' imply that Judas did approach Jesus and that he did kiss him [Lns]. In Mark 14:45 we read that Jesus permitted Judas to kiss him before he asked the question [BECNT, NIC]. This is translated as being accomplished [CEV, NLT].

QUESTION—What is indicated by the rhetorical question 'Judas, by means of a kiss are you betraying the Son of Man?'

This question indicates Jesus' surprise and sorrow that his disciple would use a sign of friendship to betray him [TG]. It was spoken in irony [BECNT]. Jesus was upbraiding Judas for using a token of friendship to deliver him to death [Arn]. The forwarded position of the phrase 'with a kiss' is emphatic [AB, Arn, ICC, My, NIGTC, Su, TH], and stresses the enormity of the betrayal in using a kiss in such a hypocritical manner [NIGTC]. The horror of betraying a friend is made all the worse by the use of a kiss to do it [NAC]. Instead of saying 'are you betraying me' Jesus said 'are you betraying the Son of Man' to remind Judas that he was betraying the Messiah [ICC]. This emphasized the seriousness of the act [BECNT, NAC]. This was an earnest warning to Judas about what he was doing [Lns, NTC].

22:49 And (when) the (ones) around him saw what was-going-to-happen they-said, Lord, if we-will-strike[a] with sword? **22:50** And a-certain-one of them struck[b] the slave of-the chief-priest and cut-off his ear, the right (one).

TEXT—In 22:49, following εἶπαν 'they said', some manuscripts add αὐτῷ 'to him'. GNT does not mention this variant. Αὐτῷ 'to him' is read by KJV.

LEXICON—a. fut. act. indic. of πατάσσω (LN 19.3) (BAGD 1.b. p. 634): 'to strike' [BAGD, LN]. The phrase 'if we will strike with sword?' is translated 'shall we strike with a sword?' [AB, NTC], 'should we strike with the sword?' [BECNT, WBC; HCSB, NASB, NRSV], 'shall we smite with the sword?' [Lns; KJV], 'should we strike with our swords?' [NIV], 'should we strike them with our swords?' [NCV], 'shall we use our swords?' [NET, REB, TEV], 'should we use our swords to fight?' [GW], 'should we attack them with a sword?' [CEV], 'shall we strike about us with a sword?' [Arn], 'should we fight? We brought the swords!' [NLT].

LUKE 22:49–50 457

b. fut. act. indic. of πατάσσω (LN **19.3**) (BAGD 1.b. p. 634): 'to strike' [BAGD, LN]. The phrase 'struck the slave of the chief priest' [Arn, BECNT; NASB, NRSV; similarly **LN**; HCSB, NET, TEV] is also translated 'struck the servant of the high priest' [NCV, NIV; similarly AB; KJV], 'did smite the slave of the high priest' [Lns], 'struck at the slave of the high priest' [WBC], 'struck at the high priest's servant' [CEV], 'slashed at the servant of the high priest' [NTC], not explicit [GW]. It is implied that a sword was used when he struck the slave [LN; CEV].

QUESTION—Who asked the question and what did they mean by εἰ πατάξομεν ἐν μαχαίρῃ 'if we will strike with sword?'

The eleven asked this question [NTC, TNTC]. The question could have been asked by more than one disciple, or possibly one disciple was the spokesman for the group [Arn]. The question was asked by one of the two disciples who were carrying the swords (22:8) [AB, Gdt, NAC]. The 'we' did not include Jesus in the question and refers only to the disciples [TG]. The singular noun 'sword' is used in a collective sense and since they had two swords, it means 'with our swords' [TH; GW]. They had leaped to the conclusion that they should use what swords they had [TNTC]. Probably their intention was to drive away the crowd rather than to kill them [TG, TH]. The question begins with εἰ 'if', but this use originates from the Septuagint and is not translated [AB]. This type of construction with 'if' is used by Luke two times in the Gospels and five times in Acts [BECNT]. The εἰ 'if' implies an ellipsis: 'tell us whether we should strike with a sword?' [Arn, BECNT, Rb]. The εἰ 'if' may simply be an interrogative particle [Lns]. It indicates that they expected a positive reply [BECNT, NIGTC] and they were not asking for permission [NIGTC]. One individual did not wait for an answer [Arn, EGT, ICC, Lns, NIC, NTC, TNTC; NET]. Or, the question was rhetorical since they didn't wait for an answer [NAC, WBC].

QUESTION—Did the disciple aim at the slave's right ear and who was the slave?

In John 18:20 we learn that 'one of them' in the next verse was Peter and the verse shows that Peter did not wait for a reply [Arn, EGT, ICC, Lns, NIC, NIGTC, NTC, TNTC]. Peter slashed at the first man in front of him [Lns]. He probably meant to severely wound or kill the man, but he only succeeded in cutting off his ear, perhaps because the man ducked when he saw the sword coming [NTC, TG]. He probably aimed at the slave's head [Arn, ICC, Lns], but when the slave dodged, only his right ear was severed [Lns]. The definite article, τὸν δοῦλον '*the* slave' puts the slave in a class by himself [Lns]. He belonged to the high priest and probably was a trusted member of the priest's household who had been sent by the priest as his personal representative and because of this he was in the front of the crowd [Lns, NICNT, WBC].

22:51 And answering Jesus said, Stop[a] more of-this! And touching[b] the ear he-healed him.

TEXT—Instead of τοῦ ὠτίου 'the ear', some manuscripts read τοῦ ὠτίου αὐτοῦ 'his ear', although GNT does not mention this reading. Τοῦ ὠτίου αὐτοῦ 'his ear' is read by KJV. 'His ear' in other translations is probably stylistic rather than textually-based.

LEXICON—a. pres. act. impera. of ἐάω (LN **68.35**) (BAGD 2. p. 212): 'to stop' [BAGD, LN], 'to quit, to cease' [LN]. The idiom ἐάω ἕως, is literally 'to leave off until' and means to cease from what one is doing and indicates strong emotion [LN]. The command Ἐᾶτε ἕως τούτου 'Stop more of this' is translated 'Stop! No more of this' [NASB, NCV], 'Stop! No more of that!' [REB], 'Stop! That's enough of this' [GW], 'No more of this!' [BAGD, BECNT, NTC; HCSB, NIV, NRSV], 'Enough of this!' [NET, TEV], 'Enough of that!' [CEV], 'Stop this' [**LN**], 'Suffer ye thus far' [KJV], 'Don't resist anymore' [NLT], 'Allow even this!' [WBC], 'Permit this far!' [Lns], 'Let them be, even this far!' [AB], 'Let them proceed! No more of this!' [Arn].

b. aorist mid. participle of ἅπτομαι, ἅπτω (LN 24.73) (BAGD 2.b. p. 103): 'to touch' [BAGD, LN]. The clause 'touching the ear he healed him' is translated 'touching the ear, he healed it' [Lns, WBC; similarly AB, Arn], 'touching his ear he healed him' [BECNT; HCSB], 'he touched his ear and healed him' [KJV, NASB, NRSV], 'he touched the man's ear and healed him' [NTC; NET, NIV, REB, TEV], 'he touched the servant's ear and healed him' [GW, NCV], 'he touched the servant's ear and healed it' [CEV], 'he touched the place where the man's ear had been and healed him' [NLT].

QUESTION—Was Jesus answering the disciples' question in 22:49, 'Lord if we will strike with sword'?

Jesus was speaking to his disciples but his 'answer' was responding to the situation [NIGTC]. 'Answering' does not refer to the question they asked in 22:49, rather it is used in response to the crucial situation brought about by Peter's action of cutting off the servant's ear [Lns].

QUESTION—What is meant by Jesus' command Ἐᾶτε ἕως τούτου 'Stop more of this!'

1. It is a command to the disciples: 'Stop, no more of this!' [BAGD, BNTC, EGT, MGC, NAC, NTC, Su, TG, TH]. Jesus wanted no more violence done by his disciples [TH]. Probably others of the disciples were getting ready to fight [TG]. It could mean simply 'Stop!' [NTC].

2. It is a command to the disciples: 'Stop, don't resist, let them do this' [Arn, BECNT, ICC, NIGTC, Rb, TNTC]. The disciples were to stop their resistance and let the police take him prisoner [Arn].

3. It is a command to the disciples: 'Stop, don't resist, let the events take their course' [AB, Crd, NIC, WBC]. 'This' refers to the arrest and he was telling them to let the events take their course, even to Jesus being arrested [AB, Crd]. 'This' refers to the whole disaster coming to Jesus' ministry

beginning with his arrest, and there is an implication that the whole development was to be accepted as God's will [WBC].
4. It is a command to the hostile crowd: 'Stop, permit me to do this' [Alf, Lns]. The crowd was about to take hold of Jesus, when Jesus asked permission to touch and heal the slave's ear and he then did so at once [Lns].

QUESTION—Where was the ear that Jesus touched?
Jesus may have picked up the ear and reattached it, or perhaps he simply touched the wound to restore the ear [BECNT].
1. Jesus touched the place where the ear had been [ICC, TG; NLT].
2. Jesus touched the ear that had been severed [Arn, ICC, Lns]. This was a complete restoration of the ear that had been cut off [ICC]. The ear was probably hanging by a shred of skin so that Jesus touched that ear to restore it perfectly [Arn, Lns].

22:52 And Jesus said to-the (ones who) had-come against[a] him, (the) chief-priests and officers[b] of-the temple and (the) elders, Have-you-come-out with swords and clubs[c] as against a-robber?[d]

LEXICON—a. ἐπί (LN 90.34): 'against' [LN]. The phrase 'who had come against him' [Arn, Lns; NASB] is also translated 'who had come out against him' [BECNT, NTC], 'who had come for him' [GW, HCSB, NIV, NRSV], 'who had come upon him' [WBC], 'who had come out to get him' [NET], 'who had come there to get him' [TEV], 'who had come to arrest him' [CEV], 'who came to arrest Jesus' [NCV], 'who had come to seize him' [REB], 'which were come to him' [KJV], 'who headed the mob' [NLT].

b. στρατηγός (LN 37.91) (BAGD 2. p. 770). 'official, commander' [LN], 'captain' [BAGD]. The phrase στρατηγὸς τοῦ ἱεροῦ 'officers of the temple' [NASB] is also translated 'Temple officers' [AB, BECNT, WBC], 'officers of the temple guard' [Arn; NET, NIV, TEV], 'officers of the temple police' [NRSV], 'commanders of the Temple' [Lns], 'commanders of the Temple guard' [LN], 'captains of the temple' [BAGD; KJV], 'captains of the temple guard' [NTC; NLT], 'soldiers who guarded the Temple' [NCV], 'temple police' [CEV, HCSB], 'temple guards' [GW, REB].

c. ξύλον (LN 6.31) (BAGD 2.b. p. 549): 'club' [BAGD, BECNT, LN, Lns, NTC, WBC; all versions except KJV, REB], 'cudgel' [BAGD; REB], 'stave' [Arn; KJV].

d. λῃστής (LN 39.37, 57.240) (BAGD 2. p. 473): 'robber' [Arn, BAGD, BECNT, LN (57.240), Lns, NTC, WBC; NASB, REB], 'highwayman' [BAGD], 'bandit' [BAGD; NRSV], 'thief' [KJV], 'outlaw' [NET, TEV], 'rebel' [LN (39.37)], 'criminal' [CEV, GW, HCSB, NCV], 'dangerous criminal' [NLT]. The clause 'as against a thief' is translated 'Am I leading a rebellion (that you come)' [NIV].

QUESTION—What was the function of Jesus' question to the crowd?

Jesus rebuked the crowd and also expressed his shock that they were arresting him as if he were violent criminal [BECNT, NIGTC]. Jesus was rebuking them by pointing out how cowardly they were behaving in coming out against such a peaceful prophet [NTC]. He wanted them to consider how ridiculous their act was [Lns].

QUESTION—What kind of a criminal is a ξύλον?

This is a robber who would waylay travelers in a country area [WBC]. A robber was the type of criminal from whom the most violent resistance could be expected and would call for such a crowd with weapons [Lns]. It can mean a highwayman, an insurrectionist, rebel, or revolutionary [NTC].

22:53 (While) I was daily with you in the temple you-did- not –stretch-out[a] (your) hands on me. But this is your hour[b] and the power[c] of-darkness.

LEXICON—a. aorist act. indic. of ἐκτείνω (LN **37.110**) (BAGD 1. p. 245): 'to lay a hand on someone' [BAGD]. The phrase ἐκτείνω τὰς χεῖρας ἐπί 'to stretch out hands on' is an idiom for taking a person into custody for an alleged illegal activity, and means 'to seize, to arrest' [LN]. The phrase οὐκ ἐξετείνατε τὰς χεῖρας ἐπ' ἐμέ 'you did not stretch out your hands on me' is translated 'you did not stretch out your hands against me' [Arn, Lns, WBC], 'you stretched forth no hands against me' [KJV], 'you did not lay hands on me' [BECNT, NTC; NASB, NRSV], 'you did not raise a hand against me' [REB], 'you did not lay a hand on me' [AB], 'you never laid a hand on me' [HCSB], 'you did not arrest me' [**LN**; CEV, NET], 'you didn't arrest me there' [NCV], 'you did not try to arrest me' [GW, TEV], 'why didn't you arrest me' [NLT].

b. ὥρα (LN 67.1) (BAGD 3. p. 896): 'hour, time' [BAGD, LN], 'occasion' [LN]. The clause αὕτη ἐστὶν ὑμῶν ἡ ὥρα 'this is your hour' [AB, Arn, BECNT, Lns, NTC, WBC; HCSB, KJV, NET, NRSV, REB] is also translated 'this is your time' [CEV, GW, NCV], 'this is your moment' [NLT], 'this is your hour to act' [TEV], 'this hour (and the power of darkness) are yours' [NASB].

c. ἐξουσία (LN 76.12) (BAGD 4.b. p. 278): 'power' [LN], 'domain' [BAGD]. The phrase καὶ ἡ ἐξουσία τοῦ σκότους 'and the power of darkness' [AB, BECNT; KJV, NRSV] is also translated 'and the rule of darkness' [NTC], 'and the dominion of darkness' [HCSB], 'and that of the power of darkness' [NET], 'and the authority of the darkness' [Lns], 'and the time for the power of darkness' [WBC], 'when darkness rules' [GW], '—when darkness reigns' [NIV, REB], '—the time when darkness rules' [NCV], 'when the power of darkness rules' [TEV], 'the time when the power of darkness reigns' [NLT], '(this hour) and the power of darkness are yours' [NASB], 'and the authority that is in control is that of darkness' [Arn] 'and darkness is in control' [CEV].

QUESTION—In what way had Jesus been with these people?
> They had all been present in the temple courts but this does not imply that they actually had personal contact with Jesus [NIGTC, TH].

QUESTION—What is the point of reminding them that while Jesus was in the temple where they were, they did not arrest Jesus?
> If Jesus had been guilty of committing any crimes, the temple police could have easily arrested him there any day [Lns, NTC]. The arrest could have been accomplished peaceably in public, so they didn't have to do this under cover of night [BECNT, NIGTC]. It amounted to saying that it was from cowardice that they hadn't arrested him while he was in the temple courts [Gdt, NAC]. It implies that there is something underhanded in this nighttime arrest away from the temple [TNTC].

QUESTION—What is meant by the statement ἀλλ' αὕτη ἐστὶν ὑμῶν ἡ ὥρα 'but this is your hour'?
1. This refers to the hour appointed by God [BECNT, Gdt, ICC, Lns, MGC, My, NAC, NIC, NIGTC, NIVS, NTC, TG, TH]. It is not difficult to explain their outrageous conduct since this hour of their success was allowed by God [ICC]. This was the hour appointed by God for them to arrest Jesus [NIGTC, TG]. It is the hour God appointed for them to do this evil deed [Lns].
2. This refers to the hour of their choice [Crd, Su]. They had chosen this hour instead of one of the daytime hours that Jesus was teaching in the temple [Su]. They had chosen the night hour to cover their deed [Crd].

QUESTION—What is meant by the final phrase καὶ ἡ ἐξουσία τοῦ σκότους 'and the power of darkness'?
> Darkness refers to Satan, the ruler of evil [Arn, ICC, NAC, NICNT, TG, WBC]. Or, darkness characterizes the rule or domain of evil [BECNT]. The expression 'the darkness' almost personifies the darkness as possessing a power as though it were a monster of evil [Lns]. It is the hour in which the power of darkness is revealed and exercises its force [NIGTC]. Darkness and all it symbolizes will hold sway [AB].
1. This hour is theirs and also it is the hour of the power of darkness [Gdt, ICC, Lns, MGC, NIC, TH, TNTC; NET]. Their hour coincides with the hour allowed to the power of darkness [ICC]. This hour is not only the hour of Jesus' human enemies, it is also the hour for the activity of the devil who rules in the darkness [TH]. Their hour is also the hour that the power of darkness operated in and through them [Lns, MGC]. They will succeed in their evil plans because in that hour Satan and his henchmen were being permitted by God to bring the Son of God into humiliation, suffering, and death [NIC]. Nighttime is when Satan puts forth his power over humanity, so it is his hour, and it is their hour because they are Satan's instruments [Gdt].
2. This hour is theirs and it is characterized by being the power of darkness [BNTC, NIBC, Su, WBC; CEV, GW, NASB, NCV, NIV, NLT, REB, TEV]. The crowd has selected the hour of darkness to arrest Jesus and it

was an appropriate time because darkness typified the nature of their act [Su]. The authorities who came to arrest Jesus were acting as representatives of Satan, the ultimate darkness [WBC]. The darkness of that night symbolizes the moral and spiritual darkness of that hour [NIBC].

DISCOURSE UNIT: 11:54–71 [AB, BECNT]. The topic is trials and denials.

DISCOURSE UNIT: 22:54–65 [NICNT; CEV, NASB, NLT]. The topic is Jesus' arrest [NASB], Peter and Jesus at the high priest's mansion [NICNT], Peter denies Jesus [NLT], Peter says he doesn't know Jesus [CEV].

DISCOURSE UNIT: 22:54–62 [NAC, NIGTC; HCSB, NCV, NET, NIV, NRSV, TEV]. The topic is Jesus' condemnation and Peter's denials [NET], Peter denies Jesus [HCSB, NRSV, TEV], Peter's denial of Jesus [NAC, NIGTC], Peter disowns Jesus [NIV], Peter says he doesn't know Jesus [NCV].

22:54a **And seizing**[a] **him they-led- (him) -away and brought (him) into the house of the chief-priest.**
LEXICON—a. aorist act. participle of συλλαμβάνω (LN 37.109) (BAGD 1.a.α. p. 776): 'to seize' [Arn, BAGD, BECNT, LN, Lns, NTC; HCSB, NIV, NRSV], 'to take' [KJV], 'to arrest' [AB, BAGD, LN, WBC; GW, NASB, NCV, NET, NLT, REB, TEV]. This active voice is also translated passively with 'Jesus' as the subject: 'to be arrested' [CEV]. This verb is a technical term for making an arrest [NAC]. The verb does not necessarily imply violence [TNTC].
QUESTION—What was the house of the chief priest?
It was the official residence of the high priest [TH]. It was part of the total temple structure [Su].

DISCOURSE UNIT: 22:54b–23:56a [Su]. The topic is Friday—a day of trial and death.

DISCOURSE UNIT: 22:54b–62 [Su, TNTC, WBC; GW]. The topic is the denials of Peter [Su, TNTC, WBC], Peter denies Jesus [GW].

22:54b **And Peter was-following from-a-distance.**[a] **22:55** **And they-having-kindled**[b] **a-fire in (the) middle**[c] **of-the courtyard and having-sat-down-together Peter was-sitting (in the)-middle**[d] **of-them.**
LEXICON—a. μακρόθεν (LN 83.30) (BAGD p. 488): 'from a distance' [BECNT], 'at a distance' [AB, BAGD, LN, NTC, WBC; all versions except KJV, NCV, NLT], 'at a considerable distance' [Arn], 'afar off' [KJV], 'from afar' [Lns], 'far behind' [NCV, NLT].
  b. aorist act. participle of περιάπτω (LN 14.65) (BAGD p. 645): 'to kindle' [AB, Arn, BAGD, BECNT, LN, NTC; KJV, NASB, NIV, NRSV], 'to light' [**LN**, Lns, WBC; GW, HCSB, NLT, REB, TEV], 'to start' [LN; NCV], 'to ignite' [LN], 'to build' [CEV], 'to make' [NET].
  c. μέσος (LN **83.10**) (BAGD 2. p. 507): 'middle' [BAGD], 'in the middle, in the midst' [LN]. The phrase ἐν μέσῳ 'in the middle' [BECNT, Lns,

NTC, WBC; all versions except KJV, NLT, TEV] is also translated 'in the center' [Arn, **LN**; TEV], 'in the midst' [KJV], 'in (the courtyard)' [NLT], not explicit [AB].

d. μέσος (LN 83.10) (BAGD 2. p. 507): 'middle' [BAGD], 'in the middle' [LN], 'in the midst' [AB, Arn, LN, Lns, NTC, WBC], 'among' [BECNT; GW, HCSB, KJV, NASB, NET, NRSV, REB], 'with' [CEV, NCV, NIV]. The clause 'Peter was sitting in the middle of them' is translated 'Peter joined them there' [NLT], 'Peter joined those sitting around it' [TEV]. It does not mean that Peter was in the exact center of the group, rather it has the more general meaning of 'among' [TG].

QUESTION—What distance did Peter keep as he followed?

He was outside the light of the torches so that he remained unnoticed [TH]. He was far enough away so that he wouldn't be arrested [TG]. The imperfect tense of the verb 'was following' is either conative or iterative and indicates that Peter was trying to keep close to Jesus [NIGTC].

QUESTION—Where was the courtyard and why was there a fire in it?

An arched passage of a gateway led into an open courtyard surrounded by rooms and perhaps the room where Jesus was brought was a kind of gallery with a view of the courtyard [NTC]. The courtyard of the house of the chief priest was a wall-enclosed area. The fire was in the middle of the outer part of the courtyard, while the Sanhedrin and Jesus were in the inner court, which was separated from the outer court by a wall about chest high [Su]. The pronoun 'they' which is the subject of the verb 'having kindled' might have been the household servants [Rb, TG], or the temple police who had arrested Jesus (22:54) [Su, TH]. A fire was needed because the nights were cold [BECNT, ICC, Lns] and the people would sit around it to keep warm [Lns]. The fire would have been made of charcoal so that there wouldn't be any smoke [Lns]. The fire would be large enough for people to sit all around it [NIGTC].

22:56 And seeing him sitting at the light/fire[a] and looking-intently-at[b] him a-certain servant-girl[c] said, Also[d] this (one) was with him. **22:57** But he-denied (it) saying, I-do- not -know[e] him, woman.

TEXT—In 22:57, following ἠρνήσατο 'denied', some manuscripts add αὐτόν 'him'. GNT does not mention this variant. Αὐτόν 'him' is added by KJV.

LEXICON—a. φῶς (LN 2.5, 14.36) (BAGD 1.b.α. p. 872): 'light' (LN 14.36), 'fire' (BAGD; LN 2.5), 'bonfire' [LN (2.5)]. The phrase καθήμενον πρὸς τὸ φῶς 'sitting at the light/fire' is translated 'sitting in the light' [Arn], 'sitting before the light' [BECNT, Lns], 'sitting in the firelight' [HCSB, NASB, NCV, NET, NIV, REB], 'as he sat in the light of the fire' [NTC], 'in the firelight' [NLT, NRSV], 'he sat facing the glow of the fire' [GW], 'sitting at the fire' [AB, WBC; TEV], 'he sat by the fire' [KJV], not explicit [CEV].

b. aorist act. participle of ἀτενίζω (LN 24.49) (BAGD p. 119): 'to look intently at' [BAGD, NTC; NASB], 'to look straight at' [LN; TEV], 'to keep one's eyes fixed on.' [LN], 'to stare at' [AB, LN, WBC; GW, NET, NLT, NRSV, REB], 'to look closely at' [Arn; HCSB, NCV, NIV], 'to look at carefully' [CEV], 'to earnestly look upon' [KJV], 'to gaze at' [BECNT], 'to gaze intently on' [Lns]. The preceding verb ἰδοῦσα 'seeing' refers to her first sight of Peter and this verb 'looking intently at' refers to a further and more intense observation [TH]. After getting a glimpse of Peter, she looked more closely to be sure of the facts before accusing him [NIGTC]. Her gaze also drew the attention of the men to Peter [Lns].

c. παιδίσκη (LN 87.83) (BAGD p. 604): 'servant girl' [AB, BAGD, BECNT, WBC; CEV, NASB, NCV, NIV, NLT, NRSV], 'serving maid' [REB], 'maid' [Arn, BAGD, Lns; KJV], 'female servant' [GW], 'servant...she (said)' [HCSB], 'female slave' [BAGD], 'slave girl' [LN; NET], 'slave woman' [LN; TEV].

d. καί (LM 89.93): 'also' [BECNT, LN, Lns, NTC; KJV, NCV, NRSV], 'too' [AB, Arn; HCSB, NASB, REB, TEV], 'surely' [WBC], not explicit [CEV, NIV, NLT].

e. perf. act. indic. of οἶδα (LN 28.1) (BAGD 2. p. 556): 'to know' [AB, Arn, BECNT, LN, Lns, NTC, WBC; all versions], 'to be acquainted with' [BAGD, LN]. Peter said that he had no knowledge of Jesus [BECNT]. This rules out any association with Jesus [TH]. Peter could have known Jesus without being a disciple, but he was saying that he did not even know him [EGT]. The word 'even' is added by some [CEV, NLT, TEV].

QUESTION—What is meant by πρὸς τὸ φῶς 'in the firelight' or 'near the fire'?

1. Peter was sitting in the light from the fire [Arn, BECNT, Lns, NTC, Rb, Su, TG, TH; all versions except CEV, KJV, TEV].
2. Peter was sitting by the fire [AB; KJV, TEV].

QUESTION—What is known about the servant girl?

This woman was the doorkeeper at the courtyard entrance (John 18:16–17) [Arn, BECNT, ICC, Lns, TNTC]. She left her station at the entry of the courtyard when she saw Peter in the firelight and looked intently at him to make sure he was the one whom she had let in at John's request [Lns, NTC].

QUESTION—Who else is referred to by καί 'also' in the woman's accusation?

1. The word καί means 'also' and indicates that the servant girl knew another person who was a follower of Jesus [AB, Arn, BECNT, ICC, Lns, NTC; HCSB, KJV, NASB, NCV, NRSV, REB, TEV]. Probably this refers to John who was also present and known to the household [BECNT, ICC, Lns]. The 'word also' implies that she knows that Jesus usually had a group of people with him [TG].
2. The word καί functions as a sentence adverb and means 'surely' instead of 'also' [WBC].

QUESTION—Whom did the servant girl address and who is the referent of the pronoun αὐτῷ 'him'?

The servant girl addressed those sitting by the fire [EGT, TG]. Her reference to 'him' was the person whom the people were all talking about [EGT].

22:58 And after a-short (while) another (one) seeing him said, You also are (one) of[a] them. And Peter said, Man, I-am not.

LEXICON—a. ἐκ (LN 63.20) (BAGD 4.a.δ. p. 236): 'one of, one among, a part of' [LN], 'belong to' [BAGD]. The clause Καὶ σὺ ἐξ αὐτῶν εἶ 'You also are one of them' [BECNT; NCV, NIV, NRSV, REB] is also translated 'You are one of them too' [Arn, Lns, NTC; HCSB, NASB, NET, TEV], 'You are one of them!' [CEV, GW], 'Thou art also of them.' [KJV], 'You too/also belong to them' [Arn, BAGD], 'Surely you are one of them!' [WBC], 'You must be one of them!' [NLT]. Being 'one of them' means being one of the disciples of Jesus [BECNT, NAC, NIC, NIGTC, TG, TH]. Or, it means 'one of those who were on the Mount of Olives with Jesus' [AB].

QUESTION—What is known about the man who spoke to Jesus?

In Mark 14:69 it says that the same servant girl again addressed Peter. In John 18:25 it says that 'they' spoke to Peter. However here in Luke, the word ἕτερος 'another' has the masculine form and Peter addresses him as 'man' [TG]. This 'different one, a man' was probably a servant [Su]. Or, 'another' does not mean that he was a slave like the servant girl, only that he was a different person [TH]. We can reconcile the statements if we understand that several persons were joining in when one stopped speaking [Rb]. Perhaps the woman gatekeeper did not address Peter himself but told the others who were present about him and one of the group spoke to Peter [NIC]. Her comments led others to take up her accusation [NIGTC]. Luke records the words of at least one male bystander who joined in with what the girl said [BECNT, Gdt, Lns, NTC]. The woman's words were substantiated by the man's assertion [Arn]. Some people were talking *to* Peter, and others were talking *about* him [NTC].

22:59 And (after) about one hour had-passed, a-certain other (man) insisted,[a] saying, In truth[b] this (one) also was with him, because he-is a-Galilean also. **22:60** And Peter said, Man, I-do- not -know[c] what you-are-saying. And immediately (while) he was- yet -speaking a-rooster crowed.

TEXT—In 22:60, instead of ἀλέκτωρ '(a) rooster', some manuscripts read ὁ ἀλέκτωρ 'the rooster', although GNT does not mention this variant. Ὁ ἀλέκτωρ 'the rooster' is translated by KJV, NIV, NLT, NRSV, although except for KJV, the readings are probably stylistic rather than textually-based.

LEXICON—a. imperf. mid./pass. (deponent = act.) indic. of διϊσχυρίζομαι (LN **33.321**) (BAGD p. 195): 'to insist' [AB, BAGD, BECNT, **LN**; CEV, GW, NCV, NET, NLT], 'to insist strongly' [TEV], 'to keep insisting' [HCSB, NRSV], 'to keep up the insistence' [WBC], 'to begin to insist'

[NASB], 'to begin to insist emphatically' [NTC], 'to strongly affirm' [Arn], 'to begin to affirm positively' [Lns], 'to maintain firmly' [BAGD], 'to confidently affirm' [KJV], 'to assert' [NIV], 'to speak more strongly still' [REB]. The imperfect tense indicates that this accuser continued what others had begun [WBC]. It indicates that the man kept on saying this to others [TG].

b. ἀλήθεια (LN 70.4) (BAGD3. p. 36): 'truth' [BAGD, LN]. The phrase κατ' ἀλήθειαν 'in truth' is an idiom meaning: 'actually, really' [LN] and it is translated 'in truth' [WBC], 'of a truth' [Lns; KJV], 'it is true' [Arn], 'truly' [BECNT], 'certainly' [NTC; HCSB, NASB, NCV, NET, NIV], 'surely' [NRSV], 'of course' [REB], 'I assure you' [AB], 'it is obvious that' [GW], 'there isn't any doubt that' [TEV], 'this must be' [NLT], '(this man) must (have been with Jesus)' [CEV]. This means that there could be no mistake about it [Su]. It contradicts the several denials made by Peter [Lns].

c. perf. act. indic. of οἶδα (LN 28.1) (BAGD 4. p. 556): 'to know' [BAGD, LN]. The clause 'Man, I do not know what you are saying' [BECNT, WBC] is also translated 'Man, I do not know what you're talking about!' [NTC; all versions except CEV, GW, KJV], 'Sir, I do not know what you are talking about!' [AB], 'I do not know what you are talking about!' [Arn; CEV, GW], 'I know not what thou sayest' [Lns; KJV].

QUESTION—How did the man know that Peter was a Galilean and how does that fact prove that Peter was with Jesus?

Galileans had a distinctive Aramaic brogue [Lns, NTC], so the man knew because of Peter's dialect [AB, Arn, BECNT, EGT, ICC, MGC, NAC, NIC, NICNT, NIVS, NTC, Su, TG, TH, TNTC, WBC; NET]. Possibly some detail of his clothing indicated this [BECNT, NICNT, WBC]. It was well known that Jesus' followers were mainly Galileans and it was improbable that there would be another Galilean among the soldiers in the courtyard that night [NIC]. A Galilean would not be present at this fire unless he was a disciple [BECNT]. Being with Jesus refers to being with him in Gethsemane [Lns].

QUESTION—What is the significance of saying 'I do not know what you are saying'?

This is a way of denying what someone else has said [TG]. It means that it is not true what the person had said [TH]. He denies a link to the disciples, but his accent prevented him from denying that he was a Galilean [BECNT]. Peter was denying that the fact that being a Galilean meant that he was a disciple of Jesus [NET]. It means something like 'I can't imagine why you are saying this' [WBC]. Or, this was an evasion rather than a direct denial [EGT].

22:61 And turning the Lord looked-at[a] Peter, and Peter was-reminded[b] of the word of-the Lord when he-said to-him, Before a-rooster crows today

you-will-deny me three (times). 22:62 **And having-gone outside he-wept bitterly.**ᶜ

TEXT—In 22:61, some manuscripts omit σήμερον 'today'. GNT does not mention this variant. Σήμερον 'today' is omitted by KJV.

TEXT—In 22:62, instead of ἔκλαυσεν 'he wept', some manuscripts read ὁ Πέτρος ἔκλαυσεν 'Peter wept' and some manuscripts omit this entire verse. GNT includes this verse (without the addition of ὁ Πέτρος 'Peter') with an A decision, indicating that the text is certain. Ὁ Πέτρος ἔκλαυσεν 'Peter wept' is read by KJV.

LEXICON—a. aorist act. indic. of ἐμβλέπω (LN **24.9**) (BAGD 1. p. 254): 'to look at' [AB, Arn, BAGD, BECNT, Lns; CEV, HCSB, NASB, NLT, NRSV, REB], 'to look straight at' [**LN**, NTC; NCV, NET, NIV, TEV], 'to look directly at' [LN; GW], 'to look intently at' [WBC], 'to look upon' [KJV]. The verb signifies a reproachful look [NIGTC].

b. aorist pass. indic. of ὑπομιμνῄσκω (LN 29.10) (BAGD 2. p. 846): 'to be reminded' [LN]. The phrase ὑπεμνήσθη τοῦ ῥήματος τοῦ κυρίου 'was reminded of the word of the Lord' [NTC] is also translated 'was reminded of the utterance of the Lord' [Lns], 'remembered the word of the Lord' [Arn, BECNT, WBC; HCSB, KJV, NASB, NET, NRSV], 'remembered the Lord's words' [REB], 'remembered the Lord's saying' [AB], 'remembered what the Lord had said' [GW, NCV], 'remembered the word the Lord had spoken to him' [NIV], 'remembered that the Lord had said to him...' [TEV], 'remembered that the Lord had said...' [CEV, NLT]. The passive form should be kept since it was Jesus' look that reminded Peter, and so 'he was reminded' is better than 'he remembered' [Lns]. The look awakened Peter's memory of Jesus' prophecy [TNTC].

c. πικρῶς (LN 25.284) (BAGD p. 657): 'bitterly' [BAGD, LN], 'with agony' [LN]. The clause 'wept bitterly' [AB, Arn, NTC, WBC; HCSB, KJV, NASB, NET, NIV, NRSV, REB, TEV] is also translated 'cried bitterly' [GW], 'crying bitterly' [BECNT; NLT], 'sobbed bitterly' [Lns], 'cried hard' [CEV], 'cried painfully' [NCV].

QUESTION—Where was Jesus that he could look at Peter?

Jesus must have been somewhere in the courtyard [AB]. Perhaps he was being guarded in the courtyard [BECNT, MGC, NIGTC]. Perhaps Jesus was passing through the courtyard as he was being taken to or from the trial with Caiaphas [ICC, MGC, NIGTC, NIVS, TNTC]. Perhaps the night trial had ended and the temple police were leading Jesus through the courtyard to a prison cell [Lns, NTC, Su]. Or, perhaps Jesus was in a gallery that looked down on the courtyard, or in a room looking out onto the courtyard [BECNT, BNTC, TG, TNTC].

QUESTION—What is meant by 'he wept bitterly'?

The ingressive aorist form of ἔκλαυσεν indicates that he burst into tears [Rb]. The verb means to sob with disappointment [Su]. The adverb 'bitterly' does not refer to the way in which Peter wept, it indicates the deep anguish and sorrow which caused him to weep [TH]. The verb refers to loud weeping and the adverb refers not to the sobbing, but to the bitterness of his contrition as he realized that he had sinned and now felt genuine sorrow because of that [Lns]. Bitterness refers to his humility and grief over his betrayal [Su]. He was remembering his brash confidence and Jesus' prediction in 22:33–34 [WBC]. Peter realized that Jesus knew of his denials and also he saw that Jesus was facing trial with no one to stand with him [BECNT]. This describes not only Peter's remorse, but it was a time of his turning back to the Lord [Alf, BNTC, NAC].

DISCOURSE UNIT: 22:63–71 [GW]. The topic is the trial in front of the Jewish council.

DISCOURSE UNIT: 22:63–65 [NAC, NIGTC, Su, TNTC, WBC; HCSB, NCV, NIV, NRSV, TEV]. The topic is the preliminary hearing before Caiaphas [Su], the mocking of Jesus [NAC, NIGTC, TNTC, WBC], the soldiers mock Jesus [NIV], Jesus is mocked and beaten [HCSB, NRSV, TEV], the people make fun of Jesus [NCV].

22:63 And the men (who) were-guarding^a him were-mocking^b him (and) beating (him),

TEXT—Instead of αὐτόν 'him', some manuscripts read τὸν Ἰησοῦν 'Jesus', although GNT does not mention this variant. Τὸν Ἰησοῦν 'Jesus' is read by KJV.

LEXICON—a. pres. act. participle of συνέχω (LN **37.122**) (BAGD 4. p. 789): 'to guard' [**LN**; CEV, GW, NCV, NIV, REB, TEV], 'to have in charge' [Lns], 'to hold in custody' [AB, BAGD, NTC, WBC; NASB], 'to hold under guard' [NET], 'to hold' [Arn, BECNT; HCSB, KJV, NRSV]. The phrase 'the men who were guarding him' is translated 'the guards in charge of Jesus' [NLT].

b. imperf. act. indic. of ἐμπαίζω (LN 33.406) (BAGD 1. p. 255): 'to mock' [Arn, BAGD, BECNT, LN, Lns, NTC, WBC; HCSB, KJV, NASB, NET, NIV, NLT, NRSV, REB], 'to ridicule' [AB, BAGD, LN], 'to make fun of' [BAGD; CEV, GW, NCV, TEV]. This verb means to make fun of someone by pretending that he is not what he is or by imitating him in a distorted manner [LN]. The imperfect tense of ἐνέπαιζον means that they *began* to mock him [AB, BECNT, NTC, Rb, WBC; HCSB, NCV, NET, NIV, NLT, NRSV]. See this word at 14:29; 18:32; 23:11, 36.

QUESTION—Who were the men who mistreated Jesus?

The men were the temple guards of 22:5 [BECNT, ICC, NAC, NIGTC, TG, TNTC, WBC]. Or, the men who had Jesus in their charge refers to the men of the Sanhedrin, and the temple police were only their minions [Lns, NICNT]. The antecedent to 'the men who were guarding Jesus' is found in 22:52 where it refers to the chief priests, the officers of the temple police, and the elders [NICNT]. Even if the underlings carried out the action, they did so with the permission and cooperation of the Sanhedrin [NTC].

LUKE 22:63 469

QUESTION—How did they mock Jesus?
They scoffed at him for the claims he had made and the things he had done to bring about this sad state of affairs [Su]. One specific way in which they mocked Jesus and beat him is described in the next verse [TH].

QUESTION—How did they beat Jesus?
They beat him by buffeting him with their palms and fists [Su, TG]. Or, this refers to striking him over his whole body [EGT]. They caused bruises and breaks in the skin [Lns]. It does not mean that they used clubs [Su]. The beating is how they mocked him [Lns]. Or, the beating was done in addition to the mocking [Su, TH]. The physical violence was in addition to the verbal mocking [Su].

22:64 and having-blindfolded him they-were-asking (him) saying, Prophesy,[a] who is the (one who) hit you? **22:65** And many other (things) they-were-saying against him, reviling/blaspheming.[b]

TEXT—In 22:64, instead of ἐπηρώτων 'they were asking', some manuscripts read ἔτυπτον αὐτοῦ τὸ πρόσωπον, καὶ ἐπηρώτων αὐτόν 'they were beating his face, and they were asking him'. GNT does not mention this variant. Ἔτυπτον αὐτοῦ τὸ πρόσωπον, καὶ ἐπηρώτων αὐτόν 'they were beating his face, and they were asking him' is read by KJV.

LEXICON—a. aorist act. impera. of προφητεύω (LN **33.459**) (BAGD 2. p. 723): 'to prophesy' [AB, Arn, BAGD, BECNT, **LN**, Lns, NTC, WBC; HCSB, KJV, NASB, NET, NIV, NRSV], 'to tell' [CEV, GW], 'to guess' [TEV]. This verb is translated as a clause: 'prove that you are a prophet, and tell us' [NCV], 'who hit you that time, you prophet?' [NLT], 'if you are a prophet, tell us who hit you' [REB]. The verb means to prophetically reveal what is hidden [BAGD], or to speak under the influence of divine inspiration, with or without reference to future events [LN].

b. pres. act. participle of βλασφημέω (LN 33.400) (BAGD 2.b.δ. p. 142): 'to revile' [LN; NET], 'to defame' [LN], 'to insult' [CEV, GW], 'to blaspheme' [BAGD, LN, Lns; HCSB, NASB], 'to utter blasphemies' [Arn], 'to blasphemously (speak against)' [KJV]. The clause 'many other things they were saying against him reviling/blaspheming' is translated 'they said many cruel things to Jesus' [NCV], 'they said many other insulting things to him' [NTC; NIV, TEV], 'they kept leveling many other insults at him' [AB], 'they threw all sorts of terrible insults at him' [NLT], 'they kept heaping many other insults on him' [NRSV], 'many other blasphemous things they were saying to him' [BECNT], 'they also said many other things to him of a blasphemous nature' [WBC]. The verb means to speak against a person or against God in such a way as to harm or injure his reputation [LN]. In relation to men the verb means to revile, to defame, or to injure the reputation of a person, and in relation to God or Christ it means to blaspheme [BAGD, NTC].

470   LUKE 22:64–65

QUESTION—What did they mean by telling Jesus to prophesy?
Since many people regarded Jesus to be a prophet, these men challenged Jesus to prove his prophetic gifts [Su, TNTC]. The guards told Jesus to use his gift of clairvoyance as a prophet [NIGTC]. In irony they were telling him to play the part of a prophet to tell them who was hitting him [TH]. In this instance 'prophesy' has the specific meaning of telling the identity of the person who struck him without being able to see him [TG].

QESTION—Does the participle βλασφημοῦντες describe reviling a man or blaspheming a divine person?

1. It is applied to a man and means reviling [Su, TG, TH; probably AB, NTC; CEV, GW, NCV, NIV, NRSV, TEV]. They said insulting things about his person or his message [TG].
2. It is used by Luke to mean blaspheming a divine person [NIGTC, NTC, WBC; probably Arn, Lns; HCSB, KJV, NASB]. This is a Christian interpretation of their mockery, seeing it as blasphemy against God and the messengers he had appointed [NIGTC].

DISCOURSE UNIT: 22:66–23:25 [NICNT; NIV]. The topic is the trial of Jesus [NICNT], Jesus before Pilate and Herod [NIV].

DISCOURSE UNIT: 22:66–71 [NAC, NICNT, NIGTC, Su, TNTC, WBC; CEV, HCSB, NASB, NCV, NLT, NRSV, TEV]. The topic is Jesus before the Sanhedrin [NAC, NICNT, NIGTC, Su, TNTC, WBC; NASB], Jesus faces the Sanhedrin [HCSB], Jesus before the council [NLT, NRSV, TEV], Jesus before the leaders [NCV], Jesus is questioned by the Council [CEV].

22:66 And when it-became day,[a] the council-of-(the)-elders[b] of-the people was-assembled, both chief-priests and scribes, and they-led-away[c] him to their council/council-room[d]

LEXICON—a. ἡμέρα (LN 67.178): 'day' [LN]. The phrase 'when it became day' [BECNT, Lns, WBC] is also translated 'when day came' [NCV, NET, NRSV, TEV], 'when day had come' [Arn], 'when it was day' [AB; NASB], 'as soon as it was day' [NTC; KJV, REB], 'when daylight came' [HCSB], 'at daybreak' [CEV, NIV, NLT], 'in the morning' [GW].

b. πρεσβυτέριον (LN 11.83) (BAGD 1. p. 699): 'council of elders' [BAGD], 'Sanhedrin, high council of the Jews' [LN]. The phrase τὸ πρεσβυτέριον τοῦ λαοῦ 'the council of the elders of the people' [NTC; NASB, NET, NIV, NLT] is also translated 'the assembly of the elders of the people' [NRSV], 'the body of elders of the people' [Arn], 'the council of the older leaders of the people' [NCV], 'the eldership of the people' [Lns, WBC], 'the council of the people's leaders' [GW], 'the elders of the people' [AB, BECNT; HCSB, KJV, REB], 'the leaders of the people' [NLT], 'the nation's leaders' [CEV], 'the elders' [TEV]. This was the highest council of the Jews [BAGD, LN] and usually this council was called the 'Sanhedrin' [BAGD].

c. aorist act. indic. of ἀπάγω (LN 15.177): 'to lead away, to lead off, to take away, to take aside' [LN]. The phrase 'assembled...and they led him away to their council chamber' [NASB] is also translated 'convened and brought him before their Sanhedrin' [HCSB], 'assembled and brought him before their council' [Arn], 'assembled, and they brought him back to their Sanhedrin' [NTC], 'gathered together and they led him into their council' [BECNT], 'was gathered together; and they brought him back into their Sanhedrin' [Lns], 'came together, and led him into their council' [KJV], 'came together and led Jesus to their highest court' [NCV], 'gathered together, and they brought him to their council' [NRSV], 'gathered together. They brought Jesus in front of their highest court' [GW]. 'gathered together. Then they led Jesus away to their council' [NET], 'got together and brought Jesus before their council' [CEV]. The verb ἀπήγαγον 'they led away' is indefinite as to who 'they' were [AB], and probably Jesus was led away by the soldiers who had been guarding him (22:63) [AB, BECNT, TG]. In view of the context, this means that they had him brought before their council [TH]. Some translations indicate that the elders did not personally lead Jesus to the council: 'assembled, and Jesus was brought before their Council' [AB], 'was gathered together; and they had Jesus brought into their council meeting' [WBC], 'met together, and Jesus was led before them' [NIV], 'met together, and Jesus was brought before the Council' [TEV], 'assembled, and he was brought before their Council' [REB], 'assembled. Jesus was led before this high council' [NLT].

d. συνέδριον (LN 11.80) (BAGD 2. p. 786): 'council' [AB, Arn, BAGD, BECNT; CEV, KJV, NET, NRSV, REB, TEV], 'high council' [BAGD; NLT], 'council meeting' [WBC], 'Sanhedrin' [BAGD, LN, Lns, NTC; HCSB], 'the council of the Jews' [LN], 'the highest court' [GW, NCV], 'them' [NIV], 'council chamber' [NASB]. This was the highest Jewish council, exercising jurisdiction in civil and religious matters, but having no power over life and death [LN]. The council was composed of high priests, elders, and scribes and met under the presidency of the high priest, but perhaps here the word council refers to the room where the council met [BAGD].

QUESTION—Were there two or three groups assembled?
1. The phrase 'both chief-priests and scribes' describes the two groups that composed the Sanhedrin [AB, BECNT, Lns, NIC, NIGTC, NTC, Rb, TNTC, WBC; HCSB, NASB, NCV, NET, NIV, NRSV]: the Sanhedrin assembled, made up of both chief priests and scribes. Luke appears to indicate that the phrase 'both chief priests and scribes' is in apposition to the 'the elders of the people' and that these two groups comprise the Sanhedrin [AB, MGC, NIGTC]. The elders are omitted from the list of groups even though Luke knew that there were three groups [NIGTC]. The Sanhedrin was composed mainly of these two groups [NAC].

2. The phrase 'both chief-priests and scribes' indicates an addition to the council of elders so that the three groups are specified [Arn, ICC, My, NAC, TH; CEV, GW, KJV, NLT, REB, TEV]: the elders assembled, along with the chief priests and the scribes. The three component parts of the Sanhedrin met so that the whole assembly was there when Jesus was brought to them [ICC]. There were three groups in the Sanhedrin, but the elders are not named along with the chief priests and scribes because the word πρεσβυτέριον 'Sanhedrin, elders' clearly includes the elders [Arn, NAC].

QUESTION—Where was Jesus brought?
1. Jesus was brought before the council, the Sanhedrin [BNTC, ICC, Lns, MGC, TH; CEV, GW, HCSB, KJV, NET, NIV, NLT, NRSV, REB, TEV]. The officials had Jesus brought before the council of which they were members [TH]. Sanhedrin is a name for the high court [Lns].
2. Jesus was brought before the Sanhedrin meeting [Arn, WBC]. This does not mean that Jesus was brought before the Sanhedrin members, but before the Sanhedrin meeting, or possibly the place where the Sanhedrin met. The Sanhedrin met in their regular meeting place and they had Jesus brought to their meeting from the chief priest's house [WBC].
2. Jesus was brought to the council room [EGT, NAC, NICNT, NIGTC; NASB]. Jesus was brought to the council chamber in which the Sanhedrin held its meetings [EGT].

22:67 saying, **If you are the Messiah, tell us. And he-said to-them, If I tell you, by-no-means will-you–believe.** **22:68** **And if I-question (you), by-no-means will-you-answer.**

TEXT—In 22:68, following ἐὰν δέ 'and if', some manuscripts add καί 'also'. GNT does not mention this variant. Καί 'also' is added by KJV.

TEXT—In 22:68, following οὐ μὴ ἀποκριθῆτε 'by no means will you answer', some manuscripts add μοι 'me' and some manuscripts add μοι ἢ ἀπολύσητε 'me or release'. GNT rejects both of these additions with a B decision, indicating that the text is almost certain. Μοι ἢ ἀπολύσητε 'me or release' is read by KJV.

QUESTION—What was behind their demand, 'If you are the Messiah, tell us'?
The word εἰ 'if' is conditional [Alf, Gdt, ICC, My, NIGTC, TH]. Probably the question of Jesus' messiahship had come up in the council [NIGTC]. The council was looking for a statement from Jesus that they could use to charge him with before the Roman court which had the authority to execute him [AB, NIGTC]. The Jews could explain to the Romans that his claim to be the Messiah meant that he was a national deliverer who would lead a revolt against Rome [ICC, MGC, NIC, Su]. They were looking for a way to accuse Jesus before the Romans, not because they really wanted to know themselves [NIC].

QUESTION—Why did Jesus answer 'If I tell you (that I am Messiah), by no means will you believe', instead of simply saying 'Yes'?

Jesus knew that they had already prejudged him and would not believe him if he said he was the Messiah [NIC]. Jesus' view of the role of the Messiah was so different from theirs that a simple 'Yes' would not be adequate [Lns, TNTC]. This reply indicates that it would be useless to give an answer since they had already made up their minds [AB, BECNT, EGT, NAC].

QUESTION—What would Jesus ask them that they would not answer?

Jesus was probably referring to a question like the one he asked in 20:44, 'David calls him Lord, then how is he his son?' [NAC, TH, TNTC]. He might ask them why they have asked him about being the Messiah [NIC, Su]. He might ask them about his qualifications for being the Messiah [TNTC]. This probably means 'If I tell you that I am the Messiah, you will not believe; and if I try to discuss the question, you will refuse to do so' [ICC]. He might ask them about the real nature of the Messiahship [TNTC]. If he showed from Scripture who the Messiah was and then asked them if this was not so, they would refuse to answer [Arn, Lns].

22:69 And from^a now (on) the Son of Man^b will-be sitting at (the) right of the power^c of God.

LEXICON—a. ἀπό (LN 67.131): 'from' [LN]. The phrase ἀπὸ τοῦ νῦν 'from now on' [AB, Arn, BECNT, Lns, NTC, WBC; all versions except KJV, NLT] is also translated 'hereafter' [KJV], 'the time is soon coming when' [NLT].

b. υἱὸς τοῦ ἀνθρώπου 'Son of Man'. This title for Christ occurs at 5:24; 6:5, 22; 7:34; 9:22, 26, 44; 11:30; 12:8, 40; 17:22, 24, 26; 18:8, 31; 19:10; 21:27, 36; 22: 22, 48; 24:7. See the discussions of this title at 5:24, 6:5, and 9:22.

c. δύναμις (LN76.1) (BAGD 1. p. 207): 'power' [LN], 'might, strength, force' [BAGD]. The phrase 'will be sitting at the right of the power of God' [Lns] is also translated 'will be seated at the right hand of the power of God' [AB, BECNT, NTC, WBC; HCSB, NASB, NET; similarly Arn, KJV], 'will sit at the right hand of the powerful God' [NCV], 'will be seated at the right hand of the mighty God' [NIV], 'will be seated at the right hand of Almighty God' [REB], 'will be seated at the right side of Almighty God' [TEV], 'will be seated at the right side of God All-Powerful' [CEV], 'will be sitting at God's right hand in the place of power' [NLT], 'will be in the highest position in heaven' [GW].

QUESTION—What is meant by ἀπὸ τοῦ νῦν 'from now on'?

The change is imminent [TNTC]. This does not mean immediately, but refers to the exaltation of Jesus after his resurrection [Su, TH]. As a result of Jesus' death, he will be exalted to honor and power with God [Arn, Lns, Su]. This means 'in the near future' [TG]. This phrase means from the very time of the fulfillment of their purpose for him [Su]. Or, Jesus' glorification had now begun [ICC]. Jesus had taken up that authority at that very moment

[NET]. From now on Jesus is the Son of man, the Lord, and he will shortly be seated at the Father's side at his ascension [BECNT].

QUESTION—What is meant by τῆς δυνάμεως τοῦ θεοῦ 'the power of God'?

The noun δυνάμεως 'power' functions as an adjective qualifying God [TG; CEV, NCV, NIV, REB, TEV]. This refers to God's majesty and greatness [NTC]. 'Power' was a word the Jews used in place of the word 'God' [BNTC, Crd, NAC, WBC], but here Luke has added 'of God' to explain the word for his Gentile readers [BNTC, Crd, NAC].

22:70 And they- all -said, Then[a] are you the Son of God? And he-said to them, You are-saying[b] that I am.

LEXICON—a. οὖν (LN 89.50) (BAGD 1.c.α. p. 593): 'then' [AB, Arn, BAGD, BECNT, LN, Lns, WBC; all versions except CEV, GW], 'so' [LN, NTC; GW], 'so then, therefore, consequently, accordingly' [LN], not explicit [CEV]. This often implies the conclusion of a process of reasoning [LN].

b. pres. act. indic. of λέγω (LN 33.69): 'to say' [LN]. The clause Ὑμεῖς λέγετε ὅτι ἐγώ εἰμι 'You are saying that I am' is translated 'You say that I am' [BECNT; HCSB, KJV, NASB, NCV, NET, TEV], 'You say I am!' [CEV], 'It is you who say I am' [AB; REB], 'You yourselves are saying that I am' [Lns], 'Do you say that I am?' [WBC], 'You say it, because I am he' [Arn], 'You are right, I am' [NTC], 'You're right to say that I am' [GW], 'You are right in saying that I am' [NIV, NLT], 'Yes I am' [NASB].

QUESTION—What relationship is indicated by οὖν 'then'?

The question is based on what Jesus has just said about being at the right hand of God [BECNT, Lns, TH]. It implies that the meaning of the Son of Man and that of the Son of God were virtually identical [Alf, TH]. Calling himself the 'Son of Man' alludes to Daniel 7:13 and they took it as a claim to divinity [ICC]. Sitting at the right hand of God was a claim to be the Son of God [NIGTC, Su], To make the claim he made in 22:69 could only mean that he claimed to be the Son of God, and the court took it as blasphemy [Su]. This statement does not indicate that they believed this, but it states the implications of what Jesus had said [AB].

QUESTION—What was the significance of the reply Ὑμεῖς λέγετε ὅτι ἐγώ εἰμι 'You are saying that I am'?

1. Jesus clearly affirmed that he was the Son of God [Arn, Gdt, Lns, NICNT, NTC, Rb; GW, NASB, NIV, NLT]. This was a Greek idiom meaning 'I am' [NIC, Rb]. It means 'I am the Son of God exactly as you are saying it in your question' [Lns]. Jesus answered their question in the affirmative [NIC] and it was taken by the Jewish council as an affirmation [Arn, NIC, NTC]. The parallel passage in Mark 14:62 is Ἐγώ εἰμι 'I am.' [NIC].

2. Jesus indirectly implied that he was the Son of God [AB, NAC, NIBC, NIGTC, Su, TNTC; NET]. The answer was not a direct affirmation nor was it a denial, so it apparently was a grudging admission that suggested that Jesus would have put it otherwise and that those who asked the

question did not understand exactly what they were asking [NIGTC]. His reply means that he did not have to say that he was the Son of God since they were saying it and what they said was true [Su]. Jesus' reply indicated that he would not put it like that, but since they have done so, he could not deny it [NTC]. It implies an affirmation, but stresses that it was their way of putting it [AB, NAC; NET], but Jesus did not quite mean what they thought [NET].
   3. Jesus did not commit himself [TG]. He avoided a direct affirmation and his answer means 'You are the ones saying this, not I' [TG].

22:71 **And they-said, Why do-we- still -have-need of-testimony?**[a] **Because (we) ourselves have-heard (it) from his mouth.**

LEXICON—a. μαρτυρία (LN 33.262, 33.264) (BAGD 2.a. p. 493): 'testimony' [BAGD, LN (33.264)], 'witness' [LN (33.262)]. The clause 'Why do we still have need of testimony?' [WBC] is also translated 'What further need do we have for/of testimony?' [AB, BECNT, NTC; NASB], 'What further testimony do we need?' [NRSV], 'Why do we need further testimony?' [NET], 'Why do we need any more testimony?' [GW, HCSB, NIV], 'Why do we still have need of witness?' [Arn], 'What need do we have for other witnesses?' [NLT], 'Why do we need more witnesses?' [CEV], 'What need we any further witness?' [KJV], 'Why have we yet need of witness?' [Lns], 'Why do we need witnesses now?' [NCV], 'We don't need any witnesses!' [TEV], 'what further need do we have for testimony?' [BECNT], 'What further evidence do we need?' [REB].

QUESTION—What do they no longer have need for?
   1. They do not now have need for any testimony of a witness [AB, Arn, BECNT, Lns, NICNT, NIGTC, NTC, Su, TG, TH, WBC; all versions except REB]. The noun 'testimony' concerns what is said by witnesses in court, or testimony given in court [TH]. They don't need any people to accuse Jesus of wrongdoing [TG]. Jesus' answer was understood to be an affirmation and a claim to be the Messiah, the Son of God [NAC], so Jesus' testimony against himself is enough and no further testimony is needed [BECNT, NAC]. This statement is odd in that Luke has not referred to the witnesses who actually gave testimony as mentioned in Mark 14:55–56 [NIGTC]. At this hearing, Jesus was the only person to give testimony and that had been enough [NICNT]. In Luke, no witnesses have given their testimony and now they have no further need of testimony [AB]. Because of Jesus' affirmation that he was the Son of God, they need no further testimony and could dispense with calling in witnesses to give testimony [Arn, Lns]. The rhetorical question implies that the answer is that no more testimony is needed because Jesus has condemned himself [BECNT].
   2. They do not need anymore evidence [NIGTC; REB]. There is no mention of witnesses in the account, so this means that they do not need any further evidence [NIGTC].

QUESTION—What relationship is indicated by γάρ 'because'?
This shows that Jesus' answer in 22:70 was taken as affirmative and it explains why no further evidence was need to condemn him [MGC, NIGTC, TG]. They now had enough evidence to accuse Jesus before Pilate [NIC].

DISCOURSE UNIT: 23:1–25 [NLT]. The topic is Jesus' trial before Pilate.

DISCOURSE UNIT: 23:1–7 [NASB]. The topic is Jesus before Pilate.

DISCOURSE UNIT: 23:1–5 [AB, BECNT, NAC, NICNT, NIGTC, Su, TNTC, WBC; CEV, NCV, NET, NRSV, TEV]. The topic is Jesus before Pilate [AB, BECNT, NAC, NICNT, NIGTC, Su, TNTC, WBC; NRSV, TEV], Jesus brought before Pilate [NET], Pilate questions Jesus [CEV, NCV].

DISCOURSE UNIT: 23:1–4 [GW]. The topic is Pilate questions Jesus.

23:1 **And having-arisen the whole group[a] of-them brought[b] him before Pilate.**

LEXICON—a. πλῆθος (LN 11.1) (BAGD 2.b.β. p. 668): 'group' [NCV, NET, TEV], 'assembly' [AB, NTC, WBC; GW, HCSB, NIV, NRSV, REB], 'council' [CEV, NLT], 'meeting' [BAGD], 'multitude' [BAGD, LN; KJV], 'body' [NASB], 'number' [Arn, BECNT], 'crowd' [LN, Lns].

b. aorist act. indic. of ἄγω (LN 15.165): 'to bring' [LN, NTC, WBC; HCSB, NASB, NET, NRSV, REB], 'to take' [GW, NLT, TEV], 'to lead' [AB, Arn, BECNT, LN, Lns; KJV, NCV], 'to lead off' [CEV, NIV]. The council members themselves took Jesus to Pilate [TG]. Or, they had Jesus brought before Pilate [TH].

QUESTION—Who comprised the ἅπαν τὸ πλῆθος αὐτῶν 'the whole group of them'?
'Them' refers to the people mentioned in 22:66 [AB, NAC, TG, TH]. It was the whole body of the Sanhedrin [Arn, Crd, ICC, Lns, NAC, NIGTC, NTC, Rb, TG, TNTC]. The word 'whole' emphasizes the group's solidarity in their action, but it is probably hyperbolic [AB, WBC]. They were all of the Sanhedrin members except Nicodemus and Joseph of Arimathea, who were not invited to the meeting [Rb]. Or, in addition to the whole council of seventy or seventy-two members, the temple guard would be included [Lns, Su].

QUESTION—Who was Pilate?
Pilate was the highest authority for the occupying power of Rome [AB]. In 3:1 Pontius Pilate is called the governor. He was the Roman procurator for Samaria and Judea [NTC], and he was responsible for maintaining law and order in the region and had charge of finances [BECNT]. In 13:1 it states that he caused some Galileans to be murdered [NTC]. Since Rome did not allow the Jews to inflict capital punishment, it was necessary for the Roman procurator to condemn Jesus in order to execute the sentence of death passed by the Jewish council [ICC]. Only Pilate had the authority to exercise the death penalty [NAC].

23:2 And they-began to-accuse[a] him saying, This (one) we-found misleading[b] our nation and forbidding taxes[c] to-be-paid to-Caesar and saying (that) he-himself is Messiah a-king.

TEXT—Instead of τὸ ἔθνος ἡμῶν 'our nation', some manuscripts read τὸ ἔθνος 'the nation'. GNT does not mention this variant. Τὸ ἔθνος 'the nation' is read by KJV.

TEXT—Instead of καὶ λέγοντα 'and saying', some manuscripts read λέγοντα 'saying'. GNT does not mention this variant. Λέγοντα 'saying' is read by KJV.

LEXICON—a. pres. act. infin. of κατηγορέω (LN 33.427) (BAGD 1.a. p. 423): 'to accuse' [AB, Arn, BECNT, LN, Lns, NTC, WBC; all versions except NLT, REB], 'to bring charges' [BAGD, LN], 'to state their case' [NLT], 'to open the case against' [REB]. This verb is used as a legal term for bringing charges against him in court [NAC, WBC]. See this word at 6:7.

b. pres. act. participle of διαστρέφω (LN **31.71, 88.264**) (BAGD 2. p. 189): 'to mislead' [BAGD]. The phrase διαστρέφοντα τὸ ἔθνος ἡμῶν 'misleading our nation' [NTC; NASB] is also translated 'misleading our people' [TEV], 'telling things that mislead our people' [NCV], 'subverting our nation' [AB; HCSB, NET, NIV, REB], 'perverting our nation' [Arn, BECNT, Lns; NRSV], 'perverting the nation' [KJV], 'trying to pervert our nation' [WBC], 'leading our people to ruin' [NLT], 'he stirs up trouble among our people' [GW], 'trying to get our people to riot' [CEV]. In LN, two alternatives are given for this verse: (1) it can mean to cause someone to believe something that is quite different, 'to cause someone to turn away from a belief, to mislead' [LN (31.71)], or (2) it can mean to cause someone to depart from correct behavior and thus engage in serious wrongdoing, 'to lead astray, to pervert, to mislead' [LN (88.264)].

c. φόρος (LN **57.182**) (BAGD p. 865): 'tax' [AB, Arn, BAGD, Lns, NTC, WBC; all versions except KJV, NET], 'tribute tax' [**LN**; NET], 'tribute' [BECNT; KJV]. This is a payment made by the people of one nation to another and implies their submission and dependence [LN].

QUESTION—Who began to accuse Jesus?

It seems to say that all those in the group began to speak out until Pilate interposed [AB, ICC]. Caiaphas and a few leaders did the speaking while the rest gave their assent [Lns]. The formal charge would have been made by only one or two members of the group [TNTC]. Probably their accusations were repeated and amplified [Arn].

QUESTION—How did they 'find' Jesus doing these things?

It is not clear whether it means that they caught him in the act or that they discovered this by investigation [ICC]. It probably means that they caught Jesus in the act of doing these things rather than discovering the facts in a formal trial [Rb, TH]. Or, 'find' is a legal term and refers to the finding of their trial by due legal procedure [Alf, Lns].

QUESTION—What is meant by the charge that Jesus was misleading the nation?

This was an unspecific charge [AB, TNTC]. The charge is vague, and perhaps serves as an introduction to the two following charges [NTC]. It probably refers to sedition [ICC, TNTC]. It means he was causing civil unrest and rebellion [NICNT]. It means that Jesus was stirring up a revolution [TG]. He was an agitator [Lns]. He was leading the people astray by his teachings and practice [Su]. He was turning the Jews against God and his Law [MGC]. In accusing Jesus before Pilate, this means that he was seducing the people away from their loyalty to the Roman empire [EGT, NAC]. He misled the people by his teachings and even subverted them [AB].

QUESTION—How are the following two charges connected with the charge of misleading the nation?

1. The following two charges are specifics of the first charge [NICNT, TG, WBC; GW, NLT; probably NCV, NIV]: he was misleading our nation by forbidding taxes and by saying he was the Messiah, a king. The first accusation is explained by the following clauses [WBC]. The following two charges are specific ways of how Jesus was stirring up a revolution [TG].
2. The following charges are additional charges so that there were three charges in all [AB, BECNT, Lns, MGC, NAC, NIBC, NIC, NIGTC; NET; probably CEV, HCSB, NASB]. The following two charges are introduced with 'and' to make all three charges coordinate, although all three were of the same kind [Lns].

QUESTION—How serious was the charge of forbidding the payment of taxes to Caesar and was it true?

If this was true, it meant that Jesus was guilty of rebellion and resistance against the Roman government [Su]. This charge was a lie and it is contradicted by the facts given in 20:20–26 [AB, ICC, Lns, NAC, NIGTC, NTC]. However, if Jesus claimed to be a king, he would naturally be expected to forbid payment to a foreign power [ICC]. This is a charge of leading the nation away from its loyalty to Caesar [NIGTC].

QUESTION—Did Jesus claim to be a king and what is meant by the phrase Χριστὸν βασιλέα 'Messiah, a king'?

Jesus had never claimed this himself [WBC]. Jesus had never wanted to be a king in the political sense [NTC]. This climatic charge was that Jesus was a Messiah-king who was capitalizing on the Jewish hope of the coming of the Messiah, a vastly more dangerous claim than being a political pretender to the throne of Israel [Lns]. The charge is true in the sense that Jesus accepted the title of Messiah in 22:69–71, but not in the sense that he planned to start a revolution [BECNT]. This charge was based on his equivocal answer before the Sanhedrin [NIGTC]. This charge was sedition, in the sense that Jesus was claiming to be a king in opposition to Caesar [NICNT]. This accusation was probably based on the event in 19:38 where the pilgrims had shouted 'Blessed is the coming one, the king, in the name of the Lord'

[MGC, NIBC]. The accusers used the Jewish title 'Messiah' and then added the Greek word 'king' in apposition as an explanation for the Gentiles [Arn, BNTC, EGT, Gdt, NAC, NICNT, NIGTC, TG, TH]. This enabled Pilate to realize the political significance of the word 'Messiah' [ICC].

23:3 **And Pilate asked him saying, You are the king of-the Jews? And answering him he said, You are-speaking.**[a] **23:4 and Pilate said to the chief-priests and the crowds, I-find**[b] **no guilt in this man.**

LEXICON—a. pres. act. indic. of λέγω (LN 33.69) (BAGD II.1.e. p. 469): 'to say, to speak' [LN], 'to maintain' [BAGD]. The clause Σὺ λέγεις 'You are speaking' is translated 'Yes, I am' [GW], 'It is as you say' [NASB], 'Yes, it is as you say' [NIV, NLT], 'You say it' [Arn, Lns; KJV], 'It is you who say this!' [AB], 'You have said it' [HCSB], 'You have said so' [BECNT], 'You say so' [NET, NRSV], 'So you say' [TEV], 'These/those are your words' [CEV, NCV], 'The words are yours' [REB]. Instead of a statement, this is translated as a question: 'Do you say so?' [WBC].

b. pres. act. indic. of εὑρίσκω (LN 27.1) (BAGD 1.c.α. p. 325): 'to find' [BAGD, LN], 'to learn, to discover' [LN]. The clause Οὐδὲν εὑρίσκω αἴτιον ἐν τῷ ἀνθρώπῳ τούτῳ 'I find no guilt in this man' [NASB] is also translated 'I find no wrong in this man' [Arn], 'I find nothing against this man' [NCV], 'I find nothing wrong with this man' [NLT], 'I find no crime in this man' [BECNT, Lns], 'I find no fault in this man' [KJV], 'I don't find him guilty of anything' [CEV], 'I can't find this man guilty of any crime' [GW], 'I find no basis for an accusation against this man' [NET, NRSV], 'I find no chargeable offense in this man' [WBC], 'I find no basis for a charge against this man' [NIV], 'I find no grounds for charging this man' [HCSB], 'I find no case for this man to answer' [REB], 'I find no reason to condemn this man' [TEV], 'I find nothing in this man that calls for his death' [AB].

QUESTION—What is indicated by fore-fronting the pronoun 'You' in Pilate's question to Jesus?

The pronoun is made emphatic by its position at the beginning of the sentence [Lns, NTC, TG, TNTC]. It implies that Jesus' appearance does not support such a claim [TG]. The sight of Jesus shows that the claim is absurd [TNTC]. There is mockery in the question [Lns, NTC].

QUESTION—What is the meaning of Jesus' statement 'You are speaking'?

1. Jesus was affirming that he was the king [ICC, Lns, NAC, NTC, Rb, Su, TNTC; GW, NASB, NIV, NLT]. Jesus meant 'Yes' or 'You have said it because it is true' [Su]. It means 'It is as you say' [NTC].
2. Jesus gave a reluctant assent similar to the answer he made in 22:70 [AB, Arn, BECNT, EGT, NIC, NIVS, TNTC]. Jesus was king of the Jews in reality, but not in the sense that Pilate had in mind [Arn, TNTC]. The reply indicates that Jesus had certain reservations [NIC].
3. Jesus was refusing to answer the question directly [MGC, TH]. The answer is 'You, not me!' and is similar to the answer in 22:70, but slightly

more evasive [TH]. The answer 'If you say' was a diplomatic answer that was not incriminating [MGC].
4. Jesus replied by asking a question, 'Do you say so?' [BNTC, WBC]. This question challenges Pilate to see for himself if Jesus was the king of the Jews or if he claimed to be the king [BNTC].

QUESTION—Why did Pilate say that he found no guilt in this man?
Since Jesus had admitted that he was a king, it seems strange that Pilate would find no fault in him, but a conversation with Jesus had brought out that Jesus did not claim to be a king in an ordinary sense [ICC], so Pilate considered Jesus to be a harmless enthusiast [AB, BECNT, ICC]. In John 18:33–38 we find that there was an interview with Jesus and Pilate had learned that Jesus' kingdom was not of this world [Alf, Arn, BECNT, Lns].

DISCOURSE UNIT: 23:5–17 [GW]. The topic is Pilate sending Jesus to Herod.

23:5 And they-were-insisting[a] saying, He-incites[b] the people teaching throughout all of-Judea, even beginning[c] from Galilee to here.

TEXT—Some manuscripts omit καί 'even'. GNT does not mention this variant. Καί 'even' is omitted by Arn, BECNT, Lns; CEV, GW, KJV, NCV, NET, NIV, NLT, REB, and TEV.

LEXICON—a. imperf. act. indic. of ἐπισχύω (LN **68.71**) (BAGD p. 302): 'to insist' [AB, Arn, BAGD, LN, Lns, NTC, WBC; HCSB, NASB, NCV, NIV, REB], 'to be insistent' [BECNT; NRSV], 'to persist in' [**LN**; NET], 'to become more forceful' [GW], 'to be more fierce' [KJV], 'to become desperate' [NLT]. The phrase 'they were insisting saying' is translated 'they all kept on saying' [CEV], 'they insisted even more strongly' [TEV]. The imperfect tense indicates that they *kept on* insisting [AB, Arn, Gdt, Lns, NTC, Rb, Su, WBC; HCSB, NASB]. They insisted by renewing the charge against Jesus [Su]. They brought on more accusations [Lns]. Since Pilate took this matter too lightly, they were more definite in their accusations [ICC]

b. pres. act. indic. of ἀνασείω (LN **39.44**) (BAGD p. 60): 'to incite' [BAGD; NET], 'to stir up' [AB, BAGD, BECNT, LN, NTC, WBC; GW, HCSB, KJV, NASB, NIV, NRSV], 'to make trouble with' [NCV], 'to arouse' [Arn], 'to excite' [Lns], 'to start a riot among' [LN; TEV], 'to cause riots' [NLT], 'to cause unrest among' [REB], 'to cause an uproar among' [LN], 'to cause trouble' [CEV]. The people who watched Jesus were filled with excitement [Su]. They were incited against Roman rule [WBC].

c. pres. act. indic. of ἄρχομαι, ἄρχω (LN 68.1) (BAGD 2.c. p. 113): 'to begin' [BAGD, LN], 'to commence' [LN]. The phrase 'even beginning from Galilee to here' is translated 'beginning from Galilee to this place' [KJV], 'beginning from Galilee even to this place' [AB], 'beginning from Galilee and reaching even to this place' [WBC], 'starting from Galilee and continuing even to this place' [NTC], 'starting from Galilee even as far as this place' [NASB], 'from Galilee where he started even to here' [HCSB], 'from Galilee where he began even to this place' [NRSV], 'also starting from Galilee till here' [Lns], 'from Galilee to this place' [BECNT], 'from Galilee to Jerusalem' [NLT], 'he started in Galilee and has come here' [GW], 'he began in Galilee and now he is here' [NCV], 'He began in Galilee and now has come here' [TEV], 'he has begun in Galilee and come till here' [Arn], 'he started in Galilee and has now come all the way here' [CEV, NIV], 'it started in Galilee and ended up here' [NET], 'it started from Galilee and now has spread here' [REB].

QUESTION—Who were insisting?

The pronoun 'they' refers to the same people in 23:2 [BECNT, TG]. They are primarily the chief priests [NIGTC], or the Sanhedrin [MGC, Su]. Probably it does not include the crowds mentioned in 23:4 [WBC]. Or, it includes the crowds as the Jewish leaders induced the ordinary people to turn against Jesus [Arn, NAC]. It refers to the chief priest and the crowd of 23:4 and they are in contrast with the 'people' in the accusation [NAC].

QUESTION—What is the function of the participle διδάσκων 'teaching'?

1. It clarifies how Jesus was inciting the people by indicating the means [AB, Gdt, MGC; GW, NET, NIV, NRSV, TEV]: he incites the people by teaching,
2. It gives the grounds for saying that he incites the people [TH]: he incites the people because he teaches.

QUESTION—What is included in 'all of Judea'?

1. This includes all of Palestine, the land of the Jews [AB, Arn, BECNT, Crd, MGC, NAC, NICNT, NTC, WBC]. Galilee is included in 'all of Judea' [Lns, NTC]. There is a contrast with 'the people' in their accusation [AB].
2. This refers to Judea proper [Gdt, Su]. This is the province under of Pilate's jurisdiction [EGT].

DISCOURSE UNIT: 23:6–12 [AB, BECNT, NAC, NICNT, NIGTC, Su, TNTC, WBC; CEV, NCV, NET, NRSV, TEV]. The topic is Jesus before Herod [AB, BECNT, NAC, NICNT, NIGTC, Su, TNTC, WBC; NRSV, TEV], Jesus is brought before Herod [CEV, NET], Pilate sends Jesus to Herod [NCV].

23:6 **And having-heard Pilate asked if the man is a-Galilean, 23:7 and having-learned that he-is of the jurisdiction^a of-Herod he-sent him to Herod, (who) himself was also in Jerusalem in these days.**

TEXT—In 23:6, following ἀκούσας 'having heard', some manuscripts add Γαλιλαίαν 'Galilee'. GNT does not mention this variant. Γαλιλαίαν 'Galilee' is read by KJV.

LEXICON—a. ἐξουσία (LN **37.36**) (BAGD 4.b. p. 278): 'jurisdiction' [AB, Arn, BAGD, BECNT, **LN**, Lns, NTC, WBC; HCSB, KJV, NASB, NET, NIV, NLT, NRSV, REB]. The phrase 'of the jurisdiction of Herod' is translated 'came from the region ruled by Herod' [CEV], 'was from the region ruled by Herod' [TEV], 'was under Herod's authority' [NCV],

'Herod ruled Galilee' [GW]. The noun means 'authority', but here it refers to the domain in which the authority was exercised [AB]. This refers to the domain or sphere over which one has authority to control or rule [LN].

QUESTION—What did Pilate hear?

In the previous verse they told him that Jesus had begun his activities in Galilee [NIBC, TNTC]. He heard that Jesus originally came from Galilee [TH].

QUESTION—Who did Pilate ask?

Pilate asked those who made the accusation in 22:56 [TG].

QUESTION—Why did Pilate send Jesus to Herod?

Probably Pilate wanted a Jewish opinion about the situation [NIGTC]. Jesus technically belonged to Herod's jurisdiction [NIGTC, TNTC]. Pilate took advantage of the presence of Herod being in the city and sent Jesus to him in hope that Herod would judge this Galilean subject of his [NIC, NICNT]. This was a gracious complement to Herod [TNTC]. Pilate wanted to pass off a bothersome case [Alf, ICC, Lns, MGC, NIBC, NIC, NTC; NET]. Probably Pilate was trying to hand over authority in this case or at least share responsibility [BECNT]. Here, the verb ἀνέπεμψεν 'he sent' means to send up for judicial examination [Arn]. The verb means to send on or up to some higher or appropriate authority [LN (15.17)]. Usually it means to remand to a higher authority, but here it cannot have that meaning since Herod was under Pilate's authority [BECNT, Crd, NAC]. In 23:11 the same verb is used when Herod sent Jesus back to Pilate [NIGTC]. It means to remand someone to another authority [AB, Lns, MGC], or to the proper authority [NTC, TH]. In 23:11 and 15 it means to 'send back' and it is best to have the same sense here in that Pilate was sending Jesus back to Herod's jurisdiction [ICC].

DISCOURSE UNIT: 23:8–12 [NASB]. The topic is Jesus before Herod.

23:8 And Herod having-seen Jesus rejoiced[a] greatly, because for a-long time he-was wanting to-see him, because (he) had-heard[b] about him and he-was-hoping to-see some sign[c] performed by him. **23:9** And he-was-questioning[d] him with many words, but he-answered him nothing.

TEXT—In 23:8, before περὶ αὐτοῦ 'about him', some manuscripts add πόλλα 'many things'. GNT does not mention this variant. Πόλλα 'many things' is added by CEV, KJV.

LEXICON—a. aorist pass. (deponent = act.) indic. of χαίρω (LN 25.125) (BAGD 1. p. 873): 'to rejoice' [BAGD, LN]. The phrase ἐχάρη λίαν 'he rejoiced greatly' [Arn, WBC] is also translated 'he was very happy' [CEV], 'he was very glad' [BECNT; HCSB, NASB, NCV, NET, NRSV], 'he was exceedingly glad' [Lns; KJV], 'he was very pleased' [AB; GW, TEV], 'he was highly pleased' [NTC], 'he was greatly pleased' [NIV, REB], 'he was delighted' [NLT].

b. pres. act. infin. of ἀκούω (LN 33.212): 'to hear' [LN]. The clause 'he had heard about him' [BECNT, WBC; all versions except CEV, KJV, NASB; similarly Arn, Lns, NTC] is also translated 'he had been hearing about him' [AB; NASB], 'he had heard many things about him' [CEV, KJV]. The verb refers to receiving information about something, normally by word of mouth [LN]. The present infinitive indicates that he kept hearing about Jesus [Lns].

c. σημεῖον (LN 33.477) (BAGD 2.a. p. 748): 'sign' [BAGD, LN]. The phrase 'some sign performed by him' [WBC; NASB] is also translated 'some sign done by him' [BECNT, Lns], 'perform some sign' [NTC; NRSV], 'the performance of some sign by him' [Arn], 'perform some miraculous sign' [NET], 'some miracle performed by him' [AB; REB], 'some miracle done by him' [KJV], 'perform a miracle' [NLT], 'perform some miracle' [NIV, TEV], 'perform some kind of miracle' [GW], 'work a miracle' [CEV, NCV]. This refers to some event that has a special meaning [LN]. See this word at 11:16, 29.

d. imperf. act. indic. of ἐπερωτάω (LN 56.14): 'to question, to interrogate, to try to learn' [LN]. The clause 'he questioned him with many words' is translated 'he questioned him in many words' [Arn], 'he continued to inquire of him in many words' [Lns], 'he questioned him at length' [NTC], 'he questioned him at some length' [BECNT; KJV, NRSV, REB], 'he questioned him at considerable length' [NET], 'he tried to question him at length' [AB], 'he asked him a lot of questions' [CEV], 'he asked Jesus many questions' [GW, NCV, TEV], 'he plied him with many questions' [NIV], 'he asked question after question' [NLT], 'he tried at length to question him' [WBC]. This refers a legal or semi-legal procedure in which an attempt is made to learn the truth about a matter, normally by interrogation [LN]. The imperfect tense indicates that this was a lengthy interrogation [NIGTC].

QUESTION—What is the significance of the use of the word σημεῖον 'sign' here?

In the Gospel of John, the word *sign* is regularly used for Jesus' miracles and it meant that the miracles pointed beyond the acts themselves to verify that Jesus was the Messiah, but Herod was interested only in seeing Jesus do some magical feats [Su]. Herod was thinking only of something spectacular and miraculous [TNTC, WBC]. He wanted to be entertained [BECNT, EGT, Lns, NTC].

QUESTION—What did Herod question Jesus about?

Herod questioned Jesus about the accusations made against him by the Sanhedrin [WBC]. He asked him about the signs [Lns, Su], whether Jesus did them, were they real, and would he do one for Herod [Lns]. He asked about Jesus' identity, his mission, and the miracles he had been doing [NIBC]. This does not seem to be a court hearing [Su].

23:10 And the chief-priests and the scribes stood (there) vehemently[a] accusing him. **23:11** And having-treated- him -with-contempt[b] also Herod with his soldiers also having-ridiculed[c] (him), having-dressed (him in) bright[d] clothing they-sent- him -back to-Pilate.

TEXT—In 23:11, instead of καὶ ὁ Ἡρῴδης 'also Herod', some manuscripts read ὁ Ἡρῴδης 'Herod' with the definite article, and some manuscripts read Ἡρῴδης 'Herod' without the definite article. GNT reads καὶ ὁ Ἡρῴδης 'also Herod' with a C decision and brackets καί 'also' in the text, indicating that the Committee had difficulty making the decision. The versions would not distinguish between the readings of Ἡρῴδης 'Herod' with or without the definite article.

LEXICON—a. εὐτόνως (LN 78.18) (BAGD p. 327): 'vehemently' [BAGD, LN], 'vigorously' [BAGD, LN], 'powerfully' [BAGD]. The phrase εὐτόνως κατηγοροῦντες αὐτοῦ 'vehemently accusing him' [BECNT, NTC; HCSB, KJV, NASB, NET, NIV, NRSV] is also translated 'strongly accusing Jesus' [NCV], 'vigorously accusing him' [AB, Arn, WBC], 'strenuously accusing him' [Lns], 'pressed the case against him vigorously' [REB], 'made strong accusations against Jesus' [TEV], 'shouting their accusations' [NLT], 'shouted their accusations against Jesus' [GW], 'accused him of all kinds of bad things' [CEV]. They talked loudly and incessantly [NTC]. This adverb implies tension and opposition [LN].

b. aorist act. participle of ἐξουθενέω (LN 88.195) (BAGD 3. p. 277): 'to treat with contempt' [AB, BAGD, BECNT, NTC, WBC; GW, NASB, NET, NRSV, REB, TEV], 'to despise' [LN], 'to make fun of' [CEV, TEV], 'to ridicule' [NIV], 'to mock' [NLT], 'to make light of' [Arn], 'to set at naught' [Lns]. The phrase 'having treated him with contempt...also having ridiculed him' is translated 'made fun of Jesus' [NCV]. This verb means to despise or disdain someone [BAGD]. It means to despise someone because he is worthless or of no value [LN].

c. aorist act. participle of ἐμπαίζω (LN 33.406) (BAGD 1. p. 255): 'to ridicule' [AB, BAGD, LN, WBC; NLT, REB], 'to mock' [Arn, BAGD, BECNT, **LN**, Lns, NTC; HCSB, KJV, NASB, NET, NIV, NRSV], 'to make fun of' [BAGD; GW, TEV], 'to insult' [CEV], 'to set at naught' [KJV]. This verb means to make fun of someone by pretending that he is not what he is or by imitating him in a distorted manner [LN]. It means to ridicule someone in word and deed [BAGD]. See this word at 14:29; 18:32; 22:63; 23:11.

d. λαμπρός (LN 79.20) (BAGD 3. p. 465): 'bright, shining' [BAGD], 'splendid, luxurious, glamorous' [LN]. The phrase ἐσθῆτα λαμπρὰν 'bright clothing' is translated 'a shining garment' [Arn, Lns], 'a brilliant robe' [HCSB], 'a gorgeous robe' [NTC; KJV, NASB, REB], 'in gorgeous apparel' [BECNT], 'a splendid garment' [WBC], 'a fine robe' [CEV, TEV], 'a kingly robe' [NCV], 'an elegant robe' [NIV, NRSV], 'in elegant clothes' [NET].

LUKE 23:10–11   485

QUESTION—Who was treating Jesus with contempt and ridiculing him?
Herod and his soldiers treated Jesus with contempt and ridicule [AB, Arn, Lns, NIBC, NTC, Su, TNTC, WBC; all versions]. Herod joined his soldiers in mocking Jesus [BECNT, NIGTC]. Herod's whole court followed his lead [Lns]. Or, Herod initiated the actions of the soldiers who treated Jesus with contempt, ridiculed him, and dressed him in bright clothing [EGT, TH].

QUESTION—Who dressed Jesus in bright clothing and sent him back to Pilate?
Herod and his soldiers dressed Jesus in the bright robe and they sent him back to Pilate [NTC, Su; CEV, GW, HCSB, KJV, NASB, NCV, NIV, NLT, REB, TEV]. Or, Herod and his soldiers dressed Jesus with the robe and after they had treated Jesus with contempt Herod sent him back to Pilate [MGC, NIC, TNTC, WBC]. Or, Herod dressed Jesus in the robe and sent him back to Pilate [AB, Arn, TH, WBC; NET, NRSV]. Herod mocked Jesus by dressing him in this clothing [BECNT]. Either Herod or someone ordered by him put the garment on Jesus [Lns]. Herod had his soldiers put the bright clothing on Jesus and then he sent him back to Pilate [NAC, TG].

QUESTION—What was the ἐσθῆτα λαμπρὰν 'bright clothing'?
Some think that the clothing was white [Gdt, Lns]. A white garment was the kind worn by the grand and illustrious men [Lns]. Jewish kings wore a white robe and so did Roman dignitaries [Gdt]. Others think it was purple to imitate the robe of a king [Crd]. If the 'bright' clothing was white, it would mock him with the toga that a king-designate would wear, and if it was royal purple in color, it would mock Jesus' claim of being a king, but in either case it refers to regal clothing or clothing of high social standing [BECNT]. The adjective 'bright' refers to its gorgeous character, not to its color, and they meant to mock Jesus' claim to be a king [EGT, ICC, Su, TNTC, WBC]. It was probably a cast-off royal robe [EGT, TNTC]. It was the dress of a dignitary and this was meant to mock the pretensions of Jesus [WBC].

23:12 And both Herod and Pilate became friends[a] with one-another on this day. Because[b] they-previously-were at enmity[c] towards themselves.

LEXICON—a. φίλος (BAGD 2.a.α. p. 861): 'friend' [BAGD, LN]. The phrase ἐγένοντο φίλοι…μετ' ἀλλήλων 'became friends with one another' [Lns, WBC; NASB] is also translated 'became friends of one another' [Arn], 'became friends with each other' [BECNT; NET, NRSV], 'were made friends together' [KJV], 'became friends' [AB, NTC; CEV, GW, HCSB, NCV, NIV, NLT, REB, TEV]. The phrase μετ' ἀλλήλων 'with one another' is redundant, but strengthens the word 'friends' [TH].

b. γάρ (LN 89.23): 'because' [Arn, LN], 'for' [BECNT, LN, Lns, NTC, WBC; KJV, NASB, NET], 'even though' [CEV], 'whereas' [AB], not explicit [GW, HCSB, NCV, NIV, NLT, NRSV, REB, TEV].

c. ἔχθρα (LN 39.10) (BAGD p. 331): 'enmity' [BAGD, LN], 'being an enemy of' [LN]. The phrase ἐν ἔχθρᾳ ὄντες πρὸς αὐτούς 'were at enmity towards one another' is translated 'they were in enmity with each other' [BECNT, Lns], 'they were at enmity between themselves' [KJV], 'they had been hostile toward one another' [WBC], 'they had been hostile toward each other' [HCSB], 'they had been enemies with each other' [NASB], 'they had been enemies' [Arn, NTC; CEV, GW, NET, NIV, NLT, NRSV, TEV], 'had always been enemies' [NCV], 'they had been at odds with one another' [AB], 'there had been a feud between them' [REB].

QUESTION—What relationship is indicated by γάρ 'because'?

The conjunction explains why they were not friends before this day [AB, TG, TH].

QUESTION—Why were Herod and Pilate enemies?

It is possible that the fact they ruled over adjacent territories caused friction [Lns]. There may have been a dispute about jurisdiction [ICC]. With their different cultural backgrounds, hostility could have arisen for various reasons [Su],

QUESTION—What made them become friends on this occasion?

By sending Jesus to Herod, Pilate showed that he recognized Herod's authority in such a matter [WBC]. Pilate recognized the return of Jesus to be a practical joke signifying that Herod deferred authority to him [Su]. Pilate had honored Herod by sending Jesus to him for his judgment and in turn Herod had honored Pilate by returning Jesus for Pilate's judgment [Alf, Lns, NTC]. They were in agreement as to Jesus' political innocence [NIBC, WBC]. They were joined in their hostility towards Jesus [NICNT], and they had both mistreated Jesus in a very shameful manner [MGC, NTC].

DISCOURSE UNIT: 23:13–25 [BECNT, NICNT, NIGTC, Su, TNTC; CEV, NASB, NCV, NET, NRSV, TEV]. The topic is bringing Jesus before the crowd [NET], the hearing before Pilate—sentenced to death [Su], Pilate seeks Jesus' release [NASB], the sentencing of Jesus [NICNT, NIGTC, TNTC], sentencing by Pilate and the release of Barabbas [BECNT], the death sentence [CEV], Jesus is sentenced to death [NRSV, TEV], Jesus must die [NCV].

DISCOURSE UNIT: 23:13–16 [AB, BECNT, NAC, WBC]. The topic is Pilate's sentence [AB, NAC], Jesus' innocence declared [BECNT, WBC].

23:13 And Pilate having-called-together the chief-priests and the rulers[a] and the people[b] 23:14 said to them, You-brought this man to-me as (one who) misleads[c] the people, and behold having-examined (him) before you I found nothing in this man (regarding the) charge[d] which you-bring against him.

LEXICON—a. ἄρχων (LN 37.56) (BAGD 2.a. p. 114): 'ruler' [Arn, BECNT, LN, Lns, NTC, WBC; GW, KJV, NASB, NET, NIV], 'authority, official' [BAGD], 'leader' [AB; CEV, HCSB, NRSV, TEV], 'Jewish leader' [NCV], 'councilor' [REB], 'other religious leaders' [NLT]. This word refers to the members of the Sanhedrin [TG, TH]. They were the other Jewish leaders besides the chief priests [NIGTC]. Or, this refers to the whole Sanhedrin, including the chief priests (22:66) and the initial

mention of the chief priests indicates that that the chief priests were the ones who had the central responsibility for what was unfolding [NICNT]. They were the social leaders who supported the religious leaders [BECNT]. See this word at 8:41; 14:1; 18:18; 23:35.
b. ὄχλος (LN 87.64) (BAGD 1.c.α. p. 466): 'people' [AB, Arn, BAGD, BECNT, Lns, NTC, WBC; all versions], 'common people, rabble' [LN]. The noun refers to the common people, in contrast with those who are rich, leaders, or authorities in the society and the use of the word often implies disdain and low esteem [LN]. The word contrasts the people with their leaders [BAGD].
c. pres. act. participle of ἀποστρέφω (LN **31.70**) (BAGD 1.a.β. p. 100): 'to mislead' [BAGD, LN], 'to cause to turn away from a belief' [LN], 'to cause to revolt' [BAGD]. The phrase 'as one who misleads the people' is translated 'as one who was misleading the people' [NET], 'as one who subverts the people' [AB; HCSB], 'as one who is/was perverting the people' [BECNT, WBC; NRSV], 'as one who incites the people to rebellion' [NTC; NASB, NIV], 'as turning away the people' [Lns], 'as someone who turns the people against the government' [GW], 'as one that perverteth the people' [KJV], 'as one that makes the people disloyal' [Arn], 'you said he was misleading the people' [**LN**], 'you said he was causing the people to turn away from their beliefs' [**LN**], 'and said that he was misleading the people' [TEV], 'and said he was a troublemaker' [CEV], 'saying he makes trouble among the people' [NCV], 'accusing him of leading a revolt' [NLT], 'on a charge of subversion' [REB]. This verb ἀποστρέφω 'mislead' is practically equivalent to the verb διαστρέφω 'mislead' in 23:2 [AB, BECNT, TG, TH]. The verb refers to turning the people away from their loyalty to the emperor and thus incite a rebellion [NTC]. It means to turn the people away from their allegiance and loyalty, thus misleading them and causing them to revolt [TH].
d. αἴτιος (LN 89.15) (BAGD 2. p. 26): 'charge' [AB, NTC; NASB, NRSV], 'complaint' [BAGD], 'reason, cause' [LN], 'things' [KJV], 'crimes' [GW, TEV]. The clause 'I have found nothing in this man regarding the charge which you bring against him' is translated 'I have found no guilt in this man concerning anything you charged against him' [BECNT], 'I have found in this man no basis for what you accuse him of' [WBC], 'I have found no basis for your charges against him' [NIV], 'I did not find this man guilty of anything you accused him of doing' [NET], 'I have not found him guilty of anything that you say he has done' [CEV], 'I have not found him guilty of what you say' [NCV], 'I have not found in him any one of those misdeeds of which you accuse him' [Arn], 'I myself found no crime in this man as to the things you are charging against him' [Lns], 'and found nothing in him to support your charges' [REB], 'and find him innocent' [NLT]. This refers to the content of the legal charges brought against someone [LN]. It refers to the cause for guilt [BECNT]. See this word at 23:22.

488   LUKE 23:13–14

QUESTION—Who were the people Pilate called together and why did he do this?

> They were the people standing around Pilate's palace [TH]. These people had gathered before the judgment hall for the usual amnesty request [Arn]. This shows that Pilate was preparing for a public announcement [NTC, TNTC]. Pilate also called the people because he hoped that they would be more kindly disposed towards Jesus and could influence their leaders [AB, ICC, Lns, MGC, Rb]. He wanted to have the people agree with his verdict of dismissing Jesus [Arn, Gdt, Lns]. Or, such motives are speculations and we only know that he gathered the people in order to make a public announcement [NTC]. The people's presence indicates that they too were culpable in Jesus' death [NAC].

QUESTION—What is meant by the phrase ὡς ἀποστρέφοντα τὸν λαόν 'as one who misleads the people'?

> This conjunction introduces the charge [BECNT, Lns]. The conjunction ὡς 'as' with the participle indicates that that this was not an established fact but a subjective charge [Rb, TH].

QUESTION—When had Pilate examined Jesus before these people?

> This shows that Luke has omitted many of the details of what took place [TNTC]. This is only a summary of what took place, since Luke's account does not include such a public examination except for a hint of it in 23:3–4 [NTC]. Or, this means that the people had seen how Pilate had taken Jesus into the judgment hall and that they had been given the opportunity to amplify the charges against Jesus [Arn].

23:15 But[a] neither (did) Herod, because he-sent-back him to us, and behold[b] nothing worthy[c] of-death has-been-done by-him.

TEXT—Instead of ἀνέπεμψεν γὰρ αὐτὸν πρὸς ἡμᾶς 'because he sent back him to us' some manuscripts read ἀνέπεμψεν γὰρ αὐτὸν πρὸς ὑμᾶς 'because he sent back him to you', some manuscripts read ἀνέπεμψα γὰρ ὑμᾶς πρὸς αὐτόν 'because I sent you to him', some manuscripts read ἀνέπεμψα γὰρ αὐτὸν πρὸς αὐτόν 'because I sent him to him', and some manuscripts read ἀνέπεμψα γὰρ αὐτὸν πρὸς ὑμᾶς 'because I sent him to you'. GNT reads ἀνέπεμψεν γὰρ αὐτὸν πρὸς ἡμᾶς 'because he sent back him to us' with an A reading, indicating that the text is certain. Ἀνέπεμψα γὰρ ὑμᾶς πρὸς αὐτόν 'because I sent you to him' is read by Gdt and KJV.

LEXICON—a. ἀλλά (LN 89.125) (BAGD 3. p. 38): 'but' [BAGD, LN]. This can be explained elliptically 'but also' [BAGD]. The clause ἀλλ' οὐδὲ Ἡρῴδης 'But neither Herod' is translated 'But neither did Herod' [BECNT], 'Neither did Herod' [NET], 'Neither has Herod' [AB, NTC; HCSB, NIV, NRSV], 'And neither has Herod' [Arn], 'Neither could Herod' [GW], 'No, nor Herod' [Lns], 'No, nor has Herod' [NASB], 'No, nor yet Herod' [KJV], 'No more did Herod' [REB], 'Nor did Herod find him guilty' [TEV], 'What is more, neither did Herod' [WBC], 'Also,

Herod found nothing wrong with him' [NCV], 'Herod didn't find him guilty either' [CEV], 'Herod came to the same conclusion' [NLT].
b. ἰδού (LN 91.13) (BAGD p. 371): 'behold' [Arn, BAGD, BECNT; NASB], 'lo' [Lns; KJV], 'look' [LN; NCV, NET], 'see' [WBC], 'as you can see' [NIV], 'listen' [LN], 'clearly' [HCSB, REB], 'obviously' [AB], 'indeed' [NTC; NRSV], not explicit [CEV, GW, NLT, TEV]. This introduces a concluding statement [TH]. It makes this statement more solemn [BECNT]. It indicates that the preceding statement was surprising [Lns].
c. ἄξιος (LN 66.6) (BAGD 1.b. p. 78): 'worthy of, proper, fitting' [LN], 'deserving' [BAGD]. The phrase 'nothing worthy of death has been done by him' [Arn, BECNT, Lns, WBC] is also translated 'nothing deserving death has been done by him' [NASB], 'he has done nothing to deserve death' [HCSB, NIV, NRSV, REB; similarly NET], 'there is nothing this man has done to deserve death' [TEV], 'nothing that deserves the death penalty was done by him' [NTC], 'this man hasn't done anything to deserve the death penalty' [GW], 'this man doesn't deserve to be put to death' [CEV], 'he has done nothing for which he should die' [NCV], 'he has done nothing that calls for his death' [AB], 'nothing this man has done calls for the death penalty' [NLT], 'nothing worthy of death is done unto him' [KJV]. The pronoun αὐτῷ in the dative case is the dative of the agent 'by him', i.e., by Jesus [Alf, NAC, NIGTC; all versions except KJV]. The KJV rendering 'done unto him' does not make good sense [ICC]. The verb means to be fitting or proper in regard to what should be expected [LN]. See this word at 23:41.

QUESTION—What is the purpose of adding ἀλλ' οὐδὲ Ἡρῴδης 'but neither Herod'?

This means 'but not only I, neither did Herod find any guilt in him' [TH]. It means 'but not even Herod' [Rb]. With the strong adversative 'but', this can be translated 'no, nor Herod' [Lns]. Since Herod was a Jewish ruler, his opinion would hold more weight among the Jews than that of the Roman judge [NIGTC]. Herod would be expected to know more about Jewish matters than Pilate [Crd, My]. Herod would know if Jesus had done something wrong in Galilee [Arn].

QUESTION—What relationship is indicated by γάρ 'because'?

It indicates the proof that Herod had not found any guilt in him [BECNT, NTC, Su]. Herod would not have acted as he did unless he was convinced that Jesus was not guilty [TNTC]. Herod would have punished Jesus since Herod governed Galilee [TG].

QUESTION—Who did Pilate refer to when he said 'he sent him back to *us*'?

1. The pronoun ἡμᾶς 'us' is the royal plural and refers only to Pilate [Lns, NICNT, WBC]. It refers to Pilate since he was speaking to people who had not been with him when Herod sent Jesus back to Pilate [WBC]. This is the plural of majesty and refers to Pilate's court [Lns].

2. This is an inclusive pronoun and includes Pilate and those to whom he was speaking [TG, TH]. It refers to Pilate, the Jewish leaders, and the people [TH]. The pronoun refers to more than Pilate and either indicates that the chief priests and scribes that were sent to Herod had already returned and were then present with Pilate, or that only a delegation had been sent to Herod to testify against Jesus while the rest remained with Pilate [NAC].

23:16 Therefore having-disciplined[a] him I-will-release[b] (him).

LEXICON—a. aorist act. participle of παιδεύω (LN **38.4**) (BAGD 2.b.γ. p. 604): 'to discipline' [AB, BAGD], 'to punish' [Arn, **LN**, NTC; NASB, NCV, NIV], 'to chastise' [Lns; KJV], 'to have him beaten' [CEV], 'to have him whipped' [GW, HCSB, TEV], 'to have him flogged' [WBC; NLT, NRSV], 'to flog him' [REB], 'to scourge him' [BECNT]. This verb means 'to educate' and it is probably used here as a euphemism for having him 'disciplined' by being whipped or scourged [TH].

b. fut. act. indic. of ἀπολύω (LN 37.127) (BAGD 1. p. 96): 'to release' [AB, Arn, BAGD, BECNT, LN, Lns, NTC, WBC; HCSB, KJV, NASB, NET, NIV, NLT, NRSV], 'to set free' [BAGD, LN; CEV, GW], 'to let go free' [NCV], 'to let him go' [REB, TEV].

QUESTION—What relationship is indicated by οὖν 'therefore'?

It seems to say that because Jesus was innocent, therefore Pilate would punish him. However this is explained differently. The whipping was not a punishment, but a warning to Jesus to be more circumspect from then on [ICC, MGC, NIBC]. Most translations seem to indicate that although Jesus did not deserve death, he did deserve to be disciplined. Pilate thought that Jesus might have been guilty of a minor misdemeanor [WBC]. The whipping was a punishment for being a nuisance [NIGTC]. It was a concession to those who accused Jesus [Arn, BECNT, Lns, NIC, NIGTC, NIVS, TH, TNTC, WBC]. If Pilate showed some judicial displeasure, the Jews might be satisfied and agree to release Jesus [TNTC]. A Roman scourging was a severe punishment [ICC, MGC, Su, TG] and could result in the death of the prisoner [TG]. Here it refers to a lighter punishment [NAC, NIGTC, TNTC; NET] which under Roman law was administered together with a warning so that the person would take greater care in the future [NIVS, TNTC].

23:17

TEXT—Some manuscripts include 23:17: ἀνάγκην δὲ εἶχεν ἀπολύειν αὐτοῖς κατὰ ἑορτὴν ἕνα 'and he had necessity to release to them at (the) feast one (person)', and some manuscripts include this verse following 23:19. GNT omits this verse with an A decision, indicating that the text is certain. It is included as 23:17 by KJV and it is included in brackets by HCSB and NASB.

DISCOURSE UNIT: 23:18–25 [AB, NAC; GW]. The topic is Jesus delivered to be crucified [AB, NAC], the crowd rejects Jesus [GW].

LUKE 23:18 491

DISCOURSE UNIT: 23:18–23 [BECNT, WBC]. The topic is the crowd's demand [BECNT], Pilate capitulates to the will of the crowd [WBC].

23:18 **And they-cried-out all-together saying, Take-away[a] this (one), and release[b] Barabbas to-us;**

LEXICON—a. pres. act. impera. of αἴρω (LN **20.65**) (BAGD 4. p. 24): 'to take away' [BAGD], 'to kill, to execute' [LN]. The clause Αἶρε τοῦτον 'Take away this one' is translated 'Take this man away!' [HCSB, NCV, NET], 'Take him away!' [GW], 'Take this one' [BECNT], 'Away with him!' [REB], 'Away with this man!' [AB, Arn, NTC; KJV, NASB, NIV], 'Away with this fellow!' [WBC; NRSV], 'Make away with this fellow' [Lns], 'Kill him!' [**LN**; NLT, TEV], 'Kill Jesus!' [CEV]. They are saying that he should be taken away from life [AB]. The verb 'to take away' means to kill or execute Jesus [BECNT, MGC, NAC, NICNT, TH] because of the charge he has been accused of [BECNT]. It means to deprive a person of his life and implies that he had been condemned by legal or quasi-legal procedures [LN].

b. aorist act. impera. of ἀπολύω (L 37.127) (BAGD 1. p. 92): 'to release, to set free' [BAGD, LN]. The clause ἀπόλυσον ἡμῖν τὸν Βαραββᾶν 'release Barabbas to us' [AB, Arn, Lns; HCSB, KJV, NIV, NLT] is also translated 'Release Barabbas for us!' [NTC, WBC; NASB, NET, NRSV], 'Free Barabbas for us' [GW], 'Set Barabbas free for us!' [TEV], 'Give us Barabbas!' [BECNT; CEV], 'Let Barabbas go free!' [NCV], 'Set Barabbas free!' [REB]. The words ἀπόλυσον ἡμῖν 'release for us' means to release him 'in answer to our request' [TG]. See this verb at 23:16.

QUESTION—Who cried out with the demand that Jesus be taken away and that Barabbas be released?

It refers to the three groups mentioned in 23:13: the chief priests, the rulers, and the people [AB, MGC, NAC, NIBC, NIC, NICNT, WBC]. The crowd joined in with their leaders [WBC]. The members of the Sanhedrin moved among the crowds and stirred them up to make this demand [BECNT, Lns, MGC, NTC].

QUESTION—Why did the people demand that Barabbas be released?

Probably verse 23:17 has been inserted in some manuscripts to explain why the people demanded the release of Barabbas [Su]. By not writing verse 17, Luke assumed that the readers knew about this tradition [NAC]. It was customary to give some prisoner amnesty at the feast of the Passover and Matt. 27:15, Mark 15:6, and John 18:39 include such an explanation [NIGTC]. There was a custom of releasing a prominent Jewish prisoner during the Passover to carry out the theme of the release of the Jews from bondage [Su].

23:19 **who was thrown into prison because of-some riot[a] having-occurred in the city and (because of) murder.[b]**

LEXICON—a. στάσις (LN 39.34) (BAGD 2. 764): 'riot, uprising, revolt' [BAGD], 'rebellion' [BAGD, LN], 'insurrection' [LN]. The phrase 'some riot' [AB] is also translated 'a certain riot' [WBC], 'a riot' [Lns; CEV, GW, NCV, TEV], 'a rebellion' [HCSB], 'an insurrection' [BECNT, LN, NTC; NASB, NET, NIV, NLT, NRSV], 'a certain uprising' [Arn], 'a rising' [REB], 'a certain sedition' [KJV]. This refers to people rising up in open defiance of authority, and it is presumed that they intend to overthrow that authority or to act in complete opposition to its demands [LN]. The riot had probably been an uprising of the people against the Roman government [TG].

b. φόνος (LN 20.82) (BAGD p. 864): 'murder' [BAGD, LN], 'killing' [BAGD]. The phrase 'and because of murder' [Lns] is also translated 'and for murder' [AB, BECNT, NTC; all versions except CEV], 'and a murder' [WBC], 'and on account of a murder' [Arn], 'and had murdered someone' [CEV].

QUESTION—Whose words are given in 23:19?

The grammar appears to attach this verse to the speech in verse 23:18, but it is not really a part of what the people were saying [TH]. The verse is added by Luke to give information about Barabbas [MGC, NIGTC, TG, TH]. It is best to translate this verse as an independent sentence [NTC; CEV]. It is enclosed within parenthesis marks to show that these are Luke's words [AB, BECNT, TH, WBC; all versions except CEV]. The parenthesis shows that this verse interrupts the narrative [TG].

QUESTION—How was Barabbas connected with the insurrection?

Barabbas had not started the insurrection, but he had played a prominent part in it [ICC]. Barabbas had something to do with it and he had murdered someone during it [TH]. He was a prisoner who been found guilty of leading an attempted revolution in which he had murdered someone and was now awaiting to be executed [Su]. The insurrection was probably not a popular movement, but was just some disturbance involving plundering [ICC]. It was a riot [TH]. Someone had been murdered during the riot [Su, TG, TH, TNTC]. Or, the grammar appears to indicate that the riot occurred in the city, but the murder had occurred elsewhere [ICC]. It is ironical that Barabbas had actually done what Jesus had been wrongly accused of [BECNT, NIBC; NET].

23:20 And again Pilate addressed^a them wishing to-release Jesus. 23:21 And they-were-crying-out^b saying, Crucify, crucify him.

TEXT—In 23:20, instead of δέ 'and', some manuscripts read οὖν 'therefore', although GNT does not mention this variant. Οὖν 'therefore' is read by KJV.

LEXICON—a. aorist act. indic. of προσφωνέω (LN 33.79) (BAGD 1. p. 720): 'to address' [AB, Arn, BAGD, LN; HCSB, NASB, NET, NRSV, REB], 'to speak to' [CEV, GW, KJV], 'to speak out to' [BAGD, LN], 'to call to' [Lns], 'to call out to' [BECNT, WBC], 'to appeal to' [NTC; NIV, TEV], 'to argue with' [NLT], 'to tell (this) to' [NCV].

b. imperf. act. indic. of ἐπιφωνέω (LN 33.77) (BAGD p. 304): 'to cry out' [BAGD, LN; KJV], 'to shout' [AB, Arn, LN, WBC; all versions except GW, KJV, NASB], 'to yell' [NTC; GW], 'to call out' [BECNT, LN; NASB], 'to call at' [Lns].

QUESTION—What did Pilate say when he addressed them?

In Matt. 27:22 (and similarly in Mark 15:12), it says that Pilate asked another question following the crowd's demand to release Barabbas: 'Then what shall I do with Jesus who is called the Messiah?' [Arn, BECNT, Lns, Su]. Or, the word πάλιν 'again' implies that he repeated what he had said in 23:14–16 [Gdt, NICNT, TG]. The words 'a third time' in 23:22 indicates that the words in verses 15–16 and verse 22 are what he also said in this verse [Gdt]. Or, the phrase 'wishing to release Jesus' implies that instead of asking a question, he told the crowd what he intended to do [NIGTC; NCV].

QUESTION—What is indicated by the use of the present participle form of θέλων 'wishing'?

This indicates Pilate's purpose in addressing them again [MGC, TH; CEV, GW, NET, NLT, TEV]: he addressed the crowd because he wished to release Jesus.

QUESTION—What is indicated by the use of the imperfect tense of ἐπεφώνουν 'they were crying out'?

The imperfect tense is durative [AB, EGT, ICC, Lns, NAC, NIGTC, NTC, Rb, TH; CEV, HCSB, NASB, NET, NIV, NRSV]: they kept on crying out. They kept up the chant of 'Crucify, Crucify him' [Su]. Or, it indicates that they *began* yelling these words [GW]: they began to cry out.

QUESTION—Why did the Jews demand death by crucifixion instead of by stoning?

The Jews had turned over to Pilate the matter of execution and the Roman execution involved crucifixion [Lns]. Crucifixion was the current method of execution and so they repeated their desire for Jesus' death in 23:18 by describing the means of carrying it out [NAC]. Crucifixion was the Roman punishment for treason and insurrection [MGC; NET]. The crowd was not satisfied with the Jewish form of a quick execution and wanted the prolonged torture involved in crucifixion [NTC].

23:22 And a third (time) he-said to them, Why,[a] what evil did- this (man) -do? I-found in him no reason[b] (worthy) of-death; therefore having-disciplined[c] him I-will-release (him).

LEXICON—a. γάρ (LN 91.1) (BAGD 1.f. p. 152): 'why' [BAGD, BECNT, Lns, NTC; all versions except CEV, TEV], 'what' [BAGD], 'then' [LN], 'but' [CEV, TEV], 'how can I, for…' [Arn], not explicit [AB, WBC]. It prefixes a question with 'why' or 'what' [BAGD]. It serves as a marker for a new sentence and can highlight the significance of the question [LN].

b. αἴτιος (LN 89.15) (BAGD 2. p. 26): 'reason, cause' [LN], 'complaint, guilt' [BAGD]. The clause 'I found in him no reason worthy of death' is translated 'I have found in him no grounds for the death penalty' [HCSB, NIV], 'I have found in him no grounds for the sentence of death' [NRSV], 'I have found in him no basis for a death penalty' [WBC], 'no basis whatever for the death penalty have I found in him' [NTC], 'I have found no crime worthy of death in him' [BECNT], 'I have found in him no guilt demanding death' [NASB], 'I have found no cause of death in him' [Arn; KJV], 'I have found no reason to sentence him to death' [NLT], 'I have found him guilty of no crime deserving death' [NET], 'I have not found him guilty of any capital offence' [REB], 'no capital crime did I find in him' [Lns], 'I have not found him guilty of anything for which he should be put to death' [CEV], 'I haven't found this man deserving of the death penalty' [GW], 'I have found nothing in him that that calls for his death' [AB], 'I cannot find anything he has done to deserve death' [TEV], 'I can find no reason to kill him' [NCV]. This word refers to the content of the legal charges brought against someone [LN]. See this word at 23:14.

c. aorist act. participle of παιδεύω (LN 38.4) (BAGD 2.b.γ. p. 604): 'to discipline' [BAGD], 'to punish' [LN]. The clause παιδεύσας οὖν αὐτὸν ἀπολύσω 'therefore having disciplined him I will release him' is identical with Pilate's words in 23:16.

QUESTION—What were the three times?

The first time is given in 23:14–16 and the second time is in 23:20 [BECNT, EGT, TG]. Or, the other two times he addressed them were at 23:4 and 23:14–15 [Gdt, NIVS]. This appears to be the fourth appeal to the people: 23:4, 15, 20, and 22 [NTC, TNTC]. The four times can be reduced to three by regarding 23:15 as referring to Herod's view [TNTC]. Or, the phrase 'a third time' means 'three times in succession' *after* Jesus returned from Herod [NTC].

QUESTION—What is indicated by γάρ 'why' in Pilate's question?

It is used to mark a new sentence and also highlights the significance of the question rather than providing a reason [LN (91.1)]. The word is little more than an intensive particle [Lns]. The word does not have its causal meaning here, but indicates an inferential or transitional sense [TH]. Or, the conjunction does have a causal meaning and indicates the impossibility of crucifying Jesus, so that the question means '*Impossible, because* what evil has this man done?' [ICC], and it can be translated idiomatically by 'why?' [BECNT, ICC, Lns, NTC; GW, HCSB, KJV, NASB, NCV, NIV, NLT, NRSV, REB]. Something is implied, such as 'I cannot have Jesus crucified, *for* what evil deed has he committed deserving crucifixion' [Arn], or 'I cannot respond to your demand *because*...' [EGT]. It means 'Crucify him? *For* he has done what evil?' [Gdt].

23:23 And they kept-on^a with-loud voices demanding (that) he be-crucified, and their voices prevailed/were-prevailing.^b

TEXT—Following αἱ φωναὶ αὐτῶν 'their voices', some manuscripts add καὶ τῶν ἀρχιερέων 'and of the chief priests' and some manuscripts add καὶ τῶν ἀρχόντων καὶ τῶν ἀρχιερέων 'and of the rulers and of the chief priests'. GNT rejects both of these additions with a B decision, indicating that the text is almost certain. Καὶ τῶν ἀρχιερέων 'and of the chief priests' is read by KJV.

LEXICON—a. imperf. mid./pass. (deponent = act.) indic. of ἐπίκειμαι (LN **68.16**) (BAGD 2.b. p. 294): 'to keep on' [**LN**; CEV, TEV], 'to persist' [AB, LN; REB], 'to go on insisting' [Lns], 'to continue insisting' [LN], 'to continue to press' [NTC], 'to keep on pressing' [WBC], 'to press upon' [Arn], 'to continue' [NCV], 'to be urgent' [BAGD], 'to be insistent' [BAGD, BECNT; KJV, NASB, NET], 'to pressure' [GW], 'to keep up the pressure' [HCSB]. This verb is also translated as an adverb: 'they insistently (demanded)' [NIV], 'they kept urgently (demanding)' [NRSV]. The phrase 'they kept on with loud voices demanding that he be crucified' is translated 'the crowd shouted louder and louder for Jesus' death' [NLT].

b. imperf. act. indic. of κατισχύω (LN 79.64) (BAGD 1. p. 424): 'to prevail, to be dominant' [BAGD], 'to have the strength to, to be able to' [LN]. The clause κατίσχυον αἱ φωναὶ αὐτῶν 'their voices were prevailing' is translated 'their voices prevailed' [AB, BECNT, NTC, WBC; KJV, NLT, NRSV], 'their voices began to prevail' [Arn; NASB], 'their shouts prevailed' [NET, NIV, REB], 'their voices won out' [HCSB], 'they finally won' [GW], 'finally their shouting succeeded' [TEV], not explicit [CEV, NCV]. Most translate this to mean that they had won [BECNT, NTC, WBC; all versions except CEV, NASB, NCV]. Some take the imperfect to mean that 'their voices *began* to prevail' [Arn, Lns; NASB] and this would mean that the battle with Pilate would not entirely be won until Pilate finally pronounced sentence [Lns].

QUESTION—What is meant by ἐπέκειντο 'they kept on'?

This summarizes the series of negotiations that are only implied by Luke and are recounted only in John 19:1–12 [Gdt].

DISCOURSE UNIT: 23:24–25 [BECNT]. The topic is Jesus' condemnation and Barabbas' release.

23:24 **And Pilate decided**[a] **(that) their demand be-done.** **23:25** **And he-released the (one) whom they were demanding,**[b] **who had-been-thrown into prison because-of an-insurrection and murder, but Jesus he-handed-over**[c] **to-their will.**

TEXT—In 23:25, following ἀπέλυσεν δέ 'and he released', some manuscripts add αὐτοῖς 'to them', although GNT does not mention this variant. Αὐτοῖς 'to them' is read by KJV.

LEXICON—a. aorist act. indic. of ἐπικρίνω (LN **30.75**) (BAGD p. 295): 'to decide' [BAGD, LN], 'to determine' [BAGD]. The phrase ἐπέκρινεν γενέσθαι τὸ αἴτημα αὐτῶν 'decided that their demand be done' is translated 'decided that their demand should be granted' [NET], 'decided that their request should be granted' [WBC], 'decided that their demand should be met' [AB], 'decided to grant their demand' [**LN**; HCSB, NIV], 'decided to give in to their demand' [GW], 'decided to give them what they wanted' [NCV], 'decided that they should have their way' [REB], 'Pilate gave in' [CEV], 'pronounced sentence that their demand be granted' [NTC; NASB], 'passed the sentence on Jesus that they were asking for' [TEV], 'gave sentence that it should be as they required' [KJV], 'gave sentence that their demand be done' [Lns], 'gave judgment for their demand' [BECNT], 'gave his verdict that their demand should be granted' [NRSV], 'ruled that their request should be granted' [Arn], 'sentenced Jesus to die as they demanded' [NLT].

b. imperf. act. indic. of αἰτέω (LN 33.163): 'to demand' [LN], 'to ask for' [AB, Arn, BECNT, LN, NTC, WBC; HCSB, NASB, NET, NIV, NRSV, REB], 'to ask as their due' [Lns], 'to request' [NLT], 'to want' [CEV, GW, TEV], 'to desire' [KJV], not explicit [NCV]. The imperfect tense is iterative [ICC, Lns, TH]: the one whom they *kept* demanding. However, many translate the verb as a simple past action [AB, Arn, BECNT; CEV, GW, NET, NIV, NLT, NRSV, REB, TEV], the one whom they demanded.

c. aorist act. indic. of παραδίδωμι (LN 37.111): 'to hand over, to turn over to' [LN]. The phrase Ἰησοῦν παρέδωκεν τῷ θελήματι αὐτῶν 'Jesus he handed over to their will' [AB] is also translated 'Jesus he delivered over to their will' [Arn; similarly WBC, HCSB, NET], 'Jesus he delivered to their will' [Lns; similarly KJV, NASB], 'Jesus he gave over to their will' [BECNT], 'Jesus he surrendered to their will' [NTC], 'he gave Jesus over to their will' [REB], 'he handed Jesus over as they wished' [NRSV], 'he delivered Jesus over to them to do as they wished' [NLT], 'he handed Jesus over for them to do as they wished' [TEV], 'he handed Jesus over to them to do with him as they wished' [NCV], 'he handed Jesus over for them to do what they wanted with him' [CEV], 'he surrendered Jesus to their will' [NIV], 'he let them do what they wanted to Jesus' [GW].

QUESTION—What is meant by Πιλᾶτος ἐπέκρινεν 'Pilate decided'?

1. The verb is used in its general sense of personally deciding to do this [AB, NAC, TH, WBC; GW, HCSB, NCV, NET, REB]. The general sense of 'decide' is likely here [WBC]. Pilate did not declare that Jesus was guilty, he decided that what the Jews wanted should be granted [NAC; NET].

2. The verb has a technical nuance of issuing an official sentence [BECNT, EGT, ICC, Lns, Rb; KJV, NASB, NLT, NRSV, TEV]. In this context, the verb means 'to decree, to pass judgment on' [NTC, Rb]. Pilate pronounced the final sentence [Rb]. He gave the sentence of death [EGT].

QUESTION—What is meant by παρέδωκεν τῷ θελήματι αὐτῶν 'he delivered to their will'?

This does not mean that Pilate delivered Jesus over to the crowd so that they could kill him, rather it means that Pilate handed Jesus over to be executed, as the Jews wanted him to do [BNTC, Lns, TG, TH]. In Mark 15:15, apparently Jesus was handed over to the soldiers to be crucified [BECNT,

NIGTC]. Pilate's soldiers crucified Jesus and that was the Jews' will [Lns]. Or, Pilate handed Jesus over to the Jewish leaders and the people to take Jesus out to be executed [WBC].

DISCOURSE UNIT: 23:26–56a [Su]. The topic is being crucified and buried.

DISCOURSE UNIT: 23:26–49 [BECNT, NICNT, NIGTC, TNTC; NET]. The topic is the crucifixion [NET], the crucifixion of Jesus [BECNT, NICNT, NIGTC, TNTC],

DISCOURSE UNIT: 23:26–43 [CEV, NCV, NIV, NLT, NRSV, TEV]. The topic is the crucifixion [NIV, NLT], the crucifixion of Jesus [NRSV], Jesus is crucified [NCV, TEV], Jesus is nailed to a cross [CEV].

DISCOURSE UNIT: 23:26–32 [AB, BECNT, NAC, WBC; GW, NASB]. The topic is the way to the cross [AB, NAC], to Golgotha [BECNT], on the way to execution [WBC], Jesus is led away to be crucified [GW], Simon bears the cross [NASB].

DISCOURSE UNIT: 23:26–31 [NICNT, NIGTC]. The topic is on the way to the crucifixion.

DISCOURSE UNIT: 23:26 [TNTC]. The topic is Simon carries the cross.

23:26 And as they-led- him -away,ᵃ having-seizedᵇ a-certain Simon a-Cyrenian coming from (the) countrysideᶜ they-put-onᵈ him the cross to-carry following Jesus.

TEXT—Instead of the predicate participle ἐρχόμενον 'coming/as he was coming' some manuscripts read the attributive participle τὸν ἐρχόμενον 'the one coming/who was coming', although GNT does not mention this variant. Strangely, the attributive participle τὸν ἐρχόμενον 'the one coming/who was coming' is rendered by GW, HCSB, NET, NIV, NLT, NRSV, and TEV, while the predicate participle ἐρχόμενον 'coming/as he was coming' is rendered by KJV, NASB, and NCV. It appears that none of these translations were governed by the textual difference between these two readings. The sense is not affected [AB].

LEXICON—a. aorist act. indic. of ἀπάγω (LN 56.38) (BAGD 2.c. p. 79): 'to lead away' [AB, Arn, BAGD, BECNT, LN, Lns, NTC, WBC; all versions except CEV, REB], 'to lead away to execution' [BAGD; REB]. This active verb is also translated passively with Simon as the subject: 'to be led away' [CEV]. This verb is used here as a legal technical term meaning 'to lead off to punishment or to death' [LN], 'to lead away to execution' [Arn, BAGD].

b. aorist mid. (deponent = act.) participle of ἐπιλαμβάνομαι (LN 18.2) (BAGD 1. p. 295): 'to seize' [Arn, BECNT; HCSB, NASB, NET, NIV, NRSV, TEV], 'to seize upon' [AB], 'to take hold of' [BAGD, LN, Lns, WBC; REB], 'to catch hold of' [NTC], 'to grasp' [BAGD, LN], 'to grab' [GW], 'to grab hold of' [CEV], 'to lay hold upon' [KJV]. This active verb is also translated passively with Simon as the subject: 'to be forced' [NLT]. The phrase 'having seized...they put upon him the cross' is translated 'they forced him to carry Jesus' cross' [NCV]. It is implied that this was done with violence [TH].

c. ἀγρός (LN 1.87) (BAGD 2. p. 14): 'countryside' [LN, WBC], 'the country' [BAGD, BECNT, Lns, NTC; all versions except CEV, GW, NCV], 'the fields' [LN; CEV, NCV], 'a/the field' [AB, Arn], 'rural area' [LN], not explicit [GW].

d. aorist act. indic. of ἐπιτίθημι (LN **85.51**) (BAGD 1.a.α. p. 303): 'to put upon/on' [AB, BAGD, **LN**; CEV, NIV, TEV], 'to put on his back' [REB], 'to place on' [Arn, LN, Lns, NTC; NASB, NET], 'to lay on' [BECNT, LN, WBC; GW, HCSB, KJV, NRSV]. The subject is changed to Simon: 'to carry' [NCV, NLT].

QUESTION—Who led Jesus away and where were they taking him?

1. The soldiers led Jesus away [Arn, EGT, Gdt, Lns, MGC, NAC, NIGTC, NTC, Su, TG, TH, WBC; GW, TEV]. Following the statement in the preceding verse, 'Jesus he delivered to their will' it would seem that the Jews led Jesus away, but the following passage shows that the soldiers led Jesus away [NIGTC, WBC]. They were Roman soldiers [TG]. However, in this case the soldiers were only carrying out the will of the ones who demanded the crucifixion [NAC]. In John 19:17–20 it says that they took Jesus outside Jerusalem to be crucified at Golgotha [Su].

2. The chief priests, scribes, and people led Jesus away [AB]. The pronoun 'they' refers to the people to whom Pilate delivered Jesus to their will in 23:25 and the Roman soldiers will eventually appear in verses 36 and 47 [AB].

3. This refers to all those who opposed Jesus: Romans, Jewish leaders, and the Jewish people [NICNT].

QUESTION—Who was Simon, the Cyrenian, and why would the soldiers seize him?

Simon came from Cyrene, a city west of Egypt, in the land that is now Libya [NTC]. Simon was a Jew from Cyrene, which was an important center for dispersed Jews in North Africa [Su]. Simon was one of the many Cyrenians who were now residents of Jerusalem [Lns]. Or, instead of being a permanent resident of Jerusalem, Simon was probably a pilgrim who was coming to Jerusalem for the Passover [WBC]. Simon had been working in the fields [Arn, Gdt], or had merely gone a Sabbath day's journey to look at his field [Arn]. It was too early in the day to be coming from working in a field, so he may have resided outside the city [NAC]. It cannot be certain that Simon was a farmer since many people had business or social connections in the country [NTC]. He was coming in from the countryside to celebrate the Passover [BECNT, NTC, Su]. The Roman army had the authority to requisition assistance from civilians and so they had the power to demand that Simon carry Jesus' cross the rest of the distance [NAC, NTC].

QUESTION—Why was the cross put upon Simon and what was this cross?

It is implied that Jesus had been carrying the cross on his back or across his shoulders until then [Lns, Su, TG]. It was the custom for the condemned man to carry his own cross to the place of crucifixion [NIGTC], so it can be assumed that Jesus was physically breaking down under its weight [AB, BECNT, ICC, Lns, MGC, NIC, NIGTC, NTC, TNTC, WBC]. Jesus had not eaten for hours and he had endured a terrible scourging, so in his weakened state he couldn't carry the cross any further [Su]. With all the ordeals that Jesus had gone through, it was a wonder that Jesus could have carried the cross that far [NTC]. Probably only the horizontal cross beam of the cross is meant [BECNT, Crd, ICC, NAC, NIC, TG]. The man to be crucified had to carry the horizontal beam to the place of the crucifixion and there that beam would be attached to the vertical beam [TG]. Sometimes only the cross piece was carried and sometimes both beams were carried to the place of crucifixion where the beams would be joined together [ICC]. Or, the complete cross was carried [EGT, Lns], although it was not as high as it is often pictured [Lns].

QUESTION—What is meant by putting the cross on Simon to carry following Jesus?

It could mean that Simon and Jesus carried the two beams together, or it might mean that Jesus carried one part in front while Simon followed him carrying the other beam. However, Mark 15:21 and Matthew 27:32 seem to imply that Simon alone carried the cross while Jesus went ahead of him [Su]. Simon alone carried the cross [EGT]. 'Put' may mean that they placed on Simon the obligation to carry the cross [NAC].

DISCOURSE UNIT: 23:27–31 [TNTC]. The topic is the daughters of Jerusalem.

23:27 **And there-were-following him a-great multitude of-the people and^a of-women who were-mourning^b and lamenting^c for-him.**

TEXT—Following αἵ 'who', some manuscripts add καί 'also', although GNT does not mention this variant. Καί 'also' is read by KJV.

LEXICON—a. καί (LN 89.92): 'and' [LN]. The phrase 'and of women who' [Arn, BECNT, NTC; KJV, NASB] is also translated 'also of women' [Lns], 'including women who' [HCSB, NIV], 'including some women who' [NCV], 'including many (grief-stricken) women' [NLT], 'and among them women who' [NET, NRSV], 'among them many women who' [REB], 'and among them were many women who' [WBC], 'many of them women who' [AB], 'among them were some women who' [TEV], 'and in the crowd a lot of women were' [CEV], 'The women in the crowd (cried)' [GW]. There were many women who were probably walking together close to him [Lns].

b. imperf. mid. indic. of κόπτομαι (LN 52.1) (BAGD 2. p. 444): 'to mourn' [BAGD, LN; HCSB, NASB, NET, NIV, REB], 'to lament' [Arn, LN], 'to cry' [CEV, GW], 'to weep' [TEV], 'to wail' [BECNT], 'to bewail' [KJV],

'to be sad for' [NCV], 'to beat their breasts' [AB, Lns, NTC, WBC; NRSV]. The phrase 'women who were mourning and lamenting for him' is translated 'grief-stricken women' [NLT]. Literally, the verb means 'to beat the breast' and this act expresses sorrow [BAGD, LN]. Beating the breast was a form of ritual mourning in Jewish funerals [NET].
c. imperf. act. indic of θρηνέω (LN **25.141, 52.2**) (BAGD 2. p. 363): 'to lament' [BAGD, BECNT, **LN** (52.2), NTC; HCSB, KJV, NASB, REB], 'to mourn' [BAGD], 'to wail' [AB, **LN** (25.141), WBC; NET, NIV, NRSV, TEV], 'to bewail' [Lns], 'to weep' [Arn; CEV], 'to cry' [NCV], 'to sing funeral songs' [GW]. The phrase 'who were mourning and lamenting for him' is translated 'who beat their breasts and lamented' [LN (52.2)]. See the preceding lexical item for NLT. They wailed at Jesus' fate [AB]. Loud demonstrations of distress and grief were customary [Su]. This was a death wail since they considered Jesus to be as good as dead [Lns]. Although using a professional mourning style, they were sincere in lamenting Jesus' fate [MGC].

23:28 **And having-turned to them Jesus said, Daughters**[a] **of-Jerusalem, do-not -weep for me, but weep for yourselves and for your children.**
LEXICON—a. θυγάτηρ (LN **11.65**) (BAGD 2.d. p. 365): 'daughter' [BAGD, LN]. The phrase θυγατέρες Ἰερουσαλήμ 'daughters of Jerusalem' [Arn, BECNT, Lns, NTC, WBC; HCSB, KJV, NASB, NET, NIV, NLT, NRSV, REB] is also translated 'women of Jerusalem' [CEV, NCV, TEV], 'you women of Jerusalem' [GW]. Here this is a figurative extension of θυγάτηρα 'daughter' (10.46) and it means a female inhabitant of a place [BAGD, **LN**, TH]. This title was used to portray these women as being representatives of the nation [NET].
QUESTION—Who were the people who followed Jesus?
They were the people of Jerusalem in general [TH]. Gatherings of curious crowds at an execution were normal [NIGTC]. The crowds that had demanded that Jesus be crucified were few enough to crowd around Pilate's judgment hall, but now there was a great number of people and it appears that many of them admired Jesus [TNTC]. These were mostly people who sympathized with Jesus [NAC, NICNT, NIGTC]. Although they were not followers of Jesus, some of the women considered Jesus to be a prophet and a benefactor and they now saw that he was suffering from the ruthless authorities [NIC]. The people included loyal followers and those who sympathized with Jesus, and perhaps some women who were members of the society of charitable women of Jerusalem [NTC].
QUESTION—What did Jesus mean when he said 'do not weep for me'?
1. Jesus told them to stop weeping for him and weep for themselves [Alf, Arn, BECNT, Lns, My, NTC, Su, WBC; NET]. He commanded them to stop what they were already doing [Lns, Su]. They were mourning for the wrong person [NET]. He appreciated their concern, but it was not the time to weep for him because his death was a necessary part of God's

redemptive purposes and it had to occur [Su]. Rather than weeping for Jesus who was prepared to be obedient to his Father and go to his appointed destiny of death and glory, they should weep about the terrible judgment of God that will befall the city [WBC]. They were not to weep for him because he was on his way to meet a glorious future while they themselves had the impending destruction of Jerusalem to face [My]. Jesus would not be suffering the torments of hell, but unless those women repented, they would [NTC].
2. This command was a literary device meaning that although it was proper to weep for him, they should realize that they had far more reason to weep for themselves [ICC, NIC, NIGTC, TNTC]. Jesus' suffering would be short, but theirs will be prolonged and end in shame and destruction [ICC]. Jesus' words have the force of 'Do not weep so much for me as for yourselves and your children' [NIGTC].

23:29 Because behold (the) days are-coming[a] in which they-will-say, Fortunate[b] (are) the barren[c] and the wombs that did- not -bear[d] and (the) breasts that did- not -nurse.[e]

LEXICON—a. pres. mid./pass. (deponent = act.) indic. of ἔρχομαι (LN 13.117) (BAGD I.1.b.α. p. 311): 'to come' [BAGD], 'to happen' [LN]. The phrase 'the days are coming' [Arn, BECNT, NTC, WBC; HCSB, KJV, NASB, NET, NLT, NRSV, REB, TEV] is also translated 'the time is coming' [AB; GW, NCV], 'the time will come' [NIV], 'there are coming days' [Lns], 'some day' [CEV].

b. μακάριος (LN 25.119) (BAGD 1.a. p. 486): 'fortunate' [BAGD; CEV, NLT], 'how fortunate' [WBC], 'how lucky' [TEV], 'blessed' [AB, Arn, BAGD, BECNT, Lns, NTC; GW, HCSB, KJV, NASB, NET, NIV, NRSV], 'happy' [BAGD, LN; NCV, REB]. See this word at 1:45; 6:20; 7:23; 10:23; 11:27; 12:37, 43; 14:14.

c. στεῖρα (LN 23.56) (BAGD p. 766): 'barren' [BAGD, LN]. The phrase 'the barren' [Arn, Lns, WBC; HCSB, KJV, NASB, NET, NRSV, REB] is also translated 'the barren women' [NTC; NIV], 'the women who couldn't get pregnant' [GW], 'the childless' [AB], 'the women who are childless' [NLT], 'the women who never had children' [TEV]. The first two types of women are combined as 'the barren wombs' [BECNT], 'the women who cannot have children' [NCV]. The three types of women are combined as 'women who never had children' [CEV]. This refers to the state of not being able to conceive and bear children [LN].

d. aorist act. indic. of γεννάω (LN 23.52) (BAGD 2. p. 155): 'to bear' [BAGD, LN], 'to give birth' [LN]. The phrase 'the wombs that did not bear' [Lns] is also translated 'the wombs that never bore' [NTC; HCSB, KJV, NASB, NIV, NRSV], 'the wombs which did not give birth' [Arn], 'the wombs that have never given birth' [AB, WBC], 'the wombs that never bore children' [NET, REB], 'the wombs that have not borne a child' [NLT], 'the women who never bore babies' [TEV], 'the women who

couldn't give birth' [GW]. The punctiliar aorist tense implies 'never once' [TH].
- e. aorist act. indic. of τρέφω (LN 23.6) (BAGD 1. p. 825): 'to nurse, to feed, to nourish' [BAGD], 'to provide food for' [BAGD, LN]. The phrase 'the breasts that did not nurse' is translated 'the breasts that never nursed' [NTC; HCSB, NASB, NET, NIV, NLT, NRSV], 'the breasts which did not give nourishment' [Arn], 'the breasts that did not give milk' [BECNT], 'the breasts that never fed one' [REB], 'the breasts that have never given suck' [AB, WBC], 'the breasts which did not suckle' [Lns], 'the paps that never gave suck' [KJV], 'the women who have no babies to nurse' [NCV], 'the women who never nursed them' [TEV], 'the women who couldn't nurse a child' [GW]. The punctiliar aorist tense implies 'never once' [TH].

QUESTION—Who are the 'they' who will say this?
This means people in general will say this [ICC, TG]. The indefinite subject refers to anybody and everybody [Lns]. The coming days will be so horrible that people will consider that it would be better not to have children than to see their children suffer so terribly [NIGTC].

QUESTION—Why will such women be blessed?
Although bearing children was the most fortunate state of womanhood, in the coming days children will be slaughtered in front of their mothers and women will be fortunate not to have children then [Su]. In the dreadful situation of those days the normal values will be reversed [BECNT, MGC, NIC, NIGTC, Su]. Normally, children were God's good gift, but in that day children will suffer so terribly that it would be better not to have children that would have to go through such suffering and death [Su]. These women will not have to see their children put to death [AB]. The statement in the form of a blessing is ironic [MGC].

QUESTION—What are the distinctions between the three states of women?
The barren are women who could not have children while the other two conditions refer to women who had not given birth to children [TH]. The three phrases about women are a vivid way of simply saying 'How fortunate are women who do not have children!' [TG; CEV]. Or, the reference to the barren women is explained by the other two statements that belong together [Lns]. The fortunate women with no children were either barren or unmarried [EGT].

23:30 Then they-will-begin[a] to-say to-the mountains, Fall[b] on us, and to-the hills, Cover[c] us.

LEXICON—a. fut. mid. indic. of ἄρχομαι (LN 68.1): 'to begin' [AB, Arn, BECNT, LN, Lns, NTC, WBC; HCSB, KJV, NASB, NET, NRSV, REB], 'to commence' [LN], not explicit [CEV, GW, NCV, NIV, NLT, TEV]. This verb has no meaning of its own here and can go untranslated [TH].
- b. aorist act. impera. of πίπτω (LN 15.118) (BAGD p. 659): 'to fall' [AB, Arn, BAGD, BECNT, LN, Lns, NTC, WBC; all versions].

c. aorist act. impera. of καλύπτω (LN 79.114) (BAGD 1. p. 401): 'to cover' [AB, Arn, BAGD, BECNT, LN, Lns, NTC, WBC; all versions except CEV, TEV], 'to cover over' [LN], 'to bury' [NLT], 'to hide' [BAGD; CEV, TEV], 'to conceal' [BAGD]. 'Cover' means to 'pile up over', 'form a heap over', or 'bury' [TH].

QUESTION—Who are the 'they' who will say this?

This refers to people in general, not just women [Arn, BECNT, ICC, My], 'everyone' [CEV]. The indefinite subject refers to the people who will experience the horrors of those days [BECNT, Lns]. They are the people who rejected Jesus [NICNT].

QUESTION—What is significant about the mention of the mountains and the hills?

Palestine was a land of mountains and hills [EGT]. These nouns also appear together in 3:5, but here they are poetically personified [TH]. Although the clauses are transposed from 'mountains cover us' and 'hills fall on us', the prophecy is found in Hosea 10:8 where Samaria was to be destroyed by the Assyrians [Alf, BNTC, Lns, MGC, NAC, NICNT, NIGTC, NTC, TG, WBC; NET]. That transposition is probably stylistic [NTC].

QUESTION—Why would people desire to have the mountains fall on them and to have the hills cover them?

1. This expresses their desire for a quick death in order to escape the coming agony [BECNT, ICC, Lns, MGC, My, NAC, NIBC, NIC, NICNT, NIVS, Su, TH, TNTC, WBC; NET]. Death is preferable to enduring such terror and misery [ICC]. Suffering a quick death is preferable to the prolonged agony at the hands of the Roman army in those days [Su]. They will wish for death and burial to put an end to the horrors coming to them [NIBC].
2. This expresses their desire for protection [Alf, Arn, TG; CEV, TEV]. This poetic language is uttered by people who will wish for a place of refuge from their punishment from God [Arn]. The Jews sought to escape death by hiding in underground passages and sewers under the city [Alf].

23:31 Because[a] if they-do these (things) when (the) firewood/tree[b] (is) full-of-moisture,[c] what will-happen[d] when (it is) dry?

LEXICON—a. ὅτι (LN 89.33): 'because' [LN, Lns], 'for' [AB, Arn, BECNT, NTC, WBC; all versions except CEV, GW, NCV], not explicit [CEV, GW, NCV].

b. ξύλον (LN **3.4, 3.61**) (BAGDS 3. p. 549): 'firewood' [**LN** (3.61)], 'wood' [AB, BAGD, BECNT, Lns, NTC, WBC; CEV, HCSB, NET, NRSV, REB, TEV], 'tree' [Arn, BAGD, **LN** (3.4); GW, KJV, NASB, NIV, NLT], not explicit [NCV].

c. ὑγρός (LN **79.78**) (BAGD p. 832): 'moist' [BAGD, **LN**], 'green' [AB, Arn, BAGD, BECNT, **LN**, Lns, NTC, WBC; all versions except NCV], not explicit [NCV]. 'Green' is used in reference to wood [LN].

d. aorist mid. (deponent = act.) subj. of γίνομαι (LN 13.107) (BAGD I.2.b. p. 158): 'to happen' [AB, Arn, BECNT, LN, NTC, WBC; all versions except KJV], 'to occur, to come to be' [LN], 'to be done' [BAGD; KJV], 'to be' [Lns].

QUESTION—What relationship is indicated by ὅτι 'because'?

It indicates the reason for predicting the horrors that will certainly come [ICC]. It is the reason that the future outlook is so bleak [NIGTC]. Jesus explains why such cries will be justified [Lns]. It introduces an explanation of the quotation in 23:30 [TH].

QUESTION—What are 'these things' that they do?

This refers to the thing being done to Jesus [TH]. 'These things' refers to what the Romans were doing to Jesus and 'what will happen' refers to what would happen to Jerusalem [Su].

QUESTION—What will happen if they do these things in the second clause?

It is a lesser to greater argument [BECNT, ICC, NAC, WBC]. It means that they will do much worse things [Lns, TG].

QUESTION—Does ξύλον mean 'firewood' or 'tree' and what does the question mean?

1. This refers to firewood [LN (3.61), NTC, TG; probably AB, CEV, HCSB, NRSV, REB, TEV which translate this as 'wood']. Firewood full of moisture refers to firewood that has not had an opportunity to dry out or is still green and wet with sap [LN]. This has nothing to do with a living tree, it refers to wood in its moist green condition [NTC]. Wood of a tree that has just been cut is green wood [TG]. The question is translated 'If they do these things to moist firewood, what will happen in the case of dry firewood?' [**LN**].

2. This refers to a tree [Arn, BECNT, LN (3.4), NIVS; GW, KJV, NASB, NET, NIV, NLT]. The question is translated 'If they do these things to a green tree, what will happen in the case of a dry one?' [**LN**]. Jesus is compared to a living tree [BECNT].

3. This is a metaphor of spring and Jesus is the green wood of fruit bearing when God's favor was extended and Israel is the dry wood of fruitlessness when God's favor was not extended [Su].

4. This question is translated without the metaphor: 'If they act like this now when life is good, what will happen when bad times come?' [NCV].

QUESTION—How is this metaphor to be interpreted?

This appears to be a proverbial saying [AB, ICC, NTC, TG, TH, TNTC, WBC] and it could have many applications [ICC]. Wood that is dry burns much more readily than wood that is green or soggy [NAC, NIGTC, NTC]. If green wood is made to burn, then of course dry wood would surely burn until completely consumed [NTC]. Jesus compared himself with damp, soggy wood which is difficult to kindle [AB, NTC, TH]. The dry wood is ready to be burned [NIC]. It is implied that the wood is burned and the fire is a symbol of judgment [WBC]. The dry wood represents the sinful Jews in Jerusalem or the nation of Israel [AB, BECNT, Crd, EGT, Gdt, MGC, NAC, NIBC, NIC, NIGTC, NTC, TG, TNTC]. This contrasts Jesus with the women of Jerusalem along with the generation that will go through the ordeals implied in 23:29–30 [TH]. There are various explanations. If Jesus, who is innocent, suffers like this, how much more the guilty Jews will suffer [TNTC]. It means that if an innocent person is punished like this, how much worse the punishment will be for wicked people who deserve punishment [Arn, Crd, My, TG]. It means that when Jesus who is innocent has to suffer death, how much more will the sinful Jews have to suffer [TH]. If God has not spared Jesus, how much less will impenitent Jews be spared God's judgment [NTC]. Or, if Jesus is punished by the Romans for being a rebel even though he always submitted to them, how much worse the Romans will treat the Jewish people who have a spirit of revolt and thus give the Romans a stronger reason for punishment [Gdt]. If God allows innocent Jesus (the green wood) to suffer what the Jews of Jerusalem have prepared for him, how much worse will be the fate of Jerusalem (the dry wood) [AB]. Or, if God has not spared Jesus from crucifixion, how much worse it will be for the impenitent nation when God brings his righteous wrath on it [BECNT, NAC, NIGTC] and he permits the Romans to destroy Jerusalem [NAC].

DISCOURSE UNIT: 23:32–43 [NICNT]. The topic is Jesus crucified and mocked.

DISCOURSE UNIT: 23:32–38 [NIGTC, TNTC]. The topic is the crucifixion.

23:32 And also there-were-led-off others, two criminals,[a] to-be-executed[b] with him.

LEXICON—a. κακοῦργος (LN **88.114**) (BAGD p. 398): 'criminal' [AB, Arn, BAGD, BECNT, NTC, WBC; all versions except KJV], 'evildoer' [BAGD, LN], 'wrongdoer, bad person' [LN], 'malefactor' [Lns; KJV]

b. aorist pass. infin. of ἀναιρέω (LN 20.71) (BAGD 1.a. p. 55): 'to be executed' [LN, NTC, WBC; GW, HCSB, NET, NIV, NLT], 'to be killed' [LN], 'to be put to death' [AB, Arn, BAGD, BECNT; CEV, KJV, NASB, NCV, NRSV, TEV], 'to be made away with' [Lns]. This verb is also translated as a noun: '(to be led out to) execution' [REB]. The verb means to kill by execution [TH].

QUESTION—What were they being led away from?

Soldiers led them out of the city [TG]. They were taken outside the city wall [NTC].

QUESTION—Does the wording ἕτεροι κακοῦργοι δύο 'others, two criminals' suggest that Jesus was also a criminal and what was their crime?

The word 'criminals' qualifies the two others, not Jesus [EGT, ICC, My, NAC, TH]. The word ἕτεροι 'others' is used in unusual way and means 'two others, namely criminals' and not 'two other criminals' [Arn]. None of the versions suggest that Jesus was also a criminal. Or, it means 'two other malefactors' [Alf], and, if so, it would be in reference to what men thought [EGT]. The noun κακοῦργος means a person who commits serious crimes [TH]. It is a general term meaning any kind of a lawbreaker [BECNT]. 'Criminal' means someone who does evil things [Su]. Their crime is not known, but since they were to be crucified for it, they must have been men who were a threat to the government, perhaps dangerous and violent men [NICNT]. Perhaps they were companions of Barabbas [Gdt, Su]. Mark 15:27 and Matt. 27:38 use the word ληστής 'robber', which means a highwayman or a revolutionary [Su], a bandit [ICC], or a thief [TNTC].

QUESTION—Why were the two criminals also crucified along with Jesus?

Perhaps the authorities arranged this in order to suggest that Jesus' crime was similar to that of the other two [ICC]. Pilate wanted everyone to see the kind of king the Jews had brought to him [Lns]. That Jesus was reckoned among transgressors fulfills the prophecy in Isaiah 53:12 [BECNT, Lns; NET]. Or, this connection to Isaiah is not likely [NICNT]. This is what Jesus foretold in 22:37 [BECNT, Lns, NAC, WBC; NET].

DISCOURSE UNIT: 23:33–65 [NASB]. The topic is the crucifixion.

DISCOURSE UNIT: 23:33–49 [GW]. The topic is the crucifixion.

DISCOURSE UNIT: 23:33–38 [AB, BECNT, NAC, WBC]. The topic is the crucifixion [AB, BECNT, NAC], Jesus crucified and mocked [WBC].

23:33 **And when they-came to the place called Skull,[a] there they-crucified[b] him and the criminals, one on (the) right, one on (the) left.**

LEXICON—a. κρανίον (LN 8.11) (BAGD p. 448): 'skull' [BAGD, LN]. The phrase 'the place called Skull' [WBC] is also translated 'the place called The Skull' [AB, NTC; all versions except KJV, NCV, NLT], 'a place called the Skull' [BECNT; NCV, NLT], 'the place called a Skull' [Arn], 'the place called Cranium' [Lns], 'the place, which is called Calvary' [KJV]. The place is called 'Golgotha' in Aramaic and that is the name used in Matt. 27:33 and Mark 15:22, but they add that this Aramaic word means 'skull' [BECNT]. In the Latin translation, the name is *Calvariae* (Calvary) [ICC, NAC], and Calvary was the name used in all English translations prior to the English Revised Version of 1881 [ICC].

b. aorist act. indic. of σταυρόω (LN20.76) (BAGD 1. p. 765): 'to crucify' [AB, Arn, BAGD, BECNT, LN, Lns, NTC, WBC; all versions except CEV, GW, NLT], 'to nail to a cross' [CEV]. The active voice is also translated passively: 'to be crucified' [GW, NLT].

QUESTION—Who are the 'they' who came to the place called Skull and who are the 'they' who crucified the men?

The pronoun 'they' in both places refer to the soldiers [TH]. Or, 'they came' refers to the whole group [MGC]. The soldiers nailed Jesus to the cross [NTC, TG, TH; CEV, NCV].

QUESTIO—How was Jesus crucified?

Luke does not mention nails, but John 20:5 and Col. 2:14 indicate that at least the hands were nailed [AB, BECNT, NAC]. It is not certain that his feet were also nailed [BECNT, ICC]. From history, we learn that first the cross was planted in the ground and a block or peg of wood was fastened to the beam for the victim to sit upon. The victim mounted the seat himself or was lifted onto it by the soldiers. The soldiers fastened the body, arms, and legs with ropes and then drove large nails through the hands and also through each foot separately. Some commentators think that Jesus' feet were not nailed, but in 24:39 Jesus says 'Behold my hands and my feet' [Lns]. Or, the vertical beam and the cross beam were attached on the ground and a small seat for the victim was added. The victim was laid on the cross and his arms and legs were tied in place. Then nails were driven through the hands and one nail through the feet which had been placed one on the other. The cross was raised and put into a hole that had been dug for it [Arn]. Or, the feet rested on a little wooden projection not far from the ground [NTC]. Three types of crosses were used in crucifixions: in the shape of an X, in the shape of a T, or in the shape of a cross, and since there was an inscription placed above Jesus' head, it was probably the third type that was used. Sometimes the feet were fixed to the beam by a nail though the superimposed feet and nails were driven through the palms or wrists. If it was through the palms, the wrists would also be tied to the cross beam to prevent the hands from tearing away. Death came from exposure, from loss of blood, and from dehydration [Su]. There were many different ways in which victims were crucified, but probably nails pierced Jesus' forearms and not his hands since when he said 'Behold my χεῖρας', the noun can mean either hands or forearms. Probably a buttocks support was not used to help prolong his life since the bodies had to be taken down before the Sabbath began [WBC].

QUESTION—Why was the place called 'Skull'?

Probably the place was a hill that that was shaped like a man's skull [AB, Gdt, ICC, Lns, MGC, My, NAC, Su, TG, TH, TNTC]. It was the shape of the hill that gave the place its name, not because skulls were lying about unburied [AB, BECNT, Gdt, ICC]. The hill was shaped like a cranium, the top part of a skull, and it was called 'Cranium', not a whole skull [Lns]. The place was a bare rounded hill [Gdt].

23:34 And Jesus said, Father, forgive them, because they-do- not -know[a] what they-are-doing. And dividing-up[b] his garments they-cast lots.[c]

TEXT—Some manuscripts omit ὁ δὲ Ἰησοῦς ἔλεγεν, Πάτερ, ἄφες αὐτοῖς, οὐ γὰρ οἴδασιν τί ποιοῦσιν 'And Jesus said, Father, forgive them, because they do not know what they are doing', other manuscripts include these words, and one manuscript includes these words with asterisks, indicating doubt. GNT favors the omission of these words with an A decision, indicating that the omission of these words is certain, yet it includes them in the text in double brackets, since even though not part of the text in Luke, Jesus apparently did say these words. This sentence is included in brackets by NET. It is omitted by AB. Others have a footnote to indicate the problem.

LEXICON—a. perf. act. indic. of οἶδα (LN 32.4): 'to understand, to be aware of, to really know' [LN]. The clause 'they do not know what they are doing' [Lns, NTC, WBC; all versions except KJV] is also translated 'they do not know what they do' [BECNT; similarly Arn, KJV].

508   LUKE 23:34

b. pres. mid. participle of διαμερίζω (LN 57.89) (BAGD 1.b. p. 186): 'to divide up' [AB, WBC; NASB, NIV], 'to divide' [Arn, BECNT, Lns; HCSB, NET, NRSV, TEV], 'to divide among themselves' [GW], 'to distribute' [BAGD, LN], 'to give each in turn' [LN], 'to part' [KJV], 'to share out' [REB], not explicit [CEV, NCV, NLT].

c. κλῆρος (LN 6.219) (BAGD 1. p. 435): 'lot' [BAGD, LN]. The phrase 'they cast lots' [AB, Arn, BECNT, WBC; HCSB, KJV, NASB, NRSV] is also translated 'they threw lots' [Lns; NCV], 'they threw dice' [NET], '(divided) by throwing dice' [GW, TEV], '(divided) by casting lots' [NIV], '(shared) by casting lots' [REB], '(gambled) by throwing dice' [NLT]. The clause 'they cast lots, distributing his garments' is translated 'they divided his clothes and cast lots' [HCSB], 'the soldiers gambled for his clothes' [CEV]. A *lot* is a specially marked object such as a pebble, a piece of pottery, or a stick and it was used for making decisions based upon chance [LN].

QUESTION—Whom did Jesus ask his Father to forgive and what was the basis for asking that they be forgiven?

1. 'Them' refers to the Jewish authorities [AB, BECNT, Gdt, ICC, My, NIC]. Their guilt was to be excused by the fact that they were ignorant of what they were doing in crucifying Jesus. [ICC].

2. 'Them' refers to the Jewish nation [BECNT, Gdt, NIC]. The prayer was primarily for the Jews as a nation since they were in error about God's activity. Jesus was asking that individuals would change their thinking and that God would not hold this act against them, and this actually happened in Acts [BECNT]. God withheld his wrath for forty years so that the people could hear the apostolic preaching and have the opportunity to repent and be saved [Gdt, NIC].

3. 'Them' refers to the Roman soldiers [Alf, Crd, Rb, Su, TH]. It could mean that the soldiers were ignorant of Jesus' innocence or guilt and were just carrying out the crucifixion on orders from an officer [Su]. 'What they are doing' means what they were doing at that very time, not what they did in general [Alf, TH]. It refers directly to the soldiers who were only doing their duty when they crucified Jesus, yet the soldiers were also the representatives of the sin of the Jewish nation [Alf].

4. 'Them' can refer to all of the above [Lns, NAC, NICNT, NIGTC, NTC, Su, TG, TNTC]. This refers either to the soldiers in particular or the crowd in general [Su, TG]. It refers to the executioners or possibly all who were involved in the crucifixion [NIGTC]. It refers to all those involved in Jesus' death and Jesus' prayer was answered by his death, which brought about the forgiveness of sins [NAC]. The soldiers did not know the significance of what they were doing and the members of the Sanhedrin, although knowing that what they did was wicked, did not comprehend the extent of that wickedness. But the Father could answer Jesus' prayer by causing them to repent so they could be forgiven [NTC]. Their sin was unwitting [NIGTC]. This forgiveness was not absolute; the fulfillment of

the prayer would be that these people would comprehend their horrible sin in putting to death God's own Son and learn of the redemption that Jesus effected through his death, and this knowledge would be the means of causing their repentance and forgiveness [Lns].

QUESTION—What was involved in casting lots for Jesus' garments?

It was usual for the executioners to get the clothing of the victim [BECNT, ICC, MGC, NAC, NIGTC, NTC, TNTC]. In John 19:23, we learn that four soldiers made up the group that cast lots [Lns, NTC]. The garments that were divided up among the four soldiers could have been a seamless tunic, headgear, sandals, and a belt [NTC]. The lots may have been marked pebbles [TG; NET], broken pieces of pottery [NET], dice [NTC, Su, TG], or this may refer to drawing names out of a helmet [Su]. Some translate the verbs as being in sequence and this gives the picture of dividing the clothing in separate piles and then casting lots to see who would get a pile: 'they divided up his garments *and* cast lots' [Arn, WBC; HCSB, KJV], 'dividing up his clothes, they cast lots for them' [AB]. Or, casting lots was the means by which they divided up his clothes: they divided up his clothes *by* casting lots [EGT, MGC; GW, NIV, NLT, REB, TEV], they cast lots *to* divide up his clothes [BECNT, NTC, TNTC; NET, NRSV], they cast lots, dividing up his clothes [NASB], in dividing up his clothes they cast lots [Lns], 'they threw lots to decide who would get his clothes' [NCV]. Setting apart the seamless tunic, the rest of the clothes (cloak, cap, girdle, and sandals) were divided up into nearly equal parts. Then lots were drawn to determine which of the four parts of the clothes each would get. Then a second drawing was made to determine which one would get the seamless tunic [Gdt]. Or, the clothing was divided among themselves and then they cast lots for the seamless tunic [TNTC].

23:35 And the people stood observing.[a] And also/even the rulers[b] were-ridiculing[c] (him) saying, He-saved[d] others, let-him-save himself if this (one) is the Messiah of-God the chosen[e] (one).

TEXT—Following οἱ ἄρχοντες 'the rulers', some manuscripts add σὺν αὐτοῖς 'with them'. GNT does not mention this variant. Σὺν αὐτοῖς 'with them' is read by KJV.

TEXT—Instead of ὁ Χριστὸς τοῦ θεοῦ ὁ ἐκλεκτός 'the Messiah of God, the chosen one' some manuscripts read ὁ Χριστὸς ὁ τοῦ θεοῦ ἐκλεκτός 'the Messiah, the chosen one of God', although GNT does not mention this variant. Ὁ Χριστὸς ὁ τοῦ θεοῦ ἐκλεκτός 'the Messiah, the chosen one of God' is read by KJV.

LEXICON—a. pres. act. participle of θεωρέω (LN 24.14) (BAGD 1. p. 360): 'to observe' [BAGD, LN], 'to watch' [BECNT; all versions except KJV, NASB, REB], 'to look' [BAGD, LN], 'to look on' [AB, Arn, NTC, WBC; NASB, REB], 'to behold' [Lns; KJV]. They were watching Jesus [CEV].

b. ἄρχων (LN 37.56) (BAGD 2.a. p. 114): 'ruler' [Arn, BECNT, LN, Lns, NTC; GW, KJV, NASB, NET, NIV, REB], 'authority, official' [BAGD], 'leader' [WBC; CEV, HCSB, NCV, NLT, NRSV], 'Jewish leader' [TEV]. Matt. 27:41 says that this refers to the chief priests, scribes, and elders [Arn, Gdt, Lns, NTC]. See this word at 8:41; 14:1; 18:18; 23:13.

c. imperf. act. indic. of ἐκμυκτηρίζω (LN 33.409) (BAGD p. 243): 'to ridicule' [BAGD, LN; NET], 'to sneer' [AB, BAGD, BECNT, LN, NTC, WBC; NASB], 'to jeer at' [REB], 'to scoff at' [HCSB, NRSV], 'to laugh and scoff' [NLT], 'to show contempt for' [LN], 'to insult' [CEV], 'to make sarcastic remarks' [GW], 'to make fun of' [NCV, TEV], 'to mock' [Arn], 'to deride' [KJV], 'to turn up the nose' [Lns]. The verb means to make fun of someone by joking or jesting about him [LN]. The imperfect tense indicates that they did this for some time and the words recorded here cover only the main things they said about Jesus [Lns].

d. imperf. act. indic. of σῴζω (LN 21.18) (BAGD 1.a. p. 798): 'to save' [AB, BAGD, BECNT, Lns, NTC, WBC; all versions], 'to deliver' [LN], 'to rescue' [Arn, LN]. The verb means to save or rescue from danger [BAGD, LN].

e. ἐκλεκτός (L 30.93) (BAGD 1.a. p. 242): 'chosen' [BAGD, LN]. The phrase ὁ Χριστὸς τοῦ θεοῦ ἐκλεκτός 'the Messiah of God the chosen' is translated 'the Messiah of God, his chosen one' [NRSV], 'the Christ of God, the Chosen one' [WBC; NIV], 'the Anointed of God, the Chosen One' [Arn], 'the Christ of God, his Chosen One' [NTC], 'the Christ of God, the elect' [BECNT, Lns], 'God's Messiah, the chosen One' [HCSB], 'God's Messiah, his Chosen One' [AB], 'God's Messiah, his Chosen' [REB], 'the Christ of God his Chosen One' [NASB, NET], 'Christ, the chosen of God' [KJV], 'God's chosen Messiah' [CEV], 'God's chosen One, the Christ' [NCV], 'God's Chosen One, the Messiah' [NLT], 'the Messiah that/whom God has chosen' [GW, TEV].

QUESTION—Does δὲ καὶ ἄρχοντες mean 'and *also* the rulers' or 'and *even* the rulers'?

  1. It means 'and also the rulers' [Alf, Arn, EGT, Lns, My, NIC, NIGTC, TH, WBC; KJV].

    1.1 This indicates that the people were ridiculing Jesus and also the rulers were ridiculing him [EGT, Gdt, NIGTC, TH]. They all were contemptuous of Jesus [TH].

    1.2 This indicates that the people were standing and also the rulers were standing by [Lns].

    1.3 This does not indicate that the rulers were doing the same as the people [NAC, WBC]. It may be listing the groups that were involved: the rulers also played a role, they sneered. Or it is possible that it is parallel with καὶ 'and' in 23:36 and means: it is the case that the rulers sneered and that the soldiers mocked [WBC].

  2. It means 'and even the rulers' [NTC, TNTC, WBC; HCSB, NASB, NIV]. As the people observed the event, the rulers ridiculed Jesus [TNTC].

QUESTION—What is meant by their taunt and did they believe that Jesus had saved others?

The verb ἔσωσεν 'he saved' means Jesus saved others from death [TH]. They mocked Jesus' ability to deliver others by working miracles on their behalf [BECNT]. He saved others by healing them and even raising some from death [NIC]. It may refer to what Jesus said about forgiving the sins of others [Su].
1. They admitted that Jesus had healed people and brought some back to life [Arn, NIC]. However the fact that Jesus did not use supernatural power to save himself proved to the rulers that he was not the Messiah [NIC].
2. They did not believe that Jesus had saved sinners [Lns, Su]. 'He saved others' indicates that his miracles were spurious since he was unable to save himself [Lns].

QUESTION—What does the genitive noun θεοῦ 'of God' modify?
1. It modifies the preceding words [AB, Arn, BECNT, BNTC, EGT, ICC, Lns, NIGTC, NTC, TH, TNTC, WBC; HCSB, NASB, NET, NIV, NRSV, REB]: he is the Messiah of God, the chosen one. God has appointed Jesus for his office [Lns]. Grammatically it goes with the preceding words, but in sense it goes with both Messiah and chosen one [NIGTC].
2. It modifies the following words [TG; GW, KJV, NCV, NLT, TEV]: he is the Messiah, the one chosen by God.

23:36 **And also the soldiers mocked[a] him approaching, (and) offering[b] him sour-wine[c]** **23:37** **and saying, If you are the king of-the Jews, save yourself.**

TEXT—Following προσερχόμενοι 'approaching', some manuscripts add καί 'and'. GNT does not mention this variant. Καί 'and' is read by KJV.

LEXICON—a. aorist act. indic. of ἐμπαίζω (LN 33.406) (BAGD 1. p. 255): 'to mock' [BAGD, BECNT, LN, Lns, NTC, WBC; HCSB, KJV, NASB, NET, NIV, NLT, NRSV], 'to join in the mockery' [REB], 'to ridicule' [AB, BAGD, LN], 'to make fun of' [Arn, BAGD; CEV, GW, NCV, TEV]. The verb means to make fun of someone by pretending that he is not what he is or by imitating him in a distorted manner [LN]. The aorist tense here is in contrast with the imperfect tense in the preceding verse and indicates that the soldiers were less persistent in their mocking than the rulers were [ICC, Rb]. Or, the difference in the tense is only for the sake of variety [TH]. See this word at 14:29; 18:32; 22:63; 23:11.
  b. pres. act. participle of προσφέρω (LN 15.192) (BAGD 1.b. p. 719): 'to offer' [AB, Arn, BAGD, BECNT, Lns, NTC, WBC; all versions except CEV], 'to bring' [BAGD, LN; CEV], 'to carry to' [LN]. Although the sour wine was offered, many think that it was offered in mockery and it wasn't actually given to Jesus to drink [Alf, Arn, BECNT, EGT, Gdt, Lns, My, NICNT, NIVS, NTC, Su, TG, TH, TNTC; NET].
  c. ὄξος (LN 6.201) (BAGD p. 574): 'sour wine' [AB, Arn, BAGD, LN, Lns, NTC, WBC; HCSB, NASB, NET, NLT, REB], 'wine' [CEV], 'cheap wine' [TEV], 'wine vinegar' [NIV], 'vinegar' [BAGD, BECNT; GW,

KJV, NCV]. This sour wine was a cheap and favorite beverage of poor people and soldiers since it relieved thirst more effectively than water [BAGD, BECNT, LN]. This was the ordinary wine used by soldiers and it was a dry wine instead of the sweet wine called οἶνος [AB, BECNT]. It was a cheap vinegar wine that was diluted with water [NET]. There is not much difference between cheap wine and vinegar, but wine is a drink while vinegar is used as a condiment [TG].

QUESTION—How did the soldiers mock Jesus?

The following clauses describe their mocking as offering Jesus the sour wine and speaking the words recorded in 23:37 [TH].

QUESTION—Why did the soldiers offer Jesus the sour wine?

1. The sour wine was offered in mockery [Alf, Arn, BECNT, EGT, Gdt, Lns, My, NICNT, NIVS, NTC, Su, TG, TH, TNTC; NET]. In Psalm 69:21 it says 'They also gave me gall for my food. And for my thirst they gave me vinegar to drink', implying that the act of giving vinegar was an hostile act, and evidently Luke considers it part of the soldiers' mockery [NIGTC, WBC]. The offer was made as a joke since it was accompanied by the words that followed [BECNT]. Offering a cheap beverage to someone who pretended to be king was an act of mockery [MGC, TH]. This was a cruel act to taunt Jesus who had had nothing to drink since the night before [Lns]. They held up of some of their own wine and invited Jesus to come down off the cross and join them in a drink [Arn, Lns, Su]. This was done as mockery and they did not actually give the drink to Jesus [My, Su]. This does not refer to the drugged wine that Jesus refused when he first arrived at Golgotha (Mark 15:23) [NTC, TNTC]. This seems to be a different act than the later incident in the other three Gospels about what happened during the hours of darkness near the end [Alf, BECNT, Lns, My, NIVS, NTC, Su, TNTC]. It is an incident that only Luke reported, or else Luke departed from the chronological order and this describes when Jesus cried out that he was thirsty and one soldier offered a sponge full of wine to Jesus' lips while the other soldiers were mocking Jesus [NTC].

2. The sour wine was offered as an act of kindness to a thirsty man [BNTC].

23:38 And there-was also an-inscription[a] over him, The king of-the Jews (is) this (one).

TEXT—Instead of ἐπ' αὐτῷ 'over him', some manuscripts read ἐπ' αὐτῷ γεγραμμένη 'over him written', others read γεγραμμένη ἐπ' αὐτῷ γράμμασιν Ἑλληνικοῖς καὶ Ῥωμαϊκοῖς καὶ Ἑβραϊκοῖς 'written over him in letters Greek and Roman and Hebrew', and others read ἐπιγεγραμμένη ἐπ' αὐτῷ γράμμασιν Ἑλληνικοῖς καὶ Ῥωμαϊκοῖς καὶ Ἑβραϊκοῖς 'inscribed over him in letters Greek and Roman and Hebrew'. GNT reads ἐπ' αὐτῷ 'over him' with an A decision, indicating that the text is certain. Γεγραμμένη ἐπ' αὐτῷ γράμμασιν Ἑλληνικοῖς καὶ Ῥωμαϊκοῖς καὶ

Ἑβραϊκοῖς 'written over him in letters Greek and Roman and Hebrew' is read by KJV.

LEXICON—a. ἐπιγραφή (LN 33.46) (BAGD p. 291): 'inscription' [AB, BAGD, BECNT, LN, Lns, WBC; HCSB, NASB, NET, NRSV, REB], 'superscription' [Arn, BAGD, NTC; KJV], 'a writing' [LN], 'a written notice' [GW, NIV], 'a sign (that said)' [CEV], 'a signboard' [NLT]. This noun is also translated as a verb phrase: 'these words were written' [NCV], 'were written these words' [TEV].

QUESTION—What is the function of this verse?

It is a parenthetical statement that helps the reader understand the preceding verse where the soldiers said, 'If you are the king of the Jews' [Lns, MGC, WBC]. Or, the conjunction καί 'also' suggests that this was an additional way of mocking Jesus [EGT, ICC].

QUESTION—How was the inscription placed over Jesus and what was its purpose?

This was a notice or placard [TH]. The words were written on a slab of wood and nailed to the vertical beam above Jesus' head [TG]. The inscription was not an announcement to let the people know who Jesus actually was, but it announced the charge for which he was being executed [NAC, NIVS, TG, TH, TNTC]. It was placed above Jesus so that people would know the crime for which he was being crucified [BECNT, ICC, Lns, TG, TNTC, WBC]. It showed that Jesus was crucified for claiming to be a king [NET]. In John 19:19 it says that Pilate had this sign written. Some think that Pilate had this sign made to take revenge on the Jewish leaders who had forced him to execute Jesus [Lns, NIC, NTC, TNTC]. Pilate was in effect saying 'Here is Jesus, the King of the Jews, the only king they have been able to produce, a king crucified at their own urgent request!' [NTC]. Or, Pilate was taunting Jesus, not the Jews [AB].

DISCOURSE UNIT: 23:39–43 [AB, BECNT, NAC, NIGTC, TNTC, WBC]. The topic is the two criminals [AB, BECNT, NAC, NIGTC], Jesus and the two criminals [WBC], the penitent thief [TNTC].

23:39 And having-been-hung[a] one of-the criminals was-blaspheming[b] him saying, Are you not the Messiah? Save yourself and us.

TEXT—Instead of οὐχὶ σὺ εἶ 'Are you not' some manuscripts read εἰ σὺ εἶ 'If you are'. GNT does not mention this variant. Εἰ σὺ εἶ 'If you are' is read by KJV.

LEXICON—a. aorist pass. participle of κρεμάννυμι (LN 18.23) (BAGD 1. p. 450): 'to be hung' [BAGD, LN], 'to be hanged' [BECNT; KJV, NASB, NRSV], 'to be crucified' [BAGD]. This passive verb is also translated actively: 'to be hanging' [WBC; CEV, GW, HCSB, NET, NLT, TEV], 'who hung (there)' [AB; NIV]; or as a locative: 'on a cross' [NCV]; or as an adjective: 'crucified (criminal)' [NTC], 'suspended (criminal)' [Arn, NTC]. The context makes it clear that he was hanging on a cross [ICC,

514 LUKE 23:39

NICNT]. The verb refers to the crucifixion here and it is used as a synonym for σταυρόω 'to crucify' [Arn, NAC, NICNT, NIGTC, TH].
- b. imperf. act. indic. of βλασφημέω (LN 33.400) (BAGD 2.b.δ. p. 142): 'to blaspheme' [Arn, BAGD, BECNT, LN, Lns], 'to revile' [LN, WBC], 'to defame' [LN], 'to insult' [AB; CEV, GW], 'to yell insults at' [HCSB], 'to shout insults at' [NCV], 'to hurl insults at' [NIV, TEV], 'to hurl abuse at' [NTC; NASB], 'to deride' [NRSV], 'to rail at' [NET], 'to rail on' [KJV], 'to scoff' [NLT]. This refers to speaking against someone in such a way as to harm or injure his reputation [LN]. It is to blaspheme against God and against the one who belongs to God [BAGD]. The imperfect tense indicates that he kept it up [Arn, Rb]. The fact that he was interrupted by the other criminal requires that the imperfect tense be used [NIGTC].

QUESTION—What is meant by one of the criminals 'blaspheming' Jesus?

The verb means that he reviled Jesus by saying evil things to him [Su]. He mocked Jesus by not taking his powers seriously [NIGTC]. Those who mocked Jesus were also mocking the power of God [NICNT].

QUESTION—What is the force of the question 'Are you not the Messiah?'

The word οὐδέ 'not' indicates that the response is expected to be in the affirmative [BECNT, Lns, NIGTC, Su, TH, TNTC; NET]. This was presented as true since it is the current opinion of people, or it is presented as true for the sake of argument [BECNT]. The question is equivalent to a conditional clause, but it is clear that the criminal did not believe that Jesus was the Messiah [NIGTC]. The question was asked in a manner that was mocking [NIGTC, Su, TG, TH], sarcastic [BECNT, NICNT, TNTC], taunting [ICC, NAC], jeering [My], contemptuous [NIC], or ironical [NET].

23:40 And the other answered (and) rebuking him said, Not-even[a] do- you -fear[b] God, because[c] you-are in the same condemnation?[d] **23:41** And we indeed justly,[e] because for (things) worthy[f] of-what we-did we-are-receiving. But this (one) did nothing wrong.

LEXICON—a. οὐδέ (LN 69.8) (BAGD 3. p. 591): 'not even' [AB, Arn, BAGD, LN, Lns, NTC, WBC; HCSB, NASB], 'not (fear)' [BECNT; CEV, KJV, NET, NIV, NLT, NRSV]. The clause 'Not even do you fear God' is translated 'Don't you fear God at all?' [GW], 'Don't you fear God even when' [NLT], 'Don't you fear God?' [TEV], 'You should fear God' [NCV]. The word οὐδέ can be taken as a combination of the negative particle οὐ 'not', and the postpositional particle δέ 'even' [LN]. This is speaking about fearing God's judgment [NIGTC].
- b. pres. pass. indic. of φοβέομαι (LN 87.14) (BAGD 1.b.α. p. 863): 'to fear' [AB, Arn, BAGD, BECNT, LN, Lns, NTC, WBC; CEV, all versions], 'to show great reverence or respect for' [LN].
- c. ὅτι (LN 89.33): 'because' [Arn, LN], 'since' [LN, NTC; HCSB, NASB, NET, NIV, NRSV], 'for' [BECNT, WBC], 'seeing' [Lns; KJV], 'after all' [AB], not explicit [CEV, NCV, NLT, TEV]. This conjunction is also translated as a phrase: 'can't you see that' [GW].

d. κρίμα (LN 56.30) (BAGD 4.b. p. 450): 'condemnation' [BAGD, LN], 'punishment' [BAGD]. The clause ἐν τῷ αὐτῷ κρίματι εἶ 'you are in the same condemnation' [Arn; KJV] is also translated 'you are in the same judgment' [Lns], 'you are under the same judgment' [BECNT], 'you are under the same sentence of condemnation' [NTC; NASB, NET, NRSV], 'you are under the same sentence' [WBC; NIV], 'you are under the same sentence yourself' [AB], 'you received the same sentence he did' [TEV], 'you're condemned in the same way that he is' [GW], 'you are undergoing the same punishment' [HCSB], 'you are getting the same punishment he is' [NCV], 'you are getting the same punishment as this man' [CEV], 'when you are dying' [NLT]. The noun means a judicial verdict, a judgment, a sentence [NTC]. This probably means that both men were condemned on the same charge of insurrection [Su]. See this word at 20:47.

e. ἔνδικος (LN **88.15**) (BAGD 2. p. 198): 'justly' [BAGD, LN], 'rightly' [LN]. This means that it is right as the result of being deserved [LN]. Their sentence is right [**LN**]. They have been justly condemned [BAGD].

f. ἄξιος (LN 66.6) (BAGD 1.b. p. 78) 'worthy of, proper, fitting' [LN], 'deserving' [BAGD]. The clause 'for things worthy of what we did we are receiving' is translated 'we receive things that are worthy of what we did' [BECNT], 'we are duly receiving things worthy of what we did' [Lns], 'we are receiving what we deserve for our deeds' [NASB; similarly NRSV], 'we are getting what we deserve for what we did' [NCV, NET, TEV], 'we are getting what we deserve' [NTC; GW], 'we're getting back what we deserve for the things we did' [HCSB], 'we are only getting what our deeds deserve' [AB; similarly NIV], 'we are receiving due deserts for what we did' [WBC], 'we receive the due reward of our deeds' [KJV], 'we receive treatment deserved by the things we have done' [Arn], 'we are paying the price for our misdeeds' [REB]. The two clauses 'and we indeed justly, because for things worthy of what we did we are receiving' are translated 'we got what was coming to us' [CEV], 'we deserve to die for our evil deeds' [NLT]. This word means to be fit or proper in regard to what should be expected [LN]. See this word at 23:15.

QUESTION—In the question Οὐδὲ φοβῇ σὺ τὸν θεόν; 'Not even do you fear God?', what does οὐδέ 'not even' go with?

1. It goes with the verb 'fear' [AB, EGT, ICC, Lns, NTC, Rb, TH, TNTC, WBC; GW, HCSB, NASB]: do you not even *fear* God? He might well have done more than fear God, but he should not have done less [TNTC]. Fear of God should restrain him from adding to his sins [ICC].
2. It goes with the pronoun 'you' [Alf, Arn, Gdt, NIGTC]: do not even *you* fear God? The first criminal is compared with all of the others who mocked Jesus and he of all men should have known better and should have feared God [NIGTC]. The criminal was not merely a spectator of the punishment like the crowd, he was undergoing it himself [Gdt].

3. It goes with God [WBC]: do you fear not even *God*? The criminal has despised human laws and justice, and even on the brink of death he shows no fear of God [WBC].

QUESTION—What relationship is indicated by ὅτι 'because' in the last clause of 23:40?

It indicates the reason why the criminal should fear [Lns]. It is the reason for an implied statement '*you should fear God* because...' [Alf, Arn, Gdt]. He should fear God's judgment because he is in the same situation of judgment as Jesus [NIGTC]. The criminal was under the same sentence of death as Jesus and was about to face God who is the judge of all the earth [MGC].

QUESTION—Who is the referent of 'we' in 23:41?

This refers to the criminal who is speaking and to the other criminal whom he is addressing, not to Jesus [TH].

23:42 **And he was-saying, Jesus, remember[a] me when you-come into[b] your kingdom.**

TEXT—Instead of ἔλεγεν, Ἰησοῦ, μνήσθητί μου 'he was saying, Jesus, remember me', some manuscripts read ἔλεγεν τῷ Ἰησοῦ, μνήσθητί μου, κύριε 'he was saying to Jesus, Remember me, Lord'. GNT does not mention this variant. Ἔλεγεν τῷ Ἰησοῦ, μνήσθητί μου, κύριε 'he was saying to Jesus, Remember me, Lord' is read by KJV.

TEXT—Instead of ὅταν ἔλθῃς εἰς τὴν βασιλείαν σου 'when you come *into* your kingdom', some manuscripts read ὅταν ἔλθῃς ἐν τῇ βασιλείᾳ σου 'when you come *in* your kingdom', another reads ἐν τῇ βασιλείᾳ σου ὅταν ἔλθῃς 'in your kingdom when you come', and one Greek and Latin manuscript reads ἐν τῇ ἡμέρᾳ τῆς ἐπελεύσεώς σου 'in the day of your coming'. GNT reads ὅταν ἔλθῃς εἰς τὴν βασιλείαν σου 'when you come *into* your kingdom' with a B decision, indicating that the text is almost certain. The reading ὅταν ἔλθῃς ἐν τῇ βασιλείᾳ σου 'when you come *in* your kingdom' appears to be taken by Alf, Arn, BECNT, EGT, Gdt, ICC, Lns, NIC, NIGTC, NTC, Su, TH, TNTC and NET.

LEXICON—a. aorist pass impera. of μιμνῄσκομαι (LN 29.7) (BAGD 1.c. p. 522): 'to remember' [AB, Arn, BAGD, BECNT, LN, Lns, WBC; all versions], 'to recall, to think about again' [LN], 'to think of, to care for, to be concerned about' [BAGD].

b. aorist act. subj. of ἔρχομαι (LN 15.81): 'to come' [LN]. The phrase 'when you come into/in your kingdom' is translated 'when you come into your kingdom' [AB, Arn, WBC; HCSB, KJV, NCV, NIV, NLT, NRSV], 'when you enter your kingdom' [GW], 'when you come to your throne' [REB], 'when you come into power' [CEV], 'when you come in your kingdom' [BECNT, NTC; NASB, NET], 'when you come in connection with your kingdom' [Lns], 'when you come as King' [TEV].

QUESTION—What does the request 'remember me' mean?

The criminal asked Jesus not only to think about him, but to do something for him [TG]. This is a request that he be included in the kingdom and not be forbidden entrance because of his sins and crimes [Lns]. It means to remember him for good [NIGTC, NTC, TNTC]. He asked Jesus to show him grace [AB, TH]. He wanted Jesus to save him [NAC]. He wanted to be among those whom Jesus would raise from the dead [EGT]. He wanted Jesus to remember his repentance and confession of faith with the result that he be forgiven and made a part of that kingdom [Su].

QUESTION—What did the criminal mean when he spoke of Jesus 'coming into his kingdom'?

The manuscript differences have a bearing on the time that the man was thinking about. The GNT reading ὅταν ἔλθῃς εἰς τὴν βασιλείαν σου 'when you come *into* (εἰς) your kingdom' refers to the present time while ὅταν ἔλθῃς ἐν τῇ βασιλείᾳ σου 'when you come in (ἐν) your kingdom refers to the future time when Jesus returns [BECNT, NAC, TNTC, WBC; NET].

1. He meant when Jesus begins to rule as king after his death [AB, BNTC, MGC, TNTC, WBC]. It refers to when Jesus will enter his royal estate by going through death to a kingdom in the next world [TNTC]. Death and exaltation will begin Jesus' kingly rule [AB, MGC]. This is the time when Jesus would be exalted at the right hand of God after his death [WBC].
2. He meant when Jesus again comes to earth as king [Alf, Arn, BECNT, EGT, Gdt, ICC, Lns, NIC, NIGTC, NTC, Su, TH, TNTC; NET]. This refers to Christ's return to earth in glory [ICC]. The preposition ἐν mean 'in' or 'with' your kingdom [Alf, NAC]. Jesus will return at the end of this age in royal glory [NTC]. This is when Jesus will come with his kingship, with his power to rule, with the authority of the kingdom [TH]. It is when Jesus comes to earth again as King and the man wants to be among the resurrected who will share the joys of that kingdom [EGT]. The request is that Jesus would let the man be among the righteous who return with Jesus [BECNT].

23:43 **And he-said to-him, Truly**[a] **I-say to-you, today with me you-will-be in paradise.**[b]

TEXT—Following αὐτῷ 'to him', some manuscripts add ὁ Ἰησοῦς 'Jesus'. GNT does not mention this variant. Ὁ Ἰησοῦς 'Jesus' is read by KJV.

LEXICON—a. ἀμήν (LN 72.6): 'truly, indeed, it is true that' [LN]. The phrase 'truly I say to you' [BECNT; NASB] is also translated 'Amen, I say to you' [Lns, WBC], 'verily I say unto thee' [KJV], 'truly tell you' [NRSV, REB], 'I tell you the truth' [NCV, NET, NIV], 'I say to you truthfully' [Arn], 'I assure you' [HCSB, NLT], 'I can guarantee this truth' [GW], 'I solemnly declare to you' [NTC], 'I promise you that' [TEV], 'I promise that' [CEV], 'believe me' [AB]. This is a strong affirmation of what is being said [LN, Su]. It introduces an important announcement [Arn].

b. παράδεισος (LN 1.14) (BAGD 2. p. 614): 'paradise' [BAGD, BECNT, LN, WBC; CEV, GW, HCSB, KJV, NET, NLT], 'Paradise' [AB, Arn, Lns, NTC; NASB, REB]. Paradise is a place of blessedness above the earth [BAGD]. It is a place where the righteous dead dwell in a state of blessedness and it is generally equated with heaven [LN].

QUESTION—What is paradise?

The word παράδεισος is from a Persian word that means 'garden' or 'park' and in the Greek Septuagint this word was used for the garden of Eden [NIGTC]. It is the abode of the righteous after death and is a place of bliss [AB, MGC, NIBC, WBC; NET]. It is man's eternal dwelling place in fellowship with Christ [Su]. Paradise is heaven [Lns, NIC, NTC, Su, TG, TH]. It is the abode of God, the angels, and the righteous who have died [Lns]. There is no support for the idea that Paradise is the abode of the righteous from the time of their death until they are resurrected, and only after their resurrection will heaven be their eternal abode. Paradise is where God is, and that is heaven [Su]. Or, paradise is that part of Hades where the faithful were assembled after death [Gdt]. It is a pleasant resting place for the saved until they are resurrected [NIVS, WBC].

QUESTION—What is the force of σήμερον 'today' in Jesus' reply?

'Today' contrasts with the future coming of Jesus when he comes as king [BECNT, Crd, NIC, Su, TH]. The criminal was thinking about attaining life at the Second Coming, but Jesus assured him that he would immediately enter paradise, the heavenly realm where the righteous are gathered [BAGD, Lns]. He won't have to wait until the messianic age but it would happen when they both died on that day [Su].

1. 'Today' means before sunset when that day ended [Alf, Arn, BECNT, Gdt, Lns, NIC, NTC]. The word 'with' states that they will both be in paradise before night sets in [Lns]. This refers to the immediate present, not a few days later when Jesus would be resurrected and would ascend to heaven since Jesus was never in limbo [BECNT]. When Jesus ascended to heaven a few days later in his human nature and resurrected body it was different from his death when his soul went immediately to the abode of God [Lns]. When Jesus died, his soul went immediately to Paradise and this is the same for those who believed in him [Arn]. Or, when Jesus descended in the depths of the earth to announce his triumph to the imprisoned spirits they were perhaps in Paradise [Alf].

2. 'Today' was not that very day, but the day when Jesus would inaugurate his messianic salvation when he was exalted by entering into his glory [AB, MGC, NAC, WBC]. The creedal teaching of Jesus' descent into Hell is a problem if this meant that very day [AB]. Three days would pass as Jesus descended into Hades after his death and afterwards be resurrected and then ascend to heaven [MGC].

QUESTION—What is the predicate of the verb ἔση 'you will be' in the statement μετ' ἐμοῦ ἔση ἐν τῷ παραδείσῳ 'with me you will be in paradise'?

1. Although there is little difference, some take the predicate of the verb to be ἐν τῷ παραδείσῳ 'in paradise' [Lns, TH]: *you will be in paradise with me*. He will be in paradise and when he is there he will be in the

company of Jesus [TH]. Jesus said that today, in company with him, the criminal would be in paradise [Lns].

2. Others seem to take the predicate to be μετ' ἐμοῦ 'with me' [ICC, NIC]: *you will be with me* in paradise. He will be in the company of Jesus and share with Jesus when they are in paradise [ICC].

DISCOURSE UNIT: 23:44–49 [AB, BECNT, NAC, NICNT, NIGTC, TNTC, WBC; CEV, GW, NCV, NIV, NLT, NRSV, TEV]. The topic is the death of Jesus [AB, BECNT, NAC, NICNT, NIGTC, TNTC, WBC; CEV, NIV, NLT, NRSV, TEV], Jesus dies [NCV], Jesus dies on the cross [GW].

23:44 **And it-was already[a] about (the) sixth hour and darkness was over the whole land[b] until (the) ninth hour**

LEXICON—a. ἤδη (LN 67.20): 'already' [AB, BECNT, LN, Lns, NTC], 'now' [WBC; HCSB, NASB, NET, NIV, NRSV], not explicit [Arn; CEV, GW, KJV, NCV, NLT, TEV].

b. γῇ (LN 1.79): 'land' [AB, LN, NTC, WBC; all versions except CEV, KJV, TEV], 'region, territory' [LN], 'country' [Arn; TEV], 'earth' [BECNT, Lns; KJV], not explicit [CEV]. The clause 'darkness was over the whole land' is translated 'darkness came upon the whole country' [Arn], 'darkness fell across the whole land' [NLT], 'darkness came upon the whole land' [WBC], 'darkness covered the whole country' [TEV], 'darkness enveloped the whole land' [NTC], 'the whole land became dark' [NCV], 'the sky turned dark' [CEV], 'darkness fell over the whole earth' [BECNT].

QUESTION—What time is meant by the sixth hour and how can this be reconciled with John's account?

The day was divided into twelve parts beginning with dawn and the hours varied in length according to the time of the year so that the sixth hour was always at midday [TNTC]. The sixth hour was noon [AB, BECNT, BNTC, ICC, Lns, NAC, NIC, NTC, Su, TG, TH, WBC; CEV, GW, HCSB, NCV, NET, NLT, NRSV, TEV]. Both Matthew and Mark agree with Luke about the hours of darkness. However, in John 19:14 it says that Pilate was preparing to sentence Jesus at the sixth hour, while Mark says that the sentencing happened at the third hour. Before the existence of clocks, people could not be as precise as we are. John could be saying that it was late morning when Pilate gave his sentence and Luke was saying that it was about midday when Jesus was crucified. Mark may mean that the morning was getting on when the sentence was given [TNTC]. A large margin of inaccuracy is allowed by the word ὡσεί 'about' [ICC]. Or, John used the Roman way of counting the hours beginning at midnight [BECNT, NIVS].

QUESTION—How far did the daytime darkness extend when it says 'the darkness was over the whole land'?

1. This refers to the land in which the crucifixion took place [AB, Arn, Gdt, ICC, MGC, NTC, TG, TH]. The phrase τὴν γῆν 'the land' probably refers to the land or the country, not the whole earth [TG]. The land was the

immediate area of Jerusalem [MGC]. The land was Palestine [AB, TH]. The word probably takes in the surrounding countries [Gdt]. It had to refer to very extensive coverage [NTC].
2. This refers to the entire earth [BECNT, Lns, Su; KJV]. When the sun fails, the entire dayside of the earth is in darkness [Lns].

23:45 the sun having-failed,[a] and the curtain[b] of-the temple was-torn[c] in-two.

TEXT—Instead of τοῦ ἡλίου ἐκλιπόντος 'the sun having failed' some manuscripts read τοῦ ἡλίου ἐκλείποντος 'the sun failing', some manuscripts read καὶ ἐσκοτίσθη ὁ ἥλιος 'and the sun was darkened', and one manuscript omits this phrase. GNT reads τοῦ ἡλίου ἐκλιπόντος 'the sun having failed' with a B decision, indicating that the text is almost certain. Καὶ ἐσκοτίσθη ὁ ἥλιος 'and the sun was darkened' is read by KJV.

LEXICON—a. aorist act. participle of ἐκλείπω (LN **68.36**) (BAGD p. 242): 'to fail' [BAGD], 'to stop, to cease' [LN]. The phrase 'the sun having failed' is translated 'the sun failing' [Lns, NTC], 'the sun's light failed' [REB], 'the sun was darkened' [Arn; KJV], 'the sun stopped shining' [**LN**; CEV, TEV; similarly GW], 'the light from the sun was gone' [NLT], 'because the sun's light failed' [HCSB, NET], 'for the sun's light had failed' [WBC], 'for the sunlight had failed' [AB], 'for the sun stopped shining' [NIV], 'because the sun did not shine' [NCV], 'because the sun was obscured' [NASB], 'while the sun was darkened' [BECNT], 'while the sun's light failed' [NRSV]. In reference to the sun the verb means 'to grow dark' or perhaps 'to be eclipsed' [BAGD].
b. καταπέτασμα (LN 6.160) (BAGD p. 416): 'curtain' [AB, BAGD, LN, Lns, NTC, WBC; all versions except KJV, NASB, NLT], 'drape' [LN], 'veil' [Arn, BECNT, LN; KJV, NASB], 'the thick veil' [NLT].
c. aorist pass. indic. of σχίζω (LN 63.26) (BAGD 1.b. p. 797): 'to be torn' [AB, Arn, BAGD, LN, NTC; NASB, NCV, NET, NIV, NLT, NRSV, REB, TEV], 'to be split' [BAGD, LN, WBC; GW, HCSB], 'to be rent' [Lns; KJV], 'to be ripped' [BECNT], 'to be divided' [LN], 'to be separated' [BAGD]. This passive verb is also translated actively: '(the curtain) split down the middle' [WBC; CEV].

QUESTION—What relationship is indicated by the use of the participle ἐκλιπόντος 'having failed'?
It indicates the reason for the darkness [AB, Lns, MGC, NIGTC, WBC; HCSB, NASB, NCV, NIV]: the darkness was over the whole land because the sun failed. Or, it indicates an attendant circumstance [NLT, NRSV]: the darkness was over the whole land while the sun failed.

QUESTION—In what way did the sun fail?
An eclipse is impossible at the full moon which determined the time of the Passover [ICC, NAC, NIGTC, NTC, Su, TNTC, WBC; NET], and an eclipse would not last for three hours [NTC]. Luke means that a darkness came that was similar to an eclipse, but no natural explanation is able to cover the

details [Su]. This does not describe an eclipse and this is simply saying that the sun stopped shining [TG]. The sun failed to give its light, and perhaps this could be the result of a sirocco wind [NIGTC]. The darkness was wholly miraculous and there is no need to search for secondary means [Lns, NTC]. We must be satisfied with the vague description of the sun failing [ICC]. The darkness could be a symbol of God's displeasure with the people who rejected Jesus [NIGTC]. It was a symbol of God's judgment of the world's sins on the dying Savior [Lns, NTC]. Or, this was a Satanic darkness that manifested Satan's work in bringing about the death of Jesus [AB, WBC]. It seemed that evil was prevailing [MGC].

QUESTION—Which curtain was torn in two?

1. It was the inner curtain that separated the Holy Place from the Most Holy Place that only the high priest could enter once each year [Arn, BAGD, Gdt, ICC, Lns, MGC, NAC, NIBC, NIC, NIVS, NTC, Su, TNTC, WBC]. Historians wrote that the curtain in this huge Temple was about eighty feet high, twenty-four feet wide, and had a thickness of several inches [Su].
2. It was the outer curtain that hung at the entrance to the Holy Place and restricted the building to priests [AB, BECNT]. Along with the other signs, this was a public event that could be seen from outside the temple [BECNT].

QUESTION—What was the significance of the curtain being torn in two?

The curtain symbolized the remoteness of God, so when it was torn to expose the Holy of Holies it indicated that Jesus' death opened the way into the presence of God [MGC, NIC, TNTC; NET]. It meant that the ministry of the high priest was at an end [Lns]. Perhaps it indicated that the Temple was no longer God's dwelling place [Gdt, TNTC]. This was a forewarning of the coming destruction of the Temple [NIGTC]. The tearing was an act of God [Lns, NICNT, NTC]. Matthew 27:51 says that it was torn from top to bottom and this indicates that it was an act of God since men would have to tear it from the bottom to the top [Su].

23:46 And having-cried-out[a] with-a-loud voice Jesus said, Father, into your hands I-entrust[b] my spirit. And having-said this he-breathed-out.[c]

LEXICON—a. aorist act. participle of φωνέω (LN 33.77) (BAGD 1.b. p. 870): 'to cry out' [BAGD, LN], 'to call out' [BAGD, LN], 'to speak loudly' [BAGD, LN], 'to shout' [LN]. The phrase 'having cried out with a loud voice' is translated 'crying out with a loud voice' [NASB, NRSV], 'crying out with a loud cry' [BECNT], 'calling out with a loud voice' [NET], 'crying with a loud voice' [Arn], 'when Jesus had cried out with a loud voice' [KJV], 'crying out with a great cry' [Lns], 'Jesus uttered a loud cry' [AB; REB]. The phrase 'having cried out with a loud voice Jesus said' is translated 'Jesus cried out in a loud voice' [WBC; GW, NCV, TEV], 'Jesus called out with a loud voice' [HCSB, NIV], 'with a loud voice Jesus cried out' [NTC], 'Jesus shouted' [CEV, NLT].

b. pres. mid. indic. of παρατίθεμαι (LN **35.47**) (BAGD 2.b.β. p. 623): 'to entrust, to commend, to give over' [BAGD], 'to entrust oneself to, to commit oneself to the care of' [LN]. The clause 'into your hands I entrust my spirit' [AB, BECNT; GW, HCSB] is also translated 'into your hands I commit my spirit' [Arn, **LN**, Lns, WBC; NASB, NET, NIV, REB], 'into your hands I commend my spirit' [NTC; KJV, NRSV], 'I entrust my spirit into your hands' [NLT], 'in your hands I place my spirit' [TEV], 'I give myself into your care' [**LN**], 'I put myself in your hands' [CEV], 'I give you my life' [NCV].

c. aorist act. indic. of ἐκπνέω (LN 23.103) (BAGD p. 244): 'to breath out' [BAGD, LN]. The clause 'he breathed out' is translated 'he breathed his last' [AB, NTC, WBC; HCSB, NASB, NET, NIV, NLT, NRSV], 'he drew his last breath' [Arn], 'he gave up the ghost' [KJV], 'he died' [CEV, GW, NCV, REB, TEV], 'he expired' [BECNT, Lns]. The verb 'to breath out' is used figuratively to refer to the final act of dying, 'to breathe out one's last, to die' [LN], 'to breathe out the life or the soul, to expire' [BAGD]. It is a euphemism for 'to die' [BAGD, BECNT, WBC].

QUESTION—What is the relationship of the phrase 'having cried out with a loud voice' with the verb 'said'?

1. Jesus cried out the words that are quoted [AB, Arn, BECNT, BNTC, Gdt, ICC, Lns, MGC, NTC, TH, WBC; CEV, GW, HCSB, NCV, NIV, NLT, TEV]. Crying out is not a separate act [TH]. The cry in Matt. 27:50 and Mark 15:37 does not mention the content of the cry, but Luke supplies it [AB, BECNT, BNTC, Gdt]. He spoke the words with a loud voice [Lns]. The fact that he said this loudly indicates that he did not die from exhaustion [Arn, ICC]. It indicates that he had secured victory over death and was still in control of his destiny [MGC].
2. The crying out was a separate act from what he said [Alf, BNTC, NIC; KJV]. After he cried out he spoke the quoted words [BNTC]. The cry is alluded to in Matt. 27:50 and Mark 15:37 [Alf]. If this interpretation is taken, the cry would be the words 'My God, my God, etc.' or 'It is finished', or both [Arn], or it could be an inarticulate cry [ICC].

QUESTION—What is meant by Jesus' πνεῦμα 'spirit'?

Jesus' spirit means his person [BECNT]. The spirit is the whole of the living person [AB, NIBC]. It was his whole spiritual nature in contrast with his dying body [My]. His spirit means his life [NAC]. The spirit is the deathless part of a person which lives apart from the body [Su, TG], but which is embodied again at resurrection [Su].

QUESTION—What is meant by Jesus entrusting his spirit into the Father's hands?

This means that Jesus placed himself in his Father's care, he committed his soul or spirit into his Father's keeping [NICNT, TG]. This was not a cry indicating distress because after he had asked 'My God, why did you abandon me?' he later had shouted in victory 'It is finished' (John 20:30). So he said these last words in peace and joy [Lns]. He spoke with a calm restfulness [Arn, NIC, NTC]. The phrase 'your hands' indicates God's care [BECNT]. The Father's hands are mighty and true [Lns]. This does not mean that at this point Jesus deliberately died by giving up his spirit, rather death came as a natural result of scourging and crucifixion [Su].

23:47 **And having-seen what had-happened the centurion[a] was praising God saying, Surely this man was righteous.[b]** **23:48** **And all the crowds (who) had-gathered-together for this spectacle,[c] having-observed what had-happened, were returning beating[d] the chests.**

LEXICON—a. ἑκατοντάρχης (LN 55.16) (BAGD p. 237): 'centurion' [AB, Arn, BAGD, BECNT, LN, Lns, NTC, WBC; HCSB, KJV, NASB, NET, NIV, NRSV, REB], 'captain' [LN], 'the captain of the Roman soldiers' [NLT], 'army officer' [GW, NCV, TEV], 'Roman officer' [CEV]. See this word at 7:2.

b. δίκαιος (LN 88.12) (BAGD 3. p. 196): 'righteous' [Arn, LN, Lns, NTC, WBC; HCSB, KJV, NIV], 'just' [BAGD, LN], 'innocent' [AB, BAGD, BECNT; GW, NASB, NET, NLT, NRSV, REB], 'good' [CEV, NCV, TEV]. See this word at 1:6, 17; 2:25; 5:32; 14:14; 15:7; 18:9; 20:20; 23:50.

c. θεωρία (LN **24.5**) (BAGD p. 360): 'spectacle' [AB, BAGD, **LN**, Lns, NTC, WBC; HCSB, NASB, NET, NRSV, REB], 'sight' [Arn, BAGD, BECNT; GW, KJV, NIV], 'unusual sight' [LN], 'terrible sight' [CEV], 'the crucifixion' [NLT]. This noun is also translated as a verb: '(gathered there) to watch' [NCV]. The noun refers to an unusual event that is observed [LN].

d. pres. act. participle of τύπτω (LN 19.1) (BAGD 1. p. 830): 'to beat, to strike' [BAGD, LN]. The phrase 'beating the chests' is translated 'beating their breasts' [AB, NTC, WBC; NASB, NET, NRSV, REB], 'they beat their breasts' [Arn, BECNT; NIV], 'striking their breasts' [Lns], 'striking their chests' [HCSB], 'smote their breasts' [KJV], 'beating their breasts in sorrow' [TEV], 'beating their chests because they were so sad' [NCV], 'in deep sorrow' [NLT], 'they felt brokenhearted' [CEV], 'they cried' [GW]. The imperfect tense indicates that they began to beat their chests when they departed [NIGTC]. The imperfect tense indicates that they continued doing this as they went away [Lns, TH]. See this word at 18:13.

QUESTION—Who was the centurion?

This officer has not been mentioned in the preceding context, but it is presumed that he presided over the crucifixion [NIGTC, TH]. The centurion commanded a hundred soldiers and he had with him a few of those soldiers to carry out the crucifixion [Su]. Perhaps there were four soldiers for each of the three persons being crucified, and probably more were there for additional safety [Lns].

QUESTION—How is 'praising God' connected with the words 'Surely this man was righteous'?
1. He praised God by saying that Jesus was righteous [ICC, NIGTC, NTC, TH, TNTC]. It is implied that the centurion praised God unwittingly when he spoke these words since he did not mention God [ICC, TH, TNTC].
2. He praised God and then spoke the following words [Su]. Seeing that God was involved in all this, he spoke of God's greatness and power [Su].

QUESTION—What did the centurion mean by saying that Jesus was δίκαιος 'righteous'?
1. He used 'righteous' in a judicial sense, meaning that Jesus was innocent [Arn, BAGD, EGT, Lns, MGC, NAC, NIGTC, TG; GW, NASB, NET, NLT, NRSV, REB]. There was nothing against Jesus [Lns]. Jesus was not guilty of any crime that should be punished by death [TG].
2. He used 'righteous' in a moral sense, meaning that Jesus was a good person [TH, TNTC, WBC; CEV, NCV, TEV]. He was righteous in that he was acceptable to God [TNTC]. The centurion had watched Jesus' steadfast commitment to God throughout his suffering [WBC].

QUESTION—What was the spectacle?
It was the act of crucifying the three men [BECNT, Su]. It was this public affair that everyone could watch [TG].

QUESTION—Why were they all beating their chests when they left the scene?
They did this in self-reproach [Alf, NTC]. They felt remorse for giving into the pressure by the priests to clamor for Jesus' death [ICC]. They felt guilt for what had been done and felt that the darkness and earthquake indicated an approaching calamity [NIC]. It was not done as a sign of repentance, it was done in grief at the execution of Jesus, perhaps in recognition that he was innocent [NIGTC]. It was done in grief and sorrow [Arn, BECNT, NICNT; NET]. In 18:13, the tax-collector beat his breast in guilt and contrition, but here it probably indicates mourning over the death of Jesus [AB]. Or, it was done in sadness and it also indicated their remorse as they realized their guilt in the affair [NAC]. The people realized that something terrible had been done when God had brought about the darkness. This tells of the general impression on the people, but there would have been varying thoughts and feelings [Lns]. 'All' is used as hyperbole [NAC].

23:49 And/but all the (ones) known[a] to-him and (the) women (who) had-followed[b] him from Galilee, stood at a-distance, seeing these (things).

TEXT—Instead of οἱ γνωστοὶ αὐτῷ 'the ones known to him', some manuscripts read οἱ γνωστοὶ αὐτοῦ 'his acquaintances'. GNT does not mention this variant. Οἱ γνωστοὶ αὐτοῦ 'his acquaintances' is read by KJV.

LEXICON—a. γνωστός (LN 34.17) (BAGD 1.b. p. 164): 'known' [BAGD], 'acquaintance, friend' [BAGD, LN], 'intimate' [BAGD]. The phrase οἱ γνωστοὶ αὐτῷ 'the ones known to him' is translated 'those known to him' [Lns], 'those who knew him' [BECNT; HCSB, NIV], 'those who knew Jesus' [NET], 'those who knew Jesus personally' [TEV], 'his friends' [GW, NLT, REB], 'those who were close friends of Jesus' [NCV], 'Jesus' close friends' [CEV], 'his acquaintances' [AB, Arn, NTC, WBC; KJV, NASB, NRSV].

b. pres. act. participle of συνακολουθέω (LN 15.157) (BAGD p. 783): 'to follow' [Arn, BAGD, BECNT, LN, Lns, NTC, WBC; all versions except CEV, NASB, REB], 'to accompany' [BAGD, LN; NASB, REB], 'to come with' [AB; CEV]. In this verse 'follow' implies being a disciple of Jesus [BAGD]. The present participle indicates that they were still following Jesus [BECNT, TH].

QUESTION—Does the conjunction δέ at the beginning of the verse mean 'and' or 'but'?

1. The conjunction is continuative [Arn, BECNT, TG; KJV, NASB, NET]: *and*. It indicates where they had been during the crucifixion and does not appear to mean that they remained when the crowds went away [TG].
2. The conjunction is contrastive [ICC, Lns, NTC, Su, TH, TNTC; HCSB, NCV, NIV, NLT, NRSV]: *but*. In contrast with the crowds who went home, Jesus' friends remained behind at the site [TH]. Only the faithful few remained [ICC, Lns].

QUESTION—Who were the people described as 'all the ones known to Jesus'?

The word 'all' is used hyperbolically [TH]. The word 'all' is used to indicate that there were many of them [Lns, Su]. 'All' is limited to those then present in Jerusalem [My]. These were disciples, a group broader than the apostles [BECNT, TG], but it includes them [Arn]. These were relatives and friends, including the disciples, from Galilee [NAC, NIGTC]. Some of the people known to Jesus were closer to the cross. Jesus spoke to John about Mary, and there is a possibility that Joseph of Arimathea and Nicodemus were also closer. Perhaps they stood far away at first and then drew closer later on when they became convinced that the soldiers would not harm them [NTC].

QUESTION—Were the women who followed Jesus also ones who were known to him?

'All the ones known to him' included the women who had accompanied him from Galilee as his disciples [MGC, NIGTC, NTC, WBC; GW, HCSB, NCV, NIV, NLT, NRSV, TEV]: all the ones known to him, *including* the women who had followed him.

QUESTION—Why were they standing at a distance?

Probably the soldiers had set the limits for people to approach the cross [Arn, Su]. Or, perhaps they feared to come any closer [Arn, Gdt, NTC].

QUESTION—Who stood at a distance and who were seeing these things?

The syntax is awkward here [WBC]. The participle ὁρῶσαι 'seeing' has a feminine ending [NTC].

1. All the ones known to Jesus, including the women who had followed him, stood at a distance and saw these things [ICC, Lns, NTC, TH; all versions except NET, REB]. The participle ὁρῶσαι 'seeing' is feminine because it gets it gender from γυναῖκες 'women' [Lns], but belongs also to οἱ

γνωστοί 'the ones known' so that it means all were seeing these things [ICC, Lns, TH].

2. All the ones known to Jesus, including the women who had followed him, stood at a distance, and the women were seeing these things [AB, EGT, WBC; NET, REB]. Only the women are *specifically* said to be watching these things, but this doesn't mean that the others did not see theses things also [WBC; REB]. The women were probably bolder and nearer to the crucifixion site [EGT].

DISCOURSE UNIT: 23:50–24:53 [NIGTC]. The topic is the resurrection of Jesus.

DISCOURSE UNIT: 23:50–56 [BECNT, NAC, NICNT, TNTC, WBC; CEV, GW, NASB, NCV, NET, NIV, NLT, NRSV, TEV]. The topic is the burial of Jesus [BECNT, NAC, NICNT, TNTC, WBC; NET, NIV, NLT, NRSV, TEV], Jesus is buried [CEV, GW, NASB], Joseph takes Jesus' body [NCV].

DISCOURSE UNIT: 23:50–56a [AB, NIGTC]. The topic is the burial of Jesus.

23:50 **And behold a man named Joseph who was a-member-of-the-council,ᵃ and a-good man and righteousᵇ**

TEXT—Instead of καὶ ἀνήρ 'and (a) man', some manuscripts read ἀνήρ '(a) man'. GNT does not mention this variant but places καί 'and' in brackets in the text, indicating doubt about including it. Καί 'and' is omitted by KJV.

LEXICON—a. βουλευτής (LN 11.85) (BAGD p. 145): 'a member of the council' [AB, Arn, BAGD, BECNT, LN, NTC, WBC; CEV, NASB, NET, NIV, NRSV, REB, TEV], 'a member of the Jewish council' [GW, NCV], 'a member of the Jewish high council' [NLT], 'a member of the Sanhedrin' [LN; HCSB], 'councilor' [Lns; KJV]. This indicates that he was a member of the Sanhedrin [Arn, BECNT, ICC, LN, MGC, NAC, NTC, Su, TH, WBC; HCSB].

b. δίκαιος (LN 88.12) (BAGD 1.b. p. 195): 'righteous' [Arn, BAGD, BECNT, LN, Lns, WBC; HCSB, NASB, NET, NLT, NRSV], 'upright' [AB, NTC; NIV, REB], 'religious' [NCV], 'honorable' [TEV], 'honest' [CEV], 'just' [KJV]. This adjective is also translated as a verb phrase: 'who had God's approval' [GW]. See this word at 1:6, 17; 2:25; 5:32; 14:14; 15:7; 18:9; 20:20; 23:47.

QUESTION—What is the function of ἰδού 'behold'?

It expresses surprise that such a prominent man would interest himself in the burial of Jesus [Arn]. It introduces a bright side of the tragic event [EGT].

QUESTION—What is meant by the description ἀγαθὸς καὶ δίκαιος 'good and righteous'?

This description is used in a moral sense and is explained by the following verse [TH]. 'Good' refers to the good act he was going to perform and 'righteous' refers to his past conduct in relation to Jesus' trial [EGT]. This refers to his life as a whole, not merely to his conduct at the present time [ICC]. The combination was a common phrase in use among the Greeks, 'good' referring to inward disposition and 'righteous' referring to observing God's rules of conduct [Arn].

23:51 —this (one) had- not -agreed-with[a] their decision[b] and action— from Arimathea a-city of-the Jews, who was-awaiting[c] the kingdom of-God,

TEXT—Instead of ὃς προσεδέχετο 'who was awaiting', some manuscripts read ὃς καὶ προσεδέχετο καὶ αὐτός 'who was awaiting also, himself also'. GNT does not mention this variant. Ὃς καὶ προσεδέχετο καὶ αὐτός 'who was awaiting also, himself also' is read by KJV.

LEXICON—a. perf. mid./pass. (deponent = act.) participle of συγκατατίθεμαι (LN **31.18**) (BAGD p. 773): 'to agree with' [Arn, BAGD, **LN**; CEV, GW, HCSB, NLT, TEV], 'to agree to' [NCV, NRSV], 'to consent to' [AB, BAGD, BECNT, NTC, WBC; KJV, NASB, NET, NIV], 'to vote for' [Lns]. The phrase 'had not agreed with' is translated 'had dissented from' [REB]. The perfect participle indicates that Joseph did not agree from the start [NET].

b. βουλή (LN 30.57) (BAGD 2. p. 145): 'decision' [AB, BAGD, NTC, WBC; NIV, NLT, TEV], 'resolution' [BAGD], 'policy' [REB], 'plan' [Arn, LN; HCSB, NASB, NET, NRSV], 'purpose' [BECNT, LN], 'intention' [LN], 'counsel' [Lns; KJV]. The phrase 'their decision and action' is translated 'what they had decided' [CEV], 'the other leader's plans and actions against Jesus' [NCV].

c. imperf. mid./pass. (deponent = act.) indic. of προσδέχομαι (LN 85.60) (BAGD 2.b. p. 712): 'to await' [LN], 'to wait for' [Arn, BAGD, LN, Lns; GW, KJV, NASB, NCV, NIV, NLT, TEV], 'to be constantly waiting for' [NTC], 'to wait expectantly for' [WBC; NRSV], 'to expect' [BAGD] 'to look for' [BECNT], 'to look forward to' [NET, REB], 'to live in expectation of' [AB]. The phrase 'who was awaiting the kingdom of God' is translated 'he was eager for God's kingdom to come' [CEV].

QUESTION—What is the function of the parenthetical comment 'this one had not agreed with their decision and action'?

Since Luke had said that Joseph was a member of the Sanhedrin in the preceding verse, it was necessary to make clear that Joseph had not shared in the verdict of his fellow members [Lns, NAC, NIGTC]. This explains how a member of the Sanhedrin which had brought about the crucifixion of Jesus, could be called good and righteous [NTC, TH].

QUESTION—What is meant by 'their decision and action'?

'Their' obviously refers to the members of the Sanhedrin [NIGTC, TH]. Their decision and action covers the way in which they brought about the death of Jesus [ICC]. This covers sentencing Jesus and getting Pilate's consent [Gdt, TG]. This means that Joseph did not go along with the council's plot with Judas, the verdict they rendered, and their sending Jesus to Pilate [BECNT]. Their decision refers to either the plot involving Judas or to the sentence that is implied when the council said that no further testimony was needed (22:71), while the action refers to handing Jesus over to Pilate (23:1) [AB]. Their decision was the plot to get rid of Jesus and their action was the act of turning Jesus over to Pilate [NAC].

QUESTION—How did Joseph not agree with the decision and action of the Sanhedrin?

Here the noun βουλή has the meaning 'resolution' or 'decision' [NIGTC]. It doesn't specify whether Joseph had absented himself from the meeting of the Sanhedrin, or abstained for voting, or voted in opposition to the Sanhedrin's decision [ICC]. Taking the noun συγκατατεθειμένον 'agreed with' to mean 'to cast one's vote', Joseph had voted against the majority of the council members [Su]. We should hope that being present at the meeting, he dissented from the proceedings [EGT]. Or, 'they *all* said' in 22:70 suggests that the vote had been unanimous, and therefore Joseph must have been absent [Alf, TNTC].

QUESTION—Where was Arimathea and how was Joseph connected with it?

Although Arimathea had once been a part of Samaria, it was now reckoned to be in Judea [Su]. The identification of the city as 'a city of the Jews' was added for the benefit of Gentile readers [ICC, NAC, NIGTC]. This identification has the name of the people who lived in it instead of the name of the country [TH]. It distinguishes the town from gentile cities in Palestine [WBC]. Some translate with the name of the country: a city of 'Judea' [CEV, NLT, TEV], or 'a Judean town' [HCSB]. Joseph was a native of Arimathea [TH], either having been born there or formerly having lived there [ICC]. This fact is mentioned to distinguish him from other men who had the same name [Su]. At this time he was not an inhabitant of Arimathea [TH]. Since he had a burial-place in Jerusalem, he apparently was now a resident of Jerusalem [AB, BECNT, Gdt, ICC, Lns, TNTC].

QUESTION—What is meant by Joseph 'awaiting the kingdom of God'?

Joseph was awaiting the arrival of the kingdom of God [MGC]. It would arrive when God established his rule of earth [TG]. Joseph was a devout Jew who, like Simeon (2:25) and Anna (2:38), was longing for the coming of the messianic kingdom to bring peace in Israel [BNTC, Su], and he had found in Jesus the one he believed would prove to be the Messiah [Su]. Jesus taught his followers to pray for the coming of the kingdom, to expect the return of the Son of Man, and to look for his coming [NAC]. In agreement with Jesus' message, he believed that God's reign was being established in human hearts and he hoped for it to be established more and more [NTC]. He thought the time was near for the spiritual rule of the Messiah and his royal rule [Lns]. This suggests that he was a disciple of Jesus [NIGTC, TNTC]. Or, it does not imply that he recognized Jesus to be the Messiah [ICC].

23:52 this (one) having-approached[a] Pilate asked-for[b] the body of-Jesus.
23:53 And having-taken-down (the body) he-wrapped it in-linen and placed it in a-hewn-out-of-rock[c] tomb where no one (had) ever been-laid.

LEXICON—a. aorist act. participle of προσέρχομαι (LN 15.77) (BAGD 1. p. 713): 'to approach' [AB, Arn, BAGD, LN; HCSB, REB], 'to go to'

[NTC, WBC; all versions except HCSB, REB, TEV], 'to go into the presence of' [TEV], 'to come to' [BECNT]. This implies that Joseph went to Pilate in the praetorium [AB, MGC]. He asked for an audience with Pilate [TG]. Being a member of the Sanhedrin, Joseph would be more likely to be granted access than one of Jesus' family or friends [NAC].
   b. aorist mid. indic. of αἰτέω (LN 33.163) (BAGD p. 25): 'to ask for' [AB, Arn, BAGD, BECNT, LN, NTC, WBC; all versions except KJV], 'to beg' [KJV]. He asked for permission to take Jesus' body and give it a proper burial [MGC, Su, TNTC]. The middle voice of this verb was used in business transactions and the Romans generally allowed relatives and friends of the executed to bury the bodies [Lns]. It is implied that Pilate granted the request [BECNT, NAC, TG].
   c. λαξευτός (LN **19.26**) (BAGD p. 466): 'hewn out of rock' [**LN**], 'hewn in the rock' [BAGD]. The phrase μνήματι λαξευτῷ 'a hewn out of rock tomb' is translated 'a rock-hewn tomb' [BECNT, NTC, WBC; NRSV], 'a rock-cut tomb' [AB], 'a tomb hewn of rock' [Arn], 'a tomb cut out of the rock' [NET, REB], 'a tomb cut into the rock' [HCSB, NASB; similarly GW, NIV], 'a tomb that had been cut out of solid rock' [CEV], 'a tomb that had been dug out of solid rock' [TEV], 'a tomb that was cut out of a wall of rock' [NCV], 'a new tomb that had been carved out of rock' [NLT], 'a sepulcher that was hewn in stone' [KJV]. The rock would have been an outcropping of rock and the tomb would have been a cave that was cut into that outcropping [LN].
QUESTION—How did Joseph take down the body?
He took the body down from the cross [NIGTC, TG]. Probably Jesus' body was lowered from the cross after they drew out the nails [Lns]. The verb 'having taken down' implies that the cross remained standing upright while Jesus' body was taken down from it. However, it would still be an appropriate verb if the cross had been first lowered to the ground before the body was removed from it [Arn]. By saying that Joseph did this, it implies that he took charge of the others who actually took down the body [Lns]. Joseph could not have done this by himself, so probably his servants helped, and John 19:39 says that Nicodemus accompanied him [NTC].
QUESTION—How did he wrap the body in linen?
The linen cloth was cut into strips [Arn, Lns, NTC, Su]. The body was wrapped in fine linen cloth that was torn into strips so it could be wrapped around the limbs and body. John 19:40 tells about sprinkling aromatic spices between the strips as they were being wrapped [Lns, NTC]. Only the head was left free to be covered with a small cloth when the body was laid in the tomb [Lns]. Or, it was a burial shroud [AB, MGC, TNTC, WBC; NET]. After the body was first wrapped with strips of cloth containing spices, a linen shroud was wrapped around all of the prepared body [NIC, TNTC].
QUESTON—What was the μνήματι λαξευτῷ 'a rock-hewn tomb'?
This was not a grave dug below the surface of the ground, but a cave that was dug into solid rock at the side of a cliff [Lns, TG]. The tomb was

probably hewn into the side of a rock face and had a small entrance maybe a yard tall [BECNT]. Tombs were caves cut into rock and had ledges or shelves carved inside for placing a number of bodies [MGC]. It is implied that this tomb was available because it was Joseph's own tomb as stated in Matt. 27:60 [NAC].

QUESTION—What is the purpose of adding that no one had ever been laid in the tomb?

It indicates that the tomb was a new one [NTC, Su; NLT]. It indicates that such a tomb was appropriate to honor such a person as Jesus [EGT, Lns, NAC, NTC, Su]. It was a fitting place for Jesus' body since it was new, with no odor of death and decay [Lns]. Instead of saying 'where no one had ever been laid', some translate 'and had never been used' [CEV, TEV], 'this tomb had never been used before' [NCV], 'a new tomb' [NLT]. Tombs like this were expensive [TNTC], so such tombs often were used to accommodate a number of bodies [NIGTC, TNTC]. It was the custom that after the flesh of a body had decomposed, a second burial took place when the bones were placed in a stone box called an ossuary [AB, MGC, NICNT].

23:54 And it-was (the) day of-preparation^a and (the) Sabbath was-dawning.^b

TEXT—Instead of καὶ ἡμέρα ἦν παρασκευῆς 'and it was (the) day of preparation' some manuscripts read καὶ ἡμέρα ἦν παρασκευή 'and it was preparation day', although GNT does not mention this variant. Καὶ ἡμέρα ἦν παρασκευή 'and it was preparation day' is read by KJV.

LEXICON—a. παρασκευή (LN 67.201) (BAGD p. 622): 'preparation' [BAGD], 'day of preparation, Friday' [BAGD]. The phrase 'the day of preparation' [Arn, WBC; NET, REB] is also translated 'the day of Preparation' [AB, BECNT; NRSV], 'the preparation day' [HCSB, NASB], 'Preparation Day' [Lns, NTC; NCV, NIV], 'that day (was) the preparation' [KJV], 'Friday' [CEV, GW, TEV], 'Friday, the day of preparation for the Sabbath' [NLT]. This was a day on which preparations were made for a sacred day or a feast day [LN]. The word παρασκευή 'preparation' was a technical term for Friday [NIC, Rb]. In the NT, this noun refers to a definite day, Friday, the day when everything had to be prepared for the Sabbath day when no work was permitted [BAGD].

b. imperf. act. indic. of ἐπιφώσκω (LN 14.41) (BAGD p. 304): 'to dawn' [BAGD, LN], 'to become light' [LN], 'to draw on' [BAGD]. The verb ἐπέφωσκεν 'was dawning' [Lns] is also translated 'was near to dawning' [WBC], 'was about to begin' [NTC; CEV, HCSB, NASB, NIV, REB, TEV], 'was beginning' [BECNT; NET, NRSV], 'was just beginning' [GW], 'was approaching' [Arn], 'was drawing near' [AB], 'drew on' [KJV], 'it was late on Friday afternoon' [NLT]. The clause 'and Sabbath was dawning' is translated 'when the sun went down, the Sabbath day would begin' [NCV]. The verb means to change from darkness to light in the early morning hours [LN]. The imperfect tense indicates that it was coming gradually [Lns].

QUESTION—What was the day of preparation?

This was the Jewish day of the week preceding the Sabbath and the day of preparation covered the time from Thursday evening to Friday evening [NIGTC]. Preparations for the Sabbath included cleaning the house, buying supplies, and cooking so that no work would be done from sunset of Preparation until sunset of the Sabbath [Su].

QUESTION—What time of day is indicated by the phrase σάββατον ἐπέφωσκεν 'Sabbath was dawning'?

The verb is not accurate, since the Sabbath began at sunset, not at dawn [ICC]. The Jews reckoned a new day to start at sunset, so the verb cannot refer to the sun shining forth at dawn. Perhaps the verb refers to the custom of lighting lamps when the Sabbath begins at sunset, but probably the verb is used in a extended sense so that 'to dawn' means 'to begin' [TH]. The phrase 'it was dawning' can easily mean 'it was beginning' when used with things that cannot 'dawn' [Alf, BNTC, Crd, ICC, My, NIC]. The verb is used figuratively for 'was approaching' [Arn]. The new day began at sunset with the 'dawning' of the first star [Lns, NIGTC, Su]. Luke intended to indicate the near arrival of sundown when the Sabbath would begin, but his use of the verb 'was dawning' is unique and the translation needs to show that it had not arrived: 'Sabbath was (near to) dawning' [WBC]. Most translations state that the Sabbath had not yet begun [AB, Arn, NTC; CEV, HCSB, KJV, NASB, NCV, NIV, NLT, REB, TEV]. However, though stating it was the day of preparation before the Sabbath, some translations appear to say that the Sabbath had begun: 'was beginning' [BECNT; NET, NRSV], 'was just beginning' [GW], 'was dawning' [Lns].

23:55 And having-followed the women, who had-come from Galilee with-him, saw the tomb and how his body was-laid,[a] **23:56a** and having-returned they-prepared spices[b] and ointments.[c]

TEXT—In 23:55, instead of αἱ γυναῖκες 'the women', some manuscripts read καὶ γυναῖκες 'women also', although GNT does not mention this variant. Καὶ γυναῖκες 'women also' is read by KJV.

LEXICON—a. aorist pass. indic. of τίθημι (LN 85.32) (BAGD I.1.a.α. p. 815): 'to be laid' [BAGD, BECNT, Lns, NTC; all versions except CEV, HCSB, TEV], 'to be put' [BAGD, LN], 'to be placed' [AB, Arn, LN, WBC; CEV, HCSB, TEV]. This passive verb is also translated actively with 'they' as the subject: 'to place' [NLT].

b. ἄρωμα (LN 6.207) (BAGD p. 114): 'spices' [AB, Arn, BAGD, BECNT, NTC, WBC; all versions except NET], 'aromatic spices' [Lns; NET], 'aromatic salves, perfumed ointment' [LN]. The phrase 'spices and ointments' is translated 'some sweet-smelling spices' [CEV]. This noun refers to anything that is highly perfumed and used in food as spices, in perfume, or in embalming a corpse [WBC]. This refers to aromatic oils or salves that were used especially for embalming the dead [BAGD, LN]. These are expensive spices in powdered form [Lns]. They are fragrant herbs [Arn].

c. μύρον (LN **6.205**) (BAGD 530): 'ointments' [AB, Arn, BAGD; KJV, NLT, NRSV], 'perfumed oil' [LN], 'perfumes' [BAGD, BECNT, **LN**, Lns, NTC, WBC; GW, HCSB, NASB, NCV, NET, NIV, REB, TEV]. This refers to a strongly aromatic and expensive ointment [LN]. These are perfumed liquids or extracts [Lns]. They are sweet-smelling ointments [Arn].

QUESTION—What is significant about the women following and seeing the tomb where Jesus was laid?

They went to see where the tomb was because they planned to come back later [Lns, NIC, TH]. They not only saw where the body was laid, but *how*, noting the insufficient washing and anointing [AB, MGC]. This fact rules out any possibility that they returned to the wrong tomb on Sunday [MGC, NAC, NIGTC]. The women followed at a distance [TG]. Some specify whom they followed: Joseph [TH; CEV, GW, NCV, NIV, TEV], Joseph and his assistants [AB, ICC], or Jesus [WBC]. They didn't go into the tomb itself [ICC].

QUESTION—Where did the women from Galilee return to?

This does not mean that they returned to Galilee [TH]. They went back to the house where they were staying in Jerusalem [NIGTC, TG, TH].

QUESTION—What was the purpose of preparing spices and ointments?

The spices and perfumes were used to slow decomposition and to counteract death's stench [BECNT]. These were rubbed on the corpse to prepare it for burial and although this was usually done before the body was wrapped in a cloth, there had been no time to do this before the Sabbath began at sunset [TG].

QUESTION—When did they prepare the spices and ointments?

1. They did this as soon as they arrived at their lodgings [Alf, Arn, BECNT, Gdt, Lns, MGC, NIC, NTC, Rb, Su, TNTC]. On their way to the house where they were staying, they obtained the materials to anoint Jesus' body so as to be ready to go to the tomb at their first opportunity on Sunday [Su]. Probably the women bought spices twice. During the short time they had before the Sabbath began, they started preparing the material, but there wasn't enough, so after the Sabbath on Saturday evening they bought what more they needed [BECNT, NIC, NTC, TNTC].
2. They did this after the Sabbath ended at sunset Saturday night [NIGTC]. Luke does not explicitly say when the material was purchased and Mark 16:1 says that they bought the material after the Sabbath ended [NIGTC].

DISCOURSE UNIT: 23:56b–24:53 [AB]. The topic is the resurrection narrative.

DISCOURSE UNIT: 23:56b–24:12 [AB, NIGTC]. The topic is the empty tomb [NIGTC], the women at the empty tomb [AB].

DISCOURSE UNIT: 23:56b [Su]. The topic is Saturday—a day of rest.

23:56b And on-the Sabbath they-rested[a] in-accordance-with[b] the commandment.

LXICON—a. aorist act. indic. of ἡσυχάζω (LN **23.82**) (BAGD 1. p. 349): 'to rest' [AB, BAGD, BECNT, **LN**, Lns, NTC, WBC; all versions], 'to keep quiet' [Arn]. It means to abstain from work [BAGD], not to be engaged in some activity [LN].

   b. κατά (LN 89.8): 'in accordance with' [LN]. The phrase 'in accordance with the commandment' is translated 'in accord with the commandment' [WBC], 'according to the commandment' [Arn, BECNT, Lns; GW, HCSB, KJV, NASB, NET, NRSV], 'as the Law commanded' [TEV], 'as the Law of Moses commands' [CEV], 'as the law of Moses commanded' [NCV], 'in obedience to the commandment' [AB, NTC; NIV, REB], 'as required by the law' [NLT].

QUESTION—How is this sentence connected with its context?

1. It is joined with verse 22:56a [Arn, BECNT, EGT, Gdt, ICC, Lns, NAC, NTC, TNTC; CEV, GW, KJV, NIV, NLT, REB]: after they returned they prepared spices and ointments and on the Sabbath they rested.
2. It is an independent paragraph [Su, WBC; NASB, NCV, NET, NRSV, TEV].
3. It is joined with verse 24:1 [AB, Alf, BNTC, GNT, NIGTC, TH]: on the Sabbath they rested and on the first day of the week they came to the tomb.

QUESTION—What is the commandment?

The commandment is found in Exodus 20:10. It is a commandment to keep the seventh day holy as a day for rest and worship, abstaining from any form of work [Su]

DISCOURSE UNIT: 24:1–53 [BECNT, NAC, NICNT, Su, TNTC, WBC; REB]. The topic is Sunday—a day of triumph [Su], the resurrection [REB], the resurrection of Jesus [TNTC, WBC], the resurrection and ascension of Jesus [BECNT, NAC], the exaltation of Jesus [NICNT].

DISCOURSE UNIT: 24:1–12 [BECNT, NAC, NICNT, Su, WBC; CEV, GW, NASB, NCV, NET, NIV, NLT, NRSV, TEV]. The topic is the empty tomb [NICNT], the women at the empty tomb [NAC], the resurrection [NASB, NET, NIV, NLT, TEV], the resurrection of Jesus [NRSV], the resurrection discovered [BECNT], the women and Peter find an empty tomb [WBC], the angelic announcement of his resurrection [Su], Jesus rises from the dead [NCV], Jesus is alive [CEV], Jesus comes back to life [GW].

DISCOURSE UNIT: 24:1–11 [TNTC]. The topic is the appearance to the women.

24:1 But/and[a] on-the first (day) of-the week[b] very early (in the) morning[c] they-came to the tomb bringing the spices (which) they-had-prepared.

TEXT—Following ἀρώματα 'spices', some manuscripts add καί τινες σὺν αὐτοῖς 'and some (others) with them'. GNT does not mention this variant. Καί τινες σὺν αὐτοῖς 'and some (others) with them' is read by KJV.

LEXICON—a. δέ (LN 89.136): 'but' [LN, Lns, NTC; NASB, NET, NLT, NRSV, REB], 'now' [KJV, NET], not explicit [Arn, BECNT, WBC; CEV, GW, HCSB, NCV, NIV, TEV]. The combination μέν...δέ in Καὶ τὸ μὲν σάββατον 'And on the Sabbath' (23:56) and τῇ δὲ μιᾷ τῶν σαββάτων 'but on the first of week' are markers of sets of items in contrast with one another, meaning 'on the one hand...but on the other hand' [LN].

b. σάββατον (LN 67.177) (BAGD 2.b. p. 739) 'week' [AB, Arn, BAGD, BECNT, LN, NTC, WBC; HCSB, KJV, NASB, NET, NIV, NRSV, REB]. The phrase 'the first day of the week' is translated 'the first day with reference to the Sabbath' [Lns], 'Sunday' [CEV, GW, NLT, TEV]. This noun refers to a period of seven days and the Sabbath Day marked the seventh day of the week with the next day being regarded as the first day of the week, our Sunday [LN].

c. ὄρθρος (LN **67.73**) (BAGD p. 580): 'early morning' [BAGD], 'dawn' [BAGD, LN], 'sunrise, daybreak' [LN]. The phrase 'very early in the morning' [WBC; HCSB, KJV, NIV] is also translated 'at early dawn' [Arn, **LN**, NTC; NASB, NET, NRSV], 'at deep dawn' [Lns], 'during the deep dawn' [BECNT], 'very early, at dawn' [NCV], 'at the crack of dawn' [AB], 'very early' [REB], 'very early (on Sunday morning)' [CEV, GW, NLT, TEV]. Probably this was during the first portion of dawn since John 20:1 says that it was still dark and Mark 16:2 says that it was early in the morning after the sun had risen [BECNT]. The women started before dawn while it was still dark and the sun was rising as they reached the tomb [Lns, NIVS, NTC].

QUESTION—What relationship is indicated by the beginning conjunction δέ?
1. It indicates a contrast with the preceding clause [AB, BECNT, EGT, ICC, Lns, NIGTC, TH]: on the Sabbath they rested, but on the first day of the week they did not rest, they went to the tomb.
2. It is a continuative [KJV, NET]: now on the first day of the week.

QUESTION—Who are included in the statement '*they* came to the tomb'?
The pronoun refers to the women who prepared the spices in 23:55–56 [AB, NTC, Su, TNTC; NET]. The women are named in 24:10 [NAC]. Besides the spices that they had prepared before the Sabbath began, Mark 16:1 indicates that they bought other spices after the Sabbath had ended [Rb].

24:2 And they-found[a] the stone rolled-away[b] from the tomb, **24:3** and having-entered they-did- not -find the body of-the Lord Jesus.

TEXT—In 24:3, instead of τοῦ κυρίου Ἰησοῦ 'the Lord Jesus', some manuscripts read τοῦ Ἰησοῦ 'Jesus' and others omit this phrase. GNT reads τοῦ κυρίου Ἰησοῦ 'the Lord Jesus' with a B decision, indicating that the text is almost certain.

LEXICON—a. aorist act. indic. of εὑρίσκω (LN 27.27): 'to find' [AB, Arn, BECNT, LN, Lns, NTC, WBC; all versions], 'to discover' [LN].

b. perf. pass. participle of ἀποκυλίω (LN 15.248) (BAGD p. 94): 'to be rolled away' [AB, Arn, BECNT, LN, Lns, NTC, WBC; all versions].

QUESTION—What stone was rolled away from the tomb?

Although a stone had not been previously mentioned, τὸν λίθον 'the stone' refers to the stone that was well known to the readers [ICC, Lns, TH]. Or, it refers to the usual stone that was used to close such tombs [Arn, ICC, NIGTC]. Such tombs usually had a huge circular stone disc set in a channel carved into the stone floor across the rectangular doorway of the tomb [AB, BECNT, MGC, NAC, NIBC]. It is possible that it was a large spherical stone that merely plugged the entrance to the tomb without a channel [BECNT, WBC]. It was a large stone that had been rolled across the entrance of the tomb to seal it [TG]. The stone closed the entrance to keep out thieves and animals [Arn]. In Mark 16:3, it tells how the women had been wondering how they could roll back the heavy stone [Su].

QUESTION—How had the stone been rolled away from the tomb?

Matt. 28:2 says that there had been an earthquake and an angel had rolled away the stone and sat upon it. Being 'rolled away from (ἀπό) the tomb' means that the stone disc had been rolled clear out of its groove as if it had been hurled away and it now lay flat on the ground [Lns].

QUESTION—Is there significance in the contrast 'they found the stone rolled away' and 'they did not find the body'?

This is a neat balance produced by using the same verb 'to find' [NIGTC]. It makes a contrast [BECNT]. We are to note what they found and what they did not find [Lns]

QUESTION—What is the significance of Luke calling Jesus 'the Lord Jesus' at this point?

Jesus was now Lord over death [MGC]. This recognizes the new status of the risen Jesus [NIGTC].

24:4 And it-happened-that while they-were-at-a-loss[a] about this behold[b] two men stood-by them in gleaming[c] clothes.

LEXICON—a. pres. mid. infin. of ἀπορέω (LN 32.9) (BAGD p. 97): 'to be at a loss, to be uncertain' [BAGD, LN]. The phrase 'they were at a loss about this' is translated 'they were perplexed about this' [BECNT, Lns, NTC; HCSB, NASB, NET, NRSV], 'they were perplexed at this' [AB], 'they were perplexed about this matter' [Arn], 'they were much perplexed thereabout' [KJV], 'they were wondering about this' [NCV, NIV], 'they were puzzling about this' [WBC], 'they were puzzled about this' [GW], 'they stood there puzzled about this' [TEV], 'they were puzzled, trying to think what could have happened to it' [NLT], 'they did not know what to think' [CEV], 'they stood utterly at a loss' [REB]. The verb means to be

in perplexity and implies serious anxiety [LN]. They were very confused and anxious [NET]. They had not expected to find an empty tomb, so they were perplexed and wondered about this situation [BECNT; NET]. They were perplexed about the missing body [MGC, NICNT].
- b. ἰδού (LN 91.13) (BAGD p. 371): 'behold' [BAGD; KJV], 'look' [LN], 'behold, suddenly' [NASB], 'lo, suddenly' [Lns] 'suddenly' [AB; all versions except KJV, NASB], not explicit [Arn, BECNT, NTC, WBC]. As they stood there wondering, the two men appeared [BECNT]. The angels had been there all the time, but now their presence was suddenly made visible to the women [Lns].
- c. pres. act. participle of ἀστράπτω (LN **14.47**) (BAGD p. 118): 'to gleam' [BAGD, LN], 'to glisten, to dazzle' [LN]. The phrase 'in gleaming clothes' [**LN**] is also translated 'in gleaming garments' [WBC], 'in gleaming robes' [AB], 'in dazzling clothes' [HCSB, NRSV], 'in dazzling clothing' [NASB], 'clothed in dazzling robes' [NLT], 'in dazzling garments' [REB], 'in dazzling attire' [NET], 'in dazzling apparel' [Lns], 'in shining apparel' [Arn, BECNT], 'in shining garments' [KJV], 'in shining clothes' [NCV], 'in bright shining clothes' [TEV], 'in clothes that gleamed like lightning' [NIC], 'dressed in garments that flashed like lightning' [NTC], 'in clothes that were bright as lightning' [GW], 'in shining white clothes' [CEV]. It means 'in white', the same as the account given in John 20:12 [Su].

QUESTION—Who were these two men?

They were men in appearance, but they wore angelic clothing [Arn, EGT, Rb; NET]. The dazzling of flashing clothing identifies them as messengers from heaven and, though angels are sexless, they had taken the form of young men [Lns]. This is a standard description of the appearance of angels [TG, TNTC]. They were angels [Lns, MGC, NIC, NIGTC, NTC, TNTC, WBC]. The two men are said to be angels in 24:23 [AB, Arn, BECNT, NAC, NIBC, TNTC]. Luke also calls angels 'men' in Acts 1:10 and 10:30.

24:5 And they became afraid and (while) bowing[a] (their) faces to the ground they-said to them, Why are-you-seeking the (one who) is-living among[b] the dead?

LEXICON—a. pres. act. participle of κλίνω (LN **17.21**) (BAGD 1.a. p. 436): 'to bow' [BAGD, LN]. The phrase 'bowing their faces to the ground' [Lns] is also translated 'bowed their faces to the ground' [BECNT, NTC, WBC; NASB, NET, NRSV], 'bowed down their faces to the earth' [KJV], 'bent their faces to the ground' [Arn], 'bowed their heads to the ground' [NCV], 'bowed down with their faces to the ground' [NIV], 'stood with eyes cast down' [REB], 'bowed low before them' [NLT], 'bowed down to the ground' [AB, **LN**; HCSB, TEV], 'bowed to the ground' [CEV, GW], 'prostrated themselves on the ground' [**LN**]. The present tense of the participle indicates the attitude of the woman when the men began to speak to them [TH].

b. μετά (LN 83.9) (BAGD A.I. p. 508): 'among, with' [BAGD, LN]. The phrase 'among the dead' [AB, Arn, BECNT, NTC, WBC; all versions except CEV, NCV, NLT] is also translated 'with the dead' [Lns], 'in the place of the dead' [CEV], 'in this place for the dead' [NCV], '(looking) in a tomb' [NLT]. The preposition μετά with a genitive object indicates location, 'among' [BAGD, LN]. Or, it indicates association: 'in association with those who are dead' or 'with those who are dead' [Lns, Su]. Tombs were for dead people [NAC, Su].

QUESTION—What is meant by the women 'bowing their faces to the ground'?
1. As the women stood there, they looked down at the ground instead of looking at the angels [BECNT, Lns, NIGTC, NTC, Su, TH, WBC; REB]. They inclined their faces to the ground [NTC]. The women looked down in order to avoid the brightness of the angels' clothing and perhaps to indicate their submission [WBC]. Bowing is a sign that they recognized that these men were heavenly beings and messengers from God [BECNT]. Rather than expressing worship, they lowered their eyes in fear or confusion [TH]. They bowed their heads in fear, and possibly to avoid the bright light [NIGTC]. The present participle indicates that they kept inclining their faces again and again, every time they tried to look up [Lns].
2. They prostrated themselves before the angels [LN]. The phrase κλινουσῶν τὰ πρόσωπα εἰς τὴν γῆν 'bowing their faces to the ground' is an idiom meaning to prostrate oneself before someone as an act of reverence or fear [LN].

QUESTION—Does the phrase 'they said to them' mean that the two angels spoke in unison?
One of the angels spoke for both of them [Lns]. If one spoke for both, the singular or the plural verb could properly be used [NTC].

QUESTION—What is the function of the question the angels asked?
It was a rhetorical question and expressed rebuke [BECNT, ICC, MGC, NICNT, NIGTC, NTC, WBC], or mild criticism [TH]. The women had a momentary lapse of faith [MGC]. It indicated that women should have remembered Jesus' assurance that on the third day he would rise from the dead [ICC, NIC]. They had no business to be there for the purpose of anointing a dead body [NTC]. Or, it was not a rebuke, but a way to bring home to the women that they had been acting in blind ignorance [Lns]. Or, it expresses surprise that they had come to a tomb to look for someone who is living [TG]. Or, it was a jubilant announcement of Jesus' victory over death [Arn].

24:6 **He-is not here, but has-been-raised/has-risen.[a] Remember how[b] he-spoke to-you (while) still[c] being in Galilee**

TEXT—Instead of οὐκ ἔστιν ὧδε, ἀλλὰ ἠγέρθη 'he is not here, but he has risen/been raised' some manuscripts read οὐκ ἔστιν ὧδε· ἠγέρθη 'he is not here; he has risen/been raised', one manuscript reads ἠγέρθη ἐκ νεκρῶν 'he has risen/been raised from (the) dead', and some manuscripts omit this phrase. GNT reads οὐκ ἔστιν ὧδε, ἀλλὰ ἠγέρθη 'he is not here, but he has risen/been raised' with a B decision, indicating that the text is almost certain. This phrase is omitted by REB. It is included as part of 24:5 by NRSV.

LEXICON—a. aorist pass. infin. of ἐγείρω (LN 23.94): 'to be raised' [AB, BECNT, WBC; NET, TEV], 'to be raised from death' [CEV], 'to be raised to life' [LN], 'to be brought back to life' [GW], 'to be made to live again' [LN], 'to be resurrected' [HCSB]. This passive voice is also translated actively: 'to rise' [Arn, NTC; KJV, NASB, NIV, NRSV], 'to arise' [Lns], 'to rise from the dead' [NCV, NLT].

b. ὡς (LN 90.21) (BAGD IV.4. p. 899): 'how' [Arn, BECNT, Lns, NTC, WBC; HCSB, KJV, NASB, NET, NIV, NRSV, REB], 'that' [BAGD, LN; CEV], 'what' [AB; GW, NCV, NLT, TEV]. It marks the discourse content [LN]. 'How' does not refer to the mode of speaking but to what was said [TH]. It indicates the wording of the statement [ICC]. It means in what terms it was said [EGT].

c. ἔτι (LN 67.128) (BAGD 1.a.b. p. 315): 'still' [AB, Arn, BAGD, BECNT, LN, NTC, WBC; HCSB, NASB, NET, NIV, NRSV, REB], 'yet' [BAGD, LN, Lns; KJV], not explicit [NCV, NLT, TEV]. 'Yet' means as early as that, and includes all the utterances from that time on [Lns]. This points to the beginning of Jesus' ministry [NET].

QUESTION—What is indicated by the passive voice of ἠγέρθη 'he was raised'?

1. The verb is to be translated as a passive [AB, BECNT, MGC, NAC, NIBC, NTC, TNTC, WBC; CEV, GW, HCSB, NET, TEV]: he was raised. The passive indicates that God raised him [AB, BECNT, MGC, NIBC, TNTC, WBC; NET].

2. This passive verb is used in the active sense [Arn, Lns; KJV, NASB, NCV, NIV, NLT, NRSV]: he has risen. Many such passives are used with an active meaning [Lns, Rb]. The fact that 24:7 uses the active sense 'rise again' governs the use of the sense here [Lns, NAC]. It is true that the resurrection is an act of God, but it is also true that it is an act of Jesus himself (Mark 9:31; Luke 18:33) [Lns]. Jesus' resurrection was his own doing [NAC].

24:7 saying that the Son of-Man[a] must be-delivered[b] into (the) hands of-sinful men and be-crucified and on-the third day rise-again.

LEXICON—a. υἱὸς τοῦ ἀνθρώπου 'Son of Man'. This title for Christ occurs at 5:24; 6:5, 22; 7:34; 9:22, 26, 44; 11:30; 12:8, 40; 17:22, 24, 26; 18:8, 31; 19:10; 21:27, 36; 22:22, 48, 69. See the discussions of this title at 5:24, 6:5, and 9:22.

b. aorist pass. infin. of παραδίδωμι (LN 37.12) (BAGD 1.b. p. 614): 'to be handed over' [BAGD, LN], 'to be turned over' [BAGD]. The phrase 'must be delivered into the hands' [NTC; KJV, NASB, NET, NIV] is also translated 'it was necessary...to be delivered up into the hands' [WBC], 'it is necessary that...be delivered into the hands' [Lns], 'had to be delivered into the hands' [Arn], 'must be delivered over into the hands' [BECNT], 'must be betrayed into the hands' [HCSB, NLT], 'must be handed over into the hands' [AB], 'must be handed over' [GW, NCV, NRSV, TEV], 'will be handed over' [CEV], 'must be given into the power of' [REB]. The phrase παραδίδωμι εἰς χεῖρας 'to give into the hands' is an idiom meaning to hand someone over into the control of others [LN]. The inclusion of the verb δεῖ 'must, it is necessary' indicates that God's will was at work [TG, TH].

QUESTION—When was this information imparted?

Before Jesus had started his journey to Jerusalem, he had spoken of his death and resurrection in 9:21–22 and 9:43–44. In 9:22 he referred to his death and that the manner of his death would be by crucifixion is implied when he said in 9:23 that a disciple must take up his cross and follow him [Su]. Here the angel clarified the kind of death Jesus had spoken of previously [MGC, NAC, NICNT]. 'Crucified' was the natural word to use in the light of what had taken place [NIGTC]. Although the occasion in 9:21–23 took place in the territory of Philip, Mark 9:3–31 says that Jesus spoke the same words to his disciples in Galilee [BECNT].

24:8 And they-remembered his words. 24:9 And having-returned from the tomb they-reported all these (things) to-the eleven and to-all the others.

QUESTION—Who were the people they reported to?

The 'eleven' were the remaining apostles after the defection of Judas [Su]. 'All the others' are the disciples in a wider sense than just the apostles [TH]. They were whatever friends and relatives that were present [Su]. It does not mean that they were all assembled together so that they could all be told at the same time. In other accounts Mary found only Peter and John, while Thomas was absent from the group for some time. The women's report reached all these disciples as the news was spread to them and probably they then met together to discuss it [Lns].

24:10 And they-were[a] Mary Magdalene and Joanna and Mary the (mother) of-James and the others with them. They-were-telling[b] these (things) to the apostles. 24:11 But these words seemed to them as nonsense,[c] and they-were-not-believing them.

TEXT—In 24:10, instead of ἦσαν δέ 'and they were', some manuscripts read ἦν δέ 'and it was' and others omit these words. GNT reads ἦσαν δέ 'and they were' with a B decision, indicating that the text is almost certain. Ἦν δέ 'and it was' is read by KJV.

TEXT—In 24:10, instead of ἔλεγον 'they were telling', some manuscripts read αἳ ἔλεγον 'who were telling'. GNT does not mention this variant. Αἳ ἔλεγον 'who were telling' is read by KJV and also translated by Arn, WBC, NCV, NET, NIV, and NRSV.

TEXT—In 24:11, instead of τὰ ῥήματα ταῦτα 'these words', some manuscripts read τὰ ῥήματα αὐτῶν 'their words'. GNT does not mention this variant. Τὰ ῥήματα αὐτῶν 'their words' is read by KJV.

LEXICON—a. imperf. act. indic. of εἰμί (LN 85.1); 'to be' [LN]. The phrase 'they were' [BECNT, Lns; NASB] is also translated 'the women were' [GW, REB, TEV], 'it was' [Arn, WBC], 'it was...who' [KJV, NCV, NET, NIV, NRSV], 'the women who went to the tomb were' [NLT], 'those who told these things were' [NTC], 'were the ones who had gone to the tomb' [CEV], not explicit [HCSB].

b. imperf. act. indic. of λέγω (LN 33.69): 'to tell' [BECNT, LN, Lns, NTC; all versions], 'to say' [LN, WBC], 'to speak' [Arn], 'to repeat' [AB]. The imperfect tense means that they kept talking about these things [Lns, Su, WBC]. The imperfect tense indicates either that they repeatedly tried to make the apostle believe them [AB, NIGTC], or that they spoke one by one [NIGTC].

c. λῆρος (LN **33.380**) (BAGD p. 473): 'nonsense' [AB, BAGD, NTC, WBC; CEV, HCSB, NASB, NCV, NIV, NLT, REB, TEV], 'pure nonsense' [**LN**; NET], 'silly talk' [Lns], 'foolish talk' [Arn], 'idle tale' [BAGD, BECNT; KJV, NRSV]. The phrase 'seemed to them as nonsense' is translated 'thought that the women's story didn't make any sense' [GW]. They didn't believe that such a resurrection was possible [Arn; NET].

QUESTION—How is the obscure syntax of 24:10 to be taken?

1. All of these women are mentioned to identify who returned from the tomb to report to the apostles, and all of these women are the subject of the new sentence 'They were telling...' [AB, BECNT, MGC, NIGTC, TH, TNTC, WBC; CEV, GW, NLT, REB, TEV]: the women who reported all these things to the apostles were Mary Magdalene, Joanna, Mary, and the other women with them. They were telling these things to the apostles. The 'other women' reinforced the message of the women who are named [WBC]. This is translated variously: 'Mary Magdalene, Joanna, Mary the mother of James, and some other women were the ones who had gone to the tomb. When they returned, they told the eleven apostles and the others what had happened' [CEV], 'The women who went to the tomb were Mary Magdalene, Joanna, Mary the mother of James, and several others. They told the apostles what had happened' [NLT], 'The women were Mary Magdalene, Joanna, and Mary the mother of James; they and the other women with them told these things to the apostles' [TEV; similarly REB]. 'The women were Mary from Magdala, Joanna, and Mary (the mother of James). There were also other women with them. They told the apostles everything' [GW].

2. This is similar to the preceding interpretation, but instead of identifying the women involved in the giving the report in the preceding verse, it identifies the women who were telling these things to the apostles in the rest of this verse [HCSB, NAC, NTC; KJV, NCV, NET, NIV, NRSV]: it

was Mary Magdalene, Joanna, Mary, and the other women with them who were telling these things to the apostles. The 'who' can be avoided: 'Mary Magdalene, Joanna, Mary the mother of James, and the other women with them were telling the apostles these things' [HCSB].
3. The phrase καὶ αἱ λοιπαὶ σὺν αὐταῖς 'and the others with them' belongs with the last part of the verse as the subject of the verb 'they were telling' [Arn, ICC; NASB]: 'the women who reported all these things to the apostles were Mary Magdalene, Joanna, and Mary. Also the other women with them were telling these things to the apostles'. The women who gave the report in the preceding verse are the women named; also the other women with them told these things to the apostles [ICC].

DISCOURSE UNIT: 24:12 [TNTC]. The topic is Peter at the tomb.

24:12 **But Peter having-gotten-up**[a] **ran to the tomb and bending-over**[b] **he-sees only the linen-cloths,**[c] **and he-departed to himself**[d] **wondering**[e] **(at) the (thing) that had-happened.**

TEXT—Some manuscripts omit this verse. GNT includes this verse with a B decision, indicating that the text is almost certain. It is omitted by REB.

TEXT—Following τὰ ὀθόνια 'the linen cloths', some manuscripts add κείμενα 'lying'. GNT does not mention this variant. Κείμενα 'lying' is read by KJV and NIV.

LEXICON—a. aorist act. participle of ἀνίσταμαι (LN 15.36): 'to get up' [AB, NTC, WBC; GW, HCSB, NASB, NCV, NET, NIV, TEV], 'to arise' [Arn, Lns; KJV], 'to rise up' [BECNT], 'to depart, to go away from, to leave' [LN], not explicit [CEV, NLT]. This means to move away from some place, possibly with the implication of 'getting up and leaving' [LN]. Rising up implies a prompt action [EGT].
  b. aorist act. participle of παρακύπτω (LN 17.31, 24.13) (BAGD 1. p. 619): 'to bend over' [BAGD; NIV], 'to bend down' [Arn, LN (17.31); NET, TEV], 'to bend down to look inside' [GW], 'to bend down and look in' [NCV], 'to stoop to look in' [HCSB], 'to stoop and look in' [LN (24.13); NASB], 'to stoop down' [LN (17.31), Lns, NTC; KJV], 'to stoop down and look in' [CEV], 'to stoop and peer in' [NLT], 'to stretch and look in' [BECNT], 'to peer in' [AB, WBC]. The action implies looking into something [BAGD, LN].
  c. ὀθόνιον (LN 6.154) (BAGD p. 555): 'linen cloth' [BAGD, LN], 'sheet' [BAGD]. The plural noun is translated 'linen cloths' [Arn, BAGD, LN, WBC; HCSB, NRSV], 'linen clothes' [BECNT; KJV], 'strips of linen' [NTC; GW, NIV], 'strips of linen cloth' [NET], 'linen bands' [Lns], 'linen wrappings' [AB; NASB], 'empty linen wrappings' [NLT], 'the cloth that Jesus' body had been wrapped in' [NCV], 'burial clothes' [CEV], 'grave cloths' [TEV]. In the NT, this noun is used only for strips of cloth that are used to prepare a corpse for burial [LN]. The noun does not indicate the shape of the cloth, and means no more than that the cloths were those in which Jesus had been wrapped [AB]. This refers to the same

linen cloth mentioned in 23:53 [NAC]. The linen cloths had wrapped several hundred pounds of spices and myrrh spices around Jesus' body and they still showed the form of the body, but without the body in the midst of the spices [Su].

    d. ἑαυτοῦ (LN 15.92): 'himself' [LN]. The phrase ἀπέρχομαι πρὸς ἑαυτόν 'to return to oneself' is an idiom meaning 'to go back to one's place or abode', but it would be misleading here to translate it 'he went back home' because Peter probably did not have a home in Jerusalem [LN]. The phrase ἀπῆλθεν πρὸς ἑαυτόν 'he departed to himself' is translated 'he went away to himself' [Lns], 'he went home' [AB, BECNT, NTC; HCSB, NET, NRSV], 'he went off to his home' [WBC], 'he went home again' [NLT], 'he went back home' [TEV], 'he went away to his home' [NASB, NCV], 'he went away to his quarters' [Arn], 'he went back to where he was staying' [LN], 'he went away' [GW], 'he returned' [CEV]. The phrase ἀπέρχομαι πρὸς ἑαυτόν θαυμάζων 'he departed to himself wondering' is translated 'he went away, wondering to himself' [NIV], 'he departed, wondering in himself' [KJV].

    e. pres. act. participle of θαυμάζω (LN 25.213) (BAGD p. 352): 'to wonder (about)' [AB, BAGD, LN, Lns, NTC, WBC; CEV, GW, KJV, NCV, NET, NIV, NLT], 'to be amazed (at)' [BECNT; HCSB, NRSV], 'to marvel (at)' [LN; NASB], 'to marvel (about)' [Arn]. He was wondering about the empty tomb [AB]. He wondered how the undisturbed linen bands could be emptied of the body [Lns]. See this word at 1:21, 63; 2:18, 33; 4:22; 7:9; 8:25; 9:43; 11:14, 38; 20:26; 24: 41.

QUESTION—What relationship is indicated by δέ 'but'?

    It marks a contrast: they did not believe, but Peter went to the tomb to see for himself [ICC, My]. This is translated 'but' [AB, Arn, BECNT, WBC; CEV, GW, NASB, NCV, NET, NRSV, TEV], and 'however' [NTC; HCSB, NIV, NLT]. Curiosity got the better of Peter [MGC].

QUESTION—Why did Peter need to bend over to look into the tomb?

    The entrance to the tomb was small, perhaps a yard tall [BECNT]. This compound verb does not include the meaning 'to stoop down' or 'to bend forward' [AB, BECNT], rather it means to peer in by stretching forward to get a good look [AB], to make some physical effort to look inside [BECNT].

QUESTION—What is meant by the phrase ἀπέρχομαι πρὸς ἑαυτόν θαυμάζων 'he departed to himself wondering'?

    1. The phrase πρὸς ἑαυτόν 'to himself' goes with the preceding verb ἀπέρχομαι 'he departed' [AB, Arn, BECNT, LN, Lns, NIGTC, NTC, WBC; all versions except KJV, NIV, REB]: he departed to himself, wondering at the things that had happened.

        1.1 It means that Peter went back to where he was staying [AB, Arn, BECNT, LN, NTC, WBC; HCSB, NASB, NCV, NET, NLT, NRSV, TEV].

1.2 It means that Peter went away by himself [Lns, NIGTC, Su]. He sought solitude as he wondered about all he knew had happened and what others had reported as having happened [NIGTC].

2. The phrase πρὸς ἑαυτόν 'to himself' goes with the following verb θαυμάζων 'wondering' [TH; KJV, NIV]: he departed, wondering in himself at the things that had happened. The phrase 'in himself' is redundant with the verb 'wondering' [TH].

DISCOURSE UNIT: 24:13–35 [AB, BECNT, NAC, NICNT, NIGTC, TNTC, WBC; CEV, GW, NASB, NCV, NET, NIV, NRSV, TEV]. The topic is the road to Emmaus [NASB], on the road to Emmaus [NIV], the walk to Emmaus [NIGTC, TNTC; NRSV, TEV], Jesus' appearance on the road to Emmaus [AB, NAC], Jesus on the road to Emmaus [NCV], Jesus walks the road to Emmaus [NET], Jesus appears to two disciples [CEV], an encounter on the road to Emmaus [NICNT, WBC], Jesus appears to disciples on a road to Emmaus [GW], the Emmaus road and a meal of discovery [BECNT].

DISCOURSE UNIT: 24:13–34 [NLT]. The topic is the walk to Emmaus.

DISCOURSE UNIT: 24:13–33 [Su]. The topic is the appearance on the road to Emmaus.

24:13 And behold two of them were traveling on the same day to a-village named Emmaus, (which) was-a-distance-of sixty stadia^a from Jerusalem. 24:14 And they were-talking^b to one-another about all these (things that) had-happened.

LEXICON—a. στάδιος (LN 81.27) (BAGD 1. p. 764): 'stade' [BAGD, LN], 'stadium' [BAGD]. The phrase 'a distance of sixty stadia' is translated 'sixty stadia' [Arn, Lns, WBC], 'about seven miles distant' [AB], 'about seven miles' [BECNT; all versions except KJV, NLT], 'seven miles' [NLT], 'eleven kilometers (about seven miles)' [NTC], 'about threescore furlongs' [KJV]. A stade was a measurement of distance, about a distance of 600 feet [LN, Su], or 607 feet [AB, BAGD, NAC].

b. imperf. act. indic. of ὁμιλέω (LN **33.156**) (BAGD p. 565): 'to talk' [AB, Arn, BECNT, **LN**, WBC; all versions except HCSB], 'to converse (with)' [BAGD, LN, Lns, NTC], 'to speak' [BAGD], 'to discuss' [HCSB].

QUESTION—What day did this happen?
   It was the first day of the week (24:1) [AB, NAC, NICNT], Sunday [Arn], the same day as the discovery of the empty tomb [NICNT, NIGTC, Su], the day of the resurrection [NTC, TNTC, WBC].

QUESTION—Who were the two men and why would they be traveling to Emmaus?
   In 24:33 we learn that they were not some of the eleven apostles [ICC, TH]. They were members of the wider group of disciples generally [ICC, My, NTC, TH]. These were two of the group of disciples mentioned in 24:9 [AB, Alf, BECNT, Crd, EGT, MGC, NAC, NIGTC]. They were part of the group of disciples who had heard the women's report but didn't believe it [Su]. Or,

544   LUKE 24:13–14

there is no reason to think that they were part of those mentioned in 24:9 [ICC]. They were returning to their home in Emmaus after the celebration of the Passover [AB, BECNT, Lns, NAC, NIC, NIGTC, NTC]. We can deduce that they lived in Emmaus from 24:28–29 [NTC]. Or, possibly they had to go to Emmaus for overnight accommodation for the remaining days of Unleavened Bread [WBC]. The site of the village of Emmaus is not now known [BECNT, MGC, NIC, NIGTC, NTC, TNTC]. There are difficulties with all of the suggested sites [TNTC]. Probably the location is at Kubeibeh, seven miles northwest of Jerusalem [ICC, NIC]. Or, probably it is the Emmaus known to Josephus which was three and a half miles northwest of Jerusalem and the mention of seven miles refers to the round-trip distance [AB, BECNT, Crd, WBC].

QUESTION—What were they talking about?

They were probably talking about the events concerning the trial, the crucifixion, and the women's report that the tomb was empty [NTC, TG]. They were speaking back and forth to one another and the main topic would have been the crucifixion and the reports that Jesus was alive [Su]. Verses 24:19–24 tells us what they were talking about [BECNT, NAC, TH, WBC].

24:15 And it-happened while they were-talking[a] and discussing[b] Jesus himself having-come-near was-accompanying[c] them,

LEXICON—a. imperf. act. indic. of ὁμιλέω (LN 33.156) (BAGD p. 565): 'to talk'. See this word at 24:14.

b. pres. act. infin. of συζητέω (LN 33.157) (BAGD 1. p. 775): 'to discuss' [BAGD, LN], 'to talk with, to converse' [LN]. The phrase 'they were talking and discussing' [AB, WBC; NASB, NCV, NRSV] is also translated 'they were talking and discussing together' [BECNT], 'they were conversing and discussing together' [NTC], 'they talked and discussed' [TEV], 'they talked and discussed these things' [NIV], 'they communed together and reasoned' [KJV], 'they were conversing and questioning together' [Lns], 'they were talking and thinking about' [CEV], 'they were talking and debating these things' [NET], 'they were talking and arguing' [Arn], 'they were discussing and arguing' [HCSB], 'they talked and argued' [REB], 'they were talking' [GW], not explicit [NLT].

c. imper. mid./pass. (deponent = act.) imperf. of συμπορεύομαι (LN 15.148) (BAGD 1. p. 780): 'to accompany' [LN], 'to go with' [BAGD, LN]. The phrase 'having come near was accompanying them' is translated 'having drawn near, began to go with them' [Lns], 'came near and began walking with them' [NCV], 'drew near and began to walk along with them' [AB, NTC; similarly HCSB, TEV], 'came near and went with them' [NRSV; similarly KJV], 'drew near and traveled with them' [BECNT], 'drew near and started to travel along with them' [WBC], 'came up and walked along with them' [NIV, REB], 'approached and traveled with them' [Arn], 'approached and began traveling with them'

[NASB], 'approached and began to accompany them' [NET], 'came near and started walking along beside them' [CEV], 'approached them and began walking with them' [GW], 'came along and joined them and began walking beside them' [NLT].

QUESTION—What is the force of the two verbs ὁμιλεῖν αὐτοὺς καὶ συζητεῖν 'they were talking and discussing'?

The second verb, 'discussing', is more forceful than the first: they were talking and even heatedly debating [TH]. The combination suggests that their discussion was lively [EGT], animated [Arn], intense [BECNT], or emotional [NET]. Or, the second verb has a weak sense [NIGTC]. They were asking questions and suggesting answers [Su]. They were not able to get any farther than asking questions [Lns].

QUESTION—How did Jesus approach them and accompany them?

As they were walking away from Jerusalem, Jesus overtook them [AB, Alf, BECNT, ICC, Lns, MGC, My, NTC, TG, TH, TNTC]. We don't know if Jesus overtook them or if he came in from a side road [Su]. After his resurrection, Jesus came and went as he desired and at this time he appeared on the road and with a few strides caught up with his disciples [Lns]. He began walking with them in the way one traveler joins a couple of other travelers on the road [Lns]. Jesus walked alongside of them [NTC]. The imperfect tense 'was accompanying' suggests that Jesus walked with them for a while without saying anything [Alf, Lns, Su]. They thought Jesus was another pilgrim to Jerusalem who was now returning home [AB, Arn, BECNT, MGC].

QUESTION—What is the function of the phrase αὐτὸς Ἰησοῦς 'Jesus himself'?

This emphasizes the fact that the very subject of their discussion was the one who joined them [Alf, ICC, My, Su].

24:16 but their eyes were-held[a] not to-recognize[b] him.

LEXICON—a. imperf. pass. indic. of κρατέω (LN 37.16) (BAGD 2.d. p. 448): 'to be held back, to be prevented, to be restrained, to be hindered' [BAGD], 'to be controlled' [LN]. The clause οἱ ὀφθαλμοὶ αὐτῶν ἐκρατοῦντο τοῦ μὴ ἐπιγνῶναι αὐτόν 'their eyes were held not to recognize him' [Lns] is also translated 'their eyes were held so as not to recognize him' [Arn], 'their eyes were held from recognizing him' [AB], 'their eyes were holden that they should not know him' [KJV], 'their eyes were prevented from recognizing him' [NASB], 'their eyes were kept from recognizing him' [BECNT, NTC, WBC; NET, NRSV], 'they were prevented from recognizing him' [HCSB], 'they were kept from recognizing him' [NCV, NIV], 'something prevented them from recognizing him' [REB], 'they did not know who he was' [CEV], 'although they saw him, they didn't recognize him' [GW], 'they saw him, but somehow did not recognize him' [TEV], 'they didn't know who he was, because God kept them from recognizing him' [NLT]. The infinitive

ἐκρατοῦντο 'held' with τοῦ may express purpose '*in order that* they should not recognize him', or function as an ablative '*from* recognizing him', or express result '*so that* they did not recognize him', the last being preferable [Lns].
   b. ἐπιγινώσκω (LN **27.61**) (BAGD 1.b. p. 291): 'to recognize' [AB, Arn, BAGD, BECNT, **LN**, Lns, NTC, WBC; all versions except CEV, KJV], 'to know' [KJV], 'to know who someone was' [CEV].
QUESTION—What is meant by 'their eyes were held not to recognize him'?
   1. God prevented them from recognizing Jesus [AB, Arn, Lns, MGC, My, NAC, NIBC, NIGTC, NIVS, TG, TH; NLT]. The passive 'ἐκρατοῦντο 'were held' implies that God caused this [AB, Alf, Lns, MGC, NAC, NIGTC, TH], just as the passive verb 'their eyes were opened' in 24:31 implies that God opened their eyes [Lns]. Even though Jesus appeared in a different form to Mary (Mark 16:9) and might have appeared now as another traveler, they would have recognized him if their eyes had not been held [Lns]. Perhaps this was God's doing, but the text does not say so and a possible translation could be 'they saw him but did not recognize him' [TG]. Because they were kept from recognizing Jesus, they were able to be taught about the necessity of Jesus' death and resurrection and how this was prophesied [NAC].
   2. Jesus prevented them from recognizing him [Alf, Su, TNTC]. It was the Lord's will that he not be recognized by them until the time he saw fit [Alf].
   3. Their failure to recognize Jesus was due to their own inability [BECNT, Gdt]. They hadn't believed the report about the resurrection (24:25) and a mysterious change had come over the person of Jesus [Gdt]. Jesus now had a resurrection body that they did not recognize [BECNT]
   4. Satan worked on the state of their minds so that they did not recognize him [WBC].

24:17 And he-said to them, What (are) these words that you-are-exchanging[a] with one-another (as) you-are-walking? And they-stood sad.[b]

TEXT—Instead of καὶ ἐστάθησαν 'and they stood' some manuscripts read καὶ ἔστε 'and you are'. GNT reads καὶ ἐστάθησαν 'and they stood' with a B decision, indicating that the text is almost certain. Καὶ ἔστε 'and you are' is read by KJV.

LEXICON—a. pres. act. indic. of ἀντιβάλλω (LN **33.160**) (BAGD p. 74): 'to exchange' [BAGD], 'to argue about, to discuss' [LN]. The clause 'What are these words that are you are exchanging with one another/each other?' [NTC; NASB] is also translated 'What are these statements which you are exchanging with each other?' [Lns], 'What is all this talk that you exchange with one another?' [AB], 'What are the matters which you are talking about with one another?' [WBC], 'What are these matters which you debate with each other?' [Arn], 'What is this conversation you are holding with each other?' [BECNT], 'What were/are you discussing?'

[LN; GW], 'What are you discussing together?' [NIV], 'What are you discussing with each other?' [NRSV], 'What are these things you are talking about?' [NCV], 'What are you talking about to each other?' [TEV], 'What were you talking about?' [CEV], 'What is the subject of your discussion?' [BAGD], 'What are these matters you are discussing so intently?' [NET], 'What is this dispute that you're having?' [HCSB], 'What manner of communications are these that ye have one to another?' [KJV], 'You seem to be in a deep discussion about something, what are you so concerned about?' [NLT], 'What is it you are debating?' [REB]. The literal translation 'throwing back and forth' indicates highly excited, heated statements and questions [Su]. Jesus was asking the subject of their discussion [MGC, NIGTC].

b. σκυθρωπός (LN 25.287) (BAGD p. 758): 'sad, gloomy' [BAGD, LN]. The phrase ἐστάθησαν σκυθρωποί 'they stood sad' is translated 'the two followers stopped, looking very sad' [NCV], 'they stood still, looking sad' [BECNT; NASB, NET, NRSV], 'they stood still, with sad faces' [TEV], 'they stood still, their faces full of sadness' [REB], 'they stood still, their faces downcast' [NIV], 'they stopped and looked very sad' [GW], 'they stopped walking and looked discouraged' [HCSB], 'they stopped walking and looked downcast' [WBC], 'they stood still, looking glum' [NTC], 'they stood there looking sad and gloomy' [CEV], 'they stopped short, sadness written across their faces' [NLT], 'they stopped momentarily, full of gloom' [AB], 'they with sad looks came to a halt' [Arn], 'they stopped, sullen' [Lns].

QUESTION—Why did Jesus ask this question?

Jesus knew what they were talking about, but he asked the question in order to arouse their interest and to provide an opportunity for explaining what the disciples needed to know [NTC]. He wanted them to state their problem so that he could solve it for them in an objective way [Lns].

QUESTION—Why did the two disciples stop and stand looking sad?

They were sad about the events they had been discussing [BNTC, NTC, TG, TH, TNTC, WBC]. The events of the last two days had filled them with sorrow and a feeling of disappointment [NTC]. They stopped with surprise and astonishment, and their displeasure is better expressed as 'sullen' instead of 'sad' [Lns]. They were sullen about being asked such a question [EGT, Lns].

24:18 And answering one by-name-of Cleopas said to him, (Are) you (the) only-one visiting/living-in^a Jerusalem and not know the (things which) have-happened in it in these days?

TEXT—Instead of εἷς 'one' some manuscripts read ὁ εἷς 'the one'. GNT does not mention this variant. Ὁ εἷς 'the one' is read by KJV.

TEXT—Instead of ὀνόματι 'by name' some manuscripts read ᾧ ὄνομα 'to whom (the name)/whose name'. GNT does not mention this variant. ᾧ ὄνομα 'to whom (the name)/whose name' is read by KJV.

LEXICON—a. pres. act. indic. of παροικέω (LN **85.71**) (BAGD 1.a., 2. p. 628): 'to inhabit a place as a stranger' [BAGD (1.a.)], 'to live for a time' [LN], 'to live in, to inhabit' [BAGD (2.)]. The phrase 'the only one visiting/living in' is translated 'the only one visiting' [NASB], 'the only visitor in' [NCV], 'the only stranger in' [AB; NRSV], 'the only stranger who stays in' [Arn], 'the only person living for a time in, the only stranger living in' [**LN**], 'the only one so strange in' [BAGD (1.a.), NTC], 'the only visitor in' [HCSB, TEV], 'the only visitor to' [WBC; NET], 'only a visitor to' [NIV], 'the only person staying in' [REB], 'the only one in' [GW], 'the only person in' [NLT], 'the only person from' [CEV], 'the only one who dwells in' [BECNT], 'dost thou dwell as an outsider in' [Lns], 'only a stranger in' [KJV].

QUESTION—Who was the other disciple with Cleopas?

Cleopas was a man, but there have been speculations about who the other disciple was. Perhaps it was the wife of Cleopas [NIGTC, TNTC], or his son [NIGTC].

QUESTION—What is meant by using the adjective μόνος 'only' in the phrase 'Are you the only one'?

The adjective logically goes with both verbs 'visiting/living in' and 'not know' [Arn, Crd, Gdt, My, TG, WBC; CEV, GW, HCSB, NCV, NET, NLT, NRSV]: the only one visiting/living in Jerusalem *who* does not know. There were many visitors and strangers in Jerusalem for the Passover, but even they would be expected to know what had happened [EGT]. This adjective implies being in isolation as well as being a stranger. Even visitors knew all about what happened, so the question asks if he lived alone so as to be the only man in Jerusalem who did not know [EGT].

QUESTION—Does the verb παροικεῖς mean *visiting* Jerusalem or *living in* Jerusalem?

The verb can mean to live somewhere as a stranger or visitor, or it can it can mean to live somewhere permanently without the connotation of being a stranger [BAGD, TG].

1. This refers to Jesus as a stranger or visitor to Jerusalem [Alf, Crd, Gdt, ICC, LN, MGC, My, NAC, NIGTC, NTC, TH, TNTC, WBC; HCSB, NASB, NCV, NET, NIV, TEV]: are you the only visitor in Jerusalem. The two travelers thought that the stranger was another pilgrim returning home [NIGTC]. They wanted to know if Jesus was such a lonely stranger that he didn't know what everyone in Jerusalem was talking about [NIGTC].
2. This refers to Jesus as a resident of Jerusalem [BNTC, Lns, Su; GW]: are you the only person residing in Jerusalem. This is a technical word that referred to a Jew who had been born outside Jerusalem but was now a resident of that city [Su]. Perhaps because of a Galilean accent, they took Jesus to be a foreign-born Jew who had become a permanent resident [Lns].

LUKE 24:19

24:19 And he-said to-them, What (things)? And they said to-him, The (things) about Jesus the Nazarene, who was a-man a-prophet powerful[a] in deed and word in-the-opinion-of[b] God and all the people,

TEXT—Instead of τοῦ Ναζαρηνοῦ 'the Nazarene' some manuscripts read the alternative form τοῦ Ναζωραίου 'the Nazarene', or possibly 'the (one) of Nazareth' (as the suffix -ιου would suggest). GNT reads τοῦ Ναζαρηνοῦ 'the Nazarene' with a B decision, indicating that the text is almost certain. some versions would probably not distinguish between these two forms.

LEXICON—a. δυνατός (LN 74.4) (BAGD 1.a.β. p. 208): 'powerful, strong, capable' [BAGD], 'competent, particularly capable' [LN]. The phrase δυνατὸς ἐν ἔργῳ καὶ λόγῳ 'powerful in deed and word' [Lns] is also translated 'powerful in word and deed' [NIV], 'powerful in action and speech' [GW], 'mighty in deed and word' [AB, BECNT, WBC; KJV, NASB, NRSV], 'mighty in word and deed' [NTC], '(considered to be) powerful in everything he said and did' [TEV]. The clause 'who was a man, a prophet powerful in deed and word' is translated 'a man who, with his powerful deeds and words, proved to be a prophet' [NET], 'he was a powerful prophet in what he did and said' [GW], 'by what he did and said he showed that he was a powerful prophet' [CEV], 'who had proved himself a prophet mighty in deed and word' [Arn], 'who, by deeds and words of power, proved himself a prophet' [REB], 'he was a prophet who said and did many powerful things' [NCV], 'He was a prophet who did wonderful miracles. He was a mighty teacher' [NLT].

b. ἐναντίον (LN 90.20) (BAGD 1.b. p. 262): 'in the opinion of' [LN], 'in the sight of' [BAGD, LN; GW, NASB, REB], 'in the eyes of' [AB, WBC], 'in the judgment of' [BAGD, LN], 'before' [Arn, BECNT, Lns; GW, KJV, NCV, NET, NIV, NRSV], 'considered by' [TEV], 'highly regarded by' [NLT]. The preposition is also translated as a verb: 'who pleased' [CEV]. Jesus won the approval of God and the people [MGC, NAC, NIGTC, Su]. See this word at 1:6.

QUESTION—How were the two disciples involved in the phrase '*they* said to him'?

This is a condensation of all that they reported and much more was said [Alf]. Both disciples spoke [Arn]. They both joined in as they told the details of the last few days [Su]. Each spoke, first one and then the other [EGT]. Or, if they didn't take turns, one acted as the spokesman for the other [Lns], one speaking and the other assenting [My].

QUESTION—What is meant by the phrase ὃς ἐγένετο ἀνὴρ προφήτης 'who was a man a prophet'?

Jesus was a 'prophetic man' [EGT, ICC], but ἀνήρ 'man' can be regarded as redundant [EGT]. Perhaps the word 'man' is used to show respect [ICC, NIGTC]. The words 'who was a man a prophet' simply mean 'who was a prophet' [Lns, TH]. The word 'man' is left out of most translations [AB, Arn, BECNT, Lns, NTC, WBC; all versions except NET]. The verb in the aorist tense is the historical aorist which makes a summary statement that

Jesus was a prophet [Alf, Lns]. Or, the verb has the force, 'he showed himself to be a prophet' [Arn, ICC, NIGTC; CEV, NET, REB]

QUESTION—What is meant by being powerful in deed and word?

The deeds were miracles and healings and the words were Jesus' teachings and preaching [TH]. God showed his approval of Jesus by enabling him to perform miracles and by giving him a message to proclaim [TG].

24:20 how our chief-priests and rulers handed-over him to a-sentence^c of-death and they-crucified him. **24:21** And we were-hoping^b that he was the (one) about to-redeem^c Israel but in-addition to all these (things) this (the) third day it/he-spends^d from which these (things) happened.

TEXT—In 24:21, following τρίτην ταύτην ἡμέραν ἄγει 'this the third day spends', some manuscripts add σήμερον 'today'. GNT does not mention this variant. Σήμερον 'today' is read by KJV.

LEXICON—a. κρίμα (LN 56.24) (BAGD 4.b. p. 450): 'sentence, verdict, judgment' [LN], 'judicial verdict, (death) sentence' [BAGD]. The phrase παρέδωκαν αὐτὸν εἰς κρίμα θανάτου 'handed him over to a sentence of death' is translated 'delivered him to the sentence of death' [NASB], 'handed him over to be sentenced to death' [AB; HCSB, NCV, NIV, REB, TEV], 'handed him over to a judgment of death' [BECNT], 'delivered him up to a death judgment' [Lns], 'handed him over to be condemned to death' [Arn; NET, NRSV], 'delivered him to be condemned to death' [KJV], 'arrested him and handed him over to be condemned to death' [NLT], 'delivered him up to be sentenced to death' [NTC, WBC], 'had him arrested and sentenced' [CEV], 'had him arrested and sentenced to death' [CEV], 'had him condemned to death' [GW]. The Sanhedrin handed Jesus over to the Roman governor for him to sentence Jesus to death [Lns, TG].

b. imperf. act. indic. of ἐλπίζω (LN **25.59**) (BAGD 2. p. 252): 'to hope' [AB, Arn, BAGD, BECNT, **LN**, Lns, NTC, WBC; all versions except KJV, NLT], 'to trust' [KJV], 'to think' [NLT]. The verb means to look forward with confidence to something good that would happen [LN]. The imperfect tense indicates a continuous action in the past: 'we were hoping' [Lns, Rb, Su]. This describes their hope during the days of Jesus' ministry [NET]. It implies that they could no longer hope for this [Arn, ICC, TG].

c. pres. mid. infin. of λυτρόομαι (LN **37.128**) (BAGD 2. p. 482): 'to redeem' [Arn, BAGD, BECNT, NTC, WBC; HCSB, KJV, NASB, NET, NIV, NRSV], 'to ransom' [Lns], 'to rescue' [BAGD; NLT], 'to liberate' [**LN**], 'to be the liberator of' [REB], 'to set free' [BAGD, LN; CEV], 'to free' [GW, NCV, TEV], 'to deliver' [AB, LN]. See the noun form at 1:68; 2:38.

d. pres. act. indic. of ἄγω (LN **67.64, 67.79**) (BAGD 4. p. 14): 'to spend (time)' [BAGD, **LN** (67.79)], 'to take place, to occur' [**LN** (67.64)]. The clause 'this the third day it/he-spends from which these (things) happened' is translated 'it's the third day since these things happened' [HCSB], 'today is the third day since these things were done' [KJV], 'today is the third day since these things happened' [Arn], 'it is (now) the third day since these things happened' [LN (67.64); NASB, NET], 'it is the third day since all this took place' [NIV], 'it is now the third day since this happened' [NCV], 'this is the third day since it happened' [REB, TEV], 'this day is the third since these things happened' [WBC], 'this is now the third day since everything happened' [GW], 'it is now the third day since these things took place' [NTC; NRSV]. 'it is three days since this happened' [AB], 'it has already been three days since all this happened' [CEV], 'that all happened three days ago' [NLT], 'Jesus is spending the third day since these things happened' [LN (67.79)], 'Jesus is spending the third day' [BAGD], 'this is the third day he has spent since all these things came to pass' [BECNT], 'he is spending the third day since these things occurred' [Lns].

QUESTION—Who were hoping for liberation by Jesus?

This is an exclusive 'we' [TG] and the pronoun may refer to the wider group of the disciples, that is, 'we Christians' [Lns, TG, TNTC]. The pronoun is emphatic [Arn, TH], contrasting them with those mentioned in the preceding verse [TH].

QUESTION—What is meant by the redemption of Israel?

They thought Jesus was the Messiah who would set Israel free from its subjection to Rome [NIBC, Rb] and Roman occupation [AB]. They expected Jesus to set the nation free from their enemies and inaugurate the kingdom of God [NIGTC, NIVS]. Some think this includes being redeemed spiritually from sin [Alf, Lns, NIC, NTC, Su]. The verb does not mean merely to save, since the saving act costs something, so if it means to save from sin, it cost a blood sacrifice, and if it means to save from danger or evil, it costs the strain and effort to do so. Therefore here it speaks of the one about to pay the ransom or price and thus deliver Israel [Lns].

QUESTION—What is meant by ἀλλά γε καὶ σὺν πᾶσιν τούτοις 'but in addition to all these things'?

The additional fact that three days now had passed explains why they had lost hope [TG].

QUESTION—What is meant by 'this the third day spends these (things) happened'?

1. The verb ἄγει 'spends' is impersonal: it is three days since this happened [AB, Arn, ICC, NAC, NTC, TG, TH, WBC; all versions].
2. The verb ἄγει 'spends' is personal, and refers to Jesus: this is the third day he (Jesus) is spending since this happened [Alf, BAGD, BECNT, Crd, Lns].

QUESTION—How are the days counted for this to be the third day?

It was two days ago and since this was Sunday, the trial and crucifixion happened on Friday [TG].

24:22 But[a] also some women among us astounded[b] us, having-been early at the tomb, **24:23** and not having-found his body they-came saying also/even[c] to-have-seen a-vision[d] of-angels, who said he is-alive. **24:24** And some of-the (men) with us went to the tomb and they-found (it) just-as the women said, but him they-did- not -see.

LEXICON—a. ἀλλά (LN 89.125) (BAGD 3. p. 38): 'but' [BAGD, LN]. The phrase ἀλλὰ καί 'but also' [BECNT; NASB] is also translated 'but furthermore' [Arn], 'furthermore' [NET], 'moreover' [HCSB, NRSV], 'in addition' [NIV], 'and another thing' [Lns], 'yea, and' [KJV], 'and' [NCV], 'and now' [REB], 'then' [NLT], 'though' [NTC], not explicit [AB, WBC; CEV, GW, TEV].

  b. aorist act. indic. of ἐξίστημι (LN **25.220**) (BAGD 1. p. 276): 'to astound' [BAGD; HCSB, NRSV, REB], 'to completely astound' [**LN**], 'to greatly astound, to astonish greatly' [LN], 'to really astound' [AB], 'to astonish' [WBC], 'to make (us) astonished' [KJV], 'to amaze' [BAGD, BECNT; NASB, NCV, NET, NIV], 'to startle' [Arn, NTC; GW], 'to dumbfound' [Lns], 'to surprise' [CEV, TEV]. The phrase 'astounded us' is translated 'they came back with an amazing report' [NLT]. The thing that had amazed them was not that the women had been at the tomb early in the morning, but their report of seeing the angels [ICC]. See this word at 2:47, 8:56.

  c. καί (LN 89.93): 'also' [BECNT, LN, Lns; KJV, NASB], 'even' [AB, LN, NTC, WBC], 'indeed' [NRSV], not explicit [Arn; all versions except KJV, NASB, NRSV].

  d. ὀπτασία (LN 33.488) (BAGD 1. p. 576): 'vision' [AB, Arn, BAGD, BECNT, LN, Lns, NTC, WBC; all versions except GW, NLT]. The phrase 'had seen a vision of angels' is translated 'had seen angels' [GW, NLT]. See this word at 1:22.

QUESTION—What is meant by ἀλλὰ καί 'but also'?

This indicates a strong contrast with the preceding verse: but in spite of this, also this happened [ICC, TH], 'not only this, but also' [BAGD]. But in spite of this disappointment, there is also something favorable to tell [ICC, NIC]. Or, it continues the report: 'and another thing' [Lns].

QUESTION—In 24:23, what is meant by καί 'also/even'?

  1. It means 'also' [BECNT, My, NIGTC, TH]. In addition to seeing the empty tomb, they also saw a vision of angels [NIGTC]. Besides the fact that they did not find the body, they also saw the vision [TH].
  2. It means 'even' [AB, NTC, WBC]: they had even seen a vision of angels.

QUESTION—What is meant by seeing a vision of angels?

This means that they had seen a divine revelation and it does not imply that what they saw was not real [TG]. They saw a supernatural vision, that is to say, they saw angels [TH]. It simply means that they had seen angels [GW, NLT].

QUESTION—Who were the men who went to the tomb?

Although Luke mentions only Peter going to the tomb in 24:12, here the masculine plural τινες τῶν σὺν ἡμῖν 'some of the men with us' tells about at least two men who went. Peter had not been alone when he went [TNTC]. From John 20:3 we know that John accompanied Peter to the tomb [Arn, EGT, Lns, MGC, NTC, Su]. Or, after Peter had visited the tomb other disciples went there also [NAC].

24:25 And he said to them, O foolish[a] (ones) and slow[b] in-heart to-believe in all that the prophets spoke.

LEXICON—a. ἀνόητος (LN 32.50) (BAGD 1. p. 70): 'foolish' [BAGD, LN], 'stupid, without understanding' [LN]. The phrase 'O foolish ones' is translated 'O foolish men' [NTC; NASB], 'O you foolish men' [Arn], 'You foolish men' [WBC], 'You foolish people' [NET], 'You are such foolish people!' [NLT], 'O fools' [KJV], 'O dullards' [Lns], 'Oh, how foolish you are' [NRSV], 'Oh you foolish' [BECNT], 'How foolish you are' [NIV, TEV], 'You are foolish' [NCV], 'How foolish you are' [AB; GW], 'how unwise' [HCSB], 'How dull your are!' [REB], 'Why can't you understand?' [CEV]. The adjective pertains to being unwilling to use one's mental faculties in order to understand [LN].

b. βραδύς (LN 67.123) (BAGD 147): 'slow' [BAGD, LN]. The phrase 'slow in heart to believe' is translated 'slow of heart to believe' [BECNT, Lns, NTC, WBC; KJV, NASB], 'how slow of heart to believe' [NIV, NRSV], 'slow in your heart to believe' [Arn], 'how slow of heart to believe' [NET], 'slow of wit to believe' [AB], 'slow to believe' [NCV], 'how slow to believe' [REB], 'you're so slow to believe' [GW], 'how slow you are to believe' [HCSB, TEV], 'how can you be so slow to believe' [CEV], 'you find it so hard to believe' [NLT].

QUESTION—Who were foolish and why did Jesus call them foolish?

Some supply 'men' in their translations [Arn, NTC, WBC; NASB]. But the two could have been man and wife [TNTC]. Some make it ambiguous by supplying 'people' in their translations [NET, NLT]. This was a rebuke [BECNT, MGC, TNTC]. It was a tender chiding [TNTC]. It expressed Jesus' disappointment in them [BECNT]. By addressing them in this way, Jesus expressed both surprise and rebuke in regard to their intelligence, because they should have known the Scriptures better [Lns]. It means that they were dull [Su, TNTC], or stupid [EGT]. The following words explain that this refers to their lack of understanding [TH]. They were dull-witted not to consider the explanation that was in Scripture [Su].

QUESTION—What is meant by the disciples being slow in heart to believe?

They were slow to believe the prophets, thinking that what the Scriptures plainly stated was absurd [Arn]. Their minds (hearts) lacked spiritual alertness so they failed to be convinced of the truth of the prophetic writings and also the Law (24:27) [TH]. It means that they were reluctant to believe the Hebrew Scriptures [TG]. Their unbelieving attitude resulted in their dejection and failure to believe the reports of the empty tomb and the vision of angels. But their attitude would have been different if they had a thorough belief in all the evidence of the Scriptures [WBC]. If they had accepted what the prophets had said, they would have believed the report of the women who went to the tomb [NIGTC]. They were foolish or dull because they failed to believe that for the Messiah the way to glory had to be through suffering [NTC].

QUESTION—What is the force of πᾶσιν 'all' in the phrase 'in all that the prophets spoke'?

The word 'all' is quite important [Arn, ICC, Lns, NIC, NTC, Su]. Of course they believed a part of the prophets' writings [Su]. They had believed in the predictions of the glory of the Messiah, but hadn't taken to heart the predictions about the suffering he had to go through [Alf, ICC, NTC, TNTC]. They believed the Scriptures in general, but did not believe the things dealing with the Messiah's suffering and death, nor in the nature of his exaltation [Arn]. Jewish teachers would apply the references of the Servant's glory in Isaiah 52:13–53:12 to the Messiah, but then apply the references of the Servant's suffering to Israel [NIC, NTC]. Or, the word 'all' is used hyperbolically, and Jesus refrained from specifying the passages of OT prophetic writings he had in mind [AB]. No specific prophets are referred to and here Jesus was referring to the whole OT in general [MGC, TG].

24:26 **Was-it- not -necessary (for) the Messiah to-suffer[a] these (things) and to-enter into his glory?[b]**

LEXICON—a. aorist act. infin. of πάσχω (LN 24.78) (BAGD 3.b. p. 634): 'to suffer' [LN], 'to endure sufferings' [BAGD]. The phrase 'to suffer these things' [Arn, BECNT, NTC, WBC; GW, HCSB, NASB, NET, NIV, TEV] is also translated 'to suffer all this' [AB], 'to suffer all these things' [NLT], '(must/should) suffer these things' [NCV, NRSV], 'to have suffered these things' [KJV], 'to suffer in this way' [REB], 'to suffer' [CEV], '(that Christ) suffer' [Lns].

b. δόξα (LN 14.49) (BAGD 1.b.a. p. 203): 'glory' [BAGD], 'brightness' [LN]. This refers to the state of being in the next life, of participating in its radiance and glory [BAGD]. The phrase 'and to enter into his glory' [Arn, NTC, WBC; KJV, NASB; similarly GW, HCSB, NET] is also translated 'and come into his glory' [BECNT], 'and that he enter into his glory' [Lns], 'and then to enter his glory' [NIV, NRSV, TEV], 'before he enters his glory' [NCV], 'before entering into his glory' [AB], 'before entering upon his glory' [REB], 'before entering his time of glory' [NLT], 'before he was given his glory' [CEV].

QUESTION—Why was it necessary for this to take place?

The necessity was based in prophecy [BECNT, Crd, EGT, Gdt, Lns, My, TNTC]. God's decree was expressed in prophecy [ICC]. Behind the prophecies was God's will and plan for the salvation of mankind [Arn, Lns,

Su]. This was God's will for Jesus [NAC, TG]. It was God's plan that suffering must precede entering into his glory [Alf; NET].

QUESTION—What is meant by the final clause, καὶ εἰσελθεῖν εἰς τὴν δόξαν αὐτοῦ 'and enter into his glory'?

1. The conjunction καί 'and' appears to indicate the second thing that was necessary, but semantically it is to be taken in the consecutive sense, '*and so* to enter' [AB, Alf, ICC, TG, TH, WBC; CEV, NCV, NIV, NLT, NRSV, REB, TEV]. Suffering was the road to glory [ICC]. Glory is the outcome of his suffering [WBC]. He had to suffer *and then* enter his glory [NIV, NRSV, TEV]. He had to suffer *before* he entered his glory [AB; CEV, NCV, NLT, REB].

2. It was necessary to both suffer *and* to enter [Arn, Lns]. The influence of 'it is necessary' extends to the last part of the verse also [Arn]. The two acts were necessary because they were both revealed and fulfilled; Jesus suffered to expiate the world's guilt by his death and he also had to enter his glory to lay this sacrifice before God [Lns]. Some translations seem to indicate that this is coordinate with 'to suffer' [Arn, BECNT, NTC, WBC; GW, HCSB, KJV, NASB, NET]. However, the use of 'and' can still be taken in the sense of outcome [WBC].

QUESTION—What was the glory that Jesus entered into and when did he enter it?

Jesus entered the realm of glory, God's dwelling place, and there shared God's power [TG]. 'Glory' describes his exaltation at the right hand of God [WBC]. This was the glory that the Son had before the world began (John 17:5) [Lns]. The aorist tense of εἰσελθεῖν indicates that Jesus had already entered into this glory [AB, BECNT, NAC]. He entered at his resurrection [NAC]. Jesus was raised to reign next to God [BECNT]. Glory is the condition in which Jesus already enjoyed the company of his heavenly Father and from there he then appeared to his disciples [AB]. Or, Jesus had not yet entered into his glory [EGT, NIGTC]. Jesus passed over the period in which he appears to his disciples and speaks as though he had passed straight from the cross to his ascension to heavenly glory [NIGTC].

24:27 And having-begun from[a] Moses and from all the prophets he-explained[b] to-them the (things) concerning himself in all the Scriptures.[c]

LEXICON—a. ἀπό (LN 90.15) (BAGD II.3.a. p. 87): 'from' [BAGD, LN]. The phrase 'having begun from Moses and from all the prophets' is translated 'having begun/beginning with Moses and with all the prophets' [Lns, NTC; NASB], 'beginning from Moses and from all the prophets' [BECNT], 'beginning with Moses and all the prophets' [AB, Arn, WBC; HCSB, NET, NIV, NRSV], 'beginning at Moses and all the prophets' [KJV], 'starting from Moses and all the prophets' [REB], 'starting with what Moses said and all the prophets had said' [NCV], 'he began with Moses' Teachings and the Prophets' [GW], 'beginning with the Law of Moses and the Books of the Prophets' [CEV], 'beginning with the books

556　LUKE 24:27

　　　of Moses and the writings of all the prophets' [TEV], '(Jesus quoted passages) from the writings of Moses and all the prophets' [NLT].
  b. aorist act. indic. of διερμηνεύω (LN **33.148**) (BAGD 2. p. 194): 'to explain' [BAGD, LN; CEV, GW, NASB, NIV, NLT, REB, TEV], 'to interpret' [AB, Arn, BAGD, BECNT, **LN**, Lns, NTC, WBC; HCSB, NET, NRSV], 'to expound' [KJV]. The verb means to thoroughly explain the meaning of something that is particularly difficult to comprehend [LN].
  c. γραφαί (LN 33.54) (BAGD 2.b.a. p. 166): 'Scriptures' [Arn, BAGD, BECNT, LN, Lns, NTC, WBC; all versions except REB], 'Scripture' [AB; REB], 'holy writings' [LN].

QUESTION—What is meant by 'having begun from (ἀπό) Moses and from (ἀπό) all the prophets'?

　　There is a grammatical difficulty; he might begin *from* Moses, but how could he begin from Moses *and from* all the prophets? [EGT].
  1. Jesus explained all the Scriptures (the OT generally), starting with the law and the prophets [NIGTC, TNTC]. Some translations can easily be taken to fit in with this interpretation [AB, NTC; all versions except NASB, NLT]. This appears to view the Scriptures to have three parts (the Law, the Prophets, and the Psalms). The phrase 'in all the Scriptures' is meant to *include* the books of Moses and the books of the prophets [NIGTC].
  2. Jesus began with the books of Moses and proceeded with the books of all of the prophets [Alf, Arn, BECNT, Crd, Gdt, ICC, Lns, TH, WBC]. This is a zeugma where 'having begun' applies to two words with a different sense for each, and it means that he began with Moses and then went through all of the prophets [Crd]. He began with Moses first, and then began with each of the prophets as he came to them [Alf, Arn, Gdt, ICC]. 'Moses and all the prophets' is a traditional coupling of the Law and the Prophets [BECNT, WBC]. The old name of the OT was 'the Law and the Prophets' [Lns]. 'Moses and all the prophets' describes the whole of Scripture [Arn, NAC, NIVS, TG; NET]. Each book of the OT was written by a prophet [Arn].
  3. Jesus *began to instruct them* from Moses and from all of the prophets [EGT]. This tells what Jesus began to do, not where he began [EGT].

QUESTION—What is meant by explaining the things concerning himself in all the Scriptures?

　　Jesus chose the passages from the OT which concerned the Messiah and showed how they should be understood [NIGTC]. The passages would concern the suffering of the Messiah, probably emphasizing the passages in Isaiah, and then there would be the passages about his glory in explaining the resurrection [Su]. The two disciples did not realize at the time that the stranger was speaking about himself as he pointed out the Messianic passages [BECNT, Su]. This should not be taken to mean that he picked out proof-texts, rather he showed that throughout the OT there was a consistent divine purpose being worked out and ending with the cross [TNTC]. He

LUKE 24:27 557

picked out the symbols and types that pointed to the Messiah's work and person [Arn].

24:28 **And they-drew-near to the village where they-were-going, and he acted-as-though^a to-go farther.**

LEXICON—a. aorist mid. indic. of προσποιέομαι, προσποιέω (LN **41.49**) (BAGD 1. p. 718): 'to act as though/if' [BAGD, BECNT, **LN**, NTC; GW, NASB, NCV, NET, NIV, TEV], 'to make as though/if' [BAGD, WBC; KJV, REB], 'to make a move to' [Arn], 'to give the impression that' [LN; HCSB], 'to make the appearance of' [Lns], 'to seem to be' [CEV], 'to pretend' [AB, BAGD, LN]. The clause 'he acted as though to go farther' is translated 'he walked ahead as if he were going on' [NRSV], 'Jesus would have gone on' [NLT].

QUESTION—What is the referent of the included 'they' in the verbs in 'they drew near to the village where they were staying'?

Only the two disciples were going to Emmaus and it was not yet settled that Jesus would be staying in the village, so 'they' refers to the two disciples [TG]. This is made explicit in some translations: 'when the two of them came near the village where they going' [CEV]. Or, the subjects of 'they drew near to the village' are the two disciples and Jesus, but the subjects of 'where they were staying' are only the two disciples [TH].

QUESTION—How did Jesus act as though he was going on farther and why did he do this?

Probably when the two disciples left the highway to go into a house, Jesus did not turn aside with them [Arn]. 'He walked ahead as if he were going on' [NRSV]. Jesus' home was not in Emmaus and it was only natural that he should go on [Su]. This was not just play-acting, since Jesus actually began to leave them and would have departed had they not asked him to stay [Gdt, ICC, Lns, NIC, NIVS, NTC, Rb, Su, TNTC]. Jesus pretended to be going on, but he was planning to stay with them [BECNT]. Although the verb could mean 'to pretend', that is saying too much since Jesus did intend to stay with them and he was just giving them an opportunity to invite him to stay [NIGTC]. The text gives the impression that Jesus knew he would be asked to stay [NET]. Jesus desired to prompt an invitation and knew what would follow [My].

24:29 **And they-urged^a him saying, Stay with us, because it-is towards evening and the day already has-begun-to-end.^b And he-entered to-stay^c with them.**

TEXT—Some manuscripts omit ἤδη 'already'. GNT does not mention this variant. Ἤδη 'already' is omitted in the translations by NTC; CEV, GW, KJV, NCV, NET, NLT, REB and TEV.

LEXICON—a. aorist mid. (deponent = act.) indic. of παραβιάζομαι (LN **33.299**) (BAGD p. 612): 'to urge' [**LN**; GW, HCSB, NASB, NET], 'to urge strongly' [AB, BAGD, NTC; NIV, NRSV], 'to prevail' [BAGD], 'to beg' [CEV, NCV, NLT], 'to press' [REB], 'to press (him to stay)'

[WBC], 'to constrain' [BECNT, Lns; KJV], 'to compel (to stay)' [Arn], 'to hold (him) back' [TEV]. The verb sometimes means that force is used, but here quiet persuasion is meant [BECNT]. By their entreaties, they pressured him to stay [ICC]. It means that they persuaded him to stay [TG]. The urging was not so much in the words they used, but by the way in which they spoke them [TH]. Their pleading was so insistent that he could not refuse them [Su].

    b. perf. act. indic. of κλίνω (LN **67.118** or **68.51**) (BAGD 2. p. 436): 'to begin to end' [LN (68.51)], 'to draw to a close' [LN (67.118)], 'to decline, to be far spent' [BAGD]. The clause 'the day already has begun to end' is translated 'the day was coming to an end' [**LN** (67.118)], 'when the day was about to end' [**LN** (68.51)], 'the day has already declined' [Arn, Lns], 'the day is now almost over' [HCSB, NASB, NIV], 'the day is almost over' [NTC; GW, REB], 'the day is almost done' [NET], 'the day is already spent' [BECNT], 'the day is already far spent' [AB, WBC], 'the day is far spent' [KJV], 'the day is now nearly over' [NRSV], 'the sun is going down' [CEV], 'it is almost night' [NCV], 'it is getting dark' [TEV]. The clause 'it is towards evening and the day already has begun to end' is translated 'it was getting late' [NLT].

    c. aorist act. infin. of μένω (LN 85.55) (BAGD 1.a.α. p. 503): 'to stay' [LN], 'to remain' [BAGD, LN]. The clause 'and he entered to stay with them' is translated 'and he entered to remain with them' [BECNT], 'and he went in to remain with them' [Arn], 'and he went in to abide with them' [Lns], 'and he went in to tarry with them' [KJV], 'so he went in to stay with them' [NTC, WBC; HCSB, NASB, NCV, NET, NIV, NRSV, REB, TEV], 'so he went to stay with them' [GW], 'so Jesus went into the house to stay with them' [CEV], 'so he went home with them' [NLT], 'so he went into the village to stay with them' [AB]. He did not merely go into the village, but he went into their house since the next verse says that he reclined to eat [Lns]. This refers to spending the night at their house [TG].

QUESTION—What is the difference between 'it is towards evening' and 'the day already has begun to end' and why was the darkness to be avoided?

    The two clauses express the same thing, that it was in the late afternoon and it would soon be dark [Su]. The clauses are virtually synonymous and some translators may have to combine them so as to avoid a tautology [TH]. One version combines them [NLT]. It was time to stop normal traveling because after dark it would be difficult to walk on the path and there might be danger from robbers [TNTC].

24:30 **And it-happened while he was-reclining[a] (at the table) with them having-taken the bread he-blessed[b] (it) and having-broken (it) he-was-giving[c] (it) to-them.**

LEXICON—a. aorist pass. infin. of κατακλίνομαι, κατακλίνω (LN 17.23) (BAGD p. 411): 'to recline, to eat, to be at table, to sit down to eat' [LN], 'to recline at dinner' [BAGD]. The phrase 'he was reclining at the table' is translated 'having reclined' [Lns], 'he was reclining at table' [NTC], 'he reclined at the table' [AB, BECNT; HCSB, NASB], 'he was at the table' [GW, NCV, NIV, NRSV], 'he had taken his place at the table' [NET], 'he sat down at table' [WBC], 'he sat down to eat' [CEV, TEV], 'he sat at meat' [KJV]. The phrase 'he was reclining at the table with them' is translated 'they sat down to eat' [NLT], 'he sat down with them' [Arn; REB].

- b. aorist act. indic. of εὐλογέω (LN 33.470) (BAGD 1. p. 322): 'to bless' [LN], 'to give thanks and praise' [BAGD]. The phrase 'he blessed it' [Arn, BECNT, Lns, NTC; CEV, GW, HCSB, KJV, NASB, NET, NRSV] is also translated 'he said a/the blessing' [WBC; REB, TEV], 'he uttered a blessing' [AB], 'he asked God's blessing on it' [NLT]. 'he gave thanks' [NASB, NIV]. Jesus offered a prayer of thanks to God [Gdt, NIC, TG].
- c. imperf. act. indic. of ἐπιδίδωμι (LN 57.75) (BAGD 1. p. 292): 'to give' [BAGD, LN]. The phrase 'he was giving it to them' is translated 'he was in the act of giving it over to them' [Lns], 'he began giving it to them' [NTC; NASB], 'he began to give it to them' [NIV], 'he gave it to them' [Arn, BECNT, WBC; all versions except NASB, NIV, REB], 'he offered it to them' [AB; REB]. The imperfect tense indicates that he was beginning to give the bread to them [Rb]. The imperfect tense indicates that in the act of giving it to them, as they were taking it from his hand, their eyes were opened [Lns]. Most translate so as to imply that the disciples received the bread.

QUESTION—What is meant by Jesus blessing the bread?

Jesus spoke the customary blessing on the bread [EGT, Gdt, ICC, Lns, My, Su, TG, TH, TNTC]. He took the role of the host instead of a guest [AB, Arn, BECNT, Gdt, Lns, Su, TG, TH, WBC]. The disciples had probably asked Jesus to assume the position of host [EGT]. Perhaps it was because he was the oldest, or it showed their respect for the man who had explained the Scriptures to them [BECNT]. From the time they spent together on the road, Jesus had established the role of teacher [EGT, Lns].

24:31 **And their eyes were-opened[a] and they-recognized[b] him. And he became invisible[c] from them.**

LEXICON—a. aorist pass. indic. of διανοίγω (LN 79.110) (BAGD 1.b. p. 187): 'to be opened' [AB, Arn, BAGD, BECNT, LN, Lns, WBC; all versions except CEV, NCV], 'to be made open' [LN]. The clause 'their eyes were opened and they recognized him' is translated 'at once they knew who he was' [CEV], 'they were allowed to recognize Jesus' [NCV].
- b. aorist act. indic. of ἐπιγινώσκω (LN 27.61) (BAGD 1.b. p. 291): 'to recognize' See translations of this word at 24:16.
- c. ἄφαντος (LN **24.28**) (BAGD p. 124): 'invisible' [BAGD, LN], 'unseen' [LN]. The clause 'he became invisible from them' is translated 'he disappeared from their sight' [**LN**; HCSB, NIV, TEV], 'he disappeared

from them' [BECNT], 'at that moment he disappeared' [NLT], 'he disappeared' [CEV, NCV], 'he vanished from their sight' [AB, NTC, WBC; GW, NASB, NRSV, REB], 'he vanished out of their sight' [KJV, NET], 'when they saw who he was, he disappeared' [NCV], 'he became hidden from them' [Lns], 'he became invisible and disappeared from them' [Arn].

QUESTION—What is meant by the statement 'their eyes were opened'?

The metaphorical description of their eyes being opened is explained in the next clause where it says that they were caused to recognize Jesus [TH]. In 24:16 it says that 'their eyes were held not to recognize him' and now the opposite had happened [Su, TG, TH]. If verse 16 means that God prevented them from recognizing Jesus, then this verse must mean that God caused them to recognize Jesus [Gdt, ICC, NAC]. This is a theological passive meaning that God caused this [AB, Arn, MGC, NIGTC]. God lifted the veil from their eyes [BECNT]. God caused them to realize the significance of Jesus action and because of this they recognized who he was [NIGTC]. The aorist tense of 'were opened' indicates that they instantly recognized him [Lns, NTC; CEV], or they fully recognized him without any doubt [Rb].

QUESTION—What is meant by the statement that Jesus became invisible to them?

Jesus was there with them and suddenly he was not with them [Su]. The place where he was reclining was empty [Lns]. The new state of Jesus' resurrection body enabled him to appear and disappear at will [Lns, MGC, NTC, Su]. In saying that Jesus became invisible *from* (ἀπό) them, instead of *to* them, it is implied that Jesus had left the house in an invisible manner [EGT]. Instead of meaning that Jesus was there but invisible *to* them, the preposition *from* implies that a supernatural disappearance had taken place in which he had left them [Alf]. Jesus' disappearance is the counterpart of his arrival in 24:15 [Lns, NICNT, WBC].

24:32 And they-said to one-another, Was not the heart of-us burning[a] in us as he-was-speaking to-us on the road, as he-was-opening-up[b] to-us the Scriptures? **24:33** And having-arisen the very hour they-returned to Jerusalem and they-found gathered-together the Eleven and the (ones who were) with them,

TEXT—In 24:32, instead of ἐν ἡμῖν ὡς ἐλάλει ἡμῖν 'in us as he was speaking to us', some manuscripts read ὡς ἐλάλει ἡμῖν 'as he was speaking to us', others read ἐν ἡμῖν 'in us', and still others omit this entire phrase. GNT reads [ἐν ἡμῖν] ὡς ἐλάλει ἡμῖν '[in us] as he was speaking to us' with a C decision, indicating that the Committee had difficulty making the decision.

LEXICON—a. pres. pass. participle of καίω (LN 14.63) (BAGD 1.b. p. 396): 'to burn' [BAGD, LN]. The phrase 'was not the heart of us burning in us' is translated 'was not our heart burning in us' [Lns], 'did not our heart burn within us' [KJV], 'did not our hearts burn within us' [BECNT; NET], 'were not our hearts burning within us' [NTC; NASB, NIV,

NRSV], 'did not our hearts burn' [Arn], 'were not our hearts on fire within us' [AB, WBC], 'were not our hearts on fire' [REB], 'weren't our hearts ablaze within us' [HCSB], 'wasn't it like a fire burning in us' [TEV], 'it felt like a fire burning in us' [NCV], 'didn't it warm our hearts' [CEV], 'didn't our hearts feel strangely warm' [NLT], 'weren't we excited' [GW].
- b. imperf. act. indic. of διανοίγω (LN 33.142) (BAGD 2. p. 187): 'to open (up)' [BAGD, BECNT, LN, Lns, NTC, WBC; KJV, NIV, NRSV], 'to open up the meaning' [GW], 'to open the sense of' [AB], 'to explain' [BAGD, LN; CEV, HCSB, NASB, NCV, NET, NLT, REB, TEV], 'to interpret' [BAGD]. We should note the use of the same verb in *opening* their eyes and *opening* the Scriptures [ICC, NAC].

QUESTION—What is meant by their hearts burning in them?

Their hearts were in an extraordinary condition of fervent commotion [My]. They felt a warm glow within them by the gradual return of their understanding, joy, and hope [Su]. The warm glow in their hearts came from what Jesus said as he opened the Scriptures [Su]. The metaphor of burning refers to experiencing: enthusiasm and expectation [TH], joy, delight, enthusiasm, and energy [TG], new faith, assurance, and joy [Lns], a feeling of wonder and holy joy [Arn], or an intense emotion of excitement and comfort [BECNT]. They had sensed that something special was happening [BECNT]. The stranger's interpretation of the Scriptures began to convince them of Jesus' resurrection [NAC]. They had seen that Jesus was really the Messiah and that the women's report must have been true [Lns]. The phrase ἡ καρδία ἡμῶν 'the heart of us' is a common idiom for the distributive singular, meaning that in each of them the heart burned [BECNT, NIGTC; NET]. It is translated 'our hearts' [AB, Arn, BECNT, NTC, WBC; CEV, HCSB, NASB, NET, NIV, NLT, NRSV, REB].

QUESTION—Who were 'the Eleven' and who were the ones with them?

'The Eleven' were formerly called 'the Twelve' until Judas betrayed Jesus and was not now counted as an apostle [BECNT, Lns]. We learn in John 20:4 that the apostle Thomas was absent, but the group of apostles was now called 'the Eleven' whether the full number was actually present or not [Arn, Lns, NTC]. The people with them were the same people as 'all the others' mentioned in 24:9 [ICC]. They were family members and friends who had heard the early morning reports that Jesus was alive and all were now bound together as a group by these events [Su].

DISCOURSE UNIT: 24:34 [Su]. The topic is the appearance to Simon Peter.

24:34 saying, The Lord really[a] was-raised[b] and he-appeared to Simon.

LEXICON—a. ὄντως (LN 70.2) (BAGD 1. p. 574): 'really' [BAGD, LN; CEV, GW, NASB, NCV, NET, NLT], 'certainly' [BAGD, LN, Lns; HCSB], 'truly' [LN], 'in truth' [BAGD], 'actually' [Arn], 'indeed' [BECNT, NTC, WBC; KJV, NRSV, TEV], 'It is true!' [NIV, REB], 'It is really true!' [AB]. This is an affirmation of a fact that they had previously doubted [TH]. It was real because Simon had actually seen Jesus [Rb].

b. aorist pass. indic. of ἐγείρω (LN 23.94): 'to be raised' [LN]. The phrase 'was raised' is translated 'has been raised' [AB, BECNT, WBC; HCSB]. This passive verb is also translated actively with the Lord as the subject: 'has risen' [Arn, NTC; NASB, NCV, NET, NIV, NLT, NRSV, REB], 'is risen' [KJV, TEV], 'did rise up' [Lns], 'has come back to life' [GW], 'was alive' [CEV]. This verb means to be caused to live again after having once died [LN]. This is a theological passive, meaning that God had raised Jesus [MGC]. Or, see 24:6 for an explanation of the passive being used in the active sense.

QUESTION—Why did they refer to Peter as Simon at this time?

Peter's old name of Simon was commonly used by his friends [Lns]. Luke seems to have a pattern that when the Twelve or the Eleven are spoken of, the name 'Simon' is used and when the Apostles are spoken of, the name 'Peter' is used [WBC]. This recalls the use of the name Simon in 22:31 [NAC].

QUESTION—Who are the people giving the report in 24:34?

Although there is an abrupt shift of subject from the two people from Emmaus to the people assembled in the house, it is that group making the report [BECNT, ICC, NAC, NICNT]. The two disciples from Emmaus found the group gathered together in conversation talking to one another about the Lord having been raised and seen by Peter [MGC]. As one person in the excited group started speaking he would be interrupted by another [BECNT].

DISCOURSE UNIT: 24:35–49 [NLT]. The topic is Jesus' appearance to the disciples.

DISCOURSE UNIT: 24:35 [Su]. The topic is the report by the two from Emmaus.

24:35 And they were-reporting[a] the (things) on the road and how he-was-made-known to-them when/by[b] the breaking of-the bread.

LEXICON—a. imperf. mid./pass. (deponent = act.) indic. of ἐξηγέομαι (LN 33.201) (BAGD p. 275): 'to report, to explain, to tell, to describe' [BAGD], 'to inform, to relate, to tell fully' [LN]. The phrase 'were reporting the things' is translated 'told what things were done' [KJV], 'told about the things that happened' [BECNT], 'told their story' [NLT], 'told what had happened' [CEV, GW, NCV, NET, NIV, NRSV], 'described what had happened' [REB], 'began to describe what had happened' [HCSB], 'explained what had happened' [AB, WBC; TEV], 'related the incidents' [Arn], 'began to relate what had happened' [NTC], 'began to relate their experiences' [NASB], 'began to rehearse the things' [Lns]. The verb means to systematically provide detailed information

[LN]. They carefully explained all of the details and told about Jesus' explanations of the writings of the prophets concerning the Messiah [Su].
  b. ἐν (LN **89.76**) (BAGD I.2. p. 258): 'by' [BAGD, **LN**], 'by means of, through' [LN], 'when' [BAGD; NCV, NET, NIV, TEV], 'as' [NLT], 'in' [AB, BECNT, NTC, WBC; HCSB, KJV, NASB, NRSV, REB], 'in connection with' [Lns], 'at' [Arn].

QUESTION—Who is giving the report now?
  The words καὶ αὐτῶν 'and they' stress the change of subject to the two disciples, 'and they on their part' [TH]. The emphatic pronoun 'they' puts their experience and report in strong contrast with the group gathered in Jerusalem [Su]. The report of the two disciples further confirmed Jesus' appearance to Peter [NICNT, NIGTC]. Both the reports from the two disciples and from Peter confirmed the women's report [NET].

QUESTION—What relationship is indicated by the preposition ἐν 'when/by'?
  1. It indicates the occasion when Jesus was made known to them [Lns, My; CEV, GW, NCV, NET, NIV, NLT, TEV]: Jesus was made known to them *when* he broke the bread. Right after their fellow-traveler broke the bread and handed it to them they realized who he was [Lns]. It means at the time of the breaking of the bread [My]. It was not when they ate the bread, but when Jesus was breaking the bread [ICC].
  2. It indicated the means by which Jesus was made known to them [Alf, BAGD, LN]: Jesus was made known to them *by* his breaking the bread. This preposition indicates the means by which one event makes another event possible [LN]. It indicates the object by which something is recognized [BAGD].

DISCOURSE UNIT: 24:36–53 [BECNT; GW]. The topic is Jesus' appearance to the apostles [GW], the commission, promise, and ascension [BECNT].

DISCOURSE UNIT: 24:36–49 [NICNT; CEV, NASB, NCV, NIV, NRSV, TEV]. The topic is other appearances [NASB], the appearance to the disciples [NICNT], Jesus appears to his followers [NCV, NIV], Jesus appears to his disciples [NRSV, TEV], what Jesus' followers must do [CEV].

DISCOURSE UNIT: 24:36–43 [AB, BECNT, NAC, NIGTC, Su, TNTC, WBC; NET]. The topic is Jesus' final appearance [NET], Jesus' appearance to the disciples in Jerusalem [AB, NAC, NIGTC, Su, TNTC, WBC], the appearance at a meal [BECNT].

24:36 And (while) they were-speaking these (things) he-himself stood in (the) midst of-them and he-says to-them, Peace[a] to-you.
  TEXT—Instead of αὐτὸς ἔστη 'he himself stood', some manuscripts read αὐτὸς ὁ Ἰησοῦς ἔστη 'Jesus himself stood'. GNT does not mention this variant. Αὐτὸς ὁ Ἰησοῦς ἔστη 'Jesus himself stood' is read by KJV.
  TEXT—Some manuscripts omit καὶ λέγει αὐτοῖς Εἰρήνη ὑμῖν 'and he says to them, Peace to you'. GNT includes it with a B decision, indicating that the text is almost certain. It is omitted by Arn, ICC; NASB, REB.

LEXICON—a. εἰρήνη (LN 22.42) (BAGD 2. p. 227): 'peace' [BAGD, LN], 'tranquility' [LN]. The clause 'Peace to you' [BECNT, Lns, WBC; HCSB] is also translated 'Peace be to you' [KJV], 'Peace be with you' [AB, NTC; GW, NCV, NET, NIV, NLT, NRSV, TEV]. The phrase 'and he says to them, Peace to you' is translated 'and greeted them' [CEV]. This was the usual Jewish greeting [Alf, Su, TG, TNTC]. It was Jesus' normal greeting to them [Su]. This noun covers a condition of peace along with the resultant feeling of peace [Lns].

QUESTION—Who were speaking these things?
'They' refers to the two disciples giving their report in 24:35 [NAC, TG, TH]. Or, 'they' refers to all the people who were there as they discussed the things reported by the two disciples [NICNT].

QUESTION—How did Jesus arrive in the midst of them?
It is implied that Jesus suddenly was standing right there in their midst [EGT, Gdt, ICC, Lns, MGC, My, NTC, TH]. In John 20:19 we learn that after the doors were locked, Jesus appeared in the room where the disciples were gathered and that is the implication here [Alf, Arn, TNTC]. Jesus appeared in the locked room by supernatural power because he now had a glorified body that was not limited as ordinary earthly bodies are [NIC]. Jesus appeared or disappeared wherever he desired and he simply was there and did not have to take steps from the door or wall to be in their midst [Lns]. Jesus was no longer limited to time and space [Arn, Su].

24:37 And being-alarmed[a] and being afraid,[b] they-thought they-were-seeing a-spirit.[c]

LEXICON—a. aorist pass. participle of πτοέομαι, πτοέω (LN **25.264**) (BAGD p. 727): 'to be alarmed' [BAGD, **LN**], 'to frightened' [Arn, BAGD, LN; CEV], 'to be fearful' [NCV], 'to be terrified' [AB, BAGD, BECNT, LN, Lns; KJV], 'to be startled' [BAGD, NTC, WBC; HCSB, NASB, NET, NIV, NRSV, REB]. The phrase 'being alarmed and being afraid' is translated 'they were terrified' [GW, TEV], '(the whole group) was terribly frightened' [NLT]. The verb refers to being terrified because of something that is startling or alarming [TH].

b. ἔμφοβος (LN 25.256) (BAGD p. 257): 'afraid' [BAGD, Lns], 'very frightened, very much afraid' [LN], 'terrified' [BAGD, LN; CEV, HCSB, NCV, NET, NRSV, REB], 'frightened' [NTC, WBC; KJV, NASB, NIV], 'filled with fear' [Arn], 'startled' [AB, BAGD, BECNT]. This is combined with the preceding verb [GW, NLT, TEV]. This means to be extremely afraid [LN].

c. πνεῦμα (LN **12.42**) (BAGD 4.b. p. 676): 'spirit' [Arn, BECNT, Lns, WBC; KJV, NASB], 'ghost' [AB, BAGD, **LN**, NTC; all versions except KJV, NASB].

QUESTION—What is the difference between the verb πτοηθέντες 'being alarmed' and the phrase ἔμφοβοι γενόμενοι 'being afraid'?

There is little difference between the two expressions [TG, TH], they just reinforce one another [TH]. Both express having great terror [TG]. Being alarmed means being terrified and being afraid means being full of fear and these descriptions concerned a fear from encountering something they didn't understand—in this case what appeared to them to be a ghost [Su].

QUESTION—What did they think they saw?

They thought they saw a spirit, that is, a disembodied person [BECNT, ICC], a bodiless Jesus [NAC]. Here the noun πνεῦμα means a ghost, that is, something that is believed to be the part of a person's personality that leaves the body at death and then appears to people in a bodily likeness [TH]. It is an unsubstantial appearance of someone without a solid material body [Lns]. They knew that it was Jesus, but could not understand how he could suddenly be there without having entered the house, so instead of thinking he was their risen Lord, they thought it was his ghost [Su]. None of them had ever seen a ghost, but it was what they thought a ghost must be like when Jesus appeared with his old familiar form now clothed in majesty and exaltation [Lns]. This impression arose because of the sudden and miraculous appearance of Jesus [Arn, Gdt, NTC]. They did not expect another appearance by Jesus and did not recognize him at first [BECNT]. They certainly did not think they saw an evil spirit [ICC].

24:38 **And he-said to-them, Why are-you greatly-distressed[a] and why (do) doubts[b] arise in your heart(s)?**

LEXICON—a. perf. pass. participle of ταράσσω (LN 25.244) (BAGD 2. p. 805): 'to be greatly distressed' [LN], 'to be perturbed' [REB], 'to be disturbed' [Arn, WBC], 'to be troubled' [BAGD, NTC; KJV, NASB, NCV, NIV], 'to be agitated' [Lns], 'to be alarmed' [AB, BECNT; TEV], 'to be frightened' [BAGD; CEV, NET, NLT, NRSV], 'to be afraid' [GW], 'to be terrified' [BAGD]. This verb focuses on their mood, their being alarmed at the presence of what they thought to be a disembodied spirit [BECNT]. See this word at 1:12.

b. διαλογισμός (LN **31.37**) (BAGD 2. p. 186): 'doubt' [BAGD, **LN**]. The question 'Why do doubts arise in your hearts?' [Arn, BECNT, Lns, WBC; HCSB, NASB, NET, NRSV] is also translated 'Why do thoughts arise in your hearts?' [KJV], 'Because of what are thoughts going up in your hearts?' [Lns], 'Why do doubts arise in your minds?' [AB; NIV, REB], 'Why are these doubts coming up in your minds?' [TEV], 'Why do you doubt?' [CEV], 'Why do you have doubts?' [GW], 'Why do you doubt what you see?' [NCV], 'Why do you doubt who I am?' [NLT]. This question focused on the lack of perception that brought on doubts due to their slowness to accept the fact of Jesus' resurrection [BECNT].

QUESTION—What is the function of this double question and what did they doubt?

They are both rhetorical questions [NIGTC]. This was a way of rebuking them and implied that the disciples should not be alarmed and should not have doubts [TG; NET]. By asking for the reason for their alarm and doubts, Jesus brought their state of mind out into the open for them to consider what caused it [Lns, TNTC]. There was no rational reason for them to feel the way they did and Jesus asked this in order to replace their frantic thoughts with something sensible [Lns]. The questions were meant to dispel their fears [MGC]. They were doubting what they could actually see [TG]. They were wondering if the Jesus they looked upon was a ghost or if he possessed a real body [NAC]. They were doubting the reality of the resurrection [NIGTC, Su], and Jesus' following questions made them consider the evidences that were available for believing that he was now alive [Su].

24:39 **See my hands^a and my feet that I am^b myself. Touch me and see,^c because^d a-spirit does- not -have flesh and bones as you-see me having.** **24:40** **And having-said this he-showed them the hands and the feet.**

TEXT—Some manuscripts omit verse 40. GNT includes this verse with a B decision, indicating that the text is almost certain. This verse is omitted by REB.

LEXICON—a. χείρ (LN 8.30) (BAGD 1. p. 880): 'hand' [AB, Arn, BAGD, BECNT, LN, Lns, NTC, WBC; all versions]. This noun means a hand or any relevant portion of the hand such as the fingers [LN]. At the crucifixion the nails would have been through his wrists, but here 'hands' are used in a broad sense to include the wrists [NIGTC].

b. pres. act. indic. of εἰμί (LN 13.4): 'to be' [LN]. The clause ὅτι ἐγώ εἰμι αὐτός 'that I am myself' is translated 'that it is I myself' [Lns, WBC; HCSB, KJV, NASB], 'see that it is I myself' [NTC; NRSV, TEV], 'and see that it's really me' [AB; GW], 'you can see that it's really me' [NLT], 'and see who I am' [CEV], 'it is I myself' [NCV, NIV, REB], 'it's me' [NET], 'because/for it is I myself' [Arn, BECNT].

c. aorist act. impera. of ὁράω (LN 24.1): 'to see' [LN]. The phrase 'and see' [AB, Arn, BECNT, Lns, NTC, WBC; HCSB, NASB, NCV, NET, NIV, NRSV, REB] is also translated 'and see for yourselves' [GW], 'and you will know' [TEV], 'and find out for yourselves' [CEV], 'and make sure that I am not a ghost' [NLT]. At the beginning of the verse this same verb means to *see with their eyes* Jesus' hands and feet, but here it means to *see with their minds* that he is not a ghost because ghosts do not have flesh and bones [EGT]. When they touch Jesus, they will realize that it really is him and not a ghost [TG].

d. ὅτι (LN 89.93): 'because' [Arn, LN; HCSB, NCV, NLT], 'for' [BECNT, LN, Lns, NTC, WBC; KJV, NASB, NRSV, TEV], not explicit [AB; CEV, GW, NET, NIV, REB].

QUESTION—Why did Jesus tell them to look at his hands and his feet?

It is not clear in the text what they were to see by looking at Jesus' hands and feet [NIGTC]. It could be that they were to look at those uncovered parts of his body so they could know that Jesus had a real physical body and was not a ghost [Alf, Lns, NAC, NTC, WBC]. However, it is implied that his hands and feet retained the evidence of being nailed on the cross and he wanted them to see those marks [AB, Alf, BECNT, EGT, Gdt, ICC, Lns, NIVS, NTC, Su, TG, TNTC]. This is made plain in John 20:25–27 [NIGTC]. Jesus pointed out the nail scars as evidence they were seeing a real body and not a spirit [Su]. The nail holes were the feature they were to see in order to prove Jesus' *identity,* that the same Jesus who had been nailed to the cross now stood there [AB, Alf, Arn, BECNT, EGT, ICC, Lns, MGC, NIGTC, TNTC]. The following invitation to touch Jesus would prove that he had a real physical body [AB, BECNT, EGT, Gdt, MGC, TG, TNTC]. Some people think that it is impossible that Jesus' glorified body would permanently retain the gaping wounds of the crucifixion, others think that only marks would be left to indicate where the wounds had been, but if Jesus wished to retain the wounds, he could certainly do so and forever show the evidence in his body of his work of redemption [Lns].

QUESTION—What relationship is indicated by ὅτι 'because' in the clause 'because a spirit does not have flesh and bones'?

It indicates the reason they can see that it is Jesus himself and not a ghost [ICC, Lns, My, TG]: you can be sure that it is I myself and not a ghost, *because* a ghost does not have flesh and bones as you can see that I have.

QUESTION—What is the connection of flesh and bones with a resurrected body?

Flesh and bones are regarded as being essential for a resurrected body, a ghostly appearance would not be a resurrection of the body [NIGTC]. Jesus' body had physical aspects, or it could at least conform to physical laws as Jesus willed [TNTC]. His resurrection body had characteristics of his physical body, but this new body would not perish, it could move through solid material, and it could appear and vanish at will [BECNT]. Or, Jesus was in a transition state and had not yet been glorified since the resurrection body will not have flesh and bones [Rb].

QUESTION—What was involved in Jesus showing them his hands and his feet in 24:40?

Jesus put them out in plain sight [TG]. Jesus wanted them not only to look at them, but to handle them as well [Lns]. Touching Jesus would prove that there was no visual deception involved [WBC].

24:41 **And (while/because) they still were-disbelieving[a] from the joy and being-amazed,[b] he-said to-them, Do-you-have some food here?**

LEXICON—a. pres. act. participle of ἀπιστέω (LN 31.39) (BAGD 1.a. p. 85): 'to disbelieve' [BAGD, LN, Lns, WBC; NRSV], 'to be in a state of disbelief' [NTC], 'to be unbelieving' [Arn, BECNT], 'to not believe' [LN;

CEV, HCSB, KJV, NASB, NCV, NET, NIV, TEV], 'to doubt' [NLT], 'to be incredulous' [AB; REB], not explicit [GW].

b. pres. act. participle of θαυμάζω (LN 25.213) (BAGD 1.a.α. p. 352): 'to be amazed' [BECNT, LN; CEV, HCSB, NCV, NET], 'to be filled with amazement' [NTC], 'to be astonished' [BAGD], 'to be astounded' [REB], 'to wonder' [AB, BAGD, LN, Lns, WBC; KJV, NRSV], 'to be filled with wonder' [NLT, TEV], 'to marvel' [Arn, LN]. This participle is also translated as a noun: 'amazement' [GW, NASB, NIV]. See this word at 1:21, 63; 2:18, 33; 4:22; 7:9; 8:25; 9:43; 11:14, 38; 20:26; 24:12.

QUESTION—What relationship is indicated by the use of the participle ἀπιστούντων 'disbelieving'?

1. It has a temporal meaning [Arn, BECNT, Lns, NTC, WBC; all versions except REB, TEV]. Some indicate this by using 'while': *while* they were still disbelieving, Jesus spoke to them [BECNT, NTC, WBC; HCSB, KJV, NASB, NCV, NET, NIV, NRSV]. Some indicate this by using 'then': 'they were disbelieving and were amazed. *Then* Jesus spoke to them' [CEV, GW, NLT]. While their joy and wonder was at their height, Jesus requested something to eat [Lns].

2. It indicates the reason Jesus spoke to them [AB, TG, TH; REB, TEV]: *because* they were still disbelieving, Jesus spoke to them. Jesus asked them for food in order to convince them that he really was Jesus [TG].

QUESTION—What relationship is indicated by the preposition ἀπό 'from' and the participle θαυμαζόντων 'being amazed' in the clause ἔτι πιστούντων αὐτῶν ἀπὸ τῆς χαρᾶς καὶ θαυμαζόντων 'still they were disbelieving from joy and being amazed'?

1. The prepositional phrase ἀπὸ τῆς χαρᾶς 'from joy' is the reason they disbelieved [AB, Arn, BECNT, NICNT, NIGTC, NTC, WBC; CEV, HCSB, KJV, NET, REB]. Joy is given as the excuse for their disbelief [AB]. This clause is translated 'they were still incredulous, overjoyed yet wondering' [AB], 'they were still unbelieving for very joy and marveling' [Arn], 'they were still unbelieving from joy and amazed' [BECNT], 'they continued in a state of disbelief for joy, and were filled with amazement' [NTC], 'they still disbelieved from joy and continued to wonder' [WBC], 'they still could not believe because of their joy and were amazed' [HCSB], 'they yet believed not for joy, and wondered' [KJV], 'they still could not believe it (because of their joy) and were amazed' [NET].

2. The prepositional phrase ἀπὸ τῆς χαρᾶς 'from joy' and the participle θαυμαζόντων 'being amazed' are joint reasons for their disbelief [Lns; CEV, GW, NASB, NCV, NIV, TEV]. This clause is translated 'they still disbelieving from joy and wondering' [Lns], 'the disciples were so glad and amazed that they could not believe it' [CEV], 'the disciples were overcome with joy and amazement because this seemed too good to be true' [GW], 'they still could not believe it because of their joy and amazement' [NASB], 'they still could not believe it because they were amazed and happy' [NCV], 'they still did not believe it because of joy and

amazement' [NIV], 'they still could not believe, they were so full of joy and wonder' [TEV].
3. The prepositional phrase ἀπὸ τῆς χαρᾶς 'from joy' is the reason they both disbelieved and were amazed [TH; REB]. This clause is translated 'they were still incredulous, still astounded, for it seemed too good to be true' [REB].
4. The prepositional phrase ἀπὸ τῆς χαρᾶς 'from joy' and the participle θαυμαζόντων 'being amazed' indicate the states that accompanied their disbelief [NLT, NRSV]. This clause is translated 'in their joy they were disbelieving and still wondering' [NRSV], 'still they stood there doubting, filled with joy and wonder' [NLT].

QUESTION—How could the disciples still not believe?

They were still not convinced [NIGTC]. This was a continued state of disbelief [Arn, Lns, MGC, NAC, NIBC, NIC, NICNT, NIGTC, NTC, Su, TH, TNTC, WBC]. In one moment they thought that this must be Jesus himself, but in the next moment they thought that it was too good to be true and that it must be a ghost [NTC]. They were still hesitant to accept what they knew to be true [NAC]. They felt it too good to be true [Arn, MGC, NAC, NIBC, NIC, NICNT, NIGTC, Su, TH, TNTC]. They were not just disbelieving, they were disbelieving because of joy [Lns]. Or, they would not be filled with joy if they actually did not believe, so here it means that they found it hard to believe that this was really happening [BECNT].

24:42 And they-gave him a-piece of-broiled[a] fish. **24:43** And having-taken (it) he-ate (it) before them.

TEXT—Following ἰχθύος ὀπτοῦ μέρος '(a) piece of broiled fish', some manuscripts add καὶ ἀπὸ μελισσίου κηρίου 'and from honeycomb of bee' and some manuscripts read καὶ ἀπὸ μελισσίου κηρίον 'and honeycomb from bee'. GNT rejects both of these additions with a B decision, indicating that the text is almost certain. One of these additions is read by KJV.

LEXICON—a. ὀπτός (LN 46.15) (BAGD p. 576): 'broiled' [AB, Arn, BAGD, BECNT, LN, Lns, NTC, WBC; all versions except CEV, REB, TEV], 'baked' [BAGD, LN; CEV], 'cooked' [TEV]. The phrase 'a piece of broiled fish' is translated 'a piece of fish they had cooked' [REB]. The fish was cooked by direct exposure to a fire or to burning coals and the main point for mentioning this is to indicate that it had been prepared for eating and was not a piece of raw fish [TG, TH].

QUESTION—Why did Jesus eat the fish as they watched?

Jesus showed them that he had a real body that could eat food [Alf, Gdt, Lns, MGC, NAC, NIVS, Su]. This does not mean that he had to eat to sustain his resurrection body as he had to before his death [Su]. Jesus did not have to eat to maintain his body, but he could eat and did so here to prove that he had a true human body and was not a ghost [Arn]. Eating this piece of fish was a cumulative proof that his physical body stood before them [Lns]. It was the final proof that he was not a ghost [NIGTC].

570   LUKE 24:44

DISCOURSE UNIT: 24:44–53 [Su]. The topic is the conclusion.

DISCOURSE UNIT: 24:44–49 [AB, BECNT, NAC, NIGTC, Su, TNTC, WBC; NET]. The topic is Jesus' final commission [NET], Jesus' commission to the disciples [AB, NAC, NIGTC], the commission, plan, and promise of the Spirit [BECNT], a summary of Jesus' teachings between his resurrection and his ascension [Su], Jesus instructs and expounds Scripture [WBC], the fulfillment of Scripture [TNTC].

24:44 And he-said to them, These (are) the words/things of-me that I-spoke to you while being with you, that all (things) written about me in the law of-Moses and the prophets and (the) psalms must be-fulfilled.[a]

TEXT—Some manuscripts omit μου 'of me', although GNT does not mention this variant. Μου 'of me' is omitted by KJV.

LEXICON—a. aorist pass. indic. of πληρόω (LN 13.106) (BAGD 4.a. p. 671): 'to be fulfilled' [Arn, BAGD, BECNT, LN, Lns, NTC, WBC; HCSB, KJV, NASB, NET, NIV, NRSV, REB], 'to see fulfillment' [AB], 'to happen' [CEV, NCV], 'to come true' [GW, NLT, TEV].

QUESTION—When did this take place?
  1. It took place while Jesus was still meeting with his disciples after he had eaten the piece of fish [AB, Lns, MGC, My, NAC, TG, WBC; NET]. It was still the evening of Resurrection Sunday in Jerusalem [TG].
  2. It may have taken place at some later time [Alf, BECNT, Crd, EGT, Gdt, ICC, NIC, NIGTC, NTC, Su, TH]. The introduction 'and he said to them' points to a break between 24:43 and 44, but it could have been a break of moments or of days [ICC, NTC]. The beginning particle δέ 'and' indicates only a general transition and it seems to follow right after the meal, yet the absence of a chronological note makes it possible that this event occurred later [BECNT]. It appears that this continues immediately after the preceding verse, but possibly it refers to another occasion since the post-resurrection scenes in this Gospel all seem to occur within a single day [EGT]. Probably Luke summarized what Jesus said to his disciples over the period covering the different resurrection appearances [Alf, NIGTC, Su]. This could not have been said on Sunday evening because after the command to stay in the city (24:49), the disciples would not have gone to Galilee as reported in John 21 [Alf]. This was at a later meeting [TH].

QUESTION—What does 'these' refer to in the statement 'these are my words that I spoke to you'?
  1. 'These' refers to the *words* Jesus had spoken before and now repeats [AB, Alf, Arn, BECNT, ICC, Lns, NAC, NIGTC, NTC, Su, WBC; all versions except REB, TEV]: the words I spoke to you before are these: that everything written about me…must be fulfilled. The pronoun 'these' points forward to the ὅτι 'that' clause [Arn]. It was not just the words that Jesus recalled for them but it was the meaning of them [AB]. This refers not to his general teachings, but to what he taught about his death and

resurrection [MGC, NAC]. Such statements were made in 9:22, 44; 17:25; 18:31–33; 22:37 [NIGTC]. This is translated 'While I was still with you, I told you that everything written about me…had to happen' [CEV], 'These are the words I spoke to you while I was still with you. I told you that everything written about me…had to come true' [GW], 'Remember when I was with you before? I said that everything written about me must happen' [NCV].

2. 'These' refers to the *events* that have taken place [Crd, EGT, Gdt, Lns, My, TH, TNTC; REB, TEV]: these things that have happened are in accord with the words that I spoke to you before. The events of the Jesus' death and resurrection fulfilled Jesus' previous statements that all that was written of him must be fulfilled [Crd, EGT]. These events involving the resurrection are the outworking of the things Jesus had taught them [TNTC]. The events that had just come to pass are the things Jesus had told them in his teaching, things that they had not understood at the time [Gdt]. This is translated 'This is what I meant by saying, while I was still with you, that everything written about me…was bound to be fulfilled' [REB], 'These are the very things I told you about while I was still with you: everything written about me…had to come true' [TEV].

QUESTION—What is the significance of the statement 'while being with you'?

This refers to the time they spent together in Jesus' ministry before Jesus had been crucified and resurrected [TG, TH]. The statement implies that his presence with them now was of a different nature from his previous presence with them [Arn, ICC, TH]. At the present time Jesus' presence was exceptional because he no longer abode on earth [TNTC]. Jesus' previous mode of associating with his disciples had ceased [NTC]. Jesus was the same person as before, but now a new period was inaugurated in which he would no longer be 'with them' [NAC].

QUESTION—What is meant by the three terms 'the law of Moses and the prophets and the psalms' and what was included by the designation 'Psalms'?

These are the three divisions of the Hebrew Bible, and by naming each part Jesus indicated that there is no part of the Scriptures that does not bear witness to him [TNTC]. 'Psalms' was used here to refer to the third part of the Hebrew Bible, which was generally called 'the Writings' [TG]. Being the first book, Psalms was named to designate all of the Writings [Arn, TG]. The Writings are here called by its principle component, the Psalms [EGT, ICC, Lns, Su, TG, TNTC]. The Book of Psalms was the best known book of the Writings and contained much about the Messiah, so it was naturally singled out as being representative of the Writings [ICC, MGC]. Elsewhere in Luke we have the designation of the OT as the Law and the Prophets (16:16), Moses and the Prophets (16:29, 31) where the third division is not specially mentioned, but nevertheless, this third division was not to be regarded as being excluded [ICC].

24:45 Then he-opened[a] their mind(s) to-understand the Scriptures. **24:46** And he-said to-them, Thus it-is-written (that) the Messiah would-suffer[b] and rise-again out-of (the) dead[c] (ones) on the third day,

TEXT—In 24:46, following γέγραπται 'it is written', some manuscripts add καὶ οὕτως ἔδει 'and thus it was necessary'. GNT does not mention this variant. Καὶ οὕτως ἔδει 'and thus it was necessary' is read by KJV.

LEXICON—a. aorist act. indic. of διανοίγω (LN **27.49**) (BAGD 1.b. p. 187): 'to open' [BAGD, LN]. The phrase διήνοιξεν αὐτῶν τὸν νοῦν τοῦ συνιέναι 'he opened their minds to understand' [Arn, BECNT, **LN**, Lns, WBC; GW, HCSB, NASB, NLT, NRSV, REB, TEV] is also translated 'he opened their minds so they could understand' [NCV, NET, NIV], 'he opened their minds to enable them to understand' [NTC], 'he opened their minds to an understanding of' [AB], 'he opened their understanding' [KJV], 'he helped them understand' [CEV]. The phrase is an idiom meaning to cause someone to be willing to learn and to evaluate fairly [LN].

b. aorist act. infin. of πάσχω (LN 24.78) (BAGD 3.a.α. p. 634): 'to suffer' [BAGD, LN]. The phrase 'would suffer' [GW, HCSB, NASB, NCV, NET] is also translated 'will/shall suffer' [AB; NIV], 'is to suffer' [BECNT, WBC; NRSV], 'should suffer' [Arn, NTC], 'must suffer' [CEV, NLT, TEV], 'it behooved (Christ) to suffer' [KJV], 'that (the Christ) suffer' [Lns], '(foretells) the suffering' [REB]. The verb is written in the aorist tense, but it is a prophecy in Scripture that was to be fulfilled in the future [TH]. The idea is, 'the Scriptures say that the Messiah must suffer and must rise from death three days later' [TG]. Luke regularly uses the verb 'suffer' to cover the whole of Jesus' passion [NICNT]. In this context, 'to suffer' means 'to die' or 'to be put to death' [TG]. See this word at 22:15.

c. νεκρός (LN 23.121): 'dead' [LN]. The phrase ἀναστῆναι ἐκ νεκρῶν 'rise again out of the dead ones' is translated 'arise/rise from the dead' [AB, Arn, Lns, WBC; HCSB, KJV, NCV, NET, NIV, NRSV, REB], 'rise again from the dead' [NTC; NASB, NLT], 'rise from death' [CEV, TEV], 'come back to life' [GW]. The active voice is also translated passively: 'is to be raised' [BECNT]. Scriptures speak of Christ raising himself (active voice) and also of the Father raising him [Lns].

QUESTION—How did Jesus open up the disciples' minds?
Jesus explained the OT in regard to how it was fulfilled in himself [NIGTC, NIVS]. Jesus interpreted the Scriptures so that they saw them in a new way [AB, NAC]. The prophecies became quite clear when the fulfillments were explained [Lns]. The disciples had failed to understand the teachings in the Scriptures about Jesus' death and resurrection, but now they came to understand as Jesus interpreted the Scriptures for them [NAC]. The disciples were given understanding and insight into God's plans [BECNT].

LUKE 24:45-46

QUESTION— How is 'and he said to them' at the beginning of verse 46 connected to verse 45?

Verse 46 is a continuation of the preceding verse [TH]. This explains how Jesus opened up their minds [ICC]. This tells what Jesus said to open their minds [NIBC]. This begins a summary of the things Jesus told his disciples during the forty days before his ascension [Gdt]. It lists the things that were prophesied in the Scriptures [NIGTC]. It gives the gist of the prophecies [EGT].

QUESTION—What does οὕτως 'thus' refer to in the statement 'thus it is written'?

1. 'Thus' refers forward to the content of what was written [AB, Arn, EGT, NAC, Su, TH]: what is written is this: *that* the Messiah would suffer.
2. It refers backward to 24:44 [BECNT, My, NIGTC]: all things written about me must be fulfilled, (because) thus it is written that the Messiah must suffer and rise again. Although both interpretations make sense, this one emphasizes design the most [BECNT].

24:47 and repentance[a] for/and (the) forgiveness of-sins would-be-preached[b] in his name to all the nations. Beginning from Jerusalem

TEXT—Instead of εἰς ἄφεσιν 'for forgiveness' some manuscripts read καὶ ἄφεσιν 'and forgiveness'. GNT does not mention this variant. Καὶ ἄφεσιν 'and forgiveness' is read by Arn, TH; KJV, Lns, NTC, NCV, NIV, NRSV, and TEV.

LEXICON—a. μετάνοια (LN 41.52) (BAGD p. 512): 'repentance'. The phrase μετάνοιαν εἰς ἄφεσιν ἁμαρτιῶν 'repentance for (the) forgiveness of sins' [AB, BECNT, WBC; HCSB, NASB, NET] is also translated 'to turn to God in order to be forgiven' [CEV], 'to turn to God and change the way they think and act so that their sins will be forgiven' [GW], 'repentance bringing the forgiveness of sins' [REB], 'repentance and (the) forgiveness of sins' [Arn; NIV, NRSV, TEV], 'conversion and forgiveness of sins' [NTC], 'a change of hearts and lives and forgiveness of sins' [NCV], 'repentance and remission of sins' [Lns; KJV], '(take this message) of repentance...There is forgiveness of sins for all who turn to me' [NLT]. See this noun at 3:3, 8; 5:32; 15:7.

b. aorist pass. infin. of κηρύσσω (LN 33.256) (BAGD 2.b.β. p. 431): 'to be preached' [BAGD, LN], 'to be proclaimed' [BAGD]. The phrase κηρυχθῆναι ἐπὶ τῷ ὀνόματι αὐτοῦ 'be preached in his name' [BECNT, NTC; KJV, NCV, NIV] is also translated 'be proclaimed in his name' [WBC; HCSB, NASB, NET, NRSV], 'in his name...shall be preached' [AB], 'in his name the message about...must be preached' [TEV], 'in his name...is to be proclaimed' [REB], 'on the basis of his name...should be preached' [Arn], 'be proclaimed on the basis of his name' [Lns], 'by the authority of Jesus people must be told' [GW], 'be told in my name' [CEV], 'with my authority take this message' [NLT]. The verb means to proclaim a religious message [BAGD], to announce religious truths and principles and urge the listeners to accept them and comply with them [LN]. It is an authoritative proclamation [TH]. The herald announces the message he gets from the one who sends him [Lns]. See this word at 3:3; 4:18, 19, 44; 8:1, 39; 9:2; 12:3.

QUESTION—How is repentance related to the forgiveness of sins?

1. When the reading is 'repentance *for* the forgiveness of sins' [AB, BECNT, ICC, NIGTC, NIVS, NTC, WBC]. This means conversion with a view to forgiveness [NTC]. Repentance leads to forgiveness [NIGTC].
2. When the reading is 'repentance *and* the forgiveness of sins' [Arn, Lns, NTC; KJV, NCV, NIV, NRSV, TEV]. On the basis of his name both repentance and the forgiveness of sins were to be preached [Arn]. It is also true that forgiveness is the benefit that results from repentance [Arn, NIVS].

QUESTION—What is meant by ἐπὶ τῷ ὀνόματι αὐτοῦ 'in his name'?

1. The phrase indicates the basis for being forgiven [Arn, ICC, Lns, NIC, NIGTC, NTC, TH, TNTC]. This is what makes repentance effectual [ICC]. 'In his name', connects repentance and forgiveness with what Christ has done [TNTC]. It means on the basis of all that Jesus' name implies [ICC, TH]. It is on the ground of Christ's work of redemption and through his saving power [NIC]. They will preach that on the basis of Christ's name, that is, on the basis of his revelation, repentance and forgiveness can be obtained [Lns].
2. The phrase indicates their authority to preach this message [TG, WBC; GW, NLT]. They are to preach as Christ's representatives having his authority [TG]. They will be acting as Christ's representatives [WBC].

QUESTION—How is the phrase 'beginning from Jerusalem' to be connected?

1. It begins a new sentence connected to the next verse [Arn, GNT; CEV]: beginning from Jerusalem, you are witnesses of these things.
2. It is connected to the preceding clause and ends the sentence [AB, BECNT, EGT, ICC, Lns, NTC, TH, TNTC, WBC; all versions except CEV]: …would be preached in his name to all the nations, beginning from Jerusalem. This implies that the ones mentioned in Scripture who would be preaching were Jesus' disciples [EGT, TH, TNTC].

QUESTION—What is meant by the phrase 'beginning from Jerusalem'?

Jesus told his disciples that they should start preaching in Jerusalem and from there they should go on to other places [TH]. The Galilean disciples were not to start their world-wide preaching from Galilee, instead they would start in Jerusalem, the heart of the Jewish nation [Lns].

24:48 you (are/are to be) witnesses[c] of/to-these (things).

TEXT—Instead of ὑμεῖς 'you' some manuscripts read ὑμεῖς δέ 'and you'. GNT does not mention this variant. Ὑμεῖς δέ 'and you' is read by KJV.

LEXICON—a. μάρτυς (LN 33.270) (BAGD 2.c. p. 494): 'witness' [BAGD, LN], 'one who testifies' [LN]. The clause ὑμεῖς μάρτυρες τούτων 'You are witnesses of these things' [Arn, BECNT, Lns, NTC, WBC; all versions except CEV, GW, REB] is also translated 'you are witnesses of this' [AB], 'you are witnesses to these things' [GW], 'you are to be witnesses to it all' [REB], 'you must tell everything that has happened' [CEV].

QUESTION—In what way were they witnesses to these things?
1. This states that they have witnessed the events concerning Jesus' suffering and resurrection and implies that now they were to testify about these things to others [AB, Lns, NAC, NIBC, NTC, WBC]: you have witnessed these things. Jesus did not need to directly tell them to be the preachers who had been foretold in the Scriptures, but by telling them that they witnessed the fulfillment of the prophecies concerning the Messiah in Jesus, it implied that they are to be witness-heralds [Lns]. They had seen what the Lord did and taught, and they had experienced the meaning of the good news, so they should now bear testimony concerning all of this [NTC]. The disciples were eyewitnesses who were to become testifiers to the ministry of Jesus, his resurrection, and all that pertained to him [AB, NAC]. The fact that they have witnessed all of this, implies that they were in a position to testify about it and should realize that they were being directed to testify about it [WBC].
2. This is simply a command to witness to others about these things [Arn, BECNT, Rb, TG, TH; CEV, GW, REB]: you are to witness to these things. This is a command to be witnesses, not a statement [TG]. It means 'you are to give testimony about these things' [TH]. Here the Apostles and other disciples are given the role of being messengers to proclaim the message of redemption and tell people what they have seen and heard [Arn]. The disciples are told that their role was to proclaim God's work in Jesus since they had seen what Jesus did and had heard what he taught [BECNT].

24:49 And behold I am-sending the promise[a] of my Father upon you. And you are-to-stay[b] in the city until you-are-clothed-with[c] power from on-high.[d]

TEXT—Instead of καὶ ἰδοὺ ἐγώ 'and behold I', some manuscripts read καὶ ἐγώ ἰδοὺ 'and I behold' and others read κἀγώ or καὶ ἐγώ 'and I'. GNT reads καὶ ἰδοὺ ἐγώ 'and behold I' with a C decision and places ἰδοὺ 'behold' in brackets, indicating that the Committee had difficulty making the decision.

TEXT—Following πόλει 'city', some manuscripts add Ἰερουσαλήμ 'Jerusalem'. GNT does not mention this variant. Ἰερουσαλήμ 'Jerusalem' is read by KJV.

LEXICON—a. ἐπαγγελία (LN 33.288) (BAGD 2.b. p. 280): 'promise' [LN], 'what was promised' [BAGD]. The phrase 'I am sending the promise of my Father upon you' [BECNT, WBC; KJV; similarly Arn] is also translated 'I am sending forth the promise of my Father upon you' [Lns; NASB], 'I am sending you what my Father promised' [GW, HCSB, NET], 'I am sending upon you what my Father promised' [AB, NTC;

NRSV], 'I will send upon you what my Father has promised' [TEV], 'I will send you what my Father has promised' [NCV, NIV], 'I am sending on you the gift promised by my Father' [REB], 'I will send you the one my Father has promised' [CEV], 'I will send the Holy Spirit, just as my Father promised' [NLT]. This will happen so soon that Jesus used the present tense [Lns]. The present tense is used for what will happen in the immediate and certain future [ICC]. Or, this present tense is a futuristic present tense, meaning 'I am going to send' [NAC, NIGTC, NTC, TH].

b. aorist act. impera. of καθίζω (LN **85.63**) (BAGD 2.a.β. p. 390): 'to stay' [BAGD, BECNT, **LN**, Lns; CEV, HCSB, NASB, NCV, NET, NIV, NLT, NRSV], 'to remain' [AB, Arn, LN, NTC], 'to wait' [WBC; GW, REB, TEV], 'to tarry' [KJV].

c. aorist mid. subj. of ἐνδύω (LN 49.1) (BAGD 2.b. p. 264): 'to be clothed' [BAGD, LN], 'to put on' [LN]. The clause 'until you are/have been clothed with power from on high' [Arn, BECNT, NTC; NASB, NET, NIV, NRSV] is also translated 'until you become clothed from on high with power' [Lns], 'until you are clothed with power from heaven' [WBC], 'until ye be endued with power from on high' [KJV], 'until you are armed with power from above' [REB], 'until you are invested with power from on high' [AB], 'until the power from above comes down upon you' [TEV], 'until you receive power from heaven' [GW], 'until you have received that power from heaven' [NCV], 'until you are given power from heaven' [CEV], 'until you are empowered from on high' [HCSB], 'until the Holy Spirit comes and fills you with power from heaven' [NLT].

d. ὕψος (LN **1.13**) (BAGD 1.b. p. 850): 'high place' [BAGD], 'high, world above' [LN], 'heaven' [BAGD, LN]. The phrase ἐξ ὕψους 'from on high' [AB, Arn, BECNT, Lns, NTC; HCSB, KJV, NASB, NET, NIV, NRSV] is also translated 'from above' [REB, TEV], 'from heaven' [WBC; CEV, GW, NCV, NLT], 'from God' [**LN**]. This refers to a place above the earth that is associated with supernatural events or beings: 'high, world above, sky, heaven, on high' and when referring to heaven, as here, it can serve as a type of substitute reference for God [LN].

QUESTION—What is it that his Father promised?

In Acts 2:33, Peter speaks about Christ 'having received from the Father the promise of the Holy Spirit' he poured out what the people had seen occur at Pentecost, so here this promise refers to the Holy Spirit [AB, Alf, Arn, BECNT, BNTC, EGT, Gdt, ICC, Lns, MGC, NAC, NIBC, NIC, NICNT, NIVS, NTC, TG, TH, TNTC, WBC; NET, NLT]. The Spirit will be the source of the power [AB, BECNT]. There is no need to make a distinction between the Spirit being the power or being the one who confers it [ICC]. It is not clear whether the Father's promise was spoken by Jesus (Luke 12:12; Matt. 10:20; John 14:16) or was written in the OT (Joel 2:28; Isa. 32:15; 44:3; Ezek. 39:29), or both [NIGTC]. The disciples had heard Jesus speak of the promise (Acts 1:4) [Crd]. The Father had promised the Spirit long ago in the OT, but Jesus was the channel through whom the Father's promise would be brought about to inaugurate the kingdom blessings [BECNT]. Jesus would send the Spirit [BECNT, ICC]. The promise was that the Holy Spirit would be sent to them after Jesus had gone away and this may refer to what John the Baptist had said about Jesus baptizing with the Spirit (3:16) or to John 14–16 about the coming of the Spirit [Su]. The promise was fulfilled on the day of Pentecost [NIVS, NTC, Su; NET].

QUESTION—What is meant by the metaphor 'clothed with power from on high'?

Like a person is wrapped up in a robe, they would be covered with the power that God would send [Su]. Receiving power from on high is a way of speaking about receiving the Holy Spirit [BECNT, TH], because power is what the Spirit supplies [BECNT]. Some omit the metaphor and simply say 'to be endued with power' [KJV], 'to be given power' [CEV], 'to be empowered' [HCSB], 'to receive power' [GW, NCV]. This power concerns empowerment for testifying [Arn, BECNT, NICNT].

QUESTION—What does the phrase ἐξ ὕψους 'from on high' modify?

1. It modifies the preceding verb 'clothed with' [Lns, Su, WBC; HCSB]: until you are clothed from on high with power. The source of their being clothed with power is heaven where God is [Su]. From his place of exaltation in heaven Jesus will send the Spirit to empower the disciples for witnessing [WBC]. This power is a gift from heaven, that is, from God and also from Jesus who will soon ascend to heaven [Lns].
2. It modifies the following noun 'power' [Arn, LN, MGC, My, TG, TH]: until you are clothed with power that comes from on high. The power is supplied from heaven, that is, by the Holy Spirit [My], or by God [Arn]. Or, 'power' is practically a synonym for the Spirit and the phrase means that they will receive the Spirit who comes from heaven [TH].

DISCOURSE UNIT: 24:50–53 [AB, BECNT, NAC, NICNT, NIGTC, Su, TNTC, WBC; CEV, NASB, NCV, NET, NIV, NLT, NRSV, TEV]. The topic is the final appearance and ascension [Su], the ascension of Jesus [AB, BECNT, NAC, NICNT, TNTC, WBC; NASB, NIV, NLT, NRSV], the departure of Jesus [NIGTC; NET], Jesus returns to heaven [CEV, NCV], Jesus is taken up to heaven [TEV].

24:50 And he-led- them -out[a] outside as-far-as Bethany, and having-raised[b] his hands he-blessed[c] them.

TEXT—Some manuscripts omit ἔξω 'outside'. GNT does not deal with this variant in the apparatus but brackets it in the text, indicating doubt about including it.

LEXICON—a. aorist act. indic. of ἐξάγω (LN 15.174) (BAGD 1. p. 271): 'to lead out' [BAGD, LN]. The phrase ἐξήγαγεν αὐτοὺς [ἔξω] ἕως 'he led them out outside as far as' is translated 'he led out them out as far as' [AB, NTC; HCSB, KJV, NASB, NET, NRSV, REB], 'he led his followers as far as' [NCV], 'he led them out of the city as far as' [TEV], 'he led his disciples out to' [CEV], 'he led them to' [NLT], 'he led them

out to near' [WBC], 'he led them out till over against' [Lns], 'he took them to a place near' [GW], 'he led them out to the vicinity of' [NIV], 'he led them out as far as the neighborhood of' [Arn], 'he led them out to the neighborhood of' [BECNT]. 'To lead *out*' means that he led them out of the city [Alf, Lns, TH], or possibly out of the house they were in [Alf].
   b. aorist act. participle of ἐπαίρω (LN 15.105) (BAGD 1. p. 281): 'to raise' [LN; CEV, GW, NCV, TEV], 'to lift up' [AB, Arn, BAGD, BECNT, Lns, NTC, WBC; HCSB, KJV, NASB, NET, NIV, NRSV], 'to lift to heaven' [NLT]. The clause 'having raised his hands he blessed them' is translated 'he blessed them with uplifted hands' [REB].
   c. aorist act. indic. of εὐλογέω (LN 33.470) (BAGD 2.a. p. 322): 'to bless' [AB, Arn, BAGD, BECNT, LN, Lns, NTC, WBC; all versions]. It means to ask God to bestow his favor on someone [LN].

QUESTION—When did this take place?

The conjunction δέ 'and' or 'then' introduces a new occasion [ICC]. Without any time frame, this seems to all happen on the same day as the resurrection [Alf, Arn, BECNT]. There is no indication of the time this took place, but from Acts 1:3 we learn that forty days elapsed from the time of Jesus' resurrection to his ascension [TNTC]. Luke knew about the interval of forty days because he wrote about it in the first chapter of Acts [Arn, Lns]. Here Luke gave only a brief account since he intended to open his story in Acts with a full account of this act and the time it occurred [Lns].

QUESTION—How far did Jesus lead his disciples?

The phrase ἕως πρὸς Βηθανίαν 'as far as Bethany' does not mean that they went into the town of Bethany [TH]. They went in the direction of Bethany, and even into the neighborhood of Bethany [Gdt]. Bethany was located on the eastern slope of the Mount of Olives [NIGTC, Su] and in Acts 1:12 it says that they returned from the Mount of Olives, which was a Sabbath day's journey from Jerusalem [NIGTC]. The scenes here and in Acts name two locations, but these locations overlap so there is no conflict [Arn, BECNT]. This does not imply that Jesus was visible to the residents of Jerusalem as he led his disciples [EGT]. We can assume that Jesus' glorified body was visible only to his disciples as he led them [Lns].

QUESTION—What was the significance of Jesus raising his hands to bless the disciples?

This was the regular gesture that accompanied prayer or blessing [TG, TH]. The high priest Aaron lifted his hands as he blessed the people in Lev. 9:22. After talking with his disciples, Jesus assumed the attitude of a priest pronouncing a blessing [Arn, Gdt, MGC, NIBC, NIC, Su]. Or, Luke does not present Jesus as a priest [BECNT, NICNT, NIGTC], but as a prophet-teacher, so raising his hands as he bestows a blessing gives a solemn closure to the proceedings [BECNT]. The blessing is reminiscent of the leave-taking of Moses (Deut. 33) and Abraham (Gen. 49) [NICNT]. Jesus' hands were outstretched [NIC]. He lifted up his hands over them [NTC].

QUESTION—What is meant by the words εὐλόγησεν αὐτούς 'he blessed them'?

Jesus called down God's favor upon them [AB]. He asked God to bless them [TG]. He spoke a word of benediction over them [Lns]. Jesus commended them to God's care in a benediction [BECNT, NIBC].

24:51 **And it-happened while he was-blessing them he-departed[a] from them and was-carried-up[b] into heaven.**

TEXT—Some manuscripts omit the phrase καὶ ἀνεφέρετο εἰς τὸν οὐρανόν 'and was carried up into heaven'. GNT includes this phrase with a B decision, indicating that the text is almost certain. It is omitted by Arn and REB.

LEXICON—a. aorist act. indic. of διΐσταμαι (LN **15.50**) (BAGD 1. p. 195): 'to depart' [**LN**], 'to leave' [LN], 'to go away' [BAGD]. The phrase 'he departed from them' [BECNT, NTC; TEV] is also translated 'he departed' [NET], 'he left them' [GW, HCSB, NIV], 'he left' [CEV], 'he parted from them' [NASB, REB], 'he was parted from them' [WBC; KJV], 'he happened to be parted from them' [AB], 'he withdrew from them' [NRSV], 'he was separated from them' [Arn; NCV], 'he separated from them' [Lns]. This verb does not indicate the direction, but the following verb gives both direction and destination [TH]. This verb indicates a movement of going away and the following verb indicates an upward movement [NICNT].

b. imperf. pass. indic. of ἀναφέρω (LN **15.206**) (BAGD 2. p. 63): 'to be carried up' [**LN**], 'be taken up' [BAGD]. The clause 'he was carried up into heaven' [AB, BECNT, NTC, WBC; HCSB, KJV, NASB, NRSV] is also translated 'he was carried into heaven' [NCV], 'he was taken up to/into heaven' [CEV, NET, NIV, TEV], 'he was taken to heaven' [GW], 'he was being borne into the heaven' [Lns], not explicit [Arn; REB]. The imperfect tense indicates that this movement continued as the disciples worshipped him in the next verse [Alf].

QUESTION—What is meant by Jesus being carried up into heaven?

Jesus was taken up by God [TG]. The verb does not require us to think that there were any agents involved in carrying him up [My]. The imperfect tense implies that his body rose higher and higher as they watched [Lns]. In Acts 1:9 it tells us that a cloud enveloped Jesus and took him out of their sight [Lns]. We should not think that Jesus continued rising inside the cloud until he was in outer space, but that timelessly his glorified body was in heaven [Lns]. This account gives the impression that Jesus went up with no visible agent lifting him until a cloud came under him and when the cloud disappeared, Jesus had disappeared [Su]. Going up into heaven signifies the finality of Jesus' departure until his Second Coming and also his glorified status [NICNT]. At other times during the forty days after the resurrection, Jesus simply vanished, but here they could see his final departure and no other mode would have left such an impression [Lns].

24:52 And having-worshipped[a] him they returned to Jerusalem with great joy **24:53** and they-were continually[b] in the temple praising[c] God.

TEXT—In 24:52, instead of προσκυνήσαντες αὐτόν 'having worshiped him', some manuscripts read προσκυνήσαντες 'having worshiped' and others omit these two words. GNT reads προσκυνήσαντες αὐτόν 'having worshiped him' with a B decision, indicating that the text is almost certain. The words are omitted by Arn, BNTC, ICC, Crd, and REB.

TEXT—In 24:53, instead of εὐλογοῦντες 'praising', some manuscripts read αἰνοῦντες 'praising' and others read αἰνοῦντες καὶ εὐλογοῦντες 'praising and blessing'. GNT reads εὐλογοῦντες 'praising' with a B decision, indicating that the text is almost certain. Αἰνοῦντες καὶ εὐλογοῦντες 'praising and blessing' is read by Gdt and KJV.

TEXT—In 24:53, following τὸν θεόν 'God', some manuscripts add ἀμήν 'amen'. GNT rejects this addition with an A decision, indicating that the text is certain. Ἀμήν 'amen' is read by KJV.

LEXICON—a. aorist act. participle of προσκυνέω (LN 53.56) (BAGD 5. p. 717): 'to worship' [AB, BAGD, BECNT, LN, NTC, WBC; all versions except REB], 'to bow down and worship' [BAGD, LN], 'to bow in worship' [Lns]. By one's attitude and possibly by his position he expresses his allegiance to and regard for deity [LN].

b. διὰ παντός (LN 67.86) (BAGD II.1.a. p. 179): The phrase διὰ παντός 'through all' is an idiom that is translated 'continually' [BECNT, Lns, NTC; HCSB, KJV, NASB, NET, NRSV], 'always' [GW], 'constantly' [AB, Arn, LN]. The clause 'they were continually in the temple' is translated 'they spent their time in the temple' [AB; CEV], 'they spent their time continually in the temple' [WBC], 'they spent all of their time in the Temple' [NLT, REB, TEV], 'they stayed continually at the temple' [NIV], 'they stayed in the Temple all the time' [NCV].

c. pres. act. participle of εὐλογέω (LN 33.356) (BAGD 1. p. 322): 'to praise' [Arn, BAGD, LN, Lns, NTC; CEV, GW, NASB, NCV, NIV, NLT, REB], 'to speak well of' [BAGD, LN], 'to bless' [BECNT, WBC; HCSB, KJV, NET, NRSV], 'to give thanks to' [TEV]. This means to speak about someone in favorable terms [LN].

QUESTION—How did they worship Jesus?

The verb means to worship, but it usually carries the sense of a person prostrating himself as an act of veneration [NICNT]. They prostrated themselves as an act of adoration to a divine being [Gdt]. They bowed down in adoration [AB]. As Jesus was speaking his blessing, the disciples bowed or knelt to receive it [Su].

QUESTION—What was the cause of their great joy?

They rejoiced in Jesus' exaltation [NTC]. All of their doubts, questions, and fears were removed [NAC]. They no longer were fearful, because they had a Lord in heaven who ruled everything and could make good his promises [Lns]. Jesus' ascension stamped God's approval on all that Jesus had done and said and it also guaranteed that his cause would triumph [Arn, Gdt].

QUESTION—How much time did they 'continually' spend in the temple and why were they there?

This is a hyperbole and means that they went often to the temple [TG]. Since this is not to be taken literally, it does not conflict with their meeting in an upper room in Acts 1 [NIGTC]. They went to the temple at every opportunity, such as the time for prayer [Alf; NIV], at the hours of worship when the temple was open [EGT, My]. They attended the daily worship at the temple and may have held meetings of their own in the temple porticos or halls [Arn, ICC]. There were many rooms in the temple complex where they could meet together [NIVS]. The Temple provided the best place to worship God and to meet together as they waited in prayer for the fulfillment of Jesus' promise of being filled with the Holy Spirit [Su].

www.ingramcontent.com/pod-product-compliance
Lightning Source LLC
Chambersburg PA
CBHW052110010526
44111CB00036B/1600